written and researched by

Mark Salter and Jonathan Bousfield

with additional contributions by

Gordon McLachlan

ROUGH
GUIDES

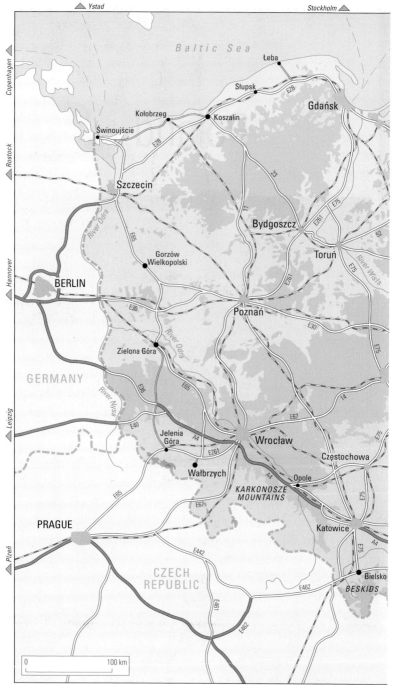

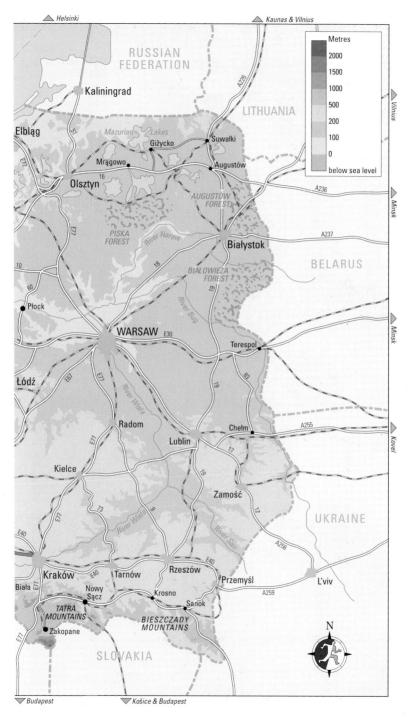

Introduction to

Poland

In many ways, Poland is one of the success stories of the new Europe, transforming itself from a one-party state to a parliamentary democracy in a remarkably short period of time. More than a decade of non-communist governments has wrought profound changes on the country, unleashing entrepreneurial energies and widening cultural horizons in a way that pre-1989 generations would have scarcely thought possible. Gleaming corporate skyscrapers have taken root in Warsaw, and private shops and cafés have established themselves in even the most provincial of rural towns. The country has a radically different look about it, having exchanged the greyish tinge of a state-regulated society for the anything-goes attitude of private enterprise – and all the billboards and window displays that go with it.

 However at the heart of modern Poland lies an all-too-familiar paradox: the very people who made the country's democratic revolution possible – militant industrial workers and anticommunist intellectuals – have found themselves marginalized in a society in which street-smart businessmen and computer-literate youth are far better poised to take advantage of the brave new Poland's burgeoning opportunities.

All this may come as a shock to those who recall the Poland of the 1980s, when images of industrial unrest and anticommunist protest were beamed

Fact file

● **Poland** occupies a vast swathe of territory in north-central Europe, bordered by Germany to the west, the Czech Republic and Slovakia to the south, and Ukraine, Belarus, Lithuania and Russia to the east.

● Much of northern and central Poland is made up of **agricultural plainland** and gently rolling countryside, although the Sudeten and Tatra **mountains** in the south provide a dramatic contrast.

● Its **population** of 38.6 million is predominantly both Polish and devoutly Catholic, although, unsurprisingly for a country which has changed its borders many times in the past, significant pockets of Ukrainians, Belarusians, Bojks and Łemks exist in the east of the country.

● Traditionally, Poland is known for its shipbuilding, coal and steel **industries**, although these days cosmetics, medicines and textile products – often made under licence for Western conglomerates – are increasingly important sources of foreign earnings.

● The vast bulk of foreign visitors head for splendid old **cities** like Kraków, or the ski resorts of the Tatras, although Baltic **beaches** and inland **lake resorts** – both much patronized by the Poles themselves – help to complete a varied tourist picture.

around the world. Strikes at the Lenin shipyards of Gdańsk and other industrial centres were the harbingers of the disintegration of communism in Eastern Europe, and, throughout the years of martial law and beyond, Poland retained a near-mythical status among outside observers as the country that had done most to retain its dignity in the face of communist oppression.

For many Poles, the most important events in the movement towards a post-communist society were the visits in 1979 and 1983 of **Pope John Paul II**, the former archbishop of Kraków. To the outside world this may have been surprising, but Poland was never a typical communist state: Stalin's verdict was that imposing communism on Poland was like trying to saddle a cow. Polish society in the postwar decades remained fundamentally traditional, maintaining beliefs, peasant life and a sense of nationhood to which the **Catholic Church** was integral. During periods of foreign oppression – oppression so severe that Poland as a political entity has sometimes vanished altogether from the maps of Europe – the Church was always the principal defender of the nation's identity, so that the Catholic faith and the

> To a great extent, the sense of social fluidity, of a country still in the throes of major transitions, remains a primary source of Poland's fascination

struggle for independence have become fused in the Polish consciousness. The physical presence of the Church is inescapable – in Baroque buildings, roadside shrines and images of the national icon, the **Black Madonna of Częstochowa** – and the determination to preserve the memories of an often traumatic past finds expression in religious rituals that can both attract and repel onlookers.

World War II and its aftermath profoundly influenced the character of Poland: the country suffered at the hands of the **Nazis** as no other in Europe, losing nearly twenty percent of its population and virtually its entire **Jewish** community. In 1945 the **Soviet**-dominated nation was once again given new borders, losing its eastern lands to the USSR and gaining tracts of formerly German territory in the west. The resulting make-up of the population is far more uniformly "Polish" than at any time in the past, in terms of both language and religion, though there are still **ethnic minorities** of Belarusians, Germans, Lithuanians, Slovaks, Ukrainians and even Muslim Tatars.

To a great extent, the sense of social fluidity, of a country still in the throes of major transitions, remains a primary source of Poland's fascination. A decisive attempt to break with the communist past as well as tenacious adherence to the path of radical market economic reforms adopted in the

Folk music in Poland

Polish **folk music** may hold a significant position in the general national consciousness, but it's especially vibrant in the folk cultures found chiefly among the country's minorities and in its southern and eastern parts. Thanks to Chopin, whose inspiration came in large part from his native **Mazovia**, music from here is probably the best known but there are other equally worthwhile traditions in **Silesia**, the **Tatras**, and the **Beskid Niski**. The festivals in **Rzeszów** and **Kazimierz Dolny** offer excellent opportunities for getting to grips with many of these rootsy rural styles, while along the **Baltic coast** the popularity of sea shanties is demonstrated in many an annual festival. For a more detailed look at Polish music see p.55 and p.714.

late 1980s have remained the guiding tenets of Poland's new political leadership – a course seemingly unaltered by the changing political complexion of successive governments. Few would question the economic and human toll reaped by Poland's attempt to reach the El Dorado of capitalist prosperity – not least among the most vulnerable sectors of society: public sector employees, farmers, pensioners and the semi- or unemployed. Despite this, the Polish people, as so often before, continue to demonstrate what to the visitor may appear an extraordinary resilience and patience. Hope springs eternal in the minds of Poles, it seems, and for all the hardships involved in establishing a new economic order – an order to which the majority of Poles retain a remarkable, if grumbling, political commitment – individual and collective initiative and enterprise of every conceivable kind is flourishing as almost nowhere else in the region.

Symbolizing a transformed geopolitical landscape, the new millennium finds Poland a member of **NATO**, the US-led military alliance of which it was – officially at least – a sworn enemy only ten years previously. Perhaps even more significantly, Poland, along with neighbours the Czech Republic and Hungary, is now decisively engaged in **EU membership** negotiations, a move that if – or more accurately, when – it actually happens promises to transform the country more profoundly than anything since the advent of communism.

Tourism is proving no exception to Poland's general "all change" rule, but despite the continuing state of flux in the country's tourist infrastructure, it is now easier to explore the country than anyone could have imagined only a few years back. This sea change is reflected in continuing and significant increases in the numbers of people visiting the country.

Encounters with the **people** are at the core of any experience of the country. On trains and buses, on the streets or in the village bar, you'll never be stuck for opportunities for contact: Polish hospitality is legendary, and there's a natural progression from a chance meeting to an introduction to the extended family. Even the most casual visitor might be served a prodigious meal at any hour of the day, usually with a bottle or two of local vodka brought out from the freezer.

Where to go

P oles delineate their country's attractions as "the mountains, the sea and the lakes", their emphasis firmly slanted to the traditional, rural heartlands. To get the most out of your time, it's perhaps best to follow their preferences. The **mountains** – above all the Carpathian range of the Tatras – are a delight, with a well-established network of hiking trails; the **lakes** provide opportunities for canoeing and a host of other outdoor pursuits; and the dozen or so **national parks** retain areas of Europe's last primeval forests, inhabited still by bison, elks, wolves, bears and eagles. Yet you will not want to miss the best of the **cities**

– Kraków, especially – nor a ramble down rivers like the Wisła for visits to Teutonic **castles**, ancient waterside towns and grand, Polish **country mansions**, redolent of a vanished aristocratic order. The **ethnic regions** offer insights into cultures quite distinct from the Catholicism of the majority, while the former centres of the **Jewish community**, and the concentration camps in which the Nazis carried out their extermination, are the most moving testimony to the complexity and tragedy of the nation's past.

> In the countryside, the golden Polish October is especially memorable, the rich colours of the forests heightened by brilliantly crisp sunshine that's often warm enough for T-shirts

Unless you're driving to Poland, you're likely to begin your travels with one of the three major **cities**: Warsaw, Kraków or Gdańsk. Each provides an immediate immersion in the fast-paced changes of the last decade or so and a backdrop of monuments that reveal the twists and turns of the nation's history. **Warsaw**, the capital, had to be rebuilt from scratch after World War II, and much of the city conforms to the stereotype of Eastern European greyness, but the reconstructed Baroque palaces, churches and public buildings of the historic centre, the burgeoning street markets and the bright shopfronts of Poland's new enterprise culture are diverting enough. **Kraków**, however, the ancient royal capital, is the real crowd puller for Poles and foreign visitors alike, rivalling the central European elegance of Prague and Vienna. This is the city where history hits you most powerfully, in the royal Wawel

complex, in the fabulous open space of the Rynek, in the one-time Jewish quarter of Kazimierz, and in the chilling necropolis of nearby Auschwitz-Birkenau, the bloodiest killing field of the Third Reich. **Gdańsk**, formerly Danzig, the largest of the Baltic ports and home of the legendary shipyards, presents a dynamic brew of politics and commerce against a townscape reminiscent of mercantile towns in the Netherlands.

German and Prussian influences abound in the **north** of the country, most notably in the austere castles and fortified settlements constructed by the Teutonic Knights at **Malbork**, **Chełmno** and other strategic points along the **River Wisła** – as the Vistula is known in Poland. **Toruń** is one of the most atmospheric and beautiful of the old Hanseatic towns here.

Over in the **east**, numerous minority communities embody the complexities of national boundaries in central Europe. The one-time Jewish centre of **Białystok**, with its Belarusian minority, is a springboard for the eastern borderlands, where onion-domed Orthodox churches stand close to Tatar mosques. Further south, beyond **Lublin**, a famous centre of Hassidic Jewry, and **Zamość**, with its magnificent Renaissance centre, lie the homelands of Ukrainians, Łemks and Boyks – and a chance to see some of Poland's extraordinary wooden churches.

In the **west**, ethnic Germans populate regions of the divided province of **Silesia**, where **Wrocław**

Seeing Poland's Jewish heritage

The history of Poland is inexorably linked to that of its **Jewish** population which, before World War II, comprised roughly ten percent (three million) of the country's total, Europe's largest Jewish community and the world's second largest. Of the current world population of fifteen million, over half are thought to be related to Polish Jewry, but up until the late 1980s those travelling to their ancestral home remained few in number due largely to fear of anti-Semitism and apprehension about travelling in communist Eastern Europe. Nowadays, **organized tours**, particularly from Israel and the US, are common, visiting the traditional focal points of Polish-Jewish life and culture. Every effort has been made in the Guide to cover sites of interest to Jews, and many of the organizations on p.29 can provide further information. For more on Jewish heritage, see the "Books" section of Contexts.

Polish vodka

The tipple most associated with Poland, **vodka** is actually in danger of being eclipsed in popularity by beer among young Poles, so it's well worth seeking out the varieties you can't find abroad before they disappear from Polish shops and bars completely. Traditionally served chilled and neat – although increasingly mixed with fruit juice – vodka can be **clear** or **flavoured** with anything from bison grass to mountain herbs to juniper berries or honey. There's even been a revival of **kosher** vodkas – although whether their rabbinic stamps of approval are kosher themselves or just a marketing gimmick isn't always obvious.

sustains the dual cultures of the former German city of Breslau and the Ukrainian city of L'viv, whose displaced citizens were moved here at the end of World War II. The other main city in western Poland is the quintessentially Polish **Poznań**, a vibrant and increasingly prosperous university town.

Despite its much-publicized pollution problems – problems it is now finally making a serious attempt to address – Poland has many regions of unspoilt natural beauty, of which none is more pristine than the **Białowieża Forest**, straddling the Belarusian border; the last virgin forest of the European mainland, it is the habitat of the largest surviving herd of European bison. Along the southern borders of the country lie the wild **Bieszczady** mountains and the alpine **Tatras** and further west, the bleak **Karkonosze** mountains – all of them excellent walking country, interspersed with less demanding terrain. North of the central Polish plain, the wooded lakelands of **Mazury** and **Pomerania** are as tranquil as any lowland region on the continent, while the Baltic coast can boast not just the domesticated pleasures of its beach resorts, but also the extraordinary desert-like dunes of the **Słowinski national park** – one of a dozen such parks.

When to go

Spring is arguably the ideal season for some serious hiking in Poland's mountainous border regions, as the days tend to be bright – if showery – and the distinctive flowers are at their most profuse. **Summer**, the tourist high season, sees plenty of sun, particularly on the Baltic coast, where the resorts are crowded from June to August and temperatures are consistently around 24°C. The major cities can get pretty stifling at these times, with the effects of the heat compounded by the influx of visitors; accommodation can be tricky in the really busy spots, but a good network of summer hostels provides a low-budget fall-back.

Autumn is the best time to come if you're planning to sample the whole spread of the country's attractions: in the cities the cultural seasons are beginning at this time, and the pressure on hotel rooms is lifting. In the countryside, the golden Polish October is especially memorable, the rich colours of the forests heightened by brilliantly crisp sunshine that's often warm enough for T-shirts.

In **winter** the temperatures drop rapidly, icy Siberian winds blanketing many parts of the country with snow for anything from one to three months. Though the central Polish plain is bleak and unappealing at the end of the year, in the south of the country skiers and other winter-sports enthusiasts will find themselves in their element. By mid-December the slopes of the Tatras and the other border ranges are thronged with holiday-makers, straining the established facilities to the limit.

Average temperatures (°F) and rainfall

	Jan		Mar		May		July		Sept		Dec	
	°F Max/Min	rain mm	°F Max/Min	rain mm	°F Max/Min	rain mm	°F Max/Min	rain mm	°F Max/Min	rain mm	°F Max/Min	rain mm
Kraków												
	32 / 22	28	45 / 30	35	67 / 48	46	76 / 58	111	67 / 49	62	38 / 28	36
Gdynia												
	35 / 27	33	40 / 30	27	59 / 44	42	70 / 58	84	64 / 51	59	38 / 31	46
Poznań												
	33 / 24	24	45 / 30	26	67 / 46	47	76 / 57	82	67 / 49	45	38 / 28	39
Przelmśyl												
	32 / 20	27	43 / 29	25	67 / 46	57	76 / 57	105	67 / 49	58	38 / 28	43
Warsaw												
	32 / 22	27	41 / 28	27	67 / 48	46	76 / 58	96	67 / 49	43	36 / 28	44

28

things not to miss

It's not possible to see everything that Poland has to offer in one trip – and we don't suggest you try. What follows is a selective taste of the country's highlights: outstanding buildings and historic sites, natural wonders and vibrant festivals. They're arranged in five colour-coded categories, which you can browse through to find the very best things to see, and experience. All highlights have a page reference to take you straight into the guide, where you can find out more.

01 **The Black Madonna of Częstochowa** Page **483** ▪ The world-famous Black Madonna should not be missed, although what you actually do get to see of the painting is limited as the figures of the Madonna and Child are always "dressed" in sets of richly decorated clothes. More impressive, perhaps, is the sense of wonder, excitement and devotion the icon inspires in the pilgrims who come here.

02 **The Tatras** Page **500** • Poland's prime highland playground is a paradise for hikers of all abilities, with relaxing rambles in subalpine meadows for the easy-going, or hair-raising mountain-ridge walks for the more experienced.

03 **Folk festivals** Page **716** • July and August are the busiest months in Poland's considerable calendar of traditional festivals. The International Festival of Highland Folklore in Zakopane is the main event to aim for, although there are numerous other regional events worth considering.

04 **Cerkiew** Page **372** • An age-old form of folk architecture still preserved in rural corners of the country. Visit some of the best examples in Jaszczurówka near Zakopane, or in the remote villages of the Bieszczady.

05 Słowinski national park

Page **645** • Trek across Sahara-like dunes just outside the seaside town of Łeba, pausing to sunbathe, birdwatch, or explore World War II rocket installations along the way.

06 Warsaw's Stare Miasto

Page **88**

Lively pavement cafés, fine restaurants and exuberant street life in a historic town centre that was faithfully reconstructed after its almost total destruction by the Nazis. As strong a symbol as any of Poland's struggle to rebuild in the aftermath of World War II.

07 Gdańsk's Ulica Długa

Page **175** • A stroll down one of Poland's most beautiful set-piece streets will take you past a string of wonderfully restored town houses, recalling the mercantile dynasties that made Gdańsk one of the great trading centres of northern Europe.

08 Solidarity

Page **183**

To get to grips with the Polish national identity, it's important to understand the country's decades of communist government and anti-communist protest – much of it led by independent trade union Solidarity, or Solidarność, commemorated by the shipyard monument in Gdańsk, built in remembrance of the workers killed by riot police in the demonstrations of 1971.

09 **Markets** Pages **132** & **461** • In order to investigate the changes wrought by free-market economics in Poland, savour the street-level commerce of the country's outdoor markets – often frequented by small-time traders from Poland's eastern neighbours – where you'll find everything from fresh fruit and veg, fake designer tracksuits and car parts to traditional smoked cheeses.

10 **Wrocław** Page **528** • There's any number of magnificent town halls in Poland, but you'd be hard pressed to find one more magnificent than the late-Gothic monstrosity at Wrocław, the centrepiece of a typically vibrant, café-splashed Rynek.

11 **Catholic festivals** Page **53** • As well as understanding Poland's politics it's essential to appreciate the religious backdrop. Attending one of the big Church festivals like Easter, Corpus Christi or Annunciation will give you a flavour of this deeply religious country.

12 **Zamość** Page **292** A model Renaissance town located deep in the countryside of eastern Poland, and stuffed with the palaces and churches built by the Zamoyskis, one of the country's leading aristocratic families.

13 Kazimierz Dolny Page 323

One of the best-preserved small towns of Poland's rural heartland, and an age-old centre of Jewish culture, now popular with the Warsaw arts-and-media set, who descend on Kazimierz enmasse on summer weekends.

14 Pałac Kultury i Nauk

Page 111 • (Palace of Culture and Sciences), Warsaw. Love it or hate it, this soaring Art-Deco monument to Stalinist ideology is still the outstanding feature of the downtown skyline.

15 The Bar Mleczny

Page 44 • A particularly Polish institution in which you can scoff both heartily and cheaply on staples like *bigos* (sauerkraut stew), *pierogi* (dumplings stuffed with meat) and *placki* (potato pancakes) in unpretentious, canteen-style surroundings.

16 Wawel

Page 428 • One of the most striking royal residences in Europe and a potent source of national and spiritual pride, Wawel is to Poles what Westminster Abbey, the Tower of London, Windsor Castle and Canterbury Cathedral are to the British – only all rolled into one.

17 Toruń Page **210** •
Birthplace of the astronomer Copernicus, and famous for the local gingerbread, Toruń is a medieval university town with a satisfying jumble of historical monuments, and a laid-back, easy-going charm.

18 Open-air museums
Pages **360**, **382** & **630** •
Poland's rich tradition of folk crafts has been pre-served in the open-air museums (or *skansen*) that gather together examples of vernacular architecture from around the country – often fea-turing the kind of timber-built farmhouses which have all but disappeared in the rest of Europe. Those in Nowy Sącz, Sanok and Lednica are particularly worth a visit.

19 Białowieża national park Page **283** • One of the most extensive areas of primeval forest in Europe, which you can explore on foot or by horse-drawn cart. Also famous for being home to a beast indigenous to Poland: the European bison.

20 **Rynek Główny, Kraków** Page **412** • A spectacular medieval market square, packed with fine architecture, in a country that's famous for them. Settle down in one of the numerous pavement cafés and soak up the atmosphere.

21 **The Mazurian Lakes** Page **227** • The central Mazurian Lakes are a hugely popular destination for Polish tourists in summer, but the further east you head into the lakeland, the closer you can get to the lakes' essence as discovered by the first visitors here – beauty and solitude.

21 **Baltic beaches** Experience the bracing sea breezes and mile upon mile of unspoilt sands in laid-back, old-fashioned seaside resorts like Hel (p.198), Międzyzdroje (p.571) and Mielno (p.651).

23 Vodka
Page **47**
The essential accompaniment to any social occasion. It has to be drunk neat and downed in one go if you want to do things properly.

24 Lublin
Page **296**
A jewel of an old town and a large student population make Lublin the liveliest and most rewarding of Poland's eastern cities – and one that's relatively undiscovered by tourists.

25 Malbork Castle
Page **203** • The Teutonic Knights lorded it over northern Poland for more than 200 years, and this – a rambling complex of fortifications on the banks of the Wisła – is their most imposing monument.

26 Poznań
Page **601**
Recharge your urban batteries in the down-to-earth, work-hard-and-play-hard city that epitomizes the invigorating mercantile bustle of the new Poland.

27 **The Sukiennice, Kraków** Page **413** • The vast cloth hall in the middle of Kraków's Rynek Główny bustles with tourists and street sellers all year round, although winter is probably the most atmospheric time at which to visit.

28 **Auschwitz-Birkenau** Page **463** • Poland was once home to one of the most vibrant Jewish communities in Europe, a presence that was all but snuffed out by the Nazis during World War II. The most notorious extermination camp of them all, Auschwitz-Birkenau, offers the profoundest of insights into the nature of human evil, and demands to be visited – few who come here will be unchanged by the experience.

contents

Using the Rough Guide

We've tried to make this Rough Guide a good read and easy to use. The book is divided into five main sections, and you should be able to find whatever you want in one of them.

front section

The front colour section offers a quick tour of Poland. The **introduction** aims to give you a feel for the place, with suggestions on where to go. We also tell you what the weather is like and include a basic country fact file. Next, our authors round up their favourite aspects of Poland in the **things not to miss** section – whether it's great food, amazing sights or a special hotel. Right after this comes the Rough Guide's **contents** list.

basics

You've decided to go and the basics section covers all the **pre-departure** nitty-gritty to help you plan your trip. This is where to find out which airlines fly to your destination, what paperwork you'll need, what to do about money and insurance, about internet access, food, security, public transport, car rental – in fact just about every piece of **general practical information** you might need.

guide

This is the heart of the Rough Guide, divided into user-friendly chapters, each of which covers a specific region. Every chapter starts with a list of **highlights** and an **introduction** that helps you to decide where to go, depending on your time and budget. Likewise, introductions to the various towns and smaller regions within each chapter should help you plan your itinerary. We start most town accounts with information on arrival and accommodation, followed by a tour of the sights, and finally reviews of places to eat and drink, and details of nightlife. Longer accounts also have a directory of practical listings. Each chapter concludes with **public transport** details for the area covered.

contexts

Read contexts to get a deeper understanding of how Poland ticks. We include a brief **history**, articles about **mountain walking** and **music**, together with a detailed further-reading section that reviews dozens of **books** relating to the country.

index + small print

Apart from a **full index**, which includes maps as well as places, this section covers publishing information, credits and acknowledgements, and also has our contact details in case you want to send in updates and corrections to the book – or suggestions as to how we might improve it.

contents ▶

basics ▶

guide ▶

contexts ▶

language ▶

index ▶

chapter map of **Poland**

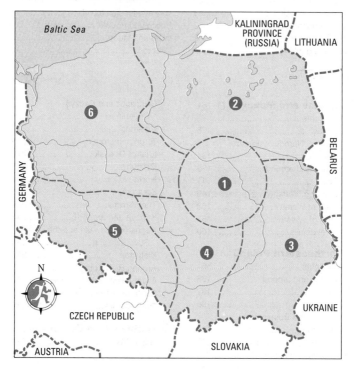

contents

contexts

673–742

language

742–760

Pronunciation 745
Useful words and phrases 746

Glossaries 751

index and small print

761–772

map symbols

symbols
maps are listed in the full index using coloured text

Motorway		Concentration camp
Paved road		Information office
Steps		Post office
Path		Bus stop
Railway		Parking
Ferry route		Metro station
River		Gate
National boundary		Church (regional)
Chapter division boundary		Synagogue
Point of interest		Wall or fortifications
Mountain peak		Stadium
Mountain range		Building
Airport		Church (town)
Campsite		Christian cemetery
Border crossing		Jewish cemetery
Accommodation		Woods or forest
Restaurant		Park

basics

basics

Getting there

There are regular services from Britain to Poland by air, train and bus, although there are no direct flights from Ireland, from where you will need to fly via London or Copenhagen. The easiest way to get to Poland from the US and Canada is to fly direct to Warsaw or, less commonly, Kraków. Alternatively, you can fly to London, or another good-value western European destination, and continue by a combination of bus, train and ferry. There are no direct flights to Poland from Australia or New Zealand, but as well as catching connecting flights you again have the option of flying into Europe and then going overland.

Barring special offers, the cheapest of the airlines' published fares is usually an **Apex** ticket, although this will carry certain restrictions: you will, most likely, have to book – and pay – at least 21 days before departure, spend at least seven days abroad (maximum stay three months), and you tend to get penalized if you change your schedule. On transatlantic routes, there are also winter **Super Apex** tickets – slightly cheaper than an ordinary Apex, but limiting your stay to between 7 and 21 days. Some airlines also issue **Special Apex** tickets to people younger than 24, often extending the maximum stay to a year. Many airlines offer youth or student fares to under 26s, though these tickets are subject to availability and can have eccentric booking conditions. It's worth remembering that most cheap return fares involve spending at least one Saturday night away and that many will only give a percentage refund if you need to cancel or alter your journey, so make sure you check the restrictions carefully before buying a ticket.

You can normally cut costs further by going through a specialist **flight agent** – either a consolidator (in North America only), who buys up blocks of tickets from the airlines and sells them at a discount, or a discount agent, who in addition to dealing with discounted flights may also offer special **student and youth fares** and a range of other travel-related services such as travel insurance, rail passes, car rentals, tours and the like. Bear in mind, though, that penalties for changing your plans can be stiff. Some agents specialize in charter flights, which may be cheaper than anything available on a

scheduled flight, but again departure dates are fixed and withdrawal penalties are high (check the refund policy). If you travel a lot, discount **travel clubs** are another option – the annual membership fee may be worth it for benefits such as cut-price air tickets and car rental.

Don't automatically assume that tickets purchased through a travel specialist will be cheapest – once you get a quote, check with the **airlines** and you may turn up an even better deal. Be advised also that the pool of travel companies is swimming with sharks – exercise caution and never deal with a company that demands cash up front or refuses to accept payment by credit card.

Regardless of where you buy your ticket, fares will depend on the **season**. It's a good idea to check the seasonal boundaries as they may differ from airline to airline and from year to year, but you can usually expect prices to be highest from around June to September, when the weather is best. They drop during the "shoulder" seasons – April to May and October to November – and you'll get the best prices during the low season, December to March (excluding Christmas and New Year when prices are hiked up and seats are at a premium). Note also that flying at weekends ordinarily adds approximately £40/US$60 to the round-trip fare. **Early booking** is always advisable, with flights filling up weeks in advance at peak times, particularly at Christmas when émigré Poles return home in force. Prices quoted are round trip, assume midweek travel, exclude **taxes**, and are subject to availability and change.

Online booking

Many airlines and discount travel websites offer you the opportunity to book your tickets **online**, cutting out the costs of agents and middlemen. Good deals can often be found through discount or auction sites, as well as through the airlines' own websites.

Online booking agents and general travel sites

ⓦ **www.cheapflights.com** Flight deals, travel agents, plus links to other travel sites.

ⓦ **www.cheaptickets.com** Discount flight specialists.

ⓦ **www.deckchair.com** Bob Geldof's online venture, drawing on a wide range of airlines.

ⓦ **www.etn.nl/discount.htm** A hub of consolidator and discount agent Web links, maintained by the nonprofit European Travel Network.

ⓦ **www.expedia.com** Discount air fares, all-airline search engine and daily deals.

ⓦ **www.flyaow.com** Online air travel info and reservations site.

ⓦ **www.gaytravel.com** Gay online travel agent, concentrating mostly on accommodation.

ⓦ **www.hotwire.com** Bookings from the US only. Last-minute savings of up to forty percent on regular published fares. Travellers must be at least 18 and there are no refunds, transfers or changes allowed. Log-in required.

ⓦ **www.lastminute.com** Offers good last-minute holiday package and flight-only deals.

ⓦ **www.priceline.com** Bookings from the US only. Name-your-own-price website that has deals at around forty percent off standard fares. You cannot specify flight times (although you do specify dates) and the tickets are non-refundable, non-transferable and non-changeable.

ⓦ **www.princeton.edu/Main/air800.html** Has an extensive list of airline toll-free numbers and websites.

ⓦ **www.skyauction.com** Bookings from the US only. Auctions tickets and travel packages using a "second bid" scheme. The best strategy is to bid the maximum you're willing to pay, since if you win you'll pay just enough to beat the runner-up regardless of your maximum bid.

ⓦ **www.smilinjack.com/airlines.htm** Lists an up-to-date compilation of airline website addresses

ⓦ **www.travelocity.com** Destination guides, hot Web fares and best deals for car hire, accommodation & lodging as well as fares. Provides access to the travel agent system SABRE, the most comprehensive central reservations system in the US.

ⓦ **www.travelshop.com.au** Australian website offering discounted flights, packages, insurance, online bookings.

ⓦ **http://travel.yahoo.com** Incorporates a lot of Rough Guide material in its coverage of destination countries and cities across the world, with information about places to eat and sleep etc.

ⓦ **www.uniquetravel.com.au** Australian site with a good range of packages and good value flights.

From Britain and Ireland

From Britain, daily direct flights link London and Warsaw and, less frequently, Kraków and Gdańsk (all around 2hr 30min). Trains (around 20hr) are only marginally cheaper, unless you're under 26, in which case you can get some discounts. Return buses – run mainly for the benefit of Polish émigrés – are an overlooked bargain, taking around 25 hours. A **budget option** worth considering is to get a cheap flight to Berlin and continue from there by train. By car, it's an all-motorway 1000-kilometre run to the Polish border from the Channel Tunnel or ferry ports, via Belgium, Holland and Germany – a surprisingly fast haul, but best covered over two days.

There are no direct flights **from Ireland** to Poland, so you will need to fly via London or **Copenhagen.** With through fares costing around IR£259, there's little to be saved by getting a cheap flight to London and shopping around there, unless you are really looking for rock-bottom prices or are considering taking the budget option via Berlin (see above).

Students and anyone under 26, should contact Usit Campus or USIT Now, which generally have the best discount deals on flights and train tickets. It's always worth trying the airlines direct, especially if you are over 26, as they often have special deals. For InterRail details see p.12.

Flights

From London **Heathrow** LOT (Polish Airlines), and, more expensively, British Airways operate around 5 daily scheduled flights (more at peak periods) to Warsaw, with connections on to all major cities throughout the country. In addition, from London **Gatwick** LOT and BA offer direct flights to Kraków (7 flights a week) and Gdańsk (2 flights a week). LOT also offers direct flights from **Manchester** to Warsaw (6 times a week).

Currently, the London–Warsaw Apex **fare** with LOT is around £140 in low season and £270 during the rest of the year, while, barring special offers, BA's Apex economy fares range from around £200 in low season to around £300 in high. However, BA's occasional offers can bring the price of a flight to Warsaw down to about £125. With all airlines, there's a slight price increase if you fly at the weekend. Return tickets average out at £130–250, depending on the season.

However, if you shop around, you should be able to come up with a cheaper discounted fare. The best **specialist agents** to try are Polorbis, the official tourist office, Fregata and the Polish Travel Centre, two established Polish-run travel outfits (see next column and overleaf). From Fregata, for instance, one-month returns cost from about £160 – or £170 to Kraków – with no advance booking needed. The Polish Travel Centre, meanwhile, occasionally has specials from £140. Although Poland is hardly a major discount destination, you'll find other **discount agents** in the classified travel sections of the national Sunday papers, London's *Evening Standard* newspaper or *Time Out* magazine, and in major regional newspapers and listings magazines. If you are a student or under 26, you may be able to get further discounts on flight prices through agents such as Usit Campus Travel or STA Travel (see overleaf).

As a cheaper alternative, you might consider **flying to Berlin** (discounted return fares can cost around £105), and continuing to Warsaw by train, an inexpensive eight-hour journey. In addition to the general discount agents listed in next column and overleaf, it's worth contacting specialists such as the German Travel Centre for competitive fares to Germany.

Airlines

Aer Lingus ☎0645/737 747; in Ireland ☎01/886 8888; ⓦwww.aerlingus.ie.
British Airways ☎0845/773 3377; in Ireland ☎0141/222 2345; ⓦwww.british-airways.com
LOT (Polish Airlines) ☎020/7580 5037; ⓦwww.lot.com.
Ryanair ☎0870/156 9569; in Ireland ☎01/609 7800; ⓦwww.ryanair.ie.

Travel and discount agents

Aran Travel International Galway ☎091/562 595, ⓕ564 581, ⓦwww.iol.ie/~aran/aranmain.htm. Good value flights to all parts of the world.
CIE Tours International Dublin ☎01/703 1888, ⓦwww.cietours.ie. General flight and tour agent.
Co-op Travel Care Belfast ☎028/9047 1717, ⓕ471 339. Flights and holidays around the world.
Destination Group ☎020/7400 7000, ⓦwww.destination-group.com. Good discount air fares, as well as Far East and USA inclusive packages.
Flightbookers ☎020/7757 2444, ⓦwww.ebookers.com. Low fares on an extensive selection of scheduled flights.
Fregata Travel 4 Tanner Street, London SE1 ☎0207/940 1700; 117 Withington Rd, Manchester M16 8EE ☎0161/226 7227. Established specialists in discounted travel and tours to Poland.
German Travel Centre 403–409 Rayners Lane, Pinner, Middlesex HA5 5ER ☎0208/429 2900. Discounted flights to Berlin.
Joe Walsh Tours Dublin ☎01/872 2555 or ☎01/676 3053, Cork ☎021/277 959, ⓦwww.joewalshtours.ie. General budget fares agent.
Lee Travel Cork ☎021/277 111, ⓦwww.leetravel.ie. Flights and holidays worldwide.
Liffey Travel Dublin ☎01/878 8322 or ☎878 8063. Package tour specialists.
The London Flight Centre ☎020/7244 6411, ⓦwww.topdecktravel.co.uk. Long-established agent dealing in discount flights.

McCarthy's Travel Cork ☎021/270 127, ⓦwww.mccarthystravel.ie. General flight agent.

Neenan Travel Dublin ☎01/676 5181, ⓦwww.neenantrav.ie. Specialists in European city breaks.

North South Travel ☎ & Ⓕ01245/608 291, ⓦwww.northsouthtravel.co.uk. Friendly, competitive travel agency, offering discounted fares worldwide – profits are used to support projects in the developing world, especially the promotion of sustainable tourism.

Polish Travel Centre 246 King St, London W6 0RF ☎0208/741 5541. Specialist in discounted flights and buses to Poland.

Polorbis Suite 530–532 Walmar House, 288/300 Regent St, London ☎0207/636 2217. UK office of the Polish tourist bureau.

Premier Travel Derry ☎028/7126 3333, ⓦwww.premiertravel.uk.com. Discount flight specialists.

Rosetta Travel Belfast ☎028/9064 4996, ⓦwww.rosettatravel.com.Flight and holiday agent.

STA Travel ☎0870/160 6070, ⓦwww.statravel.co.uk. Worldwide specialists in low-cost flights and tours for students and under-26s, though other customers welcome.

Student & Group Travel Dublin ☎01/677 7834. Student and group specialists, mostly to Europe.

Trailfinders ☎020/7628 7628; Republic of Ireland ☎01/677 7888; ⓦwww.trailfinders.com. One of the best-informed and most efficient agents for independent travellers; produce a very useful quarterly magazine worth scrutinizing for round-the-world routes.

Travel Bug 597 Cheetham Hill Rd, Manchester M8 5EJ ☎0161/721 4000. Large range of discounted tickets.

Travel Cuts ☎020/7255 2082, ⓦwww.travelcuts.co.uk. Specializing in budget, student and youth travel.

Usit Campus ☎0870/240 1010, ⓦwww.usitcampus.co.uk. Student/youth travel specialists, offering discount flights.

USIT Now Belfast ☎028/9032 7111; Dublin ☎01/602 1777 or ☎ 677 8117; Cork ☎021/270 900; Derry ☎028/7137 1888, ⓦwww.usitnow.ie. Student and youth specialists for flights and trains.

By train

Travelling by **train** to Poland can be an enjoyable way of getting there if you're intending to stop off along the way, but you'll only really save money over the cost of a flight if you're under 26, and some of the complex routeings will end up taking longer than a direct bus.

Rail Europe offers the fastest and most sensible option from London, starting with Eurostar from London Waterloo to Brussels (3hr), and then onto another (overnight) train to Warsaw via Cologne, a total journey of 21 hours. The standard fare is £295 or £291 for the under-26s (with the London–Brussels leg priced at £79, barring special offers, with £75 fares for those under 26); these must be booked between four and six weeks in advance, require you to spend Saturday night or two nights away and are non-changeable. You can get through-ticketing – including the tube journey to Waterloo – from main-line stations in Britain.

Otherwise, **regular return tickets** incorporating a ferry or catamaran crossing between Dover and Ostend are available from selected main-line train stations and travel agents, though in high season at least you don't save that much money this way, and you're talking about a journey time of around 30 hours. The ordinary return fare is £257 in low season, slightly more in high. Tickets are valid for two months and allow any number of stopovers, providing you stick to the pre-scribed route. Trains leave London's Charing Cross station, and for a comfortable journey, it's best to book a couchette before you leave.

Finally, those under 26 can purchase a discounted **BIJ** ticket, available from main-line stations or Wasteels for £157; again tickets are valid for two months, with unlimited stops en route.

InterRail passes and other offers

If you're planning to visit Poland as part of a more extensive trip around Europe, it may be worth buying an **InterRail** pass, available from any major UK train station or youth/student travel office; the only restriction is that you must have been resident in a European country for at least six months. Those aged under 26 get the best deal, with anyone older having to pay a supplementary £56–90 (depending on the pass bought) or so. With the one-zone pass there's a £56 difference, then £70 for two zones, £76 for three zones and £90 for four zones. Passes come in two main forms: the All-Zone pass (£229 under 26s/£319 others), valid for one month on all European railways, and the Zonal pass, whereby the 28 countries are split into eight zones and you choose the countries you want the pass to be valid for (the UK to Warsaw would necessitate a £276 – or £199 for under-26s – three-zone pass, valid for a month, but excluding the Eurostar, which requires a £75 supplement). In addition, all InterRail passes offer discounts on rail travel in the UK and on cross-Channel ferries.

If you're sixty or over and have a Senior Rail Card (£18 from any train station), you can get a **Rail Europe Senior Card** for £12, which gives a thirty-percent discount on rail travel between – but not within – 25 European countries, and includes Eurostar and rail-connected sea crossings; the card is valid for a year.

A better bargain, perhaps, is **Polrail passes**, which also offer unlimited travel on the entire Polish train network – these, however, do have to be used on consecutive days. An eight-day pass starts at £43/US$60 for second-class, or £64/US$90 for first-class travel, rising to £64/US$90 or £86/US$120 for fifteen days. The **Eurodomino** passes (£34–£69), valid for a month and issued for one particular European country only, can also be bought for rail travel for a certain number of days (eg 3–8) within a one-month period. It doesn't, however, work out to be cost-effective if you're travelling for a month or more.

One warning about rail travel, however. There have been reports of numerous **robberies** on international night services into Poland, especially from Berlin and Prague. Some bizarre heists have involved entire compartments being stripped while their occupants are put to sleep by gas fed through the ventilation system. Always sleep with your valuables close to you.

Rail Ticket agents

Eurostar EPS House, Waterloo Station, London SE1 8SE ☎0870/518 6186.
International Rail Enquiries ☎01354/660 222
Rail Europe ☎08705/848 848
Wasteels Victoria Station (by platform 2), London SW1V 1JY ☎020/7834 7066.

By bus

Bus travel is an inexpensive and straightforward way to get to Poland, much favoured by Poles during the holiday seasons and, with Polish drivers taking frequent cigarette breaks, not as gruelling as you might expect.

The most reliable services are operated by **Eurolines**, a division of the National Express bus company, in conjunction with **Fregata**. They run regular services from London to Warsaw, Kraków, Rzeszów, Olsztyn and a whole host of other Polish cities. Return tickets for Warsaw, for example, start at £79 (£95 in peak season), with reductions for under-26s, senior citizens and children. Tickets can be bought at any National Express office in the UK, and will include connecting fares from anywhere outside London. There's a ten-percent discount on all fares booked via its website.

In addition, a number of other Polish émigré-run companies run "buses", which can mean anything from a double-decker Mercedes to a minibus. The best established of these is the **Polish Travel Centre**, which runs buses from London to Warsaw via Amsterdam and Poznań, and to Kraków via Amsterdam, Wrocław and Katowice. Prices are from £75 return from London. **Tazab** operate similar services at similar prices, again aimed primarily at the Polish community in this country, as do **Bogdan Travel**, who also offer a service from London to Gdańsk via Szczecin. Some of these companies also do pick-ups from major northern English cities which adds £10–20 to the price of the ticket.

Bus operators

Bogdan Travel 5a Broadway, Gunnersbury Lane, London W3 8HR ☎0208/993 9997.
Eurolines ☎0870/514 3219, Republic of Ireland ☎01/836 6111, Ⓦwww.eurolines.co.uk.
Fregata Travel see p.11.
New Millennium 1665 High St, Solihull, Birmingham B91 3TB ☎01564/770 750.
Polish Travel Centre see opposite.
Tazab Travel 273 Old Brompton Rd, London SW5 9JB ☎0207/373 1186.

Border crossings

Following the break-up of the Soviet Union – and the split of neighbouring Czechoslovakia – Poland now shares **land borders** with seven countries: **Germany**, the **Czech Republic**, **Slovakia**, **Ukraine**, **Belarus**, **Lithuania** and the **Russian Federation** (Kaliningrad region). Recent political changes have made the formalities of entering Poland from Germany, the Czech Republic or Slovakia pretty straightforward, though in summer long delays often build up at the busiest customs points, as the understaffed Polish customs force search for smuggled goods – a major and growing problem, owing to big-time cigarette, alcohol and drug operations run by post-Soviet mafias.

Theoretically at least, entering or leaving Poland **from the east** via the former Soviet republics ought to be less difficult now than in the past. Despite the easing of travel restrictions, though, the actual state of affairs is pretty uneven: the mentality of many post-Soviet guards is very much "business as usual", and this, combined with the lack of properly functioning international crossing points, means that the delays (by car especially) can be considerable, a day being about average.

To keep locals up to date during the summer holiday season, Polish radio broadcasts "border reports" after the weather news, giving details of the length of the queues (anything up to 10km on a bad day) and expected waiting time (up to 60 hours). The opening of more border crossings features prominently in high-level discussions between politicians on all sides – indeed in some instances (Belarus, for example) it can be taken as a litmus test of the state of relations between the two countries. To date, however, progress has been slow, the number of new or expanded crossing points being more than matched by the volume of people wanting to travel.

Following is a list of border crossings (open 24 hours unless specified) open to international travellers. In addition there are a fair number of "local" crossing points: while these are theoretically only open to local (i.e. Polish and neighbouring country) travellers or may only be crossed on foot, some on train, and others by car, in practice some may turn out to be open to international traffic – something you're most likely to discover by turning up. In view of these uncertainties your best bet is to check with local tourist offices in the region you're planning to travel through – agencies and offices abroad are generally pretty clueless about the situation on the ground – for the lowdown on current developments (or lack of them).

Germany–Poland (north to south)

Ahlbeck–Świnoujście (Baltic coast).
Linken–Lubieszyn.
Pomellen–Kołbaskowo (Berlin–Gdańsk route).
Schwedt–Krajnik Dolny.
Bad Freienwalde–Osinów (Berlin–Gorzów Wielopolski route).
Seelow–Kostrzyn (Berlin–Gorzów Wielopolski route).

Frankfurt an der Oder–Słobice (Berlin–Warsaw route).
Frankfurt an der Oder–Świecko (Berlin–Warsaw route).
Guben–Gubin.
Forst–Olszyna (Berlin–Wrocław/Kraków route).
Bad Muskau–Łeknica.
Görlitz–Zgorzelec (Dresden–Wrocław route).
Zittau–Sieniawka.

By car

Driving to Poland means a long haul of 1000km from Calais or Ostend to the Polish border – and another 450–500km from there to Warsaw or Kraków. Flat out, and using the Channel Tunnel, you could do the journey to the border in eighteen hours, but it makes more sense to allow longer, breaking the journey in central Germany.

The Czech Republic–Poland (listed from west to east)

Habartice–Zawidów
(Prague–Gorlitz).

Harachow–Jakuszyce
(Prague–Wrocław route, via
Jelenia Góra).

Pomezni Boudy–Przelęcz Okraj
(Prague–Wrocław route, via
Wałbrzych).

Kralovec–Lubawka
(Prague–Wrocław route, via
Wałbrzych).

Nachod/Slone–Kudowa
(Prague–Wrocław route, via

Kłodzko).

Dolni Lipka–Boboszów
(Prague–Wrocław route, via
Kłodzko).

Mikulovice–Głuchłazy (Brno–Opole
route).

Krnov–Pietraszyn (Brno–Opole
route).

Bohumin–Chałupki
(Ostrava–Katowice route).

Cesky Tesin–Cieszyn
(Brno/Ostrava–Kraków route).

Slovakia–Poland (west to east)

Oravská Polkora–Korbielów.

Trstena–Chyżne
(Ruźomberok–Kraków route).

Javorina–Łysa Polana
(Poprad–Nowy Targ route, via
Tatra mountains).

Mnisek–Piwniczna (Poprad–Nowy
Sącz route, via Beskid Sądecki;
currently only Poles, Czechs and
Slovaks can cross here).

Vysny Komarnik–Barwinek
(Presov–Rzeszów, via Dukla).

Poland–Ukraine (north to south)

Dorohusk–Jahodyn (Lublin–Kowiel
route).

Hrebenne–Raba Russkaja (Lublin–L'viv
route).

Medyka–Sudowaja
Wisznia–Kraków–L'viv route).

Poland–Belarus (north to south)

Brzugi–Kuźnica (Białystok–Grodno
route).

Terespol–Briest (Warsaw-Moscow
rail route).

Sławatycze–Damachave (alternative
route to Briest).

Poland–Lithuania (north to south)

Budzisko–Kalwarija
(Warsaw–Kaunas route).

Ogrodniki–Lazdijai (Warsaw–Vilnius
route).

Sejny–Alytus (Warsaw–Kaunas
route; not 24 hours).

Poland–Kaliningrad Province (west to east)

Gronono–Mamonowo
(Elbląg–Kaliningrad rail route).

Bezledy–Bagrationovsk (Warsaw/
Olsztyn–Kaliningrad route).

Goldap–Gasev
(Csuwałki–Cerniakowsk–Kaliningrad
route).

The most convenient **Channel crossings** are on the P&O Stena services from **Dover/Folkestone to Calais**, Hoverspeed to **Ostend** (around £129–189 return for up to 5 adults and a car depending on season), or the Le Shuttle **Channel Tunnel** option from Folkestone to Calais (£180–299 for 2 adults and a car depending on season, with a fifty-percent cancellation charge, although there are frequent special offers). From either of these ports, the most popular and direct route is on toll-free motorways all the way, bypassing Brussels, Düsseldorf, Hannover and Berlin.

A more relaxing alternative, which halves the driving distance, is to catch the thrice-weekly Scandinavian Seaways ferry from **Harwich to Hamburg** (19hr) and then drive east past **Berlin**, getting to the **Polish border** in another six hours. This costs £232–292 per passenger, depending on season (including a comfortable cabin with shower and toilet) and £80–96 for a car, plus an extra £10 or so if you travel at the weekend.

Better value still is the All-in-a-Car deal where three to four adults – plus vehicle – can travel from just £260 on a low-season weekday, rising to £506 at peak periods: journeying out or back at a weekend will add £40 to the total. The most convenient ferry route from the north of England is the nightly North Sea Ferries service from **Hull to Rotterdam** (14hr), costing £240–298 with reclining seats, or £292–350 for a cabin – again, prices are for two adults and a car depending on season.

If you decide to drive into Poland, check the required **documentation**; see p.36 for more on this.

Cross-Channel operators

Brittany Ferries Ireland ☎021/277 705.
Hoverspeed ☎08705/240 241.
Irish Ferries Ireland ☎0870/517 1717 or 01407/764 261.
Le Shuttle ☎08705/353 535
ⓦwww.eurotunnel.com.
North Sea Ferries ☎08701/296 002.
P&O Stena Line ☎08705/989 0980.
Scandinavian Seaways ☎08705/333 000.

Packages and organized tours

The number of foreign visitors on **package tours** continues to outweigh independent travellers. During the communist era, Orbis, the state tourist company, now privatized, had unquestioned dominance of this market, with a couple of Polish émigré-run operators coming a distant second. However, in recent years, small travel operations have mushroomed in Poland – a recent estimate was over 2500 – and a growing number of British and other western European travel companies have set up their own programmes, often in co-operation with local private operators.

Orbis and **Polorbis** (see p.12) now operate a somewhat reduced range of mainstream tours, which are retailed overseas through Polorbis agencies. The bulk of the tours are one- or two-week packages, their busy schedules taking in Warsaw and Kraków plus a combination of places such as Gdańsk, Częstochowa, Kórnik, Poznań, and Toruń. A 10-day tour is also run to Poland, Slovakia and Hungary. At around £600 for one week, £965 for two weeks, these are pricey ways of seeing the country. More interesting, although still not cheap, are some of its specialist ventures, such as Warsaw Opera weekends, a long-weekend package starting at around £300. Its Jewish tours are run rather infrequently, depending on the number of enquiries. Polorbis also offers hiking in the Tatras, horse-riding and cycling tours.

Few of the larger general operators feature Poland in their brochures. **Fregata Travel** (see p.11) offers a range of packages along similar lines, and at similar prices, to Orbis. It also offers a package called "Poland's Great Train Journey", a rail loop starting and ending in Warsaw and visiting various cities and sites in the process, as well as a number of all-in city breaks to Warsaw, Kraków, Gdańsk and Poznań throughout the year (2 or 3 nights), starting from £235. **Polish Travel Centre**, **Tazab** and **Bogdan Travel** (see pp.12–13 for addresses), which, like Fregata, are run in Britain by Polish émigrés, also offer this kind of tour.

New Millennium (see p.13), one of the most popular operators in Britain, offers packages to the Tatras base of Zakopane, for £129–179 per person, depending on season, comprising a return bus trip plus a week's accommodation in a pension. The same deal to Kraków costs £169–234. More expensively, you can also do the same trips by air. It also operates trips combining Poland with Ukraine and other neighbouring countries.

Other UK-based specialists include **Exodus Expeditions**, 9 Weir Rd, London SW12 0LT (☎0208/675 5550, ⓦwww.exodus.co.uk/holidays/avnwho) who offer a fourteen-day tour, including Gdańsk, Warsaw and Kraków, as well as trekking holidays in the Tatras, with prices from £965 (including flights, accommodation and all transport required). They also run a tour taking in

Poland, Slovakia and Hungary for £795. Lastly, **Shearings**, Miry Lane, Wigan WN3 4AG (℡01942/244 246) are a general operator with three tours incorporating Poland.

From the US and Canada

The easiest way to get to Poland from the US and Canada is to fly direct to Warsaw or, less commonly, Kraków. Once there, LOT connects with most of the major Polish cities. Alternatively, if expense is a main consideration, you might consider flying to London, Frankfurt or another good-value western European destination, and continuing by a combination of bus, train and ferry.

Flights

From the US, LOT (Polish Airlines) flies daily nonstop to Warsaw from New York (either JFK or Newark) and six days a week from Chicago's O'Hare Airport. It also flies several times weekly from New York and Chicago to Kraków. Approximate APEX fares are: New York–Warsaw US$700 (high season) or US$450 (low); Chicago–Warsaw US$800/ 480; New York–Kraków US$750/500; Chicago–Kraków US$850/ 530. If you're coming from the West Coast, LOT will connect you with a domestic carrier. The total APEX fare from LA to Warsaw, via Chicago or New York, will be roughly US$1000/650.

Several other carriers, including BA, Northwest/KLM, Swissair, Lufthansa and Sabena have daily flights from the US to Warsaw via their European hub cities. Delta has flights connecting via Paris.

From Canada LOT operates a charter service nonstop to Warsaw from Toronto (twice a week in the winter months, 5 flights a week in the summer) and, in the summer only, from Toronto to Kraków and Edmonton to Warsaw. Tickets must be purchased via a travel agent such as Pekao (see p.19), whose cheapest fare to Warsaw from Toronto is CDN$550 in low season (senior citizens CDN$399) or CDN$990 in high.

To give you more flexibility, you might want to check out the other major airlines who fly daily to Warsaw, but require a change of plane in western Europe – British Airways flies to Warsaw via London, Lufthansa via Frankfurt, Northwest/KLM via Amsterdam and Swissair via Zürich. However, you can expect fares significantly higher than LOT's charter service. BA for instance quotes a Toronto–Warsaw fare of roughly CDN$1000 (low season) or CDN$1800 (high) and a Vancouver–Warsaw fare of CDN$1700/ 2190. Another thing you might wish to consider is that the taxes vary depending on which European airport you make your connection. For example, if you're changing planes in London you'll pay a total of approximately CDN$15 on top of the plane fare, while a Frankfurt connection will be more like CDN$30.

Airlines

British Airways ℡1-800/247-9297; in Canada ℡1-800/668-1059; ⊛www.british-airways.com
Delta Airlines ℡1-800/241-4141; in Canada ℡1-800/221-1212; ⊛www.delta.com
KLM/Northwest ℡1-800/447-4747; in Canada ℡1-514/397-0775; ⊛www.klm.com
LOT ℡1-800/223-0593; in Canada ℡1-800/668-5928; ⊛www.lot.com
Lufthansa ℡1-800/645-3880; in Canada ℡1-800/563-5954; ⊛www.lufthansa.com
Virgin Atlantic Airways ℡1-800/862-8621, ⊛www.virgin-atlantic.com

Discount agents, consolidators and travel clubs

Air Brokers International 150 Post St, Suite 620, San Francisco, CA 94108 ℡415/397-1383 or 1-800/883-3273, ⊛www.airbrokers.com. Consolidator.
Airhitch 2641 Broadway, 3rd Floor, New York, NY 10025 ℡212/864-2000 or 1-800/326-2009; ⊛www.airhitch.org. Standby-seat broker. For a set price, they guarantee to get you on a flight as close to your preferred destination as possible, within a week.
Council Travel 205 E 42nd St, New York, NY 10017 ℡212/822-2700 or 1-800/226 8624, ⊛www.ciee.com. Other branches in San Francisco, Los Angeles, Boston, Chicago, Washington DC, etc. Nationwide specialists in student travel.
Educational Travel Center 438 N Frances St, Madison, WI 53703 ℡608/256-5551 or 1-800/747-5551,

@www.edtrav.com. Student/youth and consolidator fares.

Moment's Notice 7301 New Utrecht Ave, Brooklyn, NY 11204 ☎718/234 6295, @www.moments-notice.com. Discount travel club.

Pekao International Travel and Tours, see Specialist Operators box, opposite.

STA Travel 10 Downing St, New York, NY 10014 ☎212/627-3111 or 1-800/777-0112, @www.sta-travel.com. Other branches in Los Angeles, Chicago, San Francisco, Philadelphia, Boston, etc. Worldwide discount travel firm specializing in student/youth fares; also student IDs, travel insurance, car rental, train passes, etc.

TFI Tours International 34 W 32nd St, New York, NY 10001 ☎212/736-1140 or 1-800/745-8000. Consolidator.

Travac 989 Sixth Ave, New York, NY 10018 ☎212/563-3303 or 1-800/872-8800. Consolidator and charter broker, mostly to Europe; has another office in Orlando.

Travel Avenue 10 S Riverside, Suite 1404, Chicago, IL 60606 ☎312/876-6866 or 1-800/333-3335, @www.travelavenue.com. Discount travel company.

Travel Cuts 187 College St, Toronto, ON M5T 1P7 ☎416/979-2406 or 1-800/667-2887, @www.travelcuts.com. Canadian discount travel organization, with branches in Montréal, Vancouver, Calgary, Winnipeg, etc.

Traveler's Advantage 3033 S Parker Rd, Suite 900, Aurora, CO 80014 ☎1-877/259-2691, @www.travelersadvantage.com. Discount travel club.

Travelling via Europe

If you have the time, travelling to another European capital and continuing your journey overland can be an excellent and economical way to reach Poland, allowing stopovers en route and enabling you to see much more of Europe along the way. See pp.10–17 for details of the options **from London**.

There are a variety of **rail passes** available which must be purchased before you arrive in Europe. A Eurail Pass is only likely to pay for itself if you're planning to travel widely around Europe en route to Poland. Allowing unlimited free train travel in seventeen countries, not including Poland, it will get you there from other European destinations, but not allow travel within Poland itself. The Eurail Youthpass (for under-26s) costs US\$388 for fifteen consecutive days, US\$623 for one month or US\$882 for two months; if you're 26 or over you'll have to buy a first-class pass, available in fifteen-day (US\$554), 21-day (US\$718), one-month (US\$890), two-month (US\$1260) and three-month (US\$1556) increments. The passes also come in versions which allow you to stagger your rail days over a longer period (FlexiPass) and/or with a discount for two to five persons travelling together (FlexiSaver-Pass/SaverPass).

The new European East Pass, covering Poland, Austria, Hungary, the Czech Republic and Slovakia, has no age restrictions, allowing five days' first-class travel during a one-month period for US\$210 with the option to buy up to five extra rail days for US\$24 each day. The Polrail Pass is valid for travel solely within Poland (see "Getting Around" p.34 for details).

For passes contact Rail Europe, 226 Westchester Ave, White Plains, NY 10604 (☎1-800/438-7245), the official Eurail Pass agent in North America; Orbis; or in Canada, Canadian Reservations Centre, 2087 Dundas East, Suite 105, Mississauga, ON L4X 1M2 (☎1-800/361-7245).

Packages and organized tours

With the opening up of Poland, independent travel is now easier, but the organized **package tour** still remains a popular method of seeing the country. A good place to start shopping around would be **Orbis**, the state tourist company. They have an extensive selection of tours, although they're not especially cheap, ranging from six to 21 days, including flights, accommodation, and most meals. A fifteen-day planned excursion called Panorama of Poland, which takes in the main sights of the country, will cost from US\$2209 (low season) or US\$2439 (high) if travelling from New York; you'll need to add on roughly US\$80 (from Chicago) or US\$320 (from LA) for the air fare. Southern Delight is a ten-day tour of the country's southern provinces, starting in Warsaw and visiting Kraków, Zakopane, Częstochowa, Wadowice (birthplace of the pope) and

Wola, before returning to Warsaw. From New York, this will cost you between US$1629 and US$1879, depending on the time of year. Another option is the twelve-day Castles and Palaces trip, starting at US$2019 (low season from New York) or US$2169 (high). Orbis will also help you customize specialist tours, such as explorations of Warsaw's Jewish heritage or visits to Kraków, Lublin, Auschwitz and Treblinka.

Another major operator to Poland is **PAT** (Polish American Tours), whose specialist packages include a twelve-day Best of Poland trip, as well as Historic Poland and Southern Adventure. **Tradesco** also offers several options, such as a seven-day escorted Scenic Poland tour starting at US$855 and three-day/two-night city packages of Kraków and Warsaw priced around US$100 and US$120 respectively (all land only). Otherwise **General Tours**, who operate the Eastern European division of Delta Vacations, have land/air plus sightseeing packages to Warsaw (5 days/3 nights from US$949) and Kraków (6 days/4 nights from US$1089).

All prices quoted above include hotel rates calculated for single person/double occupancy and are subject to availability and change.

If you're considering travelling independently, bear in mind that **rail tickets** for journeys within Poland should, wherever possible, be purchased inside the country, as prices for tickets reserved abroad can be up to fifty percent higher. See "Getting Around" p.32.

Specialist tour operators

Adventures Abroad 2148-20800 Westminster Hwy, Richmond, BC V6V 2W3 ☏604/303-1099 or 1-800/665-3998, ⓦwww.adventures-abroad.com. Exclusive Poland tours plus Poland/Baltics/Russia, etc. combinations.

Air Tours Poland 500 Fifth Ave, Suite 408, New York, NY 10110 ☏212/852-0243 or 1-800/223-0593. A division of LOT Polish Airlines, offering general interest escorted tours, pilgrimages, folk art, Jewish heritage tours, and so on.

Canadian Travel Abroad 80 Richmond St W, Suite 804, Toronto, ON M5H 2A4 ☏416/364-2738 or 1-800/387-1876, ⓦwww.baxter.net/cantrav. General interest, churches, pilgrimages, museums and Jewish-oriented tours to Poland.

Elderhostel 11 Avenue de Lafayette, Boston, MA 02111 ☏877/426-8056, ⓦwww.elderhostel.org. Specialists in educational and activity programmes for senior travellers.

Exotik Tours 1117 Ste Catherine St W, Suite 806, Montréal, Québec H3B 1H9 ☏514/284-3324 or 1-800/361-6164. Independent travel and motorcoach tours of Warsaw, Kraków, etc.

General Tours 53 Summer St, Keene, NH 03431 ☏603/357-5033 or 1-800/221-2216, ⓦwww.generaltours.com. City packages including Warsaw and Kraków.

International Gay and Lesbian Travel Association ☏1-800/448-8550, ⓦwww.iglta.org. Trade group with lists of gay-owned or gay-friendly travel agents, accommodations and other travel businesses.

Isram World of Travel 630 Third Ave, New York, NY 10017 ☏212/661-1193 or 1-800/223-7460. Independent city packages and escorted Jewish heritage tours.

ITS Tours 1055 Texas Ave, Suite 104, College Station, TX 77840 ☏409/764-0518 or 1-800/533-8688. Overview of Poland's most popular cities as well as comprehensive tours of its historic regions. Independent and escorted options.

Kentours 44 Victoria St, Suite 1315, Toronto, ON, M5C 1Y2 ☏416/593-0837 or 1-800/387-2615. Offers a variety of city packages and Polish heritage tours.

Kompas 2929 E Commercial Blvd, Suite 201, Fort Lauderdale, FL 33308 ☏1-800/233-6422. Warsaw and Kraków city packages and escorted tours.

Orbis Polish Travel Bureau 342 Madison Ave, New York, NY 10173 ☏212/867-5011 or 1-800/TO-POLAND, ⓦwww.orbistravel.com. Still has strong ties to the Polish State Tourist Board (now semi-privatized).

PAT Tours 1285 Riverdale St, West Springfield, MA 01089 ☏413/747-7702 or 1-800/388-0988, ⓦwww.polandtours.com. Services the large Polish-American tourist market, organizing tours and courses, often in liaison with local *emigracja* organizations.

Pekao International Travel and Tours 1610 Bloor St W, Toronto, ON M6P 1A7 (☏416/588-1988 or 1-800/387-0325;

Ⓦwww.pekao-canada.com). Émigré flight agent and tour company operating charter flights from Toronto and Edmonton to Poland.

Tradesco Tours Inc 6033 W Century Blvd, Los Angeles, CA 90045 ℡310/649-5808 or 1-800/448-4321, Ⓦwww.tradescotours .com. Independent and escorted tours to central and eastern Europe.

Travcoa 2350 SE Bristol, Newport Beach, CA 92660 ℡1-800/992-2003 or 949/476-2800, Ⓦwww.travcoa.com. City tours of Warsaw and Kraków and trips to Zakopane.

Unique World Cruises 154 Village Rd, Manhasset, NY 11030 ℡516/627-2636 or 1-800/669-0757, Ⓦwww.uniqueworldcruises.com. Two-week tour/cruise of Poland and the Czech Republic, visiting Warsaw, Kraków and Częstochowa.

From Australia and New Zealand

There are no direct **flights** to Poland from Australia or New Zealand; however, the Polish national carrier, LOT, in combination with, Qantas, British Airways and Thai Airways, has scheduled flights to Warsaw via a stopover in Asia. Aeroflot, Lauda, Lufthansa and Malaysian Airlines also fly to Warsaw via a transfer in their respective national hubs. Alternatively, you can pick up a cheap fare to Frankfurt, and then continue on to Poland by train. Round-the-world (RTW) tickets can also be structured to include Poland. The Eastern European Rail Pass covering Poland, Hungary, Austria, the Czech Republic and Slovakia covers some internal rail travel within Poland and can be purchased from Australia or New Zealand. No advance purchase rail tickets are available in Australia or New Zealand for travel exclusively within Poland. See "Getting Around", p.32 or "Travelling via Europe" p.18 for details on Polish rail passes and the Eastern Europe Rail Pass, respectively.

From Australia, the cheapest connecting fares to Warsaw are with Lufthansa via Asia and Frankfurt or Thai Aiways and Aeroflot via Asia and Moscow. Prices with these airlines start at A\$1470 low season, rising to A\$2050 high season. Lauda Air is also highly competitive with flights via Asia and Vienna starting at A\$1530 low season to A\$2200 high season.

Malaysian Airways have flights to Amsterdam with a connecting KLM flight to Warsaw starting at A\$1699. Flights via Singapore and London with Qantas/British Airways start at A\$1899. Additional airport taxes apply to these fares ranging from A\$180–230 depending on the carrier and current exchange rates.

From New Zealand, the best fare is with Qantas/British Airways/LOT, connecting twice weekly to Warsaw from Auckland via Bangkok or Singapore for NZ\$2499 low season, NZ\$2950 high season. Alternatively, fly via Sydney and pick up the less expensive Lufthansa, Qantas, British Airways, Thai Airways or Aeroflot code-share flights.

Poland can be readily included in most **round-the-world tickets**, such as British Airways/Qantas "One World" or Air New Zealand/Singapore Airlines "Star Alliance" fares. Expect to pay around A\$2599/NZ\$3099 low season to A\$3089/NZ\$3699 high season.

Airlines

Aeroflot Australia ℡02/9262 2233, Ⓦwww.aeroflot.com.
Air New Zealand Australia ℡02/9223 4666, reservations 13/2476; New Zealand ℡09/357 3000 or 0800/737 000; Ⓦwww.airnz.co.nz.
British Airways Australia ℡02/8904 8800; New Zealand ℡09/356 8690; Ⓦwww.britishairways.com.
LOT Polish Airlines Australia ℡02/9244 2466; no NZ office; Ⓦwww.lot.com.
Lufthansa Australia ℡02/9367 3888; New Zealand ℡09/303 1529; Ⓦwww.lufthansa.com.
Qantas Australia ℡13 13 13; New Zealand ℡09/357 8900, toll-free 0800/808 767; Ⓦwww.qantas.com.au.
Thai Airways Australia ℡02/9251 1922, local-call rate 1300/651 960; New Zealand ℡09/377 3886; Ⓦwww.thaiair.com.

Travelling via Europe

The **Eastern Europe Rail Pass**, covering Poland, Austria, Hungary, the Czech Republic and Slovakia, has no age restrictions, and allows five days' first-class travel during a one-month period for A\$438, six days (A\$488), seven days (A\$538), eight days (A\$588), nine days (A\$638), or ten days (A\$688). Contact the Eastern European Travel Bureau or your travel agent.

If you're planning to travel widely around Europe en route to Poland, there are several other options. A **Eurail Pass** allows unlimited train travel in seventeen countries, not including Poland. The **Eurail Youthpass** (for under-26s) starts at A$733 for fifteen days consecutive travel, A$942 for 21 days, A$1176 for one month, A$1665 for two months and A$2055 for three months; if you're 26 or over you'll have to buy a first-class pass, available in 15-day (A$1046), 21-day (A$1355), one-month (A$1680), two-month (A$2378) and three-month (A$2940) increments. Passes are available through your travel agent, who will also be able to assist with tailoring a pass to suit your particular needs.

Busabout allows unlimited travel in fourteen European countries and seventy cities, not including Poland. For those under 26 or HI members, prices for a two-week pass start at A$389, three weeks cost A$569, one month is A$749, two months A$1159, three months A$1449 and a seven-month pass A$1699. If you are 26 or over you will have to buy a standard pass available in increments of two weeks (A$439), three weeks (A$629), one month (A$839), two months (A$1289), three months (A$1579) and a seven-month pass (A$1899). Flexipasses are also available to suit your needs; speak with your travel agent.

Packages and organized tours

The **Eastern European Travel Bureau** (see next column) is the main agent for Orbis, the Polish Tourist Office, and offers a variety of accommodation packages and tours for independent travellers, excluding flights. These include two-night Warsaw and Kraków city breaks (twin share) with breakfast and airport transfers from A$202/NZ$232 and A$247/NZ$270 respectively, and a seven-day bus tour (Poland's Best), Warsaw– Kraków return visiting Zakopane and Auschwitz, from A$1580/NZ$1700.

Discount and specialist agents

Accent on Travel 545 Queen St, Brisbane ☏07/3832 1777.
Anywhere Travel 345 Anzac Parade, Kingsford, Sydney ☏02/9663 0411.
Budget Travel 16 Fort St, Auckland ☏09/366 0061, plus other city branches (nearest branch ☏0800/808 040).
Contal Travel 133 Goulburn Street, Surry Hills, Sydney ☏02/9212 5077.
Destinations Unlimited 3 Milford Rd, Milford, Auckland ☏09/373 4033.
Eastern European Travel Bureau Level 5, 75 King St, Sydney ☏02/9262 1144, ✉eetb@optusnet.com.au; 343 Little Collins St, Melbourne ☏03/9600 0299, ✉eetbmelb@netlink.com.au; 190 Edward St, Brisbane ☏07/3229 9716, ✉eetbrtcbne@AOL.com; 111 Little William St, Adelaide ☏08/8212 2233; Living Travel, 5 Mill St, Perth ☏08/9322 6812.
Flight Centres Australia: 82 Elizabeth St, Sydney ☏02/9235 3522; 19 Bourke St, Melbourne ☏03/9650 2899; plus branches nationwide (nearest branch ☏13/1600). New Zealand: 205–225 Queen St, Auckland ☏09/309 6171; plus branches nationwide (nearest branch ☏0800/FLIGHTS); ⊕www.flightcentre.com.au.
Innovative Travel PO Box 21247, Christchurch, New Zealand ☏03/3653 910, ✉innovative.travel@clear.net.nz.
Magna Carta Travel Suite C, 2 Albert Road, Strathfield ☏02/9746 9895.
Northern Gateway 22 Cavenagh St, Darwin ☏08/8941 1394, ⊕www.northernterritory.com.
Orbis Express Travel Level 1, 296 Parramatta Rd, Auburn, Sydney ☏02/9737 8099; 161 George St, Liverpool, Sydney ☏02/9822 5681.
Passport Travel 401 St Kilda Rd, Melbourne ☏03/9867 3888, ⊕www.travelcentre.com.au.
STA Travel Australia: 855 George St, Sydney ☏02/9212 1255; 256 Flinders St, Melbourne ☏03/9654 7266; plus branches nationwide (nearest branch ☏13/1776). New Zealand: 10 High St, Auckland ☏09/309 0458; 132 Cuba St, Wellington ☏04/3850561; 90 Cashel St, Christchurch ☏03/379 9098; other offices in Dunedin, Palmerston North, Hamilton and at major universities; ⊕www.statravel.com.au.
Student Uni Travel Level 8, 92 Pitt St, Sydney ☏02/9232 8444, ⊕www.sut.com.au.
Topdeck Travel 65 Grenfell St, Adelaide ☏08/8232 7222.
YHA Travel 422 Kent St, Sydney ☏02/9261 1111, ⊕www.yha.com.au.
USIT Beyond 5 Victoria St East, Auckland ☏09/379 4224 or 0800/788 336, ⊕www.usitbeyond.co.nz.

Visas and red tape

Citizens of the UK can spend up to six months in Poland without a visa. Citizens of other EU countries, some other European countries and the US may stay for up to 90 days without a visa. Nationals of many other countries – including Australia, New Zealand and Canada – still require a visa, which should be obtained prior to arriving in Poland.

Visas are valid for ninety days and must be used within six months of the date of issue. To qualify for a visa, you must have a full passport, valid for at least nine months beyond the date of your application and with at least one clear page for the authorization stamp. The visa application form can be obtained (in person or by post) from **Orbis**, **Polorbis** or from a **Polish embassy** or, though not always, **consulate**. Polorbis can also handle the whole transaction on your behalf on payment of a handling charge. You should allow two to three weeks for delivery by post, two to three days if you lodge your application in person. You need to include a passport photograph with your application. Currently the fee is CDN$70 in Canada, A$80 in Australia and NZ$80 in New Zealand.

Polish embassies and consulates abroad

Australia 7 Turrana St, Yarralumla, Canberra, ACT ℡02/6272 1000; 10 Trelawney St, Woollahra, Sydney ℡02/9363 9816.
Canada 443 Daly St, Ottawa, Ontario K1N 6H3 ℡613/789-0468; 2603 Lakeshore Blvd W, Toronto, Ontario MAV 1G5 ℡416/252-5471; 1500 Pine Ave W, Montréal, Québec H3G 1B4 ℡514/937-9481; 1177 W Hastings St, Suite 1600, Vancouver, BC V6E 2K3 ℡604/688-3530.
New Zealand 17 Upland Rd, Kelburn, Wellington ℡04/475 0453.
UK and Ireland 47 Portland Place, London W1B 1JH ℡020/7580 4324, ℮polishembassy@polishembassy.org.uk.
US 2640 16th Street NW, Washington, DC 20008 ℡202/234-3800; 223 Madison Ave, New York, NY 10016 ℡212/237 2100, ℠www.polandconsulateny.com; 1530 N Lake Shore Drive, Chicago, IL 60610 ℡312/337-8166; 12400 Wilshire Blvd, Suite 555, Los Angeles, CA 90025 ℡310/442-8500.

Polorbis offices abroad

Australia Eastern European Travel Bureau, Level 5, 75 King St, Sydney ℡02/9262 1144.
UK Suite 530-532, Walmar House, 288–300 Regent St, London W1B 3AL ℡020/7636 4701, ℠www.polorbis.co.uk.
US 342 Madison Ave, New York, NY 10173 ℡212/867-5011.

Insurance

Even though EU health care privileges apply in Poland, you'd do well to take out an insurance policy before travelling to cover against theft, loss and illness or injury. Before paying for a new policy, however, it's worth checking whether you are already covered: some all-risks home insurance policies may cover your possessions when overseas, and many private medical schemes include cover when abroad.

In Canada, provincial health plans usually provide partial cover for medical mishaps overseas, while holders of official student/teacher/youth cards in Canada and the US are entitled to meagre accident coverage and hospital inpatient benefits. Students will often find that their student health coverage extends during the vacations and for one term beyond the date of last enrolment.

After exhausting the possibilities above, you might want to contact a specialist travel insurance company, or consider the **Rough Guides travel insurance** deal we offer (see below). A typical travel insurance policy usually provides cover for the loss of baggage, tickets and – up to a certain limit – cash or cheques, as well as cancellation or curtail-ment of your journey. Most of them exclude so-called dangerous sports unless an extra premium is paid. Many policies can be chopped and changed to exclude coverage you don't need – for example, sickness and accident benefits can often be excluded or included at will. If you do take medical coverage, ascertain whether benefits will be paid as treatment proceeds or only after return home, and whether there is a 24-hour medical emergency number. When securing baggage cover, make sure that the per-article limit – typically under £500 – will cover your most valuable possession. If you need to make a claim, you should keep receipts for medicines and medical treatment, and in the event you have anything stolen, you must obtain an official statement from the police.

Rough Guides travel insurance

Rough Guides offers its own travel insurance, customized for our readers by a leading UK broker and backed by a Lloyds underwriter. It's available for anyone, of any nationality, travelling anywhere in the world.

There are two main Rough Guides insurance plans: **Essential**, for basic, no-frills cover; and **Premier** – with more generous and extensive benefits. Alternatively, you can take out **annual multi-trip insurance**, which covers you for any number of trips throughout the year (with a maximum of 60 days for any one trip). Unlike many policies, the Rough Guides schemes are calculated by the day, so if you're travelling for 27 days rather than a month, that's all you pay for. If you intend to be away for the whole year, the Adventurer policy will cover you for 365 days. Each plan can be supplemented with a "Hazardous Activities Premium" if you plan to indulge in sports considered dangerous, such as skiing, scuba-diving or trekking. Rough Guides also does good deals for older travellers, and will insure you up to any age, at prices comparable to SAGA's.

For a **policy quote**, call the Rough Guides Insurance Line on UK freefone ☏0800/015 09 06; US freefone ☏1-866/220 5588, or, if you're calling from elsewhere ☏+44 1243/621 046. Alternatively, get an online quote at ⓦwww.roughguides.com/insurance.

Health

Reciprocal arrangements between Poland and Britain mean British travellers are entitled to free basic medical care in the country; there is, however, a charge for certain imported drugs and for some specialized treatments. It's important to carry your NHS card as proof of your entitlement to free treatment; without it you will probably end up paying the full cost. However, these arrangements do not cover everything, and it is advisable for everyone to have adequate private health insurance. North Americans, Canadians, Australians and New Zealanders must arrange full insurance before leaving home.

Inoculations are not required for a trip to Poland. Tap **water** is officially classified as safe, at least in the major cities, but most people prefer to drink bottled mineral water (*woda mineralna*).

Pharmacies and hospitals

Simple complaints can normally be dealt with at a regular **pharmacy** (*apteka*), where basic medicines are dispensed by qualified pharmacists. In the cities, many of the staff will speak at least some English or German. Even in places where the staff speak only Polish, it should be easy enough to obtain repeat prescriptions, if you bring along the empty container or remaining pills. In every town there's always at least one *apteka* open 24 hours; addresses are printed in local newspapers and guides.

For more serious problems, or anything the pharmacist can't work out, you'll be directed to a **public hospital** (*szpital*), where conditions will probably be cramped, with more patients than beds, a lack of resources and occasionally insanitary conditions. Health service staff are heavily overworked and scandalously underpaid: the funding crisis in the Polish health service is currently the subject of intense political debate. Hospital patients may be required to pay for the better-quality medicines, and will probably need friends to bring food in for them. If you are required to pay for any medical treatment or medication, remember to keep the receipts for your insurance claim when you get home.

In the larger cities you can opt for **private health care**. Kraków and Warsaw now have a considerable Western expatriate population, with health centres run on Western lines. In a crisis, it may even be best to ring the 24-hour emergency service of one of these clinics rather than an ambulance; the ethics of private versus public health care aside, there are advantages to being able to talk to someone in English. See the relevant city listings – or check the local press – for details.

Travellers with disabilities

In the past, very little attention was paid to the needs of the disabled in Poland. Attitudes are slowly changing – the 1997 Constitution included provision banning discrimination against people with disabilities – but there is still a long way to go and there is not a lot of money available for improvements.

The State Fund for the Rehabilitation of the Disabled, established in 1991, now sponsors a number of programmes designed to make buildings and other **public facilities** wheelchair-accessible. **Lifts** and **escalators** are gradually becoming more common in public places and an increasing number of **hotels**, mainly in Warsaw and Kraków, have access and rooms designed for the disabled. The sadly predictable downside is that the majority of these places are expensive, meaning that such provision is still, by and large, a luxury. **Orbis** (see p.16) offers special facilities in its hotels in over fifteen cities including Poznań, Częstochowa and Zakopane. A handful of **youth hostels** also offer facilities suitable for wheelchair users; contact the Polish Youth Hostel Federation (PTSM; see p.42) for further details.

Transport is a major problem, since buses and trams are virtually impossible for wheelchairs, and although Polish Railways claims that seats in each carriage are designated for disabled passengers, this can't be relied on. Taxi drivers in eastern Europe in general are also very reluctant to lift passengers to and from their wheelchairs.

Some of the organizations that should be able to provide some help and advice are listed below.

Contacts for disabled travellers

Australia and New Zealand

ACROD (Australian Council for Rehabilitation of the Disabled) National Branch PO Box 60, Curtin, ACT 2605 (☏02/6282 4333); ACROD, NSW Division, 24 Cabarita Rd, Cabarita (☏02/9743 2699).
Disabled Persons Assembly, 173 Victoria St, Wellington (☏04/801 9100).

Britain and Ireland

Disability Action Group 2 Annadale Ave, Belfast BT7 3JH ☏01232/491011. Information and advice.
Irish Wheelchair Association Blackheath Drive, Clontarf, Dublin 3 ☏01/833 8241, ⓕ833 3873. Information and advice.
Holiday Care Service 2nd floor, Imperial Building, Victoria Rd, Horley, Surrey RH6 7PZ ☏01293/774535, ⓕ784647, Minicom ☏01293/776943. Provides free lists of accessible accommodation and information on financial help for holidays.
RADAR (Royal Association for Disability and Rehabilitation) 12 City Forum, 250 City Rd, London EC1V 8AF ☏020/7250 3222, Minicom ☏020/7250 4119). A good source of advice; its guide on European holidays will tell you everything you need to know.
Tripscope The Courtyard, Evelyn Rd, London W4 5JL ☏ 020/8580 7021, ⓕ8994 3618. This registered charity provides a national telephone information service offering free advice on UK and international transport for those with a mobility problem.

USA and Canada

Jewish Rehabilitation Hospital 3205 Place Alton Goldbloom, Chomedy Laval, Quebec H7V 1RT ☏514/688-9550, ext 226. Guidebooks and travel information.
Mobility International USA 451 Broadway, Eugene, OR 97401 (Voice & TDD: ☏541/343-1284; ⓦwww.miusa.org). Information and referral services, access guides, tours and exchange programmes. Annual membership US$35 (includes quarterly newsletter).
Society for the Advancement of Travel

for the Handicapped (SATH) 347 Fifth Ave, Suite 610, New York, NY 10016 ☏212/447-7284, ⓦwww.sath.org. Non-profit travel-industry referral service that passes queries on to its members as appropriate.
Travel Information Service ☏215/456-9600. Telephone information and referral service.
Twin Peaks Press Box 129, Vancouver, WA 98661 ☏360/694-2462 or 1-800/637-2256. Publisher of the *Directory of Travel Agencies for the Disabled*, listing more than 370 agencies worldwide; *Travel for the Disabled*; the *Directory of Accessible*

Van Rentals; and *Wheelchair Vagabond*, loaded with personal tips.

Poland

Catholic Association of the Disabled Grojecka 118, PL-02-367 Warsaw ☏022/22 8026.
Polish Society for Rehabilitation of the Disabled ul. Oleandrow 4m 10, 00629 Warsaw ☏022/25 9839, ⓕ25 7050. Open 8am–4pm. No English spoken. Go through the archway at no. 4 and it's on the right with the sign "Polskie Towarzystwo Walki z Kalectwem".

Costs, money and banks

Despite the gradual rise in prices that has accompanied the transition to a market economy, travel in Poland is still relatively cheap. Many of the essentials, such as food and drink, public transport and entrance fees, remain well below their western equivalents. Accommodation is priced on a different scale, but is still inexpensive as a rule. Note that prices are often much higher in Warsaw than in the rest of the country, and are similarly increased in places which see a lot of foreign visitors, such as Kraków, Gdańsk and Poznań.

Average costs

The reforms pursued by successive post-1989 governments continue to place economic pressure on ordinary Poles. However, for Western visitors, prices for most goods remain low. You can **eat and drink** well for £10/US$14 or less even at some of the country's best restaurants, though it's becoming increasingly easy to spend £15/US$21 or more for a meal, especially if you want to move beyond home cuisine. In a more basic restaurant, a meal can be had for not much more than £4/US$5.60, and substantial hot meals are available at milk and snack bars for even less than this – £1.50/US$2.20 will often buy a main course. Coffee or tea with cakes in a café costs a similarly nominal amount.

Prices for **public transport** are little more than pocket money – even travelling across half the length of the country by train or bus

only costs around £15/US$21. Similarly, you never have to fork out much more than £2/US$2.80 to visit even the most popular **tourist sights**, with half that the normal asking price.

Only if you go for expensive **accommodation** will your costs start to rise. Here at least there's plenty of opportunity to spend money, with international hotels in the main cities charging up to £180/US$250 per night. On the other hand, if you stick to campsites, youth and tourist hostels, you'll seldom spend much more than £5/US$7 on a bed. Budget on about twice as much for a room in a private house or in the cheapest hotels.

Currency

The Polish unit of currency is the **złoty** (abbreviated as zł). As a result of a major currency reform initiated in January 1995, a "new" złoty was introduced, and the old currency phased out. The new złoty comes in notes of 10zł, 20zł, 50zł, 100zł and 200zł; and coins in 1, 2 and 5zł denominations, subdivided into groszy (10, 20 and 50). The old złoty is no longer legal tender, so don't accept any bills with "proletariat" written on. Currently the **exchange rate** is around 5.6zł to the pound sterling and 4zł to the US dollar, and looks set to remain reasonably stable – minor fluctuations aside.

Travellers' cheques, credit cards and exchange

Although **travellers' cheques** are the safest way of carrying your money, they're also the least convenient way of getting local currency, with only main banks, Orbis offices and hotels accepting them. They are not accepted by the "kantors" or exchange offices that you see dotted about everywhere. American Express, who now have offices in Warsaw, are a useful alternative and will cash most brands of travellers' cheques, in addition to their own. The number of places providing a travellers' cheque exchange service is actually decreasing, not least with the explosion of ATMs, and transactions can often be a lengthy process. This is not a particular problem in major cities and tourist areas, but cashiers in provincial towns are often so unfamiliar with the procedure that you can be kept waiting for hours. If you're travelling in such areas, you really do need a supply of cash as a backup. Hotels usually charge a hefty commission of five percent, banks around one percent, while American Express will cash cheques free of charge (into local currency only).

Credit and **charge cards** are well established. Access/Mastercard, American Express, Diners Club, Eurocard, JCB and Visa are accepted by an increasing number of travel agents, hotels, restaurants and shops. You can also arrange a cash advance on most of these cards in big banks.

After a slow beginning, **ATMs** are now appearing all over Poland. In any reasonably sized town you'll find them dotted around the main squares, in hotels, outside banks or even inside *McDonald's*. It is now perfectly viable to arrive in the country with a plastic card and a PIN number and pull out złotys wherever you go.

Exchange

Poland's appetite for foreign currency is reflected in the ease with which it's possible to change cash.

The worst exchange rates are offered by the **banks** (usually Mon–Fri 7.30am–5pm, Sat 7.30am–2pm), who also deduct a flat-rate commission of around 3zł per transaction. Surprisingly, the little **kantors** (private banks) you see all around you offer the best rates and unlike those in the neighbouring Czech Republic, where they extract a ludicrously high commission from unsuspecting tourists, the Polish kantors charge no commission at all. They will also change all major currencies and quite a few minor ones (like Czech, Slovak and Hungarian notes). In the big cities there are a number open 24 hours a day. It's wise to avoid changing money in **hotels**; they tend to offer poor rates and charge hefty commissions.

The effective legalization of the **black-market** rate means that illicit currency transactions are definitely no longer worth the risk; the likelihood is that you'll be given counterfeit notes or swindled in some other way.

Information, websites and maps

Poland has a National Tourist Office with branches in a number of European countries and the US (see below for addresses). Within the country, however, tourist information centres of the west European kind are a relatively new phenomenon, and the level of help you will get from them remains unpredictable. Often you'll have to resort to other sources of information – commercial travel agencies or the reception staff at your hotel – in order to get a full picture of what tourist sights and facilities are on offer.

Most towns and cities now have a **tourist information centre** (known as *informator turystyczny* or IT). Sometimes these are run by the local municipality and are rather effective, offering full hotel listings, accommodation bookings, and a range of brochures and maps – which are usually for sale rather than given away free. More often than not however, IT offices are privately run travel agencies that are using the IT label to attract tourists, in order to sell them tours and travel tickets. Some of these privately run IT offices do an admirable job in finding you a bed for the night and answering your queries; others show a distinct lack of commitment to their information-giving task. In some cases, places displaying the IT logo actually gave up their tourist information responsibilities years ago, thereby adding to the frustrations of the stray tourist. Bear in mind that many provincial towns – especially those that see few tourists – have yet to establish an IT office of any kind.

National Tourist Offices

Australia Eastern European Travel Bureau Level 5, 75 King St, Sydney ☎02/9262 1144, ℻9262 4479.
UK Remo House, 1st floor, 310–312 Regent St, London W1N 5AJ ☎020/7580 8811, ℻7580 8866, ℮pnto@dial.pipex.com.
US 275 Madison Ave, Suite 1711, New York, NY 10016 ☎212/338-9412, ℻338-9283, ⓦwww.polandtour.org.

Orbis

Before 1990 all incoming travel to Poland was controlled by **Orbis**, usually known out-side the country as Polorbis. Founded in the 1920s, it was turned by the communists into a vast organization with an unusually wide range of functions, including the dispensation of tourist information. Privatized in the 1990s, Orbis has now transformed itself into a high-street travel agency that is more concerned with selling package holidays to Poles than doling out information to new arrivals. Orbis offices can still be useful, however: they sell air, rail, bus and ferry tickets, change money, arrange guided tours, car rental and special interest activities, and make hotel reservations – especially in the hotels belonging to the Orbis chain (see "Accommodation", p.39).

Abroad, the **Polorbis** branch of the company acts both as an agent for holidays in Poland and as a quasi-official tourist office (see p.22 for addresses), though in countries where National Tourist Offices exist, it has largely lost this function. Even if you're intending to visit Poland under your own steam, it's well worth writing or going along to one of their offices to pick up free promotional material in English.

PTTK and Almatur

PTTK – which translates literally as "The Polish Country Lovers' Association" – has a rather more direct responsibility for internal Polish tourism than Orbis, maintaining hiking routes and administering mountain huts, hostels and hotels. PTTK offices can be found throughout the country, providing bookings in PTTK-run accommodation and selling hiking maps. Despite signs of change, however, PTTK remains a remarkably old-fashioned organization. With a few exceptions, its offices are dingy, underfunded affairs whose resolutely monolingual staff feign bemused indifference to queries launched at them by foreigners. Its main office is at ul. Litewska 11/13, Warsaw (☎022/629 3947, ⓦwww.pttk.com.pl).

Almatur is a student and youth travel bureau which sells ISIC cards, books discounted travel tickets for the under-26s, and arranges accommodation in student hostels during July and August. The latter are open to anyone, although priority goes to students and teachers. Almatur's head office is at ul. Kopernika 15, Warsaw (☎022/826 5381, ⓦwww.almatur.pl); other addresses can be found in the Guide under the appropriate section.

The Polish emigracja

Over the last two centuries Poland's economic problems and turbulent political history have produced one of Europe's largest streams of emigrants, known in Polish as the **emigracja**.

Today's worldwide *emigracja* population is estimated as around fifteen million, encompassing both actual Polish citizens and people of Polish origin. Of these, by far the largest group are **Polish-Americans**, thought to number anywhere from seven to ten million, with a particularly strong base in Chicago, still said to have the largest Polish population in the world after Warsaw. Publicly the community's most prominent representative is the **Polish American Congress**, a thriving national organization that has lobbied the US Congress to some effect on issues such as support for Solidarity and according Polish membership of NATO.

In Europe, the largest populations are in Germany and France (around one million each). Despite its smaller size, the Polish community in **Britain** (around 200,000), the majority of whom originally came during World War II as refugees or with the Polish armed forces, held a symbolically significant position as the home of the Polish Government-in-Exile which moved to London in 1939.

Since the dawn of the post-communist era in 1989, growing numbers of original emigrants, as well as second and third generation descendants, are now returning to Poland, most to visit relatives or as "roots" tourists. All the major English-speaking countries have cultural and other **Polish organizations** which are worth contacting if you have Polish heritage and are interested in specialist tours or courses in Poland – contacting the Polish embassy in your home country should yield a healthy list of local Polish contacts. Otherwise the internet is a valuable research tool: Polonia, the organization which looks after the interests of expatriate Poles worldwide, has a useful website (ⓦwww.polonia.org) with numerous links to affiliated organizations. Some of the more active groups around the globe include the Polish Cultural Insitute in the UK (ⓦwww.polishculture.org.uk); the Polish Community in Ottawa (ⓦwww.polonianet .com); the Polish Cultural Institute in New York (ⓦwww.polishculture-nyc.org); and the Polish Community of Australia (ⓦwww .polonica.org.au).

Jewish tourism

Jews and **Jewish heritage** loom large in the history of Poland. Prior to the outbreak of World War II, Jews comprised roughly ten percent (three million) of the country's population, the largest Jewish community in Europe and the second largest in the world at the time. Of a current world population of fifteen million Jews, more than half are reckoned to have historical connections to Polish Jewry.

Up until the mid-1980s, **Jewish tourism** in Poland was a small-scale affair. Historically rooted fears of (and the real existence of) anti-Semitism, combined with generalized Western apprehension over travel to the communist East, limited the numbers prepared to make the trip to the land of their own or their ancestors' birth. The re-establishment of diplomatic relations with Israel in 1987 and the ending of the communist era in 1989 altered the situation radically. Into the 1990s **organized tour groups**, principally (though by no means exclusively) from Israel and the USA, have become an established feature in many parts of the country, particularly cities such as Warsaw, Kraków and Lublin which had the largest pre-Holocaust Jewish populations and which constituted the traditional focal points of Polish-Jewish life and culture.

Many Jewish groups come with their own prearranged schedules and guides, normally focusing on surviving Jewish monuments alongside Holocaust memorials such as Auschwitz-Birkenau and the other concentration camps. Every effort has been made in the Guide to cover sites of interest to Jews. If you find yourself hunting around the back streets of a town in search of Jewish buildings and monuments – a common experience in the further flung reaches of the country – the basic words and phrases to know when asking for directions are *bożnica* or *synagoga* (synagogue) and *cmentarz żydowski* (Jewish cemetery). However, you can't bank on everyone knowing where to find what you're looking for: generally speaking, the older the person the more likely they are to be able to point you in the right direction. Although the Guide will help you locate many Jewish sites and buildings, bear in mind that, for example, many former synagogues are now used for something totally different, and all too often, don't have any signs indicating their original use. Many of the Polish-Jewish organizations (see below) can be extremely helpful in providing further information and contacts. For more on Jewish heritage, see the "Books" section of Contexts.

Polish/Jewish organizations

Jewish Communities Federation (Związek Religijny Wyznania Mojzeszowego), ul. Twarda 6, Warsaw ✆022/620 4324, ⓦwww.jewish.org.pl. Headquarters of religious congregations throughout Poland.

Jewish Cultural Centre, ul. Meiselsa 17, Kraków ✆012/423 5595, ⓕ423 5034. Ambitious new cultural centre in the heart of the Kazimierz district, with a library, reading room, gallery, café and bookshop.

Jewish Historical Institute, ul. Tlomackie 3/5, Warsaw ✆022/827 9225. Archives, exhibitions, library and irregularly open bookshop.

Our Roots, ul. Twarda 6, Warsaw ✆ & ⓕ022/620 0556. Jewish travel agency that provides general information and local guides, produces guide books and helps with tracing family ancestry in Poland.

Ronald Lauder Foundation, ul. Twarda 6, Warsaw ✆022/620 0793, ⓦwww.lauder.pl. US-based foundation supporting Jewish cultural and religious initiatives within Poland.

Useful web sites

ⓦ**www.gopoland.com** General travel

guide and resource for Poland. Also train schedules, internet café locations, hotel discounts.

ⓦ**www.hotelspoland.com** Plenty of good discounts on selected hotels all over the country. Also cut-price air fares from the USA.

ⓦ**www.insidepoland.pl** Good general site covering plenty of historical and cultural subjects.

ⓦ**www.inyourpocket.com** Independent online travel guides to Warsaw, Wrocław, Kraków, Poznań and Gdańsk, as well as a host of other central and eastern European cities.

ⓦ**www.krakow.pl** Official Kraków city home page. Lots of useful tips and city information.

ⓦ**www.masterpage.com.pl** Popular site aimed at the foreign business community, with daily English summaries of leading stories from selected Polish newspapers, along with links to their own sites.

ⓦ**www.orbis.pl** Orbis home page. Detailed current information for all its hotels.

ⓦ**www.pkp.com.pl** National railways (PKP) site with all the major train schedules from Warsaw. Also general rail information covering the whole country.

ⓦ**www.poland.net** Compendious source of information on culture and tourism.

ⓦ**www.polandtour.org** Good National Tourist Office site, maintained by the New York office. Also contact details for NTO offices around the world.

ⓦ**www.polhotels.com** Another site specializing in discount hotel bookings only available via the internet. Prices are similar to the above site, although this one usually has a wider selection of places and towns.

ⓦ**www.polishworld.com** Useful all-round resource: discount hotel bookings, travel information, arts and entertainment, politics, news and media, plus plenty of links to other Poland-related sites.

ⓦ**www.visit.pl** General travel information, and a hotel booking service.

ⓦ**www.warsawtour.pl** Official Warsaw tourist information site. Plenty of useful practical information, city listings and public services.

ⓦ**www.warsawvoice.com.pl** Warsaw's leading English-language magazine online, with business and cultural information.

@ **www.zem.co.uk** British-based site boasting tons of Polish links, covering all aspects of society and culture, often covered in lively style.

Maps

There are now excellent maps covering all parts of Poland – just scan the appropriate shelves in any Empik bookshop. Best of the **road maps** available outside the country are Freytag & Berndt's 1:750 000 map; and the 1:800 000 Geo Centre Euro map. Geo Centre Euro also produce a useful set of 1:300 000 regional maps, covering north-east, northwest, southeast and southwest Poland respectively.

More easily available once you're inside the country are the maps produced by PPWK, the state map company. They produce an extremely good **Atlas Samochodowa** (1:300 000), published in book form and divided into regions, with supplementary schematic town plans; it's also available as a series of sixteen individual regional maps.

Should you need more detailed **city maps**, tourist offices, kiosks, street sellers, bookshops and Empik stores all seem to sell the distinctive, red-jacketed PPWK series *Plan Miasta* (City Plan). These list all streets in A–Z format, and give exhaustive listings on bus and tram routes, places of entertainment, restaurants and cafés, often in several languages, including English. Useful words to look out for are *ulica*, often abbreviated to ul. (street); *aleja* or al. (avenue); *plac* or pl. (square) and *rynek* (old town square). Bus routes are generally shown in blue, tram lines in red.

Even more essential, if you intend doing any serious walking, are the **hiking maps** of the National Parks and other tourist areas. Known as *Mapa Turystyczna*, and displaying a blue cover, these cost only a nominal amount and are very clear and simple to use: although the texts are usually only in Polish, the keys to the symbols are in several languages, including English.

Finally for **campers**, there's the *Camping in Poland* (*Camping w Polsce*) map of the whole country, available in many tourist offices and bookshops, though the *Atlas Samochodowa* (see above) will provide all the information you need.

Map and guide outlets

In Australia and New Zealand

Mapland 372 Little Bourke St, Melbourne ☎03/9670 4383, @www.mapland.com.au.
Mapworld 173 Gloucester St, Christchurch ☎03/374 5399, ℻03/374 5633, @www.mapworld.co.nz.
Perth Map Centre 1/884 Hay St, Perth ☎08/9322 5733, @www.perthmap.com.au.
Specialty Maps 46 Albert St, Auckland ☎09/307 2217, @www.ubd-online.co.nz/maps.
The Map Shop 6 Peel St, Adelaide ☎08/8231 2033, @www.mapshop.net.au.
Travel Bookshop Shop 3, 175 Liverpool St, Sydney NSW 2000 ☎02/9261 8200.
Worldwide Maps and Guides 187 George St, Brisbane ☎07/3221 4330, @info@worldwidemaps.com.au; 12 Capalaba Road, Upper Mount Gravatt, Brisbane ☎07/3349 6633.

In the UK and Ireland

Blackwell's Map and Travel Shop 53 Broad St, Oxford OX1 3BQ ☎01865/792792, @www.bookshop.blackwell.co.uk.
Easons Bookshop 40 O'Connell St, Dublin 1 ☎01/873 3811, @www.eason.ie.
Heffers Map and Travel 20 Trinity St, Cambridge, CB2 1TJ ☎01223/568 568, @www.heffers.co.uk.
Hodges Figgis Bookshop 56–58 Dawson St, Dublin 2 ☎01/677 4754, @www.hodgesfiggis.com.
John Smith and Sons 26 Colquhoun Ave, Glasgow, G52 4PJ ☎0141/552 3377, @www.johnsmith.co.uk.
James Thin Melven's Bookshop 29 Union St, Inverness, IV1 1QA ☎01463/233500, @www.jthin.co.uk.
The Map Shop 30a Belvoir St, Leicester, LE1 6QH ☎0116/2471400.
National Map Centre 22–24 Caxton St, SW1H 0QU ☎020/7222 2466, @www.mapsnmc.co.uk.
Newcastle Map Centre 55 Grey St, Newcastle upon Tyne, NE1 6EF ☎0191/261 5622, @www.traveller.ltd.uk.
Ordnance Survey Service Phoenix Park, Dublin 8 ☎01/820 6100, @www.irlgov.ie/osi/.
Ordnance Survey of Northern Ireland

Colby House, Stranmillis Ct, Belfast BT9 5BJ ☎028/9066 1244, ⊛www.osni.gov.uk.

Stanfords 12–14 Long Acre, WC2E 9LP ☎020/7836 1321, ⊛www.stanfords.co.uk; maps by mail or phone order are available on this number and via ☎esales@stanfords.co.uk. Other branches within British Airways offices at 156 Regent St, W1R 5TA ☎020/7434 4744, and 29 Corn St, Bristol BS1 1HT ☎0117/929 9966.

The Travel Bookshop 13–15 Blenheim Crescent, W11 2EE ☎020/7229 5260, ⊛www.thetravelbookshop.co.uk.

USA and Canada

Adventurous Traveler Bookstore PO Box 64769, Burlington, VT 05406 ☎1-800/282-3963, ⊛www.AdventurousTraveler.com.

Book Passage 51 Tamal Vista Blvd, Corte Madera, CA 94925 ☎415/927-0960, ⊛www.bookpassage.com.

Elliot Bay Book Company 101 S Main St, Seattle, WA 98104 ☎206/624-6600 or 1-800/962-5311, ⊛www.elliotbaybook.com.

Forsyth Travel Library 226 Westchester Ave, White Plains, NY 10604 ☎1-800/367-7984, ⊛www.forsyth.com.

Globe Corner Bookstore 28 Church St, Cambridge, MA 02138 ☎1-800/358-6013, ⊛www.globercorner.com.

GORP Adventure Library Online only ☎1-800/754-8229, ⊛www2.gorp.com.

Map Link Inc., 30 S La Patera Lane, Unit 5, Santa Barbara, CA 93117 ☎805/692-6777, ⊛www.2.gorp.com.

Map Link Inc 30 S La Patera Lane, Unit 5, Santa Barbara, CA 93117 ☎805/692-6777, ⊛www.maplink.com.

Phileas Fogg's Travel Center #87 Stanford Shopping Center, Palo Alto, CA 94304 ☎1-800/533-3644, ⊛www.foggs.com.

Rand McNally 444 N Michigan Ave, Chicago, IL 60611 ☎312/321-1751, ⊛www.randmcnally.com; 150 E 52nd St, New York, NY 10022 ☎212/758-7488; 595 Market St, San Francisco, CA 94105 ☎415/777-3131; around thirty stores across the US – call ☎1-800/333-0136, ext 2111, or check the website for the nearest store.

Travel Books & Language Center 4437 Wisconsin Ave, Washington, DC 20016 ☎1-800/220-2665, ✉travelbks@aol.com.

The Travel Bug Bookstore 2667 West Broadway, Vancouver V6K 2G2 ☎604/737-1122, ⊛www.swifty.com/tbug.

World of Maps 118 Holland Ave, Ottawa, Ontario K1Y 0X6 ☎613/724-6776, ⊛www.worldofmaps.com.

World Wide Books and Maps 1247 Granville St, Vancouver V6Z 1G3 ☎604/687-3320.

Getting around

Poland has comprehensive and cheap public transport services, though they can often be overcrowded and excruciatingly slow. As a general rule, trains are the best means of moving across the country, as all but the most rural areas are still crisscrossed by passenger lines. Buses come into their own in the remoter regions of the country, where you'll find that even the smallest of villages are served by at least one bus a day. For information on the major train and bus connections, consult the "Travel Details" section at the end of each chapter. Car rental prices are fairly reasonable, and taxis are cheap enough to be considered for the occasional inter-town journey, especially if you can split costs three or four ways (but make sure you use reliable operators – see the advice on p.36).

Trains

Polish State Railways (PKP) is a reasonably efficient organization, though its services, particularly on rural routes, have been heavily cut since the fall of communism and continue to be reduced at frequent intervals. PKP runs three main types of train (*pociąg*):

Intercity or **express** services (*ekspresowy*) are the ones to go for if you're travelling long distances, as they stop at the main cities only. Once slow by western European standards, they are getting faster, with journey times between Warsaw and Kraków a very respectable 2.5 to 3 hours. Seat reservations, involving a small supplementary charge, are compulsory; if you haven't understood the reservations system the ticket inspector can sell you one, albeit at a supplement of around £2/US$3. Expresses are marked in red on timetables, with an R in a box alongside. **Fast** trains (*pospieszny*), again marked in red, have far more stops than express trains, and reservations are optional. The **normal** services (*normalny* or *osobowy*) are shown in black and should be avoided whenever possible: in rural areas they stop at every haystack, while even on inter-urban routes it usually takes about an hour to cover 20km. In effect you go at the speed of a healthy cyclist.

Fares won't burn a hole in the pocket of even the most impoverished Westerner. Even a long cross-country haul such as Warsaw to Wrocław, Kraków or Gdańsk will set you back little more than £10/US$14. At these prices, it's well worth paying the fifty percent extra to travel first-class (*pierwsza klasa*) or make a reservation (*miejscówka*) even when this is not compulsory, as sardine-like conditions are fairly common. **Reservations** can be made up to sixty days in advance, or ninety days for return trips.

Most long intercity journeys are best done overnight; they're often conveniently timed so that you leave around 10 or 11pm and arrive between 6 and 9am. For these, it's advisable to book either a **sleeper** (*sypialny*) or **couchette** (*kaszet*) at the station counter marked with the logo of a bed, at "Polres" offices at main junctions or at Orbis offices; the total cost will probably be little more than a room in a cheap hotel. Sleepers cost about 90zł (£15/US$21) per head, in a three-bunk compartment (though it's rare that all three beds are used), complete with wash-basin, towels, sheets, blankets and a snack. At about 60zł (£10/US$14), couchettes have six bunks and also come with sheets, a blanket and a pillow. Midweek, an alternative is to buy a regular first-class ticket, as there's a good chance of the compartment being empty, allowing you to sleep on the seats. Finally, a reminder about **theft** on trains: overnight sleepers on the principal lines are prime targets for robberies. One major hazard to watch out for is night-time stops at Warsaw's Central station en route to elsewhere – thieves regularly hop on, steal what they can, and hop off again. The best advice is to keep your compartment locked and your valuables well hidden at all times.

Tickets and passes

Though not the problem it once was, buying **tickets** in the main city train stations (such as Warsaw and Poznań) can be a hassle, due to the bewildering array of counters, each almost invariably with a long snaking queue. Make sure you join the line at least 45 minutes before your train is due to leave, though usually the absolute maximum you'll have to wait is half an hour.

Tickets come in all shapes and sizes, but you won't need to think too much about them unless you have an **undated ticket**, which you must validate in a machine on the platform before departure. These are normally for journeys of 100km or less, and you can often save queuing time if you look to check that there is a special counter for these short journeys or an automatic ticket machine. If you're booking a sleeper or couchette, major stations have special counters (look for the bed logo). Since most officials don't speak any English, a good way to get the precise ticket you want is to write all the details down and show them at the counter; include destination, time of departure, class (first is *pierwsza*, second is *druga*) and whether you want a seat reservation (*miejscówka*). A nonsmoking compartment is a *wagon dla niepalących* – and if you want to smoke just write it out without the *nie*.

As an alternative to the station queues, you can buy tickets for journeys of over 100km at **Orbis** offices. The main branches of these are also a good way of booking for international journeys.

Discounted tickets (*ulgowy*) are available for pensioners and for children aged between four and ten years; those under four travel free, though they're not supposed to occupy a seat. For students, ISIC cards no longer entitle you to discounted travel within Poland – no great hardship as travel is so cheap anyway.

North Americans and Britons are eligible for the **Polrail Pass**, available from Polorbis before leaving home (see pp.12 & 18). This covers any period from eight days up to a month and gives free travel on the entire rail network, although you'd have to take an awful lot of trains to justify the outlay. An eight-day pass starts at £43/US$60 for second-class, or £64/US$90 for first-class travel, rising to £64/US$90 or £86/US$120 for fifteen days. **InterRail** passes are valid in Poland, but not Eurail.

Station practicalities

In train stations, the **departures** are normally listed on yellow posters marked *odjazdy*, with **arrivals** on white posters headed *przyjazdy*. "Ex" indicates express trains, fast trains are marked in red and normal services in black. An "R" in a square means that seat reservations are obligatory. Additionally, there may be figures at the bottom indicating the dates between which a particular train does (*kursuje*) or doesn't run (*nie kursuje*) – the latter usually underlined by a warning wiggly line. Platform (*peron*) is also indicated.

Information counters, if they exist, are usually plagued by long queues and non-English-speaking staff. If you're intending to do a lot of travelling in Poland, it makes sense to invest in the six-monthly **network timetable** (*rozkład jazdy*), which can, in theory, be bought at all main stations, although it usually sells out soon after publication.

Each **platform** has two tracks, so take care that you board the right train; usually only the long-distance services have boards stating their route, so you'll need to ask. However, electronic departure boards are increasingly common in cities, whilst small towns will only have one or two platforms, so you shouldn't really go too far wrong.

The **main station** in a city is identified by the name Główny or Centralna. These are open round the clock and usually have such **facilities** as waiting rooms, toilets, kiosks, restaurants, snack bars, cafés, a left-luggage office (*przechowalnia bagażu*) – or, in the largest cities, lockers – and a 24-hour post office.

Facilities on the trains are much poorer, though all intercity trains, and occasionally others, have a buffet car (check on the departure board) and light refreshments are available on all overnight journeys. **Ticket control** is rather haphazard, particularly on crowded services, but it does happen more often than not. If you've boarded a train without the proper ticket, you should seek out the conductor, who will issue the right one on payment of a small supplement.

Buses

The extent to which you'll need to make use of the services of PKS, the Polish national bus company, depends very much on the nature of your trip. If you're concentrating on journeys between major cities, then the trains are faster and more numerous. As soon as you start visiting provincial towns and villages however, buses are likely to be your best bet.

The **PKS** network is extraordinarily comprehensive, and buses provide an excellent means of getting around in those areas not well served by rail; especially in the mountains, along the coast, and in the Mazurian lake district. The main disadvantages of bus travel are the slow speed (in some rural areas, buses rarely exceed an average of 30km per hour) and the discomfort – buses are likely to be crammed with local schoolchildren on weekdays. Many of the older vehicles feature broken seats and bad ventilation – avoid the temptation to sit at the back; the fumes rising from the engine will have you retching within minutes.

Private bus companies like **Polski Express** (Ⓦ www.polskiexpress.pl) and **Komfort Bus** (Ⓦ www.komfortbus.pl) run fast and cheap intercity services, although these only operate on radial routes linking Warsaw with the major provincial capitals.

Tickets

In towns and cities, the **main bus station** (*dworzec autobusowy*) is usually alongside the train station. **Tickets** can be bought in the terminal building; in larger places there are several counters, each dealing with clearly displayed destinations. In a few places the terminal is shared with the train station, so make sure you go to the right counter. **Booking** in the departure terminal ensures a seat, as a number will be allocated to you on your ticket. However, the lack of computerized systems means that many stations cannot allocate seats for services starting out from another town. In such cases, you have to wait until the bus arrives and buy a ticket – which may be for standing room only – from the driver.

The same procedure can also be followed, provided the bus isn't already full to overflowing, if you arrive too late to buy a ticket at the counter. With a few exceptions, it isn't possible to buy tickets for return journeys on board. Note too that a few routes are now run by private companies; these generally leave from outside the bus station. Private travel agents like **Orbis** often sell tickets for these privately run intercity services, as well as booking seats on international routes. There are no student discounts on buses.

Timetables

Noticeboards show **departures** and **arrivals** not only in the bus stations, but on all official stopping places along the route. "Fast" buses (which carry a small supplement) are marked in red, slow in black. The towns served are listed in alphabetical order, with the relevant times set against each, and mention made of the principal places passed on the way. As at the train stations, departures are on yellow boards, arrivals on white, so make sure you're looking at the right one. If in doubt, ask at the information counter, which may – if you're lucky – be equipped with the multi-volume set of timetables listing all PKS routes. It's very rare to find an English speaker in the average Polish bus station, so it's best to write your destination down to avoid any confusion.

City transport

Trams are the basis of the public transport system in nearly all Polish cities. They usually run from about 5am to 11pm, and departure times are clearly posted at the stops. **Tickets** can be bought from a Ruch kiosk (just ask at any kiosk selling newspapers). They can only be used in the city where they were bought. On boarding, you should immediately cancel your ticket in one of the machines; checks by inspectors are rare, but they do happen from time to time. Note that some tickets have to be **cancelled** at both ends (arrows will indicate if this is so): this is for the benefit of children and pensioners, who travel half-price and thus have to cancel only one end per journey. In some cities (like Gdańsk) you pay for the time you spend on the tram, and have to keep cancelling tickets (if you're making a long journey) as if feeding a meter. In other cities (like Warsaw) you pay a flat fare for each single journey – and if you transfer from one tram to another you'll need a second ticket.

Tram tickets are valid on **municipal buses**, and the same system for validating them applies. The routes of the municipal buses go beyond the city boundaries into the outlying countryside, so many nearby villages have several connections during peak times of the day. Note that on both buses and trams, **night services** require two or three tickets.

The price of **taxis** is cheap enough to make them a viable proposition for regular use during your visit. In the new free-market economy, plenty of people have turned to taxi driving, and outside hotels, stations and major tourist attractions you often have to run the gauntlet of cabbies. Make sure you choose a taxi with an illuminated sign on its roof bearing the company name and phone number.

If you pick up a taxi in the street, you're more likely to pay above-average prices; the safest and cheapest option is to ring a quoted taxi number and order one. Generally speaking, you should pay 15–25zł for a cross-city journey, depending on your time of travel (prices are fifty percent higher after 11pm). Prices are also raised by fifty percent for journeys outside the city limits. However, costs are always negotiable for longer journeys, between towns, for example, and can work out very reasonable if split among a group. For more advice on travelling by taxi, see the Warsaw account (p.84).

Flights

The domestic network of **LOT**, the Polish national airline, operates regular flights from Warsaw to Gdańsk, Katowice, Kraków, Poznań, Rzeszów, Szczecin and Wrocław – all of which take about an hour. Some routes are covered several times a day, but services are reduced during the winter months (end Oct to mid-April). Most of the cities mentioned are also linked directly to some of the others, but Warsaw is very much the lynchpin of the system. As a general rule, **airports** are located just outside the cities, and can be reached either by a special LOT bus or by a municipal service.

Tickets can be purchased at the airport itself or from LOT and Orbis offices, where you can also pick up free timetables (ask for *rozkład lotów*). Prices are currently in the region of £110/US$150 one-way (there are no savings on returns), though advance booking and occasional promotional offers can reduce the cost substantially. Children up to the age of two travel for free, provided they do not occupy a separate seat; under-12s go for half-price. Private competitors also operate on some routes.

Boats

In summer, ferries and hydrofoils serve towns along the **Baltic coast**, notably around Szczecin and the Gdańsk area where they connect Gdańsk, Sopot and Gdynia with each other and with the Hel Peninsula. For further information contact the Polish Baltic Shipping Service at ul. Przemysłowa 1 (☎058/343 1887, ◍www .polferries.com.pl). For **international services** contact Polish Baltic Shipping Service (see above) or Stena Line, ul. Kwiatkowskiego 60, Gdynia (☎058/665 14 14, ☎◍www.stenaline.pl).

Inland, excursion boats also run along certain stretches of the country's extensive system of **canals** – most enjoyably from Augustów near Białystok and along the ingeniously constructed Elbląg Canal – and short sections of the main **rivers**, such as the Wisła. Additionally, a curious and somewhat antiquated system of chain-haul car/passenger ferries serves the upper reaches of the Wisła.

Driving

Although access to a **car** will save you a lot of time in exploring the country, **traffic** is heavy on Poland's main roads. There's a dearth of multi-lane highways on the trunk routes, ensuring that you'll spend much of your time trailing behind a stream of slow-moving cars and lorries. Poland's rural back-

roads are quiet and hassle-free by comparison, and – providing you have a decent map – present the perfect terrain for unhurried touring.

If you're **bringing your own car**, you'll need to carry your vehicle's registration document. If the car is not in your name, you must have a letter of permission signed by the owner and authorized by your national motoring organization. You'll also need your **driving licence** (international driving licences aren't officially required, though they can be a help in tricky situations), and an **international insurance green card** to extend your insurance cover – check with your insurers to see whether you're covered or not. You're also required to carry a red warning triangle, a first-aid kit, a set of replacement bulbs and display a national identification sticker. Note that rear-wheel mud flaps are obligatory in Poland.

Car rental

Car rental in Poland works out at about £70/US$100 a day and £360/US$500 a week for a Fiat Punto with unlimited mileage – though note that prices are often quoted and calculated in Deutschmarks. A Ford Escort will cost fifteen percent more, a Nissan Primera fifteen percent more again. Cars can be booked through the usual agents in the West (see opposite) or in Poland itself: all the four major operators now have their own agents in all or most of the big Polish cities. Alternatively you can rent through the main Orbis offices in large cities (see the Guide for addresses). **Payment** can be made with cash or any major credit card, and you can drop a car at a different office from the one where you rented it.

Cars will only be rented to people over 21 (or for some types of vehicle, over 25) who have held a full **licence** for more than a year. If you're planning on renting a car outside Poland and bringing it into the country you should be aware that rising levels of **car theft** (see p.38) have led several of the major rental companies to slap severe restrictions on taking their cars east.

Check the conditions carefully before renting anything – if you do take a rental car into Poland without permission it means you effectively accept the financial risk for the car's full value if it's damaged in an accident or stolen. Of the major companies, Hertz currently seems to operate the least restrictive policies, but since they (like the other majors) have agents in Poland, you're better off renting inside the country.

Car rental agencies

Australia
Avis ☏13 6333, ⓦwww.avis.com
Budget, ☏1300/362 848,
ⓦwww.budget.com
Dollar ☏02/9223 1444 or 1800/358 008,
ⓦwww.dollarcar.com.au
Hertz ☏1800/550 067, ⓦwww.hertz.com

Ireland
Avis Northern Ireland ☏028/9442 3333,
Republic of Ireland ☏01/605 7555,
ⓦwww.avis.co.uk.
Budget Northern Ireland ☏028/9442,
Republic of Ireland ☏01/878 7814,
ⓦwww.budgetcarrental.ie or
ⓦwww.budget-ireland.co.uk.
Europcar Northern Ireland ☏028/9442 3444, Republic of Ireland ☏01/614 2800,
ⓦwww.europcar.ie.
Hertz Northern Ireland ☏028/9442 2533,
Republic of Ireland 0903/27711,
ⓦwww.hertz.co.uk.
Holiday Autos ☏01/872 9366,
ⓦwww.holidayautos.ie.

New Zealand
Avis ☏09/526 5231 or 0800 655 111,
ⓦwww.avis.com.
Budget, ☏0800/ 652 227 or 09/375 2270,
ⓦwww.budget.com
Hertz ☏09/309 0989 or 0800 655 955,
ⓦwww.hertz.com

UK
Avis ☏0870/606 0100,
ⓦwww.avisworld.com.
Budget ☏0800/181181,
ⓦwww.go-budget.co.uk.
Europcar ☏0845/722 2525,
ⓦwww.europcar.co.uk.
Hertz ☏0870/844 8844,
ⓦwww.hertz.co.uk.
Holiday Autos ☏0870/400 0000,
ⓦwww.holidayautos.com.

US and Canada
Auto Europe US ☏1-800/223-5555,
Canada ☏1-888 /223-5555,
ⓦwww.autoeurope.com.
Avis US ☏1-800/331-1084, Canada ☏1-

800/272-5871, ⓦwww.avis.com.
Budget ☏1-800/527-0700,
ⓦwww.budgetrentacar.com.
Dollar ☏1-800/800-6000,
ⓦwww.dollar.com.
Europe by Car ☏1-800/223-1516,
ⓦwww.europebycar.com.
Hertz US ☏1-800/654-3001, Canada ☏1-800/263 0600, ⓦwww.hertz.com.
Kemwel Holiday Autos ☏1-800/422-7737, ⓦwww.kemwel.com.

Rules of the road

The main rules of the road are pretty clear, though there are some particularly Polish twists liable to catch out the unwary. The **basic rules** are: traffic drives on the right; it is compulsory to wear seat belts outside built-up areas; children under twelve years of age must sit in the back; right of way must be given to public transport vehicles (including trams). Drinking and driving is strictly prohibited – anyone with a foreign number-plate driving around after 11pm, however innocently, has a strong chance of being stopped and breathalyzed. From November through to March, headlights must be switched on at all times.

Speed limits are 60kph in built-up areas (white signs with the place name mark the start of a built-up area, the same sign with a diagonal red line through it marks the end), 90kph on country roads, 110kph on dual carriageways, 130kph on motorways, and 80kph if you're pulling a caravan or trailer. Fines, administered on the spot, range from the negligible up to around £20/US$30. Speed traps are common, particularly on major trunk roads, such as the Gdańsk–Warsaw route, so caution is strongly advised, especially on the approach to, and travelling through, small towns and villages.

Other problems occur chiefly at night, especially on **country roads**, where potential disasters include horses and carts, mopeds without lights and staggering inebriated peasants. In **cities**, beware of a casual attitude towards traffic lights and road signs by local drivers and pedestrians. **Road conditions** are varied: on the one hand, backroads Poland still features large stretches of near-deserted idyllic countryside routes; on the other, the rapidly expanding volume of traffic is putting an increasing strain on the country's major roads, and with few resources devoted to upkeep, a number of routes – particularly those used by lorries – are quite simply beginning to fall apart. Motorways are still confined to a couple of stretches in the south (between Katowice and Kraków, for example), and major new projects (such as the proposed motorway link with the Czech Republic) remain the subject of much discussion.

Fuel

With car ownership increasing rapidly, and operators of all kinds waking up to the economic potential of the Polish market, the old problems with finding **fuel** have largely faded away. A growing number of small-scale operators, privatized CPN fuel depots and brand new multinational outlets have added substantially to the number of service stations around. Many stations in cities and along the main routes are open 24 hours a day, others from around 6am to 10pm; almost all out-of-town stations close on Sunday. Fuel is often colour coded at the pumps: yellow – 98 octane; or green – 95 octane, available **leaded** or **unleaded** (*benzyna bezołowiowa*). **Diesel** is usually available (the pumps have an ON sign and are black). Carrying at least one fuel can permanently topped up will help to offset worries in rural areas.

Car crime

With car-related **crime** – both simple break-ins and outright theft – one of the biggest criminal growth areas in Poland today, and foreign-registered vehicles one of the major targets, it pays to take note of the following simple precautions: especially in big towns, always park your vehicle in a **guarded parking lot** (*parking strzeżony*), never in an open street – even daylight break-ins occur with depressing frequency. Never leave anything of importance, including vehicle documents, in the car. Guarded lots are not too expensive (about £5/US$7 a day, more in major city centres) and in most towns and cities you can usually find one located centrally – the major hotels almost always have their own nearby. If you have a break-in, report it to the police immediately. They'll probably shrug their shoulders over the prospects of getting anything back, but you'll need their

signed report for insurance claim purposes back home.

Breakdowns and spares

The Polish motoring association PZMot runs a 24-hour car **breakdown service**. The national HQ, which can provide some English-language pamphlets on their services, is at ul. Solec 85, Warsaw (☎022/622 9335). Anywhere else dial the national breakdown emergency number – ☎9637 – and you'll eventually be towed to a garage. If you have insurance against breakdowns, the tow will be free; otherwise it will cost you 2.5zł per kilometre. The wide range of cars now available in Poland means that you will not have problems finding spares for major Western makes like Volvo, Renault and Volkswagen. If it's simply a case of a flat tyre, head for the nearest sizeable garage.

Hitching

A by-product of the previous scarcity of private vehicles in Poland was that **hitchhiking** was positively encouraged, with a PTTK-sponsored voucher scheme and rewards for drivers taking passengers, though this is much less the case now. If you do hitch, note that the Polish convention is to stick out your whole arm – not just your thumb.

Cycling

Cycling is often regarded as an ideal way to see a predominantly rural country like Poland. Particularly on the back roads, surfaces are generally in good shape, and there isn't much traffic around – anyone used to cycling in Western traffic is in for a treat. An additional plus is the mercifully flat nature of much of the terrain, which allows you to cycle quite long distances without great effort. You'll need to bring your own machine and a supply of **spare parts**: except in a few major cities like Warsaw and Kraków, and a number of southern mountain areas like the Bieszczady, **bike rental** and spare part facilities are still a comparative rarity. In rural areas, though, bikes are fairly common, and with a bit of ingenuity you can pick up basic spares like inner tubes and puncture repair kits.

Taking your bike on **trains** isn't a problem as long as there's a luggage van on board: if there isn't you usually have to sit with it in the last carriage of the train, where if you're lucky there'll be fewer passengers; either way there's a nominal fee. Hotels will usually put your machine either in a locked luggage room or a guarded parking lot. You need to exercise at least as much caution concerning security as you would in any city at home: strong locks and chaining your bike to immobile objects are the order of the day, and always try and take your bike indoors at night.

Accommodation

Accommodation will probably account for most of your essential expenditure in Poland. The hotel market has witnessed a considerable shake-up in recent years, with the construction of new business-oriented international franchises and the privatization and refurbishment of old state-run establishments.

The overall effect of these developments has been to force prices upwards, although accommodation bargains are still easy to come by in Poland – especially in the rural resort areas favoured by the Poles themselves. Listings in the Guide have been made as wide-ranging as possible to reflect the immense diversity on offer: privately run hotels, pensions, hostels, workers' hostels, youth hostels, rooms in private houses and a good range of campsites.

One useful resource is the *Hotele, Restauracje* handbook published every year by Polish travel publisher Pascal (50zł), available from most bookshops and Empik stores, which contains details of prices, locations and facilities at hotels, pensions, motels and guesthouses throughout the country.

Accommodation price codes

All accommodation listed in the Guide (apart from youth hostels) is **price graded** according to the scale below. Unless specified otherwise, prices given are for the **cheapest** double room.

In the cheapest places (categories ❶–❷), rooms generally come without their own private bath/shower, breakfast is often not included, and in some instances (specified in the text) beds are in dorms only. In categories ❸–❺ you can normally expect breakfast and an en-suite shower/bath. Overall, room quality in the **middle ranges** is affected by the age of the building (generally speaking the newer the place, especially post-1990, the better) and its geographical location – the more popular tourist centres are improving room quality faster than the rest, and the east of the country still lags noticeably behind western regions. Into the **top bracket** hotels (categories ❽–❾) it's another story; high prices are generally matched by consistently high standards.

The majority of places will expect you to pay in złoty, though really upmarket hotels generally show prices in dollars/Deutschmarks and will accept payment in Western currencies.

❶ under 60zł (under £11/US$15)
❷ 60–90zł (£11–16/US$15–22.50)
❸ 90–120zł (£16–22/US$22.50–30)
❹ 120–160zł (£22–29/US$30–40)
❺ 160–220zł (£29–39/US$40–55)
❻ 220–300zł (£39–54/US$55–75)
❼ 300–400zł (£54–72/US$75–100)
❽ 400–600zł (£72–108/US$100–150)
❾ over 600zł (over £108/US$150)

Hotels

There's a growing range and diversity of hotel accommodation in Poland, although standards of service and value for money vary widely from place to place. The international five-star **grading system** is in use in Poland but is yet to be applied universally – and even in those cases where star ratings are in use, they aren't always an accurate guide to quality. As a general rule however, one-star hotels provide rooms with a bed and not much else; two-star hotels offer rooms with at least an en-suite shower; while three-star hotels are likely to provide you with a telephone and a TV. Anything four-star or five-star is in the international business league.

Most Polish towns and cities still retain one or two (usually unclassified) **budget hotels** offering sparsely furnished rooms in old, unrenovated buildings, customarily with shared bathroom facilities located in the hallway. Originally intended to provide cheap digs for Poles working away from home, these were almost invariably off-limits to foreigners until the fall of communism. Despite an outward air of shabbiness these places are usually clean and well run, and shouldn't be discounted if all you need is a bed for the night. They rarely cost more than £10/US$14 per person per night, although they're decreasing in number – largely because of the temptation to refurbish and upgrade these establishments as soon as investment becomes available.

Another traditional source of cheap rooms is the **sports hotel** (*Dom Sportowy*; sometimes known by the acronym *OSiR* or *MOSiR*), usually built adjacent to the town stadium (often located in a park way out from the centre) and intended for the use of visiting sporting teams – which means they're likely to be fully booked for at least part of the weekend. Sports hotels often have a mixture of en-suite rooms and rooms with shared facilities, and are likely to provide several triples and quads as well as doubles – although single travellers may be asked to share a room with a stranger.

Occupying a similar price range are the hotels run by the **PTTK** organization (see p.28), which are found in many city centres and usually go by the name of *Dom Turysty* or *Hotel PTTK*. These usually contain a mixture of dorm rooms, rooms with shared facilities and simple en-suites, with beds costing anything from £7/US$10 to £14/US$20 per person. Although the majority of PTTK places are budget-oriented establishments patronized by international and Polish youth, a few of them are being modernized and turned into mid-price hotels.

Long lacking in Poland, there are now plenty of competitively priced **mid-range hotels** which would fit comfortably into the international two- and three-star brackets. Prices and quality vary considerably in this category (see p.39), but for a standard double medium-range room in summer expect to pay £20–35/US$30–50 a night – more in Warsaw and Kraków. Breakfast is usually included in the room price. The older of these mid-range hotels often have a few cheap rooms with shared facilities as well as the standard en-suites which are invariably offered to new arrivals – there will be a substantial difference in price, so always ask.

Five-star hotels are still something of a rarity outside Warsaw, but four-star establishments are mushrooming all over the place, largely thanks to the booming numbers of business travellers roaming around post-communist Poland. Double room prices at this level can be anything from £55/US$80 to £110/US$150, although you may well find significant reductions at weekends. Many of the older hotels in this category are run by Orbis, the former state-run tourism behemoth which oversaw all incoming travel to Poland in the years before 1990. Many of Poland's most stylish, prewar hotels were gobbled up by the Orbis empire, although the vast majority of their establishments date from the last 30 years or so, and are in the anonymous communist-era slabs-of-concrete style. Traditionally Orbis hotels haven't always deserved their star ratings, due to wonky room fittings or indifferent service, but standards are gradually improving now that Orbis has to make its way as a profit-making concern. In the past few years Orbis's supremacy has in any case been threatened by the mass of new business hotels opening up in Poland's major cities, many built as joint ventures with well-known Western hotel chains. The number of Western tourists making their way to Warsaw and Kraków has encouraged the emergence of numerous flashy modern hotels offering international standards of service.

Orbis also runs a number of **motels** on the outskirts of major cities; these are usually a bit cheaper than their more central counterparts, but generally only practical if you've got your own transport.

Pensions and holiday homes

Some of Poland's best accommodation deals can be found in the growing stock of **pensions** (*pensjonaty*) situated in major holiday areas – especially in the mountains, the Mazurian lake district, and along the coast. There's no hard and fast rule governing what constitutes a pension in Poland. Some are small hotels that used to cater for workers taking rural rest cures and are now open to all; others are private houses transformed into family-run B&Bs. In all cases they tend to be cosy, informal affairs offering simple en-suite rooms, often equipped with the additional comforts of a fridge and an electric kettle. Rates hover between £16/US$23 and £22/US$30 a double. Breakfast is sometimes available at an extra cost.

Since the beginning of the 1990s, there has been a new addition to the holiday lodging scene – workers' **rest homes** (*Dom Wypoczynkowy*). These were formerly run by unions and factories for their own employees, but are increasingly being privatized and opened to general trade. They're usually located in spa resorts, but often crop up in other rural holiday areas as well. Accommodation tends towards the simple, with sparsely furnished rooms and shared bathrooms, but these establishments are invariably cheap and well run. Expect to pay £10–15/US$14–21 per person per night.

Private rooms

You can get a room in a **private house** (*kwatery prywatny*) almost anywhere in the country. In urban areas these tend to be located in shabby flats, which may be situated some way from the centre of town. You will be sharing your hosts' bathroom, and breakfast will not be included. As a rule, landlords in lake, mountain and seaside resorts are much more attuned to the needs of tourists and may provide rooms with en-suite bathroom, electric kettle, and even TV. Staying in private rooms doesn't necessarily constitute a great way of meeting the locals: some hosts will brew you a welcome glass of tea and show a willingness to talk; most

will simply give you a set of house keys and leave you to get on with it.

In big cities such as Warsaw, Kraków, Gdańsk and Poznań, a **private-room bureau** (*biuro zakwaterowania*) or one of the local travel agencies undertakes the job of allocating rooms – details of these are given in the relevant sections of the guide. In the lakes, mountains and on the coast, the local IT office will usually find you a place. Expect to pay around £6–10/US$8.50–14 per person per night, slightly more in Warsaw. In case you don't like the place you're sent to, it makes sense not to register for too many nights ahead, as it's easy enough to extend your stay by going back to the agency, or paying your host directly.

At the unofficial level, many houses in the main holiday areas hang out signs saying *Noclegi* (lodging) or *Pokoje* (rooms). It's up to you to bargain over the price; £4/US$6 is the least you can expect to pay. In the cities, you won't see any signs advertising rooms, but you may well be approached outside stations and other obvious places. Before accepting, establish the price and check that the location is suitable.

Eco-holidays in Poland

The traditional image of Poland as a fearsome environmental blackspot is changing. One of the factors behind this reassessment is a growing appreciation of the relatively unspoiled condition of much of the **rural Polish environment**. Uniquely among the former communist states of Eastern Europe, agriculture in Poland remained relatively unaffected by Stalinist-era collectivization, and a large proportion of the country is dominated by small-scale privately run holdings. Increasing numbers of these land-holders are adopting organically based farming practices, and to help supplement their incomes are turning towards small-scale tourism, mostly in the form of rural bed and breakfast.

The **accommodation** on offer is cheap though not as basic as you might imagine, and includes easy access to some of the most beautiful parts of the Polish countryside, plenty of scope for outdoor activities (for example, many farms keep horses that guests are welcome to use) and the knowledge that you're doing something to support the local rural economy. The range of accommodation is growing and also includes facilities connected with national parks, environmental organizations, and village community projects.

In most places, the local **IT office** will have a list of farms offering accommodation. A yearly **handbook** of farms throughout Poland offering holiday stays, *Gospodarstwa Gościnne*, written in English despite the title, is available from the Polska Federacja Turystyki Wiejskiej, ul. Wspólna 30 in Warsaw (☎ 022/623 23 50, ☏623 2352). Another useful source of information is the European Centre for Eco-Agro Tourism (ECEAT), a Dutch-based foundation dedicated to supporting practical initiatives in the field of eco-friendly tourism; it produces **Green Holiday Guides** to all its properties in Poland (call ☎+31/20 668 1030 or check out ⊛www.eceat.nl).

Hostels and refuges

Scattered throughout Poland are some 600 official **youth hostels** (*schroniska młodzieżowe*), identified by a green triangle on a white background. However, the vast majority of these are only open for a few weeks at the height of the summer holiday period, usually in converted school buildings, and are liable to be booked solid, especially mid-May to mid-June by school groups. Some of the permanent year-round hostels are still very much in line with the hair-shirt ideals of the movement's founders, but things are easing up a little. Preference is supposedly given to those under 26, though there's no upper age restriction. You will probably be able to rent a sheet or sleeping bag for a nominal fee. Cooking facilities are usually available.

Two plus points are the **prices** (rarely more than £5/US$7 a head) and the **locations**, with many hostels placed close to town centres. Against that, there's the fact that dormitories are closed between 10am and 5pm, you must check in by 9pm, and a 10pm curfew is often enforced (though ususally negotiable in large cities).

The most useful hostel addresses are given in the Guide, but if you need a complete list, either buy the official **International Handbook** or contact the head office of the **Polish Youth Hostel Federation** (PTSM) at ul. Chocimska 28, Warsaw (Mon–Fri 8am–3.30pm; ☎022/849 8128) for their

own comprehensive handbook (*Informator*). Though you can buy an IYHF membership card before you go (see below for addresses), it's best to get a national card once you're in Poland (70zł).

In July, August and early September **Almatur** also organizes accommodation in so-called student hostels in the main university towns. Rooms have two, three or four beds; the charges including breakfast are around £4/US$5.60 for students (proof will be required), £7/US$10 for others under 35, which is the age limit. You can eat cheaply at the cafeteria on the premises, and there are often discos in the evenings; they're also a safe bet for meeting English speakers. The location of these hostels can vary from year to year: contact an Almatur office on arrival (relevant addresses are given in the text).

In mountain areas, a reasonably generous number of **refuges** (*schroniska*), many of them PTTK-run, which are clearly marked on hiking maps, enable you to make long-distance treks without having to make detours down into the villages for the night. Accommodation is in very basic dormitories, but costs are nominal and you can often get cheap and filling hot meals; in summer the more popular refuges can be very crowded indeed, as they are obliged to accept all comers. As a rule, the refuges are open all-year round but it's always worth checking for closures or renovations in progress before setting out.

Youth hostel associations

An Óige, 61 Mountjoy St, Dublin 7 ☎01/8430/4555, ⊛www.irelandyha.org.
Hostelling International Northern Ireland, 22–32 Donegall Rd, Belfast BT12 5JN ☎028/9032 4733, ⊛www.hini.org.uk. Adult membership IR£10; under-18s IR£6; family IR£20.
Hostelling International/American Youth Hostels (HI-AYH) 733 15th St NW, Suite 840, PO Box 37613, Washington, DC 20005 ☎202/783-6161, ⊛www.hiayh.org. Annual membership for adults (18–55) is US$25, for seniors (55 or over) is US$15, and for under-18s is free. Lifetime memberships are US$250.
Hostelling International/Canadian Hostelling Association, Room 400, 205 Catherine St, Ottawa, ON K2P 1C3 ☎1-800/663 5777 or 613/237 7884,

www.hostellingintl.ca. Rather than sell the traditional 1- or 2-year memberships, the association now sells one Individual Adult membership with a 16- to 28-month term. The length of the term depends on when the membership is sold, but a member can receive up to 28 months of membership for just C$35. Membership is free for under-18s and you can become a lifetime member for C$175.

New Zealand Youth Hostels Association, 173 Gloucester St, Christchurch ℡03/379 9970, www.yha.co.nz. Adult membership NZ$40 for one year, NZ$60 for two and NZ$80 for three.

Scottish Youth Hostel Association, 7 Glebe Crescent, Stirling, FK8 2JA ℡0870/1553 255, www.syha.org.uk. Annual membership £6, for under-18s £2.50.

YHA Australia, 422 Kent St, Sydney ℡02/9261 1111, www.yha.com.au. Adult membership rate A$49 for the first twelve months and then A$32 each year after.

Youth Hostel Association (YHA), Trevelyan House, 8 St Stephen's Hill, St Albans, Herts AL1 2DY ℡0870/870 8808, www.yha.org.uk and www.iyhf.org, customerservices@yha.org.uk. Annual membership £12.50, for under-18s £6.25.

Campsites

There are some 500 **campsites** throughout the country classified in three categories: **category 1** sites usually have amenities such as a restaurant and showers, while **category 3** sites amount to little more than poorly lit, run-down expanses of grass. The most useful are listed in the text; for a complete list, get hold of the *Camping w Polsce* **map**, available from bookshops (particularly Empik stores), some travel bureaux or the motoring organization PZMot. Apart from a predictably dense concentration in the main holiday areas, sites can also be found in most cities: the ones on the outskirts are almost invariably linked by bus to the centre and often have the benefit of a peaceful location and swimming pool. The major drawback is that most are open **May–September** only, though a few do operate all year round. Charges usually work out at a little under £2/US$3 per tent/caravan space, £2/US$3 per person, and £2/US$3 per car.

One specifically Polish feature is that you don't necessarily have to bring a tent to stay at many campsites, as there are often **bungalows** or **chalets** for rent, generally complete with toilet and shower. Though decidedly spartan in appearance, these are good value at around £4/US$6 per head. In summer, however, they are invariably booked long in advance.

Camping wild, outside of the national parks, is acceptable so long as you're reasonably discreet.

If you're planning to do a lot of camping, an **international camping carnet** is a good investment. The carnet gives discounts at member sites and serves as useful identification. Many campsites will take it instead of making you surrender your passport during your stay, and it covers you for third-party insurance when camping. In the US and Canada, the carnet is available from home motoring organizations, or from Family Campers and RVers (FCRV), 4804 Transit Rd, Building 2, Depew, NY 14043 (℡1-800/245-9755, www.fcrv.org). FCRV annual membership costs US$25, and the carnet an additional US$10. In the UK and Ireland, the carnet costs £4.50, and is available to members of the AA or the RAC, or for members only from either of the following: the Camping and Caravanning Club, Greenfields House, Westwood Way, Coventry, CV4 8JH (℡024/7669 4995, wwwcampingandcaravanningclub.co.uk), or the foreign touring arm of the same company, the Carefree Travel Service (℡024/7642 2024), which provides the CCI free if you take out insurance with them; they also book ferry crossings and inspect camping sites in Europe.

Eating and drinking

Poles take their food seriously, providing snacks of feast-like proportions for the most casual visitors, and maintaining networks of country relatives or local shops for especially treasured ingredients – smoked meats and sausages, cheeses, fruits and vegetables. The cuisine itself is a complex mix of influences: Russian, Lithuanian, Ukrainian, German and Jewish traditions all leaving their mark. To go with the food, there is excellent beer and a score of wonderful vodkas.

Once, if you wanted a really good meal in Poland, you had to hope for an invitation to someone's house. Now, however, with the moves towards a market economy, the country's fast-growing number of **restaurants** – most of which specialized in ungarnished slabs of meat during the communist era – are looking up. In the cities at least, there's now a distinctly Western spread of places to eat and a cosmopolitan range of cuisines. What is undeniable still is that eating out is a bargain, with splendid meals available for under £10/US$14 a head.

Drinking habits are changing, too. Poles for years drank mainly at home, while visitors stuck to the hotels, with such other bars as existed being alcoholic-frequented dives. In recent years, though, something of a café-bar culture has been emerging in the cities, and though the old drinking dens survive, you'll find plenty of choice for a relaxing, unthreatening night out.

Food

Like their central and eastern European neighbours, Poles are insatiable **meat** eaters: throughout the austerities of the past decade, meat consumption here remained among the highest in Europe. Beef and pork in different guises are the mainstays of most meals, while hams and sausages are consumed at all times of the day, as snacks and sandwich-fillers. **Game** is also common, and **lamb** is a speciality in the mountain regions where sheep-rearing is practised. In the coastal and mountain regions, you can also expect **fish** – particularly carp and freshwater trout – to feature prominently on the menus, with lots of seafood in the Baltic region.

A meal without meat is a contradiction in terms for most Poles, and **vegetarians** will

often be forced to find solace in customary stand-bys like omelettes, cheese-based dishes and salads. Thankfully there are now a few vegetarian restaurants starting to appear in the larger cities, while an ever-increasing number of mainstream restaurants offer vegetarian dishes (*potrawy jarskie*), albeit largely unimaginative ones. The word *wegetariański* is useful, as are the phrases *bez mięsa* (without meat) and *bez ryby* (without fish). The Ⓦ www.wegetarian.com.pl site has details of vegetarian restaurants throughout the country, although it's currently in Polish only.

Breakfasts, snacks and fast foods

For most Poles, the first meal of the day, eaten at home at around 7am, is little more than a sandwich with a glass of tea or cup of coffee. A more leisurely **breakfast** might include fried eggs with ham, mild frankfurters, a selection of cold meats and cheese, rolls and jam, and this is what you are liable to encounter in hotels, but for most people this full spread is more likely to be taken as a second breakfast (*drugie śniadanie*) at around midday. This is often eaten in the workplace, but a common alternative is to stop at a milk bar or self-service snack bar (*samoobsługa*).

Open from early morning till 5 or 6pm (later in the city centres), **snack bars** are works-canteen-type places, serving very cheap but generally uninspiring food: small plates of salted herring in oil (*śledź w oleju*), sandwiches, tired-looking meat or cheese, sometimes enlivened by some Russian salad (*sałatka jarzynowa*). **Milk bars** (*bar mleczny*; often called *jadłodajnia* in Kraków) are a little more wholesome, offering a selection of solid meals with the emphasis on quantity. Milk bars and snack bars both operate as self-service cafeterias: the menu is displayed over the counter, but if you don't recognize the names of the dishes, you can just point.

Although the classic milk bar is something of a threatened institution, with many closing down in the face of fast-food competition, the style of food they offer remains enduringly popular, and looks set to remain part of the Polish snack-eating scene for some time to come. Two national specialities you'll find everywhere are *bigos* (cabbage stewed with meat and spices) and *pierogi* (dumplings stuffed with meat and mushrooms – or with cottage cheese, onion and spices in the non-meat variation, *pierogi ruskie*). Potato pancakes (*placki ziemnaczane*) – either in sour cream or covered in *goulasch* – are another filling milk-bar favourite.

Takeaways and fast food

Traditional Polish **takeaway stands** usually sell *zapiekanki*, baguette-like pieces of bread topped with melted cheese; a less common but enjoyable version of the same thing comes with fried mushrooms. You'll also find hotdog stalls, doling out frankfurter sausages in white rolls, and stalls and shops selling French fries; the latter are generally skinny and oily, sold by weight, and accompanied by sausage or chicken in the tourist resorts and some city stands, or by fish in the northern seaside resorts and lakeland areas.

Western-style **fast food**, the totemic symbol of transformation towards a market economy all over Eastern Europe, has been seized on with eager enthusiasm in Poland. Many of the major international burger/pizza chains are now established in the big cities. Stalls selling grilled chicken (*kurczak z rożna*) have long been a local favourite, and no self-respecting high street is likely to be without one. Perhaps more appetizing are the new crop of oriental fast-food stands you'll find in the bigger cities, particularly Warsaw, often equipped with a few plastic chairs for instant eating convenience.

Do-it-yourself snacks

If the snacks on offer fail to appeal, you can always stock up on your own provisions.

Most people buy their bread in **supermarkets** (*samoobsługowe*) or from market traders; **bakeries** (*piekarnia*) are mostly small private shops and still something of a rarity, but when you do find them they tend to be

very good, as the queues indicate. The standard loaf (*chleb zakopiański*) is a long piece of dense rye bread, often flavoured with caraway seeds. Also common is *razowy*, a solid brown bread sometimes flavoured with honey, and *mazowiecki*, a white, sour rye bread. Rolls come in two basic varieties: the more common is the plain, light white roll called a *kajzerka*, the other is the *grahamka*, a round roll of rougher and denser brown bread.

Supermarkets are again a useful source for fillers, with basic **delicatessen counters** for cooked meats and sausages, and fridge units holding a standard array of hard and soft cheeses. **Street markets** will be cheaper for fruit and vegetables. Few market stalls supply bags, so bring your own.

Coffee, tea and sweets

Poles are inveterate tea and coffee drinkers, their daily round punctuated by endless cups or glasses, generally with heaps of sugar.

Tea (*herbata*), which is cheaper and so marginally more popular, is drunk Russian-style in the glass, without milk and often with lemon. In most places, you'll get hot water and a tea bag, though occasionally it will come *naturalna* style – a spoonful of tea leaves with the water poured on top.

Coffee (*kawa*) in Poland has improved immeasurably thanks to *Pożegnanie z Afryką* (*Out of Africa*), the chain of coffee bars that has spread throughout the main cities, and a real treat for the coffee connoisseur. Remember that coffee is served black unless you ask otherwise, in which case specify with milk (*z mleckiem*) or with cream (*ze śmietanką*). Many cafés (*kawarnia*) offer only *kawa naturalna*, which is a strong brew made by simply dumping the coffee grounds in a cup or glass and pouring water over them. Espresso and capuccino, usually passable imitations of the Italian originals, are now available in the more modern cafés and restaurants. In cafés and bars alike a shot or two of vodka or *winiak* (locally produced cheap brandy) with the morning cup of coffee is still frequent practice.

Cakes, sweets and ice cream

Cakes, pastries and other **sweets** are an integral ingredient of most Poles' daily consumption, and the cake shops (*cukiernia*) – which you'll find even in small villages – are as good as any in central Europe. Cheesecake is a national favourite, as are poppyseed cake, *drożdówka* (a sponge cake, often topped with plums), and *babka piaskowa* (marble cake). In the larger places you can also expect to find *torcik wiedeński*, an Austrian-style *schlagtort* with coffee and chocolate filling, as well as *keks* (fruitcake) and a selection of eclairs, profiteroles and cupcakes.

Poles eat **ice cream** (*lody*) at all times of the year, queueing up for cones at street-side kiosks or in *cukiernia*. The standard kiosk cone is watery and pretty tasteless, but elsewhere the selection is better: decent cafés offer a mouthwatering selection of ices.

Restaurant meals

The average **restaurant** (*restauracja*) is open from late morning through to mid-evening. Until recently, all but the smartest closed early, winding down around 9pm in cities, earlier in the country, although these days there's more variety and most cities now boast several late-opening options (particularly at weekends). Bear in mind that the total shutdown principle, applied around religious festivals and public holidays, often applies to restaurants. In smaller towns, the big hotels may be the only place open.

Although many restaurant **menus**, particularly in the bigger cities, are in both Polish and English, those in smaller, rural places will usually be in Polish only. Menus are broken up into courses with separate headings: *zupy* (soups); *przekąski* (starters/hors d'oeuvres); *dania drugie* (main course); *dodatki* (side dishes); *desery* (desserts); and *napoje* (drinks). The language section on p.745 should provide most of the cues you'll need. While the list of dishes apparently on offer may be long, in reality only things with a price marked next to them will be available, which will normally reduce the choice by fifty percent or more. If you arrive near closing time or late lunchtime, the waiter may inform you there's only one thing left.

There are no hard and fast rules about **tipping**, although it's increasingly common to leave an additional ten to fifteen percent, or round the bill up to the nearest convenient figure.

Soups and starters

First on the menu in most places are **soups**, definitely one of Polish cuisine's strongest points, varying from light and delicate dishes to concoctions that are virtually meals in themselves.

Best known is *barszcz*, a spicy beetroot broth that's ideally accompanied by a small pastry. Other soups worth looking out for are *żurek*, a creamy white soup with sausage and potato; *botwinka*, a seasonal soup made from the leaves of baby beetroots; *krupnik*, a thick barley and potato soup with chunks of meat, carrots and celeriac; and *chłodnik*, a cold Lithuanian beetroot soup with sour milk and vegetable greens, served in summer.

In less expensive establishments, you'll be lucky to have more than a couple of soups and a plate of cold meats, or herring with cream or oil to choose from as a **starter**. In better restaurants, though, the hors d'oeuvres selection might include Jewish-style gefilte fish, jellied ham (*szynka w galarecie*), steak tartare (*stek tatarski*), wild rabbit paté (*pasztet ze zająca*), or hard-boiled eggs in mayonnaise, which sometimes come stuffed with vegetables (*jajka faszerowane*).

Main courses and side dishes

Snack-bar favourites such as *bigos*, *pierogi* and *placki* also form a large part of the average restaurant menu, although here they're served in larger portions and with slightly more style. Otherwise, the basis of most **main courses** is a fried or grilled cut of meat in a thick sauce, commonest of which is the *kotlet schabowy*, a fried pork cutlet. Another favourite is *flaczki* (tripe cooked in a spiced bouillon stock with vegetables – usually very spicy), while also worth trying are *gołąbki* (cabbage leaves stuffed with meat, rice and occasionally mushrooms) and *golonka* (pig's leg with horseradish and pease pudding). Duck is usually the most satisfying poultry, particularly with apples, while carp, eel and trout are generally reliable fish dishes, usually grilled or sautéed, occasionally poached. Pancakes (*naleśniki*) often come as a main course, too, stuffed with cottage cheese (*ze serem*).

Main dishes come with some kind of **vegetables**, normally boiled or mashed potatoes and/or cabbage, either boiled or as sauerkraut. Wild forest mushrooms (*grzyby*), another Polish favourite, are served in any number of forms, the commonest being fried or sautéed. **Salads** are generally a regulation issue plate of lettuce, cucumber and tomato in a watery dressing. If available, it's better to go for an individual salad dish like *mizeria* (cucumber in cream), *buraczki* (grated beetroot) or the rarer *ćwikła* (beetroot with horseradish).

Desserts

Desserts are usually restricted to a selection of cakes and ice creams. If it's available try *kompot*, fruit compote in a glass – in season you may chance upon fresh strawberries, raspberries or blueberries. Pancakes are also served as a dessert, with jam and sugar or with *powidła*, a delicious plum spread.

Drinks

Poles' capacity for alcohol has never been in doubt, and drinking is a national pursuit. Much of the **drinking** goes on in restaurants, which in smaller towns or villages are often the only outlets selling alcohol.

In the cities and larger towns, there's a far greater range of atmospheric and pleasant drinking holes than there used to be a few years ago, with a convivial crop of privately run **bars** (*bary*) and **café-bars**, plus the odd faux-Irish, Scottish or English **pub**. As a result, **hotel bars** – once the preserve of Westerners or wealthier Poles – have lost their stranglehold on the tourist market and are largely the preserve of businessmen and prostitutes. You'll still come across traditional **drink bars** – basic and functional, these are almost exclusively male terrain and generally best avoided: the haunt of wide boys and hardened alcoholics, they reflect the country's serious alcohol problems, caused in part by the traditional preference for spirits over beer or wine. Among the younger generation, however, things are changing – not least as a result of a massive advertising campaign by the breweries – with beer rapidly replacing vodka as the tipple of choice.

Beer

The Poles can't compete with their Czech neighbours in the production and consumption of **beer**, but there are nevertheless a number of highly drinkable, and in a few cases really excellent, Polish brands.

Most beer is sold on draught – ask for *jedno duże* ("a big one") if you want the full half-litre; *jedno małe* ("a small one") will get you a 33cl glass. The biggest Polish breweries are all owned by multinational companies now, and produce a palatable lager-style beer. Żywiec is by far the most widespread brand, although Okocim, Tyskie and EB (long considered the Trabant among Polish beers, but now improving) are also fairly ubiquitous. There's also an assortment of regional beers you'll only find in the locality, Dojlidy (Białystok) being one of the most highly rated.

Vodka and other spirits

It's with **vodka** that Poles really get into their stride. Such is its place in the national culture that for years the black-market value of the dollar was supposed to be directly pegged to the price of a bottle. If you thought vodka was just a cocktail mixer you're in for some surprises: clear, peppered, honeyed – reams could be written about the varieties on offer. And although younger Poles are increasingly adopting the Western habit of mixing it with fruit juice (apple juice is a particular favourite), traditionally – and ideally – vodka is served neat, well chilled, in measures of 25 or 50 grams (a *czysta* – 100 grams – is common, too) and knocked back in one go, with a mineral water chaser. A couple of these will be enough to put most people well on the way, though the capacities of seasoned Polish drinkers are prodigious – a half-litre bottle between two or three over lunch is nothing unusual.

Best of the **clear vodkas** are Żytnia, Krakus and Wyborowa. A perfectly acceptable everyday substitute is Zwykla or ordinary vodka, such as Polonez, one of the most popular brands and the one you're most likely to encounter in people's houses and in the average restaurant. Of late there's been a revival of kosher vodkas – whether their rabbinic stamps of approval are all entirely authentic is a matter of some debate.

Many of the **flavoured vodkas** are now exceedingly hard to get hold of, having been forced off bar counters and supermarket shelves by imported spirits. One that you won't have any trouble in finding is Żubrówka, a legendary vodka infused with the taste of bison grass from the eastern Białowieża forest – there's a stem in every bottle. Some say the bison have urinated on the grass first, but don't let that put you off. Tatrzańska, the Tatra mountain equivalent, flavoured with mountain herbs is harder to find, but excellent. Also worth seeking out are Pieprzówka, which has a sharp, peppery flavour, and is supposed to be good at warding off colds. The juniper-flavoured Myśliwska tastes a bit like gin, while the whisky-coloured Jarzębiak is flavoured with rowanberries. Others to look out for are Wiśniówka, a sweetish, strong wild cherry concoction; Krupnik, which is akin to whisky liqueur; Cytrynówka, a lemon vodka; and Miodówka, a rare honey vodka. Last but by no means least on any basic list comes Pejsachówka, which, at 75 percent proof, is by far the strongest vodka on the market and is rivalled in strength only by home-produced *bimber*, the Polish version of moonshine.

Other popular *digestifs* are *śliwowica*, the powerful plum brandy that is mostly produced in the south of the country, and *miód pitny*, a heady mead-like wine. Commonest of all in this category however is *winiak*, a fiery Polish brandy you'll find in many cafés and restaurants.

Soft drinks

The range of **soft drinks** on offer in Poland is pretty much the same as in any other European country, with international brands widely available – alongside locally produced equivalents.

Poland's own sparkling **mineral water** (*mineralna*) from the spas of the south is highly palatable and available throughout the country; the commonest brand name is Nałęczowianka. Well water, taken from different levels underground, is available in shops, together with a few Western brands like Perrier. If you order mineral water in a pub, it usually comes with ice and a twist of lemon.

Communications and the media

Post offices and the mail

Post offices in Poland are identified by the name Urząd Pocztowy (Poczta for short) or by the acronym PTT (Poczta, Telegraf, Telefon). Each bears a number, with the head office in each city being no. 1. Theoretically, each head office has a poste restante (general delivery) facility: make sure, therefore, that anyone addressing mail to you includes the no. 1 after the city's name. This service works reasonably well, but don't

expect complete reliability. Mail to the UK currently takes four days, a week to the US, and is a day or so quicker in the other direction. It currently costs 1.90zł to send a card or letter to the UK, 2.10zł to the USA and 2zł to Australia or New Zealand. Always mark your letters "Par avion", or better still "Lotnicza", or pick up the blue stickers with both on from post offices; if you don't, they may take longer. Post boxes are red.

Opening hours of the head offices are usually Mon–Fri 7/8am–8pm, with some open on Saturday mornings. Other branches usu-

Time

Poland is one hour ahead of GMT, nine hours ahead of US Pacific Standard Time and six hours ahead of Eastern Standard Time. Clocks go forward one hour at the end of March and an hour back at the end of October.

ally close at 6pm, often earlier in rural areas. A restricted range of services is available 24 hours a day, seven days a week, from post offices in or outside the main train stations of major cities.

Telephones

The antiquated **telephone** system bequeathed by the communist system was long one of the biggest obstacles to Poland's economic development. Fortunately, things have improved immeasurably in recent years, though the omnipresence of mobile phones implies that many Poles have found their own solutions to the communication problem.

Making calls

Currently, two types of public payphone are in existence. By far the best are the blue **cardphones**, which are operated by a card (*karta telefoniczna*), bought at post offices and Ruch kiosks, the latter usually marginally more expensive. Cards come in denominations of 25, 50 or 100 units, and cost 10, 18 and 37zł respectively. Trim off the top corner of the card before you insert it into the machine. The second, increasingly rare, type of payphone is the grey, yellow and rectangular blue ones requiring **tokens** (*żetony*), which can also be bought at kiosks. These come in two types: the small A tokens (currently costing 0.35zł) are for local calls lasting three minutes; the larger C tokens (currently 3.55zł) for long distance calls. When dialling, place the token on the slide, but do not insert it until someone answers at the other end – otherwise you'll lose it and be cut off.

Local calls, and dialling from one city to another, should present few problems, and the recent standardization of the country's area codes has helped a great deal (see the codes on p.50), which now usually apply to the surrounding area as well as the cities themselves). You can also make **long-distance calls** from the main post offices in large cities, phoning from a booth with the time monitored and paying the cashier after you've made your call.

Making **international calls**, at least within Europe, is far less of a problem these days than it was. Use cards rather than tokens, and buy those with a maximum number of credits. Though local calls are cheap, international calls are not – 50 units will buy just a three-minute connection to the UK.

Emergency calls (police ☏997, fire ☏998, ambulance ☏999) are free. To make a **collect call**, go to a post office, write down the number you want and "Rozmonta R" and show it to the clerk – persistence, and above all, patience will eventually pay off. Remember, too, that calls from hotels are usually far more expensive than calls from a payphone.

Travellers with GSM **mobile phones** will find that almost all of Poland enjoys coverage – apart from the odd remote mountain valley. Before using your mobile phone abroad you will need to ask your phone company to switch on your international access, and you'll probably have to pay a hefty deposit against future bills.

Calling home from abroad

One of the most convenient ways of phoning home from abroad is via a **telephone charge card**. Using access codes for the particular country you are in and a PIN number, you can make calls from most hotel, public and private phones that will be charged to your own account. While rates are always cheaper from a residential phone at off-peak rates, that's normally not an option when you're travelling (if you do use a calling card in conjunction with a residential phone, when you're staying as a guest, for instance, you will be paying the calling card company's rates, which will usually be dearer than the local operator's). You may be able to use it to minimize hotel phone surcharges, but don't depend on it. However, the benefit of calling cards is mainly one of convenience, as rates aren't necessarily cheaper than calling from a public phone while abroad and can't compete with the discounted off-peak times many local phone companies offer. But since most major charge cards are free to obtain, it's certainly worth getting one at least for emergencies; enquire first though whether your destination is covered.

In the **USA** and **Canada**, AT&T, MCI, Sprint, Canada Direct and other North American long-distance companies all enable their customers to make credit-card calls while overseas. Call your company's customer service line to find out if they provide service from Poland, and if so, what the toll-free access code is. Calls made from overseas will automatically be billed to your home number.

Phone codes

Calling Poland from abroad

Dial the international access code
   (given below) + 48 (country code)
   + area code (minus initial 0) +
   number.
Australia ☎0011
Canada ☎011
Ireland ☎010
New Zealand ☎00
UK ☎00
USA ☎011

Phoning abroad from Poland

Dial the country code (given below)
   + area code (minus initial 0) +
   number
Australia ☎0061
Canada ☎001
Ireland ☎00353
New Zealand ☎0064
UK ☎0044
USA ☎001

Polish phone codes

Białystok ☎085
Kielce ☎041
Rzeszów ☎017
Bielsko-Biała ☎033
Kraków ☎012
Szczecin ☎091
Bydgoszcz ☎052
Łódź ☎042
Tarnów ☎014
Częstochowa ☎034
Lublin ☎081
Toruń ☎056
Elbląg ☎055
Olsztyn ☎089
Warsaw ☎022
Gdańsk/Gdynia/Sopot ☎058
Opole ☎077
Wrocław ☎071
Katowice ☎032
Poznań ☎061
Zakopane ☎018
Zamość ☎084

In the **UK** and **Ireland**, British Telecom (☎0800/345 144, ⊛www.chargecard.bt.com/) will issue free to all BT customers the BT Charge Card, which can be used in 116 countries; AT&T (Dial ☎0800/890 011, then 888 641 6123 when you hear the AT&T prompt to be transferred to the Florida Call Centre, free 24 hours) has the Global Calling Card; while Cable & Wireless (☎0500/100505) issues its own Global Calling Card, which can be used in more than sixty countries abroad, though the fees cannot be charged to a normal phone bill.

To call **Australia** and **New Zealand** from overseas, telephone charge cards such as Telstra Telecard or Optus Calling Card in Australia, and Telecom NZ's Calling Card can be used to make calls abroad, which are charged back to a domestic account or credit card. Apply to Telstra (☎1800/038 000), Optus (☎1300/300 937), or Telecom NZ (☎04/801 9000).

Email and the internet

One of the best ways to keep in touch while travelling is to sign up for a free internet **email** address that can be accessed from anywhere, for example YahooMail or Hotmail – accessible through ⊛www.yahoo.com and ⊛www.hotmail.com. Once you've set up an account, you can use these sites to pick up and send mail from any internet café, or hotel with internet access.

Internet cafés are springing up all over Poland, and are listed in the Guide where relevant. Outside Warsaw and Kraków however, connections tend to be slow – making the sending and receiving of emails a patience-sapping process. ⊛www.kropka.com is a useful website giving details of how to plug your laptop in when abroad, phone country codes around the world, and information about electrical systems in different countries.

The media

The Polish **media** scene has long been one of the most lively in Eastern Europe, not least because of the popularity enjoyed by semi-official and dissident publications during the communist period.

Newspapers and magazines

Among Polish-language **daily newspapers**, most popular is the tabloid-sized *Gazeta*

Wyborcza (🌐www.gazeta.pl), Eastern Europe's first independent daily, set up in 1989. Forced to abandon the Solidarity logo from its masthead following a bitter dispute between its editor, veteran dissident and intellectual Adam Michnik, and Lech Wałęsa, the paper has gone from strength to strength, with a daily circulation (500,000, rising to 750,000 at weekends) that puts it among the top-ten-selling European dailies. *Gazeta* is strong on investigative journalism, has a liberal political stance and, in a bid to further enhance its popularity, now comes with regional supplements and colour magazines. Even if you don't read Polish it's worth getting for its cultural listings – especially on Fridays, when the week's attractions are previewed in the *Co jest Grane?* supplement.

Other national daily papers include *Rzeczpospolita*, originally the official voice of the communist government, now a highbrow independent paper with a strong following among business people and government officials because of its good economic coverage. *Trybuna*, once the official newspaper of the communist party, is still pursuing a leftist agenda and supporting the post-communist-led SLD. However, local rather than national papers are what most of the population read: though generally pretty unexciting, they're often useful for current events and cultural listings.

Weekly papers comprise a colourful mix of the specialist, the political and the sensationalist. Top sellers in the latter category include *Skandale*, which features the usual diet of sex, violence and pure invention; and *Nie*, edited by the flamboyant and outspoken Jerzy Urban, spokesman for the communist government throughout most of the 1980s.

Of the political organs, the theoretically inclined *Polityka* is another former communist mouthpiece (in this case for the liberal wing of the party), while its main rival *Wprost* is a well-respected, liberal-leaning alternative. Circulation of the once hugely popular *Tygodnik Powszechny*, a liberally minded Catholic weekly that used to be the country's only officially published independent newspaper, has declined rapidly following some rather misjudged forays into the political domain during the Mazowiecki government era.

Glossy **monthly magazines** are devoured as eagerly in Poland as anywhere else in the developed world. Home-grown women's magazines like the best-selling *Twój Styl*

have been joined by Polish-language versions of *Cosmopolitan*, *Marie-Claire* and others; the worldwide explosion in mens' lifestyle magazines has been mirrored here too. *Machina* provides the best overall view of Polish popular culture, covering pop, rock and dance music as well as video games and cinema – although the latter is given exhaustive coverage by a whole raft of specialist titles, *Film*, *Kino* and *Cinema* among them.

There's a mind-boggling number of **periodicals** dealing with cultural, social and intellectual concerns, including *Midrasz* (🌐www.midrasz.home.pl), a lively monthly devoted to Polish-Jewish issues.

English language publications

There are a number of **English-language publications**. Longest established is the *Warsaw Voice* (🌐www.warsawvoice .com.pl), a Warsaw-based weekly that's widely available throughout the country. It's readable and informative, with good listings, though noticeably slanted towards the business community. The increasingly ubiquitous *In Your Pocket* people publish useful A5-format guides to Warsaw, Kraków, Gdańsk and Wrocław (🌐www.inyourpocket.com); although the best choice in this genre is probably the monthly *Warsaw Insider*, written for the capital's 20,000-strong expatriate community and invaluable for the visitor.

Western newspapers and magazines are now available the same day in the big cities. Most common are the *Guardian International Edition*, the *Financial Times*, *The Times* and the *Herald Tribune*, plus magazines like *Newsweek*, *Time* and *The Economist*.

Ruch and other **kiosks** are the main outlets for papers and magazines, with a wide selection also available in Empik stores. The latter usually stock a reasonable choice of international, English-language glossies – especially the leading fashion, lifestyle and pop music titles.

TV and radio

Poland's **TV network** has improved by leaps and bounds in recent years, with the previously rather staid state-run channels now competing for viewers with a plethora of private stations. The regular diet of game shows, soap operas and American films doesn't differ that much from anywhere else in Europe, although Polish TV has managed to preserve a few quirks of its own – notably the tendency for foreign imports to be dubbed by a single *lektor*, who reads all the parts in the same voice. For increasing numbers of Poles satellite and, in the big cities, cable TV are popular additions to the range of viewing options. Most hotels now carry a selection of international cable/satellite channels, although German-language stations tend to be more common than English.

Most popular Polish **radio stations** are Warsaw-based Zet, and Kraków's RFM FM (both of which now broadcast to other cities on a variety of different frequencies), offering a varied and often rather imaginative diet of pop, rock and other contemporary musical styles. A number of local stations broadcast occasional English-language news bulletins, although for a full English-language service you'll have to track down BBC World Service, for which you'll need a shortwave radio; Ⓦ www.bbc .co.uk/worldservice lists all the World Service frequencies around the globe.

Opening hours and holidays

Most shops are open on weekdays from approximately 10am to 6pm. Exceptions are grocers and food stores, which may open as early as 6am and close by mid-afternoon – something to watch out for in rural areas in particular. On Saturdays, most shops will have shut by 2 or 3pm;, while there's a minority trade on Sunday afternoons.

Other idiosyncrasies include Ruch **kiosks**, where you can buy newspapers and municipal transport tickets, which generally open from about 6am; some shut up around 5pm, but others remain open for several hours longer. Increasing numbers of **street traders** and makeshift kiosks also do business well into the evening, while you can usually find one or two **shops** in most towns offering late-night opening throughout the week (in the cities this is no problem). Additionally, in the cities, there are increasing numbers of **night shops** (*sklepy nocne*), generally all-purpose stores, many of which really do stay open throughout the night (in Warsaw there are currently fourteen); the most useful are listed in the Guide.

As a rule, **tourist information offices** are open from 9 or 10am until 5pm (later in major cities) during the week; hours are shorter on Saturdays and Sundays.

Tourist sites

Visiting **churches** seldom presents any problems: the ones you're most likely to want to see are open from early morning until mid-evening without interruption. However, a large number of less famous churches are fenced off beyond the entrance porch by a grille or glass window for much of the day; to see them properly, you'll need to turn up around the times for Mass – first thing in the morning and between 6 and 8pm. Otherwise it's a case of seeking out the local priest (*ksiąz*) and persuading him to let you in.

The current visiting times for **museums** and **historic monuments** are listed in the text of the Guide. They are almost invariably closed one day per week (usually Mon) and many are closed two days. The rest of the week, some open for only about five hours, often closing at 3pm, though 4pm or later is more normal.

Public holidays

The following are national **public holidays**, on which you can expect some shops, restaurants and most sights to be closed. It's well worth checking if your visit is going to coincide with one of these to avoid frustrations and disappointments. It's particularly worth noting that because Labour Day and Constitution Day are so close together, most businesses (including the majority of banks and shops) give their employees a full 4 days of holiday.

January 1 New Year's Day
March/April Easter Monday

May 1 Labour Day
May 3 Constitution Day
May/June Corpus Christi
August 15 Feast of the Assumption
November 1 All Saints' Day
November 11 National Independence Day
December 25 & 26 Christmas

Festivals, entertainment and sports

One manifestation of Poland's intense commitment to Roman Catholicism is that all the great feast days of the Church calendar are celebrated with wholehearted devotion, many of the participants donning the colourful traditional costumes for which the country is celebrated.

This is most notable in the mountain areas in the south of the country, where the **annual festivities** play a key role in maintaining a vital sense of community. As a supplement to these, Poland has many more recently established **cultural festivals**, particularly in the fields of music and drama. As well as a strong ethnic/folk **music** scene, contemporary music in Poland is intriguing, if a little inaccessible to outsiders.

Religious and traditional festivals

The highlight of the Catholic year is **Easter** (Wielkanoc), which is heralded by a glut of spring fairs, offering the best of the early livestock and agricultural produce. **Holy Week** (Wielki Tydzień) kicks off in earnest on **Palm Sunday** (Niedziela Palmowa), when palms are brought to church and paraded in processions. Often the painted and decorated "palms" are handmade, sometimes with competitions for the largest or most beautiful. The most famous procession takes place at Kalwaria Zebrzydowska near Kraków, inaugurating a spectacular week-long series of mystery plays, re-enacting Christ's Passion.

On **Maundy Thursday** (Wielki Czwartek) many communities take symbolic revenge on Judas Iscariot: his effigy is hanged,

dragged outside the village, flogged, burned or thrown into a river. **Good Friday** (Wielki Piątek) sees visits to mock-ups of the Holy Sepulchre – whether permanent structures such as at Kalwaria Zebrzydowska and Wambierzyce in Silesia, or ad hoc creations, as is traditional in Warsaw. In some places, notably the Rzeszów region, this is fused with a celebration of King Jan Sobieski's victory in the Siege of Vienna, with "Turks" placed in charge of the tomb. **Holy Saturday** (Wielka Sobota) is when baskets of painted eggs, sausages, bread and salt are taken along to church to be blessed and sprinkled with holy water. The consecrated food is eaten at breakfast on **Easter Day** (Niedziela Wielkanocna), when the most solemn Masses of the year are celebrated. On **Easter Monday** (Lany Poniedziałek), girls are doused with water by boys to "make them fertile" (a marginally better procedure than in the neighbouring Czech Republic where they're beaten with sticks). Even in the cosmopolitan cities you'll see gangs of boys waiting in the streets or leaning out of first-floor windows waiting to throw water bombs at passing girls.

Seven weeks later, at **Pentecost**, irises are traditionally laid out on the floors of the house, while in the Kraków region bonfires are lit on hilltop sites. A further eleven days on comes the most Catholic of festivals,

The list below is not exhaustive, so contact the Polish National Tourist Office for a list of upcoming events before you leave home. The listings in *Gazeta Wyborcza* or the *Warsaw Insider* will provide an idea of what's on once you arrive.

January
Warsaw Traditional jazz
Wrocław Solo plays

February
Poznań Boys' choirs
Wrocław Polish contemporary music

March
Częstochowa Violin music
Łódź Opera; student theatre

April
Kraków Organ music
Kraków Student song

May
Bielsko-Biała International puppet theatre (every even-numbered year)
Gdańsk "Neptunalia" (student festival)
Hajnówka Orthodox choirs
Kraków "Juvenalia" (student festival)
Łącko (near Nowy Sącz) Regional folk festival
Łancut Chamber music

Warsaw Festival of Sacred Songs
Wrocław Contemporary Polish plays (May/June)
Wrocław Jazz on the Odra

June
Brzeg Classical music
Kamień Pomorski Organ and chamber music (June/July)
Kazimierz Dolny Folk bands and singers (June/July)
Krynica Arias and songs
Kudowa-Zdrój Music of Stanisław Moniuszko
Opole Polish pop songs
Poznań Festival of contemporary theatre
Płock Folk ensembles
Toruń Contact festival of modern drama
Warsaw Summer Jazz Days

July
Gdańsk-Oliwa Organ music (July/Aug)
Gdynia Summer Jazz Days

Corpus Christi (Boże Ciało), marked by colourful processions everywhere and elaborate floral displays, notably in Łowicz. Exactly a week later, the story of the Tartar siege is re-enacted as the starting point of one of the country's few notable festivals of secular folklore, the **Days of Kraków**.

St John's Day on June 24 is celebrated with particular gusto in Warsaw, Kraków and Poznań; on the night of June 23/24 at around midnight, wreaths with burning candles are cast into the river, and there are also boat parades, dancing and fireworks. July 26, **St Anne's Day**, is the time of the main annual pilgrimage to Góra Świętej Anny in Silesia.

The first of two major Marian festivals on consecutive weeks comes with the **Feast of the Holy Virgin of Sowing** on August 8 in farming areas, particularly in the southeast of the country. By then, many of the great pilgrimages to the Jasna Góra shrine in Częstochowa have already set out, arriving for the **Feast of the**

Assumption (Święto Wniebowzięcia NMP) on August 15. This is also the occasion for the enactment of a mystery play at Kalwaria Pacławska near Przemyśl.

All Saints' Day (Dzień Wszystkich Świętych), November 1, is the day of national remembrance, with flowers, wreaths and candles laid on tombstones. In contrast, **St Andrew's Day**, November 30, is a time for fortune-telling, with dancing to accompany superstitious practices such as the pouring of melted wax or lead on paper. **St Barbara's Day**, December 4, is the traditional holiday of the miners, with special Masses held for their safety as a counterweight to the jollity of their galas.

During **Advent** (Adwent), the nation's handicraft tradition comes to the fore, with the making of cribs to adorn every church. In Kraków, a competition is held on a Sunday between December 3 and 10, the winning entries being displayed in the city's Historical Museum. On **Christmas Eve** (Wigilia) fami-

Jelenia Góra Street theatre (July/Aug)
Koszalin World Polonia Festival of Polish Songs (every 5 years – next 2006)
Kraków Jewish culture
Międzyzdroje Choral music
Międzyzdroje "Stars on Holiday" Film Festival
Mrągowo Country Picnic (Country and Western music)
Nowy Sącz Festival of ethnic/electronic crossover music
Rzeszów Festival of Polonia Music and Dance Ensembles Groups (every 3 years – next 2002)
Sanok Festival of Alternative and Art Films
Świnoujscie Fama Student Artistic Festival

August
Duszniki-Zdrój Music of Frédéric Chopin
Gdańsk Dominican fair
Jarocin Rock festival
Kazimierz Dolny Film Festival
Kraków Classical music
Sopot International songs
Zakopane Highland folklore
Zielona Góra International song and dance troupes

Żywiec Beskid culture

September
Bydgoszcz Classical music
Gdańsk Polish feature films
Słupsk Polish Piano Competition
Toruń International Old Music Festival
Warsaw Contemporary music
Wrocław "Wratislavia Cantans" (choral music)
Zamość Jazz Festival

October
Kraków Jazz music
Warsaw Baroque Opera Festival
Warsaw Chopin Piano Competition (every 5 years – next 2000)
Warsaw International Film Festival
Warsaw Jazz Jamboree

November
Gdynia Film festival
Poznań International Violin Competition (every 5 years – next 2006)
Warsaw Ancient Music Festival

December
Toruń Camerimage International Film Festival (specializing in camerawork)
Warsaw Theatre festival
Wrocław Old music

lies gather for an evening banquet, traditionally of twelve courses to symbolize the number of the Apostles; this is also the time when children receive their gifts. **Christmas Day** (Boże Narodzenie) begins with the midnight Mass; later, small round breads decorated with the silhouettes of domestic animals are consumed. **New Year's Eve** (Sylwester) is the time for magnificent formal balls, particularly in Warsaw, while in country areas of southern Poland it's the day for practical jokes – which must go unpunished. The Christmas period winds up with **Epiphany** (Dzień Trzech Króli) on January 6, when groups of carol singers move from house to house, chalking the letters K, M and B (symbolizing the Three Kings Kaspar, Melchior and Balthazar) on each doorway as a record of their visit. The chalk marks are usually left untouched throughout the coming year, thereby ensuring good fortune for the household.

Folk music

Though less dynamic than some of its eastern European neighbours, Polish **folk music** nevertheless plays a noteworthy role in national cultural life. Traditional folk comes in (at least) two varieties: a bland, sanitized version promoted by successive communist governments and still peddled, with varying degrees of success, principally for foreign consumption: and a rootsier, rural vein of genuine and vibrant folk culture, which you chiefly find among the country's minorities and in the southern and eastern parts of the country. Thanks in part to Chopin, who was profoundly influenced by the music of his native **Mazovia** (Mazowsze), Mazovian folk music is probably the best known in the country, traditional forms like the mazurka and polonaise offering a rich vein of tuneful melodies and vibrant dance rhythms. Other regions with strong traditional folk music cultures include

Silesia, the **Tatras**, whose music-loving *górale* (highlanders) have developed a rousing polyphonically inclined song tradition over the centuries, and the Lemks of the **Beskid Niski**, whose music bears a tangled imprint of Ukrainian, Slovak and Hungarian influences. Among the notable showcases for Polish folk music of all descriptions are the triennial Festival of Polonia Music and Dance in **Rzeszów**, which draws a welter of *emigracja* ensembles from the worldwide Polish diaspora, and the annual summer folk festival bash in **Kazimierz Dolny**.

In the north of the country along the **Baltic coast** the popularity of sea shanties is a surprising discovery, with annual festivals during the summer in many towns.

For a detailed account of Polish folk music see Contexts, p.714.

Classical music

The nation's wealth of folk tunes have found their way into some of the best of the country's **classical** music, of which Poles are justifiably proud, the roster of Polish composers containing a number of world-ranking figures, including Chopin, Moniuszko, Szymanowski, Penderecki, Panufnik, Lutoslawski and the 1990s runaway best-seller Henryk Górecki. The country has also produced a wealth of classical musicians, mostly in the first half of the twentieth century when pianists Artur Rubinstein and musician-premier Ignacy Paderewski gained worldwide prominence. A cluster of Polish **orchestras**, notably the Polish Chamber Orchestra, the Warsaw and Kraków Philharmonics, and the Katowice-based Radio and TV Symphony Orchestra, have made it into the world league and are regularly in demand on the international touring circuit.

All the big cities have music **festivals** of one sort or another, which generally give plenty of space to national composers, the international Chopin Piano Competition in Warsaw (held every five years) being the best known and most prestigious of the events. Throughout the year it's easy to catch works by Polish composers since the repertoires of many regional companies tend to be oriented towards national music.

Jazz

Jazz has a well-established pedigree in Poland ever since the 1950s, when bebop broke

through in a country hungry for Western forms of free expression. This explosion of interest in jazz brought forth a wealth of local talent, most notably **Krzystof Komeda**, who wrote edgy, experimental scores for Roman Polański's early movies during the sixties. Other home-grown musicians who made it into the international big league include tenorist **Zbigniew Namysłowski**, singer **Urszula Dudziak**, violinist **Michał Urbaniak** and trumpeter **Tomas Stanko**. Namyślowski and Stanko are still very much around on the gig circuit, and CD reissues featuring all the above names can be picked up in Polish record shops. The annual **Warsaw Jazz Jamboree** in October is well established as a major international event that always attracts a roster of big names. There's a reasonably healthy jazz **club** scene in the major cities – especially Kraków, which regards itself as the spiritual home of Polish jazz.

Rock and pop

There was a time when Poland was the Liverpool of Europe, producing a stream of guitar-wielding mop-tops and warbling starlets whose music was then exported all over the Soviet bloc. It started in the early Sixties, when a whole raft of groups emerged to cover the skiffle, rock-and-roll and rhythm-and-blues hits that had entered the country via the long-wave radio transmissions of Radio Luxembourg. Aided by the emergence of a nightclub scene in Gdańsk and Sopot, and the inauguration of the Festival of Polish Song in Opole (see p.580), Poland developed a home-grown version of western pop which went under the name of **Bigbeat** – with groups like **Czerwone Gitary** and **Skaldowie** providing the local answer to the Beatles and the Rolling Stones. However the biggest name to emerge from the sixties was **Czesław Niemen**, a national institution who is still regularly voted the best Polish singer-songwriter of all time. Moving from saccharine pop to earthy rhythm-and-blues, psychedelia, then prog-rock, Niemen introduced a new breadth of vision to Polish pop, although his voice – a cross between Otis Redding and a castrated wildebeest – is very much an acquired taste. In the 1970s intellectual art-rock held sway (**Marek Grechuta** and his group **Anawa** are the names to look out for if you're shopping for CDs), while in the 1980s punk and reggae came to the fore, the popularity of both due in part to their latent espousal of political protest

– anything gobbing at authority or chanting down Babylon went down particularly well in post-martial-law Poland. Nowadays the Polish pop scene resembles that of any other European country, with hardcore, rap, reggae and death-metal subcultures coexisting with a mainstream diet of techno – the Polish version of which, leavened with a few folksy influences, rejoices in the name of **Disco-Polo**. In a music industry that's so vibrant and varied it's difficult to pick out acts for specific attention, although **Kazik Staszewski** (a veteran of punk group Kult, his latest project has been to cover the songs of Kurt Weil) is probably the one big-selling album artist who gets bags of respect from the critics. The most striking development in recent years has been the eagerness to mix traditional folk music with pop and rock styles, with albums by crossover specialists **Brathanki** and **Golec uOrkestra** (of which more in Contexts; see p.714) selling by the bucketload. Another peculiarly Polish phenomenon is the emergence of a new brand of church-sanctioned pop: you'll find **Arka Noego**, a massively successful group of children singing Catholic nursery rhymes, hard to avoid.

There's a regular **gig circuit** in the major cities, and an underground scene in most places with a large student population. **Clubs** that host regular live music are listed in the relevant sections of the guide. Fly posters, or the Friday edition of *Gazeta Wyborcza*, are the best sources of information about up-and-coming events. In summer, **open-air concerts** (often featuring Western acts) take place in parks or sports grounds – again, posters advertising these events are plastered up just about everywhere. These summer stadium gigs are beginning to eclipse the importance of the annual **festival** in Jarocin, 75km southeast of Poznań (late July or early Aug; ⓦ www.start-festival.com) which, despite being the main annual showcase for Polish rock bands since the mid-1980s, has been cancelled at least once in recent years due to poor ticket sales.

Cinema

Cinemas (*kino*) are cheapish (£2–3/US$4) and generally comfortable. They can be found in almost every town in Poland, however small, showing major international films (especially anything American) as well as the home-produced ones. Only foreign films for children are dubbed into Polish (since they may have problems reading subtitles), otherwise films will be subtitled. The month's listings are usually fly-posted up around town or outside each cinema with the titles translated into Polish (the *Warsaw Insider* has a useful, regularly updated list of the original titles next to the Polish translations). The film's country of origin is usually shown – WB means British, USA American.

Based around the famous Łódź film school, postwar Polish cinema has produced a string of important directors, the best known being **Andrzej Wajda**, whose powerful *Człowiek z żelaza* ("*Man of Iron*") did much to popularize the cause of Solidarity abroad in the early 1980s. As in all the ex-communist countries the key issue for Polish film-makers used to be getting their work past the censors: for years they responded to the task of "saying without saying" with an imaginative blend of satire, metaphor and historically based parallelism whose subtle twists tend to leave even the informed Western viewer feeling a little perplexed. In the case of Wajda and other notables like **Agnieszka Holland**, **Krzysztof Zanussi** and **Krzysztof Kieślowski**, though, a combination of strong scripting, characterization and a subtle dramatic sense carries the day, and all these directors enjoy high prestige in international film circles.

In the 1990s, the picture looked a little different, concerns over the censor now replaced by the more conventional film-maker's headache of securing funding (whatever else the communists did wrong, they did, as some directors ruefully recall now, guarantee a level of film financing) and responding to a profoundly changed political and social reality. Post-communist efforts like **Krzysztow Kieślowski**'s award-winning *The Double Life of Véronique*, his masterful *Red*, *White* and *Blue* trilogy, and Wajda's *Korczak* pointed towards an artistically productive future for Polish cinema, although the local public showed more enthusiasm for the kind of home-grown historical blockbusters that rarely won international prizes. The outstanding example of this was **Jerzy Hoffman**'s 1999 adaptation of Henryk Sienkiewicz's patriotic novel *With Fire and Sword*, an extravagant costume drama that soon became the most succesful Polish film of all time – but sank without trace outside the country.

Theatre

Theatre in Poland is popular and cheap (£4/US$6), and most towns with a decent-sized population have at least one permanent venue with the month's programme pinned up outside and elsewhere in the town. The serious stuff tends to go on in the often sumptuous fin-de-siècle creations established by the country's trio of Partition-era rulers – Habsburg opulence if you're in Kraków, Russian-tolerated classicism in Warsaw, Prussian austerity in Gdańsk. Aside from the odd British or US touring company, there's little in English, though the generally high quality of Polish acting combined with the interest of the venues themselves – Poles go as much for the interval promenade as the show itself – usually makes for an enjoyable experience.

Theatre's special role in Polish cultural life dates from the Partition-era, when it played a significant role in the maintenance of both the language and national consciousness. In recent decades **Jerzy Grotowski**'s experimental Laboratory Theatre in Wrocław (disbanded in 1982 when he emigrated to Italy) gained an international reputation as one of the most exciting and innovative trends in theatrical theory and practice to emerge since Stanislavski's work in Moscow in the early part of this century. Theatre companies like the excellent **Teatr Ósmego Dnia** (Theatre of the Eighth Day) from Poznań, who also moved to Italy subsequently, carried the torch through the trials of martial law in the early 1980s, developing a probing, politically engaged theatre that closely reflected the struggles of the period. Till his death in 1992, **Tadeusz Kantor**, an experimental director and performance artist of international stature and long based in Kraków, was another figure at the creative forefront of contemporary Polish theatre. Among a handful of companies currently in demand internationally is **Gardziennice**, a consistently innovative experimental group based in a village near Lublin of the same name who specialize in field trips to villages throughout eastern Europe where oral cultural traditions are kept alive. The resulting productions, led by the company's founder and director **Włodzimierz Staniewski**, a close collaborator with Grotowski in the 1970s, are inspirational part-improvised, part-scripted happenings drawing on a wealth of dramatic resources.

In the late 1990s Polish experimental theatre companies like the **Wierszalin** group from Białystok became internationally renowned, carrying off prizes at the Edinburgh Festival, for instance.

Sport

The Polish media devote a vast amount of coverage to team games as diverse as **basketball** (*koszykówka*), **handball** (*handy-ballski*) and **volleyball** (*siatkówka*). One sport that enjoys major popularity in Poland is **speedway** (*żużel*), which basically involves motorbikes repeatedly racing each other around an oval track. Most major cities boast a team and a stadium, although it's in the industrial conurbations of the southwest that the sport arouses the greatest passions. Events usually take place on Saturdays; street posters advertise times and venues.

Football (*piłka nóżna*) remains the only sport that commands a genuine mass following nationwide. Franz Beckenbauer described the Polish national side as "the best team in the world" in 1974's World Cup, when they were unlucky to finish only in third place. The Poles remained a major force in the world game for the next decade, with players such as Grzegorz Lato, Kazimierz Deyna and Zbigniew Boniek becoming household names. Since then it's mostly been downhill, although the national team's impressive performance in qualifying for the 2002 World Cup suggested a turn in fortunes.

Despite receiving blanket coverage from the country's private TV stations, Polish **league football** is currently in the doldrums: few clubs are rich enough to pay the wages of top players, and the country's best talents ply their trade in Germany, Italy or elsewhere. Warsaw club Legia enjoys the biggest countrywide following, although they've been edged out of the league title in recent years by capital-city rivals Polonia, and the Kraków team Wisła. Other teams with proud historical pedigrees are the Silesian trio of GKS Katowice, Ruch Chorzów and Górnik Zabrze; and the two Łódź sides, LKS and Widzew. The season lasts from August to November, then resumes in March until June. Some of the top teams have equipped their stadia with plastic seating in order to comply with UEFA safety guidelines; elsewhere wooden benches, or uncovered concrete terraces, remain the rule. Inside, grilled sausages and beer are the order of the day. Regular league fixtures suffer from pitifully low attendance figures, not least because the emergence of a serious hooligan problem has scared many stadium-goers away.

Unsurprisingly, you shouldn't have trouble buying tickets (£4/US$6) on the gate for most games, although you may be asked to show ID before being subjected to a spot of vigorous security frisking. For details of results and fixtures, check out the Polish Football Federation's **website**, Ⓦ www.pzpn.pl.

Outdoor activities

For a growing number of visitors, it's the wide range of outdoor pursuits Poland has to offer, as well as its better-known cultural and architectural attractions, that constitute the country's chief lure. Most obvious of these are the hiking opportunities provided by the extensive national (and regional) parks, several of which incorporate authentic wilderness areas of great beauty.

Equally attractive for **skiers** are the slopes of the Tatra mountains – long the country's most developed, but by no means its only, ski resort area. Lakes and rivers offer generous opportunities for water-based activities. **Riding** enthusiasts will find plenty of scope for pursuing a pastime that remains a favourite among wealthier Poles, while **anglers** can sample Poland's significant collection of pristine fishing areas, notably in the outlying eastern regions of the country.

Hiking

Poland has some of the best **hiking** country in Europe, specifically in the sixteen areas designated as national parks and in the mountainous regions on the country's southern and western borders. There's a full network of marked **trails**, the best of which are detailed in the Guide. Many of these take several days, passing through remote areas served by *schroniska* (refuges; see "Accommodation" p.42). However, much of the best scenery can be seen by covering sections of these routes on one-day walks.

Unless you're in the High Tatras (see p.513 for some important tips), few of the one-day trails are especially strenuous and, although specialist **footwear** is recommended, well-worn-in sturdy shoes are usually enough. An account of hiking in the Tatras is included in

Contexts on p.724.

Skiing

Poland's mountainous southern rim provides some good **skiing** opportunities, seized on, in season, by what can often seem like the country's entire population. The best and not surprisingly, most popular ski slopes are in the Tatras, the highest section of the Polish Carpathians, where the skiing season runs from December through into March.

Poland's national parks

Although still in the shadow of the Alps and other well-known European resorts, Zakopane, the resort centre of the **Tatras**, has acquired a strong and growing international following, not least in the UK, where a variety of travel operators specialize in cheap, popular skiing packages. Though the skiing facilities in and around Zakopane may still leave a little to be desired, both in volume and quality, they have improved considerably over the last few years, not least in the provision of ski-lifts. Certainly, you shouldn't have any problems renting skiing gear in Zakopane itself.

Less dramatic alternatives to the Tatras include: the **Beskid Sudety**, notably the resorts at Karpacz and Szklarska Poręba; the Beskid Śląski resort of Szczyrk; and the **Bieszczady** (a favourite with cross-country skiers). One great advantage with all these is that they are relatively unknown outside Poland, although, consequently, facilities are fairly undeveloped – usually involving a single ski lift and a limited range of descents. As yet relatively free from package hotels, these smaller resorts are perhaps better suited to individual tourists than Zakopane, which can be jam-packed with groups from late December to the end of March.

Kayaking, sailing and windsurfing

Large stretches of lowland Poland are dotted with lakes, especially Mazuria (see p.239) in the northeast of the country, and it's relatively easy for travellers to rent a variety of **water craft** – from simple kayaks to luxury yachts – once they arrive. Most people content themselves with a day or two on the water, although the number of navigable waterways in Mazuria ensures there's a host of lengthy **canoeing and kayaking** itineraries to choose from, often involving overnight stops at campsites or hostels en route. The most popular of these are the nine-day traverse of the Mazurian lakes (see p.238), and the 3-day journey down the Czarna Hańcza river (see p.255). Well-equipped marinas at Mikołajki (see p.247), Giżycko (p.252) and Ruciane-Nida (p.250) are packed with **sailing** folk in the summer months. Simple sailing boats are easy enough to rent at these places; although at least one member of your party will have to

have sailing experience if you want to rent out a bigger craft.

Given the short duration of the Baltic summer, Poland's northern coast doesn't offer the kind of water sports opportunities that you'll find in the Mediterranean. However there's an established **windsurfing** scene in Łeba (see p.643), and in the resorts on the southern side of the Hel peninsula (p.197).

Riding

Horses and **riding** have a special place in the affections of many Poles. In a country that takes great pride in its military traditions, horses are associated with the dashing cavalry regiments for which the country was long famous. Even today, equestrian prowess is regarded as one of the higher art forms. Long established horse-breeding traditions, particularly at the stud farms begun in the nineteenth century, continue unabated, with internationally known centres such as Janów Podlaska rearing what connoisseurs view as some of the world's finest full-bloods, in particular classical Arabian purebreds. The annual autumn auctions at Janów are pretty big news in the horse world, with visiting celebrities including Jane Fonda and Rolling Stones' drummer Charlie Watts bidding for the best mounts.

Equestrian holidays in Poland are becoming a real draw. There's a wide and growing selection of state-owned stud farms, horse farms and other horse-riding and equestrian centres to choose from, encompassing easy-going family-oriented packages through to more strenuous holidays for the serious enthusiast. All the holiday deals are reasonably priced, and generally include meals, accommodation and the availability of riding instruction.

Orbis has a good range of stud farms and riding centres detailed in their brochure *Horse-riding Holidays*, while many of the farms offering eco-holidays (see p.41) offer riding among their attractions. If you're staying in Warsaw and simply fancy a day or two's riding nearby, the riding centre Pa-Ta-Taj at Grodzisk Mazowiecki in Pruszków (☎022/758 5835) offers horses at 20zł per hour, while the training centre at Paszków, 20km from the centre, offers rides with an instructor for 35zł per hour (☎022/729 8336).

Fishing

Especially in the more outlying regions of the country, where the rivers are generally less polluted, **fishing** is a popular pastime. The season effectively runs all year in one form or another, with winter fishing through holes in the ice and on the major Mazurian lakes, and fishing for lavaret with artificial spinners in summer.

The best fishing areas include the Mazurian lakes (pike and perch), the Bieszczady, notably the River San and its tributaries (trout), and the southeast in general. Pick up the *Yachting, Rowing and Angling* **brochure** produced by the State Sport and Tourism administration, ul. Świętokrzyska 12, Warsaw (☎022/694 4140), or for really comprehensive advice, including details on how to buy compulsory fishing **licences**, contact The Polish Fishing Association, ul. Twarda 42, Warsaw (☎022/620 5089, ☎620 5088), the National Tourist Board or Polorbis (see p.28 and p.12).

Cultural hints

In a country in which rural life continues to play a major role (over thirty percent of the population still lives in the countryside), mainstream Polish culture remains fundamentally conservative in outlook. The divide between city and country is pronounced: while the major cities such as Warsaw, Kraków, Wrocław and Gdańsk increasingly tune in to urban Western lifestyles and habits, the picture is very different in rural areas, particularly the further east you travel, where traditional peasant-based lifestyles remain the norm.

Despite the inroads of the communist era in relation to work practices, traditional **gender roles** are still dominant, with women shouldering responsibility for the home and rearing children, and men generally occupying the main breadwinner role.

With international **fashion** now followed by the bulk of Polish youth, you're unlikely to look out of place because of what you wear, although modest attire is advised when visiting churches. Although Warsaw now has its first **nudist beach**, in other areas, like the beaches of the Baltic coast or Mazurian lakesides, nude or topless sunbathing will attract attention and sometimes direct protest.

Polish **hospitality** is proverbial. "A guest is God in the house" runs the traditional saying, and if your visit involves any kind of home-based encounter with Poles you're more than likely to experience this at first hand. Home is the important word here. One of the more corrosive social effects of the communist era was to heighten the division between public and private life. Straitened economic circumstances resulted in the descent of the public sphere into a grinding, often ruthless struggle to secure the basic necessities of life for one's family, with public interactions a necessary but despised aspect of life. By contrast, the private, meaning the home, friends and family, became the place where Poles really came into their own. The economic and political circumstances may have changed but the public/private division persists. If your encounters with Poles are restricted to waiters, shop assistants and hotel receptionists, you'll have a very different experience of the country than if you manage to establish some more personal encounters. The good news for those who don't have friends or family awaiting them is that it isn't difficult to establish contact, especially among people of younger Western-oriented generations.

Social conventions are important to get a grip on. Poles are inveterate handshakers, even the most casual street encounter with second cousins three times removed is prefaced and ended by a short, firm handshake. If you're invited to somebody's home, a bouquet of flowers for your hostess (size is not important) is an indispensable item of traditional etiquette.

Polish attitudes to **time** are fairly relaxed: lateness for social appointments is fairly standard, at least within a half-hour margin, but not turning up at all definitely constitutes a sin of the first order, particularly if you've been invited to someone's house: in true Polish style, people will have made an effort for you, and will be offended if this is not at least minimally reciprocated.

Gay and lesbian travellers

For the **gay** and especially the **lesbian** visitor accustomed to the energetic sub-cultures flourishing in cities in the United States, Britain and other western European countries, the Polish gay scene may seem a bit of a disappointment, though as in any other country it depends where you are. Warsaw definitely has a scene, Kraków and Gdańsk are developing one, and other cities will follow. There's little in the way of gay media, but contacts can easily be made through agencies, pubs and clubs (details are given in the Guide).

Unlike the grim juridical situation prevailing in much of the former Soviet Union, homosexuality is not proscribed under the provisions of Poland's 1963 criminal code. The statutory age of consent is 15, irrespective of the sexual orientation of the partners. Indeed, in this regard Polish **laws** governing sexual behaviour are actually relatively more liberal than those in Britain, not to mention those in nearly half of the states in the USA whose statutes continue to outlaw gay sexual relations altogether. Polish gays and lesbians also are legally free to establish clubs and newspapers and all of the other paraphernalia sexual minorities seeking a voice in, say, New York or London employ.

Though the exact figures are not known, Poland has the highest incidence of **AIDS** in eastern Europe. The Church's influence has been something of a hindrance in combating the disease, but helplines are now established in the major cities, and there is a higher level of "safe sex" and AIDS awareness in Polish society now that information and good condoms are readily available (see the "Directory", p.65).

As in other homophobically inclined cultures, too, caution is generally the watchword – gay-bashings do occur outside places known to be frequented by homosexuals.

Contacts for gay and lesbian travellers

The Ⓦ www.gay.pl **website** has details of gay contacts and clubs throughout the country. One organization worth contacting before or during a visit to Poland is **Lambda**, a national network of gay and lesbian organizations, with branches in several major cities; its Warsaw branch is at ul. Czerniakowska 178, lok. 16. (Tues & Wed 6–9pm, Fri 4–10pm; ℡022/628 5222, Ⓔlambdawa@polbox.com).

For more on the Polish Women's Movement, see "Directory", p.66. Otherwise, the organizations listed below should be able to help out with information.

Australia and New Zealand

Gay and Lesbian Travel
Ⓦwww.galta.com.au. Directory and links for gay and lesbian travel in Australia and worldwide.
Gay Travel Ⓦwww.gaytravel.com. The site for trip planning, bookings, and general information about international travel.
Parkside Travel 70 Glen Osmond Rd, Parkside, SA 5063 ℡08/8274 1222 or 1800/888 501, Ⓔhwtravel@senet.com.au. Gay travel agent associated with local

branch of Hervey World Travel; all aspects of gay and lesbian travel worldwide.

Pinkstay ⓦwww.pinkstay.com. Everything from visa information to finding accommodation and work around the world.

Silke's Travel 263 Oxford St, Darlinghurst, NSW 2010 ☏02/9380 6244 or 1800/807 860, ⓔsilba@magna.com.au. Long-established gay and lesbian specialist, with the emphasis on women's travel.

Tearaway Travel, 52 Porter St, Prahan, VIC 3181 ☏03/9510 6344, ⓔtearaway@bigpond.com. Gay-specific business dealing with international and domestic travel.

UK

ⓦ**www.gaytravel.co.uk** Online gay and lesbian travel agent, offering good deals on all types of holiday. Also lists gay- and lesbian-friendly hotels around the world.

In USA and Canada

Damron Company PO Box 422458, San Francisco CA 94142 ☏1-800/462-6654 or 415/255-0404, ⓦwww.damron.com. Publisher of the *Men's Travel Guide*, a pocket-sized yearbook full of listings of hotels, bars, clubs and resources for gay men; the *Women's Traveler*, which provides similar listings for lesbians; the *Road Atlas*, which shows lodging and entertainment in major US cities; and *Damron Accommodations*, which provides detailed listings of over 1000 accommodations for gays and lesbians worldwide. All of these titles are offered at a discount on the website. No specific city guides – everything is incorporated in the yearbooks.

Ferrari Publications PO Box 37887, Phoenix, AZ 85069 ☏1-800/962-2912 or 602/863-2408, ⓦwww.ferrariguides.com. Publishes *Ferrari Gay Travel A to Z*, a worldwide gay and lesbian guide; *Inn Places*, a worldwide accommodation guide; the guides *Men's Travel in Your Pocket* and *Women's Travel in Your Pocket*, and the quarterly *Ferrari Travel Report*.

International Gay/Lesbian Travel Association 4331 N Federal Hwy, Suite 304, Ft Lauderdale, FL 33308 ☏1-800/448-8550, ⓦwww.iglta.org. Trade group that can provide a list of gay- and lesbian-owned or friendly travel agents, accommodation and other travel businesses.

Police and trouble

Nothing epitomizes recent political change in Poland better than what's happened to the police. Gone now is the secret police structure and the ZOMO, the hated riot squads responsible for quelling the big demonstrations from martial law onwards. What's left is the milicja, or, as they've been diplomatically renamed now, the policja, who are responsible for everyday law enforcement.

Transforming the ethos of a force accustomed to operating outside the bounds of public control is a difficult task, and all in all the *policja* seem to be in a pretty demoralized state, with the entire force supposedly being put through retraining programmes. In common with other East European countries, Poland has experienced a huge increase in crime in recent years, the police seemingly unable or unwilling to do much about it. Sales of alarms, small firearms and other security paraphernalia are on the increase, and residents of Warsaw's high-rise blocks have resorted to organizing their own night watches to stem the flood of car break-ins.

For Westerners, the biggest potential hassles are from **petty crime**: notably hotel-room thefts, and pickpocketing in crowded places such as train stations (especially in Warsaw) and in markets. A few common-sense precautions should help you avoid trouble: display cameras, fancy mobile phones and other signs of affluence as little as possible, never leave valuables in your room, and keep large sums of cash in a (well hidden) moneybelt. Guard against opportunistic thefts on overnight trains by booking a couchette or sleeper and keeping it well locked. If you're travelling in the regular carriages, try not to fall asleep.

Theft of Western **cars** and/or their contents is something of a national sport in Poland. Avoid leaving cars unattended anywhere in town centres – and if you do have to park in the street for a short time, remove valuable items from the vehicle or ensure they are hidden from view. It's invariably worth paying to park in a guarded lot *(parking strzeżony)*; most hotels will have one of these, or will at least direct you to the nearest one available.

Your best protection against crime is to take out **travel insurance** before you go (see p.23). If you do have anything stolen, report the loss to the police as soon as possible, and be patient – the Polish police rarely speak English, and filling out a report can take ages. The chances of getting your gear back are virtually zero.

Poles are obliged to carry some form of ID with them at all times: you should always keep your **passport** with you, even though you're unlikely to get stopped unless you're in a car; Western numberplates provide the excuse for occasional unprovoked spot checks. It's a good idea to carry a photocopy of the final, information-bearing page of your passport. This will help your consulate to issue a replacement document if you're unlucky enough to have it stolen.

Sexual harassment

Sexual harassment is less obviously present than in the West, but lack of familiarity with the cultural norms means it's easier to misinterpret situations, and rural Poland is still extremely conservative culturally: the further out you go, the more likely it is that women travelling alone will attract bemused stares.

Polish women tend to claim that men leave off as soon as you tell them to leave you alone, but this isn't always the case, particularly with anyone who's had a few drinks. However, if you do encounter problems, you'll invariably find other Poles stepping in to help – the Polish people are renowned for their hospitality to strangers and will do much to make you feel welcome. The only particular places to avoid are the hard-drinking haunts in provincial towns and big-city suburbs, which still tend to be male-only preserves; and hotel nightclubs, where plenty of men will assume you're a prostitute.

Work and study

Despite the booming international business scene in cities like Warsaw, Gdańsk and Poznań, it's extremely unlikely that you'll pick up casual work in Poland – or indeed that you'll want to, given that the average monthly wage is still below US$400. The fact that all non-Polish citizens (officially at least) require a work permit before commencing employment provides a further disincentive.

The popularity of learning **English** has mushroomed in recent years, leading to a constant demand for native-language English teachers both in the state education system and in the private language schools that seem to have sprung up all over the country. However you'll probably need a TEFL certificate or equivalent in order to secure a job at any but the most fly-by-night organizations. Vacancies are sometimes advertised in the education supplements of western newspapers; otherwise it's a question of touting your CV around the language schools and making use of local contacts once you arrive.

Study

Summer **language courses** are run by the universites of Kraków, Poznań, Lublin (KUL) and Łódź. Courses last from two to six weeks, covering all levels from beginners to advanced; a six-week course with full board and lodging will cost in the region of £500/US$800. Information on these courses can be obtained from the Polish Cultural Institute, 34 Portland Place, London WC1N 4HQ (☎020/7636 6032, ⓦwww.polishculture.org.uk) or Polish consulates abroad.

In addition, many private language schools in Poland are beginning to offer language courses to the growing army of expatriate Westerners keen to learn Polish. In Kraków, Poliglota (ⓦwww.poliglota.pl); and Prolog (PNTA, ul. Starowiślna 56/34 (☎421 6066, ⓦwww.prolog.edu.pl) offer 2- and 4-week intensive courses, and longer ones lasting a term or more. Similar courses are operated in Warsaw by Linguarama (ul. Sniadeckih 17, 00654 Warsaw (☎22/628 7291, ⓦwww.linguarama.com); and in the Tri-City area by Centrum Językowo-Szkoleniowe, ul. Starowiejska 41/43, 81363 Gdynia, (☎058/781 9885, ⓦwww.lcs.pl). Prices for all the above are worked out on an ad-hoc basis, depending on how many people show an interest.

For humanities graduates seeking an opportunity for further study, the Jagiellonian Univesity in Kraków offers an MA programme – taught in English – on central European history and society (ⓦwww.ces.uj.edu.pl).

Directory

ADDRESSES The street name is always written before the number. The word for street (ulica, abbreviated to ul.) or avenue (aleja, abbreviated al.) is often missed out – for example ulica Senatorska is simply known as Senatorska. The other frequent abbreviation is pl., short for plac (square). In towns and villages across the country, streets named after the stars and dates of Polish and international communism have almost all been retitled, more often than not by the ubiquitous Jan Paweł II. See Contexts for details on the most common street names.

AIDS There is a 24-hour advice helpline on ☎022/622 5051. Those who are HIV positive can also phone ☎022/628 3285 (Mon & Thurs 1–6pm). There's advice on AIDS and venereal disease generally on ☎022/629 7977 (daily 4–9pm); ask for an English speaker.

BOTTLES Some drinks still come in bottles which have a deposit on them. Shops will accept bottles from other outfits providing they stock the type you're trying to fob off on them.

CIGARETTES American brands are being pushed hard in Poland, driving out the cheaper (and admittedly nastier) Polish brands, of which Sobieski and Mars are the main representatives. Apart from familiar names like Marlboro and Camel, West and Prince are the main Western brands. Matches are zapałki. Smoking is banned in all public buildings and on all public transport within towns.

CONTRACEPTIVES Condoms (*prezerwatywy*) are purchased from street kiosks or high-street pharmacies, with familiar Western brand names widely available. The Catholic mores in operation do not affect their sale.

DRUGS Hard drug abuse – principally amphetamines, *kompot*, a locally produced opium derivative, and heroin – is on the rise. Marijuana and hashish are fairly common, and possession of small quantities of soft drugs is currently legal, though selling or trading in them is not.

ELECTRICITY is the standard Continental 220 volts. Round two-pin plugs are used, so UK residents will need to bring an adaptor.

EMBASSIES AND CONSULATES All foreign embassies are in Warsaw, though a number of countries maintain consulates in Gdańsk and Kraków. See respective listings for addresses.

EMERGENCIES Police ☎997; fire ☎998; ambulance ☎999. There are private ambulance services in Warsaw and other big cities; see listings in the Guide.

FILM Familiar western brands of print film are widely available and are preferable to the locally-produced stuff, which is of poor quality. Outside major cities, the choice of transparency and black and white film is limited, so stock up before leaving home. Colour prints can be developed in high-street print shops in most cities and tourist resorts.

JAYWALKING is illegal but everyone does it, since you can grow old waiting for some of the lights to turn green. If caught you'll be fined on the spot.

LAUNDRY Self-service facilities are virtually nonexistent in Poland – although most towns do boast a *pralnia* (laundry), these tend to concentrate exclusively on dry cleaning. Some of them offer service washes too, although this might take up to three days. You can get things service-washed in the more upmarket hotels within 24 hours, but at a cost.

LEFT LUGGAGE Most train and bus stations of any size have a left-luggage office, or *przechowalnia bagażu*. In big-city train stations these are often open 24hr; elsewhere, take note of opening and closing times.

STUDENT CARDS Carrying an ISIC card will save you about 50 percent in admission fees to museums and galleries, and also qualifies you for cut-price city transport tickets in Warsaw and Kraków.

TAMPONS Polish shops supply all the main international brands of sanitary towels (*podpaski hygieniczne*) and tampons (*tampony*).

TIME Poland is one hour ahead of GMT, nine hours ahead of US Pacific Standard Time and six hours ahead of Eastern Standard Time. Clocks go forward one hour at the end of March and an hour back at the end of October.

TOILETS Public toilets (*toalety*, *ubikacja* or WC) are few and far between (except in the biggest cities) and would win few design awards; restaurants or hotels are a better bet. Once in, you pay a fixed amount to the attendant, usually 0.5zł, and paper and towels are freely available. The days when you had to buy toilet paper by the sheet are numbered, but there may be a rural toilet somewhere in Poland where it still happens. Gents are marked ▼, ladies ● or ▲.

WOMEN'S MOVEMENT Following the demise of communism and concurrent with the growing ascendancy of Catholic mores in the country's social and political life, the status of women is on the political agenda – in particular, what many see as their treatment as second-class citizens. The biggest single cause of this is the heated debate about abortion sparked by government moves to criminalize abortion in all but the most exceptional circumstances. After a move towards liberalization which allowed abortion up to twelve weeks into pregnancy on grounds of financial or emotional difficulties, the law was tightened in 1996 to restrict abortion to cases of rape, incest, a damaged foetus or a threat to the mother's health. As a result the number of miscarriages in the country shot up to 45,000, most a product of illegal and botched backstreet abortion efforts. Highly controversial as the subject is, most Poles consider further liberalization inevitable as the Church's grip on society weakens. A feminist women's movement is weak at the popular level, ironically part of the reason being a widespread adverse reaction to campaigns for sexual equality as a relic of communist-era sloganeering. The website Ⓦwww.oska.org.pl has details of national and regional organizations; while Ⓦwww.kobiety.pl has more general news on women's issues in English.

guide

guide

Warsaw and Mazovia

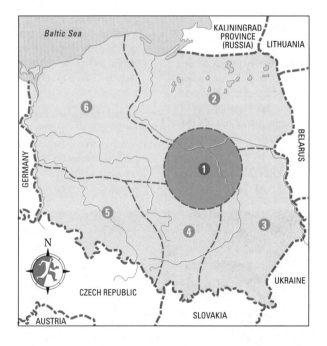

CHAPTER 1 **Highlights**

* **Warsaw's Stare Miasto** A testament to Poland's postwar efforts to reconstruct itself after World War II, this historic town centre was recreated from almost nothing after being razed by the Nazis. **See p.88**

* **Zamek Królewski** The sumptuous palace of Poland's seventeenth- and eighteenth-century kings is a treasure trove of Baroque over-statement. **See p.90**

* **Pałac Kultury i Nauk** A colossal monument to the ideological certainties of the Stalinist period, this imposing neo-Baroque monolith is still the defining feature of downtown Warsaw's skyline. **See p.111**

* **Park Łazienkiowski** The most elegant of Poland's urban parks, criss-crossed with oaklined promenades and a favourite with strollers whatever the time of year. **See p.115**

* **Wilanów** Warsaw grandest palacs, tucked away in the almost rural surroundings on the southern outskirts of the city. **See p.118**

* **Żelazowa Wola** Chopin's birthplace, and nowadays a national shrine; there's a museum dedicated to the composer and you can even attend summertime piano recitals in the surrounding park. **See p.136**

* **Łódź** Poland's second city is an endearingly gruff industrial centre that boasts fine nineteenth-century architecture and a vibrant cultural and social scene. **See p.141**

Warsaw and Mazovia

Warsaw has two enduring points of definition: the Wisła River, running south to north across the Mazovian plains, and the Moscow–Berlin road, stretching across this terrain – and through the city – east to west. Such a location, and four hundred years of capital status, have ensured a history writ large with occupations and uprisings, intrigues and heroism. Warsaw's sufferings, its near-total obliteration in World War II and subsequent resurrection from the ashes, has lodged the city in the national consciousness and explains why an often ugly city is held in such affection. In the latest era of political struggle – the emergence of Solidarity, fall of communism and the re-establishment of electoral democracy – Warsaw has at times seemed overshadowed by events in Gdańsk and the industrial centres of the south, but its role has been a key one nonetheless, as a focus of popular and intellectual opposition to communism, the site of past and future power and, increasingly, as the centre of the country's rapid economic transformation.

Likely to be most visitors' first experience of Poland, Warsaw makes an initial impression that is all too often negative. The years of communist rule have left no great aesthetic glories, and there's sometimes a hollowness to the faithful reconstructions of earlier eras. However, as throughout Poland, the pace of social change is tangible and fascinating, as the openings provided by the post-communist order turn the streets into a continuous marketplace. Many of the once grey and tawdry state shopfronts of the city centre have given way to a host of colourful new private initiatives, while the postwar dearth of nightlife and entertainments has become a complaint of the past now that a mass of new bars, restaurants and clubs have established themselves.

You're unlikely to find many outward manifestations of modernity in the villages of **Mazovia** – **Mazowsze** in Polish – the plain which surrounds the capital. Mazovia is historically one of the poorer regions of Poland, its peasant population eking a precarious existence from the notoriously infertile sandy

Accommodation price codes

The accommodation listed in this book has been given one of the following price codes, based, unless stated otherwise, on the cost of the cheapest double room in high season. For more details see p.39.

❶ under 60zł	❹ 120–160zł	❼ 300–400zł
❷ 60–90zł	❺ 160–220zł	❽ 400–600zł
❸ 90–120 zł	❻ 220–300zł	❾ over 600zł

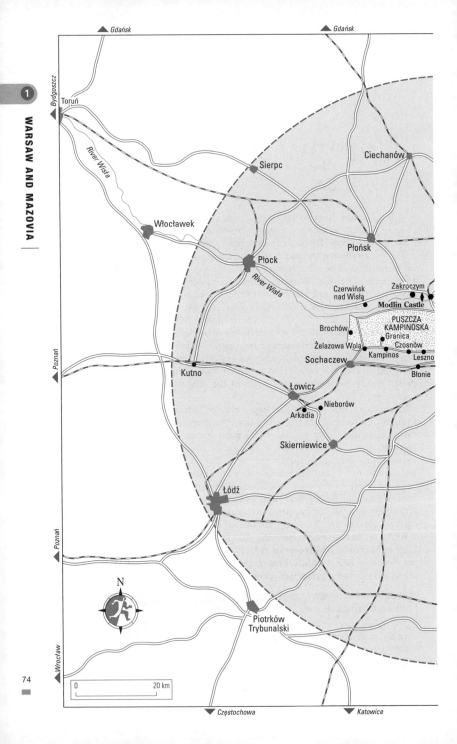

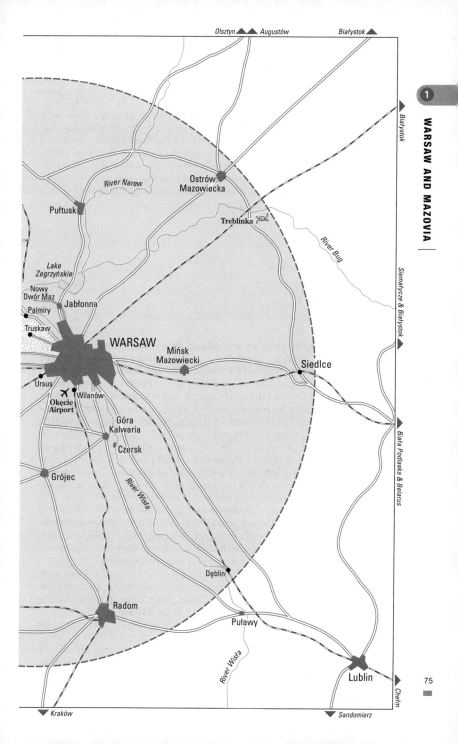

Olsztyn ▲▲ Augustów   Białystok ▲

Białystok ▶

Siemiatycze & Białystok ▶

River Narew

Ostrów-Mazowiecka

Pułtusk

Treblinka

River Bug

Lake Zegrzyńskie

Nowy Dwór Maz
Jabłonna

Palmiry

Truskaw

WARSAW

Mińsk Mazowiecki

Siedlce

Ursus

Okęcie Airport   Wilanów

Góra Kalwaria

Czersk

Biała Podlaska & Belarus ▶

Grójec

River Wisła

Dęblin

Radom

Puławy

River Wisła

Lublin

Chełm ▶

▼ Kraków   ▼ Sandomierz

soil. It is not the most arresting of landscapes, but contains a half-dozen rewarding day-trips to ease your passage into the rural Polish experience. The **Park Narodowy Puszcza Kampinoska** (Kampinoski Forest National Park), spreading northwest of Warsaw, is the remnant of the primeval forests that once covered this region, with tranquil villages dotted along its southern rim. A little further west is **Żelazowa Wola**, the much-visited birthplace of Chopin, and on the opposite side of the river, the historic church complex at **Czerwińsk nad Wisłą**. **Łowicz** is well known as a centre of Mazovian folk culture, while the palace at **Nieborów** is one of the finest and best-preserved aristocratic mansions in the country. A hundred kilometres southwest of the capital lies industrial **Łódź**, the country's second city and an important cultural centre, while to the north there are historic old Mazovian centres, notably the market town of **Pułtusk**. Finally, fans of Secessionist art won't want to miss the outstanding museum at **Płock**, west along the river.

Warsaw

Travelling through the grey, faceless housing estates surrounding **WARSAW** (**WARSZAWA**) or walking through the grimy Stalinist tracts that punctuate the centre, you could be forgiven for wishing yourself elsewhere. But a knowledge of Warsaw's rich and often tragic history can transform the city, revealing voices from the past in even the ugliest quarters: a pockmarked wall becomes a precious prewar relic, a housing estate the one-time centre of Europe's largest ghetto, the whole city a living book of modern history. Among the concrete, there are reconstructed traces of Poland's imperial past, including a castle, a scattering of palaces and parks, and the restored streets of the historic Stare Miasto, while the headlong rush into the embrace of capitalist culture is already throwing up its own particular architectural legacy, some of it familiar – towering skyscrapers and plush Western shopfronts – some more original – Party headquarters turned stock exchanges, Stalin-era palaces transformed into business centres. Indeed, new construction is everywhere: many of the areas of waste ground left untouched since the destruction of World War II have disappeared under gleaming new office blocks, while many public squares (notably pl. Defilad and pl. Bankowy) are receiving extensive facelifts in order to make room for brand-new metro stations, department stores or corporate headquarters.

Wending its way north towards Gdańsk and the Baltic Sea, the **Wisła** river divides Warsaw neatly in half: the main sights are located on the western bank, the eastern consists predominantly of residential and business districts. Marking the northern end of the city centre, the busy **Stare Miasto** (Old Town) provides the historic focal point. Rebuilt from scratch after World War II like most of Warsaw, the magnificent Zamek Królewski (Royal Castle), ancient Archikatedra św. Jana (St John's Cathedral) and the Rynek Starego Miasta (Old Town Square) are the most striking examples of the capital's reconstruction. Baroque churches and the former palaces of the aristocracy line the streets west of the ring of defensive walls, and to the north, in the quietly atmospheric **Nowe Miasto** (New Town).

West of the Stare Miasto, in the **Muranów** and **Mirów** districts, is the former **ghetto** area, where the Nożyck Synagogue and the ul. Okopowa cemetery bear poignant testimony to the lost Jewish population. South from the Stare Miasto lies **Śródmieście**, the city's commercial centre, its skyline dominated by the Pałac Kultury i Nauk (Palace of Culture), Stalin's permanent legacy to the citizens of Warsaw. Linking the Stare Miasto and Śródmieście, **Krakowskie Przedmięscie** is dotted with palaces and Baroque spires, and forms the first leg of the **Trakt Królewski** (Royal Way), a procession of open boulevards stretching all the way from plac Zamkowy to the stately king's residence at **Wilanów** on the southern outskirts of the city. Along the way is **Park Łazienkowski**, one of Warsaw's many delightful green spaces and the setting for the charming Pałac Łazienkowski (Łazienki Palace), surrounded by waterways and lakes. Further out, the city becomes a welter of high-rise developments, but among them, historic suburbs like **Żoliborz** to the north and **Praga** to the east give a flavour of the authentic life of contemporary Warsaw.

Warsaw is a much livelier and more cosmopolitan place than it's given credit for in the West. It is a little-known fact, for instance, that there are up to thirty thousand Americans living in Warsaw – much the same number as in Prague – and since they're not all trying to write the Great American Novel, their contribution to the Polish capital has been more marked in terms of cuisine and practical facilities. It's an eye-opening experience for many people to walk the bustling, vibrant streets, though a notable side-effect of this influx of new money are the **beggars** that you'll encounter every few steps, from the limbless and blind to the headscarved elderly bent double against the elements.

For those arriving without personal connections or contacts, Warsaw can seem forbidding, with much of the place still shutting down within a few hours of darkness, but Varsovians are generous and highly hospitable people: no social call, even to an office, is complete without a glass of *herbata* and plate of cakes. Postwar austerity has strengthened the tradition of home-based socializing, and if you strike up a friendship here (and friendships in Warsaw are quickly formed) you'll find much to enrich your experience of the city.

Some history

For a capital city, Warsaw entered history late. Although there are records of a settlement here from the tenth century, the first references to anything resembling a town at this point on the Wisła date from around the mid-fourteenth century. It owes its initial rise to power to the Mazovian ruler **Janusz the Elder**, who made Warsaw his main residence in 1413 and developed it as capital of the Duchy of Mazovia. Following the death of the last Mazovian prince in 1526, Mazovia and its now greatly enlarged capital were incorporated into **Polish** royal territory. The city's fortunes now improved rapidly. Following the Act of Union with Lithuania, the Sejm – the Polish parliament – voted to transfer to Warsaw in 1569. The first election of a Polish king took place here four years later, and then in 1596 came the crowning glory, when **King Sigismund III** moved his capital two hundred miles from Kraków to its current location – a decision chiefly compelled by the shift in Poland's geographical centre after the union with Lithuania.

Capital status inevitably brought prosperity, but along with new wealth came new perils. The city was badly damaged by the **Swedes** during the invasion of 1655 – the first of several assaults – and was then extensively reconstructed by the **Saxon** kings in the late seventeenth century. The lovely Ogród Saski (Saxon Gardens), in the centre of Warsaw, date from this period, for example. Poles tend to remember the **eighteenth century** in a nostalgic haze as the

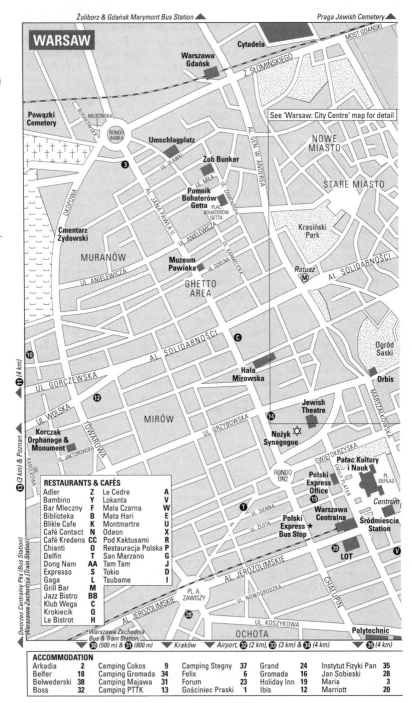

WARSAW

Żoliborz & Gdańsk Marymont Bus Station ▲

Praga Jewish Cemetery ▲

MOST GDAŃSKI

Cytadela

Warszawa
Gdańsk

Z. SŁOMIŃSKIEGO

See 'Warsaw: City Centre' map for detail

Powązki
Cemetery

MŁOCIŃSKA

BURAKOWSKA

RONDO
BABKA

Umschlagplatz

UL. SŁAWKI

Żob Bunker

UL. MIŁA

AL. GEN. W. ANDERSA

NOWE
MIASTO

STARE MIASTO

Pomnik
Bohaterów
Getta

PLAC
BOHATERÓW
GETTA

UL. ZAMENHOFA

Krasiński
Park

Cmentarz
Żydowski

OKOPOWA

AL. JANA PAWŁA II

UL. ANIELEWICZA

MURANÓW

UL. ANIELEWICZA

Muzeum
Pawiaka

UL. DZIELNA

UL. KARMELICKA

GHETTO
AREA

Ratusz Ⓜ

AL. SOLIDARNOŚCI

AL. SOLIDARNOŚCI

Ⓒ

Ogród
Saski

⑩

⑪ (4 km)

UL. GORCZEWSKA

⑫

TOWAROWA

UL. WOLSKA

MIRÓW

Hala
Mirowska

UL. GRZYBOWSKA

Orbis

MARSZAŁKOWSKA

Jewish
Theatre

⑭

Korczak
Orphanage &
Monument

UL. JAKTOROWSKA

KAROLKOWA

⑬ (3 km) & Poznań

Nożyk ✡
Synagogue

UL. GRZYBOWSKA

ŚWIĘTOKRZYSKA

RONDO
ONZ

Pałac Kultury
i Nauk

PL.
DEFILAD

Polski
Express
Office
⑲

EMILII PLATER

Centrum

RESTAURANTS & CAFÉS

Adler	Z	Le Cedre	A
Bambino	Y	Lokanta	V
Bar Mleczny	F	Mala Czarna	W
Biblioteka	B	Mata Hari	E
Blikle Cafe	K	Montmartre	U
Café Contact	N	Odeon	X
Café Kredens	CC	Pod Kaktusami	R
Chianti	O	Restauracja Polska	P
Delfin	T	San Marzano	G
Dong Nam	AA	Tam Tam	J
Expresso	S	Tokio	D
Gaga	L	Tsubame	I
Grill Bar	M		
Jazz Bistro	BB		
Klub Wega	C		
Krokiecik	Q		
Le Bistrot	H		

UL. SIENNA

Ⓣ

Polski
Express
Bus Stop ★

UL. ZŁOTA

Warszawa
Centralna

Warszawa
Centralna

Śródmieście
Station

⑳

LOT

Ⓥ

CHAŁUBIN

AL. JEROZOLIMSKIE

Dworzec Centralny Pks (Bus Station)
Warszawa Zachodnia (Train Station)

PL. A.
ZAWISZY

AL. JEROZOLIMSKIE

UL. NOWOGRODZKA

UL. KOSZYKOWA

OCHOTA

Polytechnic

㉘

Warszawa Zachodnia
Bus & Train Station,
㉚ (500 m) & ㉛ (800 m)   ▼ Kraków   ▼ Airport, ㉜ (2 km), ㉝ (3 km) & ㉞ (4 km)   ▼   ㉟ (4 km)

ACCOMMODATION

Arkadia	2	Camping Cokos	9	Camping Stegny	37	Grand	24	Instytut Fizyki Pan	35
Belfer	18	Camping Gromada	34	Felix	6	Gromada	16	Jan Sobieski	28
Belwederski	38	Camping Majawa	31	Forum	23	Holiday Inn	19	Maria	3
Boss	32	Camping PTTK	13	Gościniec Praski	1	Ibis	12	Marriott	20

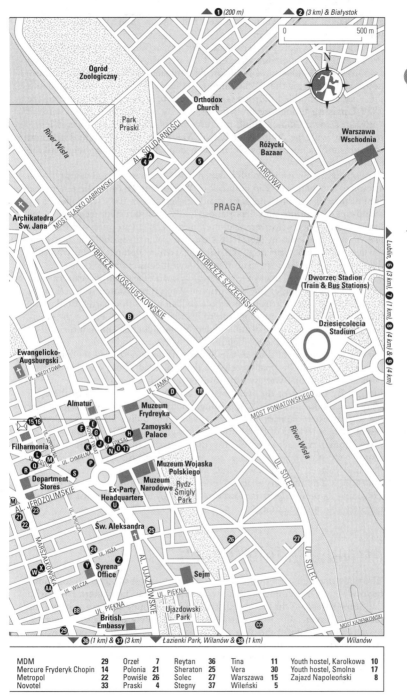

1 (200 m) **2** (3 km) & Białystok

0 — 500 m

N

Ogród
Zoologiczny

Orthodox
Church

Park
Praski

Różycki
Bazaar

Warszawa
Wschodnia

River Wisła

AL. SOLIDARNOŚCI

4 A

5

TARGOWA

PRAGA

MOST ŚLĄSKO DĄBROWSKI

Archikatedra
Św. Jana

WYBRZEŻE SZCZECIŃSKIE

WYBRZEŻE KOŚCIUSZKOWSKIE

Dworzec Stadion
(Train & Bus Stations)

B

Dziesięciolecia
Stadium

Ewangelicko-
Augsburgski

UL. KREDYTOWA

UL. TAMKA

D

18

MOST PONIATOWSKIEGO

River Wisła

Almatur

Muzeum
Frydreyka

Zamoyski
Palace

UL. SPYTALNA

15 16

F E
G
J H
N O **17**
K
P

NOWY ŚWIAT

FOKSAL

Filharmonia

UL. CHMIELNA

L M
R Q
U

UL. WIDOK

S

Muzeum Wojska
Polskiego

Department
Stores

Muzeum
Narodowe

Rydz-
Śmigly
Park

Ex-Party
Headquarters

AL. JEROZOLIMSKIE

M

21
23
22

MARSZAŁKOWSKA

Św. Aleksandra

25

26

27

UL. SOLEC

24

UL. HOŻA

Z

W X

Y

Syrena
Office

UL. KRUCZA

AL. UJAZDOWSKIE

Sejm

AA

UL. WILCZA

UL. PIĘKNA

BB

UL. PIĘKNA

Ujazdowski
Park

British
Embassy

29

MOST KAZIENKOWSKI

CC

36 (1 km) & **37** (3 km)   Łazienki Park, Wilanów & **38** (1 km)   Wilanów

Lublin, **6** (3 km), **7** (1 km), **8** (4 km) & **9** (4 km)

WARSAW AND MAZOVIA | Warsaw

1

MDM	29	Orzeł	7	Reytan	36	Tina	11	Youth hostel, Karolkowa	10
Mercure Fryderyk Chopin	14	Polonia	21	Sheraton	25	Vera	30	Youth hostel, Smolna	17
Metropol	22	Powiśle	26	Solec	27	Warszawa	15	Zajazd Napoleoński	8
Novotel	33	Praski	4	Stegny	37	Wileński	5		

79

golden age of Warsaw, when its concert halls, theatres and salons were prominent in European cultural life.

The **Partitions** abruptly terminated this era, as Warsaw was absorbed into Prussia in 1795. Napoleon's arrival in 1806 gave Varsovians brief hopes of liberation, but the collapse of his Moscow campaign spelled the end of those hopes, and, following the 1815 Congress of Vienna, Warsaw was integrated into the Russian-controlled **Congress Kingdom of Poland**. The failure of the **1830 Uprising** brought severe reprisals: Warsaw was relegated to the status of "provincial town" and all Polish institutes and places of learning were closed. It was only with the outbreak of **World War I** that Russian control began to crumble, and late in 1914 the **Germans** occupied the city, remaining until the end of the war.

Following the return of Polish independence, Warsaw reverted to its position as capital; but then, with the outbreak of **World War II**, came the progressive annihilation of the city. The Nazi assault in September 1939 was followed by round-ups, executions and deportations – savagery directed above all at the Jewish community, who were crammed into a tiny ghetto area and forced to live on a near-starvation diet. It was the Jews who instigated the first open revolt, the **Ghetto Uprising** of April 1943, which resulted in the wholesale destruction of Warsaw's six-centuries-old Jewish community.

As the war progressed and the wave of German defeats on the eastern front provoked a tightening of the Nazi grip on Warsaw, **resistance** stiffened in the city. In August 1944, virtually the whole civilian population participated in the **Warsaw Uprising**, an attempt both to liberate the city and ensure the emergence of an independent Poland. It failed on both counts. Hitler, infuriated by the resistance, ordered the total elimination of Warsaw and, with the surviving populace driven out of the city, the SS systematically destroyed the remaining buildings. In one of his final speeches to the Reichstag, Hitler was able to claim with satisfaction that Warsaw was now no more than a name on the map of Europe. By the end of the war, 850,000 Varsovians – two-thirds of the city's 1939 population – were dead or missing. Photographs taken immediately after the **liberation** in January 1945 show a scene not unlike Hiroshima: General Eisenhower described Warsaw as the most tragic thing he'd ever seen.

The momentous task of **rebuilding** the city took ten years. Aesthetically the results were mixed, with acres of socialist functionalism spread between the Baroque palaces, but it was a tremendous feat of national reconstruction nonetheless. The recovery that has brought the population up to 1.7 million, exceeding its prewar level, is, however, marred by a silence: that of the exterminated Jewish community.

Arrival and information

The wide open expanse of the Wisła River is the most obvious aid to **orientation**. Almost everything you will want to see lies on the western bank, with the **Stare Miasto** (Old Town) squatting on high ground to the north, and the modern commercial heart of Warsaw, the **Śródmieście** district, stretching out to the south. Linking the two is the two-kilometre-long street known as **Krakowskie Przedmieście** (which changes name to **Nowy Świat** in its lower reaches), the city's main artery of tourist traffic, which cuts through the centre from north to south. The main points of arrival are all within easy reach of the city centre.

The city's notorious **taxi** drivers are at their worst at the airport – even the officially registered ones may well try to sting you for up to 100zł for the ride into town. Settle the price (which shouldn't be more than around 20zł by day, 30zł at night) before setting off. The cheapest way of getting a taxi into town is to order one from MPT (☎919) or Super Taxi (☎9622) – they usually turn up within ten minutes, and charge a fair rate. If you choose to flag down a cab, get one bearing the name of the company followed by "taxi" and the number; the dodgier ones just say "taxi". For more information, see p.84.

By plane

Okęcie airport, handling both international and domestic flights, is 8km southwest of the city. **Bus #175** takes you into the centre in about 35 minutes, passing Warszawa Centralna train station (see below) and Krakowskie Przedmeście on the way. From about 11pm to 5am, night bus #611 heads from the airport to Warszawa Centralna. Buy your tickets (currently 2.40zł one way) from the Ruch kiosk inside the terminal building, or from the driver; you have to buy an extra ticket for each large item of luggage – see p.84 for ticket information. Watch out for **pickpockets** all the while – newly arrived visitors often prove easy prey for the professional gangs working the buses to and from the airport.

By train

Warszawa Centralna, the main train station (☎9436), is just west of the central shopping area, a ten-minute bus ride (#175) or a thirty-minute walk from the Stare Miasto. A confusing, cacophonous hive serving all international routes and the major national ones, it has the feel of a vast indoor market and is definitely not a place to hang around in: keep a close eye on your luggage at all times and never leave it unattended. There's a 24-hour **left-luggage** office just downstairs from the main ticket hall, and computerized lockers in which you can store luggage for up to ten days for a nominal fee. Most trains also stop at **Warszawa Wschodnia** (East) station, out in the Praga suburb, or **Warszawa Zachodnia** (West), in the Ochota district – the latter is also the site of the main bus station (see below). Both stations have regular connections to Centralna.

Trains coming in from the north also stop at **Warszawa Gdańska** (ul. Buczka 4), those from the east and north at **Warszawa Zachodnia** (ul. Towarowa 1), and those from the west at **Warszawa Wschodnia** (ul. Lubelska 1). **Śródmiescie** station, just east of Warszawa Centralna, handles local traffic to and from Łowicz, Pruszkow and Skierniewice.

By bus

Warsaw's **main bus station** (☎022/9433), 3km west of the centre on al. Jerozolimskie, handles all international services from western Europe and the Baltic States, as well as those from major domestic destinations in the south and west. Although officially known as Dworzec Centralny PKS, this bus station is usually referred to as **Warszawa Zachodnia** (Warsaw West), because it's housed in the same building as the Warszawa Zachodnia train station (see above). From here, a short train ride will take you in to Warszawa Centralna – virtually every east-bound municipal bus will take you to Warszawa Centralna too; #127 continues on to plac Bankowy on the fringes of the Stare Miasto. Some buses from eastern Poland terminate at **Dworzec Stadion** on the east bank of the Wisła, next to the enormous Stadion market; from here either tram #12 or a suburban train will take you to Warszawa Centralna. Inter-city buses run by private companies like Polski Express and Komfort Bus drop off on **aleja Jana Pawła II**, just behind Warszawa Centralna train station.

Information

Warsaw's municipal **tourist office** (☎022/9431, Ⓦwww.warsawtour.pl) operates a number of **tourist information centres** (Informacja Turystyczna, or IT) in the city, the most useful and most central of which stands at the entrance to the Stare Miasto at pl. Zamkowy 1 (Mon–Fri 9am–6pm, Sat 10am–6pm, Sun 11am–6pm). The English-speaking staff provide information on accommodation throughout Warsaw, handle hotel bookings, have plenty of brochures to give away and sell maps. There are less well-stocked branches at the Warszawa Centralna train station (in the main ticket hall; daily 8am–8pm); at the Warszawa Zachodnia bus and train station (daily 8am–8pm); and in Okęcie airport's arrivals hall (daily 8am–8pm).

The growing influx of Western tourists and the large number of English-speaking expatriates has resulted in a number of English-language publications in the city. Most useful of these is *Warsaw in Your Pocket* (6zł; Ⓦwww.inyourpocket .com), a bi-monthly, A5-format **listings** magazine that gives critical coverage of hotels, restaurants and bars as well as addresses of all kinds of useful services. It's available from bookshops and a few newspaper kiosks. Less info-packed but with more feature-based content is the booklet-sized monthly *Warsaw Insider* (9zł), available from the IT offices and bigger bookshops around town. The weekly newspaper *Warsaw Voice* (Ⓦwww.warsawvoice.com) is good on local politics and business news, has tourism-related features, and carries a reasonable amount of concert listings. If you read Polish, you can't beat the Warsaw edition of the national daily *Gazeta Wyborcza* for news of what's on in town, especially on Fridays, when the *Co jest grane* entertainment supplement covers cinema, concert and clubbing listings for the coming week. Other good Polish-language sources of listings information are the monthly, tabloid-sized *City Magazine*, and the fortnightly glossy *Aktiwist* (Ⓦwww.aktiwist.pl) – both of which are given away free in the trendier bars and clubs.

The most comprehensive **map** of the city is undoubtedly the book-format *Warszawa – Plan Miasta* (12zł), available at tourist offices, booksellers and Ruch kiosks. However, unless you're going to trawl the suburbs or are in accommodation some way from the centre, your needs will be adequately met by the perfectly good maps in *Warsaw In Your Pocket*, the *Warsaw Insider*, or in this guide.

City transport

Warsaw can boast a reliable and well-integrated **bus**, **tram** and **metro** network (Ⓦwww.ztm.waw.pl for timetable information). Buses and trams cover most of the city, while the relatively new Warsaw metro consists of a single, fourteen-stop line running from Ratusz (on plac Bankowy, just west of the Stare Miasto) in the north to suburban Kabaty 14km to the south. The major points where overground and underground public transport lines meet are **plac Bankowy** itself, and **Centrum** in the modern commercial centre, a loosely defined area around the Pałac Kultury i Nauk, just 400m east of the Warszawa Centralna train station.

All services get very crowded at peak hours, but are by and large remarkably punctual. Regular bus, tram and metro routes close down around 11–11.30pm; from 11.15pm to 4.45am **night buses** leave from behind the Pałac Kultury i Nauk on ul. Emilii Plater at 15 and 45 minutes past the hour.

△ Tram, Warsaw

Tickets (*bilety*) for trams, buses and the metro are bought from any newspaper or tobacco kiosk sporting the "MZK" logo, or from ticket machines at some of the central stops. They can also be bought from drivers but this is a slightly more expensive way to buy them. Prices have proved extremely volatile over the past decade and will certainly continue to go up. A single flat-fare ticket (changing trams or buses requires a new ticket) currently costs 2.40zł (or 1.20zł for ISIC card holders) – three single tickets are required for a journey on a night bus. It's more economical to buy a **day pass** (*bilet jednodniowy*; 7.20zł; ISIC holders 3.60zł) or **week pass** (*bilet tygodniowy*; 26zł; ISIC holders 13zł): the day pass is usually available from all kiosks, but the week pass is harder to get hold of – try the MZK offices at pl. Bankowy 4 or ul. Senatorska 37 (both Mon–Fri 7.30am–3pm).

Punch your tickets in the machines on board or at the metro entrance – pleas of ignorance don't cut much ice with inspectors, who'll fine you 120zł on the spot if they catch you without a validated ticket. You also need to stamp an extra ticket for each large item of **luggage** – backpacks included – that you carry on board. Failure to do so will land you a 48zł fine if you're caught, and checks are visited on foreigners with increasing frequency.

Taxis

For Poles, recurrent price increases have made **taxis** a bit of a luxury, though for Westerners they're still reasonable, and easy to get. As a guide to **fares**, there's an initial charge of 6zł followed by 6zł per kilometre travelled in the city centre, with the price falling to 3 zł per kilometre in the suburbs. There's a fifty-percent mark-up at weekends and after 10pm. That said, you need to be aware that a small but significant proportion of Warsaw's cab drivers will take every opportunity to rip you off, especially at night or from hotels, the airport and the train stations. Checking in advance what you ought to be paying by asking hotel receptions, IT points or even locals, is always a help, but you may have to resign yourself to paying up. There's no point insisting that the meter's on – they can be fixed.

The most reliable cabs bear the name of the company followed by "taxi" and a number (the dodgier cabs just say "taxi"). There are plenty of these on **ulica Emilii Plater**, a quiet side road a few yards from the main station, or you can call for a pick-up: try MPT (☎022/919), Bialź (☎022/9668) or Super Taxi (☎022/9622). Drivers generally speak a little English, though it helps if you can pronounce the street you want and the place you're going to.

Accommodation

There's an ever-widening range of accommodation choices in Warsaw, but prices are creeping inexorably upwards – with the result that many options seem overpriced in relation to the standards on offer. Hotels serving the top end of the market are pretty reliable: the city's growing importance as a central European commercial centre has ensured the emergence of numerous **upscale establishments** which are on a par with anything in western Europe. For **budget** and **mid-range** travellers, however, standards are much more unpredictable, and new arrivals in the city often find themselves paying over the odds for a level of accommodation that fails to meet their expectations. Good-value options do exist, but you'll need to book them in advance to avoid disappointment.

For those who arrive without a reservation, the IT offices at the airport, train and bus stations (see "Information" above) will arrange hotel and hostel rooms, although they're beset by long queues in summer, and the staff may not be well informed about standards in the places they're recommending.

Warsaw's stock of **youth hostels** and **private rooms** aren't as cosy and welcoming as they might be, but at least provide tolerable budget accommodation for a stay of a day or two. **Camping** in Warsaw's suburbs is a reasonably good option if you don't mind being a lengthy public-transport ride away from the centre.

Hotels

Warsaw's **hotel** scene represents both the best and worst of post-communist Poland. While there's no shortage of new, Western-financed hotels offering high standards for high prices, there are still a large number of communist-era hotels peddling overpriced, unrenovated rooms coupled with old-fashioned ideas of customer service.

It's difficult – though not impossible – to find a double room in central Warsaw for anything below the 200zł mark, and most establishments charge considerably more than this, regardless of whether their rooms are up to scratch. You'll often find yourself paying in excess of 400zł to be sure of international standards of comfort. Bargains are still to be had however: many of the more business-oriented central hotels offer reductions of about thirty percent at weekends – be sure to ask when you phone.

In the handful of inexpensive options still remaining in the **centre**, you'll have to book in advance in order to secure a bed – a task made all the more difficult by the fact that reception staff in the cheaper places rarely speak English. Otherwise finding a budget place to stay involves settling for something some way from the centre. The suburb of **Praga**, east of the centre just over the Wisła, is the best place to look, although there's a scattering of hotels in the **southern** and **western suburbs** too. The main disadvantage of staying outside the centre is the relative lack of amenities: there's little in the way of reliable restaurants, bars and shops once you move outside the main downtown areas. In addition, some suburban areas (Praga in particular) have a reputation for being unsafe at night, and you may find yourself spending more money on taxis than you bargained for.

The city centre

Belfer ul. Wybrzeże Kościuszkowskie 31/33 ☎022/625 5185. Just downhill from the centre, near the Wisła. Pretty basic place with careworn feel and communist-era colour schemes. One of the few cheapies in this part of town, though. En-suites and rooms with shared facilities available. ❺–❻

Europejski Krakowskie Przedmieście 13 ☎022/826 5051, ✉europej@orbis.pl. Belle-époque exterior and reasonable interiors make this the best of the numerous hotels run by the Orbis chain. It is also very central. ❽

Forum ul. Nowogrodzka 24/26 ☎022/621 0271, ✉waforum@orbis.pl. Unmissable yellow-brick skyscraper, full of businesspeople conferencing, on the corner of busy Marszałkowska and al. Jerozolimskie. Comfortable and with high stan-

dards of service. Some rooms come with good views over the city. ❽

Grand ul. Krucza 28 ☎022/583 2100, ✉wagrand @orbis.pl. Hulking grey Orbis-owned hotel that has been completely revamped inside. Now a respectable three-star, charging four-star prices on account of its location. Within walking distance of both the central train station and the town centre. ❽

Gromada pl. Powstańców Warszawy 2 ☎022/625 1545, ⊛www.gromada.pl. Central, reliable and comfortable middle-of-the-range provision in a large modern building. Revamped and much improved since its previous incarnation as *Dom Hłopca*. Popular as a conference venue. ❽

Harenda Krakowskie Przedmieście 4/6 ☎022/826 0071, ✉hh@hotelharenda.com.pl. Located centrally just below the university campus with a great ranch-like pub next door. The comfortable en-suites are recommended for this price range: book ahead if possible. **❼**

Holiday Inn ul. Złota 48/54 ☎ 022/022/697 3999, ✉ holiday@orbis.pl. Towering monument to the international business traveller, right by Warszawa Centralna train station. **❾**

Ibis al. Solidarności 165 ☎ 022/520 3000, ✉ h2894@accor-hotels.com. Gleaming modern place that is one of the few hotels in Warsaw to offer international comforts at a realistic price. Already a tourist and business favourite: book ahead. Two kilometres west of the Stare Miasto, but numerous trams running along al. Solidarności speed you into the centre. Ask about weekend discounts. Trams #22 and #24 from Warszawa Centralna. **❼**

Jan Sobieski pl. Artura Zawiszy ☎ 022/579 1000, ⓦ www.sobieski.com.pl. Expensive Austrian-backed hotel in Ochota, 800m west of Warszawa Centralna. The wacky exterior colour was a local source of contention when it was first built, although the originally brash yellows and pinks have now weathered sufficiently to blend in to their surroundings. Swish rooms with all mod-cons. **❾**

Le Meridien Bristol Krakowskie Przedmieście 42/44 ☎ 022/625 2525, ⓦ www.bristol.polhotels.com. If you simply can't stay in a hotel that doesn't come complete with liveried doormen, then the magnificently swanky *Bristol* is the place for you. A legendary prewar establishment, completely modernized and now offering the level of comfort and service you would expect at this price. Superbly central too. Reductions at weekends. **❾**

Maria al. Jana Pawła II 71 ☎ 022/838 4062, ✉ hotmaria@optimus.waw.pl. Small, well-run hotel on the northwestern fringe of the city centre. Tram #16, #17 or #19 from Warszawa Centralna. **❼**

Marriott al. Jerozolimskie 65/79 ☎ 022/630 6306. Looming glass monstrosity that's one of the city's top hotels, right opposite Warsawa Centralna, and in the heart of the modern business district. Swimming pool on site. **❾**

Mazowiecki ul. Mazowiecka 10 ☎ 022/687 9117, ⓦ www.mazowiecki.com.pl. Centrally located former soldiers' overnighter turned into a hotel open to all. Rooms are musty and careworn, but habitable. En-suite doubles plus rooms with shared facilities in the hallway. **❺**

MDM pl. Konstytucji 1 ☎ 022/621 6211, ✉ hotel.mdm@syrena.com.pl. Rooms are quieter and pleasanter than the hotel's location and external appearance might otherwise suggest. Quite pricey for what it is, though. Handy location for the main business/shopping districts and Park Łazienkowski. **❽**

Mercure Fryderyk Chopin ul. Jana Pawła II 22 ☎ 022/620 0201, ✉ mercure@perytnet.pl. Brash, modern and stylish four-star place, part of a French chain, with a couple of good restaurants. Doubles from **❾**

Metalowcy ul. Długa 29 ☎ 022/831 4021. Spartan but acceptable former workers' hostel a few steps west of the Stare Miasto. A mixture of singles, doubles and quads, most with shared facilities – although some of the quads come with en-suite shower. You really need to book in advance – but be prepared for Polish-only speaking reception staff. **❸**

Metropol ul. Marszałkowska 99a ☎ 022/621 4354. An impersonal high-rise within easy walking distance of Warszawa Centralna – hence the inflated prices. Rooms have TV and bath but rejoice in dowdy colour schemes. **❽**

Polonia al. Jerozolimskie 45 ☎ 022/628 7241. Just round the corner from the similar *Metropol*, on a noisy street. Again, the unspectacular ensuites are overpriced due to proximity to the train station. Modern art buffs may care to know that the *Polonia* was the site of Russian Suprematist Kazimir Malevich's first ever exhibition outside the USSR in 1927. **❼**

Powiśle ul. Szara 10a ☎ 022/628 0014. High-rise hotel in a leafy area just southeast of the centre, handy for Park Łazienkowski. Rooms feature frumpy communist-era decor and matching bathrooms. Breakfast costs 20zł extra. **❻**

Solec ul. Zagórna 1 ☎ 022/625 4400, ✉ solec@orbis.pl. One of the better Orbis hotels, located just south of the centre, near the river, handy for strolling in the parks. **❽**

Sheraton ul. Prusa 2 ☎ 022/657 6100, ⓦ www.sheraton.com/warsaw. Hotel with impeccable standards handily located in the attractive pl. Trzech Krzyży district. **❾**

Vera ul. Bitwy Warszawskiej 16 ☎ 022/822 7421, ✉ vera@orbis.pl. Another Orbis hotel, 3km west of the centre but handy for the Warszawa Zachodnia bus and train stations. Up to international business standards, but not cheap. **❾**

Victoria Inter-Continental ul. Królewska 11 ☎ 022/657 8011, ✉ warsaw@interconti.com. Ugly pile built for communist dignitaries that has reinvented itself as an international, five-star place. Overlooks the huge expanse of pl. Piłsudskiego. **❾**

Warszawa pl. Powstańców Warszawy 9 ☎ 022/826 9421, ✉ hotel.warszawa@syrena.com.pl. Just off Świętokrzyska. Monumental Stalinist design lends an attractive ugliness to this soaring building, that's dowdy but clean inside. Most rooms are en-suite, although there are some perfectly accept-able doubles with shared facilities ⑥–⑦

Praga and the eastern suburbs

Arkadia ul. Radzymińska 182 ☎022/678 5055. Decent quality hotel, 5km east of the Stare Miasto on the edge of the Praga Północ district. It's a small place, so reserve ahead. Acceptable restau-rant. Bus #512 from Warszawa Centralna. ⑤

Felix ul. Omulewska 24 ☎022/610 2182 or 870 4519. Big, bland suburban hotel with comfortable if unspectacular rooms, 6km east of the centre on the Lublin road. Tram #9 or #24 from Warszawa Centralna. ⑥

Gościniec Praski ul. Bródnowska 13 ☎022/618 7230, ℮phthot@polbox.com. Hotel in Praga offer-ing sparsely furnished, functional but clean rooms. Tram #32 from pl. Bankowy. ③

Orzeł ul. Podskarbińska 11 ☎022/810 5060. Smallish eighteen-room sports hotel in southern Praga, with its own restaurant and bar. The spar-tan rooms are often booked up by groups, so call ahead. Bus #102 from Centrum. ③

Praski al. Solidarności 61 ☎022/818 4989, ℮ph-thot@polbox.com. In the Praga district, but only one tram stop from the heart of the Stare Miasto. Pleasantly situated opposite the Praski park, and with a great Lebanese restaurant next door. Tram #4 from Centrum. Rooms have both shared and en-suite facilities. ⑤–⑥

Wileński ul. Kłopotowskiego 36. ☎022/818 5780. Friendly place down a quiet side street in the run-down Praga quarter: take tram #4 from Warszawa Centralna to the Praga Orthodox church, then walk a short way southeast. An odd mixture of clean, well-equipped en-suites and dirty, unrenovated rooms with shared facilities. ③–④

Zajazd Napoleoński ul. Płowiecka 83 ☎022/815 3068. Small luxury inn reputedly frequented by

Napoleon, 8km southeast of the centre on the Lublin road. Bus #525 from Warszawa Centralna. ⑦

The western and south-ern suburbs

Belwederski ul. Sulkiewicza 11 ☎022/840 4011. Comfortable new mid-range hotel right by the southern reaches of Park Łazienkowski. Buses #131 from Centrum and #180 from Nowy Świat pass right by. ⑦

Boss ul. Żwanowiecka 20 ☎022/872 9953, ℮hotboss@polbox.com. Cosy, quietly situated hotel on the rural southeastern outskirts of the city. Bus #521 from Centrum to the Miedzeszyn stop. Nice restaurant too. ⑥

Instytut Fizyki Pan al. Lotników 32/46 ☎022/843 2424. Moderately priced hotel 5km south of the centre in Mokotów offering sparsely furnished but reasonable en-suites. Bus #524 from Centrum. ⑤

Novotel ul. 1 Sierpnia 1 ☎022/575 6000, ℮nwarszaw@orbis.pl. Smart, modern business-oriented place with swimming pool, 6km south-west of the centre, and 1km short of the airport. Bus #175 stops right by it. ⑧

Reytan ul. T. Rejtana 6 ☎022/646 3166, ⓦwww.polhotels.com/warsz/reytan. Modern, smart, comfortable place 2km south of the main downtown business and shopping area. Tram #4 from Centrum passes the end of the street. ⑦

Stegny ul. Inspektowa 1 ☎022/842 2768. A sports hotel, built beside a stadium and traditional-ly used by visiting teams, 5km south of the centre in Mokotów. Triples (110zł) and quads (150zł) only, with one bathroom to every two rooms. Bus #503 from Nowy Świat.

Tina ul. Górczewska 212 ☎022/664 9720, ⓦwww.zrew.com.pl. Friendly place 6km west of the centre in the Wola district. Reasonable quality rooms, as well as a decent restaurant. Tram #10 from Warszawa Centralna. ⑥

Hostels

Warsaw has only two **IYHF hostels**, monstrous underprovision for a city of its size, both imposing lockouts from 10am to 5pm and a curfew of 11pm. These restrictions make cost their only advantage, apart from the social con-tacts brought by shared misery. The hostel at ul. Karolkowa 53a (☎022/632 8829, ℉632 9746) is out in the western Wola district – take tram #12 or #24 from Warszawa Centralna to the Centrum Wola department store. There's a 3zł charge to rent a sleeping bag, along with some en-suite doubles (③), and dorm beds 25–35zł. The hostel at ul. Smolna 30 (☎ & ℉022/827 8952) has a great location on the fourth floor of a grey concrete building just a five-minute bus ride along al. Jerozolimskie from the central station – any bus heading towards Nowy Świat will drop you at the corner of the street. There are a few doubles

(**❸**) as well as multi-bed dorms (30zł per person, sheet rental 3zł). Reservations here are taken two days in advance only.

From late June to mid-September, the Almatur-run **international student hostels** – basically student halls of residence vacated for the summer – are another inexpensive possibility. The Almatur office at ul. Kopernika 23 (**☎**022/826 3512 or 826 4592, **❿**www.almatur.com.pl) has current details. You can call the halls of residence directly, of course, though you'll be lucky if the conversation's in English. Best bets are the *Dom Studenta* at ul. Spiska 16 (**☎**022/849 6722) or the two student halls at ul. Żwirki I Wigury 95 and 99 (**☎**022/822 2407).

Private rooms

The main source of **private rooms** in Warsaw is the Syrena travel agency at ul. Krucza 17 (Mon–Fri 9am–7pm, Sat 11am–7pm, Sun 2–7pm; at weekends you may have to ask someone at the next-door *Lokomotywa* pub to open up the office for you; **☎**022/628 7540 or 629 0537, **❢**office@syrena-pl.com), a fifteen-minute walk – or two-stop tram ride – east from Warszawa Centralna. They will fix you up with a single (70zł) or double (100zł) room in someone's flat – some of these are superbly situated in the city centre, others may be some way out, so check locations carefully. In addition, be warned that security-conscious Warsaw landladies may refuse to give you a set of keys to the flat, preferring to let you in and out themselves – which effectively places you under a (negotiable) curfew.

Campsites

Even in Warsaw, **camping** is extremely cheap and popular with Poles and foreigners alike. On the whole, site facilities are reasonable and several offer bungalows (around 20zł per person per night).

Camping Gromada, ul. Żwirki i Wigury 32 **☎**022/825 4391). Best and most popular of the Warsaw campsites, 7km southwest of the centre on the way out to the airport – bus #188 or #175 will get you there. As well as tent space the site has a number of cheap bungalows. Extra charges for a tent and for linen. May–Sept.

Cokos SC, ul. Grochowska 1 **☎**022/610 6366). Seven kilometres out of town in the Praga Południe district, on the main road to Lublin, Terespol and the Ukrainian border. Plenty of cabins. Trams #9 or #24 from Warszawa Centralna. May–Sept.

Majawa, ul. Bitwy Warszawskiej 15/17 **☎**022/823

3748). About 600m south of the Warszawa Zachodnia bus and train station. Less crowded than the *Gromada* site. Some bungalows and the usual small extra charges for linen, tents, electricity, car or motorcycle parking, and so on. Open all year.

PTTK Camping, ul. Połczyńska 6a. **☎**022/664 6736). Six kilometres west of the centre in the Wola district, on the Poznań road. Cabins available. Trams #8 or #10 from Warszawa Centralna.

Stegny, ul. Inspektowa 1 **☎**022/842 2768). Next to the *Hotel Stegny*; see p.87 for details. May–Sept.

The Stare Miasto

The **Stare Miasto** (Old Town) is in some respects a misnomer for the historic nucleus of Warsaw. Fifty years ago, this compact network of streets and alleyways lay in rubble – even the cobblestones are meticulously assembled replacements. Yet surveying the tiered houses of the main square, for example, it's hard to believe they've been here only decades. Some older residents even claim that the restored version is in some respects an improvement.

Plac Zamkowy (Castle Square), on the south side of Stare Miasto, is the obvious place to start a tour. Here the first thing to catch your eye is the bronze

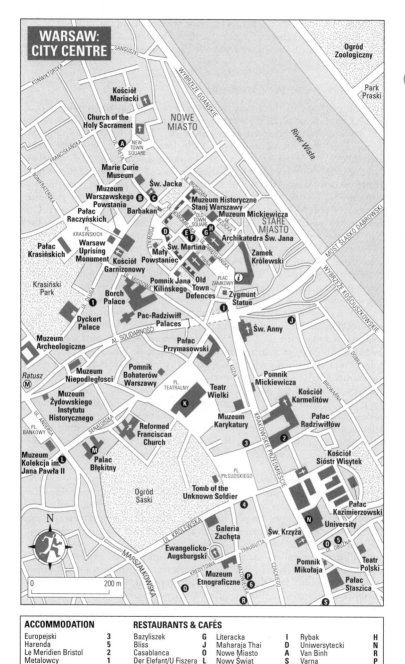

WARSAW: CITY CENTRE

SANGUSZKI

KONWIKTORSKA

Ogród Zoologiczny

Park Praski

Kościół Mariacki

Church of the Holy Sacrament

NOWE MIASTO

NEW TOWN SQUARE

UL FRETA

FRANCISKANSKA

UL BONIFRATERSKA

WYBRZEŻE GDAŃSKIE

River Wisła

Marie Curie Museum

Św. Jacka

Muzeum Warszawskego **B** **C** Powstania

Pałac Raczyńskich

Barbakan

UL BRZOZOWA

Muzeum Historyczne Stanj Warszawy

Muzeum Mickiewicza

STARE MIASTO

OLD TOWN SQUARE

KOZMA LOJOLA

PL KRASIŃSKICH

D **E** **F** **G** **H**

Archikatedra Św. Jana

MOST SLASKO DABROWSKI

Pałac Krasińskich

Warsaw Uprising Monument

Kościół Garnizonowy

Mały Powstaniec

Sw. Martina

Zamek Królewski

WYBRZEŻE KOŚCIUSZKOWSKIE

Krasiński Park

UL DŁUGA

UL MIODOWA

Borch Palace

1

Pomnik Jana Kilińskiego

Old Town Defences

PLAC ZAMKOWY

Zygmunt Statue

i

Dyckert Palace

Pac-Radziwiłł Palaces

AL. SOLIDARNOŚCI

Pałac Przymasowski

Św. Anny

J

UL DOBRA

Muzeum Archeologiczne

Ratusz **M**

Muzeum Niepodległości

Pomnik Bohaterów Warszawy

Pomnik Mickiewicza

BRÓWARNA

Muzeum Żydowskiego Instytutu Historycznego

PL TEATRALNY

Teatr Wielki

Kościół Karmelitów

SENATORSKA

K

Muzeum Karykatury

Pałac Radziwiłłów

KRAKOWSKIE PRZEDMIEŚCIE

PL BANKOWY

M

Reformed Franciscan Church

3

2

Kościół Sióstr Wisytek

Muzeum Kolekcja im. Jana Pawła II **L**

Pałac Błękitny

PL PIŁSUDSKIEGO

Ogród Saski

Tomb of the Unknown Soldier

4

Pałac Kazimierzowski

N University

N

UL KRÓLEWSKA

Galeria Zachęta

Św. Krzyża

O **5**

UL OBOŻNA

Teatr Polski

Ewangelicko-Augsburgski

TRAUGUTTA

Pomnik Mikołaja

MARSZAŁKOWSKA

KREDYTOWA

MAZOWIECKA

CZACKIEGO

P **6**

Muzeum Etnograficzne

Pałac Staszica

Q

R

S

0   200 m

statue of Sigismund III, the king who made Warsaw his capital. Installed on his column in 1640, Sigismund suffered a direct hit from a tank in September 1944, but has now been replaced on his lookout; the base is a popular and convenient rendezvous point.

The Zamek Królewski

On the east side of the square is the former **Zamek Królewski** (Royal Castle), once home of the royal family and seat of the Polish parliament, much of which is now occupied by a **museum** (Tues–Sat 10am–4pm, Sun 11am–4pm, last admission 3pm; 14zł; free on Sun; ⓦwww.zamek-krolewski.art.pl). What you can see in the castle is divided into two separate "routes" – the **blue route**, which covers the bulk of the castle, and the **yellow route**, which includes the Royal Apartments and can only be visited in the company of the official guide – so you may have to wait until the requisite number of people (usually 25) turn up before setting off on this part. On Sunday you can follow the **Sunday route**, which features the highlights of the blue and the yellow routes, but not the entirety of each route.

Dynamited by German troops in the aftermath of the Warsaw Uprising, the seventeenth-century castle was rebuilt as recently as the 1970s. In July 1974 a huge crowd gathered to witness the clock of the domed Sigismund Tower being started up again – the hands set exactly where they were stopped by the first Luftwaffe attack. The castle was perceived as a crucial symbol of independent nationhood – Poles from all over the world donated money to finance its rebuilding, and hundreds of volunteers helped with the labour. Though the structure is a replica, many of its furnishings are originals, scooted into hiding by percipient employees during the first bombing raids. Parallel with its tourist role these days, the castle regularly serves as a glorified reception hall for myriad dignitaries visiting the country.

Entry is through the Senatorial Gate and a vaulted hallway. As with many royal palaces, once inside it's something of a hotchpotch of international luminaries (busts of Molière and Voltaire here, a Gainsborough portrait of George III there) and somewhat over the top (check out the ceiling painting in the north wing entitled *Apotheosis of the Genius of Poland*), but there are clear explanations in English throughout and a range of interesting artefacts.

The blue route

The **blue route** takes you through the **Jagiellonian Rooms**, overlooking the river from the northeast wing. Originally part of the residence of eighteenth-century monarch Augustus III, they are adorned with portraits of the Jagiellonian royal families and some outstanding Flemish tapestries, including the ominously titled *Tragedy of the Jewish People*.

Next are the chambers where the Sejm (parliament) used to meet. Beyond the chancellery, which features more tapestries and portraits of the last dukes of Mazovia, comes the **Old Chamber of Deputies**, formerly the debating chamber. During parliamentary sessions, the deputies sat on benches on the left side of the chamber, with the Speaker in the centre of the room, while members of the public could stand and listen on the right-hand side. Democracy as practised here was something of a mixed blessing. On the one hand, the founding decree of the Polish Commonwealth, hammered out here in 1573, demonstrated an exceptionally tolerant attitude to religious differences; on the other, it was also here that the principle of *liberum veto* – unanimity as a prerequisite for the passing of new laws – was established in 1652, often seen as the beginning of the end of effective government in Poland. Arguably the Sejm's finest hour, however, came precisely at the moment when political developments threatened it and the country's very existence: the famous **Third of May Constitution**, passed here in 1791, being one of the radical highpoints of European constitutional history (see Contexts, p.681). The painted pillars and heraldic emblems adorning the chamber are recently completed reconstructions of the original decorations by Baptista Quadro (of Poznań Town Hall fame – see p.607) in the Italianate style typical of much Polish architecture of the period.

The blue route culminates with the **Matejko rooms** in the north wing, crammed with paintings by the doyen of nineteenth-century Polish painters, Jan Matejko. A romantic visionary consumed by a sense of patriotic mission, Matejko specialized in grandiose history paintings (many of which are on show here) commemorating key moments in Poland's past. *Rejtan* shows a bare-breasted deputy blocking the path of a group of deputies preparing to accept the First Partition, imploring them to kill him rather than Poland, while *The Third of May Constitution* (see above) celebrates an enlightened moment in a similarly intense vein.

The yellow route

The **yellow route** takes you to the most lavish section of the castle, the **Royal Apartments of King Stanisław August Poniatowski**. Amid all the pomp and circumstance, it can be hard to remember that this is all a reconstruction of the eighteenth-century original – in this case, postwar architects had to rely on archival sources from Dresden to rebuild the rooms from scratch. Through two smaller rooms you come eventually to the magnificent **Canaletto Room**, with its views of Warsaw by Bernardo Bellotto, a nephew of the famous Canaletto – whose name he appropriated to make his pictures sell better. Marvellous in their detail, these cityscapes provided invaluable information for the architects involved in rebuilding the city after the war. Next door is the richly decorated **Royal Chapel**, designed and decorated by Domenico Merlini in the 1770s, where an urn contains the heart of Tadeusz Kościuszko, swashbuckling leader of the 1794 insurrection, and hero of the American War of Independence (see box on p.448). Like many other rooms on this floor, the **Audience Chamber** has a beautiful parquet floor as well as several original furnishings. The four pictures on display here are by Bacciarelli, court painter to Stanisław August, and symbolize the cardinal virtues of Courage, Wisdom, Piety and Justice, while the room itself was again designed by Merlini, a good example of solid Polish Neoclassicism.

The **King's Bedroom**, another lavishly decorated setup, is followed by the **Study Room**, decorated with paintings by the last Polish king's court artists, where Napoleon is supposed to have slept during his short stay – apparently he had Stanisław's bed moved in here, not wishing to sleep in the bedroom occupied so recently by a deposed ruler.

From here you proceed through to the reception rooms, where the sumptuous **Marble Room** is dominated by portraits of the 22 Polish monarchs, including a much-reproduced portrait of Stanisław August in his coronation robes. Highlight of the parade of royal splendour is the **Ballroom**, the largest room in the castle, with its aptly titled ceiling allegory by Bacciarelli, *The Dissolution of Chaos*. Napoleon met the elite of Warsaw society here in 1806, the occasion on which he made his comments (legendary in Poland) about the beauty of Polish women – his mistress-to-be Countess Maria Walewska included, presumably.

North of the Zamek Królewski

Shops, bars, restaurants and upmarket souvenir shops line **Piwna** and **Świętojańska**, the two narrow cobbled streets leading northwards from plac Zamkowy. Each street has a church worth a stopoff as well. On Piwna there's **Kościół św. Martina** (St Martin's Church), a fourteenth-century church whose Baroque interior was carefully restored after the war. Among those buried here is Adam Jarzibski, king's musician and author of the first guide to Warsaw – written in verse. You should take the opportunity to nip down to **plac Kanonia** at this point (lodged behind ul. Jezuitska, just north of the castle), where the narrowest house in Warsaw puts even the equivalents in Amsterdam to shame.

On Świętojańska is the entrance to **Archikatedra św. Jana** (St John's Cathedral), the main city church, an early fourteenth-century structure built on the site of an earlier wooden shrine, and subsequently remodelled in the local Mazovian Gothic style. Some of the bitterest fighting of the 1944 Warsaw Uprising took place around here. German tanks entered the church after destroying its southern side, and you can see sections of their caterpillar tracks built into the wall along **ul. Dziekania**. After the war, a lot of money was invested in rebuilding the cathedral in its original brick Gothic style.

For all the hard work, though, the cathedral's a bare, rather cold sort of place. Most of the interest is provided by the tombstones of the dukes of Mazovia, a sixteenth-century crucifix from Nürnberg with real hair on the head, and a

Adam Mickiewicz (1789–1855)

If one person can be said to personify the Polish literary Romantic tradition it is **Adam Mickiewicz**. A passionate, mystically inclined writer, Mickiewicz's unabashedly patriotic writings have long served as a central literary (and sometimes, in times of crisis, political) reference point for generations of Poles. Quotations from and references to Mickiewicz's considerable volume of writings litter subsequent Polish literature and politics – even the avowedly unacademic Lech Wałęsa has been known to cite a line or two from the hugely popular epic poem, *Pan Tadeusz* – and performances of his plays are still numbered among the most popular in the country. More controversially, there's an increasing (though muted) discussion of the man's "ethnic" origins, with several scholars now claiming that at least one of Mickiewicz's parents was **Jewish**, a view that might go some way, it is argued, to accounting for the sympathetic portrayal of Jews – notably the musical innkeeper, Jankiel – in a work like *Pan Tadeusz*: aired publicly to the average Pole, this view provokes plenty of controversy. Despite the fact that the best of Mickiewicz's writings rank among the finest outpourings of nineteenth-century Romanticism, he's still relatively unknown in the West, a situation not helped by the general lack of decent, readily available translations of his works.

Born in Lithuania of an impoverished Polish *szlachta* (gentry) family, Mickiewicz studied at **Vilnius University** where he, like many of his generation, was rapidly drawn into conspiratorial anti-Russian plotting. Already a budding writer (*Poezye*, his first collection of ballads and romances based on Lithuanian folklore, appeared in 1822), Mickiewicz was arrested along with fellow members of a secret student organization on suspicion of "spreading Polish nationalism" and was deported to Russia in 1823, where he remained, mostly in **Moscow**, for the rest of the decade, befriending a number of Russian writers, Pushkin included. Notable works of this period include *Dziady* ("Forefather's Eve"), the innovative patriotic drama whose Warsaw performance in spring 1968 sparked subsequent student protests, and *Konrad Wallenrod*, a popular epic poem depicting the medieval struggle between Teutonic Knights and Lithuanians, in reality a thinly disguised allegory of the age-old Polish–German conflict.

number of famous Poles lodged in the crypt. Notable among these are Nobel Prize-winning writer **Henryk Sienkiewicz**, former primate of Poland **Cardinal Wyszyński** and, the most recent addition, former pianist and prime minister **Ignacy Paderewski**, whose remains were installed here with much ceremony in July 1992 in the presence of presidents Lech Wałęsa and George Bush Senior, a fulfilment of the exile Paderewski's last wish that his body only be returned to a free Poland. The Catholic-dominated governments of the post-communist era have seen to it that the church's old official functions are revived, so, especially at weekends, there's a fair chance of your visit being cut short by the arrival of a visiting foreign dignitary (and the building is closed anyway between 11am and 2pm).

Next to the cathedral is the **Kościół Jezuitski** (Jesuit Church), a popular shrine dedicated to Our Lady of Charity, the city's patron saint. Its high belfry is the tallest in the Stare Miasto area, standing out for miles around.

Rynek Starego Miasta and around

The compact Old Town Square, **Rynek Starego Miasta**, is one of the most remarkable bits of postwar reconstruction anywhere in Europe. Flattened during the Warsaw Uprising, the three-storey merchants' houses surrounding the square have been scrupulously rebuilt to their seventeenth- and eighteenth-century designs, multicoloured façades included. By day the buzzing Rynek teems with visitors, who are catered for by buskers, artists, cafés, moneychangers and

Following the failure of the **November 1830 Uprising**, Mickiewicz moved to exile in **Paris**, like many Polish intellectuals, and quickly immersed himself in émigré politics. It was here too that Mickiewicz wrote *Pan Tadeusz* (1834), his greatest epic poem; modelled on the novels of Walter Scott, it is a masterful, richly lyrical depiction of traditional gentry life in his native Polish–Lithuanian homeland, a region dear to many Polish writers – Miłosz and Konwicki are two contemporary examples – both for its outstanding natural beauty and powerful historical Polish associations.

The remaining years of Mickiewicz's life read like a litany of personal and political disappointments. Appointed to a professorship in Lausanne in 1839, Mickiewicz resigned in the following year to teach Slavonic literature at the Collège de France. Increasingly drawn to mystical and theosophical doctrines, the uncompromising Mickiewicz was suspended from his post in 1844. With the outbreak of the **1848 revolutions** in central Europe, the "Springtime of the Nations" that briefly appeared to herald a new dawn for the oppressed nations of the region, Mickiewicz travelled to Rome to try and persuade the new pope, Pius IX, to come out in support of the cause of Polish independence. Later the impassioned Mickiewicz also organized a small Polish military unit to fight with Garibaldi's forces – the nucleus, he hoped, of a future Polish national liberation army – and assumed editorship of the radical agit-prop newspaper *Tribune des Peuples* ("Tribune of the Peoples"), a move which led to dismissal from his tenure at the Collège de France by Napoleon III.

The writer's life came abruptly to an end in 1855 when Prince Adam Czartoryski, a leader of the Paris exile community, sent Mickiewicz on a mission to Turkey to try and resolve the factional quarrels bedevilling the Polish military forces that had volunteered to fight against Russia in the approaching Crimean War: having contracted typhus soon after his arrival, Mickiewicz died in November 1855 in **Istanbul**, and is commemorated in a museum there. He was already a national hero of almost mythic proportions, and his remains were eventually brought back to Poland and placed, along with other Polish "greats", in the crypt of Kraków's cathedral on Wawel Hill.

doroski, the traditional horse-drawn carts that clatter tourists around Stare Miasto for a sizeable fee. Plumb in the centre are two nineteenth-century water pumps; for years the only creatures capable of stomaching their offerings were the *doroski* horses, but now following the installation of a filter system, the one that works is a good alternative to the overpriced drinks in the square's cafés.

The **Muzeum Historyczne Starej Warszawy** (Warsaw Historical Museum; Tues & Thurs 11am–6pm, Wed & Fri 10am–3.30pm, Sat & Sun 10.30am–4pm; 5zł, free on Sun) takes up a large part of Strona Dekerta, the north side of the square; entrance is through a house called the Pod Murzynkiem ("Under the Negro"), a reference to the inn sign that used to hang above the doorway. Exhibitions here cover every aspect of Warsaw's life from its beginnings to the present day, crammed tightly into a warren of rooms on three floors – there are excellent views over the parasol-crowded Rynek from the upper storeys. The early history of the city is told in didactic words-and-pictures style, but things improve the further on into the museum you get. Daily life in prewar Warsaw is evocatively recalled with a display of old photographs, theatre posters and fashion magazines, and there's a particularly moving chronicle of everyday resistance to the Nazis – an uplifting complement to the wartime horrors documented in the film shown in Polish on the hour, but in English at 3pm only.

On the square's east side, Strona Barssa, the **Muzeum Mickiewicza** (Mickiewicz Museum; Mon, Tues & Fri 10am–3pm, Wed & Thurs 11am–6pm, Sun 11am–5pm; 5zł, free on Thurs) is a temple to the national Romantic poet. Among a stack of first editions, contemporary newspapers and family memorabilia, there's actually a shrine room, with portrait and crucifix enveloped in church-like gloom.

The west side of the Rynek, **Strona Hugo-Kołłątaja**, named after the co-author of the 1791 Constitution, features a number of fine reconstructed residences, notably the Dom Fukiera (Fukier House) at no. 27, longtime home of one of the city's best-known *winiarnia* or wine cellar and still going strong, and the Klucznikowska mansion at no. 21, which includes a carefully reconstructed Gothic doorway among its features.

West of the Rynek, the narrow cobbled streets and alleyways bring you out to a long section of the old **city walls**, split-level fortifications with ramparts, rebuilt watchtowers and apple trees lining their grassy approaches (but currently undergoing renovation). Along Podwale, the open path surrounding the walls and a favourite with evening strollers, an array of plaques commemorates foreigners who supported the Polish cause, including the French poet Alfred de Vigny. Here, as in many places around the city, the fresh flowers laid on the ground mark places where the Nazis carried out wartime executions. The most poignant of the memorials, however, is the **Mały Powstaniec** (Little Insurgent), a bronze figure of a small boy with an oversized helmet carrying an automatic rifle – a solitary figure commemorating the children and young people killed fighting in the Warsaw Uprising, personifying all that was heroic and singularly tragic in the city's resistance to the Nazis (see box, pp.98–99). During term-time it is usually thronged by schoolchildren on class outings.

From the Rynek, ul. Nowomiejska runs north towards the sixteenth-century **Barbakan**, 200m beyond, which formerly guarded the Nowomiejska Gate, the northern entrance to the city. The fortress is part of the Stare Miasto defences, running all the way round from plac Zamkowy to the northeastern edge of the district. In summer, the Barbakan attracts street artists, buskers and hawkers of kitsch souvenir jewellery – credit cards accepted. Walk east along the walls to the Marshal's Tower, and you have a good view over the river to the Praga district (see p.122). Conversely, some of the best views of Stare Miasto itself are from the **Praga waterfront**: take any tram over Most Śląsko-Dąbrowski, the bridge immediately south of Stare Miasto, get off at the first stop and cross into **Praski Park**, then down to the riverbank.

The Nowe Miasto

Across the ramparts from the Barbakan is the **Nowe Miasto** (New Town) district, which, despite its name, dates from the early fifteenth century, although it wasn't formally joined to Warsaw until the end of the eighteenth. At that time, the wooden buildings of the artisan settlement were replaced by brick houses, and it's in this style that the area has been rebuilt.

Along ul. Freta to the Rynek Nowego Miasta

From the Barbakan, **Ulica Freta** – the continuation of Nowomiejska – runs north through the heart of the Nowe Miasto. Before progressing too far however it's worth making a short detour to the left, where ul. Długa leads to the eighteenth-century **Pałac Raczyńskich** (Raczyński Palace), used as one of several field hospitals in the city centre during the Warsaw Uprising. A tablet near the corner of ul. Kilińskiego commemorates over 400 wounded insurrectionists murdered in their beds when the Nazis marched into the Stare Miasto. It's now an archive.

Returning to ul. Freta and heading north soon brings you to the **Kościół św. Jacka** (St Jacek's Church), a Dominican foundation, which is an effective blend of Gothic and early Baroque. The adjoining monastery, the largest in Warsaw, was another field hospital and was heavily bombed as a consequence; hundreds died here when the Nazis regained control in October 1944. There is a pleasant café with outdoor tables at ul. Freta 3, while the **Asian Gallery** at no. 5 (Galeria Aziatycka; Tues–Sun 11am–5pm) holds occasional exhibitions of Asian and Pacific art, shown alongside a small permanent collection. For a time, the German Romantic writer E.T.A. Hoffmann lived at ul. Freta no. 5, and no. 16 was the birthplace of one of Poland's most famous women, **Marie Skłodowska–Curie**, the double Nobel Prize-winning discoverer of radium (see box, overleaf). Inside there's a small but fascinating **museum** (Tues–Sat 10am–4pm, Sun 10am–2pm; 5zł) dedicated to her life and work, where photographs of her with other scientists are reminders of the male preserve she had to break into.

Ul. Freta leads to the **Rynek Nowego Miasta** (New Town Square) – once the commercial hub of the district. Surrounded by elegantly reconstructed eighteenth-century facades, this pleasant square makes a soothing change from the bustle of Stare Miasto. Tucked into the eastern corner is the **Church of the Holy Sacrament**, commissioned by Queen Maria Sobieska in memory of her husband Jan's victory over the Turks at Vienna in 1683 (see Contexts p.680); as you might expect, the highlight of the remarkably sober interior is the Sobieski funeral chapel. The architect of the church, Tylman of Gameren, was the most important figure in the rebuilding of Warsaw after the destruction of the Swedish wars in the 1660s. Invited to Poland from Utrecht by Count Jerzy Lubomirski, he went on to redesign what seems like half the city in his distinctive, rather austere Palladian style.

Marie Curie (1867–1934)

Nobel Prize-winning scientist **Marie Curie** is a good example of the "famous person/anonymous Pole" syndrome – Joseph Conrad being the other obvious one. To anyone brought up on a conventional diet of school science it comes as something of a surprise to discover that unlike her French husband, Pierre, and despite France being her adoptive country, Curie (née **Maria Skłodowska**) was a Pole through and through, and a strongly patriotic one at that. Born into a scientifically oriented Warsaw family, with her father a physics teacher, the young Maria ("Manya" to her friends) showed academic promise from the start. After completing her secondary education at the city's Russian lyceum, Curie travelled to Paris in early 1890 to follow the lectures of the prominent French physicists of the day at the Sorbonne.

The intellectually voracious Curie threw herself into the Parisian scientific milieu, landing a job in the laboratory of the noted physicist Gabriel Lipmann and meeting fellow researcher Pierre Curie, whom she married in 1895. Thus began a partnership that was to result in a number of spectacular scientific achievements, most famously the discovery of **polonium** – so named in honour of her native country – in summer 1898, and soon afterwards, **radium**. Following her colleague Henri Becquerel's discovery of the phenomenon she eventually dubbed "radioactivity", Curie set to work on systematic research into the revolutionary new wonder, work which eventually gained worldwide recognition in the **Nobel Prize for Physics** which she, Pierre Curie and Becquerel were awarded jointly in 1903. Pierre's sudden death in 1906 was a heavy emotional blow, but one which led to Curie's appointment to the professorship her husband vacated, making her the first woman ever to teach at the Sorbonne. A **second Nobel Prize**, this time in chemistry, came in 1911 for the isolation of pure radium.

Despite the upheavals of World War I, with the assistance of one of her two daughters Curie worked on developing the use of **X-rays** and was a prime mover in the founding of the famous **Institut de Radium** in 1918, which rapidly developed into a worldwide centre for chemistry and nuclear physics. By now a figure of world renown, and deeply committed to developing the medical applications of the new radiological science, Curie and her daughters visited the US in 1921, receiving a symbolic gram of prized radium from the president, Warren G. Harding, in the course of the visit. During the rest of the 1920s Curie travelled and lectured widely, founding her own **Curie Foundation** in Paris and eventually realizing a long-standing ambition, the setting up of a Radium Institute in her native Warsaw in 1932, of which her sister Bronia was appointed director. Constant exposure to radiation began to have its effect, however, and in early 1934 it was discovered that Curie had **leukaemia**, of which she died only a few months later, in July 1934. The scientific community in particular mourned the loss of one of its outstanding figures, a woman whose research into the effects of radioactivity pioneered both its medical and research-oriented applications, simultaneously paving the way for subsequent developments in nuclear physics.

Just off the northern edge of the square, the early fifteenth-century **Kościół Mariacki** or **N.M.P** (Church of the Virgin Mary), one of the oldest churches in Warsaw and once the Nowe Miasto parish church, has retained something of its Gothic character despite later remodellings. The adjoining belfry is a Nowe Miasto landmark, easily identifiable from the other side of the river. Staggered rows of benches provide a wonderful viewing point across the water.

Plac Krasińskich

The streets west of the square lead across ul. Bonifraterska to ul. Gen. W. Andersa, a main thoroughfare which marks the boundaries of the Muranów area (see p.100). South, ul. Bonifraterska leads to the large **plac Krasińskich**, now augmented by the Warsaw Uprising **monument**, a controversial piece commissioned by the communist authorities and viewed with mixed feelings by many Varsovians. Built on the spot where AK (Home Army) battalions launched their assault on the Nazis on August 1, 1944, it's a memorably dramatic piece (though now dwarfed by the glass and concrete monstrosity built to house the National Court), the large metal sculpture depicting AK insurgents surfacing from streetside manholes to begin their attack on the Germans, as well as their final forlorn retreat into the sewers of the city. Just beyond the monument, on the corner of ul. Miodowa, is the **Muzeum Warszawskego Powstania** (Museum of the Warsaw Uprising; Tues–Sat 10am–5pm) currently housed in the office of the Union of Warsaw Insurgents, the surviving combatants from the Uprising. The small exhibition (free, but contributions are welcome) details the course of the 63-day assault in different parts of the city, showing, among other things, how the AK used old aerial maps of the city to plan their initial attacks on German positions. Material is provided in English as well as Polish. Additionally, a short but sobering film chronicling the events of the Uprising is shown downstairs regularly throughout the day. Following the fiftieth anniversary of the Warsaw Uprising in August 1994, plans were announced for a permanent, fully fledged Uprising museum in a new complex on nearby ul. Bielańska, built on the site of the prewar Bank Polski, a key insurgents' stronghold. Work on the site, hampered by lack of money, is nowhere near completion.

Immediately opposite the Uprising monument is the **Kościół Garnizonowy** (Garrison Church), the soldiers' main place of worship, with the key Uprising symbol, a large anchor, and a streetside tablet with a roll call of World War II battles in which Polish units participated. Overlooking the west side of the square is the huge and majestic **Pałac Krasińskich** (Krasiński Palace), built for regional governor Jan Krasiński by the tireless Tylman of Gameren, its facade bearing fine sculptures by Andreas Schlüter. Most of the palace's collection of documents – forty thousand items in all – was destroyed in the war, so today's collection comes from a whole host of sources. Theoretically, the building is only open to official visitors, but enquiries at the door should get you in to see at least some of the library. The inside of the palace is splendid, the Neoclassical decorations being restored versions of the designs executed by Merlini in the 1780s. Behind the palace are the **gardens**, now a public park, and beyond that the ghetto area. If you've got the stomach for it then you could visit the **Muzeum Pawiaka** (Pawiak Prison Museum; Wed 9am–5pm, Fri 10am–5pm, Thurs & Sat 9am–4pm, Sun 10am–4pm; 4zł), ten minutes' walk west at ul. Dzielna 24/26, which tells the grim story of Warsaw's most notorious prison from tsarist times to the Nazi occupation.

Ulica Długa and around

Back on pl. Krasińskich, at the corner of **ulica Długa** and ul. Miodowa, is a small streetside **plaque**, one of the least conspicuous yet most poignant memorials in the city. It commemorates the thousands of half-starved Varsovians who attempted to escape from the besieged Stare Miasto through the sewer network during the Warsaw Uprising. Many drowned in the filthy passageways, were killed by grenades thrown into the tunnels, or were shot upon emerging, but a hundred or so did make it to freedom. The bitter saga was the subject of Andrzej Wajda's film *Kanal*, the second in his brilliant war trilogy. The first film of the three, *A Generation*, was also about the Uprising; while the last one, *Ashes and Diamonds*, dealt with the communist takeover in 1945 and the futile nature of resistance. Made during the cultural thaw that followed Gomułka's rise to power in 1956, they're the kind of movies that regularly crop up in art-house retrospectives around the world, and they're also widely available on video and DVD (in Polish only, though) once you get here.

A number of old patrician residences can be seen west along ul. Długa, which leads to the **Muzeum Archeologiczne** (Archeological Museum; Mon–Fri 9am–4pm, Sun 10am–4pm; 6zł), housed in the seventeenth-century arsenal.

The 1944 Warsaw Uprising

Of the many acts of resistance to the savage Nazi occupation of Poland, the **1944 Warsaw Uprising** was the biggest. Almost sixty years on, the heroic, yet ultimately tragic, events of the autumn of 1944 remain firmly lodged in the national memory, at once a piece of history whose interpretation remains controversial and a potent source of national self-definition.

The immediate circumstances of the Uprising were dramatic. With Nazi forces reeling under the impact of the determined push west launched by the Red Army in mid-1944, a German withdrawal from Warsaw began to seem a possibility. The **Armia Krajowa** (Polish Home Army) or AK as they were commonly known, the largest of the Polish resistance forces (indeed, with over 400,000 soldiers, the largest resistance force anywhere in Europe) were thereby confronted by an agonizing dilemma. On one side, they were being strongly urged by the Allies to co-operate actively with advancing Soviet forces in driving back the Nazis. On the other, news of the treatment being meted out to AK units in areas of eastern Poland already liberated by the Red Army served to confirm the long-held suspicion that there was little, if any, room for the AK or its political backing – the Polish government-in-exile in London – in the Soviet scheme of things to come, a fact chillingly symbolized in news of the Soviet detention of AK units in the ex-Nazi concentration camp at Majdanek.

Throughout the second half of July, AK Commander **Tadeusz Komorowski**, known as **Bór**, hesitated over which course of action to take. With the arrival of the first Soviet tanks in the eastern suburbs of the city (Praga), the decision to launch a single-handed attack on the Germans was taken and on August 1, the main Warsaw AK corps of around 50,000 poorly armed troops sprang an assault on the city centre. For the first few days the element of surprise meant AK forces were able to capture large tracts of the city centre. By August 5, however, the tide was already beginning to turn against them. Supported by dive bombers and hastily drafted reinforcements, Nazi troops under the command of ruthless General von dem Bach-Zelewski began the task of clearing out the insurgents. Partisans and civilians alike were treated as legitimate targets for reprisals by the fearsome collection of SS and Wehrmacht units – including three battalions of half-starved Soviet POWs, an "anti-partisan" brigade made up of pardoned criminals and the notorious RONA Red Army deserters brigade – assembled for the task. The Nazi recapture of the **Wola district,** the first to be retaken on August 11, was followed by the massacre of over 8000 civilians. Even worse followed in **Ochota**, where over 40,000 civilians were murdered. Hospitals were burned to the ground with all their staff and patients; during the initial attack, women and children were tied to the front of German tanks to deter ambushes, and rows of civilians were marched in front of infantry units to ward off AK snipers.

With German troops and tanks systematically driving the beleaguered partisans into an ever diminishing pocket of the city centre, the decision was made to abandon the by now devastated Stare Miasto. On September 2, around 1500 of the surviving AK troops, along with over 500 other wounded, headed down into the city sewers through a single manhole near pl. Krasiński – an event imprinted firmly on the national consciousness as much thanks to Wajda's legendary film *Kanał*, a stir-

Starting with Neolithic, Palaeolithic and Bronze Age sites, the museum continues through to early medieval Polish settlements, the highlight being a reconstruction of the early Slav settlements in Wielkopolska and records of forty other excavations from around the country, notably the Jacwingian cemetary site at Jegleniec near Suwałki (see p.259).

A little way east from the museum, at 62 al. Solidarności, on the traffic island, is the **Muzeum Niepodległości** (Museum of Independence; Tues–Fri

ring 1950s rendition of the Uprising, as to its symbolic depiction in the contemporary Warsaw Uprising monument. Fighting continued for another month in the suburbs and pockets of the city centre until October 2, when General Bór and his troops finally surrendered to the Germans, 63 days after fighting had begun. Heavy AK casualties – around 20,000 dead – were overshadowed by the huge losses sustained by the city's civilian population, with over 225,000 killed during the fighting.

With the AK and eventually almost the entire population of Warsaw out of the way, Nazi demolition squads set about the task of fulfilling an enraged Hitler's order to wipe the city off the face of the map, dynamiting and razing building after building until the city centre had to all intents and purposes ceased to exist, as confirmed in the photos taken when the Soviets liberated Warsaw in January 1945.

Of the many controversial aspects of the Uprising, the most explosive, in Polish eyes at least, remains that of the **Soviet role**. Could the Red Army have intervened decisively to assist or save the Uprising from defeat? Throughout the postwar years, the official Soviet line combined the (arguably accurate) claim that the Uprising was a mistimed and strategically flawed diversion from the goal of driving the Germans west in 1944 with absurd ideological denigrations of the AK as reactionary, anti-Soviet nationalists whose actions were a betrayal of the anti-Nazi cause. Certainly Soviet action, or lack of it, during August 1944 was fertile ground for subsequent Polish misgivings about Stalin's real intentions. The Soviet tanks that had reached Praga, for example, sat idly by throughout September 1944 as the Germans pounded the city across the river. Equally significantly, on several occasions the Soviet authorities refused Allied access to Soviet airbases for airlifts of supplies to the beleaguered insurgents, and the secret telegram correspondence between Stalin, Roosevelt and Churchill at the time reveals a Stalin deeply scornful of the whole operation, arguing on one occasion that sooner or later "the truth about the handful of criminals who started the Warsaw disturbance to take over power, will become known to all".

Crudely stated, a common Polish interpretation of all this was that Stalin had simply allowed the Germans to do what his future plans for Poland would have anyway necessitated – the systematic annihilation of the sections of Polish society that formed the core of the AK forces with their uncompromising commitment to a free, independent postwar Poland. With sentiments like these around, it's not surprising that the Warsaw Uprising has remained, if no longer a taboo subject, then certainly a continuing area of disagreement in Polish–Russian relations.

Tensions surfaced visibly during the solemn **fiftieth anniversary commemorations** of the start of the Uprising, held in the city throughout August 1994. In a move widely criticized in Poland, particularly among older sections of Polish society, President Wałęsa invited his Russian and German counterparts to participate at the opening ceremony held in Warsaw on August 1. While the German President **Roman Herzog** accepted the invitation (reportedly under the mistaken impression that the 1943 Ghetto Uprising was being commemorated) and made a speech asking Polish forgiveness for the country's treatment at the hands of the Nazis, Russian President **Boris Yeltsin** declined the invitation, sending a lower-level aide instead, giving rise to the wry popular quip that the Russians had accepted the invitation but decided to stay in Praga instead.

10am–5pm, Sat & Sun 10am–4pm; 5zł), housed in a charming old Neoclassical pile. The museum features changing displays on the theme of the national struggle for independence. The absence of concessions to the faint-hearted (or the non-Polish speaker, for that matter) make this a museum for the dedicated, as demonstrated in the above average quotient of elderly Poles among the visitors.

Ulica Miodowa and around

South from plac Krasińskich, along **ulica Miodowa**, you find yourself in the heart of aristocratic old Warsaw. The palaces lining Miodowa mainly date from the prosperous pre-Partition era, when this section of the city hummed with the life of European high society. Next door to the **Borch** palace – now the residence of the Catholic Primate, Cardinal Glemp – stands the **Pałac Radziwiłłów** (Radziwiłł Palace), designed by Tylman of Gameren, and adjoined by the later **Pałac Paca** (Pac Palace; the resulting agglomeration is sometimes known simply as the Pac-Radziwiłł Palace), with its distinctive frieze-topped entrance. Across the street is the Basilan church and monastery, the city's only Greek Catholic (Uniate) church, designed with an octagonal interior by Merlini in the 1780s.

A few steps down ul. Miodowa to the southwest is the late seventeenth-century **Kościół Kapuczynski** (Capuchin Church), repository of the heart of Jan Sobieski, while off to the left, at the bottom of ul. Kapitulna on ul. Podwale, the **Pomnik Jana Kilińskego** (Jan Kiliński Monument) commemorates another stirring figure in the country's history. During the 1794 Insurrection, it was the shoemaker Kiliński who led the citizens of Warsaw in their assault on the tsarist ambassador's residence on this street. His special place in local consciousness was amply demonstrated during World War II after the Nazi governor took down the uncomfortably defiant-looking monument and locked it up in the Muzeum Narodowe – the next day this message was scrawled on the museum wall: "People of Warsaw, here I am! Jan Kiliński."

Returning to ul. Miodowa, and continuing about 200m further southwest towards ul. Miodowa's continuation, ul. Kozla, you'll come across the **Pałac Przymasowski** (Przymasowski Palace), another imposing monument to the Neoclassical tastes of Poland's eighteenth-century aristocracy.

Muranów and Mirów

Like Łódź, Białystok and Kraków, Warsaw was for centuries one of the great Jewish centres of Poland. In 1939 there were an estimated 380,000 Jews living in and around the city – one-third of the city's total population. By May 1945, around 300 were left. Most of **Jewish** Warsaw was destroyed after the Ghetto Uprising (see box, p.103), to be replaced by the sprawling housing estates and tree-lined thoroughfares of the **Muranów** and **Mirów** districts, a little to the west of the city centre. However, a few traces of the Jewish presence in Warsaw do remain, along with a growing number of newly erected monuments to the notable personalities of the city's historic Jewish community. Equally important, there's a small but increasingly visible Jewish community here – well supported by its exiled diaspora.

Virtually all the Jewish monuments and memorials you will find today are enclosed within the confines of the wartime ghetto area, sealed off from the city's "Aryan" population by the Nazis in November 1940. Warsaw Jews actually lived in a considerably larger part of the city before World War II. The

Our Roots

To cater for the increasing number of Jews from around the world now visiting Poland, a specialist agency-cum-foundation, **Our Roots**, was set up in 1987. Located directly in front of the Nożyk Synagogue at ul. Twarda 6 (9am–5pm; ☎ & ℱ 022/620 0556), the agency stocks a range of detailed guides to Jewish monuments in various parts of the country (including the useful *Guide to Jewish Warsaw* by Jan Jagielski and Robert Pascieczny); offers **guided tours** of Warsaw and elsewhere, by arrangement; and helps visitors trace their Jewish ancestry in Poland. The staff, young Polish Jews, generally speak English.

wholesale obliteration of the area both during and after the 1943 Ghetto Uprising meant that several of the streets changed their name, course or simply disappeared altogether after the war, often making it difficult for the visitor to gain a meaningful impression of what the ghetto area once looked like.

The Nożyk Synagogue

First stop on any itinerary of Jewish Warsaw is the **Nożyk Synagogue**, a stately ochre structure hidden behind a white office block on ul. Twarda, the only one of the ghetto's three synagogues still standing. The majestic Great Synagogue on ul. Tłomackie – which held up to three thousand people – was blown up by the Nazis, and in a gesture of crass insensitivity, the Polish authorities decided to build a flashy skyscraper on the site, now the Sony building.

The Nożyk, a more modest affair built in the early 1900s, was used as a stable, a food store and then gutted during the war, reopening in 1983 after a complete restoration. The refined interior is officially only open to tourists from 10am to 3pm on Thursdays, but in practice it's possible to get in at other times with a little diplomacy. The **Jewish Theatre**, rehoused just east of the synagogue on plac Grzybowski, continues the theatrical and musical traditions of the ghetto.

Before you leave the area walk across plac Grzybowski to **Próżna**. This street has somehow survived the ravages of war and (in some cases) reconstruction, and stands scaffolded but surviving as a testimony to prewar red-bricked Warsaw.

Plac Bohaterów Getta and the Path of Remembrance

Fifteen minutes' walk north of the synagogue is the **Pomnik Bohaterów Getta** (Ghetto Heroes Monument), actually built from blocks ordered from Sweden by Hitler in 1942 to construct a monument to the Third Reich's anticipated victory. Unveiled in 1948 on the fifth anniversary of the Ghetto Uprising, the stark monument recalls both the immense courage of the Jewish resistance and the helplessness of the deportees to moving effect. Once at the heart of the ghetto area, the plac Bohaterów Getta itself is a wide-open green expanse surrounded by drab apartment buildings, with, as in much of the ghetto area, only the occasional rubble-filled bump disturbing the surface to remind you of what used to be there. Plans to build a major new museum complex dedicated to the history of Polish Jewry in the nearby district were announced in spring 1995, though by 2001 they'd not progressed beyond a billboard.

The decline of communism enabled local Jewish groups to actively commemorate their history in a way that had been officially discouraged before, and beginning in the late 1980s, a series of memorial plaques, known as the **Path of Remembrance** was laid out, starting from plac Bohaterów Getta, then north along ul. Zamenhofa and up to the Umschlagplatz on ul. Stawki. The plaques, nineteen simple granite blocks engraved in Polish and Hebrew, honour important individuals and events of the ghetto. Those commemorated by name include ghetto historian Emmanuel Ringenblum (stone 5; see "Books", p.731); Szmul Zygielbojm (stone 8), Jewish Bund representative of the wartime Polish government-in-exile in London, who committed suicide in May 1943 in protest at Allied passivity over the destruction of Warsaw Jewry during the Ghetto Uprising; Mordechai Anielewicz (stone 10), legendary commander of the Jewish Combat Organization (ŻOB) and leader of the Ghetto Uprising (see box opposite); and Janusz Goldszmidt, better known as Janusz Korczak (stone 15), the writer-doctor who voluntarily went with the children of his famous Warsaw orphanage to the Treblinka gas chambers in 1942 (see also opposite).

Along the way, the route takes you past the grass-covered memorial mound covering the site of the **ŻOB Bunker** at ul. Miła 18 (see box opposite) – the mound's height representing the level of rubble left after the destruction of the ghetto area. In many of the surrounding streets you'll find houses built on a similar level, as the postwar communist authorities simply went ahead and constructed new housing blocks on the flattened remains of the ghetto. Continuing on up ul. Zamenhofa soon brings you to the junction with ul. Stawki.

A short way west from the junction, on the edge of a housing estate is the **Umschlagplatz**, where Jews were loaded onto cattle wagons bound for Treblinka and the other death camps. The simple white marble monument standing here, raised in the late 1980s and designed to resemble the cattle trucks used in the transportations, is covered inside with a list of four hundred Jewish first names, the chosen way of symbolizing the estimated 300,000 Jews deported from here to the death camps. A stone stands at the exact point from which the trains departed, while across the road, one of the few surviving prewar buildings (no. 5/7) was the house of the SS commander supervising operations at the Umschlagplatz. It now houses a university psychology department.

The Cmentarz Żydowski and the Korczak orphanage

West along ul. Stawki and down ul. Okopowa (about fifteen minutes' walk in all), the large **Cmentarz Żydowski** (Jewish Cemetery; Mon–Thurs & Sun 9am–3pm, Fri 9am–1pm, closed Sat), established in 1806, contains the graves of more than 250,000 people, and is one of the very few Jewish cemeteries still in use in Poland today – though worrying instances of desecration have led to temporary closures. The tombs range from colossal Gothic follies to simple engraved stones. This site was left almost untouched during the war, the reason being that, unlike in smaller Polish towns, the Nazis didn't need the materials for building new roads.

Scattered among the plots are the graves of eminent Polish Jews like **Ludwig Zamenhof**, the inventor of Esperanto (see p.271), early socialist activist **Stanisław Mendelson** and writer **D.H. Nomberg**. Also worth seeking out is a powerful sculpted monument to Janusz Korczak (see opposite), erected in his honour in the 1980s. The caretaker at the entrance lodge has detailed guidebooks to the tombstones for anyone wanting to know more (information is also available from the Jewish Historical Institute and the Our Roots Foundation offices; see p.101).

The Warsaw Ghetto and the Ghetto Uprising

In 1940, on the order of Ludwig Fisher, the governor of the Warsaw district, 450,000 Jews from Warsaw and the surrounding area were sealed behind the walls of the Nazi-designated ghetto area, creating the largest **ghetto** in Nazi-occupied Europe. By 1941, nearly one and a half million Jews from all over Poland had been crammed into this insanitary zone, with starvation and epidemics the predictable and intended consequence. By mid-1942, nearly a quarter of the ghetto population had died from disease and hunger, a plight communicated to the Allied command by a series of seeringly forthright reports from the budding Polish underground.

Deportations to the death camps from Umschlagplatz began in summer 1942, with 300,000 taken to Treblinka in that summer alone. After further mass round-ups, the Nazis moved in to "clean out" the ghetto in January 1943, by which time there were only 60,000 people left. Sporadic resistance forced them to retreat, but only until April, when a full-scale Nazi assault provoked the **Ghetto Uprising** under the leadership of the Jewish Combat Organization (ŻOB). For nearly a month, Jewish partisans battled against overwhelming Nazi firepower, before ŻOB's bunker headquarters on the corner of ul. Miła and Zamenhofa was finally surrounded and breached on May 9, following the suicide of the legendary Mordechai Anieliewicz and his entire staff. A few combatants survived and escaped to join up with the Polish resistance in the "Aryan" sector of the city. Of those remaining in the ghetto, 7000 were shot immediately, the rest dispatched to the camps. On May 15, Jürgen Stroop, commander-in-chief of the German forces, reported to Himmler, "The Jewish quarter in Warsaw no longer exists".

The Ghetto Uprising has remained a potent symbol both of the plight of Jews under Nazi tyranny and – contrary to the dominant received images – of the absolute will to resist under conditions of systematic terror manifested by a small but significant minority of the Jewish community. The dual nature of the Uprising's legacy was amply attested to in the fiftieth anniversary commemorations held in Warsaw in May 1993, attended by a broad assembly of Jewish and Gentile dignitaries from around the world including a handful of survivors of the Uprising, notably Marek Edelman, the only ŻOB commander still alive today.

From the cemetery entrance, a twenty-minute walk south down ul. Towarowa and then west along ul. Jaktorowska brings you to the site of the prewar **orphanage** set up by **Janusz Korczak**, the focus of one of Andrzej Wajda's better films of the 1990s, *Korczak*. Set back from the road, and still functioning as an orphanage, the original building, which survived the war, has a Korczak memorial plaque on the outside and a monument to him in the main hall. The caretaker will let you have a look inside, and there's also a small selection of souvenirs on sale at the reception. Most powerful of all, though, is the simple statue of Korczak in front of the building – here at least, the city's Jewish past has been done justice.

The Muzeum Żydowskiego Instytutu Historycznego and the Ghetto Wall

The **Muzeum Żydowskiego Instytutu Historycznego** (Jewish Historical Institute), near the site of the former Great Synagogue at ul. Tłomackie 3/5, stands on the site of the prewar Judaic Library, and is part museum (Mon–Fri 8.30am–3pm; donation requested), part library and research archive (Mon–Fri 8am–4pm). The museum details life in the wartime ghetto, a fascinating and moving corrective to the familiar images of passive victims. The international section of the library and archive includes English-language books and journals about Polish Jewry and related issues, as well as a large collection of books rescued from Lublin at the outset of World War II. The archival section contains documents of Jewish life in Poland going back to the seventeenth century, along with an extensive collection of over thirty thousand photos. To meet an increasing demand, the Institute also stocks the indispensable *Guide to Jewish Warsaw* (10zł).

Finally, anyone with a sense of historical symbolism should make their way downtown to ul. Złota at the southern edge of the wartime ghetto area. Wedged between ul. Sienna 55/59 and ul. Złota 62 is one of the very few surviving fragments of the three-metre-high wartime **ghetto wall** (to reach it, use the buzzer at no. 59 or walk through the archway at no. 55 and continue despite the growing conviction that you're trespassing). Tucked away in a backyard, in between modern tenement buildings, the short section of brick wall stands as a poignant testimony to the rude separation of the ghetto – so close, and yet so far from life (and death) on the other side of the wall. The isolation was never absolute – post and phone communication with the Aryan sector continued long into the Nazi occupation, and food was continually smuggled into the starving ghetto, despite the threat of instant execution for anyone, Pole or Jew, caught doing so. A small commemorative plaque records the removal of two bricks from the wall to the Holocaust Museum in New York, and another plaque records the president of Israel's official launch of the monument in 1992. The wall now provides a useful spot on which to perch satellite dishes.

Śródmieście

Śródmieście, the large area that stretches from the Stare Miasto down towards Park Łazienkowski, is the increasingly fast-paced heart of Warsaw. However, in keeping with the Polish spirit of reverence for the past, the sector immediately below the Stare Miasto contains an impressive number of reconstructed palaces, parks, churches and museums, all contributing to a distinctive atmosphere of faded grandeur that's been spruced up. The broad boulevard known as **Krakowskie Przedmieście** (which becomes **Nowy Świat** in its southerly reaches) is the main artery of the Śródmieście, a popular promenading route lined with cafés, boutiques and private galleries. To the west, the brash shopfronts, office blocks and fast-food stands around **ul. Marszałkowska** are overshadowed by the looming form of the **Pałac Kultury i Nauk**, an architectural monument to Stalinist megalomania. Further west still, a modest collection of post-communist **skyscrapers** epitomizes the changing face of Warsaw city life. Immediately beyond the Pałac Kultury i Nauk, **al. Jerozolimskie** cuts through the Śródmieście from west to east – a chaotic strip of trams and traffic which nevertheless provides access to the impressive collections of the **Muzeum Narodowe**.

Plac Teatralny and around

Running west from plac Zamkowy is ul. Senatorska, once one of Warsaw's smartest shopping streets, now studded with wall plaques recording the civilian victims of Nazi street executions. The pseudo-classical giant dominating the nearby **plac Teatralny** is the **Teatr Wielki** (Grand Theatre), the city's main venue for serious drama, opera and ballet. Designed by Corazzi in the 1820s, it boasts a fine classicist facade decorated with Greek sculptures. Rebuilt and enlarged after wartime destruction, the main theatre now holds almost two thousand people, though even then it regularly sells out in summer. Inside, the elegant entrance hall has a sumptuous rotunda overhead and an intricate parquet floor – worth a look even if you're not planning to attend one of the lavish operas, theatre or ballet productions that are staged here throughout the year (see "Nightlife, entertainment, activities and sport", p.128).

The north side of pl. Teatralny is one of the city areas currently receiving a major facelift. A Citibank hides its business concerns behind a facade that has sensitively re-created that of the **Stary Ratusz** (Old Town Hall), though the block of postwar high-rise housing nearby rather ruins the effect. The redoubtable sword-waving goddess who once rose from the stone plinth on the other side of the square, Nike, otherwise known as the **Pomnik Bohaterów Warszawy** (Warsaw Heroes Monument), the state's tribute to the war dead, has been moved to make way for redevelopment. She now stands directing the traffic on the highway under the Stare Miasto – walk down Miodowa from the Nowe Miasto and she's on the right. Continuing west along Senatorska, the Baroque **Kościół Franciszkański** (Franciscan Church) – a quiet place with restful cloisters – is followed by the **Pałac Mniszech** and the **Pałac Błękitny** (Blue Palace), where Chopin gave one of his earliest concerts at the age of six. Tragically, the palace's destruction in 1944 engulfed the fabulous Zamoyski library of over 250,000 books and manuscripts.

Plac Bankowy

Senatorska ends at **plac Bankowy**, formerly plac Dzierżyńskiego: the giant statue of its former namesake Felix Dzierżyński, the unloved Polish Bolshevik and founder of the NKVD, was removed in 1990 to public rejoicing. A rather more unassuming-in-size statue of Romantic poet **Juliusz Słowacki** is set to take its place. On the northeast corner of the square is a tall, silver-looking tower known locally as the Blue Skyscraper, or **Błękitny Wieżowiec**, that's long been a talking point: built on the former site of the Great Synagogue (see p.101) – and cursed, according to local legend, as a consequence – from its inception in the early 1970s, it took over twenty years to complete this lumbering Yugoslav-financed giant of a project, now the Sony building. The west edge of the increasingly smart-looking square is taken up by a palatial early-nineteenth-century complex designed by Antoni Corazzi, and originally housing Congress Kingdom-era government offices (see p.682). This grand building has been the seat of the city's administrative authorities since the destruction of the original town hall in 1944. On the southwest corner of the square is the old **National Bank** building, until recently the official Museum of the Workers' Movement but now taken over by the **Kolekcja I. Jana Pawła II**.

The Muzeum Kolekcji im. Jana Pawła II

The **Muzeum Kolekcji im. Jana Pawła II** (John Paul II Museum; Tues–Sun 10am–5pm, last entry 4pm; 7zł) comprises a large art collection – some 400 paintings in all – assembled by the wealthy émigré Carroll-Porczyński family in the early 1980s and donated to the Polish Catholic church a few years later, with works ranging from the fourteenth to the twentieth century, and a heavy emphasis on religious subjects. The museum has proved controversial: sections of the academic art world are doubtful about the value of the collection, and the Porczyńskis went to great – and ultimately unsuccessful – lengths to try to block the publication of an article by a leading Polish art expert claiming that several of the more famous paintings, in particular the early Italian works, are actually fakes. Alongside the museum's unquestionably high artistic aspiration, there's an unabashedly catachestic tone to the place, the portraits of the pope and current Catholic Primate Cardinal Glemp placed at the entrance reminding you of whom the collection is supposed to be in honour. Most of the collections, too, are arranged according to themes drawn from the Catholic theological canon – the Bible and Saints, the Life of Mary, Myth and Allegory, Motherhood and the like – the rest being set up on the basis of national "schools" of art and artistic themes, like "Still Lifes and Landscapes". The museum entrance is round the side of the building, next to the pope's statue.

Italian and German works

Most visitors begin with the main ground-floor room, a large domed auditorium once occupied by the Warsaw Bourse that now doubles as a concert recital hall – hence the chairs filling the body of the building. The large collection of portraits lining the walls is divided into national "schools", as are most of the ground-floor collections. The **Italian school** features a fine *Death of Lucretia* from the Titian school, as well as a notable *Sacrifice of the Dead Abraham* from the Caravaggio workshop, probably a replica of a smaller painting of the same title housed in the Uffizi in Florence. Highlights of the **German** collection include portraits of Luther and his wife Catherine by Cranach the elder, and one of the oldest known versions of the lost *St Anne* by Albrecht Dürer, dated 1523.

Flemish and Dutch works

The big guns of **Flemish and Dutch** Baroque provide some of the museum's leading works, with self-portraits of Rubens and Rembrandt, the latter placed alongside the thoughtful *Portrait of a Nobleman* by van Dyck beneath the impassive bust of patron John Paul peering out over the auditorium. Additionally there are a couple of works by Jordaens, while *Farm in Hoogeveen*, a typically brooding early Van Gogh, is one of several works in the "Still Lifes and Landscapes" section housed in an adjoining room, which also features a Constable still life and an evocative pair of landscapes by the French-born English painter Alfred Sisley: here as elsewhere in the collection, enjoyment is somewhat marred by the neck-wrenching height at which the pictures have been hung.

French, English and Spanish works

The **French** collection is particularly strong on portraiture, featuring a wealth of courtly eighteenth-century aristocracy, a fine portrait of Henry IV, a Renoir picture of his son Pierre, and a plaster mould head of John the Baptist by Rodin. The same goes for the **English** section: notable works here include Sir Joshua Reynolds' penetrating *Portrait of Miss Nelly O'Brien* – one of three he painted of the Irish woman – and a noble-looking self-portrait. **Spanish** artists provide some of the most powerful works in the auditorium, particularly the self-portraits by Murillo and Velázquez, Ribera's hauntingly intense *Portrait of a Philosopher,* and *Woman Carrying Water*, a powerful later Goya work.

The upper floors

The upper floors of the building house the theologically oriented "theme" rooms, including the art-crammed "Mother and Child" section populated by the inevitable welter of fleshy-looking Baroque cherubs. The upper sections contain plenty of notable works too, with **Italian** artists providing the earliest (and most controversial) works, especially a fine *Jesus' Offertory in the Temple* from the circle of Jacopo Bellini, a mid-fourteenth-century *Virgin and Child* from the Marches school (the oldest painting in the collection), a *Madonna and Child* by Carucci, Titian's *Child from the Medici Family*, and a *Last Supper* by Tintoretto. Works from other countries include another *Last Supper* by Brueghel the Younger, a dreamy *Ecstasy of St Francis* by David Teniers, and an outstanding Mannerist *Crucifixion* by Cornelis van Haarlem housed in the "crucifixion room" whose centrepiece is a huge, dramatic depiction of Calvary by the Polish nineteenth-century artist Wojciech Gerson.

Plac Piłsudskiego, the Ogród Saski and around

Returning to plac Teatralny, the way south leads onto an even larger square, **plac Piłsudskiego** (previously Zwycięstwa), once the site of a beautiful Orthodox church which was torn down in a wave of anti-Russian feeling in the 1920s. In the 1980s a huge flower cross was laid here by Varsovians as a protest against the imposition of martial law. After the authorities had cleared the cross away, the whole area was closed off for public works for years, presumably to prevent embarrassing demonstrations happening in full view of the tourists staying in the *Victoria* and *Europejski* hotels. These days the military guard in front of the **Tomb of the Unknown Soldier** here is the only permanent security presence, and bollards keep the centre of the spacious square traffic-free.

Beyond the tomb stretch the handsome and well-used promenades of the **Ogród Saski** (Saxon Gardens), laid out for August II by Tylman of Gameren in the early 1700s, and landscaped as a public garden in the following century. The **royal palace** built in the gardens by August II was blown up by the Nazis in 1944 and never rebuilt; the Tomb of the Unknown Soldier is the only surviving part of the building. Other sections of the park were luckier, notably the scattering of Baroque sculptures, symbolizing the Virtues, Sciences and Elements, an elegant nineteenth-century fountain pool above the main pathway, the old **water tower** (Warsaw's first) built by Marconi in the 1850s and the park's fine crop of **trees**, over a hundred species in all. Long one of Warsaw's most popular green areas, the gardens are now very well kept.

Immediately south of the gardens on plac Małachowskiego, to the west of the plush *Victoria* hotel, is the **Galeria Zachęta** (Tues–Sun 10am–6pm; entry fee varies according to what's on; Ⓦwww.zacheta-gallery.waw.pl), built at the turn of the twentieth century as the headquarters of the Warsaw Fine Arts Society, and one of the few buildings in central Warsaw left standing at the end of World War II. The stucco decoration in the entrance gives a taste of the building's original qualities. The gallery's considerable original art collection (Matejko's *Battle of Grunwald* included) was packed off into hiding in the Muzeum Narodowe at the start of the war, subsequently forming part of that museum's permanent collection. The Zachęta is now the nation's leading contemporary art gallery, staging a wealth of high-quality exhibitions by international artists. The gallery's commitment to showcasing up-to-the-minute trends in art have helped turn it into something of a political football of late, with many conservative critics arguing that the gallery's frequently controversial exhibitions are unworthy of such an important, state-funded institution.

Krakowskie Przedmieście

Of all the long thoroughfares bisecting central Warsaw from north to south, the most important is the one often known as the **Trakt Królewski** (Royal Way),

△ Street vendor, Nowy Swiat, Warsaw

which runs almost uninterrupted from plac Zamkowy to the palace of Wilanów. **Krakowskie Przedmieście**, the first part of the Trakt Królewski, is lined with historic buildings. **Kościół św. Anny** (St Anne's Church), directly below pl. Zamkowy, is where Polish princes used to swear homage to the king; founded in 1454, the church was destroyed in 1656 by the besieging Swedes, then rebuilt in Baroque style in the following century. All that remains of the original church is the Gothic brick presbytery adjacent to the nave and Baroque chapel dome. There's a fine view over the Wisła from the courtyard next to the church, though your enjoyment of it is somewhat marred by the traffic thundering through the tunnel below. By 1983, the second year of martial law, resourceful oppositionists had assembled a new flower cross to this courtyard after the authorities removed the huge one from plac Piłsudskiego (see p.107). These days, the courtyard is filled with a busy outdoor café and a pizzeria that are at least as popular with Polish sightseers as the cross used to be. For an even better view, you can climb the **belfry** on the northern side of the courtyard (May–Sept daily 10am–5pm; 2zł).

South of St Anne's the bus-congested street broadens to incorporate a small green. The **Pomnik Mickiewicza** (Mickiewicz Monument) stuck in the middle of it is the first of many you'll see if you travel round the country – he's a hero with whom everyone seems comfortable, communist governments included (see pp.92–93). It was unveiled on the centenary of the poet's birth, before a twelve-thousand-strong crowd (the Russians were enforcing a ban on rallies and speeches at the time).

Just south of the statue stands the seventeenth-century **Kościół Karmelitów** (Carmelite Church) whose finely wrought facade, complete with a distinctive globe of the world, is one of the first examples of genuine classicism in Poland. Next door in the **Pałac Radziwiłłów** – Radziwiłł Palace; another building belonging to the Polish-Lithuanian aristocrats who also built the Pałac Radziwiłłów on ul. Miodowa, see p.100 – is where the Warsaw Pact was formally created in 1955, at the height of the Cold War. Thirty-four years later, it hosted another equally momentous event in the spring 1989 "Round Table" talks between the country's communist authorities and the Solidarity-led opposition. In front of the palace's large courtyard is a statue of another national favourite, Józef Poniatowski, nephew of the last king of Poland and a diehard patriot who fought in the 1794 Insurrection.

West of the main street on ul. Kozia, a quiet, atmospheric cobbled backstreet, is the **Muzeum Karykatury** (Museum of Caricatures; Tues–Sun 11am–5pm; 4zł; free on Thurs) at no. 11, a quirky but enjoyable setup featuring exhibitions of work by Polish cartoonists. The main feature for some time to come is likely to be a large display of work by the late Eryk Lipiński, the veteran cartoonist, honoured in a plaque on the wall, whose satirical portraits seem to cover just about every famous Pole you're likely to have heard of, and many more besides. The overall tone of his pictures is hearteningly irreverent – no one is sacrosanct, not even the pope or other national icons past and present.

Back on Krakowskie Przedmieście, two grand old hotels face each other a little further down the street: the **Europejski**, Warsaw's oldest hotel, and the **Bristol**. Begun in the 1850s, the *Europejski* was badly hit in World War II, and though the exterior has been restored well enough to preserve at least a hint of *fin-de-siècle* grandeur, the rooms inside have been eviscerated and lack character. After years out of action, the *Bristol*, a neo-Renaissance pile completed in 1899, is now back in business as part of the Meridien chain. Once owned by musician-premier Ignacy Paderewski and a legendary prewar journalist's hangout, it's now been transformed into a super-luxury hotel. Some of the interior charm has been retained, and this is probably the one hotel in the luxury bracket that's worth it. Both hotels are listed in "Accommodation" pp.85–87.

Even in a city not lacking in Baroque churches, the triple-naved **Kościół Sióstr Wizytek** (Nuns of the Visitation) stands out, with its columned, statue-topped facade; it's also one of the very few buildings in central Warsaw to have come through World War II unscathed. The church's main claim to fame, in Polish eyes, is that Chopin used to play the church organ here, mainly during services for schoolchildren.

The university

Most of the rest of Krakowskie Przedmieście is taken up by Warsaw's **university**. Established in 1818, it was closed by the tsar in 1832 as part of the punishment for the 1831 Insurrection, and remained closed till 1915. During the Nazi occupation, educational activity of any sort was made a capital offence, and thousands of academics and students were murdered. However, clandestine university courses continued throughout the war – a tradition revived in the 1970s with the "Flying University", when opposition figures travelled around the city giving open lectures on politically controversial issues. Nowadays you're less likely to notice public debates than the host of beggars who patrol the area – old women bent double outside the churches, mothers with children on the pavements, gangs of kids at the bus stops. The cafés, restaurants and milk bars just down the street and round the corner on ul. Oboźna are established student hangouts.

On the main campus courtyard, the **library** stands in front of the seventeenth-century **Pałac Kazimierzowski** (Kazimierz Palace), once a royal summer residence and now home to the rector and associated bureaucrats, while across the street from the gates is the former **Pałac Czapskich** (Czapski Palace), now home of the Academy of Fine Arts. Just south is the twin-towered Baroque **Kosciół św. Krzyża** (Holy Cross Church), which was ruined by a two-week battle inside the building during the Warsaw Uprising. Photographs of the distinctive stone figure of Christ left standing among the ruins became poignant emblems of Warsaw's suffering, and now hang inside the church entrance, whilst outside a statue of a broken Christ with a crown of thorns exhorts passers-by to "*Sursum Corda*" ("Lift up your Hearts"). Another factor increases local affection for this church – an urn containing **Chopin**'s heart stands on a pillar on the left side of the nave.

Biggest among Warsaw's consistently big palaces is the early-nineteenth-century **Pałac Staszica** (Staszic Palace), which virtually blocks the end of Krakowskie Przedmieście. Once a Russian boys' grammar school, it's now the headquarters of the Polish Academy of Sciences. In front of the palace is the august **Pomnik Mikołaja Kopernika** (Copernicus Monument), designed by the Danish sculptor Bertel Thorvaldsen in the 1830s and showing the great astronomer holding one of his revolutionary heliocentric models. Past the monument down the narrow ul. Oboźna is the **Teatr Polski** (Polish Theatre) building.

Ulica Marszałkowska and around

The area below the Ogród Saski and west of Krakowskie Przedmieście is the city's busiest commercial zone. **Marszałkowska**, the main road running south from the western tip of the gardens, is lined with department stores and clothes shops. South of ul. Świętokrzyska, in the long narrow streets surrounding Chmielna and Zgoda, it's worth scouting around for good-quality items like heavy winter coats and hand-crafted leather goods; **Chmielna**, recently pedestrianized, is particularly recommended.

North of ul. Świętokrzyska, on ul. Kreditowa, the eighteenth-century **Ewangelicko–Augsburgski** (Lutheran) church is topped with Warsaw's largest dome. The building's excellent acoustics have long made it popular with musicians – Chopin played a concert here at the age of fourteen, and the church still holds regular choral and chamber concerts (see "Nightlife, entertainment, activities and sport", p.128). Opposite, stands the **Muzeum Etnograficzne** (Ethnographic Museum; Tues, Thurs & Fri 10am–4pm, Wed 11am–6pm, Sat & Sun 10am–5pm; 4zł, free on Wed), whose collection of over 30,000 items was virtually destroyed in the war. They've done pretty well to revive the place since then, restocking with African tribal artefacts, Latin American outfits and local folk items. Polish objects take up much of the second floor, a highlight being an absorbing collection of traditional costumes from all over the country. Folklore enthusiasts will enjoy the section devoted to straw men, winter processions and a host of other arcane rural customs.

Towering over everything in this part of the city is the **Pałac Kultury i Nauk** (Palace of Culture and Sciences, or PKiN – pronounced "pay-kin" – for short), a gift from Stalin to the Polish people, and not one that could be refused. Officially dubbed "an unshakeable monument to Polish-Soviet friendship" during the communist era but popularly known as "the Russian cake", this neo-Baroque leviathan provokes both intense revulsion and admiration for its sheer audacity – city residents maintain that the best **views** of Warsaw are from the Pałac Kultury i Nauk's top floor – the only viewpoint from which one can't see the palace. A lift whisks visitors up to the thirtieth-floor platform (daily 9am–6pm; 10zł), from where, on a good day, you can see out into the plains of Mazovia. Long despised by Varsovians for casting a Stalinist shadow over their city, the palace is increasingly seen as the grand old lady of the downtown skyline – especially when compared to the rather functional skyscrapers that are beginning to sprout from neighbouring streets. The palace has in any case been shorn of much of its ideological symbolism: slick marketing slogans have replaced the admonitions from Marx and Lenin on the banners over the giant entrance, up the steps from the expansive **plac Defilad** – recently the subject of an international design competition. The winning proposal – to fill the area with small-scale buildings and a pedestrian boulevard, but leave the palace essentially untouched – has angered many Varsovians, a good few of whom support the idea of demolishing the whole thing. The debate still rages, and parts of the area still resemble a huge building site, but the landscaped entrance to the new Centrum metro station has pacified some critics. The cavernous interior contains offices, cinemas, swimming pools, some good foreign-language bookshops, and, the ultimate capitalistic revenge, a casino. It's also the site of one of Warsaw's most important congress venues and concert venues, the **Zala Kongresowa**, which provides a home for visiting pop stars as well as the city's two major **jazz festivals** (see p.128). One truly epoch-defining gig to take place here was the appearance of the Rolling Stones in 1967 (a time when Western groups hardly ever made the trip to Eastern Europe), an event which kick-started the Polish beat boom of the sixties.

South and west of the palace lie the areas of Warsaw that have experienced the most intense development in the years following the introduction of the free market. High-rise office blocks seem to be shooting up everywhere along the main westbound highway **Aleja Jerozolimskie**, and in the streets surrounding Warszawa Centralna train station. The gleaming chrome and glass of the LOT building on al. Jerozolimskie has long been the major landmark here, although its supremacy has recently been challenged by the **Warsaw Tower** (known as the Daewoo Tower when the Korean conglomerate first built it in 1997) a little further west along ul. Sienna – second only to the Pałac Kultury i Nauk in height, it's a haughtily elegant structure whose combination of smooth curves and angular straight lines ensures that it has a different profile from whichever direction you look at it.

South of the Pałac Kultury i Nauk, the busy tramlined strip of ul. Marszalęowska leads south towards **plac Konstitucji**, crowded on either side by department stores, glitzy shops and the cultural institutes of other erstwhile communist countries. Cross-streets such as Hoża and Wilcza comprise a residential area whose discreetly well-heeled inhabitants are served by increasing numbers of chic little stores and snazzy café-bars.

Nowy Świat and around

South of the Pałac Staszica (Staszic Palace; see p.110), Krakowskie Przedmieście becomes **Nowy Świat** (New World), an area first settled in the mid-seventeenth century. This wide boulevard, is currently being redeveloped, giving way to shops and **cafés**. The *Nowy Świat* café, on the corner with Świętokrzyska, has long been a favoured meeting point for the city's cultural elite, while the *Blikle* further down still produces the cakes for which it's been famed since 1869. For more on both places, see "Cafés and bars", pp.126–128.

Numerous cultural luminaries have inhabited this street, the most famous being Joseph Conrad, who once lived at no. 45. A left turn down ul. Ordynacka brings you to the **Muzeum Fryderyka Chopina** (Chopin Museum; daily except Tues 10am–2pm; 5zł), housed in the late-seventeenth-century Palac Ostrogski on ul. Okólnik, which also forms the headquarters of the Towarzystwo im. Fryderyka Chopina (Chopin Society). Memorabilia on display include the last piano he played, now used for occasional concerts. Monday evening concerts are held here throughout the summer months (May–Sept) and there are also regular performances in Park Łazienkowski (see p.115) and at Żelazowa Wola (see p.136). The Society organizes the International Chopin Piano Competition held every five years.

The neo-Renaissance **Zamoyski Palace**, off to the left of Nowy Świat at the end of ul. Foksal, is one of the few Warsaw palaces you can actually see inside. In 1863, an abortive attempt to assassinate the tsarist governor was made here; as a consequence the palace was confiscated and ransacked by Cossacks, who hurled a grand piano used by Chopin out of the window of his sister's flat in the palace. These days it's a suitably elegant setting for an architectural institute, boasting a restaurant and a nice quiet café open to the public, with terrace seating in the summer. Round one side of the palace, an outwardly unassuming building houses the **Galeria Foksal** (Mon–Fri noon–5pm), one of the better contemporary galleries in the city, with a regular programme of temporary exhibitions by artists both Polish and foreign. It's been something of a cult place for arty avant-gardists ever since the early 1960s, when it became the first Warsaw gallery to host happenings arranged by renowned Cracovian performance artist and theatre director Tadeusz Kantor.

Further down Nowy Świat, the concrete monster on the southern side of the junction with al. Jerozolimskie was for decades the headquarters of the now defunct Polish **communist party**. After a pleasingly ironic stint as the new Warsaw Stock Exchange (now relocated to premises nearby), it is now leased out to various private companies who sport their logos from the roof.

The Muzeum Narodowe

Immediately east along al. Jerozolimskie from the old communist HQ is the **Muzeum Narodowe** (National Museum; Tues–Wed & Fri 10am–4pm, Thurs noon–5pm, Sat & Sun 10am–5pm; last entry 45min before closing; 13zł, free on Sat), a daunting grey-brown building that was considered a masterpiece of modern functionalism when first built in the 1930s, and one of the few central Warsaw buildings to survive World War II intact.

The displays begin to the right of the entrance with the department of ancient art – assorted **Egyptian**, **Greek**, **Roman** and **Etruscan** finds. These, however, are completely overshadowed by the stunning array in the corresponding wing to the left of art from Faras, a town in **Nubia** (the present-day Sudan), excavated by Polish archeologists in the early 1960s. There are capitals, friezes, columns and other architectural fragments, together with 69 murals dating from between the eighth and thirteenth centuries. The earliest paintings – notably *St Anne, The Archangels Michael and Gabriel* and *SS Peter and John Enthroned* – are direct and powerful images comparable in quality with the much later productions of the European Romanesque, and prove the vibrancy of African culture at this period. No less striking are the later portraits such as the tenth-century *Bishop Petros with St Peter* and the eleventh-century *Bishop Marianos*.

In the rooms off the central hall, in which stand notable sculptures by Adrian de Vries, Bernini and Canova, is the museum's other star collection, that of **medieval art**, which is dominated by a kaleidoscopic array of carved and painted altarpieces. Although all the objects come from within the modern borders of Poland, the predominance of works from Silesia and the Gdańsk area suggests that most were created by German or Bohemian craftsmen, whose style was closely imitated elsewhere. Highlights include a lovely late-fourteenth-century "Soft Style" polyptych from the castle chapel in Grudziądz; the monumental fifteenth-century canopied altar from St Mary in Gdańsk; and the altar from Pławno depicting the life of St Stanisław, painted by Hans Süss von Kulmbach, a pupil of Dürer who spent part of his career in Poland.

Much of the first floor is given over to **Polish painting**, beginning with a number of examples of what is a quintessential national art form, the coffin portrait. There's a comprehensive collection of works by nineteenth-century and modern artists, many of them relatively little known; an important section is the group of works from the turn-of-the-twentieth-century Młoda Polska school. Stanisław Wyspiański's intense self-portraits stand out, as do Jacek Malczewski's haunting images of Death disguised as an angel. Matejko is represented by some of his most heroic efforts, notably the huge *Battle of Grunwald*, which depicts one of the most momentous clashes of the Middle Ages, the defeat of the Teutonic Knights by combined Polish-Lithuanian forces.

The left wing of the first floor, plus all of the second floor, are given over to the extensive but patchy department of foreign paintings. In the **Italian section**, look out for some notable Renaissance panels, such as the tondo of *The Madonna and Child with St John* from the workshop of Botticelli, *Portrait of a Venetian Admiral* by Tintoretto and *Christ among the Doctors* by Cima da Conegliano. Among the **French paintings** in the following rooms are a badly damaged little canvas called *The Polish Woman* attributed to Watteau and Ingres' sensual *Academic Study*. Upstairs, the **German Renaissance** is represented by a fine group of works – including *Adam and Eve, The Massacre of the Innocents* and *Portrait of a Princess* – by Cranach, and *Hercules and Anteus* by Baldung. From the same period in the **Low Countries** are an impressive *Ecce Homo* triptych by van Heemskerk and the satirical *Moneychangers* by van Reymerswaele. Later Dutch works include *Queen Sylvia,* a brilliant Mannerist composition by Goltizius and a couple of striking examples of Tenebrism: *King David Playing the Harp* by Terbrugghen and *Boy Blowing Charcoal* by Rembrandt's collaborator, Jan Lievens.

Occasional temporary exhibitions – like a mammoth French Impressionist retrospective that toured all Poland's major cities in 2001 – spice up the normal fare, and there's a good café on site, too.

The Muzeum Wojska Polskiego

The **Muzeum Wojska Polskiego** (Army Museum; Wed–Sun 10am–4pm; 4zł, free on Fri), next door to the Muzeum Narodowe, was established in the 1920s and is devoted to an institution that has long played a pivotal role in national consciousness, as much, many Poles would argue, for its role in preserving national identity during periods of foreign occupation as for militaristic self-glorification. Greeting you outside the museum is an intimidating collection of heavy combat equipment, from sixteenth-century cannons through to modern tanks and planes. A unique item is *Kubuś*, as it's affectionately known, an improvised truck-cum-armoured car cobbled together by Home Army forces and used to notable effect during the Warsaw Uprising. Inside there's a wide array of guns, swords and armour from over the centuries. Exhibits include an eleventh-century Piast-era helmet (the oldest exhibit); early cannon prototypes produced by the Teutonic Knights; fearsome Hussar "whistling" feather headgear; and scythes of the type used in combat by Polish peasants during the Partition-era struggles. All in all the museum is a must for avid amateur military historians (and there are plenty of them in Poland), though the appeal of the insistently militarist ambience wears a little thin by the end of the exhibits.

Plac Trzech Krzyży, the Sejm, the Senat and around

South of the museum, **plac Trzech Krzyży** (Three Crosses), with the Pantheon-style **Kościół św. Aleksandra** (St Alexander's Church) in the centre, leads to the tree-lined pavements and magisterial embassy buildings of al. Ujazdowskie. Past the unattractive US embassy and off to the left down ul. Jana Matejki, is the squat 1920s **Sejm** (Parliament) and **Senat** (Senate) building. A feeble institution stuffed with government-approved yes-men until the epoch-making elections of July 1989, these days it's where veteran Solidarity-era oppositionists jostle for power as much among themselves as with their former communist (now dubbed post-communist) political opponents.

Many of the streets in this and other areas confront you with dull postwar frontages plastered over the pockmarks of World War II gunfire. However, many of these unprepossessing edifices mask red-brick or stone buildings a century or more old, some also featuring elaborate shrines to the Virgin Mary; step through the archways ul. Mokotowska 65 or 73, just south of plac Trzech Krzyży, for examples of these rarely touristed corners of the city.

Further south along al. Ujazdowskie and over the junction with al. Armii Ludowej is the grim **Muzeum Walki i Męczeństwa** (Museum of Struggle and Martyrdom; Wed–Sun 9am–4pm; donation requested), al. Szucha 25. Housed in the former Gestapo headquarters, now occupied by government ministries, the basement museum commemorates the thousands tortured and murdered here during World War II.

Ujazdowski and Łazienki parks

Parks are one of Warsaw's distinctive and most attractive features. South of al. Jerozolimskie lies one of the best stretches of greenery the city has to offer, an unequalled strolling area that begins immediately behind the Muzeum Narodowe (see p.113) with **Park Rydza-Śmigłego** (Rydz-Śmigły Park) and continues almost unbroken for 2.5km, passing through **Park Ujazdowski** (Ujazdowski Park) before arriving at the most luxuriant public space of them all, **Park Łazienkowski** (Łazienki Park). If you haven't got the time to walk the whole distance, the numerous buses running along al. Ujazdowskie on the parks' western fringes provide a good way of getting around.

Park Ujazdowski

Al. Ujazdowskie itself is one of the city's more elegant thoroughfares, with opulent nineteenth century villas (most of which are now occupied by foreign embassies) lining its western side, and the regimented flowerbeds of Ujazdowski Park on the other. Lurking on **Park Ujazdowski**'s eastern side is the **Pałac Ujazdowski** (Ujazdowski Palace), a Renaissance structure once inhabited by King Sigismund August's Italian-born mother Bona Sforza. It's now home to the **Centrum Sztuki Współczesnej** (Contemporary Art Centre; Tues–Thurs & Sat–Sun 11am–5pm, Fri 11am–9pm; 10zł, free on Thurs; Ⓦ www.csw.art.pl), the city's leading venue for modern art shows after the Galeria Zachęta (see p.107). As well as organizing themed exhibitions, the centre mounts innovative theatre, film and video events. Occupying the terrace on the eastern side of the palace, the centre's café-**restaurant** *Qchnia Artystyczna* (see p.107) commands an excellent view down towards the Wisła.

South from Pałac Ujazdowski, on the far side of ul. Agrykola, the **Ogród Botaniczny** (Botanical Gardens; Mon–Sat 9am–7pm, Sun 10am–7pm; 4zł) boast an impressive collection of carefully landscaped shrubs and trees, with a sizeable rose garden, and a knot garden crammed full of fragrant medicinal herbs.

Park Łazienkiowski

South and east of here lie several entrances to the main body of **Park Łazienkowski** (Łazienki Park; open daily 8am–sunset). Once a hunting ground on the periphery of town, the area was bought by King Stanisław August in the 1760s and turned into an English-style park with formal gardens. A few years later the slender Neoclassical **Pałac Łazienkowski** was built across the park lake. Designed for the king by the Italian architect Domenico Merlini, in collaboration with teams of sculptors and other architects, it's the best memorial to the country's last and most cultured monarch. Before this summer residence was commissioned, a **bathhouse** built by Tylman of Gameren for Prince Stanisław Lubomirski stood here – hence the name, "Łazienki" meaning simply "baths".

The oak-lined promenades and pathways leading from the park entrance to the palace are a favourite with both Varsovians and tourists. On summer Sunday lunchtimes and afternoons, concerts and other events take place under the watchful eye of the ponderous Chopin Monument, just beyond the entrance. These are an enjoyable introduction to Polish culture in populist form – stirring performances of Chopin *études* or *mazurkas*, declamatory readings from Mickiewicz and other Romantics, and so on. On the way down to the lake you'll pass a couple of the many buildings designed for King Stanisław by Merlini: the Nowa Kordegarda (New Guardhouse), just before the palace, is now a pleasant terrace **café** serving great ice cream. There's another café next to the amphitheatre.

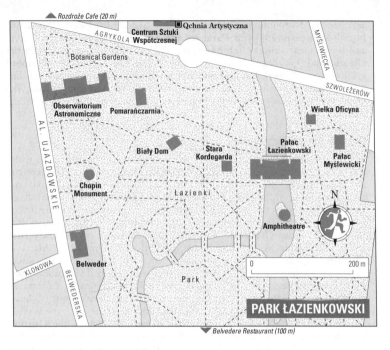

Rozdroże Cafe (20 m)

Qchnia Artystyczna

Centrum Sztuki Współczesnej

A G R Y K O L A

MYŚLIWIECKA

Botanical Gardens

SZWOLEŻERÓW

Obserwatorium Astronomiczne

Pomarańczarnia

Wielka Oficyna

AL. UJAZDOWSKIE

Biały Dom

Stara Kordegarda

Pałac Łazienkowski

Pałac Myślewicki

Chopin Monument

Łazienki

N

Amphitheatre

KLONOWA

BELWEDERSKA

Belweder

0   200 m

Park

PARK ŁAZIENKOWSKI

Belvedere Restaurant (100 m)

Pałac Łazienkowski

There are always queues for tours of the **Pałac Łazienkowski** (Łazienki Palace; Tues–Sun 9am–4pm; 11zł, free on Thurs) – often referred to as the Island Palace or Pałac na Wyspie due to its water-bound location – so get there early or be prepared for a long wait. Nazi damage to the rooms themselves was not irreparable, and most of the lavish furnishings, paintings and sculptures survived the war intact, having been hidden during the occupation.

On the ground floor are rooms incorporated from the earlier bathhouse; the baths themselves are long gone, but the bas-reliefs decorating the walls serve as a reminder of their original water-bound function. In the main section of the palace, the stuccoed **ballroom**, the largest ground-floor room, is a fine example of Stanisław's classicist predilections, lined with a tasteful collection of busts and sculptures. As the adjoining **picture galleries** demonstrate, Stanisław was a discerning art collector. The Nazis got hold of some of the best pieces – three Rembrandts included – but a large collection drawn from all over Europe remains, with an accent on Dutch and Flemish artists.

Upstairs are the **king's private apartments**, most of them entirely reconstructed since the war. Again, period art and furniture dominate these handsome chambers: a stately and uncomfortable-looking four-poster bed fills the royal bedroom, while in the study a Bellotto canvas accurately depicts the original Łazienki bathhouse. An exhibition devoted to the history of Łazienki completes the tour.

The rest of the park

The buildings scattered round the park are all in some way connected with King Stanisław. Across the lake from the palace, and north along the water's edge, is the **Stara Kordegarda** (Old Guardhouse; Tues–Sun 9am–4pm; free), built in the 1780s in a style matching the north facade of the main palace, which features regular exhibitions of contemporary art. Immediately next to it is the so-called **Wielka Oficyna** (Great Outbuilding), another Merlini construction, the former officers' training school where young cadets hatched the anti-tsarist conspiracy that resulted in the November 1830 Uprising. The building now houses the **Muzeum J. Paderewskiego i Wychodżstwa Polskiego** (Ignacy Jan Paderewski and Polish Expatriates in America Museum; Tues–Sun 10am–3pm; 6zł, free on Thurs) inaugurated during the summer 1992 celebrations surrounding the return of the composer's body to Warsaw from the US. Much of the museum's collection consists of items bequeathed to the country by the exile Paderewski in his will. Pride of place goes to the grand piano he used at his longtime home on the shores of Lake Geneva. Standing on it, as during the man's lifetime, are the improbably paired autographed photos of fellow composer Saint-Saëns and Queen Victoria, while the walls are decorated with Paderewski's personal art collection. Adjoining rooms contain the dazzling array of prizes, medals and other honours awarded to him during his distinguished musical and political career, as well as his fine personal collection of assorted Chinese porcelain and enamel ware. To finish off there's a section devoted to mementoes of the Polish *emigracja*, detailing the Polish experience of America.

Immediately next to the museum is the **Pałac Myślewicki** (Myślewicki Palace; daily except Tues 9.30am–4pm; 4zł), a present from the king to his nephew Prince Józef Poniatowski, which imitates the studied decorum of the main palace. In summer the Greek-inspired **amphitheatre**, constructed for the king on an islet on the other side of the palace, still stages the occasional open-air performance (check with the tourist office for details, see p.82); rustling trees and the background duck chorus can make it hard to hear the proceedings on occasion, however.

Back up towards the main park entrance, past the guardhouse, is the **Biały Dom** (White House; Tues–Sun 9am–3.30pm; 5zł) built in the 1770s by Merlini for King Stanisław August to live in while the main palace was being finished. It retains the majority of its original eighteenth-century interiors, including a dining room decorated with a wealth of grotesque animal frescoes, and an octagonal-shaped study which features enjoyable trompe l'oeil floral decoration.

Just beyond it, the main **Pomarańczarnia** (Orangery; Tues–Sun 9am–3pm; 6zł), sometimes known as the Stara or "Old" Pomarańczarnia due to the existence of a smaller, newer greenhouse in the south part of the park, contains a well-preserved wooden theatre (one of the few in Europe to retain its original eighteenth-century decor), with room for over two hundred people, royal boxes not included. To complete the classical pose, pieces from King Stanisław's extensive sculpture collection fill the long galleries behind the auditorium. Finally, there's the **Obserwatorium Astronomiczne** (Astronomical Observatory; Tues–Sun 9.30am–3.30pm), a fine construction built in the early nineteenth century.

Back out on al. Ujazdowskie, south from the Chopin monument, stands the **Belweder** (Belvedere), another eighteenth-century royal residence redesigned in the 1820s for the governor of Warsaw, the tsar's brother Konstantine. Official residence of Polish heads of state since the end of World War I (with a brief interlude as home of the Nazi governor Hans Frank), it was used for ten years by General Jaruzelski, in turn supplanted by Lech Wałęsa, the country's first freely elected president in over fifty years. In 1995, Wałęsa announced that he was moving the presidential residence to the Namiestnikowski Palace on

Krakowskie Przedmieście, and his successor has remained there. The Belvedere is now used to house foreign dignitaries, but a new museum dedicated to **Józef Piłsudski**, the country's venerated president for much of the interwar period, and a former resident, is planned.

The **Trakt Królewski** (Royal Way) slopes gently down from here towards the Mokotów district, passing the huge **Russian embassy** building, its security looking a lot more relaxed these days. The Trakt Królewski then continues a few kilometres south to Wilanów, its ultimate destination.

Wilanów

The grandest of Warsaw's palaces, **Wilanów** (Mon & Wed–Sat 9.30am–2.30pm, Sun 9.30am–4.30pm; 15zł; Ⓦ www.wilanow-palac.art.pl) is tucked away in almost rural surroundings on the outskirts of Warsaw, and makes an easy excursion from the city centre: buses #116, #130, #165, #180 and #522 run to the station just over the road from the palace entrance, beside the inevitable *McDonald's*. Sometimes called the Polish Versailles, it was originally the brainchild of King Jan Sobieski, who purchased the existing manor house and estate in 1677. He spent nearly twenty years turning it into his ideal country residence, which was later extended by a succession of monarchs and aristocratic families. Predictably, Wilanów was badly damaged during World

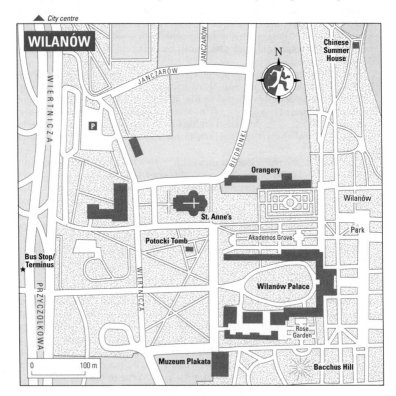

War II, when the Nazis stole the cream of the art collection and tore up the park and surrounding buildings. In 1945, the palace became state property, and for eleven years was extensively renovated and its art collection refurbished. It's now a tourist favourite, visitable only on a group **guided tour** (in Polish, setting off every 20 minutes or so), and with an average summertime queue of half an hour.

The approach to the palace takes you past former outhouses, including the smithy, the butcher's and an inn. Also close at hand are some decent cafés, welcome refuges after the palace tour. The domed eighteenth-century **Kościół św. Anny** (St Anne's Church) and ornate neo-Gothic Potocki mausoleum across the road lead to the **entrance gates**, where you buy your tickets.

The palace

Laid out in a horseshoe plan with a central core flanked by a pair of projecting wings, the classical grandeur of the **facade**, complete with Corinthian columns, Roman statuary above the pavilions and intermingled Latin inscriptions, reflects Sobieski's original conception. The centrepiece of the main facade – a golden sun with rays reflecting from decorated shields bearing the Sobieski coat of arms – clarifies the essential idea of the palace: the glorification of Sobieski himself.

Despite extensive wartime damage, the essentials of the interior design have remained largely unchanged. Among the sixty or so rooms of Wilanów's **interior** you'll find styles ranging from the lavish early Baroque of the apartments of Jan Sobieski and John III, to the classical grace of the nineteenth-century Potocki museum rooms. Some might find the cumulative effect of all this pomp and glory rather deadening – even the official guides seem to recognize this, easing off with the facts and figures in the last part of the guided tour.

Several flights of stairs lead to the **portrait galleries**. After the opening set of rooms, which are among the oldest, outlining the history of the palace, the galleries contain a number of casket images, intended to be interred with the subject, but sometimes removed from the coffin before burial. They are part of a total collection of over 250 portraits, most of which are hung in long corridor galleries – an intriguing introduction to the development of Polish Sarmatian fashion, with its peculiar synthesis of Western *haute couture* and Eastern influences such as shaved heads and wide sashes. If you've already visited other museums, the portrait of Jan Sobieski in the **Sobieski Family Room** will probably look familiar – the portly military hero most often crops up charging Lone Ranger-like towards a smouldering Vienna, trampling a few Turks on the way. Here as in the later galleries, the presence of portraits of the (aristocratic) great and good of Polish history provides the opportunity for the impromptu history lessons administered to local tour groups by the guides – naturally enough with an emphasis on insurgents, uncompromising oppositionists and other heroes of the struggle for independence over the centuries. One of the undoubted highlights of the collection is the great masterpiece of Neoclassical portraiture, *Stanisław Kostka Potocki on Horseback* by Jacques-Louis David.

After Sobieski's **Library**, with its beautiful marble-tiled floor and allegorical ceiling paintings, you come to the **Faience Room**, clad in blue with white Delft tiles and topped by an elegant copper-domed cupola surrounded by delicate period stucco mouldings, the centrepiece an eagle raising aloft the ubiquitous Sobieski coat of arms. The **August Locci Room**, named after Sobieski's chief architect, who designed most of the early interiors is one of several where the fine original seventeenth-century wooden beams have been uncovered. Many of the rooms on this floor offer excellent views over the palace gardens. The **Painted Cabinet Room**, next door, features recently uncovered eighteenth-century frescoes, notably a turbaned black man carrying a parrot in a cage. In contrast, restoration work in the **Quiet Room** has uncovered seventeenth-century frescoes of preening Greek goddesses.

Next comes another series of long **portrait galleries**, mostly from the Enlightenment era, including Kościuszko (see box p.448), the architects of the Third May Constitution, and a benign looking Stanisław Poniatowski, Poland's last king, and family. Another flight of stairs takes you up into the nineteenth-century portrait galleries, much used by the guides-cum-teachers with tour groups, with a suitably demure Maria Walewska, Napoleon's mistress, next to a bust of the general himself.

Downstairs again brings you to the other main set of apartment rooms. First comes the grand **Great Crimson Room**, as colourful as its name suggests, replete with a fabulously ornate ceiling filled with decorative cherubs and medallions and lashings of period art and furniture, including a massive dining table big enough to seat at least fifty people. Continuing on, you pass through the **Etruscan Study**, filled with third- and fourth-century BC vases from the Naples region, collected by nineteenth-century palace owner Stanisław Potocki during his regular architectural excursions. The **Lower North Gallery** further on links the two wings to the main building. Converted into a mini-museum of antiquities by Potocki in the 1820s to show off his archeological finds, it's now been restored to its original early-eighteenth-century state, murals included, though the classical sculptures have remained.

The end of the gallery brings you into the **Queen's Apartments** originally used by Maria Kazimierza, Sobieski's wife, the most impressive of which are the **Antechamber**, containing two cabinets of fine late-seventeenth-century porcelain, an inevitably sumptuous bedchamber, and the **Great Vestibule**, a three-storeyed affair of marble pillars and classicist mouldings connecting the royal apartments. The King's Bedchamber sports a great four-poster bed surrounded by period military trappings – precisely the kind of things the indefatigably warfaring Sobieski probably dreamed about. Past the **Chapel**, a simple shrine built by Potocki to commemorate his royal predecessor, you pass through further galleries containing more of Potocki's collection of classical sculpture, including some Roman sarcophagi, and a prize plaster **Sobieski Monument** of the corpulent king striking his customary pose charging a horse over the hapless Turks on his way to lifting the Siege of Vienna.

Last, but by no means least, comes the **Grand Hall of August II**, also known as the **White Hall**. Designed in the 1730s for King August II and thoroughly renovated after 1945, the mirrors on the walls combine to create a feeling of immense space. Box galleries, with balconies for the royal musicians, stand above the fireplaces at both ends, though the hall is more often used for piano recitals these days.

The palace gardens

If your energy hasn't flagged after the palace tour, there are a couple of other places of interest within the grounds. The gate on the left side beyond the main entrance opens onto the stately **palace gardens** (daily 9.30am–dusk). Overlooking the garden terrace, the graceful well-proportioned rear palace facade is again topped by statuary featuring a golden sundial on the southern side. Designed by Gdańsk astronomer Jan Hevelius, whose relief sits on the opposite side of the facade, the dial has Saturn, god of time, holding out the mantle of the heavens, on which both the time and the season's astrological sign are displayed. The fresco sequence punctuating the facade shows scenes from classical Greek literature, notably the *Aeneid* and *Odyssey*. Strolling along the back terrace, it's easy to appreciate the fine synthesis between regal residence and country mansion achieved by the palace.

The gardens reach down to the waterside, continuing rather less tidily along the lakeside to the north and south; in autumn this is a fine place for a Sunday afternoon scuffle through the falling oak leaves. Beyond the **Orangery** is the **English Park** – so-called because it was modelled on the landscaped gardens beloved of eighteenth-century British aristocrats – whose main feature is a Chinese summer house exhibiting pottery and other pieces of decorative art. Just down from the main gates, the **Muzeum Plakatu** (Poster Museum; Tues–Sun 10am–4pm; 5zł), has a mishmash of the inspired and the bizarre, from an art form that has long had major currency in Poland.

The suburbs

For most visitors anything outside the city centre and Trakt Królewski remains an unknown quantity. While not visually attractive, some of the Warsaw **suburbs** – notably **Żoliborz** and **Praga** – are worth visiting both for their atmosphere and for their historic resonance, while at its furthest limits the city merges into the villages of the Mazovian countryside, with head-scarved peasants and horse-drawn carriages replacing the bustle of city life.

Żoliborz

Until the last century, the **Żoliborz** district (whose name comes from a corruption of the French "joli bord"), due north of the centre, was an extension of the Kampinoski forest (the Bielany reserve in the northern reaches of the city today is a remnant), but then evolved into a working-class stronghold. The district's heart is the large square near the top of **ulica Mickiewicza** – the northern extension of Marszałowska and Gen. Andersa. Officially restored to its prewar name, **plac Wilsona** (reached on trams #15, #36 and #45 from Centrum) has a gritty, down-to-earth feeling that contrasts strongly with the gentrified airs of the city centre. Politics are gritty here too: the tough campaign fought by local resident and veteran oppositionist-turned-government-minister Jacek Kuroń in the 1989 elections, led to several sizzling confrontations with his political opponents before packed audiences at the old Wisła cinema on the square. The district remains a touchstone of political feeling in the city.

The **Church of St Stanisław Kostka**, off to the west side of plac Wilsona, was Solidarity priest Jerzy Popiełuszko's parish church until he was murdered by militant security police in 1984 – a major event in Polish political life of the 1980s that ensured his popular canonization. After Popiełuszko's funeral, attended by over half a million people, his church developed into a major Solidarity sanctuary and focus for popular opposition. Although Western politicians no longer troop here, the custom of newlyweds dropping by to pay their respects at Father Jerzy's shrine continues. The basement houses a poignant memorial to **Jerzy Popiełuszko** (open erratically; ask in the church for current times). In the grounds there's a Via Dolorosa – a path marking the Stations of the Cross – taking you through the major landmarks of modern Polish history.

South of plac Wilsona, bordering on the Nowe Miasto, is an altogether more sinister place, the fearsome **cytadela** (Citadel). These decaying fortifications are the remains of the massive fortress built here by Tsar Nicholas I in the wake of the 1831 Uprising. Houses were demolished to make way for it, and Varsovians even had to pay the costs of the intended instrument of their punishment, whose function was to control and terrorize the city as opposed to guarding it. For the next eighty years or so, suspected activists were brought here for interrogation and eventual imprisonment, execution or exile. Those held here included the later president, Józef Piłsudski.

The large steps up the hill lead to the grim **Gate of Executions**, where partisans were shot and hanged, with particular regularity after the 1863 Uprising. Uneasy with so obvious a symbol of Russian oppression and Polish nationalist aspirations, the postwar communist party attempted to present the Cytadela as a "mausoleum of the Polish revolutionary, socialist and workers' movement": thus, alongside the plaque commemorating the leaders of 1863, there are memorials to the tsarist-era Socialist Party, the Polish Communist Party and "the proletariat". Part of the prison is now a **historical museum** (Tues–Sun 9am–3.30pm; 4zł), with a few preserved cells and some harrowing pictures by former inmates depicting the agonies of Siberia. The wagon in the courtyard is a reconstruction of the vehicles used to transport the condemned to their bleak exile.

Praga

Across the river from the Stare Miasto, the large **Praga** suburb was the main residential area for the legions of tsarist bureaucrats throughout the nineteenth century – particularly the Saska Kempa district, south of al. Waszyngtona. Out of range of the main World War II battles and destruction, the area still has some of its prewar architecture and atmosphere, and an increasingly bohemian reputation.

Immediately across from the Stare Miasto is the **Ogród Zoologiczny** (Warsaw Zoo; daily 9am–sunset; 8zł), whose run-down yet attractive park-like expanses house a varied collection of animals including elephants, hippos and bears. The **Cerkiew św. Cyryla i Metodego** (Orthodox Church of SS Cyril and Methodius; services daily at 5pm) just beyond, on al. Solidarności, is one remaining sign of the former Russian presence. A large neo-Byzantine structure topped by a succession of onion domes, its original mid-nineteenth-century interior decoration remains intact. Pretty much the only way to get to see inside is to turn up during services, when you can hear the excellent **choir** in action.

Praga's most notorious connection with Russia stems from the time of the Warsaw Uprising (see box on pp.98–99). At the beginning of September 1944, Soviet forces reached the outer reaches of Praga. Insurrectionists from the besieged town centre were dispatched to plead with them to intervene against the Nazis – to no avail. Throughout the Warsaw Uprising, Soviet tanks sat and waited on the edges, moving in to flush out the Nazis only when the city had been virtually eradicated. For the next forty years, the official account gave "insufficient Soviet forces" as the reason for the nonintervention; as with the Katyn massacre, every Pole knew otherwise. A **monument** to the Soviet arrival, alongside the highway behind the Orthodox church, features four somnolent-looking Red Army soldiers known locally as the "Four Sleepies".

On a lighter note, Warsaw's best-known and longest-running flea market – the **Bazar Różyckiego** – is five minutes' walk south from the Orthodox church on ul. Ząbkowska, though it has been on its last legs now for some time, and is largely limited to selling illegal goods like guns. If you do go, keep all valuables well in hand – pickpockets are numerous and skilful. Further south along the river, close to the Poniatowski bridge, is the **Dziesęciolecia** stadium, once the city's largest sports stadium and now taken over by a sprawling outdoor market (see "Markets and bazaars", p.132).

Praga was once home to a significant proportion of the city's Jewish population. Directly over the Śląsko-Dąbrowski bridge, south of the leafy Park Praski, there are a number of streets, notably **ulica Kłopotowskiego** and **ulica Sierakowskiego** where you can still see some typical old Jewish residences. As elsewhere in the city there are numerous archways leading to extraordinary red-brick buildings from an earlier age, often bearing signs of wartime shrapnel. Try the streets behind Targowa such as **ulica Środkowa** (nos. 18 and 130).

A little further out, in the Brodno district, is the **Cmentarz Żydowski** (Jewish Cemetery; entrance at the corner of ul. Odrozona and ul. Wincentego; take tram #3 from Targowa in Praga), founded in the 1780s. It was badly damaged by the Nazis, who used many of the stones for paving. Restoration work is in progress on the thousand or so graves remaining.

Eating and drinking

Warsaw is one of the best places to eat in central Europe. Alongside a good smattering of **restaurants** specializing in traditional Polish cuisine, there's a welcome trend towards culinary variety – modern European and Mediterranean-influenced dishes have made their way onto most restaurant menus, and ethnic establishments offering anything from Jewish to Japanese cuisine are well established.

In the **café** scene also, a wealth of new or renovated places has sprung up in the past few years, offering everything from the most calorific haunts to down-to-earth student hangouts. Cakes and pastries, worthy of the best of central Europe, are easy to come by, and if you follow the traditional local example, you'll doubtless find yourself passing many hours musing over the edge of a cup of coffee or, Russian-style, a glass of tea. And now you can surf the internet while you sup, too.

Bars of all sorts are everywhere. Alongside the ubiquitous traditional "drink-bars" serving hard spirits to hard-drinking locals, there's now a wide choice of newer, Western-influenced places, serving big-name German beers and other European brands alongside an increasing range of local brews, aimed partly at the tourists, partly at the city's young and upwardly mobile. There are also "ethnic" pubs, bars in wooden ranch-type shacks in the city's parkland, theme bars and simple, friendly, unpretentious local haunts. In short, everything you need.

The distinction between Warsaw's eating and drinking venues is inevitably blurred, with many of the latter offering both snacks and full meals as well as booze – so bear in mind that many of the places listed under "Cafés and bars" below are also good places for a bite to eat.

Places to eat

Warsaw's Stare Miasto and central business districts are packed with places to eat, many of which invitingly offer outdoor chairs and tables during the summer months. Snack bars and cheap restaurants' **opening times** may be as early as 8–9am for the benefit of those seeking breakfast or brunch, although it's more common for manstream restaurants to open at around 11am. A few restaurants, especially cheaper places, still follow the traditional practice of having relatively early **closing times** of 9–10pm, though most shut around 11pm–midnight. Cheaper places tend to close even earlier due to their snack-bar nature, which is why we've listed the closing times for these in the listings below. Foreign-language **menus** are available in most restaurants, but don't count on it; refer to pp.749 and p.751 for help.

Warsaw is the most expensive city in Poland, and restaurant prices are slowly edging towards those charged in the West. A small number of the famously **cheap** milk bars – canteen-style places doling out filling Polish staples for well under 10zł a head – still survive in Warsaw, and you can also get good budget food (much of it traditionally Polish) at innumerable cheap eateries and self-service restaurants. Otherwise, restaurants below have been listed as **moderate** (around 28–55zł a head for main course and drink) and **expensive** (55–110zł or more). Wherever you choose to eat however, traditional Polish dishes like *barszcz* (beetroot soup), *placki* (potato pancakes) and *kotlet schabowy* (pork chop) invariably work out cheaper than the fancier items on the menu. We've included telephone numbers for those restaurants where **reservations** – especially at weekends – are a good idea.

Fast-food joints – the big Western names and their Polish imitators – are now firmly established all over the city; as well as burgers and hot dogs you'll find pizza – both Italian and the Polish variant of *zapiekanki*, a half-baguette type morsel liberally sprinkled with cheese. Numerous kiosks dole out sandwiches (*kanapki*) and tasty take-out salads, and the number of snack bars offering cheap Vietnamese and other Oriental dishes is on the increase.

Cheap

Bambino ul. Krucza 21. Traditional communist-era milk bar down from the *Grand* hotel with a huge sign above the pavement. Lashings of greasy stodge at rock-bottom prices. Mon–Fri till 7pm, Sat till 5pm.

Bar Mleczny Nowy Świat 39. Another milk bar-style survivor: a basic café with plastic flowers serving solid fare. Mon–Fri till 8pm, Sat & Sun till 5pm.

Café Contact ul. Foksal 21. Deli-style place with very few seats – good for takeaway sandwiches, salads and other snacks. Mon–Fri till 7pm.

Expresso ul. Bracka 18. Cheap, no-nonsense café-restaurant serving up pizzas and Polish standards. Till 10pm.

Gaga ul. Zgoda 6. Self-service, fuss-free pizzeria, with outdoor seating in summer. Till 10pm.

Grill Bar ul. Zgoda 4. Classy and comfortable budget diner, serving good, filling meals – grilled meats a speciality. Till 10pm.

Klub Wega al. Jana Pawła II 36a. Café serving up solid, filling and cheap vegetarian dishes. Till 6pm.

Krokiecik ul. Zgoda 1. Fast service in a useful downtown shoppers' location, offering salads, grilled dishes and the house speciality – stuffed potato croquettes. Till 8pm.

Mata Hari Nowy Świat 52. Intimate little café offering vegetarian cuisine with a strong Indian slant. Mon–Fri till 7pm, Sat till 5pm, closed Sun.

Uniwersytecki Krakowskie Przedmieście 20. Milk bar much frequented by students, just up from the university gates. Mon–Fri till 8pm, Sat & Sun till 5pm.

Van Binh ul. Mazowiecka 11. Cheap and filling Chinese-Vietnamese meals in unpretentious, fast-food surroundings. Till 10pm.

Moderate

Argo ul. Lwowska 17. Cheap and filling Georgian dishes like *lobia* (spicy black-eyed beans) and *hatchapuri* (flatbread filled with runny cheese). Friendly and relaxed, even when busy. In the southern end of the downtown area, just east of the Polytechnic.

Bliss ul. Boczna 3. In a square below pl. Zamkowy, which gives it atmosphere. Fair prices for Asian specialities.

Blue Cactus ul. Zajączkowska 11. Big, boisterous place serving filling Tex-Mex food – egg rolls, enchiladas and the like. In a side street just south-west of the far end of Łazienkowski Park. [off the map]

Cafe Kredens ul. Przemysłowa 36 ☎022/625 1578. Greek and Italian fare. Decor looks as if someone's just emptied the attic. Reservations advisable.

Der Elefant/U Fiszera pl. Bankowy 1. Extended opening hours (Mon–Fri & Sun 1.30am, Sat 2am) make the restaurant with two names a good place for a late-night grill. Portions aren't as large as the name might suggest, but the food is generally up to scratch.

Dong Nam ul. Marszałkowska 45/49. Reliable source of good-value Asian food, with Thai cuisine on the ground floor, Chinese and Vietnamese upstairs.

Jazz Bistro ul. Piękna 20. Café-restaurant aimed at downtown office workers serving up tasty grills and pasta dishes in artfully sparse surroundings. Sultry sounds (either live or on tape) in the evenings.

Lokanta ul. Nowogrodzka 47a. Turkish café-restaurant with stylish modern decor, and great food direct from the charcoal grill.

Maharaja Thai ul. Szeroki Dunaj 13. Dependable Thai food served until midnight near the Stare Miasto.

Nowe Miasto Rynek Nowego Miasta 13/15. Trendy, self-styled "ecological" restaurant – ignore the rainforest furniture for the good, mostly vegetarian menu. A bit much atmosphere-wise – there's a "salad theatre", for instance, with dishes based on Shakespeare's plays.

Odeon ul. Marszałkowska. Themed "nostalgia" restaurant with antique-shop bits and pieces strewn around the place. International menu: lots of pasta dishes and a wide range of cocktails.

Pod Samsonem ul. Freta 3/5. Open till 10pm. Popular Nowe Miasto restaurant offering a cheap, good-quality Polish menu with a sprinkling of Jewish dishes.

Qchnia Artystyczna al. Ujazdowski 6. Wonderful location in the Ujazdowski Castle, next to Park Łazienkowski, with quirky decor (it shares premises with the Centrum Sztuki Współczesnej) and a great outdoor terrace. Modern European food, with several vegetarian options.

San Marzano Nowy Świat 42. Swanky pizzeria owned by the international Pizza Express chain offering reliable, inexpensive fare – grill dishes as well as pizzas and (vegetarian-friendly) pastas. Other central branches at ul. Świętokrzyska 18 and Puławska 19/21. Till 11pm.

Tam Tam ul. Foksal 18. Funky, African-themed venue that's a café, restaurant, bar and club depending which floor you're on and what night it is. Good atmosphere, and great food with a Mediterranean/North African twist.

Tandoor Palace ul. Marszałkowska. One of the best curry houses in Poland, with a decent range of Mediterranean options too. Good for vegetarians. Down at the southern end of this busy street.

Varna ul. Mazowiecka 12. Bulgarian restaurant offering a nice line in Balkan dishes – from *kebapcheta* (grilled mincemeat patties) and *kavarma* (meat braised in a pot) through to roast lamb.

Stuffed peppers a speciality. Frequent folk-influenced live music in the evenings.

Expensive

Adler ul. Mokotowska 69 ☎022/628 7384. Bavarian food with Polish modifications, in intimate, folksy surroundings. Atmospheric and popular – you should reserve.

Bazyliszek Rynek Starego Miasta 3/9 ☎022/831 1841. Traditional Polish cuisine, with an emphasis on fish (eels and carp) and game (boar and wild pig) in glamorous old-world surroundings. Reservations advised.

Belvedere Park Łazienkowski's Pomarańczarnia, see p.117 ☎022/841 4806. Beautiful building and expensive fine food, the cheapest being the Polish dishes – and even they will set you back 160zł.

Biblioteka University of Warsaw Library, ul. Dobra 56/66 ☎022/552 7195. Imaginative, modern-European menu in swish, modernist surroundings. Currently favoured by art and media types.

Chianti ul. Foksal 17 ☎022/828 0222. Candle-lit cellar restaurant with intimate feel and great Italian food.

Delfin ul. Twarda 42 ☎022/620 5080. Straightforward little place widely regarded as the best fish restaurant in town. Fish are priced according to weight; "*mała ryba*" means "small fish".

Flik ul. Puławska 43 ☎022/849 4434. Highly popular with Varsovians and expats alike. Solid traditional Polish food and plenty of international dishes. Inexpensive lunchtime buffet. About 2km south of the Pałac Kultury i Nauk area (follow ul. Marszałkowska to the end and bear right, or catch tram #4).

Fukier Rynek Starego Miasta 27 ☎022/831 1013. Top-notch Stare Miasto restaurant with a strong line in imaginatively reinterpreted traditional Polish cuisine, and candlelight after dark. Open noon until midnight. Reservations advised.

Garret ul. Marszałkowska 55/73 ☎022/621 9675. Expensive end of moderate, but good Polish food, including delicious mushroom soup and steak tartare. Down towards the southern end of the street.

Karczma Gessler Rynek Starego Miasta 21/21A ☎022/831 4427. Endless labyrinthine cellars and a range of Polish dishes, including Jewish specialities. Check out the photographs of famous customers at the entrance. Reservations advised.

La Boheme pl. Teatralny 1 ☎022/692 0681. Excellent, modern French-influenced food in the Teatr Wielki; the café here is a useful stopoff during the day.

Las ul. Niepodległości 43 ☎022/843 6008. Open till midnight. Korean specialities, with a reasonable choice of vegetarian options. About 3km south of the Pałac Kultury i Nauk area, near Wierzbno metro station.

Le Bistrot ul. Foksal 2. ☎022/827 8707. French and other food in a delightful setting, with a terrace in summer. After dinner you can move on to the Cul de Sac nightclub in the same building. Open till midnight (closed Sun).

Le Cedre, al. Solidarności 61 ☎022/670 1166. Open till 11pm. Great Lebanese restaurant in the Praga district, next to the Hotel Praski. Takeout service available.

Maharaja Indian, ul. Marszałkowska 34/50 ☎022/621 1392. Genuinely hot curries. Towards the southern end of modern Warsaw's main thoroughfare.

Montmartre, Nowy Świat 7 ☎022/628 6315. Delightful French restaurant that's spacious, chic and central. Open till midnight.

Restauracja Polska, Nowy Świat 21 ☎022/826 3877. The best Polish cooking in the city. Sumptuous surroundings and impeccable service.

Rybak Rynek Starego Miasta 3/9 ☎022/635 3769. In the same building as Bazyliszek, and stuffed with nautical trinkets, this is the place for seafood in the Stare Miasto.

Santorini ul. Egipska 7 ☎022/672 0525. Excellent, atmospheric place for Greek food in the southern part of the Praga district, just across the Łazienkowski bridge.

Tokio ul. Dobra 17 ☎022/827 4632. Japanese restaurant with a high-quality sushi bar. Reservations advised. Frustratingly, closes at 10pm.

Tsubame ul. Foksal 16 ☎022/826 5127. Excellent Japanese restaurant and accompanying sushi bar off Nowy Świat. A bit pricier than Tokio, though with cheap lunchtime menus. Open till midnight daily.

Vivaldi Błękitny Pałac Ogród Saski, at ul. Senatorska 37 ☎022/826 3038. Italian restaurant with extraordinary decor comprising a collection of theatre props. Great pasta, excellent seafood.

Yesterday ul. Szkolna 2/4 ☎022/826 1060. Friendly staff, traditional Polish food and dancing at the weekend; as old-fashioned as the name – unintentionally, probably – suggests.

Cafés and bars

Warsaw can boast a vivacious **café** life, though interest is as much social as gastronomic. Establishments vary between cosy haunts serving *ciastka* (cakes) and *lody* (ice cream) – the traditional choice for browsing through newspapers in the morning or relaxing with shopping in the afternoon – to trendier, modern joints offering a range of fancy coffees and an international menu of snacks. Many of the latter stay open well into the night, competing for custom with the mushrooming number of **bars**, which range in style from hip designer joints to raucous beer halls with live bands and dancing. With a few exceptions, **pubs** are bland affairs that have little in common with their British or Irish namesakes.

Drink prices in Warsaw are significantly higher than elsewhere in Poland, but still compare favourably with western Europe – providing you stick to domestic beer and spirits rather than the imported variety.

Most cafés and bars are concentrated in the Stare Miasto and in the modern centre to the south, although there are few obvious strolling areas where you'll find one establishment after another – so it's best to plan your evening's boozing itinerary before setting out. In summer, head for the fair-weather alfresco bars along Wybrzeże Gdańskie, just below the Stare Miasto on the western bank of the Wisła; or in Pole Mokotowskie, an area of parkland southwest of the centre (easily reached from the Pole Mokotowskie metro station) which is bustling with Varsovians on balmy evenings.

Cafés

Blikle Cafe Nowy Świat 33. The oldest cake shop in the city, open since 1869 and famous for its doughnuts (*pączki*). An elegant place in which to enjoy coffee and desserts on the main drag; also does excellent – though pricey – breakfasts. Till 11pm.

Brama ul. Marszałkowska 8. Trendy if grungy hangout with good snacks, Mediterranean-influenced main courses and a no-smoking policy. Located towards the southern end of the modern centre's main street. Daily till 11pm.

Casablanca Krakowskie Przedmieście 4/6. One of the few internet cafés that's more than just a place to check your emails – it's also a stylish and relaxing place for a drink and a bite to eat. For more on internet access, see p.133. Till midnight.

Galeria Nowa ul. Puławska 37/39. Arty café with a theatre theme inside the Teatr Nowy building. Also doubles as a late-night bar, open till 2am. About 2km south of the Pałac Kultury i Nauk area, it can be reached on tram #4.

Literacka ul. Krakowskie Przedmieście 87/9. Atmospheric, romantic place with quiet jazz at weekends. Serves toothsome snacks and shuts shortly after midnight.

Mała Czarna ul. Hoża 54. Modern-style coffee bar with a generous choice of brews and a decent line in sandwiches. Till 9pm.

Nowy Świat Nowy Świat 63. Sumptuous, roomy café famous for being a favourite meeting place for the cream of Warsaw society. With formal service and officious cloakroom staff, it still feels like a wondrous relic from another era. Till 11pm.

Pod Kaktusami ul. Chmielna 32. Unpretentious but cosy café offering a wide range of drinks, cakes and sweets – and cacti (to look at, not to eat). A convenient bolt hole if you're in the Pałac Kultury i Nauk area. Till 10pm.

Pożegnanie z Afryką ul. Freta 4/6. Translating as "Out of Africa", this is one of a nationwide chain of cafés, with an attached store selling high-quality coffee. For nonsmokers only and therefore a bit useless as a café proper. Till 9pm.

Rozdroże al. Ujazdowskie 6. Just across the road from the Botanical Gardens, a glass and concrete pavilion that was all the rage when first built in the 1960s. Still serves up decent cakes and ice cream, alongside more substantial hot meals. Handy for the Łazienkowski and Ujazdowski parks.

TriBeCa ul. Bracka 22. Pastel-coloured coffee palace which also offers a good selection of sandwiches and salads. One of the few places where you can buy decent coffee to take out. Till 9.30pm.

Bars

Baumgart/Libera al. Ujazdowskie 6. Cliquey café-bar in the Centrum Sztuki Współczesnej, patronized by bohemian intellectuals and hosting occasional themed DJ nights and happenings. Till midnight or later depending on what's going on.

Browar Soma ul. Foksal 19. Ultra-trendy café-bar and restaurant that brews its own beer, located just off Nowy Świat. Has a busy bar area where in-house DJs play cutting edge dance sounds, and a loungey chill-out room. Till 4am.

Café Rytm ul. Piękna 28/34. Simple but stylish place with upstairs bar and moody cellar downstairs. A wide range of food on offer, reggae disco once or twice a week, and occasional live bands. Till 1am.

Champions Sport Bar al. Jerozolimskie 65/70. Large, garish international-style bar on the ground floor of the *Marriott* hotel (see p.86). Best place in town to catch football and other sporting events on TV, but beer prices are on the expensive side. Till midnight.

Czternastka ul. Wąski Dunaj 20. Three storeys of late-night drinking on the edge of the Stare Miasto. The counter used to be part of a grand piano. Till 5am.

Empik ul. Nowy Świat 15/17 (entrance round the corner on Jerozolimskie). Smallish bar in the basement of the Empik Megastore offering a regular programme of live music – mostly pop-rock covers and blues. Worth dropping by to see what's on. Till midnight.

Giovanni Krakowskie Przedmieście 24. Pub near the university favoured by art students. In summer, there's a large beer garden in the courtyard round the back, as well as frequent live music. Till 1am (3am Fri–Sat).

Harenda Krakowskie Przedmieście 4/5. Roomy, ranch-style bar with a big open-air beer garden in summer. Occasional live rock, jazz or DJs – when there may be a cover charge. Till 3am.

Lolek Rokitnica 20. One of several watering-holes in the middle of Pole Mokotowskie. Barbecue-type food, beer and live music in and around an overgrown log cabin. Pole Mokotowskie metro station. Till dawn.

Metal Bar Rynek Starego Miasta 8. One of the few establishments to bring nightlife to the Stare Miasto area, all metal and glass and with bar snacks like *chleb z smalcem* (bread and dripping). Till midnight, 2am at weekends.

Między Namy ul. Bracka 20. Hip but relaxed place with two levels of seating, hosting an easy-going gay and straight clientele. Full food menu includes excellent salads, while in-house DJs occasionally spin discs in the evenings. No sign outside, so look for the pale grey awnings. Till midnight.

Modulor pl. Trzech Krzyży 8. Sleek, glass-fronted café-bar with a good range of wholesome meals. Till midnight.

Morgan's Pub Okólnik 1. Irish joint that has built its reputation on friendly atmosphere and good service rather than faux-pub decor. Popular with the younger ex-pats. Occasional live music. Till midnight.

Muza ul. Chmielna 9. Spacious basement bar with fashionable clientele, groovy sounds and frequent live music. Till 4am.

Nora ul. Krakowskie Przedmieście 20/22. Boozy, smoky, studenty, and the crush along the benches means you'll definitely meet people. Till midnight.

Patrick's Irish Pub Nowogrodzka 31. Faux-rustic

beer hall with good downtown location, open-ended hours, and a dance floor where you can bop to live cover bands – which range from the enjoyable to the atrocious. Open 24hr.

Piwnica pri Hożej ul. Hoża 50. Beer cellar in the downtown streets south of the Pałac Kultury i Nauk. Lots of cosy nooks and crannies – a good place for a drink and a chat. Till midnight, 2am Fri–Sun.

Pod Baryłką ul. Gabarska 5/7, down from pl.

Zamkowy. For those who go to a pub to savour beer, with 14 draught varieties on offer. Till midnight.

Szpilka, pl. Trzech Krzyży 18. Designer café-bar popular with Warsaw yuppies and expats. Seating on two levels, and an imaginative menu of main courses and sweets. Till 5am.

Tonic, Marszałkowska 77/79. Cool café-bar with minimalist decor and a young, hip clientele. Open 24hrs.

Nightlife, entertainment, activities and sport

After decades in the wilderness, there's a reasonable – if not amazing – **club** scene in Warsaw now, with a fair spread that should cater for most tastes. If Chopin **concerts** or avant-garde **drama** (including some in English) is your idea of a good night out, you're unlikely to be disappointed. In summer especially, high-quality theatre productions, operas and recitals abound, many of them as popular with tourists as with Varsovians themselves. They are also extremely cheap, particularly if you buy tickets that entail taking whatever seats are available after the third and final call (it sounds risky, but there are always places).

For up-to-date information about what's on, check the current **listings** sections of the *Warsaw Insider* or *Warsaw Voice* (see p.82). Regular Warsaw **festivals** include the excellent Warsaw Summer Jazz in June, the Jazz Jamboree in October (a major bash at which everyone from Duke Ellington to Miles Davis have appeared in their time), the biennial Warsaw Film Festival, the Festival of Contemporary Music held every September, the prestigious Mozart Festival every June, and the five-yearly Chopin Piano Competition – always a launchpad for a major international career and next to be held in 2005. The tourist office will have details of these and other upcoming events.

Clubs and gigs

In addition to the numerous late-night bars boasting in-house DJs (see p.127), there's a reasonable range of **clubbing** opportunities in Warsaw, with new venues opening all the time – *Warsaw in Your Pocket* and the *Warsaw Insider* will have details (see p.82). The accent is on commercial techno, although you'll find that there's always something else going on on any given night of the week – be it a reggae, hip-hop, Latin or golden oldies night – if you scour the listings magazines closely enough.

Decent **live music** is much harder to find in Warsaw. You'll come across easy listening jazz, or ropey rock-pop cover bands, in many of the venues listed under "Eating and drinking" on p.123, but little in the way of a regular gig circuit catering for dedicated musical youth. There are a number of alternative-leaning clubs which put on irregular concerts, while established bands (whether Polish or foreign) play in the larger discotheques, or in venues such as the Sala Kongresowa in the Pałac Kultury i Nauk. In summer, big Western pop-rock acts may play outdoor gigs in sports stadiums – if so, the posters announcing their arrival will be hard to avoid.

As for **opening hours**, while gigs often start quite early (typically 7–8pm), there's not much point in turning up to clubs before 10pm, and things may not really get going until after midnight. **Admission** to gigs and club nights can cost anything between 5zł and 30zł depending on the prestige of the club and the night of the week. Tickets to see visiting western DJs or bands often cost much more. Gleaning what's on from Polish-language fly posters is easy enough: otherwise your best sources of information are the free fortnightly magazine *Aktiwist* and the Friday edition of *Gazeta Wyborcza* (see p.82).

Apetyt Architektów ul. Koszykowa 55. Roomy cellar venue next to the restaurant of the same name, specializing in reggae, world music and off-beat music nights featuring DJs and – occasionally – live performers.

B65 ul. Bema 65. Rough-and-ready basement club set back from the main road catering for under-ground musical tastes – punk, ska and metal for the most part. About 2km west of the Pałac Kultury i Nauk area and not open every night, so check listings or look for posters before setting out. Tram #8 or #10 from Warszawa Centralna to the Sokolowska stop.

Barbados ul. Wierzbowa 9. Warsaw's ultimate yuppie experience, filled with beautiful people and an attendant cast of expats. Fancy food restaurant – mussels and lamb with raspberry sauce, for example – upstairs. Bouncers are employed to keep out the unwashed: if you don't look like a film star, eating in the restaurant first will gain you admittance to the club. Wed–Sat.

Centralny Dom Qultury Burakowska 12. Favourite gathering point for a bohemian nonconformist crowd eager to shake their booties to underground dance music rather than the top-40 variety. Frequent themed party nights. A little way off the beaten track, 1.6km northwest of the Stare Miasto just beyond the Rondo Babka roundabout. Open Fri & Sat only.

Hybrydy ul. Złota 7/9. Popular, youthful and friend-ly club handily located in the Pałac Kultury i Nauk

area, offering a familiar mix of techno at weekends and more offbeat styles during the week.

Park al. Niepodległości 196. In the Piłsudski Park, southwest of the town centre. Regular late-night dancing; some live bands, too. Studenty and cheap. Mon–Sat.

Piekarnia ul. Młocińska 11, Żoliborz. One of the best clubs for mainstream techno and house, attracting a young and beautiful crowd. Just north-west of the centre, near to Rondo Babka. Mon–Sat.

Proxima ul. Żwirki i Wigury 99a (☎022/822 8702). Very cheap, very big, very studenty, very close to the dorms. Southwest of the centre. Bus #175 from Centrum. Mon–Sat.

Stodoła ul. Batorego 10 (☎022/25 86 25). Student disco and gig venue of many years' stand-ing, a 10-min walk from *Park*. Large dance floor. Major Polish acts and visiting Western bands are likely to play here – in which case you'll see fly posters all around town. Pole Mokotowskie metro station.

Tygmont ul. Mazowiecka 6/8. Currently the city's top jazz club, with a regular gig roster and a styl-ish, upmarket clientele.

Underground Music Café Marszałkowska 126/134. Roomy drinking and dancing venue near the Pałac Kultury i Nauk, offering mainstream house, soul and funk, sometimes with big-name DJs. There's usually something going on here every night of the week.

Opera and concerts

Opera is a big favourite in Warsaw, and **classical** concerts – especially any-thing with a piano in it (preferably Chopin) – tend to attract big audiences, but despite this concerts are rarely sold out and they are remarkably cheap. **Tickets** for many concerts are available from the theatre ticket office, Kasa Teatralny (Mon–Fri 11am–6pm, Sat 11am–2pm; ☎022/621 9454 or 621 9383), at al. Jerozolimskie 25, just along from the *Forum* hotel. Other useful ticket sources are the Estrada offices at ul. Szpitalna 8 (Mon–Fri 9am–7pm; ☎022/827 1747), and Mazurka Travel, in the *Forum* hotel lobby (Mon–Sat 8am–6pm; ☎022/829 1249); the latter specializes in tickets for the Teatr Wielki and Opera Kameralna (particularly useful during the annual summer Mozart Festival).

Akademia Muzyczna ul. Okólnik 2 (☎022/827 7241). Regular concerts by talented students. Free entry.

Filharmonia ul. Jasna 5 ☎022/827 7479, ⓦ www.filharmonia.pl. The main concert venue, with regular performances by the

excellent National Philharmonic Orchestra as well as visiting ensembles. This is also the venue for the International Chopin Piano Competition held every five years. Tickets from the box office at ul. Sienkiewicza 10 (10am–3pm), though you can always get very cheap stand-by tickets just before the performance.

Kościół Ewangelicko-Augsburgski (Evangelical Church) pl. Małachowskiego. Focuses on organ and choral music, often with visiting choirs. Excellent acoustics.

Muzeum Fryderyka Chopina, see p.112 ☎022/827 5441, ⓦwww.chopin.pl. Summer piano recitals and other occasional performances organized by the Towarzystwo im. Fryderyka Chopina (Chopin Society).

Opera Kameralna al. Solidarności 76b ☎022/831 2240. Chamber opera performances in a magnificent white and gold stucco auditorium. Also a key venue during the Mozart Festival. Box office 10am–2pm & 4–7pm.

Park Łazienkowski see p.115. Varied summer

programme of orchestral, choral and chamber concerts at the weekend, often held beside the Chopin monument, in the Orangery, or inside the Palace.

Teatr Roma, ul. Nowogrodzka 49 ☎022/628 03 60, ⓦwww.roma.warszawa.pl. Opera, operetta and popular musicals. Box office 9am–1pm & 2–6pm.

Teatr Wielki (National Theatre) pl. Teatralny 1 ☎022/826 32 88, ⓦwww.teatrwielki.pl. The big opera, ballet and musical performances – everything from Mozart to contemporary Polish composers – in suitably grandiose surroundings. Box office Mon–Sat 9am–7pm, Sun 10am–7pm.

Towarzystwo Muzyczne Warszawskie (Warsaw Music Society) ul. Morskie Oko 2 ☎022/849 5651. Frequent piano and guitar recitals.

Theatre and cinema

Theatre is one of the most popular high-brow forms of entertainment in Warsaw, and still receives generous state subsidies. Not speaking Polish is, of course, an obstacle, but the all-round quality of performance and set design ensures that it's worth considering a performance at one of the major theatres. Theatre tickets cost about 15zł.

Warsaw's **cinemas** offer a generous mixture of mainstream Western pictures, global art-house movies and home-grown hits. Films are shown in the original language with Polish subtitles. You can find lists of cinemas and current releases all over the city; try also the "Kino" section of the *Gazeta Wyborcza* (see p.82). Cinema tickets cost about 20–25zł, with reductions in some cinemas on Mondays.

Theatres

Centrum Sztuki Współczesnej Pałac Ujazdowski ☎022/628 1271, ⓦwww.csw.art.pl. Plays host to many international theatre and dance performances.

Syrena, ul. Waryńskiego 12 ☎022/660 9875, ⓦwww.teatrsyrena.art.pl. Modern drama in Polish.

Teatr Buffo ul. Marii Konopnickiej 6 ☎022/625 4709, ⓦwww.studiobuffo.com.pl. Concerts, musicals, avant-garde plays. Has performances in English at times.

Teatr Dramatyczny Pałac Kultury i Nauk ☎022/620 2102 or 656 6844 respectively. Two venues – one for big productions, another for intimate studio performances – in this huge arts complex, both staging plays in Polish, with the studio more avant-garde.

Teatr Powszechny ul. Zamoyskiego 20 ☎022/818 2516, ⓦwww.powszechny.art.pl. Often does musicals.

Teatr Żydowski pl. Grzybowski 12/16 ☎022/620 7025. Warsaw's Jewish theatre, with performances usually in Yiddish.

Cinemas

Atlantik ul. Chmielna 33 ☎022/827 0894. Modern multiplex showing first-run films and the odd arty choice.

Iluzjon ul. Narbutta 50a ☎022/646 1260. National Film Archives venue, screening cinema classics from all over the world.

Kino Lab al. Ujazdowskie 6 ☎022/628 1271, ⓦwww.kinolab.independent.pl. Art movies and assorted cinematic weirdness in the Centrum Sztuki Współczesnej.

Kinoteka Pałac Kultury i Nauk, pl. Defilad 1 ☎022/826 1961. Mixture of commercial and art films in this extraordinary Stalinist building (see p.111).

Kultura ul. Krakowskie Przedmieście 21/3 ☎022/826 3335. Late-night screenings at weekends and good Dolby sound system. The Rejs cinema in the same complex (same telephone number) shows specialist films.

Relax, ul. Złota 8 ☎022/828 3888, ⓦwww.relax.echocinema.pl. Comfy downtown cinema showing the latest releases.

Wars Rynek Nowego Miasta 5/7 ☎022/831 4488,

Gay Warsaw

Forget the horror stories about the iron hand of Catholicism. There is a **gay scene** in Warsaw. There is even a gay clerical scene. And the Poles would no more let themselves be told what to do by the Catholic Church (deeply religious though many of them are) than by the communists. For **information** check sites such as ⓦ www.warsaw.subnet.dk or ⓦ www.gay.net.pl. For gay and lesbian **literature**, check out the Odeon bookshop at ul. Hoża 19.

Like anywhere else, the scene changes rapidly in Warsaw. Though there are **gay pubs** (the most well-known is the *Koźla Pub* at ul. Koźla 10/12), most people meet in gay-friendly pubs with a mixed clientele. The current favourite is *Między Nami* (meaning "between ourselves") at ul. Bracka 20 (see p.127); ignore the sign at the door announcing that "cards must be shown" – it's just a ruse to keep numbers controlled at weekends.

A couple of **clubs** stand out: *Paradise*, Skra stadium, ul. Wawelska 5, which has a friendly all-night disco (Thurs–Sat) with a great combination of acts – lesbian George Michael impersonators, drag queens and so on – with a few self-conscious straights snogging in the corner; and *Klub M*, ul. Wałbrzyska 11 (ⓦ www.mykonos2.com.pl), which has a daytime bar and an evening disco, a good 5km south of the centre, near Sułżew metro station.

Activities and sports

If you fancy **ice skating**, then you could try your luck with the blink-and-you-miss-them opening hours at the winter ice rink at Torwar, ul. Łazienkowska 6 (Mon–Fri 8–9pm, Sat–Sun 11am–12.30pm & 6–7.30pm; ☎022/621 6207) or at the open-air rink at ul. Inspektowa 1, in Stegny (Mon–Fri 5–6.30pm, Sat & Sun noon–2pm, 3–5pm & 6–8pm; ☎022/842 2768). You can rent skates at both places for a nominal fee.

The best of the city's **swimming** centres is at Wodny Park Warszawianka, 4km south of the centre at Merliniego 4, where there's an Olympic-sized pool as well as water slides and children's areas (Mon–Fri 6.30am–10pm, Sat & Sun 8am–10pm; ⓦ www.wodnypark.com.pl; buses #505, #514, #516, #524 from Centrum). In summer, there's an open-air pool at WOW Wisła, in the Praga suburb at Namysłowska 8 (Jul–Aug daily 9am–7pm; tram #32 from pl. Bankowy).

As for spectator sports, your best bet is **football**. Legia Warszawa, the army club with a nationwide following, play at Stadion Wojska Polskiego, just southeast of the centre at ul. Łazienkowska (buses #155, #159 and #166). Their biggest rivals, Polonia, are less well supported but were league champions in 2000 – they play at ul. Konwiktorska 6, a ten-minute walk north of Stare Miasto (or tram #2 from Centrum).

Shopping

Shopping in Warsaw has changed dramatically since 1989. The old state-owned shops were one of the first things to go at the end of the communist era, replaced in the majority of cases by a wide array of private concerns, both Polish and Western-owned, that now adorn the streets of the capital. Shopping here today is not very different from shopping in any other major European city. There's no shortage of goods, with specialist stores catering to most consumer whims, alongside the regular general and department stores. And since the English-speaking expatriate community in Warsaw is as large as that in Prague, you won't find yourself lost for a newspaper or book in English, or struggling to keep variety in your diet or to buy clothes. A specific touch of Polishness is provided by the welter of markets, bazaars and street traders that you'll find around the capital.

Biggest of the central department stores is the **Galeria Centrum** on Marszałkowska, opposite the Pałac Kultury i Nauk. The pedestrianized **ul. Chmielna**, running east from here, has its fair share of clothes shops and boutiques.

Bookshops, newsagents and record stores

Academic Bookstore ul. Grzybowska 37A Ⓦ www.abe.com.pl. Huge bookshop with over 20,000 titles in English.
Akademia Krakowskie Przedmieście 5. Some English books and some Polish literature in English translation.
American Bookstore Nowy Świat 61 Ⓦ www.americanbookstore.pl. Good range of fiction and guidebooks. Stocks the *Warsaw Insider*.
Empik junction of Nowy Świat and al. Jerozolimskie, and ul. Marszałeowska 116/122. Chain of department stores offering the biggest across-the-board range of books and CDs in the city. Also foreign-language newpapers and magazines.
Księgarna Językowa Akademia Traugutta 3. Foreign-language bookshop, including plenty of books about Poland in English.
Odeon ul. Hoża 19. Wide range of titles, with a good selection of lesbian and gay literature.
Pelta Świętokrzyska 16. A haven for boys of all ages, with books on cars, bikes, trains and planes and militaria – good for Polish military history. Plastic model kits upstairs.
Zachęta pl. Małachowskiego 3. Shop inside the art gallery of the same name, selling books on the whole gamut of Polish art and architecture, as well as arty cards and gifts.

Crafts and antiques

Ambra ul. Piwna 15. One of the better amber jewellery stores on a street that's stuffed full with them.
Antyki ul. Wiejska 17. Poky place packed with antique-shop jumble of all kinds and periods.
Cepelia central branches at Nowy Świat 35, Krucza 23/31, and Marszałkowska 99/101. Chain of handicraft shops specializing in Polish ceramics, textiles and woodcarving – as well as more tacky souvenirs.
Desa Galeria Rynek Starego Miasta 4/6 and Nowy Świat 51. Upmarket antiques and paintings.
Galeria Zapiecek ul. Zapiecek 1. Contemporary Polish art for the serious enthusiast.

Markets and bazaars

At weekends, traditional **market** areas like the Hala Mirowska, on pl. Mirowski, west of the Ogród Saski (see p.107), are packed with stalls and worth visiting for the atmosphere alone. However, now that there's more in the shops, markets aren't what they used to be, and most comprise a few seedy stalls selling porn videos and guns.

Dziesięciolecia stadium Praga district, near Poniatowski bridge. Biggest of the outdoor city markets and reckoned to be Europe's largest. It's held in a sports stadium, where many street vendors moved when the city authorities cleared them out of the city centre. Everything you could imagine anyone thinking of selling – Soviet bric-a-brac, cars, rifles, fur coats and all things in between. The best bargains tend to be on the higher levels, as opposed to the more organized lower section.
Hala Mirowska pl. Mirowski, west of the Ogród Saski.
Koło Bazaar ul. Obozowa, in the Wola district (near the end of tram lines #1, #13, #20 and #24, or bus #159, #167 and #359). Held on Sundays, this is the main antiques and bric-a-brac market, with everything from sofas and old Russian samovars to genuine Iron Crosses on offer. On Monday mornings, there's a pets market selling everything from hamsters to carnivorous turtles and beyond.

Listings

Airlines Aeroflot, al. Jerozolimskie 29 ☎022/621 1611; Air France, ul. Krucza 21 ☎022/628 1281; American Airlines, al. Ujazdowskie 20 ☎022/625 3002, ⓦwww.aa.com; British Airways, ul. Krucza 49 ☎022/529 9000, ⓦwww.britishairways.com; LOT, al. Jerozolimskie 65/79 ☎022/630 5007, ⓦwww.lot.pl); Lufthansa, Warsaw Towers, ul. Sienna 39 ☎022/338 1300, ⓦwww.lufthansa.pl; SAS, see Lufthansa (ⓦwww.scandinavian.net); and Swissair, ul. Sienna 39 ☎022/850 0440, ⓦwww.swissair.com. See p.81 for airport information.

American Express Krakowskie Przedmieście 11 ☎022/551 5152. There's another branch at the *Marriott* hotel. No fee on American Express travellers' cheques. Mon–Fri 9am–6pm.

Banks and exchange There are exchange kantors and ATMs all over the city. Handy central banks include Pekao, on the corner of al. Jerozolimskie and ul. Marszałkowska, and at pl. Bankowy 2.

British Council, al. Jerozolimskie 59 ☎022/628 7401. English-language books and newspapers. Mon–Fri 8.30am–7pm, Sat 8.30am–1pm.

Buses Warszawa Zachodnia (see p.81), handles all international departures to western Europe and the Baltic States, as well as major domestic destinations to the south and west. Dworzec Stadion (see p.81), is the departure point for buses to Belarus and Ukraine, as well as services to eastern Poland. International tickets can be purchased through Orbis offices (see "Travel agents" overleaf) as well as from international counters at bus stations. Domestic inter-city buses run by the private Polski Express (☎022/620 0326, ⓦwww.polskiexpress.pl) are faster and more comfortable than their nationalized counterparts, though slightly more expensive; they operate from a stop on al. Jana Pawła II, just behind Warszawa Centralna train station. Note that there's a single hut selling tickets, and little in the way of food or drink-buying opportunities – come early and well prepared. For information on services operated by the state-run PKS bus company call ☎022/9433; for Warsaw city transport services, call ☎022/9484.

Camera repairs Foto and Video Service, ul. Marszałkowska 84/92.

Car rental Avis (ⓦwww.avis.pl), at the airport (☎022/650 4872) and at the *Marriott* (see p.86; ☎022/630 7316); Budget: at the airport (☎022/650 4062) and the *Marriott* (☎022/630 7280); Hertz (ⓦwww.hertz.com), at the airport (☎022/650 2896) and ul. Nowogrodzka 27 (☎022/621 0239).

Disabled information ☎022/828 0802.

Embassies Australia, ul. Nowogrodzka 11 ☎022/521 34 44, ⓦwww.australia.pl; Belarus, ul. Ateńska 67 ☎022/617 8441; Canada, al. Jerozolimskie 123 ☎022/584 3100; Czech Republic, ul. Koszykowa 18 ☎022/628 7221; Germany, ul. Dąbrowiecka 30 ☎022/617 3011, ⓦwww.ambasadaniemiec.pl; Ireland, ul. Humańska 10 ☎022/849 6633; Lithuania, al. Szucha 5 ☎022/625 3368; New Zealand, ul. Migdałowa 4 ☎022/645 1407; Russia, ul. Belwederska 49 ☎022/621 5575; UK, Al. Róż 1 ☎022/628 1001, ⓦwww.britishembassy.pl; Ukraine, al. Szucha 7 ☎022/625 0127; USA, al. Ujazdowskie 29 ☎022/628 3041.

Hospitals and emergencies The English-speaking American Medical Centre, ul. Wilca 23/29 (Mon–Fri 8am–6pm, Sat 9am–3pm; ☎022/545 6161) is expensive but good, and has a 24-hour emergency service; the C.M. Medical Centre, 3rd floor of the *Marriott* hotel (see p.86; Mon–Fri 7am–9pm, Sat 8am–8pm, Sun 9am–1pm; ☎022/630 3030), offers a similar service. Most central of the main hospitals is the State Clinical Hospital, ul. Marszałkowska 24 (☎022/621 3241). The emergency ambulance number is ☎022/999, but the private Falck ambulance service (☎022/9675) will also respond, and you've more chance of being understood in English.

Internet Internet cafés are springing up all over Warsaw. Reliable, centrally located ones include Casablanca, ul. Krakowskie Przedmieście 4/6 (daily 9am–midnight); Empik, ul. Marszałkowska 116/122 (Mon–Fri 9am–10pm, Sun 11am–7pm); Relax Cinema, ul. Złota 8 (daily 10am–10pm); Silverzone, ul. Puławska 19/21 (daily 9am–11pm); and W Sieci, ul. Freta 49/51 (daily 9am–11.30pm). Expect to pay about 10zł an hour in all these places.

Laundry ul. Karmelicka 17. Mon–Fri 9am–5pm, Sat 9am–1pm.

Left luggage There are left-luggage facilities at Warszawa Centralna train station (see p.81).

Lost property On city transport, ul. Słowackiego 45a ☎022/663 3297; 7am–3pm.

Pharmacies There are 24-hour *apteka* on the top floor of Warszawa Centralna train station; at Warszawa Wschodnia station; al. Solidarności 149; ul. Puławska 39; and ul. Wilcza 31.

Police Report crimes at the police office at ul. Wilcza 21; include a full list of stolen items and their value.

Post offices The main office is at ul. Świętokrzyska 31/33. It handles fax, poste restante (at window no. 12: postcode 00-001) and is open

24hr. Warszawa Centralna station also an office (postal services Mon–Fri 8am–8pm, Sat 8am–2pm; phones 24hr): go to the main upstairs hall and it's behind the train information board at the far end from the escalators.

Trains Warszawa Centralna serves all international routes and the major national ones. Northbound trains also stop at Warszawa Gdańska, west- and southbound at Warszawa Zachodnia, and eastbound at Warszawa Wschodnia. Śródmieście station, just east of Warszawa Centralna, handles local traffic to Łowicz, Pruszkow and Skierniewice; all station details are listed on p.81. For international tickets, an alternative to queuing at Warszawa Centralna's *kasa międzynarodowa* (international counters), which are upstairs on the second floor, is to book at Orbis offices (see "Travel agents" below). For train information call ☎022/9436 or 9431.

Telephone and fax facilites Both are found in main post offices, while there are also phone boxes on the street. There are also fax facilities at some internet cafés (see above).

Travel agents Almatur, ul. Kopernika 23 (Mon–Fri 9am–7pm, Sat 10am–2pm; ☎022/826 2639 or 826 3512, ⓦwww.almatur.com.pl) organize cheap student travel. Mazurkas, inside the *Forum* hotel at ul. Nowogrodzka 24/26 (☎022/629 1878, ⓦwww.polhotels.com/tours/mazurkas) organize Warsaw sightseeing trips and excursions to outlying attractions, notably Chopin's birthplace at Żelazowa Wola (see p.136). Orbis, at ul. Bracka 16 (☎022/827 7265), ul. Marszałkowska 142 (☎022/827 0875), and ul. Świętokrzyska 20 (☎022/826 2016) sell air and international train and bus tickets; both are open Mon–Fri 8am–7pm and Sat 9am–3pm.

Airport information Information ☎022/650 39 43.

Western Union Operates through Prosper Bank SA, Krakowskie Przedmieście 55 ☎022/826 2021. Mon–Fri 8am–6pm, Sat 9am–1pm.

Mazovia

Mazovia – the plain surrounding Warsaw – is not the most attractive of landscapes, but it does have several rewarding day-trips to ease your passage into the rural Polish experience. If time is limited, then at least take a break outside the city in the beautiful forest of the **Puszcza Kampinoska** national park, or to Chopin's birthplace at **Żelazowa Wola**. Southwest of the capital, the great manufacturing city of **Łódź** offers a major dose of culture. Other towns south of Warsaw are less inviting, and industrial centres such as **Skierniewice** and **Radom** are likely to be low on most people's priorities. **Płock**, under two hours by train west of the city, is altogether more enticing, with a historic Stare Miasto complex and a couple of notable museums. The northern stretches of Mazovia offer some good day excursions, chiefly the palace at **Jabłonna** and the market town of **Pułtusk.**

Just about everywhere covered in the following section can be reached from Warsaw on local **buses** and **trains**. Łódź is particularly well served by regular express trains, making a day's outing from Warsaw an easy option.

The Park Narodowy Puszcza Kampinoska

With its boundaries touching the edge of Warsaw's Żoliborz suburb, **Park Narodowy Puszcza Kampinoska** – Kampinoski Forest National Park – stretches some 30km west of the capital, a rare example of an extensive woodland area coexisting with a major urban complex. Now protected as a national park, this open forest harbours the summer houses of numerous Varsovians, and in autumn is a favoured weekend haunt for legions of mushroom-pickers. As with all national parks, the forest's nature reserves are carefully controlled to help preserve the rich plant and animal life. Elks, wild boars, beavers (reintroduced here from the northeast of the country) and lynx (reintroduced in the early 1990s) are sighted from time to time, and the park is rich in bird life – watch out for storks, cranes and buzzards. Access for walkers and cross-country skiers is pretty much unrestricted. Beware that it's all too easy to get lost in the woods, so stick to marked routes: signposts at the edge of the forest show clearly the main paths.

Originally submerged under the waters of the Wisła, which now flows north of the forest, the picturesque park landscape intersperses dense tracts of woodland – pines, hornbeams, birch and oaks are the most common trees – with a patchwork terrain of swamp-like marshes and belts of sand dune. Though most of the forest is now under local forestry commission management, a few parts of the area still retain the wildness that long made them a favourite hunting spot with the Polish monarchy.

Truskaw and Palmiry

Buses from pl. Wilson in the Warsaw suburb of Żoliborz (to get to pl. Wilson, catch **tram** #15, #36 or #45 from Centrum) take you 10km out to **TRUSKAW**, a small village on the eastern edge of the forest. It's a rapidly developing place, home to the headquarters of the park authorities. The small museum here details the often bloody history of the forest (for more on which, see below) as well as a section devoted to the local flora and fauna. From Truskaw, it's a pleasant five-kilometre walk to the hamlet of **PALMIRY**, along sandy paths that seem a world removed from the bustle of the city. People in the scattered older houses will give you well-water if you ask, and may have jars of the excellent local honey for sale.

The forest's proximity to town made it a centre of resistance activity – notably during the 1863 Uprising and World War II – and also made it an obvious killing ground for the Nazis. The **war cemetery** that you pass on the Truskaw–Palmiry walk contains the bodies of about 2000 prisoners and civilians, herded out to the forest, shot and hurled into pits. To get back into Warsaw, walk the one-kilometre track north from Palmiry to the main road bus stop and take any bus back towards Żoliborz.

If you're not in a hurry to get back, it's worth crossing the main road by the bus stop and continuing on a couple of kilometres east to the village of **DZIEKANÓW POLSKI** on the banks of the Wisła. The area round the village is one of several noted bird-watchers' haunts in and around the national park, a fact explained by the forest's location along one of the country's main bird migration routes. Among the birds regularly sighted here is the **white stork**, whose nests are common in and around the village – some of the telegraph poles here sport special platforms to which the storks return each year to raise their young. Further into the fields and dense undergrowth closer to the river you may be able to catch the call of the **lapwing**, while on the water, you can spot brilliantly coloured **kingfishers** and **bluethroats** as well as a variety of gulls, terns and ducks.

Leszno and Kampinos

On the southern side of the park, you can head further into the forest from the villages of **ZABORÓW** (which has a nineteenth-century palace and church), **LESZNO** or **KAMPINOS**, all of which are sited along the main road to Żelazowa Wola (see overleaf). Numerous **buses** run to the villages from Warszawa Zachodnia (most buses to destinations such as Wyszogród, Kamion

Frédéric Chopin (1810–49)

Of all the major Polish artists, **Frédéric Chopin** – Fryderyk Szopen as he was baptized in Polish – is the one whose work has achieved the greatest international recognition. He is, to all intents and purposes, the national composer, a fact attested to in the wealth of festivals, concerts and, most importantly, the famous international piano competition held in his name. Like other Polish creative spirits of the nineteenth century, the life of this brilliantly talented composer and performer reflects the political upheavals of Partition-era Poland. Born of mixed Polish–French parentage in the Mazovian village of Żelazowa Wola, where his father was a tutor to a local aristocratic family, Frédéric spent his early years in and around Warsaw, holidays in the surrounding countryside giving him an early introduction to the Mazovian folk tunes that permeate his compositions. Musical talent began to show from an early age: at six Chopin was already making up tunes, a year later he started to play the piano, and his first concert performance came at the age of eight. After a couple of years' schooling at the Warsaw lyceum, the budding composer – his first polonaises and *mazurkas* had already been written and performed – was enrolled at the newly created Warsaw Music Conservatory.

Chopin's first journey abroad was in August 1829, to Vienna, where he gave a couple of concert performances to finance the publication of some recent compositions, a set of Mozart variations. Returning to Warsaw soon afterwards, Chopin made his official **public debut**, performing the virtuoso Second Piano Concerto (F Minor), its melancholic slow movement inspired, as he himself admitted, by an (unrequited) love affair with a fellow Conservatory student and aspiring opera singer. In the autumn of 1830 he travelled to Vienna, only to hear news of the **November Uprising** against the Russians at home. Already set upon moving to Paris, the heartbroken Chopin was inspired by the stirring yet tragic events in Poland to write the famous *Revolutionary Étude*, among a string of other works. As it turned out, he was never to return to Poland, a fate shared by many of the fellow exiles whose Parisian enclave he entered in 1831. He rapidly befriended them and the host of young composers (including Berlioz, Bellini, Liszt and Mendelssohn) who lived in the city. The elegantly dressed, artistically sensitive Chopin soon became a Parisian high society favourite, earning his living teaching and giving the occasional recital. Some relatively problem-free years followed, during which he produced a welter of new com-

and Gostynin drop off in the villages, but this is not always indicated clearly on the departures board – so be prepared to ask). Start out early from Warsaw, as return buses stop at about 6pm, after which the only option is a **taxi**, charging double for journeys outside the city.

There are a number of **walking** options. One of the best is to get off at Leszno and take the marked forest path to Kampinos, an easy-going, twelve-kilometre walk in all. Walking north through the village on the marked path, you soon reach the swampy edges of the forest. In summer you'll need to watch out for the particularly bloodthirsty mosquitoes, but the forest itself is a treat, with acres of undisturbed woodland and only very occasional human company.

Five kilometres northwest of Kampinos (and accessible on foot), the park **museum** (Tues–Sun 9am–3.30pm; 3zł) in the village of **GRANICA** provides a thorough overview of the flora and fauna of the region.

Żelazowa Wola

Fifty kilometres west of Warsaw, just beyond the western edge of the Park Narodowy Puszcza Kampinoska, is the little village of **ŻELAZOWA WOLA**, the birthplace of composer and national hero, **Frédéric Chopin**. The journey through the rolling Mazovian countryside makes an enjoyable day out from

positions, notably the rhapsodic *Fantaisie-Impromptu*, a book of études and a stream of nationalistically inspired polonaises and mazurkas.

Chopin's life changed dramatically in 1836 following his encounter with the radical novelist **George Sand**, who promptly fell in love with him and suggested she become his mistress. After over a year spent hesitating over the proposal in the winter of 1838, Chopin – by now ill – travelled with her and her two children to Majorca. Though musically productive – the B Flat Minor Sonata and its famous funeral march date from this period – the stay was not a success, Chopin's rapidly deteriorating health forcing a return to France to seek the help of a doctor in Marseille. Thereafter Chopin was forced to give up composing for a while, earning his living giving piano lessons to rich Parisians and spending the summers with an increasingly maternal Sand at her country house at **Nohant**, south of Paris. The rural environment temporarily did wonders for Chopin's health, and it was in Nohant that he produced some of his most powerful music, including the sublime *Polonaise Fantasie*, the Third Sonata and several of the major ballades. Increasingly strained relations with Sand, however, finally snapped when she broke with him in 1847. Miserable and almost penniless, Chopin accepted an invitation from an admiring Scottish pupil Jane Stirling to visit **Britain**. Despite mounting illness, Chopin gave numerous concerts and recitals in London, also making friends with Carlyle, Dickens and other luminaries of English artistic life. Increasingly weak, and unable either to compose or return Stirling's devoted affections, a depressed Chopin returned to Paris in November 1848.

Just a few months later, he finally succumbed to the tuberculosis that had dogged him for years, and died in his apartment on place de Vendôme in central Paris: in accordance with his deathbed wish Mozart's *Requiem* was sung at Chopin's funeral, and his body was buried in the **Père-Lachaise Cemetery**, the grave topped, a year later, with a monument of a weeping muse sprinkled with earth from his native Mazovia. Admired by his friends yet also criticized by many of his peers, the music Chopin created during his short life achieved a synthesis only few fellow Polish artists have matched – a distinctive Polishness combined with a universality of emotional and aesthetic appeal. For fellow Poles, as well as for many foreigners, the emotive Polish content is particularly significant: many, indeed, feel his music expresses the essence of the national psyche, alternating wistful romanticism with storms of turbulent, restless protest – "guns hidden in flowerbeds", in fellow composer Schumann's memorable description.

the city: unless you've got a car, you'll need to take a **bus** from Warszawa Zachodnia (direction Sochaczew or Kamion) or take a train from Warszawa Śródmieście or Warszawa Zachodnia to the town of Sochaczew, from where bus #6 trundles to Żelazowa Wola. Alternatively, book up on one of the many excursions offered by Orbis and others.

The house where Chopin was born is now a **museum** (Tues–Sun 10am–4pm; 10zł) surrounded by a large, tranquil garden. The Chopin family lived here for only a year after their son's birth in 1810, but young Frédéric returned frequently to what was long his favourite place, and one which gave him contact with the Polish countryside and, most importantly, the folk musical traditions of Mazovia. Bought by public subscription in 1929, the Chopin family residence was subsequently restored and turned into a museum to the composer run by the Warsaw-based Chopin Society. The Society also organize **piano recitals** here throughout the summer (late May to end Sept: Sun at 11am and 3pm; additional concerts on Sat at 11am July & Aug) – check Warsaw listings sources or the Chopin Society (based at Warsaw's Muzeum Fryderyka Chopina; see p.112) for the current programme details. Tickets for the recitals can be booked through the Chopin Society; additionally, the concerts are sometimes included in the tours offered by Warsaw travel agents (notably Mazurkas; see p.134).

The Sochaczew–Wilcz Tulowskich railway

Ten kilometres southwest of Żelazowa Wola, the unremarkable town of **Sochaczew** (reached by local train from Warsaw's Śródmieście station) is the starting point for steam-hauled narrow-gauge railway excursions to the village of **Wilcz Tulowskich**, a scenic journey which takes you through the forests on the western fringes of Kampinoski national park. Services run every Saturday between May and October, departing at 9.40am and returning 3pm. The narrow-guage train station in Sochaczew has a Museum (May–Oct: Tues–Sun 10am–3pm; 5zł) devoted to the line – formerly used to transport logs out of the forest – which features an impressive line-up of narrow-gauge rolling stock. Further details about train running times are available from the Muzeum Kolej Wąskotorowy (Sochaczew Narrow-Gauge Railway Museum; ☎046/862 5975), ul. Towarowa 7, 95-500 Sochaczew.

The house itself is a typical *dwór*, the traditional country residence of the *szlacta* (gentlefolk) class, numerous examples of which can be found all over rural Poland – Mazovia and Małopolska in particular. All the rooms have been restored to period perfection and contain a collection of family portraits and other Chopin memorabilia. Through the main entrance way the old **kitchen**, the first room on your right, has an attractively painted characteristic nineteenth-century Mazovian ceiling.

Next along is the **music room**; the exhibits here including a caseful of manuscripts of early Chopin piano works as well as a plaster cast of the virtuoso pianist's left hand. If you've come for the popular weekend piano recitals – often by noted international performers who consider it an honour to play at the house – this is where they're held, performed on a luxury Steinway grand donated by wealthy Polish-Americans. On fine days, the audience sits outside, the music wafting through the open windows – an eminently uplifting and pleasurable experience.

The **dining room** walls sport some original Canaletto copper-worked views of Warsaw, while upstairs is the **bedroom** where the infant Frédéric was born, now something of a Chopin shrine. Back outside it's worth taking a leisurely stroll through the magnificent house grounds, turned into a sort of **botanical park** (closes dusk in winter, 7pm in summer) following the place's conversion into a museum. In spring or autumn you'll catch the scented blossoms of the rich variety of trees and bushes donated from botanical gardens around the world. The moderately priced *Pod Wierzbami* **restaurant**, on the corner of the main road, will fix you up with anything from simple soups to roast duck.

If you're travelling by car (although many of the bus tours also stop here), you could consider making a brief detour 11km north into the countryside to the village of **BROCHÓW**. The imposing brick parish **church**, a fortified sixteenth-century structure, became the Chopin family place of Sunday worship following the parents' marriage here in the early 1800s. The original of young Frédéric's birth certificate is proudly displayed in the sacristy, along with assorted other Chopin family records. Just down the road from the church, a Chopin "complex" is under construction in a renovated nineteenth-century manor house; once completed it will hold a concert hall, hotel, studios and teaching centre.

Łowicz and around

At first sight **ŁOWICZ**, 30km southwest of Żelazowa Wola, looks just like any other small, concrete-ridden central Polish town, but this apparently drab place is, in fact, a well-established centre of folk art and craft. Locally produced handicrafts, handwoven materials, carved wood ornaments and *wycinanki* – coloured paper cut-outs – are popular throughout the country, the brilliantly coloured local Mazowsze costumes (*pasiaki*) being the town's best-known product. Historically Łowicz has not been without importance, for several centuries providing the main residence of the archbishops of Gniezno, normally the Catholic primates of all Poland, who endowed Łowicz with its scattering of historic buildings – chiefly **churches**.

The ideal time to come here is at **Corpus Christi** (late May/early June) – or, failing that, during one of the other major Church **festivals** – when many of the women turn out in beautiful handmade traditional costumes for the two-hour procession to the collegiate church here. Wearing full skirts, embroidered cotton blouses and colourful headscarves, they are followed by neat lines of young girls preparing for their first Communion. The crowds gathered in the main square may well contain a sizeable contingent of camera-clicking foreigners, but they are never numerous enough to ruin the event's character and sense of tradition.

The Town

The old **Rynek**, ten minutes from the train station, is the pivot of the town, along with the vast **collegiate church**, a brick fifteenth-century construction, remodelled to its present form in the mid-seventeenth century. Size apart, its most striking features are the richly decorated tombstones of the archbishops of Gniezno and former Polish primates, and the ornate series of Baroque chapels.

The other attraction is the local **museum** across the square (Tues–Sun 10am–4pm; 4zł, free on Sat), housed in a Baroque missionary college designed by Tylman of Gameren and rebuilt following wartime destruction. The upstairs floor contains an extensive and carefully presented collection of regional folk artefacts, including furniture, pottery, tools and costumes whose basic styles are the same as those still worn on feast days. Downstairs, as well as a section devoted to local history and archeology, the former seminary **chapel** houses a notable collection of Baroque art from all over the country, the vault of the chapel itself adorned with frescoes by Michelangelo Palloni, court painter to King Jan Sobieski. Many houses around the square contain examples of the distinctive coloured cut-out decorations on display in the museum too. The back of the museum is a kind of mini-*skansen*, containing two old cottages complete with their original furnishings. If you're intrigued by the local craftwork, there's a generally reasonable selection on sale at the Cepelia shop on the main square. Of the clutch of historic buildings dotted around the town centre, the most notable are the Baroque former **Piarist church**, with some enjoyable ceiling paintings, and the remains of the **castle** on ul. Zamkowa, originally the bishop's residence until it was razed to the ground by marauding Swedes in the mid-seventeenth century.

Practicalities

Łowicz is a ninety-minute **train** journey from Warsaw and there's a regular local service from Śródmieście station (see p.81). Other than a summer-only **youth hostel** at Grunwaldzka 9 (☎046/837 3703; 20zł), the only real options for an overnight stay are the well-kept *Zacisze* hotel at ul. Kaliska 5 (☎046/837 3326; ❹), which has protected parking facilities, a restaurant and café, or the atmospheric *Zajazd Łowicki* hotel at ul. Blich 36 (☎046/837 41 64; ❸), on the Poznań road on the west side of town, which also has a decent **restaurant**. There's also good food at the *Polonia* on the main square, though it closes at 9pm.

Arkadia and Nieborów

A short distance east of Łowicz are a couple of sights redolent of the bygone Polish aristocracy, the landscaped park of **Arkadia**, and seventeenth-century palace at **Nieborów**. They combine for an easy and enjoyable day-trip from Warsaw: Arkadia is an easy ten-minute walk from **Mysłaków**, a minor train station served by Warsaw–Łowicz **trains**; while Nieborów can be accessed by **bus** from either Mysłaków or Łowicz.

Arkadia

Ten kilometres southeast of Łowicz, the eighteenth-century **Arkadia** park (Tues–Sun: May–Sept 10am–6pm; Oct–April 10am–4pm) is as wistfully romantic a spot as you could wish for an afternoon stroll. Conceived by Princess Helen Radziwiłł as an "ancient monument to beautiful Greece", the classical park is dotted with lakes and walkways, a jumble of reproduction classical temples and pavilions, a sphinx and a mock-Gothic house that wouldn't look out of place in a Hammer House film production. Many of the pieces were collected by the princess on her exhaustive foreign travels, and the air of decay – the place hasn't been touched since World War II – only adds to the evocation of times long past, consciously created by the princess, who was caught up in the cult of the classical that swept through the Polish aristocracy in the latter half of the eighteenth century.

Nieborów

Five kilometres further east lies the village of **NIEBORÓW**, whose country **palace** was designed by the ever-present Tylman of Gameren and owned for most of its history, like the park, by the powerful Radziwiłł clan – just one of dozens this family possessed right up until World War II. Now part of the Muzeum Narodowe (see p.113), the Palac Nieborów is one of the handsomest and best-maintained in the country, surrounded by outbuildings and a manicured **park** and **gardens**.

The palace **interior** (Tues–Sun: May–Sept 10am–6pm; Oct–April 10am–4pm; 5zł), restored after the war, is furnished on the basis of the original eighteenth- and nineteenth-century contents of the main rooms – a lavish restoration that makes you wonder whether Polish communists suffered from a kind of ideological schizophrenia. Roman tombstones and sculptural fragments fill a lot of space downstairs, gathered about the palace's prize exhibit, a classical-era sculpture known as the **Nieborów Niobe**. The grandest apartments (including a library with a fine collection of globes) are on the first floor, reached by a staircase clad in finely decorated Delft tiles. It all has an air, these days, of studied aristocratic respectability, somewhat belying Radziwiłł history. Karol Radziwiłł, for example, head of the dynasty in the late eighteenth century, used to hold vast banquets in the course of which he'd drink himself into a stupor, and, as often as not, kill someone in a brawl. He would then, as historian Adam Zamoyski puts it in his book *The Polish Way* (see "Books", p.730), "stumble into his private chapel and bawl himself back to sobriety by singing hymns". A far cry from today's genteel environment, which, in the spring, is host to a much publicized series of **classical concerts** by international artists – the tourist office in Warsaw will be your most likely source of information on these.

There's a **café/restaurant** in the palace itself, while Nieborów village offers a couple of regional-style restaurants, a seasonal **youth hostel** (Jul–Aug; ☎046/838 5694; 24zł per person) and a **campsite** 1km west of the palace (☎046/838 5692).

Łódź

Mention **ŁÓDŹ** (pronounced "Woodge") to many Poles and all you'll get is a grimace. Poland's second city, 110km southwest of Warsaw, is certainly no beauty, but it does have a significant place in the country's development, and a unique atmosphere that grows on you the longer you stay – especially with its newly pedestrianized swath of **ulica Piotrkowska** in the centre of town, which now teems with life day and night. Essentially a creation of the Industrial Revolution, and appropriately nicknamed the Polish Manchester, Łódź is still an important manufacturing centre. Much of it survives unchanged – the tall, smoking chimneys of the castellated red-brick factories; the grand historicist and Secessionist villas of the industrialists; the theatres, art galleries and philanthropic societies; and the slum quarters, all caked in a century and a half of soot and grime. It served as the ready-made location for Andrzej Wajda's film *The Promised Land*, based on the novel by Nobel Prize-winning author Władysław Reymont, depicting life in Industrial Revolution-era Poland.

International business and trade fairs account for a fair slice of Łódź's visitors, but its cultural and social scene is pretty lively as well. The **orchestra** is one of the best in the country, and there's an impressive array of cinemas, theatres, museums, opera houses and art galleries here. The Łódź **film school** is also internationally renowned, attracting aspiring movie-makers aiming to follow in the footsteps of alumni such as Wajda, Polański, Kieślowski and Zanussi.

Some history

Missionaries came to the site of Łódź in the twelfth century, but the first permanent settlement does not seem to have taken root until a couple of hundred years later, and at the end of the 1700s it was still an obscure village of fewer than two hundred inhabitants. Impulse towards its development, strangely enough, only came during the Partition period, with the **1820 edict** of the Russian-ruled Congress Kingdom of Poland, which officially designated Łódź as a new industrial centre and encouraged foreign weavers and manufacturers to come and settle.

People poured in by the thousand each year, and within twenty years Łódź had become the nation's second largest city, a position it has maintained ever since. Despite being the imperial rulers, the Russians played little more than an administrative role, though they adopted a higher profile following the failed nationalist insurrection of 1863. The true political elite consisted in the main of **German entrepreneurs**, most of them Protestant, who founded large textile factories which made vast fortunes within a very short period of time. These were operated principally by **Polish peasants** enticed by the prospect of a better standard of living than they could claw from their meagre patches of land. By the end of the century, the urban proletariat had swelled to over 300,000. Industrialization brought politicization, and Łódź, like other new cities such as Białystok, had become a centre for working-class and anti-tsarist agitation.

The **Jews** were another highly significant community. When they first arrived, they functioned mainly as artisans and traders, but a number managed to rise to the status of great industrial magnates, notably the Poznańskis, whose luxurious homes now house many of the city's institutions. The Jewish contribution to the cultural life of Łódź was immense, two of the city's most famous sons being the pianist Artur Rubinstein and the poet Julian Tuwim.

Łódź's reputation as a melting-pot of four great peoples and religions was only marginally affected by the fall of the tsarist empire, but was dealt a termi-

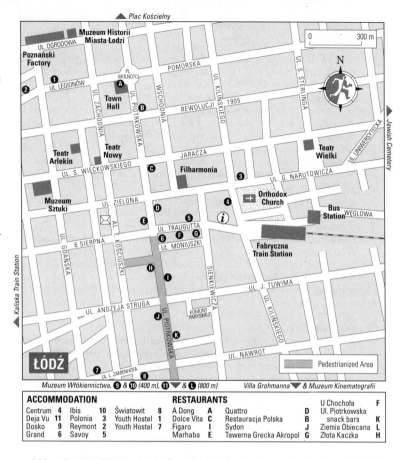

Plac Kościelny

LÓDŹ

Pedestrianized Area

Muzeum Włókiennictwa, **9** & **10** (400 m), **11** ▼ & **1** (800 m)   Villa Grohmanna ▼ & Muzeum Kinematografii

ACCOMMODATION				RESTAURANTS					
Centrum	4	Ibis	10	Światowit	8	A Dong	A	Quattro	D
Deja Vu	11	Polonia	3	Youth Hostel	1	Dolce Vita	C	Restauracja Polska	B
Dosko	9	Reymont	2	Youth Hostel	7	Figaro	I	Sydon	J
Grand	6	Savoy	5			Marhaba	E	Tawerna Grecka Akropol	G

U Chochoła	F
Ul. Piotrkowska	
snack bars	K
Ziemia Obiecana	L
Złota Kaczka	H

nal blow by **World War II**. At first, the Nazis aimed to make it the capital of the rump Polish protectorate, the so-called General Government, but, incensed by the largely hostile stance adopted by the powerful local German community, incorporated it into the Reich. In the process, they renamed it "Litzmannstadt" in honour of a somewhat obscure general who had made a breakthrough against the nearby Russian line in 1914, and established the first and longest-lasting of their notorious urban ghettos (see box pp.144–145).

For all the visual similarities, postwar Łódź has been, in an important sense, a spectre of its former self; nearly all the Jews were wiped out, while most of the German expatriates fled west, leaving only a tiny minority behind.

More recently the city has also acquired a reputation (perhaps linked to its industrial landscape) as Poland's capital of **techno music**, with an annual Parada Wolności (Freedom Parade), developed in imitation of Berlin's Love Parade, taking over ul. Piotrkowska during the last weekend of September.

Arrival and information

The main **train station**, Łódź Fabryczna, on the eastern fringes of the town centre, handles services to and from Warsaw and other destinations in northern and eastern Poland. Trains from the west, notably Poznań and Wrocław, terminate at Łódź Kaliska, 2km west of the city centre and connected by tram #12 or bus #99. The main **bus station** is right next to Łódź Fabryczna.

There's an **information office** run by the municipal Dom Kultury (Cultural Centre) at ul. Traugutta 18 (entrance round the back; Mon–Fri 8.30am–4.30pm, Sat 10am–2pm; ☎042/633 7299, ⓦwww.ldk.lodz.pl), whose primary *raison d'être* is to publicize cultural events, but it also acts as a friendly source of tourist information as well. Their bimonthly pocket-sized publication *Kalejdoskop* (2.5zł, although many hotels give it away for free) is a good source of local **listings**. There are **internet cafés** on the north side of Hotel Centrum (Mon–Fri 9am–11pm, Sat 10am–midnight, Sun 11am–11pm), and at Piotrkowska 81 (24hr).

Accommodation

Łódź is off the beaten track as far as many visitors are concerned, which means that many of its grander and plusher hotels are relatively cheap. There are two **youth hostels**, at ul. Zamenhofa 13 (open Fri–Sun only; ☎042/636 6599) and ul. Legionów 27 (☎042/630 6680), both central and open all year, and charging about 25zł per head. You can **camp** at *Stawy Jana*, 5km south of the centre at ul. Rzgowska 247 (tram #4 from Kilińskiego to the end of the line; ☎042/646 1551; bungalows ❷); or *Na Rogach*, a similiar distance northeast at ul. Łupkowa 10/14 (bus #60 from ul. Narutowicza; ☎042/659 7013; bungalows ❷).

Centrum ul. Kilińskiego 59/63 ☎042/632 8640 ⓔcentrum@hotelspt.com.pl. Unatmospheric concrete pile saved by its proximity to the train station. ❻

Deja-Vu ul. Wigury 4/6 ☎042/636 2060. Exclusive pension that aims to re-create the living quarters of a Łódź entrepreneur in the 1920s. Pleasant if you want to pay extra for historical ambience rather than another ten satellite channels. ❻

Dosko ul. Piłsudskiego 8 ☎042/636 0428. Simple no-frills place located on the top floor of a downtown tower block. En-suites as well as rooms with shared facilities. ❶–❹

Grand ul. Piotrkowska 72 ☎042/633 9920, ⓔlo-grand@orbis.pl. A *belle époque* establishment that for once really does live up to its name. Varying room rates due to partial renovation. ❼

Ibis al. Piłsudskiego 11 ☎042/638 6700, ⓔH3096@accor-hotels.com. Spotless modern business hotel with good service. Worth asking about weekend discounts. Breakfast 25zł extra. ❻

Polonia ul. Gabriela Narutowicza 38 ☎042/632 8773, ⓦwww.hotelspt.com.pl. Reasonably priced; a century of grime on the outside, pleasanter inside. A choice of en-suites or rooms with shared facilities. ❸–❹

Reymont ul. Legionów 81 ☎042/633 8023. Army-owned hotel. Reasonably central, with fairly standard en-suites with TV, but on a dowdy street. ❺

Światowit al. Kościuszki 68 ☎042/636 3637, ⓔswiatowit@hotelspt.com.pl. Good value in a twelve-storey downtown lump. Ask about weekend reductions. ❺

Savoy ul. Traugutta 6 (☎042/632 93 60, ⓦwww.hotelspt.com.pl). Clean, close to the station and pleasant. ❺

The City

The first sight for visitors arriving at the central train station – is the **Orthodox church** across the road. Once used by the city's Russian rulers, it's a compact example of nineteenth-century Orthodox architecture, which is something of a rarity in central Poland; though it's generally kept locked, you can get into it on Saturday mornings. A couple of blocks west of here is **ulica Piotrkowska**, a three-kilometre-long boulevard that bisects the city from north to south. Its pedestrianization and cleaning up have created a thoroughfare that now teems with life day and night and forms the clear heart of the city's activity, boasting most of the city's sights and a wide range of places to eat, drink and relax. **Rickshaws** – a relatively new addition to the urban transport scene – will whisk you from one end of Piotrkowska to the other for a few złotys. All around the Piotrkowska area you'll come across the mansions and tenements of the city's former *haute bourgeoisie*, some still peeling with age and neglect, others restored to their former splendour.

Plac Kościelny and around

Plac Kościelny, the old market square way up at the top of ul. Piotrkowska, is dominated by the twin brick towers of the neo-Gothic **Church of the Assumption**. On the other side is the rather forlorn Stary Rynek, which soon lost its original function as the hub of everyday life when the city rapidly expanded southwards.

From here, walk one block south and another west to the junction of ul. Zachodnia and ul. Ogrodowa, where you'll find one of the most complete complexes to have survived from the Industrial Revolution anywhere in Europe. On the corner itself is the haughty stone bulk of the **Pałac Poznański**, formerly the main residence of the celebrated Jewish manufacturing family. Right alongside is their still-functioning "Poltex" **factory**, behind whose monumental mock-Gothic brickwork facade are weaving and spinning mills, plus a number of warehouses, while across the street are the tenement flats of the workforce.

The Łódź Ghetto

The fate of the **Jews** of Łódź, who numbered over a quarter of a million in 1939, is undoubtedly one of the most poignant and tragic episodes of World War II, particularly as a pivotal role was played by one of their own number, **Chaim Rumkowski**. He has become the most controversial figure in modern Jewish history, widely denounced as the worst sort of collaborator, yet seen by others as a man who worked heroically to save at least some vestiges of the doomed community to which he belonged.

Within two days of the Nazi occupation of the city on September 8, the first definite anti-Semitic measures were taken, with Jews hauled at random off the streets and forced to undertake seemingly pointless manual tasks. The following month, Rumkowski, a former velvet manufacturer who had made and lost fortunes in both Łódź and Russia before turning his attentions towards charitable activities, was selected by the Nazis as the "elder" of the Jews, giving him absolute power over the internal affairs of his community and the sole right to be their spokesman and negotiator. Plans were made to turn the entire Jewish community into a vast pool of slave labour for the Nazi war machine, and the run-down suburb of **Bałuty** to the north of the centre was earmarked for this **ghetto**, partly because this was where the bulk of the Jews lived. Those who resided elsewhere were rounded up into barracks or else chosen for the first transportations to the death camps. By the following spring, the ghetto area had been sealed off from the rest of the city, and anyone who dared come near either side of its perimeter fences was shot dead.

Rumkowski soon made the ghetto a self-sufficient and highly profitable enterprise, which pleased his Nazi masters no end, even though this conclusively disproved a key tenet of their racist ideology, namely that Jews were inherently lazy and parasitical. He ruled his domain as a ruthless petty **despot**, attended by a court of sycophants and protected by his own police force and network of informers; his vanity extended to the minting of coins and manufacturing of stamps bearing his own image. Anyone who crossed him did so at their peril, as his omnipotent powers extended to the distribution of the meagre food supplies and to selecting those who had to make up the regular quotas demanded by the Nazis for deportation to the concentration camps. He cultivated a variation on the oratorical style of Hitler for his

The palace, now designated the **Muzeum Historii Miasta Łodzi** (City Historical Museum; Tues & Thurs–Sun 10am–2pm, Wed 2–6pm; 6zł, free on Sun), is an excellent example of the way Łódź's nouveaux riches aped the tastes of the aristocracy, transferring, both inside and out, the chief elements of a Baroque stately home to an urban setting. Downstairs are temporary exhibitions of modern art and photography, while up the heavily grand staircase are the showpiece chambers, the dining room and the ballroom, along with others of more modest size which are now devoted to displays on different aspects of the city's history. Archive photographs show the appearance of prewar Łódź, including the now-demolished synagogues, while there's an extensive collection of memorabilia of **Artur Rubinstein**, one of the greatest pianists of the last century. He was particularly celebrated for his performances of Chopin, and his recordings remain the interpretive touchstone for this composer. A quintessential hedonist, he was reputed to have played more music, loved more women and drunk more champagne than any other man – yet he was able to keep up the itinerant lifestyle of the modern concert virtuoso almost to the end of his ninety years.

One block southwest of the museum is the circular **plac Wolności**, with the Neoclassical town hall, regulation Kościuszko statue, and a lovely domed Greek cross-plan Uniate church, currently subject to a renovation that renders it green on the treated side, flaky blue on the other. At no. 14 on the square, the

frequent addresses to the community. The most notorious and shocking of these was his "Give me your children" speech of 1942, in which he made an emotional appeal to his subjects to send their children off to the camps, in order that able-bodied adults could be spared.

Whether or not Rumkowski knew that he was sending people to their deaths is unclear. There is no doubt that he saw the ghetto as at least the embryonic fulfilment of the **Zionist** ideal and believed that, after the Nazis had won the war, they would establish a Jewish protectorate in central Europe, with himself as its head. He also seems to have had few qualms about his role, insisting he would be prepared to submit himself for trial to a Jewish court of law once the war was over. It seems that his repeated claims to have cut the numbers demanded for each quota were true, and it's also the case that the ghetto was far from being a place with no hope. On the contrary, there was a rich communal life of schooling, concerts and theatre, and many inhabitants were inspired to make detailed diaries recording its history.

The Łódź ghetto was **liquidated** in the autumn of 1944, following a virulent dispute at the top of the Nazi hierarchy between Speer, who was keen to preserve it as a valuable contributor to the war effort, and Himmler, who was determined to enforce the "Final Solution". Some one thousand Jews were allowed to remain in Łódź to dismantle the valuable plant and machinery; Rumkowski voluntarily chose to go with the others to Auschwitz, albeit armed with an official letter confirming his special status. He died there soon afterwards, though there are three versions of how he met his end: that he was lynched by his incensed fellow Jews; that he was immediately selected for the gas chambers on account of his age; and that he was taken on a tour of the camp as a supposedly honoured guest, and thrown into the ovens without being gassed first. Had he remained in Łódź, he would have been among those who were **liberated** by the Red Army soon afterwards. Perhaps not surprisingly, the staunchest apologists for Rumkowski's policies have come from this group of survivors.

A large and fascinating collection of extracts from diaries kept by members of the ghetto, along with transcriptions of Rumkowski's speeches and many photographs, including some in colour, can be found in *The Łódź Ghetto*, edited by Alan Adelson and Robert Lapides (see "Books" in Contexts, p.730).

Muzeum Archeologiczne i Etnograficzne (Archeology and Ethnography Museum; Tues, Thurs & Fri 10am–5pm, Wed 9am–4pm, Sat 9am–3pm, Sun 10am–3pm; 5zł, free on Tues) has a wide-ranging collection of local artefacts, costumes and archeological finds.

The Muzeum Sztuki
A couple of blocks further south is the **Muzeum Sztuki** (Modern Art Gallery; Tues 10am–5pm, Wed & Fri 11am–5pm, Thurs noon–7pm, Sat & Sun 10am–4pm; 5zł, free on Thurs), at ul. Więckowskiego 36, installed in a mock-Renaissance palace with lovely stained-glass windows, which once belonged to the Poznański clan. Founded in 1925, when it was one of the world's first museums devoted to the avant-garde, it is the finest modern art collection in the country (though it also contains some earlier pieces). Major artists represented include Chagall, Mondrian, Max Ernst and Ferdinand Léger, but there's also an excellent selection of work by modern Polish painters such as Strzeminski (quite a revelation if you've not come upon his work before), Wojciechowski, Witkowski, Witkiewicz and the Jewish artist Jakiel Adler. From a memorable collection of Stalinist-era Socialist Realism, the lower-floor displays move on to the 1960s and 1970s, where, for some reason, British artists are strongly represented. The ground floor includes an assortment of "events" by contemporary artists – colour effects, bricks, rotating boxes and other everyday objects – guaranteed to raise a laugh and infuriate traditionalists. Be warned, however, that there are occasions when the permanent collection is packed away completely and replaced by a temporary loan exhibition.

Lower Ulica Piotrkowska and around
Back on **ulica Piotrkowska**, behind the *Grand* hotel, it's worth taking a detour along **ulica Moniuszki**, an uninterrupted row of plush neo-Renaissance family houses. Some six blocks south, on the east side of ul. Piotrkowska, is the large Olympia factory, followed by several more villas of the old industrial tycoons, often set in spacious grounds and showing an eclectic mix of architectural styles.

Across from them are two of the city's most important churches. The neo-Gothic **cathedral**, dedicated to St Stanisław Kosta, looks rather unprepossessing from the outside, mainly because of the cheap yellow bricks used in its construction. The interior, with its spacious feel and bright stained-glass windows, is altogether more impressive.

A little further south is the Lutheran **Kościół Św Macieja** (St Matthew's Church), a ponderous mid-nineteenth-century temple used by the descendants of the old German oligarchy. Frequent recitals are given on its Romantic-style organ, the finest instrument of its kind in Poland.

Towards the end of ul. Piotrkowska, around a thirty-minute walk from the centre, the huge **Biała Fabryka** (White Factory), at no. 282, is the oldest mechanically operated mill in the city. Part of it is now given over to the **Muzeum Włókiennictwa** (Textile Museum; Tues–Fri 9am–4pm, Sat–Sun 11am–4pm; 5zł, free on Fri), which features a large number of historic looms, documentary material on the history of the industry in Łódź and an impressive exhibition of contemporary examples of the weaver's art.

East of the centre
Łódź's newest museum, the **Księży Młyn** (Tues 10am–5pm, Wed & Fri noon–5pm, Thurs noon–7pm, Sat & Sun 11am–4pm; 5zł), is situated in the eastern part of the city at ul. Przędzalniana 72. To get here from the White Factory, it's a fifteen-minute walk along ul. Przbyszewskiego, followed by a left

Łódź's cemeteries

Perhaps appropriately, the most potent reminders of the cultural diversity of Łódź's past are its **cemeteries**. The two most worthwhile are some way from the centre of town, but are worth the effort of getting there. Of these, the Christian **Necropolis** is the more accessible in every sense: it's kept open throughout the day, and is a ten-minute walk west from the Poznański factory along ul. Ogrodowa. Of its three inter-connected plots, by far the largest is the Catholic cemetery, whose monuments, with rare exceptions, are fairly simple. Even less ostentatious is its Orthodox counterpart, containing the graves of civil servants, soldiers and policemen from the tsarist period. In contrast, the Protestant cemetery is full of appropriately grandiose memorials to deceased captains of industry. Towering over all the other graves, though now crumbling and boarded up, is the **Scheibler family mausoleum**, a miniaturized Gothic cathedral with a soaring Germanic openwork spire.

The **Jewish Cemetery**, the largest in Europe with some 180,000 tombstones (and twice as many graves), including many of great beauty, is situated on ul. Bracka, right beside the terminus of trams #1, #15 and #19. Unfortunately, due to occasional acts of desecration, it's kept locked; there will usually be someone there to let you in, though to make doubly sure ask for the key at the city centre synagogue and prayer house at ul. Zachodnia 78 before setting out.

---

turn once you reach its junction with ul. Przędzalniana; from the centre of town walk along al. Piłsudskiego and then turn right into ul. Przędzalniana; alternatively, take tram #9 and alight when you reach the palace's lakeside park. The building, which belonged to one of the leading German families, outwardly resembles the Renaissance villas built by Palladio in northern Italy. Its interiors – with the grand public rooms downstairs, the intimate family ones above – are evidence of decidedly catholic tastes, with influences ranging from ancient Rome via the Orient to Art Nouveau. The ballroom, which was added as an afterthought, is an effective pastiche of the English Tudor style.

A few minutes' walk west of here on ul. Tylna, and likewise at the corner of a park, is the **Villa Grohmanna** which is now an informally run **artists' museum** and studio (erratic hours), with a motley collection of local works and occasional exhibitions. Due north from here is the vast plac Zwycięstwa, which spans both sides of the busy al. Piłsudskiego. Its southern side is almost entirely occupied by the fortress-like Pałac Scheiblera, the former home of the most powerful of the German textile families. Part of it now houses the **Muzeum Kinematografii** (Cinematography Museum: Tues noon–5pm, Wed–Sun 10am–3pm; 4zł, free on Tues), which celebrates Łódź's status as one of Europe's major training grounds for film-makers with changing exhibitions on the history of Polish film.

Eating, drinking and entertainment

Things have improved greatly in Łódź's **restaurant**, **bar** and **café** scene, and the days when in order to have a good meal you had to make use of the hotels are over. The newly pedestrianized stretch of ul. Piotrkowska in the centre of town is the heart of the action, a two-kilometre-long strip of dining, drinking and dancing emporia.

Restaurants and snack bars

A Dong ul. Legionów 2. Trusty source of Oriental eats, with a cheap self-service section facing pl. Wolności, and a plusher restaurant on the first floor.

Dolce Vita ul. Piotrkowska 91. Basic pizzeria with filling food but not much atmosphere.

Figaro ul. Piotrkowska 92. Fancy café-restaurant offering a selection of modern European snacks and main meals in brightly lit, over-designed surroundings.

Marhaba ul. Piotrkowska 69. Indian food as well as steak-and-chips-type meals. Open late.

Quattro Piotrkowska 62. Inexpensive pizzeria and spaghetteria.

Restauracja Polska ul. Piotrkowska 12. Traditional Polish restaurant serving everything from *golonka* to rabbit, and not too expensive.

Sydon ul. Piotrkowska 103/105. Elegant sit-down place serving up meaty grill specialities with a middle-eastern theme.

Tawerna Grecka Akropol ul. Traugutta 9. Smartish place with a good range of Greek food.

U Chochoła ul. Traugutta 3. Folklore-themed restaurant with wooden bench seating, herbs hanging from the rafters, and traditional, reasonably priced Polish dishes including fish and game.

Ulica Piotrkowska 138/140. A collection of small snack bars grouped in a yard just off the main street, including Chinese, Near Eastern and European fare. Good for a lunchtime fill-up of cheap kebabs, falafel and so on.

Ziemia Obiecana ul. Wigury 4/6 ☎042/636 7081. Attatched to the *Deja Vu* pension, this is one hotel restaurant that *is* worth visiting, in a romantic, atmospheric 1920s palace with terrace seating in good weather. Not cheap, though, and reservations are a good idea.

Złota Kaczka, ul. Piotrkowska 79. Fairly smart Chinese restaurant, offering a takeaway service.

Bars and cafés

Bagdad Cafe ul. Jaracza 45. Tucked between two chemists not far from the Teatr Wielki, this is the legendary home of Łódź bohemians – although nowadays a laid-back studenty hangout, good for billiards. DJ nights at the weekend.

Blikle ul. Piotrkowska 128. Not up to the Warsaw original, but fine for coffee and dessert.

Dublin Pub ul. Struga 6/10. First-floor mega-pub featuring a roomy bar area, and a palm court-style

terrace with wicker chairs. Lots of cocktails and a varied selection of snacks.

Esperanto inside the *Grand*, see p.143. Unpretentious coffee bar (not to be confused with the hotel's grander *kawiarna* on the other side) offering up good, cheap brews and excellent cakes and ice cream.

Fabryka ul. Piotrkowska 80. Incredible pub in a former textile factory, with the longest bar in Europe, if not the world. Live rock and open late, so a good place in the early hours. Go through the archway at ul. Piotrkowska 80 and turn left at the end of the alley.

Forum Fabrikum ul. Legionów 2. Late bar-cum-club, attracting an arty clientele, and featuring anything from jazz concerts to house nights.

Irish Pub ul. Piotrkowska 77. Usually heaving, with an incredibly kitsch terrace (bales of hay, storks in nests and so on) and expensive Guinness, but lapped up by the locals as a cult venue.

JazzGa ul. Piotrkowska 17. Homely dive in an off-street courtyard, featuring a small bar area and a bigger room where jazz bands play at the weekend.

Łódź Kaliska ul. Piotrkowska 102. Wonderful pub full of mirrors and curios, hidden down an alley, but easy to find thanks to a large Statue of Liberty belonging to the disco next door.

Sęglowa 4 Sęglowa 4. Late-night drinking dive near Fabryczna train station with different styles of music on different nights and frequent DJ-driven events (look out for posters).

Wall Street pl. Komuny Paryskiej 6. Theme pub with barmen in red braces, copies of the *Wall Street Journal* lying around, and occasional karaoke.

West Side Piotrkowska 102. The main downtown weekend disco venue, with commercial techno and themed party nights, right next to the *Łódź Kaliska* bar (see above).

Entertainment

Łódź can hold its own when it comes to culture. For **theatre** there's the highly rated Teatr Nowy at ul. Więckowskiego 15 (☎042/633 4494) and the Teatr Wielki on plac Dąbrowskiego 1 (☎042/633 9960), which also presents **opera**; visiting foreign companies regularly perform at both venues. Among regular special events are the **opera festival** (March), a **ballet festival** (Lódzkie Spotkania Baletowe; May–June every odd-numbered year), and a **student theatre festival** (March). The **concert** programmes of the Philharmonic orchestra at ul. Piotrkowska 243 (☎042/637 2653) feature soloists of international renown, while the Teatr Muzyczny, ul. Połnocna 47/51 (☎042/678 3511), is the main venue for operetta and musicals.

For children, there are **puppet shows** at Arlekin, ul. 1 Maja 2 (☎042/633 0894), and Pinokio, ul. Kopernika 16 (☎042/636 6924), a couple of streets east of the ul. Zamenhofa youth hostel. There are also many **cinemas** in the city, the most centrally located being the Polonia at ul. Piotrkowska 67, the Silver Screen multiplex next to the Ibis hotel on al. Piłsudskiego, and the Bałtyk at ul. Narutowicza 20.

Check at the box office at ul. Moniuszki 5 for current **listings**, or pick up the monthly *Kalejdoskop* from the Dom Kultury's information office (see p.143).

West from Warsaw

Northwest of Warsaw, the Mazovian countryside is dominated by the meandering expanse of the **Wisła** as it continues its trek towards the Baltic Sea. Many of the towns ranged along its banks still bear the imprint of the river-bound trade they once thrived on. Of these, the most important is **Płock**, one-time capital of Mazovia, and a thriving industrial centre, that's recently been attracting some of the biggest new Western investments in Poland. With a major museum and an enjoyable historic complex, it makes an eminently worthwhile outing from Warsaw. Closer to the capital is the ancient church complex at **Czerwińsk nad Wisłą**, serviced by occasional **boat trips** along the Wisła.

Modlin Castle

Some 36km northwest of Warsaw, at the intersection of the Wisła and the Narew rivers, stand the eerie ruins of **Modlin Castle** – you can see them from the northbound E81 road to Gdańsk. A huge earth and brick fortress raised in the early nineteenth century on Napoleon's orders, the already large complex was restored and extended by Russian forces in the 1830s and 1840s; at its height, the huge complex accommodated a garrison of some 26,000 people. It was devastated during the early part of World War II, but you can still wander through the atmospheric ruins of the castle, which offer a pleasant view over the river below.

Czerwińsk nad Wisłą

CZERWIŃSK NAD WISŁĄ, around 70km from Warsaw along the main Płock turn-off just beyond Modlin, is a placid riverside village overlooking the banks of the Wisła. What pulls the crowds (and there can be plenty of them in summer) to this idyllic, out-of-the-way setting is the Romanesque church and monastery complex, one of the oldest, and finest, historic ensembles in the Mazovia region.

Sitting atop the hill above the village is the ancient **church complex**. Founded by the monks who were brought here in the early twelfth century by the dukes of Mazovia to hasten along the conversion of the region, it retains much of its original Romanesque structure, still visible amid the later Gothic and Baroque additions. The entrance, flanked by high twin towers, is through a delicately carved, brick Romanesque **portal** inside the brick facade added onto the building in the seventeenth century, its original ceiling decorated with some delightful geometrically patterned frescoes, featuring plant motifs and representations of the Virgin Mary. Inside the building, a couple of fine Romanesque stone columns have survived, as has a remarkable selection of early polychromy, notably in the **chapel** off the east aisle – its luminous Romanesque frescoes were uncovered in the 1950s during renovation work on the building. The late Gothic **bell tower** near the church, whose powerful bells are among the oldest in the country, was once the gateway to the town. If you're here during the summer season, you should be able to climb this, or one of the church towers, for a panoramic view over the flat pastoral surroundings. Round the back of the church is the **monastery complex**, now occupied by a Salesian Fathers seminary, some of whose members act as guides in summer – if you ask, you should be able to get hold of someone who speaks English to take you round. It's also worth asking to see round the **cloisters**, which contain a fine Gothic refectory and a small **museum** of local ethnography and church art (10am–dusk; 4zł), the quiet toing and froing of the seminarists blending in with the restful, contemplative feel of the whole place. There is also a parochial museum (same hours) containing sculpture, painting and craftwork.

If you haven't climbed one of the towers, there's a nice view over the river from the terrace in front of the church. With time to spare, it's also worth taking a stroll down the hill into the tumbledown **village**, which has a notable predominance of wooden houses, and on down to the riverbank, as peaceful a rural setting as you could wish for. Local **buses** to Czerwińsk run from Warszawa Zachodnia via Nowy Dwór (6 daily), a journey of an hour and a half approximately each way. Despite the summer tourist crowds, no one in the village has thought to start up a restaurant or snack bar yet, so unless the seminary invites you in for a meal, the village **shop** is the only place you'll find anything to eat.

Płock

Initial impressions of **PŁOCK**, the major town of western Mazovia, located some 115km west of Warsaw, suggest there aren't going to be many reasons to hang around for very long. First appearances can be deceiving, though, for in the midst of the sprawling industrial conurbation spread along the banks of the Wisła lies a charming **Stare Miasto**, its predominantly low-rise centre characterized by spruced-up nineteenth-century facades and quiet, flower-bedded squares.

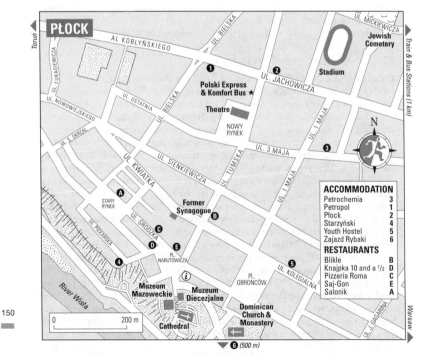

The oldest urban settlement in Mazovia, Płock became the seat of the Polish kings in the eleventh century, and remained so for nearly a hundred years. An important bishopric, and one of the number of strategically located riverside towns that grew fat on the medieval Wisła-bound commercial boom, Płock felt the full weight of mid-seventeenth-century Swedish invasions – the Płock bishopric's valuable library was purloined and taken to Uppsala, where it remains. A modern industrial centre, whose huge petrochemical works and oil refinery located just north of the town centre add a definite tang to the local air, Płock's strategic location and large workforce have made both the town and surrounding region a prime target for foreign investment, multinational jeans giants Levis among those who've established major new plants in the area.

The Stare Miasto

Nestling on a clifftop overlooking the wide expanses of the Wisła, the **Stare Miasto** area, a small central part of modern-day Płock, provides the town's main point of interest. Known locally as "little Kraków", because the important buildings are grouped together at the top of a hill, the Stare Miasto area has undergone recent excavations which have unearthed an ancient (c.400 BC) stone altar and pillar, indicating the early presence of pagan cults here. Walking down to the Stare Miasto from either the bus or train station takes you along **ulica Tumska**, a busy pedestrianized thoroughfare and the town's main shopping area. Crossing ul. Kollegialna, Tumska leads directly into the ancient core of the town.

The cathedral

First stop is the medieval **cathedral** (Mon–Sat 10am–5pm, Sun 2–5.30pm: sightseeing discouraged outside these hours), a magnificent Romanesque building begun after the installation of the Płock bishopric in 1075 and completed in the following century. A monumental basilical structure with an imposing cupola almost worthy of St Paul's in London, the cathedral was clearly intended to dominate the surroundings, an effect it definitely achieves. Successive rebuildings, the most significant of them being the classicist remodelling undertaken by Italian architect Merlini in the mid-eighteenth century, mean there are few traces left of the building's original character. The sumptuous interior decoration, however, including some ornate choir stalls and a magnificently carved pulpit, all indicate that the old-time bishops of Płock were a wealthy bunch.

Other notable features of the building are the **royal chapel** containing the Romanesque sarcophagi of Polish princes **Władysław Herman** (1040–1102) and his son, **Bolesław the Wrymouth** (Krzywousty; 1086–1138), and the Secessionist frescoes decorating parts of the building. The sculptured **bronze doors**, probably the cathedral's most famous feature, were the subject of a major piece of architectural detective work. The Romanesque originals commissioned by the bishop of Płock from the Magdeburg artist Riquin in the mid-twelfth century went missing for over six centuries, when King Władysław Jagiełło gave them to his Russian counterpart as a present, around the time his own brother became Prince of Novgorod. Subsequently hung in the entrance to the Orthodox church of St Sophia in Novgorod, and adorned with fake Cyrillic inscriptions identifying them as booty from a twelfth-century Russian expedition to Sweden, the doors were located in 1970 by a Polish academic. He had noticed the Latin inscriptions mentioning Płock on a late-nineteenth-century gypsum copy of the doors hanging in the Historical Museum in Moscow. A further bronze copy of the originals (still in Novgorod) was made for the cathedral after the discovery, and it's these you see today, two dozen **panels** filled with a magnificent series of **reliefs** depicting scenes from the Old Testament and the Gospels as well as a number of allegorical pieces. Back from the building, the skyline is dominated by the twin brick Gothic **Zegarowa** and **Szlachecka towers** beside the cathedral – the former the cathedral belfry – the best-preserved fragments of the fourteenth-century castle that once stood here.

The Muzeum Mazoweckie and the Muzeum Diocezialne

A short way from the cathedral is Płock's other major monument, the Gothic former Mazovian dukes' castle, home of the **Muzeum Mazoweckie** (Regional Museum: mid-May to Sept Tues–Thurs & Sun 9am–4pm, Fri & Sat 10am–5pm; Oct to mid-May Wed–Fri 9am–3pm, Sat & Sun 9am–4pm; 4zł), one of the oldest such exhibitions in Europe, established here by the local Historical Society in 1820. The main reason for traipsing round this museum is the superb selection of turn-of-the-twentieth-century **Secessionist** work. Art Nouveau in all its various artistic forms is represented here, with a wide array of paintings, ceramics, sculpture, glass and metalware both from the Młoda Polska movement in Poland and from other countries – Austria and Germany included – where the style gained a strong following. Anyone drawn to the sensuous curves, intricate colouring and flowing figures of *fin-de-siècle* central European art will have a field day wandering around the rich collection of objects assembled here. The really outstanding feature, however, is the re-creation of several rooms furnished and decorated as they would have been when Art Deco was in vogue. For anyone whose principal acquaintance with the style is via the architecture of Vienna and other central European cities, it will come as a revelation to see how the style was applied to the ordinary everyday business of living. Additionally, the collection of Młoda Polska-era art is hugely impressive, featuring works by Wyspiański, Witkiewicz, Mehoffer, Malczewski and Tetmajer, a veritable gallery of turn-of-the-twentieth-century Polish artists.

Directly across from the cathedral entrance is the **Muzeum Diecezjalne** (Diocesan Museum: Tues–Sat 10am–3pm, Sun 10am–4pm; 3zł), very much the Stare Miasto's "other" collection, but housing a worthy exhibition of sacral art both Polish and foreign, local archeological finds and wooden folk art nonetheless. Back up along ul. Tumska and west past the former bishop's palace, halfway down ul. Małachowskiego, is the **Płock Lyceum**, the oldest school in the country, founded in the 1180s and still going strong 800 years later. Next to it is a gallery sitting on the foundations of two recently uncovered Romanesque pillars located in the west wing of the school.

The waterfront

As you turn back towards the cathedral you'll see the **terrace** to the left of the building, overlooking the Wisła waterfront. An open, blustery spot on a fine day, it offers huge panoramas over the wide expanse of the river below, at its widest around Płock. A wooded path leads off in both directions along the clifftop, the Wisła spread below you along with the sandy promontories running out into the mainstream of the river. Walking west, refreshments can be taken at the *Hotel Starzyński*, with its terrace offering a marvellous view of the river. If you're here in summer, you'll see townsfolk stretched out on the expansive sandy **beach** just down the hill from here. Walking east from the cathedral terrace and down through the park, brings you to the Klasztor Dominikański, or **Dominican church and monastery**, a thirteenth-century edifice originally built for Duke Konrad of Mazovia, later given a predictably ornate classicist treatment. A Protestant church up until 1945, it sits isolated from the town in the middle of a park, part of the rolling woodland that covers much of the waterfront below the Stare Miasto.

Finally, there are reminders of the city's vanished Jewish population in the former **synagogue** at ul. Kwiatka 7, west of ul. Tumska, built in 1810 but now boarded up, peeling and left to go to ruin, and the untended, overgrown **Jewish cemetery** on ul. Mickiewicza, fifteen minutes' walk northeast of the centre, which contains a monument honouring local Jews who perished in the concentration camps.

Practicalities

The most convenient way of getting to Płock by public transport is to use the Warsaw-Bydgoszcz bus services run by Komfort Bus and Polski Express – both companies pick up and drop off on the Nowy Rynek, just north of the Stare Miasto. Otherwise, the regular **bus and train stations** are next to each other on the northeastern side of town, a twenty-minute walk (or a short ride on bus #20) from the centre. The PTTK office, in the Stare Miasto at (Mon–Fri 9am–5pm, Sat & Sun 9.30am–1.30pm; ☎024/262 9497) handles **tourist information**.

Most people treat Płock as a day-trip from Warsaw, although there's a reasonable choice of **accommodation** in town, beginning with the marvellously placed *Starzyński*, overlooking the river at ul. Piekarska 1 (☎024/262 4061, Ⓦwww.starzynski.com.pl; ❻), with an attached restaurant, and a disco from 10pm. The other options are the basic but friendly *Płock*, just north of the centre at al. S. Jachowicza 38 (☎024/262 9393, Ⓔhotelplock@plocman.pl; ❸); the Orbis-run *Petropol*, just down the road at no. 49 (☎024/262 4451, Ⓔpetropol@orbis.pl; ❻); the offputtingly named but spacious and comfortable *Petrochemia*, ul. 3 Maja 33 (☎024/262 4033; ❺); and the cosier, pension-style *Zajazd Rybaki* inn down by the riverbank at ul. Mostowa 5 (☎024/264 5658; ❺). Finally, there's a summer-only **youth hostel** at ul. Kolegialna 19 (☎024/262 3817; 22zł).

Both the *Zajazd Rybaki* and the *Starzyński* hotels have decent **restaurants**. Otherwise, most eating takes place in the pleasantly pedestrianized Stare Miasto area just west of the cathedral. If you're in the market for a cheap fill-up, then either *Saj-Gon*, pl. Narutowicza 1, with tasty Vietnamese and Chinese dishes in fast-food surroundings; or the fairly basic, order-at-the-counter *Pizzeria Roma* at Grodzka 13, should do the trick. *Knajpka 10 and a 1/2*, on the corner of Grodzka and Narutowicza, serves up similarly inexpensive pizzas and grills in a nice courtyard; while *Café-Restaurant Salonik*, Stary Rynek 19, concentrates on a more substantial Polish meat-and-potatoes repertoire. *Blikle*, Tumska 14, is the place for cakes and ice cream.

Drinking venues include *Rock 69*, in the same courtyard as *Knajpka 10 and a 1/2* (see above), a friendly bar that has regular live music; and *Chimera*, Tumska 5 (in the courtyard off the street), which features swirly psychedelic decor, a laid-back crowd, and occasional live music. In summer, the Stary Rynek can boast a fair sprinkling of pavement cafés, and there's a rash of outdoor bars downhill from the Stare Miasto on the banks of the Wisła – the perfect place for boozing on warm evenings, although you may have to fend off midges and other airborne creatures.

South of Warsaw

South of the city, the Wisła again provides the enduring point of definition to the flat, agricultural landscape that rapidly opens up as you leave the outer suburbs. Of the towns of the area, the legendary Hassidic centre of **Góra Kalwaria**, and the nearby Gothic castle at **Czersk**, offer the prospect of an enjoyable and eminently manageable day-trip from Warsaw.

Góra Kalwaria

Thirty-four kilometres south of Warsaw (1hr by bus from the PKS Mokotów station, close to Racławicka metro station) is **GÓRA KALWARIA**, a dusty provincial Mazovian town with a forlorn end-of-the-world feel to it, and on

In the court of the Rebbe of Góra Kalwaria

The German writer **Alfred Döblin** visited Góra Kalwaria in the 1920s. The following excerpts from his account of the visit in *Journey to Poland* (see "Books" in Contexts) gives a glimpse of the powerful atmosphere of Hassidic fervour that once enveloped the town:

One morning before seven o'clock, I set out from Warsaw with my companion; we are travelling to see the great rebbe of Gura Kalwarja. The church portals are open, beggars huddle outside, people sing inside. In the cool gray morning, we drive through the silent Sunday city; the car fills up with men in long black coats and black skullcaps. They all carry and lift packages, pouches, whole sacks, crates. We don't know where the railroad station is, but all we have to do is follow the black procession of men, the young, old, black-bearded, red-bearded Jews, whole scores of whom are now trotting along the street.

The trolley passengers gaped at the Jews, whispered, smiled: "Gura!" Now, coarse, sturdy Poles sit in the railroad carriage, with dogs and hunting rifles. At a few stations, they joke around, yell: "Gura!" but the Jews ignore them. People curiously eye me and my companion, we are both wearing European clothes; he addresses them in Yiddish, and the Jews become friendly. But will I, I get to see the rebbe: their heads sway, they whisper, they're very skeptical. These people come from far away; one of them – with a fine intelligent face – wears a round black velvet hat. He's from East Galicia; the rebbe of Gura has a large following there.

When the little train has swum along for two hours, it stops in Gura, emptying out completely. And, once again, we don't have to ask the way to the village. As we turn into the broad main street, a fantastic unsettling tableau heaves into view. This swarm of pilgrims in black – those who came with us and others – with bag and baggage, teeming along the lengthy street. These black skullcaps bobbing up and down. The yellow trees stand on either side, the sky above is pale gray, the soil tawny – between them, an almost frightening, bustling black throng moves along, hundreds of heads, shoulders serried together, an army of ants plods along, inches along. And from the other side, people trudge toward them, look down from the windows of the cottages, wave.

But the men and boys who await the travelers and come to meet them are a very special breed. They have long hair, their curls shake; the curls, twisted as tight as corkscrews, drop sideways from under the skullcaps and dangle in front of their ears, next to their cheeks, on their throats. I get a picture of what earlocks are; what a proud adornment. How proudly these men, youths, boys stride along in clean black caftans, in high shiny black caps; they look romantic, rapturous, medieval. Their faces have an extraordinary look, an earnest stillness. Some of them boast free, proud expressions. The handsome boys are festive in white stockings and beautiful slippers.

"Where is the rebbe's court?" At every step we take, we are surrounded by men (no woman walks here) who gape at us, talk among themselves. Their eyes are distrustful, chilly. It doesn't help that my companion speaks Yiddish to them nonstop. New ones keep sizing us up. I feel as if I've come upon an exotic tribe; they do not want me, me or my companion, they regard us as intruders. At the left, amid the small houses, a huge wooden gate is open. We go over there with the others, find ourselves in a vast crowded rectangular courtyard. It is closed off by a clean, simple, sprawling wooden house, one floor.

We are in the vestibule of the house. Men with raised arms emerge from the left-hand door; some men swirl towels: beyond the door lies a room for prayer and assembly.

first impressions, little to recommend the place. As often, awareness of the place's history is what gives the place its primary interest.

The Bishop of Poznań, Stefan Wierzbowski, purchased the original village in the 1660s, and set about developing the site as a pilgrimage centre, building a town on the layout of a Latin crucifix, with a long central Way of the Cross

More and more keep pouring into the room. We are the butt of universal attention. People keep coming over to me. Since I cautiously hold my tongue, my companion instantly steps in. This doesn't go on for long. Because soon we are completely wedged in, and it's every man for himself. A dreadful, incredible mobbing has begun at the door. Silently, they push, squeeze. Silently, they all press against the narrow door, which opens from time to time and closes again. This is much worse, much worse than any urban crowd that I have ever experienced. I can say nothing. I keep wishing they'd let me out. But when I see the way they cling to one another, this fierce mute doggedness, I give up. I do not jam along, I hang between the others, who pant into the back of my neck, into my ears. I let my feet hang loose, I draw up my knees, and I am carried.

Slowly – I'm almost done for – I see the crack in the door coming nearer. The door now remains open; the man inside, the doorman, is no longer able to shut it. The big bearded men in skullcaps have reached over the heads of the other, and their hairy hands have grabbed the door hinges, the door jambs; with red faces, they wordlessly pull themselves over to the door. And no one complains, no one curses. They moan.

A long arm strikes out at the men ahead of me. I see the big doorman pushing against the mass. With his left shoulder, he pushes the first few back, his long right arm beats, bangs on the fingers thrust into the door hinges, on the shoulders, on the black skullcaps. The hands let go. I cringe, he's about to reach me. But instead, he punches the chest of the man next to me, reaches out, grabs my arm. He yanks me inside. I'm at the head of the line, I see my companion standing inside, he waves me over. Another step, I'm inside the room.

An enormous, completely empty room, wooden floor, wooden walls. My companion stands in front of me with an elderly man, who points toward the window, at the right. I look there, walk over. There is a table at the window. And at the table, with his back to the light, sits a stocky, pudgy man. He keeps rocking to and fro, incessantly, now less, now more. A round black skullcap perches on the crown of his head. His head is completely wreathed in a tremendous mass of curls, dark brown, with touches of gray. Thick sheaves of curls tumble over his ears, over his cheeks, along the sides of his face all the way down to the shoulders. A full fleshy face surges out from the curls. I can't see his eyes; he doesn't look at me, doesn't look at my companion, as we stand next to the plain wooden table. The rabbi's thick hands burrow through a heap of small papers lying in front of him; slips of paper; with writing on them. He and my companion are conversing. The rabbi stops rocking, he keeps rummaging through the papers. His expression is ungracious, he never looks up for even an instant. He shakes his head. All at once, my companion says: "He says you can ask him something." I think to myself: Impossible, that's not what I'm after; I want to speak to him, not question him. But the rebbe is already speaking again, softly; I can't understand a single word of this very special Yiddish. Then, suddenly, I have his hand, a small slack fleshy hand, on mine. I am astonished. No pressure from his hand; it moves over to mine. I hear a quiet "*Sholem*," my companion says: "We're leaving." And slowly, we leave. Someone else has already come in, he puts down a slip of paper, says a few words, goes out, backward, facing the small rocking figure at the window.

Reprinted by permission of I.B. Tauris.

modelled on Jerusalem's Mount Calvary. This was a popular innovation at the time, examples of which can be found dotted around the country, notably at Kalwaria Zebrzydowska (see p.471). Legions of chapels and devotional shrines were erected on and around the two principal town axes, today's ul. Kalwarijska and Dominikańska, the majority of which were destroyed during World War II, though the basic plan remains clear. Devotional buildings that survived the Nazis include **Kaplica Pilata** (Pilate's Chapel) on ul. Dominikańska, a relatively restrained Baroque ensemble with a characteristic period cycle of Passion paintings, and the late-Baroque **Bernardine church**, now the parish church, which retains most of its original ornamentation.

However, it's the town's **Jewish connections** that really set the imagination – and at one stage, arguably, the European world – alight. Following the decision to allow Jews to settle here in 1745, Góra went on to become the seat of the famous **Hassidic dynasty** founded in the early nineteenth century by **Tzaddik (Rebbe) Meir Alter**. The fame of the rebbe spread fast among the growing ranks of the Hassidim, and by the 1850s, they were flocking to his court in Góra (known popularly as "New Jerusalem" or "Gura") from all over the western regions of the Russian Empire. The dynasty continued into this century, culminating in the leadership of **Tzaddik Abraham Mordechai Alter**, grandson of Meir Alter and founder of the deeply conservative Agudas Israel party who promoted the court at Góra as a rallying point for Orthodox Jews of all persuasions, committed to the goal of preserving traditional Orthodox Judaism from modernizing influences, Zionism included. Rebbe Alter narrowly managed to escape to Palestine before hostilities broke out in 1939: the dynasty has continued up to the present time, directed from Jerusalem.

Armed with this knowledge, a visit to Góra becomes a fascinating, though in many ways also depressing, experience. Both the **synagogue** and many of the buildings of the Hassidic court are still here today, though you certainly won't find any signs informing you where to look. The once proud squat brick synagogue is now a dilapidated old furniture workshop tucked away at the back of a filthy courtyard off ul. Pijarska (entry through the gate to no. 10) – you'll be able to make out the frame of a Star of David up in one of the windows and a small commemorative tablet on the wall. If you're brave enough to persevere, the caretaker of the adjoining building, formerly part of the Hassidic court complex, may let you in to have a look around, though there really isn't a lot to see now. Wandering through the dusty courtyards of the surrounding streets under the inquiring gaze of local residents, it requires an effort of the imagination to picture what things must have been like here when Hassidim filled the streets and houses.

If you have your own transport, or feel up to a reasonable stroll, the well-fenced and irregularly open **Jewish cemetery**, out of town past the Catholic graveyard at the end of al. Kalwarija, provides the only other tangible reminder of Jewish presence in the town – a monument to Kalwaria Jews murdered by the Nazis is visible from the roadside.

Czersk

Three kilometres east of Góra stands the village of **CZERSK**, set back from the river. From Góra, there's a picturesque six-kilometre route leading east of town down to the riverside, and south through the orchards along the banks of the Wisła to the village. If ever there were a case of having seen better days, this is it. An important medieval cloth-producing centre straddling the vital river-bound trade route, and guarded by a once-mighty **castle**, Czersk was one of the principal towns of the then independent principality of Mazovia. Decline set in from the mid-fifteenth century, when changes in the course of the Wisła eventually left the town stranded a few kilometres from the river bank and, hence, adrift from its main source of commercial opportunity. Things went from bad to worse, culminating in the devastation wreaked on the town in the course of the Swedish invasions of the mid-seventeenth century, when much of Czersk was razed to the ground. By this stage, Warsaw was on the ascent as the newly established capital of the country, and the chance of ever again aspiring to regional dominance had disappeared for good. By the early 1800s, Czersk had been reduced to a village, and to crown the humiliation, its municipal status was revoked in 1869. Aside from some brief action and destruction during World War II, things have been pretty quiet since then.

The castle

The most potent symbol of Czersk's once lofty status are the splendid ruins of its medieval **castle** (Tues–Sun 8am–8pm; 5zł), located on the edge of the town, up the road from the market square. A towering Gothic brick structure, reached by a solid bridge built in the 1760s to replace the medieval drawbridge, a considerable portion of the original fortifications are intact. Chief among these are the eight-metre-thick walls surrounding the castle and a formidable-looking set of bastions, originally somewhat lower and raised to their current towering height in the mid-1500s, when the **northeast tower** was redesigned as a gate watch. This tower, the best preserved of the three, serves as venue for **exhibitions** of regional painting, tapestry and sculpture. Moving round the inner castle area, the western tower is the only one that can be reached directly from the courtyard. It's worth climbing the staircase leading up to the very top of the **eastern tower** for the grandstand view over the surrounding countryside. Formerly the castle prison, Prince Konrad of Mazovia kept his brother Henryk the Bearded, prince of Silesia, and nephew Bolesław the Chaste, locked up in the tower's dungeons. Back in the castle courtyard, you can see the foundations of the twelfth-century castle chapel, recently uncovered by archeologists. The concerts held here at weekends in the summer are a favourite with local visitors, and there are occasional summer medieval theme fairs in the castle courtyard, complete with crossbow competitions and jousting, arranged by the mysterious sounding Warsaw Sword and Crossbow Brotherhood.

North of Warsaw

North of Warsaw, the main routes whisk you through the suburbs and out into the flat Mazovian countryside, its scattered farmland bisected by the Wisła from the west and by the smaller, and less polluted, River Narew to the east. Close to Warsaw, and popular with the increasing number of city commuters, the towns and villages are beginning to show signs of benefiting from the country's economic transformation – small industrial units, new villas and advertising boards are appearing. Slightly further afield, but still in striking distance of Warsaw, are a number of older centres, notably **Pułtusk** and **Ciechanów**, which retain the rustic feel of a traditional Mazovian market town. **Transport links** are pretty straightforward this close to the capital, a well-serviced network of **local buses** providing the most convenient way of getting around.

Pułtusk

Sixty kilometres north of Warsaw along the west bank of the River Narew stands **PUŁTUSK**, a lively provincial Mazovian market town that's a popular day-tripper's outing from Warsaw. One of the earliest towns founded in the region, and established on the site of an earlier trading settlement, for many years Pułtusk was a leading grain-trading centre on the river route to Gdańsk, the town's political influence stemming from the presence of the powerful bishops of Płock, whose seat the town was for several centuries. Pułtusk twice hit the headlines in the nineteenth century, first in 1806 when Napoleonic and Russian forces fought a major battle here – a French victory recorded alongside Bonaparte's other notable triumphs on the walls of the Arc de Triomphe – and later, in 1868, when a huge meteorite, known, unsurprisingly, as the Pułtusk meteorite, fell near the town. Badly damaged, like much of northern Mazovia, during the Soviet advance of winter 1944–45 when eighty percent of the buildings were destroyed, the town has nevertheless managed to retain its old-time market-town atmosphere, thanks, in part, to a major postwar reconstruction programme.

The Town

As often, the **Rynek** provides the main focus of the town. In the large cobbled area – at nearly 400m long, the square is claimed to be one of the biggest in Europe – a number of the original eighteenth- and nineteenth-century burghers' houses are still in evidence. These apart, the square mostly consists of surpassingly tasteful postwar reconstruction.

The imposing high Gothic brick tower tacked onto the town hall, in the middle of the square, houses the enjoyable regional **museum** (Tues–Sat 10am–4pm, Sun 10am–2pm; 4zł). Erected in the 1400s, the tower was originally part of the town's defences, subsequently serving as a craftsman's storehouse, Jesuit boarding-school house and local prison. Inside, the first-floor exhibitions cover the wealth of archeological finds uncovered when the square and surroundings were systematically excavated in the 1970s. The mostly medieval objects on display include reconstructed early wooden sailing vessels, military paraphernalia, silver and metalwork, and some fine decorated tiles from the castle area. The collection of folk art and craft on other floors comes mostly from the forested Kurpie region to the east of the town, an area noted for its strong folk artistic traditions. It's worth climbing the full six floors of the tower for the panoramic view over the town and surroundings from the top of the building – binoculars are available at the entrance.

The monumental collegiate **church** at the north end of the square is a Gothic brick basilica, remodelled in the sixteenth century by the Venetian architect Giovanni Battista. A striking feature is the arched vault of the nave, the design motif of circles connected by belts being a characteristic ornamental element of Renaissance-era churches in the Mazovia and Podlasie regions. The Renaissance Noskowski chapel modelled on the Wawel kaplica Zygmuntowska (see p.430), is a beauty, featuring a Renaissance copy of Michelangelo's famous *Pietà*, and some delicate original polychromy. More eccentric is the main rear chapel, stuffed with local Catholic standards for use on Holy Day processions and lined from floor to ceiling with blue Dordrecht tiles.

Off the southern end of the square is the town **castle**, one-time residence of the bishops of Płock, an oft-rebuilt semicircular brick structure straddled across an artificial raised mound, overlooking the banks of the Narew. A wooden fortification was in place here by the early 1300s, destroyed soon after (along with the rest of the town) by marauding Lithuanians. Rebuilt from scratch in the 1520s, the arcaded bridge leading up to the brick castle was added a century later, only to be pummelled by the Swedes in the 1650s. The castle's claim to historical fame is as the site of the first public theatre in Poland, opened here by the Jesuits in 1565. As with many towns in Mazovia, there's a Napoleonic connection too: Bonaparte stayed here with his brother Jérôme in 1806, prior to the nearby battle against Russian forces, and again in 1812 during the disastrous retreat from Moscow. It's also one of several places where he is supposed to have first met his lover-to-be, Maria Walewska.

In the 1970s, the castle was taken over by Polonia, the state-sponsored organization dedicated to maintaining links between émigré Poles and their home country. As a result the **Dom Polonii**, the official seat for all expatriate Poles, has now been converted into a luxury hotel and holiday/conference centre for the huge Polish diaspora, with émigré Poles young and old from all over the world – the USA and Germany in particular – taking part in events here throughout the year.

The **gardens**, laid out when the moat was drained and covered in the sixteenth century, lead down to the water's edge – a pleasant, tranquil place for a stroll, with sailing and other aquatic activities much in evidence during the summer season. In summer there's also a café open by the water. Back out towards the main square is the old castle **chapel**, a Renaissance structure largely rebuilt after wartime destruction.

Practicalities

The **bus station**, on the Nowy Rynek, is a ten-minute walk from the Rynek. For anyone tempted by a stay out in the country, the Dom Polonii's **hotel**, the *Zamek* (☎023/692 9000; ❻), in the castle, is an obvious but expensive option. The castle **restaurant**, housed in a magisterial dining room, is also reasonably pricey, but again worth trying, especially for the traditionally prepared duck dishes. There are some cheaper local restaurants and cafés around the main square.

Ciechanów

Continuing northwest for 40km brings you to **CIECHANÓW**, a largish, dowdy-looking Mazovian town on the main rail line to Gdańsk, where life passes slowly – someone forgot to give the place a centre. There's nothing here to get the crowds stampeding in, but if you happen to be passing through, it's worth stopping off to see the remains of the imposing fourteenth-century **Mazovian dukes' castle** stuck out on a limb on the eastern edge of town, one of the scattering of fortifications around the region originally occupied by the medieval rulers of Mazovia. A redoubtably solid-looking brick structure (the walls are over 55m high), the interior houses a minor **museum** (Tues–Sun 10am–4pm; 3zł), the main point of going being for the chance to look around the castle itself. Totally unlike the Teutonic castles of the Gdańsk region, the castle has only two towers of the original building still standing. Back into town, over the river and past the solemn neo-Gothic town hall, the **local museum**, on central ul. Sienkiewicza (Tues–Sun 10am–4pm; 4zł), is a rather unimaginatively presented display of nevertheless colourful local crafts and folk items.

The **Kościół św. Jozefa** (St Joseph's), off what passes for the main town square, is a good example of Mazovian Gothic, a high brick structure with a tiered facade arranged in thin pointed layers. The vaulted interior boasts some solid chunky-looking Gothic pillars – locally it's known as the church that writer **Ignacy Krasiński** attended regularly. Next door to the church you'll find something of a Polish rarity, a local Catholic teetotallers' club. Immediately north of town, the countryside is scattered with **military cemeteries**, a reminder of the major battle fought here in September 1939, where German forces attempting to push straight to Warsaw encountered some stiff resistance from the retreating Polish Army.

The centrally located **tourist office** at ul. 17 Stycznia 7 (Mon 9am–5pm, Tues–Fri 8am–4pm; ☎023/672 2613) can provide information on the local **accommodation** options, of which the central *Zacisze* hotel, ul. Mikołaczyka 8A (☎023/672 2046; ❷) is your best bet. For **restaurants**, try the *Zacisze* hotel or *U Bony*, ul. Sienkiewicza 81, for cheap, straightforward Polish fare.

Travel Details

Trains

Warsaw to: Białystok (12 daily; 3–4hr); Bydgoszcz (6 daily; 3hr 30min–5hr); Częstochowa (10 daily; 3–5hr); Gdańsk/Gdynia (16 daily; 3hr 30min–5hr); Jelenia Góra (4 daily; 10hr; couchettes); Katowice (14 daily; 3hr); Kielce (12 daily; 3–4hr); Kraków (18 daily; 3–6hr); Krynica (1 daily; 10–13hr; couchettes); Lublin (10 daily; 2hr 30min–3hr); Łódź (Mon–Fri hourly; Sat & Sun every 2hrs; 1hr 30min–2hr 30min); Olsztyn (8 daily; 3–5hr); Poznań (18 daily; 4hr); Przemyśl (3 daily; 6–8hr); Rzeszów (4 daily; 5–6hr); Suwałki (4 daily; 4–6hr); Świnoujście (3 daily; 10 hr; couchettes); Szczecin (5 daily; 6–8hr); Toruń (6 daily; 3–4hr); Wrocław (16 daily; 5–6hr; couchettes); Zagórz, for Sanok (2 daily; 11hr); Zakopane (2 daily; 6hr).
Łódź to: Częstochowa (4 daily; 2hr 30min–3hr 30min); Katowice (4 daily; 4hr); Kraków (1 daily; 5hr); Lublin (5 daily; 4–6hr); Warsaw (Mon–Fri hourly, Sat & Sun every 2hr; 1hr 30min–2hr 30min).

Buses

Łódź to: Warsaw (7 daily; 2hr); Bydgoszcz (3 daily; 4hr); Ciechocinek (5 daily; 3hr); Częstochowa (10 daily; 2hr 15min); Kraków (4 daily; 4hr 30min); Płock (10 daily; 2hr 30min); Toruń (4 daily; 3hr 20min).
Płock to: Bydgoszcz (7 daily; 2hr 30min); Łódź (10 daily; 2hr 30min); Toruń (10 daily; 1hr 45min).
Warsaw, Dworzec Stadion, to: Białystok (5 daily; 4hr); Lublin (6 daily; 4hr); Przemyśl (4 daily; 8hr); Suwałki (4 daily; 6hr); Zamość (2 daily; 7hr).
Warsaw, Dworzec Warszawa Zachodnia, to: Krosno (1 daily; 7hr); Mrągowo (1 daily; 5hr); Olsztyn (3 daily; 5hr); Rzeszów (1 daily; 8hr); Toruń (1 daily; 3hr 30min); Zakopane (1 daily; 7hr); Żelazowa Wola (5 daily; 1hr 40min).
Warsaw, Polski Express stop on al. Jana Pawła II, to: Białystok (3 daily; 3hr 30min); Bydgoszcz (hourly; 4hr 30min); Ciechocinek (2 daily; 3hr 30min); Częstochowa (2 daily; 4hr); Gdańsk (2 daily; 5hr); Gdynia (2 daily; 5hr 40min); Lublin (7 daily; 3hr); Łódź (7 daily; 2hr); Płock (hourly; 1hr 45min); Szczecin (2 daily; 8hr); Toruń (hourly; 3hr 40min).

Flights

Warsaw to: Gdańsk (2–4 daily; 1hr); Kraków (3–4 daily 1hr); Wrocław (1 daily; 1hr).

International trains

Warsaw to: Berlin (5 daily; 6hr 30min); Budapest (2 daily; 10hr); Cologne (1 daily; 13hr 30min); Dresden (1 daily; 10hr 30min); Kiev (2 daily; 24hr); Minsk (3 daily; 10hr); Moscow (2 daily; 21hr); Prague (2 daily; 10hr); St. Petersburg (1 daily; 30hr); Vienna (1 daily; 10hr); Vilnius (3 weekly; 11hr).

International buses

Warsaw (Warszawa Zachodnia) to: Amsterdam (2 weekly; 22hr); Berlin (1 daily; 8hr); Frankfurt (1 daily; 19hr); London (1 daily; 27hr); Paris (6 week-ly; 23hr); Prague (3 weekly; 12hr); Rome (4 week-ly; 28hr); Vilnius (2 daily; 9hr).

International flights

Warsaw to: Amsterdam (4 daily; 2hr 15min); Berlin (1 daily; 1hr 40min); Budapest (daily; 1hr 15min); Frankfurt (3 daily; 2hr); London (4 daily; 2hr 40min); Moscow (daily; 3hr); Paris (4 daily; 2hr 30min); Prague (2 daily; 1hr 45min); Riga (4 weekly; 2hr); Stockholm (5 weekly; 1hr 45min); Vienna (6 weekly; 1hr 30min).

Northeastern Poland

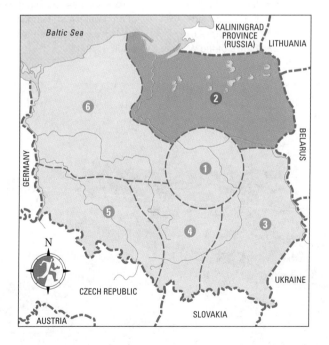

CHAPTER 2 **Highlights**

✳ **Gdańsk** An archetypal north European maritime city, full of gothic architecture, fog-bound quays, and buzzing nightlife. **P.168**

✳ **Hel** This quaint fishing village provides easy access to mile upon mile of pristine white-sand beaches. **P.198**

✳ **Malbork** The erstwhile capital of the Teutonic Knights, where their rambling red-brick castle still sprawls along the banks of the Wisła river here. **P.203**

✳ **Toruń** A lively university town packed with a jumble of medieval buildings. **P.210**

✳ **Mikołajki** Poland's prime venue for yachting, kayaking, and generally messing about in boats, situated in the heart of the Mazurian lake district. **P.247**

✳ **Białowieża national park** Europe's largest surving area of primeval forest, famous for its large population of bison. **P.283**

Northeastern Poland

ven in a country accustomed to shifts in its borders, **northeastern Poland** presents an unusually tortuous historical puzzle. Successively the domain of a Germanic crusading order, of the Hansa merchants and of the Prussians, it's only in the last forty years that the region has really become Polish. Right up until the end of World War II, large parts of the area belonged to the territories of East Prussia, and although you won't see the old place names displayed any more, even the most patriotic Pole would have to acknowledge that Gdańsk, Olsztyn and Toruń have made their mark on history under the German names of Danzig, Allenstein and Thorn. Twentieth-century Germany has left terrible scars: it was here that the first shots of World War II were fired, and the bitter fighting during the Nazi retreat in 1945 left many historic towns as sad shadows of their former selves.

Gdańsk, **Sopot** and **Gdynia** – the **Trójmiasto** (Tri-City) as they are collectively known – dominate the area from their coastal vantage point. Like Warsaw, historic Gdańsk was obliterated in World War II but it now boasts many reconstructed quarters, a booming economy and a place in history as the cradle of Solidarity. It makes an enjoyable base for exploring neighbouring **Kashubia**, to the west, with its rolling hills, lakeside forests and distinctive communities of Prussianized Slavs. While waters around the Trójmiasto are a dubious though ever-improving proposition, the **Hel Peninsula** and the coast further west make a pleasant seaside option. On the other side of the Trójmiasto, attractive, historic **Frombork**, chief of many towns in the region associated with the astronomer Nicolaus Copernicus, is an attractive and historic lagoon-side town across the water from the **Wiślana Peninsula**, a beachside holiday-makers' favourite.

South from Gdańsk, a collection of Teutonic castles and Hanseatic centres dot the banks of the Wisła and its tributaries. Highlights include the huge medieval fortress at **Malbork**, long the headquarters of the Teutonic Knights, and **Toruń**, with its spectacular medieval ensemble. Eastwards stretches

Accommodation price codes

The accommodation listed in this book has been given one of the following price codes, based, unless stated otherwise, on the cost of the cheapest double room in high season. For more details see p.39.

1 under 60zł   **4** 120–160zł   **7** 300–400zł

2 60–90zł   **5** 160–220zł   **8** 400–600zł

3 90–120 zł   **6** 220–300zł   **9** over 600zł

Mazury, Poland's biggest lakeland district, long popular with Polish holiday-makers and, increasingly, with the Germans. Canoe and yacht rental are the main attractions of its resorts, but for anyone wanting to get away from the crowds, there are much less frequented patches of water and nature to explore, both in Mazury and, above all, in the neighbouring **Suwalszczyna** and **Augustów** region.

South again, lakes give way to the forests, open plains and Orthodox villages of **Podlasie**, the border region with Belarus, centred on the city of **Białystok**.

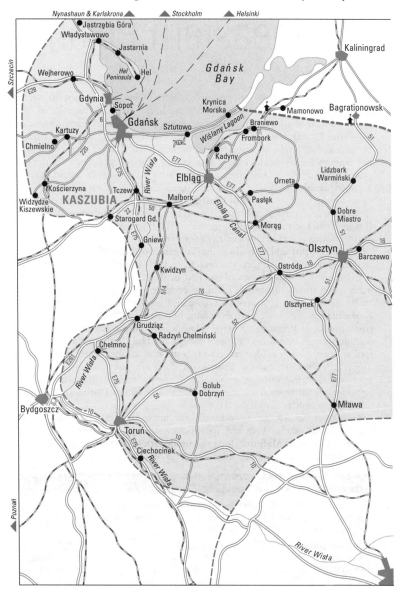

This is the obvious jumping-off point for journeys into the **Białowieża national park**, a unique area of virgin forest and home to a famous bison reserve. The Podlasie region maintains one of Poland's most fascinating ethnic mixes, with a significant **Belarusian** population and smaller communities of **Tatars**. The Nazis wiped out the **Jewish** population, but their history is important in these parts too, with one of Poland's finest synagogues well restored at **Tykocin**.

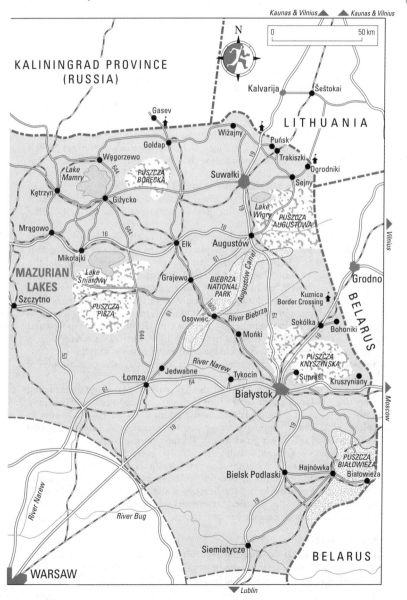

The area is covered with an extensive **public transport** network, although progress can be painfully slow once you get beyond the Gdańsk region – so you should allow plenty of time if you're keen on exploring the rural northeast. Gdańsk itself offers generous bus and train links with almost everywhere in this chapter; while Olsztyn (and to a lesser extent Mrągowo) serves as the main gateway to Mazury; and Białystok offers services to almost everywhere you'll want to visit in the east.

Gdańsk and around

For outsiders, **GDAŃSK** is perhaps the most familiar city in Poland. The home of Lech Wałęsa, Solidarity and the former Lenin Shipyards, its images flashed across a decade of news bulletins during the 1980s. Expectations formed from the newsreels are fulfilled by the industrial landscape, and suggestions of latent discontent, radicalism and future strikes are all tangible. That said, ten years of rapid economic development have given Gdańsk fresh sources of prosperity, and an image of industrial decline based on the problems of shipbuilding would not do justice to the city.

What is surprising, at least for those with no great knowledge of Polish history, is the cultural complexity of the place. Prewar Gdańsk – or **Danzig** as it then was – was forged by years of Prussian and Hanseatic domination, and the reconstructed city centre looks not unlike Amsterdam, making an elegant and bourgeois backdrop. What has changed entirely, however, is the city's demography. At the outbreak of the last war, nearly all of the 400,000 citizens were German-speaking, with fewer than 16,000 Poles. The postwar years marked a radical shift from all that went before, as the ethnic Germans were expelled and Gdańsk became Polish for the first time since 1308. Germans are returning in numbers now, chiefly as tourists and businesspeople, making an important contribution to the city's rapid emergence as one of the economic powerhouses of the country's post-communist development.

With a population of over 750,000, the **Trójmiasto** (Tri-City) conurbation comprising **Gdańsk** (itself with more than 470,000 residents), **Gdynia** and **Sopot**, ranks as one of the largest in the country. It's an enjoyable area to explore, with ferries tripping between the three centres and up to the **Hel Peninsula**, and offering a good mix of Poland's northern attractions: politics and monuments in Gdańsk, seaside chic in Sopot, gritty port life in Gdynia and sandy beaches and clean water up at the Hel Peninsula. The lakes and forests of **Kashubia** are just an hour or two from Gdańsk by bus, as are the castles of **Malbork** and **Frombork**, and the beaches of the Wiślana Peninsula. As you'd expect, Gdańsk also has excellent **transport connections** with the rest of Poland, with a host of buses, trains and flights.

Some history

The city's position at the meeting point of the Wisła and the Baltic has long made Danzig/Gdańsk an immense strategic asset: in the words of Frederick the Great, whoever controlled it could be considered "more master of Poland than any king ruling there". First settled in the **tenth century**, the city assumed prominence when the Teutonic Knights arrived in 1308, at the invitation of a population constantly threatened from the west by the Margraves of Brandenburg. The knights established themselves in their accustomed style, massacring the locals and installing a colony of German settlers in their place.

The city's economy flourished, however, and with the ending of the knights' rule in the **mid-fifteenth century** – accompanied by the brick-by-brick dismantling of their castle by the city's inhabitants – Danzig, by now an established member of the mercantile Hanseatic League, became to all intents and purposes an independent city-state, with its own legislature, judiciary and monopolies on the Wisła trade routes, restricted only by the necessity of paying homage and an annual tax to the Polish monarch. The key elements of Danzig/Gdańsk history were thus emerging: autonomy, economic power, cultural cosmopolitanism and German-Polish rivalry for control of the city.

The city's main period of development occurred between the **sixteenth century** and the Partitions of the **late eighteenth century**. An indication of the scale of the city's trading empire is given by statistics showing that the Danzig Eastland Company had a bigger turnover than even London's mighty East India Company. (One of their major exports was wood, specifically spruce, the very name of which derives from the Polish *Z Prus*, meaning "from Prussia".) Most of the important building took place at this time, as the burghers brought in Dutch and Flemish architects to design buildings that would express the city's self-confidence – hence the strikingly Hanseatic appearance. From the Renaissance period also dates a tradition of religious toleration, a pluralism that combined with trade to forge strong connections with Britain: a sizeable contingent of foreign Protestant merchants included a significant Scottish population, many of them refugees from religious persecution at home, who were granted land and rights and who lived in the city districts still known as Stare and Nowe Szkoty – Old and New Scotland. The following century, a time of continuing economic development for the city, yielded two of Gdańsk's most famous sons – astonomer Jan Heweliusz (Johannes Hevelius), who spent most of his life in the city, and Daniel Fahrenheit, inventor of the mercury thermometer.

Prussian annexation of the city, following the Partitions, abruptly severed the connection with Poland. Despite the German origins of much of the population, resistance to Prussianization and support for Polish independence were as strong in **early-nineteenth-century** Danzig as elsewhere in Prussian-ruled Poland. In 1807, a Prussian campaign to recruit soldiers to fight Napoleon yielded precisely 47 volunteers in the city. Even as German a native of Danzig as the philosopher Schopenhauer was castigated by the Prussian authorities for his "unpatriotic" attitudes. The biggest impact of Prussian annexation, however, was economic: with its links to Poland severed, Gdańsk lost its main source of trading wealth, Polish wheat.

Territorial status changed again after **World War I** and the recovery of Polish independence. The Treaty of Versailles created the semi-autonomous Free City of Danzig, terminus of the so-called Polish Corridor that sliced through West Prussia (an area heavily dominated by Germans during the nineteenth century) and connected Poland to the sea. This strip of land gave Hitler one of his major propaganda themes in the 1930s and a pretext for attacking the city: the German assault unleashed on the Polish garrison at Westerplatte on September 1, 1939 – memorably described by Günter Grass in *The Tin Drum* – was the first engagement of **World War II**. It was not until March 1945 that the city was liberated, after massive Soviet bombardment; what little remained was almost as ruined as Warsaw.

The **postwar era** brought communist rule, the expulsion of the ethnic German majority, and the formal renaming of the city as Gdańsk. The remains of the old centre were meticulously reconstructed and the traditional shipping industries revitalized. As the **communist era** began to crack at the edges, however, the shipyards became the harbingers of a new reality. Riots in Gdańsk and neighbouring Gdynia in 1970 and the strikes of 1976 were important precursors to the historic 1980 Lenin Shipyards strike, which led to the creation of **Solidarity**. The shipyards remained at the centre of resistance to General Jaruzelski's government, the last major strike wave in January 1989 precipitating the Round Table negotiations that heralded the end of communist rule. Following the traumas of "shock therapy", the reform programme pursued with vigour in the **early 1990s**, the city blossomed economically until it ranked second only to Warsaw in terms of foreign investment. Such new-found economic optimism didn't extend to the famous shipyards however, which were on the verge of bankruptcy in **1997**, when a wave of workers' protests prevented a "post-communist" government from closing down the yards altogether. This time popular sympathy for the unions didn't extend to all-out support, and the Polish prime minister felt able to publicly admonish the workers for trying to turn the country into "a new Albania" rather than a "a new Japan". The shipyards remain a powerful emotional symbol of today's Poland, but with orders falling, and with Solidarity entering the **new millennium** with its political strength in decline, it's difficult to see how they can survive in the long term.

Arrival and information

The main **train station** (Gdańsk Główny) is a ten-minute walk west of the core of the old city. The traffic speeding along Wały Jagiellońskie, the wide main road running immediately in front of the station is lethal, so be sure to take the pedestrian underpass on your way into the centre and to get to the island tram stops in the middle of the same road. The **bus station** (Dworzec PKS) is located right behind the train station across ul. 3 Maja. The city **airport** (Gdańsk-Rębiechowo; information on ☎058/348 1163), at ul. Slowackiego 200, is about 15km west of the city, a thirty-minute bus journey (#B). A taxi into town will set you back 40–45zł.

Coming **by car**, signposting into the city centre is reasonably clear, although the last leg of the journey in from Warsaw takes you along a rather tortuous approach road which gets heavy with lorries and buses. If you're arriving **by boat** from Scandinavia, you'll find yourself disembarking at the Nowy Port ferry terminal, 6km north of the city centre; ignore the unscrupulous taxi drivers congregating outside and head for the Nowy Port ferry terminal train station, 500m walk south and take one of the regular local trains into town.

Information

The helpful **tourist information centre** is at ul. Heweliusza 27 (Mon–Fri 9am–4pm; ☎058/301 4355), a five-minute walk from the train station, and has a good supply of maps and brochures, and can make hotel reservations. The **PTTK office** at ul. Długa 45, bang in the centre of the Stare Miasto (Mon–Sat 9am–6pm; ☎058/301 9327, ⓦwww.pttk.gdansk.com.pl), is very helpful between May and September when it drafts in English-speakers, though for the rest of the year it is of little use. **Almatur**, also in the centre of town at Długi

Targ 11/13 (Mon–Fri 9am–5pm, Sat 10am–2pm; ☎058/301 2931), is friend-ly and offers a similar service, arranging accommodation in student hostels (see p.173). General **online information** about the Trójmiasto is avaialable at Ⓦwww.trojmiasto.pl.

The small-format English-language **listings** guide *Gdańsk In Your Pocket* (6zł; Ⓦwww.inyourpocket.com), available from newsstands, is your best source of information on hotels, restaurants and bars throughout the Trójmiasto area. More detailed entertainment and clubbing listings appear in Polish-language publications such as the monthly *City Magazine* (given away free in bars) or the Friday edition of the daily newspaper *Gazeta Wyborcza*.

Orientation and getting around

Orientation is fairly straightforward, the main sites of interest being located in three historic districts: Główne Miasto, Stare Miasto and Stare Przedmieście. **Główne Miasto** (Main Town), the central area, is in easy walking distance of the main station. The main pedestrianized avenues, ul. Długa and its continua-tion Długi Targ, form the heart of the district, which backs east onto the attrac-tive and, in summer, very lively waterfront of the Motława Canal and the island of Spichlerze. To the north is the **Stare Miasto** (Old Town), bounded by the towering cranes of the shipyards, beyond which the suburbs of Wrzeszcz, Zaspa and Oliwa sprawl towards Sopot. South of the centre stands the quieter **Stare Przedmieście** (Old Suburb).

Travelling within the city area is pretty straightforward. A regular local **train** service, Szybka Kolej Miejska (SKM; colloquially known as the Kolejka), between Gdańsk Główny (the SKM platforms are immediately north of the main-line platforms), Sopot and Gdynia, with plenty of stops in between, runs roughly every ten minutes in the middle of the day, with services thinning out to once every hour or so in the early hours. **Tickets**, which must be validated before you get on the train, can be bought in the passage beneath the main sta-tion or at any local station (most have ticket machines). Total journey time from Gdańsk to Gdynia is 35 minutes.

Trams run within all districts of Gdańsk, and **trolleybuses** in Sopot and Gdynia, but services do not connect between the districts. **Buses**, however, operate right across the conurbation – #117, #122 and #143 connect with Sopot, #171 connects with Gdynia, while #181 connects Gdynia with Sopot. The large-scale map of Gdańsk available from kiosks and some bookshops gives all bus and tram **routes**. Tickets for both trams and buses can be bought from any kiosk, street vendor or from the driver and must be validated upon entry. You can change buses as often as you like during the period your ticket is valid, on all buses, trams and trolleybuses. The **tariffs** on trams and buses depend on the length of your journey and are unaffected by transfers – the current rate is 1zł for up to 10 minutes, 2zł for up to 30 minutes, 2.50zł for up to 45 minutes and 3zł for up to an hour; in effect you have to feed the machine when your time is up if you want to stay legal. Alternatively, an all-day ticket costs 5zł.

Ferry services, chiefly aimed at tourists, operate between Gdańsk and a number of local destinations, notably Westerplatte, Sopot, Gdynia and further out to Hel and Jastarnia (see p.197). The Gdańsk landing stage is on the main waterfront (Długie Pobrzeże) close to the Green Gate, below the waterfront promenade. In Sopot and Gdynia, it's on the pier. Current timetables (adjusted seasonally) are posted at all landing stages. **Tickets** are sold at the landing stages

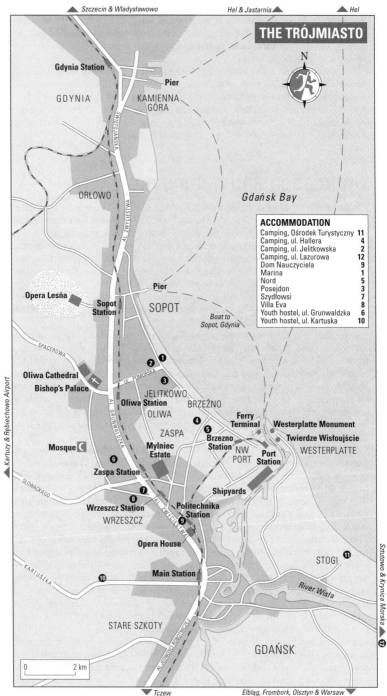

Szczecin & Władysławowo

Hel & Jastarnia

Hel

THE TRÓJMIASTO

N

Gdynia Station

Pier

GDYNIA

KAMIENNA GÓRA

ORŁOWO

Gdańsk Bay

ACCOMMODATION

Camping, Ośrodek Turystyczny	11
Camping, ul. Hallera	4
Camping, ul. Jelitkowska	2
Camping, ul. Lazurowa	12
Dom Nauczyciela	9
Marina	1
Nord	5
Posejdon	3
Szydłowsi	7
Villa Eva	8
Youth hostel, ul. Grunwaldzka	6
Youth hostel, ul. Kartuska	10

Opera Leśna

Sopot Station

Pier

SOPOT

Boat to Sopot, Gdynia

SPACEROWA

Oliwa Cathedral

Bishop's Palace

JELITKOWO

BRZEŹNO

Oliwa Station

OLIWA

ZASPA

Ferry Terminal

Westerplatte Monument

Twierdze Wisłoujście

WESTERPLATTE

Mosque

Mylniec Estate

Brzezno Station

NW PORT

Port Station

Zaspa Station

Shipyards

Wrzeszcz Station

Politechnika Station

WRZESZCZ

Opera House

STOGI

Main Station

River Wisła

STARE SZKOTY

GDAŃSK

Kartuzy & Rębiechowo Airport

Sztutowo & Krynica Morska

0   2 km

Tczew

Elbląg, Frombork, Olsztyn & Warsaw

or, occasionally on the boat itself; as an example of price, the current run between Gdańsk and Gdynia is 17zł one-way, 25zł return, with children under four travelling free. Further **information** is available on ⓣ058/301 4926.

Accommodation

As in the other big tourist cities, **accommodation** in Gdańsk ranges from the ultra-plush to the ultra-basic – and rooms in the centre are at a premium in summer. At the top end of the scale, Orbis runs a string of **hotels** aimed very firmly at Western tourists and business people. Lower down the price scale, hotels in the centre are thicker on the ground than they used to be, but if you're prepared to stay a little further out, the range of options increases considerably.

Private rooms (❷) can be arranged either with the efficient, if occasionally frosty, Gdańsk Tourist, in the mall opposite the train station at Podwale Grodzkie 8 (Mon–Fri 9am–6pm, Sat 10am–2pm). There are three **youth hostels** open year-round, all of them usually full in season when you can instead turn to the **student hostels** and **dormitories** managed by Almatur at Długi Targ 11/13 (Mon–Fri 9am–5pm, Sat 10am–2pm; ⓣ058/301 2931). All of the city's **campsites** are open from May to September.

Hotels and pensions

Dom Aktora ul. Straganiarska 55/56 ⓣ058/58/301 5901. Simple but cosy *pensjon* with good central location. Rooms are en-suite and come with TV. ❻.

Dom Harcerza ul. Za Murami 2/10 ⓣ058/58/301 4936, ⓦwww.domharcerza.prv.pl. Simple but clean rooms above a gloomy reception area shared with the Watra-Syrena cinema. Has rooms to accommodate large numbers dormitory-style (25zł), frugal doubles with shared bathrooms, and a small number of en-suite doubles with kitchenettes. ❸–❺

Dom Nauczyciela ul. Upenhaga 28 ⓣ058/341 9116. Nice location out in Wrzeszcz – a five-minute walk north of Gdańsk-Politechnika station – in a quiet side street, with a restaurant and guarded car park. Some basic singles and three-to four-person rooms, as well as en-suite doubles and doubles with shared facilities. ❷–❹

Hanza ul. Tokarska 6 ⓣ058/305 3427, ⓦwww.hanza-hotel.com.pl. Luxury hotel with lots of atmosphere right by the Motława canal. Some rooms come with dockside views. Doubles from 600zł. ❾

Hewelius ul. Heweliusza 22 ⓣ058/321 0000, ⓔhevelius@orbis.pl. Big, yellowish Orbis showpiece five minutes from the central station, with tastefully refurbished rooms, some of which have great views of the Stare Miasto. ❽

Holiday Inn Podwale Grodzkie 9 ⓣ058/300 6000, ⓦwww.holidayinn.pl/gdansk/. As comfortable and well run as you would expect from the international chain. Bang opposite the station. Doubles start at 640zł. ❾.

Jantar Długi Targ 19 ⓣ058/301 2716. Excellent location in the heart of the Stare Miasto. The decoration is socialist flashback, which adds atmosphere if of a rather dowdy kind. WCs are in the hallway. The breakfast room doubles as a ballroom at weekends with easy-listening crooning and dancing. Rooms with shower or just with sink. ❹–❺

Marina, ul. Jelitkowska 20 ⓣ058/553 2079, ⓔmarina@orbis.pl. Nine-storey white cube right on the administrative border between Gdańsk and Sopot. Rooms are bland but comfortable – and the beach is a mere 200m away. Swimming pool, tennis courts and kiddies' play area are on site. Take tram #2, #6 or #8 from the train station to the Jelitkowo terminus (a 40min ride). ❽

Nord Al. Hallera 245 ⓣ058/343 5700. Cheap, clean and basic en-suites (all with TV) in a converted 1970s apartment block in a rather uninspiring part of the Brzeźno district. Only 300m from the beach, but half an hour from the train station on tram #13. ❺

Novotel ul. Pszenna 1 ⓣ058/300 2750, ⓔngdansk@orbis.pl. A typical mid-range business hotel, though Orbis-run. Expensive for what you get. Within easy walking distance of the Stare Miasto, although the hotel itself is oddly stranded between busy highway and scruffy parking lots. ❼

Posejdon ul. Kapliczna 30 ⓣ058/511 3100,

ⓔposejdon@orbis.pl. Eight kilometres northwest of the centre in the seaside suburb of Jelikowo, this is arguably the nicest Orbis hotel in town. Balconied rooms, some with a sea view, others looking onto the woods. Indoor swimming pool and fitness centre. It's near a pleasant stretch of beach, along which you can walk to Sopot. Directions as for the *Marina* (see above). ⑥
Szydłowski Al. Grunwaldzka 114 ☎058/345 7040, ⓦwww.hotel-szydlowski.com.pl. Newish upmarket choice with plush rooms and attentive staff. Five kilometres west of the Stare Miasto on the bustling main street of the Wrzeszcz suburb. Tram #6 or #12 from the main train station or SKM train to Gdańsk-Wrzeszcz. ⑦
Villa Eva, ul. Batorego 28 ☎058/341 6785, ⓔvilla-eva@hotmail.com. Upmarket bed-and-breakfast in a quiet suburban street in Wrzeszcz. ⑥
Zaułek, ul. Ogarna 107/108 ☎058/301 4169. Sparsely furnished, slightly musty but essentially clean rooms bang in the Stare Miasto centre and very popular. Bathrooms in the hallway. ②

Hostels

Student hostels ul. Wyspiańskiego 5 (☎058/341 0955), 7 (☎058/341 4985) & 9 (☎058/341 1536). Cheap rooms in student lodgings.
Ul. Grunwaldzka 244 ☎058/341 1660. Near Oliwa in the northern Wrzeszcz suburb; take tram #6 or #12 from the central station. A decent-quality hostel inside a sports centre, with a restaurant and conference centre, which means it tends to get booked up by schools. Mostly quads (20zł per person) and doubles (②). SKM train to the Gdańsk-Zaspa station.

Ul. Kartuska 245b ☎058/302 6044. Hostel 4km west of the Stare Miasto offering beds from just 9zł per person in dorms, although there are some doubles (②). Tram #10 or #12 from the train station, or buses #161, #167 and #174 from ul. 3 Maja.
Ul. Wałowa 21. ☎058/301 2313. The closest to the centre, with prices from 11zł a night in ten-person dorms. Also some singles and doubles (①). Usually overrun with groups, so ring ahead.

Campsites

Ośrodek Turystyczny ul. Wydmy 1 ☎058/307 3915. Self-proclaimed "Tourist Centre" in the Stogi district close to the sea. About 10zł per person. Tram #13 from the train station.
Ul. Hallera 234 ☎058/343 5531. In the suburb of Brzeżno, just north of the town centre; trams #13 and #15 pass nearby from the central station. Sites cost 10zł each, and there are a few bungalows for 20zł. There's a small charge to keep cars or motorbikes overnight.
Ul. Jelitkowska 23 ☎058/553 2731. Near the beach at Jelitkowo. Regular camping facilities plus bungalows – at around 20zł a bed, a bargain if you can get one. It's a short walk from the terminus of trams #2, #4 and #6 which run from the central station.
Ul. Lazurowa 5 ☎058/308 3915. Known as the Baltic Youth Centre. Even further out in Orle, east of the city along the Martwa Wisła; bus #112 passes it. Near to a lonely beach in the middle of woods, this is definitely the campsite with the nicest location. About 10zł per person.

The City

The **Główne Miasto**, the largest of the historic quarters, is the obvious starting point for an exploration of the city; the **Stare Miasto**, across the thin ribbon of the Raduna Canal, is the natural progression. The third, southern quarter, **Stare Przedmieście,** cut off by the Podwale Przedmieskie, has its main focus for visitors in the National Museum. Moving north, out towards Sopot, is the **Oliwa** suburb with its cathedral – one of the city's most distinctive landmarks – and botanical gardens.

North along the canal, **Westerplatte** – and its monument commemorating the outbreak of World War II – can be reached by **boat** from the central waterfront (as can Gdynia, Sopot and the Hel Peninsula), a trip that allows good views of the famous **shipyards**.

The Główne Miasto

Entering the **Główne Miasto** (Main Town) is like walking straight into a Hansa merchants' settlement. The layout, typical of a medieval port, comprises a tight network of streets, bounded on four sides by water and main roads – the Raduna and Motława canals to the north and east, Podwale Przedmieskie and Wały Jagiellońskie to the south and west. The ancient appearance of this quarter's buildings is deceptive: by May 1945 the fighting between German and Russian forces had reduced the core of Gdańsk to smouldering ruins. A glance at the photos in the town hall brings home the scale of the destruction and of its reversal.

Ulica Długa and Długi Targ

Ulica Długa, the main thoroughfare, and **Długi Targ**, the wide open square on the eastern part of it, form the natural focus of attention. As with all the main streets, huge stone gateways guard both entrances. Before the western entrance to Długa, take a look round the outer **Brama Wyżynna** (Upland Gate) and the recently renovated Gothic **prison tower** which contains a gruesome museum of prison exhibits (opening hours unpredictable), some of them displayed in the torture chambers. The gate itself, built in the late sixteenth century as part of the town's outer fortifications, used to be the main entrance to Gdańsk. The three coats of arms emblazoned across the archway – Poland, Prussia and Gdańsk – encapsulate the city's history.

This gate was also the starting point of the "royal route" used by Polish monarchs on their annual state visits. After the Upland Gate they had to pass through the richly decorated **Brama Złota** (Golden Gate), reminiscent of a Roman triumphal arch, alongside **Dwór św. Jerzego** (St George's Court), a fine Gothic mansion appropriately housing the architects' society, with a statuette of St George and the Dragon on its roof – a copy of the original now housed in the National Museum in the Stare Przedmieście (see p.184). From here, ul. Długa leads down to the town hall, with several gabled facades worth studying in detail – such as the sixteenth-century **Dom Ferberów** (Ferber Mansion; no. 28), and the imposing Lwi Zamek (Lion's Castle; no. 35), where King Władysław IV entertained local dignitaries.

One of the few houses along this stretch to be open to the public is the **Dom Uphagena** at ul. Długa 12 (Uphagen Mansion; Tues–Sat 10am–4pm, Sun 11am–4pm; 5zł), former home of a leading Gdańsk merchant dynasty, rebuilt and refurnished in late-eighteenth-century style. The second-floor reception rooms are particularly lavish, each boasting wallpaper designs devoted to a particular theme: one room has butterflies, another flowers, while a third is decked out with pictures of exotic birds. Paintings of arcadian scenes from Graeco-Roman legend, and an impressive collection of Delft and Meissen porcelain, complete the picture of domestic luxury.

The town hall

Topped by a golden statue of King Sigismund August, which dominates the central skyline, the huge and well-proportioned tower of the **town hall** makes a powerful impact. Originally constructed in the late fourteenth century, with the tower and spire added later, the building was totally ruined during the last war, but the restoration was so skilful you'd hardly believe it. "In all Poland there is no other, so Polish a town hall" observed one local writer, though the foreign influences on the interior rooms might lead you to disagree. They now house the **historical museum** (Tues–Sat 10am–4pm, Sun 11am–4pm; 5zł), their lavish decorations almost upstaging the exhibits on display.

From the entrance hall an ornate staircase leads to the upper floor and the main council chamber, the **Red Room** (Sala Czerwona). Interior decoration was obviously one thing that seventeenth-century Gdańsk councillors could agree on: the colour red completely dominates the room. The chamber's sumptuous decor, mostly from the late sixteenth century, is the work of various craftsmen: its furniture was designed by a Dutch fugitive who became municipal architect of Gdańsk in the 1590s; Willem Bart of Ghent carved the ornate fireplace – note the Polish-looking Neptunes in the supports – while most of the ceiling and wall paintings were produced by another Dutchman, Johan Verberman de Vries. The central oval ceiling painting, by another Dutchman, Isaac van den Block, is titled *The Glorification of the Unity of Gdańsk with Poland*, a period panorama of the city, stressing its Polish ties. The council used this chamber only in summer; in winter they moved into the adjoining

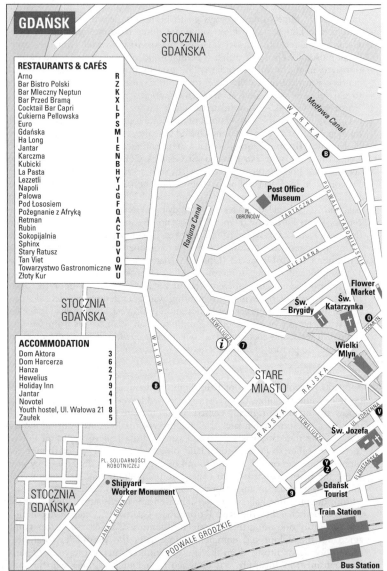

GDAŃSK

STOCZNIA GDAŃSKA

RESTAURANTS & CAFÉS

Arno	R
Bar Bistro Polski	Z
Bar Mleczny Neptun	K
Bar Przed Bramą	X
Cocktail Bar Capri	L
Cukierna Pellowska	P
Euro	S
Gdańska	M
Ha Long	I
Jantar	E
Karczma	N
Kubicki	B
La Pasta	H
Lezzetli	Y
Napoli	J
Palowa	G
Pod Łososiem	F
Pożegnanie z Afryką	Q
Retman	A
Rubin	C
Sokopijalnia	T
Sphinx	D
Stary Ratusz	O
Tan Viet	V
Towarzystwo Gastronomiczne	W
Złoty Kur	U

ACCOMMODATION

Dom Aktora	3
Dom Harcerza	6
Hanza	2
Hewelius	7
Holiday Inn	9
Jantar	4
Novotel	1
Youth hostel, Ul. Wałowa 21	8
Zaułek	5

STOCZNIA GDAŃSKA

STOCZNIA GDAŃSKA

Motława Canal

WARTKA

Raduna Canal

PODWALE STAROMIEJSKIE

TARTACZNA

PL. OBROŃCÓW

OLEJARNA

Post Office Museum

Flower Market

POMIN

Św. Brygidy

Św. Katarzynka

J. HEWELIUSZA

WALOWA

Wielki Młyn

STARE MIASTO

RAJSKA

RAJSKA

J. HEWELIUSZA

UL. KORZENNA

Św. Jozefa

ELBLĄSKA

PL. SOLIDARNOŚCI ROBOTNICZEJ

Shipyard Worker Monument

Gdańsk Tourist

JANA Z KOLNA

PODWALE GRODZKIE

Train Station

Bus Station

▼ *Wrzeszcz, Gdynia & Sopot*

smaller room, entered through the wooden door to the right of the fireplace.

As well as another reconstructed seventeenth-century fireplace, the next room, the **court room**, contains a haunting photomontage of the ruins of Gdańsk in 1945. The "before and after" illustrations show just how much reconstruction was necessary. One floor up, the **archive rooms** now house permanent exhibitions including a display of prewar Gdańsk photographs, plus temporary shows such as the display of engravings by the city's best-known

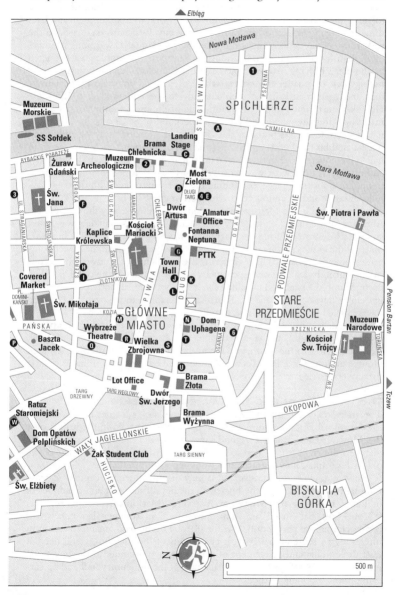

writer, Günter Grass. The old municipal finance office contains a pair of paintings by van den Block, one a forbidding representation of the Flood, and a statue of King Jagiełło taken from the neighbouring Arthur's Court.

Dwór Artusa

Immediately east of the town hall is **Dwór Artusa** (Arthur's Court; Tues–Sat 10am–4pm, Sun 11am–4pm, sometimes closed for functions; 5zł): even in a street lined with many fine mansions, this one is impressive. Recently opened to the public following extensive renovation work, the building encapsulates some fascinating aspects of the history of the city. Its origins date back to the early fourteenth century, a period marked by a widespread awakening of interest in British Arthurian legends among the European mercantile class. Attracted by the ideals of King Arthur's fabled court at Camelot, merchants began establishing their own latter-day courts, where they could entertain in the chivalrous and egalitarian spirit of their knightly forebears. Founded in 1350, the Gdańsk Court grew rapidly to become one of the most fabulous and wealthy in Europe. Initially occupied by the Brotherhood of St George, by the 1500s it had become a focal point of the city, with a growing array of guild- and trade-based brotherhoods establishing their own meeting benches in the main hall. The court's development was encouraged (and financed) by the city authorities, creating what was effectively northern Europe's first nonsectarian, nonpolitical meeting place, combining the functions of guild house, civic hall, judicial court and reception centre for foreign guests.

Reconstructed in the 1480s, with the main facade reworked by the ever-present Abraham van den Block in the early seventeenth century, the building was almost completely destroyed during the Nazi retreat in spring 1945. Mercifully, however, much of the court's rich interior was spirited away in advance of the Soviet bombardment and thus saved. Today it forms the highlight of the cavernous, reconstructed main hall and adjoining chamber, notably sections of the original ceiling decoration in the main hall including the starred vaulting, supported on a brace of graceful granite columns, and the Renaissance ceramic heating oven used to keep the assembled burghers of Gdańsk from freezing during the winter.

Immediately outside Arthur's Court is the wonderful **Fontanna Neptuna** (Neptune Fountain), the god standing, like Botticelli's *Venus*, in his shell. Continuing just to the south, you'll come to the **Złota Kamienica** (Golden House), an impressive Renaissance mansion named after the luminous gilding that covers its elegant four-storeyed facade.

The waterfront and the Muzeum Morskie

The archways of the **Brama Zielona** (Green Gate), a former royal residence for the annual visit, open directly onto the **waterfront**. From the bridge over the Motława canal you get a good view of the old granaries on Spichlerze island to the right (there used to be over 300 of them), and to the left of the old harbour quay, now a tourist hang-out and local promenade.

Halfway down is the massive and largely original fifteenth-century **Żuraw Gdański** (Gdańsk Crane), the biggest in medieval Europe; it and a number of buildings make up the **Muzeum Morskie** (Maritime Museum; Tues–Fri 9.30am–4pm, Sat–Sun 10am–4pm, closes 6pm in summer, last tickets 1hr before closing; 4zł per section, 10zł for all), one of the best-organized and most interesting in the country. To visit all sections of the museum, you'll need at least three hours and an element of patience when it comes to the ticket system: as there are different stubs for each part of the museum, you'll end up carrying round a bundle of them.

The crane itself houses a colourful and well-laid-out collection of **marine-life** specimens from around the world, a selection of sea birds, swordfish, dried starfish, delicate coral, seashells and some huge lobsters greeting you from the corners. Like their countryman Joseph Conrad, Poles have long been avid seafarers and explorers: mementoes of some of their travels around the world have been gathered together, the exhibition animated by some rollicking recordings of Polish sea shanties playing in the background. An additional bonus is the bird's-eye view of the inner workings of the massive crane from the museum rooms.

Across the street, another building houses an anthropological collection of **boats** from around the world: again, well thought out and presented. There's an enjoyable selection of vessels here, many of them painted canoes, catamarans, barques and other fishing vessels from Africa, Asia and Polynesia.

The main part of the museum is housed in three recently renovated Renaissance granaries (*spichlerze*) across the water on Ołowianka island. To get across you can take a short boat trip in the vessel moored at the waterside beneath the crane (included in the all-in ticket). The boat leaves as soon as it's full, the journey offering you a good view back onto the houses along the city waterfront. The stout-looking granaries – known as "Panna" (Virgin), "Miedź" (Copper) and "Oliwski" (Oliwa) respectively – recall the days when the bustling, international Gdańsk port reached right into the city centre.

Entitled *Polska nad Bałtykiem*, or "Poland and the Baltic Sea", the **exhibition** in the granaries comprises a rich array of items connected in some way to the city's maritime past. Everything the maritime enthusiast could want is here: model ships, paintings on stirring sea themes, ship fittings, instruments, old binoculars and compasses, and an extensive display devoted to the various stages of the traditional shipbuilding process. The biggest room houses a fearsome display of cannons mounted on their wooden rollers, a good proportion seemingly Swedish weapons dating from the mammoth assaults on the city of the 1650s and 1660s. Colourful mastheads recovered from ships, including the decorative Polish *Artus* figurehead, decorate the walls, and a series of maps illustrate the struggle for control of the Baltic over the centuries. Mannequins in sailors' outfits from different centuries provide a charming distraction, as does the rich fragrance of the wooden floors. Appropriately enough, the exhibition concludes with a display devoted to the modern struggles of the Gdańsk shipyards, the birth of Solidarity in particular.

Back out of the granaries, there's the chance to clamber around the solid-looking *Sołdek*, the first **steamship** built in Gdańsk after World War II, moored in front of the granaries. The trek through the ship's holds, crew cabins, engine and boiler rooms culminates in a display devoted to the 1980 strikes in the Gdańsk shipyards and the advent of Solidarity.

All the streets back into the town from the waterfront are worth exploring. Next up from Brama Zielona is **ulica Chlebnicka**, reached through the fifteenth-century **Brama Chlebnicka** (Bread Gate), built during the era of Teutonic rule. The Dom Angielski (English House) at no. 16, built in 1569 and the largest house in the city at the time, is a reminder of the strong Reformation-era trading connections with Britain. Close by, the **Schlieff House** (no. 16), a graceful early-sixteenth-century Gothic mansion is minus its original facade, which was spirited off to Potsdam by the Prussian ruler, Wilhelm III, where it remains.

Kościół Mariacki and around

Running parallel to ul. Chlebnicka to the north is **ulica Mariacka**, a charmingly atmospheric and meticulously reconstructed street of spindly iron railings and dragon-faced gutter spouts, its gabled terraced houses now occupied by expensive clothes and amber jewellery shops. At its western end stands the gigantic **Kościół Mariacki** (St Mary's Church), reputedly the biggest brick church in the world. Estimates that it could fit 20,000 people inside were substantiated during the early days of martial law, when huge crowds crammed the cold whitewashed interior. Overall, the building is beginning to lose some of its austerity thanks to the gradual return of elements of original decoration removed to the National Museum in Warsaw after the war. The south aisle is dominated by a copy of the miraculous **Madonna of the Gates of Dawn** from Wilno (now Vilnius in Lithuania), a city whose Polish inhabitants were encouraged to emigrate in 1945 – many of them ending up in Gdańsk, where they replaced the departing German population. Beside it, there's a memorial to the Polish Home Army fighters who liberated Wilno in 1944 – only to be rounded up and deported by the Red Army. The **high altar**, totally reconstructed after the war, is a powerful sixteenth-century triptych featuring a *Coronation of the Virgin*. Of the chapels scattered round the church, two of the most striking are the **Chapel of 11,000 Virgins**, which has a tortured Gothic crucifix for which the artist apparently nailed his son-in-law to a cross as a model, and the **St Anne's Chapel**, containing the wooden *Beautiful Madonna of Gdańsk* from around 1415. A curiosity is the reconstructed fifteenth-century **astronomical clock**, which tells not only the day, month and year but the whole saints' calendar and the phases of the moon; when completed in 1470 it was the world's tallest clock.

If you're feeling fit, make sure you climb up the church **tower** (Mon–Sat 9am–5pm, Sun 9am–1pm; 2zł). The 402 steps are graphically described in the Polish guide, which warns against anyone with claustrophobia or heart problems attempting this "cold spell of hell" as "after 130 steps you'll wish you'd given up smoking, after 150 that you'd visited the crypt instead . . .", it warns. On a good day the view over Gdańsk and the plains is excellent; for 0.5zł per minute you can hire binoculars.

After the bareness of the church, the Baroque exuberance of the domed late-seventeenth-century **Kaplica Królewska** (Royal Chapel), directly opposite on ul. Św. Ducha, and designed by Tylman of Gameren for use by the city's then minority Catholic population, makes a refreshing change, though it's often shut. The **Muzeum Archeologiczne** (Archeological Museum; Tues–Fri 9am–4pm, Sat & Sun 10am–4pm; 3zł), at the east end of ul. Mariacka, is a bit of a disappointment, perhaps unavoidably after the Maritime Museum: the exhibitions are dry and lifeless, with only the Peruvian finds lightening the tone.

From the Wielka Zbrojownia to the flower market

Ulica Piwna, another street of high terraced houses west of the church entrance, ends at the monumental **Wielka Zbrojownia** (Great Arsenal), an early seventeenth-century armoury facing the **Targ Węglowy** (Coal Market), whose appearance underscores its Flemish ancestry. Now a busy shopping centre, the coal market leads north to the Targ Drzewny (Wood Market), and on to the Stare Miasto over the other side of the canal. Ul. Szeroka, first off to the right, is another charming old street with a nice view of St Mary's from the corner with ul. Furty Groba.

The Dominican-run **Kościół św. Mikołaja** (St Nicholas' Church) on ul. Świętojańska is another fourteenth-century brick structure, the only city centre church to come through the war relatively unscathed. The interior houses a rich array of furnishings, in particular some panelled early Baroque choir stalls, a massive high altar and a fine Gothic *Pietà* in one of the nave bays, while

△ Solidarity shipyards

the **Kościół św. Jana** (St John's Church), further down the same street, is a reputedly beautiful Gothic building badly damaged during World War II and still closed for restoration. Continuing north towards the canal, at the edge of pl. Obrońców Poczty Polskiej, stands the **old post office** building immortalized by Günter Grass in *The Tin Drum*. Rebuilt after the war, it's here that a small contingent of employees of the Free City's Poczta Polska (Polish Post Office) battled it out with German forces in September 1939. As at Westerplatte the Germans clearly weren't anticipating such spirited resistance; despite the overwhelmingly superior firepower ranged against them the Poles held out for nine hours, finally surrendering when the Nazis sent in flamethrowers. Official postwar accounts maintained that the survivors were taken to the nearby Zaspa cemetery and summarily shot. At least two appear to have survived, in fact, surfacing in recent years to tell their own story.

The spiky-looking monument on the square in front of the building commemorates the event that has played an important role in the city's postwar communist mythology, the Poles' heroic resistance presented as a further vindication of the claimed "Polishness" of the city. Inside the post office there's a small **museum** (Mon & Wed–Fri 10am–4pm, Sat–Sun 10.30am–2pm; 2.50zł) mainly devoted to the events of 1939, including copies of Nazi photos of the attack on the building, and, most preciously, an urn full of soil soaked in the defenders' blood. Additionally there's an exhibition of local postal history underscoring the importance of postal communications to the city ever since its early trading days.

The terraced houses and shops tail off as you approach the outer limits of the main town, marked by several towers and other remnants of the **town wall**. **Baszta Jacek**, the tower nearest the canal, stands guard over ul. Podmłyńska, the main route over the canal into the Stare Miasto. The area around the tower provides the focus of the annual Dominican fair (Jarmark) in August (see "Entertainment", p.191). The **flower market** opposite is a fine example of the Polish attachment to the finer things of life – even when there was nothing in the food shops, you still found roses or carnations in one of the stalls here. The appeal has been somewhat diminished by the spate of stark new brick buildings erected in place of the old stalls, though nothing has yet conspired to stop the group of withered-looking traders that cluster round the market hall selling their farm produce.

The Stare Miasto and the Stocznia Gdańska

Crossing the canal bridge brings you into the **Stare Miasto** (Old Town), altogether a patchier and less reconstructed part of town characterized by a jumbled mix of old and new buildings. Dominating the waterside is the sevenstorey **Wielki Mlyn** (Great Mill), built in the mid-fourteenth century by the Teutonic Knights and another Gdańsk "largest" – in this case the biggest mill in medieval Europe. Its eighteen races milled corn for 600 years; even in the 1930s it was still grinding out 200 tons of flour a day, and local enthusiasts see no reason why it couldn't be doing the same again. The building has been converted into an upmarket shopping centre complete with glass lifts. Traces of the original building are still in evidence, notably the old foundations.

The **Kościół św. Katarzyny** (Church of St Catherine), the former parish church of the Stare Miasto, to the right of the crossway, is one of the nicest in the city. Fourteenth-century – and built in brick like almost all churches in the region – it has a well-preserved and luminous interior. The astronomer Jan Hevelius and his family are buried here in a tomb in the choir. Nearby **Kościół**

św. Brygidy (St Bridget's Church) became a local Solidarity stronghold in the 1980s, and was the local church of Lech Wałęsa, the Solidarity leader. The oil painting of the Black Madonna in a T-shirt sporting the *Solidarność* logo accurately captures the aura of what now seems like a bygone era. Although the political importance of the church is diminishing in tandem with the new political configurations of the post-communist order, it's still worth visiting places like this – ideally on a Sunday – to experience the specifically Polish mixture of religion and politics that is personified in the man whose statue watches over the church, Karol Wojtyła, aka John Paul II.

Moving further into the Stare Miasto, the merchants' mansions give way to postwar housing, the tattier bits looking like something off the set of *1984*. The most interesting part of the district is just west along the canal from the mill, centred on the **Ratusz Staromiejski** (Old Town Hall), on the corner of ul. Bielanska and Korzenna. Built by the architect of the main town hall, this delicate Renaissance construction, until recently occupied by four local government offices, has now been smartened up and converted into the new **Nadbałtyckie Centrum Kultury** (Upper Baltic Cultural Centre; daily 10am–6pm). The main ground-floor room houses a lively changing series of exhibitions, devoted to local and regional cultural and historical themes. There's also a pleasant café and bookshop, again with a historical bent. When it's not being used for receptions and other events, the place is fully open to the public – all in all, an inspired venue fully deserving of the support it has already garnered. The bronze figure in the entrance hall is of Jan Hevelius, the Polish astronomer after whom Orbis has named its nearby skyscraper hotel. Like the better-known Mr Fahrenheit, he was a Gdańsk boy.

Continuing west from the town hall, Gothic churches of **Kościół św. Jozefa** (St Joseph's Church) and **Kościół św. Elżbiety** (St Elizabeth's Church) – facing each other across ul. Elżbietańska – and the Renaissance **Dom Opatów Pelplińskich** (House of the Abbots of Pelplin) make a fine historic entourage. From here you're only a short walk through the tunnels under the main road (Podwale Grodzkie) from the train station.

The Stocznia Gdańska

Looming large in the distance are the cranes of the famous **Stocznia Gdańska** (Gdańsk Shipyards), once known as the Lenin Shipyards – Lenin's name was dropped in the late 1980s. With the Nowa Huta steelworks outside Kraków, this was the crucible of the political struggles of the 1980s.

Ten minutes' walk or one tram stop north along the main road brings you to the shipyard gates on pl. Solidarności Robotniczej. In front of them stands an ugly set of steel crosses, a **monument** to workers killed during the 1970 shipyard riots; it was inaugurated in 1980 in the presence of Party, Church and opposition leaders. A precursor to the organized strikes of the 1980s, the 1970 riots erupted when workers took to the streets in protest at price rises, setting fire to the Party headquarters after police opened fire. Riots erupted again in 1976, once more in protest at price rises on basic foodstuffs, and in August 1980 Gdańsk came to the forefront of world attention when a protest at the sacking of workers rapidly developed into a national strike.

The formation of **Solidarity**, the first independent trade union in the Soviet bloc, was a direct result of the Gdańsk strike, instigated by the Lenin Shipyards workers and their charismatic leader **Lech Wałęsa**. Throughout the 1980s the Gdańsk workers remained in the vanguard of political protest. Strikes here in 1988 and 1989 led to the Round Table Talks that forced the communist party into power-sharing and, ultimately, democratic elections.

Standing at the gates today, you may find it hard to experience this as the place where, in a sense, contemporary Poland began to take shape. Yet ironically the shipyards remain at the leading edge of political developments: unlike those at nearby Gdynia, the sprawling Gdańsk yards have always been unprofitable, and it was a post-communist government that attempted to modernize them, bitterly opposed by President Wałęsa (as he had by then become). Attempts to interest foreign investors collapsed because of the insistence that the full local workforce must be retained by any buyer. When the post-communists went ahead with "downsizing" in 1997, protests and even riots followed. Successive Polish governments have been faced by a quandary; they cannot appear hostile to Solidarity, yet they are left supporting a shipyard which, from a capitalist point of view, is a lame duck.

Of course one possibility would be to turn the whole complex into a tourist attraction. So far there's only an information hut near the main gates, a sporadically open souvenir shop and an entry gate with a few fluttering Solidarity ribbons and faded pictures of John Paul II. Best view of the yards is via a cruise to Westerplatte (see p.186).

The Stare Przedmieście

Stare Przedmieście (Old Suburb) – the lower part of old Gdańsk – was the limit of the original town, as testified by the ring of seventeenth-century bastions running east from plac Wałowy over the Motława.

The main attraction today is the **Muzeum Narodowe** (National Museum; Tues–Fri 9am–4pm, Sat & Sun 10am–4pm; Ⓦ www.muzeum.narodowe.gda.pl; 5zł), housed in a former Franciscan monastery at ul. Toruńska 1. There's enough local Gothic art and sculpture here to keep enthusiasts going all day, as well as a varied collection of fabrics, chests, gold and silverware – all redolent of the town's former wealth. The range of Dutch and Flemish art in the "foreign galleries" – Memling, the younger Brueghel, Cuyp and van Dyck are the best-known names – attests to the city's strong links with the Netherlands.

The museum's most famous work is Hans Memling's colossal *Last Judgement* (1473), the painter's earliest known work – though he was already in his thirties and a mature artist. The painting has had a more than usually chequered past, having been commissioned by the Medici in Florence, then diverted to Gdańsk, looted by Napoleon, moved to Berlin, returned to Gdańsk, stolen by the Nazis and finally, after being discovered by the Red Army, hidden in the Thuringian hills, to be returned to Gdańsk by the Russians in 1956.

Adjoining the museum is the old monastery, **Kościół św. Trójcy** (Holy Trinity Church), a towering brick Gothic structure with characteristic period net vaulting. One of the best-preserved Gothic churches in the city, the interior features a fine high altar, an assemblage of triptych pieces cobbled together following the wartime destruction of Isaac van Blocke's original, a delicately carved pulpit (the only Gothic original left in the city) and an array of other period furnishings, notably a pair of winged altar pieces.

Twierdza Wisłoujście

A half-hour bus journey from the city centre out along the Westerplatte peninsula is the old **Twierdza Wisłoujście** (Gdańsk Fortress), from which the local *kaper* defence force (see box opposite) used to guard the city port. Long neglected, it's recently been substantially renovated and is due to become a section of the city historical museum, although there's no indication of when it might open.

The kaper of Gdańsk

In a city with a tradition of cosmopolitan and independent-minded attitudes the story of Gdańsk's one-time mercenary naval defence force is instructive. Right from the city's early days, the citizen merchants of Gdańsk appreciated the need for some form of sea-based protection to keep potential invaders out. The first Polish king to try and establish a proper navy was Kazimierz Jagiełłończyk (1444–92), during his thirteen-year-long war with the Teutonic Knights. A significant portion of his navy actually consisted of local mercenaries – **kaper**, as they came to be known, after *kaap*, the Old Dutch for "ship" – who agreed to work on contract for the king, but not officially as his representatives.

The **crews** on the *kaper* vessels were a mixed bunch, the contingent of locals from the Gdańsk and Elbląg regions supplemented by an assortment of Swedish, Flemish, Scottish and Kashubian adventurers. Skilled sailors keen on risk, the *kaper* were ostensibly employed to guard the Gdańsk merchant fleet, which by the late fifteenth century was already nearly 100 vessels strong. In 1482 the newly constructed fortress at Wisłoujście became the base of their operations. Protecting the harbour aside, the *kaper* clearly weren't averse to a bit of adventuring-cum-piracy. Under the designation "the king's maritime military", King Sigismund Stary employed a *kaper* force for his assault on Moscow in 1517; their main interest, however, was actually in the Baltic port of Memling, which the *kaper* captured single-handedly under the leadership of one Adrian Flint, an English adventurer.

By the mid-sixteenth century, with their own base, ships and uniforms, the increasingly ill-disciplined *kaper* appear to have developed into a fully fledged paramilitary naval outfit capturing twenty vessels in one year (1568) alone. Recognizing that the Gdańsk *kaper* were flourishing in the vacuum left by the absence of a proper navy, King Sigismund Wasa set about creating a standing force and in 1600 asked *kaper* to work for him. It was left to King Jan Sobieski, however, to rein the *kaper* in fully, and finally to integrate them into an official Polish navy.

Designed by Dutch architects using the octagonal zigzag defence plan popular at the time, the first fortifications for the two-storey fortress were put up in the 1480s, with additions built on throughout the following century. Doubling as the main port lighthouse, the whole construction was enlarged to its current size in the mid-eighteenth century, and reinforced by Napoleon's forces in the early nineteenth. (Napoleon himself visited the place on his way to Moscow.) The city's Partition-era Prussian masters used the fortress as a jail, notably for Polish political prisoners – Jósef Piłsudski included – which probably explains why they didn't dismantle it along with all the other port fortifications in the 1870s.

Despite years of modern neglect the fortress still looks formidable: through the heavily fortified entrance you enter the main courtyard, with the high former lighthouse tower – as featured on the local Kaper beer label – in the centre. Clamber up to the top of the tower, the walls of which are lined with prints of the old Prussian plans of the fortress, for an excellent view out over the city, with the shipyards to the south and Westerplatte and beyond it the Hel Peninsula out to the north.

Back down to ground level you can wander around the ramparts, stopping now and then to peer out through the menacing cannon holes looking out onto the waters of the harbour approach – not a pretty sight for any passing assailant.

You can wander through the dank, old, sixteenth-century kitchens as well as the former commandant's room, currently being refurbished (like much of the building), and due to be converted into a tourist café/restaurant. Finally you can wander through the cavernous fortress cellars reaching down to, and in some places below, the water's edge. Big enough to hold supplies to keep the *kaper* going for a whole year, these days the smoke-blackened cellars are piled high with barrels of strawberries for jam-making, a commercial revival, apparently, of an old mercenary pastime.

There are a number of ways of getting to the fortress: after passing the huge local sulphur factory, **bus** #106 from outside the main station stops close by, continuing on to Westerplatte; a more attractive alternative is to take a **tram** or bus to Nowy Port, then a **ferry** (every half-hour in summer) across to the fortress.

Westerplatte

It was at **Westerplatte**, the promontory guarding the harbour entrance, that the German battleship *Schleswig-Holstein* fired the first salvo of World War II, on September 1, 1939. For a full week the garrison of 170 badly equipped Poles held off the combined assault of aircraft, heavy guns and over 3000 German troops, setting the tone for the Poles' response to the subsequent Nazi–Soviet invasion. The ruined army guardhouse and barracks are still there, one of the surviving buildings housing a small **museum** (May–Oct daily 9am–4pm; 3zł) chronicling the momentous events of September 1939. Beyond the museum it's a fifteen-minute walk to the main **Westerplatte Monument**, a grim, ugly-looking 1960s slab in the best Socialist Realist traditions, whose symbolism conveys a tangible sense of history. The green surroundings of the exposed peninsula make a nice, if generally blustery, walk to the coast, with good views out onto the Baltic.

You can get to Westerplatte by bus #106 or #158 from the centre, but a much better way is to take one of the tourist **boats** from the main city waterfront, just north of the Brama Zielona. (There are boats to several destinations – Gdynia, Sopot and Hel included – so make sure you're on the right one.) Taking about thirty minutes each way, the trip provides an excellent view of the **shipyards** and the array of international vessels anchored there.

Oliwa

The modern Oliwa suburb, the northernmost area of Gdańsk, has one of the best-known buildings in the city, its **cathedral**. To get here, take the local train to Gdańsk-Oliwa station, walk west across the main Sopot road, and carry on through the park.

Originally part of the monastery founded by the Danish Cistercians who settled here in the mid-twelfth century at the invitation of a local Pomeranian prince, the cathedral has seen its fair share of action over the years. First in a long line of plunderers were the Teutonic Knights, who repeatedly ransacked the place in the 1240s and 1250s. A fire in the 1350s led to a major Gothic-style overhaul, the structural essence of which remains to this day. The wars of the seventeenth century had a marked impact on Oliwa, the Swedish army carrying off much of the cathedral's sumptuous collection of furnishings as booty in 1626, the church bells and main altarpiece included. The second major Swedish assault of 1655–60 eventually led to the Oliwa Peace Treaty (1660), signed in the abbey hall: the following century brought lavish refurbishment of the building, (notably the organ, begun in 1755), most of which you can still see today. The Prussian Partition-era takeover of Gdańsk spelled the end of the fabulously wealthy abbey's glory days, the monastery finally being officially abolished in 1831. Unlike most of its surroundings, the cathedral miraculously came through the end of World War II largely unscathed, though the retreating Nazis torched the abbey complex. Today the complex is a remarkable sight, both the cathedral and the abbey having been thoroughly renovated and restored.

The cathedral

Approached from the square in front of the building, the towering main **facade** combines twin Gothic brick towers peaked with Renaissance spires and dazzling white Rococo stuccowork to unusually striking effect. The fine, late-seventeenth-century portal brings you into the lofty central **nave**, a dazzlingly exuberant structure topped by a star-spangled vaulted ceiling supported on arched pillars. Past the side chapels filling the two side aisles, the eye is immediately drawn to the **high altar**, a sumptuous Baroque piece from the 1680s containing several pictures from the Gdańsk workshops of the period, including one ascribed to Andreas Schlüter the Younger. Above the altar rises a deliciously over-the-top decorative ensemble, a swirling mass of beatific-looking cherubs being sucked into a heavenly whirlpool, surrounded by angels and with gilded sun rays breaking out in all directions, the whole thing leading towards a central stained-glass window.

Apart from some fine Baroque choir stalls and the old Renaissance high altarpiece, now in the northern transept, the building's finest – and most famous – feature is the exuberantly decorated eighteenth-century **organ** which completely fills the back of the nave. In its day the largest instrument in Europe – seven men were needed to operate the bellows – the dark heavy oak of the organ is ornamented with a mass of sumptuous Rococo woodcarving, the whole instrument framing a stained-glass window of Mary and Child, a mass of supporting angels and cherubs again filling out the picture. It's a beautiful instrument with a rich, sonorous tone and a wealth of moving parts, trumpet-blowing angels included. The 110 registers of the organ allow for an extraordinary range of pitch, and there are frequent ribcage-rippling recitals to show it off (Mon–Sat noon; free).

Passing through the gateway round the edge of the cathedral brings you into the old **Pałac Opatów** (Abbot's Palace), originally the abbey buildings. The stately main palace building now houses the **Wystawa Sztuki Współczesnej** at ul. Cystersów 15a (Modern Art Museum; Tues–Sat 9am–4pm, Sun 10am–4pm; 5zł, free on Sat). Upstairs is an enjoyable gallery of twentieth-century Polish art, the centrepiece being a large selection of 1960s Pop Art, conceptual sculptures and installations – all going to show how postwar Polish art succesfully escaped the ideological fetters of communist cultural policy. There's a whole room of works by Henryk Staszewski (1894–1988), a leading Constructivist of the interwar years who enjoyed a new lease of life from the 1950s onwards, churning out bold abstract paintings that stood in haughty opposition to the rather feeble, government-approved figurative paintings of the period. Other leading Polish avant-gardists get a look in, notably theatre director and performance artist Tadeusz Kantor, represented here by a series of trashed umbrellas; and the sculptor Władysław Hasior, whose enigmatic series of totem poles seem to draw on Catholicism, communism and consumer culture for inspiration.

Across the courtyard from the palace, an old granary contains an **ethnographic museum** (same hours; 5zł), a smallish collection of local exhibits taking you through the district's complicated historical heritage, including a section of Kashubian folk art and some icons.

Surrounding the complex is the old palace **park**, a pleasant, shaded spot verging on a botanical garden with an enjoyable collection of exotic trees, hanging willows and a stream meandering through the middle – a pleasant place for an afternoon stroll. Unfortunately the one tree you won't find here is the olive whose branches the Cistercians adopted as their symbol and after which they named the monastery they founded here. Olive motifs do crop up in the cathedral decorations around, however, most notably on the back of the high south window.

If you happen to be here on **All Souls' Day** (Nov 1), the large **cemetery** over the road is an amazing sight, illuminated by thousands of candles placed on the gravestones. Whole families come to visit the individual graves and communal memorials to the unknown dead, in a powerful display of remembrance which says much about the intertwining of Catholicism and the collective memory of national sufferings.

Around the cathedral

Like several Polish cities, Gdańsk has a small, low-profile **Tatar** community (see also "Białystok", p.268). They've recently put the finishing touches to a new **mosque** south of the cathedral; already in use by local Muslims, including the Arab student population, the mosque is at the south end of ul. Polanki, on the corner with ul. Abrahama (nearest station Gdańsk-Zaspa; trams #6, #12 and #15 also run nearby). Further up the same road, the attractive, late-eighteenth-century mansion at number 122 is where **Arthur Schopenhauer** (1788–1860), the Danzig/Gdańsk-born philosopher, grew up.

North of the cathedral is the **Trójmiejskie Park Krajobrazowy**, a hilly patch of forest behind the city, with trails and, when there's a break in the trees, refreshing views.

Eating, drinking and entertainment

In a city accustomed to tourism, finding a place to eat is relatively straightforward: there's a good range of **cafés** and **snack bars**, an increasing number of local Western **fast-food** lookalikes, and some genuinely recommendable **restaurants**. Though tourist numbers are increasing, supply more than keeps up with demand, and you should have no problem finding places. As for local specialities, fish dishes are obviously worth sampling.

Drinking in the city centres on a number of bars and cafés on ul. Długa and parallel streets to the north. In summer the attractive terrace cafés of ul. Chlebnicka and Mariacka make the ideal place to sit out and enjoy the sun – and more often than not a decent espresso. The waterfront is the centre of activity, however, with a few good spots to sit and a lot of rather tacky ones.

The **clubbing** scene in Gdańsk is constantly growing, thanks in large part to the Trójmiasto's large student population – in addition, several of the places listed as bars below offer live music and/or dancing at weekends. Dedicated clubbers should note that there's also a good range of nightlife opportunities in the **Sopot** area (see p.195).

Snack bars and cafés

Bar Mleczny Neptun ul. Długa 33. Reliable milk bar with a range of cheap meals on the menu, though a lot of them are unavailable.

Bar Bistro Polski Podwale Grodzkie 8. Bright and breezy café in the mall opposite the train station, offering scrambled-egg and pancake breakfasts,

and a lot more besides.

Bar Mleczny Syrena ul. Grunwaldzka 73, Wrzeszcz. Not in the centre, but the best place to stock your tray with wholesome Polish food.

Bar Przed Bramą Targ Sienny 1. Fast-food joint just across the main road from the Upland Gate, with good salad bar, and French fries with a range of imaginative toppings.

Cocktail Bar Capri ul. Długa 59/60. Outdoor seating in summer, good coffees and the best place in town for ice cream. Till 10pm.

Cukierna Pellowska Podwale Staromiejskie 82. Comfy sit-down café on the northwestern fringes of the Stare Miasto offering excellent coffee, scrumptious cakes, and fresh bread from the accompanying bakery. Till 7pm.

Lezzetli Podwale Grodzkie 8. Cheap kebab and pizza joint in glass-sided pavilion above the shopping mall. Comfy chairs and pot plants conjure up a loungy atmosphere.

Pożegnanie z Afryką ul. Kołodziejska 4. Part of the *Out of Africa* chain, serving good coffee till 10pm.

Sokopijalnia ul. Długa 11. Good place for fresh carrot juice, served until 8pm.

Stary Ratusz ul. Korzenna 33/5. Housed inside the Ratusz Staromiejski next to the Upper Baltic Cultural Centre, this is a good café with marble tables and a madeleine with your coffee.

Wielki Błękit ul. Jantarowa 8, at the Brzeżno pier between Gdańsk and Sopot. Spacious seafood café, with self-service counter and pleasant decor. The perfect stopoff on a beach walk from Brzeżno to Sopot.

Złoty Kur ul. Długa 4. A decent cheap restaurant/glorified milk bar, depending on your point of view, in a central location, with Delft tiles for decoration.

Restaurants

Arno ul. Tkacka 1. Straightforward cellar with some Italian dishes. Cheap and reliable.

Euro ul. Długa 79/80 (℡058/305 2383). Cosy, slightly kitsch Rococoesque place serving expensive European food, like veal escalopes with fettucine in a cream sauce. Worth splashing out on.

Gdańska ul. Świętego Ducha 16 (℡058/301 03 22). Another fairly expensive option for a good meal out; the advantage of this place is that it's open till midnight.

Ha Long ul. Szeroka 37/39. One of the best of the new central Chinese restaurants.

Jantar *Hotel Jantar*, ul. Długa 19. Pre-revolutionary decor and decent food, including breakfast. dancing at weekends

Karczma ul. Długa 18. Great-value Polish food served in folksy, wooden-bench surroundings.

Kubicki ul. Wartka 5. Generous helpings of good food in slightly murky maritime-influenced surroundings. Popular with foreign sailors, hence the multilingual menus. Till 10pm.

La Pasta ul. Szeroka 32. Unpretentious order-at-the-counter restaurant with cheap and tasty pizza and pasta dishes. Till 10pm.

Margherita ul. Cysterstów 11, Oliwa. Worth the trip to this northern suburb for fine pizzas from a brick oven. Handy if you've just been to visit Oliwa cathedral. Till 10pm.

Napoli ul. Długa 62/63. Central pizzeria with plenty of room and fast service.

Palowa ul. Długa 47. Situated underneath the Town Hall, handsome rather than cosy, and with a suitably municipal atmosphere. Meals as solid as the furnishings.

Pod Łososiem ul. Szeroka 52/3 (℡058/301 7652). One of the most luxurious restaurants in town, so you may have to book, though it's not as pricey as you might think. Specializing in seafood, it's also known locally as originator of Goldwasser vodka liqueur, a thick yellow concoction with flakes of real gold that's as Prussian as its name suggests.

Retman ul. Stągiewna 1 (℡058/301 9248). Situated by the waterfront just over from the Brama Zielona, specializing in fish dishes. A bit pricey, but the best choice for a meal out. Open till midnight.

Rubin ul. Długie Pobrzeże. Near the Brama Zielona, this floating restaurant is for refuelling at the waterfront rather than relishing a meal. Polish food.

Sphinx Długi Targ 31/32. One of the ever-growing chain of Egyptian-themed restaurants, offering hearty portions of grill food, including a few Middle Eastern specialities. Also takeaway kebab fare served from a hole in the wall. Till midnight.

Tan Viet ul. Podmłyńska 1/5. Presentable Vietnamese/Chinese restaurant close to the town centre. Open till 11pm. A little pricey.

Towarzystwo Gastronomiczne ul. Korzenna 33/35. Imaginative range of modern European cuisine served up in the basement of the Ratusz Staromiejski, catering for an arty local clientele. Diners usually linger for a spot of late-night drinking and dancing at weekends

Bars and pubs

Blue Café ul. Chmielna 103/104. Spacious modern café-bar featuring live jazz and blues, and DJ nights at weekends (anything from acid jazz to golden oldies), when there's a cover charge.

Casablanca ul. Długa 59. Pleasantly spacious café-bar located on the upper floors of the Stare Miasto's main cinema, with some comfortable couches, pool tables and Bogart-based decor. Teenage and twentysomething clientele. Open till 2am.

Celtic Pub ul. Lektykarska (off ul. Długa). Big basement pub with homely wooden benches, giant screen for music videos, and live music and dancing at weekends. Open till 2am.

Cotton Club ul. Złotników 25/29. Spacious bar/nightclub on two levels, good for billiards, and with room to sit and drink or to dance.

Gospoda pod Wielkim Młynem ul. Na Piaskich 1. Behind the Great Mill. Atmospheric place on an island between two canals feeding the mill. Good on warm nights.

Gazeta Rock Café ul. Tkacka 7/8. Friendly and fashionable basement bar decked out with pop memorabilia – styles itself as the "Museum of Polish rock". Djs and dancing at weekends.

Herbaciarnia Cztery Pory Roku ul. Ogarna 73/75. Ultra-hip (or at least ultra-hippy) tea shop with "music and oil" also on offer. Down an alley off Długi Targ. Open till midnight Tues–Sun.

Irish Pub ul. Korzenna 33/5. Cavernous venue underneath the Ratusz Staromiejski, lined with church pews and full of students. Frequent live music, and discos at weekends.

Jazz Club Długi Targ 39/40. All-ages jazz haunt with great live jazz at weekends, tacky cocktail-bar piano music and golden oldies disco on other nights. Open till 1am.

Kamienica ul. Mariacka 37/39. Cosy intimate café on two floors, good for a daytime coffee break or an evening drinking session.

Piwnica Pub ul. Podgarbary 1. Relaxed bar in a lovely barrel-vaulted cellar just off ul. Długa – one of the few pub-style places that actually feels like a real pub.

Scruffy Murphy's ul. Grunwaldzka 76/78, Wrzeszcz. Decent pub grub, decent beer, part of a pub chain that's the drinking person's *McDonald's*. Useful place to know about if you're in the

Wrzeszcz district, but not worth a special trip. Open till midnight.

Vinifera ul. Wodopój 7. A nice canal-side bar-cum-café in a doll-size house (indeed this is the little doll's house referred to in Günter Grass's *The Call of the Toad*). Open till midnight.

Vins Seńkclauze ul. Teatralna, behind Teatr Wybrzeże. The best place in town for a good glass of wine, perfect for settling down quietly with a book and a Bordeaux.

Clubs

Escape ul. 3 Maja 9a. Student disco and gig venue behind the main train station. Wed–Sat.

Iks, ul. Polanki 66. Student club beneath the dorms, a little way out of town in the Oliwa district. Thurs–Sat. Gdańsk-Przymorze SKM station.

Kazamaty ul. Doki 1. A huge all-night disco that holds 5000 and has eight bars. Cheap and crazy. Best place for a wild night out.

Kwadratowa ul. Siedlicka 4. Good-time student disco serving up a mainstream dance menu at weekends, rock and retro styles during the week. Tues–Sat.

Medyk ul. Dębowa 7. Another fun student-oriented joint, 1km west of the main train station, concentrating on top-40 hits and commercial techno. Thurs–Sat.

Olimp ul. Czyzewskiego 29. Spacious student disco in Oliwa (nearest station Gdańsk-Zabianka) concentrating on techno and chart hits. Occasional live acts.

U Boot ul. Do Studzienki 32. Yet another hedonistic student-oriented disco specializing in techno and house, in the suburb of Wrzeszcz.

Entertainment

The National Philharmonic and Opera House, al. Zwycięstwa 15 (nearest station Gdańsk-Politechnika) is one of the best **classical venues** in the country, with a varied programme of classical performances and occasional ballet productions. Information and ticket reservations are available from the box office (☎058/341 0563). In addition, there are frequent chamber music recitals at the Akademia Muzyczna, ul. Łankowa 1/2 (☎058/300 9201); in the Nadbaltyckie Centrum Kultury, ul. Korzenna 33/35 (☎058/301 1051), which is also the venue for small-scale drama productions. The main city centre **theatre** is the Wybrzeże, just behind the Wielka Zbrojownia at ul. Św. Ducha 2 (☎058/301 1328).

The principal centre-of-town **cinema** complex is at ul. Długa 57, where three separate screens, the Neptun (☎058/301 8256), Kameralne (☎058/301 5331) and Helikon (☎058/301 5331) show recent Hollywood productions with subtitles. Watra-Syrena, occupying the same building as the Dom Harcerza hotel at za Murami 2/10 (☎058/305 4564) is more art-oriented. A little way northwest of the centre, Multikino, al Zwycięstwa 14 (☎058/340 3099, ⓦwww.multikino.pl), is a brand new multiplex on the road to Wrzeszc.

The Trójmiasto boasts a variety of **festivals** and other major cultural get-togethers. The Jarmark Dominikański (Dominican Fair) held annually in the first three weeks of August is an important local event, with artists and crafts-people setting up shop in the centre of town, accompanied by street theatre and a wealth of other cultural events. Jarmark Mikołaja (St Nicholas's Fair) in the first three weeks of December is a pre-Christmas variation on the same theme. Musically there's the annual international Chamber Music Festival timed to coincide with the Jarmark Dominikański, an International Choral Festival, held in the town hall, or *ratusz* (June–Aug), and the Festival of Organ Music in Oliwa's cathedral during July and August. For film buffs, the Gdańsk Film Festival takes place in late September. Alongside the regular festivals, there's an increasing number of lively one-offs.

The main city **football** team Lechia Gdańsk have plummeted down the divisions in recent years, although they still command a hard core of local support. They play at the BKS Lechia stadium at ul. Traugutta 29; nearest station is Gdańsk-Politechnika.

There are a number of worthwhile diversions and entertainments for children in town. The open-air Cricoland **amusement park** just north of the main train station has all the usual fairground attractions: stalls, roller coasters, ghost trains, and a hall of mirrors. You pay for the rides with tokens. The **Lazurkowa** centre in Gdynia has a children's paddling pool, with open-air terraces surrounding it for parents to keep an eye on things from. The Miniatura **puppet theatre**, ul. Grunwaldzka 16 (☎058/341 94 83), is excellent: performances every Saturday and Sunday with weekday morning performances for schools. Buy tickets one hour in advance – there's a nice theatre interior, and children love the performances. Cinemas often have matinees. Check the local paper for details of performances. Finally there's the **zoo** in Oliwa at Karwińska 3, set in enjoyably forested, hilly surroundings and reached by bus #122 (open 10am–7pm summer, 10am–4pm winter).

For what's-on **listings**, check out *Co jest Grane?*, the free supplement given away with the Friday edition of *Gazeta Wyborcza*.

Listings

Airline offices LOT, ul. Wały Jagiełłońskie 2/4 ☎058/301 1161; SAS, at the airport, see p.170 ☎058/341 3111.

Airport information ☎058/348 1163.

Banks and exchange ATMs are everywhere. Kantor shops are fine for regular foreign exchange and charge no commission. The Bank Gdański inside the railway station will handle major credit cards and American Express. If you have to use travellers' cheques, use a bank, such as Narodowy Bank Polski at ul. Okopowa 1.

Books, maps and newspapers For maps, guidebooks and English-language papers and periodicals try the Empik stores on Podwale Grodzkie (opposite the central station) and at Długi Targ 25/7.

Car rental Avis, ul. Długa 76 ☎058/301 8818; Budget, at the airport, see p.170 (☎058/348 1298).

Consulates Finland, ul. Jana z Kolna 25, Gdynia ☎058/621 6852; Germany, al. Zwycięstwa 23 ☎058/341 4366; Netherlands, al. Jana Pawła II 20 ☎058/346 7618; Norway, ul. Jana z Kolna, Gdynia ☎058/621 6216; Russia, ul. Batorego 15 ☎058/341 1088; Sweden, ul. Chmielna 101/102 ☎058/300 9500; UK, ul. Grunwaldzka 100/102 ☎058/341 4365. No US consulate – the embassy in Warsaw is the nearest (see p.133).

Ferries Ferries to and from Nynashavn, Sweden, use the Novy Port terminal, opposite Westerplatte (see p.186), and are operated by Polish Baltic Shipping, ul. Przemysłowa 1 ☎058/343 1887, ⊛www.polferries.com.pl. Ferries to and from Karlskrona, Sweden, use the ferry terminal in Gdynia and are operated by Stena Line, ul. Kwiatkowskiego, Gdynia ☎058/665 1414, ⊛www.stenaline.pl. Ferry tickets are also available from Orbis, ul. Heweliusza 22 ☎058/301 4544.

Gay and lesbian contacts Lambda Gdańsk, PO Box 265, 81–806 Sopot 6. Alternatively ring the office in Warsaw (☎022/628 5222) and ask for local contacts.

Hospitals Main casualty department at al. Zwycięstwa 49 in the suburb of Wrzeszcz ☎058/302 3076.

Left luggage At the train station (daily 8am–10pm).

Parking Guarded parking is available at the main Orbis hotels and is available to non-guests for a fee: *Hewliusz*, ul. Heweliusza 22; *Marina*, ul. Jelitkowska 20; *Novotel*, ul. Pszenna 1; *Posejdon*, ul. Kapliczna 30.

Pharmacy All-night pharmacy at the main train station (Dworcowa, on the second floor) or at ul. Zwycięstwa 49 in the Wrzeszcz district, and ul. Pilotów 21 in the Zaspa district.

Police City headquarters, ul. Okopowa 15 ☎058/301 6221 or 301 1940.

Post office The main office, Poczta Główna, with poste restante (general delivery) available, is at ul. Długa 23/28 (Mon–Fri 8am–8pm, Sat 9am–3pm).

Shopping If you want to browse round a market, then the Hala Targowa on ul. Pańska has vegetables and fresh chickens outside, loads of small stalls inside. Podwale Grodzkie, opposite the train station, is the best of the modern shopping malls; ul. Długa is the place to browse for (admittedly expensive) antiques and souvenirs; and ul. Mariacka is good for amber and other jewellery.

Taxi In Gdańsk, call ☎058/9197 for Hallo Taxi; in Gdynia, call ☎058/9191 for Hallo Komputer Taxi; in Sopot call ☎058/551 0101 for Inter Taxi.

Train tickets International train tickets are available from Orbis, ul. Heweliusza 22; and from the main stations in Gdańsk and Gdynia.

Sopot

One-time stamping ground for the rich and famous, who came from all over the world to sample the casinos and the high life in the 1920s and 1930s, **SOPOT** is still a beach resort popular with landlocked Poles, and is increasingly attractive to Westerners – Germans and Swedes in particular. It has an altogether different atmosphere from its neighbour: the fashionable clothes shops and bars scattered round ul. Bohaterów Monte Cassino, the main street, seem light years away from both historic central Gdańsk and the industrial grimness of the shipyards. Sopot has always enjoyed a special position in Polish popular culture, not least because it's the place where media personalities traditionally come to see and be seen. In the early 1960s Sopot witnessed the birth of Polish beat music, with most of the era's top names beginning their careers in the *Non Stop* discotheque – Poland's answer to Liverpool's *Cavern Club*. Today, Sopot's position slap in the middle of the Trójmiasto ensures that it's more than just a summertime seaside resort. It's a year-round nightlife centre servicing the big-city populations of both Gdynia and Gdańsk, as well as a growing business centre and an enduringly fashionable place in which to live. In terms of local affluence and outside investment, it's probably been the fastest growing town in Poland over the past decade.

Arrival, information and accommodation

The simplest way to get to Sopot is by SKM **train** from Gdańsk, a twenty-minute journey. The **tourist office**, diagonally opposite the train station at ul. Dworcowa 4 (summer daily 10am–6pm; winter Mon–Fri 8am–4pm; ☎058/550 3783, ⓦwww.sopot.pl), will guide you towards private rooms (②) as well as advising on pensions and hotels. Sopot's holiday popularity means that rooms can be scarce, and during July and August, prices are often considerably increased. Best of the **campsites** are Kamienny Potok, at the northern end of the resort near the Kamienny Potok SKM station (☎058/550 0445); and *Sopot Camping* (☎058/551 6523), close to the beach at Bitwy Pod Płowcami 79, about a kilometre south of the pier.

There's an **internet** café, the *Net Cave*, in a courtyard off ul. Bohaterów at ul. Pulaskiego 7a (daily noon–9pm; ⓦwww.cave.hq.pl).

Hotels

Amber ul. Grunwaldzka 45 ☎058/550 0042. Plush, modern hotel that's is small enough to feel intimate, cosy and characterful. Only 100m south of the main street. ⑥, rising to ⑧ in July & Aug.

Chemik ul. Bitwy pod Płowcami 61 ☎058/551 1209. Frumpy concrete box with simple, spick-and-span rooms. Set back slightly from the beach, some 2km south of the pier. Bus #143 (direction Gdańsk-Oliwa) from ul. Kościuszki to the Złoty Kłos stop. A choice between en-suite rooms or those with shared facilities. ③–④

Eden ul. Kordeckiego 4/6 ☎058/551 1503. A good low-budget option, well located in the park just south of the pier, with a nautical theme. Smallish, so arrive early or ring ahead. All rooms have shared facilities. ④

Grand Hotel ul. Powstańców Warszawy ☎058/551 0041, ✉sogrand@orbis.pl. Built in the 1920s in regal period style, the *Grand* was a favourite with President de Gaulle, Giscard d'Estaing and the shah of Iran. Tarted up to suit the demands of an increasingly prominent local nouveau-riche clientele, it retains some of its former magnificence, with huge old rooms making this an enjoyable indulgence. ⑧

Irena ul. Chopina 36 ☎058/551 2073. A small, reasonably priced and well-kept *pensjonat* a short way down the hill from Sopot station. All rooms are en-suite. ⑤

Maryla ul. Sępia 22 ☎058/551 0034. A converted country maisonette with beautiful views of trees and the sea. Book early. Near Kamienny Potok SKM station; otherwise walk north along ul. Powstanców Warszawy then bear left onto Sępia, or catch bus #122 (direction Kamienny Potok) from outside the Grand Hotel. ⑥

Wanda ul. Poniatowskiego 7 ☎058/550 5725. Upmarket pension in a lovely villa right on the beach, 800m south of the pier. Difficult to get a place in July and August unless you commit yourself to a seven-day stay. ⑤

WDW (Wojskowy Dom Wypoczynkowy) ul. Kilińskiego 12 ☎058/551 0685. Big, army-owned rest home that is now a moderate-price hotel open to all-comers. Near the beach, about 1km south of the pier. En-suite rooms with shared facilities. ③–④

Zatoka ul. Emilii Plater 7/9/11 ☎058/551 2367. Reasonably priced B&B in a quiet street, right on the seaside walkway 1200m south of the Molo. All rooms are en-suite. ④

Zhong Hua al. Wojska Polskiego 1 ☎058/550 2020. Well-located upmarket hotel, right on the beach just south of the pier. Housed in a spectacular wooden building which used to be used as a bathhouse for spa tourists, and is now a Chinese restaurant. Good views from spacious rooms; worth the extra expense. ⑧

Złoty Kłos ul. Bitwy pod Płowcami 62 ☎058/551 3201, ✉zlotyklos@dech.com.pl. Concrete monster, bit like a Spanish resort hotel, on the opposite side of a busy highway from the beach, 2km south of the pier. Good facilities inside, but beware that some of the singles have shared toilets. Directions as for the *Chemik* (see above). ⑤

The Town

Most life in Sopot revolves around **ul. Bohaterów Monte Cassino**, the largely pedestrianized strip which slopes down towards the sea, and acts as both the main venue for daytime strolling and the centre of the summer nightlife scene. The street culminates in a supremely well-manicured stretch of seaside gardens which mark the entrance to Sopot's famous **pier** (*molo*). Constructed in 1928 but later rebuilt, at just over 500m it's by far the longest in the whole Baltic area – and a walk to the end is considered an essential part of the Sopot experience for visitors. Long sandy beaches stretch away on both sides; on the northern section you'll find ranks of bathing huts, some with marvellous 1920s wicker beach chairs for rent. On the southern side, a foot- and bike path leads all the way back to the northern suburbs of Gdańsk, passing endless sands and fried-fish stalls on the way – a wonderfully bracing one-hour stroll if you're so inclined.

Upper Sopot, as the western part of town is known, is a wealthy suburb of entrepreneurs, architects and artists. Here, and in other residential areas of Sopot, many of the houses have a touch of Art Nouveau style to them – look out for the turrets built for sunrise viewing. The **park** in upper Sopot offers lovely walks in the wooded hills around Łysa Góra, where there's a ski track in winter.

There's a rental service for **sailing** next to the *Grand Hotel* (see p.193), and **tennis** courts at the Klub Tenisowy, ul. Haffnera 57. For **windsurfing** go to the Sopot Sailing Club on the seaside bike path below the *Hotel Marina* at ul. Bitwy pod Płowcami 67. **Biking** along the shoreline is very pleasant; rental operations alongside the bike path in Sopot or Jelitkowo will provide cycles for a substantial deposit.

Eating, drinking and entertainment

There's a pleasing spread of **restaurants** in Sopot, both Polish and international. In summer especially, the **pier area** is full of bars, coffee shops and pleasant old milk bars, with Western-style fast-food joints making noticeable inroads of late. With the student halls not far away in the Oliwa district, and most of the pubs and cafés conveniently concentrated in the ul. Bohaterów Monte Cassino, Sopot scores over Gdańsk and Gdynia for a buzzing **nightlife**.

The open-air **Opera Leśna**, in the peaceful hilly park in the west of Sopot, hosts large-scale productions throughout the summer, including an **International Song Festival** in August which includes big names from the Western rock scene alongside homegrown performers; for tickets and current details of what's on, check with the Orbis office. The "Friends of Sopot" hold **chamber music** concerts every Thursday in the Dworek Sierakowskich, ul. Czyżewskiego 12 (off al. Bohaterów), in a room where Chopin is said to have played.

Restaurants

Balzac ul. 3 Maja 7 ☎058/551 7700. French food, luxurious surroundings, commensurate prices. Competes with *Villa Hestia* (see below) for the title of best restaurant in town.

Bar Elita ul. Podjazd 3. Cheap and stodgy Polish favourites served up milk-bar-style in unassuming surroundings just behind the train station.

Bar Przystań al. Wojska Polskiego 11. Seaside seafood café, pleasant and cheap, about 1.5km south of the pier on the path to Gdańsk. Open till at least 8pm, depending on the season and weather.

Derby Restaurant ul. Polna 70. Fine food in a swanky restaurant that does an excellent line in Polish classics and local fish.

Greenway ul. Powstańców Warszawy 2/4/6. Smart, comfortable and stylish vegetarian restaurant, housed in the Rotunda of the Sopot art gallery.

Pizzeria Brawa ul. Grunwaldzka 18. Cheap and reliable pizzeria. The place for a quick refuelling stop rather than a dinner date.

Rozmaryn ul. Ogrodowa 8 ☎058/551 1104. Mediterranean decor and a good, if pricey, pasta-based menu. Reservations recommended.

Sai-Gon ul. Grunwaldzka 8. A popular, reasonably priced Vietnamese restaurant serving up consistently reliable food.

Villa Hestia ul. Władysława IV 3/5 ☎058/551 2100. Hotel restaurant offering up a sublime mixture of Polish, French and Italian cuisine in opulent surroundings. The perfect place for a special meal if money's no object.

Zhong Hua al. Wojska Polskiego 1 ☎058/550 2019. Excellent Chinese cooking with seats outdoors and views of the sea. Not cheap, but well worth splashing out on.

Cafés and Bars

Błękitny Pudel ul. Bohaterów Monte Cassino 44. Kitsch but cosy café-pub on the main strip. Always full in the evenings.

Dworek Sierakowskich ul. Czyżewskiego 12. Refined daytime café housed in an art gallery just off ul. Bohaterów Monte Cassino. Best place in town for tea and cakes.

Galeria Kińsky ul. Kościuszki 10. Bar with antique clutter, intimate atmosphere and good coffee. Something of a shrine to crazed German actor Klaus Kinski, who was born on the premises.

Kawiaret ul. Bohaterów Monte Cassino 57/59. Café by day, bar by night. Live jazz and blues at weekends.

Language Pub ul. Pulaskiego 8/1. Cosy home-from-home pub with a Scottish theme, in the side streets just south of ul. Bohaterów Monte Cassino. Decent international beers, good crack.

Lili Marlene ul. Powstańców Warszawy 6. Open till 2am and quieter than the other bars; as there's nothing beyond it but the pier, this makes a good choice for a nightcap.

Pubkin Grunwaldzka 55. Eccentrically decorated little pub with cosy intimate feel – ring the bell for entrance.

Wieloryb ul. Pojazd 2. Upmarket bar which also does food, decked out in undersea grotto style.

Clubs

Enzym ul. Mamuszki 21. In the Park Północny, about 500m north of the Grand Hotel. The place to go for a taste of alternative-leaning, studenty dance culture. Evenings devoted to reggae and rap, plus there are ravey weekend sessions.

Galaxy Łazienki Północne. In the Park Północny, just before you get to *Enzym* (see above). A hedonistic weekend disco venue catering for the commercial end of the spectrum.

Non Stop ul. Powstańców Warszawy 2/4.

Mainstream disco doling out top-40 hits and techno to a youngish crowd. Sadly, nothing like the famous *Non Stop* club of the 1960s – that used to be located in the *Grand Hotel*.

Sfinks ul. Powstancow Warszawy 18. Art gallery-cum-club located in a pavilion in the park just beyond the Grand Hotel. Superbly atmospheric bar that's a magnet for bohemians and arty types. Live gigs and top DJ nights (cutting-edge dance music rather than the mainstream stuff) feature regularly. Sometimes operates a private-club-style door policy: ring the bell and charm the bouncer with your perfect English.

Gdynia

The northernmost section of the Trójmiasto, **GDYNIA** was originally a small Kashubian village, and the property of the Cistercian monks of Oliwa from the fourteenth to the eighteenth century. Boom time came after World War I, when Gdynia, unlike Gdańsk, returned to Polish jurisdiction. The limited coastline ceded to the new Poland – a thirty-two-kilometre strip of land stretching north from Gdynia and known as the "Polish Corridor" – left the country strapped for coastal outlets, so the Polish authorities embarked on a massive port-building programme, which by the mid-1930s had transformed Gdynia from a small village into a bustling harbour, which by 1937 boasted the largest volume of naval traffic in the Baltic region. The injustice of the Corridor's existence provided Hitler with one of his major propaganda themes, and following Gdynia's capture in 1939, the Germans deported most of the Polish population, established a naval base and, to add insult to injury, renamed the town Gotenhafen. Their retreat in 1945 was accompanied by wholesale destruction of the harbour installations, which were subsequently rebuilt from scratch by the postwar authorities. The endearingly run-down, almost seedy atmosphere of today's port makes an interesting contrast to the more cultured Gdańsk. In the 1990s, Gdynia underwent something of a transformation too: rapid privatization of state-owned shops. Thanks to Gdynia's historical position within Polish territory it's a much easier business than in the old Free City, where establishing retroactive property rights is still proving a tricky business. But in the centre of town, shopping streets like ul. Starowiejska with a brash facelift, are helping to develop Gdynia's position at the forefront of the country's burgeoning economic transformation and development.

Arrival, information and accommodation

Gdynia is half an hour's SKM journey from central Gdańsk (trains every 5–10min). You can also get there by **ferry**, calling at Sopot on the way from the Motława waterfront (2 daily; 90min; 20zł). Gdynia's **tourist office**, lurking in a corner of the main train station (Mon–Fri 10am–5pm, Sat 10am–3pm; ☎058/628 5466), can fill you in on local accommodation and sightseeing possibilities. There's an **internet café**, *websites.pl*, at ul. Świętojańska 135 (daily 8am–10pm), across the main road from the Gdynia Wgórze SKM station.

Accommodation

There's a fair spread of beds in town, most of them acceptable if not outstanding. **Private rooms (❷)** are organized by the Turus bureau diagonally opposite the train station at ul. Sarowiejska 47 (Mon–Fri 8am–6pm, Sat 10am–6pm; ☎058/621 8265). The main **youth hostel**, open all year, is at ul. Morska 108C (☎058/627 0005; ❶); take the SKM train to Gdynia-Grabówek.

Antracyt ul. Korzeniowskiego 19 ☎058/620 6571, ⓔgdynia@antracyt.home.pl. Modern medium-rise place on a bluff above the beach, in a quiet residential area 1500m south of the centre. Simple en-suites with TV on the lower floors, roomier accommodation with balconies and sea views higher up. ❺–❻

Dom Marynarza al. Piłsudskiego 1 ☎058/622 0025. Former Polish navy hostel just down the hill from the *Antracyt*. The en-suite rooms are a bit sparsely furnished for the price, although seventies nostalgia buffs will like the green/brown colour-clash interiors. ❺

Gdynia ul. Armii Krajowej 22 ☎058/666 3040, ⓔgdynia@orbis.pl. Flashy modern Orbis joint for the rich sailing contingent who hang out here in the summer. The rooms are comfy if uninspiring, and there's a decent swimming pool on site. ❼

Lark ul. Sarowiejska 1 ☎058/621 8047. Outwardly unappealing but acceptable budget place just down the hill from the station. Shared bathrooms and WCs in the hallway. ❸

Nadmorski ul. Ejsmonda 2 ☎058/622 1542, ⓦwww.nadmorski.pl. Smart ultramodern en-suites in a Bauhaus-style building right by the sea, five minutes south of the Dom Marynarza. ❼

The City

Betraying its 1930s origins, sections of the **city centre** are pure Bauhaus, with curved balconies and huge window fronts, many now on the receiving end of a much-needed facelift: the contrast with the faceless postwar concrete jungle that envelops much of the rest of the centre couldn't be more striking. The place to head for is the **port area**, directly east across town from the main station. From the train and bus stations walk down bustling ul. Starowiejska past the fountains – and, at no. 30, an interesting museum of the city's early history, the **Domek Abrahama** (Tues–Sun 10am–4pm; 2zł) – and you'll find yourself at the foot of the large southernmost **pier**. Moored on its northern side is the *Błyskawica*, a World War II destroyer now a miniature **maritime museum** (Tues–Sun 10am–4.30pm; 6zł). The sailors manning the ship are quick to point out to British visitors the decktop plaque commemorating the vessel's year-long wartime sojourn in Cowes on the Isle of Wight, where it helped to defend the port against a major German attack in May 1942. Anchored in the yacht basin beyond the ferry embarkation point is another proudly Polish vessel, the three-masted frigate *Dar Pomorża,* built in Hamburg in 1909 and now a training ship; guided tours are given when it's in dock (summer daily 10am–6pm; winter Tues–Sun 10am–4pm; 5zł), and there is an exhibition of Polish wanderlust entitled "Poles at Cape Horn". At the very end of the pier, a hamfisted monument to Polish seafarer and novelist Joseph Conrad stands near the **aquarium** (daily 9am–6.30pm; 7.50zł), home to piranhas, barracudas, sharks, and a couple of educative exhibitions. A walk along the north side of the pier takes you past the welter of yachts kept here by the growing number of seriously wealthy Poles.

If you want more local maritime history, the **naval museum** at ul. Sedzickiego 3, south of the pier (Tues–Sun 10am–5pm; 3zł), fills in the details of Polish seafaring from early Slav times to World War II, though its value to foreigners is limited by the minimal, Polish-only captioning. To complete the tour there's a nice view over the harbour from the hilltop of Kamienna Góra, a short walk south of the town centre.

Eating, drinking and entertainment

Gdynia is the least affluent part of the Trójmiasto, with a more run-down air than its neighbours. As a consequence it lacks the range of **eating and drinking** venues enjoyed by Sopot and Gdańsk, though there are a few places worth seeking out. For a quick bite, there are several fish-and-chip huts down by the pier.

The **Teatr Muzyczny** (Musical Theatre), pl. Grunwaldzki 1, near the *Gdynia* hotel, is a favourite venue with Poles and tourists alike, featuring quality Polish musicals, as well as all-too-frequent productions of the Andrew Lloyd Webber oeuvre. Tickets (hard to find in the summer season) are available from the box office (☎058/620 9521) or the Orbis bureau in the *Gdynia* hotel. Emphasizing the naval connection there's also an annual Sea Shanty **festival** held here in August. Silver Screen, Waszyngtona 21 (☎058/628 1800, ⓦwww.silver-screen.com.pl), is the main multiplex **cinema**.

Restaurants

Ameryka ul. 10 Lutego 27. As the name suggests, T-bone steaks are the big deal here. Pricey.

Anker al. Piłsudskiego 50. Busy budget restaurant, usually packed at lunchtimes, serving up anything from pizza through crepes to chicken dishes.

Kwadrans ul. Kościuszki 20. Good breakfasts, pizzas, salads and spaghettis in spacious surroundings.

La Gondola ul. Portowa 8 ☎058/620 5923. Good Italian food, just north of the centre. Reservations recommended. Open till midnight.

Monte ul. Świętojańska 50. No-nonsense pizzeria on the main shopping street.

Santorini ul. Świętojańska 61. Rather good Greek restaurant with soothing decor, good service, and satisfying eats.

Smok al. Piłsudskiego 36/38. Well-regarded Vietnamese place with good-value set lunches. Closes at 9pm.

Żółty Melon ul. Abrahama 11. Very pleasant café-cum-pub that also serves meals. Opens noon till midnight.

Cafés and Bars

Cyganeria ul. 3 Maja 27. All distressed walls, mirrors and antique furniture, this is a good café by day and a pleasant pub by night. Shuts midnight or later.

Delicje ul. 10 Lutego 27. Daytime café just east of Gdynia Główna station. The strange Art Deco interior makes this look like a coffee shop from outer space. Good pastries.

Donegal ul. Zgoda 10. Pretty authentic-feeling Irish pub based around a cosy suite of dark, woody rooms. Packed at weekends.

Dziupla al. Piłsudskiego 56. Lively café and late-night bar with occasional live music. Decent food from breakfast onwards.

Zoom ul. Świętojańska 135. Prime stomping ground of alternative-leaning youth. Good place to listen to cutting-edge music or watch (occasional) gigs. About 1km south of the centre, near the Gdynia-Wzgórze SKM station.

Clubs

Bukszpryt ul. Morska 81/87. Club with big dancefloor offering cheap weekend discos aimed at teens and students.

Orange Club Skwer Kościuszki. Weekend discos for serious house and techno clubbers.

Space Cube ul. Jana z Kolna 55. Unsophisticated, good-fun cheesy discos.

North of the Trójmiasto

If the prospect of escaping from the rigours of the city appeals, head for the **Hel Peninsula**, a long thin strip of land sticking out into the Baltic Sea some 35km north of Gdańsk as the crow flies. As in several places along the Polish section of the Baltic coast, the peninsula was formed over the centuries by the combined action of current and wind. The sandy beaches dotted along the north side of the peninsula are well away from the once poisonous Wisła outlet, making the water around here as clean as you'll get on the Baltic coast; what's more, they are easily accessible and, away from the main resorts, never overcrowded, providing one of the Trójmiasto's increasing number of holiday spots popular with foreigners – most rewarding of the settlements along the peninsula is the fishing village of **Hel** itself.

Władysławowo and Jastrzębia Góra

The peninsula joins the mainland at **WŁADYSŁAWOWO**, a small but busy fishing port 40km north of Gdynia. From the **train** station (the **bus** station is

100m northwest) head left and left again, crossing the railway tracks, to find the resort area of town, where ul. Morska slopes down through a grid of low-rise streets towards a splendid stretch of dune-backed beach. It's a low-key family resort which can't compete with Hel in terms of charm, but if you do want to stay, the *Biuro Zakwaterowań* (☎058/674 0533), immediately opposite the train station at ul. Hallera 4, will help with **private rooms** (❶). If it's closed, ul. Morska and the lateral side streets branching off from it are full of houses advertising vacancies with *pokoje* signs. There's a generous selection of alfresco **fish bars** on the streets backing onto the beach.

If the idea of getting away from it all appeals, head for the village of **CHŁAPOWO**, about 3km out of town on the Jastrzębia Góra road (Jastrzębia Góra **buses** pass by), where there's a string of clifftop **campsites** overlooking the shore.

From Władysławowo, all trains and most buses continue eastwards onto the peninsula. However some bus services head ten kilometres west along the coast to **JASTRZĘBIA GÓRA**, once the playground of the interwar Polish elite, Józef Piłsudski included. Perched on top of crumbling cliffs, the place lacks a defining tourist focus save for the beach, but it's a reposeful and leafy place nevertheless, especially once you get past the soulless strip of rest homes and hotels that characterizes the eastern entrance to the resort. **Buses** stop near the intersection of Rozewska, the main east–west thoroughfare, and Promenada Światowida, the pedestrianized street which runs down to the sea. **Private rooms** (❶–❷) can be obtained by hunting around for *pokoje* signs or by calling in at *Pensjonat Damian*, Rybacka 53 (☎058/674 9142; ❹), which maintains a list of vacancies as well as offering simple en-suite rooms of its own. Elsewhere, the popularity of the resort with well-heeled Trójmiasto folk is reflected in the quality and price of accommodation. *Willa Jasna*, Bałtycka 24 (☎058/674 9698; ❺), is a lovely house hard up against the woods in the western part of town, with cosy en-suite rooms with TV, a sizeable garden, and a restaurant in the basement. *Ara*, Rozewska 4a (☎058/674 9600; ❺), is another swish modern place, offering en-suites with TV and fridge; it also has a popular weekend disco. Also in the centre is the rather posher *Onyks*, Słowackiego 5 (☎058/674 9746; ❻), offering snazzy apartments with sitting room and kitchenette. Most **eating** and **drinking** takes place in the inevitable line of fish-fry huts along Rozewska and Promenada Światowida. The place to head for if you're after a bit more style is *Café Kredens* on Promenada Światowida, serving up T-bone steaks, salads, pasta dishes and drinks in an interior liberally strewn with driftwood and fishing nets.

Hel

HEL, the small fishing port at the tip of the peninsula, is the main destination and a day-trippers' favourite. Despite heavy fighting – a German army of 100,000 men was rounded up on the peninsula in 1945 – the town retains some nineteenth-century fishermen's cottages, sturdy one-storey brick-built affairs which add character to the resort's compact centre. It's a fast-developing place, with souvenir shops and amber jewellery stores aplenty, but it retains enough old-world appeal to distinguish it from the majority of Baltic holiday spots, and access to miles of beach is a major plus.

From the train station (where buses from Gdynia also stop), walk down ul. Dworska to reach the northwestern end of Wiejska, the pedestrianized main street on which most of the town's amenities are located. It's here that you'll find Hel's **Muzeum Rybołówstwa** (Maritime Museum; Tues–Fri 9am–4pm, Sat & Sun 10am–4pm; 4zł), housed in the fifteenth-century Gothic Kościół św

Piotra (St Peter's Church). Inside are plenty of model ships and fishing tackle displaying the history of the fishing industry in this area, as well as some local folk art. There is a good view of the bay from the observation deck. As on the adjoining mainland, the people of the peninsula are predominantly Kashubian, as evidenced in the local dialect and the distinctive **embroidery** styles on show in the museum. At the eastern end of ul. Wiejska, ul. Leśna darts northwards, passing a graceful lighthouse before pressing on through the woods towards Hel's most valued tourist attraction, the **beach** – a luxurious, semolina-coloured ribbon of sand that extends as far as the eye can see.

Practicalities

In summer, direct **trains** run to Hel from Gdańsk train station, but there's a wider range of year-round services from Gdynia, which boasts regular train and **bus** services – as well as faster minibuses (departing when full), which run from the northern side of Gdynia bus station. In summer, tourist **boats** run to Hel several times a day from both Gdynia and Gdańsk (the latter providing excellent views of the Gdańsk shipyards); expect to pay around 45zł one-way. For times check with the local tourist offices or call Żegluga Gdańska on ☎058/301 6335 (Ⓦwww.zegluga.gda.pl).

There are numerous **private rooms** (❶–❷) in Hel, and you may well be propositioned by prospective landladies upon arrival at the train station. If not, the area around Sikorskiego (just south of the station, at the northwestern end of Wiejska) is the place to look for *wolne pokoje* signs. Of the **hotels**, the sparsely furnished rooms (en-suite or with shared facilities) at the impersonal *Riviera*, ul. Wiejska 130 (☎058/675 50528; ❶–❷) will suffice, although you'd be better off shelling out a little more to stay in smaller family-run establishments such as the *Helios*, Lipowa 2 (☎058/675 0103; ❹); *Captain Morgan*, Wiejska 21 (☎058/675 0091; ❸); and *Gwiazda Morza*, Leśna 7 (☎058/675 0859; ❸), all of which offer cosy en-suites.

There are any number of snack food joints along Wiejska doling out fried fish at reasonable prices: the local halibut is particularly good. In addition, there are a growing number of more formal **eating** joints, most of which are beginning to resemble each other in terms of ambience: chunky wooden furniture and ceilings hung with fishing nets are very much the order of the day. *Maszoperia*, Wiejska 110, offers an intimate candle-lit interior; while *Fiszeria*, Wiejska 100, is a fancy place with the full range of fish and meat dishes. Most convivial place for **drinking** is the *Captain Morgan*, a popular pub-style meeting place crammed with antique maritime junk.

Kashubia

The large area of lakes and hills to the west of Gdańsk – **Kashubia** (Kaszuby) – is the homeland of one of Poland's lesser-known ethnic minorities, the **Kashubians**. "Not German enough for the Germans, nor Polish enough for the Poles" – Grandma Koljiaczek's wry observation in *The Tin Drum* – sums up the historic predicament of this group.

Originally a western Slav people linked ethnically to Poles, and historically spared the ravages of invasion and war, thanks to their relative geographical isolation, the Kashubians were subjected to a German cultural onslaught during the Partition period, when the area was incorporated into Prussia. The process was resisted fiercely: in the 1910 regional census, only six out of the 455 inhabitants of one typical village gave their nationality as German, a pattern of resistance continued during World War II.

However, the Kashubians' treatment by the Poles has not always been better, and it's often argued that Gdańsk's domination of the region has kept the development of a Kashubian national identity in check. Certainly the local museums are sometimes guilty of consigning the Kashubians to the realm of quaint historical phenomena, denying the reality of what is still a living culture. You can hear the distinctive Kashubian language (supposedly derived from the original Pomeranian tongue) spoken all over the region, particularly by older people, and many villages still produce such Kashubian handicrafts as embroidered cloths and tapestries.

Żukowo and Kartuzy

The old capital of the region, Kartuzy, is tucked away among the lakes and woods 30km west of Gdańsk. From the main Gdańsk station a bus climbs up through **ŻUKOWO**, the first Kashubian village. The fourteenth-century Norbertine **church** and **convent** here has a rich Baroque interior and organ, resembling a country version of St Nicholas in Gdańsk. The arrangement of buildings – church, convent, vicarage and adjoining barns – has a distinctly feudal feel.

Though it can be reached in just under an hour on the same bus, the dusty, rather run-down market town of **KARTUZY** feels a long way from Gdańsk. The **Muzeum Kaszubskie** on ul. Kościerska (Kashubian Regional Museum; May–Sept Tues–Fri 8am–4pm, Sat 8am–3pm, Sun 10am–2pm; Oct–April Tues–Sat 8am–3pm; 5zł) will introduce you to some of the intricacies of Kashubian domestic, cultural and religious traditions. The Gothic **church**, part of a group of buildings erected in 1380 on the northern edge of town by Carthusian monks from Bohemia, is a sombre sort of place. The building itself is coffin-shaped – the original monks actually used to sleep in coffins – while the pendulum of the church clock hanging below the organ sports a skull-like angel swinging the Grim Reaper's scythe and bears the cheery inscription "Each passing second brings you closer to death". Apart from the church, nothing much remains of the original monastery. More appealing are the paths leading through the beech groves which surround nearby **Lake Klasztorne**, a nice place to cool off on a hot summer's day.

If you decide to make a night of it, the **tourist office**, Rynek 2 (Mon–Fri 9am–5pm, Sat 9am–1pm; ✆058/684 0201), will point you in the direction of **private rooms** (❶), although most of these are in the surrounding countryside and you'll need your own transport. The *Rugan*, ul. 3 Maja 36 (✆058/681 1635; ❺), is the only **hotel** in town, and its **restaurant** is the best source of passable sit-down food. *Be-mol*, just off the Rynek at Kościuszki 19, offers cheap pasta and pizza dishes named after different styles of music – a dub reggae pizza comes with tuna fish and peas, just in case you were wondering.

In the postwar years, Kashubia has gathered some wealth through the development of strawberry production: if you want to sample the crop, the June **strawberry festival** held on a hill 2km out of Kartuzy (anyone will direct you) provides an ideal opportunity. The occasion is part market, part fair – a little like a German *Jahrmarkt* – with the local farmers bringing baskets of strawberries to the church at nearby Wygoda.

Around Kashubia

Behind Kartuzy the heartland of Kashubia opens out into a high plateau of low hills and tranquil woodland dotted with villages and the occasional small town.

Running round the whole area is the **Ostrzydkie Circle**, an Ice Age hill formation that folds itself around several picturesque **lakes**. The lake resort of **Chmielno**, just west of Kartuzy, is one of the more obvious tourist targets, while the open-air museum at **Wdzydze Kiszewskie** is the place to aim for if you're at all interested in Kashubian folk culture. Being an intensely religious region, Kashubia is especially worth visiting during any of the major Catholic **festivals** – Corpus Christi for example, or Marian festivals such as the Assumption of the Virgin (Aug 15).

If you've got your own **transport** it's worth considering doing a round trip, taking in Chmielno and Wdzydze before heading back to Gdańsk, passing through some wonderful hilly countryside on the way. Travelling by bus, a day each for both destinations seems more reasonable. In summer, additional bus excursions are usually on offer from Gdańsk to Wdzydze Kiszewskie and elsewhere; ask at Orbis or the Gdańsk tourist offices for details of current offers.

Chmielno and Sierakowice

CHMIELNO, at the western edge of the Ostrzydkie Circle, is the most idyllic of several holiday centres around the area, and also the easiest to get to, lying some 12km west of Kartuzy and easily reachable by bus. Set in tranquil, beautiful surroundings overlooking the shores of three lakes – Białe, Rekowo and Kłodno – the waterside nearest the village is dotted with former "workers' rest centres", many of them now holiday homes and *pensjonaty*. Chmielno is a centre of traditional Kashubian ceramics, and the **Muzeum Ceramyky Kaszubskiej** at ul. Fr. Necla 1 (Museum of Kashubian Ceramics; Mon–Sat 9am–4pm; 2zł), puts the craft into context. Despite the village's holidaytime popularity, you shouldn't have any trouble finding somewhere to stay. The **tourist office**, right by the **bus** stop in the village cultural centre (Mon–Fri 9am–5pm; ☎058/684 2205), will fix you up with a **private room** (❶). Up from the museum at ul. Gryfa Pomorskiego 68, *U Czorlińskiego* (☎058/684 2278; ❷) is a homely **hotel** with a restaurant serving local food, while of the **pensions**, the *Dorota* at ul. Grździckiego 10 (☎058/684 2237; ❷), has en-suites available. Walking east from the village centre, between lakes Białe and Rekowo, will bring you round to the far shore of Lake Kłodno, where there are a couple of **campsites** renting out boats and kayaks. Back in the centre, *U Świętopełka*, downhill from the bus stop on ul. Świętopełka, is another good **restaurant** serving traditional Kashubian fare (potatoes with everything).

Moving west, the town of **SIERAKOWICE**, 15km further on, borders on a large expanse of rolling forestland, some of the prettiest in the region, and deservedly popular hiking country. **MIRACHOWO**, a ten-kilometre bus journey northeast across the forest, is a good base for walkers. The village has several traditional half-timbered Kashubian houses similar to those featured at the *skansen* at Wdzydze Kiszewskie (see below). The same holds for **ŁEBNO**, some 15km north, and many of the surrounding villages, a firm indication that you're in the heart of traditional Kashubian territory.

Kościerzyna and Wdzydze Kiszewskie

Continuing south through the region, **KOŚCIERZYNA**, the other main regional centre, some 40km south of Kartuzy, is an undistinguished market town – bus change or a bite to eat on the way to Wdzydze aside, there's no particular reason for stopping over here.

Sixteen kilometres on through the sandy forests south of Kościerzyna brings you to **WDZYDZE KISZEWSKIE**: if your tongue has trouble getting round this tongue-twister of a name, simple "*skansen*" will probably do the trick when asking for the right bus. Feasible as a day-trip from Gdańsk (72km) – in summer **buses** travel direct, at other times you have to change in Kościerzyna – the *skansen* here (mid-April to mid-Oct Tues–Sun 9am–4pm; mid-Oct to mid-April Mon–Fri 9am–3pm; last tickets half an hour before closing; 7zł) is one of the best of its kind, bringing together a large and carefully preserved set of traditional Kashubian **wooden buildings** collected from around the region. Established at the beginning of the twentieth century, it was the first such museum in Poland. Spread out in a field overlooking the nearby Lake Goluń, the *skansen's* location couldn't be more peaceful. After the real towns and villages of the region there's a slightly artificial "reservation" feel to the place, however – buildings without the people. That said the *skansen* is clearly a labour of love, an expression of local determination to preserve and popularize traditional Kashubian folk culture. Most people join the hourly **guided tours** round the site (English- and German-speaking guides are available in summer) since most of the buildings are kept locked when a guide's not present.

The panoply of buildings, most culled from local farms, range from old windmills and peasant cottages to barns, wells, furnaces, a pigsty and a sawmill with a frame saw so big that it was originally driven by a steam engine. The early eighteenth-century **wooden church** from the village of Swornegacie in the southwest of the region, renovated on the *skansen* grounds, is a treat: topped by a traditional wood-shingled roof, the interior is covered with regional folk-baroque designs and biblical motifs, with the patron St Barbara and a ubiquitous all-seeing Eye of God peering down from the centre of the ceiling. The thatched cottage interiors are immaculately restored with original beds and furniture to reflect the typical domestic setup of the mostly extremely poor Kashubian peasantry of a century ago. Even the old-style front gardens have been laid out exactly as they used to be. Finances permitting, there are plans to expand the collection of buildings to reflect a broader selection of regional architectural styles.

Skansen aside, lakeside Wdzydze Kiszewskie is another popular local holiday spot. In summer, **private rooms** are on offer in the houses by the lake, and there's a seasonal **youth hostel** and a number of **camping sites**.

The Wisła delta

Following the **Wisła** south from Gdańsk takes you into the heart of the territory once ruled by the **Teutonic Knights**. Physically, the river delta is a flat plain of isolated villages, narrow roads and drained farmland, while the river itself is wide, slow-moving and dirty, the landscape all open vistas under frequently sullen skies. Towns are an occasional and imposing presence, mostly comprising a string of fortresses overlooking the river from which the religio-militaristic Teutonic order controlled the lucrative medieval grain trade – it was under their protection that merchant colonists from the northern Hanseatic League cities established themselves down the Wisła as far south as Toruń. The knights' architectural legacies are distinctive red-brick constructions: tower-churches, sturdy granaries and solid burghers' mansions surrounded by rings of defensive walls and protected by castles. **Malbork**, the knights' headquarters, is the prime example – a town settled within and below one of the largest fortresses of medieval Europe. Continuing downriver a string of lesser fortified towns – **Kwidzyn**, **Gniew**, **Grudziądz** and **Chełmno** – lead to the ancient city of **Toruń**.

During the Partition era – from the late eighteenth century up until World War I – this upper stretch of the Wisła was **Prussian** territory, an ownership that has left its own mark on the neat towns and cities. After 1918, part of the territory returned to Poland, while part remained in East Prussia. During World War II, as throughout this region, much was destroyed during the German retreat.

Travel connections aren't too bad in the area, with buses and trains between the main towns (and cross-river ferries at several points along the Wisła), all of which are within reasonable striking distance of Gdańsk.

Malbork

For Poles brought up on the novels of Henryk Sienkiewicz, the massive riverside fortress of **MALBORK** conjures up the epic medieval struggles between Poles and Germans that he so vividly described in *The Teutonic Knights*. Approached from any angle, the intimidating stronghold dominates the town, imparting the threatening atmosphere of an ancient military headquarters to an otherwise quiet, undistinguished and, following war damage, predominantly modern town.

The history of the town and castle is intimately connected with that of the **Teutonic Knights** (see box overleaf), who established themselves here in the late thirteenth century and proceeded to turn a modest fortress into the labyrinthine monster whose remains you can see today. After two centuries of Teutonic domination, the town returned to Polish control in 1457, and the knights, in dire financial difficulties, were forced to sell the castle to the Czechs, who in turn sold it to the Polish Crown. For the next three hundred years the castle was a royal residence, used by Polish monarchs as a stopover en route between Warsaw and Gdańsk. Following the Partitions, the **Prussians** turned the castle into a barracks and set about dismantling large sections of the masonry – a process halted only by public outcry in Berlin. The eastern wings aside, the castle came through World War II (when it was used as a POW camp) largely unharmed. The sections destroyed during the Soviet assault in 1945, when much of the old town was unnecessarily smashed, have been painstakingly restored to something resembling their original state.

Other than the castle, there is little to say about Malbork, whose Stare Miasto was virtually razed in World War II. Evidence of the intense fighting which took place in these parts can be seen in the **Commonwealth War Graves** on the edge of the town.

The fortress

The approach to the main **fortress** (Tues–Sun: May–Sept 8.30am–5pm; Oct–April 9am–2.30pm; 13zł) is through the old outer castle, a zone of utility buildings that was never rebuilt after the war. Entrance is by (Polish-language) guided tour only; they tend to depart as soon as a sufficient number of people arrives.

The Teutonic Knights

The Templars, the Hospitallers and the **Teutonic Knights** were the three major military-religious orders to emerge from the Crusades. Founded in 1190 as a fraternity serving the sick, the order combined the ascetic ideals of monasticism with the military training of a knight. Eclipsed by their rivals in the Holy Land, the Knights – the **Teutonic Order of the Hospital of St Mary**, to give them their full title – established their first base in Poland at Chełmno in 1225, following an appeal from Duke Konrad of Mazovia for protection against the pagan Lithuanians, Jacwingians and Prussians. The Knights proceeded to annihilate the Prussian population, establishing German colonies in their place. It's ironic that the people known as Prussians in modern European history are not descendants of these original Slavic populations, but the Germanic settlers who annihilated them.

With the loss of their last base in Palestine in 1271, the Teutonic Knights started looking around for a European site for their headquarters. Three years later they began the construction of Malbork Castle – **Marienburg**, "the fortress of Mary", as they named it – and in 1309 the Grand Master transferred here from Venice.

Economically the Knights' chief targets were control of the Hanseatic cities and the trade in Baltic amber, over which they gained a virtual monopoly. **Politically** their main aim was territorial conquest, especially to the east – which, with their **religious zealotry** established in Palestine, they saw as a crusade to set up a theocratic political order. Although the Polish kings soon began to realize the mistake of inviting the Knights in, until the start of the fifteenth century most European monarchs were still convinced by the order's religious ideology; their cause was aided by the fact that the Lithuanians, Europe's last pagan population, remained unconverted until well into the fourteenth century.

The showdown with Poland came in 1410 at the **Battle of Grunwald**, one of the most momentous clashes of medieval Europe. Recognizing a common enemy, an allied force of Poles and Lithuanians inflicted the first really decisive defeat on the Knights, yet failed to follow up the victory, and allowed them to retreat to Malbork unchallenged. It wasn't until 1457 that they were driven out of their Malbork stronghold by King Kazimierz Jagiełło. The Grand Master of the Order fled eastward to Königsberg.

In 1525, the Grand Master, Albrecht von Hohenzollern, having converted to Lutheranism, decided to dissolve the order and transform its holdings into a **secular duchy**, with himself as its head. Initially, political considerations meant he was obliged to accept the Polish king as his overlord, and thus he paid homage before King Sigismund in the marketplace at Kraków in 1525. But the duchy had full jurisdiction over its internal affairs, which allowed for the adoption of Protestantism as its religion. This turned out to be a crucially important step in the history of Europe, as it gave the ambitious Hohenzollern family a power base outside the structures of the Holy Roman Empire, an autonomy that was later to be of vital importance to them in their ultimately successful drive to weld the German nation into a united state.

Passing over the moat and through the daunting main gate, you come to the **Middle Castle**, built following the knights' decision to move their headquarters to Malbork in 1309. Spread out around an open courtyard, this part of the complex contains the Grand Master's palace, of which the **main refectory** is the highlight. Begun in 1330, this huge vaulted chamber is one of the few rooms still preserved in pretty much its original condition; the elegant palm vaulting, supported on slender granite pillars, shows the growing influence of the Gothic cathedral architecture developed elsewhere in Europe. Displays of weaponry are arranged round the refectory, but more interesting is the painting that fills one of the walls: *The Battle of Grunwald* is archetypal Matejko romanticism, a heroic, action-packed interpretation of a key moment in Polish history.

Leading off from the **courtyard** are a host of dark, cavernous chambers. The largest ones contain collections of ceramics, glass, sculpture, paintings and, most importantly, a large display of Baltic **amber**, the trade which formed the backbone of the order's fabulous wealth. Innumerable amber pieces of all shapes and sizes are on show here – everything from beautiful miniature altars and exotic jewellery pieces to an assembly of plants and million-year-old-flies encased in the precious resin. If you're visiting in summer, the main courtyard provides the spectacular backdrop for the castle's son et lumière shows.

From the Middle Castle a passage rises to the smaller courtyard of the **High Castle**, the oldest section of the fortress, which dates from the late thirteenth century. Climbing up from the courtyard you enter a maze of passages leading to turrets whose slit windows scan the approaches to Malbork. The religious focus of the knights' austere monasticism was the vast **Castle Church**, complete with seven-pillared refectory and cloisters; features from the church's delicately sculptured **Golden Gate** are mirrored in the portals of the **Chapel of St Anne**, a later extension of the main structure. The knights' spartan sleeping quarters are nearby, down the passageway running to the Gdańsko Tower – the castle toilet.

You can also climb the main square tower in the centre of the castle – the views both of the castle complex and the flat surrounding countryside are excellent. On the way up you can also peer into the castle chapel, still under long-term restoration. When you've finished looking round inside, head over the newly built wooden **footbridge** leading from the castle to the other side of the river (technically the Nogat – a tributary of the Wisła), where the view allows you to appreciate what a Babylonian project the fortress must have seemed to medieval visitors and the people of the surrounding country.

Practicalities

The **train station** and **bus station** are sited next to each other about ten minutes' walk south of the castle; Malbork is on the main Gdańsk–Warsaw line: the plethora of trains from Gdańsk (30–40min), as well as a regular bus service, ensures that it's easy to treat Malbork as a day-trip. There's a **tourist office** (with unpredictable hours; ☏055/272 5599) at the southeastern side of the castle at Piastowska 15 – you'll pass it if approaching the castle from the train and bus stations – which will direct you towards the small number of **private rooms** (❷) in town.

Of the many **hotels**, the best and priciest by far is the *Zamek* (☏055/272 8400; ❻), just outside the entrance to the castle, whose comfortable en-suites are furnished in ponderous socialist-era style (although there's something charming about the worn brown easy chairs and heavy curtains), and there's a swanky restaurant housed in the Gothic refectory. The hotel is already an established tourist favourite, so it's best to book ahead. Of the other places in town, the *Zbyszko*, between castle and stations at ul. Kościuszki 43 (☏055/272 2640; ❹), is a more modern affair with plain but respectable en-suites with TV; while the *Parkowy*, next to a small football stadium 1500m north of the castle at ul. Portowa 3 (☏055/272 2413; ❸), offers exceedingly neat and cosy en-suites (loud carpets notwithstanding) with TV, alongside several simpler triples and quads. Presiding over the housing estates 2km south of the town centre on the Iława road, the concrete *Hotel Dedal*, ul. General de Gaulle'a 5 (☏055/272 6850; ❺), also belongs to the everything-must-be-brown school of interior decoration, but its TV-equipped en-suites are perfectly serviceable. As a last resort, the *Szarotka*, near the bus and train stations at ul. Dworcowa 1 (☎055/270 1444; ❶), offers careworn but clean rooms with shared facilities; and there's a spartan, summer-only **youth hostel,** 500m south of the castle at ul. Żeromskiego 45 (☎055/272 2408). There's a decent **campsite** at ul. Portowa 3 (June–Sept; ☎055/272 2413), next to the *Parkowy*; bungalows taking three cost 120zł.

For a quick meal there are several **snack stalls** around the castle entrance, including a couple of floating bar-restaurants moored on the riverbank below. The **restaurant** of the *Hotel Zamek* is a very good source of traditional Polish fare, as is the *Restauracja Piwniczka*, entered through the river-facing side of the castle walls. The self-explanatory *Pizza*, on ul. Kościuszki diagonally opposite the Zbyszko hotel, offers simple and filling pizza pies, pasta dishes, and truly excellent *pierogi*.

Kwidzyn and around

Set in the loop of a tributary a few kilometres east of the Wisła, **KWIDZYN** is a smallish fortified town amid a sprawling, dirty industrial belt. The first stronghold established by the Teutonic Knights – in the 1230s, some forty years before the move to Malbork – its original fortress was rapidly joined by a bishop's residence and cathedral. Three hundred years on, the castle was pulled down and rebuilt, but the cathedral and bishop's chapterhouse were left untouched: unlike the rest of the Stare Miasto area, the entire complex survived the fierce fighting in 1945 unscathed, after which it was the subject of some careful restoration work.

Most of the **castle** is poised on a hilltop over the River Liwa, but the immediately striking feature is the tower stranded out in what used to be the river-bed, connected to the main building by means of a precarious roofed walkway – it looks more like the remains of a bridge-builder's folly than a solid defensive structure. Originally the castle toilet, the best views of it and the castle as a whole are from the other side of the river.

Ranged around a large open courtyard, the castle houses a rather run-down local **museum** (Tues–Sun 10am–4pm; last tickets 3pm; 4zł), charting the early development of human settlements along the length of the Wisła basin, with additional sections on folklore, natural history and the tangled ethnography of the region. Despite later reconstructions the large, moody **cathedral**, adjoining the castle, retains several original Gothic features, the most noteworthy being a beautiful late-fourteenth-century mosaic in the southern vestibule.

There's no particularly good reason to stop over in what – cathedral and castle apart – is a pretty undistinguished sort of place. If you need to stay, most convenient of the **hotels** are the *Kaskada*, near the train station at ul. Chopina 42 (☎055/279 3731), which has en-suites (❹) or simple doubles with shared facilities (❷); or the *Miłosna*, a quiet and comfy pension 3km south of town at ul. Miłosna 5 (☎055/279 4052; ❺). For eating, the **restaurant** at the *Kaskada* hotel is a passable option, though the best is the *Pomezania* at ul. Chopina 27, offering fine Polish dishes until 10pm. The town has regular **bus** services to Tczew, Malbork and Grudziądz. **Trains** run to Gdańsk twice daily (1hr 30min).

West from Kwidzyn

If you're travelling by car, it's worth continuing west from Kwidzyn some 20km through the lush farmland of the Wisła delta to the riverbanks just beyond the village of Janowo and the **ferry** crossing over to **Gniew**. "Ferry" (*prom*) in this case means an amazingly dilapidated old contraption operated by an extraordinary mechanical chain system. It's one of three similarly archaic-looking vessels in operation along the northern stretches of the Wisła. All run from early morning till around sunset (seasonally adjusted). The trip costs nothing, since by law the local authorities are obliged to provide free transportation wherever a river "breaks" a road. The boats aren't large – the maximum car load at Janowo is four at a time – so especially in summer car passengers may face a bit of a wait for the blustery ten-minute boat trip. It's an experience not to be missed though, giving you probably your only chance to see the river – and the sadly polluted state of it – from close up.

Gniew

Sixty-five kilometres south of Gdańsk, the little town of **GNIEW** is one of the most attractive and least known of the former Teutonic strongholds studding the northern shores of the Wisła, an out-of-the-way place that's worth a stopover. Clearly visible from the ferry, thanks to the Wisła's changing course, the town has been left stranded on the top of a hill a kilometre back from the river. Gniew's original strategic location overlooking the river led the Teutonic Knights to set themselves up here in the 1280s, taking the place over from the Cistercian Order and completing the requisite castle within a few years. Untouched by wars, it's a quiet and, by Polish standards, remarkably well-preserved country town, one of those places modern history seems simply to have passed by. It's also a curiously unknown spot – the standard tourist literature barely mentions the town – so you're unlikely to encounter many other visitors, the odd German tour group excepted. However, the place's popularity is gradually increasing thanks to the activities of the enthusiastic group of locals who have now started organizing medieval jousting tournaments and costume battle re-enactments during the summer months – check with the Gdańsk tourist offices for current details.

At the centre of the Stare Miasto the solid-looking brick **town hall** provides the focus of such action as the deserted surrounding square sees – mostly kids kicking their footballs against the building. The atmosphere is enhanced, however, by the many original sixteenth- and eighteenth-century dwellings lining the square. West of here, the Gothic **parish church** is a typically dark, moody building filled, as often, with wizened old characters reciting their rosaries. A short walk east of the square brings you to the battered remains of the **castle** (May–Oct Tues–Sun 10am–4pm; 3zł), a huge deserted ruin of a place that would make an ideal Gothic horror movie set, its cavernous heights dimly hinting at the past glories of the place. A little way behind the castle perched on the spur overlooking the river – the **Pałac Marysienkich** (Marysieńki Palace), added on by King Jan Sobieski in the late seventeenth century for his wife – is a real find: a reasonably priced and scenically situated **hotel**, the *Pałac Marysieńki* (☎069/135 2537; ❺), an excellent restaurant and a view over the Wisła from the hotel balcony that's one of the best in the region. There's also a summer-only **hostel**, the *Dormitorium*, occupying a wing of the castle (☎069/135 2537).

Reasonably regular **buses** to and from Gdańsk (1hr 20min), Tczew and Grudziądz stop off at Gniew from the shelter on the western edge of the town centre.

Grudziądz and Radzyń Chełmiński

The garrison town of **GRUDZIĄDZ**, 35km downriver of Kwidzyn, was another early Teutonic stronghold and is again flanked by unprepossessing industrial development, with a huge power station dominating the town centre. Years of Prussian control explain the Germanic feel of the town, which despite the damage of the war retains several old buildings. A bustling provincial centre which boasts an impressive riverside position, Grudziądz is a convenient stop off en route to Toruń and Bydgoszcz (both of which are easily reached from here by bus), but hardly merits an overnight stop.

In the **Stare Miasto**, the tidy arrangement of the charming **Rynek** bespeaks Prussian orderliness and sense of proportion. Most of the sights are a few minutes' walk from here. The Gothic **parish church**, to the north, is a typically Teutonic high brick construction, with an equally typical Baroque overlay applied to the interior. The most striking feature is a finely carved Romanesque font in the sacristy. A short way south on ul. Ratuszowa, are the former **Jesuit Church and College**, founded in 1622, the church an aisleless Baroque structure with lavish chinoiserie decoration adorning the interior. To the south, the **Benedictine Monastery** houses a **museum** (Tues & Fri 10am–6pm, Wed & Thurs 10am–3pm, Sat 10am–4pm, Sun 10am–2pm) that's as interesting for the exhibitions by local artists as for the established displays recounting the town's history.

Above the river, the **granaries** built into the hillside fortifications are a reminder of the importance once attached to the grain trade. Together with the **mansions** topping the walls they form the centrepoint of the famous view of the town from the other side of the river; one of the best vantage points is from the train to or from Bydgoszcz and Gdańsk.

As with Malbork, the area surrounding Grudziądz is peppered with **war memorials**. A particularly moving one, in the forest near the village of **Grupa**, 3km out of town on the west bank of the river, commemorates more than 10,000 local Poles, most of them civilians, who were murdered here by the Nazis between 1939 and 1945.

Grudziądz practicalities

Trains run frequently to Toruń and Malbork, and there are good **bus** connections with Kwidzyn, Chełmno and Bydgoszcz. Bus and train terminals are fifteen minutes' walk southeast of the Stare Miasto. For an overnight stay in the town, the *U Karola*, a short walk south of the Stare Miasto at ul. Toruńska 28 (☎056/643 0333; ❷–❹), is definitely the **hotel** to go for, offering a mixed bag of habitable en-suites, some with TV, some without; while the *Adriano*, south of the train station at ul. Gen. Hallera 4 (☎056/465 6999; en-suites ❹, rooms with shared facilities ❷), is also reasonable if you don't mind being a little further from the centre. The **youth hostel**, 2km south of the centre at ul. Gen. Hallera 37, is one of the few in Poland with facilities for the disabled. As for **food**, there's a reasonable pizzeria, the *Tomato*, just off the Rynek at ul. Szewska 5, and the rather posher *Ratuszowa*, ul. Ratuszowa 1, whose mixture of Polish and French cuisine makes it the best place for a slap-up evening meal.

Radzyń Chełmiński

For every well-known Teutonic castle in the region there's at least one other that's a neglected ruin. The fortress at **RADZYŃ CHEŁMIŃSKI** 20km south of Grudziądz (some, but not all, Toruń-bound buses pass through) is a particularly memorable example of the phenomenon. Stuck out at the edge of a nondescript little town, in its time the castle here was the largest Teutonic stronghold after Malbork. Surrounded by a large dry moat, the walls of the ruins, which you can wander around the edge of, have a lost but rather epic feel to them. The "keep out" sign stuck up on the gateway claiming that the castle will open as soon as reconstruction is completed has obviously been there for years, though as the tourist brochure points out, it has at least been "preserved as a permanent ruin".

Chełmno

The hilltop town of **CHEŁMNO**, another important old Prussian centre, escaped World War II undamaged and has remained untouched by postwar industrial development. Perhaps the most memorable thing about the place is its atmosphere – an archetypal quiet rural town, steeped in the powerful mixture of the Polish and Prussian that characterizes the region as a whole.

Although a Polish stronghold is known to have existed here as early as the eleventh century, Chełmno really came to life in 1225 with the arrival of the Teutonic Knights. They made the town their first political and administrative centre, which led to rapid and impressive development. An academy was founded in 1386 on the model of the famed University of Bologna and, despite the damage inflicted by the Swedes in the 1650s, the town continued to thrive right up to the time of the Partitions, when it lapsed into provincial Prussian obscurity.

The Stare Miasto

To enter the Stare Miasto area pedestrians pass through the **Grudziądz Gate**, a well-proportioned fourteenth-century Gothic construction topped by fine Renaissance gables; cars have to park outside. Continue along ul. Grudziądzka and you're soon amid the Prussian ensemble of the **Rynek**, a grand open space at the heart of the grid-like network of streets. Gracing the centre of the square is the brilliant-white **town hall**, its facade exuding a real hat-in-the-air exuberance. Rebuilt in the 1560s on the basis of an earlier Gothic hall, its elegant facade, decorated attic and soaring tower are one of the great examples of

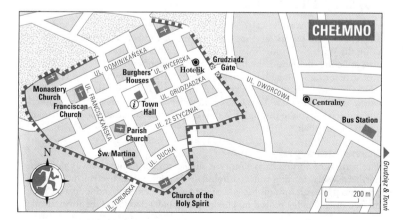

Polish Renaissance architecture. Inside there's a fine old courtroom and an appealing local **museum** (Tues–Sun 10am–4pm; 3zł), whose exhibits include an intriguing section devoted to brick production – traditionally the main building material in this part of Poland – with examples of how each individual brick was painstakingly smoothed down to the required size by hand. At the back of the town hall is the old Chełmno measure, the **pręt**, used up until the nineteenth century. Employed in the original building of the town, it explains why all the streets are the same width. Clearly a town of individual predisposition, it also used to have its own unique system of weights.

Most of Chełmno's seven churches are Gothic, their red-brick towers and facades punctuating the streets of the Stare Miasto at regular intervals. Best of the lot is the **parish church** standing just off the Rynek to the west, an imposing thirteenth-century building with a fine carved doorway. The interior retains sculpted pillars, a Romanesque stone font and fragmentary frescoes. Further west, past St James's Church, is an early fourteenth-century **monastery**, former home to a succession of Cistercian and Benedictine orders, and now to Catholic sisters who run a handicapped children's hostel here. Its church, whose Baroque altar is reputed to be the tallest in the country, features some original Gothic painting and a curious twin-level nave. The church backs onto the western corner of the town walls, crumbling but complete and walkable for excellent views over the Wisła and low-lying plains.

Practicalities

The **bus station** is on ul. Dworcowa, a fifteen-minute walk to the west of the Stare Miasto, where you'll find a small municipal **tourist office** at Rynek 28 (Mon–Fri 9am–5pm; ☎056/686 2104; ⓦwww.chelmno.pl). Central accommodation options boil down to the rather basic *Centralny*, just up from the bus station at ul. Dworcowa 23 (☎056/686 0212; ❶), which specializes in simple rooms with shared bathroom facilities; and the small, family-run *Hotelik*, just inside the Grudziądz Gate at Podmurna 3 (☎056/676 2030; ❹), which has a couple of cosy en-suites. Both of them have restaurants; otherwise you'll be dependent for food and drink on the huddle of cafés ranged around the Rynek.

Toruń and around

Poles are apt to wax lyrical on the glories of their ancient cities, and with **TORUŃ** – the biggest and most important of the Hanseatic trading centres along the Wisła – it's more than justified. Miraculously surviving the recurrent wars afflicting the region, the historic centre remains one of the country's most evocative, bringing together a rich assembly of architectural styles. The city's main claim to fame is as the birthplace of **Nicolaus Copernicus** (see p.225), whose house still stands. Today, it is a university city: large, reasonably prosperous and – once you're through the standard postwar suburbs – one with a definitely cultured air.

Some history

The pattern of Toruń's early history is similar to that of other towns along the northern Wisła. Starting out as a Polish settlement, it was overrun by Prussian tribes from the east towards the end of the **twelfth century**, and soon afterwards the Teutonic Knights moved in. The knights rapidly developed the town, thanks to its access to the burgeoning river-borne grain trade, a position further consolidated with its entry to the Hanseatic League. As in rival Gdańsk, economic prosperity was expressed in a mass of building projects through the **thirteenth century**; together these make up the majority of the historic sites in the city.

Growing disenchantment with the Teutonic Knights' rule and heavy taxation in the **fifteenth century**, especially among the merchants, led to the formation of the Prussian Union in 1440, based in Toruń. In 1454, as war broke out between the knights and Poland, the townspeople destroyed the castle in Toruń and chased the Order out of town. The 1466 Treaty of Toruń finally terminated the knights' control of the area.

The **sixteenth** and **seventeeth centuries** brought even greater wealth as the town thrived on extensive royal privileges and increased access to goods from all over Poland. The Swedish invasion of the 1650s was the first significant setback, but the really decisive blow to the city's fortunes came a century later with the Partitions, when Toruń was annexed to Prussia and thus severed from its hinterlands, which by now were under Russian control. Like much of the region, Toruń was subjected to systematic Germanization, but as in many other cities a strongly Polish identity remained, clearly manifested in the cultural associations that flourished in the latter part of the **nineteenth century**. The **twentieth century** saw Toruń returned to Poland under the terms of the 1919 Versailles Treaty as part of the "Polish Corridor" that was to so enrage Hitler, and was liberated from the Nazis in 1945.

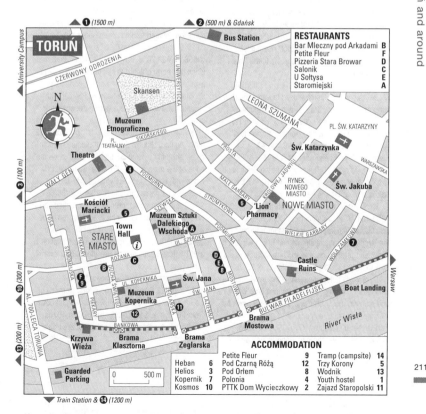

Arrival, information and accommodation

The main **stations** are on opposite sides of the Stare Miasto. Toruń Główny, the main **train station**, is south of the river: leave the station by the subway on the north (left) of the entrance, emerging a short way from the bus stop for the centre; buses #22 and #27 (every 20min) run over the bridge to pl. Rapackiego, on the west of the Stare Miasto. Some trains (but not most expresses) stop at Toruń Miasto, about 1km east of the centre. The **bus station** is on ul. Dąbrowskiego, a short walk north of the centre.

The well-organized municipal **tourist office**, in the town hall at Rynek Staromiejski 1 (Mon & Sat 9am–4pm, Tues–Fri 9am–6pm, plus Sun 9am–1pm in summer; ☎056/621 0931), doles out free brochures and maps and is a useful source of information for the whole region. There is a **youth hostel** at ul. Józefa 22/4 (☎056/654 4580; ❶), although it's 2km northwest of the Stare Miasto – bus #11 from the stop opposite the train station access road passes by. The PTTK Dom Wycieczkowy (see below) has a small number of cheap dorm beds. The *Tramp* **campsite** at ul. Kujawska 14 (☎056/654 7187), a short walk west of the train station, has some bungalows for rent (❶) as well as tent space – and a partly wooded setting near the river.

Hotels

Heban ul. Małe Garbary 7 ☎058/56/652 1555, ⓦwww.hotel-heban.com.pl. Historic town house in the centre with plush rooms, the larger ones decorated in lavish Second-Empire style. ❼

Helios ul. Kraszewskiego 1/3 ☎058/56/619 6550, ⓔhelios@orbis.pl. Orbis-run high-rise monster northwest of the centre, offering standard three-star comforts. ❼

Kopernik ul. Wola Zamkowa 16 ☎058/56/659 2573. An old army hotel housed in a grey block 5 minutes' east of the Stare Miasto with simple, cramped but eminently civilized rooms with TV; some come with sink only, some with sink and WC, others with shower and WC. ❷–❹

Kosmos ul. ks. Popiełuszki 2 ☎058/56/622 8900, ⓔkosmos@orbis.pl. The second-string Orbis joint in town: slightly less plush than the Helios, but enjoys a pleasant site near the river. ❼

Petite Fleur ul. Piekary 25 ☎058/56/663 4400 or 633 5454, ⓔhotel@hotel.torun.com.pl. Small-sized hotel with intimate feel a stone's throw from the Rynek. Rooms are simple and bright with pine floors and furnishings, and modern bathrooms. ❺

Pod Czarną Różzą ul. Rabiańska 11 ☎056/621 9637, ⓦwww.hotel.jade.pl. Another small and cosy Stare Miasto choice. All rooms come with TV and shower; most come with reasonably plush furnishings and warm colours. ❺

Pod Orłem ul. Mostowa 17 ☎056/622 5024, ⓔpodorlem@hotel.torun.pl. Good-value en-suites

with TV, in a central location. The walls and ceilings are paper-thin, however. ❹

Polonia pl. Teatralny 5 ☎056/622 3028. Time-worn downtown place that's due for a revamp, so call in advance to check prices. For the time being, rooms come with shared facilities or en-suites. ❷–❸

PTTK Dom Wycieczkowy ul. Legionów 24 ☎058/56/622 3855. Basic but clean and well-run place just north of the bus station. Cramped 4- or 5-person dorms for 30zł per person, or simple doubles. Bathrooms in the hallway. Popular with students and school groups during the academic year. ❷

Trzy Korony Rynek Staromiejski 21 ☎058/56/622 6031. Ageing, slightly gloomy but ultimately clean establishment enjoying an enviable location on the edge of the main square. En-suite rooms with TV, those with shared facilities without. ❸–❺

Wodnik ul. Bulwar Filadelfijski 12 ☎058/56/661 3226, ⓔosir@ascomp.torun.pl. Whitewashed concrete building that looks a bit like a Mediterranen package hotel, right by the river just west of the centre. Rooms are functional but all have shower and TV. Hotel residents can use the outdoor swimming pool next door. ❺

Zajazd Staropolski ul. Żeglarska 10/14 ☎058/56/622 6060, ⓔzstaropolska@gromada.pl. Comfortable place conveniently situated just down from the Rynek. Some rooms retain their 1970s brown colour schemes, although most are bright and modern in style. ❻

The City

The historic core of Toruń is divided into Stare Miasto and Nowe Miasto areas, both established in the early years of Teutonic rule. Traditional economic divisions are apparent here, the Stare Miasto quarter being home for the merchants, the other for the artisans; each had its own square, market area and town hall.

Overlooking the river from a gentle rise, the medieval centre constitutes a relatively small section of the modern city and is clearly separated from it by a ring of signs pointing to the centre: ask for the way to the Stare Miasto. For motorists, the Stare Miasto centre's impenetrable one-way system is pretty much a case of "abandon hope all ye who enter here" – you're better off walking.

The Stare Miasto

The **Stare Miasto** (Old Town) area is the obvious place to start looking around – and as usual it's the **Rynek**, in particular the **town hall**, that provides the focal point. Town halls don't come much bigger or more striking than this: raised in the late fourteenth century on the site of earlier cloth halls and trading stalls, it's a tremendous, if rather austere, statement of civic pride. A three-storey brick structure topped by a sturdy tower, its outer walls are punctuated by indented windows, framed by a rhythmic succession of high arches peaking just beneath the roof, and complemented by graceful Renaissance turrets and high gables.

The south side entrance leads to an inner courtyard surrounded by fine brick doorways, the main one leading to the **town museum** (Tues–Sun: May–Sept 10am–6pm; Oct–April 10am–4pm; 6zł), which now occupies much of the building. Over the centuries Toruń's wealth attracted artists and craftsmen of every type, and it's their work that features strongest here. Most of the ground floor – once the wine cellar – is devoted to medieval artefacts, with a gorgeous collection of the **stained glass** for which the city was famed and some fine **sculptures**, especially the celebrated "Beautiful Madonnas" – in which the Virgin is portrayed swooning in an S-shaped posture of grace. Also housed on this floor is an extensive archeological section, bringing together highlights of a vast array of Neolithic and early Bronze Age relics uncovered in this region. On the first floor, painting takes over, with rooms covered in portraits of Polish kings and wealthy Toruń citizens. A small portrait of the most famous city burgher, Copernicus, basks in the limelight of a Baroque gallery. Before leaving, it's worth the couple of złotys to climb the **tower** for the view of the city and the course of the Wisła, stretching into the plain on the southern horizon.

Lining the square itself are the stately mansions of the Hansa merchants, many of whose high parapets and decorated facades are preserved intact. The finest houses flank the east side of the square. Number 35, next to one of the Copernicus family houses, is the fifteenth-century **Pod Gwiazdą**, with a finely modelled late Baroque facade; inside, a superbly carved wooden staircase ends with a statue of Minerva, spear in hand. The house is now a small **Muzeum Sztuki Dalekiego Wschodu** (Far-Eastern Art Museum; Wed–Sun 10am–4pm; 3zł), based on a private collection of art from China, India and other Far Eastern countries. There is a separate gallery in the basement belonging to the "U Kalimacha" cultural society.

Off to the west of the square stands the **Kościół Mariacki** (St Mary's Church), a large fourteenth-century building with elements of its early decoration retained in the sombre interior. There's no tower to the building, supposedly because the church's Franciscan founders didn't permit such things; monastic modesty may also help to explain the high wall separating the church from the street. Back across the square, on the other side of the town hall, a blackened but noble **statue** of Copernicus watches over the crowds scurrying round the building.

South of the square, on the dusty, narrow and atmospheric ul. Żeglarska, is **Kościół św. Jana** (St John's Church), another large, magnificent Gothic structure, whose clockface served as a reference point for loggers piloting their way downstream. The presbytery, the oldest part of the building, dates from the 1260s, but the main nave and aisles were not completed till the mid-fifteenth century. Entering from the heat of the summer sun, you're immediately enveloped in an ancient calm, heightened by the damp, chilly air rising from the flagstones and by the imposing rose window. The tower, completed late in the church's life, houses a magnificent fifteenth-century bell, the *Tuba Dei*, which can be heard all over town and which is in fact the largest bell in Poland outside Kraków. Opening hours depend on when a service is being held. Check the notice board outside for current details, which will include at least one daily service.

West from the church runs ul. Kopernika, halfway down which you'll find the **Muzeum Kopernika** (Copernicus Museum; Tues–Sun: May–Sept 10am–6pm; Oct–April 10am–4pm; 5zł), installed in the high brick house where the great man was born. Restored in recent decades to something resembling its original layout, this Gothic mansion contains a studiously assembled collection of Copernicus artefacts: priceless first editions of the momentous *De Revolutionibus*, models of gyroscopes and other astronomical instruments, original household furniture and early portraits. Authenticity is abandoned on the upper floors, which are given over to products of the modern Copernicus industry: Copernicus coins, badges, stamps, even honey pots and tea labels. There's also a son et lumière display (performance times posted at the ticket desk; an additional 9zł required) on the city's evolution, worth seeing for the fascinating model of medieval Toruń.

Ulica Kopernika and its atmospheric side streets, lined with crumbling Gothic mansions and granaries, blend past glory and shabbier contemporary reality. Further down towards the river, the high, narrow streets meet the old defensive **walls**, now separating the Stare Miasto from the main road. These fortifications survived virtually intact right up to the late nineteenth century, only for some enterprising Prussian town planners to knock them down, sparing only a small section near the river's edge. This short fragment remains today, the walls interspersed by the old gates and towers at the ends of the streets.

To the west, at the bottom of ul. Pod Krzywą Wieżą, stands the mid-fourteenth-century **Krzywa Wieża** (Crooked Tower), followed in quick succession by the **Brama Klasztorna** (Monastery Gate) and **Brama Żeglarska** (Sailors' Gate), all from the same period, the last originally leading to the main harbour.

Heading east, past the large **Brama Mostowa** (Bridge Gate), brings you to the ruins of the Teutonic Knights' **castle**, sandwiched between the two halves of the medieval city. While not in the same league as the later Malbork fortress, the scale of the ruins here is enough to leave you impressed by the Toruń citizenry's efforts in laying waste to it. For a few złotys you can wander through the ruins and get some idea of the extent of the original. The castle grounds are the location for occasional summertime concerts (folk and classical) – check with the tourist offices for details – and there is always an open-air café during the warm months. A little further east along the river bank is a landing stage, from which in summer you can take a ninety-minute **boat trip** downriver and back.

The Nowe Miasto

Following ul. Przedzamcze north from the castle brings you onto ul. Szeroka, the main thoroughfare linking the Stare and Nowe Miasto districts. Less grand than its mercantile neighbour, the **Nowe Miasto** still boasts a number of illustrious commercial residences, most of them grouped around the **Rynek Nowomiejski**. On the west side of this square, the fifteenth-century *Pod Modrym Faruchem* inn (no. 8) and the Gothic pharmacy at no. 13 are particularly striking, while the old *Murarska* inn at no. 17, on the east side, currently houses an art gallery (closed on Sunday) displaying children's work from all over the country.

The fourteenth-century **Kościół św Jakuba** (St James's Church), south of the market area of the Rynek, completes the city's collection of Gothic churches. Unusual features of this brick basilica are its flying buttresses – a common enough sight in western Europe but extremely rare in Poland. Inside, mainly Baroque decoration is relieved by occasional Gothic frescoes, panel paintings and sculpture – most notably a large fourteenth-century crucifix.

North of the square, ul. Prosta leads onto Wały Sikorskego, a ring road which more or less marks the line of the old fortifications. Across it there's a small park, in the middle of which stands the former arsenal, now the **Muzeum Etnograficzne** (Ethnographic Museum; Mon, Wed & Fri 9am–4pm, Tues, Thurs, Sat & Sun 10am–6pm; 8zł; free on Mon) dealing with the customs and crafts of northern Poland. The displays covering historical traditions are enhanced by imaginative attention to contemporary folk artists, musicians and writers, whose work is actively collected and promoted by the museum. The surrounding park houses an enchanting *skansen* containing an enjoyable and expanding collection of traditional wooden buildings from nearby regions, including a blacksmith's shop, windmill, water mill and two complete sets of farm buildings from Kashubia.

West of the centre

If you're feeling the need for a bit of tranquillity, there's a pleasant **park** along the water's edge west of the city centre, reached by tram #3 or #4 from pl. Rapackiego. At weekends you'll be joined at the waterside by picnickers and the odd group of horse-riders, and there's a riverbank walk that's very enjoyable, particularly the section between the two great bridges straddling the mighty Wisła.

North of the park, the **Bielany** district houses the main section of the university campus, largely unmemorable by itself, but it's the location of several of the really lively student clubs and discos (see p.216). To get here, take bus #11 or #15.

Eating, drinking and entertainment

There's a growing choice of **places to eat** in Toruń. Traditional fast food is available from *Bar Mleczny pod Arkadami*, on the corner of Różana and Św. Ducha, which serves up filling *barszcz*, bean soups, pancakes, and takeaway waffles (*gofry*). It's impossible to walk the streets of the Stare Miasto without bumping into a cheap pizza joint every 100m or so; best of the sit-down places

Toruń gingerbread

Don't leave town without picking up some **gingerbread** (*piernik*), a local speciality already popular here by the fourteenth century – as attested by the moulds in the town museum. It comes in ornate shapes: stagecoaches, eighteenth-century figures and Copernicus are among the most popular. Numerous shops round the Stare Miasto sell the stuff, notably the one at ul. Żeglarska 25. Watch your teeth, though: the traditional type intended for display is rock hard, while the edible variety usually comes shaped in small cakes or biscuits.

are *Pizzeria Stara Browara*, Mostowa 17, a student favourite where it takes as long to make sense of the enormous menu as it does to eat what you've ordered; and the slightly plusher *Staromiejski*, Szczytna 2/4, which has a bigger range of pasta dishes. *Salonik*, on the south side of the Rynek Staromiejski, is a dependable source of standard Polish meat-and-potatoes fare; although *U Sołtysa*, ul. Mostowa 17, has a lot more atmosphere, with wooden bench seating, dried herbs hanging from the rafters, and a range of traditional fare served up with folk staples such as *kasza* (buckwheat) instead of the usual fries. For something slightly more formal and expensive, the restaurant of the *Petite Fleur* hotel is a great place for classic Polish and European meat dishes.

Cafés and **bars** are in good supply, with daytime pavement-café places on streets such as ul. Szeroka providing an opportunity to enjoy the atmosphere of the Stare Miasto. The riverbank also provides good outdoor café spots on warm summer nights. Otherwise, best of the evening haunts is *Pod Aniołem*, Rynek Staromiejski, a wonderfully atmospheric, vaulted cellar under the town hall, and often featuring live music, cabaret performances or DJs at weekends. *U Szwejka*, on the eastern side of the Rynek at nos. 34–38, is another roomy cellar bar catering for boisterous pleasure-seekers at weekends; while the nearby *Guinness* at no.33 is a much cosier little place in which to spend an evening. *Krzywa Wieża*, Pod Krzywą Wieżą 1/3, is a tremendous little bar nestling in the Stare Miasto battlements. *Art.café*, Szeroka 35, is a disco-bar specializing in techno and house; and *Żmija*, Podmurna, is a basement pub with frequent live music.

Some of the best **nightlife** in town happens in the university district, clustered on and around ul. Gagarina. The *Imperial*, Gagarina 17, is a cult student club of many years' standing that currently serves as a weekend disco and live music venue; while *Od Nowa*, Gagarina 37a, is a theatre and rock/jazz venue (☎058/611 4593).

Entertainment

The grand old Toruń **theatre**, on pl. Teatralny 1 (box office ☎056/622 5021), is home to one of the country's most highly regarded repertory companies. It's also worth checking the listings in the local newspaper for occasional classical **concerts** in the town hall and regular ones given by the Town Chamber Orchestra in the Dwór Artusa at Rynek Staromiejski 6 (☎056/655 4939, Ⓦwww.artus.torun.pl).

The city has a number of regular **festivals**, notably the International Theatre Festival (May), which is the most prestigious theatrical event in Poland; a folk festival (June); and an international festival of film camerapeople (late Nov/early Dec). Contact the tourist office for details.

Golub-Dobrzyń

About 35km east of Toruń, the elegant facades of the castle at **GOLUB-DOBRZYŃ** are a traditional Orbis poster favourite. While the town itself is nothing to write home about, the Renaissance **Castle**, located high up on a hill overlooking the town, is an impressive sight. Coming in on the long, straight approach road from Toruń, the castle is signposted off to the right just before you enter the town – if you're coming by bus ask the driver to drop you off near the castle (*zamek*). There's a regular **bus** service from Toruń (hourly on weekdays, somewhat less frequent at weekends).

A Teutonic stronghold raised in the early 1300s on the site of an early Slav settlement overlooking the River Drwęca, the original castle was built on the square ground-plan with arcaded central courtyard that survives today. Following the conclusion of the Treaty of Toruń (1460) the place fell into Polish hands; the real changes to the building came in the early 1600s, when Anna Waza, sister of King Sigismund III, acquired the castle. The king's redoubtable sister, a polyglot and botanical enthusiast reputed to have imported the first tobacco to Poland and planted it on the hills near the castle, had the whole place remodelled in Polish Renaissance style, adding the elegantly sculptured facades and Italianate court-yard you see today. After taking a severe battering during the Swedish wars of the 1650s the abandoned castle was left to crumble away, restoration work beginning following the town's final return to Polish territory in the postwar era.

The castle buildings

Past the large cannons greeting you at the entrance the castle **museum** (Tues–Sun: June–Sept 9am–7pm; Oct–May 9am–4pm; 4zł) begins unpromis-ingly, with a small regional section housed in one of the ground-floor rooms containing a routine collection of straw shoes, local costumes and assorted wooden objects, many of them related to the river economy.

Upstairs on the second floor things get more interesting. The classy main **banqueting hall** sports the coats of arms of all the major old Polish aristo-cratic families – the Jaruzelski clan included – as well as the emblem of the cas-tle's last eighteenth-century owners, the Dutch Van Doren family. In recent years the castle has begun hosting invitation-only New Year medieval banquets with everyone turning up dressed in period costume.

The former castle **chapel** next door is anything but religious in atmosphere, being filled to the brim with replicas of Polish battle standards from the Battle of Grunwald as well as an amazing array of old cannon, from tiny fourteenth-centu-ry pieces to monster seventeenth-century contraptions – and just about everything in between. The original Gothic structure built by the Teutonic Knights under-went substantial alterations in Anna Waza's time, her strict Protestant convictions possibly accounting for the severe feel of the place. The rest of the rooms on this floor once comprised the knights' living quarters: apparently everyone used to ride their horses straight up the stairs to their rooms, the resulting local legend holding that anyone who merely walks up the stairs is liable to break out in unexpected public fits of neighing. Out of the castle it's worth strolling to the viewpoint at the edge of the field next to the building for the view over the surroundings.

The upper rooms of the castle are now a fairly basic **hotel** (☎056/683 2455) run by PTTK, which has a couple of doubles (❷) but is mostly given over to dorms. A better bet is the *Kaprys* at ul. Kilińskiego 7 (☎056/683 2447; ❷), although it's also pretty small – so ring ahead if you can. The *Kaprys* has a rea-sonable Polish **restaurant**.

Every July (usually around the middle of the month) the field here is the scene of a major international **chivalry tournament**, with national teams of jousters battling it out on horseback: a spectacular event by all accounts, it's worth trying to catch the event if you're in the area at the time.

Ciechocinek

Twenty kilometres southeast of Toruń, and reached by frequent buses, **CIECHOCINEK** has rather more life about it than the normal run of Polish spas. The main feature of town is the **Park Zdrojowy** (Spa Park), just down from the bus station, which features floral gardens, tree-lined avenues and the usual spa buildings – pump room, a wooden open-air concert hall and band-stand. Far more intriguing, however, is the chance to stroll around **Park Tężniówy** (dawn–dusk; 2zł) immediately to the west. Here, in three separate sections stretching for over 1.5km, is the massive wall of wooden poles and twigs which makes up the **saltworks** (*tężnie*), begun in 1824 but not completed until several decades later. It's an extraordinary sight and is all the more remarkable in that it can still be seen functioning as originally intended. The technology behind it is very simple: water from the town's saline springs is pumped to the top of the structure, from where it trickles back down through the twigs. This not only concentrates the salt, it also creates a reputedly recuperative atmosphere in the covered space below. Formerly, patients would walk through the interior of the structure, breathing in deeply as they went, but for conservation reasons this is unfortunately no longer permitted. You can climb onto the top of the saltworks for an extra 3zł, but somehow this seems a poor substitute.

East of the spa gardens, about 1km out along Wojska Polskiego, lies a dainty, turquoise-painted **Orthodox church**, erected in wood by carpenters from the Urals in the nineteenth century. A bold ochre bell tower was added in the 1990s. Unfortunately the interior is usually only accessible at service times (Sun 8.45am; Wed 4pm).

Once you've pottered around the parks and paused at one of the numerous ice cream/grilled sausage/beer huts, you'll probably be ready to head back to Toruń. However there's plenty of **accommodation** on hand if you want to stick around: the tourist office on ul. Zdrojowa (Biuro promocja Ciechocinka; Mon–Fri 9am–5pm) will find you a place to stay in a private room (❶) or a pension (❷). Hotels worth considering include the modern and well-appointed *Hotel Restaurant Amazonka* at the end of ul. Traugatta 5 (☎054/283 1274; ❻); or the cheaper and more cramped *Chemik* at ul. Widok 18 (☎054/83 3494; ❹). There are a number of **restaurants** in the town centre: *Przy Grzybie*, on the corner of Zdrojowa and Kościuszki, serves up simple meat-and-potatoes standards on the verandah of a rickety wooden building; while the *Amazonka* provides the best (and costliest) national dishes.

East of Gdańsk

East from Gdańsk a short stretch of Baltic coastline leads up to the Russian border and, beyond, to Kaliningrad. An attractive and largely unspoilt region, the beaches of the **Wiślana Peninsula** and its approaches are deservedly popular seaside holiday country with Poles and, increasingly, returnee Germans – **Krynica Morska** is the resort to aim for if the idea of a few days on the beach appeals. Inland the lush rural terrain, well watered by countless little tributaries of the Wisła, boasts a host of quiet, sturdy-looking old Prussian villages, and more ominously, the Nazi concentration camp at **Sztutowo (Stutthof)**. This is the region most closely associated with astronomer **Nicolaus Copernicus**, and several towns, notably the medieval coastal centre of **Frombork**, bear his imprint. Of the other urban sites, **Elbląg** is a major old Prussian centre which has lost much of its old character, but remains an important transport hub.

As for **transport**, cross-country bus links are generally good in this part of the country, with the additional option of a scenic coastal train route along the southern shore of the **Wiślany Lagoon** and short-hop ferry services in several places.

The Wislany Lagoon and around

Through the flatlands of the former Wisła basin, the coast road east passes the popular local seaside resort of **STOGI**, the only place in the immediate vicinity of Gdańsk where the water has always been clean enough to swim in: additionally there's a nudist beach 2km east of the main resort. Continuing east, there's a ferry crossing over one of the small Wisła tributaries at **Świbno**. Over the other side, with your own transport, it's worth making a short detour 6km south to **DREWNICA**, where there's a fine example of the old wooden windmills that used to cover the area. If you happen to be heading south along the main Elbląg–Warsaw road instead, the *Złota Podkowa* restaurant in the village of **PRZEJAZDOWO**, 8km out of town, is well worth a stopoff; the house speciality is excellently prepared local duck.

Back on the main coastal road 15km further east you come to **STEGNA,** an attractive spot with a charming, half-timbered brick church that wouldn't look out of place in a Bavarian village, the ornate Baroque frescoes decorating the interior enhancing the feel of an archetypal German country church. Elsewhere in the village the smattering of "*Zimmer frei*" signs in the windows tell you you've hit what's now become a popular German holiday centre.

Stutthof (Sztutowo) concentration camp

May our fate be a warning to you – not a legend. Should man grow silent, the very stones will scream.

Franciszek Fenikowski, Requiem Mass, quoted in camp guidebook.

Two kilometres further east on the main coastal road, the sense of rural idyll is rudely shattered by the signs pointing north to the gates of the Nazi concentration camp site at **Stutthof (Sztutowo)**. The first camp to be built inside what is now Poland (construction began in August 1939, before the German invasion), it started as an internment camp for local Poles but eventually became a Nazi extermination centre for the whole of northern Europe. The first Polish prisoners arrived at Stutthof early in September 1939, their numbers rapidly swelled by legions of other locals deemed "undesirables" by the Nazis. The decision to transform Stutthof into an international camp came in 1942, and eventually, in June 1944, the camp was incorporated into the Nazi scheme for the "Final Solution", the whole place being considerably enlarged and the gas ovens installed. Although not on the same scale as other death camps, the toll in human lives speaks for itself: by the time the Red Army liberated the camp under a year later, in May 1945, an estimated 65,000 to 85,000 people had disappeared here.

Both Gdańsk-Krynica Morska and Elbląg-Krynica Morska **buses** pass by the short access road to the camp, which is at the western end of Sztutowo village – you can't miss the Sztutowo-Museum sign pointing to the site.

The camp

In a large forest clearing surrounded by a wire fence and watchtowers, the peaceful, completely isolated setting of the **camp** (May 1–Sept 15 8am–6pm; Sept 16–April 30 8am–3pm; no guides Mondays, children under 13 not allowed) makes the whole idea seem unreal at first. In through the entrance gate, though, like all the Nazi concentration camps, it's a shocking place to visit. Rows of stark wooden barrack blocks are interspersed with empty sites with nothing but the bare foundations left. Much of the camp was torn down in 1945 and used as firewood; the narrow-gauge rail line still crisscrossing the site reminds you of the methodical planning that went into the policy of mass murder carried out here.

A **museum** housed in the barracks details life and death in the camp, the crude wooden bunks and threadbare mats indicating the "living" conditions the inmates had to endure. A harrowing gallery of photographs of gaunt-looking inmates brings home the human reality of what happened here: name, date of birth, country of origin and "offence" are listed below each of the faces staring down from the walls, the 25 nationalities present including a significant contingent of political prisoners, communists and gays. Over in the far corner of the camp stand the gas ovens and crematoria, flowers at the foot of the ovens, as well as a large monument to the murdered close by. "Offer them a rose from the warmth of your heart and leave – here lies infamy": the words from Polish poet Jan Górec-Rosiński's elegy on visiting the camp, quoted in the official guidebook, seem an appropriate response. During the summer, the museum cinema provides further evidence of the atrocities.

The Wiślana Peninsula

East from Sztutowo, the coast road leads onto the **Wiślana Peninsula** (Mierzeja Wiślana), a long, thin promontory dividing the sea from the **Wiślana**

Kaliningrad

Kaliningrad – formerly Königsberg – the longtime capital of East Prussia, annexed by the Soviet Union at the end of World War II, was left cut off from the rest of the Russian Federation following the collapse of the Soviet Union. Although the Kaliningrad territory's continued political status as an integral part of Russia is beyond question, its geographical position – squeezed between Poland and Lithuania – looks set to generate considerable problems in the years to come.

A heavily **militarized area** often referred to as Russia's "western aircraft-carrier", Kaliningrad occupied an important place in Soviet strategic military thinking. A key air-defence centre, the region also houses the main base of the former Soviet (now Russian) Baltic Fleet at Baltysk, as well as a number of infantry divisions. A drive through the Kaliningrad *oblast* (region) confirms the weight of local military presence: in between the crumbling Prussian villages you can easily spot a welter of air-defence installations, some camouflaged, some not. Estimates of current force levels vary widely – there were thought to be at least 150,000 troops remaining in the mid-1990s, though this has certainly been reduced since.

The former threat of military confrontation may have subsided, but while agreeing that troop levels should be reduced to "reasonable" levels, the Russian authorities have so far stopped short of accepting Polish and Lithuanian calls to demilitarize the region completely. As with earlier negotiations on troop withdrawals in eastern Europe, behind this stance lurks the genuine and difficult issue of what to do with returning soldiers in a country already deep in the throes of a serious economic crisis, not least suffering from a chronic lack of employment and housing opportunities. Kaliningrad's military importance has in any case been enhanced by **NATO** enlargement and the potential threat that this poses to the Russians – Poland is already a member, and Lithuania (a country through which Russian military personnel must be allowed transit if the Kaliningrad garrison is to remain viable) is a candidate to join.

The problematic position of Kaliningrad has also been thrown into sharp relief by the growth of the **European Union** (EU). With both Poland and Lithuania on course to become EU members in the near future, the danger is that Kaliningrad will become even further isolated. The territory's one-million-strong population is already far poorer than that of its neighbours, eking out a living on an average monthly wage of some $55 dollars a month – half the size of average earnings in the rest of Russia, and minuscule in comparison with neighbouring Lithuania and Poland. The Kaliningrad region was declared a special economic zone in 1996, in the hope of encouraging Western investment by giving tax breaks to foreign importers, although this has had little significant effect on the local economy.

Lagoon (Zalew Wiślany), a land-locked tract of water known as the "Frische Haff" in Prussian times that continues some 60km up towards Kaliningrad. On the northern side of the peninsula a dense covering of mixed beech and birch forest suddenly gives way to a luxuriant strip of sandy shore, while to the south, the marshy shore beyond the road looks out over the tranquil lagoon – 15km across at its widest – and beyond that to Frombork and the mainland. A naturalist's paradise, the peninsula forest is idyllic walking country, while the northern coastline offers some of the best and most unspoilt beaches on the Baltic coast. The main resort, **Krynica Morska**, is full of hotels and pensions, and camping sites dotted along the peninsula provide an alternative source of local accommodation.

Kąty Rybackie

Four kilometres beyond Sztutowo, **KĄTY RYBACKIE** is an uneventful little resort town and fishing port with long sandy beaches stretching out as far as

It's estimated that fifty percent of Kaliningrad's income is derived from **black market** activities. Many Kaliningrad Russians make ends meet by travelling to Poland to sell cigarettes or vodka on local markets, returning home with a few dollars' profit. Polish membership of the EU, and the introduction of visa fees for non-EU citizens, will wipe these profits out. Generally speaking, Poles and Lithuanians are keen to retain a lenient system of border controls with Kaliningrad, conscious that cross-border trade has proved beneficial to all sides in the years following the breakup of the Soviet Union. However this view is unlikely to be shared by EU bigwigs in Brussels, who tend to view Kaliningrad as a reservoir of potential economic migrants, and will insist on the introduction of tougher frontier regulations. To make matters worse, Kaliningrad is increasingly notorious as a city with soaring **crime** rates, a growing tuberculosis problem, and unusually high rates of **drug abuse** and **HIV infection** – increasing the likelihood that the territory will be isolated from, rather than integrated with, the rest of Europe as the EU tightens up its borders.

Visiting Kaliningrad

There's actually not a great deal worth seeing in Kaliningrad, since most of the city was first flattened by Allied bombing raids, then by the fighting around the city in 1945, and afterwards rebuilt in what seems like the crassest and ugliest way the Soviets could come up with. In the old city only the ruins of the medieval **cathedral** survive, with a special stone marking the grave of **Immanuel Kant**, the city's most famous philosopher and about the only one deemed acceptable by the postwar Soviet authorities. Moving out into the suburbs, however, the uniform concrete blocks begin to give way to sections of characteristic old Prussian houses which can be found throughout former East Prussia.

In order to visit Kaliningrad you'll need a Russian **visa**, which can only be obtained from Russian embassies or consulates in your home country; applying to Russian consulates in Poland won't do much good.

Regular **buses** run from Warsaw, Gdańsk and Olsztyn to Kaliningrad, crossing the border at Bezledy–Bagrationovsk, about 40km north of Lidzbark Warmiński. There are also border crossings at Gronowo–Mamonowo and Gołdap–Gasev. The journey takes about 10 hours from Warsaw and 5.5 hours from Gdańsk and Olsztyn.

In summer, tourist **hydrofoils** operated by Zegluga Gdańska (✪www.zegluga .gda.pl) run to Kaliningrad from Hel (twice weekly) and Elbląg (daily).

the eye can see along the coast up by the harbour. It's an easy place to get to, with Gdańsk–Krynica **buses** dropping off at a number of stops along Kąty's main street. An **information board** at the western entrance to the village points the way towards Europe's largest **cormorant sanctuary**, which can be reached in 25 minutes by taking the path into the forest immediately opposite. Beautifully situated in the middle of thick woodland and sandy scrub, the sanctuary is a bird-watchers' delight, with every chance of spotting the large flocks of cormorants. Trails head round the reserve before continuing northwards to hit the western end of Kąty's beach.

Krynica Morska

Twenty-five kilometres on, the road brings you to **KRYNICA MORSKA**, a few kilometres short of the Russian border and the main holiday resort on the peninsula. A relatively small-scale, under-commercialized resort patronized by Poles and a smattering of Germans, Krynica straggles along a single main street, Gdańska, with a cluster of factory-owned rest homes on the wooded spine of the peninsula just above, beyond which lies an alluring white-sand beach.

Buses from Gdańsk come to a halt at the eastern end of Gdańska, just below the agglomeration of cafés and boutiques that passes for the village centre on ul. Portowa. The beach is 15 minutes' walk north of here. Numerous houses in town offer **private rooms** (❶–❷), and the **tourist office**, just off Gdańska at ul. Bosmańska 1 (Mon–Sat 10am–10pm, Sun 2–10pm; ☎055/247 6444, ⓦwww.mierzeja.pl) will make reservations both here and in other villages along the peninsula. Of the many **pensjonaty** in town, the *Polonia*, ul. Świerczewskiego 19 (☎055/247 6097; ❸) is nice and central with a restaurant on site; while the *Pod Lwem*, at the eastern end of the village at ul. Wodna 10 (☎055/247 6141; ❹), is plusher, but still intimate in feel. Comfiest of all is the *Kahlberg* **hotel**, next to the tourist office and clearly visible from the main road through town at ul. Bosmańska 1 (☎055/247 6017, ⓦwww.kahlberg.mierzeja.pl; ❺).

As in most Polish seaside resorts, **eating** out in Krynica revolves around unpretentious snack-food outlets rather than snazzy sit-down restaurants. There's a knot of fish-and-chip stalls around the central streets of Portowa and Świerczewskiego, although one of the best places to try local fish from the Wiślany lagoon is the homely *Tawerna Yachtowa*, by the yachting harbour on the lagoon side of town. Cheap meals are also available from *Koga*, a bar on Gdańska built in the shape of a beached sailing ship, which is also one of the best places in town to drink.

Elbląg

The ancient settlement of **ELBLĄG**, after Gdańsk the region's most important town, was severely damaged at the end of World War II: its Stare Miasto centre, reputed to have been Gdańsk's equal in beauty, was totally flattened in the bitter fighting that followed the Nazi retreat in 1945. After languishing for decades in a postwar architectural limbo, at the beginning of the 1990s Elbląg finally started to get the regenerative pick-me-up it badly needed, and the Stare Miasto area is now being sympathetically and imaginatively rebuilt on the principle that investors copy the feel, if not necessarily the precise architectural details, of the city's prewar architecture. Though still not complete, enough is in place for you to judge the results.

The Town

Surrounded by an undistinguished postwar urban sprawl, the **Stare Miasto** is a small section at the heart of modern Elbląg. Some parts of the old city walls remain, most notably around the old **Brama Targowa** (Market Gate) at the northern entrance to the area. Elbląg played an important role in Hitler's wartime plans, specifically as a centre of U-boat production – the city's easy access to the sea, via the Wiślana Lagoon, made it a perfect spot. The empty area between the Brama Targowa and the cathedral hides the ruins of the dry docks where scores of newly produced submarines were launched into wartime action – no wonder the Soviets hammered the place.

Standing out rather incongruously, the **cathedral**, rebuilt after the war, is another massive brick Gothic structure, its huge tower the biggest in the region. Despite the restorers' efforts to give the building back some of its former character, the job was clearly a bit of an uphill struggle. A couple of fine original Gothic triptychs and statues, and some traces of the original ornamentation aside, the interior is mostly rather vapid postwar decoration, leaving the place with a sad, empty feel to it. The area immediately surrounding the cathedral is a combination of old Prussian-style mansions and new restaurants, bars and cafés, mostly catering for the busloads of (principally German) day-trippers piling in throughout the summer season.

Not far from the cathedral is the Gothic St Mary's Church: no longer consecrated, the building houses a small, rather downbeat **modern art gallery** (Mon–Fri 10am–5pm, Sat & Sun 10am–4pm; 2zł) in the cloisters. More interesting than the pictures on display are the old gravestones and tablets lining the walls, notably that of Samuel Butler, one of the many English merchants who settled here as a result of the city's strong Reformation-era Anglo-Polish commercial links, symbolized in the establishment of the Eastland Company's headquarters here in 1579.

South along the river, the local **museum** is located at ul. Bulwar Zygmunta Augusta 11 (Tues, Wed & Fri 8am–4pm, Thurs, Sat & Sun 10am–6pm; 3zł) which features the usual displays dedicated to local history and archeology, as well as an absorbing collection of photos of the German city from the prewar era and beyond.

Practicalities

Elbląg's **bus and train stations** are close to each other, a fifteen-minute walk east of the Stare Miasto centre or a short ride on trams #1 or #2. Decent onward bus connections to either the Wiślana peninsula or Frombork ensure that you're unlikely to want to stay in town, although there's a reasonable range of hotel **accommodation** for those who get stuck here. Cheapest of the bunch is the *Galeona*, just off the central pl. Słowiański at ul. Krótka 5 (☎055/232 4808), which has careworn doubles with shared bathrooms (❷) and some tidier-looking en-suites (❸); while the Dworcowy, ul. Grunwaldzka 49 (☎055/233 8049; ❸), offers prim en-suites with TV which are slightly overpriced due to their location just across the road from the stations. Better in quality are the swish *Elzam Gromada*, pl. Słowiański 2 (☎055/234 8111; ❸), an old communist party hotel close to the cathedral and clearly aimed at German tourists, which also has facilities for the disabled; and *Boss*, ul. Św. Ducha 30 (☎055/239 3730, ✉boss@elblag.com.pl; ❸), an upmarket pension just round the corner from the cathedral whose bijou rooms come with sparkling WCs.

For **eating** you can savour cheap and filling fare at *Pizzeria Monte Cristo*, near the cathedral on the Stary Rynek, or indulge in faux-Mexican eats in the rather fun *Pod Aniołami*, also on the Stary Rynek. For a quality Polish meal with good service, the *Rattanowa* restaurant inside the *Elzam Gromada* hotel (see above) is probably your best bet.

East of Elbląg

Continuing east towards the Russian border, the high morainic inclines of the Elbląg plateau (Wzniesienie Elbląskie) stretch east along the high ridge overlooking the coast. Most traffic (including the vast majority of eastbound buses) follow the main road inland before rejoining the lagoon at the cathedral town of Frombork, some 30km from Elbląg. An alternative route involves following the minor road that loops northeast along the coast, passing through some stunningly beautiful scenery on the way. Twenty kilometres out of Elbląg, the village of **KADYNY** (Cadinen) conceals one of the region's real surprises: German Kaiser Wilhelm II's personal **stables and stud farm**. Established in 1898 as part of the Kaiser's summer residence here, the stables are still going strong, with 170 high-quality horses kept in trim for use by a predominantly German tourist clientele. Along with the stables the half-timbered buildings of the Kaiser's **palace** have recently been bought up by a US company, restored to their former Prussian opulence and converted into a luxury **hotel** (☎055/231 6120, ℱ231 6200; ❼). The rooms are small, though equipped with all the usual Western accessories, and the grounds hold tennis courts, sun lounges and a swimming pool. The excellent but pricey hotel **restaurant**, the *Stara Gorzelnia* (*Old Distillery*), housed inside the old stable brewery, still has its old cast-iron staircases and large windows. The hotel's already proving very popular, with plenty of group bookings in summer, so if you want to stay you'd be well advised to reserve well in advance. Up behind the palace it's worth wandering up to see the Kaiser's private **chapel**: it's kept locked, but ask at reception and they'll organize entry.

The magnificent **stables** are mostly for use by hotel guests, but turn up early enough and you could probably negotiate for a day's riding, with or without escort. The main riding routes are along the coast and up along the plateau: reports from riding enthusiasts indicate that the plateau routes in particular make for some exhilarating riding. To make enquiries ring ☎055/231 6133 (a knowledge of Polish and German will probably stand you in better stead than one of English). The village is also famous for **Jan Bażyński's Oak**, one of the oldest trees in Poland, 25m high and 10m in circumference.

To get to Kadyny, take the bus from Elbląg (25min) or the local train on the coastal line between Elbląg and Braniewo – although the latter boasts a meagre two departures per day.

Frombork

A little seaside town 90km east along the Baltic coast from Gdańsk, **FROM-BORK** was the home of **Nicolaus Copernicus** (see box opposite), the Renaissance astronomer whose ideas overturned Church-approved scientific notions, specifically the earth-centred model of the universe. Most of the research for his famous *De Revolutionibus* was carried out around this town, and it was here that he died and was buried in 1543. Just over a century later, Frombork was badly mauled by marauding Swedes, who carted off most of Copernicus' belongings, including his library. The town was wrecked in World War II, after which virtually none of the Stare Miasto was left standing. Today it's an out-of-the-way place, as peaceful as it probably was in Copernicus' time, though of late the town has been rocked over land ownership – the Church, which owned much of the town centre before World War II, is now claiming the whole place back.

Nicolaus Copernicus

Nicolaus Copernicus – Mikołaj Kopernik as he's known to Poles –- was born in Toruń in 1473. The son of a wealthy merchant family with strong Church connections, he entered Kraków's Jagiellonian University in 1491 and subsequently joined the priesthood. Like most educated Poles of his time, he travelled abroad to continue his studies, spending time at the famous Renaissance universities of Bologna and Padua.

On his return home in 1497 he became administrator for the northern bishopric of Warmia, developing a wide field of interests, working as a doctor, lawyer, architect and soldier (he supervised the defence of nearby Olsztyn against the Teutonic Knights) – the archetypal Renaissance man. He lived for some fifteen years as canon of the **Frombork** chapterhouse and here constructed an observatory, where he undertook the research that provided the empirical substance for the *De Revolutionibus Orbium Caelestium*, whose revolutionary contention was that the sun, not the earth, was at the centre of the planetary system. The work was published by the Church authorities in Nuremberg in the year of Copernicus' death in 1543; it was later banned by the papacy.

Around the cathedral

The only part of Frombork to escape unscathed from the last war was the **Wzgórze Katedralne** (Cathedral Hill), up from the old market square in the centre of town. A compact unit surrounded by high defensive walls, its main element is the dramatic fourteenth-century Gothic **cathedral** (daily: May–Sept 9am–5pm; Oct–April 9am–3.30pm), with its huge red-tiled and turreted roof. Inside, the lofty expanses of brick rise above a series of lavish Baroque altars – the High Altar is a copy of the Wawel altarpiece in Kraków. The wealth of tombstones, many lavishly decorated, provide a snapshot of Warmian life in past centuries; Copernicus himself is also buried here. The seventeenth-century Baroque **organ** towering over the nave is one of the best in the country, and the Sunday afternoon and occasional weekday recitals in summer are an established feature: check the concert programme at the tourist office in Gdańsk. If you like organ music but can't make it to a concert, you can obtain recordings (and much else) from the ticket office at the entrance.

To the west of the cathedral, the **Wieża Kopernika** (Copernicus Tower; May–Sept only: Mon–Sat 9.30am–5pm), the oldest part of the complex, is supposed to have been the great man's workshop and observatory. Doubting that the local authorities would have let him make use of a part of the town defences, some maintain that he's more likely to have studied at his home, just north of the cathedral complex. The **Wieża Radziejowskiego** (Radziejowski Tower; same times as the cathedral), in the southwest corner of the walls, houses an assortment of Copernicus-related astronomical instruments and has an excellent view from the top of the Wiślana Lagoon stretching 70km north towards Kaliningrad. Further equipment and memorabilia of the astronomer are to be found in the **Muzeum Kopernika** (Copernicus Museum; Tues–Sun: May–Sept 9am–4.30pm; Oct–April 9am–3.30pm) in the Warmia Bishops' Palace, across the tree-lined cathedral courtyard. Among the exhibits are early editions of Copernicus' astronomical treatises, along with a number of his lesser-known works on medical, political and economic questions, a collection of astrolabes, sextants and other instruments, plus pictures and portraits.

A word of warning about the sights in this area: although you can pay to see all of them – a **combined ticket** (8zł) is sold from the ticket office at the entrance to the cathedral complex – you cannot always wander around at will. Thus you may find the cathedral locked and have to wait until a guide has collected enough people to open it up, after which you can wander around freely until the guide is minded to lock it up again.

Practicalities

Frombork's **bus** and **train stations** – neither of which seem to display any timetable information – are located next to each other not far from the seafront. The Elbląg–Frombork train service has been cut to the bone in recent years, but plenty of Gdańsk–Braniewo and Elbląg–Braniewo buses pass through here. It's certainly feasible to treat Frombork as a day-trip from Gdańsk; if there's no direct bus back, take one to Elbląg and change there. The rudimentary IT **information office** in the souvenir shop just above the bus stop will help with public transport information and direct you towards the town's stock of **private rooms** (❶–❷) – otherwise look out for signs advertising *pokoje* on and around the main street. Best of the accommodation choices are the *Rheticus* at ul. Kopernika 10 (☎055/243 7800; ❺), a charming **pension** boasting neat modern en-suites and some family rooms with kitchenette; and the larger, concrete **hotel**, the *Kopernik*, ul. Kościelna 2 (☎055/243 7285; ❺), with cramped but spic-and-span en-suite doubles. Cheaper options include the decent-quality PTTK **hostel** at ul. Krasickiego 2 (☎055/243 7252; ❷), in the park just a few yards west of the Cathedral Hill, which has a passable café/restaurant, the summer-only *Copernicus* **youth hostel**, just west of the bus stop at ul. Elbląska 11 (☎055/243 7453), and **PTTK camping** (May 15–Sept 15), some way from the centre on the Braniewo road at ul. Braniewska 14.

Apart from some summer takeaway bars and hotel restaurants, the best **place to eat** is *Akcent*, ul. Rybecka 4, which serves up traditional treats like *żurek*.

The Kanał Ostrodzko–Elblaski

Part of the network of canals stretching east to Augustow and over the Belarus border, the 81-kilometre-long **Kanał Ostrodzko–Elblaski** (Elbląg–Ostróda Canal) was constructed in the mid-nineteenth century as part of the Prussian scheme to improve the region's economic infrastructure. Building the canal presented significant technical difficulties (it took over 30 years to complete the project), in particular the large difference in water level (over 100m) between the beginning and end points. To deal with this problem, Prussian engineers devised an intricate and often ingenious system of locks, chokepoints and slipways: the **slipways**, the canal's best-known feature, are serviced by large rail-bound carriages that haul the boats overland along the sections of rail tracks that cover the sections of the route where there's no water. Five of these amazing Fitzcarraldo-like constructions operate over a ten-kilometre stretch of the northern section of the canal, located roughly halfway between Elbląg and the village of Małdyty.

If you feel like travelling on the canal, **day-trips** along the whole stretch of the route operate daily from mid-May to the end of September, although departures are sometimes cancelled if fewer than 20 people turn up; incidentally, bird fanciers should note that the first leg of the cruise on the Drużno Lake is a nature reserve rich in waterfowl. Bear in mind, too, that you'll need to bring your own food – only drinks are served on board. Boats start at 8am from Elbląg, arriving in **OSTRÓDA**, at the southern tip of the canal, in the early evening (a total journey time of 11–12 hours): alternatively you can travel in the other direction on the boat leaving Ostróda at the same time and finishing up in Elbląg in the evening. If you don't feel like trekking the whole distance, you can at least follow a section of the canal from **MAŁDYTY**, an attractive village just east of the main Elbląg–Ostróda road, some 40km south of Elbląg. If you're travelling by car and want to glance at the slipways, turn west off the main road at **Marzewo**, a few kilometres north of Małdyty, and you'll meet the canal 5km down the road.

At certain times of the year, the canal becomes a tourist attraction for other reasons – if you're here in July watch out for the "Canal Trophy" when world records are set for inner-tube racing, and the "Canal Blues", a waterside blues festival.

The lakes

The woodlands that open up to the east of the Elbląg plateau signal the advent of **Mazury,** or **Mazuria,** the "land of a thousand lakes" that occupies the northeast corner of the country, stretching for some 300km towards the Lithuanian border. Geologically, the region's current form was determined by the last Ice Age, the myriad lakes a product of the retreat of the last great Scandinavian glacier. A sparsely populated area of thick forests and innumerable lakes and rivers, Mazury is one of the country's main holiday districts – and rightfully so. It's a wonderful haunt for walkers, campers, water sports enthusiasts or just for taking it easy.

Coming from Gdańsk, **Olsztyn** is the first major town and provides a good base for exploring the lesser-known western parts of Mazury, a landscape of rolling woodland interspersed with farming villages. Enjoyable as this area is, though, most holidaymakers head east to the area around lakes **Mamry** and **Śniardwy** – the two largest of the region – and to more developed tourist towns like **Giżycko, Mrągowo** and **Mikołajki**. Further east still, up beyond **Ełk**, is the **Suwalszczyzna**, an area of mixed forest and undulating pastureland tucked away by the border, in many ways the most enchanting part of the region. As with other border areas there is a minority population, in this case Lithuanians.

Transport links within the region are reasonably well developed if slow. Local trains and/or buses run between all the main destinations: further afield, notably in the Suwalszczyzna, the bus service becomes more unpredictable, so you may have to rely on hitching – which is not too much of a problem in the holiday season. Approaching Mazury from the south can be tricky, however, as the lakelands were in a different country until 45 years ago. Olsztyn and Augustów are on main rail lines from Warsaw; anything in between may involve a couple of changes, so the (summer-only) bus from Warsaw to Mikołajki may be a better idea if you're heading direct to the central lakes.

For **trekking** or **canoeing**, a tent, a sleeping roll, food supplies and the right clothing are essential – and are available for hire if you don't want to lug your own over. Canoe (and sometimes kayak or even yacht) rental can usually be organized by Almatur or PTTK, and sometimes by Orbis.

Ostpreussen

Present-day Warmia and Mazuria make up the heartlands of what until more than forty years ago was called **Ostpreussen** (East Prussia). Essentially the domains ruled by the Teutonic Knights at the height of their power, the whole area was originally populated by pagan Baltic and Borussian (later known as Prussian) tribes, most of whom were wiped out by the Teutonic colonizers. **Warmia** (Royal Prussia), the main part of the territory, whose name derives from the Prussian tribe of the Warms that once lived here, passed into Polish control following the Treaty of Toruń (1466), after which Polish settlers began moving into the area in numbers. It remained part of Poland until the First Partition (1772) when it was annexed by Prussia.

Mazuria proper, the eastern part of the territory – Ducal Prussia as it eventually became known – has been **German**-ruled for most of its modern history. Following the secularization of the Teutonic Knights' lands in 1525, the Brandenberg Hohenzollern family acquired the region as a hereditary duchy, though they were still obliged to pay homage to the Polish king.

This was not the end of the original "German question", however, for in 1657, under the pressure of the Swedish wars, King Jan Kazimierz released the branch of the powerful Hohenzollern family ruling Ducal Prussia from any form of Polish jurisdiction, allowing them to merge the province with their own German territories. By 1701 Elector Frederick III was able to proclaim himself king of an independent Ducal Prussia, and impose limits on Polish settlement in the region: the way was now cleared – from the Polish point of view – for the disastrous slide to Frederick the Great and Partition-era Prussia.

From the German point of view Prussia's first real setback in centuries came at the end of **World War I**, when the region was reduced to the status of a Land within the Weimar Republic and subjected to a series of plebiscites to determine whether Germany or Poland should have control of several parts of the territory. As it turned out, both the Warmian and Mazurian provinces voted to remain in Germany, with the easternmost area around Suwałki going to Poland. Heavily militarized during the course of **World War II**, in 1945 East Prussia was sliced across the middle, the northern half, including the capital Königsberg, designated a new province of the Russian Federation (though separated from it by Lithuania), the southern half becoming part of Poland.

Prusso-German culture had a strong impact on the character of the area, as evidenced by the many Protestant churches and German-looking towns dotted around – Olsztyn was once known as Allenstein, Elbląg as Elbling, Ełk as Lyck. Today the most obvious sign of Prussian influence is the influx of Germans who flock to the major lakeside holiday resorts in the summer. Many of the older visitors had family roots here until 1945, when – as in other areas of newly liberated Poland – everybody of German origin was ordered to leave. Most fled to West Germany, joining the millions of other displaced or uprooted peoples moving across Europe in the immediate postwar period.

A particularly sad example of the Polish government's rigid displacement policy occurred with the peasant minority from the villages around **Olsztyn**. Like the other historic peoples of Warmia, they were of Baltic origin, but unlike the original Baltic Prussians they survived the onslaughts of the Teutonic Knights, only to be strongly Germanized then Polonized during the Polish rule of Ducal Prussia. Yet after centuries of tending the forests, they were pressurized into leaving the Olsztyn area for good on account of the German taint in their history.

Olsztyn

Of several possible stepping-off points for the lakes, **OLSZTYN** is the biggest and the easiest to reach, and owing to the summertime tourist influx it's well kitted out to deal with visitors, most of whom stop here en route for points further east. The town itself is located in pleasant woodland, but owing to wartime destruction – Soviet troops burnt the place down in 1945 after the fighting had ceased – much of the old centre has the usual residential postwar greyness. Nestled among the concrete blocks and dusty main thoroughfares, though, quiet streets of neat brick houses built by the city's former German inhabitants remain, and there are relaxing tree-lined riverside walks around the main Stare Miasto area, with ongoing reconstruction slowly returning a sense of neat prettiness to the centre.

Olsztyn was something of a latecomer, gaining municipal status in 1353, twenty years after its castle was begun. Following the 1466 Toruń Treaty, the town was reintegrated into Polish territory, finally escaping the clutches of the Teutonic Knights. Half a century later, Nicolaus Copernicus took up residence as an administrator of the province of Warmia, and in 1521 helped organize the defence of the town against the Knights.

Coming under Prussian control after the First Partition, it remained part of East Prussia until 1945. Resistance to Germanization during this period was symbolized by the establishment here, in 1921, of the Association of Poles in Germany, an organization dedicated to keeping Polish culture alive within the Reich. With Hitler's accession, the Association became a target for Nazi terror, and most of its members perished in the concentration camps. The town also suffered, roughly forty percent being demolished by 1945.

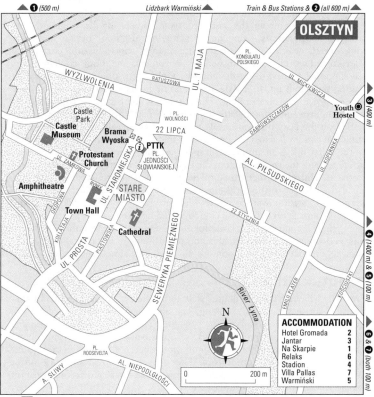

Nonetheless, postwar development has established Olsztyn as the region's major industrial centre, with a population of 160,000. Ethnically they are quite a mixed bunch: the majority of the German-speaking population, expelled from the town after World War II, was replaced by settlers from all over Poland, particularly the eastern provinces annexed by the Soviet Union, and from even further afield – such as a small community of Latvians.

The Town

The main places to see are concentrated in the **Stare Miasto**, and you won't need more than a couple of hours to take in the main sights. **Plac Wolności** is the town's main square, with the Gothic **Brama Wysoka** (High Gate) – the entrance to the Stare Miasto – a short walk away at the end of ul. 22 Lipca. Once through the gate, ul. Staromiejska brings you to the **Rynek**, currently a mass of rebuilding work, which retains a few of its old buildings, most notably the Prussian-looking town hall, appearing rather stranded in its centre.

Over to the west is the **castle**, fourteenth-century but extensively rebuilt, surveying the steep little valley of the River Łyna. Its **museum** (Tues–Sun: June–Sept 9am–5pm; Oct–May 10am–4pm; 5zł) is an institution with an ideological mission: defining the region's historical record from an unashamedly Polish perspective. The ethnography section contains a good selection of folk costumes, art and furniture, while the historical section stresses the Warmians' general resistance to all things German. There's also a large archeological collection, including objects from ancient burial grounds – look out for the mysterious granite figure in the castle courtyard, a relic of the original Slavic Prussians. **Copernicus**' living quarters, on the first floor of the southwest wing, are the castle's other main feature: along with a wistful portrait by Matejko and several of the astronomer's instruments, the rooms contain a sundial supposed to have been designed by Copernicus himself. It's also worth making the climb up the **castle tower** (same hours and ticket) for the view over the town and surroundings. Directly below the castle is a large open-air **amphitheatre**, used for theatre and concert performances in summertime, nestled on the leafy banks of the River Łyna. Coming out of the back of the castle you can stroll across the bridge over the gently coursing river to the park on the other side – an atmospheric spot, particularly at sunset.

Back towards the centre, up from the castle entrance there's a stern neo-Gothic Protestant **church**, formerly used by the predominantly non-Catholic German population. To get to the early-fifteenth-century – and Catholic – **cathedral**, whose high brick tower dominates the surroundings, walk back across the Rynek. Originally a grand parish church, including an intricately patterned brick ceiling that's among the most beautiful in the region and a powerful Crucifixion triptych hanging over the high altar, this retains some of its original Gothic features: despite extensive renovations it's still a moodily atmospheric place.

Practicalities

The Stare Miasto is fifteen minutes' walk to the west of the **bus** and **train stations**; as an alternative to walking, just about any bus heading down al. Partyzantów will drop you at plac Wolności. The **tourist office** (Mon–Fri 9am–5pm, Sat 10am–4pm; ☎089/535 3565), beside the High Gate on pl. Jedności Słowianskiej, will fill you in on most aspects of tourism in the region, but doesn't book accommodation. The next door PTTK/Mazury office (Mon–Fri 9am–5pm, Sat 9am–2pm) organizes boat rental and accommodation for the Krutynia kayaking route (see box p.238).

There's a reasonable choice of cheap to moderate **hotels**, kicking off with the *Jantar*, ul. Kętrzyńskiego 5 (☎089/553 5452; en-suites ❸, rooms with shared bathroom ❷), a former workers' hotel near the train station; and the *Stadion*, 2km east of the centre next to the football ground at ul. Piłsudskiego 69A (☎089/533 5968; bus #13, #15 or #20 from the centre; or #2, #26 or #28 from the stations), which offers grotty rooms with shared bathrooms (❷) and a couple of snazzily renovated en-suites (❹). *Relaks*, 1km south of the train and bus stations at Żołnierska 13A (☎089/527 7336; ❹), is a slightly tatty medium-rise block with clean and comfortable en-suites, some with TV; while *Na Skarpie*, Gietkowska 6A (☎089/526 9211; ❸-❹ depending on level of renovation) is very similar in style but less convenient in location, a twenty-minute walk northwest of the centre but well signposted. Right opposite the train and bus stations, the *Hotel Gromada*, Plac Konstytucji 3 Maja 4 (☎089/534 5894, ⓕ534 6330; ❻), offers smart comfortable rooms and guarded parking; although it's not as comfortable as the more central *Warmiński*, Głowackiego 8 (☎089/522 1400 or 522 1500, ⓦwww.hotel-warminski.com.pl; ❻), which offers fully refurbished en-suites with TV; or the *Villa Pallas*, Żołnierska 4 (☎089/535 0115, ⓕ535 9915; ❼), a nicely restored old house within walking distance of the centre. The all-year **youth hostel** is handy for both the town centre and the stations at ul. Kopernika 45 (☎ & ⓕ089/527 6650).

As so often in provincial Poland, central Olsztyn boasts several places which are good for a quick bite, but little in the way of slap-up **restaurants**. *Bar Dziupla*, Stare Miasto 9/10, is the place to go for a generous plateful of *pierogi*; while *Eridu*, slightly downhill at ul. Prosta 3/4, offers excellent sit-down or take-away *shawarma*, shish kebabs, *kibbeh* and falafel. *Lipka*, Okopowa 21, is an unatmospheric but serviceable pizzeria. Fans of traditional Polish cooking will be happy at the excellent *Retro*, ul. Okopowa 20.

For **drinking**, the enjoyable *Sarp* café at ul. Kołłątaja 14, housed in a restored granary, is the local Architects' Society hangout; *Zoom*, a pub-like bar with small beer garden at Piastowska 44, is a popular meeting point for Olsztyn youth. *Irish Pub*, at the eastern end of ul. Zamkowa, caters for a slightly older and less boisterous clientele; although *Journal*, just off the Rynek at Kołłątaja 25/4, is the ideal place for an intimate drink. In summer, *Pod Sową*, beside the castle walls on ul. Zamkowa, is an open-air bar whose DJ-evenings and film shows attract a more bohemian crowd.

North of Olsztyn

If you're not eager to press straight on to the lakes, it's worth considering a day-trip to one of the historical towns in the attractive countryside north of Olsztyn. **Morag**, site of an impressive regional museum, is easily accessible by train, while the churches and castles of **Orneta** and **Lidzbark Warmiński** lie an easy bus ride away from Olsztyn.

The forty-kilometre journey to Lidzbark Warmiński takes you through the open woodlands and undulating farmland characteristic of western Mazury, and if you've caught an early bus there's enough time for a stopoff en route at **DOBRE MIASTO**, a small town with a vast Gothic **church** – the largest in the region after Frombork cathedral – rising majestically from the edge of the main road. Baroque ornamentation overlays much of the interior, and there's a florid late-Gothic replica of Kraków's Mariacki altar; the collegiate buildings round the back house a minor local museum.

△ Street market trader, Gdańsk

Lidzbark Warmiński

Set amid open pastureland watered by the River Łyna, **LIDZBARK WARMIŃSKI** started out as one of the numerous outposts of the Teutonic Knights. When they'd finished conquering the region, they handed the town over to the bishops of Warmia, who used it as their main residence from 1350 until the late eighteenth century. Following the Toruń Treaty, Lidzbark came under Polish rule, becoming an important centre of culture and learning – Copernicus lived here, just one member of a community of artists and scientists. A later luminary of the intellectual scene in Lidzbark was **Ignacy Krasicki** (1735–1801), a staunch defender of all things Polish; after Prussian rule had done him out of his job as archbishop, he turned his attention to writing, producing a string of translations, social satires and one of the first Polish novels.

Sadly, much of the old town centre was wiped out in 1945, only the parish church, town gate and a few sections of the fortifications managing to survive the fighting. Lidzbark's impressive Teutonic **castle**, however, came through unscathed, a stylish, well-preserved, riverside fortress which ranks as one of the architectural gems of the region. Used as a fortified residence for the Warmian bishops, it has the familiar regional period look to it: the square brick structure echoes Frombork cathedral in its tiled roof, Malbork in the turreted towers rising from the corners.

Moving through the main gate you find yourself in a courtyard, with arcaded galleries rising dreamily above, while at ground level there are Gothic cellars with delicate ribbed vaulting. Inside the main structure, fragments of fifteenth-century frescoes are visible in places, and the **chapel** retains its sumptuous Rococo decorations. But the chief interest comes from the exhibits in the **regional museum** (Tues–Sun: June–Sept 9am–5pm, Oct–May 9am–4pm) that now occupies much of the building. The displays begin with excellent Gothic sculpture in the **Great Refectory**, featuring the tombstones of several Warmian bishops, whose heraldic devices still cover the walls. On the second floor are a collection of modern Polish art, not very riveting, and an exquisite exhibition of **icons**. These come from the convent at Wojnowo (see p.251), where the nuns are members of the strongly traditionalist Starowiercy (Old Believers) sect, a grouping which broke away from official Orthodoxy in protest at the religious reforms instigated by Peter the Great.

The east wing of the castle was demolished in the mid-eighteenth century to make way for a bishop's palace and gardens. The **winter garden** opposite the approach to the castle is the most attractive bit left, with a Neoclassical orangery that wouldn't be out of place in a royal residence. Into the town centre the tall **Parish church** is another Gothic brick hall structure, similar in style to Dobre Miasto: the aisles off the vaulted nave reveal some fine Renaissance side altars and old tombstones. The old Protestant church in town is now an Orthodox **cerkiew** used by the Eastern settlers who moved here following the postwar border shifts.

The *Pizza Hotel* **pension**, (℡089/767 5259; ❷), located on the northern side of the town centre at ul. Spółdzielców 2B, is a cheap and cosy alternative to the more upmarket *Pod Kłobukiem* **hotel**, 2km southwest of town at ul. Olsztyńska 4 (℡089/767 3002; ❺). Both places have restaurants.

Orneta

Just under 50km northwest of Olsztyn lies **ORNETA**, a small market town that boasts one of the finest of the many Gothic brick churches scattered around Warmia. Arriving in town by bus brings you almost immediately into the attractive old market square, at one end of which stands the Gothic brick **town hall**, with a snazzy new *kawiarnia* and billiard hall tucked away in its dimly lit medieval cellars.

Off the other end of the square stands the magnificent, robust-looking Gothic **Kościół św. Jana** (St John's Church). Here, for once, the austere brick facade customary in the Gothic churches of northern Poland is transformed by some imaginative and exuberant decoration. A welter of tall slender parapets rises up on all sides of the building, while close inspection of the carved walls reveals sequences of grotesquely contorted faces leering out at the world – the masons obviously retained their sense of humour. Above them a set of five menacing-looking dragon heads jut out from the roof edge, jaws agape and spitting fire down on the onlooker. Surmounting the church is a characteristic high brick tower, thicker and stockier than usual, lending solidity to the ensemble.

After the fabulous exterior, the interior lives up to expectations, the highlight being the complex geometrically patterned decorations on the brick vault soaring above the high nave. An even more than usually ornate high altarpiece and pulpit are matched by the large, solid-looking Baroque organ astride the entrance portal. A fine Gothic triptych stands in the right-hand aisle and Gothic and Renaissance murals decorate several of the side chapels, one sporting a colourful portrait of Renaissance-era Warmian cardinal Stanislaus Hosius. One of the most satisfying Gothic buildings in the region, it's well worth the detour to get here.

By **bus** the town's a one-and-a-half-hour journey from Olsztyn, making it another feasible day-trip. Like Dobre Miasto, it's also on the Olsztyn–Braniewo rail line, with services running a couple of times a day in each direction.

Morąg

Fifty kilometres west of Olsztyn, **MORĄG** is another notable old Prussian settlement. Historically its chief claim to fame is as birthplace of the German Enlightenment poet and philosopher **Johann Gottfried Herder** (1744–1803), a thinker known for his generally pro-Slav sympathies, a fact which explains German President Richard von Weizsäcker's decision to stop off at the town during his first state visit to Poland, specifically to inspect the great man's birthplace.

Ten minutes' east of the train and bus stations, the **Stare Miasto** centre, in slightly better shape than many neighbouring places, provides the focus of interest of an otherwise unmemorable postwar sprawl: the entrance to the empty-looking Gothic **town hall** in the middle of the main square sports a pair of French cannon captured by German forces during the 1870 Franco-Prussian War. The brick-vaulted Gothic parish **church** immediately south of the square received the usual heavy-duty Rococo-Baroque treatment, though overall there's a distinctly Protestant feel to the building – which is what it was until 1945. Later additions aside, some sections of Renaissance polychromy are still visible in the presbytery, and there's a memorial tablet to Herder at the back. Just outside, a newish-looking **statue** of Herder – it hasn't always been exactly kosher to commemorate famous Germans born inside the borders of modern Poland – stands opposite the house where he was born. Behind the church the ruins of the Teutonic Knights' **castle**, embedded in the Stare Miasto walls, afford a fine view over the surrounding countryside, nearby Lake Skiertąg included.

Continuing the Herder theme, the elegant seventeenth-century **Dohna Palace** off the southwestern side of the square, destroyed during the war and rebuilt to the original design, is now a branch of the Warmia and Mazury **regional museum** (Tues–Sun 9am–5pm; 3.50zł). The first room contains an exhibition of the **life of Herder**: first editions of his work, manuscripts, paintings, busts and other contemporary memorabilia place the man firmly in his historical context, emphasizing Herder's extensive network of contacts with other Enlightenment thinkers around Europe – a testament to the eminent sanity and level-headedness of an internationalist-minded philosopher. Herder devoted much of his life to collecting and publishing the folk songs of the Baltic and Slav peoples, in an attempt to demonstrate that they possessed a deep and dignified culture that had been artificially hidden by the feudal social order. Paradoxically, Herder's discovery and promotion of folk-based national cultures provided the intellectual underpinning for the extreme right-wing ideologies of the twentieth century – something that would have horrified the man himself. A large chunk of the rest of the museum is devoted to some impressive and well-displayed collections of art, furniture and handicrafts including porcelain, glass and metalwork culled from four artistic schools – Baroque, Biedermeier, Secessionist and Second-Empire style. If you like lamps, tea sets and other period household paraphernalia you're in for a treat. Last but by no means least comes the museum's artistic showpiece, a large collection of Dutch seventeenth-century portraits and landscapes by, among others, the Honthorst brothers, Pieter Nason and Caspar Netscher. The historical connection with Warmia is underlined by the portraits of the Dohna family, a branch of which moved to Warmia in the seventeenth century and built the palace here. The current exhibition, it turns out, substantially reassembles the palace's own prewar family portrait collection, carefully restored in the 1970s and 1980s at the castle museum in Olsztyn.

The town is easy enough to get to by **train**, lying on the main Olsztyn-Elbląg-Malbork-Gdańsk line. In addition, there are infrequent **bus** connections to Elbląg, Gdańsk and Olsztyn. There's little in the way of **accommodation** in the town, the *Hotel Morąg*, 2km north of the centre at ul. Żeromskiego 36 (☎089/757 4212; ❷), close to the picturesque Lake Narwie, being the only obvious choice. The *Adria* **restaurant**, near the museum at ul. Dąbrowskiego 52, is a reliable source of decent Polish food.

South from Olsztyn

South of Olsztyn takes you into more of the attractive rolling countryside for which the approaches to Mazuria are known. For most people, however, the main reason for heading this way is the battlefield at **Grunwald**, the well-kept *skansen* at **Olsztynek** providing an additional worthwhile stopoff.

Olsztynek and around

OLSZTYNEK, 26km south of Olsztyn, is home to an excellent **skansen** dating from 1941 (Tues–Sun: June–Aug 9am–5pm; May & Sept–Oct 9am–4pm; Nov–April 9am–3pm). Located on the northern edge of the small town, the park is devoted to eighteenth- and nineteenth-century folk architecture from Warmia, Mazuria and, surprisingly, Lithuania as well. Many fine examples of sturdy regional architecture have been gathered here: take a close look at the joints on some of the half-timbered cottages and you'll appreciate the superb workmanship that went into these buildings. Alongside the assorted farm buildings, barns, workshops, and a water mill, there's a fine, early eighteenth-century wooden Protestant church with a thatched roof. The highlight of the lot, though, is undoubtedly the group of old windmills, two of them over two hundred years old. With its huge coloured blades and sturdy plank frame, the **Lithuanian mill** at the edge of the park, known as Paltrak, is a picture-postcard favourite.

For an **overnight stay** in Olsztynek – the town makes a good base if you're going on to Grunwald – the *Mazurski*, ul. Park 1 (☏089/519 2885, ℱ519 2703; ❸), is the obvious venue: there's also a good **restaurant** here, with the excellent local fish dishes a house speciality. The only other place to stay is the smaller and less salubrious *Karczma Świętojańska*, ul. Świętojańska 1 (☏089/519 2005; ❷), which also boasts a passable restaurant.

The Mauzoleum Hindenburga

About a kilometre west of the *skansen* close to the village of Sudwa lie the ruins of the notorious **Mauzoleum Hindenburga** (Hindenburg Mausoleum). The original monument was built here by the German army after World War I to commemorate victory under the command of Field Marshal Paul von Hindenburg over Russian forces at the battle of Tannenberg in August 1914. After Hindenburg's death in 1934, Hitler ordered the monument's transformation into a huge mausoleum for one of the nation's favourite Prussian military figures. With defeat in sight the retreating Nazis moved his remains to Worms Cathedral in Germany in 1945. The mausoleum was obliterated by Soviet forces soon afterwards, the stones eventually being used for a Soviet war monument near Olsztyn. The site isn't marked on the road, but you'll find it in the forest behind the village, a large enclosure marking the site of what was by all accounts a massive structure.

Grunwald

If there's one historical event every Polish schoolchild can give you a date for it's the **Battle of Grunwald** (1410). One of the most important European battles of the medieval era, the victory at Grunwald came to assume the mythological status of a symbol of the nation's resistance to – and on this occasion triumph over – German militarism. Predictably, the reality of the battle was rather more complicated. Commanded by King Władysław Jagiełło, the combined Polish–Lithuanian army opposing Grand Master Ulrich von Jungingen and his knights included plenty of other nationalities among its ranks – Czechs, Hungarians, Ruthenians, Russians and Tatars. In an era when the modern concept of the nation-state was far from established the straight Polish–German struggle proposed in latterday nationalist interpretations of the event seems something of an oversimplification. What is certain is the fact that Grunwald was one of the biggest – over 30,000 men on each side – and bloodiest of medieval battles. The eventual rout of the knights left the Grand Master and 11,000 of his men dead, with another 14,000 taken prisoner. The defeat at Grunwald finally broke the back of the knights' hitherto boundless expansionist ambitions and paved the way for the first of a succession of peace treaties (1411) with Poland-Lithuania that decisively weakened their control over the northern and eastern territories.

The battlefield

The **battle site** lies 20km southwest of Olsztynek. It's not easy to get here without your own vehicle – by public transport local buses run from Olsztynek and, less frequently, Olsztyn. Stuck out in the middle of the pleasant, tranquil Warmian countryside, it's hard to square the surroundings with your idea of a major battle site. The odd modern farmhouse apart, though, the battlefield probably doesn't look that different today from the site that greeted the opposing armies 580-odd years ago. Walking up from the bus stop past the souvenir kiosk brings you to the centrepiece of the site, an imposing thirty-metre-high steel monument that looks uncannily like the Gdańsk Shipyard memorial, set on a hilltop overlooking the battlefield. To help you visualize the whole thing in context, just beyond the monument there's a large stone diagram set out on the ground illustrating the battle positions of the two armies and their movements throughout the fighting.

Back behind the monument the Grunwald **museum** (daily: May–Sept 9am–6pm; Oct–April 10am–4pm; 2.50zł) contains a heavyweight display of armour, weapons, standards and other military paraphernalia from the battle, some original, most later copies. The shield inscribed "Grunwald 1410, Berlin 1945" says much about the postwar Polish state's appropriation of Grunwald for its own specific ideological ends.

Barczewo

Seventeen kilometres east of Olsztyn, set back from the main E16 road into Mazuria, is **BARCZEWO**, another dusty old provincial town where nothing much seems to be changing: the main reason most Poles have heard of the place is the fact that the notorious former Nazi Gauleiter of Mazuria, **Jozef Koch**, was imprisoned here until his death, aged 92, in the early 1980s.

Surprisingly, for a town of this size, Barczewo boasts two attractive Gothic churches. Altar triptychs apart, the austere interior of **Kościół św. Anny** (St Anne's Church), a chunky brick edifice overlooking the river, looks as though it was given a thorough Prussian Protestant reworking. By contrast **Kościół św. Andrzeja** (St Andrew's Church), a fourteenth-century Franciscan foundation off the square, is basic Gothic with a strongly Baroque overlay, the main feature being a delicately sculptured marble Renaissance memorial to Warmian bishop Andreas Batory and his brother Balthazar, designed by Dutch architect Wilhelm van den Blocke of Gdańsk fame. Batory's actual remains aren't here, however, but lost in the Moldavian countryside, where he died in the early 1600s fighting for the independence of his Transylvanian homeland.

Mazuria's not a region usually associated with **Jewish culture**, though until the Nazi era there were in fact plenty of Jews living in the region. South of the square on ul. Kościuszki stands the mid-nineteenth-century former **synagogue**, one of the very few in the region to survive the war. A wartime Nazi ammunition dump, the synagogue was converted into a *Dom Kultury* after 1945.

In 1980 it also became the workshop of local textile artist Barbara Hulanicka, who lives next door at no. 13 – call at her place to get into the synagogue. A skilled weaver with an impressive track record of international exhibitions, Hulanicka has devoted herself to reviving and promoting the folk-weaving traditions of Warmia and Mazuria. Using some wonderful old nineteenth-century looms she's rescued from surrounding villages, Hulanicka produces unusual tapestries, often with themes drawn from different world religions, and several of which you'll find adorning the walls of the building. A mine of information about the region, she's always pleased to show visitors round the workshop, fellow artists in particular.

If you decide to **stay** over, your only options are *Grill Bar Gyros* at ul. Warmińska 56 (☎089/514 8381; ❸), a motel with a restaurant, or the *Hotel Barczewo* in ul. Olsztyńska (☎089/541 4545; ❸).

If you like messing about in boats, one of the best and most exciting ways of exploring the region is from the water. The vast complex of **lakes**, **rivers** and **waterways** means there are literally thousands of options to choose from. For those who haven't lugged their canoes, kayaks and yachts on trailers all the way across Poland – and increasing numbers of Scandinavians and Germans are joining Poles in doing so every summer – the key issue is getting hold of the necessary equipment. With the tourist trade opened up to private operators it's becoming easier to turn up and rent yourself a canoe on the spot. On the more popular routes, however, demand is increasingly high in season, so it would definitely pay to try and organize yourself a boat in advance.

A good resource here is the **PTTK office** in Olsztyn, ul. Staromiejska 1 (☎089/527 5156), which arranges **kayak hire** and advance **accommodation bookings** on some of the more popular kayaking routes. Plenty of detailed **maps** of the region appropriate for canoeists have come on the market; the most useful general ones are the 1:120,000 *Wielkie Jezioro Mazurskie* and a new Polish/English language 1:300,000 *Warmia and Masuria*.

Sorkwity and the Krutynia route

SORKWITY, 12km west of Mrągowo, is the starting point for a beautiful and popular canoeing run which ends 90km downstream at Lake Bełdany, adjoining the western edge of Lake Sniardwy. As well as the PTTK in Olsztyn, the Orbis hotel in **Mrągowo** can help sort out canoe rental for the trip, but in summer advance notice is virtually essential. Accommodation along the route is provided by PTTK-run river stations (*stanica wodna*; usually open from mid-April to Sept); basically these are kayak and canoe depots which also have bungalows and camping space.

Canoeists generally start from the *stanica wodna* at the edge of Sorkwity village. Known as the **Krutynia route**, after the narrow, winding river that makes up the last part of the journey, the route takes you through a succession of eighteen lakes, connected by narrow stretches of river, the banks often covered with dense forest. The journey usually takes anything from nine days upwards, with Ruciane-Nida or Mikołajki the final destination, though you can also shorten the route to a five-day trip ending at Krutyń. The Krutynia route is very popular in high summer, so the best time to make the trip is either in spring (April–May) or late summer (late August–September). Overnight stops are generally in the following places (in *stanice wodne* unless specified):

day one BIEŃKI (15km)
day two BABIĘTA (12km), there's also a youth hostel (July–Aug) here
day three SPYCHOWO (12.5km)
day four ZGON (10.5km)
day five KRUTYŃ (14km)
day six UTKA (18.5km), the first stop on the Krutynia river itself
day seven NOWY MOST (6.5km)
day eight KAMIEŃ (10.5km) on the beautiful Lake Bełdany
day nine ending up at RUCIANE-NIDA (13.5km; see p.250).

If this ambitious excursion sounds appealing, the **Olsztyn PTTK** offers ten-day kayak trips along the route including overnight stops for under $200. In summer, only groups are eligible, so you may have to arrange to tag along with others. You will need to provide your own gear for the trip though, including a sleeping bag. For **advance booking** (strongly recommended in summer) write or even call – if you do there's usually someone there who speaks English or, more likely, German. Other popular routes are the **Czarna Hańcza** kayak route (see p.255) which starts in Stary Folwark on Lake Wigry leading to the Augustowski Canal (100km) or the **Biebrza** route starting in Lipsk and passing through the Biebrzański National Park.

The Mazurian Lakes

East of Olsztyn, the central Mazury lakeland opens out amid thickening forests. In summer the biggest lakes – **Mamry** and **Śniardwy** – are real crowd-pullers, with all the advantages and disadvantages that brings. On the plus side, tourist facilities are well developed in many places, and you can rent sailing and canoeing equipment in all the major resorts. If the weather's good, Mazury can get pretty busy on summer weekends, and accommodation can be hard to find in the main centres. If solitude and clean water are what you're after, the best advice is to get a detailed map and head for the smaller lakes: as a general principle, tranquillity increases as you travel east.

Among highlights, **Mikołajki**, commanding the approaches to Lake Śniardwy in the centre of the region, is arguably the most pleasant and most attractively located of the major-league lakeside resorts; while **Giżycko** and **Węgorzewo**, both perched on the rim of Lake Mamry to the north, attract yachters and canoeists and are useful bases for exploring the lakes. **Ruciane-Nida** provides access to the lakes and waterways of southern Mazury, and has a pleasantly laid-back, forest-shrouded feel. **Mrągowo**, the most westerly of the major towns and a useful transport hub, is nowadays better known for its Country and Western Festival than for general touristic appeal. As well as lakeside pursuits, Mazury also boasts a wealth of historic churches and castles, including the famous monastery complex at **Święta Lipka** and the Gothic ensembles at **Reszel**. A detour into the region's tangled ethnic history is provided by the Orthodox nunnery at **Wojnowo**. In addition, Mazury hides one of the strangest and most chilling of all World War II relics, Hitler's wartime base at **Gierłoz** – a short bus ride away from the attractive small town of **Kętrzyn**.

On the whole, **transport** around the lakes isn't too problematic. While a car is a definite advantage for venturing into the further-flung reaches, **bus** connections between the main centres are more than adequate. Olsztyn is the usual jumping-off point if you're heading this way; while Mrągowo and Giżycko offer most in the way of onward connections to smaller resorts once you arrive. In addition there are a grand total of three **rail lines** from Olsztyn to **Ełk** in the east of Mazury, one of which goes through Kętrzyn and Giżycko en route, another through Mrągowo and Mikołajki, and the third through Ruciane-Nida – services on these lines tend to be less frequent than buses.

As well as the usual spread of hotels, there's an expanding range of private rooms and B&B-style *pensjonaty* in Mazury, especially in burgeoning resorts like Mikołajki. Bear in mind that the accommodation rates quoted in this guide are for the high season (July–Aug): prices drop by about twenty percent in spring and autumn and thirty–forty percent in winter. The tourism-oriented website Ⓦ www.mazury.com.pl is a useful resource if you're looking to book accommodation in advance.

Mrągowo

MRĄGOWO, situated on the main Olsztyn–Augustów road, is one of the principal centres of the district, a busy town ranged around the shores of Lake Czos – a small expanse of water that can't really compete in terms of either natural beauty or holiday activities with the bigger lakes further east. It's best to pick up onward buses to Mikołajki, Ruciane-Nida or Kętrzyn rather than stick around, although there's a pleasant town centre just up from the edge of the lake if you've an hour or two to spare. Here the local **museum** (Tues–Sun

10am–3pm), housed in the old town hall on the Rynek, features an extensive collection of local wooden chests and cabinets alongside some elegant eighteenth-century furniture pieces from around Prussia. A display centring on **Krzysztof Mrongoviusz** fills you in on the locally born priest and nineteenth-century champion of Polish culture after whom the town – originally Sensburg – was renamed in 1945.

The one event that really brings Mrągowo to life is the acclaimed Piknik

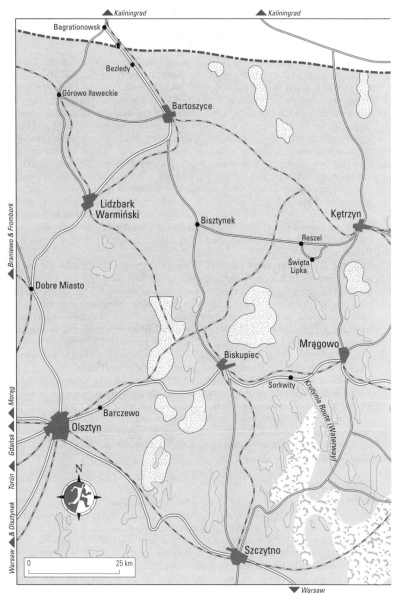

Country Festival on the last weekend in July, held in an amphitheatre on the opposite side of the lake from the town centre. The festival, which has been running since 1983, attracts country music fans from all over Poland, and is an opportunity for aspiring Slav Hank Williamses and Dolly Partons to croon their hearts out in front of large, appreciative audiences. Alongside the local bands, there's always at least a couple of big-name stars from the US – advance info is usually available on www.polcountry.medianet.pl.

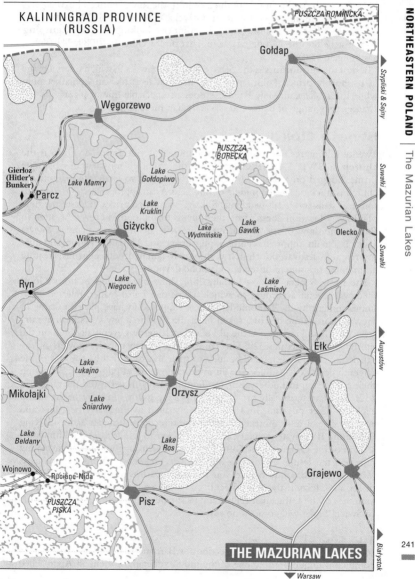

KALININGRAD PROVINCE
(RUSSIA)

PUSZCZA ROMINCKA

Gołdap

Węgorzewo

PUSZCZA
BORECKA

Gierłoż
(Hitler's
Bunker)
Parcz

Lake Mamry

Lake
Gołdopiwo

Lake
Kruklin

Giżycko

Wilkasy

Lake
Wydmińskie

Lake
Gawlik

Olecko

Ryn

Lake
Niegocin

Lake
Laśmiady

Ełk

Lake
Łukajno

Orzysz

Mikołajki

Lake
Śniardwy

Lake
Beldany

Lake
Ros

Wojnowo
Ruciane-Nida

Grajewo

PUSZCZA
PISKA

Pisz

THE MAZURIAN LAKES

Warsaw

Szypliski & Sejny

Suwałki

Suwałki

Augustów

Białystok

241

Practicalities

Mrągowo's **train station** is on the western fringes of town: walk downhill from here for ten minutes to find the **bus station**, where you turn left to reach the town centre (another 10min). The MAT travel agency, near to the museum at ul. Ratuszowa 5 (Mon–Fri 9am–4pm, Sat 10am–3pm; ☎089/741 8151), will fix you up with a **private room** (➊) or **pensjonat** (➋–➌) – reasonable examples of the latter include the *Edyta* at ul. Laskowa 10 (☎ & ℻089/741 4366; ➌) and the *Ewa* at ul. Jaszczurca Góra 14 (☎ & ℻089/741 3116; ➌), both on the far side of the lake from the town centre. The *Mrongovia* **hotel**, near the amphitheatre at ul. Giżycka 6 (☎089/741 3221, ✉mron-gov@orbis.pl; ➐), is a plush Orbis-run joint overlooking the lake. **Camping C-3**, just below the Mrongovia at ul. Jaszczurcza Góra 1 (☎089/741 2533), has bungalows (➊).

Best of the **restaurants** is the *Stara Chata*, Warszawska 9, which offers a range of reasonably priced Polish specialities in what feels like an upmarket pub; while the *Lastalla*, ul. Mały Rynek 1, does a respectable line in pizzas, and has a rather tasty range of pastas and classic Italian meat dishes.

Święta Lipka

Twenty kilometres north and a forty-minute bus ride from Mrągowo is the **church** at **ŚWIĘTA LIPKA**, probably the country's most famous Baroque shrine. Lodged on a thin strip of land in between two lakes, the magnificent church is stuck out in the middle of nowhere. As an approach area stuffed with souvenir stalls and locals peddling "folk art" at inflated prices suggests, the out-of-the-way location doesn't stop the tourists turning up in droves. As often in Poland, the draw of the church isn't purely its architectural qualities; Święta Lipka is also an important centre of pilgrimage and Marian devotion, and during religious festivals the church is absolutely jammed with pilgrims, creating an intense atmosphere of fervent Catholic devotion.

The name Święta Lipka – literally "holy lime tree" – derives from a local medieval legend according to which a Prussian tribal leader, released from imprisonment by the Teutonic Knights, is supposed to have placed a statue of the Virgin in a lime tree as a token of thanks. Within a few years healing miracles were being reported at the place, and a chapel was eventually built on the site by the knights in 1320. The fame and supposed curative powers of the shrine increased by leaps and bounds, to such an extent that by the end of the fifteenth century it had become an important centre of pilgrimage. Following their conversion to Lutheranism, the Teutonic Knights destroyed the chapel in 1526, in characteristically brutal fashion placing gallows in front of the site in a bid to deter pilgrims. In 1620 Poles managed to purchase the ruins, and another chapel was constructed under the direction of Stefan Sadorski, King Sigismund II's private secretary, and handed over to Jesuits from the Lithuanian section of the Order in the 1630s. With pilgrims turning up in ever-increasing numbers the Jesuits decided to build a new and more ambitious sanctuary. Work on the Baroque edifice you see today was begun in 1687 under the direction of Jerzy Ertly, an architect from Vilnius, so to anyone familiar with the churches of the Lithuanian capital and its surroundings, the "Eastern" Baroque of Święta Lipka will come as no surprise.

The church

In a country with a major predilection for Baroque richness the Święta Lipka complex is unquestionably one of the most exuberant of them all. Approached from a country road, the low cloisters, tapering twin towers of the church **facade** and plain yellow and white stucco covering the exterior are quintessential eastern Polish Baroque. **Entrance** to the complex (Mon–Sat 8am–6pm, Sundays in between Masses) is through a magnificent early-eighteenth-century wrought-iron gate designed by Johann Schwartz, a local from Reszel, the surrounding cloisters topped by 44 stone statues representing the genealogy of Christ.

Through the main door you enter the body of the building, a rectangular structure with a long central nave, side aisles divided from the nave on each side by four sets of pillars supporting overhanging galleries and a presbytery. The first thing to catch the eye is the superb **fresco** work covering every inch of the ceiling, the work of one Maciej Meyer from nearby Lidzbark Warmiński, which draws on a wide range of themes ranging from the lives of Christ and Mary and Old Testament stories, to depictions of Jesuit missions and the Marian cult of Święta Lipka itself. Young Meyer was sent off to Rome in the early 1700s to improve his craft, in particular the execution of three-dimensional and trompe l'oeil effects. He clearly learned a thing or two: particularly in the central nave's vaulted ceiling the polychromy is a triumph, several of the frescoes employing the newly acquired trompe l'oeil techniques to powerful effect.

Towering above the nave the lofty main **altarpiece**, an imposing wooden structure completed in 1714, has three levels; the upper two contain pictures on biblical themes, the lowest a seventeenth-century icon of the Madonna and Child – the Holy Mother of God of Święta Lipka as it's known locally – based on an original kept at Santa Maria Maggiore in Rome. Much revered by Polish pilgrims, the Madonna figure was adorned with its crown in the 1960s by the then Polish Catholic primate Cardinal Wyszyński, with a certain Karol Wojtyła (the future Pope John Paul II) in attendance. Imitating the original medieval shrine, a rather grubby-looking eighteenth-century lime tree stands to the left of the altar, topped by a silver statue of the Virgin and Child, the base smothered in pennants pinned there by virtuous pilgrims.

Filling virtually the entire west end of the building is the church's famous Baroque **organ**. Built in 1720 by Johann Mozengel, a Jew from Königsberg – many of the church artists and sculptors came from the old East Prussian capital – it's a huge, fantastically ornate creation, decked with two layers of blue gilded turrets topped by figures of the saints. Renovated by one of the Jesuit brothers during the 1960s, the instrument is in fine shape, producing a marvellously rich sound. When enough people are around, short concerts are given by one of the brothers, the real show-stopper being the exhibition pieces when the instrument's celestial assortment of moving parts are brought into action: the whole organ appears to come alive, gyrating angels blowing their horns, cherubs waving, stars jingling and cymbals crashing – Bach fugues with a heavenly back-up group in accompaniment. It's certainly an extraordinary sight and sound, worth capturing on one of the tapes or CDs you can pick up from the kiosk outside the church. Additionally there are special evening organ concerts every second and fourth Friday of the month from June to August, the second Friday of the month only in September.

Back out of the main building, the **cloisters** are a nice calm spot to recuperate in after the exertions of the church, the ceilings featuring more sumptuous polychromy by Meyer, most notably in the domed cupolas ornamenting the four corners of the structure.

Practicalities

There are a couple of daily buses to Święta Lipka from Mrągowo; otherwise head for Kętrzyn and change there – about fifteen daily Kętrzyn-Reszel services call in at Święta Lipka on the way. If you plan to **stay overnight**, the *Dom Pielgrzyma* in the monastery (☎089/755 1481; ❶) is where pilgrims usually lodge. Accommodation is frugal, with simple rooms (seven doubles and several dorms), and shared facilities, but around the time of any major festivals – and for much of the summer – it's generally full. You'll find plenty of snack bars offering basic food and drink grouped around the monastery entrance.

Reszel

Four kilometres west of Święta Lipka is the historic Warmian centre of **RESZEL**. Seat of the bishops of Warmia for over five centuries, from the establishment of Christianity in the region (1254) until the First Partition (1772), Reszel is also one of Copernicus' many old regional haunts. These days the town is another quiet end-of-the-world provincial hang-out, the main attraction being the small old-town area that sits atop a plateau overlooking the surroundings. Served by numerous daily buses from Kętrzyn, it's also easily accessible by bus from Mrągowo or Olsztyn.

Of the many Gothic country churches in Warmia, Reszel's **Church of St Peter and St Paul** is one of the most immediately striking. Hardly the most elegant of buildings from the exterior, what the church lacks in delicacy it certainly makes up for in sheer size – perhaps that's how those bishops preferred things on their home patch. The monster **church tower** is visible for miles around, and from close up you feel almost as dwarfed as in Kościół Mariacki in Gdańsk (see p.179). The **altarpiece** is a fine piece of Neoclassical elegance, the nave vaulting displaying some of the intricate geometric brick patternwork common throughout the region. On a more delicate note, early Renaissance polychromy using enjoyable plant and animal motifs is still in evidence on the pillars and arches of the nave.

Bulk is also the name of the game in the fourteenth-century **bishop's castle**, just up from the church, an impressive hulk surrounded by the ruins of the old town walls. The castle now houses a rather superior **art gallery** (Tues–Sun 10am–4pm; 4zł) featuring regular exhibitions – generally of the "disturbed and alienated" variety – by well-known contemporary artists, both Polish and foreign. In fact painters and sculptors are regularly invited to live and work in the castle for a few months, so in summer particularly the place is a mine of creative activity. For those mere mortals who aren't offered a castle bedroom of their own, there's the possibility of climbing up the castle tower (same hours as the gallery) for the view over the surroundings. The chic café inside the castle courtyard is exactly what you'd expect of an artists' centre – more *Quartier Latin* than back-of-the-woods Warmia.

Places to stay in town boil down to the rather basic *Rema*, ul. Krasickiego 6A (☎089/755 0273; ❶), and the summer-only **youth hostel** at no. 7 in the same street (☎089/755 0012). Both are close to the bus station, a short walk north of the Old Town.

Kętrzyn and around

Known as Rastenburg until its return to Polish rule in 1945, **KĘTRZYN**, 15km east of Święta Lipka, is a quiet, unexceptional town whose main interest lies in its proximity to Gierłoz – Hitler's **Wilczy Szaniec** (Wolf's Lair).

A short walk up the hill from the bus and train stations stands the old Teutonic town complex, itself built on the site of an earlier Prussian settlement. Badly destroyed in 1945, the well-restored Gothic **Teutonic Knights' castle** is home to a regional **museum** (Mon–Sat 11am–6pm, Sun 10am–5pm; 3zł) housing an exhibition combining local archeology and wildlife. If you don't get to see boars, beavers or badgers in the Mazurian wild you'll find plenty of stuffed ones here, alongside a selection of similarly preserved birds, eagles, owls and cormorants. The second floor is largely devoted to **Wojciech Kętrzyński**, a nineteenth-century local historian and patriot, the epitome of the sort of characters after whom the postwar Polish authorities renamed the Mazurian towns.

Just uphill from the castle the Gothic **Kościół św. Jerzego** (St George's Church), also rebuilt after 1945, is a rather barren, sorry-looking place, a couple of old Prussian memorial tablets all that's left of the original interior decoration. The small fourteenth-century chapel next door, rebuilt in the seventeenth century, and a small house down the hill are both Protestant chapels. North of here the town centre gathers itself around pl. Grunwaldzki, while on ul. Mickiewicza, there's an early nineteenth-century freemasons' lodge, now a Polish-German Cultural Centre (Polsko-Niemeckie Dom Kultury)

With Święta Lipka, the Wolf's Lair and Giżycko well within striking distance, Kętrzyn makes for a convenient – if somewhat laid-back – touring base. The IT **information office**, sharing premises with Orbis at pl. Piłsudskiego 1 (Mon–Fri 9am–4pm; ☎089/751 2040, ⓦwww.ketrzyn.com.pl), will fill you in on private room possibilities (**❶-❷**), although most of these are in outlying farms. Kętrzyn's **hotels** include the *Zajazd pod Zamkiem*, right beside the castle at ul. Struga 3a (☎089/752 3117), which only has quads for 45zł per person – although they're available for double occupancy too (**❹**); and the *Wanda*, about 500m north of the centre at al. Wojska Polskiego 27 (☎089/751 8584; **❹**), which features uninspiring but habitable en-suites. *Koch*, bang in the centre of town at ul. Traugutta 3 (☎089/752 2058, ⓔkoch@post.pl; **❺**), is a touch plusher, with smart and comfortable en-suites firmly geared towards the predominantly German clientele. It also hires out bikes. The *Zajazd pod Zamkiem* has a good **restaurant** with outdoor terrace serving up trusty Polish fare; while the menu at *Loża*, a refined café-restaurant in the Polish-German Cultural Centre, is more adventurous, featuring salads and pasta dishes.

Gierłoz

GIERŁOZ lies 8km east of Kętrzyn and can be reached from there by a regular municipal bus service (#1; June–Sept only), or by Kętrzyn-Węgorzewo buses, some (but not all) of which pass the site. Be careful to check return times, and allow 2 hours for a tour of the site. If you're driving here from Kętrzyn, watch carefully for signposts – the route is badly marked.

Here, deep in the Mazurian forests, Hitler established his military headquarters in the so-called **Wilczy Szaniec** (Wolf's Lair; Tues–Sun 8am–6pm; 10zł), a huge underground complex from which the Germans' eastward advance was conducted. Other satellite bunker complexes were built for the army and Luftwaffe and are spread out in a forty-kilometre radius round the site, mostly now overgrown ruins.

Encased in several metres of concrete were private bunkers for Göring, Bormann, Himmler and Hitler himself, alongside offices, SS quarters and operations rooms. The 27-acre complex was camouflaged by a suspended screen of vegetation that was altered to match the changing seasons, and was permanently mined "in case of necessity". In 1945 the retreating army fired the detonator, but it merely cracked the bunkers, throwing out flailing tentacles of metal reinforcements. Most of today's visitors come in tourist groups – an English-speaking guide is generally on hand to take you round, but costs (call ☏089/751 4467, any day after 6pm, to make sure).

Peering into the cavernous underground bunkers today is an eerie experience. You can see the place, for example, where the assassination attempt on Hitler failed in July 1944 (see box below), the SS living quarters, the staff cinema and other ancillaries of domestic Nazi life. Gruesome photographs and films remind visitors of the scale of German atrocities, but as so often with such material, there's a tendency to resort to horrifying images at the expense of information and critical understanding.

The **airstrip** from which Stauffenberg departed after his abortive assassination attempt is a couple of kilometres east from the main site, a lone runway in the middle of some heathland – you'll need a guide to show you the way.

For anybody wanting to **stay**, there's a simple hotel at the bunker site, *Wilcze Gniazdo* (☏ & ⓕ089/752 4429; ❷), which also has a rather good **restaurant**.

The July Bomb Plot

In the summer of 1944, the Wolf's Lair was the scene of the assassination attempt on Adolf Hitler that came closest to success – the **July Bomb Plot**. Its leader, **Count Claus Schenk von Stauffenberg**, an aristocratic officer and member of the General Staff, had gained the support of several high-ranking members of the German army. Sickened by atrocities on the eastern front, and rapidly realizing that the Wehrmacht was fighting a war that could not possibly be won, von Stauffenberg and his fellow conspirators decided to kill the Führer, seize control of army headquarters in Berlin and sue for peace with the Allies. Germany was on the precipice of total destruction by the Allies and the Soviet Army: only such a desperate act, reasoned the plotters, could save the Fatherland.

On July 20, Stauffenberg was summoned to the Wolf's Lair to brief Hitler on troop movements on the eastern front. In his briefcase was a small bomb, packed with high explosive: once triggered, it would explode in under ten minutes. As Stauffenberg approached the specially built conference hut, he triggered the device. Taking his place a few feet from Hitler, Stauffenberg positioned the briefcase under the table, leaning it against one of the table's stout legs no more than six feet away from the Führer. Five minutes before the bomb exploded, Stauffenberg quietly slipped from the room unnoticed by the generals and advisers, who were listening to a report on the central Russian front. One of the officers moved closer to the table to get a better look at the campaign maps and, finding the briefcase in the way of his feet under the table, picked it up and moved it to the other side of the table leg. Now, the very solid support of the table leg lay between the briefcase and Hitler.

At 12.42 the bomb went off. Stauffenberg, watching the hut from a few hundred yards away, was shocked by the force of the explosion. It was, he said, as if the hut had been hit by a 155mm shell; there was no doubt that the Führer, along with everyone else in the room, was dead.

Stauffenberg hurried off to a waiting plane and made his way to Berlin to join the other conspirators. Meanwhile, back in the wreckage of the hut, Hitler and the survivors staggered out into the daylight: four people had been killed or were dying of their wounds, including Colonel Brandt, who had moved Stauffenberg's briefcase and thus unwittingly saved the Führer's life. Hitler himself, despite being badly shaken, suffered no more than a perforated eardrum and minor injuries. After being attended to, he prepared himself for a meeting with Mussolini later that afternoon.

It was quickly realized what had happened, and the hunt for Stauffenberg was on. Hitler issued orders to the SS in Berlin to summarily execute anyone who was

Mikołajki

Hyped in the brochures as the Mazurian Venice, **MIKOŁAJKI** is unquestionably the most attractive of the top Mazurian resorts. Straddled across the meeting point of two attractive small lakes – the Tałty and Mikołajskie – the small town has long provided a base for yachting enthusiasts on popular nearby Lake Śniardwy. Legend associates the town's name with a monster creature, known as the King of the Whitefish, that terrorized the local fishermen and destroyed their nets. The beast finally met its match in a young local called Mikołajek who caught the huge fish in a steel fishing net. Despite being the most popular resort in Mazury among well-heeled Varsovians, present-day Mikołajki has succeeded in retaining its low-rise, fishing-village appearance. There's been a rash of new construction work in recent years – mostly in the form of luxury flats and shops – but new buildings have by and large blended in with their surroundings, aping the half-timbered styles of the past. Although there's an abun-

slightly suspect, and dispatched Himmler to the city to quell the rebellion. Back in the military Supreme Command headquarters in Berlin, the conspiracy was in chaos. Word reached Stauffenberg and the two main army conspirators, generals Beck and Witzleben, that the Führer was still alive: they had already lost hours of essential time by failing to issue the carefully planned order to mobilize their sympathizers in the city and elsewhere, and had even failed to carry out the obvious precaution of severing all communications out of the city. After a few hours of tragicomic scenes as the conspirators tried to persuade high-ranking officials to join them, the Supreme Command HQ was surrounded by SS troops, and it was announced that the Führer would broadcast to the nation later that evening. The coup was over.

The conspirators were gathered together, given paper to write farewell messages to their wives, taken to the courtyard of the HQ and, under the orders of one **General Fromm**, shot by firing squad. Stauffenberg's last words were "Long live our sacred Germany!" Fromm had known about the plot almost from the beginning, but had refused to join it. By executing the leaders he hoped to save his own skin – and, it must be added, knowingly saved them from the torturers of the SS.

Hitler's ruthless revenge on the conspirators was without parallel even in the bloody annals of the Third Reich. All the colleagues, friends and immediate relatives of Stauffenberg and the other conspirators were rounded up, tortured and taken before the "People's Court", where they were humiliated and given more-or-less automatic death sentences. Many of those executed knew nothing of the plot and were found guilty merely by association. As the blood lust grew, the Nazi Party used the plot as a pretext for settling old scores, and eradicated anyone who had the slightest hint of anything less than total dedication to the Führer. General Fromm, who had ordered the execution of the conspirators, was among those tried, found guilty of cowardice and shot by firing squad. Those whose names were blurted under torture were quickly arrested, the most notable being **Field Marshal Rommel**, who, because of his popularity, was given the choice of a trial in the People's Court – or suicide and a state funeral.

The July Bomb Plot caused the deaths of at least five thousand people, including some of Germany's most brilliant military thinkers and almost all of those who would have been best qualified to run the postwar German government. Within six months the country lay in ruins as the Allies and Soviet Army advanced; had events been only a little different, the entire course of the war – and European history – would have been altered incalculably.

dance of decent accommodation, it can still be hard work finding a place to stay on summer weekends.

The Town

Most activity centres on the waterfront, just downhill from the main Rynek. Here you'll find an extensive **marina**, thronging with yachting types over the summer, and a generous collection of outdoor cafés and bars. Working your way west along the waterfront, towards the two bridges (one for pedestrians, the other for the main road to Mrągowo), brings you to the passenger jetty used by the **excursion boats** operated by Żegluga Mazurska (see "Boat Trips on the Main Lakes" box opposite). There's also a **beach** of sorts on the other side of the lake (basically a grassy area with a couple of wooden piers), reached by crossing the footbridge and bearing left.

Unusually for modern Poland, the main church in town is the Protestant **Kościół św. Trójcy** (Holy Trinity Church), overlooking the shores of Lake Tałty. Designed by German architect Franz Schinki, this solid-looking early-nineteenth-century structure is the centre of worship for the region's Protestant community. Portraits of two early pastors apart, it's a fairly spartan place, light years away in feel from the usual Catholic churches.

Prime out-of-town attraction is the nature reserve round **Lake Łukajno**, 4km east of town, the home of one of Europe's largest remaining colonies of wild swans. It's an easy walk across rolling countryside, following the signed road which heads eastwards just uphill from Mikołajki bus station. The best viewing point is the **Wieża Widokowa** tower, signposted off the road and located at the lake's edge, though even here, it's very much a hit-and-miss issue whether you get to see the birds. Best time to be here is July–August, when the birds change their feathers – from a distance, the surface of the lake can look like a downy bed.

Practicalities

The **train station** is twenty minutes' walk northeast of the centre, but with only two daily train services from Olsztyn and Mrągowo you're more likely to arrive at the **bus station**, just west of the centre next door to the Protestant church. A five-minute walk down ul. 3 Maja will bring you to the main square, pl. Wolności, where the **tourist office** at no.3 (May–Sept only; Mon–Fri 9am–5pm; ☎087/421 6850; ⓦwww.mikolajki.pl) will direct you towards **private rooms** (❶) and **pensjonaty** (❷); otherwise it's a question of looking for the numerous *wolne pokoje* signs hanging outside private houses: ul. Kajki, the main street running east from the square, is a good place to start looking. Among the *pensjonaty* worth trying are the *Mikołajki*, ul. Kajki 18 (☎087/421 6437, ⓔpens.mik@pro.onet.pl; ❸–❺ depending on whether you get a lake view), a creaky but comfortable house that backs right onto the lakeside promenade; and *Na Skarpie* at ul. Kajki 96 (☎087/421 6418; ❹–❺), a slightly more modern building which enjoys a similarly convenient position. There's an increasing number of **hotels** to choose from: the *Mazur*, pl. Wolności 6 (☎087/421 69 41 and 421 69 42; ❻), has stylish en-suites right on the main square, and is a good deal more cosy than the mammoth-proportioned, 500-room *Gołębiewski*, northwest of town on the Mrągowo road at ul. Mrągowska 34 (☎087/429 0700, ⓦwww.golebiewski.pl; ❼, ask about week-end discounts), which is very much a resort in itself, complete with its own lake access, shopping mall, indoor pool and tennis courts. Main **campsite** is the *Wagabunda*, perched on a hill above town at ul. Leśna 2 (☎087/421 6018), a large tree-shaded site with bungalows (❶) and plenty of space for tents and caravans. In addition, numerous private gardens across the footbridge from the town centre accept tent-campers in summer (look for "*Pole namiotowe*" signs).

Boat trips on the main lakes

From mid-April to October the Żegluga Mazurska boat company runs regular **ferry services** on the main lakes. Numerous itineraries are on offer, ranging from short circuits around a particular lake, to longer trips linking Mazuria's main towns. They're intended as tourist excursions rather than as a means of public transport, but they represent a scenic and leisurely way of getting around. Prices are about 20zł per person for the shorter trips, rising to about 60zł per person for a long trip through the whole lake system. Some of the more important routes are as follows:

Giżycko–Mikołajki (3hr–4hr 30min)
Węgorzewo-Giżycko–Mikołajki (7hr 30min)
Mikołajki–Ruciane (2hr 30min)
Giżycko–Węgorzewo (2hr 30min)

At peak season (June–Aug) boats depart daily; otherwise, depending on demand, it's likely to be weekends and national holidays only. Often packed, the boats are mostly large, open-deck steamers with a basic snack bar on board for refreshments. **Tickets** are purchased at the passenger jetties at each stop, or on the boats themselves. **Timetables** (*rozkłady*) for departures are posted by the jetties at all the major lakeside stopoff points, and should also be available from the tourist offices in both Mikołajki and Giżycko. Otherwise contact Żegluga Mazurska's main office in Giżycko at al. Wojska Polskiego 8 (☎087/428 5332, ⊛www.gizycko.com.pl/zegluga _mazurska).

For **eating**, the *Cukiernia* at ul. 3 Maja 6 is the best place to stock up on bread and pastries, and also does a roaring trade in waffles (*gofry*) piled high with fruit and cream. *Café Mocca*, between pl. Wolności and the lakefront at Kowalska 4, does a decent set breakfast, alongside cheap lunches and good ice cream. There are any number of stalls along the lakefront offering cheap fried fish; *Okoń*, just beneath the main road bridge into town, is one of the more stylish of the fry-up joints. Slightly inland, *Cinema Quick Wojtek*, pl. Wolności 10, serves up a good-quality meat-and-fish menu in movie-themed interior, and has a terrace from which you can observe goings-on on the square; while *Pizzeria Królewska*, Kajki 5, serves up serviceable pizzas and grill-snacks in a brace of subterranean rooms. **Drinking** takes place in the impromptu fish-fry stalls along the lakefront until about midnight, when people gravitate towards the unpretentious *ABC* **disco** in the Dom Kultury on ul. Kolejowa.

Enquire at the tourist office about **kayak** and **boat rental**. Most of the lakeside hotels also have their own stock of canoes and water sports equipment for use by guests, some also extending to bicycles.

South from Mikołajki

Travelling south from Mikołajki you're soon into the depths of the **Puszcza Piska** (Pisz Forest), a characteristic Mazurian mix of woodlands and water. A huge tangle of crystal-clear lakes, lazy winding rivers and dense forest thickets, it's the largest *puszcza* in the region, one of the surviving remnants of the primeval forest that once covered much of northeastern Europe. The forest is mainly pine, many of the trees reaching thirty to forty metres in height, with some magnificent pockets of mixed oak, beech and spruce in between. A favourite with both canoers – the Krutynia River (see p.238) runs south through the middle of the forest – and walkers, who use the area's developed network of hiking trails, the Puszcza Piska is a delightful area well worth exploring, with the forest lakeside resort of **Ruciane-Nida** providing the obvious base.

Ruciane-Nida

Twenty-five kilometres south of Mikołajki along a scenic forest road is the lakeside resort of **Ruciane-Nida**. Actually two towns connected by a short stretch of road, it's an understandably popular holiday centre, offering a combination of forest and lakeland. Despite its forest location, the town is fairly accessible, with regular **trains** from Olsztyn, and **buses** from Mrągowo and (less frequently) Mikołajki.

Arriving by train from the Olsztyn direction, **RUCIANE** is the first stopoff point – although buses sometimes drop off at Nida first before terminating at Ruciane train station. Walk just south of the station and you're at the water's edge, in this case the narrow canal connecting the two lakes nearest the town: the jetty with the sign marked *Żegluga Mazurska* is the boarding point for excursion boats on the Giżycko–Mikołajki–Ruciane line, the boats travelling through the connecting series of lakes culminating in Lake Nidzkie running south from the town. If you're staying in town, there are also daily summertime excursions round the lake itself.

A kilometre further down the lakeside road, **NIDA** is a disappointment: largely made up of greying postwar blocks, it has little of the laid-back resort atmosphere of its neighbour.

Much of the **accommodation** is located on ul. Wczasów, the forest-fringed main road that links the two towns: it's here that you'll find the lakeside *Perła Jezior* at no.17 (☎ & 🖷 087/423 1044), which has holiday bungalows (❶) as well as camping space; and Wodnik at no.2 (☎087/423 1075), which has four-person wooden cabins for 90zł.

The Old Believers

In a country characterized by a proliferation of historic religious groups, the Orthodox sect of **Old Believers** – *Starowiercy* or *Staroobrzędowcy* as they are known in Polish – are among the smallest and most archaic. The origins of the group lie in the liturgical reforms introduced into the Russian Orthodox Church by Nikon, the mid-seventeenth-century patriarch of Moscow. Faced with the task of systematizing the divergent liturgical texts and practices by then in use in the national church, Nikon opted to comply with the dominant contemporary Greek practices of the time, such as the use of three fingers instead of two when making the sign of the cross and the use of Greek ecclesiastical dress.

Widespread opposition to **the reforms** focused around a group of Muscovite priests led by archpriest Avvakum Petrovich, for which he and a number of others were eventually executed. In many instances, opponents of the reforms were motivated not so much by opposition to the substance of the changes as by the underlying assumption that the contemporary Greek church represented the "correct" mode of liturgical practice.

The stern attitude of the church authorities, who swiftly moved to endorse Nikon's reforms, anathematize dissenters and pronounce acceptance of the changes "necessary for salvation", ensured that compromise was out the question, and for the next two centuries, dissenters, appropriately dubbed "Old Believers", were subjected to often rigorous persecution by the tsarist authorities. Initially strongest in the northern and eastern regions of the Russian empire (they also eventually gained a significant following in Moscow itself), the dissenters or **Raskolniki**, already divided into numerous, often opposing sects, strenuously opposed all attempts at change. This included the **Westernizing reforms** introduced in the early 1700s by Peter the Great, whom they regarded as the Antichrist. Under constant pressure from the authorities, groups of Old Believers began to move west, establishing themselves in the Suwałki region around Sejny (then on the borders of the Russian empire) around the time of the late-eighteenth-century **Polish Partitions** – as far as possible from Moscow's reach. A few

The Wojnowo Nunnery

For much of the last two centuries the area round Ruciane-Nida has been populated by communities of Orthodox **Old Believers**. The quiet seclusion of the forests and the proximity to water made the area an obvious choice for a habitually shy and retiring people. Slowly but surely the local Old Believers are dwindling in numbers, but you'll still find some of them living in the villages north of the town.

Some 6km west of Ruciane, however, is the best-known monument to their presence in the region, the **nunnery** at **WOJNOWO**. Established in the mid-nineteenth century as a centre for promoting and preserving the old-style Orthodox faith in Mazuria, the nunnery has had its ups and downs. Decline forced it to close down in 1884, after which an energetic young nun was sent from the community in Moscow to revive the place. Her efforts led to a revival which continued until World War I, after which, decline set in again. Today this once-thriving community is down to two nuns, both well over eighty, who are cared for by a local fellow-believer. Coming up the track leading off from the Ruciane–Babięta road the first impression is that you must have entered a local farm by mistake. Through the gateway it turns out to be the nunnery after all, the main building set between farmyard barns and stables on one side and a plain white church on the other.

At their age, the nuns are past showing anyone round, but knock at the main door and you should find the caretaker who'll be able to take you up to the church. If you have to wait while she finishes off in the kitchens, you could take a short stroll up to the community's **cemetery**, a small rather melancholy

of these early settlements, including their original *molenna* (places of worship) survive in the region, notably in Suwałki, Wodziłki, Pogorzelec and Gabowe Grądy.

In the 1820s, a new wave of emigration saw the Old Believers moving further west into Prussian-ruled Mazuria, establishing the convent at Wojnowo (see overleaf) that became the spiritual focal point of the Old Believers in the surrounding regions. Life became easier for members of the sect following the tsar's April 1905 **Edict of Toleration**, and they were able to continue their religious practices relatively undisturbed in the Soviet Union, newly independent Poland, and Prussia. The advent of World War II, however, dealt a severe blow to the Polish Old Believer community within Poland. Under the pressure of Nazi persecution – the habitually long-bearded male members of the sect were often mistakenly identified as rabbis, for example, and subjected to all sorts of humiliations as a consequence – most of the rest fled to Lithuania, where they remain to this day in the Klaipeda region. Following the end of World War II, a few returned to their old settlements, but the soul had effectively been ripped out of the community. Today, it's estimated that no more than 2000 remain in Poland, a number that continues to diminish year by year, and at this rate the long-term future of the community definitely looks to be in doubt.

Despite the numerical decline, the rudiments of Old Believer faith and practice remain as they have long been. In liturgical matters, the sect is egalitarian, rejecting the ecclesiastical hierarchy of conventional Orthodoxy, electing their clergy and sticking firmly to the use of Old Church Slavonic for services. Strict social rules are also (at least theoretically) applied – no alcohol, tobacco, tea or coffee, many families still live in unmodernized wooden rural houses, the older people speak a curious mixture of Polish and old-fashioned Russian, and the community as a whole tends towards the shy and retiring. Outwardly, at least, the one place where they really come into their own is during their services, characterized by the use of distinctive and hauntingly beautiful trance-like hymns and chants.

enclosure of Cyrillic-inscribed gravestones which overlooks the banks of the Krutynia. The setting is wonderful though, the swaying trees, tall waterside rushes and graceful contours of the river making this a peaceful and memorable spot.

The **church interior** is laid out on the conventional Orthodox pattern, with a notable iconostasis and accompanying collection of old icons. It's actually only a small part of the community's icon collection, the rest having been moved some years ago to the castle museum at Lidzbark Warmiński (see p.233) once the dwindling community of nuns no longer felt able to look after them. You're not allowed to take pictures, but if you ask, the caretaker will sell you a postcard.

Giżycko and around

Forty kilometres north of Mikołajki, and squeezed between Lake Niegocin and the marshy backwaters of Lake Mamry, **GIŻYCKO** is one of the main lakeland centres. It was flattened in 1945, however, and the rebuilding didn't create a lot of character: if greyish holiday-resort architecture lowers your spirits, don't plan to stay for long before heading out for the lakes. Wilkasy (see opposite) is a much more pleasant base.

From the adjacent train and bus stations, head uphill to reach the modern town centre around ul. Warszawska, or head west to reach an attractive waterside area on the shores of Lake Niegocin, characterized by grassy open spaces and occasional stands of trees. Here you'll find the passenger jetty for **boat trips** (see box p.249), and a swanky yachting marina further on. Carry on westwards for about a kilometre and you'll reach Giżycko's only real historical sight, **Twierdza Boyen** (Boyen Fortress), an enormous star-shaped affair built by the Prussians in the mid-nineteenth century to shore up their defences against the tsarist empire. It's usually open during daylight hours, when you can ramble around the slightly unkempt, park-like interior.

The **tourist office**, ul. Warszawska 7 (Mon–Fri 9am–4pm; ☎087/428 5265, ⓦwww.gizycko.ceti.com.pl), will point you in the direction of the private rooms (❶); otherwise the cheapest option is the **youth hostel** near the bus and train stations at ul. Kolejowa 10 (☎087/428 2244). Of the **hotels**, the *Jantar*, ul. Warszawska 10 (☎087/428 5415; ❺) is a small downtown place on the main street; while the *Zamek*, between the centre and the fortress at ul. Moniuszki 1 (☎087/428 2419; ❸), offers tidy little rooms in an attractive wooded area near the lake. Plushest of the lot is the *Wodnik*, ul. 3 Maja 2 (☎087/428 3872, ⓦwww.cmazur.elknet.pl; ❺–❻), a big concrete affair just off ul. Warszawska. There's a **campsite** next to the *Hotel Zamek* (May–Sept; same tel).

For **eating** there's a basic pizzeria, *Nicola*, at ul. Warszawska 14, Polish fare at the restaurant attached to the *Hotel Wodnik*, and, best of all, a range of fish dishes at *Pod Złotą Rybką,* ul. Olztyńska 15, the most expensive option but still a bargain.

Giżycko is one of the main bases for **yacht charter** companies, with craft being rented out from the beginning of May to end Sept – although bear in mind that in peak periods (July & Aug), yachts often cannot be chartered for anything less than a 7-day period. Places at which to make enquiries include Marina Bełbot, ul. Smętka 20a (☎087/428 7135, ⓦwww.marina.com.pl); and Wiking, ul. Królowej Jadwigi 10/9 (☎060/2303 588, ⓦwww.wiking .mazury.info.pl). Depending on whether you're looking for a 4- or 6-person craft, you'll be paying around 240–310zł per day in high season, 100zł less in May and September.

Wilkasy

Five kilometres west of Giżycko, and served by Giżycko-Mikołajki buses, **WILKASY** is a pleasingly laid-back holiday resort sprawled around the north-western shoulder of Lake Niegocin. If you want to experience how Poles (who overrun the place in summer) take their Mazurian holidays, this is the place to head for, with its assortment of lakeside rest homes, holiday cabins and hostels – and may make for a more restful base than Giżycko itself. Apart from some nice enclosed swimming areas by the lake, the other attraction of Wilkasy is that it's much easier to **rent canoes** or **kayaks** here. Before they are allowed to set oar to water, Poles have to produce an official card proving they can swim, but you should be able to persuade the attendants to let you aboard. It makes for a pleasant day, paddling round the lake, hiving off into reed beds or canals as the fancy takes you.

Best place to **stay** for an activity-based holiday is the *Country Club Wilkasy*, ul. Niegocińska 7 (☎087/428 0454, ✉wilkasy@orbis.pl), a sizeable settlement of simple chalets (❷) and well-appointed hotel blocks (❺), complete with tennis courts, horse-riding facilities and boat-rental. Other alternatives include the Tajty, ul. Przemysłowa 17 (☎087/428 0194, ✉tajty@polbox.com; ❹), a medium-sized hotel with respectable en-suites; and the *Fregata*, a swish but cosy *pensjonat* in the southwestern part of the resort beside the Mrągowo road at Olsztyńska 86 (☎087/428 0202; ❹). Plenty of fish-and-chip stalls sprout up during the summer, and both the Country Club and the Tajty have solid **restaurants**.

Węgorzewo

Twenty-five kilometres north of Giżycko on the furthest edge of Lake Mamry is **WĘGORZEWO**, another former Teutonic stronghold established on the site of an earlier Prussian settlement, and one of the major holiday centres for the northern Mazurian lakelands. Despite the enjoyable rural setting, however, like its bigger cousin Giżycko, the town itself is a formless, unprepossessing sort of place, the only real reason to come here being the access it offers to Lake Mamry, the second largest in the region. The town is set back 2km from the lakefront, so there's not much promenading pleasure on offer to the passing tourist unless you follow the path which heads south from the town centre, following the channel which connects Węgorzewo to the open water – you'll pass the passenger jetty for Żegluga Mazurska boats, and a small yachting marina, on the way.

Decent accommodation options include the simple but adequate PTTK hotel, by the yachting marina at ul. Wańkowicza 3 (☎087/427 2443; ❷); and the nearby Pensjonat Nautic, ul. Słowackiego 14 (☎087/427 2080; ❹), which offers comfier en-suites with TV. For campers there's the *Rusałka* (May–Sept), a good site with restaurant nicely situated on the shores of Lake Święcajty, signed off the Giżycko road 4km south of the town (☎087/427 2191). Best of a basically undistinguished selection of restaurants is that of the *Nautic*, with some Italian and French as well as Polish dishes.

Ełk

EŁK, the easternmost main town of Mazury, is a major train interchange, straddling the crossover point between lines connecting Olsztyn in the west with Suwałki and Białystok in the east. Established by the Teutonic Knights as a base from which to "protect" the locals and keep an eye on the heathen Lithuanian hordes, the town was colonized by Poles in the sixteenth century, before becoming an East Prussian border post during the Partitions.

It remained an important East Prussian centre until 1945 – German novelist Siegfried Lenz, whose work touches on the history and traditions of the region, was born here – and suffered comprehensive damage during the war. The main street, ul.Wojska Polskiego, running along the edge of the town lake, leads to the **parish church**, originally a Gothic construction rebuilt from scratch in the nineteenth century. Beyond it, on an island, stand the ruins of the old **Teutonic castle**, built in the early 1400s.

However, many visitors don't get much further than the shabby square below the train station; there really isn't much to detain you in the sprawling, tatty town centre. If you're forced to spend the night here, head for the *Grunwald* **hotel**, ul. Królowej Jadwigi 21 (☎087/610 2262; ❹); or the slightly fancier *Horeka*, by the lakefront at ul.Wojska Polskiego 63 (☎087/621 3768; ❺), both of which have en-suites with sat-TV. The restaurant at the Grunwald has a decent range of local fish; otherwise the *Horteks*, ul.Armii Krajowej 7, is worth trying for traditional Polish dishes.

Augustów, Suwałki and the Suwalszczyna

The region around the towns of **Augustów** and **Suwałki** is one of the least visited parts of Poland: even for Poles, anything beyond Mazury is still pretty much *terra incognita*. An area of peasant farmers and tortuous ethnic and religious loyalties, as with most parts of eastern Poland, the region north of Suwałki – the **Suwalszczyna** – is little developed economically. Like the Bieszczady Mountains (see p.361), its counterpart in obscurity, the Suwalszczyna is also one of the most beautiful, unspoilt territories in Europe. Once a part of the tsarist empire, much of the region's older architecture – most notably in the regional capital, **Suwałki** – has a decidely Russian feel to it. **Jews** were long a major element of the region's fluid ethnic mix, almost the only surviving sign of this being the **cemeteries** you find rotting away at the edge of numerous towns and villages throughout the area. The region's proximity to Lithuania is reflected, too, in the sizeable **Lithuanian** minority concentrated in the northeast corner of the region.

Visually the striking feature of the northern part of the Suwalszczyna is a pleasing landscape of rolling hills and fields interspersed with crystal-clear lakes – often small, but extremely deep – the end product of the final retreat of the Scandinavian glacier that once covered the area. Much of the southern stretch of this region is covered by the **Puszcza Augustówska**, the remains of the vast forest that once extended well into Lithuania. In the north, by contrast, wonderfully open countryside is interspersed with villages and lakes – some reasonably well known, like **Lake Hańcza** (the deepest in Poland), others, often the most beautiful, rarely visited. Wandering through the fields and woodland thickets you'll find storks, swallows, brilliantly coloured butterflies and wild flowers in abundance, while in the villages modern life often seems to have made only modest incursions, leaving plenty of time to sit on the porch and talk.

Getting around isn't exactly straightforward: buses operate in most of the region, but frequency declines the closer you get to the Lithuanian border. Suwałki and Augustów both have main-line train connections to Warsaw, and, slowly but surely, a fledgling network of rail, bus and air connections on into Lithuania is developing.

Augustów and around

The region around **AUGUSTÓW** was settled at some indistinct time in the early Middle Ages by Jacwingians, a pagan Baltic Slav tribe. The evidence suggests that the Jacwingians had a fairly advanced social structure; what's sure is that they posed a major threat to the early Mazovian rulers, persistently harrying at the edges of Mazovia from their northern domain. By the end of the thirteenth century, however, they had been effectively wiped out by the colonizing Teutonic Knights, leaving as testimony only a few sites such as the burial mound near Suwałki (see p.259) and a scattering of place names. The area remained almost deserted for the next two centuries or so, until the town's establishment in 1557 by King Sigismund August (hence the name) as a supply stopoff on the eastern trade routes from Gdańsk. It only really developed after the construction of the **Augustów Canal** in the nineteenth century. A hundred-kilometre network of rivers, lakes and artificial channels, this waterway was cut to connect the town to the River Niemen in the east, providing a transport route for the region's most important natural commodity, wood. Still in use today, the canal offers the most convenient approach to the heart of the forest (see p.257).

Canoeing along the Czarna Hańcza River

Along with the Krutynia (see p.238) the **Czarna Hańcza River** is one of the most beautiful – and popular – **canoeing routes** in the northeast Polish lakelands, and part of the five percent of Polish rivers still designated as grade 1 ("clean") water. If you've ever had a hankering for a backwater canoeing expedition this is as good a chance as any to satisfy it.

Rising in Belarus, the 140-kilometre-long river, a tributary of the Niemen, flows into the Puszcza Augustówska, winding its way through the Wigry National Park up to Lake Hańcza, 15km northwest of Suwałki. On the usual canoe route, the first leg of the journey starts from **Augustów**, following the Augustów Canal (see above) east to the point where it meets the Czarna Hańcza, a few kilometres short of the Belarusian border: from there the route continues on up the river to **Suwałki** and, stamina allowing, beyond to **Lake Hańcza**.

An alternative route involves exploring **Lake Wigry** and the surrounding national park. This trip heads east from Augustów along the canal, turning north at **Swoboda** and continuing 12km into **Lake Serwy**, an attractive forest-bound tributary. From here the canoes are transported across land to the village of **Bryzgiel,** on the southern shores of Lake Wigry. Three days are given over to exploring the peaceful and unspoilt lake and its protected surroundings. Overnight camps are on the island of **Kamien**, one of several on the lake, and by the lakeside at **Stary Folwark** (see p.260) with a trip up to the monastery included. Leaving Wigry near the **Klasztorny peninsula**, the canoes re-enter the Czarna Hańcza, heading south through a spectacular forest-bound section of the river before rejoining the Augustów Canal and making their way back to Augustów.

Both the above trips can be organized through the PTTK offices in Augustów and Suwałki, and take ten or eleven days, with accommodation – mostly in *stanice wodne* (waterside hostels) – and meals provided throughout: you'll need to provide your own sleeping bag, rubber boots (ideally) and appropriate clothing. The current cost for both trips is around £140/US$200 – a bargain. Contact the **PTTK offices** in Suwałki, ul. Kościuszki 37 (☎087/566 5961), or Augustów, ul. Nadrzeczna 70a (☎087/644 3850), or the Sirocco agency in Augustów, ul. Zarzecze 5a (☎087/643 3118), or Necko in Augustów, ul. Chreptowicza 3/39 (☎087/644 5639, ✉necko@augustownet.com.pl).

Thanks to its location on the edge of the *puszcza* and the surrounding abundance of water, Augustów has carved out a growing niche for itself as a holiday centre. As a town it's no great shakes, but it does allow immediate access to **Lake Necko**, which lies immediately north of the centre. Heading west from the Rynek along ul. Nadrzeczna leads after fifteen minutes or so to a small beach and boat rental facilities. However the best of the lakeside terrain lies north of the centre: head east from the Rynek and north across the bridge to find a small tourist **port** on ul. 29 Listopada, the departure point for sightseeing **boats** in the summer, and a pleasant spot from which to admire the swan- and duck-filled waterscapes of the lake. Beyond here, a network of woodland **walks** lead round the shore of the lake, passing several stretches of beach (the shore itself is grassy, but the lake bottom itself is quite sandy), and a waterskiing centre.

Practicalities

Augustów's **bus** station is right in the middle of town on Rynek Zygmunta Augusta. The main **train** station is 3km to the northeast: regular buses run into town. Some slower Osobowy train services also stop at Augustów Port (not to be confused with the tourist port as mentioned above), a small halt 1km west of the main train station which is slightly closer to the centre – although there's not much in it. Online **information** is available from ⓦ www.um.augustow.pl or ⓦ www.augustowski.home.pl, while the tourist information centre, just east of the Rynek at ul. 3 Maja 31 (July & Aug: Mon–Sat 9am–5pm; Sept–June Mon–Fri 9am–3pm; ☎087/643 2883), is reasonably well organized, and can help sort you out with a private room (❶–❷). Other **places to stay**, most of which are concentrated in the norhern part of town, midway between the centre and the train station, include the *Dom Nauczyciela* at ul. 29 Listopada 9 (☎087/643 2021; ❸), a medium-sized place offering neat and tidy en-suites next to the tourist port; and the *Hetman*, a rather functional hotel right by the lake at ul. Sportowa 1 (☎087/644 5345; en-suites ❸, rooms with shared facilities ❷), designed in the late 1930s by Maciej Nowicki, one of the architects responsible for the UN building in New York – although you'd never be able to tell from the barrack-like building on display here. Slightly more comfortable are the *Krechowiak*, ul. I Pułku Ułanów Krechowieckich 2 (☎087/643 2033, ⓔ krechowiak@home.pl; ❸), a modern block with prim en-suites a short walk east of the lake; and the upmarket *Warszawa*, ul. Zdrojowa 1 (☎087/643 2805, ⓦ www.hotelaugustow.home.pl; ❻), offering snazzy en-suites in a prime location, with the lake on one side and dense woodland on the other. There's a **campsite** at ul. Sportowa 1, next to the *Hetman*; and a seasonal **youth hostel** (July–Aug) at ul. Konopnickiej 9.

Eating out in Augustów revolves around the kind of fish-fry stalls common to all of Poland's lake resorts. You'll find a couple next to the tourist port, as well as several along ul. Mostowa, which heads north from the main Rynek. *Bella Italia*, just east of the Rynek at ul 3 Maja 21, is the best of the sit-down pizza joints; while the café-restaurant of the *Dom Nauczyciela* hotel offers up meat- and fish-based staples in simple surroundings. Best of the restaurants is the *Kolumnowa*, inside the Hotel Warszawa, where you'll find a mixture of Polish and modern European cuisine, a few vegetarian choices, and bearable prices.

You can also get snacks at the al-fresco cafés which sprout up around the Rynek in summer, and serve as handy daytime **drinking** venues. *Hades Rock Café*, Mostowa 12a, is a basement bar with guitar-based noise on the sound system, and is a lot friendlier than the bats-and-skulls decor suggests; while *Pub Bab*, Rynek 7, is an animated, welcoming cellar pub which also does substantial food.

For **kayak** and **canoe rental**, try the main tourist office (see above); the PTTK office at ul. Nadrzeczna 70a (☎087/644 3850); Sirocco, ul. Zarzecze 5a (☎087/643 3118); or Necko, ul. Chreptowicza 3/39 (☎087/644 5639, ⓔnecko@augustownet.com.pl). All of these rent out craft by the day for around 20zł, and also organize trips of longer duration down the Czarna Hańcza river (see box on p.255).

The forest and the canal

The combination of wild forest, lakes and narrow winding rivers around Augustów has made the *puszcza* a favourite with canoeists, walkers, cyclists and naturalists alike. Following in the footsteps of their partisan ancestors, whose anti-tsarist forces found shelter here during the nineteenth-century insurrections, adventurous Poles spend days and sometimes weeks paddling or trekking through the forest. Such expeditions require substantial preparation, so for most people the practical way to sample the mysteries of the forest is to take a **day-trip** from Augustów along the **canal system**. Boats leave from the tourist port on ul. 29 Listopada (see opposite) – *żegluga* (meaning, very loosely, "boats") is the key word when asking the way. There are usually about seven different excursions per day on offer in the height of the season (July & Aug), falling to a couple per day in May, June and September. First departure is at 9.30am, and you should get there early to queue for tickets. It's also a good idea to take some food: most boats don't carry any, and restaurant stops on the way are unpredictable.

The shortest trips – a couple of hours – go east through the **Necko**, **Białe** and **Studzieniczne** lakes to **Swoboda** or **Sucha Rzeczka**, giving at least a taste of the beauty of the forest. Other boats go onward to **Plaska** and the lock at **Perkuc**, returning in the evening. Beyond this point, the canal is for canoeists only, and even they can only go another twenty or so kilometres to the Belarusian border.

The **forest** is mainly coniferous, but with impressive sections of elm, larch, hornbeam and ancient oak creating a slightly sombre atmosphere, particularly along the alley-like section of the canal between Swoboda and Sucha Rzeczka – the tallest trees blot out the sun, billowing reeds brush the boat, and the silence is suddenly broken by echoing bird calls. Among the varied wildlife of the forest, cranes, grey herons and even the occasional beaver can be spotted on the banks of the canal, while deeper into the *puszcza* you might glimpse wild boar or elk.

If exploring the highways and byways on wheels appeals, the Puszcza Augustówska makes for some enticing **cycling** territory. There are plenty of decent paths and roads, although they're not always particularly clearly marked. The *Puszcza Augustówska* **map** (1:70,000) shows all the main routes through the forest, right up to the Belarusian border. Several places in town rent out bikes – ask the tourist office (see opposite) for details.

Gabowe Grądy

Six kilometres south of Augustów down a track through the woods (the nearest bus stop is about a kilometre east), the village of **GABOWE GRĄDY** is populated by a sizeable number of Russian Orthodox "**Old Believer**" or *Starowierców* families (see box on pp.250–251). The wizened old characters with flowing white beards sitting by their front gates indicate you've arrived in the right place. People apart, the main interest here is the church (*molenna*) at the north end of the village, one of three remaining places of Orthodox worship in the region. The Gabowe Grądy *molenna* boasts a superb all-women **choir**, the only such group in the country: you can usually hear them at the Sunday morning service, the only time you're guaranteed to be able to get into the place anyway. For anyone interested in Orthodox music this is a must, the sonorous harmonies of the old liturgical chants intermeshing with the full-throated exuberance of the melodizing.

Suwałki and around

Founded as late as the 1720s, **SUWAŁKI** is another slow-paced provincial town with a decidedly Eastern ambience. For all its distance from the country's centre – less pronounced in previous Polish geographical configurations, it should be remembered – it and the surrounding region occupy an important place in contemporary Polish cultural consciousness. Nobel Laureate **Czesław Miłosz**'s childhood home is in Krasnogruda, hard up by the Lithuanian border; film director Andrzej Wajda stood for election in Suwałki in the landmark 1989 elections, and continues to take an active interest in the region; and the novelist Tadeusz Konwicki filmed his wonderful adaptation of Miłosz's *Dolina Issa* (The Issa Valley) around Smolniki. The town itself isn't much more than a stepping stone to the surrounding countryside. Few people stop off here for long, and the cross-border traffic between Poland and nearby Lithuania has had little appreciable effect on the place.

A rambling, unfocused sort of place, Suwałki presents a mix of fine Neoclassical architecture and Russian-looking nineteenth-century buildings, with the usual postwar buildings around the outskirts. Religion is a mixed business here as well: the majority Catholic population uses the stately Neoclassical Parish Church of St Alexandra on pl. Wolności, but there's also an Evangelical church, further down on the main ul. Wolności, and the **molenna**, a small wooden building serving the town's Old Believer population and retaining some fine original icons. It is tucked away on a side street off al. Sejneńska close to the train station; the only reliable time to gain entry is during the Sunday morning service.

The jumbled ethnic mix that characterized Suwałki up until the outbreak of World War II is clearly illustrated in the town **cemetery** on the west side of town, on the corner of ul. Bakałarzewska and ul. Zarzecze, overlooking the Czarna Hańcza River. As in Lublin and other eastern Polish towns, the cemetery is divided up into religious sections – Catholic, Orthodox, Protestant, Tatar and Jewish, the Orthodox housing a special section for Old Believers. The Tatar gravestones have almost disappeared with the passage of time, while the Jewish cemetery was predictably devastated by the Nazis – a lone memorial tablet now standing in the middle of the area.

Back in the town centre, the somewhat humdrum local **museum** at ul. Kościuszki 81 (Tues–Fri 8am–4pm, Sat & Sun 9am–5pm; 3zł) contains a number of archeological finds relating to the Jacwingians.

Practicalities

The **train station** lies east of the centre – take bus #1, #8 or #12 into town. The **bus station**, on ul. Utrata, is also on the east side of town, but closer to the centre. The **tourist office**, conveniently located at ul. Kościuszki 45 (Mon–Fri 8am–4pm; ☎087/566 5494, ⓦwww.suwalki-turystyka.info.pl) is a good example of an emerging new brand of Polish tourist office: amply stocked with helpful information and friendly, foreign language-speaking staff in equal measures. The management are particularly keen on promoting agro/eco-tourism in the region, and can book you into **farmhouse B&Bs** (❶–❷) in the surrounding countryside – you'll need your own transport to get there though. Best of the **hotels** are the *Dom Nauczyciela* (ZNP), ul. Kościuszki 120 (☏087/566 6900, ⓦwww.domnauczyciela.suwalki.pl; ❹); and the Suwalszczyzna, ul. Noniewicza 71a (☏087/565 1900; ❺), both of which are central and offer comfy en-suites with TV. Slightly more basic but still comfortable is the *Hańcza*, ul. Wojska Polskiego 2 (☏087/566 6644; ❹), near the river on the southern edge of town; while the nearby *Motel Private*, ul. Polna 9 (☏087/566 5362; ❹), is a small, well-furnished *pensjonat* overlooking the river. There's a summer only (June–Aug) **youth hostel** at ul. Klonowa 51 (☏087/566 5140), 2km northeast of the town centre.

There's no great range of **places to eat**: the *Galeria*, Kościuszki 75, is the best of the central pizzerias; while the restaurant of the Dom Nauczyciela is the most comfortable place for a good-quality Polish meal with all the trimmings. *Pub Kuźnia*, just off ul. Kościuszki at Chłodna 9, is one of the few decent **places to drink** in the centre, and also does food.

The Cementarzysko Jacwingów and Soviet War Cemetery

The ancient Jacwingian burial ground, 4km north of Suwałki, dated between the third and fifth centuries AD, is one of the few sites left by these ancient people, and a must for lovers of mystic sites. To reach it take bus #7 to Szwacjaria, or the Jeleniewo road by car: in both cases you'll see a sign at the roadside pointing you to the **Cementarzysko Jacwingów** (Jacwingian Cemetery). A short walk through the fields and over an overgrown ridge brings you to the round, variably sized burial mounds (the largest is 20m wide), discernible through a tangled mass of trees and undergrowth, just beyond the large Soviet war cemetery on the right-hand side of the road. Excavations around the sites have revealed a little about the Jacwingians – burying horses with their masters seems to have been a common practice. In general, though, little is known of this pagan people, but stay long enough in this beautiful and peaceful spot and you conjure up your own images of how they might once have lived.

The **Soviet War Cemetery**, established close to the site of the POW camp, Stalag 68, set up by the Nazis in 1941, contains the graves of over 45,000 inmates who died here in appalling conditions, as well as several thousand Soviet troops killed in the fighting that raged around Suwałki in the latter stages of World War II. The shoddy, unkempt state of the place says much about the enduring tension between Poland and its erstwhile Soviet/Russian neighbour.

Lake Wigry and the national park

Lake Wigry, the district's largest lake, lies 11km southeast of Suwałki. The lake and a large part of the surrounding area were designated a **national park** in 1989, an unspoilt area of nearly 15,000 hectares comprising a mixture of lake, river, forest land and agricultural territory. The lake in particular is a stunningly beautiful spot, a peaceful haven of creeks, marshes and lakeside woods with the occasional village in between. A wealth of wildlife shelters largely undisturbed in and around its waters, the lake itself harbouring over twenty species of fish – lavaret, whitefish, smelt and river trout included – while in the shoreland woods you can find stag, wild boar, elk, martens and badgers. Wigry's most characteristic animal, however, is the **beaver**, and particularly round the lake's southern and western shores you'll find plenty of evidence of their presence in the reservations set aside for the creatures. The park is also a rambler's paradise, with a good network of **marked trails** running through much of the area. For anyone tempted by the idea of exploring the region on foot the *Wigierski Park Narodowy* **map** (1:46,000), which shows all the main trails, is a must. The longest route, marked green, takes you round the entire lake – nearly 50km in total – but there are also plenty of good shorter routes. **Cycling** is another more challenging option: the trails take in narrow forest paths and sandy roads, which can make the going hard. Bike rental is theoretically possible from the PTTK (see below) or via the tourist office in Suwałki. Finally, the lake itself is an angler's dream. To cast your rod you'll need a local **fishing licence**: the Suwałki tourist office will put you onto the local branch of the Polish Angling Association – Polski Związek Wędkarski (PZW) – who issue the requisite licences.

For access to the park from Suwałki, take a local bus to the holiday centre of **STARY FOLWARK**, a quiet spot on the shores of the lake some 9km from town (buses to and from Suwałki run roughly every hour). The main places to stay are the *Aga Pensjonat* (☎087/563 7894; ❷); the *Holiday Hotel* (☎087/563 7120; ❹), and a **campsite** near the water. For a bite to **eat** you can choose between the restaurant of the *Holiday Hotel*, or the *Pod Sieją*, both of which serve freshwater fish from the lake. You can **rent canoes** from a couple of outlets down by the water.

If you do get hold of a boat, head across the lake from Stary Folwark to **Wigry Church**, part of a Camadolese monastery (see p.449) founded here by King Władysław IV Waza in the 1660s, on what was originally an island later linked to the shore. The monks were thrown out by the Prussians following the Third Partition and their sizeable possessions – 300 square kilometres of land and several dozen villages – sequestered. The church is a typical piece of Polish Baroque, with exuberant frescoes in the main church and monks' skeletons in the catacombs (guided visits only), standard practice for the death-fixated Camadolese. The monastery itself has been turned into a popular conference-centre-cum-**hotel**, the *Dom Pracy Twórcej* (☎087/563 7019; ❸–❹), with a good **restaurant**, and rooms in the main building or, more cheaply, in the group of one-time hermitages beyond the church.

The Suwalszczyna

North of Suwałki the forests give way to the lush, rolling hills of the **Suwalszczyna**. Two roads take you through the heart of the region: the first heads due north then veers west through sporadic villages towards the Russian border; while the other runs some way to the east, covering the 30km to **Puńsk**. Both routes are served only sporadically by **buses**, and car-less travellers bound for Puńsk might do better by making a detour to **Sejny**, due east of Suwałki, and picking up public transport connections there.

North from Suwałki

The great appeal of this route lies in getting right off the beaten track – and tracks don't get much less beaten than that to **WODZIŁKI**, tucked away in a quiet wooded valley, around 10km north of Suwałki. The hamlet is home to a small community of Orthodox **Old Believers**, whose original wooden *molenna* is still in use, along with a nearby *bania* (sauna); for more on the Old Believers, see the box on pp.250–251.

Life in this rural settlement seems to have changed little since the first settlers moved here in the 1750s: the houses are simple, earth-floored buildings with few concessions to modernity, the old men grow long white beards, the women don't appear to cut their hair, the children run barefoot. If you're lucky

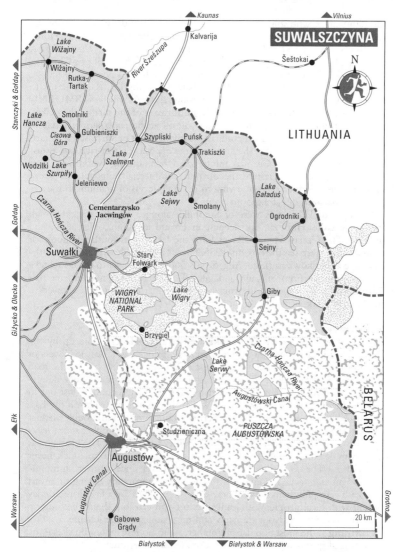

enough to get invited into one of their homes, you'll see amazing collections of icons, rosaries, Bibles and other precious relics. The easiest way to get to the hamlet is to take the bus through Jeleniewo. If possible, take one that's turning off to Turtul Rutka, from where it's thirty minutes' walk north to Wodziłki; otherwise get off at Sidorówka, the next stop after Jeleniewo, which leaves five kilometres' walk west, skirting **Lake Szurpiły**. The lake itself is great for swimming, and an ideal camping spot, provided the mosquitoes aren't out in force.

The next bus stop after Sidorówka is **GULBIENISKI**, the point of access for the hill called **Cisowa Góra** (258m), known as the Polish Fujiyama. It was the site of pre-Christian religious rituals, and it's rumoured that rites connected with Perkunas, the Lithuanian firegod, are still observed here. Bear in mind that the Lithuanians, who still make up a small percentage of the population of this region, were the last Europeans to be converted to Christianity, in the late fourteenth century – Czesław Miłosz's semi-autobiographical novel *The Issa Valley*, set in neighbouring Lithuania, bears witness to the durability of pre-Christian beliefs here. Whatever the historical reality of the hill, it's a powerful place.

North of Gulbieniski the road divides: Wiżajny to the left, Rutka Tartak to the right. Continuing along the Wiżajny route, the next village is **SMOLNI-KI**, just before which there's a wonderful **panorama** of the surrounding lakes: if you're on the bus ask the driver to let you off at the *punkt wyściowy* (viewpoint). If you happen to have a compass with you, don't be surprised if it starts to go haywire around here – the area has large deposits of iron-rich ore, as discovered by disoriented German pilots based here during World War II at Luftwaffe installations. Despite the obvious commercial potential, the seams haven't been exploited to date owing to the high levels of uranium in the ore and the risks from direct exposure to it.

A couple of kilometres west of Smolniki, along a bumpy track through woods, is **Lake Hańcza**, the deepest in Poland at 108m, quiet, clean and unspoilt. The Czarna Hańcza River joins the lake on its southern shore; for more on this river, see the box on p.255. There's a **youth hostel** on the southeast edge at Błaskowizna (June–Aug; ☏087/566 1769). To get to the hostel take the Wiżajny bus from Suwałki and get off at Bachanowo, a kilometre past Turtul Rutka; it's a short walk from here. Note that camping isn't allowed in the Suwałki Park, of which this area is part.

Stańczyki

If you're travelling by car, **Stańczyki**, west of Lake Hańcza close up by the Russian border on the edge of the Puszcza Romincka, is a must for lovers of the bizarre – follow the main route west of Wiżajny, turning left off the road about 4km past Zytkiemy. The reason for coming is to admire the huge deserted twin **viaduct** straddling the Błędzianka River valley, seemingly lost out in the middle of nowhere. Before World War II this hamlet was right on the East Prussian–Polish border: in 1910 the Germans built a mammoth double viaduct here as part of a new rail line, one side scheduled to carry timber trains leaving Prussia, the other, trains entering the country from Poland. The viaduct was duly completed, the only problem being that the promised rail track never materialized. The crumbling viaducts have stood ever since, a towering monument to an architect's and engineer's folly, no one apparently having the heart – or cash – to pull them down. These days the viaducts are a favourite Sunday outing with local people. With a bit of effort you can join them climbing up onto the viaducts to savour the view and the madness of the scheme.

Camping is the most popular option here, with no restrictions on sites – the most prized spot being right under the arches of the viaduct.

Suwałki to Puńsk

Lithuanians are one of Poland's minorities, most of the 40,000-odd community living in a little enclave of towns and villages north and east of Suwałki. The further you go into the countryside the more common it becomes to catch the lilt of their strange-sounding tongue in bars and at bus stops.

The village of **Puńsk**, close to the border, has the highest proportion of Lithuanians in the area and is surrounded by some of the loveliest countryside. There are two ways of covering the 30km from Suwałki. The first is to take the twice-daily **train** to **Trakiszki** (departs at 8.45am and 1.30pm) and walk the last couple of kilometres. The journey takes you through ancient meadows

– their hedgerows a brilliant mass of flora – and fields tilled by horse-drawn ploughs. Keep your passport handy as the border police are sometimes in Trakiszki to check what you're up to. The other option is to travel by **bus**, taking one of the two daily services from Suwałki, or four daily services from Sejny.

On to Lithuania

With cross-border **travel between Poland and Lithuania** easier than at any time in the postwar period, a trip over the border to the Lithuanian capital, Vilnius, is now a genuinely feasible option.

Situated around 160km east of Suwałki, along with Ukrainian L'viv, **VILNIUS** (in Polish, Wilno) is one of the great former Polish cities of the east – not a point to emphasize when you're there, incidentally – with a large old-town complex that ranks among the finest in Europe. Anyone expecting an orderly Protestant Hansa town on the lines of Baltic neighbours Riga, Tallinn or even Helsinki, though, will be disappointed. Vilnius is unmistakeably central European and Catholic in feel and atmosphere, a jumbled mix of cobbled alleyways, high spires, Catholic shrines and Orthodox churches. Originating as the medieval capital of the Lithuanian grand dukes, Vilnius was for centuries a multinational city which served as an important cultural centre for many different peoples – Lithuanians, Poles and Belarusians included. On the eve of World War II, the Jews made up the biggest ethnic group in the city – a fact that is skated over by present-day Lithuanian and Polish historians.

Largely unscarred by World War II, Vilnius's best-known monuments include the so-called **Gates of Dawn** (known to Polish pilgrims as Ostra Brama or the "pointed gate"), a street gallery shrine housing Eastern Catholicism's most venerated icon of the Madonna; and the fabulous **St Anne's Church**, an extraordinarily exuberant Gothic masterpiece which Napoleon is supposed to have contemplated dismantling and moving to Paris.

Vilnius is much more tourist-friendly than most Polish cities, and recent years have witnessed an explosion in the number of cafés, bars, restaurants and hotels. There's a **tourist information centre** bang in the middle of the old town at Pilies 42 (Mon–Fri 10am–7pm, plus Sat & Sun 10am–4pm in summer; call ☎370 2 626 470 from Poland); while bimonthly listings publications like *Vilnius in Your Pocket* (Ⓦwww.inyourpocket.com) and *City Paper* (which also covers Riga and Tallinn; Ⓦwww.balticsworldwide.com), both available from news kiosks, will fill you in on just about everything else you need to know. Lithuanians are a friendly and hospitable lot on the whole, and anyone tempted by the prospect of making the journey east will find it's well worth the effort.

Practicalities

Citizens of the EU, USA, Canada, New Zealand, Australia and the Nordic countries can enter Lithuania without a **visa** – nationals of other countries should contact the Lithuanian embassy or consulate in their home country for current requirements – or head for the Lithuanian embassy in Warsaw, al. Szucha 5 (☎022/625 3368).

There are several options for **travel** to Vilnius. With the opening of the new border crossing at Budzisko–Kalwarija, travelling **by car** has become a lot easier. Passport control is still slow, especially in summer, so be prepared for tailbacks at the border. There's a direct **train** from Warsaw to Vilnius three times a week; otherwise head for Suwałki, from where there are two trains a day to Šestokai on the Lithuanian side of the border, each of which is met by a connecting service on to Vilnius.

Going **by bus** is a reasonable option: most comfortable are the daytime buses from Warsaw to Vilnius (daily; 8hr), although there are also night-time services from Gdańsk (daily; 11hr) and Olsztyn (5 times weekly; 8hr). There's also one weekly bus from Białystok (currently leaving on Fridays), which calls at Augustów and Suwałki on the way.

Puńsk

Tucked away a few kilometres from the Lithuanian border, **PUŃSK** used to be sunk in complete obscurity, but since 1989 has been the object of unprecedented attention. The reason is the village's **Lithuanians** – some seventy percent of

Poles and Lithuanians

In Poland's relations with its eastern neighbours, none are as fraught with paradox and misunderstanding as those with **Lithuania**. This is almost entirely due to the fact that the two countries have large chunks of history and culture in common, but can rarely agree on which bits of the Polish-Lithuanian heritage belong to whom.

Dynastically linked by the marriage of Polish Queen Jadwiga to the Lithuanian Grand Duke Jogaila (or Jagiełło, as he is known in Polish) in 1386, the two countries coexisted in curious tandem, and embarked on mutual conquests, until the **Union of Lublin** finally bound them together in a single state – the so-called **Commonwealth** – in 1569. They were to stay together until the **Partitions** of Poland brought the Commonwealth to an end at the close of the eighteenth century. However the precise nature of the Polish-Lithuanian state has always been a source of disagreement to both sides: the Lithuanians tend to regard it as a mutual enterprise undertaken by equal partners, while the Poles reserve for themselves the leading role.

One of the reasons why the Poles traditionally looked upon Lithuania as a constituent part of a Polish-dominated state was that the Lithuanian aristocracy had become almost wholly Polish-speaking by the sixteenth century, and increasingly identified with the courtly culture of Warsaw and Kraków rather than their own native ways. Lithuanian language and culture was reduced to the status of quaint folklore, spoken of rapturously by nineteenth-century romantic poets like Adam Mickiewicz (see pp.92–93), but hardly ever taken seriously by the educated elite. This left Lithuanians with an inferiority complex vis-à-vis their overbearing Polish neighbours, an outlook that was transformed into outright hostility by the national struggles of the twentieth century.

When the end of **World War I** put the resurrection of the Polish state back on the political agenda, Polish leaders (Marshal Piłsudski, himself a Polish-Lithuanian aristocrat, included) were consumed by dreams of resuscitating the Polish-Lithuanian Commonwealth of old. However the Lithuanians, eager to escape from Polish tutelage, rushed to declare an independent state of their own. The two sides came to blows over the status of **Vilnius** which, as the medieval capital of Lithuania, was regarded by the Lithuanians as a natural part of their heritage. The Poles pointed to the city's large Polish-speaking population, and annexed it by force in 1920. The Lithuanians broke off diplomatic relations, and the border between the two countries remained closed throughout the 1920s and 1930s. Lithuania's forced incorporation into the **Soviet Union** in 1940 and the postwar imposition of communism in Poland enforced a new type of isolation between the two countries, with official Party-based relations about the only sanctioned source of contact right up into the mid-1980s.

The **glasnost** era, the collapse of communist power in Poland and the Lithuanian achievement of independence in 1991 opened the way for a new era in relations between the countries, although they were almost immediately soured by conflicts regarding the **national minorities** residing in both countries.

Mostly located in the border area between Sejny and Puńsk, Poland's 40,000-strong **Lithuanian minority** continues to demand better educational and cultural resources for the community, in particular increased provision for native-tongue teachers, books and classes in primary and secondary schools in the region. With the notable exception of the 1989–91 struggle for Lithuanian independence, when local demonstrations in Puńsk were a regular news-feature on Polish TV, the Lithuanian community tends to be a quiet, rather introverted bunch, happy to remain in Poland as long as there's no problem in visiting relatives and maintaining contacts across the border.

the population – who, despite their small numbers, maintain a Lithuanian cultural centre, choir and weekly newspaper, giving the place a decidedly un-Polish feel. In the summer of 1989 Lithuanian flags and the symbol of Sajudis (the Lithuanian Popular Front) became common sights here, and when the

Lithuania's **Polish minority** is altogether a different story. Numbering around a quarter of a million, the Poles are a significant national force – some seven percent of the total population, the largest minority grouping after Russians. The majority of them live in the eastern part of the country, in particular in the rural districts surrounding Vilnius. Lithuanian Poles initially saw Lithuanian independence – and the rather bombastic promotion of Lithuanian language and culture that accompanied it – as a threat to their own identity. Prompted by evidence that local Polish officials had actively collaborated with the organizers of the August 1991 Moscow coup, the Lithuanian authorities actually suspended Polish-run local councils for a period in the early 1990s.

Polish-Lithuanian relations suffered greatly as a result of this, and didn't really recover until the signing of a **Friendship and Co-operation Treaty** by Lech Wałęsa and his Lithuanian counterpart, Algirdas Brazauskas, in April 1994. Predictably, perhaps, even here history continued to niggle, with the Lithuanians demanding that the treaty contain an explicit condemnation of the Polish occupation of the Vilnius region in 1920 – the issue that initially stymied agreement. Resolved by a compromise that the text make no reference to past events, the demand was nonetheless implicitly restated by Brazauskas during the signing ceremony. Addressing the Seimas (parliament) in the company of Wałęsa, Brazauskas stressed the Lithuanian character of Vilnius and reiterated the claim that the city and surrounding region belonged to the interwar Polish state "in fact if not in law". Though clearly irritated, the Polish delegation resisted the temptation to get drawn into further arguments, and the treaty was duly ratified.

In practical terms, the signing of the treaty engendered movement towards the resolution of several issues, notably the situation of the Polish minority in Lithuania, whose legal and administrative status is now explicitly "normalized" for the first time. Equally important, it finally paved the way for the long overdue construction of a **new border crossing** between the two countries at Budzisko–Kalwarija – the most modern on Poland's eastern border to date – which opened to passenger traffic during a Lithuanian state visit to Poland in September 1995.

Currently the relations between the two countries are as good, if not better, than at any point since the days of the Commonwealth, due largely to a shared enthusiasm for the benefits of **EU** and **NATO** enlargement. Poland, already a member of NATO and a strong candidate to join the EU, is keen to see Lithuania accepted into both of these bodies as soon as possible, thereby helping to secure Poland's eastern borders against a potentially resurgent Russia. The Lithuanians, in turn, see the Poles as their most vociferous international advocates – a situation they are more than keen to encourage. The fact that Poland is Lithuania's most important trading partner has not gone unnoticed by either side. Top-level governmental contacts are cordial and frequent: each newly appointed Lithuanian prime minister usually jets off to see his Polish counterpart before meeting any other foreign leader. Poland has lobbied succesfully for Lithuanian inclusion in NATO-led peacekeeping missions in the Balkans, and a combined Polish-Lithuanian infantry batallion – which rejoices in the rather predictably prosaic name of Litpolbat – has been formed in order to drive home the message that the two states have common defence interests.

On a personal level, individual Poles and Lithuanians continue to display a staggering ignorance and indifference towards each others' cultures, and yet frequently make use of the new freedom of travel to visit each others' countries to sightsee or shop – proof, of a sort, that they are both well on the way to becoming normal European neighbours.

Soviet blockade of Lithuania began in March 1990, the response in Puńsk was immediate: it became the collection point for supplies to Lithuania from all over Poland, and demonstrations in support of Lithuanian independence were held after Mass every Sunday. Now that independence has been achieved, things have quietened down. Locals still gripe at the logistical restraints on crossing the border to visit relatives, though the recent opening of the nearby border at Budzisko will undoubtedly ease the situation, as well as bring more economic activity and money into the village.

The neo-Gothic parish **church** might look nothing special as a building, but turn up on a Sunday at 11am and you'll find the place packed for Mass in Lithuanian. If it's a major feast day, you may also see a procession afterwards, for which the women, especially, don the curiously Inca-like national costume. Enquiries in the bar or shops should track down Juozas Vaina, who set up the local **Zbiory Etnograficzne** (Lithuanian Ethnographical Museum), ul. Szklona, on the edge of the village. Inside there's an interesting collection of local ethnography, including some wonderful decorative fabrics and crafts, bizarre-looking farm implements, and prewar Lithuanian books and magazines, as well as maps that illuminate the tangled question of the Polish-Lithuanian border. As well as Lithuanians, Puńsk was for centuries home to another minority – Jews. Almost every Jew from this region was either slaughtered or uprooted, but a few signs of the past – ignored in the official Polish guides and maps – are still left. The Dom Handlowy on the main street in Puńsk used to be the rabbi's house, and the older locals can point you in the direction of the abandoned **Jewish cemetery**, on the northern edge of the village, where a few Hebrew inscriptions are still visible among the grass and trees.

There's no regular accommodation in the village. The *Sodas* **café**, at ul. Mickiewicza 17, handles food-and-drink duties, including excellent *blynai* (Lithuanian pancakes).

Sejny

Instead of returning directly to Suwałki, you might try the bus-trip via the market town of **SEJNY**, 25km south of Puńsk, a cross-country journey that's a treat in itself. Sejny is dominated by a Dominican **monastery** at the top of the town, which contains a grandiose late-Renaissance church refurbished in Rococo style in the mid-eighteenth century. The fourteenth-century Madonna carved from limewood, located in the main side chapel on the right, is a long-standing object of popular veneration: on feast days the body of the statue is opened to reveal an intricately carved Crucifixion scene inside. The crown on the Madonna's head was put in place by the then bishop of Kraków, **Karol Wojtyła**, in 1975.

At the other end of the short main street, ul. Piłsudskiego, is the **former synagogue**, its size indicating the importance of the former Jewish population here. Built in the 1860s and devastated by the Nazis who turned it into a fire station, it has since been carefully restored and turned into a **museum** and cultural centre (Mon–Fri 11am–4pm; free) run by the Borderland Foundation (Fundacja "Pogranicze"), dedicated to promoting the culture, music and art of "the borderland nations". Started in the early 1990s, the Foundation organizes cultural events aimed at bringing together the peoples of the region – Poles, Lithuanians, Belarusians, Ukrainians and Russians – publishes books relating to intercultural tolerance and understanding, and also runs a Klezmer band in honour of Sejny's Jewish heritage. It's no accident that the Foundation was chosen by Polish-Jewish historian Jan Tomasz Gross to be the publisher of his controversial book "Neighbours" (see box on the Jedwabne pogrom; pp.276–277). For details of these activities, contact the Foundation's office directly opposite the museum, ul. Piłsudskiego 37, 16500 Sejny (☎087/516 2765, ⓦhttp://pogranicze.sejny.pl). Its highly knowledgeable staff can fill you in on local history, particularly issues relating to the history of the Lithuanian, Jewish and Old Believer minorities.

The main **hotel** in town is the recently revamped *Skarpa* at ul. Piłsudskiego 13 (☎087/516 2187), which has rooms with shower but no WC (❶), or fully equipped en-suites (❷), and also boasts a restaurant. You can also stay at the Lithuanian cultural centre, the *Dom Litewski/Lietuviu Namai*, ul. 22 Lipca 9 (☎087/516 2908, ⓔltnamai@kki.net.pl; ❹), which has well-appointed en-suites, and a café-bar serving Lithuanian snacks.

Białystok and the Belarusian borderlands

As you head south from the lakes or east from Warsaw, you find yourself in a region of complex ethnicity, situated right up against the borders of Belarus. The Poles call the area **Podlasie** – literally "Under the Trees" – which gives little hint of its landscape of wide, open plains, tracts of primeval forest and dark skies. Even without the increasing presence of onion-domed Orthodox churches, it would feel Eastern, more like Russia than Poland. The whole area also feels extremely poor, and is one of the most neglected regions of the country, with an overwhelmingly peasant population. On the long potholed country roads you see as many horsecarts as cars, in the fields as many horse-drawn ploughs as tractors. In the **Białowieża Forest** the isolation has ensured the survival of continental Europe's last belt of virgin forest – the haunt of bison, elk and hundreds of varieties of flora and fauna, and home, too, of the wondrous Żubrówka "bison grass" vodka.

Belarusians are the principal ethnic minority, numbering some 200,000 in all. Before the war, Polish territory stretched far across the current Belarusian border, and today communities on either side are scarcely distinguishable, save that those on the eastern side are, if anything, poorer still. Another historic, but declining, minority are the **Tatars**, who settled here centuries ago and whose wooden mosques at **Bohoniki** and **Kruszyniamy** are one of the sights of the Polish east: there are several more over the border. Long a melting-pot of cultures, **Białystok** and the surrounding region were also one of the main areas of **Jewish** settlement in Poland. Before the war almost every town in the region boasted at least one synagogue, often more: many of these were wooden structures, whose exuberant design clearly reflected the influence of the indigenous folk architecture. Sadly, all the wooden synagogues – pictures suggest many of them were spectacular – were burned down by the Nazis. A wealth of brick and stone **Jewish monuments** survive, though, and on any journey through the outlying towns and villages, you'll encounter former synagogue buildings and crumbling Jewish cemeteries. Of these, the restored synagogue complex at **Tykocin** is one of the most evocative Jewish monuments in the country – as in the rest of the region, the community itself was wiped out by the Nazis.

Once again, local **transport** consists mainly of buses, with services diminishing the nearer the border you get.

Białystok

Even the habitually enthusiastic official Polish guidebooks are mute on the glories of **BIAŁYSTOK**, industrial centre of northeast Poland; it's not a beautiful place and its main development occurred during the industrialization of the nineteenth century. Uniquely among major Polish cities today, however, it has kept the healthy ethnic and religious mix – Poles, Belarusians and Ukrainians, Catholic and Orthodox – characteristic of the country before the war, though the Jews, of course, are absent. And for all the industry, it's curiously one of the country's least polluted cities.

Despite the heavy wartime destruction, a number of characteristic examples of the regional **wooden architecture** have survived in parts of the city, most notably in the houses along streets such as ul. Grunwaldzka, Żelazna and Mazowiecka down from the train station in the southern section of the centre, and in the ramshackle old Bojary and Skorupy districts in the eastern part of the city.

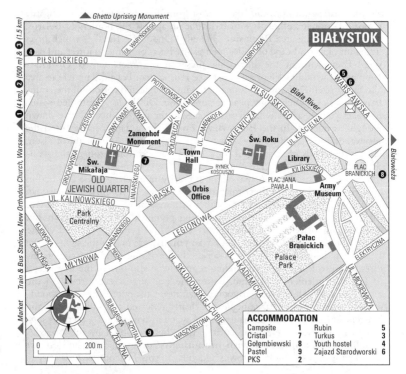

Some history

According to legend, Białystok was founded in 1320 by the Lithuanian Grand Duke Gediminas (or **Gedymin** as he's known in Polish), but its emergence really began in the 1740s when local aristocrat Jan Branicki built a palace in the town centre. Partitioned off to Prussia and then to Russia, Białystok rapidly developed as a textile city, in competition with Prussian-dominated Łódź. In both cities, industrialization fostered the growth of a sizeable urban proletariat and a large and influential **Jewish community**. Factory strikes in the 1880s demonstrated the potency of working-class protest, as did the anti-tsarist demonstrations which broke out here in 1905. Echoing protests in other parts of the Russian empire, they elicited a similar response – an officially instigated pogrom, during which many Białystok Jews lost their lives. Fifteen years later, anticipating a victory that never came against Piłsudski's apparently demoralized forces, Lenin's troops installed a provisional government in Białystok led by **Felix Dzierżyński**, the notorious Polish Bolshevik and creator of the first ever Soviet secret police force – forerunner of the KGB.

World War II brought destruction and slaughter to Białystok. Hitler seized the town in 1939, then handed it over to Stalin before reoccupying it in 1941 – which is when the Jewish population was herded into a ghetto area and deported to the death camps. The heroic Białystok **Ghetto Uprising** of August 1943 (the first within the Reich) presaged the extinction of the city's Jewry. Nor was the killing confined to Jews. By 1945, over half the city's population was dead, with three-quarters of the town centre destroyed.

Following the end of the war, the authorities set about rebuilding the town and its industrial base. From a strictly utilitarian point of view they succeeded: today Białystok is a developed economic centre for textiles, metals and timber, with a population of over 250,000. The aesthetic cost has been high, though – the usual billowing smokestacks, ugly tower blocks and faceless open streets of postwar development. But Białystok has its share of historic sights – mostly associated with its Orthodox Belarusian community – and it makes an ideal base for exploring the border region to the east.

Arrival and information

The main **train station**, a dingy pink building that wouldn't look out of place in Moscow, is a five-minute bus ride (#2, #4 or #21) west of the city centre – supposedly it was built outside the centre as a punishment for anti-tsarist protests in the city. Close by, on ul. Bohaterów Monte Cassino, is the large, modern **bus station**.

In the absence of a regular IT office, there's no reliable source of information in town, although you might try **Orbis**, Rynek Kościuszki 13 (Mon–Fri 9am–5pm); or **Almatur**, ul. Zwierzyniecka 12 (Mon–Fri 9am–4pm; ☎085/742 89 43), on the southern side of the centre (bus #10 from the train station), which may help with accommodation in **student hostels** (open June–Aug), whose venues change year by year. Otherwise, you could try going online for information at ⓦwww.bialystok.pl.

Accommodation

As with other major cities, the supply of hotels in Białystok is slowly but surely growing to include reasonable options in all price brackets, with the emphasis on the upper – read "business" – range. In addition there are dorm beds (25zł per person) in the all-year **youth hostel**, al. Piłsudskiego 7b (reception open 8am–8pm; ☎085/652 4250), a quaint wooden house squeezed between tower blocks a fifteen-minute walk east of the train station – buses #1, #9, #12, #18 and #20 pass by. **Campers** have only one real option, the *Gromada* site next to the *Lęmy* hotel on al. Jan Pawła II – bus #4 will take you there.

Hotels

Cristal ul. Lipowa 3 ☎085/742 5061, ⊛www.cristal.com.pl. Good-quality upmarket hotel in a central location. The pricey restaurant is open till late. Weekend discounts. ❻

Gołębiewski ul. Pałacowa 7 ☎085/743 5435, ⊛www.golebiewski.pl. Best place in town in the business and upper bracket tourist stakes. Located directly across from the Pałac Branickich. Weekend discounts. ❻

Pastel ul. Waszyngtona 24a ☎085/744 2744, ⊛www.kasol.com.pl. Small-sized modern hotel offering all the creature comforts. Hidden behind a group of tower blocks, but within easy walking distance of the centre. ❺

PKS ul. Bohaterów Monte Cassino 10 ☎085/742 7614. Budget place housed in a gloomy-looking

building right next to the bus station. Rooms (all with shared facilities) are sparsely furnished but bright and clean. No breakfast. ❷

Rubin ul. Warszawska 7 ☎085/677 2335. Old-fashioned but friendly overnighter in a fine classicist building located 10 minutes' walk east of the Rynek. Popular with trade tourists. No breakfast. Rooms with showers and TV or shared facilities. ❷–❸

Zajazd Starodworski ul. Warszawska 7a ☎085/653 7418. Smallish, pension-style place offering a limited number of cosy en-suites, featuring iron bedsteads and eccentric, homely furnishings. Reception is sometimes closed during the day, so ring in advance. ❺

Turkus, ul. Jan Pawła II 54 ☎085/651 1211. Medium-priced hotel offering simple en-suites with TV, 1km west of the train station. ❹

The Town

Białystok's historic centrepoint is the **Rynek**, an unusual triangular-shaped space with a large Baroque town hall in the middle. The main sights are situated on and around **ul. Lipowa**, the main thoroughfare cutting from east to west across the city centre. Immediately west of the Rynek, the **town hall**, a small, squat eighteenth-century building, was reconstructed from scratch after the war: these days it houses the **Muzeum Podlaskie** (Podlasie Museum; Tues–Sun 10am–5pm; 4zł). A good selection of works by some of the better-known nineteenth- and twentieth-century artists – Malczewski, Witkiewicz, Krzyzanowski and the like – is complemented by an enjoyable collection of local art, the portraits and landscapes displaying a strong feeling for the distinctive character of the region. In addition, the museum has regular temporary thematic exhibitions of works culled from other national museums, the imagination with which they're presented suggesting a serious attempt to get on the national art map.

A further 300m to the east along ul. Lipowa, the **Cerkiew św. Mikołaja** (St Nicholas's Church) was built in the 1840s to serve the swelling ranks of Russian settlers. A typically dark, icon-filled place of Orthodox devotion, its ornate frescoes are careful copies of those in the Orthodox cathedral in Kiev. It is filled to capacity for the Sunday services – worth coinciding with to hear the choir. A kiosk inside the entrance sells replica icons while the one outside sells books, cassettes and CDs of Orthodox music. Further down ul. Lipowa the **Orthodox cemetery** contains another enchanting *cerkiew* – though your only chance of getting in to look around is during the Sunday morning service.

Catholic competition comes from the huge **parish church** nearby and the imposing 1920s **Kościół św. Roku** (St Roch's Church), at the western end of the street. With its high spaceship-like towers, the parish church is something of a historical curio: next to it is a small seventeenth-century church built by the Branicki family, while the main structure is a vast 1900 neo-Gothic building, almost twenty times the size and only permitted by the tsarist authorities because its official request billed it as an "addition". The streets south of ul. Lipowa comprise part of the old **ghetto area**. A tablet in Polish and Hebrew

Ludwik Zamenhof and the Esperanto movement

Białystok's most famous son is probably **Ludwik Zamenhof** (1859–1917), the creator of **Esperanto**, the artificial language invented as an instrument of international communication. Born in what was then a colonial outpost of the tsarist empire, Zamenhof grew up in an environment coloured by the continuing struggle between the indigenous Polish population and its Russian rulers – both of whom were apt to turn on the Jews as and when the occasion suited them.

Perhaps because of this experience, from an early stage Zamenhof, an eye doctor by training, dedicated himself to the cause of racial tolerance and understanding. Zamenhof's attention focused on the fruits of the mythical Tower of Babel, the profusion of human languages: if a new, easily learnable **international language** could be devised it would, he believed, remove a key obstacle not only to people's ability to communicate directly with each other, but also to their ability to live together peaceably. On the basis of extensive studies of the major Western classical and modern languages, Zamenhof – Doktoro Esperanto or "Doctor Hopeful" as he came to be known – set himself the task of inventing just such a language, the key source being root words common to European, and in particular Romance, languages.

The first primer, *Dr Esperanto's International Language,* was published in 1887, but Zamenhof continued to develop his language by translating a whole range of major literary works, *Hamlet*, Goethe's and Molière's plays and the entire Old Testament included. The new language rapidly gained international attention, and the world's first **Esperanto congress** was held in France in 1905. In the same year Zamenhof completed *Fundamento de Esperanto* (1905), his main work, which soon became the basic Esperanto textbook and the one still most commonly in use today.

Even if it has never quite realized Zamenhof's dreams of universal acceptance, Esperanto – **Linguo Internacia** as it calls itself – has proved considerably more successful than any other "invented" language. With a worldwide membership of over 100,000 and national associations in around fifty countries, the *Universala Esperanto Associo* represents a significant international movement of people attracted to the universalist ideals as much as the linguistic practice of Esperanto. In Białystok itself there's a thriving **Esperanto-speaking community**, with an office just southwest of the Rynek at ul. Piękna 3 (☏085/745 4600).

on the side of a building opposite the local court house on ul. Suraska commemorates the one thousand Jews burned to death in June 1941 when the Nazis set fire to the Great Synagogue, reputedly one of the finest in Poland, which used to stand on this site.

For a town whose population was roughly seventy-percent Jewish at the turn of the twentieth century there are precious few other Jewish monuments left. Though you'd hardly guess so from today's uniform blocks, the streets leading north of ul. Lipowa were all mainly Jewish-inhabited before the war. Across the road from the town hall, in the leafy little park on the edge of ul. Malmeda, a **statue** commemorates the town's most famous Jewish citizen, **Ludwik Zamenhof**, the founder of Esperanto (see box, above), as does a plaque at the southern end of the same street. Continuing northwest over busy ul. Piłsudskiego and through streets of high concrete buildings brings you to another park, off ul. Żabia. Seemingly in the middle of nowhere, a monument to the **Białystok Ghetto Uprising** (Aug 16, 1943) recalls an important moment in the wartime history of the town. As with many Jewish war monuments in Poland, it's easy to miss – there's no sign and the place isn't even named on the city map – but the older local inhabitants usually know where to point you if you ask.

The most striking building in the town centre is the **Pałac Branickich** (Branicki Palace), destroyed by the Nazis in 1944 but rebuilt on the lines of the eighteenth-century building commissioned by Jan Branicki – itself a recon- struction of an earlier palace. The main building is now a medical academy, whose classical grandeur you can wander in and admire without much trouble if you look the student part: anyone, however, can stroll unhindered through the surrounding park and admire the palace from a distance. Look out, too, for the main front balcony, the so-called **Dzierżyński balcony**, from which Felix Dzierżyński and associates proclaimed the creation of the Polish Soviet Socialist Republic in 1920. There's also a pleasant outdoor café in the inner palace courtyard.

East of the palace across the busy main road is the **army museum** at Kilińskiego 7 (Tues–Sun 9.30am–5pm; 4zł). Among the usual collection of military items there's an interesting set of photos, newspapers and other docu- ments from the wartime era of Soviet occupation (1939–41), the original proclamation of the 1944 Białystok Ghetto Uprising and one of the Nazi "Enigma" code machines that the Polish resistance successfully cracked, much to the Allied war effort's benefit. Opposite the museum is a **monument** to the AK (Home Army) – one of a number you can find spread around the city now – this time to the AK forces in the former Eastern Polish borderlands, now within Lithuania and Belarus.

Białystok's proximity to the Belarusian border ensures it a key place among the growing number of Polish towns heavily involved in "trade tourism". On Sunday mornings the open-air **market** – located on ul. Kavaliejska – is thronged with Belarusians, Ukrainians and others from across the border ply- ing a strange assortment of consumer goods: gold, clothes, hi-fis, antiques, cos- metics, anything that Poles are prepared to buy. If you want **caviar**, this is the place to buy it, as the nearer the border you get, the lower the price: Gdańsk is fifty percent higher, Warsaw seventy-five. Pay in dollars only if you have to, be prepared to haggle, buy glass containers (not metal), and bear in mind that taking caviar out of Poland is illegal. Keep in mind, too, that the crowds are a haven for **pickpockets**.

Perhaps the saddest reminder of the city's onetime Jewish population is the **Jewish cemetery**, off ul. Wschodnia on the northeast edge of the city. Starting from Rynek Kościuszki in the centre of town bus #3 drops you close by just west of the cemetery – get off at the junction of ul. Władysława Wysockiego and ul. Władysława Raginisa, a 10–15-minute journey. With Catholic cemeter- ies on both sides, an Orthodox church under construction at the back, and children playing along the walls, the large and badly neglected cemetery looks and feels a beleaguered place. The few surviving gravestones are scattered around in the undergrowth, some of them still legible, but if things carry on this way there may not be any left in the not-too-distant future.

There's no bigger contrast imaginable than the massive new **Orthodox church** on ul. Antoniuk Fabryczny, 3km out of the centre in the northwest outskirts of the city (bus #5 will take you there). It's a vivid testament to the new-found confidence of the Orthodox Church in Poland's eastern border- lands, although the interior of this towering edifice – the largest Orthodox building in the country – is still to be fully decorated, giving the place an unusually cold, impersonal feeling. It's still worth visiting for the overall impression of a new style of Orthodox architecture that combines elements of the old with the new: when it's finally finished the result will undoubtedly be spectacular. You can usually get in around Mass times; otherwise the priest liv- ing behind the church may open it up for you.

Eating, drinking and entertainment

There are plenty of **places to eat** on and around ul. Lipowa. For something quick, *New York Bagels*, Lipowa 12, does a range of bagel and sandwich snacks and has a decent salad bar; while *Hocus Pocus*, Kilińskiego 12, is an unpretentious place serving up filling pizza, spaghetti and pancakes. *Pruszynka*, Malmeda 1, offers Polish basics like *bigos*, alongside a range of cheap and dependable pizzas. For something a bit more stylish, *Balzac*, Kilińskiego 8, is a classy bar-restaurant with good, pricier-than-average food; and *Sabatino*, Sienkiewicza 3, specializes in Mediterranean cuisine, including scrumptious seafood, served up in an interior that looks like something out of a design magazine. *Ulice Świata*, ul. Warszawska 30b, has different rooms devoted to different national cuisines – Polish, Italian, Mexican and Chinese; and finally *Ananda*, behind the *Gołębiewski* hotel at Warszawska 30, is a quiet, soothingly decorated vegetarian eatery with an imaginative line in salads and is also a good place for a drink.

As far as **drinking** is concerned, fans of quality caffeine injections should check out the *Pożegnanie z Afryką* at ul. Częstochowa 6, one of a chain offering a large range of coffees from around the world. Otherwise, *Red Velvet* (summer only), in the courtyard of the town hall, is the best place for al-fresco daytime drinking. *Kawiarna Lalek*, in the same building as the puppet theatre at ul. Kalinowskiego 1, is a lively place for an evening drink and has an outdoor patio in summer. *Odeon*, ul. Akademicka 10, is a popular bar in an octagonal glass pavilion which has occasional live jazz or blues; while *Gospoda Mandala*, Kilińskiego 15, is a relaxed and cosy pub-like place whose predominantly youthful clientele usually ends up dancing on weekend evenings.

Central **nightlife** options revolve around *Fama*, ul. Legionowa 5, a teen disco-bar which hosts occasonal live gigs; and *Metro*, ul. Białówny 9A, which offers mainstream dance music at the weekends, and more specialized styles (reggae, jungle) on week-nights. For **classical music** the Filharmonia, ul. Podleśna 2 (☏058/741 6557) runs concerts usually at least once a week. If you can cope with the language barrier, Wierszalin is an internationally known Białystok-based **theatre** group that sometimes puts on performances in town (check local listings). The Teatr Lalek at ul. Kalinowksiego 1 (☏058/742 5033, ⓦwww.btl.bialystok.pl) is a popular puppet theatre, while the city theatre, Teatr Dramatyczny, is at ul. Elektryczna 12 (☏058/741 5740, ⓦwww.teatrdramatyczny.bialystok.pl). The Pokój, ul. Lipowa 14, is the most central of the **cinemas**.

Around Białystok

A handful of trips into the city's immediate surroundings are worth considering, notably the fine icon museum in **Supraśl**, north of the city, the Branicki Palace at **Choroszcz** and the synagogue of **Tykocin**. The countryside offers some decent walking country too, chiefly the tranquil **Puszcza Knyszyńska** stretching east of the town, a popular weekend haunt with city folk. All of these are accessible using local bus connections. Further afield is the **Biebrza national park**, a rural idyll that's particularly popular with bird-watchers.

Supraśl and the Puszcza Knyszyńska

A sixteen-kilometre bus journey northeast of Białystok is **SUPRAŚL**, a sleepy provincial eastern hangout on the edge of the Puszcza Knyszyńska. The chief attraction here is the **Pałac Opatów** (Abbots' Palace), a grand, crumbling seventeenth-century structure now used as a school. Slap in the middle of the palace courtyard is a large early sixteenth-century brick Orthodox *cerkiew*, built by Grand Hetman of Lithuania Aleksander Chodkiewicz for the Orthodox Order of St Basil, which became one of the spiritual centres of Orthodoxy in the Polish–Lithuanian Commonwealth. Said to have boasted a fine interior combining Gothic and Byzantine styles – the Nazis mauled the place during the war – the whole building is currently being completely (and painstakingly slowly) renovated.

Improbably for such an out-of-the-way place, the former palace chapel contains a small but stunning Orthodox **museum** (theoretically, Wed–Sun 10am–4pm, though the lone caretaker has a habit of closing an hour or so earlier), housing some of the original frescoes and icons taken from the main *cerkiew*.

The works gathered here encompass a range of themes and images: scenes from the lives of Mary and Jesus, benign-looking early church fathers and saints, ethereal archangels and cherubim – a wonderful panorama of Orthodox art and spirituality and one in which, particularly in the frescoes, the art historians detect a strong Serbian Orthodox influence.

Poles and Belarusians

Poles and Belarusians have a long history of living together, but also one of long-suppressed cultural and political antagonisms, which have recently begun to surface. In the communist era, minorities were actively recruited into the party and state security apparatus, and their religion given active state backing – so long as the community kept its separatist or nationalist impulses in check. Use of the Belarusian language was forbidden in public, and there were no concessions to the culture in schools or cultural institutions. Despite this, a handful of Belarusian *samizdat* publications circulated during the communist years.

The result of these years of active state co-option, inevitably, was to reinforce Catholic Polish suspicion of their neighbours, which, with the state controls off, is surfacing in occasional bouts of openly expressed hostility. Meanwhile, for Belarusians, the new Polish political climate and freedoms, the disintegration of the Soviet empire and attendant emergence of an independent Belarusian state, along with ever-burgeoning Polish nationalism have reawakened their own search for a meaningful national identity. In Białystok, nationalist Belarusian candidates ran against Solidarity in the 1989 elections, and in the first post-communist decade the community has taken significant steps to re-establish its language, culture and overall sense of a distinctive identity.

The radical changes of the early 1990s – most importantly, of course, the emergence of Belarus as an independent state – added a whole new dimension to the situation faced by the **Polish-Belarusian community**, whose size is currently estimated to be 250,000–300,000 (under one percent of the population), one of the largest minority groups after the Germans and Ukrainians. The cautious line previously adopted by many community leaders has given way to a much more self-confident, assertive attitude. Cultural, political and religious associations are flourishing, Belarusian newspapers, magazines and books are published in abundance, while the local radio station established in central Białystok in the early 1990s, with Orthodox Church backing, has finally given Belarusians their own independent access to the media. Inevitably, a key concern for the Belarusians is the question of cross-border ties with the Belarus "homeland" itself, a concern echoed by the substantial Polish minority in Belarus, an estimated 420,000-strong and likewise concentrated in the border regions.

At the official political level, relations were long complicated by Belarusian

The Puszcza Knyszyńska

If you've come by bus from Białystok you could consider hiking back through the **Puszcza Knyszyńska**, a popular walking area with Białystok residents. The sandy local terrain is pretty easy-going underfoot, but the lack of signs once you get into the forest makes a local map, such as *Okolice Białegostoku* 1:150,000, readily available in Białystok, essential.

On a good day it's attractive and enjoyable walking country, the silence of the forest broken at intervals by cackling crows overhead or startled deer breaking for cover. Starting from the southern edge of Supraśl, a marked path takes you south through the lofty expanses of forest to the village of **Ciasne**, ending up by the bus stop near **Grabówka** at the edge of the main road back into Białystok – a twelve-kilometre hike in total.

Choroszcz

The highways and byways of eastern Poland hide a wealth of neglected old aristocratic piles, most of them relics of a not-so-distant period when a small group of fabulously wealthy families owned most of the eastern part of the country.

demands that Białystok and its surroundings be declared an ethnic Belarusian region – a demand rejected by the Polish side on the grounds that its acceptance would undermine the territorial cohesion of the country. Relations improved visibly in the wake of the breakup of the USSR and the emergence of an independent Belarus in 1991. As with Poland's other eastern neighbours things progressed reasonably smoothly over the next few years, especially following the signing of an economic and trade agreement in October 1991, followed by a further official Friendship and Co-operation Treaty in June 1992. A number of new **border-crossing points** were established, the most important being the crossing at Sławatycze–Damachava, an old military bridge now opened to civilian traffic.

As in other borderlands, the key underlying issue for the Belarusian community is how far government policy on minorities will go beyond rhetorical declarations towards active support for their development. At the political level, **relations** between Belarus and Poland have been severely strained by the behaviour of President Alyaksandr Lukashenka, whose increasingly confrontational and authoritarian style has won him few friends either at home or abroad (and his easy victory in the Belarusian presidential elections of 2001 suggests that he'll be around for some time). A foreign policy that emphasizes a new customs union with the Russian Federation and generally reviving ties with Moscow runs firmly against Poland's preoccupations with NATO and European integration, which hardly helps matters. Domestically, Lukashenka's Soviet-style treatment of political dissent and opposition has led to vocal Polish campaigns in support of the Belarusian opposition reminiscent of the Solidarity era. The setting up of a "Polish-Belarusian Civic Education" in February 1998 based in Białystok and led by veteran oppositionists such as Jacek Kuroń and Zbigniew Bujak, with the specific goal of "opening up" Belarus to Europe, prompted fierce official denunciation, notably from the head of the Belarusian KGB, who claimed that spying on the country had now become Polish state policy. The practical result of all this is a marked **weakening in co-operation** between the two countries, not least in the practical domain of opening up new border crossings, improving efficiency at existing ones – private cars still regularly wait for days to cross in both directions – and regulating visa regimes.

The eighteenth-century **Lietna Rezydencja Branickiego** (Branicki Summer Palace) at **CHOROSZCZ,** located 10km west of Białystok off the main Warsaw road, is a fine example of this phenomenon, the key difference being that the palace here has been completely renovated and converted into a **museum** (Tues–Sun 10am–3pm; 3zł; free on Sun). To get here, catch a local **bus** from Białystok; the palace is on the west side of town, just a short walk from the main stop.

The palace

After Białystok, you'll find that the elegant statue-topped **palace** facade makes quite a contrast to the architectural rigours of the city, with the tranquil coun-try location on the edge of the grounds of the local hospital another agreeable

The Jedwabne Pogrom

The village of **Jedwabne**, 35km north of Tykocin, would have remained an insignif-icant rural backwater were it not for the recently rediscovered fact that a major anti-Jewish **pogrom** took place here on July 10 1941. The dark secrets of Jedwabne came to light as a result of Jan Tomasz Gross's account of the pogrom in his book *Sąsiedzi* ("*Neighbours*"), a work that shocked the Polish public on its publication in 2000, and has remained the cause of controversy ever since.

It had long been known that something unpleasant had happened in Jedwabne in the summer of 1941. With the Red Army in full retreat and German forces moving in to take control, Jewish communities throughout eastern Poland were being faced with forced explulsions, beatings, and arbitrary murder – the Jews of Jedwabne were no exception. However it had always been assumed that crimes against the Jews had been committed by German soldiers, or local Poles acting under German duress. By talking to survivors of the Jedwabne pogrom, and piecing together a detailed chronology of events, Gross came to the disturbing conclusion that the local Poles had killed their Jewish neighbours without waiting for Nazi orders.

Relations between Poles and Jews had become strained as a result of the **Soviet occupation** of eastern Poland in 1939, with many Poles accusing the Jews of collab-oration with the communist authorities. It's true that many younger Jews were attract-ed to communism, not least because it seemed to promise racial equality and an end to the anti-Semitic measures enacted by the Polish government in the late 1930s. The Soviet security forces recruited a higher proportion of Jews than Poles, strengthening the popular belief that the Jews were essentially pro-Bolshevik and felt little loyalty towards Poland. When Nazi Germany declared war on the Soviet Union in June 1941, Soviet power in eastern Poland melted away, leaving Jews to be scape-goated by a Polish population humiliated by two years of communist occupation.

A massacre of Jews by Poles certainly took place in **Radziłów**, a small town 20km north of Jedwabne, on July 7. Whether the locals did this on their own initiative, or because they feared German reprisals if they left the Jews alone, remains the subject of much conjecture. The Poles of Jedwabne, meanwhile, decided to take action against their Jewish fellow citizens on July 10 – according to Gross, there were no German troops in town at the time. The Jews were forced from their homes and driven to the Rynek, where they were forced to demolish a statue of Lenin erected by the Soviets. They were then led along the road towards the Jewish cemetery on the outskirts of the village, with the majority being herded into a nearby stable – which was then set alight. Gross estimates that as many as 1500 died in the stable. Only a handful of Jedwabne's Jews survived, mostly by hiding out in the fields as the round-ups began.

Gross's account came as a profound shock to Polish society, not least because it sug-gested that Poles in wartime were just as capable of cruelty as the German occupiers. The concept of Poland as a heroic victim of Nazism had been an important plank of the country's identity in the half-century following 1945, and the idea that Poles could at the same time be the perpetrators of Nazi-style crimes was simply incomprehensible to

feature. Few of the building's original furnishings remain, most of them having been replaced by period replicas of the kind of things the Branickis are supposed to have liked. The main ground-floor room is the **salon**, its sedate parquet floor complemented by a choice collection of period furniture. Along with a number of family portraits, one of the original master of the house, Jan Branicki, hangs in the hallway, the finely wrought iron balustrades of the staircase illuminated by a lamp held aloft by a rather tortured-looking classical figure. The **second floor** is equally ornate, featuring a number of meticulously decorated apartment rooms, a dining room with a fine set of mid-eighteenth-century Meissen porcelain and a **Chippendale room**.

Back out of the building it's worth taking a stroll along the canal running

many. The effect of Gross's book was to split Polish society down the middle, with conservative opinion claiming that the historian's writings constituted a grotesque slur on the Polish nation, and left-liberal circles countering that the Jedwabne controversy offered a golden opportunity to face up to the past in a spirit of tolerance and forgiveness.

The response of the Polish establishment was measured and dignified. President Kwaśniewski made it clear that he would mark the 50th anniversary of the tragedy, scheduled for July 10 2001, by issuing an **apology** on behalf of the Polish nation – a position supported by almost all major politicians. However the idea that Polish honour had been besmirched retained a strong hold over the popular imagination. In Jedwabne itself, Poles who had spoken out about the pogrom were ostracized by the local community, and the local priest encouraged the distribution of anti-Semitic pamphlets. The Catholic hierarchy struggled to appease all factions in the dispute. A **remembrance service** for the victims of the pogrom was organized at All Saints' Church in Warsaw – a venue chosen because it was sited next to the wall of the wartime Warsaw ghetto – but was scheduled for May 27, 2001, in order to distance the service from President Kwaśniewski's official "apology", due to be delivered some weeks later. When the service at All Saints' took place, the Rabbi of Warsaw made his excuses and stayed away. At around the same time Cardinal Glemp made comments in a widely distributed interview that seemed to reinforce many of the prejudices directed against Poland's Jews – namely that the Jews took a leading role in communist security forces (and should therefore apologize to the Poles rather than the other way round), and that world Jewry was leading a campaign against Poland in an attempt to make Poles admit guilt for the Holocaust.

In the lead up to the July 10 commemoration, the site of the pogrom was subjected to intense examination, with investigators concluding that no more than 300 victims could have died at the stable, and that ammunition found at the site pointed to German involvement. While slightly diminishing the effect of Gross's book, these investigations nevertheless served to confirm that a mass murder had indeed taken place here. A new **memorial** was planned for the site, but the precise wording of the inscription caused the inevitable disagreements. Ultimately it was decided to specify that the victims were indeed Jews, but the identity of the killers was skated over. A planned sentence referring to hatreds generated by "German Nazism" was omitted after complaints from the German community.

The memorial was unveiled on 10 July 2001, at a commemoration attended by a host of Polish and Jewish dignitaries – although the Polish Catholic Church declined to send a representative. Kwaśniewski delivered the kind of statesmanlike performance that was expected of him, declaring that "as a citizen and as President of Poland, I beg pardon. I beg pardon in my own name, and in the name of those Poles whose conscience is shattered by this crime." Officially at least, the Jedwabne controversy was brought to an end, although the vexed question of Polish-Jewish relations looks set to remain the subject of debate for a long time to come.

from beneath the salon windows at the back of the palace, the overgrown **palace grounds** stretching out in all directions. From the bridge over the canal you have a good view of the whole feudal-like palace ensemble, the old lodge house and manor farm included.

Tykocin

Forty kilometres west of Białystok, north of the main Warsaw road (E18), is the quaint, sleepy little town of **TYKOCIN**, set in the open vistas of the Podlasie countryside. Tykocin's size belies its historical significance: as well as the former site of the national arsenal, it also has one of the best-restored **synagogues** in Poland today, much visited by Jewish tourist groups, a reminder that this was once home to an important Jewish community. It's a one-hour journey from the main bus station in Białystok; services depart roughly hourly throughout the day.

The bus deposits you in the enchanting **town square**, bordered by well-preserved nineteenth-century wooden houses. The **statue** of Stefan Czarnecki in the centre of the square was put up by his grandson Jan Branicki in 1770, while he was busy rebuilding the town and his adopted home of Białystok.

The Baroque **parish church**, commissioned by the energetic Branicki in 1741 and recently restored, has a beautiful polychrome ceiling, a finely ornamented side chapel of the Virgin and a functioning Baroque organ. The portraits of Branicki and his wife, Izabella Poniatowska, are by Silvester de Mirys, a Scot who became the resident artist at the Branicki palace in Białystok. Also founded by Branicki was the nearby Bernardine convent, now a Catholic seminary. Next to the church looking onto the river bridge is the **Alumnat**, a hospice for war veterans founded in 1633 – a world first. Continue out of town over the River Narew and you'll come to the ruins of the sixteenth-century **Pałac Radziwiłłów** (Radziwiłł Palace), where the national arsenal was once kept; it was destroyed by the Swedes in 1657.

Jews first came to Tykocin in 1522, and by the early nineteenth century seventy percent of the population was Jewish, the figure declining to around fifty percent by 1900. The original wooden **synagogue** in the town centre was replaced in 1642 by the Baroque building still standing today. Carefully restored in the 1970s following the usual severe wartime damage by the Nazis, it now houses an excellent **museum** (Tues–Sun 9am–4pm; 5zł; free on Sun), where background recordings of Jewish music and prayers add to a mournfully evocative atmosphere. Information sheets in English and German give detailed background on both the building and the history of Tykocin Jewry. Beautifully illustrated Hebrew inscriptions, mostly prayers, adorn sections of the interior walls, as do some lively colourful frescoes. Most striking of all is the large Baroque bimah, and there's a fine, ornate Aron Kodesh in the east wall as well. Valuable religious artefacts are on display, as well as historical documents relating to the now-lost community. Over the square in the old Talmud house there's a well-kept **local history museum** (same hours and ticket), featuring an intact apothecary's shop. The **Jewish cemetery** on the edge of town is gradually blending into the surrounding meadow – as so often, there's no one able or willing to take care of it. Among the eroded, weather-beaten gravestones, however, a few preserve their fine original carvings.

The only official **accommodation** is the youth hostel on ul. Kochanowskiego (July & Aug only; ☎085/718 1685), although private rooms are a possibility: ask in the Jewish museum for current information. The *Tejsza* **restaurant**, behind the musuem at ul. Kozia 2, is pretty unexceptional, despite admirable attempts to reproduce some traditional Jewish dishes.

Biebrzański Park Narodowy

Northeast of Tykocin the River Narew flows into one of Poland's unique natural paradises, a large area of low-lying marshland encompassed within the **Biebrzański Park Narodowy** (Biebrza National Park), added to the country's stock of officially protected areas in 1993, and, at around 600 square kilometres, the largest. Running through the area is the Biebrza River, which has its source southeast of Augustów close to the Belarusian border, the mainstay of an extensive network of bogs and marshes that constitutes one of Europe's most extensive and unspoilt **wetland** complexes. The scenic river basin landscape is home to richly varied flora and fauna. Important animal residents include otters, a large beaver population, wild boar, wolves and several hundred elk. The plant community includes just about every kind of marshland and forest species to be found in the country, including a rich assortment of rare mosses. The park's bird life – over 260 species have been recorded to date, many of them with local breeding habitats – is proving a major attraction with birdwatchers from all over Europe. **Spring** is the time to come, when floodwaters extend for miles along the river valley, making an ideal habitat for a large number of waterfowl, including such rarities as the pintail, shoveler, teal, black tern and, most prized of all, the aquatic warbler.

The park is divided into three sections corresponding to portions of the river. The **Northern Basin**, the smallest, and least easily accessible, lies in the upper part of the river, and is not much visited. The **Middle Basin** encompasses a scenic section of marshland and river forest, notably the **Red Marsh** (*Czerwone Bagno*) area, a stretch of strictly protected peatbog located some distance from the river valley floodlands that is home to a large group of elk as well as smaller populations of golden and white-tailed eagles. The area is off-limits to anyone not accompanied by an official guide (see below). The **Southern Basin**, coursed by the broad, lower stretches of the river consists of a combination of peatbogs and marshland, and is the most popular bird-watching territory on account of the large number of species to be found here.

Park practicalities

The obvious starting point for any visit to the area is the national park (BPN) **headquarters** (May–Sept daily 7.30am–7pm; Oct–April Mon–Fri 7.30am–3.30pm; ☏086/272 0620, ⊚www.biebrza.org) in **Osowiec**, a couple of hundred metres off the main Ełk–Białystok road from the train station – trains run every couple of hours in both directions. As well as selling the nominally priced **ticket** required for entrance to the park area the helpful office staff, some of whom speak English, can arrange guides (40zł an hour), guided tours for groups, and rowing boats – popular with bird-watchers – as well as help with sorting out local **accommodation**. For wildlife enthusiasts and others planning to explore less accessible sections of the park the network of basic but inexpensive forester's lodges (*leśniczówki*) dotted around the area are a vital resource – the BPN office has the details. They also have a good stock of books, brochures and **maps**, of which the *Biebrzański Park Narodowy* (1:120,000), produced with support from the Worldwide Fund for Nature, is particularly useful for bird-watchers.

If you've only limited time, the village and its surroundings make a good starting point for exploration. Back up to the main road, the twisted ruin of a concrete bunker just over the other side of the railway is a reminder of a fierce World War II battle between German and Russian forces. A ring of fortifications, remnants of a tsarist-era fortress, covers the area, many of them used these days as nesting platforms for the park's bird population. Just beyond the bunker there's an observation point that provides a good panorama over the marshes beyond.

A good deal of the park can be explored **on foot**, easily accomplished thanks to an extensive network of maintained and signposted trails, taking you through areas rich in natural attractions. Alternatively, and more adventurously, you can go **by boat**, especially worthwhile if you want to head beyond the immediate vicinity of Osowiec. The most ambitious locally organized excursion takes you along the Biebrza and Narew rivers all the way from Rajgród in the north down as far as Łomza – a 5–7-day trip involving stopovers at camping sites and forester's lodges along the river route. Check with the BPN office for current details.

Kruszyniamy and Bohoniki

Hard up near the Belarusian frontier, the old Tatar villages of **Kruszyniamy** and **Bohoniki** are an intriguing ethnic component of Poland's eastern borderlands, with their wooden mosques and Muslim graveyards. The story of how

The Tatars

Early in the thirteenth century, the nomadic Mongol people of Central Asia were welded into a confederation of tribes under the rule of Genghis Khan. In 1241 the most ferocious of these tribes, the **Tatars**, came charging out of the steppes and divided into two armies, one of which swept towards Poland, the other through Hungary. Lightly armoured, these natural horsemen moved with a speed that no European soldiery could match, and fought in a fashion as savage as the diet that sustained them – raw meat and horse's milk mixed with blood. On Easter Day they destroyed Kraków, and in April came up against the forces of the Silesian ruler, Duke Henryk the Pious, at Legnica. Henryk's troops were annihilated, and a contemporary journal records that "terror and doubt took hold of every mind" throughout the Christian West. Before the eventual withdrawal of the Tatar hordes, all of southern Poland was ravaged repeatedly – Kraków, for example, was devastated in 1259 and again in 1287.

Within a generation, however, the Tatars had withdrawn into central Russia and the Crimea, ceasing to pose a threat to the powers of central Europe. By the late fourteenth century the Tatars of the Crimea had come under the sway of the Grand Duchy of Lithuania – a vast east-European empire which became dynastically linked to Poland after 1386. Lithuanian ruler Vytautas the Great drafted Tatar units into his armies, and a contingent of Tatars helped the Polish-Lithuanian army defeat the Teutonic Knights at the Battle of Grunwald in 1410 (see p.204). Over the next few centuries communities of Tatars continued to migrate into the Grand Duchy of Lithuania (which at the time covered most of Belarus and parts of present-day eastern Poland). In time, Poland effectively absorbed Lithuania and its peoples (for more on which, see p.264). In the late seventeenth century, King Jan Sobieski granted additional lands in eastern Poland to Tatars who had taken part in his military campaigns, creating further pockets of Tatar settlement in the region, many of which – Kruszyniamy and Bohoniki included – have remained up to this day.

Today some six thousand descendants of these first Muslim citizens of Poland are spread all over the country, particularly in the Szczecin, Gdańsk and Białystok areas. Though thoroughly integrated into Polish society, they are distinctive both for their Asiatic appearance and their faith – the Tatars of Gdańsk, for example, have recently completed a mosque. Apart from the mosques and graveyards at Bohoniki and Kruszyniamy, little is left of the old settlements in the region east of Białystok, but there are a number of mosques still standing over the border in Belarus.

these people came to be here is fascinating in itself (see box on previous page), and a visit to the villages is an instructive and impressive experience.

Getting to them is no mean feat. Direct **buses to Kruszyniamy** from Białystok are scarce: the alternative is to take the bus to **Krynki** (about 40km) and wait for a connection to Kruszyniamy. If there aren't any of these, the only thing left to do is hitch. The only **buses to Bohoniki** are from **Sokółka** an hour's train journey north of Białystok. If you're trying to visit both villages in the same day, the best advice is to go to Kruszyniamy first, return to Krynki (probably by hitching) then take a bus towards Sokółka. Ask the driver to let you off at **Stara Kamionka**, and walk the remaining 4km east along the final stretch of the Szlak Tartarski ("Tatar Way"), which runs between the two villages. To get back to Białystok, take the late afternoon bus to Sokółka, then a train back to the city – they depart regularly up until around 10pm.

The villages

Walking through **KRUSZYNIAMY** is like moving back a century or two: the painted wooden houses, cobbled road and wizened old peasants staring at you from their front porches are like something out of Tolstoy. Surrounded by trees and set back from the road is the eighteenth-century **mosque**, recognizable by the Islamic crescent hanging over the entrance gate, though the architecture is strongly reminiscent of the wooden churches of eastern Poland. The elderly caretakers, who live right next door to the mosque, will let you in if you're properly dressed, which means no bare legs or revealing tops. Of late, too, they've become even more than usually cautious about opening up the building to visitors due to a depressing number of break-ins and thefts – including of valuable copies of the Koran – so you may need to be persuasive.

Though the Tatar population is dwindling – currently the village musters only seven people for the monthly services conducted by the visiting imam from Białystok – the mosque's predominantly wooden interior is well maintained. A glance at the list of Arab diplomats in the visitor's book explains where the money comes from, and the caretakers won't refuse a donation from you either. The building is divided into two sections, the smaller one for women, the larger and carpeted one for men, containing the *mihrab*, the customary recess pointing in the direction of Mecca, and a *mimber* (pulpit) from which the prayers are directed by the imam.

The **Muslim cemetery**, five minutes' walk beyond the mosque, contains a mixture of well-tended modern gravestones and, in the wood behind, old stones from the tsarist era. Despite the Tatar presence, the population of the village is predominantly Belarusian, a fact reflected in the presence of an Orthodox church, an uninspiring concrete structure that replaced the wooden original, destroyed by fire. The grimy looking **bar** in the village is the only place you'll get anything to eat in either of the villages and there's no accommodation.

The mosque in remoter **BOHONIKI** is a similar, though smaller, building, colourwashed in bright green on the outside, and stuffed with cosy-looking carpets within. Enquiries on the village's single street should establish the whereabouts of the mosque's current caretaker.

In the **Tatar cemetery**, hidden in a copse half a kilometre south of the village, gravestones are inscribed in both Polish and Arabic with characteristic Tatar names like Ibrahimowicz – in other words, Muslim names with a Polish ending tacked on. Search through the undergrowth right at the back of the cemetery and you'll find older, tumbled-down gravestones inscribed in Russian, from the days when Bohoniki was an outpost of the tsarist empire.

Tatars from all over Poland are still buried here, as they have been since Sobieski's time.

South from Białystok

Moving south of Białystok you're soon into the villages and fields of **Podlasie**, the heartland of the country's Belarusian population – you'll see the Cyrillic lettering of their language on posters (though not as yet on street signs) throughout the area. It's a poor, predominantly rural region that retains a distinctively Eastern feel, and for visitors the best-known attraction is the ancient **Puszcza Białowieska** (Białowieża Forest) straddling the border with neighbouring Belarus, with **Hajnówka**, a regional focus of Orthodox worship providing an intriguing gateway to the area. **Bielsk Podlaski**, the regional capital, and **Siemiatycze** are both worth investigating, the latter being near the extraordinary convent at **Grabarka**, focal point of Orthodox pilgrimage in Poland.

Buses represent the best way of getting round the region. A plenitude of services trundle south from Białystok to Hajnówka, Bielsk Podlaski and Siemiatycze: change in Hajnówka for the Białowieża Forest; and in Siemiatycze for Grabarka. On the way through the flat, wooded greenery of the Podlasie countryside you'll probably see more Orthodox onion domes than Catholic spires, a sure indication of the strength of the Belarusian population in the surrounding region.

Hajnówka

For most visitors to these parts **HAJNÓWKA**, some 70km southeast of Białystok, only registers as an entry point to the enticing Białowieża forest stretching east of the town. If you have the time, however, there's good enough reason to stop off in this unhurried spot in the form of a significant Belarusian minority presence. As in other Belarusian-dominated parts of the region, Hajnówka has been the focus of a significant revival of Orthodox traditions and spirituality. The prime testimony to this is the **Cerkiew Świętej Trójcy** (Church of the Holy Trinity), a magnificent *cerkiew* begun in the early 1970s and completed amid much fanfare in 1992. An imposing, unconventionally shaped structure with a curving roof punctured by a pair of onion-domed towers topped by Orthodox crucifixes, the interior boasts a fine iconostasis, a luminous series of frescoes, and a fine set of stained-glass windows from Kraków. As usual in Orthodox churches the place is generally only open during services, which in this case is quite often. Failing that, during regular daylight hours you should be able to persuade one of the priests living in the presbytery opposite the main entrance to open up the church for you.

Symbolizing the church's standing in the world of Polish Orthodoxy, once a year in early May it and the nearby *Dom Kultury*, ul. Białostocka 2 (☎085/682 3202), play joint hosts to a week-long **festival** of Orthodox choral music, attracting top-notch Orthodox choirs from around the world and broadcast nationally on radio. There's also a small **museum of Belarusian culture** at ul. 3 Maja 42 (Tues–Sun: June–Sept 9am–4pm; Oct–May 10am–3pm; 2zł), housing a modest but informative collection on the subject.

Having seen the church and the museum, your best bet is to continue eastwerds towards the Białowieża forest. If you need a **place to stay**, the *Orzechowski*, ul. Piłsudskiego 14 (☎085/682 2758; ❻), is a newish place aimed squarely at international tourists and offering all mod cons; while the *Dom Nauczyciela*, ul. Piłsudskiego 6 (☎085/682 2585; ❶), has simple rooms with shared facilities, but is pretty small – don't bank on getting a place. The main **eating** options are the cheap *Biała Róża*, ul. 3 Maja 42, which spices up a traditional Polish menu with a few Chinese dishes; and the restaurant of the *Orzechowski*, which is rather grander.

The Puszcza Białowieska

One hundred kilometres southeast of Białystok, the **Puszcza Białowieska** (Białowieża Forest) is the last major tract of primeval forest left in Europe. Covering 1260 square kilometres and spreading way over the border into Belarus, a large part of the forest is included in the **Białowieski park narodowy** (Białowieża national park), the first national park to be established in Poland and the only one currently numbered among UNESCO's World Natural Heritage sites. As well as being an area of inestimable beauty, the forest is also famous for harbouring one of the largest surviving populations of **European bison** – examples of which can be glimpsed in a special reserve.

For centuries Białowieża was a private hunting ground for a succession of Lithuanian and Belarusian princes, Polish kings, Russian tsars and other potentates – patronage which ensured the forest survived largely intact. Recognizing its environmental importance, the Polish government turned large sections of the *puszcza* into a national park in 1921, not least to protect its bison herds, which had been eaten almost to extinction by famished soldiers during World War I. Like most *puszcza*, Białowieża has hidden its fair share of partisan armies, most notably during the 1863 Uprising and World War II: monuments scatter the area, as no doubt do the bones of countless unknown dead.

Nearly forty percent of the forest located on the Polish side of the border belongs to a so-called "**strict reserve**" (*rezerwat ścisły*), a tightly controlled area clearly marked on the maps that can only be visited accompanied by a guide. Although subject to the usual national park regulations the rest of the area is open for **visits** (with or without guides). If you're planning on spending any time in this part of the country the extraordinary, primeval feel of the forest makes even a day-trip an experience not to be missed.

The place to aim for is **Białowieża** village, starting point for guided tours of the strict forest reserve, and also within walking distance of the bison reserve. There's one daily **bus** from Białystok to the village; if you miss this, catch one of the (roughly hourly) buses to Hajnówka, where you can pick up one of the eight daily buses to Białowieża. If you start reasonably early in the day, you can treat the forest as a day-trip and be back in Białystok by nightfall. However there's plenty of **accommodation** in Białowieża, and the idea of a reposeful night or two in this beautiful landscape has undoubted appeal.

Białowieża and the Palace Park

BIAŁOWIEŻA, a mere 2km from the Belarusian border, is a sleepy agricultural village full of the single-storey wooden farmhouses that characterize Poland's eastern borderlands. Colourwashed in a variety of ochres, maroons and greens, they're a picture of domestic tidiness, although the tumbledown, weather-blackened barns that lurk in most back gardens – picturesque though they are – suggest a story of rural stagnation and depopulation only partially alleviated by tourism.

Buses terminate at the eastern end of the village, opposite a red-brick Catholic church, although you'll save time by getting off earlier – either at the

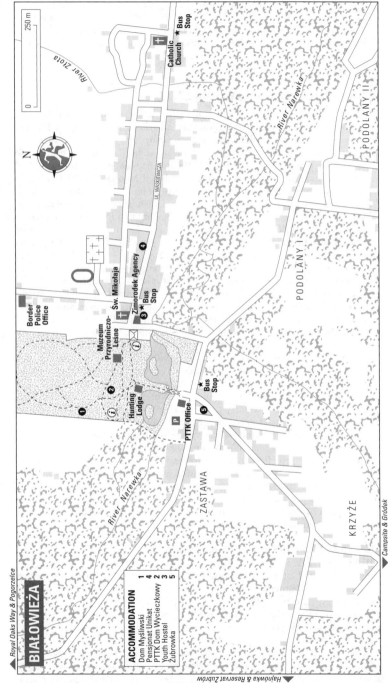

BIAŁOWIEŻA

ACCOMMODATION
Dom Myśliwski — 1
Pensjonat Unikat — 4
PTTK Dom Wycieczkowy — 2
Youth Hostel — 3
Żubrówka — 5

Border Police Office

Muzeum Przyrodniczo-Leśne

Hunting Lodge

PTTK Office

Św. Mikołaja

Zimorodek Agency

Bus Stop

Bus Stop

Bus Stop

Catholic Church

River Złota

UL. WASKIEWICZA

River Narewka

River Narewka

PODOLANY II

PODOLANY I

ZASTAWA

KRZYŻE

N

250 m

Royal Oaks Way & Pogorzelce

Hajnówka & Rezerwat Żubrów

Campsite & Gródek

southern gate of the **Park Pałacowy** (Palace Park), near the disused train station; or at the eastern entrance to the Park, opposite a typical late-nineteenth-century Orthodox **Cerkiew św. Mikołaja** (Church of St Nicholas), which boasts a unique and very attractive tiled iconostasis.

The park itself is not part of the strict reserve, and you're free to wander round it during daylight hours. It was laid out in the 1890s to accompany an impressive palace, built at Tsar Alexander III's behest and destroyed by the retreating Nazis in 1944. Containing a brace of ornamental lakes and an agreeably strollable collection of tree-lined walkways, the park also harbours the **Muzeum Przyrodniczo-Leśne** (Forest Museum; Tues–Sun: June–Sept 9am–5pm; Oct–May 9am–3.30pm; 5zł), which provides an impressively detailed and well-presented introduction to the forest, including examples of the amazingly diverse flora and fauna. If you're at all interested in natural history you should definitely put an hour or two aside for the visit. Just downhill from the museum to the west is the lime-green **Dworek** (Little Palace; Mon–Fri 8am–4pm; 2zł), a timber-built former hunting lodge which now hosts art and photography exhibitions, usually with an ecological theme.

Visiting the forest

The parts of the forest most people want to see belong to the "strict reserve" to the north and west of the village, which can only be visited in the company of an **official guide**, although "non-strict" parts, such as the **Reservat Żubrów** and the **Szlak Dębów Królewskich**, can be freely accessed whether you have a guide or not. The hiring of guides is handled by the PTTK office at the southern entrance to the Palace Park (Mon–Fri 8am–4pm, Sat & Sun 8am–3pm; ☎085/681 2295, ✉pttkbialowieza@sitech.pl).

Horse-drawn cart tours are the most popular way of travelling into the forest. Only eleven carts are permitted in a day, which makes booking a day ahead a sound policy in summer. For standard (2–3hr) trips to the bison reserve reckon on paying about 100zł for the cart, 120zł for more extended trips (4hr), 150zł for a day-trip (around 7hr) round the entire reserve. The cost of a Polish-speaking guide is included in the price; an English-speaking guide will cost an additional 100zł.

Dedicated enthusiasts maintain that exploring the forest **on foot** is the best way to experience its charms, especially if it's the animals that you want to see. Licensed guides are allowed to take groups of up to 25 people on walking tours (4hr) including the strict reserve: the usual tour takes you through the core of the forest's protected areas. Here your only costs will be for the guide (120zł per group) and the **ticket** (5zł) everyone entering the strict reserve, by whatever means of transport, is required to purchase.

However you decide to enter the strict reserve, it's likely to be a magical experience. At times the serenity of the forest's seemingly endless depths is exhilarating, then suddenly the trunks of oak, spruce and hornbeam swell threateningly to a dense canopy, momentarily pierced by shafts of sunlight that sparkle briefly before subsiding into gloom. Apart from the rarer animals such as elk and beaver, the forest supports an astounding profusion of **flora and fauna**: over twenty species of tree, twenty of rodents, thirteen varieties of bat, 228 of birds – all told over 3000 species, not counting around 8000 different insect species.

The Reservat Żubrów

Situated some 4km west of the village on the road to Hajnówka, and accessible on foot along the green and yellow marked trails that start at the southern entrance to the Park Pałacowy, the **Reservat Żubrów**, or bison reserve (Tues–Sun: June–Sept 9am–5pm; Oct–May 9am–3.30pm; 4zł), is a large fenced area where some of the 250 specimens of the forest's largest and most famous inhabitant can be seen lounging around – the rest are out in the wilds. It's not part of the strict reserve, so individual tourists can come here without a guide – although the standard three-hour carriage tours usually call in here too. Don't be fooled by the often dozy-looking appearance of the bison: when threatened, the bison – *żubr* in Polish – can charge at over 50km an hour, which makes for a force to be reckoned with when you bear in mind that the largest weigh in excess of 1000kg. The stout, sandy-coloured horses with a dark stripe on their backs that you can also spot in the reserve area are wild **tarpans**, relations of the original steppe horses that died out in the last century. The tarpans are gradually being bred back to their original genetic stock after centuries of interbreeding. In neighbouring enclosures you can see examples of other forest animals, including elk, wild boar, stag and the *żubroń*, a somewhat improbable-looking cross between bison and cow that's been specially bred here.

The Szlak Dębów Królewskich

One of the most memorable parts of the forest that's not in the strict reserve is the **Szlak Dębów Królewskich** (Royal Oaks Way), located 3km north of the bison reserve along a yellow marked trail. It consists of a group of forty-metre-high oaks, the oldest of which are over four hundred years old. Each of the brooding, venerable specimens ranged along the forest path is named after one of the monarchs of the Polish-Lithuanian Commonwealth, a sign of the respect which forest-dwellers have long accorded the trees.

Park practicalities

The park **information centre**, just inside the eastern entrance to the Park Pałacowy (daily 9am–5pm; ☎085/681 2306), gives away English-language leaflets detailing the attractions of the forest, sells local maps, and keeps a list of **private rooms** (reckon on 35zł per person) in the village. There are a couple of **hotels** within the Palace Park itself: the *PTTK Dom Wycieczkowy*, just west of the museum (☎085/681 2505; ❶–❷), is a basic place located in the former palace stable, with a rudimentary café but no restaurant. Marginally better is the *Myśliwski* (☎085/681 2584; ❷), a short walk north of the *PTTK*, which offers large rooms in a tranquil setting although again, no restaurant, but kitchen facilities are available. Alternative options are spread around the village. The *Unikat* at ul. Waszkiewicza 39 (☎085/681 2774; ❸), a short walk east of the palace park, is a good-quality, family-run *pensjonat*; while the *Żubrówka*, ul. Olgi Gabiec 6 (☎085/681 2303, ⓦwww.hotel-zubrowka.bialowieza.pl; ❸), is a fairly new place with comfortable en-suites – the plush modern annexe currently under construction aims to offer deluxe rooms in the (❻) bracket. The decent-sized all-year **youth hostel**, just opposite the Orthodox church at ul. Waszkiewicza 6 (☎085/681 2560, ⓦwww.paprotka.com.pl), has dorm rooms at 20zł per bed and some doubles (❶). There's also a basic **campsite** (May–Sept) 2km south of the village, and an increasing number of villagers are allowing camping in their gardens during the summer – look for *Pole namiotowe* ("tent ground") signs.

The *Unikat* has a wholesome **restaurant** in the basement offering good Polish staples; although the restaurant of the *Żubrówka* offers more choice, including some vegetarian options.

Bielsk Podlaski

Fifty-five kilometres south of Białystok lies **BIELSK PODLASKI**, a dusty old market town imbued with the old-world peasant feel of the surrounding countryside. By car or train the route from Białystok takes you through the attractive open Podlasie landscape, with opportunities for stopping off at the often beautiful Orthodox *cerkwie* you'll find in villages along the way. The town itself has a couple of places of interest, but it's the atmosphere, as much as buildings, that lend the place a certain down-at-heel charm.

The Town

The sights worth seeing are scattered round the rather diffuse town centre intersected from north to south by ul. Mickiewicza, the main shopping street. At the north end of Mickiewicza is the Stare Miasto **Rynek**, with some attractive examples of the local wooden architecture in evidence among the older houses ringing the square. The chunky Baroque **town hall** at the centre of the square houses a small **museum** (Tues–Sat 10am–5pm; 3zł) featuring local craft work and occasional art exhibitions. Just west of the square stands the Neoclassical **Catholic parish church**, built in the 1780s at Izabella Branicki's behest, while north of the Rynek is a good example of a local speciality, the impromptu **open-air market**. This one's a muddy patch generally swarming with Belarusians and other "trade tourists" from across the border, camped around their cars, flogging motley assortments of clothes, jewellery, hi-fis and other knick-knacks to the locals. Just beyond the market is the seventeenth-century **Carmelite church and monastery**: a characteristic Polish Baroque structure, the interior has recently been completely renovated to good effect.

South along ul. Mickiewicza brings you to the ornate **Cerkiew św. Mihała** (Church of St Michael), a large, bulbous blue *cerkiew* and the main centre of Orthodox worship in town. As often, the building's nearly always closed, except during services, so you'll have to ask next door at the parish house to get in and see the fine iconostasis.

Practicalities

The **bus** and **train station** is ten minutes' walk south of the town centre. There's not much in the way of decent **accommodation**, the best bet being the hotel *Unibus*, ul. Widowska 4 (☎085/730 0302, ⓦwww.unibus.com.pl; ❸), on the northeast edge of town, with the *Przyszłość*, ul. Dąbrowskiego 3 (☎085/730 7770; ❷), a lesser alternative. For a **meal** the *Podlasianka*, ul. Mickiewicza 37, complete with regular evening dance-band, is about the best on offer, while the *Hajduczek*, ul. Mickiewicza 25, is a presentable enough *kawiarnia* serving up cheap Polish staples.

Siemiatycze and around

Fifty kilometres south on through the quiet Podlasie countryside brings you to **SIEMIATYCZE**, a scruffy-looking place with all the hallmarks of a town suffering from the severe depression currently afflicting the rural Polish economy. As usual the main square forms the focal point of the town. The **Catholic parish church** is ornate early Baroque with a triumphal-looking altarpiece and the characteristic yellow and white stucco decoration. Following the Red Army's invasion of eastern Poland at the outbreak of World War II, the people of Siemiatycze found themselves inside Soviet territory, a fact recalled in the new plaque inside the church commemorating the "Operation Bursa" ("*Akcja*

Bursa"), in the course of which Soviet forces attacked and liquidated AK (Home Army) bases in the forests east of the town, rounded up many local people and deported them to Siberia, most of them never to return. Just down the hill is the main local Orthodox **Cerkiew św. Piotra i Pawła** (Church of SS Peter and Paul), a typical nineteenth-century *cerkiew* that's looking much the better for a recently completed restoration.

Orthodox aside, the other main religious community here used to be **Jews**: typically for the region, before the war Jews comprised some forty percent of the town's population. South of the square off ul. Pałacowa is the former town **synagogue**, an eighteenth-century brick building that somehow survived the depredations of the Nazis. Following wartime use as an arsenal, the synagogue was restored in the 1960s and turned into the local *Dom Kultury*. If you ask, the staff can point out surviving features of the building's original architecture. As often, the **Jewish cemetery**, east past the bus station on ul. Polna, is run-down and wildly overgrown. Back in town the local **museum** on ul. 11 Listopada (Tues–Sun 10am–4pm; 2.50zł), south of the centre, has a presentable collection of local exhibits enhanced by some displays devoted to local Jewish themes.

For a **place to stay**, the *U Kmicica* (☎085/655 2432; ❷), well south of the centre at ul. 11 Listopada 139, is about the only option, with the *Oleńka*, just off the main square at ul. Grodzieńska 7, the only reliable **restaurant**.

The Grabarka convent

Hidden away in the woods round Siemiatycze, the **convent** near the village of **GRABARKA**, 10km east of town, is the spiritual centre of contemporary Polish Orthodoxy: primarily a site of pilgrimage, it occupies a place in Polish Orthodox devotions similar to that of Częstochowa for Catholics. The contrast between the two religious centres couldn't be more striking, however: where the Jasna Góra monastery is all urban pomp and majesty, the Grabarka site is steeped in a powerful aura of rural mystery. If you've become accustomed to processions of Catholic sisters on the streets of Polish cities, the sight of the twenty or so Orthodox-robed nuns making their way to the church in Grabarka comes as quite a surprise. Sisters of the convent established here in 1947 to bring together all Orthodox women's religious communities within the country, they carefully – and understandably – guard their privacy from the hordes of pilgrims who descend for the major festivals of the Orthodox calendar.

Approached by a sandy forest track, the hill up to the small convent leads to the community buildings next to the main **church**: whether by accident or design – local opinion is divided on the issue – the church was burnt to the ground in 1991, a cause of great sadness among the Belarusian and Orthodox communities for whom it's long been a treasured shrine. Workmen set to work rebuilding it – judging by the brass plating used on the onion-domed roof, no expense was spared either – and a new brick building is now fully functional. The best-known and certainly most striking feature, however, is the thicket of **wooden crosses**, the oldest dating back to the early eighteenth century, when pilgrims drawn by stories of miracles said to have occurred during a local epidemic of cholera first began coming here, packing the slopes below the church. A traditional gesture of piety carried by pilgrims and placed here on completing their journey, the literally thousands of characteristic Orthodox crucifixes clustered together in all shapes and sizes are an extraordinarily powerful sight: with all this wood around, the "no lighting-up" signs sprinkled among the crosses come as no surprise.

Despite the convent's backwoods location, groups of devotees can be found visiting the place at most times of the year. The biggest pilgrimages, however, centre round major Orthodox feast and holy days, notably August 19, the **Przemienienia Panskiego (Spasa)** – Feast of the Transfiguration of the Saviour – when thousands of Orthodox faithful from around the country flock to Grabarka, many by foot, for several days of celebrations beginning with an all-night vigil in the immediate run-up to the main feast day. As much celebrations of cultural identity as their Catholic counterparts are for Poles, the festivals at Grabarka offer a powerful insight into the roots of traditional, predominantly peasant Orthodox devotion.

If you don't have your own transport, **buses** run to Grabarka village – roughly half a kilometre from the convent – two or three times a day from Siemiatycze, more often in summer. Alternatively you can take a **train** from Hajnówka or Białystok to the village of Sycze, and walk the approximately 1km distance remaining though the woods up to the convent.

Travel details

Trains

Białystok to: Gdańsk (2 daily; 9hr; couchettes); Kraków (1 daily; 9hr; couchettes); Lublin (1 daily; 9hr); Olsztyn (5–6 daily; 6hr); Poznań (1 daily; 10hr); Suwałki via Augustów (4–5 daily; 2hr 30min–3hr); Warsaw (8 daily; 2hr).

Gdańsk to: Białystok (2 daily; 8–9hr); Bydgoszcz (hourly; 2–3hr); Częstochowa (2 daily; 7–8hr); Elbląg (11 daily; 1–2hr); Hel (July–Aug 3 daily; 3hr 15min); Katowice (8 daily; 7–8hr; couchettes); Kołobrzeg (4 daily; 4–5hr); Koszalin (13 daily; 3–4hr); Kraków (7 daily; 6–10hr); Łódź (3 daily; 5hr 30min–7hr); Lublin (1 daily; 7hr 30min); Malbork (20 daily; 1hr–1hr 30min); Olsztyn (6 daily; 3hr 30min); Poznań (6 daily; 4hr); Przemyśl (1 daily; 13hr); Rzeszów (1–2 daily; 11–14hr; couchettes); Szczecin (3 daily; 4hr 30min–6hr); Toruń (5 daily; 3–4hr); Warsaw (12 daily; 3–4hr); Wrocław (4 daily; 7–8hr; couchettes); Zakopane (1 daily; 13hr; couchettes).

Gdynia to: Hel (8 daily; 2hr 15min); Władysławowo (8 daily; 1hr 25min).

Grudziądz to Malbork (6 daily; 1hr 20min); Toruń (8 daily; 1hr 30min).

Hel to: Gdynia (8 daily; 2hr 15min); Władysławowo (8 daily; 50min).

Mikołajki to: Ełk (1 daily; 1hr 40min); Mrągowo (2 daily; 40min); Olsztyn (2 daily; 2hr 30min).

Mrągowo to: Ełk (1 daily; 2hr 20min); Mikołajki (2 daily; 40min); Olsztyn (5 daily; 1hr 50min).

Olsztyn to: Białystok (4 daily; 5–7 hr); Elbląg (10 daily; 1hr 30min–2hr); Gdańsk (6 daily; 3–4hr); Kraków (2 daily; 7–12hr); Mikołajki (2 daily; 2hr 30min); Mrągowo (5 daily; 1hr 50min); Poznań (4 daily; 5hr); Suwałki (2 daily; 5–6hr); Szczecin (5 daily; 8–10hr); Toruń (8 daily; 3–4hr); Warsaw (8 daily; 3–5hr); Wrocław (2 daily; 7–8hr); Zakopane (1 daily; 16hr).

Suwałki to: Białystok (4 daily; 2hr 30min–3hr 30min); Kraków (1 daily June–Sept; 12hr); Olsztyn (2 daily; 6–8hr); Warsaw (4–6 daily; 4–8hr; couchettes June–Sept).

Toruń to: Bydgoszcz (12 daily; 30min–1hr); Gdańsk (5 daily; 3–4hr); Kraków (3 daily; 7–8hr); Łódź (12 daily; 2–4hr); Olsztyn (5 daily; 2–3hr); Poznań (5 daily; 2–3hr); Warsaw (6 daily; 3–5hr); Wrocław (2 daily; 5–6hr).

Buses

Augustów to: Białystok (12 daily; 2hr 10min); Ełk (9 daily; 1hr); Giżycko (1 daily; 3hr); Sejny (4 daily; 50min); Suwałki (20 daily; 45min); Warsaw (3 daily; 5hr).

Białystok to: Augustów (12 daily; 2hr 10min); Biała Podlaska (1 daily; 3hr 30min); Białowieża (1 daily; 3hr); Bielsk Podlaski (hourly; 1hr 10min); Choroszcz (every 30min; 30min); Hajnówka (18 daily; 1hr 30min); Lublin (2 daily; 4hr); Olsztyn (2 daily; 4hr); Suwałki (8 daily; 2hr 30min); Tykocin (18 daily; 40min); Warsaw (8 daily; 4hr).

Chełmno to: Bydgoszcz (14 daily; 1hr); Grudziądz (12 daily; 1hr); Toruń (12 daily; 1hr 10min).

Elbląg to: Krynica Morska (20 daily; 1hr 20min).

Gdańsk to: Białystok (1 daily; 9hr); Braniewo (5 daily; 2hr 50min); Chmielno (5 daily; 1hr 20min); Chojnice (5 daily; 2hr); Elbląg (every 30min; 1hr 20min); Frombork (5 daily; 2hr 30min); Gyżicko (2 daily; 7hr 30min); Kamień Pomorski (1 daily; 7hr); Kartuzy (hourly; 50min); Kętrzyn (4 daily; 5hr 45min); Kołobrzeg (1 daily; 5hr 30min); Koszalin (1 daily; 4hr 45min); Kąty Rybackie (14 daily; 1hr 20min); Krynica Morska (14 daily; 1hr 40min); Lębork (6 daily; 2hr); Lidzbark Warmiński (5 daily;

5hr); Malbork (8 daily; 1hr 15min); Olsztyn (3 daily; 5hr 30min); Sztutowo (18 daily; 1hr 15min); Świnouscie (1 daily; 9hr); Toruń (1 daily; 3hr 30min); Warsaw (2 daily; 5hr 30min).

Gdynia to: Hel (8 daily; 2hr); Jastrzębia Gora (July–Aug 15 daily; Sept–June 5 daily; 1hr 30min); Łeba (July–Aug 4 daily; Sept–June 2 daily; 2hr 30min); Warsaw (2 daily; 5hr 40min).

Giżycko to Gdańsk (2 daily; 7hr 30min); Kętrzyn (10 daily; 40min); Mikołajki (6 daily; 1hr); Mrągowo (16 daily; 1hr 40min).

Giżycko to Gdańsk (2 daily; 7hr 30min); Kętrzyn (10 daily; 40min); Mikołajki (6 daily; 1hr); Mrągowo (16 daily; 1hr 40min).

Grudziądz to: Bydgoszcz (10 daily; 2hr); Chełmno (12 daily; 1hr); Toruń (7 daily; 2hr 30min).

Hajnówka to: Białowieża (8 daily; 30min); Białystok (18 daily; 1hr 30min).

Hel to: Gdynia (8 daily; 2hr); Jastrzębia Góra (July–Aug 1 daily; 1hr 15min).

Kartuzy to: Chmielno (Mon–Fri 10 daily; Sat & Sun 6 daily; 20min).

Kętrzyn to: Gdańsk (4 daily; 5hr 45min); Giżycko (10 daily; 40min); Mrągowo (20 daily; 45min); Olsztyn (20 daily; 1hr 30min); Reszel (20 daily; 25min); Węgorzewo (16 daily; 50min).

Mikołajki to: Ełk (7 daily; 2hr); Giżycko (6 daily; 1hr); Mrągowo (14 daily; 30min); Olsztyn (3 daily;

2hr); Pisz (3 daily; 50min); Suwałki (1 daily; 3hr 20min); Tałty (4 daily; 15min); Warsaw (4 daily in summer; 5hr 40min).

Mrągowo to: Białystok (2 daily; 4hr); Gdańsk (1 daily; 5hr 30min); Gyżicko (16 daily; 1hr 40min); Kętrzyn (20 daily; 45min); Olsztyn (24 daily; 1hr 30min); Pisz (8 daily; 1hr); Ruciane-Nida (8 daily; 40min); Suwałki (4 daily; 3hr 50min); Warsaw (1 daily; 5hr).

Olsztyn to: Białystok (2 daily; 4hr); Gdańsk (3 daily; 4hr); Lidzbark Warmiński (8 daily; 1hr 10min); Kętrzyn (20 daily; 1hr 30min); Mikołajki (3 daily; 2hr); Mrągowo (24 daily; 1hr 30min); Warsaw (3 daily; 4hr).

Sejny to Puńsk (4 daily; 35min).

Suwałki to: Augustów (20 daily; 45min); Mikołajki (1 daily; 3hr 20min); Mrągowo (1 daily; 3hr 50min); Puńsk (5 daily; 50min); Sejny (15 daily; 50min); Warsaw (4 daily; 6hr).

Toruń to: Bydgoszcz (hourly; 50min); Chełmno (12 daily; 1hr 10min); Ciechocinek (every 30min; 30min); Golub-Dobrzyn (Mon–Fri 12 daily; Sat & Sun 6 daily; 1hr); Grudziądz (7 daily; 2hr 30min); Łódź (4 daily; 3hr 20min); Warsaw (hourly; 3hr 40min); Włocławek (12 daily; 1hr 10min).

Władysławowo to Jastrzębia Góra (July–Aug 20 daily; Sept–June 7 daily; 25min).

Ferries

Gdańsk to: Hel (mid-June to end Aug 4 daily; May to mid-June & Sept 1 daily)

Gdynia to: Hel (mid-June to end Aug 8 daily; May to mid-June & Sept 2 daily)

International Trains

Gdańsk to: Berlin (1 daily; 9hr).

Suwałki to: Šestokai (2 daily).

International Buses

Białystok to: Minsk (1 daily; 7hr), Vilnius (1 weekly; 9hr).

Gdańsk to: Kaliningrad (2 daily; 7hr); Vilnius (daily; 11hr).

Kętrzyn to: Kaliningrad (1 daily; 4hr).

Mrągowo to: Vilnius (5 weekly; 8hr).

Olsztyn to: Vilnius (5 weekly; 9hr).

Suwałki to: Vilnius (1 weekly; 6hr).

Southeastern Poland

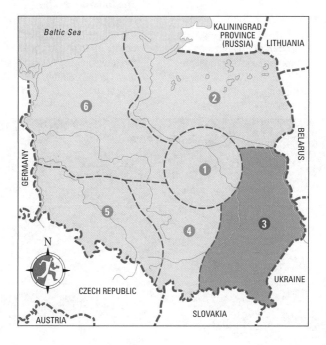

Baltic Sea

KALININGRAD
PROVINCE
(RUSSIA)

LITHUANIA

BELARUS

GERMANY

N

CZECH REPUBLIC

SLOVAKIA

UKRAINE

AUSTRIA

CHAPTER 3   Highlights

Southeastern Poland

T he **southeast** is the least populated and least known part of Poland: a great swath of border country, its agricultural plains punctuated by remote, backwoods villages and a few market towns. It is peasant land, the remnants of the great European *latifundia* – the feudal grain estates – whose legacy was massive emigration, from the late 1800s until World War II, to France, Germany and, above all, the USA.

Borders have played an equally disruptive role in recent history. Today's **eastern frontier**, established after the last war, sliced through the middle of what was long the heartland of the Polish **Ukraine**, leaving towns like Lublin (and L'viv, inside the Ukraine) deprived of their historic links. As border restrictions ease, the prewar links are reasserting themselves in the flood of ex-Soviet "trade tourists" – small-time merchants – who give an international touch to the street markets of towns like Przemyśl and Rzeszów. Burgeoning cross-border trade has established itself as a major source of income and employment for all concerned, although this is under threat from the tougher border controls Poland's entry into the EU requires. In the genuine wilderness of the **highland areas** you come upon a more extreme political repercussion of the war, with the minority **Lemks** and **Boyks** just beginning to re-establish themselves, having been expelled in the wake of the civil war that raged here from 1945 to 1947. In addition, this area's ethnic diversity is further complicated by divisions between Catholic, Uniate and Orthodox communities.

None of this may inspire a visit, yet aspects of the east can be among the highlights of any Polish trip. Main town of the region is bustling, self-confident **Lublin**, a major industrial centre that also boasts one of Poland's most magical Stare Miasto areas. The smaller towns, particularly the old trading centres of **Kazimierz Dolny** and **Sandomierz** along the Wisła River, are among the country's most beautiful, long favoured by artists and retaining majestic historic centres. Much favoured as a holiday retreat by the Warsaw middle classes, Kazimierz in particular is one of the liveliest summertime destinations that

Accommodation price codes

The accommodation listed in this book has been given one of the following price codes, based, unless stated otherwise, on the cost of the cheapest double room in high season. For more details see p.39.

❶ under 60zł
❷ 60–90zł
❸ 90–120 zł
❹ 120–160zł
❺ 160–220zł
❻ 220–300zł
❼ 300–400zł
❽ 400–600zł
❾ over 600zł

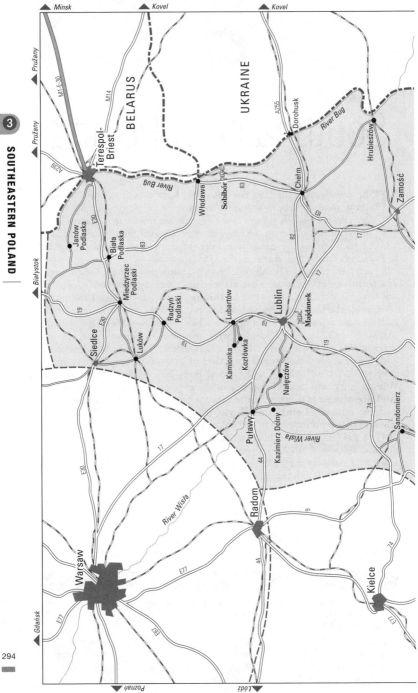

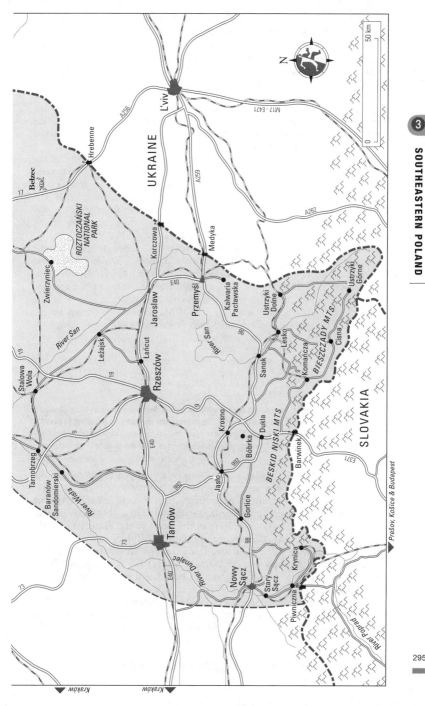

3

rural Poland has to offer. Over to the east, **Zamość** has a superb Renaissance centre, miraculously preserved from the war and well worth a detour, while in the south there's the stately **Łancut Castle**, an extraordinary reminder of pre-war, aristocratic Poland. Each summer the castle hosts a chamber music festival, one of the most prestigious Polish music events. The most intriguing festival, however, takes place at nearby **Rzeszów** in June and July every third year, when folklore groups from *emigracja* communities get together for a riot of singing, dancing and nostalgia. Other towns of note in the region include **Tarnów**, much of its medieval centre intact; while beer-lovers will probably want to make a beeline for **Leżajsk**, whose honeyed local brew is at least as popular with visitors as the annual pilgrimages to its renowned church.

The mountains of the far southeast, though not as high or as dramatic as the Tatras to the west, are totally unexploited. A week or so hiking in the **Bieszczady** is time well spent, the pleasures of the landscapes reinforced by easy contact with the locals – a welcoming bunch, and drinkers to match any in the country. The **Beskid Niski**, to the west, has some great rewards too: in particular its amazing wooden **churches** or *cerkwie*, whose pagoda-like domes and canopies are among the most spectacular folk architecture of central-eastern Europe.

This part of Poland is rich in **Jewish heritage** too, although historical sites and synagogues are not always maintained and made accessible. Kazimierz Dolny, Sandomierz and **Jarosław** form a procession of formerly Jewish-dominated towns situated along the old East–West trading routes. Lublin was one of the most important Jewish centres in Poland before World War II, which probably explains why the Lublin suburb of **Majdanek** was chosen by the Nazis as the site of one of the Third Reich's most notorious death camps – a chilling place that demands to be visited.

Lublin

In the shops, oil lamps and candles were lit. Bearded Jews dressed in long cloaks and wearing wide boots moved through the streets on the way to evening prayers. The world beyond was in turmoil. Jews everywhere were being driven from their villages. But here in Lublin one felt only the stability of a long established community.

Isaac Bashevis Singer, *The Magician of Lublin*

The city of **LUBLIN**, the largest in eastern Poland, is one of the most alluring urban centres in the whole country, thanks in large part to the evocative hive of alleys that constitute its magnificent Stare Miasto. New arrivals are sometimes put off by the sprawling high-rise buildings and Stalinist smokestacks of the suburbs, but once you're in the heart of the place, it's all cobbled streets and dilapidated mansions – a wistful reminder of the city's past glories. The fabric of this old quarter came through World War II relatively undamaged, and although years of postwar neglect left it in a pretty shambolic state, recent restoration programmes have left the city centre ripe for tourist discovery.

In among the numerous churches you'll find reminders that for centuries Lublin was home to a large and vibrant **Jewish community**, a population exterminated in the Nazi concentration camp at **Majdanek**, 6km from the city centre.

Some history

Like many eastern towns, Lublin started as a **medieval** trade settlement and guard post, in this case on the trade route linking the Baltic ports with Kiev

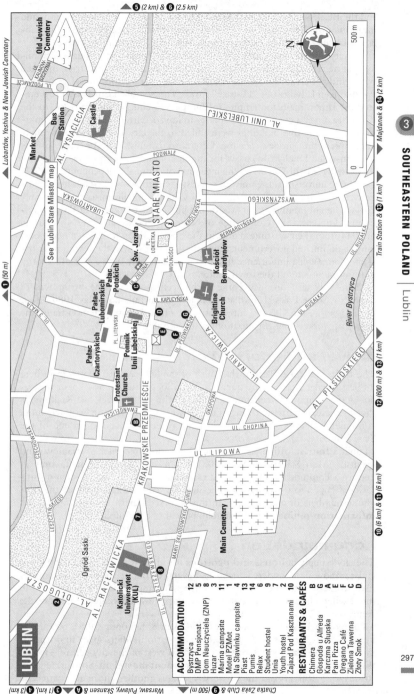

LUBLIN

STARE MIASTO

See 'Lublin Stare Miasto' map

Old Jewish Cemetery

Bus Station

Castle

Market

Św. Jozefa

Pałac Lubomirskich

Pałac Potockich

Pałac Czartoryskich

Protestant Church

Pomnik Unii Lubelskiej

Kościół Bernardynów

Brigittine Church

Katolicki Uniwersytet (KUL)

Ogród Saski

Main Cemetery

River Bystrzyca

PODWALE

KRÓLEWSKA

BERNARDYŃSKA

UL. RUSAŁKA

WYSZYŃSKIEGO

AL. UNII LUBELSKIEJ

AL. PIŁSUDSKIEGO

UL. NARUTOWICZA

UL. CHOPINA

UL. LIPOWA

MARII SKŁODOWSKIEJ-CURIE

UL. RADZISZEWSKIEGO

KRAKOWSKIE PRZEDMIEŚCIE

AL. RACŁAWICKA

AL. DŁUGOSZA

LESZCZYŃSKIEGO

CZECHOWSKA

UL. LUBARTOWSKA

AL. TYSIĄCLECIA

UL. PODZAMCZE

UL. KALINOWSZCZYZNA

UL. KLONOWICA

UL. ZIELONA

PL. ŁOKIETKA

PL. WOLNOŚCI

UL. KAPUCYŃSKA

PL. LITEWSKI

UL. PENIWAKÓW

EWANGELICKA

DOLNA 3 MAJA

OKOPOWA

UL. RUSAŁKA

(2 km) & *(2.5 km)*

(50 m)

Lubartów, Yeshiva & New Jewish Cemetery

(1 km), *(1 km)*, *(3 km)*

Warsaw, Puławy, Skansen &

(500 m)

Chatka Żaka Club & *(500 m)*

(6 km) & *(6 km)*

(600 m) & *(1 km)*

Train Station & *(1 km)*

(1 km) & *(1 km)*

Majdanek & *(2 km)*

N

500 m

0

ACCOMMODATION

Bystrzyca	12
DMP Pensjonat	5
Dom Nauczyciela (ZNP)	8
Huzar	3
Marina campsite	11
Motel PZMot	1
Na Sławinku campsite	4
Piast	13
Pumis	14
Relax	6
Student hostel	9
Unia	7
Youth hostel	2
Zajazd Pod Kasztanami	10

RESTAURANTS & CAFÉS

Chimera	B
Gospoda u Alfreda	G
Karczma Słupska	A
Pani Pizza	E
Oregano Café	F
Zielona Tawerna	C
Złoty Smok	D

and the Black Sea. Somehow managing to survive numerous depredations and invasions – the fearsome Tatar onslaughts in particular – Lublin was well established by the **sixteenth century** as a commercial and cultural centre.

The city's finest hour came in 1569 when the Polish and Lithuanian nobility met here to set a seal on the formal union of the two countries, initiated two centuries earlier by the marriage of Lithuanian grand duke Jagiełło and Polish queen Jadwiga (see "History" p.677). This so-called **Lublin Union** created the largest mainland empire in Europe, stretching from the Baltic to the Black Sea. Over a century of prosperity followed, during which the arts flourished and many fine buildings were added to the city. The **Partitions** rudely interrupted this process, leaving Lublin to languish on the edge of the Russian-ruled Duchy of Warsaw for the next hundred years or so.

Following **World War I** and the regaining of national independence in 1918, a Catholic university – the only one in eastern Europe – was established, which grew to become a cradle of the Polish Catholic intelligentsia, most notably during the communist era. It was to Lublin, too, that a group of Polish communists known as the Committee of National Liberation (PKWN) returned in **1944** from their wartime refuge in the Soviet Union to set up a new communist-dominated government. Since the end of the war, the town's industrial and commercial importance has grown considerably, with a belt of factories mushrooming around the town centre.

Lublin may also one day come to be seen as one of the birthplaces of Solidarity. Some Poles claim that it was a strike in Lublin in May **1980** – four months before the Gdańsk shipyard sit-ins – that decisively demonstrated the power of workers' self-organization to the country.

Arrival and information

The **train station** is 2km to the south of the Stare Miasto centre; from here it's best to take a taxi (if the queue isn't too long), bus #1 or #13, or trolleybus #150 – it's a fifteen-minute ride to the main street, ul. Krakowskie Przedmieście, otherwise a long walk. The main **bus station** is much more conveniently located, lying just below the castle at the northern end of the Stare Miasto.

Lublin's **tourist office**, in the Stare Miasto on the corner of Bramowa and Jezuitska (Mon–Sat 10am–6pm; ☎081/532 4412), has helpful staff, comprehensive accommodation listings, and can tell you which of the student dormitories are open to tourists during the summer. They can also provide the telephone numbers of guides expert in the history of Jewish Lublin. You can get **information online** at ⓦwww.lublin.pl, and ⓦwww.um.lublin.pl.

Accommodation

The city's supply of **hotels and pensions** has improved over the last few years, and can now be considered adequate. Several of the newer places are former state workers' hotels now open for tourists. It's important to bear location in mind when choosing a place to stay – quite a few hotels are well out of the centre.

The **youth hostel**, ul. Długosza 6 (6–10am & 5–10pm; ☎081/533 0628; bus #13 or trolleybus #150 from the train station), offers space in dorms or in triples (25–32zł per person) and is 1.5km west of the city centre – it's off the street but well signed. The all-year **student hostel**, ul. Sowińskiego 17 (☎081/525 1081; ❷) in the university area, is another cheap alternative.

Lublin's main **campsite** is the *Na Sławinku*, 5km west of the centre at ul. Sławinkowska 46 (June–Sept; ☎081/741 2231), beyond the Botanical Gardens, is pretty grim. There are bungalows (❶) as well as tent places, but you'll be lucky to get one; take bus #18 from the bus station, #20 from the train station. Preferable, but slightly further out, is the *Marina*, at the edge of Lake Zemborzycki, 7km south of the centre at ul. Krężnica 6 (May–Sept; ☎081/744 1070; bus #8 from ul. Narutowicza; May–Sept).

Hotels and pensions

Bystrzyca al. Zygmuntowskie 4 ☎081/532 3003. Decent enough, but stranded in an area of scruffy parks between the train station and the centre. One bathroom to every two rooms. Breakfast costs extra. ❷

DMP Pensjonat ul. Przyjaźni 17 ☎081/746 2838. Small, high-quality new hotel established by the Daewoo car firm to cater for their business guests, so advance booking is advisable. Almost all the rooms are singles. Decent restaurant as well. It's 1.5km southeast of the centre, so take bus #34 from the train station. ❻

Dom Nauczyciela (ZNP) ul. Akademiczka 4 ☎081/533 8285. A cheap, basic teachers' hotel near the university that's often full, so try and ring in advance. Bus #150 from the train station. En-suites, rooms with shared facilities, and some triples and quintuples. ❸–❹

Huzar ul. Spadachroniarzy 7 ☎081/ 742 3070. Recently renovated former soldiers' hotel with its own restaurant, in a tranquil location 3km west of the city centre. Take bus #3, #5, #10, #18 or #20 from Krakowskie Przedmieście to the Spadachroniarzy stop. ❺

Motel PZMot ul. Prusa 8 ☎081/533 4232. Within walking distance of both the bus station and the Stare Miasto, this is a perfect base for sightseeing, and (despite the Motel tag) is not just an overnighter for motorists. Neat en-suites, most with new furniture. Plenty of (guarded) parking space. ❹

Piast ul. Pocztowa 2 ☎081/532 2516. A cheap former state employees' hotel directly across from the main train station. Facilities in the hallway. An acceptable overnighter if nothing else is available. Breakfast not included. ❷

Pumis ul. Pogodna 36 ☎081/744 8631. Basic, decently maintained ex-workers' hotel 2km southeast of the centre just off the road to Majdanek. Buses #7 and #37 from Krakowskie Przedmieście or from ul. Fabryczna – a ten-minute walk northeast of the train station. En-suites as well as rooms with shared facilities. ❷–❺

Relax Melgiewska 7/9 ☎081/748 8500. Plain but reasonable hotel out among the industrial estates 3km east of town, built to house visitors to the next-door automobile factory. Bus #1 from the train station; bus #1, #10 or #11 from the bus station. En-suites and rooms with shared facilities. ❶–❹

Unia al. Raclawickie 12 ☎081/533 2061, ✉unia@orbis.pl. Seriously overpriced Orbis hotel, recently modernized and with a decent restaurant. Popular with upper-bracket tour groups. ❽

Zajazd Pod Kasztanami ul. Krężnica 94a ☎081/750 0390, ✇www.zajazd.lublin.pl. Comfortable place 7km south of town on the banks of Lake Zemborzycki, a popular recreation area, offering well-equipped en-suites. Bus #8 from in front of the Brigittine church on ul. Narutowicza. ❺

The Stare Miasto and around

The busy plac Łokietka forms the main approach to the **Stare Miasto** (Old Town), with an imposing nineteenth-century **Nowy Ratusz** (New Town Hall) on one side. Straight across the square is the fourteenth-century **Brama Krakowska** (Kraków Gate), one of three gateways to the Stare Miasto. Originally a key point in the city's defences against Tatar invaders, this now houses the **Muzeum Historyczne** (Historical Museum Wed–Sun 9am–4pm; 4zł); the contents aren't greatly inspiring, but the view of the new town from the top floor makes it worth a visit to orient yourself.

The Stare Miasto

A short walk round to the right along ul. Królewska brings you to the **Wieża Trinitarska** (Trinity Tower), home of a minor **Muzeum Diecezjalne** (Diocesan Museum; Tues–Sat 10am–4pm; 3zł) with another good top-floor view, this time over the Stare Miasto. Opposite is the **cathedral**, a large six-teenth-century basilica with an entrance framed by ornate classical-looking pillars. The interior decoration features a notable series of Baroque trompe l'oeil frescoes by the Moravian artist Joseph Meyer. The peculiar acoustic properties of the **Whispering Room** (Tues–Sun 10am–2pm & 3–5pm; 2zł) – part of the former sacristy adjoining the Treasury, with ebullient frescoes by Meyer depicting the "triumph of faith over heresy" – allow you to hear even the quietest voices perfectly from the other side of the chapel. Through the tower, a gate opens onto the Rynek, dominated by the outsized **Stary Ratusz** (Old Town Hall), the subject of a complete recent overhaul. Built in 1389, it later became the seat of a royal tribunal, and was given a Neoclassical remodelling in 1781 by Merlini, the man who designed Warsaw's Łazienki Palace. The well-restored cellars underneath the building house the **Muzeum Trybunału Koronnego** (Crown Tribunal Museum; Tues–Sat 9am–4pm, Sun 10am–5pm; 3zł), devoted to the history of the city, including a selection of ceramics and decorative objects unearthed in the course of the continuing renovation of the houses around the Rynek.

Getting round the square is tortuous, as a lot of the buildings are under reconstruction – judging by current progress, a state of affairs that's likely to remain for years to come. Of the surrounding burghers' houses, the **Konopnica House** (no. 12) – where Charles XII of Sweden and Peter the Great were both once guests – has Renaissance sculptures and medallions of the original owners decorating its as yet unrestored facade, while the **Lubomelski House** (no. 8) – now housing the *Piwnica Pod Fortuną* restaurant – hides some racy fourteenth-century frescoes in its large triple-tiered wine cellars. The **Cholewiński House** (no. 9), on the southeast corner of the square, features further lively Renaissance decoration on the facade, with a faded but fierce-looking pair of lions.

East of the square, down the narrow ul. Złota, lies the fine Dominican **church and monastery**, founded in the fourteenth century and reconstructed in the seventeenth. The church suffers from the familiar Baroque additions, but don't let that deflect you from the Renaissance Firlej family **chapel** at the end of the southern aisle, built for one of Lublin's leading aristocratic families, nor from the eighteenth-century panorama of the city just inside the entrance. Round the back of the monastery is a popular puppet theatre, the **Teatr im. Andersen**, one of the oldest theatres in the country, offering a good view over the town from the square in front.

The Stare Miasto's other theatre, **Studio Teatralne**, near the centre at ul. Grodzka 32, has a gallery featuring local artists. Grodzka was part of the **Jewish quarter** and several of the buildings on the street bear memorials in Polish and Yiddish to the former inhabitants. Lublin was one of the main centres of Hassidic Jewry and its *yeshiva* (Talmudic school) – now a medical academy – was the world's largest Talmudic school right up to the war (see pp.305–307).

The castle

On a hill just east of the Stare Miasto is the **castle**, an offbeat 1820s neo-Gothic edifice built on the site of Kazimierz the Great's fourteenth-century fortress, and linked by a raised, recently renovated pathway from the Brama Grodzka (Castle Gate) at the end of ul. Grodzka.

The castle houses a sizeable **museum** (Wed–Sat 9am–4pm, Sun 9am–5pm; Ⓦ www.zamek-lublin.pl; 10zł), the high points of which are the **ethnography** section, including a good selection of local costumes, religious art and wood-

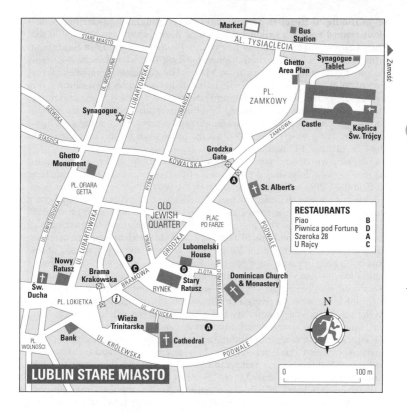

RESTAURANTS

Piao	**B**
Piwnica pod Fortuną	**D**
Szeroka 28	**A**
U Rajcy	**C**

LUBLIN STARE MIASTO

carving, and the **art gallery**, where moody nineteenth-century landscapes and scenes of peasant life mingle with portraits and historical pieces to form a virtual textbook of modern Polish history – helpfully, most of the pictures are now labelled in both Polish and English. Among the historical works, look out for two famous and characteristically operatic works by Matejko: the massive *Lublin Union* portrays Polish and Lithuanian noblemen debating the union of the two countries in 1569; the equally huge *Admission of the Jews to Poland* depicts the Jews' arrival in Poland in the early Middle Ages, the two sides eyeing each other suspiciously. Another upstairs room contains an excellent collection of eighteenth- and nineteenth-century Orthodox **icons** from the Brest (formerly Brześć) area, now just over the other side of the Belarusian border. The section of the museum devoted to World War II recalls the castle's use by the Nazis as a prison and interrogation centre. Civilian prisoners were shot in the courtyard and thousands more, including many Jews, were detained here before being sent to Majdanek or other concentration camps.

The castle chapel

Among the best reasons for visiting Lublin is the **Kaplica św. Trójcy** (Chapel of the Holy Trinity), an elegant two-storey Gothic structure located at the back of the castle complex behind one of its two remaining towers (one of them thirteenth-century Romanesque). Entrance to the chapel is via the castle museum (included in the ticket price; same times). The reason is the stunning set of **medieval frescoes** covering cross-ribbed vaulting supported on a single octagonal pillar – a striking architectural device similar to that used in the Holy Cross Church in Kraków (see p.420). Painted by a group of Ruthenian artists from the Ukraine commissioned by King Władisław Jagiełło – exceptionally for the time, the main artist, Master Andrew, signed his name and the date of completion, August 10, 1418, in the dedication to his royal patron – the frescoes are one of the outstanding and rare examples of early Slavic-Byzantine church art. Accidentally uncovered by builders at the end of the nineteenth century, they were subject to sporadic bursts of restoration over the next hundred years, but it wasn't until 1995 that the project was finally completed with the help of some EU funding.

In keeping with the principles of Byzantine iconography the frescoes are divided into sections illustrating a progression of themes, beginning with depictions of God the Father and moving on through the cosmic hierarchy to scenes from the life of Jesus and the saints, images of the archangels and other spiritual entities and ending with the risen Christ. There's an engrossing wealth of detail to take in here, which the well-produced English-language guide sheet available in the chapel will help you through. Highlights include the vivid sequence of scenes from the life of Christ and the Virgin Mary covering the upper section of the nave and choir, in particular a powerful Passion cycle, along with an intriguing pair of frescoes involving King Jagiełło, the first depicting him kneeling in humble supplication before the Virgin, the second showing the king mounted on a galloping horse while receiving a crown and crucifix from an angel – a reference to the man's legendary missionary zeal. Overlooking the whole ensemble from the choir vaulting is a triumphal depiction of *Christus Pantocrator*.

Restoring the frescoes to something approaching their original state has been a taxing business. Certain sections have been lost irrevocably and the chapel has to be kept inside a narrow temperature band to preserve the extant frescoes. **Entrance** is limited: groups of up to 25 are let in at half-hourly intervals, with a fifteen-minute break in between to ensure that the ventilation system does its job. An entrance time is written on the back of your ticket when you purchase it from the castle entrance office. During summer you may have to wait some time to get in, so purchasing your ticket in advance is a good idea.

The market

Before making your way back through the Stare Miasto, check out the **market** on the opposite side of the main road from the castle: you may find something interesting among the mixture of junk and contraband. As in many eastern towns, the squat peasants with stand-out accents selling caviar, gold and radios for dollars are from just over the border. They're what are euphemistically known as "trade tourists", an enduring eastern European practice involving itinerant traders buying and selling products cheaper, or items unobtainable in neighbouring countries.

West of the Stare Miasto

West of pl. Łokietka stretches **Krakowskie Przedmieście**, a busy shop-lined thoroughfare pedestrianized for a chunk of its length and with a number of sites worth taking in on and around its vicinity. Immediately west of the Nowy Ratusz is the **Kościół św. Ducha** (Church of the Holy Spirit), a small, early fifteenth-century structure with the familiar Baroque overlay and a quiet, restful feel to it.

Immediately opposite the church, a turn to the south takes you onto pl. Bernardyński, a car-jammed square surrounded by building activity. The fifteenth-century **Bernardine church** on the south side of the square, a large Gothic construction with a sumptuously ornate Baroque interior, has a good view over the southern rim of the city from the platform at the back of the building. On the eastern edge of another square, southwest along ul. Narutowicza, the **Brigittine church**, raised in the early fifteenth century by King Władysław Jagiełło as a gesture of thanks for victory at the battle of Grunwald, is another Gothic structure with the customary high brick period facade. Opposite the church stands the **Teatr im. Juliusz Osterwy** (Juliusz Osterwa Theatre; see "Entertainment" p.309), an enjoyable *fin-de-siècle* playhouse with an august old stage.

Back onto Krakowskie Przedmieście, north of the main street on ul. Zielona, a narrow side passage contains the tiny **Kościół św. Jozefa** (St Joseph's Church), founded by Greek Catholic merchants in the 1790s and used by the local Uniates into this century, though there's nothing now there to inform you of this. Just beyond, on the corner of ul. St Staszica, is the crumbling eighteenth-century Pałac Potockich (Potocki Palace), one of several patrician mansions in this part of the city.

Krakowskie Przedmieście soon brings you to **plac Litewski**, a large open square with lots of people milling about and, in summer, a host of chess games in progress. The monuments ranged along the edge of the square include the cast-iron **Pomnik Unii Lubelskiej** (Monument of the Union of Lublin), marking the Polish–Lithuanian concordat established here in 1569, and the 1791 **Pomnik Konstytucji 3-ego Maja** (Third of May Constitution Monument), commemorating another important event in the country's history. The north side of the square features two of the city's old aristocratic palaces, both currently used by the university: first is the former **Pałac Czartoryskich** (Czartoryski Palace), in the northeast corner, a smallish building occupied by the Lublin Scholarly Society. Next is the fading seventeenth-century **Pałac Lubomirskich** (Lubomirski Palace), with a Neoclassicist facade designed by Marconi in the 1830s. The imperial-looking building to its left is just that, the old tsarist-era city governor's residence built in the 1850s.

If it's open, the eighteenth-century Protestant **church** on ul. Ewangelicka, further along to the north of Krakowskie Przedmieście, is worth a brief look in. An austere, Huguenot-style temple with classicist stylings, it has memorial tablets ranged around the walls, mostly to the church's former German-speaking congregation.

Continuing west along Krakowskie Przedmieście turn south on ul. Lipowa, and a five-minute walk brings you to the gates of the **main cemetery**. A stroll round this peaceful, wooded graveyard provides an absorbing insight into local history. The cemetery is separated into confessional sections; to the north the predictably large **Catholic section**, with a group of "unknown soldier" graves from both world wars, is flanked by the Protestant and Orthodox cemeteries. The **Orthodox section**, with its own mock-Byzantine chapel, contains more wartime graves – Russian soldiers this time – as well as a sprinkling of older, tsarist-era Cyrillic tablets, including many of the city's one-time imperial administrators and rulers. The graves in the **Protestant section** reveal many German-sounding names, and many of the stones date from before and during World War I, when the city was occupied for several years by the Kaiser's forces. Finally, inspection of the group of plain tombstones without crucifixes in the western section of the graveyard reveals them to belong to those local Party members committed enough to the atheist cause to refuse Catholic burial.

Back up onto Krakowskie Przedmieście and a short distance west along its continuation, al. Racławickie, stands the **Katolicki Uniwersytet** or KUL

(Catholic University), a compact campus housed on the site of an old Dominican monastery. One of the KUL's more famous professors was **Karol Wojtyła**, who taught part-time here from the 1950s up until his election as pope in 1978. He is commemorated in a bronze statue in the main courtyard, accompanied by his predecessor as primate of Poland, Cardinal Wyszyński.

Directly opposite the University building lie the **Ogród Saski** (Saxon Gardens), the city's most luxuriant open space, with fastidiously tended flowerbeds sloping down towards wilder, densely wooded sections in the park's northern reaches.

The skansen

Three kilometres northwest of the Ogród Saski, out along al. Warszawska (bus #5 or #10 from al. Racławickie), an attractive jumble of rural buildings from surrounding villages have been reassembled to form the **Muzeum Wsi Lubelskiej**, usually referred to by the generic name for such collections, **skansen** (June–Aug daily 9am–6pm; April–May & Sept–Oct daily 9am–5pm; Nov–Dec Fri–Sun 9am–3pm; 6zł), providing a wonderfully rustic contrast to the downtown area. The interiors of the buildings are only open if you pay for a guided tour (25zł extra), but a visit here will be rewarding whether you opt for this or not. Highlights include a manor house from the village of Zyrzyna, crouching beneath an organic-looking mansard roof covered in wooden shingles; and an Orthodox church (*cerkiew*) from Tarnoszyna, which sports an exotic trio of bulbous domes.

Jewish Lublin

For anyone interested in Lublin's **Jewish history**, a scattering of monuments around the city's former Jewish quarters are worth visiting, most of them marked by tablets in Hebrew and Polish, although these are rather hard to spot.

Starting in the **Stare Miasto** – much of it long Jewish-inhabited – are a couple of buildings with wartime Jewish connections: on the corner of ul. Noworybna, east of the square, is the small house where the first **Committee of Jewish War Survivors** was set up in November 1944. Continuing on down to ul. Grodzka, at no. 11 is another plaque, commemorating the Jewish **orphanage** in operation here from 1862 until March 1942, when the Nazis removed about two hundred staff and children and shot them in the fields behind the Majdanek camp.

Continuing along Grodzka and down to pl. Zamkowy, a plaque on a raised pedestal, at the foot of the stairs up to the castle, shows a detailed plan of the surrounding **Podzamcze** district, the main Jewish quarter destroyed by the Nazis in 1942 (see box, pp.306–307). The Nazi devastation was so thorough that it's hard to visualize the densely packed network of houses, shops and synagogues that used to exist in the streets around what's now a noisy main road (al. Tysiąclecia), a tatty square, the adjoining main bus station and the Orthodox **cathedral** – a dark, icon-filled structure with a notable iconostasis that's the only remaining Orthodox place of worship in town, originally a Uniate building – immediately east of it.

The old Jewish cemetery

Continue east along al. Tysiąclecia and opposite the bus station, on the approaches to the castle, you'll find another plaque marking the prewar site of the main **Maharszal and Maharam synagogue**, originally constructed in the 1560s and razed, along with all the surrounding buildings, in 1942.

Cross the main road and walk along cobbled ul. Kalinowszczyzna, take the first right off ul. Lwowska and you find yourself at the **old Jewish cemetery**, a small walled area which covers a ramshackle, overgrown hill, set in almost rural surroundings.

Unless a group happens to be there at the time, you'll have to contact the **caretaker**, Pan Józef Honig, at ul. Dembowskiego 4, apt. #17 (☎081/747 8676), across from the main cemetery entrance, to get in; he'll expect you to make a financial contribution, and prefers opening up for groups rather than individuals. Despite the Nazis' best efforts to destroy the oldest-known Jewish cemetery in the country – literally thousands of the gravestones were used for wartime building purposes – the small groups of surviving tombstones display the full stylistic variety of Jewish monumental art.

Alongside the oldest, dating from 1541, is a fine range of Renaissance, Baroque and Neoclassical ornamental tombstones. The oldest section of the cemetery houses the graves of many famous Jews, among them the legendary Hassidic leader **Yaakov Yitzchak Horovitz**, one of several here regularly covered with pilgrims' candles, and **Shalom Shachna**, the renowned sixteenth-century master of the Lublin *yeshiva* (Talmudic school). Climbing to the top of the cemetery hill gives you a fine view back over the Stare Miasto and the old Jewish quarter.

The new Jewish cemetery and mausoleum

Leaving the cemetery and heading north along ul. Lwowska and into ul. Walecznych brings you to the entrance of the **new Jewish cemetery**. Established in 1829 in what was then the outskirts of town, the cemetery was predictably plundered and destroyed by the Nazis, who also used it for mass executions. The cemetery you see today covers a fragment of the original plot, the northern section having been cleared and levelled in the 1970s to make way for a trunk road (ul. Somorawińskiego).

There are precious few graves left inside, most of them dating from the late nineteenth century and the postwar years, as well as a number of collective graves for Nazi wartime victims. The whole cemetery has been renovated in the past few years with financial support from the Frenkel family, whose relatives died in Majdanek.

The domed **mausoleum** (unpredictable hours, so check at the tourist office; donation), recently erected behind the cemetery entrance, houses a small but engrossing exhibition detailing the history of the Lublin Jewry.

The yeshiva and Jewish hospital

Out of the cemetery and west along ul. Unicka brings you to the corner of ul. Lubartowska, a long, straight thoroughfare running through the heart of the prewar Jewish quarter. The large classical-looking yellow building at the top corner of Lubartowska is the site of the prewar **yeshiva** – The School of the Sages of Lublin as it was once known – a palatial structure now occupied by the local medical academy. Built in the late 1920s using funds collected from Jewish communities around the world, the Lublin *yeshiva* was set up as an international Talmudic school to train rabbis and other senior community functionaries. It functioned for just over nine years until 1939, when the Nazis closed it down and eventually plundered and destroyed the huge library. To any but the trained eye there's precious little evidence of the building's former use, a simple plaque on the outside wall briefly stating the historical facts.

Next building down on the same side of Lubartowska (no. 81) is another fine palatial-looking building, erected in 1886 – the former **Jewish hospital**, still an obstetric clinic. A plaque outside commemorates the hospital staff and patients murdered in March 1942 in the course of a Nazi liquidation *Aktion*.

Along with Kraków, L'viv and Wilno (now Vilnius in Lithuania), Lublin ranked as one of the major – if not *the* most important – Jewish centres in Poland: at its peak the Lublin Jewry exerted a Europe-wide influence, dispatching locally trained rabbis to serve communities as far away as Spain and Portugal.

The **first recorded account** of Jews in Lublin dates from 1316, though it's quite possible that merchants had established themselves here considerably earlier. King Kazimierz's extension of the **Statute of Privilege** for Jews to the whole territory of Poland in the mid-fourteenth century paved the way for the development of the first major Jewish settlement in the **Podzamcze** district, located below the castle walls. Originally a marshy river delta, the area was bought up by Jewish merchants, who drained the waters and established a community there. The first brick **synagogue** and **yeshiva** (Talmudic school) were built in the mid-sixteenth century: from then on synagogues and other religious buildings proliferated – by the 1930s there were more than a hundred synagogues in operation inside the city area. Lublin's increasingly important position on trade routes resulted in its choice as one of two locations (Jarosław was the other) for meetings of the **Council of the Four Lands**, traditionally the main consultative body of Polish Jewry, a position it retained up to the 1760s.

Occasional outbreaks of Church-inspired ritual-murder accusations apart, local Jewish–Christian relations seem to have been fairly tolerant at this stage, the main blows coming in the form of outside assaults, notably the **Chmielnicki Insurrection** (1648), when Cossacks slaughtered thousands of Jews throughout eastern Poland, and the Russian siege of the city in 1655, when much of the Podzamcze district was razed. The whole area was subsequently rebuilt, this time with an emphasis on solid, brick buildings.

In the 1790s Lublin emerged as an important centre of **Hassidism**, the ecstatic revivalist movement that swept through Eastern Jewry in the latter part of the eighteenth century. The charismatic Hassidic leader, **Yaakov Yitzchak Horovitz**, settled in town in the 1790s, drawing crowds of followers from all over Poland – by all accounts, the Hassids were no respecters of Poland's Partitions-era borders – to his "court" in the Podzamcze district. Always a controversial figure – contemporary opponents, for example, claimed that Horovitz died of "excessive alcohol consumption" – Jews from all over the world continue to make the pilgrimage to his grave in the old Jewish Cemetery.

In the mid-nineteenth century, with the town's Jewish population increasing rapidly, Jews began moving into the Stare Miasto area, also occupying much of the new district that developed around ul. Lubartowska, to the north of the Stare Miasto. At the close of the century Jews numbered around 24,000 – a little over fifty percent of the town's expanding population.

The old ghetto district

Continuing south along Lubartowska takes you through the heart of the old **ghetto district**; a grubby, lively area of shops and tenement houses. While there are no Jews left to speak of, wandering through the arched entrance ways into the back courtyards or scanning the small shops you can imagine what it must have been like here half a century ago. Right up towards the top of the street – a 1.5-kilometre walk – a backroom at no. 10 houses the city's only functioning **synagogue** (the entrance is through the gateway round the side of no. 8, and up the stairs). It's officially open Sunday 1pm to 3pm, but the caretaker pops in and out, so you could either try your luck or telephone him in advance (he's also the caretaker of the old Jewish cemetery; see p.305).

Established in 1920 by the local undertakers' guild, it became the principal synagogue for the city's surviving Jews after World War II. It is still in use today and visiting Jewish tourist groups regularly hold services here. An informative

Following the trials of **World War I**, during which many Lublin Jews died fighting in both the Russian and Austro-Hungarian armies, Lublin Jewry flourished in the **interwar years**, developing an active web of religious and cultural associations, publishing houses, newspapers (notably the Yiddish-language daily *Lubliner Sztyme* – "Lublin Voice"), trade unions and political organizations.

Following their capture of the town in September 1939, the **Nazis** quickly set about the business of confining and eventually murdering the nearly 40,000-strong Lublin Jewry. By December 1939 transports of Jews were being brought into the city from other parts of Europe, and in early 1940 Lublin was chosen as the coordinating centre for the Nazis' efforts to liquidate the Jewish population of the *Général Gouvernemen* – those portions of Poland that were under German administration (but not directly incorporated into the German Reich) after September 1939. With the Stare Miasto area already filled to bursting with destitute Jews, an official **ghetto area** was established in March 1941 by Governor Hans Frank.

Construction of the **Majdanek death camp** in a southern suburb of the city began in July 1941, and in spring 1942 the hideous business of liquidating the ghetto population began in earnest. After initial expulsions at the end of March 1942, Jews were driven to the ghetto square (next to the modern main bus station): the old and sick were shot on the spot, the rest taken to waiting rail wagons and transported to the death camp at **Belzec**, as the first victims of the notorious camp commander, Christian Wirth. Over the next few months, the remaining population was either taken and shot in the **Krępiecki Forest** on the outskirts of the city or moved to a new ghetto area established close to Majdanek. The effective end of over six hundred years of traditional Jewish life in Lublin came on November 3, 1943, when the remaining 18,000 ghetto inhabitants were taken to Majdanek to be exterminated after an *Aktion* (a ghetto raid followed by mass round-ups) codenamed *Erntfest* – "Harvest Festival". Following the *Aktion*'s conclusion, the Nazis systematically demolished the buildings of Wieniawa, an outlying Jewish settlement, and the Podzamcze district.

The city was liberated by Soviet troops in July 1944, after which **Jewish partisan groups** began using Lublin as their operational base. At the end of the war several thousand Jewish refugees resettled in Lublin: as a result of **anti-Semitic outbreaks** around Poland in 1945–46, however, many of them emigrated, others following in the wake of the anti-Semitic purges of 1968, as in Kraków and Warsaw. The tiny remaining Jewish population keeps a low profile, many now too old to take an active role in the revival of local Jewish life encouraged by the increasing number of Western Jews visiting the city.

collection of photos and other archival materials relating to the Lublin Jewry lines the walls, along with a small collection of ritual religious objects and some plaques dedicated to local Poles who protected Jews during World War II.

Finally, at the top of Lubartowska, on the approach to the old city, is **plac Ofiar Getta** (Ghetto Victims), a bustling square that used to be one of the main Jewish marketplaces. A simple monument to the ghetto victims stands in the square centre, engraved with the legend "Honour to the Polish citizens of Jewish nationality from the Lublin region, whose lives were bestially cut short by the Nazi fascists during World War II. The people of Lublin."

Majdanek

The proximity of **Majdanek concentration camp**, just 4km southeast of the city centre, is a shock in itself. Established on Himmler's orders in October 1941, this was no semi-hidden location that local people could claim or strive to remain in ignorance of – a plea that is more debatable at Auschwitz and Treblinka. Marked from the main road by a large monument erected in 1969 on the twenty-fifth anniversary of its liberation by the Red Army, the huge camp compound is more shocking inside. Wandering among the barbed wire and watchtowers, staring at crematoria and rows of shabby wooden barracks, it's hard to take in the brutal fact that over 200,000 people of more than fifty nations were murdered here, a significant number of them Jews. Between November 3 and 5, 1943, the Nazis concluded their extermination of local Jewry by machine-gunning over 43,000 inhabitants of the nearby ghetto district; 18,000 were killed in a single day. The **camp museum** (May–Sept Tues–Sun 8am–5pm; Oct–April closes 3pm) in a former barracks tells the terrible story in detail. At the end of the main path through the site, a domed mausoleum contains the ashes of many of those murdered here. The entrance building has a cinema showing a short documentary about Majdanek at regular intervals (last showing in English at 3pm) as well as a bookshop selling maps, brochures and other publications in several languages.

Bus #23 from ul. Królewska or trolleybuses #153 and #158 from ul. Lipowa run to the monument marking the entrance to the camp (30min). For more on the concentration camps in postwar Poland, see p.464.

Eating and drinking

The **restaurant** scene in Lublin is looking up, with a range of eateries establishing themselves in the recently spruced-up mansions of the Stare Miasto. There's also a fair sprinkling of food options in the side streets leading off either side of Krakowskie Przedmieście, which is itself emerging as the town's prime night-time promenading ground. It's along Krakowskie Przedmieście and around the Stary Rynek that you'll find most of the outdoor **café**-life in summer, and the growing number of late-night drinking establishments in the Stare Miasto provide ample opportunity for an extensive **bar**-crawl.

Restaurants

Chimera ul. Krótka 3. Upmarket Italian restaurant offering delicious fare, attentive service and higher than average prices.

Gospoda u Alfreda ul. Peowiaków 5. Solid, mid-priced Polish repertoire in folksy surroundings.

Karczma Słupska al. Racławickie 22. Old-fashioned dining-and-dancing venue just west of the Ogród Saski (see p.304), specializing in *kołduny* (Lithuanian ravioli) and meaty Polish dishes. Cheesy live music most nights.

Oregano Café ul. Kościuszki 5. Stylish bistro-type eatery specializing in Mediterranean fare – expect to encounter some familiar Greek and Italian dishes. Pricey by Lublin standards.

Pani Pizza ul. Kościuszki 3. Functional but friendly little place offering filling pizzas as well as fried fish, a decent salad bar, and home-made cakes. Order at the counter.

Piao ul. Olejna 3. Standard, reasonably authentic Chinese place in an alleyway just off the Rynek. Outdoor seating in the courtyard.

Piwnica pod Fortuną Rynek 8. Elegant restaurant occupying a series of subterranean chambers decorated with medieval-style frescoes. The usual range of Polish meat dishes augmented by a few duck and goose recipes. Slightly more expensive than the other places in the Stare Miasto.

Szeroka 28 next to the Brama Grodzka at ul. Grodzka 19 ☏081/534 4610. Stylish café/restaurant aimed squarely at international tourists, it re-creates the look and feel of prewar Lublin, even taking its name from the building's prewar street address in the Jewish quarter. Pricey meat dishes, and plenty of inexpensive snacks, salads and pancakes. There's a back terrace with a good view onto the castle, and regular live kletzmer concerts.

U Rajcy Rynek 2. Unpretentious mid-price place with a standard menu of pork and beef favourites as well as a stupendously stodgy range of potato pancakes (*placki*) with various toppings. Outdoor seating in a galleried courtyard.

Zielona Tawerna corner of ul. Zielona and ul. Staszica. Unpretentious café-bar with a nice line in sandwiches and cheap set lunches.

Złoty Smok in the courtyard off Krakowskie Przedmieście 30. Popular and intimate mid-price Chinese restaurant in a cosy subterranean location.

Bars, pubs and clubs

Arcus ul. Okopowa 8. Cosy student pub eccentrically decked out in thatched-hut decor. Not well marked – it's in the archway on the left.

Café Artystyczna Hades ul. Peowiaków 12, in the Dom Kultury just round the corner from the Philharmonia, has a restaurant, bar, pool hall and also hosts regular club nights and alternative gigs. Usually Thurs–Sun only.

Chata Zaka ul. Radziszewskiego 16. University cultural centre housing smoky student café, and a combined disco and gig venue – the *Art Bis Club* – round the back.

Koniec Świata ul. Peowiaków 8. Atmospheric, rock-oriented cellar pub just off Krakowskie Przedmieście, with occasional live bands.

Koyot, Krakowskie Przedmieście 26. Animated basement bar with rock music on the sound system.

Magma ul. Grodzka 18. Smallish bar in the Stare Miasto whose arty-industrial decor blends rather nicely with the barrel-vaulted Baroque ceiling. An amenable place to sink a few pints.

Odlot pl. po Farze. Under-lit turquoise parlour with space age-gothic furnishings, a hip young clientele, and dance music on the sound system.

Old Pub, ul. Grodzka 8. Fancy pub-restaurant with upmarket leanings, offering a wide though pricey range of draught beers, including the established selection of international brews – Guinness, Pilsner Urquell and the like.

U Szewca ul. Grodzka 20. Relaxing pub with a range of Polish, English and Irish beers, comfy settees, and a varied, mid-price menu of bar food.

Złoty Osioł, ul. Grodzka 5a. Multipurpose café, bar, restaurant and art gallery housed in a stylish suite of medieval rooms. Lots of wicker furniture to lounge around in, and a laid-back atmosphere. Serves mid-price traditional Polish food.

Entertainment

The Lublin Philharmonia, ul. Skłodowskiej 5, has a regular programme of high-quality **classical concerts** (ticket office ☎081/532 1536), and the Teatr im. Juliusz Osterwy, ul. Narutowicza 17 (☎081/532 4244), offers an imaginative and varied programme of modern and classical Polish **drama** – the contemporary stuff might be worth seeing even if you don't speak the language, largely because movement and stagecraft tend to be just as important as the text. The same can be said of the internationally reputed experimental theatre group Gardzienice, based in the village of the same name 30km south of the city, which has an office in the Stare Miasto at ul. Grodzka 5a (☎081/532 9840 or 532 9637). When they're not off touring abroad they occasionally give performances out at Gardzienice or, even more rarely, in Lublin itself – an experience not to be missed if you have the chance.

Listings

Airline LOT, Krakowskie Przedmieście 53.

Banks Pekao, ul. Królewska 1 (Mon–Fri 7.30am–6pm, Sat 10am–2pm); PKO, Krakowskie Przedmiescie 14/16 (Mon–Fri 8am–6pm, Sat 8am–1pm).

Books, newspapers and maps Empik, Krakowskie Przedmieście 61.

Cinemas Bajka, next to the Dom Nauczyciela at ul. Radziszewskiego 8; and Kosmos, north of the Ogród Saski at ul. Leszczyńskiego 60. Both show mainstream first-run movies.

Internet access *So@NET*, ul. Świętoduska 16 (Mon–Fri 11am–7pm, Sat 10am–3pm); *www.café*, Rynek 8 (top floor; daily 10am–10pm).

Pharmacy Apteka, ul. Bramowa 8. Big well-stocked place open 24hr (ring the bell 8pm–8am).

Post office Main office at Krakowskie Przedmieście 50 (24hr).

Travel agents Almatur, ul. Langiewicza 10 (☎081/533 3238), deals with youth and student travel. Orbis, ul. Narutowicza 31/33 (☎081/532 2256) is useful for air and rail tickets.

North from Lublin

North of the city takes you into the **Biała Podlaska** region, a pleasant agricultural area of ramshackle old market towns and sparsely populated villages that still retains a markedly old-world Eastern feel. Like most of eastern Poland, this region has its share of grand old palaces, many of them showing the effects of decades of neglect. The palaces at **Lubartów**, **Kozłówka**, **Radzyń Podlaski** and **Biała Podlaska**, the regional capital, all offer striking examples of the phenomenon, well worth checking out if you like rural aristocratic piles. A range of Catholic, Orthodox, Jewish and occasional Tatar monuments provide the region's mixed ethnic and religious profile. In a country of traditional horse-lovers, the breeding stables at **Janów Podlaski**, hard up by the Belarus border, are perhaps the area's best-known attraction.

As in many of the country's further-flung regions, local **buses** are the main form of transport. For motorists heading east, the main route from Warsaw to Moscow runs across the region, reaching the border at **Terespol**, east of Biała Podlaska.

Lubartów

Twenty-five kilometres north of Lublin, the market town of **LUBARTÓW** is a historical curio worth a brief stop on your way elsewhere. A small, undistinguished market centre facing the banks of the Wieprz River to the east, Lubartów is a good example of an eastern town effectively created by a big-league local magnate, in this case the Firlej family who moved here in the 1540s. The place was originally known as Lewartów after the family's coat of arms the "Lewart".

The fine sixteenth-century **Pałac Firleja** (Firlej Palace) in the town centre is the most tangible reminder of the local grandees. A large white-stuccoed building currently occupied by local government offices, the fading facade boasts four elegant sets of double pillars surmounted by a large classical frieze. The palace **park** behind the building is a pleasant spot with some traces of its former grandeur, the orangery included, in evidence. The **parish church** next to the palace is classic Polish Baroque (a Renaissance doorway excepted), with numerous funeral tablets – in this case, mainly of the Sanguszko family, who took over the palace in the eighteenth century – covering the interior. The local **museum** (Wed–Fri 8am–3pm, Sun 10am–3pm; 3zł), down to the right of the church on ul. Kościuszki, is also worth a brief look, with regularly changing exhibits.

As in all the Lublin region, Jews were longtime inhabitants of the town: first mentioned in 1567, they comprised some 45 percent of the local population at the start of World War II. The entire **Jewish population** was deported to the death camps at Bełzec and Sobibór in October 1942, and most of the community buildings, including two synagogues on ul. Lubelska, were destroyed. A memorial built out of tombstone fragments and thirty or so extant tombstones are all that remains of the **Jewish cemetery** at the corner of ul. Cicha and ul. 1 Maja, on the southern side of town.

Lubartów is a half-hour **bus** journey along the main Lublin–Białystok road – Lublin–Białystok and Lublin–Biała Podlaska buses pass through. For an **overnight stay** you're really limited to the uninspiring *Ambar*, ul. Kleberga 14 (T081/855 4754; ❷). The *Max*, centrally located at Rynek 11, is a solid if basic **restaurant**.

Kozłówka

Nine kilometres west of Lubartów – 35km if you're coming direct by bus from Lublin – the **Pałac Zamojskich** (Zamoyski Palace) at **KOZŁÓWKA** is among the grandest in the region. Fully restored in the 1990s, the palace is the recipient of a good deal of tourist hype – hence the processions of day-tripper buses already lining up outside the entrance gates. All in all it's a good example of the nostalgia for the "good old days" of the prewar era that's in vogue in Poland now. With admiration of and aesthetic preference for all things grand and aristocratic back at the forefront of officially sanctioned culture, it's hardly surprising to find places like this being emphasised: whether you're taken with this kind of opulent aristocratic overload is very much a question of personal taste.

Kozłówka is served by about five **buses** a day from Lublin – although bear in mind that Kozłówka is an intermediate destination on bus routes bound elsewhere, so it won't be listed on the departure boards at Lublin bus station and you'll have to ask at the information counter for details.

The palace

Built in the 1740s by the Bieliński family, after they inherited the local estate, the original two-storey Baroque **palace complex**, surrounded by a courtyard to the front and gardens at the back, was reconstructed and expanded in the early 1900s by its longtime owner, Count Konstanty Zamoyski, whose family took over the property in 1799 and kept it up to the beginning of World War II. Zamoyski's remodelling retained the essentials of the original Baroque design, adding a number of fine outbuildings, the iron gateway, chapel and elegant porticoed terrace leading up to the entrance to the building.

The interior

The palace **interior** (Mar–Nov: Tues, Thurs & Fri 10am–4pm; Wed, Sat & Sun 10am–5pm; 5zł; Ⓦwww.muzeumkozlowka.lublin.pl) can only be visited as part of a **guided tour**, so individuals will have to wait until a large enough herd of visitors assembles (35 is usually the number they allow to accumulate). Tours are conducted in Polish – English-language guides can be booked in advance for an extra 40zł (☎081/852 7091).

Once inside, you're immediately enveloped in a riot of artistic elegance. The whole place is positively dripping in pictures, mostly family portraits and copies of Rubens, Canaletto and the like, along with a profusion of sculptures and period furniture, every corner of the richly decorated building crammed with something decorative. First port of call is the **hallway**, the gloom partially lightened by sumptuous lamps and the delicate stucco work of the ceiling. Past the huge Meissner stoves and up the portrait-lined marble **staircase** brings you to the main palace rooms. On through **Count Konstanty's private rooms** the procession of family portraits and superior repro art continues relentlessly, the elaborate Czech porcelain toilet set in the bedroom suggesting a man of fastidious personal hygiene. After the countess's bedroom and its handsome selection of Empire furniture, the tour takes you into the voluminous **Red Salon**, an impressive ensemble with embroidered canopies enveloping the doors and a mass of heavy red velvet curtains. The portraits are at their thickest here, the emphasis being on kings, hetmans and other national figures collected by Count Konstanty during the Partition years as a personal gesture of patriotic remembrance.

The rest of the palace is pretty much more of the same; the **Exotic Room** houses a fine selection of chinoiserie, while the **dining room** is sumptuous, heavy Baroque with a mixture of Gdańsk and Venetian furniture and enough period trinkets to keep a horde of collectors happy. As you'd expect, the **library** contains endless shelves full of books ranged around a classic old billiard table lit by a kerosene lamp in the middle. The **chapel**, out round the side of the palace, is a fine though rather cold place partly modelled on the royal chapel in Versailles and built in the early 1900s.

The museum

After overdosing on opulence, the **museum** (same hours and ticket) housed in the one-time palace theatre makes for a real surprise. Entitled "Art and Struggle in Socialism", the exhibition brings together a large collection of postwar Polish Socialist Realist art and sculpture, most of it culled from museums around the region and kept here out of harm's way once its subjects had become politically unacceptable. The whole pantheon of international Stalinist iconography is here: Bolesław Bierut, Mao, Ho Chi Minh, Kim Il Sung and a beaming Stalin himself. Alongside the leaders, there's a gallery of sturdy proletarian and peasant types building factories, heroically swathing corn, implementing the Five Year Plan, joining the Party and other everyday communist activities. Highlight of the statues is black American singer Paul Robeson declaiming in full voice, a particularly effective piece of agitprop sculpture. If you need a walk after all the viewing, the elegantly contoured **palace gardens** stretching out behind the back of the building provide the necessary space. Refreshments are available at the palace **café** back out near the entrance gate.

Radzyń Podlaski

Forty kilometres north of Lubartów on the main Lublin–Białystok road is **RADZYŃ PODLASKI** (served by regular Lublin–Białystok and Lublin–Biała Podlaska buses), another sleepy provincial market town marked by its historic association with Polish aristocracy, in this case the powerful Potocki family, who descended on the town in the early eighteenth century and built one of their many eastern palaces here on the site of an earlier castle belonging to the Mniszek family. Badly damaged in 1944, the **Pałac Potockich** (Potocki Palace), dubbed the Podlasian Versailles in direct competition with the Branicki Palace in Białystok (see p.272), was said in its heyday to be one of the finest Rococo residences of the East. Despite the fact that it was never fully repaired after the war – much of the palace is local administrative offices now – walking round the large inner courtyard you can still sense something of the building's former grandeur. Although pretty overgrown the gardens, designed in the 1750s by royal architect Jacob Fontana, in the course of his thorough transformation of the palace, are now the **town park**, a soothing spot to cool off in on a summer's day. These days the graffiti-covered orangery is a Dom Kultury, with *Roch*, a pizza joint colonized by local teenagers, in the cellar basement. Across the road from the palace, the eighteenth-century **parish church** is a fine Mannerist building whose architecture echoes the Collegiate churches in Zamość and Kazimierz Dolny.

Biała Podlaska

The provincial capital, **BIAŁA PODLASKA**, offers a curious mixture of both the old and the new Poland. Weighing heavily on the town today is its strategic position along the main high road from Warsaw to the eastern border (the train station is similarly placed on the main Warsaw–Moscow line). Day and night, transit lorries thunder along the road to and from the border crossing at Terespol, forty-odd kilometres east, and the income generated by the town's border location is beginning to show through in the number of cafés and shops beginning to emerge around the recently spruced-up Rynek. There are a number of things worth seeing in the town, many of them associated with the pow-

△ Town hall, Zamość

erful Radziwiłł family, the town's fifteenth-century founders and longtime aristocratic benefactors.

The Town
Inevitably for a town established by aristocracy, the former **Zamek Radziwiłłów** (Radziwiłł Castle), west of the main square, provides the town's main focus of historic interest. Left, like most other such complexes, to go to

Crossing the eastern border

Despite the rapidly increasing volume of traffic, travel across Poland's **eastern borders** in any form – car especially – is still liable to be a major hassle. Behind the socialist unity rhetoric of the postwar era, up until the early 1990s the reality was a strictly controlled border, at least as strongly policed at major crossing points as the former East–West Germany border. The political climate may have changed radically, but in practical terms getting into (or out of) Belarus and Ukraine from Poland remains fraught with practical complications, and is likely to remain so for the foreseeable future. For more information on heading east from Poland, see "On to Lithuania" (p.263) and "On to L'viv" (p.356).

Crossing points
For motorists the key problem is lack of crossing points, a problem compounded by the ponderous Soviet-style customs set up on the eastern side of the border and the sheer volume of traffic attempting to get across. Two major border crossings – **Terespol–Briest** near Biała Podlaska and **Medyka** near Przemyśl – were adequate as long as few people were able to travel. With the recent explosion of travel facilitated by the new political situation it's now absurd, as everyone recognizes. The response to date has been sluggish to say the least: two new crossing points to Belarus accessible to private cars, at **Połowce**, east of Siemiatczye, and **Kukuryki**, just north of Terespol; and three with Ukraine, at **Dorohusk**, east of Chełm, **Hrebenne**, near Tomaszów Lubelski, 70km northeast of L'viv, and **Korczowa**, east of Jarosław. Amazing stories of border incidents abound: one legendary story that did the rounds in Poland a few years back was of a car stopped at customs on account of the peculiar smell emanating from the vehicle. Close examination of a back-seat passenger revealed that he had died (from a stroke) during the long wait: not wanting to lose their precious place in the queue, the other passengers had decided to keep the body in the car until they crossed the border.

EU requirements
A new factor in the equation is Poland's drive to obtain EU membership, due to occur sometime in the early 2000s. If and when Poland enters the EU, its eastern borders – over 2000km of them all-told – will effectively become the EU's new eastern frontier. Worried about a potential influx of illegal immigrants, drugs and cut-price goods, Brussels has signalled that tightened controls on the border with neighbours Kaliningrad, Lithuania, Belarus and Ukraine are a necessary condition of Polish EU membership. To meet this demand new, stricter **border controls** were implemented at the beginning of 1998. In particular, for the first time visa requirements were introduced for citizens of Belarus and Russia, whose governments have so far failed to conclude legal agreements on the return of illegal immigrants refused entry into Poland – a key EU condition.

At a stroke the number of Belarusians and Russians visiting Poland fell dramatically – Ukrainians and Lithuanians, whose governments have signed the necessary return agreements, were not affected. The move caused an immediate uproar in the east of the country, notably in towns such as Białystok whose massive open-air bazaars are heavily dependent on cross-border trade tourism, with furious local residents organiz-

seed in the postwar era, much of the damage was actually done earlier, the main palace section of the original seventeenth-century complex having been destroyed by the tsarist authorities in the 1870s. The main building, currently being renovated, is a combined school and music academy – most of the rest is a public library – while the old Tower House contains the well-organized **Muzeum Południowego Podlasia** (Museum of Southern Podlasie; late June–early Sept Tues–Fri 9.30am–4.30pm, Sat 10am–4pm, Sun 10am–5pm;

ing mass blockades of border roads in protest. Initially the Polish government remained unbowed, with Foreign Minister Bronisław Geremek stating that the estimated US$3 billion in cross-border trade the country stood to lose as a result of the new restrictions was a "worthy sacrifice" for the cause of integration into the EU.

Following much diplomatic toing and froing, however – not least to Brussels – the new visa restrictions were eventually eased, although not altogether eliminated, in spring 1998. The question of visas continues to loom large over the borderlands however – their introduction for Russians, Belarussians and Ukrainians (but not Lithuanians, because they, unlike the others, are also being groomed for EU membership) is unavoidable if Poland wishes to complete its negotiations to join the EU on schedule (currently timetabled for the end of 2002). In the meantime, with an eye on the future, the EU has increased its financial support for the modernization of the country's antiquated eastern border crossings, including training schemes for border guards and customs inspectors in EU norms and techniques. Overall, the long-term effect of all this is likely to be highly significant. But for the moment at least, for Westerners and Easterners alike, visa controls, border tailbacks and bureaucratic messiness remain the rule rather than the exception at crossings such as Terespol-Brest.

By car
Motorists can still expect waits of anything from two to four days at the major crossings in the several-kilometre-long queues backed up round the clock on both sides of the border. In summer particularly, conditions at Terespol-Brest verge on the nightmarish – there are no roadside toilet or washing facilities to speak of, with food and other supplies coming from the vendors in vans parked up on the side of the road. Thousands of stationary cars – especially those with Western number-plates – are a sitting target for robbers, so you're well advised to keep a close watch on your vehicle at all times. Protracted negotiations between the Polish and Ukrainian authorities are due to result in the opening up of at least a couple of new purpose-built border crossings in the near future. If this actually happens, the situation will undoubtedly improve for motorists.

By bus
Crossing the border **by bus** is a different story: all PKS buses get special treatment, so unless there's trouble with customs as a result of some of the passengers' "baggage" – a not infrequent occurrence – you should be through the border in a matter of hours as opposed to days. For any cross-border bus journey, it's a good idea to buy your ticket in advance.

By train
By train you probably won't face such a long wait – though even here a caveat is needed since if you've arrived without a visa, purchasing one at the border can be a long and drawn-out affair. To date, Ukrainian officials are proving better in this respect than the Belarusians, though it's important to stress that everything remains in a state of flux. In the final analysis, apart from a few sensible precautions, it's very much a case of turning up and seeing what happens.

rest of year Tues–Fri 9am–4pm, Sat 9am–3pm, Sun 10am–4pm; 3zł). Judging by the illustrations displayed here, the original castle complex was a very grand affair. The exhibitions on the upper floor feature an interesting display of local ethnography, including textiles, folk tapestries and examples of the pagan-influenced "sun" crucifixes typical of the Lithuanian part of the old Commonwealth. The artwork housed in the next room reflects traditional regional themes – hunting, horses, soldiers and the old Jewish marketplace. The former palace gatehouse contains a small but lively **art gallery-cum-café** (Tues–Sat 11am–6pm) which also puts on the occasional jazz concert. The whole ensemble is surrounded by an agreeable, largely deserted park which makes a nice spot for a leisurely stroll.

Of a number of churches in town, the basilica-shaped **Kościół św. Anny** (St Anne's Church), just up from the palace, is the most striking, an exuberant late-sixteenth-century structure with twin cupolas and a richly decorated side chapel devoted to the Radziwiłłs, as well as one curiously Celtic-looking tombstone in the graveyard outside, a contrast to the kitschy electric Marian shrine standing nearby.

The statue across the road, standing on the corner of ul. Brzeska, is of the popular writer **Józef Ignacy Kraszewski** (1821–87), who attended the 350-year-old local school, the old Akademia Bialska (Biała Academy), which was originally affiliated with the Kraków Academy and later with the Academy in Wilno (Vilnius).

Finally, 1km north of the Rynek on the northern side of ul. Nowa, there's a large, grassed-over **Jewish cemetery**, which seems to be used by the local drunks as a venue for liquid picnics. There's a recently erected memorial to Biała's Jews at the entrance to the cemetery, but elsewhere the mournful scattering of crumbling tombstones stands in poignant contrast to the well-kept Catholic cemetery immediately opposite.

Practicalities

The **train station** is on the southern side of the town, a five-minute bus ride from the centre, with the **bus station** on pl. Wojska Polskiego, a little to the east of the main Rynek along ul. Brzeska. For **accommodation**, the *Capitol*, in residential streets immediately west of the Rynek at ul. Reymonta 3 (☎083/344 2358, ✉hotel@hotelcapitol.com.pl; ❹) is a newly built, privately run venture with a good selection of rooms and one of the town's better restaurants. The *Merkury*, ul. Kolejowa 31b (☎081/342 3771; ❹), its main rival, is a smaller but similar type of new, privately run setup, situated close to the railway station, also with its own restaurant. The *Sportowy*, a ten-minute walk north of the Rynek at ul. Piłsudskiego 38 (☎081/343 4550; ❸) is a basic sports hotel with faded but acceptable en-suites next to the town stadium.

Best **place to eat** in town is the restaurant of the *Capitol*, although the *Forteca* at Brzeska 19 runs it a close second. In the summer months there's a smattering of civilized outdoor **café-bars** spread around the edge of the Rynek, and a more boisterous late-night **disco-pub**, *Night*, ten minutes' northwest of the Rynek on the opposite side of the stadium from the *Sportowy* hotel.

Janów Podlaski

Twenty kilometres north of Biała Podlaska close up by the Belarus border, formed from here southwards by the River Bug, the town of **JANÓW PODLASKI** is home to the country's most famous **stud farm**, specializing in the rearing of thoroughbred Arab horses. Located 2km east of the town centre (clearly signposted from the Rynek and served by local bus), the stables are regularly visited by luminaries of the world horse scene, principally during the annual international auctions which are usually held in August or September.

Established by Tsar Alexander I in 1817 in order to replace horses killed during the Napoleonic wars, the stud was intended to produce top-quality horses for his personal use. The farm has gone through its ups and downs: the stock was badly decimated by German soldiers in the latter stages of World War I, and again taken over by the Nazis during World War II, when the horses were transported to Germany, many dying in the notorious Allied bombing of Dresden in February 1944. The elegant stable complex you see today is essentially that designed by the Warsaw architect Marconi in the 1830s and 1840s. Janów horses are highly prized in the equestrian world, although it remains to be seen how the breeding programme will develop now that the stables are up for privatization – and will need to make a living from horse sales alone rather than relying on state subsidies.

There's always the option of having a look around the stable area and surrounding grounds. **Visiting the stables** without an appointment – preferably made directly with the stables (☎083/341 3009 or 341 3062, ℱ341 3360) – is not wildly popular, although the staff will generally let you at least walk around the grounds if you are unobtrusive or simply persuasive.

From its founding in the 1420s the town itself became an important stopoff point on the main Kraków to Vilnius road. The solid, imposing Baroque collegiate **church** with adjoining bell tower stands as a reminder of better days.

Janów is easy to reach from Biała Podlaska, with twelve **buses** a day making the thirty-minute journey. For a bite to **eat**, there's the *Janowianka* on pl. Partyzantów, the main square, while for **accommodation** the *Dom Wycieczkowy* (☎083/341 3314; ❷), at ul. Brzeska 6, is the only presentable option other than at Stadnia Koni, the stud farm's stables, though this option is generally reserved for people here on riding holidays – phone for details (see above).

East of Lublin

East of Lublin stretches an expanse of the sparsely populated agricultural lowland characteristic of Poland's eastern borders. In the midst of the region lies the recently established **Polesie** national park, a scenic area of marshy swamps and ancient, largely untouched peat bogs, and the most westerly part of a huge expanse of similar terrain stretching far beyond the border into Ukraine and Belarus, known collectively as Polesie before World War II, when the majority of the region was still within Polish territory.

For those interested in the religious and cultural mix of Poles, Ukrainians and Jews historically associated with southeastern Poland, **Chełm**, the regional capital, and the border town of **Włodawa** offer the prospect of an appealing if low-key diversion. Although both are well off the beaten track, a combined visit to both merits the backroads detour required.

Chełm

Sixty-five kilometres east of Lublin is the town of **CHEŁM**, a tranquil rural centre with a typically timeless eastern Polish feel to it. Like much of the surrounding area the town centre sits on a deep-running bedrock of **chalk**, providing Chełm with its best-known export and with a local landmark hill characteristically formed by limestone deposits. Rudely shunted into rural borderside oblivion by the postwar shifts in the country's frontiers, Chełm is currently experiencing something of a revival thanks to the growth in local cross-border traffic with neighbouring Ukraine, resulting from the opening of an international border crossing at Dorohusk, 30km east of town on the main Kowel–Kiev road. Chełm is served by frequent trains and buses from Lublin; getting here from Zamość is more tricky, with only a handful of direct buses – if you miss one, catch a bus to Krasnystaw and change there.

Historically, Chełm is one of eastern Poland's oldest urban settlements. Established in the early tenth century to protect the eastern borders of the nascent Piast-ruled domains, from the start Chełm was embroiled in a protracted contest for domination of the surrounding region between the Duchy of Kiev, the forerunner of Muscovy, and the Polish Piast monarchs. Control passed decisively to the Polish crown in 1387, soon after which the town was granted its charter by Ladislaus (Władysław) II Jagiełło. Formerly home to one of the oldest **Jewish communities** in Poland – Jews arrived here in the 1440s, possibly even earlier – they constituted roughly half of the town's population right up till 1939, enjoying legendary status in Jewish folklore as original simpletons and as such the butt of many a popular joke.

Following the local Orthodox acceptance of Rome's jurisdiction sealed in the 1596 Union of Brest, Chełm also emerged as a stronghold of **Uniate** (Greek Catholic) devotion, a position it retained until the suppression of the local Uniates and their enforced reconversion to Russian Orthodoxy ordered by the tsarist authorities in the 1870s. After the town's liberation by the Red Army in summer 1944, Chełm briefly enjoyed the dubious honour of being the first base of the Soviet-appointed Polish Committee of National Liberation (PKWN) sent into Poland by Stalin to establish a new communist-led government.

The Stare Miasto

Everything worth seeing is concentrated within the relatively tight confines of the Stare Miasto. Starting from the central pl. Luczowskiego, a brisk climb along the path up **Góra Zamkowa**, the hill overlooking the town from the east and the site of the original fortified settlement brings you to the former **Uniate Cathedral** complex, a grandiose set of buildings including the Greek Catholic cathedral turned Roman Catholic church, an imposing twin-towered Baroque structure from the 1740s with a fine high facade, the Uniate bishop's former residence and a seventeenth-century Basilian monastery. Back out of the complex it's worth climbing the fifteen-metre-high mound, the only remains of the original Slavic settlement, rising from the northern side of the hill, for the grandstand views over the town. A short walk northwest down the slopes of Góra Zamkowa brings you to another erstwhile Uniate complex, this time comprising a former seminary and the early-eighteenth-century Baroque **Kościół św. Mikołaja** (St Nicholas's Church), these days the home of the town museum's **art collection** (Tues–Fri 10am–5.30pm, Sat & Sun 11am–3pm; 3zł), holding several Uniate icons and a jumble of nineteenth-century furniture.

Back towards the centre along ul. Młodowskiej is the **Orthodox church**, a white brick nineteenth-century *cerkiew* with an impressive iconostasis. As usual though, the place is generally locked except when there's a service going on, so at any other time you'll have to persuade the priest, who lives close by, or one of his acolytes to open up and let you look inside. South down ul. Kopernika, at the corner with ul. Krzywa, stands the former **synagogue**, the only one of several that remains. Today it's a bank and there's nothing to inform you of the place's one-time function, though, if you're at all attuned to local synagogue architecture, its outward appearance is an immediate giveaway.

West along ul. Krzywa and onto ul. Lubelska brings you to the **town museum** at no. 56 (Tues–Fri 10am–3.30pm, Sat & Sun 11am–3pm; 3zł). The ground floor displays focus on the history of the town, notably the Partition-era Russian occupation, while the upstairs floor houses a collection of local wildlife as well as an extraordinary, and presumably less local selection of a wide variety of molluscs. East along ul. Lubelska stands the **parish church**, a Piarist foundation from the 1750s, designed by Italian architect Paolo Antonio Fontana. An extravagant piece of Baroque exuberance, the walls and vaults of the interior boast a fine series of trompe l'oeil paintings and frescoes by Joseph Meyer, similar in style to the ones that adorn Lublin Cathedral, this time illustrating scenes from the Life of the Virgin and in, the side chapels, the exploits of St Joseph Calasanza, founder of the Piarist order.

The chalk cellars

Immediately west of the parish church at ul. Lubelska 55a is the entrance to the town's major curiosity, a labyrinthine network of **underground tunnels** hewn out of the chalk bedrock – the only such system of chalk tunnels in Europe (daily: May–Aug 9am–6pm; Sept–April 9am–4pm; 8zł). **Entrance** is by guided tour only, and individual tourists may have to wait until a large enough group of visitors assembles; English or German guides are available by advance appointment (☎ 082/565 2530; ✉ labirynt@ptt.pl). The unusual purity of the local chalk, combined with a growing appreciation of its commercial building value, resulted in the development of an amateur chalk-mining industry here as far back as the fifteenth century. Little if any control was exercised over the pattern of the mining, the result being a seemingly uncoordinated maze of tunnels and mine shafts hacked out by succeeding generations of local entrepreneurs. Eventually, however, much of the fifteen-kilometre network of passageways – the deepest going down fifteen metres – fell into neglect and disuse. In the 1960s, in an effort to halt the rot, the deepest sections were silted up and a two-kilometre section of tunnels twelve metres deep was cleaned up and opened to tourists.

These days the standard **tour** lasts about forty minutes, more than enough for most people, given the cold. The insulating properties of chalk are such that the tunnels maintain a temperature of exactly 9°C regardless of the season, so you'll need to bring a jacket or sweater with you for the tour. As you would expect, there's a stock of historical anecdotes as well as legends of spirits and demons, all of which the torchlight-bearing guide will dutifully provide on demand.

Practicalities

The main **train** stations lie on opposite sides of the Stare Miasto centre. The larger of the two, Chełm Główny, is a good 2km northeast of the centre (regular buses shuttle into town), so it's preferable to alight at Chełm Miasto, a fifteen-minute walk west of pl. Luczowskiego, the main square. The **bus station** is on ul. Lwowska, a five-minute walk south of the centre.

The **tourist information office**, centrally located at ul. Lubelska 63 (July–Aug Mon–Fri 8am–5pm, Sat & Sun 9am–2pm; Sept–June Mon–Fri 8am–4pm, Sat 9am–2pm; ☎082/565 3667, ⊛www.um.chelm.pl/it) is well stocked with maps and other information, including a number of English-language brochures.

Chełm doesn't go overboard on **places to stay**, either in number or quality. The only real hotels are the *Kamena*, situated halfway between Chełm Miasto train station and the town centre at ul. Armii Krajowej 50 (☎082/565 6401; ❹), with decent-quality en-suites and a similarly passable restaurant and café; the *Relax*, ul. 11 Listopada 2 (☎082/563 0395; ❷), a simple overnighter offering rooms with shared facilities 2km east of the centre; and the *MOSIR*, just east of the centre by the sports stadium at ul. 1 Pułku Szwoleżerów 15 (☎082/563 0286; ❷), which has en-suite doubles as well as more basic triples and quads. There's an all-year **youth hostel** at ul. Czarneckiego 8 (lock-out 10am–5pm; ☎082/564 0022; 15zł per person), handily located a couple of blocks north of pl. Luczowskiego. For food, your best bet is the *Kamena* hotel **restaurant**, with the *Lotos*, al. Piłsudskiego 14, and *Pizzeria Romantica*, ul. Kopernika 2, the best of the alternatives.

Włodawa

Hard up by the Belarusian border, 50km north of Chełm, sits the sleepy little town of **WŁODAWA**. Situated on top of a low hill overlooking the banks of the River Bug, which here, as for about 100km in either direction, forms the national border established in 1945, Włodawa gets its as yet underdeveloped tourist stars from the presence of one of the best-preserved synagogues in the country. As with many towns in this region, Jews formed a clear majority of the town population up till World War II, when virtually all of them perished in the concentration camp at Sobibór, established by the Nazis in May 1942, 12km south of town.

Built in the 1760s on the site of an earlier wooden structure, the main **synagogue**, one of the many one-time Jewish buildings dotted around the centre, is a typically solid-looking late Baroque construction with a palatial main facade dominated by a high central section and topped by some typically Polish mansard roofing. Despite severe damage by the Nazis, and postwar conversion into a warehouse, the synagogue was thoroughly and well restored in the 1960s, since when it's functioned as a local **museum** (Tues–Sun 10am–3pm; 3zł). In the main interior room, the prayer hall, four pillars supporting the barrel-cross vaulting indicate the spot where the bema once stood. The major surviving original feature is the restored **Aron ha Kodesh**, a colourful, triple-tiered neo-Gothic structure raised in the 1930s and covered with elaborate stucco decoration. Ranged round the walls is a photo exhibition of life in the wartime Warsaw Ghetto, while the upstairs gallery of the synagogue holds a separate display of local ethnography – folk costumes, ploughs and the like (same opening hours) – that seems a little out of keeping with the rest of the building. Across the courtyard from the main synagogue is another smaller house of worship from the mid-nineteenth century, currently under reconstruction, which has preserved sections of the original polychromy as well as its Aron ha Kodesh. Plans are afoot eventually to integrate it and the main synagogue into a more comprehensive museum of local Jewish culture. For the moment, only the ticket office is located here.

If you've the inclination for a stroll around the rest of town, there are a couple of other buildings worth looking in on: the **parish church**, a curiously squat-looking late-Baroque building designed like its counterparts in Lubartów (see p.310) and Chełm (see p.319) by Paolo Antonio Fontana in the mid-1700s, with some rich Rococo interior polychromy; and across the opposite side of the main square, the Neoclassical Orthodox Church, built in 1842 with funds from the Zamoyski family. Here, as ever, the building's kept locked except for services, so you'll need to rouse the priest, who lives next door, if you want to get in to look at the building.

In the unlikely event of getting stranded here and needing **accommodation**, the basic *OSiR*, ul. Szkolna 4 (☎082/572 2584; ❷), is an unpretentious sports hotel with sparsely furnished en-suites; while the *Car Polesia*, ul. Sokołowa 4 (☎082/572 4574; ❷), is a marginally cosier small hotel, which also has a decent **restaurant**. Otherwise the top place to eat in town is probably the *Prima* at ul. Partyzantów 12a. There's a gaggle of more basic snack bars on ul. Czerwonego Krzyża, the street leading off from the square up towards the synagogue.

West to Kazimierz

The Lublin–Warsaw route has a major attraction in the town of **Kazimierz Dolny**, an ancient and highly picturesque grain-shipping centre set above the Wisła. Of all the small towns in rural Poland this is – by a long stretch – the best preserved, and continues to swallow up ever-growing numbers of tourists as a result. To reach it on public transport, the easiest approach from Warsaw is to go by train to **Puławy** and catch a connecting bus from there; from Lublin there are direct buses via the old spa town of **Nałęczów**.

Nałęczów

Twenty-five kilometres west of Lublin, **NAŁĘCZÓW** (most, but not all, Puławy-bound buses pass through here) saw its heyday at the end of the last century, when Polish writers and artists, including the popular novelists Bolesław Prus and Stefan Żeromski and pianist-prime minister Ignacy Paderewski, came here, the quality of the local air and water helping establish it as one of the country's most popular holiday spa towns.

Even today the **spa** is still renowned for its therapeutic waters, heart specialists and generally medicinal climate, and the town retains much of its old-time appearance and atmosphere. You'll see the locally produced mineral water, Nałęczowianka, on supermarket shelves throughout the country.

A leisurely stroll through the attractively landscaped spa park brings you to the Neoclassical **Pałac Małachowskego** (Małachowski Palace), an elegant Rococo structure from the 1770s, which is part health centre and part **museum** (Tues–Sun 10am–3pm; 4zł), devoted to Prus and the "Positivist" literary movement he promoted in reaction to traditional insurrectionary Romanticism. Particularly impressive is the palace ballroom, which boasts some exquisite period stucco decoration. Nearby is the Sanatorium, fronted by a monument to Żeromski, and the neo-Gothic **Pavilion Angielski** (English Pavilion), now the spa office building. For an instant iron-deficiency remedy, you can taste the local waters in the pavilion, next to a duck-filled lake in the middle of the park. Back out through the main gate, opposite the bus stop on ul. Ponatowskiego, a short way up Żeromskiego is the **Żeromski villa**, the writer's Podhale-style residence built at the turn of the twentieth century, and now housing a small museum (Tues–Sun 10am–3pm) devoted to the man's life and works.

Of the **hotels** in town, the *Przepiórecka*, near the bus station at ul. 1 Maja 8 (☎081/501 4129; ❷), provides the bare essentials; while the more upmarket *Energetyk*, 2km from the centre on the Kazimierz Dolny road at Paderewskiego 10 (☎081/501 4604, ⓦwww.cswenergetyk.lublin.pl; ❺) offers en-suite rooms with satellite TV, and kitchenettes in some rooms. Additionally, there is a wide selection of **rest homes** aimed at people here on sanitorium rest cures –

though you don't have to be enrolled in one to stay. Some good options are the *Willa Raj*, ul. Lipowa 15 (☎081/501 4193; ❷), and the good-quality *Ewelina*, across the road at ul. Lipowa 16 (☎081/501 4076; ❷), both of which offer simple en-suites. If you want to stay in a fully fledged sanatorium complete with spa treatments and medical staff on hand, you could do much worse than opt for the comfortable *Fortunat*, ul. Kościuski 7 (☎081/501 4356, ⓦwww.uzdrowisko-naleczow.com; ❸). There are simple **restaurants** at both the *Przepióreczka* and the *Ewelina*.

Puławy

Sprawling over the eastern banks of the Wisła, 20km west from Nałęczów, is **PUŁAWY**, a featureless, medium-sized industrial centre with seemingly little going for it. In Polish consciousness, however, the place is indelibly associated with the Czartoryski family, the noted aristocratic dynasty who moved to the town in the 1730s and made it their base. Best known in the line of residents are **Prince Adam Czartoryski** and his wife **Izabella**, passionate devotees of the arts who, by the end of the eighteenth century, had succeeded in transforming the palace here into one of the country's most dynamic cultural and intellectual centres, accumulating a huge library and noted art collection in the process. Despite the advent of the Partitions and the imposition of Russian rule, the family stuck determinedly to its guns throughout the early 1800s, Izabella founding a national museum here – the first of its kind in Poland – and continuing to patronize and cultivate the arts. This was not, however, to last. The failure of the 1830 Uprising (see Contexts, p.683) and the Czartoryski's involvement in its planning, resulted in the confiscation of the entire family estate, the enraged tsarist authorities even going as far as to rename the town New Alexandria. The Czartoryskis fled into exile in Paris and their huge art collection was spirited away secretly along with them, where it remained until its return to the family palace in Kraków, where it forms the core of today's museum there (see p.421).

Pałac Czartoryskich and the park

The only thing really worth making the effort to seek out, in an otherwise undistinguished town, is the **Pałac Czartoryskich**, approached from a large pond-filled courtyard off the intersection of al. Królewska and ul. Czartoryskich – a twenty-minute walk south from the main bus station. Built in the 1670s by the veteran Warsaw architect Tylman of Gameren, the main building subsequently underwent a number of remodellings (and significant damage during World War II), the result being the curiously leaden Neoclassical pile you see today. Converted into a scientific research institute in the postwar years, nobody seems to object to you strolling in for a look around the place during regular office hours. Through the main entrance and up the grand cast-iron staircase, the majestically arcaded **Gothic Hall** and **Music Hall** offer hints of the former grandeur of the place. An elegant statuetted marble balcony offers an enjoyable view over the palace park, and beyond it the Wisła river.

Designed and developed by the industrious Izabella Czartoryska over a twenty-year period (1790–1810), the meandering palace **park** is quintessentially Romantic in feel and conception. A large expanse filled with a widely variegated collection of trees, both Polish and foreign, the walkways are dotted with the hotchpotch of "historical" buildings and monuments, many of them in the classical mode, popular with the Polish aristocracy of the period (see, for example, Arkadia, p.140). Southeast of the palace down a tree-lined avenue, the **Dom Gotycki** (Gothic House), a square, two-storey building with a graceful portico, originally part of the Czartoryski museum, now houses a small exhibition (May–Nov Tues–Sun 10am–4pm; 3zł) devoted to the family, including a changing selection of exhibits from the family museum in Kraków. Opposite is the **Świątynia Sybilli** (Temple of Sibyl), consciously echoing the temple of the same name in Tivoli, near Rome, and containing another small exhibition (same opening hours and ticket), this time devoted to national historical themes along the lines of the museum initiated by Izabella, including the 1830 and 1863 Uprisings.

If you feel like strolling further afield, there are a number of follies and other assorted buildings to detain you on the way along the edge of the park lake, including a Chinese pavilion, Roman gate, the marble Czartoryski family sarcophagus and assorted imitation classical statuary.

Practicalities

Getting here is easy – Puławy is on a major train line from Warsaw (2hr) and has regular bus connections with Lublin (1hr). The main **train station** (Puławy Miasto) is 2km northeast of the centre on ul. Żyrzyńska, while the **bus station**, at the junction of ul. Lubelska and ul. Wojska Polskiego, is closer. You're unlikely to want **a place to stay** in Puławy, especially seeing as the region's main tourist attraction – Kazimierz Dolny – is a mere twenty-minute bus ride to the south. Of the various options, the newly established *Centrum Szkoleniowo-Kongresowe*, a ten-minute walk from the palace at al. Królewska 17 (☎081/887 7306, ✉csk@jung.pulawy.pl; ❷), is the best option in town – although it's often booked solid with conferences. Usually with rooms to spare is the dowdy *Izabella*, ul. Lubelska 1 (☎081/886 3041; ❹), a supposedly upmarket tourist haunt near the bus station offering gloomy en-suites and an unprepossessing restaurant. The *Dom Nauczyciela*, ul. Kołłątaja 1 (☎081/887 4277; ❷), is a good budget bet, as is the *PTTK Dom Turysty* at ul. Rybacka 7 (☎081/887 4048; ❸), 1km west of the palace, near the river.

Hotel **restaurants** aside, there are a number of other undistinguished eating and drinking establishments on and around the central ul. Piłsudskiego. *Sybilla*, ul. Królewska 17, is a pleasant café-restaurant midway between the bus station and the palace.

Kazimierz Dolny and around

Don't be surprised if your first impression of **KAZIMIERZ DOLNY** is one of *déjà vu*: recognizing celluloid potential when they see it, numerous film directors – and not just Polish ones – have used the scenic backdrop of this well-preserved town for historical thrillers and tragic romances. Artists, too, have long been drawn to Kazimierz's effervescent light and ancient buildings. These days the town is unquestionably established as a major tourist venue, a fact reflected in the wealth of hotels and restaurants continuing to spring up. Poles as well as foreign tourists are drawn by the town's memorable combination of historic architecture, rustic backstreets and riverside setting – definitely not one to miss.

Historically, the place is closely associated with its royal namesake, **Kazimierz the Great** (1333–70), who rescued Poland from dynastic and economic chaos and transformed the country's landscape in the process. It is said of him that he "found a wooden Poland and left a Poland of stone", and Kazimierz Dolny (Lower Kazimierz) is perhaps the best remaining example of

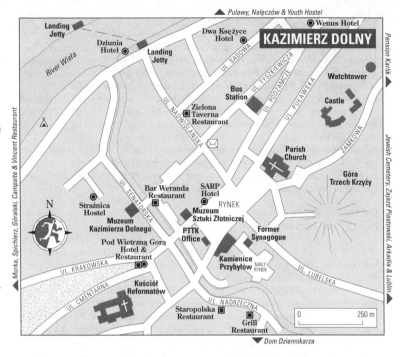

his ambitious town-building programme. Thanks to the king's promotion of the Wisła grain and timber trade, a minor village was transformed into a prosperous mercantile town by the end of the fourteenth century, gaining the nickname "little Danzig" in the process, on account of the goods' ultimate destination. Much of the money that poured in was used to build the ornate burghers' houses that are today's prime tourist attraction.

It was during this period, too, that **Jews** began to settle in Kazimierz and other neighbouring towns, grateful for the legal protection proclaimed for them throughout Poland by King Kazimierz. Dynamic Jewish communities of traders and shopkeepers were integral to the character of towns like Kazimierz for over five hundred years: at one time eighty percent of the inhabitants of Kazimierz were Jewish. With most of the town's inhabitants perishing in the death camps, Kazimierz entered the postwar era as an empty shell of a place, only to regenerate itself once the urban elite of Warsaw had discovered its irresistable rural charm. Nowadays it's thronging with tourists over the summer and at weekends throughout the year. However Kazimierz's popularity with Poland's artistic set has bestowed a relaxed, bohemian feel on the place, and despite overcrowding during summer cultural festivals (of which more on p.328), the town never has the feel of being oppressively over-touristed.

Arrival and information

Despite lying some way off the main inter-city road routes, Kazimierz Dolny is easy to reach by **bus**, with two daily departures from Warsaw, and as many as fourteen from Lublin. Alternatively you can catch a **train** to Puławy (on the Warsaw–Lublin line) and pick up a Kazimierz-bound bus (suburban bus #12 from the train station, or one of the regular PKS services from the bus station) from there. The Kazimierz bus station – really just a drop-off point – is on ul. Podzamcze, within spitting distance of the Rynek.

There's a helpful though under-resourced **PTTK office** at no. 27 on the Rynek (May to mid-Oct Mon–Fri 8am–6pm, Sat & Sun 10am–5.30pm; mid-Oct to April Mon–Fri 8am–4pm, Sat & Sun 10am–2.30pm; ☎081/881 0046, ⓔpttk_kazimierz_dolny@poczta.onet.pl) which can sort out **private rooms**, some centrally located but many further out – reckon on 25–30zł per person. Otherwise, numerous households throughout the town have *noclegi* and *pokoje* signs hanging outside. (ⓦwww.kazimierz-dolny.pl)

If you're taken by the idea of exploring the charming surrounding countryside, **bike rental** is available from the sports shop at ul. Sadowa 7A, the *Dwa Księżyce* hotel, and the *Zajazd Piastowski* (both listed under Accommodation, below).

Accommodation

Kazimierz's accommodation situation has improved by leaps and bounds in the last few years, chiefly due to the number of new privately run places now available. Even so, the deluge of visitors descending on the town in summer means that it can still be hard to find a bed, so booking ahead is a good idea – especially during the massively popular Folk Groups and Singers Festival, which takes place here in late June or early July. The main **youth hostel**, *Pod Wianuszkami*, ul. Puławska 64 (☎081/881 0327), 2km north of town in an old riverside granary, has dorms (30zł per person) as well as a few doubles (❷); it's open year-round but often full due to the popularity of Kazimierz Dolny with Polish school trips. The alternative is the newer *Strażnica*, in the fire station building at ul. Senatorska 23 (☎081/881 0427), which also fills up quickly. For **campsites** it's a choice between the site behind the *Hotel Spichlerz* at Krakowska 59/61 (May–Aug; ☎081/881 0401) and the much smaller one at the *Strażnica* (May–Aug; same tel as the hostel), closer to the centre and correspondingly noisier.

Arkadia ul. Czerniawy 1 ☎081/881 0074. Cheap, reasonably sized and popular teachers' hotel a twenty-minute walk east of the centre, offering sparsely furnished rooms with shower. ❶

Dom Architektowy (SARP) Rynek 20 ☎081/881 0544. Excellent though noisy location, bang on the square, in a holiday home belonging to the Union of Architects – it's often fully booked by their members at peak times. Full board usually a requirement, with a discount for longer stays. ❺

Dom Dziennikarza ul. Małachowskiego 17 ☎081/881 0162, ⓔddsp@lublin.top.pl. Modern three-storey building belonging to the Union of Journalists (so it's often full of them during the high season), with modernized en-suites, and an outdoor summer pool. In a good position in an area of thick forest just 10 minutes' walk south of the Rynek. A popular conference venue, which means it's often full. ❺

Dwa Księżyce ul. Sadowa 15 ☎081/881 0761. Medium-sized hotel in a posh-looking house on a quiet street in the town centre, offering rather stylish en-suites. ❺

Góralski, ul. Krakowska 47 ☎081/881 0263.

Reasonable quality *górale* chalet-style *pensjonat* overlooking the river – some rooms are en-suite, others use a bathroom in the hallway. Not many rooms, so ring in advance. ❷

Hotel na Wodzie "Dziunia" Przystań ☎0603/635 746. Boat moored beside the ferry jetty at the end of ul. Nadwiślańska, offering cosy cabins with bunk beds and pristine bathrooms. ❷

Murka ul. Krakowska 59 ☎081/881 0037, ⓦwww.redwan.com.pl. Comfortable, small-sized place in an attractive, mansard-roofed mansion 1.5km east of town. En-suites with TV. ❹

Pod Wietrzną Górą ul. Krakowska 1. Smallish, centrally located *pensjonat* with cosy en-suites and a good restaurant. ❺

Spichlerze ul. Krakowska 61 ☎081/881 0036, ⓦwww.redwan.com.pl. Larger sister establishment to the *Murka* offering plusher rooms, located in a large, refurbished riverside granary, with its own restaurant. ❹

Wenus ul. Tyszkiewicza 25a ☎081/882 0400. Modern medium-sized hotel on the northeastern fringes of the centre offering all the creature comforts. ❺

Zajazd Piastowski ul. Słoneczna 31
℡081/881 0351. Large hotel with some holiday bungalows, a swimming pool, bike rental

and horse riding plus a good restaurant. It's
2km south of town past the Jewish Cemetery
(bus #12 passes close by). **4**

The Town

The **Rynek**, with its solid-looking wooden well at the centre, is ringed by an
engaging mixture of original buildings, the opulent town houses of rich
Kazimierz merchants rubbing shoulders with more folksy structures, many
boasting first-floor verandahs which jut out from underneath plunging, shin-
gle-covered roofs. Most striking of the merchants' residences around the square
– all of which were restored after the war – are the **Kamienice Przybyłów**
(Przybyła Brothers' Houses), both on the southern edge. Built in 1615, they
bear some striking Renaissance sculpture; the guidebooks will tell you that the
largest one shows St Christopher, but his tree trunk of a staff and zodiacal
entourage suggest something more like a Polish version of the Green Giant.
Next door is the former **Kamienica Lustigowska** (Lustig House) – once
home to a notable local Jewish mercantile dynasty, its beams displaying the only
surviving original Hebrew inscription in town, a quotation from the Psalms.
On the western side of the square stands the late-eighteenth-century
Kamienica Gdańska (Gdańsk House), a sumptuous Baroque mansion originally owned by grain merchants. Immediately north is the **Muzeum Sztuki
Złotniczej** (Silverware Museum), which is currently closed for renovation –
for the time being its collection is on display at the Town Museum (Muzeum
Kazimierza Dolnego; see below).

Other houses still carrying their Renaissance decorations can be seen on ul.
Senatorska, which runs alongside the stream west of the square. Of these, the
Kamienica Celejowska (Celejowski House; no. 17), has a fabulous high attic
storey, a balustrade filled with the carved figures of saints and an assortment of
imaginary creatures, richly ornamented windows and a fine entrance portal
and hallway. It houses the town museum, the **Muzeum Kazimierza
Dolnego**; Tues–Sun: May–Sept 10am–5pm; Oct–April 10am–3pm; 4zł), which
along with paintings of Kazimierz and its surroundings, documents the history of the town's Jewish community. The nineteenth-century paintings in the
collection focus partly on the Jews – a kind of Orientalist fascination seems to
have gripped the predominantly Gentile Polish painters who formed the
town's artist community. Together with the selection of works by local Jewish
artists such as Samuel Finkenstein they evoke an almost palpable atmosphere of
Kazimierz in its heyday. The collection of the Silverware Museum (on display
here temporarily; see above) contains a highly impressive collection of ornamental silverwork and other decorative metal pieces dating back to the seventeenth century – a must if you are even remotely interested in this craft. A
notable feature is the collection of Jewish ritual objects and vessels, many from
the town itself. Several floors of the building also house temporary summer
exhibitions aimed at the seasonal tourist population. At the time of writing the
museum was being renovated and the silver exhibitions temporarily moved
over to the town museum, a state of affairs which looks set to last some time.

On the streets of the town, specifically Jewish buildings are scarce. The old
synagogue is sited off ul. Lubelska, to the southeast of the Rynek; constructed in King Kazimierz's reign, it was once a fine building. Following wartime
destruction by the Nazis, it was rebuilt in the 1950s and converted into a cinema. Of the decoration only the octagonal wooden dome, characteristic of
many Polish synagogues, and the women's gallery have been reconstructed.

Crossing the stream and following ul. Cmentarna up the hill brings you to the late-sixteenth-century **Kościół Reformatów** (Reformed Franciscan Church), from where there's a nice view back down over the winding streets and tiled rooftops. Up the hill on the other side of the square is the **parish church**, remodelled impressively in the early seventeenth century. The interior boasts a magnificent organ, a Renaissance font and fine stuccoed vaulting. The restored church bell tower nearby houses a small **gallery** (Tues–Sun: May–Sept 10am–4pm; Oct–April 10am–3pm; 4zł) displaying a changing set of quirky but enjoyable themed exhibitions.

Further up, there's an excellent view from the ruins of the fourteenth-century **castle**, built by King Kazimierz and destroyed by the marauding Swedish forces during the ferocious invasion of the country in the mid-1650s. The panorama from the top of the **watchtower** above the castle is even better, taking in the Wisła and the full sweep of the countryside. Another popular alternative is the vantage point from the top of **Góra Trzech Krzyży** (Three Crosses Hill). A steepish climb fifteen minutes east of the square (there's also a path leading directly here from the castle), the crosses were raised in memory of the early eighteenth-century plague that wiped out a large part of the local population.

On the southeastern side of town, a two-kilometre walk along ul. Czerniawa brings you to the Czerniawa Gorge, the site of the main **Jewish cemetery**. First mentioned in 1568, the cemetery was destroyed by the Nazis, who ripped up the tombstones and used them to pave the courtyard of their headquarters in town. In the 1980s the tombstones scattered around the area were collected here and assembled into a Wailing Wall-like monument – six hundred fragments in all – to moving and dramatic effect. A jagged split down the middle symbolizes the dismemberment of the local Jewish population, making this one of the most powerful Jewish memorials in the country. Wander up the hill behind the monument and you'll find decaying remnants of the former cemetery sprouting up from among the trees.

Spread out alongside the main road to Puławy northeast of town lie several of Kazimierz's sixteenth- and seventeenth-century **granaries** (*spichlerze*) – sturdy affairs with Baroque gables, they attest to the erstwhile prosperity of the town's merchants. One of these, a ten-minute walk from the centre, now houses the **Muzeum Przyrodnicze** (Natural History Museum; Tues–Sun: May–Sept 10am–4pm, Oct–April 10am–3pm; 4zł), a didactic collection of stuffed animals from the region.

Eating and drinking

The range of places to eat and drink in town has expanded in tandem with the rising number of visitors. Most of the hotels have decent **restaurants**, and there's a fair sprinkling of open-air **bars** by the river offering cheap fried fish and beer. For a novel **snack**, snap up some *koguty* (bread buns baked in the form of a cockerel) from the numerous stalls around the main Rynek. They're also on sale from Piekarna Sarzyński, a smart patisserie at ul. Nadreczna 4 that offers numerous other pastry-snacks and **cakes**.

Most **drinking** takes place in the restaurants or in the café-bars grouped around the Rynek – of which *U Radka* is one of the best.

Bar Weranda opposite the museum on ul. Senatorska. Simple Polish milk-bar dishes like *pierogi* and *placki*, on a shady terrace coralled with pot plants.

Grill ul. Nadrzeczna 24. Despite the unassuming title and rather plain outdoor courtyard, this is a wonderful place to sample delicious fried fish, and has the added attractions of a salad bar and an extensive wine list.

Pod Wietrzną Gorą ul. Krakowska 1. Restaurant belonging to the pension of the same name (see p.325), offering traditional meat dishes, fresh fish and a decent range of omelettes, served up on an attractive Mediterranean-looking patio.

Staropolska ul. Nadrzeczna 14. Long-established restaurant with a good line in mid-price traditional Polish cuisine.

Vincent ul. Krakowska 11. Flashy but enjoyable place serving up Polish and modern European cuisine to a stylish Warsaw crowd.

Zielona Taverna ul. Nadwiślańska 4. Excellent but not overpriced restaurant with a relaxing country-house interior, a delightful garden, and a wider range of vegetarian choices than anywhere else in this part of Poland.

Entertainment

Throughout the summer the Rynek is pressed into service as a venue for **outdoor concerts**, some of which are timed to coincide with the **summer film festival**, which focuses on Polish films old and new, in mid-July (information on ☎022/636 7083).

However the main event in town is the annual **Folk Groups and Singers Festival**, a wildly popular national event that takes place here in late June or early July. Unless you have a tent, expect to rough it if you're in town then, as the meagre accommodation is snapped up instantly. Now into its thirty-third year, the festival is undoubtedly the country's premier folk music event – and the only one to which performers from all over the country regularly come. Everyone's welcome to play, usually amounting to six or seven hundred performers over the week. Of late, the festival has been spearheading something of a revival of interest in Polish roots music, particularly in regional styles and songs that only a decade ago seemed on the verge of extinction. Highlight of the week are the rural dance parties held on the main square. Awards are presented at the festival, with the winners featuring on CDs put out by Polskie Radio 2 – well worth picking up.

Around Kazimierz

There's some good **walking** territory around Kazimierz. If you really want to get the feel of the town's gentle surroundings, follow one of the marked paths from the town centre: either the five-kilometre green path that takes you southwest past the PTTK hostel and along the river cliff to **Mecmierz**; or the four-kilometre red path that heads northeast to the ruined castle of **Bochotnica**. King Kazimierz is said to have built the castle here for one of his favourite mistresses, a Jewess called Esterka, with a secret tunnel connecting the fortresses in Kazimierz and Bochotnica.

Another option is to take the **ferry** from the Kazimierz riverfront near the western end of ul. Nadwiślańska (every 30min 9am–7pm May–Sept; 5zł) to the village of **JANOWIEC**, known for the ruins of the Firlej family **castle**, perched on a hill a half-hour walk from the landing point and currently being restored. In its heyday this imposing early-sixteenth-century fortress is reputed to have been one of the grandest in the country, with no less than eight ballrooms. Today, apart from the fine views it affords, the castle's most striking feature is its zany exterior decoration consisting of alternating red-and-white-painted stripes and occasional contorted human figures. Also of interest is the freshly cleared well in the castle courtyard, allegedly the ancient entrance to a secret passage joining this fortress to that of Kazimierz. The castle **interior** (Tues–Sun 10am–4.30pm; 6zł), meanwhile, though pleasantly restored in places, has a long way to go before it's anything more than a ruin. Back down in the village there's a fine Gothic parish **church** that contains the Firlej family tomb, designed by Italian Renaissance architect Santi Gucci of Kraków fame (see p.432).

If for any reason the ferries aren't running, you'll be forced to take the circuitous route via Puławy; scheduled **buses** run every hour from the village square on the 20km route to Puławy, from where you can take a regular local bus back to Kazimierz.

Sandomierz and beyond

SANDOMIERZ, 80km south of Kazimierz along the Wisła, is another of those small towns described as "quaint" or "picturesque" in the brochures. Its hilltop location certainly fits the bill, though the charm is dented by the evil stench rising from the polluted Wisła. However, a visit is definitely worthwhile, and access is straightforward, with regular train services from Warsaw and buses from Lublin. The one problem is accommodation: the town gets a lot of summer tourists and rooms in season can be very tricky to find; if you're energetic, it's a conceivable day-trip from Lublin.

Like other towns in the southeast, Sandomierz rose to prominence through its position on the medieval trade route running from the Middle East, through southern Russia and the Ukraine, into central Europe. The town was sacked by the Tatars (twice) and the Lithuanians, in the thirteenth and fourteenth centuries respectively, then completely rebuilt by **Kazimierz the Great**, who

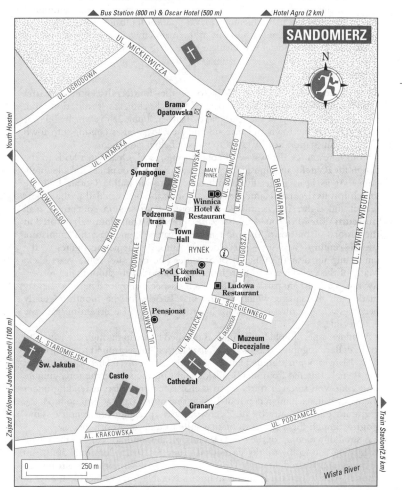

gave it a castle, defensive walls, cathedral and town plan – still visible in the Stare Miasto. Subsequently, Sandomierz flourished on the timber and corn trade, with its links along the Wisła to the Baltic ports. It was also the scene of one of the key religious events in Polish history. In 1570, while Catholics and Protestants were slitting each other's throats in the rest of Europe, members of Poland's non-Catholic churches met here to formulate the so-called **Sandomierz Agreement**, basis for the legally enshrined freedom of conscience later established throughout the country.

Physically, Sandomierz suffered badly at the hands of the Swedes, who blew up the town castle in 1656, and it was only thanks to a minor miracle that it survived World War II intact. In August 1944, as the **Red Army** pushed the Germans back across Poland, the front line moved closer and closer to Sandomierz. A popular story in the town relates how one Colonel Skopenko, an admirer of Sandomierz, managed to steer the fighting away from the town. He was later killed further west: his last wish, duly honoured, was to be buried in the town cemetery. Sadly, the anti-Soviet/Russian sentiments of the post-communist era transformed the man's memory into a political football – the statue in his honour erected after the war in front of the main city gate was recently moved to the out-of-town Soviet War Cemetery, the place of his burial.

The Town

The entrance to the **Stare Miasto** is the fourteenth-century **Brama Opatowska** (Opatowska Gate), part of King Kazimierz's fortifications and. The climb to the top of the gate (daily 10am–5.30pm; 2zł) is worthwhile for the view over the town and surrounding area; local buses coming into town from the bus station northwest of town (see below) stop here.

From here on it's alleyways and cobblestones, as ul. Opatowska leads to the delightful **Rynek**, an atmospheric square with plenty of places for a leisurely coffee. At its heart is the fourteenth-century **town hall**, a Gothic building which had its decorative attic, hexagonal tower and belfry added in the seventeenth and eighteenth centuries. The ground floor section contains a small **museum** (Tues–Fri 9am–4pm, Sat 9am–3pm, Sun 10am–2pm; 3zł) devoted to the history of the town, the most notable feature being an artful miniature twelfth-century chess set – the oldest in Europe – depicting figures of the saints, dug up near the Church of St James (see opposite) some years back. Many of the well-preserved **burghers' houses** positively shout their prosperity: nos. 5 and 10 are particularly fine Renaissance examples. There's a Tuesday market on the square, which, on the first Tuesday of the month, regularly becomes a major rural event, with livestock and produce driven in from the countryside.

A hidden aspect of old Sandomierz is revealed by a trip through the wine and grain **cellars** (signposted as the *podzemna trasa*, or "underground tourist route"; daily 10am–5.30pm – guided Polish-language tours only; 6.50zł) located under the Rynek. Entered from ul. Olesnickich, just off the square, the forty-minute tour takes you through thirty or so Renaissance-era cellars extending under the town hall, reaching a depth of 12m at one point. Back at ground level, the registrar's office on nearby ul. Żydowska was an eighteenth-century **synagogue**, though there is – as so often – little to indicate its origins.

A stroll down either of the streets leading off the southern edge of the square will bring you to the murky **cathedral** (Tues–Sat 10am–2pm & 3–5pm, Sun 3–5pm) constructed around 1360 on the site of an earlier Romanesque church, with substantial Baroque additions. Notable features include the set of early fifteenth-century Russo-Byzantine **murals** in the presbytery, probably by the same artist who painted the Kaplica św, Trójcy in Lublin (see p.301), although these ones haven't been restored anything like as sensitively. Unfortunately they're also kept roped off and unlit most of the time, so unless you strike lucky you'll have to crane your neck to catch a glimpse of them. There are no such problems with the gruesome series of eighteenth-century paintings surrounding the nave, charmingly entitled "The Torture Calendar" and depicting early church martyrs being skewered, decapitated or otherwise maimed in every conceivable way. As if this wasn't enough blood and guts, there's also a group of murals underneath the organ depicting violent scenes from the town's past, including Tatars seemingly enjoying a massacre of the local populace in 1259, Swedes blowing up the castle four centuries later, and more controversially, an incident of supposed Jewish child sacrifice from the same era – a standard theme of popular anti-Semitic discourse of the time – studiously ignored by the local guides.

Set back from the cathedral, the **Muzeum Diecezjalne** (Diocesan Museum; April–Oct Tues–Sat 9am–4pm, Sun 1–4pm; Nov–March Tues–Sat 9am–noon, Sun 1–3pm; 4zł) and its peaceful, well-tended garden was the home of **Jan Długosz** (1415–80), author of one of the first histories of Poland. The building is filled to bursting with an absorbing, well-presented collection of religious art, ceramics, glass and other curios, the latter including a rare early-seventeenth-century portable organ that still works, a collection of Renaissance locks and keys, and a wonderful old pipe supposed to have belonged to Mickiewicz. Among the artistic works there's a fine set of fifteenth- and sixteenth-century altarpieces and other religious art from Małopolska churches, a powerful Romanesque *Madonna and Child* stone carving, a delicate early-fifteenth-century *Three Saints* triptych from Kraków, a *John the Baptist* attributed to Caravaggio, and a notable collection of nineteenth-century icons from the town's former Orthodox church, abandoned by the retreating Russians in 1915.

Downhill from the cathedral is the **castle**, where the large open terrace affords good views back over the Stare Miasto. It's also used for open-air concerts and theatre performances in summer. The **museum** here (Tues–Sun 10am–5pm; 4zł), occupying part of the building, holds a pretty undistinguished permanent collection, although the high-profile temporary exhibitions mounted here over the summer usually make up for the disappointment. Towards the river stands a medieval **granary**; others are to be found north along the river. Aleja Staromiejska runs from in front of the castle to the **Kościól św Jakuba** (St James's Church), a lime-shaded late-Romanesque building that's thought to be the first brick basilica in Poland – its restored entrance portal is particularly striking. Inside, the **Martyrs' Chapel** (Mon–Sat 9am–1pm & 3–5pm, Sun 11am–1pm & 3–5pm) has a vivid painting of the martyrdom of local Dominicans by the Tatars in 1260, while in the northern nave there are glass cases said to contain the bones of the murdered monks.

The area around the church was the site of the original town, destroyed by the Tatars. Archeological digs in the area have uncovered a wealth of finds including the twelfth-century chess set now on display in the town museum (see opposite). Since the 1960s, this whole southern district has had to be shored up, owing to subsidence caused by the network of tunnels and cellars dug for grain storage and running for hundreds of metres through the soft undersoil.

Head back down the path in front of St James and you re-enter the town walls through the **Ucho Igielne**, a small entrance shaped like the eye of a needle.

Practicalities

The **train** and **bus stations** are on opposite sides of town (3km south over the other side of the river and 1.5km northwest respectively), a bus ride (#8 or #11 respectively) from the centre. For the time being, **tourist information** is handled by the PTTK office at Rynek 26 (May–Aug daily 8am–3pm; Sept–April Mon–Fri only; ☎015/832 2305), which has a list of private rooms (❶) in town and might ring them up on your behalf if the staff are in a good mood.

In the town centre at least, **accommodation** is in fairly short supply. At the top end of the scale, the *Hotel Pod Ciżemką*, Rynek 27 (☎015/832 0550; ❻), is an intimate, small hotel offering plush en-suites; while the family run *Królowej Jadwigi*, down the hill past the castle at ul. Krakowska 24 (☎015/832 2988; ❹) offers a similarly low number of cosy, well-appointed rooms at half the price. The *Oscar*, ul. Mickiewicza 17 (☎015/832 1144; ❹), is another reasonable-quality place, improbably situated on the top floors of an office block just down from the bus station. The *Winnica*, ul. Maly Rynek 2 (☎015/832 3130; ❷), is a restaurant right by the main square which lets out simple rooms with shared facilities.

The other options, most of them well out of the town centre, are the *Zacisze*, ul. Portowa 3a (☎015/832 1905; ❸), a small, clean overnighter 3km south of town; and the *Agro*, ul. Mokoszyńska 5 (☎015/833 3106; ❷), which has a mixture of en-suites and rooms with shared bathrooms in a quiet park 2km north of the centre, off the Lublin road. Finally, there's a summer-only **youth hostel** at ul. Krępniaki 6 (July–Aug; ☎015/832 2652; 20zł per person), an easy walk west of the Stare Miasto.

There are plenty of **places to eat** and **drink** around the Rynek, many of which boast attractive outdoor terraces for people-watching. *Kawiarna Staromiejska* on the southern side of the square doles out light meals like *pierogi* and soups as well as coffee and cakes; while the next-door *Trzidiesatka* offers a more filling range of Polish standards. Just off the northern end of the square, the *Ha Noi*, ul. Sokolnickiego 8, offers decent Vietnamese fare, including inexpensive lunchtime set meals. The first-floor restuarant of the *Pod Ciżenką* is as good as any in town (see above); while slightly further afield, the restaurant of the *Królowej Jadwigi* offers traditional home-cooking in endearingly chintzy surroundings (see above).

For **entertainment** the *Lapidarium*, a cellar club beneath the town hall, has regular discos and occasional live gigs. The town puts on an annual week-long **music festival** from late June to early July, featuring a variety of classical, folk and jazz concerts; check with the PTTK office for this year's details.

South from Sandomierz

South of Sandomierz along the Wisła basin you soon find yourself heading into the gritty landscape of **TARNOBRZEG**, a major industrial centre with similarly dim surroundings. Although it was previously a poor and neglected rural backwater, since World War II the region has been transformed by the growth of the mining industry built up as a result of the large sulphur deposits discovered around the town.

The sulphur may have done wonders for the local economy, but its exploitation has had serious effects on the environment; travelling through you can see and smell the stuff everywhere. Similar comments apply to **STALOWA WOLA**, 30km east of Tarnobrzeg, another major industrial city created round a burgeoning steel and metal industry in the late 1930s. The castle at **Baranów Sandomierski**, significantly affected by the pollution, will be most people's main reason for visiting the area.

Baranów Sandomierski

Fifteen kilometres south of Tarnobrzeg on the eastern bank of the Wisła, **BARANÓW SANDOMIERSKI**'s chief claim to fame is the spectacular castle located at the edge of the town.

Erected on the site of a fortified medieval structure owned by the Baranów family, the exquisitely formed and well-preserved Renaissance **castle** (Tues–Sat 9am–3pm, Sun 9am–4pm; 5zł), thought to have been designed by Santi Gucci (see Kraków, p.404) is as fine a period piece as you'll come across anywhere, well worth the out-of-the-way trek needed to get here. The epithet "castle" is actually a bit of a misnomer – behind an elegant Italianate facade the rectangular building is really a glorified palace with some fortifications added onto the front for appearance's sake. The place's sumptuously palatial feel is confirmed, too, by a wander through the carefully manicured gardens on the south side of the building. Built in the 1590s for the wealthy Leszczyński family, the castle is constructed on a rectangular plan with an inner courtyard, corner towers and a gateway. The facade is crowned by an attic with a cheerful frieze decoration. In through the gateway you find yourself in a delicately cool, animated Italianate courtyard surrounded on three sides by two tiers of sinuously arcaded passageways, their ceilings decorated with a wealth of family emblems. To reach the upper level you climb the sweeping outer staircase – a later addition – on the southern side of the courtyard. Before doing that it's worth studying the entertaining collection of face-pulling grotesques, many of them animal figures, that decorate the base of the rosette-topped pillars ranged around the courtyard. Inside the building, you can view a section of the ground floor that has retained its ornate period furnishings. Down in the castle basement there's a small **museum** displaying exhibits relating to the local sulphur industry – hardly surprising, since the castle was taken over after World War II by one of the major Tarnobrzeg industrial sulphur concerns.

The lavishly decorated rooms of the upper floors of the castle are occupied by a luxury **hotel**, the *Zamkowy* (☎015/811 8039, ⓦ www.baranow.motornik .com.pl; ❺) with a high-quality **restaurant** used for banquets. Though fairly expensive, the place is understandably popular, so particularly in summer you'd be well advised to book ahead. A cheaper and perfectly acceptable alternative is the *Zajazd Wisła*, about 1km out of town, on ul. Dąbrowskiego (☎015/811 0383; ❷), with its own restaurant.

Unless you've your own transport the only way to get to the castle is by **bus**: local services run fairly regularly from Tarnobrzeg, which is accessible by bus from Sandomierz, or by train from Lublin or Rzeszów. On arrival in Baranów, buses drop off at a stop beyond the castle entrance gates before continuing to the main bus terminal on the Rynek, a ten-minute walk from the castle.

Zamość

The old towns and palaces of southeast Poland often have a Latin feel to them, and none more so than **ZAMOŚĆ**, 96km southeast of Lublin. The brainchild of the dynamic sixteenth-century chancellor Jan Zamoyski, the town is a remarkable demonstration of the way the Polish intelligentsia and ruling class looked towards Italy for ideas, despite the proximity of Russia. Zamoyski, in many ways the archetypal Polish Renaissance man, built this model town to his own ideological specifications close to his childhood village, commissioning the design from Bernardo Morando of Padua – the city where he had earlier studied. Morando produced a beautiful Italianate period piece, with a wide piazza, grid-plan streets, an academy and defensive bastions. These fortifications were obviously well thought out, as Zamość was one of the few places to withstand the seventeenth-century "Swedish Deluge" that flattened so many other Polish towns. Strategically located on the major medieval trading routes linking Kraków and Kiev from west to east, Lublin and L'viv from north to south, the town attracted an international array of merchants from early on, notably Jews, Armenians, Greeks, Scots, Hungarians and Italians, whose presence remains embedded in the diverse architecture of the city.

War returned to Zamość early the twentieth century, when the area was the scene of an important battle during the Polish–Russian war of 1919–20. The Red Army, which only weeks before had looked set to take Warsaw, was beaten decisively near the town, forcing Lenin to sue for peace with his newly independent neighbours. Somehow, Zamość managed also to get through World War II unscathed, so what you see today is one of Europe's best-preserved Renaissance town centres, classified by UNESCO as an outstanding historical monument. Chiefly due to its off-the-beaten-track location, the town

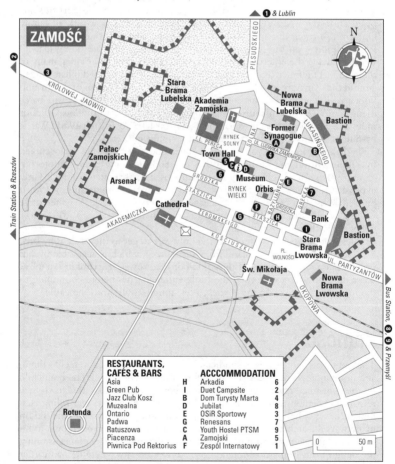

RESTAURANTS, CAFÉS & BARS		ACCCOMMODATION	
Asia	H	Arkadia	6
Green Pub	I	Duet Campsite	2
Jazz Club Kosz	B	Dom Turysty Marta	4
Muzealna	D	Jubilat	8
Ontario	E	OSiR Sportowy	3
Padwa	G	Renesans	7
Ratuszowa	C	Youth Hostel PTSM	9
Piacenza	A	Zamojski	5
Piwnica Pod Rektorius	F	Zespól Internatowy	1

hasn't yet assumed the prominence it deserves on the tourist trail, though this is beginning to change as a result of the increasing hype being created by tourist authorities in Poland and abroad.

Arrival and information

Fewer and fewer trains seem to use the **train station** located 1km southwest of the centre off ul. Akademiczka, so it's easiest to approach Zamość by bus from Lublin. The main **bus station** is roughly 2km east of the town centre (buses #10, #22 or #59 will take you in). Zamość's well-stocked and helpful **tourist office**, underneath the town hall at Rynek 13 (May–Sept Mon–Fri 8am–6pm, Sat 10am–4pm, Sun 10am–3pm; Oct–April Mon–Fri 10am–4pm; ☎084/639 2292, ✉zoil@zamosc.um.gov.pl) will provide information on the small number of private rooms (❶–❷) in town, and will advise on other accommodation possibilities as well. The nearby **Orbis office** at ul. Grodzka 18 (Mon–Fri 9am–5pm; ☎084/638 5775) deals with advance bus and train tickets.

Accommodation

There's still not enough centrally located **accommodation** to satisfy the growing demand, although the situation looks to be gradually improving. There's a wider variety of places to choose from if you're prepared to stay some way out from the Stare Miasto area. A decent **youth hostel**, *PTSM*, is located between the bus station and Stare Miasto at ul. Zamoyskiego 4 (July–Aug; ☎084/627 9125; 22zł per person). The *Duet* **campsite** on ul. Królowej Jadwigi (☎084/639 2499), 2km west of the town centre, has a few bungalows (❷), but they fill up quickly.

Hotels

Arkadia Rynek 9 ☎084/638 6507. Intimate hotel in a prime second-floor location overlooking the main square, offering comfortable en-suites with TV. Only has six rooms, so competition for them is likely to be fierce in summer. ❹

Dom Turysty Marta ul. Zamenhofa 11 ☎084/639 2639. Smallish but superbly central hotel-cum-hostel with nine rooms, most of which are dorms. One double (❶) if you can get it, otherwise it's 20zł per person in the dorms. Breakfast not included. ❶

Jubilat ul. Wyszńskiego 52 ☎084/638 6401. Owned by the same company as the *Renesans* (see below). Similarly classy and aimed at international tourist groups though the location, just behind the bus station, is definitely a step down from its partner. Weekend discounts. ❺

OSiR Sportowy ul. Królowej Jadwigi 14 ☎084/638 6011. Recently renovated athletes' hotel located in a sports complex, 500m west of

the centre next to the football stadium. Roomy en-suites, but breakfast isn't included – there is, however, a café on site. ❸

Renesans ul. Grecka 6 ☎084/639 2001. Reasonably comfortable Stare Miasto hotel option in an outwardly ugly concrete building handily close to the Rynek. Weekend discounts. ❺

Zamojski ul. Kołłątaja 2/4/6 ☎084/639 2516, ✉zamosc@orbis.pl. Spanking new hotel with plush rooms located in a historic town house just off the Rynek. Definitely the hotel of choice if you're prepared to fork out the readies. Twenty-percent discounts at weekends. ❻

Zespól Internatowy ul. Koszary 7 ☎084/638 4842. University-run guesthouse offering neat and tidy en-suites with TV. About 1km north of the Stare Miasto, next to a barracks: follow ul. Piłsudskiego (the main Lublin road) north and turn right when you see a jet fighter mounted on a plinth. ❷

The Stare Miasto

Regulation-issue urban development surrounds Zamość's historic core, and both **bus** and **train stations** are sited some way from the centre. It's worth taking a bus or taxi to the edge of **plac Wolności**, bordering the Rynek. Once there, you should have no problem finding your way around the Renaissance grid.

The Rynek

The **Rynek**, also known as pl. Mickiewicza, is a couple of blocks in from pl. Wolności and the partly preserved circuit of walls. Ringed by a low arcade and the decorative former homes of the Zamość mercantile bourgeoisie, the geometrically designed square – exactly 100m in both width and length – is a superb example of Renaissance town architecture, a wide open space whose columned arcades, decorated facades and breezy walkways exude an upliftingly light, airy warmth. Dominating the ensemble from the north side of the square is the **town hall**, a soaring showstopper that's among the most photographed buildings in the country. A solid, three-storey structure topped by a tall clock tower and spire, the original, lower construction designed by Morando acquired its present Mannerist modelling in the 1640s, the sweeping, fan-shaped double stairway jutting out from the entrance being added in the following century. Successive renovations have kept the building in reasonable shape – though now the peeling plasterwork on the staircase has been repaired, it would be good to see the main tower finally receiving a new coat of paint. The floodlighting used at night in summer heightens the power of the building, combining with the visual backdrop of the square to undeniably impressive effect. Occupied by local government offices, the town hall doesn't offer much to see inside; even the room commemorating the pivotal socialist-feminist theorist Rosa Luxemburg, born east of the square at ul. Staszica 37, has now been removed.

The Dom Wilczeka and town museum

From the town hall the vaulted arcade stretching east along ul. Ormiańska features several of the finest houses on the square. Once inhabited by the Armenian merchants who moved here under special privilege in 1585, the houses are fronted by facades that are a whirl of rich, decorative ornamentation, with a noticeable intermesh of Oriental motifs. First along is the splendid **Dom Wilczeka** (Wilczek House), built by an early professor at the Zamość Academy, with some fine decorated bas-reliefs of Christ, Mary and the Apostles gracing the upper storey of the facade. Number 26 sports similarly exuberant decoration, this time using animal themes, lions and dragons included. It and the adjoining mansions house the town **museum** (Tues–Sun 10am–4pm; 4zł): inevitably, the exhibitions focus on the Zamoyskis, with plenty of portraits of the town's founder and other assorted family memorabilia. An additional plus is the interior, with much of the original decoration, wooden ceilings, carved portals and fresco decoration well restored and preserved. Back out of the museum the sumptuous facades continue, no. 24 (part of the museum) featuring a prim-looking Renaissance couple peering down from between the windows, and no. 22 next door bearing a relief of a beatific Mary trampling a fierce-looking dragon underfoot.

The Morando Kamienica

The east side of the square, once another haunt of Armenian merchants and teachers at the Academy, is similarly enjoyable: here as all around the square it's well worth wandering along the vaulted passageways and in through the doorways (many are now shops and several of them beautifully decorated), notably at no. 6, a bookshop, and no. 2, a 350-year-old apothecary. The southern side of the square contains some of the oldest and most obviously Italian-influenced mansions, two-storey buildings with regularly proportioned facades, several designed by Morando himself.

The **Morando Kamienica** (Morando Tenement House) at no. 25, where the great architect himself used to live, boasts an impressive facade with exuberant Mannerist friezes, while the PTTK office at no. 31, in the corner of the square, features some fine stuccowork in the vestibule and another beautifully decorated portal and surrounding vault.

West of the square

Moving west of the square, first port of call is the towering collegiate church, recently cleaned up and upgraded to a **cathedral**, a magnificent Mannerist basilica designed by Morando to Zamoyski's exacting instructions. A three-aisled structure with numerous side chapels, thin, delicate pillars reaching up to the ceiling and a fine vaulted presbytery, the whole interior is marked by a strong sense of visual and architectural harmony, a powerful expression of the self-confidence of the Polish Counter-Reformation.

The **presbytery** houses a finely wrought eighteenth-century Rococo silver tabernacle, as well as a series of paintings of scenes from the life of St Thomas attributed to Domenico Tintoretto. The Zamoyski family **chapel**, the grandest in the building, contains the marble tomb of Chancellor Jan topped by some elegant Baroque stuccowork by the Italian architect, J.B. Falconi. Adjoining the main building is a high **bell tower**, the oldest and biggest of its bells – known as Jan after its benefactor – over three hundred years old. As with the town hall the whole site is floodlit in summer, creating another impressive ensemble.

West across the main road, ul. Akademiczka, are two buildings that played a key role in the historic life of the town. As its name implies the **Arsenał** (arsenal), built by Morando in the 1580s, is where the town's ample stock of weaponry used to be kept alongside Zamoyski spoils of war. These days it houses a small **military museum** (Tues–Sun 9am–4pm; 3zł) where, among the pictures of Polish soldiers through the ages, you can view a scale model of the seventeenth-century town, surrounded by defensive bastions arranged in the shape of a seven-pointed star .

The massive **Pałac Zamojskich** (Zamoyski Palace) beyond the arsenal is a shadow of its former self, the original Morando-designed building having undergone substantial modification after the Zamoyskis abandoned the place in the early nineteenth century, when it was taken over by the army and later became a hospital. The shabby old palace courtyard at the back of the building hints at former glories, but otherwise it's a rather mournful, run-down looking place, currently occupied by the town court.

Returning to the Arsenał and heading southwest along Akademiczka, you'll arrive after five minutes at the **Wystawa Plenerna** (May–Oct: Tues–Sun 9am–8pm; 2zł), the open-air section of the Arsenał museum, a tiny scrap of parkland where a helicopter and several post-World War II artillery pieces are parked for your perusal. Ten minutes further on, opposite the train station, the town **zoo** (daily 9am–7pm; 4zł) is worthy of a stroll as much for the neatly trimmed horticultural splendour of the park-like grounds as for the animals themselves.

The former Jewish quarter

Continuing north along ul. Akademiczka, west of the main street is the **Stara Brama Lubelska** (Old Lublin Gate), oldest of the entranceways dotted around the Stare Miasto fortifications, and long since bricked up. These days the gate is stranded on the edge of school playing fields, the bas-relief uncovered during renovation earlier this century providing a glimpse of earlier glories.

The impressive-looking former **Akademia Zamojska** (Zamoyski Academy) across the street, built in the 1630s and an important Polish centre of learning until its enforced closure at the start of the Partitions era, is now a school, albeit on a humbler scale than originally. Beyond it, much of the northern section of the Stare Miasto belongs to the former **Jewish quarter**, centred around ul. Zamenhofa and Rynek Solny. As in so many other eastern towns, Jews made up a significant portion of the population of Zamość – some 45 percent on the eve of World War II. The first Sephardic Jews from L'viv settled here in the 1580s, their numbers subsequently swelled by kindred settlers from Turkey, Italy and Holland, to be displaced subsequently by the powerful local Askenazi community. With much of eastern Polish Jewry in the grip of the mystical Hassidic revival, uniquely in the Lublin region Zamość developed as a centre for the progressive *Haskalah*, an Enlightenment-inspired movement originating in Germany that advocated social emancipation, the acceptance of "European" culture and scientific and educational progress within the Jewish community. Among its products were **Itzak Peretz** (1851–1915), a notable nineteenth-century Yiddish novelist born here, and **Rosa Luxemburg** (1870–1919), though it's as a radical communist theorist and activist rather than Jewish progressive that she's primarily known.

Virtually the entire old Jewish quarter is currently being renovated – another *remont* that looks set to run and run – but from the edge of the building site you can still peer through at some of the old Jewish merchants' houses ranged around the small square. The most impressive Jewish monument, however, is the **former synagogue**, now a shabby looking public library, a fine early-seventeenth-century structure built as part of Zamoyski's original town scheme. Following wartime devastation by the Nazis, who used the building as a carpentry shop, the synagogue was carefully renovated in the 1960s, and its exterior elevations reconstructed. Traces of the dazzling original decoration have survived too, notably the rich polychromy that once filled the interior, sections of which are still visible behind the stacks of library books filling the main body of the building, the ceiling vaulting and the stone **Aron ha Kodesh**.

The town fortifications

East across ul. Łukasińskiego takes you over onto the former town fortifications. Designed by Morando, the original Italian-inspired fortifications consisted of a set of seven **bastions** interspersed with three main gates with wide moats and artificial lakes blocking the approaches to the town on every side. After holding out so impressively against the Cossacks and the Swedes, the whole defensive system went under in 1866, when the Russians ordered the upper set of battlements to be blown up and the town fortress liquidated. A park area covers much of the battlements now, leaving you free to wander along the tops and see for yourself why the marauding Swedes drew a blank at Zamość. The ornamental **Stara Brama Lwowska** (Old Lvov Gate), another Morando construction, bricked up in the 1820s, and the **Nowa Brama Lwowska** (New Lvov Gate), added at the same time, complete the surviving elements of the fortifications.

Across pl. Wolności, the former Franciscan church, part of an old monastic complex and now an art school, is only half the building it used to be, having lost its Baroque towers in the 1870s. Into the southern section of the Stare Miasto the former Orthodox **Cerkiew św. Mikołaja** (Church of St Nicholas), at the bottom of ul. Bazylianska, a small domed building originally used by the town's many Eastern merchants, still has some of its fine original Renaissance stucco, uncovered during recent renovations of the interior.

The Rotunda

The Nazis spared the buildings of Zamość, but not its people. In the **Rotunda**, a nineteenth-century arsenal ten minutes' walk south of the Stare Miasto on ul. Wyspiańskiego, over eight thousand local people were executed by the Germans; a simple **museum** housed in its tiny cells (Tues–Sun: May–Sept 9am–8pm; Oct–April 10am–1pm) tells the harrowing story of the town's wartime trauma. In fact, Zamość (preposterously renamed "Himmlerstadt") and the surrounding area were the target of a brutal "relocation" scheme of the kind already carried out by the Nazis in Western Prussia. From 1942 to 1943 nearly three hundred villages were cleared of their Polish inhabitants and their houses taken by German settlers – all part of Hitler's plan to create an Aryan eastern bulwark of the Third Reich. The remaining villages were apparently left alone only because the SS didn't have enough forces to clear them out. Reflecting the opening up of other previously taboo subjects, three cells in the complex have recently been dedicated to the Soviet-instigated wartime massacre of Polish army officers at Katyń, as well as a sombre chapel in memory of local people deported to Siberia following the Soviet occupation of eastern Poland in 1939.

The Jewish cemetery

There's a tiny surviving **Jewish cemetery** at the north end of ul. Prosta, a fifteen-minute walk northeast of the Stare Miasto. A monument made out of gravestones uprooted by the Nazis commemorates the many thousands of the town's Jewish population they murdered. Interestingly, the monument was erected in 1950, a good deal earlier than in many Jewish centres in Poland.

Eating, drinking and entertainment

Under the influences of privatization and a growing tourist trade, restaurant and bar life in the Stare Miasto is flourishing. Outside the summer season, though, most places shut early in the evening, and anytime after about 8pm you may be hard-pressed to get a meal. There are numerous places on the main Rynek which seem to combine the roles of **café** and **restaurant** in a single establishment, all of which move tables out onto the square in summer. The slick *Ratuszowa*, strategically placed under the town hall, is top of the new-look crop of cafés, serving daytime meals as well as decent cappuccinos and cakes. Other obvious choices include the appropriately named *Padwa*, Rynek 23, which has a wonderful original ceiling, a posh cellar restaurant and a pleasant back courtyard section as well as the stylish café fronting the square. *Muzealna*, Rynek 30, also does the standard range of Polish food; while the *Asia* on the south side of the Rynek at ul. Staszica 10 is a cheap source of filling Chinese fare – and pizzas. For more of the latter, *Piacenza*, Zamenhofa 10, is a cosy little pizzeria-pub located in a basement just off the square to the north. *Ontario*, on the corner of Pereca and Bazyliański, is a brash mixture of fast-food joint (serving everything from goulash to pizza), pool hall and youth-oriented pub.

For **drinking**, most people opt for the al-fresco bars girdling the Rynek in summer. Of the indoor venues, the *Piwnica Pod Rektorius*, Rynek 2, is the best of several basement beer halls around the square; while *Green Pub*, a short distance east at Staszica 2, has a suave, upmarket cocktail bar feel, and also does restaurant-quality food. *Jazz Club Kosz*, ul. Zamenhofa 5 (entrance through the rear courtyard), periodically hosts live jazz and blues gigs, and is a pleasant place for moodily sprawling around on dark couches on other nights – it also has a small snack-food menu.

If you happen to be in town at the right time there are several annual cultural happenings worth checking out. The **Zamość Jazz Na Kresach** ("Borderlands") festival, usually held in the last week of May or early June, is popular with Polish and other Slav jazzers, as is the **International Meeting of Jazz Vocalists** in the final week of September. **Theatrical Summer**, a drama festival held in the latter part of June and early July, features some excellent theatre groups from all over the country, many of whom perform on the stairway in front of the town hall. The tourist office (see p.335) will have details of all the above.

Southwest from Zamość

Southwest of Zamość lies more of the open, sparsely populated countryside characteristic of much of the country's eastern borderlands. The agricultural monotony is broken by occasional forests, the few surviving swaths of the *puszcza* that once covered the whole area. The biggest of these, now protected by the bounds of the **Roztoczański national park**, offers a glimpse of something akin to the original untamed wilderness. A couple of enjoyable minor towns, **Szczebrzeszyn** and **Zwierzyniec**, provide the area's additional attractions.

Szczebrzeszyn

Twenty kilometres southwest of Zamość lies **SZCZEBRZESZYN**, a sleepy little town whose rural anonymity is belied by its tongue-twister of a name – even Polish children have difficulty with this one. Despite the usual historical depredations – in their time Cossacks, Swedes, Turks and Nazis have all had a go at the place – there are enough historical monuments to justify a stopoff, if you happen to be passing this way. The Stare Miasto square provides the focus of attention. On the west side **Kościół św. Katarzyny** (St Catherine's Church), an exuberant piece of Mannerist architecture modelled on the Cathedral (see p.337) in Zamość, has a fine Renaissance doorway and soothing, vaulted interior laced with rich stuccowork. **Kościół św. Mikołaja** (St Nicholas's Church), on the other side of the square, is from the same era but with rather fewer of its original fittings, a result of Cossack plundering during their assault on the town in 1648. The town's best-known building, however, is the **former synagogue** on the northwest side of the square, an imposing early-seventeenth-century brick structure – in fact one of the country's largest – likewise ransacked by the Cossacks, which served the large Jewish population up until World War II. Turned into a cultural centre following its postwar reconstruction from the ruins left by the Nazis, elements of the original synagogue decoration are still visible in the main hall, including the bema and parts of the decorative frieze work. A recently erected tablet outside the building recalls its original use as well as the wartime slaughter of the town's 3000-strong Jewish community. Five hundred metres up the hill behind the synagogue, past the abandoned-looking Orthodox Church, is the **Jewish cemetery**, as overgrown and lonely as any you'll find in this part of the country but with an unusually large number of tombstones still standing among the ruins, the oldest dating back to the early 1700s.

Practicalities

Szczebrzeszyn is hardly overflowing with tourist facilities, and after looking round its monuments you'd be well advised either to press onwards to Zwierzyniec or head back to Zamość – both places are served by regular **buses** from the station just off the main square. If you need **a place to stay**, the *Zajazd pod Bażantem*, Zwierzyniecka 19A (☎084/682 1297; ❷), is a small pension-style hotel with restaurant attached 2km southwest of the square on the main road to Zwierzyniec.

Zwierzyniec

Eleven kilometres further south from Szczebrzeszyn is **ZWIERZYNIEC**, whose main function, for visitors at least, is as principal gateway to the **Roztoczański national park** (see below). Frequent local bus connections to and from Zamość make a day-trip to the forest a feasible option. This tiny town owes its existence to sixteenth-century chancellor Jan Zamoyski, who purchased the surrounding forests in 1589 and commissioned Bernardo Morando (of Zamość fame) to build him a country palace here. The palace was pulled down in the 1830s, but the village that had grown up around it remained, as did elements of the original palace complex, some of which you can still see today. Chief among these is the Zamoyski **chapel**, a delicate Baroque construction scenically located on one of a series of islands in the willow-fringed palace lake, reached by a bridge. Beyond the lake, ul. Browara curves past the grand early-nineteenth-century town brewery to the national park museum, the **Ośrodek Muzealny RPN** (Tues–Sun: May–Oct 9am–5pm, Nov–April 9am–4pm; 2zł), which contains a display of stuffed birds from around the world, as well as an information desk where you can pick up advice and maps before heading into the park itself.

Practicalities

The **bus station** is five minutes north of the lake, on the far side of an unkempt town park. The only dependable **accommodation** option is the National Park-run *Jodła*, ul. Parkowa 3a (☎084/687 2012; ❷–❸), an attractive ensemble of three villas right beside the bus station offering en-suites and rooms with shared facilities. Otherwise there's a seasonal **youth hostel** in a former school one block north of the bus station at ul. Partyzantów 3 (May–Sept; ☎084/87 2142; 18zł per head) and the Echo **campsite** at ul. Biłgorajska 3 (☎084/687 2314), which also has some three- and six-bed cabins (50zł per person).

For **eating**, *Karczma Młyn*, facing the lake on ul. Aleksandry Wachniewskiej, serves up a reasonable selection of meaty Polish favourites in homely timber surroundings. The café-bar at the Zwierzynec brewery, just round the corner, is the best place to sample the local beer, a smooth lager-style brew that is extremely difficult to find outside the region.

The Roztoczański national park

Twenty kilometres southwest of Zamość, the wild expanses of the **Roztoczański national park** are a must for both walkers and naturalists. Part of the huge former Zamoyski family estate that used to cover much of the Zamość region, the park, created in 1974, covers an area of almost eighty square kilometres of the Roztocze district, a picturesque region of undulating, forest-covered hills, rising to 390m at their highest point. The existence of an immensely varied and colourful flora and fauna, including over 190 different species of birds, 30 types of tree and 40 species of protected plant can be traced back to Jan Zamoyski. After purchasing the area in 1589 he turned the forest into a prototype nature reserve, as opposed to the more usual aristocratic hunting ground. His plan even included a section of enclosed game reserve: among the animals kept here were the last of the original tarpans (see Białowieża, p.283), who died out in the nineteenth century, only to be reintroduced in the 1980s in the genetically bred modern variant enthusiastically promoted as a tourist attraction by the park authorities.

Cutting across the heart of the park is the beautiful and largely uncontaminated **River Wieprz**, which has its source just east. Most of the park consists of forest and woodland, with pine, fir and pockets of towering beeches (up to 50m high) the commonest trees. Grey storks, cranes, lizards, wild horses, a wealth of butterflies and, along the banks of the Wieprz, beavers, are among the creatures populating the area.

Walking in the park

Maps and detailed information about **hiking routes** in the park are available from the national park office located in the Ośrodek Muzealny RPN (see p.341) where you can also buy the **ticket** (2zł) required for entering the area. The park is easily navigable with the help of a local map, with several short walks branching off from the museum itself. The easiest of these leads southeast through pine forest to the reed-shrouded Echo lake (15min), the northern banks of which boast a wonderful, sloping sandy **beach**. Another popular trail traces the old palace path southwest to Bukowa Gora (20min), an upland area of dense woodland where daylight is almost blotted out by the thick canopy of beech and firs. On the far side of Bukowa Gora lies an area of sandy-soiled heath and some fine views southwards: from here you can work your way eastwards towards Echo lake in about twenty minutes.

Rzeszów

Roughly 170km south of Lublin, **RZESZÓW** was essentially a postwar attempt to revive the southeast, providing industry and an administrative centre for an area that had seen the previous half-dozen decades' heaviest emigration. The city's population of over 100,000 is evidence of some sort of success, even if this rapid expansion has produced a soulless urban sprawl. Yet the hinterland still consists of the small villages characteristic of this corner of Poland for centuries, which explains why in 1980 Rzeszów became a nucleus of Rural Solidarity, the independent farmers' and peasants' union formed in the wake of its better-known urban counterpart. A decade on from the fall of communism, moreover, it's a prime example of the way the new economic order is gradually penetrating those eastern reaches of the country traditionally most resistant to change: some way behind Kraków or Warsaw, perhaps, but a marked improvement nonetheless. If the above suggests you might not want to spend Christmas in Rzeszów, there's little that a visit will do to persuade you otherwise: essentially this is a city to see in transit.

Rzeszów has good bus connections to the rural towns of the Beskid Nisky to the south, and the Bieszczady region to the southeast; it's also the obvious jumping-off point for the palace at **Łańcut**, 20km to the east.

Arrival and accommodation

The **bus** and **train stations** are adjacent to each other, a short walk north from the centre. Most of the **hotels** are reasonably close to the stations. The *Polonia*, right opposite the train station at ul. Grottgera 16 (℗017/852 0312; ❹), offers 1970s furnishings and en-suite facilities; the *Sportowy*, fifteen minutes' walk west of the stations at ul. Jałowego 23a (℗017/862 4935; ❷–❸), is

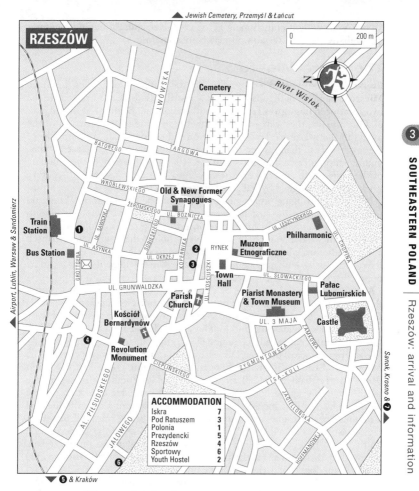

a cheap, no-frills sports hotel, offering en-suites and rooms with shared facilities; and the *Iskra*, ul. Dąbrowskiego 75 (☎017/854 9740; ❸), is a recently renovated mid-range place an inconvenient 2km south of the centre on the Sanok road. Moving up in quality, a recent overhaul has transformed the large *Rzeszów*, al. Cieplińskiego 2 (☎017/853 3389, ⒺRzeszow@hotelesemako .com.pl; ❻), from a notoriously dingy communist-era haunt into a respectable, if pricey, hotel – though the rooms haven't got any bigger. The conveniently central *Pod Ratuszem*, just off the Rynek at ul. Matejki 8 (☎017/852 9780, Ⓦwww.hotelpodratuszem.rzeszow.pl; ❺) offers cosy and bright en-suites with TV, although it's a small place and you should reserve in advance if possible. The plushest option in town is the *Prezydencki*, ul. Podwisłocze 48 (☎017/862 6835, Ⓔprezydencki@hotelesemako.com.pl; ❼), a bland but serviceable businessman-friendly slab of concrete some 2km south of the centre.

The all-year **youth hostel** (☎017/863 4430; 23zł per person) is bang in the square at Rynek 25, the major disadvantage being the nonstop noise from the pizzeria and all-night bar on the ground floor.

There's currently no functioning IT office in Rzeszów, although the municipal **website** (Ⓦwww.rzeszow.pl) may be of some use.

The Stare Miasto

Everything worth seeing is located within the compact confines of the **Stare Miasto** area, south of the main stations across al. Piłsudskiego. First stop are the two **former synagogues** facing each other along ul. Bożnicza at the edge of pl. Ofiara Getta, the heart of the old ghetto area and all that remains of the town's formerly sizeable Jewish population – the monument in the middle of the square isn't to them, as you might expect, but a typical 1960s piece of communist agitprop erected in honour of the "1000th anniversary of the founding of the Polish state (1967)". The new synagogue, a large seventeenth-century brick building designed by Italian architect Giovanni Bellotti, is now an artists' centre with a changing display of exhibitions on the ground floor. Wander up to the *kawiarnia* on the first floor and you'll probably find someone able to point out the surviving features of the original synagogue. The old synagogue, over a century older and gutted by the Nazis, houses the town archives as well as a recently formed research institute devoted to the history of the Rzeszów Jewry. Both these buildings are looking decidedly tatty these days, so it's to be hoped that the ongoing city clean-up programme will extend to them.

A short walk south brings you to the Rynek, a bustling, chaotic place two-thirds of the way through major restoration: if work ever finishes it will be a fine location. Plumped in the square centre, as ever, is the **town hall**, very much the town's trademark, and looking all the better for a recent facelift. A squat sixteenth-century edifice remodelled in the nineteenth century, it looks like an engaging cross between Disney-cartoon castle and Baroque church. The **Muzeum Etnograficzne** (Ethnographic Museum; Tues–Thurs & Sun 9am–2pm, Fri 9am–5pm; 3zł), in one of the older burghers' houses on the south side of the square, contains a small but well-presented collection of local ethnography. Exhibits include a fine set of the colourful Eastern-influenced traditional local costumes and some good examples of the naive folk art of the region, as well as a couple of complete wayside shrines of the kind you find dotting local highways and byways. The statue of Kościuszko on the square, removed by the Germans in 1940, was finally replaced in 1980, thanks to the efforts of the local Solidarity committee.

Directly west of the Rynek is the main **parish church**, a Gothic structure that was given its current Baroque overlay in the eighteenth century, notable exceptions being the fine Renaissance decoration in the vaulted nave ceiling and a number of early tombstone tablets up by the altar. South down ul. 3 Maja, the main shopping thoroughfare, brings you to a former Piarist monastery complex, home of the well-stocked **town museum** (Tues & Fri 10am–5pm, Wed & Thurs 10am–3pm, Sun 9am–3pm; 3zł) ranged around the monastery courtyard. As well as Polish and European painting, the collection includes the frescoes that once decorated the former cloister arcade and a revealing set of exhibits detailing the mass emigrations from the region in the late nineteenth century. Inevitably, the exhibition finishes with details of both local resistance and Nazi atrocities against the town's Jewish population during World War II. The **monastery church** next door has a typically elegant Baroque facade fashioned by Tylman of Gameren in the early 1700s, and a small but well-proportioned interior.

On to the bottom of ul. 3 Maja, past the post office, takes you past the **Pałac Lubomirskich** (Lubomirski Palace), another early-eighteenth-century Tylman of Gameren creation set in a small, quiet park away from the town bustle. An elegant-looking palace originally owned by one of the country's most powerful aristocratic clans, it's now occupied by the local music academy. From here it's a short way further south to the walls of the Stare Miasto's **castle**, a huge seventeenth-century edifice also once owned by the Lubomirskis. The castle was converted into a prison by the Austrian rulers of Galicia – of which Rzeszów was a part – at the turn of the twentieth century and is now the law courts.

Finally, back up in the northwest corner of the Stare Miasto is the **Kościół Bernardynów** (Bernardine Church), another sumptuous early seventeenth-century structure considerably more attractive than the nearby **monument** to the Revolutionary Movement, a typically ugly, grey communist-era offering that has thankfully now finally been removed from the front of local tourist brochures. Quite how long the monument will survive is debatable, the anti-communist graffiti scrawled all over it these days suggesting a limited future.

Moving out of the Stare Miasto area, the large **Jewish cemetery** 1km southeast of the centre off ul. Rejtana (entrance on ul. Dołowa: the old man living next door to the car-repair workshop opposite has the key) is overgrown, having been completely destroyed by the Nazis. The group of three memorial chapels (*ohels*) to famed local *tzaddiks* of the past, and maintained by the national Jewish monuments committee, are a regular place of pilgrimage for visiting Hassidic Jews.

Eating, drinking and entertainment

For **eating**, *Syty Bar*, immediately on the left as you exit the train station at Kilińskiego 6, is a clean snack-bar alternative to the chaotic muddle of fast-food stalls that characterize this part of town; while *Dexter*, Rynek 9, is a simple order-at-the-counter pizzeria.

Among the more civilized sit-down places, the *Czarny Kot*, just off the Rynek at Mickiewicza 4, advertises itself as a pub but really functions as a plush café-restaurant with some fine Polish and international food; while *Ksania*, Rynek 4, offers a similar menu in a high-tech crypt; and *Prohibicja*, next door at Rynek 5, offers excellent if pricey meals, and an impressive range of cocktails, in over-designed speakeasy-style surroundings. Ethnic variety is provided by the *Ha-Long* on the western edge of the Rynek, ul. Matejki 2, a swanky Chinese place with good food and service.

Cafés and **bars** represent one of the city's growth industries, with both the Rynek and bustling ul. 3 Maja, the main shopping street, already boasting a number of bright new Western-style hang-outs. *Kazamaty*, Rynek 7, is a flash, brash pub with plenty of outdoor seating, although in summer it's really a question of strolling around the main square to see which of the al-fresco bars has a free table. *Bohema*, ul. Okrzej 7, is a roomy, faux-rustic tavern which serves up good Polish food and has a regular programme of live jazz.

If you fancy a night out dancing, the highly popular *Akademia* (ⓦ www.akademiaclub.pl), next to the Europa shopping centre at al. Piłsudskiego 34 , is the place to go for mainstream techno **clubbing**; *El Greco*, 2km out of the centre on the Sanok road at ul. Dąbrowskiego 83, has a more alternative programme of dance nights and live music.

Appropriately enough for a town with such a long history of emigration, the **Festival of Polonia Music and Dance Ensembles** takes place in Rzeszów in June and July every third year (next one is in 2002). It's a riotous assembly of groups from *emigracja* communities all over the world, including Britain, France, the USA, Argentina and Australia.

East from Rzeszów

From Rzeszów the main road and rail line head towards the Ukrainian borderlands. A characteristic eastern mix of villages, farmsteads and wayside shrines is the region's main feature, along with a smattering of historic towns and aristocratic palaces, notably at Łańcut, Leżajsk and Jarosław. All are within easy travelling distance of Rzeszów, a mix of local bus and train services providing the main means of **transport** around the area.

Łańcut

First impressions of the **castle** palace complex that dominates the centre of **ŁAŃCUT** (pronounced "Winesoot"), 17km east of Rzeszów, suggest that it

---

The devil of Łańcut

In an era replete with tales of rapacious brigands and swashbuckling freedom-loving heroes, the figure of **Stanisław Stadnicki** (c.1560–1616) stands out from the crowd. Brought up in a remote Carpathian outpost by independent-minded parents – his father, after whom Stanisław was named, was a staunch Arian eventually excommunicated for his religious incalcitrance, while his mother came from the Zborowskis. After his parents' early deaths, the young Stadnicki, together with his six brothers, inherited the family's properties. A sign of things to come was provided by his adoption of the motto *Aspettate e odiate* ("Wait and hate").

After several years participating in military expeditions in Hungary and Muscovy, acquiring a commendation for conspicuous bravery in the field, Stadnicki returned to Poland. Angered by lack of payment for his services Stadnicki seized the estate at Łańcut, which became the base for his life of audacious banditry. Nothing was spared his vicious attentions: passing travellers were attacked, properties inexplicably razed to the ground, and local traders and markets systematically terrorized and eventually forced to operate to his benefit through the unlicensed fair he started at nearby Rzeszów. With the help of a motley assortment of spies, torturers, thugs and mercenaries, he extended his grip on the terrorized local populace. Inevitably, Stadnicki's illicit activities eventually caught the attention of the authorities and in 1600 he was sued at the Crown Tribunal in Lublin by another local magnate over his illegal operations at the Rzeszów fair, to which Stadnicki responded by leading an armed raid on his opponent's nearby estate. The conflicts surrounding Stadnicki multiplied. An active participant in the nobles' *rakosz* (rebellion) against Zygmunt III in 1605, his public denunciations of the king as a "perjurer, sodomite and cardsharper" can hardly have endeared him to the authorities.

One of Stadnicki's favourite ways of goading his opponents was to circulate libellous verses about them. Eventually, this proved too much for one of his intended victims. In 1608 the nobleman **Łukasz Opaliński**, the subject of a withering Stadnicki broadside entitled "A Gallows for my Guest", retaliated by storming the castle at Łańcut, where prodigious quantities of loot were discovered in the cellars, and massacring everyone there – except Stadnicki, who in characteristic fashion just managed to escape in time. Bloodied, but unbowed, Stadnicki eventually returned to the area in a bid to pick up his malevolent career once more. Things were never the same again, however: pursued relentlessly by Opaliński's Cossack guard and eventually given away in the hills by his personal servant, a mortally wounded Stadnicki was finally beheaded with his own sword. Symptomatically for a country where the "Golden Freedom" was cherished so highly among the nobility, the references to Stadnicki from his contemporaries suggest that the man's claimed independence and Wild West-style championing of the spirit of liberty were at least as significant for many as his vindictive destructiveness.

must have seen rather more high-society engagements than military ones. The first building on the site, constructed by the Pilecki family in the second half of the fourteenth century, was, however, burnt down in 1608 when royal troops ambushed its robber-baron owner Stanisław Stadnicki, known by his contemporaries as "The Devil of Łańcut" (see box opposite). The estate was then bought by Stanisław Lubomirski, who set about building the sturdier construction that forms the basis of today's palace. Following contemporary military theory, the four-sided palace was surrounded by a pentagonal outer defence of moat and ramparts, the outlines of which remain.

The fortifications were dismantled in 1760 by Izabella Czartoryska (see Puławy, p.322), wife of the last Lubomirski owner, who turned Łańcut into one of her artistic salons, laid out the surrounding park and built a theatre in the palace. Louis XIII of France was among those entertained at Łańcut during this period, and the next owners, the Potocki family, carried on in pretty much the same style, Kaiser Franz Josef being one of their guests. Count Alfred Potocki, the last private owner, abandoned the place in the summer of 1944 as Soviet troops advanced across Poland. Having dispatched six hundred crates of the palace's most precious objects to liberated Vienna, Potocki himself then departed, ordering a Russian sign reading "Polish National Museum" to be posted on the gates. The Red Army left the place untouched, and it was opened as a museum later the same year.

The palace

Forty or so of the **palace**'s hundreds of rooms are open to the public (mid-April to mid-Sept Tues–Sat 9am–4pm, Sun 9am–3pm; mid-Jan to mid-April & mid-Oct to mid-Dec Tues–Sun 9am–3pm; entry by guided tour only, last entry 60min before closing), and in summer they are crammed with visitors. The **ticket office** is in a building at the western entrance to the park: there's a combined ticket for the palace and the Carriage and Religious Art museums (16zł) and a separate one for the synagogue (3zł from mid-June to mid-Sept; difficult to visit out of season; see p.348). If you're with company consider booking one of the English-speaking **guides** to take you round: they're well worth their fee of 100zł per group for the anecdotes – and if you're really lucky your guide might be the highly knowledgeable English-speaking museum curator. Ask at the ticket office for guide details, or in summer consider booking one in advance (℡017/225 2338). Otherwise you'll have to join one of the Polish-speaking **tours** – with this account and the detailed English-language guidebook on sale at the ticket office you won't miss much.

Most of the interesting rooms are on the **first floor** (though not all of them are always kept open), reached by a staircase close to the entrance hall, which is large enough to allow horse-drawn carriages to drop off their passengers. The **corridors** are an art show in themselves: family portraits and busts, paintings by seventeenth-century Italian, Dutch and Flemish artists, and eighteenth-century classical copies commissioned by Izabella. Some of the nearby bedrooms have beautiful inlaid wooden floors, while the bathrooms have giant old-fashioned bathtubs and enormous taps.

Moving through the **Chinese apartments**, remodelled by Izabella at the height of the vogue for chinoiserie, and through the **ballroom** (setting for the big Łańcut festival concerts – see p.349) and **dining room**, you reach the **old study**, decorated in frilliest Rococo style – all mirrors and gilding – and with a fine set of eighteenth-century French furniture. In the west corner of this floor, the domed ceiling of the **Zodiac Room** still has its Italian seventeenth-century stucco decorations. Beyond is the old **library**, where among the leather tomes you'll find bound sets of English magazines like *Country Life* and *Punch* from the 1870s – which only goes to show how the old European aristocracy stuck together.

On the **ground floor**, the **Turkish apartments** contain a turbaned portrait of Izabella and a suite of English eighteenth-century furniture. Don't miss the extraordinary eighty-seater **Łańcut theatre** commissioned by Izabella: as well as the ornate gallery and stalls, the romantic scenic backdrops are still there, as is the stage machinery to crank them up and down.

The **Carriage Museum** (same hours and ticket as the palace) in the old coach house is a treat, including over fifty horse-drawn vehicles for every conceivable purpose, from state ceremonies to mail delivery. Next door, the old stables contain the **Slavic Religious Art museum** (same hours and ticket as the palace), housing a large and fabulous collection of Ruthenian icons, the majority of them removed from the Uniate and Orthodox churches of the surrounding region in the years following the notorious Operation Vistula of 1947 (see p.368). Part of the vast collection is displayed for viewing, with the rest of the icons hanging from the walls in huge, densely packed racks. Among the choice items on show there's a complete eighteenth-century iconostasis, a superb, meditative fifteenth-century *Mandilion* and a poignant, suffering *Christus Pantocrator*, reflecting the humanizing influences of Roman Catholic art on later Uniate and Orthodox iconography. In addition there's a fine collection of vestments, Bibles and other Cyrillic scripts.

The Town

Łańcut town has one other main point of interest: the old **synagogue**, close to the castle, just off the main square on ul. Zamkowa, which now houses a newly renovated Jewish **museum** (June 15–Sept 15 Tues–Sun 10.30am–4pm; rest of year by special request; tickets sold at the palace ticket office, see p.347). A simple cream-coloured structure built in the 1760s on the site of an earlier wooden synagogue, the interior survived the Nazi era relatively intact, preserving an authentic and virtually unique taste of what scores of similar such synagogues throughout Poland would have looked like in the pre-World War II era. The walls and ceiling are a mass of rich, colourful decoration including stucco bas-reliefs, frescoes, illustrated Hebrew wall prayers, zodiacal signs and false marble ornamentation. In the centre of the building stands the *bimah*, its cupola decorated with some striking frescoes of biblical tales and a memorable depiction of a leviathan consuming its own tail – a symbol for the coming of the Messiah – adorning the inner canopy. In addition, there's a small collection of Torah scrolls, menorah and other religious artefacts on display. It's worth noting that outside the summer season (when it's just 3zł), you'll be expected to stump up the "group price" of 60zł to get into the synagogue – an outrageous rip off of which the palace management, who administer admissions, should be thoroughly ashamed.

The Hassidic movement that swept through Eastern Europe in the nineteenth century took strong hold among the Jews of Łańcut. The **old Jewish cemetery**, fifteen minutes' walk north of the palace complex off ul. Moniuszki houses the recently rebuilt *ohel* (tomb) of **Reb Horovitz**, a noted nineteenth-century *tzaddik* whose grave remains a much-visited place of Hassidic pilgrimage. The key to the cemetery is kept by the family living at ul. Jagiellońska 17, round the corner from the entrance. The overgrown **new Jewish cemetery**, ten minutes south of the Rynek off ul. Armii Krajowej, is larger, but more destroyed. A small memorial garden and monument nearby marks the spot where large numbers of local Jews were shot by the Nazis during World War II.

Practicalities

Łańcut's **train station** is a short taxi ride or a two-kilometre walk north of the centre; the **bus station**, however, is only five minutes' walk from the castle in the same direction. If you're planning to stay overnight, first choice is the wonderful *Zamkowy* **hotel** (☎017/225 2671; ❸–❺), offering en-suites and rooms with shared facilities, a period piece occupying the south wing of the castle, which is predictably popular – in the summer you won't get in unless you've booked in advance. Although its location isn't as good, the *Pałaczyk*, five minutes' walk south of the synagogue at ul. Paderewskiego 18 (☎017/225 2043; ❹), offers comfortable en-suites in a rather grand-looking turn-of-the-twentieth-century *dwór*-type mansion, and boasts a fairly posh restaurant. The only other option is the PTTK-run *Dom Wycieczkowy* in the former Dominican monastery at ul. Dominikańska 1 (☎017/225 4512; ❶), just north of the Rynek, which has a handful of spartan doubles, as well as dorm beds from 20zł per person.

The **restaurant** of the *Zamkowy* has a decent and not too expensive selection of traditional Polish dishes, although it's a bit gloomy in comparison to the al-fresco **cafés** just west of the castle on Łańcut's main Rynek – *Caffe Antico* at no.3 serves up decent coffee and cakes as well as a selection of main meals.

Every May, the palace hosts the prestigious **Łańcut Music Festival**, now approaching its fortieth year, an increasingly popular event on the international circuit, with a focus on chamber music – expect hotels to be booked solid at this time. Festival **tickets** are sold via the State Philharmonic Concert Office in Rzeszów (☎017/862 8507), though some are available an hour before each concert, either from the office in the palace vestibule or outside the concert venue itself. Finally, in the summer international master classes for aspiring young instrumentalists are held at the palace.

Leżajsk

Thirty kilometres northeast of Rzeszów on the verges of the River San, **LEŻAJSK** is at first sight a typical bustling market town with a main square, a church and precious little else to show for itself. For many, though, the town's name at least will be familiar thanks to the local brewery, long-established producer of one of the country's leading – and best – range of beers. For Catholic pilgrims, and lovers of organ music, the monastery church in the north of town makes the place the subject of a special journey.

Leżajsk's main attraction is some way north of the town centre: arriving by bus or train at the combined central station it's a two-kilometre walk or bus ride north to the vast Bernardine **church** and **monastery**. Built in the late 1670s inside a fortress-like defensive structure, the vast Baroque basilica is an established and important centre of pilgrimage thanks to an icon of the Madonna and Child placed here, venerated for centuries by Catholics as a miracle-worker. On religious holidays, notably the Feast of the Assumption (Aug 15), the church draws huge crowds. At just about any time of year you're likely to find buses full of schoolchildren or OAPs doing the rounds of the church and Stations of the Cross situated in the woods behind the building. The cavernous church interior is a mass of Baroque decoration, with numerous side altars, religious paintings, some finely carved wooden choir stalls and a huge gilded main altarpiece.

Pride of place, however, goes to the monster Baroque **organ** filling the back of the nave, one of the finest – and certainly one of the most famous – in Poland. With nearly six thousand pipes, four manuals and over seventy different registers, the exquisitely decorated instrument produces a stunning sound more than capable of filling the building. Now that the funds have been raised, some badly needed restoration work has begun to combat the destructive effects of wood-eating parasites on the organ.

Services apart, you can also get to hear the organ at the concerts held regularly in summer – check with the tourist offices in Rzeszów for details. The **International Organ Festival** held here every May is a magnet for fellow players and a major musical event well worth coinciding with.

Just south of the monastery gates over ul. Klasztorna is the **Leżajsk Brewery**. You can try the draught version of the tasty local brew at the roadside bar along with the hardened local consumers, or stock up on cans of the stuff at the shop next door. Back into the town centre, the late Renaissance **Parish Church**, east of the square, is worth a quick look, featuring some fine early fresco work in the nave.

Practicalities

It's easy enough to get here from Łańcut, with **buses** running every hour or so; otherwise there are five daily services from Rzeszów. For **accommodation**, the hotel options are the *71*, ul. Mickiewicza 80 (☎017/242 8098; ❸), which proffers plain but habitable en-suites; and smaller *U Braci Zygmuntów*, ul. Klasztorna 2e (☎017/242 0472; ❸), which at least has TV in all the rooms. Both hotels have serviceable **restaurants**. Virtually every **bar** or takeaway joint in town serves at least one of the good range of beers produced by the Leżajsk brewery.

Jarosław

Nestled at the foot of the San river valley on the main road east to the Ukrainian border, the town of **JAROSŁAW** is one of the oldest in the country. An urban settlement is known to have been established here by the mid-twelfth century, on the site of a stronghold raised by a Ruthenian prince known as Jarosław the Wise some two centuries earlier. The town's strategic location at the nexus of major medieval international trade routes led to its rapid development as a commercial settlement.

In their medieval heyday the fairs held in Jarosław were second only to those of Frankfurt in size, drawing merchants from all over the continent. The most tangible reminder of the mercantile glory days is the old **market** complex at the centre of town, which has preserved the essentials of its medieval layout. Like many towns in the region, Jarosław's large and dynamic local **Jewish population** suffered badly at the hands of the Nazis. Jews established themselves here early on, and the importance of the town fairs to Jewish commercial life throughout Poland was such that the **Council of the Four Lands** (see Lublin, p.306) met regularly here during the seventeenth and eighteenth centuries. Into the present, sad to say, the drive to smarten up the country's architectural legacy – in evidence in neighbouring towns such as Rzeszów or Tarnów – hasn't reached Jarosław yet: if the tatty looking town centre ever gets the thorough sprucing up it deserves, the place might become more appealing.

The Town

Focal point of the medieval town centre is the breezy, open central square where the fairs used to be held. Filling the centre is the Gothic **town hall**, a handsome-looking building topped by a tall spire that was burnt down, like much of the town centre, in 1625 and subsequently remodelled in Baroque and later in neo-Renaissance style, when the raised balcony was added. On several sides the square is lined with the arcaded merchants' houses: while not as grand as those in Zamość, some of the houses are impressive nonetheless, most notably the Renaissance **Kamienica Orsettich** (Orsetti Mansion) on the south side. Built in the 1670s by a wealthy family of Italian merchants, the building has a beautifully decorated upper attic and a typically open, airy arcade. It's also the home of the **town museum** (Tues–Thurs 10am–2pm, Fri 9am–4pm, Sat 10am–1pm; 3zł), which contains an enjoyably offbeat collection of portraits of local priests of all denominations and the local aristocratic Potocki dynasty, period furniture and a brilliant collection of early typewriters, gramophones and polyphones. Looking round also gives you a chance to admire the fine original polychromy decorating several of the grand, wooden-beamed rooms.

The clearest evidence of the town's mercantile past comes from the honeycomb of **cellars** stretching beneath the town square. Originally built as storage space for the merchants trading on the square above, the network of cellars served as an effective hide-out for local people during successive assaults on the town, most notably the Tatar raids of the fourteenth century. The cellars were gradually abandoned during later centuries, but a 150-metre-long section of the (by then) flooded cellars was cleared out by miners in the early 1960s and opened to visitors a decade later.

Subject to demand (there's a 5-person minimum), **tours** through the cellars are conducted on the hour by one of the staff at the museum ticket office (same times as the museum; 3zł); call ahead if you want to be sure of getting a guide (☎016/621 4337). The entrance is through one of the merchants' houses on the eastern side of the square: from here you descend into the brick-walled passageways – many of the walls are original – and wind your way through the gloom down to a depth of twenty metres at the lowest point, eventually re-emerging where you started. The chill down below is explained by the ingeniously constructed and still-functioning ventilation system, good enough to allow meat to be kept here.

North of the square, a short walk along the bumpy, cobbled streets to pl. Skargi is the **parish church**, an imposing late-sixteenth-century Renaissance construction with a fine façade. A short way further north is the **Klasztor Sióstr Benedyktynek** (Benedictine Convent), a fine early-seventeenth-century complex surrounded by its own set of fortified walls. If you are here when it's open, the *cerkiew* down the hill east of the square, a colourful eighteenth-century construction now in use again by its former Uniate occupants, is also worth a look. Completing the tour of religious architecture, the former **synagogue** northwest off the square on the corner of ul. Opolska, built in 1810, now a school building, is one of several that served the town's once thriving Jewish population. Despite the signs warding them off, the **wiała targowa** (covered market) on ul. Grodzka, leading west off the square, is popular with Ukrainian and Russian traders from across the border, who've set up an improvised marketplace of their own on the south side of the building.

Practicalities

The combined **bus** and **train station**, at the bottom of ul. Słowackiego, is a fifteen-minute walk southwest of the Stare Miasto. There's no IT office, but the town website (🌐www.jaroslaw.pl) carries a modicum of tourist **information**. Accommodation options include the *Turysta* **hotel**, Rynek 25 (☎016/623 1344; ❸), which offers comfy en-suites, but has a limited number of rooms so advance reservations are advisable; and the similarly central but rather more modest *Turkus*, ul. Sikorskiego 5a (☎016/621 2640; ❶), most of whose rooms come with shared facilities. There's a summer-only **youth hostel**, ul. Reymonta 1 (July–Aug; ☎016/621 4190), east of the stations.

Central Jarosław isn't exactly awash with **restaurants**: the Chinese-Vietnamese fare on offer at the enduringly popular *Azyatyka*, Rynek 1, is probably your best option on the main square. Otherwise there's a scattering of cafés in and around the Rynek where you can get good simple meals, including the *Pod Arkadami*, a popular bar on the Rynek with a billiards table; and the *Taras*, ul. Trybunalska 3, a pleasant courtyard café off the southern edge of the square. For a taste of local **nightlife** the *Joker* on ul. Grodzka, open till midnight, is the main diversion.

Przemyśl and around

Overlooking the River San, just 10km from the Ukrainian border, with the foothills of the Carpathians in the distance, the grubby but haunting border town of **PRZEMYŚL** has plenty of potential. Climbing the winding streets of the old quarter is like walking back through history to some far-flung corner of the Habsburg empire. As yet, it's very little visited by Westerners, although there are encouraging signs that the benefits of economic transition are beginning to make themselves felt even in these far-flung reaches. Access is straightforward though, with both trains and buses from Rzeszów, Łańcut and points beyond.

Founded in the eighth century on the site of a documented prehistoric settlement, Przemyśl is the oldest town in southern Poland after Kraków, and for

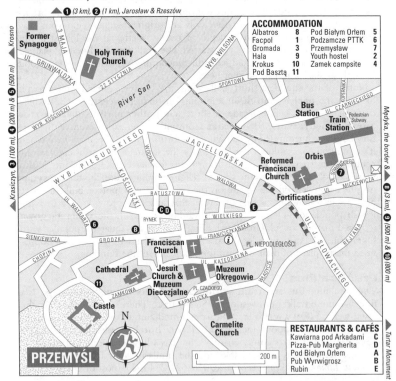

▲ ❶ (3 km), ❷ (1 km), Jarosław & Rzeszów

ACCOMMODATION
Albatros	8	Pod Białym Orłem	5
Facpol	1	Podzamcze PTTK	6
Gromada	3	Przemysław	7
Hala	9	Youth hostel	2
Krokus	10	Zamek campsite	4
Pod Basztą	11		

RESTAURANTS & CAFÉS
Kawiarna pod Arkadami	C
Pizza-Pub Margherita	D
Pod Białym Orłem	A
Pub Wyrwigrosz	B
Rubin	E

PRZEMYŚL

0   200 m

its first few centuries its location on the borders between Poland and Ruthenia made it a constant bone of contention. Only under Kazimierz the Great did Poles establish final control of the town, developing it as a link in the trade routes across the Ukraine. Przemyśl maintained a commercial pre-eminence for several centuries, despite frequent invasions (notably by the Tatars), but as with many Polish towns, economic decline came in the seventeenth century, particularly after Swedish assaults in the 1650s. Much of the town's character derives from the period after the First Partition, when Przemyśl was annexed to the Austrian empire. In 1873 the Austrians added a huge castle to the town's defences, creating the most important fortress in the eastern Austro-Hungarian Empire. During World War I this region was the scene of some of the fiercest fighting between the Austrians and Russians: throughout the winter of 1914 Russian forces besieged the town, finally starving the city into surrender in March 1915, then losing it again only two months later. The devastation of both town and surrounding region was even more intense then than during the Nazi onslaught 25 years later; the castle was totally destroyed and only small sections of the sturdy fortifications survived the siege, though the old town centre escaped, mercifully unscathed by the intense bombardments.

In more recent times Przemyśl's proximity to the Ukrainian border has made it a prime target for trade tourists from the fomer Soviet Union, most of whom congregate at the local bazaar west of the train station along the river. Some of the international flavour of the town is evident at the bus station, where crowds of Ukrainian traders wait to board buses to Lwów and beyond. Be warned that it isn't a place to hang around at night, especially if carrying luggage: as with most of the main-line eastern border transit points, mafia-type gangs are well established in the area, increased police presence notwithstanding.

Arrival and information

Przemyśl's elegant Habsburg-era **train station** is ten minutes' walk northeast of the centre; the **bus station** is on the far side of the tracks from the train station, to which it is linked by pedestrian underpass. There's a left-luggage office at the train station (daily 8am–8pm) if you're just passing through.

There's a **tourist information** counter doling out leaflets on the surrounding region inside the Gromada travel agency on the corner of ul. Franciskańska and pl. Niepodległośsi (Mon–Fri 9am–5pm), although the arrangement has a temporary air about it – be prepared for changes. The **Orbis** office, just outside the train station at pl. Legionów 1 (Mon–Fri 9am–5pm; ☎016/678 3366), is another useful resource, particularly when it comes to booking travel tickets.

Accommodation

There's a fair spread of hotels and *pensjonaty* in Przemyśl that's largely developed on the back of the cross-border tourist trade. The town's **youth hostel**, north of the Stare Miasto at ul. Lelewela 6 (☎016/670 6145), stays open throughout the year, as does the *Zamek* **campsite** at Wybrzeże Piłsudskiego 8a (☎016/678 5642), about half a mile west of the Stare Miasto just behind the *Gromada* hotel, which also has bungalows (**❶**).

Albatros ul. Ofiar Katynia 26 ☎016/678 0870. Large hotel over 3km east of town off the Medyka road, aimed squarely at the business traveller. Functional en-suites. Bus #21 passes by. **❹**
Facpol ul. Armii Krajowej 6b ☎016/670 9105.

Good-quality place in scenic park location overlooking the city, 4km north of the centre off the Rzeszów road. Decent restaurant, too. **❹**
Gromada Wyb. J. Piłsudskiego 4 ☎016/676 1111, ⦿www.hotelprzemysl.republika.pl. Large

business-standard place just west of the town centre, on the banks of the river. Twenty-five-percent discount at weekends. **❺**

Hala ul. Mickiewicza 30 ☎016/678 3849. Basic overnighter a 5min walk east of the train station. Looks run-down from the outside but the dowdy rooms are habitable. Rooms range from spartan doubles with a sink to en-suites with TV **❶**–**❷**.

Krokus ul. Mickiewicza 47 ☎016/678 5127. Just beyond the *Hala* and slightly better quality, providing cosy en-suites – as long as you don't object to the frumpy brown decor. No breakfast, but you can scoff heartily at the frontier guards' canteen across the road. **❸**

Pod Basztą ul. Królowej Jadwigi 4 ☎016/678 8268. Cheap six-room hotel located close to the castle, offering simple rooms with shared

facilities. **❷**

Pod Białym Orłem ul. Sanocka 13 ☎016/678 6107. Intimate medium-sized place occupying futuristic modern villa, in a peaceful location 1.5km west along the river from the centre (bus #10 or #10A). Comfy en-suites with TV, and the restaurant serves good home-cooked specialities. **❹**

Podzamcze PTTK ul. Waygarta 3 ☎016/678 5374. Very basic place close to the cathedral, offering dorms (20zł per person) and sparsely furnished doubles. **❶**

Przemysław ul. Sowińskiego 4 (☎016/678 4032 or 678 4033). A stone's throw from the train station, a very basic bed-and-breakfast place, popular with the Ukrainian "trade tourist" brigade and generally full in season. **❷**

The Town

Advancing into town from the train and bus stations you'll pass the recently spruced-up **Reformed Franciscan church** on the corner of ul. Mickiewicza, opposite which fragments of the Austrian **fortifications** can be seen on the approach to the Stare Miasto. From here ul. Franciszkańska brings you to the scruffy, sloping **Rynek**, where the mid-eighteenth-century **Franciscan church** offers a florid demonstration of unbridled Baroque, including a wealth of sumptuous interior decoration and a fine columned facade. Round the corner and slightly uphill stands the seventeenth-century **Jesuit church**, formerly used by the Austrian garrison stationed here in Habsburg times. The recent beneficiary of a pleasingly custard-coloured paint job, the church's facade gives you a good idea of how splendid central Przemyśl will look if and when the money is found to restore its other principal monuments. The church became the focus of national attention in 1991, following the Polish Catholic hierarchy's decision (approved directly by the pope) to hand the building over to the sizeable local Greek Catholic (Uniate) population, hitherto deprived of their own place of worship. The move sparked a wave of local protest, with incensed Roman Catholic parishioners blockading the church and refusing to hand it over. Catholic defiance was quickly met with equally spirited opposition, and for a while the situation looked as if it might develop into a serious confrontation, with disturbing ethnic undertones and old Ukrainian-Polish scores and prejudices coming to the fore. After several weeks of tense negotiations, the Roman Catholics finally agreed to give the local Uniates free use of the building, and the latter now appear to be well established. Although the main body of the church is usually locked outside service times, you can admire the gilt iconostasis, displaying the full panoply of saints, from the vestibule. Partisans of Catholic religious paraphernalia can still find solace in the **Muzeum Diecezjalne** (Diocesan Museum; May–Oct: daily 10am–3pm; 3zł) in the college adjacent to the church, which nuns take you round.

Immediately east of here is the **Muzeum Okręgowie** (Tues & Fri 10.30am–7.30pm, Wed, Thurs, Sat & Sun 10am–2pm; 4zł) housed inside the grand old Uniate bishop's palace. Main attraction is the excellent collection of fifteenth- to seventeenth-century icons removed from the Uniate and Orthodox churches of the surrounding region after World War II – one of a series of such collections in the southeast of the country (see pp.348, 358 &

382). The influence of Catholic art and theology on these essentially Orthodox-derived pieces is most evident in the later works, in particular the Madonna and Child icons, the "Christus Pantocrator" figures also being decidedly Roman in feel. Highlights include a mystical early-eighteenth-century *Assumption of Elijah*, a fabulously earthy *Day of Judgement* from the same era, which has a team of prancing black devils facing off against a beatific angelic host, and some wonderful sixteenth-century depictions of saints and holy men, including the intrepid św. Paraskeva, the patron saint of "engaged couples, happy households and commerce". For anyone keen to know more about the churches from which the icons were taken, *Church in Ruins* by Canadian-Ukrainian Oleh Iwanusiw (see "Books" in Contexts), provides an encyclopedic illustrated overview.

Immediately up the hill from here is the **Carmelite church**, the other half of the equation in the interdenominational controversy. A fine late-Renaissance structure designed by Gelleazo Appiani in the early 1600s, it functioned as the Uniate cathedral for nearly 150 years until 1945, when it was handed back to the (Roman Catholic) Carmelites by the new authorities. Understandably, this was the building whose return local Uniates agitated for in the late 1980s before settling for the other. Rightly or wrongly they didn't get it, so the sumptuous Baroque interior decoration remains, most notably an extraordinary pulpit shaped like a ship, complete with rigging.

From here ul. Katedralna twists its way down towards the **cathedral** (10am–noon & 2–4pm), its sturdy 71-metre bell tower pointing the way. Remnants of the first twelfth-century rotunda can be seen in the crypt, and there's a fine Renaissance alabaster *Pietà* to the right of the main altar, but Baroque dominates the interior, most notably in the Fredro family chapel. Up beyond the Cathedral, a steeply climbing path leads through a park (open until sunset) to the **castle**, the remains of the fourteenth-century construction built by King Kazimierz the Great and given a thorough Renaissance remodelling a century later. The conifer-stuffed courtyard contains evidence of an eleventh-century Rotunda and adjoining palace, thought to be associated with Poland's Piast monarchs. The castle's most striking architectural feature is the pair of newly renovated Renaissance towers, tubby cylinders topped with a ring of decidedly un-military-looking baubles. One of them can be scaled (Tues–Sun: April–Sept 10am–6pm; Oct–March 10am–4pm; 2zł) to reveal a panoramic view over the city. The terrace of the *Artystyczna* **café**, just outside the castle walls, is particularly pleasant in summer.

Fifty years ago Przemyśl had much greater ethnic diversity than today: old guidebooks indicate that the area around the Carmelite Church was the **Ruthenian district**. There are three **Orthodox churches** still functioning in the east of the town, the main one fifteen minutes' walk east of the train station off ul. Mickiewicza. The **Jewish quarter** was more to the north of the old centre. Numbers 33 and 45 in ul. Jagiellońska were both synagogues before World War II, and there was another across the river – just off ul. 3 Maja on pl. Konstitucji, now part of a garage workshop. The decaying **Jewish cemetery**, 2km south of the centre on ul. Słowackiego, whose lock appears to have fallen off recently, still contains a couple of hundred tombs and gravestones, including a number of postwar monuments.

Eating and drinking

For **eating** and **drinking** you really need do no more than head for the *Pub Wyrwigrosz*, Rynek 20, a bar-restaurant with a big enough menu to suit most tastes, and a large terrace overlooking the (admittedly drab) main square.

There's no better illustration of the current revival of cross-border ties in Poland than the growing tourist influx to **L'VIV**, 60km across the Ukrainian border. Alongside its cultural cousin, Vilnius, L'viv (Lwów to Poles) was long one of the main eastern centres of Poland: like the Lithuanian capital, too, traditionally this was a city characterized by a diverse, **multicultural population** – three cathedrals, Armenian, Orthodox and Catholic, are still there today. In Polish terms, the city's greatest ascendancy was during the Partitions era, when it became at least as important a centre as Kraków: during the interwar years, too, Polish culture flourished in the city. The postwar loss of the city to the Soviet Union was a cruel blow to Poles – L'viv still has a significant Polish-speaking population – who've always remained strongly attached to the place, as evidenced by the scores of old photo albums and prewar guidebooks you can find in the bookshops these days. The liberalization of border controls in the early 1990s let in a large influx of Polish visitors, thankfully unaccompanied by demands for the "return" to Polish control of a city that was at the forefront of the recent Ukrainian struggle for independence.

For the time being at least, neither Ukrainians nor Poles need a visa to visit each other's countries, and a wealth of **transport** links (currently 7 buses and 3 trains a day) have grown up between Przemyśl and L'viv to cater for trippers on either side. If the idea of an **excursion** to L'viv appeals, however, be warned that most people (including citizens of EU countries, Australia, New Zealand and the US) need a **visa** to enter Ukraine – something that you're strongly advised to sort out in your home country before setting out, as they're not available on the border. At the time of writing, the Ukrainian authorities will only grant a tourist visa to those who already have a letter or fax of invitation from a Ukrainian hotel, tourist company or private individual – an absurdly bureaucratic system that effectively dissuades independent travellers from bothering to go there. Visa costs are also high (contact your nearest Ukrainian embassy for precise details): by the time you've paid both the visa fee and the additional "administration charge", you'll have shelled out over $100 US.

The address for the Ukrainian embassy in Australia is 4 Bellevue Road, Bellevue Hill, NSW 2023 (☎02/9388 9577); in Canada, 310 Somerset St West, Ottawa, Ontario K2P OJ9 (☎613/230 2961, ☎230 2400); in the UK, 60 Holland Park Rd, London W11 3SJ (☎020/7727 6312, ☎7792 1708); and in the US, 3350 M St NW, Washington DC 20007 (☎202/333 0606, ☎333 0817, ☎www.ukremb.com).

Otherwise, *Kawiarna pod Arkadami*, Rynek 5, is a serviceable daytime café which also serves up traditional dishes like *bigos*, *barszcz* and *pierogi*; while *Pizza-Pub Margherita*, Rynek 4, is a trusty source of decent pizza, spaghetti and risotto in a subterranean setting. The *Rubin*, ul. Kazimera Wielkiego 10, is a small, family-run bar-restaurant with a good selection of the usual Polish favourites, although for a slap-up meal of good home cooking you should really head for the restaurant of the *Białym Orłem* hotel (see p.354). The *Wyrwigrosz* aside, the only decent bar in the town centre is the cosy *Pub Zoodiak*, just off the Rynek at Serbańska 3.

Around Przemyśl

For an excellent view, especially towards the Carpathians, the **Kopiec Tartarski** (Tartar Monument) on the southern outskirts of Przemyśl is worth a trip: buses #28 and #28a deposit you at the bottom of the hill. Legend says the monument at the top marks the burial place of a sixteenth-century Tatar khan who is reputed to have died nearby. The route there takes you past a number of **World War I cemeteries**, Russian, Austrian and German included, reminders of the massive battles fought in and around the town in the first years of the conflict. Close to the monument there are also the remnants of one of the **bastions** in an extensive ring of fortifications thrown up round the town by the Austrians from the 1870s onwards, consisting of an inner ring located in the immediate vicinity of the town and an outer ring pushing far out into the countryside. If you have your own transport you could have a fascinating time exploring the network of fortifications with the help of a map titled *Twierdza Przemyśl* ("Fortress of Przemyśl") available from the tourist office. One of the best preserved is at **Siedliska**, right up by the Ukrainian border – a clear indication of the size of the enterprise.

On the northern outskirts of town, a couple of kilometres out of the centre, you'll see signposts to **Bolestraszyce**, a pleasant, leafy arboretum with a good vantage point overlooking the town. There's a good little hotel here, the *Facpol* (see p.353), which offers a restful alternative to staying in town.

For a slightly longer excursion from Przemyśl, the obvious destination is **Krasiczyn castle**, a ten-kilometre ride west of town by bus #5. Built in the late sixteenth century for the Krasicki family by Italian architect Gallazzo Appiani, the castle is a fine example of Polish Renaissance architecture, though it's currently in the middle of an extensive and painfully slow restoration. You can however explore the courtyard and three of the four cone-shaped corner towers named after the pillars of the contemporary order, to wit, the Pope, the King, the Nobility and the Almighty. The wooded **park** that shelters the castle makes a cool, relaxing spot for a stroll. There's a plush **hotel** next to the castle, the *Zamkowy* (☎016/671 8316, ⓦwww.krasiczyn.motornik.com.pl; ❻), with its own **restaurant**.

The Sanok region

The main routes south from Przemyśl and Rzeszów towards the **Bieszczady** head towards the provincial town of **Sanok**, passing through an increasingly rustic landscape of wooded foothills. It's a journey that's particularly alluring in spring and autumn, the sun intensifying the green, brown and golden hues of the beech forests. If you've the time to spare, consider stopping off at picturesque little towns such as **Bircza** or **Tyrawa Wołoska** (both on the Przemyśl-Sanok road) to soak up the atmosphere; a number of villages with wooden *cerkwie* are tucked away in easy walking distance of Tyrawa. A little way off the road to the east, close to the Ukrainian border, lies the village of **Arłamów**, site of the decommissioned army HQ where ex-president/former Solidarity leader Lech Wałęsa was imprisoned during the early days of martial law. A luxury palatial-looking complex that used to double as a Party members' hunting lodge has now transformed itself into a posh country hotel – the hunting facilities are currently utilized by classier holiday groups. Further east still, right on the border itself, a large, wooded area west of the popular pilgrimage centre of **Kalwaria Pacławska** is in the process of being designated as a national park – an additional reason to explore the region further.

Sanok and around

Perched up on a hilltop above the San valley, **SANOK** looks a sleepy sort of place. Best known within Poland for its rubber and bus factories, whose AutoSan vehicles can be seen all over the country, of late the town has begun to pick up economically, largely on the back of increased cross-border trade flowing into the surrounding region. For the southbound traveller, though, the important thing about Sanok is that it's the last real town before the Bieszczady, which loom through the mists on the horizon.

The Town

A number of things in and around the town make it a place worth visiting in its own right, too. The reconstructed fourteenth-century parish **church** on the edge of the Rynek hosted the wedding of King Władysław Jagiełło in 1417, while a short way down the hill is the Orthodox **cathedral**, an imposing late-eighteenth-century edifice with a fine, and mercifully complete, iconostasis that's well worth a visit (open for Sunday services at 10.30am & 5pm; at other times guided tours are organized by the PTTK office).

Perched halfway up the hill between the two, the town's major focal point of interest is the **castle**, a sixteenth-century construction later remodelled by the town's Habsburg-era rulers that could pass for the ancestral pile of some Scottish laird, built on the site of the original twelfth-century fortress that guarded the main highway running through the town from the southern Carpathians on into the Baltic. Its current renovation project has thrown up some interesting discoveries: sections of Gothic walls underneath the nineteenth-century Austrian overlay, bits of an early wooden fortress on top of a thirteenth-century cemetery, and possibly the foundations of a Romanesque church. Inside the main building, the **museum** (mid-June to mid-Sept Mon noon–3pm, Tues–Sun 9am–5pm; mid-Sept to mid-June Mon noon–3pm, Tues & Wed 9am–5pm, Thurs–Sun 9am–3pm; 6zł) contains a smattering of archeological finds. Most interestingly, there's a display of finds from the excavations in progress at Trepcza, 5km northwest of Sanok. The discovery of an early medieval stronghold here has evoked considerable interest in the archeological world, as it's reckoned to provide major new insights into Western Byzantine/Orthodox culture as it developed in this region following the eleventh-century schism between Rome and Constantinople. Among the items on display are pieces of jewellery, religious artefacts including crucifixes, and detailed reconstructions of the site, notably the wooden eleventh- to twelfth-century Orthodox church and cemetery recently unearthed there.

The Icon Museum

The fabulous **Sanok Icon Museum**, in the castle (same hours and ticket as castle museum), is the largest collection of Ruthenian icons in the world after the Tretyakov Gallery in Moscow. Though most of the pieces on display date from the sixteenth and seventeenth centuries, the oldest comes from the mid-1300s, so the collection gives a clear impression of the development of the **Ukrainian school** of painting, which evolved in tandem with an autonomous and assertive local Church.

Unlike Russian and Greek Orthodox iconography, however, much of the work on display here is still pretty unknown to anyone but art historians and specialists, despite its quality. The best of the early icons have both the serenity and severity of Andrei Rublev's greatest works. In contrast, later icons manifest the increasing influence of Western Catholicism – which culminated in the formation of the Uniate Church in 1595 (see box on pp.368–369) – both in their style and subject matter, with an encroaching Renaissance approach to the portraiture. In a few cases, the figures show strong Tatar influences too. Look out too for a large *Icon of Hell*, an icon of a type traditionally housed in the women's section of Orthodox churches: such lurid depictions of the torments of the underworld must have kept a few people in check.

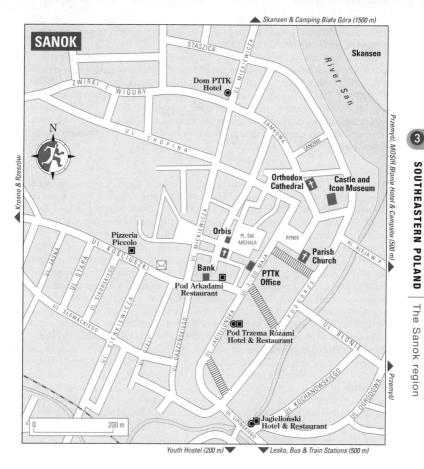

SANOK

STASZICA

ZWIRKI I WIGURY

UL. MICKIEWICZA

Dom PTTK Hotel

Skansen

River San

UL. CHOPINA

ZAMKOWA

SANOWA

N

Krosno & Rzeszów

Orthodox Cathedral

Castle and Icon Museum

Pizzeria Piccolo

Orbis

PL. ŚW. MICHAŁA

RYNEK

Parish Church

AL. ALEJA W. P.

UL. JASNA

UL. STARA

UL. KOŚCIUSZKI

UL. SIKORSKIEGO

UL. MICKIEWICZA

Bank

Pod Arkadami Restaurant

UL. 3-GO MAJA

PTTK Office

PODGÓRZE

UL. SŁOWACKIEGO

UL. SIENKIEWICZA

UL. LELI

UL. DASZYŃSKIEGO

UL. JAGIELLOŃSKA

Pod Trzema Różami Hotel & Restaurant

UL. BŁONIE

Przemyśl

UL. KOCHANOWSKIEGO

UL. OGRODOWA

0   200 m

UL. LIPIŃSKIEGO

Jagielloński Hotel & Restaurant

As with the related collections in Łańcut (see p.348), Przemyśl (see p.354) and Nowy Sącz (see p.382), the presence of these icons is related to postwar "resettlements". With many local villages deserted in the aftermath of Operation Vistula (see box on p.368), their wooden *cerkwie* neglected and falling apart, the oldest and most important icons were removed to museums. Genuine artistic concern prompted their removal, but now that local people are returning to the villages and using the churches again, in places where their security can be assured, it's high time to consider handing at least some of the icons back – not a view shared by the museum curators, it should be added.

The Beksiński Gallery

The other main part of the castle collection is the **Beksiński Gallery** (same hours and ticket as castle museum), devoted to the work of Zdzisław Beksiński, the noted modern Polish artist born in, and long-time resident of, Sanok. An intriguing selection of his vivid, imaginative canvases is on display here, though many of the best have long since been bought up by museums abroad. While renovation of the castle is in progress the gallery seems to be acting as a replacement town museum, putting on a continuous selection of moving exhibitions of art from around the country.

As with most towns in the area, for centuries Jews were an integral part of local life. Nazi wartime destruction put paid to the main synagogue and cemetery, along with most of the several-thousand-strong Jewish population. Virtually all that remains is the overgrown **new Jewish cemetery**, about 1km west of the town centre on ul. Kiczury, just beyond the main Catholic cemetery. A monument erected among the few surviving gravestones in 1988 by the Nissenbaum Foundation commemorates "Jews, Poles and Ruthenians murdered here".

The skansen

Also worth a visit is the **skansen** in the Biała Góra district, well signposted 2km north of the centre (daily: May–Sept 8am–6pm; April 9am–4pm; Oct 8am–4pm; Nov–Mar 9am–2pm; 6zł); if you don't want to walk, take a bus north along ul. Mickiewicza to the bridge over the river – the *skansen* is on the other side, spread along the riverbank. This open-air museum, one of the best in the country, brings together examples of the different styles of all the region's main ethnic groups – Boyks, Lemks, Dolinianie ("Inhabitants of the Valley") and Pogorzanie. If you want detailed ethnography, an English guidebook is available at the entrance. It's pretty large too, so you'll need a couple of hours to see everything. As many of the buildings are only open when there's a guide on hand, even if your Polish doesn't stretch very far it may be a good idea to tag along with one of the official guided tours held on the hour.

Specimens of every kind of country building have been (and still are) carefully moved and reassembled here: smithies, inns, granaries, windmills, pigsties and churches. Up on the hillside in the Boyk section, a couple of typical eighteenth-century *cerkwie*, one with a complete iconostasis, nestle peacefully in the shade of the trees. There's a good view from the top here over the town and river valley. The neighbouring Lemk section has a good set of farmhouses, while the Dolinianie area features a quaint old fire station, complete with nineteenth-century fire engines, a number of churches in the process of being installed, and a fine range of rural dwellings from stately *dwór* right down to the humblest and poorest cottages. In the nineteenth-century school building, you'll find some amazing old textbooks: note too the carefully preserved maps of pre-1914 Poland, showing this area as a region of the Austro-Hungarian province of Galicia – hence the portrait of Kaiser Franz Josef behind the teacher's desk.

Practicalities

The **bus station** is close to the **train station**, about fifteen minutes' walk southeast of the town centre; most buses from here will take you up to the main square. Of the **tourist offices**, the most helpful are the PTTK office at ul. 3-go Maja 2 (Mon–Fri 8am–4pm; ☎013/463 2171, ⓕ463 2512), with a reasonable stock of maps and general information about hiking in the Bieszczady, and the **Orbis** office, at ul. Grzegorza 2 (Mon–Fri 9am–5pm ☎013/463 0938), which deals with travel tickets.

The town centre offers a small but reasonable range of **places to stay** – sufficient to meet demand at the moment, but only for as long as the mountains beyond remain off the beaten track. They include the *Dom Turysty PTTK*, just downhill from the town centre at ul. Mickiewicza 29 (☎013/463 1439), with frumpish-looking but perfectly comfortable en-suites (❶–❸ depending on how modern the bathroom is), and some hostel-style triples (25zł per person);

the *MOSiR Błonie*, just east of the centre at al. Wojska Polskiego 1 (☏013/463 0257; ❶), offering sparsely furnished doubles and triples with en-suite facilities; and the *Pod Trzema Różami*, ul. Jagiellońska 13 (☏13/0463 0922; ❸), which offers comfy en-suites with TV right in the town centre. Best of the bunch is the *Jagielloński*, ul. Jagiellońska 49 (☏013/463 1208; ❹), already a foreigners' favourite on account of the comfortable, spacious en-suites, friendly management and good-quality cellar restaurant – reservations are a good idea, especially in summer. There's a spartan **youth hostel** (July–Aug) at ul. Konarskiego 10 (☏013/463 0925; 15zł per head), the street off the Lesko road directly opposite the *Jagielloński*. You can pitch a tent or park a caravan at the *AutoCamping* **campsite** attached to the *MOSiR Błonie* (see above); while *Camp Biała Góra* (013/463 2818), on a hilltop overlooking the river just next to the *skansen*, offers A-frame chalets sleeping two to five (18–25zł per person).

When it comes to **restaurants**, the one in the *Jagielloński* hotel tops most people's lists, locals included. The *Pod Trzema Różami* has a small restaurant specializing in cheap pizzas, although it's probably inferior to the Pizzeria Piccolo, just beyond the post office at ul. Kościuszki 28, in terms of choice. The Pod Arkadami, ul. Grzegorza 2, has a reasonable choice of inexpensive beef and chicken dishes, and also functions as the main late-night **drinking** venue for the town's youth.

If you're here in July, it's worth asking about the **Sanok Film Festival**, a relatively new event (inaugurated in 2001) designed to showcase underground and non-mainstream films from Poland and abroad. Details are available from the Sanok Dom Kultury (☏013/463 1042, ⓦwww.ffsanok.wp.pl).

Ulucz and Czerteż

If you have your own transport the **wooden church** (*cerkiew*) in **ULUCZ**, a tiny village 20km north of Sanok on the River San, is worth seeking out. Built in 1510, it's the oldest, and among the finest, of the Boyk *cerkwie* located within Polish territory (others of a similar vintage are all in Ukraine). A graceful, well-proportioned building poised on a hilltop, it boasts a large bulbous dome, fine Baroque iconostasis (though sadly several icons, including the entire middle row, were stolen a few years back) and mural paintings of the Passion and Crucifixion. The key is kept in a house marked by a sign at the village entrance.

At **CZERTEŻ**, immediately north of the main Krosno road, 6km west of Sanok, there's another beautiful Boyk *cerkiew* from 1742, hidden in a clump of trees up above the village. It houses another fine iconostasis, although Roman Catholics have now taken over the church as a place of worship.

The Bieszczady

The valleys and slopes of the **Bieszczady** were cleared of their populations – over eighty percent Boyks – in 1947 by Operation Vistula (see box, p.368), the majority of the native population being forcibly displaced into the Ukraine. Today, these original inhabitants and their descendants are coming back, but the region remains sparsely populated and is largely protected as national park or nature reserves. The majority of the area is part of the **East Carpathian biosphere reserve** that was established in 1991 with support from the World Bank, which also incorporates similar territory across the border in Slovakia and Ukraine. The reserves are carefully controlled to protect the wildlife, but are open to the public – quite a change from a decade ago, when

BIESZCZADY REGION

the communist party elite still maintained various sections for its own high-security hunting lodges. Ecologically, the area is of great importance, with its high grasslands and ancient forests of oak, fir and, less frequently, beech. Among the rarer species of fauna inhabiting the area you may be lucky enough to sight **eagles**, **bears**, **wolves**, **lynx** and even **bison**, introduced to the Bieszczady in the 1960s. Even the highest peaks in the region, around 1300m, won't present many **hiking** problems, as long as you're properly kitted out. Like all mountain regions, however, the **climate** is highly changeable throughout the year: on the passes over the *połonina* (meadows) for example, the wind and rain can get very strong. The best time to visit is late autumn: here, as in the Tatras, Poles savour the delights of the "Golden October". Mountain temperatures drop sharply in winter, bringing excellent skiing conditions.

The main place to aim for is the hiking base-camp of **Ustrzyki Górne** – direct buses run here from Rzeszów and (more frequently) Sanok, although you can also pick up these services en route in Lesko and Ustrzyki Dolne. Extra buses are laid on in July and August, but there's a scramble for seats at all times of year – buying a ticket in advance may not save you from having to stand.

Lesko and the foothills

East from Sanok the southbound road passes through Zagórz, the hub of local rail connections, and continues a further 6km to **LESKO**, a tranquil and long-established foothills town that seems to be doing increasingly well out of its strategic tourist location. South off the approach road from Sanok is what remains of the old sixteenth-century town **castle**, now a fairly posh, but extremely reasonably priced, hotel (see below).

Lesko's other attractions relate to the town's one-time **Jewish community**, who made up over fifty percent of the population immediately prior to World War II. Just east off the main square stands the **former synagogue**, a solid-looking Renaissance structure, originally part of the town's defensive system, with a vivacious, finely sculptured facade emblazoned with a quotation from the Torah. The whole building was reconstructed in the early 1960s, following wartime destruction, and converted into a local **art gallery** (daily 10am–4pm; 2zł). Alongside the worthy local art exhibition you can also view the converted synagogue interior, including the few elements of the original decoration still visible. A small exhibition in the entrance hall has some good prewar photos of the synagogue, records of local families murdered by the Nazis and a detailed list of the location and size of Jewish communities throughout Galicia (the region of Poland occupied by the Habsburg Empire during the Partitions era – see Contexts p.681).

Head down the hill behind the building and bear right to reach the **Jewish cemetery**, one of the most beautiful and evocative in the whole country. Hidden from a distance by the trees covering the hillside cemetery, the steps up from the roadside – the Star of David on the rust-coloured gate tells you you're at the right entrance – take you up through a tangled knot of twisted tree trunks and sprawling undergrowth to the peaceful hilltop cemetery site, around which are scattered two thousand-odd gravestones, the oldest dating back to the early 1500s. As in other major surviving cemeteries there's a wealth of architectural styles in evidence, notably a number of ornately decorated Baroque tablets with characteristic seven-branched candelabra, recurring animal motifs and often a pair of hands reaching up in prayer towards the heavens from the top of the stone. It's the setting as much as the stones that makes this cemetery so memorable, a powerful testimony to centuries of rural Jewish presence. A multilingual memorial tablet was erected in 1995 following a ceremony during which, as it states, "the ashes of Jews from Galicia and other lands murdered in [the death camp at] Bełżec were interred here".

Lesko's **bus** station is on the Sanok road, about 1km downhill from the main Rynek. Occupying a low concrete pavilion beside the Rynek's town hall, the **tourist information** centre (Mon–Fri 8am–4pm; ☎013/469 6695), has a wealth of leaflets on the region and has details of **private rooms** in farmhouses (*agroturystika*) in nearby villages – although you'll need your own transport to get to these. The sole reliable **hotel** is the *Zamek*, in the castle (☎013/469 6268; ❹) – if the conferences it now hosts regularly aren't occupying the whole place, you should be able to pick up a room. Otherwise there's a hard-to-find all-year **youth hostel** (☎013/469 6269), the *Baza Noclegowa Bartek*, 1.5km out on the northern outskirts of town, off the Sanok road at al. Jana Pawła II 18a, with dorm accommodation from 10zł per person. There's also a **campsite** (☎013/469 6689), nicely situated beneath the castle on the banks of the San, which also has some bungalows (❷). The best **places to eat** are the *Zamek* hotel's restaurant, and the *Pizzeria Roma*, on the corner of the Rynek and ul. Piłsudskiego.

South from here the bus continues through **UHERCE**, where many Polish tourists veer off towards **Jezioro Solińskie**, a fjord-like artificial lake created in the 1970s for hydroelectric power and water sports purposes. The custom-built lakeside villages of **SOLINA**, **POLAŃCZYK** and **MYCZKÓW** have more restaurants than anywhere else in the area, but there's little else to recommend them apart from their access to the water. In all three your best bets for **accommodation** now are the numerous workers' holiday houses and camping sites ranged across the water's edge. The *Jawor*, a bulky former Polish army rest home in Solina (☎013/468 8145, ⓦwww.jawor.org.pl; ❷), is a reliable year-round source of rooms that also offers bike and boat rental. **Yachts** and **kayaks** can be rented from the Biała Flota boat centre (☎013/476 1821) by the lakeside in Solina.

Ustrzyki Dolne

Back on the main road, **USTRZYKI DOLNE**, 25km east of Lesko, is an important staging post en route for the mountains, swarming in summer with backpacking students and youth groups. Otherwise this is a pretty featureless agricultural town with a small **museum**, on ul. Bełzka immediately north of the Rynek (Tues–Sat 9am–5pm; plus Sun July & Aug 9am–2pm; 2zł) covering the flora and fauna of the national park and just a scattering of minor monuments: a synagogue, reconstructed beyond all recognition, now a library, a *cerkiew* – both from the nineteenth century – and several memorials commemorating the Polish soldiers who fell in the struggle against the Ukrainian resistance (see box, pp.368–369). There are a couple of worthwhile hiking routes in the low hills either side of town, although you'd do better to press on towards the more inviting walking territory to the south.

Ustrzyki Dolne's **train** and **bus stations** are a ten-minute walk east of the Rynek, where the Bieszczadzkie Centrum Informacji i Promocji at Rynek 16 (Mon–Fri 8am–5pm, Sat 9am–5pm; ☎013/471 1130) offers a wealth of local **information** and sells hiking maps. Best bets for **accommodation** are the *Laworta* at ul. Nadgórna 107 (☎013/461 1178; ❷), the biggest place in town and so most likely to have a room, ten minutes' walk north from the stations; the smaller *Strwiąz* off the main square at ul. Sikorskiego 1 (☎013/461 1468; ❶); and the *Hotel Bieszczadzka*, on the western side of the Rynek at no. 19 (☎013/461 1072; ❶–❷), which offers en-suites with showers or rooms with shared facilities. There's plenty of **camping** space, both at the dingy official site on ul. PCK, a kilometre or so north of the Rynek, and in the fields around the edge of town. The **restaurant** of the *Bieszczadzka* hotel concentrates on cheap pizza fare. *Bar Lukasz*, on the southern side of the Rynek, does a nice line in cheap snacks like *bigos* and *pierogi*.

Krościenko

Nine kilometres north of Ustrzyki Dolne is the village of **KROŚCIENKO**, last train stop before the Ukrainian border (local buses run here too). The Bieszczady region is full of surprises, and this is one of them. Following the outbreak of civil war in Greece, a small community of Greek partisans and their families escaped to Poland in 1946 and settled in this area. The monument in the village centre is to **Nikos Balojannis**, a Greek resistance hero executed by the generals in Athens soon after his return in 1949. Not expecting to stay long they never made much effort to do up their houses, hence the shabby look of the place. Only a few Greeks remain these days, the younger generation having mostly elected to return to their home country. The chief reminder of their presence is the village **cemetery**, a tranquil, wooded spot 1km east off the road to the Ukrainian border. Back in the village, there's a fine late-eighteenth-century *cerkiew* just over the river, while just north of Krościenko on the edge of the Przemyśl road is a **Protestant cemetery**, all that remains of an earlier generation of local German settlers, who named the area Obersdorf.

From Ustrzyki Dolne to Ustrzyki Górne

The main road south out of Ustrzyki Dolne – a section of the so-called Bieszczady loop route built in the 1970s to open up this hitherto largely untouched area to tourism – winds south through the mountain valleys towards Ustrzyki Górne, an eighty-minute (50km) journey by bus. If you've developed an enthusiasm for the wooden churches of this area, you've time to spare, and have your own transport, you could consider a diversion a few kilometres east off the road to the border villages of **Jałowe**, **Równia** and **Moczary** (the first two are also reachable by bus or hiking from Ustrzyki Dolne) to see the fine examples of Boyk architecture there. Back on the main road, you'll also find Boyk churches at **Hoszów**, **Czarna Górna**, **Smolnik** (one of the few remaining places of Orthodox worship in the region), and – on a road off to the east – at **Bystre** (now disused) and **Michniowiec** (bus from Czarna Górna).

Coming over the hill into the old market town of **LUTOWISKA** you'll see makeshift barracks and drilling rigs, signs of the oil industry that has developed here sporadically since the last century. Locals insist that the Soviets for years blocked full development of the region's resources, fearing Polish economic independence. Even in these remote parts, Jews constituted over half the local population, up until 1939. The abandoned Jewish cemetery east of the main road contains several hundred tombstones, most from the nineteenth and twentieth centuries, while, near the village church, there's a collective **monument** to the 650 or so local Jews shot here by the Nazis in June 1942. The main reason to stop off in Lutowiska is to call in at the Ośrodek Informacyjno-Edukacyjny BPN (Bieszczady National Park Information and Education Centre; Mon–Fri 9am–5pm; ☎013/461 0165, ✉bdpn@radiostacja.pl), beside the main road, which has **information** on accommodation in the the park, and sells maps.

Ustrzyki Górne

Spread out along the bottom of a peaceful river valley and surrounded by the peaks of the Bieszczady, **USTRZYKI GÓRNE** has an end-of-the-world feel to it, being little more than a bus stop girdled by snack bars and a sparse collection of holiday villas. There's nothing to do here but **hike**: luckily, well-marked trails start right next to the bus stop, getting you up onto the forest-carpeted hillsides within a matter of minutes. You can treat Ustrzyki Górne as a day-trip from Sanok if you just want to get the feel of the place (and the bus ride through the foothills is enough on its own to make the excursion worthwhile), although you'd be well advised to spend a couple of nights hereabouts if you want to make it up onto the surrounding summits.

Accommodation choices in Ustrzyki Górne are still limited. First on the comfort list is the PTTK-run *Hotel Górski* (☎013/461 0604; ❷), in a good riverside location at the north end of the village, offering comfortable if sparsely furnished en-suites, a sauna, mountain-bike rental, and a respectable restaurant. Other options are the *Kremenaros*, a cheerful but basic all-year PTTK **hostel** (☎013/461 1036, ext. 105; 20zł per person), 100m south of the bus stop, which guarantees to find you at least some floor space, however crowded it gets. The marginally better *Dom Biały* (☎013/461 0641; 23zl per person), run by the BPN and signposted to the southeast of the bus stop, is a similar setup. There are **camping sites** next to the *Hotel Górski* or *Kremenaros*: the former also has a number of basic cabins (❷) available. A student camp (signposted "*baza studentowa*") operates in the summer months near the *Górski*: you can probably get a mattress in a tent here.

Riding in the Bieszczady

Walking and wintertime skiing aside, there are other ways of exploring the wilder parts of the Bieszczady region. Traditionally the plateaux and high paths of the region have been the natural habitat of *hucule*, an ancient breed of **wild horses** found throughout the Carpathians and named after the equally temperamental people of the eastern stretches of the mountains. Recent years have seen a renewed interest in these captivating beasts, not least because of the tourist potential they represent – and a number of places are now offering **riding holidays** in the mountains.

Your best points of contact are the Bieszczady Information Centre in Ustrzyki Dolne (see p.364) or the BPN Information and Educational Centre in Lutowiska (see p.365), who will put you on to the local stables. Best established of the horse-breeding and riding centres is the BPN's own stable (Zachowawcza Hodowla Konia Huculskiego BPN; ☏013/461 0650) in Wołostati, 6km southeast of Ustrzyki Gorne.

Besides the **restaurant** in the *Górski*, there's a line of **snack bars** opposite the bus stop offering hearty staples such as *bigos* and *kiełbasa* (sausage), as well as local trout – although they tend to close early if there are few tourists around. The main village **shop** has a basic range of food but plentiful supplies of Leżajsk beer: a small but devoted band of locals seem to spend most of their time camped round the next-door bar.

Hiking routes in the Bieszczady

Walking and winter skiing are the main reasons for coming to the Bieszczady region. From Ustrzyki there are a number of **hiking** options, all of them attractive and accessible for anyone reasonably fit; route durations given below are reckoned for an average walker's speed, including regular stops. The best **map** for hikers is the *Bieszczady Mapa Turystczyna* (1:75,000) available from shops in Sanok and Ustrzyki Dolne, or from the BPN huts at the entrance to the park.

The remoteness and rapid changes of weather that characterize the Bieszczady region make it more than usually essential for hikers to equip themselves well, particularly when planning more extended hikes. At any time of year, your **equipment** should include waterproof clothing and a rucksack; a reasonable quantity of basic food supplies; a detailed map; compass; and warm clothing. As far as **weather conditions** go, outside of the summer months (and even, sometimes including them), it is important to keep a check on things: particularly up on the *połonina*, terrific storms often appear seemingly from nowhere. Generally, locals advise you not to set out alone on extended hikes, as the area's overall remoteness means the chances of your being spotted if you have an accident are slim in many places. The BPN now charges all hikers a small **entry fee** (2zł), collected at the huts at the area's main access points.

East to Tarnica and the Ukrainian border

There are two initial routes east from Ustrzyki, both leading to the high Tarnica valley (1275m). The easier is to follow the road to the hamlet of **Wołosate** (there's a **campsite** just beyond at Beskid, right on the border) then walk up via the peak of Hudow Wierszek (973m) – about four hours all in. Shorter but more strenuous is to go cross-country via the peak of Szeroki Wierch (1268m), a three-hour hike. **Tarnica** peak (1346m) is a further half-hour hike south of the valley.

From Tarnica valley you can continue east, with a stiff up-and-down hike via **Krzemien** (1335m), **Kopa Bukowska** (1312m) and **Halicz** (1333m; 3hr) to **Rozsypaniec** (1273m), the last stretch taking you over the highest pass in the range. This would be a feasible day's hike from the Beskid campsite; the really fit could do an outing from Ustrzyki to Krzemien and back in a day.

Adventurous walkers could consider trekking into the region to the north of Tarnica valley in search of the **abandoned Ukrainian villages** and tumbled-down *cerkwie* scattered along the border (delineated by the River San). Some, like Bukowiec and Tarnawa Wyznia, are marked on the map, but others aren't, so you have to keep your eyes peeled. Many villages were razed to the ground, the only sign of their presence being their orchards. The Polish **border police** who shuttle around the area in jeeps are nothing to worry about as long as you're carrying your passport, and have a plausible explanation of what you're up to. The Ukrainians who watch this area are a different proposition, though, so don't on any account wander into Ukrainian territory – police detention of hikers in L'viv has been known.

A couple of kilometres west of Tarnawa Niżna, on the narrow road back to Ustrzyki Górne at **Muczne**, is another abandoned site, this time of a secret hunting **hotel** that used to be used by the communist party leadership and international guests including French president Giscard d'Estang and Romanian leader Nicolae Ceauşescu. It's now being touted as an upmarket mountain getaway (☎013/461 0122, ✉muczne@kki.net.pl; ④).

West to the Slovak border
There are some easy walks west to the peak of **Wielka Rawka** (1307m), flanked by woods on the Slovak border. One option is to go along the Cisna road and then left up the marked path to the summit (3hr). Another is to head south to the bridge over the Wołosate river, turn right along a track, then follow signs to the peak of Mała Szemenowa (1071m), from where you turn right along the border to the peaks of Wielka Szemenowa (1091m) and Wielka Rawka (4hr).

Northwest of Ustrzyki
The best-known walking areas of the Bieszczady are the **połonina**, or mountain meadows. These desolate places are notoriously subject to sudden changes of weather: one moment you can be basking in autumn sunshine, the next the wind is howling to the accompaniment of a downpour. The landscape, too, is full of contrasts: there's something of the Scottish highlands in the wildness of the passes, but wading through the tall rustling grasses of the hillsides in summer you might imagine yourself in the African savannah. Walking the heights of the passes you can also begin to understand how Ukrainian partisans managed to hold out for so long up here; even for the most battle-hardened Polish and Soviet troops, flushing partisan bands out from this remote and inhospitable landscape must have been an onerous task.

Skiing in the Bieszczady

Although nowhere near as popular a **skiing** area as, say, the Tatras, the Bieszczady provides some of the country's most enjoyable – and certainly most uncrowded – skiing terrain. While the **slopes** are rarely very dramatic, the **cross-country routes** are tranquillity itself. The principal slopes and routes are in and around Lesko, Jawor, Komańcza, Bystre, Cisna, Polańczyk and both the Ustrzykis. Infrastructure is basic and the availability of skiing **equipment** for hire still limited – the vast majority of skiers bring their own. Most of the major slopes fall within the national park area, and in view of the park's authorities' emphasis on environmental preservation it's probably a good idea to contact the national park office in the museum in Ustrzyki Dolne (see p.364) to find out about current rules and regulations before heading out.

Boyks, Lemks and Uniates

Up until World War II, a large part of the population of southeast Poland was classified officially as **Ukrainian**. For the provinces of L'viv, Tarnopol and Volhynia, in the
eastern part of the region (all in Ukraine today), this was accurate. However, for the
western part, now Polish border country, it was seriously misrepresentative, as this
region was in fact inhabited by **Boyks** (Boykowie) and **Lemks** (Łemkowie). These
people, often collectively called "Rusini" in Polish, are historically close to the
Ukrainians but have their own distinct identities, both groups being descendants of
the nomadic shepherds who settled in the **Bieszczady** and **Beskid Niski** regions
between the thirteenth and fifteenth centuries. Geographically speaking, the Boyks
populated the region east of Cisna, while the Lemks inhabited the western part of
the Bieszczady, the Beskid Niski and part of the Beskid Sądecki.

For centuries these farming people lived as peacefully as successive wars and
border changes allowed. Their real troubles began at the end of World War II, when
groups of every political complexion were roaming around the ruins of Poland, all
determined to influence the shape of the postwar order. One such movement was
the **Ukrainian Resistance Army** (**UPA**), a group fighting against all odds for the
independence of their perennially subjugated country. Initially attracted by Hitler's
promises of an autonomous state in the eastern territories of the Third Reich, by
1945 the UPA were fighting under the slogan "Neither Hitler nor Stalin", and had
been encircled by the Polish, Czech and Soviet armies in this corner of Poland. For
almost two years small bands of partisans, using carefully concealed mountain hide-
outs, held out against the Polish army, even killing the regional commander of the
Polish army, General Karol Swierczewski, at Jabłonki in March 1947.

This is where the story gets complicated. According to the official account, UPA
forces were fed by a local population more than happy to help the "Ukrainian fascists". The locals give a different account, claiming they weren't involved with the
UPA, except when forced to provide them with supplies at gunpoint. The Polish
authorities were in no mood for fine distinctions. In April 1947 they evacuated the
entire population of the Bieszczady and Beskid Niski regions in a notorious operation code-named **Operation Vistula** (Akcja Wisła). Inhabitants were given two hours
to pack and leave with whatever they could carry, then were "resettled" either to the
former German territories of the north and west in the case of many Lemks, or to the
Soviet Union with most of the Boyks.

From the Gorlice region of the Beskids, a traditional Lemk stronghold, an estimated 120,000–150,000 were deported to the Soviet Union and a further 80,000 were
scattered around Poland, of whom about 20,000 have now returned. The first arrived
in 1957, in the wake of Prime Minister Gomułka's liberalization of previously hard-line

Note that you can save walking time in this region by taking a **bus** from
Ustrzyki Górne though Wetlina, Dołzyca and Cisna. If you've only got a very
short time, you could take just a brief detour off the road north from Ustrzyki
Górne to Ustrzyki Dolne. Take the bus a couple of kilometres west to the
Przelec Wyzniańska pass, the first stop, from where a marked path leads up
through the woods on the right-hand side of the road to the **Połonina
Caryńska** (1107m) – a steep climb of roughly 45 minutes. You'll have time to
walk along the pass a short way to get a feel for the landscape, and then get
back down to catch the next bus on.

For a more extended trip from Ustrzyki Górne, take the steep trail marked
in red and green north through the woods up to the eastern edge of the
Połonina Caryńska, and walk over the top to the western edge (1297m; 2hr
30min). Continue down the hill to the village of Brzegi Górne where there's
a **campsite** near the road. From here you can either take a bus to Ustrzyki

policy. (Rumour has it that this was Gomułka's way of thanking the Lemks who had helped him personally during the war.) The trickle of returnees in the 1960s and 1970s has, since the demise of communist rule, become a flow, with Lemks and a few Boyks reclaiming the farms that belonged to their parents and grandparents. This return to the homeland brought a new level of political and cultural self-assertion. In the June 1989 elections, Stanisław Mokry, a Solidarity candidate from near Gorlice, openly declared himself a Lemk representative. Boyks and Lemks lost no time in pressing for official condemnation of the postwar deportations – a demand partially met by the Senate in August 1990 when it passed a resolution condemning Operation Vistula, though the Sejm failed to follow suit. Like other minorities in Poland, Lemks and Boyks want their own schools, language teaching and the right to develop their own culture – although there's been little significant progress in these areas so far.

The question of self-identity in the Bieszczady is entangled by the religious divisions within the community. Like their Ukrainian neighbours, in the seventeenth century many previously Orthodox Boyks and Lemks joined the **Uniate Church**, which was created in 1595 following the Act of Union between local Orthodox metropolitans and Catholic bishops. The new church came under papal jurisdiction, but retained Orthodox rites and traditions – including, for example, the right of priests to marry. Today the majority of Lemks in the Bieszczady and Beskid Niski classify themselves as Uniate (or "Greek Catholic", as Poles know them). Encouraged both by the Pope's appointment of a Polish Uniate bishop and political changes in Ukraine, where Uniates are finally coming into the open after years of persecution, Lemk Uniates have succesfully adopted a much higher religious profile.

The Uniates' revival in Poland is still hampered, however, by the vexed question of restitution of property confiscated in the wake of Operation Vistula, in particular the 250-odd churches in the region taken away from the Uniates and mostly given to the Roman Catholics and Orthodox. The dispute over the Carmelite Cathedral in Przemyśl that broke out in spring 1991 was resolved only after a nasty local dispute with distinctly anti-Ukrainian undertones, and a row that temporarily threatened to jeopardize newly developing Polish-Ukrainian political relations. The Uniates have still not recovered most of their former Church property. A further twist is added in the case of Orthodox-occupied buildings – the Church in Rzepedź (see p.372) is a good example – since like Ukrainians, the Lemk and Boyk communities are divided between the two faiths.

If you want to find out more about the Carpathian communities, the English-language Ⓦwww.lemko.org and Ⓦwww.carpatho-rusyn.org websites are useful sources of **information**.

Górne (or on to Sanok), or take the red-marked path which takes you up the wooded hill to the right to the all-year PTTK **hostel** on the eastern edge of the **Połonina Wetlińska** (1228m; 1hr 30min from Brzegi) – the views from this windswept corner are spectacular. Sleeping arrangements are basic and comprise mattresses in ten-person rooms; theoretically you should bring your own food, but the couple who run the place will probably be happy to feed you from the communal pot.

Beyond the hostel there's an excellent walk over the Połonina Wetlińska to **Przelec Orłowicza** (1075m), where the path divides into three. A sharp left takes you down the hill to **WETLINA** (2hr 30min from the hostel), a scenically located and popular holiday centre where **accommodation** is easy to find. As well as plenty of private rooms (❶), several of them part of the local *agroturystyka* network (see Lesko private rooms, p.363), there's a good PTTK hostel (with dorm beds from 15zł per person) and campsite, open all year and run by an extremely friendly local character; the *U Rumcajsa pensjonat* (☎013/468 4633; ❶), with a few en-suite doubles as well as several hostel-style triples and quads; the *Górski* **hotel** (☎013/468 4634; ❸), a reasonable, PTTK-run hotel on the southern outskirts of the village, with a passable restaurant; and the *Leśny Dwór* (☎013/468 4654; ❺), an upmarket family-run *pensjonat* with an equally commendable restaurant situated on a side track at the north end of the village, off the Cisna road. Hotel **restaurants** apart there's the basic *Smak* and a few snack-bar type joints dotted along the main road.

Buses from here take you north to Sanok or south to Ustrzyki Górne. The middle path goes to **Smerek** (1222m) and down through the woods to the **bus** stop in Smerek village (2hr). The right-hand path is for the long-distance hike via Wysokie Berdo (940m), Krysowa, Jaworzec, Kiczera, Przerenina and Fałówa to Dołżyca (7hr; there's a PTTK hostel here), or even further on to the villages of Jabłonki and Baligród (see p.373). West of Smerek, a little-travelled highland road passes through sleepy Przysłup (eastern terminus of the narrow-gauge rail line (see below) before descending towards Dołżyca, where motorists have a choice of onward routes – north to Lesko and Sanok via Jabłonki and Baligród (see p.373), or west to Cisna and Majdan.

Cisna, Majdan and Nowy Łupków

Continuing west from Dołżyca brings you to **CISNA**, a smallish village that saw some bitter fighting during the 1945–47 civil war, when the UPA (see box on pp.368–369) had one of their main bases nearby, a struggle commemorated by the large graffiti-covered monument overlooking the village. The village and surrounding area were ruthlessly emptied during Operation Vistula; today's population of just under two thousand is only a fraction of the 60,000 or so who lived here before 1939. There's a reasonable supply of **accommodation**, most of it pretty rudimentary, and mainly aimed at the hikers stopping over on their way across the mountains. Options include the *Okrąglik*, a basic, centrally located tourist hostel (18zł per head) with a campsite next to it; the *Bacówka Pod Honem*, a dirt-cheap mountain hut with a snack bar, on a path up above the village; a summer-only youth hostel (15zł per head) in the village school and a couple of old workers' holiday homes – the *Perełka* (☎013/468 63 25, ⓦwww.pkp-dus.com.pl; ❹), which also has well-appointed bungalows (❹); and the *Wolosań* (☎013/468 6373; ❷), which also offers dorm-style triples and quads. A kilometre to the southwest is **MAJDAN**, little more than a group of houses and the main boarding point for the **narrow-gauge rail line** running from west to east through the forests along the Slovak border. In addition to carrying passengers, these days the line forms part of a network of tracks through the forest which are used by the local forestry industry for wood transportation. Although its dependence on hefty local subsidies makes the line economically insecure – it was temporarily forced to close down in the mid-1990s – for now, at least between April and October, it's a regular tourist attraction.

Currently, the diesel-powered train, accompanied by a couple of old passenger carriages, operates two short stretches of track: one running 20km east of Majdan to the mountain pass of Przysłup, just beyond Cisna; the other running about 30k west to Wola Michowa. **Trains** for Przysłup leave Majdan at 10am (July–Aug daily; May, June & Sept Mon–Fri & public hols), arriving in Przysłup at around 11.10am and setting off on the return leg once you've had a chance to stretch your legs and take some pictures. Trains for Wola Michowa only run at weekends and on public holidays in July and August, departing from Majdan at 1pm. All in all you'd be well advised to check the **timetables** beforehand either directly at Majdan station or by calling the Bieszczady Railway

Preservation Foundation offices during business hours (☎013/468 6335), although you're unlikely to find an English-speaker. The majority of this memorable and out-of-the-way route passes through uninhabited hillside forests filled with a gloriously rich and diverse flora, the beautiful views over the valleys adding a touch of mountain thrill to the experience. The train crawls along at a snail's pace for much of the journey, which is all it can manage on the steep hills it has to negotiate at regular intervals. You can pick the train up at several points along the way, and the driver can usually be persuaded to stop for a while en route if anyone wants to take a longer look at the scenery. At weekends the train is liable to be joined by contingents of local drinkers who spend the journey getting absolutely plastered, in many cases falling off the train at regular intervals and clambering drunkenly back on again.

Heading west from Majdan by road brings you to **NOWY ŁUPKÓW**, some 20km distant, a tiny place whose name is familiar to Poles for the nearby internment camp, to which many prominent Solidarity leaders were consigned during martial law. If you have access to transport, there's an interesting Uniate **cerkiew**, now a Roman Catholic church, which is worth a visit at the village of Smolnik, just to the east.

The western Bieszczady

There is a choice of routes out of the western Bieszczady back to Sanok. The main one runs from Nowy Łupków through **Komańcza** and a series of tiny Uniate villages such as **Rzepedż**. The other is a more obscure, winding road north from Cisna, via **Jabłonki** and **Baligród**. **Buses** run along both roads, while **trains** serve only the main route.

Komańcza and Rzepedż

North from Nowy Łupków, buses and PKP trains take you to the village of **KOMAŃCZA**, whose churches illustrate graphically the religious divisions of the region. West of the main Sanok road is a modern church with an attractive iconostasis constructed in the 1980s by the majority local Lemk **Uniate** population – curiously, the ethnic cleansing effected by Operation Vistula on the surrounding region seems not to have touched Komańcza itself. Round the back of the church is a **museum** of Lemk culture (ask at the presbytery if the building's not open), housed in a traditionally decorated farm building, and with a small but enjoyable collection of traditional costumes, religious artefacts and wooden farming implements. Further up the same road, hidden away in the woods on the edge of the hill is a beautiful early-nineteenth-century *cerkiew*, used by the tiny local **Orthodox** community, while back on the main road, opposite the railway station, is the **Roman Catholic** church, built in the 1950s for the village's Polish settlers – a rare commodity around here up until World War II. Roughly 1km further north, on a track leading uphill to the left under the railway bridge, is the **Nazarene Sisters' Convent**, something of a shrine for Polish tourists: it was here that Cardinal Wyszyński, the redoubtable ex-primate of Poland, was kept under house arrest in the mid-1950s during the Stalinist campaign to destroy the independence of the Catholic Church. The PTTK-run *Podkowiata* (☎013/462 5211 ext. 13; ❶) with an adjacent seasonal **campsite**, has a reasonable supply of **rooms**, as does the convent **hostel** (☎013/462 5211 ext. 56; ❶), though the number of pilgrims that flock to the latter, particularly in summer, mean it's advisable to book here. The only place worth speaking of for a bite to **eat** is the *Pod Kominkiem*, back in the centre on the main road.

The cerkiew of the Polish Carpathians

Despite a modern history characterized by destruction and neglect, both the Bieszczady and neighbouring Beskid Niski regions still have a significant number of villages that boast the wooden Uniate churches – **cerkwie** (singular, **cerkiew**) as they and Orthodox places of worship are known in Polish – traditional to this part of Europe.

Some of the most remarkable date from the eighteenth century, when the influence of Baroque was beginning to make itself felt, even among the carpenter architects of the Carpathians. The simpler constructions with a threesome of shingled onion domes also encountered in the Bieszczady region – a structure common to most Uniate churches – have their origin in the later, **Boyk**-derived architectural styles. Finally in the Lemk-inhabited districts of the Beskid Niski you'll often encounter grander, showier structures wth a marked Ukrainian influence, built in the 1920s and 1930s at the height of Ukrainian self-assertion within Poland.

Without your own transport, the possibility of reaching many of the churches *in situ* is limited, though several of the small towns mentioned in this chapter have *cerkwie* within reasonable walking distance. The easiest way of having a close look is to visit the *skansens* at Sanok or Nowy Sącz, both of which contain complete churches. If, on the other hand, you do make it out to some of the more remote villages you'll need to ask around for the key (*klucz*), which is more likely than not to be in the hands of the local priest (*ksiądz*) or the person living nearest the building.

The dark and intimate **interior** of a Uniate church is divided into three sections from west to east: the narthex or entrance porch, the main nave and the naos or sanctuary. Even the smallest of the Uniate churches will boast a rich iconostasis all but cutting off the sanctuary, which will contain the familiar icons of (working from left to right) St Nicholas, the Madonna and Child, Christ Pantocrator and, lastly, the saint to whom the church has been dedicated. Above the central door of the iconostasis (through which only the priest may pass) is the representation of the Last Supper, while to the left are busy scenes from the great festivals of the church calendar – the Annunciation, the Assumption and so on. The top tier of icons features the Apostles (with St Paul taking the place of Judas). Typically, the Last Judgement covers the wall of the narthex, usually the most gruesome of all the depictions, with the damned being burned, boiled and decapitated with macabre abandon.

Locations of a number of *cerkwie* are indicated throughout the chapter. The current pattern of ownership varies: following the expulsions of Operation Vistula, many Uniate buildings were taken over by Roman Catholics and some by Orthodox worshippers. Despite the recent upsurge in Uniate activity, Roman Catholics still retain many of these buildings. Some have been returned – grudgingly you feel – to the Uniates, others are shared by both branches of Catholicism, while a good many still remain abandoned.

You could have a fascinating time searching the Komańcza area for **cerkwie**: modern maps of the region mark them clearly (Uniate buildings are identified in the keys as "churches in ancient orthodox churches".) There's a particularly fine and typically **Lemk-style Uniate Church** – this far north is firmly outside Boyk territory – from the 1820s just beyond at **RZEPEDŹ**, roughly fifteen minutes on foot from the train station. Nestled away on a hillside surrounded by tranquil clusters of trees, the church merges into the landscape – a common quality in *cerkwie* that may explain how they escaped the destruction of Bieszczady villages in the wake of Operation Vistula (see p.368). Surprisingly, this one only closed down for ten years after World War II, reopening for Uniate worship in 1956. The interior of the church gives a sense of the twin strands of Uniate worship: on the one hand Western Madonnas and insipid oil paintings; on the other the Eastern iconostasis, the absence of an organ (in the Orthodox tradition the choir provides all the music), the pale blue Ukrainian saints, and Ukrainian-script wall inscriptions. If you're planning on **staying** here, there are a couple of former workers' holiday centres, the *Nad Osławą* (☎013/462 5511 ext. 14; ❶) and the *Pod Suliłą* (☎013/467 8341; ❶) at hand in the village.

Turzańsk, 1.5km east of the village along the Baligród road, has another fine *cerkiew* in the most peaceful location imaginable; built in the 1830s, its interior decoration is preserved almost intact, a fine Rococo iconostasis included.

Jabłonki and Baligród

From Cisna, buses head to Lesko and Sanok, through a region which was the scene of some of the heaviest fighting between the Polish Army and the Ukrainian resistance. At **JABŁONKI** there's a large monument to **General Karol Swierczewski**, the veteran Spanish Civil War commander whose assassination in March 1947 goaded Poland's newly established communist authorities into a decisive all-out assault on the UPA, culminating in Operation Vistula (see p.368). Long a regulation stopoff point for Polish bus tour groups, these days the monument's looking decidedly neglected. The **natural history museum** across the road (Tues–Sun 9am–5pm; 3zł) provides some rewarding insights into the rich local flora and fauna. For accommodation there's a **youth hostel** (☎013/469 8641; 18zł per head), open year round, while the basic *Letnia* **snack bar** is the only eating option.

Continuing north, in the larger village of **BALIGRÓD** there's further evidence of wounds still festering from the Polish-Ukrainian conflict. A recently erected **monument** opposite the former Uniate church on the edge of the Rynek commemorates a notorious UPA-instigated massacre of 42 local Poles on August 6, 1944. Another monument in the middle of the square honours Polish soldiers who fell during the fighting – but not, as yet, the Ukrainians. Baligród was the headquarters of the Polish Army during the Polish-Ukrainian conflict, and if you root around in the surrounding hills, you'll see fortifications and the sites of various villages cleared in 1947. Finally, the only evidence of the village's other major prewar ethnic population group lies in the **Jewish Cemetery**, a short walk northwest of the square; around a hundred tombstones remain, the oldest dating back to 1718. There's a basic **bar-café** on the north side of the square, but as things stand, the place has the dubious distinction of having absolutely nowhere to stay – good enough reason for moving on rapidly elsewhere.

Sticking to the main road north out of Baligród brings you to Lesko after about 20km, where you join the main road back to Sanok.

The Beskid Niski

West from Sanok the main road, closely tracked by the slow rail line, heads towards Gorlice through the Wisłok valley, a pleasant pastoral route, with a succession of wooden villages set back in the hills of the **Beskid Niski** to the south. There's not a great deal to detain you, though, until you get west of Krosno, to the medieval town of **Biecz** and on to **Gorlice**, the centre for Beskid Niski hikes.

Also covered in this section is **Dukla**, an isolated old town that has long controlled the Przełec Dukielska pass into Slovakia – the most important crossing point in the east of the country.

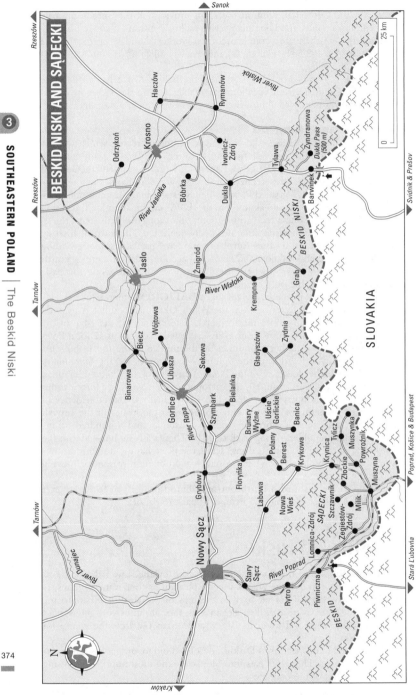

BESKID NISKI AND SĄDECKI

SLOVAKIA

25 km

0

▲ Sanok

◀ Rzeszów

◀ Rzeszów

◀ Tarnów

◀ Tarnów

◀ Kraków

▶ Svidník & Prešov

▶ Poprad, Košice & Budapest

▶ Stará Ľubovňa

River Wisłok

River Jasiołka

River Wisłoka

River Ropa

River Poprad

River Dunajec

BESKID NISKI

SĄDECKI

BESKID

N

Haczów
Rymanów
Odrzykoń
Krosno
Iwonicz-Zdrój
Tylawa
Żydranowa
Dukla Pass (500 m)
Barwinek
Bóbrka
Dukla
Jasło
Żmigród
Grab
Krempna
Wójtowa
Żydnia
Biecz
Libusza
Sękowa
Gładyszów
Binarowa
Gorlice
Szymbark
Bielanka
Brunary Wyżne
Uście Gorlickie
Banica
Polany
Berest
Krykowa
Tylicz
Muszynka
Krynica
Powroźnik
Grybów
Floryńka
Złockie
Muszyna
Łabowa
Nowa Wieś
Szczawnik
Milik
Żegiestów-Zdrój
Łomnica-Zdrój
Nowy Sącz
Stary Sącz
Rytro
Piwniczna

Krosno and around

At the heart of the country's richest oil reserves, **KROSNO**, the regional capital, is also the **petroleum** centre of Poland, but for the moment the resource is under-exploited, and the town seems more rooted in the past than expectant of future riches. Prior to the discovery of oil, which helped the town grow fairly wealthy in the late 1800s, Krosno had quite a record of mercantile prosperity. In particular, the town's favourable position on the medieval trade routes east meant it rapidly became one of the wealthiest Renaissance-era towns in the country, as evidenced by the sturdy burghers' mansions lining the square. Nowadays it's a tired-looking place which seems to have been bypassed by the economic developments going on elsewhere – a town from which to catch buses southwards into the Beskid Niski rather than stay the night.

The Town

From the adjacent train and bus stations, head downhill and turn right onto the main road, which leads to the hilltop-hugging Stare Miasto after about ten minutes. Ranged around the compact-looking **Rynek** are the Italianate merchants' houses fronted by arcaded passages – reconstructed in the nineteenth century in this case – characteristic of several towns in the southeast. Notable among these is the early sixteenth-century **Kamienica Wojtówska** (Wojtówska Mansion; no. 12) on the southwest side of the square, which boasts a finely decorated Renaissance portal, underscoring the town's mercantile Italian connections. South of the Rynek on ul. Franciszkańska is the brick-facaded late-Gothic **Kościół Franciszkanów** (Franciscan Church), notable features being some Renaissance tombstones of various local dignitaries, and, when it's open, which isn't often, the Baroque **Oświęcim family chapel**, a sumptuously ornate piece designed by Italian architect Falconi, with a particularly impressive ceiling, located in the north aisle of the building.

South from the Rynek along ul. Sienkiewicza, a statue on pl. Konstytucji 3 Maja commemorates **Ignacy Łukasiewicz**, the local boy who sank what's claimed to be the world's first oil well in 1854 in the village of **Bóbrka**, 10km south of town (see overleaf). North of the square along ul. Piłsudskiego, the main shopping street, is the **parish church**, a large Gothic structure with an overlay combining Renaissance and Baroque decoration to impressive effect, including a notable set of richly carved choir stalls and some fine polychromy above the nave. Unsurprisingly the regional museum, the **Muzeum Podkarpacie** (Tues–Sun: May–Oct 10am–4pm; Nov–April 10am–2pm; 2zł), in the sixteenth-century former bishops' palace at the top of the street, is mostly devoted to the local oil-mining trade, the highlight being a large and lovingly polished collection of early kerosene lamps, the revolutionary device of which Łukasiewicz was the inventor, including an elegant set of Secessionist lamps culled from around Europe.

The town had a thriving **Jewish community** (Jews first arrived here in the fifteenth century) up until the outbreak of World War II. Most of them perished in the Bełżec concentration camp during 1942. The Jewish Cemetery, northwest of the Stare Miasto, across the River Wisłok on ul. Okerzej, still contains a hundred or so gravestones and a monument to those murdered by the Nazis.

Practicalities

Accommodation options boil down to the *Hotel Śnieżka*, ul. Lewakowskiego 22 (☎013/432 3449, ✉sniezka1@polbox.com; ❷), which has a small number of rooms with shared facilities and is handy for the stations; the similarly basic

Elenai, ul. Łukasiewicza 3 (☎013/436 4334; ❸); and the business-oriented con-crete-and-glass palace that is the *Krosno-Nafta*, ul. Lwowska 21 (☎013/436 6212, ⓦwww.hotel.nafta.pl; ❼), southwest of town on the main road to Sanok. There's a summer-only **youth hostel** (☎013/432 1009; 20zł per head), 2km northwest of the centre at ul. Konopnickiej 5.

You'll find a sprinkling of **eating** and **drinking** opportunities on the main square: the Royal, Rynek 5, has a decent selection of Polish standards; while the nearby Piccolo Mondo at Rynek 6 has pizzas alongside a few more ambi-tious stabs at Italian cuisine like *Saltimbocca alla Romana*; and the *Wójtowska* at Rynek 7 is a decent eatery and *piwnica* (beer cellar) with a nice square-side location.

Around Krosno

The area around Krosno holds a number of worthy diversions, most of which are linked to Krosno by **bus**, even if there may only be the odd service a day (and none at all at weekends) to the more out-of-the way villages. Historic sites of the petroleum industry may not rank high on most people's must-see lists, but the intriguing **skansen museum** (Tues–Sun: May–Sept 9am–5pm; Oct–April 9am–3pm; 4zł) at **BÓBRKA**, a tiny village 10km south of Krosno, makes a good stab in that direction. Its chief claim to fame rests on the pres-ence of what's widely reckoned to be the world's first proper oil well, sunk here in 1854 by local pioneer Ignacy Łukasiewicz. The highlight of the *skansen*, devoted to the development of the oil industry that flourished in the eastern Carpathian foothills in the latter part of the nineteenth century, is the enjoy-able collection of early drilling derricks and rigs, the oldest built in wood, pre-served complete and several of them still in operation. At "Franek", the oldest specimen built in 1860, you can still see the crude oil bubbling away at the bot-tom of its well, while "Janina", ten years younger, is still in low-level commer-cial operation. Clambering up onto the platforms of some of these antiquated setups helps you appreciate the demands – and dangers – involved in extract-ing one of the planet's primary energy resources.

At the far end of the area, which takes a good half-hour to walk around, is a set of old workshops along with Łukasiewicz's former offices, converted into an informative museum; highlights include a chart of the first oil field com-plete with the locations of the first drill shafts, and a fine collection of Art Deco kerosene lamps, including Łukasiewicz's prototype, made in 1853. To get to the *skansen* from Krosno, you'll have to take a local **bus** from Krosno to the village and walk the remaining 2km through the forest. If you want to stay over in the village there's a **youth hostel** (May–Oct; ☎013/431 3097; 15zł per head) with cooking facilities, though apart from a basic **café**-type place at the *skansen*, there's not a restaurant in sight.

Elsewhere in the region, the ruins of the fourteenth-century **Kamieniec**, one of the oldest fortresses in the Carpathian Mountains, can be seen at **ODRZYKOŃ**, 8km north of Krosno. At **HACZÓW**, 12km east, a medieval town settled by Swedes and Germans in the fourteenth century, there's a beau-tiful mid-fifteenth-century Gothic **church**, the oldest wooden structure in the country, with a fine sequence of scenes of the Passion of Christ and the lives of the Virgin Mary and the saints, arranged in several layers, illuminating the walls of the nave. Some elements of the original decoration have been moved over to the new church immediately opposite, including a justly famed early-fifteenth-century *pietà*, carved in wood. While the wooden church is normally kept locked the local priest, who lives opposite, will open it up for you if you turn up at a reasonable time of day.

IWONICZ-ZDRÓJ, 11km southeast of Krosno, off the main Sanok road, is one of the most agreeable of a succession of pleasant little spa towns nestled in the river-coursed valleys of the Beskid Niski, the range of lower-lying hills stretching west of the Bieszczady that make up the continuation of the Carpathians chain. The town's strategic setting also makes it a good base for **walks** in the scenic surrounding *beskidy* (hills), with a couple of good hilltop routes leading westwards to Dukla (see below), some 6km away from town.

The main town thoroughfare, leading off from the only road into town, is a genteel promenade filled in season by crowds of holiday-makers, many of them staying in the plentiful *pensjonaty* available for takers of the supposedly healthy local waters. The main **hotel** choices are the *Pod Jodłą*, al. Torosiewicza 1 (☎013/435 0115; ❺), a popular, classy joint up beyond the main sanitorium marred by the curious lack of a restaurant; the similar *Energetyk*, ul. Piwarskiego 26 (☎013/435 0311; ❹); and the *Klimat*, al. Parkowa 2 (☎013/435 0767; ❷), a humbler alternative offering simple en-suites on the main street with its own restaurant – beware the "dance band" though. **Restaurant** options include the *Iwoniczanka*, al. Słoneczna 16, where you'll also have to watch out for the inevitable appearance of the house dance band, and the *Pizzeria Joanna* at al. Słoneczna 7. In season there are plenty of **drinking** establishments, mostly fairly down at heel, open on and around the main promenade.

Dukla and around

DUKLA, 24km south of Krosno, was for centuries the main mountain crossing point on the trade route from the Baltic to Hungary and central Europe. The location has also ensured an often bloody history, the most savage episode occurring during World War II, in August 1944, when more than 60,000 Red Army soldiers and 6500 Czech and Slovak partisans died during an (eventually successful) attempt to capture the mountain pass from its Nazi defenders, an event still commemorated on both sides of the nearby Slovak border.

Today, rebuilt after the comprehensive damage inflicted during the fighting, Dukla is a windy, quiet and rather bleak place – every bit the frontier town with its eerie, stage-set main square. There are two sights of interest: the reconstructed parish **church**, a warm, pastel-coloured Baroque edifice with a pleasing Rococo interior; and the former Mniszech family palace across the road, badly battered in 1944 and now home to a local **museum** (Tues–Sun: May–Sept 10am–5pm, Oct–April 10am–3pm; 3zł). As you might expect, the chilling story of fighting in the wartime "Valley of Death" is the focus of attention here – even the surrounding park contains a collection of Soviet and Polish military hardware.

For an **overnight stay** it's a choice between the basic PTTK *Dom Wycieczkowy* at no. 18 on the main square (☎013/433 0046), which offers simple doubles (❶) as well as dorm beds (20zł per person); or the seasonal **youth hostel** at Trakt Węgierski 14 (July–Aug; ☎013/433 0008; 20zł per head), or **private rooms** (ask at the PTTK). There are also a couple of places in **Lipowica** 1.5km south of town on the road to Barwinek and the Slovak border, notably the pleasant *Rysieńka*, (☎013/433 0149; ❷), where you can also get a bite to eat. For **food and drink** in town, check out the rudimentary restaurant in the PTTK hotel, the *Basztowa*, opposite the squat town hall in the main square, or the slightly better *Granicze* round the corner on ul. Kościuszki.

Around Dukla

Twenty-five kilometres south of Dukla, off the road to Barwinek, the village of **ZYNDRANOWA**, really no more than a collection of farmhouses, is the location of another of the region's diverse collection of *skansen*s. This one, right near the Slovak border, is devoted to local **Lemk culture** (Tues–Sun: May–Sept 9am–4pm; Oct–April 10.30am–3.30pm; 4zł). Established in 1966 by Teodor Gocz, an energetic local guardian of Lemk culture and customs, in a set of wooden farm buildings themselves typical of Lemk rural architecture, the *skansen* houses a vivid collection of folk religious art, traditional costumes and venerable old agricultural implements, a display detailing the results of Operation Vistula (see p.368), and, equally poignantly, a set of Soviet uniforms and other military leftovers from the 1944 Battle of Dukla Pass, picked up in the surrounding woods over the past few decades. Interestingly, 200 metres down the road a recently renovated **Jewish village house** (*chata*) has now been added to the *skansen*'s collection of buildings, containing a small but informative and well-presented exhibition about rural Jewish life and culture – a worthy and unusual enterprise. Getting here without your own transport isn't easy. The only option is to take a local **bus** from Dukla to the signposted turnoff from the main road, just south of **Tylawa**, and walk or thumb a lift the remaining 5km.

West of Dukla, one or two buses a day cover the backwoods route to **Gorlice**, taking you along the edge of the hills. If you have transport, or have time to **hike**, the tiny roads leading south into the Beskid Niski are well worth exploring.

Biecz and around

BIECZ is one of the oldest towns in Poland and was the conduit for nearly all the wine exported north from Hungary in medieval times. This thriving trade continued until the middle of the seventeenth century, when the "Swedish Deluge" flattened the economy – but fortunately not the town. These days it's a placid rural backwater living in the midst – but not, as yet, making the most – of its past architectural glories.

Trains and buses both stop near the centre, with the Stare Miasto a short walk up on the top of the hill. The **Rynek** is dominated by the fifty-metre tower of the late Renaissance **town hall**, which will look all the better when current renovations are completed. West along ul. Węgierka the parish **church**, a massive Gothic brick structure complete with a forty-metre fortified bell tower, contains Renaissance and Gothic pews, a fine seventeenth-century high altar and a noteworthy pulpit from the same era decorated with musicians, located in one of the side aisles. Not that it's easy to get in and see all this: the place only seems to be open during services, which means Sunday Masses and the occasional weekday service: check the notice board for details. Over the road, the well-organized town **museum** (May–Sept Tues–Fri 9am–5pm, Sat 8am–4pm, Sun 9am–2pm; Oct–April Mon–Sat 8am–3pm, Sun 9am–2pm; 2zł), housed in an early-sixteenth-century burgher's mansion once part of the town fortifications, is wide-ranging, eccentric and occasionally fanatically completist. The intriguing collection of local artefacts includes an excellent set of Baroque musical instruments, notably some venerable old bagpipes and hurdy-gurdys, a selection of eighteenth-century farming implements and carpenters' tools, a huge early-seventeenth-century Hungarian wine vat with a capacity of 9000 litres, and the entire contents of the old pharmacy – sixteenth-century medical books, herbs and prescriptions included. For the record, guides inform you that Biecz once had a school of public executioners. They were kept busy: in 1614, for example, 120 public executions took place in the square. There's another section of the museum, at ul. Kromera 1 on the other side of the church, detailing the town's chequered history (same opening times).

For an overnight stay there are two **hotel** options: the *Grodzka*, ul. Kazimierza Wielkiego 35 (☏013/447 1121; ❷), a former synagogue close to the train station on the main Krosno road; and the considerably more upmarket *Centennial*, a haven of luxury at Rynek 8 (☏013/447 1576; ❺). There's also a good-quality all-year **youth hostel**, uphill from the Grodzka at ul. Parkowa 1 (☏013/447 1829), on the top floor of a school building. **Places to eat** include the *U Becza*, a reasonable restaurant in a fine old beamed mansion on the Rynek, or the restaurant of the *Centennial*, which features French and Mediterranean cuisine at high prices. There are also a number of other more basic options on and around the square.

Around Biecz

Several villages in the vicinity of Biecz have beautiful wooden churches. If you've got time for only one sortie, go to **BINAROWA**, 5km northwest of Biecz (local bus or taxi). Constructed around 1500, the timber **church** here has an exquisitely painted interior, rivalling the better-known one at Dębno in the Podhale (see p.515); the polychromy is part original, part eighteenth-century additions, and all meriting close attention – notably, the marvellous pictures near the altar of devils with huge eyes and long noses cowering in the background at Christ's Resurrection, and the Last Judgement scenes, again populated by fearsome devilish creatures on the north wall.

Gorlice and around

GORLICE is an improbable base for the Beskid Niski, the westerly extension of the Bieszczady: you'll know when you're approaching the town by the suddenly foul air. Like Krosno, the town has for a century been associated with the oil industry, Ignacy Łukasiewicz having set up the world's first refinery here in 1853. If you want further doses of petroleum history, the local **museum**, just south of the battered old Rynek on ul. Wąska (Tues–Fri 9am–4pm, Sat & Sun 10am–2pm) – ring the bell to get the place opened up for you – is devoted to Łukasiewicz and the oil industry generally. The town's other points of interest are strictly historical. Gorlice was the site of a major World War I battle between Russian and Austro-Hungarian forces. The legacy of the bloody combat, which lasted over four months and caused over 20,000 casualties is the series of **war cemeteries** dotted around the approaches to the town. Examples can be found west of the Rynek near ul. Krakowska, 3km south of town off ul. Łokietka; and largest of all, in the Korczak district, roughly 2km northwest of the centre, a sombre, walled enclosure on a peaceful hilltop – like several other places, the subject of ongoing renovation. Looking around the 850 gravestones you'll find names of soldiers from virtually every nation in the region, Russians, Poles, Hungarians and Czechs included. A short walk south is the **Jewish cemetery**, a remnant of the town's long-standing Jewish community, who made up nearly half the population before World War II. A monument commemorates local Jews murdered by the Nazis in the local forests or in the death camp at Bełżec.

The **bus and train stations** are both close to the centre on the northern side of town. The train station is the terminus of the Krosno line – trains to Tarnów and on to Kraków leave from Gorlice Zagorzany, 2km up the line (frequent train and bus connections). **Tourist information** is available at the IT office on ul. Legionów 3 (☏Mon–Fri 9am–5pm; ☏018/353 5091). Accommodation options include the *Dom Nauczyciela* teachers' **hostel** at ul. Wróblewskiego 10 (☏018/353 5231; ❶), a short walk north of the Rynek (reception open from 5pm); the *Max* **hotel** at ul. Legionów 6d (☎018/352 1628; ❸); or the *Hotel Lipsk*, 2km out in the Krosno direction at ul. Chopina 43 (☎018/353 6766, ✉wczasy@glinik.gorlice.pl; ❷). There's a summer-only **youth hostel** at ul. Wyszyńskiego 16 (☎018/353 5746; 16zł), on the outskirts of town. For **places to eat** try the *Biesiadna*, ul. Piłsudskiego 6, for traditional Polish fare and local fish; or the *Patio*, Rynek 3, which serves up decent pasta dishes. For a snack, there's the *kawiarnia* in the town hall basement.

Sękowa and Gładyszów

If you're not in a hurry to move on it's worth stopping off at **SĘKOWA**, 7km southeast of Gorlice, home of one of the region's many beautiful wooden churches and straddling the historic borderline between the ethnic Polish and Lemk populations. A graceful early-sixteenth-century structure added onto – and in the case of World War I Austro-Hungarian soldiers who pillaged it for firewood, taken away from – several times in subsequent centuries, it has the sloping shingle roofs, high bell tower and protective surrounding verandah characteristic of wooden Roman Catholic churches in the south of the country. A Baroque high altar aside, the interior has sadly lost much of its original decoration. The church is frequently locked, but the nuns who live opposite will usually open it up for you. Local buses (#17) run here from Gorlice, dropping you a half-kilometre from the church.

Finally, horse-riding enthusiasts will want to consider visiting the **stables** at **Gładyszów**, 25km or so southeast of Gorlice (the best route, via the Uście Gorlickie, is slightly longer). A group of Carpathian horses (*hucule*) is bred and maintained here, and the stables organize very reasonably priced horse-riding excursions in the surrounding hills; contact Stadnina Koni Huculskich Gładyszów, 38-309 Gładyszów, Woj. Nowy Sącz (☎ & ☏ 018/351 0018).

South of Gorlice

The Beskid Niski are a hilly rather than mountainous range, less dramatic than the Bieszczady, but nevertheless excellent walking country. The people – predominantly **Lemks** (see box pp.368–369) – provide a warm welcome to the relatively few hikers who do get to this area, and many of their settlements have fine examples of the region's characteristic **wooden churches**. As a rule you'll find these deliberately tucked away amid the trees, their rounded forms and rustic exteriors seeming almost organic to the landscape. The earliest date from the fifteenth century, most from the eighteenth and beyond. For security reasons the churches are usually only open during services, although the local priest or caretaker will usually be prepared to open the place up for you. In the Gorlice area, a noticeable feature of most **cemeteries** is the international collection of names on the tombstones, a legacy of the momentous battle between the Austro-Hungarian and Russian armies fought here in 1915 (see p.379). If you want more detail, there's a useful Polish-language guide, *Galicyjskie Cmentarze Wojenne, tom 1: Beskid Niski i Pogórze* by Roman Frodyna (Rewasz, 1995) available in bookshops around the region.

Details of all hill walks are given in the PTSM youth hostel **handbook** (see Basics, p.42), and should be provided by the tourist offices in towns such as Krosno and Gorlice. A good local **map** will greatly increase your enjoyment of this region: again, you should be able to find the best one, *Beskid Niski i Pogórze* (1:125,000) in local bookshops or tourist offices. The most ambitious **route**, marked in blue on the map, runs some 80km from Grybow, 12km west of Gorlice, along the Czech border to Komańcza (see p.371). **Youth hostels** (July & Aug) are strategically placed at twenty- or thirty-kilometre intervals at Uscie Gorlickie and Hańczowa (day 1), Grab (day 2), Barwinek (day 3) and Rzepedź (day 4), all with **bus stops** nearby (served irregularly from Gorlice and Nowy Sącz).

Bielanka and Zydnia

The physical return of the Lemk and Boyk minorities to their roots has been accompanied by a revival of interest in their cultural and linguistic traditions. **BIELANKA**, 10km southwest of Gorlice, is the base of the **Lemkownya Music and Dance Ensemble**, which has already toured the Ukraine, Canada and the USA. Though less active of late, you can occasionally catch them rehearsing in the village hall at the weekends. Another route into the intriguing folk music of the region is provided by the annual **Lemk and Ukrainian Festival** (*Vatra*), a three-day bash held every July in **ZYDNIA**, a remote village 15km southeast of Bielanka, near the Slovak border – a showcase for music from all over the Carpathian region, Ukraine and Slovakia included.

The Beskid Sądecki

West from Gorlice the hills continue through a range known as the **Beskid Sądecki**, another low-lying stretch of border slopes sheltering a sizeable Lemk population and – enticingly – a wealth of old wooden churches. **Nowy Sącz**, the regional capital, is the obvious base for the area, which otherwise mostly comprises very small market towns, scattered villages and traditional peasant farms. Spa towns, notably the well-known cure centre of **Krynica**, are the region's other main attraction. If you're considering exploring the region in more detail you'd be well advised to invest in a copy of the *Beskid Sądecki: Mapa Turystyczna* (1:75,000), widely available and particularly helpful when searching out the numerous *cerkwie* scattered in and around the hills and valleys.

Nowy Sącz

NOWY SĄCZ, the main market town of the Beskid Sądecki and the regional capital, nestles on the banks of the River Dunajec, an out-of-the-way place these days and ideal as a base for exploring the hills. It was once better known, having been a royal residence from the fourteenth to the seventeenth centuries, and in the fifteenth century having seen the birth of the **Kraków-Sącz school** of painters, the first recognized Polish "school". After a long period of decline beginning at the end of the seventeenth century and lasting through to the late 1800s things began to pick up. The town expanded – not least its burgeoning Jewish population, eventually wiped out by the Nazis – on the back of the development of the railways in Austrian-ruled Galicia. Following the major wartime damage inflicted on the town by the Nazis, Poland's new communist authorities poured plenty of resources into reconstruction and expansion. Perhaps due to its favoured position as regional top-dog, into the post-communist era Nowy Sącz seems to be enjoying something of a resurgence. Renovation of the Stare Miasto is proceeding apace and at least in the centre there are plenty of signs of new-found prosperity, although you'd still be hard put to describe the place as a thriving metropolis.

The Town

The centre of the spacious **Rynek**, in the Stare Miasto, is occupied by the incongruous neo-Gothic **town hall**, which hosts occasional chamber music concerts as well as council meetings. At least in summer the Rynek boasts quite a collection of open-air terrace cafés and bars, lending the place an animated, bustling atmosphere it hasn't seen for generations. The much reconstructed Gothic **Kościół św Małgorzata** (St Margaret's Church), a cavernous edifice off the east side of the square, has the familiar Baroque overlay, two Renaissance altars excepted. It and many of the burghers' houses lining the square are looking a lot less shabby as a result of the systematic and extensive programme of restoration currently being pursued around the Stare Miasto.

Over the road on ul. Lwowska, the sixteenth-century Canonical House contains the **town museum** (Tues–Thurs 10am–3pm, Fri 10am–5pm, Sat & Sun 9am–2.30pm; 3zł), which displays those few pieces from the Kraków-Sącz school that haven't been taken off to the national museums in Kraków and Warsaw. The influence of Orthodox-inspired themes, albeit mediated via "Westernized" Uniate artistic trends, is strongly evident in these locally produced works, many of which also retain the naive proportions of popular religious art. Other rooms hold a collection of icons gathered from *cerkwie* in the surrounding region – not as extensive as that in Sanok but amply demonstrating the distinctive regional style of icon painting, and including some wonderful examples of the *Hodigitria* (Holy Virgin and Child) theme popular in Uniate iconography, and a complete iconostasis. There's plenty of folk art on show too, including some typically Polish *Christus Frasobliwy* sculptures, showing a seated Christ propping his mournful face on one hand.

The seventeenth-century **former synagogue** on ul. Berka Joselewicza, in the former Jewish quarter north of the Rynek, where the popular nineteenth-century tzaddik Chaim Ben Halberstam had his base, houses a contemporary art gallery (Wed & Thurs 10am–3pm, Fri 10am–6pm, Sat & Sun 9am–2.30pm; 3zł); the building has been so well modernized that there's virtually nothing visibly Jewish left. By way of compensation there's a small photo exhibition of local Jewish life – before World War II the 10,000-strong community made up over thirty percent of the town's population. An English-language brochure provides details of the layout of the Stare Miasto Jewish quarter: the north section of ul. Kazimierza Wielkiego alone used to have no less than four synagogues, although again there's not much evidence of the fact today. The surrounding area was also the location of a Nazi wartime ghetto, eventually liquidated in August 1942, when its residents were either shot or transported to Bełżec concentration camp. The recently renovated *ohel* of Ben Halberstam rests in the predictably overgrown **Jewish cemetery** on ul. Rybacka, over the river on the northern edge of Stare Miasto; a monument here commemorates the place where mass executions of local Jews were carried out by the Nazis.

Back across the river on the northern edge of the Stare Miasto, the ruins of the **castle**, built during Kazimierz the Great's reign, give a good view over the valley below. After being used for mass executions of local civilians, the castle was blown up by the Germans in 1945. Further south, on ul. Lwowska, the daily **Russian market**, known locally as Red Square, is worth a look – particularly for the adventurous shopper. There are some permanent kiosk-type setups, but the real deals can be found on the long tables or plastic dropcloths spread out on the ground. Keep an eye on your wallet and you may find some bargains.

About 3.5km east of town (or a brisk 40-minute walk; or bus #14 or #15 from the train station, bus station or ul. Lwowska), the **skansen** on ul. Długoszewskiego 83 (May–Sept Mon–Sat 10am–5pm, Sun 10am–2pm; 5zł) has an extensive and

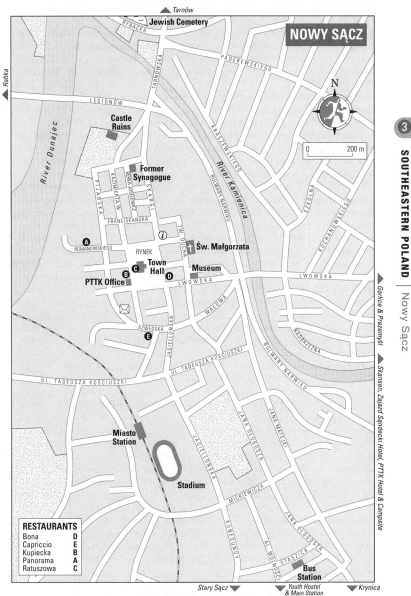

NOWY SĄCZ

Jewish Cemetery

Castle Ruins

Former Synagogue

Św. Małgorzata

RYNEK

Town Hall

Museum

PTTK Office

Miasto Station

Stadium

RESTAURANTS

Bona	**D**
Capriccio	**E**
Kupiecka	**B**
Panorama	**A**
Ratuszowa	**C**

Bus Station

Stary Sącz ▼   Youth Hostel & Main Station ▼   *Krynica* ▼

still growing collection of regional peasant architecture. If you've already visited the *skansen* at Sanok, the buildings in the Lemk and Pogorzanie sections here will be familiar, a couple of recently erected wooden churches included. What you won't have seen before, however, are buildings like the fragments of a Carpathian Roma hamlet – realistically situated some distance from the main village – and the assortment of manor houses, including a graceful seventeenth-century specimen from Małopolska, complete with its original interior wall paintings.

There are two **train stations**: the Miasto station, near the Stare Miasto, only handles local *osobowy* trains to Chabówka on the Kraków-Zakopane route; all other services use the Dworzec Główny station, 2km south of town. Local buses shuttle between the Dworzec Główny and town centre, via the **bus station** on ul. Staszica.

Online **information** can be found at ⓦ www.nowy-sacz.pl, while the main **tourist office**, located at ul. Piotr Skargi 2 (Mon–Fri 9am–5pm, Sat 9am–2pm; ☎018/443 5597) has a decent supply of maps and brochures. The PTTK office at Rynek 9 (Mon–Fri 9am–5pm; ☎018/443 7457) is useful for local **hiking** information, while the Poprad bureau in the *Hotel Panorama* (see below) may have details of **rafting** trips in the Dunajec gorge (see p.517). The Empik bookstore, Rynek 17, stocks all the local hiking **maps**.(ⓦ www.nowy-sacz.pl)

The choice of **accommodation** is reasonable. Aside from the handful of **private rooms** (❶–❷) the tourist office has at its disposal, the *Panorama* at ul. Romanowskiego 4a (☎018/443 7145; ❹) is top choice – central, cheaper and more congenial than the Orbis-run *Beskid Hotel*, a seven-storey concrete affair near the train station at Limanowskiego 1 (☎018/443 5770, ✉beskid@ orbis.pl; ❼–❽). Other options are the rather plain *Zajazd Sądecki*, stranded beside a main road junction 3km east of town at ul. Król. Jadwigi 67 (☎018/443 6717; ❷), and offering basic en-suites; and the spartan, barrack-block *PTTK Hotel*, situated a similar distance from the centre in the same direction at ul. Jamnicka 2 (☎018/441 5012; ❷), with frugal doubles and triples with shared facilities; take bus #14 or #15 from the train station. There's an all-year **youth hostel** on ul. Batorego 72 (☎018/442 3241), a short walk north of the main train station. For **camping**, there's tent space next to the PTTK hotel in summer.

Restaurants are pretty good. Currently the smartest places in town are the *Ratuszowa*, Rynek 11 (☎018/443 5615), offering quality Polish and international dishes in elegant rooms underneath the town hall; and the *Kupiecka*, roughly opposite at Rynek 10 (☎018/442 0831), an intimate cellar restaurant with a decent wine list (still a Polish rarity) open till midnight; for both restaurants, booking is recommended on summer weekends. The cookery-school-assisted *Bona*, on the east edge of the main square, serves an appetizing range of local specialities such as *placki* (potato pancakes), as well as serviceable pizzas, though it's only open till 9pm. Other reasonable places include the *Panorama* hotel's restaurant (see above), which provides excellent and inexpensive Polish standards; and *Capriccio*, south of the Rynek at ul. Szwedzka 3, a popular pizzeria-cum-bar housed in renovated medieval cellars, which also does decent lasagne and salads.

Assorted **drinking** dives are all over town, especially on and around the Rynek. *Pod Sklepowronem*, Jagiellońska 1, is an elegant underground café-bar stuffed with comfy wicker chairs, with a summer terrace at ground level; while *Czarna Wdowa* is a rough-and-ready but friendly basement bar further south along the same street.

The road around the Beskid Sądecki

The **Poprad River** – which feeds the Dunajec just south of Nowy Sącz – creates the broadest and most beautiful of the **Beskid Sądecki valleys**. A minor road runs its length to the Slovak border, which it then proceeds to trail for the best part of 25km. Meandering along this route is as good an experience of rural Poland as you could hope for, through fields where farmers still scythe the grass, with forests covering the hills above. Tracks lead off to remote hamlets, ripe for a couple of hours' church-hunting, while along the main body of the valley you can boost your constitution at Habsburg-looking spa towns like **Krynica**. North of Krynica, the road follows another valley to Nowy Sącz, making a satisfying circuit.

Travelling into the Beskid Sądecki by public transport, there are regular **trains** plying the route from Nowy Sącz through the Poprad valley to Krynica, stopping at numerous village halts en route. Most Nowy-Sącz-Krynica **buses**, however, by-pass the Poprad valley entirely, taking the more direct Kamienica valley route to the north.

Stary Sącz

Nowy Sącz's smaller cousin town of **STARY SĄCZ**, 10km south (buses #10, #11 or #43 from Nowy Sącz train station; or train on the Krynica line), is the oldest urban centre of the region. It grew around the convent founded by Princess Kinga, the public-spirited widow of thirteenth-century King Bolesław Wstydliwy ("the Shy") who was long the centre of a local cult, before finally being declared a saint by Pope John Paul II in 1999. The town squats atop a hill between the Dunajec and Poprad rivers, whose confluence you pass soon after leaving Nowy Sącz.

Like its modernized neighbour, the town's ancient cobbled **Rynek** – one of the few such remaining – has an expansive feeling to it, the main difference being in the height of the buildings – none of the eighteenth-century houses round the Stary Sącz square has more than two storeys. Even in a town this small, though, you still find two thirteenth-century churches: an imposing fortified Gothic **parish church** south of the square, subjected to the full Baroque treatment, and the convent **Church of the Poor Clares**, to the east, its nave decorated by sixteenth-century murals depicting the life of the Blessed Kinga, who founded the convent in 1270 and subsequently entered it in 1280 following her husband's death, to whom the side chapel with a statue of her on the altar is dedicated. The eccentrically cobbled together **town museum** at Rynek 6 (Tues–Sat 10am–5.30pm, Sun 10am–1pm; 2zł), a fine seventeenth-century mansion, will kill half an hour. On the other side of the square, it's worth looking inside the building at Rynek 21 to see the ceilings covered with murals by local artists in the characteristic local naive style, notably former owner-artist Józef Racek, who died a few years back.

Accommodation is limited to basic rooms at the *Szalas* (☎018/146 0077; ❸), 1.5km north of the centre on the Nowy Sącz road, the **youth hostel** (July–Aug; ☎018/146 0584; 20zł per person) at ul. Kazimierza Wielkiego 14, and the Poprad **campsite**, behind the *Szalas* on ul. Byłych Więźników Politycznych (May–Sept; ☎018/146 1197), which also has a few bungalows (❶).

The only real **restaurant** is the *Staropolska* on the Rynek (closes 9pm) and still a fairly basic dive, while the tallest of the Rynek's houses has a good *kawiarnia*-cum-restaurant upstairs, the *Marysienka*, with an enjoyable view over the square.

The Poprad Valley

By local train or bus it's a scenic two-hour ride along the deep, winding **Poprad Valley** from Stary Sącz to Krynica, and if you're not in too much of a hurry, there are one or two places worth breaking your journey at before you reach the terminus.

At **RYTRO**, 16km down the line, there are ruins of a thirteenth-century castle, and lots of hiking trails up through the woods into the mountains; there's a PTTK hotel-cum-hostel, the *Pod Roztoką* (☎018/446 9151; ❷), offering en-suite doubles, triples and quads; as well as a number of *pensjonaty* and workers' holiday homes here too. Radziejowa summit (1262m), which is reached by following a ridge path to the southwest, is one of the more popular destinations, about two hours' walk from the village. The stretch of the river after nearby **PIWNICZNA** forms the border between Poland and Slovakia, and is one of the most attractive parts of the valley, with trout-filled water of crystalline clarity. If you're not hoping to catch the fish yourself, call in at the *Karczma Poprad* restaurant in **ZEGESTIÓW-ZDRÓJ**, a lovely spa town further down the valley, for some excellent poached trout. The old village, some distance uphill from the station and beyond the restaurant, makes for an enjoyable, leisurely post-lunch stroll.

MUSZYNA, next along the valley, has sixteen mineral springs, spa buildings, and the ruins of a thirteenth-century castle, just north of the train station. The **town museum** (Wed–Sun 9.30am–3pm; 2zł), installed in a seventeenth-century tavern, focuses on local woodwork, agricultural implements in particular. With their own transport, fans of wooden churches can have a field day in this area, bearing in mind the usual caveats about access and opening hours. There are *cerkwie* worth seeking out in **Milik**, **Andrzejówka**, **Złockie** – a characteristic three-towered Lemk structure from the 1860s with an impressive iconostasis and collection of religious art – and **Szczawnik**, now a Roman Catholic church. From Muszyna the Poprad runs south and the railway heads off to the north towards Krynica, passing through the village of **Powroźnik**, which has a low-ceilinged seventeenth-century *cerkiew* with a fabulous iconostasis.

Krynica

If you only ever make it to one spa town in Poland, **KRYNICA** should be it. Redolent of *fin-de-siècle* central Europe, its combination of woodland setting, rich mineral springs and moderate altitude (600m) have made it a popular resort for over two centuries. In winter the hills (and a large skating rink) keep the holiday trade coming in.

From the train and bus stations at the southern end of town, ul. Novotarskiego heads towards the flowerbed-filled centre of the resort, where you'll come across a fine array of **sanatoria**, including pump rooms ancient and modern, assorted "therapeutic centres", and mud-bath houses. The main place to try the local waters is the **Pijalnia Wód Mineralnych** (Pump Room; daily 6.30am–6pm; entrance free, but it costs a złoty or two to take the waters) a remarkably ugly 1960s concrete monstrosity on the outside, but boasting fountains and huge indoor plants within. Rent or buy a tankard from the desk before heading for the taps, where the regulars will urge you to try the purply-brown Zuber. Named after the professor who discovered it in 1914, it is reckoned to be the most concentrated mineral water in Europe – it's certainly the worst-smelling. Zdrój Główny, a mixture of three or four different waters, is one of the more palatable brews. Somewhat improbably there's a concert hall located up on the second floor that sees plenty of action during the summer season. After all this, the nearby **Stary Dom Zdrojowy**, an imposing Habsburg-era monument, makes for a welcome change of style.

The town's other place of interest is the recently established **Muzeum Nikiforsa** (Tues–Sun 10am–1pm & 2–5pm; 3zł), occupying a nineteenth-century villa on Bulwary Dietla, just behind the Stary Dom Zdrojowy. As you'd expect, the exhibitions are mainly devoted to the life and work of the self-taught Lemk artist Nikifors (1895–1968), known locally as the "Matejko of Krynica", whose paintings bear inscriptions in spidery, childlike handwriting (he didn't learn to write until late in life), and are often reminiscent of Lowry's scenes of industrial northern England.

At the northern end of the promenade, past a statue of Mickiewicz and a small church, a **funicular train** (roughly every 30min Mon 10am–6.45pm, Tues–Sun 10am–7.45pm; 4zł each way) ascends the nearby Góra Parkowa (741m) and drops you at the top for an enjoyable overview of town.

Practicalities

Tourist **information** is dealt with by Jaworzyna, at the northern end of the centre at Pilsudskiego 8 (Mon–Fri 9am–5pm, Sat 10am–2pm, longer hours in summer; ☎018/471 5654), who also rent out **private rooms** (❶) and sell raft-ing trips on the Poprad and Dunajec rivers.

Another source of cheap **accommodation** is the FWP (Fundusz Wczasów Pracowniczych) bureau at Pułaskiego 7 (☎018/471 2842, ⓦwww.fwp-wczasy.krynica.pl), which will allocate rooms in one of the ten rather old-fash-ioned spa rest-homes they've got scattered throughout the resort – expect rooms wth shared facilities from about 25zł per person. Otherwise, there are innumer-able *pensjonaty* in Krynica – you'll find plenty along Zdrojowa, uphill from the town centre to the west, or on Pułaskiego and Świdzinskiego, uphill from the town centre to the east – often with their room rates advertised on signboards outside. Reasonably characterful are the *Willa Janka*, Pułaskiego 28 (☎018/471 2057; ❶–❷), a family-run place with en-suites and rooms with shared facilities surrounded by a well-tended garden; and the larger and more upmarket *Witoldówka*, ul. Bulwary Dietla 10 (☎081/471 5577, ⓔwitoldowka@pro.onet.pl; ❺), in a fine old wooden building at the northern end of the main drag, with comfortable en-suites with TV. Those with serious intentions of taking the cure should consider the *Panorama*, ul. Wysoka 15 (☎018/471 2885, ⓕ471 5415; ❺), a 100-room behemoth on a hillside just north of the centre, featuring neat en-suites, indoor pool and spa treatments; or the *GeoVita Znicz*, Ul. Leśna 15 (☎081/471 2866, ⓕ471 5665; ❼), a well-appointed hotel-sanatorium offering the full range of spa treatments and medical staff on hand.

For **eating and drinking**, *Lilianka*, Piłsudskiego 9, is a simple café that serves up the best pastries and cakes in town; while *Krynica*, Bulwary Dietla, is an unpretentious restaurant with a good line in inexpensive Polish staples. Nearby, the slightly smarter *Pizzeria-Kaviarnia Węgerska Korona*, Bulwary Dietla, offers so-so pizzas, good pasta and risotto dishes, and excellent ice cream in its café section. *Zielona Gorka* is a lively pizzeria and pub-style **bar** at the northern end of Nowotarskiego.

East from Krynica

The hill region **east from Krynica** towards the Slovak border is particularly rich in attractive villages and *cerkwie*, including some of the oldest in the coun-try. Those in **Wojkowa**, which boasts a fine Rococo iconostasis, **Muszynka** and **Tylicz** are all worth a visit, although the last, a Uniate building across the square from the Roman Catholic church, is generally closed. Tylicz and its sur-roundings figure in Polish history as base camp of the Confederates of the Bar (1768–72), a failed aristocrat-led revolt against growing tsarist control of the country (see Contexts). Local buses run occasionally from Krynica, or you could take a taxi – especially with company, it won't break the bank.

North from Krynica

North from Krynica buses run to Nowy Sącz and Grybów, to the west of Gorlice. For the first 6km both routes follow the main road to Krzykowa, where the road divides. For Nowy Sącz you continue through the wooded groves of the Sącz Beskids, via villages such as Nowa Wieś and Łabowa.

The **Grybów road** is an even more attractive backroads route, due north through open countryside. The village of **BEREST**, 5km north of the main Nowy Sącz road, is a real treat. Set back from the road in pastoral surroundings, it has an eighteenth-century *cerkiew*, an archetype of the harmonious beauty of this region's wooden churches. The doors, opened by a huge metal key that's kept by an ancient peasant caretaker, creak open to release a damp draft from inside; muted scufflings from the priest's small herd of goats will probably be the only sounds to break the silence. Just a couple of kilometres up the road is **POLANY**, where a contemporary icon painter named Eugeniusz Forycki has a workshop in an old Lemk house; in summer you can visit his workshop – a sort of private *skansen*. From here to Grybów the valley is a gorgeous riverside route; if you have a car, a brief detour south to Brunary-Wyzne, then on to the border villages of Banica and Izby, is worthwhile, as all three have magnificent wooden *cerkwie*. From **GRYBÓW**, you have the choice of frequent buses and trains west to Nowy Sącz or east to Gorlice, or trains north to Tuchow and Tarnów.

Tarnów

First impressions of **TARNÓW** are less than promising. A major regional centre with a population close on 100,000, much of the city is decidedly lacking in character. At the heart of Tarnów, though, is a medieval Stare Miasto area that more than makes up for the rest in interest. As you'd expect, the background story here is essentially commercial. Founded in the 1330s, like several towns in the southeast of the country, Tarnów rapidly grew fat on the back of the lucrative trade routes running east from Kraków down into Hungary and east on into the Ukraine. Long the seat of the wealthy local Tarnowski family, it remained a privately owned town right up to the end of the eighteenth century. Under their patronage it grew to become an important Renaissance-era centre of learning within the Polish Commonwealth, a branch of the Jagiellonian University in Kraków being set up here in the mid-1500s.

Later centuries of wars and partition brought the inevitable decline, and in this century, Tarnów's significant and long-standing Jewish population was a particular target for the Nazis. Today, the city's notable scattering of surviving Jewish monuments combine with the historic Stare Miasto centre to provide an enjoyable short visit, with enough here to detain you for a good day's sightseeing.

The Stare Miasto

The well-preserved central **Stare Miasto** area, only a small part of modern Tarnów, retains all the essentials of its original medieval layout. A chequerboard network of angular streets, cobbled alleyways and open squares, the oval-shaped Stare Miasto is ringed by the roads built over the ruins of the sturdy defensive walls, pulled down by the Austrians in the late nineteenth century. Within the area, the compact medieval ensemble retains its original two-tier layout, stone stairways connecting the lower and upper sections of the area.

The Rynek

Approached from the south side of town the steps up from the lower level lead on to the **Rynek**. Overall there's an enjoyably relaxed feel to the place, the ambience further heightened by the cleanup operation recently performed on most of the square's buildings, and the new terrace cafés dotting the edges –

banning cars from the square has helped, too. Centrepiece of the square is the fifteenth-century **town hall**, a chunky, single-storey building with a roofed circular tower and an arched Renaissance brick parapet topped by a series of sculpted grotesque heads, a device reminiscent of the Sukiennice in the town's former trading rival, Kraków. Arcaded Renaissance burghers' mansions occupy all sides of the square, notably the trio of parapeted houses on the **north** side, the facades adorned with their colourful original friezes. The central building of the three (no. 21) is the entrance to the **town museum** (Tues & Thurs 10am–5pm, Wed & Fri 9am–3pm, Sat & Sun 10am–2pm; 4zł), some of whose impressive wood-beamed rooms still retain their Renaissance fresco decoration. Largest of the exhibition halls houses a gallery of Polish seventeenth- and eighteenth-century portraits, members of the wealthy local Rzewuski and Sanguszko families sporting Eastern-influenced period Sarmatian dress being well to the fore. In addition there's a wealth of exhibits relating to local hero Józef Bem (see box overleaf) and his military wanderings, other rooms containing a largish assortment of European furniture, porcelain, art and sculpture of the same era.

The cathedral, diocesan museum and around

West of the Rynek on pl. Katedralny stands the Gothic **cathedral**, a cheerful-looking statue of the pope greeting you near the entrance. Though much rebuilt in subsequent centuries, the rather gloomy interior still has a fair bit of its early Gothic and Renaissance decoration. As well as the early six-

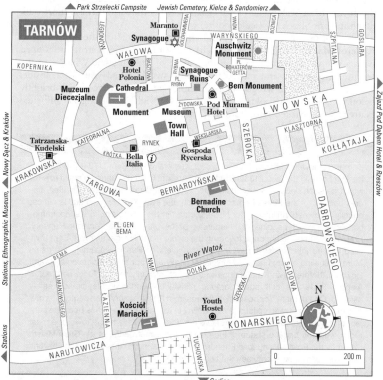

teenth-century entrance portal (featuring some fine stone polychromy topped by a figure of Christ and the Madonna), the cathedral boasts a fine collection of Renaissance tombstones, a number executed by the group of noted Italian sculptors employed at the royal court in Kraków. Particularly impressive are the grand sixteenth-century memorial to **Jan Tarnowski**, designed by Giovanni Maria Mosca and surrounded with friezes representing his military triumphs; the magnificent tomb of Barbara Tarnowska in the nave, the slender relief by Bartolomeo Berecci with a frame by Mosca; and the Mannerist Ostrogski family monument, a sumptuous marble ensemble with sculpted representations of family members kneeling beneath a crucifix at the centre.

Back out on the square, the former collegiate buildings on a quiet, atmospheric side street round the back of the cathedral house the **Muzeum Diecezjalne** (Diocesan Museum; Tues–Sat 10am–3pm, Sun 9am–2pm; 3zł), the oldest and one of the biggest such collections in the country; notable exhibits here include a couple of roomfuls of Gothic religious art, sculpture and other artefacts chiefly from the local Kraków–Sącz artistic school, the highlight being a graceful set of fourteenth- and fifteenth-century wooden *pietà*. Out behind the museum, as at several points around the Stare Miasto area, you can see surviving sections of the Stare Miasto walls.

South of the Stare Miasto and across ul. Bernardyńska, on the bustling market square below the main road is the birthplace of **Józef Bem**, after whom the square is named, a plaque on a house on the north side of the square commemorating the fact. There's a **statue** to the man back in the Stare Miasto at the corner of ul. Wałowa and Forteczna, while his **mausoleum** is a short walk north in Park Strzelecki (see opposite).

Following ul. NMP south from pl. Bema brings you after fifteen minutes to **Kościół Mariacki** (St Mary's Church), a charming wooden structure topped with a steep shingle roof, built in the village of Przedmieście Większe in the seventeenth century and moved to Tarnów two hundred years later. Inside, there are two Gothic winged altars on either side of the nave – each brightly coloured in reds and golds – the one on the right displaying an animated Nativity scene packed with hordes of saintly onlookers.

Józef Bem

Born in Tarnów in the early Partition years, General **Józef Bem** (1794–1850) was a leading figure in the failed 1830–31 Uprising against Poland's tsarist rulers, a role for which he soon became widely celebrated. A prototype of the dashing military figures beloved of the Polish Romantic tradition, the swashbuckling general is almost equally renowned in Hungary for his heroic part in the 1848 rising in Vienna, immediately after which he joined the leadership of the anti-Habsburg forces in Hungary. Heroic adventurer to the core, following the failure of the Hungarian revolt Bem travelled east to join Turkish forces in their struggle with Russia, assuming the name Murat following a rapid (and doubtless tactically appropriate) conversion to Islam. However, before having the chance to do much militarily for the Turks he died, in Aleppo, Syria, his cult status among resistance-minded Poles already safely assured. One of many "oppositional" figures from Polish history the country's former communist rulers were anxious to play down, in recent years Bem has been the subject of a welter of monuments that have gone up around his home town, the most recent addition being a statue of the man on the eastern edge of the Stare Miasto raised by the Polish–Hungarian Friendship Society, a move illustrative of the historic sense of communality between the two countries.

The Muzeum Etnograficzne

A ten-minute walk west of the Stare Miasto along busy ul. Krakowska brings you to the outstanding local **Muzeum Etnograficzne** (Ethnographic Museum; Tues & Thurs 9am–5pm, Wed & Fri 9am–3pm, Sat & Sun 10am–2pm; 4zł). The focal point of interest here is the set of exhibits relating to Poland's **Roma** (gypsy) population, claimed to be the only permanent exhibition of Roma in Europe. A handy English-language booklet produced by regional museum director Adam Bartosz, a local ethnographer and advocate for Roma rights, will fill you in on the details. Although Roma arrived in Poland at an early stage historically, they have never settled in the country in the same way, for example, as they have in the neighbouring Czech and Slovak republics. From a pre-World War II population estimated at 50,000, their numbers declined dramatically at the hands of the Nazis, with up to 35,000 perishing in the concentration camps – part of the estimated half-million Roma, equivalent to half their entire population, murdered during the course of the war. In the 1990s, the population was swelled by influxes from nearby countries, notably Slovakia and Romania – for the most part, these newcomers are still here. The Tarnów region has long been a centre for Roma in Poland, and it's this that explains the exhibition. Along with the general historical sections, there's a good collection of costumes, folk art and archival photographs of Polish Roma, a sombre account of their treatment at the hands of the Nazis and, bravely, a section detailing contemporary ill-treatment of and prejudice against Roma in Polish society. There's also memorabilia relating to **Papusza**, a gifted Polish Roma poetess whose work was "discovered" and translated into Polish in the 1970s. To round off, there are a group of four traditional painted Roma caravans displayed in the yard at the back of the museum. In summer (usually June), a traditional Roma camp is re-created in the yard, accompanied by occasional folklore shows and mini-festivals.

Park Strzelecki

Five minutes' walk north of the centre along ul. Piłsudskiego, **Park Strzelecki** (literally "Shooters' Park", a reference to the rifle associations that used to practice here in the early nineteenth century) is the town's main weekend strolling ground, a tranquil kilometre-long stretch of manicured flowerbeds and landscaped woodland. At it's northern end stands the **mausoleum** of General Bem, an arresting Neoclassical structure built to house the relics of the hero on their return to Poland from Aleppo in 1929. The general's funeral casket, bearing inscriptions in Hungarian and Ottoman Turkish as well as Polish, is held aloft by six slender Corinthian columns, the whole ensemble occupying an island in the middle of a lily pond patrolled by fat grey fish.

Jewish Tarnów

East of the Rynek takes you into what used to be the **Jewish quarter** of the town, a fact recalled in the names of streets such as ul. Żydowska and Wekslarska ("moneychangers"). Jews have a long history in Tarnów: the first settlers arrived here in the mid-fifteenth century, and right into the pre-World War II era Jews constituted roughly forty percent of the town's population. The town also became an important centre of Hassidism during the nineteenth century. Following their capture of the town in 1939 the Nazis rapidly established a ghetto area to the east of the Stare Miasto, filling it with all local Jews as well as many transported in from other parts of the country. At its height the population of the massively overcrowded ghetto area rose to 40,000. Between June 1942 and September 1943, virtually the entire ghetto population was either shot or deported to the death camps, principally Auschwitz, and most of the area itself was destroyed. A few Jewish monuments, however, remain in and around the Stare Miasto area.

Architecturally the moody, narrow streets around ul. Żydowska, all of which escaped wartime destruction, are essentially as they were before the war, with traces of the characteristic mezuzah boxes visible in a couple of doorways. The battered **bimah**, covered by a four-brick-pillared ceiling that stands forlornly in the middle of a small empty square north of ul. Żydowska, is what remains of the magnificent sixteenth-century synagogue that stood here until the Nazis gutted it in November 1939. At the corner of the street is a memorial tablet to the local Jewish residents murdered here in the course of a brutal *Aktion* carried out in June 1942. Over ul. Wałowa into ul. Goldhammer, named after a prominent local politician from the turn of the twentieth century, no. 1 houses the town's only remaining functioning **synagogue** (Sun 1–3pm), while no. 5, a classicist building from the 1890s, is the former home of the local Jewish Credit Company. Turning east into ul. Waryńskiego, past the corner with ul. Kupiecka, where the gate to the Nazi ghetto area stood, the corner of ul. Nowa is the former site of the New Synagogue, the biggest and most ornate in the town. Also known as the "Jubilee of Franz Joseph Synagogue" (it was consecrated on the emperor's birthday in 1908), the place burned for three days in 1939 before the Nazis finally resorted to blowing up the remains. The bottom of ul. Nowa leads onto pl. Bohaterów Getta. Across the square is the Moorish-looking **ritual bathhouse**, now a brash new shopping arcade-cum-office block: it was from here that a group of 728 local people were transported to Auschwitz in June 1940 to become the first inmates of the camp, a fact commemorated by the monument off the square on the corner of ul. Dibowa and Bożnica.

Final stop is the **Jewish cemetery**, a fifteen-minute walk north along ul. Nowodąbrowska. One of the largest and oldest Jewish graveyards in Poland, the cemetery was established as early as the 1580s, though the oldest surviving gravestone dates from considerably later. Surprisingly untouched by the Nazis, and still in pretty good shape, the overgrown cemetery contains a large number of tombstones, the emphasis being on the traditional type of tablet in which biblical and other illustrative reliefs are used only sparingly. Next to the entrance way on ul. Słoneczna (the cemetery's original gates are now in the Holocaust Museum in New York), stands a monument to the Jews of Tarnów incorporating a column from the devastated New Synagogue.

Practicalities

The main **bus and train stations** are situated next to each other on the southwest side of town, a twenty-minute walk from the Stare Miasto centre – bus #41 drops you on the edge of pl. Katedralna at the southern side of the Stare Miasto.

An extremely helpful **tourist office** at Rynek 7 (Mon–Fri 8am–7pm, Sat 9am–5pm; ☎014/627 8735 or 627 8736, ⓦwww.turystyka.tarnow.pl) has a wealth of information on the Tarnów region and sells local maps. They also offer **accommodation** in the shape of four guest rooms (❷) above the office; clean and modern en-suites which are well worth snapping up if you arrive early enough in the day. The only other centrally located alternative is the spartan, PTTK-run *Hotel Pod Murami*, ul. Żydowska 16 (☎014/621 6229), which has a mixture of bare-looking doubles (❶) and 4- to 5-person dorms (25zł per person). Tarnów's top hotel is the *Tarnovia*, near the train and bus stations at ul. Kościuszki 10 (☎014/621 2671, ⓦwww.hotel.tarnovia.com.pl; ❺), an outwardly grotty five-storey affair which nevertheless harbours neat en-suite rooms with TV. *Zajazd Pod Dębem*, 3km east of the centre, just off the main road to Rzeszów at ul. H. Marusarz 9B (☎014/626 9620; ❹), has plain but adequate en-suites and a bar-restaurant on site. There's a **youth hostel** just south of the Stare Miasto at Konarskiego 17 (☎014/621 6916; 10–15zł per person). The town **campsite**, fifteen minutes' walk north of the centre at Piłsudskiego 28A (or bus #30 from the train station; ☎014/621 5124) offers four-person cabins (❶), and tent/caravan pitches in an attractive apple orchard.

Tarnów doesn't exactly bristle with good **restaurants**, although there are plenty of places in the centre doling out snacks, pizzas and the like. *Maranto*, ul. Wałowa 4, is probably the best of the pizza places, and has a leafy outdoor terrace; while *Gospoda Rycerska*, just off the Rynek at Wekslarska 1, mixes pizza fare with grill food and Polish standards, served up in a cosy wooden interior. *Bella Italia*, Rynek 5, offers a similar Italian-Polish culinary mix, and has outdoor seating overlooking the square. *Kawiarnia Tatrzanska-Kudelski*, Krakowska 1, serves the best cakes, pastries and ice cream in town. Evening **drinking** centres on the cafés around the Rynek, which spread out onto the pavement in the summer months. *Art Café*, just off the square at ul. Żydowska 20, is a cosy subterranean café-bar with bohemian clientele.

Travel details

Trains

Krynica to: Nowy Sącz (10 daily; 2hr).
Łańcut to: Jarosław (10 daily; 1hr); Przemyśl (10 daily; 1–2hr); Rzeszów (12 daily; 30min).
Lublin to: Białystok (1 daily; 9hr); Chełm (8 daily; 2hr); Gdańsk (2 daily, including 1 overnight with sleepers; 8hr); Katowice (4 daily; 6–7hr); Kielce (5 daily; 3–4hr); Kraków (3 daily including 1 overnight with couchettes; 6–8hr); Przemyśl (1 daily; 6hr); Warsaw (11 daily; 2–3hr); Zamość (4 daily; 3–4hr).
Nowy Sącz to: Kraków (10 daily; 2–3hr); Krynica (10 daily; 2hr); Muszyna (14 daily; 1hr 40min); Tarnów (12 daily; 1hr–1hr 30min).
Przemyśl to: Kraków (10 daily; 3–6hr); Lublin (1 daily; 4hr 30min); Opole (3 daily; 7–9hr); Rzeszów (12 daily; 1–2hr); Tarnów (10 daily; 4–6hr); Warsaw (4 daily; 7–8hr); Wrocław (1 daily; 10hr).
Rzeszów to: Gdańsk (2 daily; 11hr); Kraków (12 daily; 2–4hr); Krosno (2 daily; 3hr); Przemyśl (12 daily; 1–2hr); Tarnów (16 daily; 1–2hr); Warsaw (2 daily; 5–7hr).
Sandomierz to: Kielce (2 daily; 2–3hr); Rzeszów (4 daily; 1hr 30min–2hr); Warsaw (3 daily; 4–6hr).
Sanok to: Kraków (1 daily; 5–7hr); Krosno (5 daily; 2hr).
Tarnów to Kraków (every 30min; 1hr 30min–2hr); Krynica (8 daily; 3hr 30min); Novy Sącz (16 daily; 1hr 30min–2hr); Rzeszów (20 daily; 1hr 30min–2hr); Warsaw (7 daily); Zamość (2 daily; 5–7hr).
Zamość to: Kraków (2 daily; 6–10hr); Lublin (1 daily; 2hr); Warsaw (1 daily; 7hr).

Buses

Biała Podlaska to: Białystok (3 daily; 3hr 10min); Bielsk Podlaski (3 daily; 2hr 10min); Janow Podlaski (12 daily; 30min); Siemiatycze (hourly; 1hr 20min).
Kazimierz Dolny to: Lublin (14 daily; 1hr 40min); Rzeszów (1 daily; 4hr); Sandomierz (1 daily; 2hr); Warsaw Stadion (1 daily; 3hr); Warsaw Zachodnia (2 daily; 3hr 30min).
Krosno to: Bóbrka (Mon–Fri 10 daily; 20min); Dukla (Mon–Fri 8 daily, Sat & Sun 3 daily; 40min); Haczów (Mon–Fri 8 daily, Sat 4, Sun 2; 20min); Iwonicz-Zdrój (every 30min; 30min); Rzeszów (14 daily; 1hr 30min); Sanok (12 daily; 1hr); Ustrzyki Dolne (2 daily; 2hr); Ustrzyki Gorne (Jul–Aug 3 daily; 3hr 30min).
Krynica to: Nowy Sącz (every 30min; 1hr).
Lublin to: Biała Podlaska (hourly; 3hr); Chełm (10 daily; 1hr 40min); Kazimierz Dolny (14 daily; 1hr 40min); Kielce (3 daily; 4hr); Kozłówka (5 daily; 1hr); Lubartów (Mon–Fri 12 daily; Sat & Sun 2 daily; 45min); Nałęczów (24 daily; 50min); Puławy (every 30min; 1hr 30min–2hr); Przemyśl; Radzyn Podlaski (Mon–Fri 16 daily; Sat & Sun 10 daily; 2hr); Sandomierz (5 daily; 2hr 15min); Siemiatycze

(hourly; 1hr 30min); Zamość (every 30min; 2hr).
Nowy Sącz to: Gorlice (10 daily; 1hr 10min);
Katowice (5 daily; 3hr 20min); Kraków (hourly; 2hr
10min); Krynica (every 30min; 1hr); Lublin (4 daily;
6hr); Muszyna (5 daily; 1hr 30min); Sanok (1 daily;
3hr 15min); Rzeszow (1 daily; 3hr 30min);
Szczawnica (10 daily; 1hr 20min); Warsaw (2 daily;
7hr); Zakopane (8 daily; 2hr 30min).
Rzeszów to: Krosno (14 daily; 1hr 30min); Łańcut
(Mon–Fri 24 daily, Sat 14 daily, Sun 8; 30min);
Krosno (12 daily; 1hr 45min); Lublin (8 daily; 4hr);
Przemyśl (12 daily; 1hr 40min); Sanok (10 daily;
2hr); Ustrzyki Dolne (4 daily; 3hr 20min); Ustrzyki
Gorne (Mon–Fri 2 daily; Sat & Sun 1 daily; 5hr
10min); Zamość (2 daily; 4hr 15min).
Sandomierz to: Kazimierz Dolny (1 daily; 2hr);
Kielce (8 daily; 2hr); Lublin (5 daily; 2hr 15min);
Rzeszów (4 daily; 2hr); Warsaw Zachodnia (8 daily;
5hr 45min).

Sanok to: Cisna (July–Aug 4 daily, rest of year 2
daily; 2hr); Krosno (12 daily; 1hr); Lesno (12 daily;
25min); Przemyśl (5 daily; 2hr); Rzeszów (10 daily;
2hr); Ustrzyki Dolne (4 daily; 1hr 10min); Ustrzyki
Gorne (Mon–Fri 2 daily, Sat & Sun 1 daily; additional services in July & Aug; 2hr 40min).
Tarnów to: Kielce (4 daily; 2hr 45min); Kraków (20
daily; 1hr 30min); Krynica (5 daily; 2hr 45min);
Nowy Sącz (16 daily; 1hr 45min); Sanok (4 daily;
3hr); Warsaw (4 daily; 6hr); Zakopane (3 daily;
4hr).
Zamość to Lublin (every 30min; 2hr);
Szczebrzeszyn (16 daily; 30min); Rzeszów (2 daily;
4hr 15min); Zwierzyniec (Mon–Fri 10 daily, Sat &
Sun 6 daily; 45min).
Przemyśl to: Jarosław (12 daily; 40min); Łańcut
(12 daily; 1hr 10min); Rzeszów (12 daily; 1hr
40min); Sanok (5 daily; 2hr); Zamość (1 daily;
4hr).

International trains

Nowy Sącz to: Bucharest; Budapest.
Przemyśl to: L'viv; Bucharest; Sofia.

Rzeszów to: Kiev; L'viv.

International flights

Nowy Sącz to: Bucharest (1 daily); Budapest (1
daily); Košice (4 daily); Pécs (1 daily).

Tarnów to: Bucharest (1 daily); Budapest (1 daily);
Košice (4 daily).

International buses

Biała Podlaska to: Brest (3 daily; 4hr).

Przemyśl to: L'viv (7 daily; 5hr).

Kraków, Małopolska and the Tatras

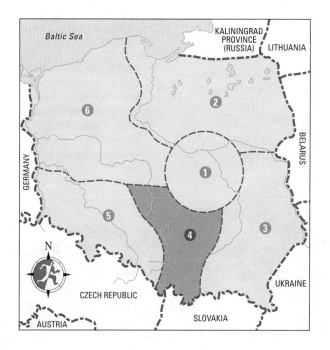

CHAPTER 4

Highlights

✳ **Krakow's Stare Miasto** One of the most wonderfully preserved old-town complexes in Europe. **P.412**

✳ **Kazimierz** The old Jewish quarter of Kraków, now the subject of much refurbishment, is still quiet enough to feel as though you're away from the crowds. **P435**

✳ **The Wawel** Kraków's hilltop castle-and-cathedral complex was for centuries the political heart of the nation . **P.428**

✳ **Ojców national park** This beautiful area of woodland makes for a great day out from Kraków. **P.476**

✳ **Częstochowa** This shrine to the Black Madonna, is the most popular Catholic pilgrimage site in Poland. **P.479**

✳ **Auschwitz-Birkenau** The infamous Nazi death camp, on the outskirts of Oświęcim, is a compelling memorial to man's inhumanity. **P.463**

✳ **The Tatras** Poland's most grandiose mountain range offers all the skiing and hiking possibilities that you could ask for. **P.512**

✳ **Górale folk music** The *górale* (highlanders) who live in the foothills of the Tatras have preserved folk and music traditions to a much greater extent than their lowland compatriots. **P.519**

4

Kraków, Małopolska and the Tatras

he Kraków region attracts more visitors – Polish and foreign – than any other in the country, and the attractions are clear enough from just a glance at the map. The **Tatras**, which form the border with Slovakia, are Poland's grandest and most beautiful, snowcapped for much of the year and markedly alpine in feel. Along with their foothills, the **Podhale**, and the neighbouring, more modest peaks of the **Pieniny**, they have been an established centre for hikers for the best part of a century. And with much justice, for there are few ranges in Europe where you can get so authentic a mountain experience without having to be a committed climber. The region as a whole is perfect for low-key rambling, mixing with holidaying Poles, and getting an insight into the culture of the indigenous *górale*, as the highlanders are known. Other outdoor activities are well catered for, too, with raft rides down the Dunajec Gorge in summer and some fine winter skiing on the higher Tatra slopes.

With a population of just under one million, **Kraków** itself is equally impressive: a city that ranks with Prague and Vienna as one of the architectural gems of central Europe, with a Stare Miasto which retains an atmosphere of *fin-de-siècle* stateliness. A longtime university centre, its streets are a cavalcade of churches and aristocratic palaces, while at its heart is one of the grandest of European squares, the Rynek Główny. The city's significance for Poles goes well beyond the aesthetic though, for this was the country's ancient royal capital, and has been home to many of the nation's greatest writers, artists and thinkers, a tradition retained in the thriving cultural life. The Catholic Church in Poland has often looked to Kraków for guidance, and its influence in this sphere has never been greater – Pope John Paul II was archbishop of Kraków until his election

Accommodation price codes

The accommodation listed in this book has been given one of the following price codes, based, unless stated otherwise, on the cost of the cheapest double room in high season. For more details see p.39.

❶ under 60zł
❷ 60–90zł
❸ 90–120zł

❹ 120–160zł
❺ 160–220zł
❻ 220–300zł

❼ 300–400zł
❽ 400–600zł
❾ over 600zł

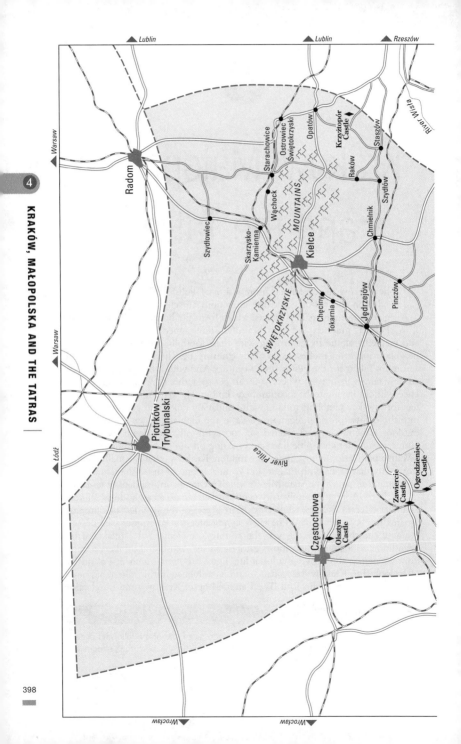

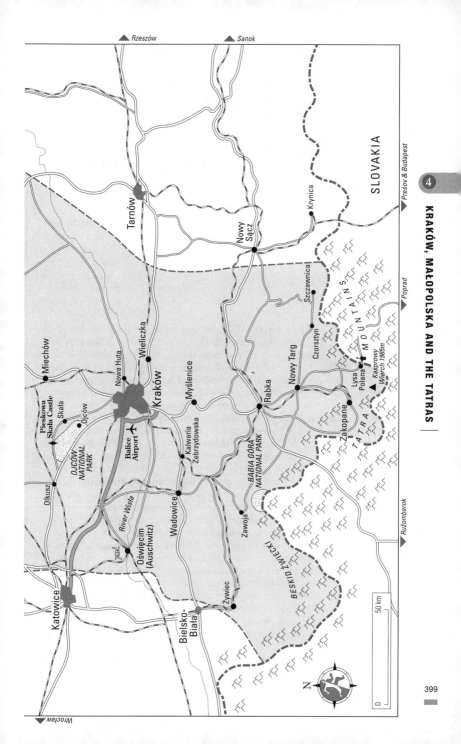

4

Rzeszów

Sanok

SLOVAKIA

Prešov & Budapest

Krynica

Tarnów

Nowy Sącz

Poprad

Szczawnica

Wieliczka

Czorsztyn

MOUNTAINS

Miechów

Nowa Huta

Kraków

Myślenice

Rabka

Nowy Targ

Łysa Polana

Kasprowy Wierch 1985m

Pieskowa Skała Castle

Skała

Ojców

OJCÓW NATIONAL PARK

Balice Airport

Kalwaria Zebrzydowska

BABIA GÓRA NATIONAL PARK

Zakopane

TATRA

Ružomberok

Olkusz

River Wisła

Wadowice

Zawoja

Oświęcim (Auschwitz)

BESKID ŻYWIECKI

Katowice

Żywiec

Bielsko-Biała

50 km

N

0

Wrocław

in 1978. Equally important are the city's **Jewish roots**. Until the last war, this was one of the great Jewish centres in Europe, a past whose fabric remains clear in the old ghetto area of Kazimierz, and whose culmination is starkly enshrined at the death camps of **Auschwitz-Birkenau**, west of Kraków.

This chapter also takes in an area which loosely corresponds to **Małopolska** – a region with no precise boundaries, but which by any definition includes some of the historic heartlands of the Polish state. Highlights here, in countryside characterized by rolling, open landscape, market towns and farming villages, include **Kielce**, springboard for hikes into the **Świętokrzyskie Mountains**, the magnificent ruins of **Krzyżtopór Castle** and the pilgrim centre of **Częstochowa**, home of the Black Madonna, the country's principal religious symbol.

Kraków

KRAKÓW, the ancient capital of Poland and residence for centuries of its kings, was the only major city in the country to come through World War II essentially undamaged. Its assembly of monuments, without rival in Poland, is listed by UNESCO as one of the world's twelve most significant historic sites. The city is indeed a visual treat, with the **Wawel** being one of the most striking royal residences in Europe, and the old inner town a mass of flamboyant monuments. For Poles, these are a symbolic representation of the nation's historical continuity, and for visitors brought up on grey Cold War images of Eastern Europe they are a revelation. All the more ironic, then, that the government of the 1970s had to add a further tag, that of official "ecological disaster area" – for Kraków's industrial suburbs represent the communist experiment at its saddest extreme.

Until the war, the city revolved around its **Jagiellonian University**, founded back in the fourteenth century, and its civic power was centred on the university's Catholic, conservative intelligentsia. The communist regime, wishing to break their hold, decided to graft a new working class onto the city by developing one of the largest steelworks in Europe, **Nowa Huta**, on the outskirts. Within a few decades its effects were apparent as the city fabric began to crumble. Consequently, in recent times, Kraków has been faced with intractable economic and environmental problems: how to deal with the acid rain of the steelworks, how to renovate the monuments, how to maintain jobs. Throughout the 1990s steady progress was made on environmental issues, and local initiatives in pollution reduction – combined with Western funding – mean that Kraków is now cleaner than it has been for decades, recent figures suggesting that air pollution levels are seventy percent below those of the mid-1980s.

Nowa Huta has played a significant role in Poland's recent **political history**. It was here – along with the Lenin Shipyards in Gdańsk – that things started to fall apart for the communist government. By the 1970s, the steelworkers had become the epitome of hostility to the state, and with the birth of Solidarity in 1980, Nowa Huta emerged as a centre of trade union agitation.

Working-class unity with the city's Catholic elite was demonstrated by Solidarity's call to increase the officially restricted circulation of *Tygodnik Powszechny*, a Kraków Catholic weekly which was then the only independent newspaper in Eastern Europe. It was in Kraków, as much as anywhere in the country, that the new order was created, and today, it is in Kraków that the economic fruits of that order are most visible.

Some history

The origins of Kraków are obscure. An enduring legend has it that the city was founded by the mythical ruler **Krak** on Wawel Hill, above a cave occupied by a ravenous dragon. Krak disposed of the beast by offering it animal skins stuffed with tar and sulphur, which it duly and fatally devoured. In reality, traces of human habitation from prehistoric times have been found in the city area, while the first historical records are of **Slavic peoples** settling along the banks of the Wisła here in the eighth century.

Kraków's position at the junction of several important east–west trade routes, including the long haul to Kiev and the Black Sea, facilitated commercial development. By the end of the tenth century, it was a major market centre and had been incorporated into the emerging **Polish state**, whose early **Piast** rulers made Wawel Hill the seat of a new bishopric and eventually, in 1038, the capital of the country. Subsequent development, however, was rudely halted in the mid-thirteenth century, when the Tatars left the city in ruins. But the urban layout established by **Prince Bolesław the Shy** in the wake of the Tatar invasions, a geometric pattern emanating from the market square, remains to this day.

Kraków's importance was greatly enhanced during the reign of **King Kazimierz**. In addition to founding a **university** here in 1364 – the oldest in central Europe after Prague – Kazimierz rebuilt extensive areas of the city and, by giving Jews right of abode in Poland, paved the way for the development of a thriving **Jewish community**. The advent of the Renaissance heralded Kraków's emergence as an important European centre of learning, its most famous student (at least, according to local claims) being the young **Nicolaus Copernicus**. Part and parcel of this was a reputation for religious tolerance at odds with the sectarian fanaticism then stalking sixteenth-century Europe. It was from Kraków, for example, that King Sigismund August assured his subjects that he was not king of their consciences – bold words in an age of despotism and bloody wars of religion.

King Sigismund III Waza's decision to move the capital to Warsaw in 1596, following the Union of Poland and Lithuania, was a major blow. The fact that royal coronations (and burials) continued to take place on Wawel for some time after was little compensation for a major loss of status. Kraków began to decline, a process accelerated by the pillaging of the city during the Swedish invasion of 1655–57.

Following the **Partitions**, and a brief period as capital of a tiny, notionally autonomous republic, the Free City of Kraków (1815–46), the city was incorporated into the **Austro-Hungarian** province of Galicia. The least repressive of the occupying powers, the emperor granted Galicia autonomy within the empire in 1868, the prelude to a major revival. The relatively liberal political climate allowed Kraków to become the focus of all kinds of underground political groupings. **Józef Piłsudski** began recruiting his legendary Polish legions here prior to World War I, and from 1912 to 1914 Kraków was **Lenin**'s base for directing the international communist movement and the production of *Pravda*. Artists and writers attracted by the new liberalism gathered here too. Painter **Jan**

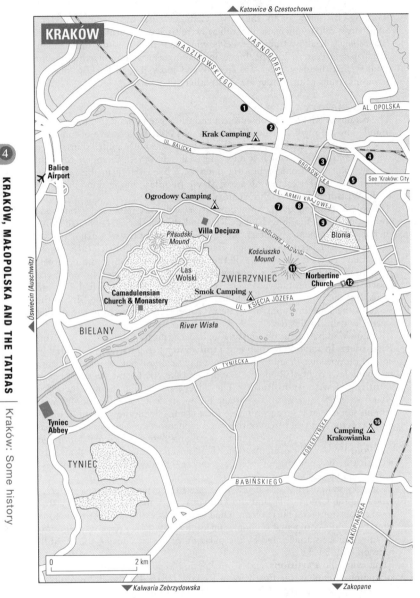

KRAKÓW

Katowice & Częstochowa

Balice Airport

Krak Camping ❷

Ogrodowy Camping

Villa Decjuza

Piłsudski Mound

Las Wolski

ZWIERZYNIEC

Camadulensian Church & Monastery

Smok Camping

Kościuszko Mound

Norbertine Church ⑫

Błonia

See 'Kraków: City

BIELANY

River Wisła

Tyniec Abbey

TYNIEC

Camping Krakowianka ⑯

0   2 km

Kalwaria Zebrzydowska   Zakopane

Matejko produced many of his stirring paeans to Polishness during his residency as art professor at the Jagiellonian University, and the city was centre of the **Młoda Polska** (Young Poland) movement – an Art-Nouveau-inspired flowering of the arts led by Stanisław Wyspiański and Jacek Malczewski.

The brief interlude of independence following World War I ended for Kraków in September 1939 when the **Nazis** entered the city. Kraków was soon designated capital of the so-called General Government, which covered

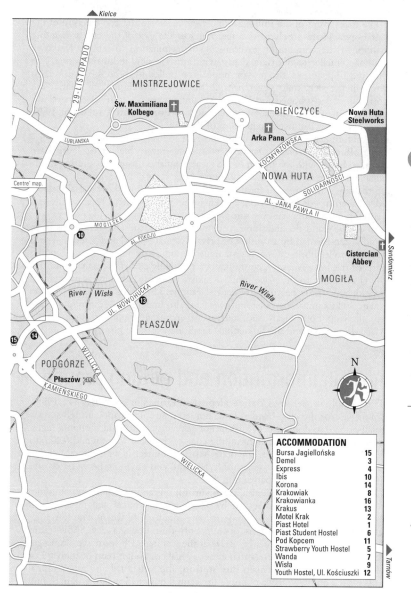

ACCOMMODATION

Bursa Jagiellońska	15
Demel	3
Express	4
Ibis	10
Korona	14
Krakowiak	8
Krakowianka	16
Krakus	13
Motel Krak	2
Piast Hotel	1
Piast Student Hostel	6
Pod Kopcem	11
Strawberry Youth Hostel	5
Wanda	7
Wisła	9
Youth Hostel, Ul. Kościuszki	12

all those Polish territories not directly annexed to the Reich. Hans Frank, the notorious Nazi governor, moved into the royal castle on Wawel Hill, from where he exercised a reign of unbridled terror, presaged by the arrest and deportation to concentration camps of many professors from the Jagiellonian University in November 1939. The elimination of the **Kraków ghetto**, most of whose inhabitants were sent to nearby Auschwitz (Oświęcim), was virtually complete by 1943.

The main event of the immediate postwar years was the construction of the vast **Nowa Huta steelworks** a few miles to the east of the city, a daunting symbol of the communist government's determination to replace Kraków's Catholic, intellectually oriented past with a bright new industrial future. The plan did not succeed: the peasant population pulled in to construct and then work in the steel mills never became the loyal, antireligious proletariat the communist party hoped for. Kraków's reputation as a centre of conservative Catholicism was enhanced by the election of **Pope John Paul II** in 1978, who until then had been archbishop of Kraków.

An unforeseen consequence of the postwar industrial development is a serious **pollution** problem. Over the years dangerously high toxic levels have wreaked havoc with the health of the local population, as well as causing incalculable damage to the ancient city centre. After years of prevarication, cleaning up the city is now a major local political issue: in 1989 Kraków actually elected a Green mayor for a period, and environmental problems have remained a central political concern ever since.

Since 1989 and the transition to democratic rule, the city centre has been rapidly transformed by an influx of private capital – local and foreign – with Western-style shops, cafés and restaurants springing up in abundance, lending parts of the Stare Miasto a cosmopolitan, decidedly affluent feel that confirms the city's return to the place proud Kraków residents have always maintained it belonged, in the heartland of central Europe. The historic ensemble of the square and its immediate surroundings have also undergone a thorough cleanup, allowing both locals and tourists to appreciate buildings such as the Mariacki Church and the Sukiennice in all their pristine beauty.

Arrival, information and getting around

The recently modernized **Balice airport** (information on ☎012/411 1955), 15km west of the city, handles both domestic and international flights. It's a small place – so don't expect a wealth of cafés, restaurants and shopping malls. Buses #152 (to Basztowa, right on the edge of the Stare Miasto) and #208 (to pl. Nowy Kleparz, north of the Stare Miasto) connect it with the city centre (30–40min). Taxis are always available, too, and cost anything between 40 and 70zł depending on your bargaining skills.

Kraków Główny, the central **train station**, a grand Habsburg-era building, recently modernized and served by all principal national and international lines, is within walking distance of the Stare Miasto (Old Town). The **left-luggage** office at the station is open twenty-four hours a day. Some trains (overnight services particularly) arrive at the southern **Płaszów** station: to get to the city centre from here, catch either a local commuter train or tram #3 or #6. **Dworzec PKS**, the main **bus station**, also a national and international hub, is sited on ul. Worcella opposite the central train station. For where to find train and bus information and tickets, see p.406.

Arriving by car, major roads from all directions are well signposted, though once in the centre, you'll need to cope with trams, narrow streets, heavy daytime traffic, and in much of the centre, heavily enforced **zonal parking restrictions**, including wheel clamps on illegally parked vehicles. The Rynek Główny and much of its immediate surroundings are now completely closed to private vehicles, and the local police no longer show much sympathy even for wayward foreigners. If this is where you're headed for, use one of the official **guarded car parks** on plac św. Ducha and plac Szczepański – fairly expensive (currently 60zł per 24hr period) and it's often hard to get a space. Other guarded car parks in the central city area include those at al. Focha, ul. Armii Krajowej, ul. Karmelicka, ul. Królewska 55 and ul. Powiśle. Furthermore, although they are technically for hotel guests only, you could also try the *Cracovia*, *Continental* and *Wanda* hotel guarded car parks (see "Hotels," below), further out but slightly cheaper.

Information and maps

Possibly in response to the sheer number of visitors, provision of **tourist information** in Kraków is better organized than in most other Polish cities. The **municipal tourist office**, occupying a circular pavilion in the Planty between the train station and the Stare Miasto (Mon–Fri 8am–8pm, Sat & Sun 9am–5pm; ☎012/430 2646, ⓦwww.krakow.pl) can give advice on accommodation possibilities and sells maps; while the Małopolksa **regional tourist office**, Rynek Główny 1/3 (on the eastern side of the Sukiennice; Mon–Fri 8am–6pm, Sat 8am–4pm; ☎012/428 3600, ⓦwww.mcit.pol), gives out information on Kraków and the surrounding region as well as booking accommodation and selling tickets for cultural events. Most useful of the travel agencies is Orbis, Rynek Główny 41 (Mon–Fri 9am–6pm, Sat 9am–2pm, Sun 10am–2pm; ☎012/422 4035, ⓦwww.orbis.travel.krakow.pl), who organize **tours** to Auschwitz, Wieliczka, the Dunajec gorge and elsewhere, as well as selling international air, train and bus tickets.

The Centrum Informacji Kulturalnej (Cultural Information Centre), at ul. św. Jana 2, just off the Rynek (Mon–Fri 10am–7pm, Sat 11am–7pm; ☎012/421 7787, ⓦwww.karnet.krakow2000.pl), provides a pretty comprehensive supply of information and **tickets** for current and upcoming concerts, theatre and other cultural events. Most of the staff are English-speaking. Otherwise, your best source of information is likely to be *Kraków in your Pocket* (from the tourist offices or from newsstands; 5zł), a remarkably comprehensive English-language **listings** booklet that is published five to six times a year. There are two glossy English-language monthly magazines available from the tourist office, Orbis hotels and certain bookshops, *Welcome to Kraków* and *Kraków: What, Where, When* – both of which boast nice colour pictures, but are hopeless as sources of up-to-date information. Better is *Karnet* (3zł), a small-format Polish- and English-language cultural listings booklet produced by the Centrum Informacji Kulturalnej (see above), with a decided bias towards mainstream events – not much use for gigs, in other words.

If you can read Polish, the Kraków edition of *Gazeta Wyborcza* carries local listings in the *Co jest grane* supplement on Fridays. For a low-down on the bar and club scene consult the monthly, tabloid-sized *City Magazine*, or the glossier, fortnightly *Aktivist* (ⓦwww.aktivist.pl), both of which are given away free in the trendier bars and cafés.

If you plan a longer stay, or are staying out in the suburbs, it might be worth investing in the fold-out 1:20,000 *Plan Miasta* with the red cover, available at the tourist offices, Ruch kiosks, bookshops or street vendors – for a wider range of local **maps**, head for the Empik megastore, Rynek Główny 25.

Orientation and getting around

Kraków is bisected by the **River Wisła**, though virtually everything of interest is concentrated on the north bank. At the heart of things, enclosed by the **Planty** – a green belt following the course of the old ramparts – is the **Stare**

Miasto, the Old Town, with its great central square, the **Rynek Główny**. Just south of the Stare Miasto, looming above the riverbank, is **Wawel**, the royal castle hill, beyond which lies the old Jewish quarter of **Kazimierz**. This whole central area is compact enough to get around **on foot**; recently introduced restrictions mean that much of the Stare Miasto – including the Rynek – is virtually car-free.

Exploring further afield, the **inner suburbs** have more character than usual thanks to the lack of wartime damage, the modern apartment blocks being interspersed with the odd villa and nineteenth-century residential area. Coming in from the east, you'll see and smell the steelworks at **Nowa Huta**, the chimneys mercifully working rather less hard on acid rain production these days thanks to the installation of effective filter systems. **Trams** in and out of these areas are plentiful, start early and run till late at night – routes radiate out from the Planty to the suburbs, and useful services are detailed in the text. **Buses**, which complement the trams and keep similarly long hours (with night buses taking over from around 11pm to 5am), provide the main links with outer suburbs and local towns such as Wieliczka. **Tickets** are purchased at kiosks and shops displaying the MPK symbol, or from the driver, for a 0.50zł surcharge. You can buy single tickets valid for one journey (2.20zł); tickets valid for one hour and allowing for any number of changes in that time (2.80zł); day tickets (*bilet dzienny*; 9zł); or week tickets (*bilet tygodniowy*; 22zł). Unless you have one of the latter, you'll need a separate ticket to travel on night buses (5zł). There are also a range of **group tickets**, of which the one-day, four-person family ticket (*bilet rodzinny*; 9zł) is probably the most useful. Students with ID travel half-price in Kraków. Bear in mind that public transport is subject to regular price hikes, so expect changes. Remember to punch your ticket at both ends on entering the bus or tram – if you're caught without a valid ticket, you'll be fined 40zł on the spot. Annoyingly, large pieces of luggage (including backpacks) require their own individual ticket (holders of day or week tickets are exempt from this): failure to follow this arcane regulation will incur a 20zł fine.

Taxis are still affordable for visitors, though as elsewhere in the country they are highly priced for the local economy. Remember to make sure the driver turns on the meter, and that from 11pm to 5am, rates go up by half. There are ranks around the centre of town at plac św. Ducha, Mały Rynek, plac Dominikański, plac Szczepański, plac Wszystkich Świętych, ul. Sienna (by the main post office) and at the main train station. Calling a radio taxi, such as Wawel Taxi (☏9666) or ExpresTaxi (☏9629), can work out significantly cheaper. There's a special subsidized taxi service for people with disabilities, using a small fleet of **minibuses** adapted for **wheelchair access** (6am–10pm; ☏9633 or 644 5555).

Local train services can be handy for trips out of the city centre, such as to Płaszów – we've given details of whenever these come in useful.

Accommodation

Kraków is becoming one of central Europe's prime city destinations, so you're well advised to book ahead with **hotels**, particularly during the summer. **Prices** for hotel rooms are higher than in most Polish cities, especially in the Stare Miasto area where the top-grade places charge rates on a par with central Europe's priciest. Price is not always an accurate guide to quality, with many of the older unrenovated hotels charging similar prices to the newer,

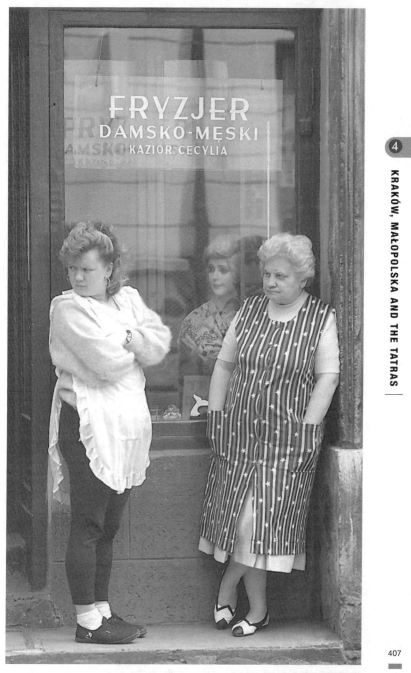

△ Hairdressers, Kraków

international-style establishments. It's rare (but not entirely impossible) to find a hotel room in or around the Stare Miasto for under 300zł a double, so budget travellers who aren't camping will have to be content with hotels well outside the centre, hostels or private rooms.

The **Waweltur office**, near the train and bus stations at ul. Pawia 6 (Mon–Fri 8am–8pm, Sat 8am–2pm; ☎012/422 1921), organizes **private rooms** (❸), which can be a good bet, especially during the summer when other budget accommodation options may be booked solid. Ask carefully about addresses, as many tend to be a long way out. Alternatively, especially in the train station area you're likely to be approached by any number of locals offering rooms, sometimes at markedly lower prices (and of a correspondingly lower standard) than those quoted at the Waweltur office. Before you formally accept, apply the obvious rules: establish the exact location, don't hand over any money until you've actually seen the place, and be prepared to engage in some haggling over the price, particularly if you're planning to stay for a longer period.

Hotels

Many of the city's **hotels** are located in and around the Stare Miasto area, with a cluster within striking distance of the train station. Generally speaking, the closer you get to the Rynek, the pricier and noisier it gets, although the really upmarket places tend to be on quieter side streets or around courtyards. Note that **Kazimierz** is a growth area for hotels, thanks to the heightened pull of the former Jewish quarter post *Schindler's List*. Expect new places, the majority aimed principally at Jewish visitors, to continue opening up over the next few years.

Note that a number of hotels – particularly upper-bracket places – may have significant **discounts** on rooms during the off-season period: the main tourist offices can supply you with details of what's on offer currently.

Near the train and bus stations

Atrium ul. Krzywa 7 ☎012/430 0203, ⓦwww.hotelatrium.com.pl. Modern, comfortable and stylish place – imagine a Scandinavian furniture showroom and you'll know what the rooms look like. Just off the bustling ul. Długa, and within minutes of both the stations and the Stare Miasto. ❼

Europejski ul. Lubicz 5 ☎012/423 2510, ⓦwww.he.pl. Undistinguished mid-range place close to the train station, and accordingly popular. Old-fashioned rooms come with parquet floors and furnishings that have been around a bit, but the bathrooms are sparkly new. En-suites and rooms with shared facilities. ❻–❼

Mistia ul. Szlak 73a ☎012/633 2926, ⓦwww.mistia.org.pl. Decent budget hotel owned by a Polish local government institute ten minutes' walk north of the stations. Rooms are narrow and sparsely furnished but they're clean and well looked after throughout. Rooms with en-suite shower or with shared facilities. ❹–❺

Polonia ul. Basztowa 25 ☎012/422 1233, ⓦwww.hotel-polonia.com.pl. Best of the hotels close to the train station, although rooms come in various stages of modernization. At least the en-suites have clean bathrooms and TV; the rooms with shared bathrooms are a bit less salubrious. ❹–❼

Warszawski ul. Pawia 6 ☎012/424 2100. Good location right across from the train station, but a mixed bag of rooms: renovated ones are plush and pricey, while the older rooms are gloomy in comparison and often don't come with bathrooms. ❻–❼

The Stare Miasto

Bursa Pigonia ul. Garbarska 7a ☎012/422 3008, ⓦwww.uj.edu.pl. Sedate university guesthouse just beyond the Planty in the Piasek district, with a small number of decently furnished rooms and a restaurant. ❼

Campanile ul. św. Tomasza 34 ☎012/424 2600, ⓦwww.envergure.fr. Brand new French-run place on the northeastern edge of the Stare Miasto with small but snazzy en-suites – each comes with tea/coffee-making facilities. ❼

Classic ul. św. Tomasza 32 ☎012/424 0303, ⓦwww.hotel-classic.pl. Thoroughly modern place with bright en-suites done out in orange and avocado colours. ⑧

Copernicus ul. Kanonicza 16 ☎012/431 1044, ⓦwww.hotel.com.pl. Medium-sized luxury joint on the way to Wawel, offering supreme levels of comfort and service. Worth the high price tag. ⑨

Cracovia al. Focha 1 ☎012/422 8666, Ⓔcracovia@orbis.pl. Oldest, ugliest and best located of the Orbis hotels, a ten-minute walk west of the Stare Miasto. ⑧

Dom Gościnny ul. Floriańska 49 ☎429 1789, ⒺDGUJ@if.uj.edu.pl. Good-value and well-run university guesthouse with large rooms, in an excellent central location. It's much used by visiting academics, which makes advance booking near essential at most times of the year. ⑦

Elektor ul. Szpitalna 28 ☎012/423 2317, ⓦwww.bci.krakow.pl/elektor. Recent addition to the city's growing stock of smart hotels. Fine central location, swish apartment-style rooms, upmarket bar and restaurant, all with prices to match. ⑨

Floryan ul. Floriańska 38 ☎012/431 1418, ⓦwww.floryan.com.pl. Small hotel offering very stylish downtown rooms with modern furnishings. Recommended if you want a change from the faded glories on offer elsewhere. Prices depend on room size. ⑦–⑧

Fortuna ul. Czapskich 5 ☎4012/22 3143, ⓦwww.hotel-fortuna.com.pl. Enjoyable, reasonably priced little hotel with simply furnished rooms in easy walking distance west of the university district. ⑦

Fortuna Bis ul. Piłsudskiego 25 ☎012/430 1025, Ⓔinfo@hotel-fortuna.com.pl. Small but plush annexe of the *Fortuna* (see above), offering en-suites that wouldn't look out of place in any international three-star, and the building itself has a lot of character; two houses knocked together to create a maze of staircases and landings. Stylish pub-restaurant on site. ⑧

Francuski ul. Pijarska 13 ☎012/422 5122, Ⓔfrancusk@orbis.pl. Elegant, comfortable old hotel, recently renovated though still retaining some of its retro feel. A well-established favourite with upmarket travellers. ⑨

Grand ul. Sławkowska 5–7 ☎012/421 7255, ⓦwww.grand.pl. Luxury hotel in a good central location. Habsburg-era fittings add a touch of class. ⑨

Logos ul. Szujskiego 5 ☎012/632 3333, ⓦwww.interkom.pl/logos. Modern building aimed at business people and tourists alike, featuring fully equipped but rather sparse rooms. An easy walk west of the Stare Miasto. Weekend discounts. ⑦

Pod Różą ul. Floriańska 14 ☎012/422 1244, Ⓔpod-roza@hotel.com.pl. Venerable, once-atmospheric place which preserves a *belle-époque* sumptuousness in the reception areas and restaurant, and has largish, decent-quality rooms. ⑧

Pollera ul. Szpitalna 30 ☎012/422 1044, ⓦwww.pollera.com.pl. Charming hotel with good central location, Art Nouveau decor – notably the original Wyspiański stained-glass window in the foyer – and increasingly popular. Mixed bag of old-fashioned, parquet-floored rooms and modern, carpeted ones. ⑦

Polski Pod Byałym Orłem ul. Pijarska 17 ☎012/422 1144, ⓦwww.podorlem.com.pl. A very central and quiet location. Room standards are gradually improving following a return to private ownership, but the en-suite doubles remain on the small side. Not as great a place as the price tag suggests. ⑧

PTTK Wyspiański ul. Westerplatte 15 ☎012/422 9566, ⓦwww.hotel-wyspianski.pl. Thoroughly modernized hotel with en-suite rooms decorated in warm colours. Bigger, balconied rooms cost a few extra złotys. ⑦

Rezydent ul. Grodzka 9 ☎012/269 1408, ⓦwww.rthotels.com.pl. Newish hotel just off the Rynek Główny, offering swish modern rooms in a medieval building. ⑧

SARP ul. Floriańska 39 ☎ & Ⓕ012/429 1778. Tiny top-floor hotel in a former architects' centre, offering just five doubles with shared facilities. The prime centre-town location means you'll be lucky to get a room though. ⑥

Saski ul. Sławkowska 3 ☎012/421 4222. Art Nouveau-era building (and featuring an old cage-lift still in working order) in useful but noisy central location with comfy rooms furnished with a mixture of old and new. En-suites with TV, as well as rooms with shared facilities. ⑤–⑦

Wawel Tourist ul. Poselska 22 ☎012/422 1301, ⓦwww.wawel-tourist.com.pl. Unspectacular place in a central location south of the Rynek. Simple en-suite rooms with an odd jumble of furniture – you'll feel as if you're either in the 1960s or the 1860s depending on which room you get. ⑥

Wit Stwosz ul. Mikołajska 28 ☎012/429 6026, ⓦwww.wit-stwosz.hotel.krakow.pl. Bright, comfortable rooms with a few chintzy touches in a Stare Miasto house just off the Mały Rynek. ⑦

Around Wawel

Maltański ul. Straszewskiego 14 ☎012/431 0010, ⓦwww.maltanski.com. Top-quality hotel with an intimate, pension-like feel. Rooms boast a nice blend of modern and traditional furnishings and come with TV, video player and minibar – and most of the bathrooms have tubs. ⑧

Monopol ul. św. Gertrudy 6 ☏012/422 7015. A good, well-maintained budget choice even if the corridors are a little gloomy and the rooms come with standard-issue 1970s brown furnishings. En-suites as well as rooms with showers but shared WCs. ⑤–⑥

Retro ul. Barska 59 ☏012/266 0708. Cheap *pensjonat* on the left bank of the Wisła, just up from the *Sofitel* hotel offering en-suite doubles alongside several triples and quads. Good views of Wawel. ④

Royal ul. św. Gertrudy 26–29 ☏012/421 3500, ⓦwww.royal.com.pl. Smart, recently renovated former army officers' hotel close to Wawel, popular with small tour groups. Rooms in the plush western wing are more expensive than the standard en-suites in the eastern wing. ⑦–⑧

Rycerski pl. na Groblach 22 ☏012/422 6082. Simply furnished *pensjonat* on the northern edge of Wawel Hill with a mixed bag of rooms, varying in price depending on whether you get en-suite shower, TV etc. Very small, so reserve in advance. ⑥–⑦

Sofitel ul. Konopnickiej 28 ☏012/261 9212, ⓔkrsofitel@orbis.pl. Luxury Western-style business travellers' haunt, much used by tour groups, on the opposite side of the river from Wawel. East-facing rooms have great views of the castle, west-facing ones enjoy vistas of the hotel car park. ⑨

Kazimierz

Alef ul. Szeroka 17 ☏012/421 3870, ⓦwww.alef.pl. Tiny hotel with five rooms, all of which are decked out in pre-World War II style, complete with authentic furnishings and nicknacks. Restaurant with frequent live Kletzmer music on site. ⑦

Eden ul. Ciemna 15 ☏012/430 6565, ⓦwww.hoteleden.pl. Cosy place with plush, tastefully decorated rooms, and an upmarket cellar-pub downstairs. ⑧

Ester ul. Szeroka 20 ☏012/429 1188, ⓦwww.hotel-ester.krakow.pl. Plush, upmarket and stiffly formal hotel in renovated building in heart of Kazimierz. The rooms are pretty much what you would expect from this price range, and there's a decent Jewish-oriented restaurant too. ⑧

Franciszek ul. Miodowa 15 (☏012/430 6506, ⓦwww.franciszekhotel.com.pl. Newish, medium-sized place with small but pleasant pastel en-suites, all with TV and tea/coffee-making facilities. Good value for the area, and there are weekend reductions. ⑥

Kazimierz ul. Miodowa 16 ☏012/421 6629, ⓦwww.hk.com.pl. Recently renovated hotel with intimate feel just east of the Tempel synagogue.

Rooms are comfortable and fully equipped. ⑦

The suburbs

Demel ul. Głowackiego 22 ☏012/636 1600, ⓦwww.demel.com.pl. Modern hotel with all the facilities but well out of the centre, 3km west in the Łobzów district. Tram #14 from the train station. ⑦

Ibis ul. Przy Rondzie 2 ☏012/421 8188, ⓔibiskrk@kr.onet.pl. Standards of comfort and service that you would expect from the international chain, at a price that's just about right. As in other Ibis hotels, all rooms come with proper double beds. Located by a main roundabout, a short way east of the main station. ⑦

Korona ul. Kalwaryiska 9/15 ☏012/656 1780, ⓕ656 1566. Located out in the southern Podgorze district, on the edge of the wartime ghetto area, this is a cheap, lesser-known sports hotel. Tram #10 from the train station. En-suites and rooms with shared bathrooms. ④–⑤

Krakowiak ul. Armii Krajowej 9 ☏012/637 7304. Modestly priced teachers' hotel on the west side of town, lurking below the flanks of the much more prominent *Novotel*. The en-suite rooms are simple in the extreme, but are bright and clean. Breakfast not included, but there's a student canteen next door. Bus #208 or #228 from the train station to the Continental stop. ④

Krakowianka ul. Żywiecka Boczna 2 ☏012/268 1135. A last resort – well south of the centre. Also has bungalows and a campsite. A selection of doubles and triples, all with shared facilities. Tram #8 from pl. Wszystkich Świętych. ④

Krakus ul. Nowohucka 33 ☏012/652 0202, ⓔkpusit@kraknet.pl. Recently renovated place well east of town in Płaszów district offering unexciting but serviceable en-suites. Bus #115 from the train station passes close by. ⑤

Motel Krak ul. Radzikowskiego 99 ☏012/637 2122, ⓕ637 2532. Well outside the city – see "Campsites", opposite, for transport details. Its advantages are a swimming pool and bungalows. ⑥

Piast ul. Radzikowskiego 109 (☏012/637 9708, ⓔwimos@kr.onet.pl. Newish privately run motel with lots of rooms, 5km northwest of town, beyond the *Motel Krak*. ⑧

Pod Kopcem al. Waszyngtona 1 ☏012/427 1355, ⓔhotelFM@polished.net. Housed in the old Habsburg-era fortress surrounding the Kopiec Kościuszko (see p.446), 3km west of the centre. A delightfully peaceful hotel that's recently been refurbished by the local RMF-RM radio station located next door – for once, well worth its upper-bracket price tag. The top-floor rooms have excellent views over the city. Bus #100 from pl. Matejki. ⑧

Wanda ul. Armii Krajowej 15 ☏012/637 1677, wanda@orbis.pl. Modern business-style place with a friendlier, more intimate feel than its immediate neighbour, the *Novotel*. Directions as for the *Krakowiak* (see above). ❼

Wisła ul. Reymonta 22 ☏012/615 1535. Another sports hotel, set in a pleasant park in the western Czarna Wieś district, next to the main football stadium. Bus #144 (from the main bus station) passes close by. Triples only (80zł per person).

Student hostels, youth hostels and campsites

Despite representing one of the cheapest ways of staying in the city, official **youth hostels** in Kraków tend to be subject to curfews, therefore seriously curtailing your enjoyment of the city's nightlife. A preferable, though often more expensive, option is to aim for the **student hostels**, which are open to nonresidents throughout the summer months (July–Aug) and will rent out rooms at other times if space allows. The student hostels listed below are solid bets – other university dorms are likely to open their doors to tourists in season, but locations change from one year to the next, so ask the municipal tourist office for details. There's a reasonable choice of suburban **campsites** in Kraków, and although they're invariably several kilometres from the centre, all are well served by public transport.

Youth hostels

Ul. Kościuszki 88 ☏012/422 1951. HI hostel attractively sited in a former convent overlooking the river, 2km southwest of the centre (tram #2 from the train station). Open all year. 11pm curfew. Dorms from 25zł per person.

Ul. Oleandry 4 ☏012/633 8822. Kraków's main HI hostel, a large greying construction behind the *Żaczek* student hostel, and usually full up during the summer. Open all year. 11pm curfew. Tram #15 or #18 from the train station. Beds in 8-room dorms as low as 25zł per person, although there are some quads and triples, and even some en-suite doubles. ❸

Student and other hostels

Bursa Jagiellońska ul. Śliska 14 ☏012/656 1266, ⓦ www.bursa.krakow.pl. Clean and comfortable university student dorm south of the river on the western edge of the Podgórze district. Tram #10 from the train station to the Smolki stop. ❸

Express ul. Wrocławska 91 ☏ & ⓕ012/633 8862. Highly popular hostel-cum-*pensjonat*, 2km northwest of the centre – it's initially difficult to spot, located slightly uphill from the main road, next to the railway line. Reservations virtually essential, especially in summer. Bus #130 from the train station. Doubles or dorm beds (25zł per person). ❷

Piast ul. Piastowska 47 ☏012/637 4933. A large university dormitory 3km west of the centre popular with summer language students. Lots of regular student accommodation plus some higher-grade rooms with own bathroom. There's a cafeteria on site, plus it's the only place in Kraków with a

self-service laundry. Tram #4 from the train station to the Wawel stop followed by a 10min walk down Piastowska. En-suite doubles and rooms with shared facilities. ❸–❹

Strawberry Youth Hostel ul. Racławicka 9 ☏012/636 1500. Seasonal hostel in student dorms offering comfy doubles and triples and communal kitchen. Open early July to end August only. Trams #4, #12 or #40 from the train station. ❸

Żaczek al. 3 Maja 5 ☏012/633 5477, ⓕ633 1914. Busy university student hostel close to the main youth hostel: easiest to get rooms during the summer months. Tram #15 or #18 from the train station. Simple doubles with shared facilities as well as en-suites. ❷–❹

Campsites

Krak Camping ul. Radzikowskiego 99 ☏012/637 2122. Near the motel of the same name (see opposite), 5km northwest of the centre on the Katowice road, and with its own restaurant. The most popular and best-quality campsite in Kraków. Buses #118, #173, #208, # 218 and #223 pass the motel. May–Sept.

Krakowianka ul. Żywiecka Boczna ☏012/266 4191. Part of the *Krakowianka* hotel complex, usefully located in a pleasant setting on the Zakopane road, 6km south of town. Includes bungalows and a restaurant. Tram #8 from pl. Wszystkich Świętych. May–Sept.

Ogrodowy ul. Królowej Jadwigi 223 ☏622 2011 ext. 67. Decent privately run campsite 5km west of the centre on the road to Balice airport, near the Villa Decjusza. Buses #B, #102, #134.

The City

The heart of the city centre is the **Stare Miasto**, the Old Town, bordered by the lush, tree-shaded city park known as the **Planty**. The **Rynek Główny** is the focal point, with almost everything within half an hour's walk of it. A broad network of streets stretches south from here to the edge of **Wawel Hill**, with its royal residence, and beyond to the Jewish quarter of **Kazimierz**. Across the river, on the edge of the **Podgórze** suburb, is the old wartime ghetto. And finally, a little further out to the west, **Kopiec Kościuszki** (Kościuszko's Mound) offers an attractive stretch of woods and countryside, just a ten-minute bus ride from the centre.

Rynek Główny

The **Rynek Główny** was the largest square of medieval Europe – a huge expanse of flagstones, ringed by magnificent houses and towering spires. Long the marketplace and commercial hub of the city, it's an immediate introduction to Kraków's grandeur and stateliness. By day the square hums with crowds and commercial bustle, its size being such that no matter how much is going on, you're never left feeling cramped for space. While appreciation of the architectural ensemble can become obscured by the crowds, venture into the square late at night and you can immerse yourself in its subtler, historic resonances. Architecturally the square is pretty much unchanged since its *fin-de-siècle* heyday, boasting as fine a collection of period buildings as any in central Europe and beyond. This, combined with echoes of the events played out here, such as Kościuszko's impassioned rallying call to the defence of national independence in 1794 (see box, p.448), provides an endlessly renewable source of interest and inspiration. Once hooked, you'll find yourself constantly gravitating back towards the place. By night or by day, too, it's also worth exploring the stately network of passageways and recently restored Italianate courtyards leading off from the front of the square, many of them enlivened by cafés and restaurants that have colonized the area since the advent of the market economy.

The square is more open today than it used to be. Until the last century, much of it was occupied by market stalls, a tradition maintained by the flower sellers and ice-cream vendors, and by the stalls in the **Sukiennice**, the medieval cloth hall at the heart of the square dividing it into west and east sections, the latter dominated by the **Kościół Mariacki** (St Mary's Church).

Around the square

In the east section, the focus is a statue of national poet **Adam Mickiewicz** (see box, pp.92–93), a facsimile of an earlier work destroyed by the Nazis, and a favourite meeting point. To its south, the copper-domed **Kościół św. Wojciecha** (St Adalbert's Church), is the oldest building in the square and the first church to be founded in Kraków. The saint was a Slav bishop, reputed to have preached here around 995 AD before heading north to convert the Prussians, at whose hands he was martyred. In the basement (reconstructed in the eighteenth century), you can see the foundations of the original tenth-century Romanesque building. Traces of an even earlier wooden building, possibly a pre-Christian temple, and an assortment of archeological finds are also on display.

Many of the **mansions** ranged around the square are associated with artists, writers and wealthy local families, though these days most of them are in use as shops, offices or museums. On the eastern side are some of the oldest buildings in the city. The **Kamienica Szara** (Grey House; no. 6) on the corner of ul. Sienna, for example, despite its later appearance, has many of its Gothic rooms intact; its ex-residents include Poland's first elected king, Henri de Valois, and Tadeusz Kościuszko, who used the house as his headquarters during the 1794 Uprising. The neighbouring **Kamienica Montelupich** (Montelupi House; no. 7), with a monumental Renaissance portal, was the site of the country's first-ever post office, established by its Italian owners in King Sigismund August's reign. The Gothic **Kamienica Bonerowska** (Boner House; no. 9) was for some time the home of the Kraków writer and painter Stanisław Wyspiański, while the house at no. 15, in the southeast corner, is home to the city's oldest and most famous restaurant, the **Wierzynek** (see "Restaurants", p.456), founded in 1364 and claiming an unbroken culinary tradition. It also holds its original charter from King Kazimierz the Great. Political heavyweights who've dined here in recent years include presidents de Gaulle, Nixon, Mitterrand and Bush (the elder).

Continuing round the south section of the square, the **Pałac Potockich** (Potocki Palace; no. 20), with a small courtyard with loggias at the back, is a good example of a classical Kraków mansion, while the **Pałac Pod Baranami** (no. 27), on the western side, is another aristocratic home, constructed from four adjacent burghers' houses in the sixteenth century. The nucleus of nineteenth-century social life, it's nowadays used as a cultural centre (see p.458). Further along the western edge of the square, an orderly collection of shopfronts and restaurants added on to the old houses, ends at the **Pałac pod Krzysztofory** (Krzysztofory Palace; no. 35) on the corner of ul. Szczepańska, another well-preserved mansion created by fusing burghers' houses into a single building with a fine courtyard at the back. Today it's part of the **Muzeum Historyczne Krakowa** (Kraków History Museum; Tues, Wed & Fri 9am–3.30pm, Thurs 11am–6pm; 4zł). The first floor houses a large and varied collection relating to the historical development of the city. Interspersed among the historical exhibits is an interesting spread of paintings by artists with connections with the city, including some fine works by Witkiewicz and Małczewski. On the top floor are the museum's prize exhibits, a collection of *szopki*, amazingly colourful and detailed model buildings produced for the annual Christmas contest (see "Festivals", p.460). The main display is staged during the winter, but at any time of the year you'll find a couple of examples, generally winners of past competitions, on display. Completing the exhibits is a large, jumbled collection of clocks and other timepieces.

The tall **tower** (daily 9am–6pm; 4zł), facing the Pod Baranami, is all that remains of the original, fourteenth-century **town hall**, pulled down in the 1820s by the authorities as part of a misguided improvement plan. It's worth the climb up for an excellent overview of the city. The top floor of the tower features occasionally illuminating local exhibitions.

The Sukiennice

The medieval **Sukiennice**, rebuilt in the 1550s, is one of the most distinctive sights in the country – a vast cloth hall, topped by a sixteenth-century attic dripping with gargoyles whose splendour is heightened by a recently com-

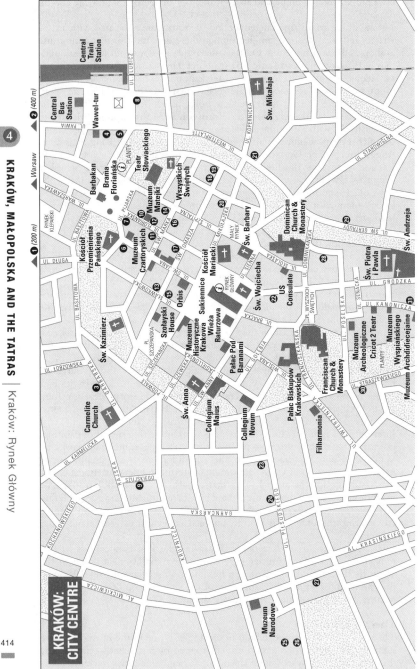

KRAKÓW: CITY CENTRE

Central Train Station

Central Bus Station

Wawel-tur

Barbakan

Brama Floriańska

Teatr Słowackiego

Wszystkich Świętych

Muzeum Matejki

Kościół Przemienienia Pańskiego

Muzeum Czartoryskich

Orbis

Szołayski House

Św. Kazimierz

Carmelite Church

Św. Anna

Muzeum Historyczne Krakowa

Św. Barbary

Sukiennice

Wieża Ratuszowa

Kościół Mariacki

Św. Wojciecha

US Consulate

Dominican Church & Monastery

Św. Mikołaja

Collegium Maius

Collegium Novum

Pałac Pod Baranami

Pałac Biskupów Krakowskich

Franciscan Church & Monastery

Filharmonia

Muzeum Archeologiczne

Cricot 2 Teatr

Muzeum Wyspiańskiego

Muzeum Archidiecezjalne

Św. Piotra i Pawła

Św. Andrzeja

Muzeum Narodowe

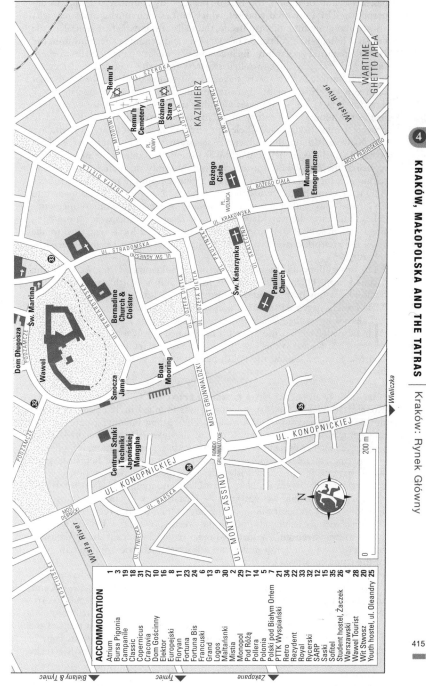

▶ Wieliczka

N

0   200 m

ACCOMMODATION

Atrium	1
Bursa Pigonia	3
Campanile	19
Classic	18
Copernicus	31
Cracovia	27
Dom Gościnny	10
Elektor	16
Europejski	8
Floryan	11
Fortuna	23
Fortuna Bis	24
Francuski	6
Grand	13
Logos	9
Maltański	30
Mistia	2
Monopol	29
Pod Różą	17
Pollera	14
Polonia	5
Polski pod Białym Orłem	7
PTTK Wyspiański	21
Retro	34
Rezydent	22
Royal	33
Rycerski	32
SARP	12
Saski	15
Sofitel	35
Student hostel, Żaczek	26
Warszawski	4
Wawel Tourist	28
Wit Stwosz	20
Youth hostel, ul. Oleandry	25

Wawel

Dom Długosza

Św. Martina

Bernadine Church & Cloister

Smocza Jama

Boat Mooring

Centrum Sztuki i Techniki Japońskiej Manggha

Remu'h

UL. SZEROKA

Remu'h Cemetery

Bóżnica Stara

KAZIMIERZ

Bożego Ciała

Muzeum Etnograficzne

Św. Katarzyna

Pauline Church

UL. BOŻEGO CIAŁA

UL. KRAKOWSKA

UL. STRADOMSKA

UL. KONOPNICKIEJ

UL. MONTE CASSINO

Wisła River

Wisła River

WARTIME GHETTO AREA

pleted cleanup operation, the first in decades. Its commercial traditions are perpetuated by a **covered market**, which bustles with tourists and street sellers at almost any time of year. Inside, the stalls of the darkened central arcade display a hotchpotch collection of tourist tat and genuine craft items from the Podhale region. Popular buys include amber jewellery, painted boxes in every shape and size and thick woollen sweaters from the mountains. Prices are inevitably inflated, so if you're travelling on to the south, it's better to wait until you get to one of the Tatra-region markets, such as the one in Nowy Targ (see p.503). The colonnades on either side of the Sukiennice were added in the late nineteenth century in an attempt to smarten up the Rynek and provide a home for a brace of elegant terrace cafés, most famous of which is the **Noworolski** on the Sukiennice's eastern side. The centre of Kraków social life in the years before World War I (Lenin was one of the more famous regulars), the café boasted a series of sumptuously decorated Art-Nouveau salons, of which one – with a separate entrance from the rest – was a ladies'-only tea room. The café was confiscated by the Nazis in 1939 and made into a German-only club, but resumed its status as Kraków's prime coffee-and-cakes venue after the war. Many of the *belle-époque* interiors were renovated in the 1990s, making it well worth a visit – although the locals who used to idle away the afternoon over tea and *sernik* have been almost totally replaced by tourists.

The **art gallery** on the upper floor of the Sukiennice (Tues, Wed, Fri–Sun 10am–3.30pm Thurs 10am–6pm; 7zł, free on Sun) is worth a visit for its collection of works by nineteenth-century Polish artists, among them Matejko, Małczewski, Gierymski and Chełmonski. The Matejkos here include two political heavyweights, the *Homage of Prussia* and the stirring *Kościuszko at Racławice*. As usual with Matejko, the impact is heightened if you appreciate the historical reference points, in this case the homage of the Teutonic Knights in 1525 (see Malbork, p.203) and the Polish peasant army's victory over the Russians in 1794.

Kościół Mariacki and plac Mariacki

Kościół Mariacki (St Mary's Church) was founded in 1222 and destroyed during the mid-century Tatar invasions. The current building, begun in 1355 and completed fifty years later, is one of the finest Gothic structures in the country. The taller of its towers, a late-fifteenth-century addition, is topped by an amazing ensemble of spires, elaborated with a crown and helmet. Legend has it that during one of the early Tatar raids the watchman positioned at the top of this tower saw the invaders approaching and took up his trumpet to raise the alarm; his warning was cut short by a Tatar arrow through the throat. The legend lives on, and every hour on the hour a lone **trumpeter** plays the sombre *hejnał* melody, halting abruptly at the precise point the watchman was supposed to have been hit. The national radio station broadcasts the *hejnał* live at noon every day and Polish writers are still apt to wax lyrical on the symbolism of the trumpet's warning.

First impressions of the **church** are of a cavernous, somewhat gloomy expanse. What little light there is comes from the high windows at each end, the ancient altar window facing the stained glass of the west end, an Art-Nouveau extravaganza by Kraków artist Stanisław Wyspiański. Walking down the nave, you'll have to pick your way past devotees kneeling in front of the fifteenth-century **Chapel of Our Lady of Częstochowa**, with its copy of the venerated image of the Black Madonna. Locals claim that this is actually older than the original.

Veit Stoss

As with Copernicus, the issue of the nationality of the man who carved the Mariacki altar – unquestionably the greatest work of art ever created in Poland – was long the source of a rather sterile dispute between Polish and German protagonists. Although his early career remains something of a mystery, it now seems indisputable that the sculptor's original name was **Veit Stoss**, and that he was born between 1440 and 1450 in Horb at the edge of the Black Forest, settling later in Nuremberg, where a few early works by him have been identified. He came to **Kraków** in 1477, perhaps at the invitation of the royal court (the Polish queen was an Austrian princess), though more likely at the behest of the German merchant community, a sizeable but declining minority in the city, who worshipped in the Mariacki and paid for its new altar by subscription.

Despite being his first major commission, the **Mariacki altarpiece** is Stoss's masterpiece. It triumphantly displays every facet of late-Gothic sculpture: the architectural setting, complete with its changing lights, is put to full dramatic effect; there is mastery over every possible scale, from the huge figures in the central shrine to the tiny figurines and decoration in the borders; subtle use is made of a whole gamut of technical devices, from three different depths of relief to a graded degree of gilding according to the importance of the scene; and the whole layout is based on a scheme of elaborate theological complexity that would nevertheless be bound to make an impression on the many unlettered worshippers who viewed it. It would seem that it is mostly Stoss's own work: gilders and joiners were certainly employed, but otherwise he was probably only helped by one assistant and one apprentice.

While engaged on the altarpiece, Stoss carved the relief of *Christ in the Garden of Gethsemane*, now in the City Art Museum. Made of sandstone, a material he later used for the Mariacki crucifix, it is indicative of his exceptional versatility with materials. This is further apparent in consideration of the works he created after finishing the altarpiece: the tomb of King Kazimierz the Jagiellonian in the Wawel cathedral is of Salzburg marble, the epitaph to Philippus Buonaccorsi in the Dominican Church is of bronze, while his two other key Polish commissions – the episcopal monuments in the cathedrals of Gniezno and Włocławek – are both of Hungarian marble. These sculptures made Stoss a great Polish celebrity, and he rose far above his artisan status to engage in extensive commercial activities, and to dabble in both architecture and engineering. The forms of the Mariacki altarpiece and his monuments were widely imitated throughout Poland, and continued to be so for the next half-century.

It therefore seems all the more curious that he returned to **Nuremberg** in 1496, remaining there until his death in 1533. His homecoming was a traumatic experience: Nuremberg was well endowed with specialist craftsmen, and Stoss was forced to follow suit, concentrating on producing single, unpainted wooden figures. Attempts to maintain his previous well-to-do lifestyle led him into disastrous business dealings, which culminated in his forging a document, as a result of which he was branded on both cheeks and forbidden to venture beyond the city. He never really came to terms with the ideals of the Italian Renaissance, which took strong root in Nuremberg, nor did he show any enthusiasm for the Protestant Reformation, which was supported by nearly all the great German artists of the day, most notably his fellow townsman, Albrecht Dürer. Yet, even if Stoss never repeated the success of his Kraków years, he continued to produce memorable and highly individualistic sculptures, above all the spectacular garlanded *Annunciation* suspended from the ceiling of Nuremberg's church of St Lorenz.

Continuing down the high Gothic nave, under arched stone vaulting enhanced in blue and gold, the walls, like those surrounding the high altar, are decorated with **Matejko friezes**. Separating the nave from the aisles are a succession of buttressed pillars fronted by Baroque marble altars. The aisles themselves lead off to a number of lavishly ornamented chapels, fifteenth-century additions to the main body of the building. Focal point of the nave is the huge stone **crucifix** attributed to Veit Stoss, hanging in the archway to the presbytery.

The biggest crowds are drawn by the majestic **high altar** at the far east end. Carved by the Nuremberg master craftsman **Veit Stoss** (Wit Stwosz, as he's known in Poland; see box on p.417) between 1477 and 1489, the huge limewood polyptych is one of the finest examples of late-Gothic art in Europe. The outer sides of the folded polyptych feature illustrations from the life of the Holy Family executed in gilded polychromy. At noon (Sundays and saints' days excluded) the altar is opened to reveal the inner panels, with their reliefs of the Annunciation, Nativity, Adoration of the Magi, Resurrection, Ascension and Pentecost; for a good view, arrive at least a quarter of an hour before the opening. These six superb scenes are a fitting backdrop to the central panel – an exquisite **Dormition of the Virgin** in which the graceful figure of Mary is shown reclining into her final sleep in the arms of the watchful Apostles. Like most of the figures, the Apostles, several of them well over lifesize, are thought to be based on Stoss's contemporaries in Kraków. Certainly there's an uncanny mastery of human detail that leaves you feeling you'd recognize their human counterparts if you met them in the street. Other features of note in the chancel are the Gothic stained-glass windows, the Renaissance tabernacle designed by Giovanni Maria Mosca, and the exuberant early Baroque stalls.

Plac Mariacki and Kościół św. Barbary

The side door on the south side of the chancel brings you into **plac Mariacki** (St Mary's Square), a small courtyard replacing the old church cemetery closed down by the Austrians in the last century. On the far side of the courtyard stands the fourteenth-century **Kościół św. Barbary** (St Barbara's Church; rarely open except during services), among its contents a remarkable late-Gothic *pietà* group, sculpted in stone and attributed to the anonymous local artist known as "Master of the Beautiful Madonnas". During the Partitions, the ruling Austrians took over the Mariacki, so the locals were forced to use this tiny place for services in Polish. The back of the church looks onto the tranquil **Mały Rynek**, whose terrace cafés make an enjoyable venue for postcard sessions or a quiet beer.

From Mały Rynek, the narrow **ul. Sienna** offers an alternative route back to the main square. On the street outside no. 5 there's usually a bunch of students touting political books and badges, alternately amusing, informative or impenetrable to the foreigner. The first floor of the building houses the local branch of the **Catholic Intellectuals Club** (KIK), an organization that's more approachable than it sounds. Founded in the wake of the post-Stalinist political thaw of the 1950s, the KIK was for over thirty years one of the few officially sanctioned independent structures in the country, and its national network played an important part in the last decade's political events. It was to the KIK offices in Kraków, for example, that local steelworkers and farmers came for help when setting up the first Solidarity organizations in 1980. Today, a number of KIK people are now prominent politicians, ex-prime minister Tadeusz Mazowiecki included.

Around the Stare Miasto

Like the Rynek, the streets of the Stare Miasto still follow the medieval plan, while their **architecture** presents a rich central European ensemble of Gothic, Renaissance and Baroque. They are a hive of commercial activity, too, with a welter of boutiques, fast-food joints and other privately owned shops that render the old state enterprise outlets almost a figment of past imagination. West of the Rynek, the atmosphere is generated by the academic buildings and student haunts of the **university district**.

South of the main square, the busy **ul. Grodzka** leads down towards **plac Dominikański**, one of the pivotal points of the Stare Miasto, and on to Wawel Hill. The historic streets combine the increasingly fast-paced bustle of the city's commercial life with the tranquillity and splendour of myriad ancient churches, palaces and mansions. Additionally, there's a brace of museums worth exploring.

Ulica Floriańska

Of the three streets leading north off the Rynek, the easternmost, **ul. Floriańska** is the busiest and most striking. In among the myriad shops, cafés and restaurants are some attractive fragments of medieval and Renaissance architecture. At no. 5, for example, a beautiful early Renaissance stone figure of the *Madonna and Child* sits in a niche on the facade of the Brama Floriańska (Floriańska Gate; see below). At no. 14, **Pod Różą**, the oldest hotel in Kraków, has a Renaissance doorway inscribed in Latin, "May this house stand until an ant drinks the oceans and a tortoise circles the world" – it doesn't seem to get much attention from the moneyed revellers who flock to the hotel's reopened casino. Famous hotel guests of the past include Franz Liszt, Balzac and the occasional tsar.

Further up the street, at no. 41, is the sixteenth-century **Dom Jana Matejki** (Matejko House; Tues–Thurs & Sat–Sun 10am–3.30pm, Fri 10am–6pm; 5zł, free on Sun), home of painter Jan Matejko until his death in 1893. An opulent, slightly gloomy three-storey mansion of the type favoured by the wealthy turn-of-the-twentieth-century Kraków bourgeoisie, it houses a museum with a range of Matejko family memorabilia, parts of the man's extensive personal art collection and a number of his own paintings and assorted other artistic outpourings.

The first-floor parlour and a couple of other rooms remain pretty much as the Matejko family kept them, attractive old fireplaces included. The second and third floors house Matejko's private art gallery, notably a number of Renaissance pictures and triptychs. The rest of the exhibition is mostly Matejko's own work, including the sketches of the windows he designed for the Mariacki Church. There's also a collection of old costumes and armour that he used as inspiration for several of his more famous pictures, notably *Sobieski at Vienna*. Not a wildly exciting museum, it's a popular enough place with Matejko freaks, of whom there still seem to be plenty in the country.

Further along, Western fast-food culture has come to town in the form of the *McDonald's* at no. 55, more or less welcomed by local residents depending on who you speak to, though plans to build another restaurant right on the revered main square are proving a good deal more controversial.

The **Brama Floriańska** (Floriańska Gate), at the end of the street, marks the edge of the Stare Miasto proper. A square, robust fourteenth-century structure, it's part of a small section of fortifications saved when the old defensive walls were pulled down in the early nineteenth century. The walls lead east to the fifteenth-century Haberdashers' (Pasamoników) Tower and west to the Joiners' (Stolarska) Gate, which is separated from the even older Carpenters' (Cieśli) Gate by the Arsenal. The original fortifications must have been an impressive sight – three kilometres of wall ten metres high and nearly three metres thick, interspersed with 47 towers and bastions. The strongest-looking defensive remnant is the **Barbakan**, just beyond Floriańska Gate. A bulbous, spiky fort, added in 1498, it's unusual in being based on the Arab as opposed to European defensive architecture of the time. The covered passage linking the fort to the walls has disappeared, as has the original moat – all of which leaves the bastion looking a little stranded.

One notable recent development is the opening up of Kraków's extensive network of **medieval cellars**. The first stone buildings to go up were usually simple constructions consisting of a ground floor, first floor and attic: basements were not added on account of the shallow foundations used. As often, over time these buildings were gradually absorbed into newer houses, and as newer layers of road were progressively added to the streets of the city centre they were transformed into basements, largely ignored or forgotten by their owners. A further twist to the picture was provided by communist-era property laws, which in the Stare Miasto as elsewhere circumscribed ownership and thus control of a building's use. As a result, up until the late 1980s only two buildings on and around the Rynek Główny – the Krzysztofory and Pod Baranami palaces – had cellars that were actually accessible to the public.

All that has, however, changed rapidly in the post-communist era. Radical changes in property laws have resulted in a large number of Stare Miasto cellars being opened up, renovated and put to an assortment of uses, notably as bars, restaurants and galleries. At a stroke, Kraków has thus (re)acquired a large slice of its architectural heritage. And as anyone who visits the city today can testify, it's been well worth the wait: many of the cellars are notable, solid brick constructions, more often than not with their medieval stone ceiling decoration still virtually intact.

Ulica Szpitalna and around

Immediately east of ul. Floriańska is **ul. Szpitalna**, another mansion-lined thoroughfare. At no. 24, the city's **Orthodox church** is housed upstairs in a building that used to serve as a synagogue. As usual, the icon-filled church is only open during services (currently Saturday at 5pm, and Sunday at 10am), but there's an interesting display of Orthodox-inspired religious art in the entry lobby and ground-floor art gallery, featuring works by the contemporary Polish artist Jerzy Nowoselski.

Further up the street, across pl. św. Ducha is the **Kościół św. Krzyża** (Church of the Holy Cross) a fabulous building that's thankfully now open outside services (daily 11am–4pm). The most impressive feature is the beautifully decorated Gothic vaulting, supported by a single exquisite palm-like central pillar, an extremely unusual architectural phenomenon, built at the time of the reconstruction of the original fourteenth-century Gothic edifice in the 1520s. The graceful fifteenth- and 'sixteenth-century murals decorating the nave and choir were restored at the turn of the twentieth century by Wyspiański among others, who was passionately devoted to the building, regarding it as one of the city's finest Gothic churches. When the church is closed, you can catch a glimpse of the palm vaulting through the iron grille, but it's definitely worth the effort of coming back when it's open. Service times are posted on the board outside.

Immediately before the church is the **Teatr im. J. Słowackiego** (Słowacki Theatre), built in 1893 on the site of the ancient Church of the Holy Ghost complex demolished amid loud protests from Matejko and other local luminaries. Modelled on the Paris Opéra, the richly ornate theatre, named after the much-loved Romantic poet and playwright Julius Słowacki, established itself as one of Kraków's premier theatres, a position it still enjoys (see "Entertainment", p.458). The interior has been renovated recently, accentuating the splendour of a setting also used for occasional large-scale opera productions.

The Pałac Czartoryskich and Kamienica Szołajskich

Back to Floriańska Gate and past the reproduction Pop Art collections displayed on the old walls, a left turn down the narrow **ul. Pijarska** brings you to the corner of ul. św. Jana and back down to the main square. On the way, on your right, is the Baroque **Kościół Przemienienia Pańskiego** (Church of the Holy Transfiguration), with a facade modelled on the Gesù Church in Rome; on your left, linked to the church by an overhead passage, is the Czartoryski Palace.

The Muzeum Czartoryski

A branch of the Muzeum Narodowe, the **Pałac Czartoryskich** (Czartoryski Palace) houses Kraków's finest art collection, the **Muzeum Czartoryskich** (Tues–Thurs, Sat & Sun 10am–3.30pm, Friday 10am–6pm; 7zł, free on Sun). Its core was established by Izabella Czartoryska at the family palace in Puławy (see p.322) and was then moved to Kraków following the confiscation of the Puławy estate after the 1831 Insurrection, in which the family was deeply implicated. The family were legendary collectors, particularly from the Paris salons of the seventeenth and eighteenth centuries, and it shows, despite the Nazis' removal, and subsequent loss, of many precious items, including Raphael's famous *Portrait of a Young Man*, which has never been recovered.

The **ancient art** collection alone contains over a thousand exhibits, from sites in Mesopotamia, Etruria, Greece and Egypt. Another intriguing highlight is the collection of **trophies** from the Battle of Vienna (1683), which includes sumptuous Turkish carpets, scimitars, tents and other Oriental finery.

The **picture galleries** contain a rich display of art and sculpture ranging from thirteenth- to eighteenth-century works, the most famous being Rembrandt's brooding *Landscape with the Good Samaritan* and Leonardo da Vinci's *Lady with an Ermine*. A double pun identifies the rodent-handler as Cecilia Gallerani, the mistress of Leonardo's patron, Lodovico il Moro: the Greek word for this animal is *galé* – a play on the woman's name – and Lodovico's nickname was "Ermelino", meaning ermine. There is also a large collection of Dutch canvases and an outstanding array of fourteenth-century Sienese primitives, the whole thing arranged following nineteenth-century tradition to form distinct artistic and decorative groupings. As in all Polish museums, you may find several galleries closed off, ostensibly for lack of staff.

Plac Szczepański and the Kamienica Szołajskich

On down ul. św. Jana towards the Rynek, there are more wealthy Stare Miasto residences, such as the Neoclassical Pałac Lubomirskich (Lubomirski Palace) at no. 15 and the eighteenth-century Kamienica Kołłątajowska (Kołłątaj House) at no. 20, once a meeting place for the cultured elite. Back onto the square and west along ul. Szczepańska, the modest **Kamienica Szołajskich** (Szołajski House), on the eastern edge of **plac Szczepański**, houses a small but important section of the city **art museum** (closed for renovation in 2001; reopening date uncertain), featuring a significant collection of Gothic and Renaissance Polish art and sculpture, much of it taken from churches in the Małopolska region. The best-known exhibit here is the fourteenth-century *Madonna of Krużlowa*, an exquisite Gothic sculpture of the "Beautiful Madonna" school. Unearthed in a local village church attic, this wonderful piece depicts a typically dreamy Mary with a cheerful-looking Christ perched on her shoulder. Other pieces here include a beautiful figure of Christ riding on a donkey from 1470, used in Palm Sunday processions, an expressive cycle of late-fifteenth-century altarpieces from the local Augustine and Dominican churches, and a powerful *Christ in the Garden of Gethsemane*, a sandstone relief carved by Veit Stoss for the cemetery beside the Mariacki Church, as well as a small wooden *Crucifixion* attributed to his workshop. The works by Nicholas Haberchrack, a lesser-known local artist are likewise impressive, notably a fine *Christ Washing the Disciples' Feet* and *Adoration of the Magi*. After the joys of this superb selection of Gothic sculpture the later-era art housed on the second floor is a bit of an anticlimax, though the portraits of kings Jan Sobieski and Sigismund August will be familiar enough to anyone who's already trailed round the Wawel collections. It's interesting too to note the distinctive icon-like Uniate influences in many of the pieces gathered from churches in eastern Małopolska, including the triptychs from places such as Dębno (see p.515).

Also on this square are two impressive turn-of-the-twentieth-century buildings in the Viennese Secessionist style: the decorative **Stary Teatr** to the south (see "Entertainment", p.458), the city's best known theatre used by Oscar-winning cinema director Andrzej Wajda for his exemplary theatrical productions of Polish classics, and the **Pałac Sztuki** (Palace of Arts; daily 8am–8pm; price depends on what's on) to the west, a stately structure with reliefs by Małczewski and niches filled with busts of Matejko, Witkiewicz and other local artists. The latter, adorned with a mosaic frieze, features high-profile art exhibitions, often featuring major international works on loan from abroad. Just round the corner on Podwale Dunajewskiego is the **Bunkier Sztuki** (Art Bunker; Tues–Sun 11am–6pm; ⓦ www.bunkier.com.pl; price depends on what's on), a brutally modernist concrete building which is the city's main venue for large-scale contemporary art shows.

The university district

Head west from the Rynek on any of the three main thoroughfares – ul. Szczepańska, ul. Szewska or ul. św. Anny – and you're into the **university area**. The main body of buildings is south of ul. św. Anny, the principal Jewish area of the city until the early 1400s, when the university bought up many of the properties and the Jews moved out to the Kazimierz district.

The Gothic **Collegium Maius** building, at the intersection of ul. św. Anny with ul. Jagiellońska, is the historic heart of the university complex. The university got off to something of a false start after its foundation by King Kazimierz in 1364, foundering badly after his death six years later, until it was revived by King Władysław Jagiełło in the early fifteenth century, when the university authorities began transforming these buildings into a new academic centre.

Through the passageway from ul. Jagiellońska you find yourself in a quiet, arcaded **courtyard** with a marble fountain playing in the centre, an ensemble that, during the early 1960s, was stripped of neo-Gothic accretions and restored to something approaching its original form. The cloistered atmosphere of ancient academia makes an enjoyable break from the city in itself, though actually getting into the building is not so easy. Now renamed and known as the **Muzeum Uniwerzytecki** (University Museum), the Collegium is open to guided tours only (every 30min Mon–Fri 11am–2.20pm, Sat 11am–1.20pm; 7zł, free on Sat), for which you theoretically need to book places in advance (☎012/422 0549). In practice you can usually just turn up and talk your way onto a tour, although this can prove more difficult in summer. While most tours are in Polish there are usually a limited number of English- and French-speaking guides on hand, so it's worth waiting to try and get on their tours. The shop in the courtyard arcade has caught onto the logo craze, selling mugs, pens, sweatshirts and other items sporting the Jagiellonian

University crest. Entrance is via the first floor ticket office, reached via the staircase on the far side of the courtyard.

Inside, **tours** proceed through the elaborately decorated first-floor rooms, several of which retain the mathematical and geographical murals once used for teaching, as well as an impressive library of old books. The professors' common room, which also served as their dining hall, boasts an ornate Baroque spiral staircase and a Gothic bay window with a replica statuette of King Kazimierz. In the **Treasury** rooms, the most valued possession is the copper Jagiellonian globe, constructed around 1520 as the centrepiece of a clock mechanism and featuring the earliest known illustration of America – labelled "a newly discovered land". Additionally, there's a collection of old scientific instruments thought to have been used by Copernicus during his astronomical experiments, a venerable old astrolabe and a prototype telescope from the 1480s included. The **Aula**, the grand principal assembly hall, has a Renaissance ceiling adorned with carved rosettes and portraits of Polish royalty, benefactors and professors; its Renaissance portal carries the Latin inscription *Plus Ratio Quam Vis* – "Wisdom rather than Strength". Bizarrely, there's also a carved wooden door leading onto the street that's never opened: to get out you have to make your way back through the rooms. If you find old scientific instruments interesting, ask the guide if you can see the other old laboratories and globe rooms.

Several other old buildings are dotted round this area. The university **Kościół św. Anny** (St Anne's Church), was designed by the ubiquitous Tylman of Gameren. A monumental Baroque extravaganza, built on a Latin cross plan with a high central dome, it's widely regarded as Gameren's most mature work, the classicism of his design neatly counterpoised by rich stucco decoration added by the Italian sculptor Baldaggare Fontana. The **Collegium Minus**, just round the corner on ul. Gołębia, is the fifteenth-century arts faculty, rebuilt two centuries later; Jan Matejko studied and later taught here. On the corner of the same street stands the outsize **Collegium Novum**, the neo-Gothic university administrative headquarters, with an interior modelled on the Collegium Maius. The Copernicus **statue**, in front of the Collegium Novum, on the edge of the Planty, commemorates the university's most famous supposed student – some local historians doubt that he really did study here.

West of the University district: the Muzeum Narodowe and the Dom Mehoffera

Housed in a large concrete block at al. 3 Maja 1, a couple of minutes west of the university district along ul. Piłsudskiego, the **Muzeum Narodowe** (National Museum; Mon noon–6pm, Tues–Sun 10am–6pm; 5zł) features permanent exhibitions of a wide selection of painting and sculpture from the 1890s and beyond. The turn-of-the-twentieth-century Młoda Polska movement is particularly well represented here, with a number of notable works by Wyspiański, including the designs for his windows in Wawel cathedral, as well as a number of other major Polish artists including Mehoffer, Witkiewicz and Ślewiński. The museum also presents a diverse range of roving exhibitions, some of them major national cultural events, so it's always worth checking what's on in the local listings.

Another essential stopoff on any Młoda Polska tour of Kraków is the **Dom Mehoffera** (Mehoffer House), a short walk north of the Muzeum Narodowe at Krupnicza 26 (Tues, Thurs–Sun 10am–3.30pm, Wed 10am–6pm; 5zł; free on Sun). Occupying the house where Wyspiański's friend and professional rival Józef Mehoffer lived and worked, it's stuffed with *belle-époque* furnishings, pictures of old Kraków, and Mehoffer's own artworks. Portraits of contemporaries cover the walls of rooms decked out in Art Nouveau-inspired curtains and wallpaper (most designed by Mehoffer himself), and among several larger, symbolist works, there's a stained-glass allegory of the immortality of art in which smiling muses hover fairy-like above the pale form of a dying maiden.

The Dominican church and monastery

Ulica Grodzka stretches south of the Rynek, crossing the tram lines circling the city centre at plac Dominikański. East across the square stands the large brick-work basilica of the thirteenth-century **Dominican church and monastery**. Constructed on the site of an earlier church, following its destruction during the fearsome Tatar raid of 1241, the modest original Gothic brick church grew to become one of Kraków's grandest churches. Much of the accumulated splendour, however, was wiped out during a fire in 1850, which seriously devastated the church and much of the surrounding quarter, the Franciscan church included (see below). The appearance of both churches has improved markedly thanks to a recent much-needed cleanup.

Today, the dominant atmosphere is one of uncluttered, tranquil contemplation – like most Polish churches, the main purpose of the building is worship, not display, a fact attested to by the continual stream of services held here on almost any day of the week. However, there is a wealth of architectural detail to appreciate. Adjoining the main nave, redecorated in an airy neo-Gothic style, are a succession of chapels, many of which survived the 1850 fire in better shape than the rest of the building. Oldest of them all, up a flight of steps at the end of the north aisle, is **St Hyacinth's chapel**, dedicated to the joint founder and first abbot of the monastery. Based on the design of the Sigismund Chapel in Wawel cathedral, the chapel boasts some rich stuccowork on the dome above the freestanding tomb, both by Baldassare Fontana. The other notable feature is a sequence of paintings portraying the life of the saint by Thomas Dolabella. The Baroque **Myszkowski family chapel** in the southern isle is a fine creation from the workshop of Santi Gucci (see box, p.432), the exuberantly ornamented exterior contrasting with the austere, marble faced interior, with busts of the Myszkowski family lining the chapel dome. Similarly noteworthy is the **Rosary chapel**, built as a thanks-offering for Sobieski's victory over the Turks at Vienna in 1683, and housing a supposedly miracle-producing image of Our Lady of the Rosary. A fine series of **tombstones** survives in the chancel, notably those of the early-thirteenth-century prince of Kraków Leszek Czarny (the Black), and an impressive bronze tablet of the Italian Renaissance scholar Filippo Buonaccorsi, built to a design by Veit Stoss and cast at the Nuremberg Vischer works.

Through the Renaissance doorway, underneath the stairs leading up to St Hyacinth's chapel, are the tranquil Gothic **cloisters**, whose walls are lined with memorials to the great and good of Kraków, leading in the north wing to a fine Romanesque refectory with a vaulted crypt. The Dominicans have a long tradition of involvement with the city's student population, and during the 1980s, the cloisters were a focus of independent cultural and political activism, notably exhibitions of art frowned upon or banned by the authorities. The tradition is maintained in the student art exhibitions still displayed in the cloisters.

Franciscan church and monastery

On the west side of plac Dominikański is the **Franciscan church and monastery**, home to the Dominicans' long-standing rivals in the tussle for the city's religious affections. Built soon after Franciscan friars first arrived from Prague in 1237, the church was completed some thirty years later. As one of Kraków's major churches it has witnessed some important events in the nation's history, notably the baptism in 1385 of the pagan grand duke of Lithuania Prince Jagiełło, prior to (and as a condition of) his assumption of the Polish throne. A plain high brick building, the church's somewhat murky, brooding atmosphere forms a stark contrast to its Dominican neighbour. The most striking feature is the celebrated series of Art Nouveau **murals** and **stained-glass windows** designed and executed by Stanisław Wyspiański in 1900, following the gutting of the church in the fire fifty years earlier (see opposite). An exuberant outburst of floral and geometric mural motifs extol the naturalist creed of St Francis, culminating in the magnificent **stained-glass** depiction of God the Creator in the large west window, the elements of the scene seemingly merging into each other in a hazy, abstract swirl of colour. By contrast, the floral motif depiction of St Francis and the Blessed Salomea in the window behind the altar conjures up an altogether more restrained, meditative atmosphere, while the **north chapel** contains a flowing set of Stations of the Cross by another Młoda Polska adherent, Jacek Mehoffer. The **south chapel** contains a fine early-fifteenth-century image of the Madonna of Mercy, a popular local figure. The Gothic **cloisters**, reached from the southern side of the church are worth a visit for the series of portraits of the bishops of Kraków dating back to the mid-fifteenth century and continuing up to the present day, notably the portrait of Bishop Piotr Tomicki from the early 1500s. To complete the ecclesiastical picture, the archbishop of Kraków's residence, once inhabited by Karol Wojtyła, stands across from the Franciscan Church.

South from plac Dominikański

On down ul. Grodzka, past the gilded stone lion above the **Kamienica Podelwie** (House Under the Lion; no. 32), the oldest such stone emblem in the city, turn right into ul. Poselska to find the house, at no. 12, where novelist **Joseph Conrad** spent his childhood: a commemorative plaque in the corner carries a quotation from his work.

Further down ul. Poselska, through the garden entrance at no. 3 and past the top of ul. Senacka, is the **Muzeum Archeologiczne** (Archeological Museum; Mon–Wed 9am–2pm, Thurs 2–6pm, Fri & Sun 10am–2pm; 7zł; free on Thurs). Housed in a building with a chequered history – it was originally an early medieval stronghold, then successively a palace, monastery and Habsburg-era prison; before becoming a museum – the collections feature an array of Egyptian, Greek and Roman objects alongside a large group of local finds, including an extensive set of Neolithic painted ceramics considered to be among the best in Europe. Even if you're not totally sold on hoards of old coins and pottery there's one totally unmissable object here, the famed figure of a pagan Slavonic god, known as **Światowit**, the only image of a Slav pagan deity ever discovered. An extraordinary carved stone idol standing 2.5m high and sporting what looks like a top hat, its crude decoration includes a face on each side (one for each of the winds, it is thought).

The route south continues down ul. Grodzka, past another run of churches before ending up at the busy crossroads in the shadow of Wawel. The first, the austere twin-domed **Kościół św. Piotra i Pawła** (Church of SS Peter and Paul), a little way back from the street, is fronted by imposing statues of the two Apostles, actually copies of the pollution-scarred originals, now kept elsewhere for preservation's sake. The church's exterior recently received a thorough cleanup, the much reduced pollution levels in the inner city meaning that the distinctive statues should be able to keep their current shine for a while to come. Modelled on the Gesù in Rome, it's the earliest Baroque building in the city, commissioned by the Jesuits when they came to Kraków in the 1580s to quell Protestant agitation. A notable feature here is the **crypt** of Piotr Skarga (Mon–Fri 9am–5pm; 3zł) down the steps in front of the altar, where there are piles of slips of paper filled with the prayers of the devout. A noted Jesuit preacher and Polish champion of the Counter-Reformation, Skarga delivered anti-Protestant sermons here at the close of the sixteenth century. Fine stuccowork by Giovanni Falconi in the chapels on either side of the nave helps to relieve the severity of the place.

Immediately in front of the church stands one of Kraków's more controversial cultural monuments, a **statue of Skarga** erected in 2001 to provide a focal point for the recently tidied-up plaza that leads from here through to ul. Kanoniczna (see below). A clumsy piece of work which makes the much revered priest look more like a comic-book superhero than a spiritual leader, the sculpture is totally out of keeping with the Baroque splendours that surround it, and has proved profoundly unpopular with the *krakowski* cultural elite as a consequence.

Next comes the Romanesque **Kościół św. Andrzeja** (St Andrew's Church), remodelled in familiar Polish Baroque style, where the local people are reputed to have holed themselves up and successfully fought off marauding Tatars during the invasion of 1241; it looks just about strong enough for the purpose. The early-thirteenth-century mosaic icon of the Virgin from Constantinople stored in the Treasury is credited with having helped out. A little further on, **Kościół św. Marcina** (St Martin's Church), built in the seventeenth century on the site of a Romanesque foundation, now belongs to Kraków's small Lutheran community.

The route to Wawel Hill

The traditional route used by Polish monarchs when entering the city took them through the Brama Floriańska, down ul. Floriańska to the Rynek, then south down ul. Grodzka – part of the old trade route up through Kraków from Hungary – to the foot of Wawel Hill. The alternative route for the last leg of the walk to Wawel Hill leads off ul. Grodzka via ul. Senacka and down **ul. Kanoniczna**, a quiet, dusty cobbled backstreet, unquestionably one of the most atmospheric in the city. Restoration work on the string of Gothic mansions lining the street is now almost complete, lending the ensemble a meditative aura that takes ready hold on the imagination.

First of the street's pair of museums, two doors down from the legendary Tadeusz Kantor's **Cricot 2** theatre at no. 5 (now home to an archive devoted to his work), is the **Muzeum Wyspiańskiego** (Wyspiański Museum; Wed & Fri–Sun 10am–3.30pm; Thurs 10am–6pm; 5zł; free on Sun) devoted to the life and works of the brilliant writer/artist and longtime Kraków resident. The ground floor fills you in on the man's background and early development (there's a helpful set of English-language guide sheets you can borrow from the ticket office), and on the staircase there's an arresting set of **photos** of the Kazimierz district, a number taken by Wyspiański himself around the turn of the century, offering a view of life in the ghetto as seen by a Gentile outsider. The second floor houses a collection of paintings by Wyspiański and Młoda Polska movement contemporaries such as Jacek Małczewski and Włodymir Tetmajer. Other notable exhibits here are the models that formed the basis of Wyspiański's plan to refashion and enlarge the Wawel complex as a Polish Acropolis – a bizarre, haunting vision given full reign in his play of the same name. In addition there are sketches from the conservation work carried out on the Kościół św. Krzyża (see p.420) by Wyspiański in the 1890s, then in a very dilapidated state, and some fine examples of the **stained-glass windows** he produced for the Dominican Church on plac Dominikański. Proof of Wyspiański's endless inventiveness is provided by the display of wacky furniture he made for leading literary figure Tadeusz Boy-Żeleński – chunky, jagged-edged stools which look like film props from the set of some gothic epic.

Almost at the bottom of the street, housed in an impressive pair of recently renovated mansions from the late 1300s, belonging to the archbishop of Kraków (nos. 19/21), is the archdiocesan **museum** (Tues–Fri 10am–4pm, Sat & Sun 10am–3pm; 5zł), an engaging newcomer to the city's already extensive set of museums. Like the Szołajski House, the wealth of religious art displayed here comes from the churches of the surrounding Małopolska region, much of it never previously put on public show. As well as the permanent collections, the museum is planning to hold a regular series of temporary exhibitions of further treasures from the obviously vast local ecclesiastical collection.

Highlight of the collection in the first gallery is a set of **Gothic sculptures**, including a wonderful early-fifteenth-century *Madonna and Child* in the "Beautiful Madonna" style, from the Orawa region, a powerful late-Gothic *Martyrdom of St Stephen*, from the Kraków school of the early 1500s and an exquisite relief of the *Adoration of the Magi* dating from the 1460s taken from the Mariacki Church. As with the best of Veit Stoss's work, what's most striking here is the human realism of the figures, the gentle, expressive faces reaching out across the centuries.

The second hall features a notable cycle of pictures by Hans Suess of Kulmbach, illustrating the legend of St Kathryn of Alexandria, executed in 1514 for the Boner family chapel in Mariacki and a notable *Annunciation* by Jakob Mertens from 1580, alongside a wealth of assorted religious artefacts. On into the third gallery there's yet more Gothic art from the region, including a fine early-sixteenth-century pentaptych from the St Nicholas Church in Kraków. Rounding off the exhibitions is a room dedicated to Karol Wojtyła, its one-time resident in his days as a humble priest in Kraków. As usual with Polish exhibitions devoted to the man, there's a string of papal memorabilia, much of it donated by the pope himself, including sets of his old vestments and to round it all off, a pair of pre-papal shoes.

Back out on the street, the Ukrainian **bookshop** (no. 20) is worth a look for the occasional displays of contemporary Orthodox and Uniate art. At the very end of the street, the fifteenth-century **Dom Długosza** (Długosz House) at no. 25, named after an early resident, the historian Jan Długosz, originally served as the royal bathhouse. Local legend has it that in preparation for her marriage to Lithuanian Grand Duke Władysław Jagiełło, the future Queen Jadwiga sent one of her most trusted servants to attend the duke during his ablutions and report back over rumours of the grotesque genital proportions of the pagan Lithuanians. Exactly what the servant told her is not revealed, but at any rate the queen went ahead and married the man.

At this point, most people head straight up to the Wawel by the obvious route across the road. If you can't face the crowds swarming up this path in summer, a quieter (though considerably longer) alternative route is to continue round the southern edge of the complex, and turn either up the castle approach to the right or along ul. Bernardyńska, both of which lead you to the entrance to the complex at the **Brama Bernardyńska** (Bernardine Gate). The absence of tourist-trinket hawkers aside, the advantage of these routes, particularly the latter, is the fine **view** back onto Wawel cathedral. At the foot of Wawel, along ul. Bernardyńska, in the square of the same name is the **Bernardine church**, a Baroque basilica built on the site of an earlier Gothic church containing a wealth of lavish period furnishings, notably a graphic depiction of the *Dance of*

Death in the main aisle, a well-known local favourite, and a fine sculpture of St Anne with the Virgin and Child attributed to the workshop of Veit Stoss in one of the side chapels.

Wawel Hill: the castle, cathedral and around

For over five hundred years, the country's rulers lived and governed on **Wawel Hill**, whose main buildings stand pretty much as they have done for centuries. Even after the capital moved to Warsaw, Polish monarchs continued to be buried in the cathedral, and it's at Wawel that many of the nation's venerated poets and heroes lie in state within a set of buildings that serve as a virtual textbook of Polish history. As such, Wawel represents a potent source of national and spiritual pride, and unusually in Kraków, there are always far greater crowds of Poles than foreigners looking around, many of them in large organized groups making a near-obligatory pilgrimage to the fount of national memory. In more recent times Wawel has been associated with an additional reason for making a pilgrimage here – the belief that one of the walls in the inner castle courtyard stands upon one of the world's main centres of spiritual energy. It became customary for cultists and followers of the chakra to come here and lean against the wall for a few minutes in order to recharge their spiritual batteries – until the area was roped off in 2001. A conservationist desire to protect the wall from the public was touted as the main reason for this, although there's no doubt that the cathedral hierarchy's distaste for New Age tourism also played a part.

At the top of the cobbled path leading up the hill, a typically dramatic statue of Tadeusz Kościuszko – a copy of the one destroyed by the Nazis – stands before

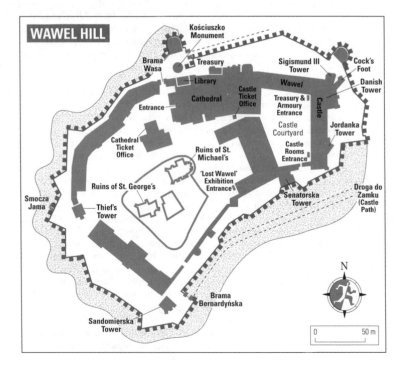

the sixteenth-century Brama Wazów (Waza Gate). As you emerge, the cathedral rears up to the left, with the castle and its outbuildings and courtyards beyond. Directly ahead is a huge, open square, once the site of a Wawel township, but cleared by the Austrians in the early nineteenth century to create a parade ground.

The cathedral and castle have separate official opening hours, but times do vary, so it's a good idea to check beforehand at one of the tourist offices or in the local listings newspapers and magazines (see p.405). Keep in mind, too, that Wawel is extremely popular at all times of year – for any chance of avoiding the summer crowds, you'll need to get there well before opening time and queue up for your tickets. **Tickets** for the royal tombs and cathedral Treasury are bought near the cathedral entrance; while tickets for the castle chambers and exhibitions are available from a separate box office inside the castle inner courtyard. In each case, state clearly which bits of the complex you want to visit, and bear in mind that your ticket may well be stamped with a time-frame within which you will be allowed to enter the exhibition – a strategy designed to regulate the flow of visitors and prevent bottlenecks.

English-speaking **guides** for small groups are available for hire from the PTTK office near the entrance to the complex; Orbis also arranges **tours** of the Stare Miasto, castle and cathedral, complete with tickets, as do a number of other local tourist offices. If there's one place where it would be worth coughing up for your own guide, this is it. With so much to see, and the crowds to navigate your way through, a reliable local hand can definitely ease the experience.

The cathedral

"The sanctuary of the nation . . . cannot be entered without an inner trembling, without an awe, for here – as in few cathedrals of the world – is contained a vast greatness which speaks to us of the history of Poland, of all our past." So was the **cathedral** (Tues–Sat 9am–3pm, Sun noon–3pm) evoked by former Archbishop Karol Wojtyła of Kraków. As with Westminster Abbey or St Peter's, the moment you enter Wawel, you know you're in a place resonant to the core with national history.

The first cathedral was built here around 1020 when King Bolesław the Brave established the Kraków bishopric. Fragments of this building can still be seen in the west wing of the castle and the courtyard between the castle and the cathedral, while the St Leonard's crypt survives from a second Romanesque structure. The present brick and sandstone basilica is essentially Gothic, dating from the reigns of Władysław the Short (1306–33) and Kazimierz the Great (1333–70), and adorned with a mass of side chapels, endowed by just about every subsequent Polish monarch and a fair number of aristocratic families too.

As you enter the cathedral, look out for the bizarre collection of **prehistoric animal bones**, supposedly the remains of the Krak dragon (see p.401), but actually a mammoth's shinbone, a whale's rib and the skull of a hairy rhinoceros, in a passage near the main entrance. As long as they remain, so legend maintains, the cathedral will too.

The view down the nave of the cathedral, with its arched Gothic vaulting, is blocked by the **Mauzoleum św. Stanisława**, an overwrought seventeenth-century silver sarcophagus by the Gdańsk smith Peter van der Rennen commemorating the bishop who is supposed to have been murdered by King Bolesław at Skałka in Kazimierz (see p.444) in 1079 for his opposition to royal ambitions. The remains of the bishop-saint, who was canonized in 1253, were moved to Wawel the following year, and his shrine became a place of pilgrimage. Below the shrine, on the right, is the **Sarkofag Władysława Jagiełło** (tomb of King Władysław Jagiełło), a beautiful marble creation from the mid-1400s with a fine

Renaissance canopy added on by the king's grandson, Sigismund the Old (Zygmunt I Stary) a century later. Beyond stands the Baroque **high altar** and choir stalls. However, most people are drawn immediately to the outstanding array of side chapels which punctuate the entire length of the building.

The Groby Królewskie

All bar four of Poland's forty-five monarchs are buried in the cathedral, and the royal tombs and chapels, or **Groby Królewskie** (Tues–Sat 9am–3pm, Sun noon–3pm; 6zł) are a directory of central European architecture, art and sculpture of the last six centuries.

Beginning from the right of the entrance, the Gothic **Kaplica Świętokrzyska** (Holy Cross Chapel) is the burial chamber of King Kazimierz IV Jagiełło (1447–92). The boldly coloured Byzantine-looking paintings on the walls and ceiling were completed by artists from Novgorod, one of a small group of such murals in Poland, while the king's red marble tomb is the characteristically expressive work of Veit Stoss, of Mariacki fame. Two carved Gothic altars and a beautiful triptych of the Holy Trinity in the side panels round off a sumptuously elegant masterpiece.

Moving down the aisle, the next two chapels celebrate aristocratic families rather than kings: the **Potocki** (a Neoclassical creation) and **Szafraniec** (a Baroque ensemble at the foot of the Silver Bells tower). They are followed by the majestic, if gloomy, **Kaplica Wazów** (Waza Chapel), a Baroque mausoleum to the seventeenth-century royal dynasty whose design is based on the Sigismund Chapel (see below). Protecting the chapel are some elaborately worked **bronze doors** displaying the dynastic coats of arms along with those of all their territories. The **Kaplica Zygmuntowska** (Sigismund Chapel), whose shining gilded cupola – its exterior regularly replated owing to the corrosive effects of pollution – dominates the courtyard outside. Designed for King Sigismund the Old (1506–48) by the Italian architect Bartolomeo Berrecci and completed in 1533, it's an astonishing piece of Renaissance design and ornamentation, widely regarded as one of the artistic gems of the period, with intricate sandstone and marble carvings, and superb sculpted figures above the sarcophagi of the king, his son Sigismund August and his wife Queen Anna. The two altarpieces are spectacular, too: the silver *Altar of the Virgin* was designed by craftsmen from Nuremberg and includes Passion paintings by George Pencz, a pupil of Dürer. Opposite the chapel is the modern **tomb of Queen Jadwiga**, wife of King Władysław Jagiełło and one of the country's most loved monarchs – in reality, her remains are buried nearby beneath her own favourite crucifix.

Venerable fourteenth-century bishops occupy several subsequent chapels, while the Gothic red Hungarian marble **tomb of King Kazimierz the Great**, immediately to the right of the high altar, is a dignified tribute in marble and sandstone to the revered monarch, during whose reign the cathedral was actually consecrated. The fourteenth-century **Kaplica Mariacka** (St Mary's Chapel), directly behind the altar and connected to the castle by a passage, was remodelled in the 1590s by Santi Gucci to accommodate the austere black marble and sandstone tomb of King Stefan Batory (1576–86). The **tomb of King Władysław the Short** (1306–33), on the left-hand side of the altar, is the oldest in the cathedral, completed soon after his death; the reclining, coronation-robed figure lies on a white sandstone tomb edged with expressive mourning figures.

The Muzeum Katedralne, Wieża Zygmuntowska and crypts

The highlights of the **Muzeum Katedralne** (Cathedral Museum; Tues–Sun 10am–3pm; 5zł), in the northeast corner, behind the sacristy, includes a collection of illuminated texts and some odd items of Polish royal and ecclesiastical history – St Maurice's spear (a present to King Bolesław the Brave from Emperor Otto III when they met at Gniezno in 1000 AD), an eighth-century miniature of the four Evangelists, and King Kazimierz the Great's crown. An ascent of the fourteenth-century **Wieża Zygmuntowska** (Sigismund Tower; same hours and ticket as Groby Królewskie), access again from the sacristy, gives a far-reaching panorama over the city and close-up views of the five medieval bells. The largest, an eight-tonne monster known as "Zygmunt", cast in 1520, is two and a half metres in diameter, eight in circumference, and famed for its deep, sonorous tone, which according to local legend, scatters rain clouds and brings out the sun. These days it doesn't get too many chances to perform, as it's only rung on Easter Sunday, Christmas Eve and New Year's Eve.

Back in the cathedral, the **crypt** (in the left aisle) houses the remains of numerous Polish kings and queens, many encased in pewter sarcophagi, notably the Sigismunds and Stefan Batory. Also buried here are the poets **Adam Mickiewicz** and **Juliusz Słowacki**, while the early-twelfth-century **Krypta św. Leonarda** (St Leonard's crypt), part of a long network of vaults reached from near the main entrance, contains the tombs of national heroes Prince Józef Poniatowski and Tadeusz Kościuszko. The equally sanctified prewar independence leader Józef Piłsudski lies in a separate vault nearby. Standing with the crowds filing past this pantheon, you catch the passionate intensity of Polish attachment to everything connected with past resistance and independent nationhood. The exit from the crypt takes you back out of the building and onto the main Wawel courtyard.

The castle

Entering the tiered courtyard of the **castle**, you might imagine that you'd stumbled on an opulent Italian palazzo. This is exactly the effect Sigismund the Old intended when he entrusted the conversion of King Kazimierz's Gothic castle to a Florentine architect in the early 1500s. The major difference from its Italian models lies in the response to climate: the window openings are enlarged to maximize the available light, while the roof is sturdier to withstand snow. A spate of fires, and more recently the corrosive effects of Kraków's atmosphere, have taken their toll on the building, but it still exudes a palatial bravura.

After the capital moved to Warsaw, the palace started to deteriorate, and was already in a dilapidated state when the Austrians pillaged it and turned it into barracks. Reconstruction began in earnest in 1880, following Emperor Franz Josef's removal of the troops, and continued throughout the interwar years. Wawel's nadir came during World War II, when Governor Hans Frank transformed the castle into his private quarters, adding insult to injury by turning the royal apartments over to his Nazi henchmen. Luckily, many of the most valuable castle contents were spirited out of the country at the outbreak of war, eventually being returned to Wawel from Canada in 1961, after years of wrangling. Alongside many pieces donated by individual Poles at home and abroad – some of these, incidentally, items plundered by the Nazis but subsequently spotted at art auctions – they make up the core of today's ample and well-restored collection.

The castle is divided into four main sections: the **Komnaty Królewskie** (State Rooms), **Skarbiec** (Royal Treasury and Armoury), and the **Sztuka Wschodu** (Orient of the Wawel) and **Wawel Zaginiony** (Lost Wawel) exhibitions – remember that tickets for the state rooms and treasury won't gain you admittance to the other two sights, for which you'll need to pay separately. The state rooms are the section to focus on if time is limited, as the best of the art collections – accumulated by the Jagiellonian and Waza dynasties – are to be found here.

Poland's long history of contacts with Italy was particularly fruitful in the artistic sphere, and an amazingly high proportion of the country's principal monuments were created by **Italians** who were enticed there by lucrative commissions offered by the royal court and the great rural magnates. One consequence of this is that Poland, and Kraków in particular, possesses some of the finest **Renaissance architecture** to be found outside Italy itself. Although the architects remained true to the movement's original classical ideals, they nonetheless modified their approach to suit the local climate and tradition. The result is a distinctive national Renaissance style which is purer than the derivatives found anywhere else north of the Alps.

The Renaissance was introduced to Poland as a direct result of the Jagiellonians' short-lived dynastic union with Hungary. **Franciscus Italus** (d.1516, and tentatively identifed as Francesco della Lora), who had been employed at the Hungarian court since the 1480s, was summoned to Kraków to reconstruct the royal palace which had been badly damaged by fire in 1499. Work on this occupied him until his death, but it was far from complete by then, as King Sigismund subsequently decided on a complete rebuild.

The present appearance of the complex is due mainly to Franciscus' fellow Florentine and successor as the royal architect, **Bartolomeo Berrecci** (c.1480–1537), who seems to have invented the highly original form of the courtyard. Its first two storeys are reminiscent of the celebrated Palazzo Strozzi in Florence, but the third tier is at twice the normal height, with the columns, which are moulded into bulbous shapes at the normal position of the capital, rising straight to the huge overhanging wooden roof, omitting the usual entablature in between. In his other key commission, the Sigismund chapel in the Wawel cathedral, Berrecci showed similar ingenuity. The basic shape he chose – a cube divided internally by paired pilasters, and surmounted by a dome, octagonal outside and cylindrical inside, with eight circular windows – represents the Italian ideal. Yet the overall appearance, with its profuse furnishings in a wide range of materials and elaborate surface decoration filling every available space on the walls, is totally unlike anything to be found in Italy. Berrecci built nothing else of significance, as his life was cut short by an assassin's knife.

Many other Italian craftsmen worked on the interior of the Sigismund chapel, the most prominent being **Giovanni Maria Mosca** (c.1495–1573), generally known as "Il Padovano" on account of having been born in Padua. The recruitment of Mosca was seen as a major artistic coup, as he had already established a formidable reputation for himself in his native city and in Venice. Primarily a sculptor, it is probable that he was entrusted with carving the effigy of Sigismund himself; he also made the two memorials to bishops in the chantry chapels of the east end. In addition, he struck four royal medals, carved the tabernacle in the Mariacki, and made many other funerary monuments in Kraków and elsewhere, notably those of the Tarnowskis in Tarnów cathedral. As an architect, his main work was the addition of the attic and parapet to the medieval Sukiennice, giving it a pronounced Renaissance appearance in a transformation reminiscent of that wrought by Palladio on the Basilica in Vicenza just a few years before.

The outsized savage masks on the Sukiennice were carved by the Florentine **Santi Gucci** (c.1530–1600), who was also responsible for some of the tombs in the Sigismund chapel. Gucci subsequently came to prominence in his own right as court artist to Stefan Batory, adapting the Wawel's Lady Chapel into a lavish chantry in his honour. He also seems to have built a number of country houses; not all of those documented have survived, but he is thought to have been responsible for the most spectacular one remaining intact, at Baranów Sandomierski. By the time of his death, Italian Renaissance architects had been dominant in Kraków for exactly a century. The style was to remain popular elsewhere in Poland for a considerable time yet, but in Kraków it was supplanted by the Baroque — introduced, once again, by Italians.

The centrepiece of the art collections in the **Komnaty Królewskie** (State Rooms; Tues & Fri 9.30am–6pm, Wed, Thurs & Sat 9.30am–3pm, Sun 10am–3pm; 12zł, free on Wed) is King Sigismund August's splendid assembly of **Flanders tapestries**, scattered throughout the first and second floors. The 136 pieces – about a third of the original collection – are what remains from the depredations of tsarist, Austrian and Nazi armies. Outstanding are three series from the Brussels workshops of the "Flemish Raphael", Michel Coxie, the first and most impressive of which is a group of eighteen huge Old Testament scenes, featuring a lyrical evocation of Paradise and a wonderfully detailed tapestry of Noah and family in the aftermath of the Flood. The oldest tapestry in the castle is the mid-fifteenth-century French *Story of the Swan Knight* displayed in Sigismund the Old's first-floor bedroom.

In the northwest corner of the first floor is a remnant of the original Gothic castle, a tiny two-roomed **watchtower** named the Cock's Foot Tower. In contrast to other parts of the castle, the rooms of the north wing are in early Baroque style, the result of remodelling following a major fire in 1595. Of the luxurious apartments in this section, the **Silver Hall**, redesigned in 1786 by Domenico Merlini (of Warsaw's Łazienki Park fame), achieves a particularly harmonious blending of the old architecture with period classicism.

The state rooms on the top floor are among the finest in the building, particularly those in the **east wing** where the original wooden ceilings and wall paintings are still visible. A glance upwards at the carved ceiling of the **Audience Hall** at the southern end of the wing will tell you why it's nicknamed the Heads Room. Created for King Sigismund in the 1530s by Sebastian Tauerbach of Wrocław and Jan Snycerz, only thirty of its original array of nearly two hundred heads remain, but it's enough to give you a feeling for the contemporary characters, from all strata of society, on which they were based. The frieze by Hans Dürer, brother of the famous Albrecht, illustrates *The Life of Man*, a sixteenth-century retelling of an ancient Greek legend, while the magnificent tapestries of biblical stories – the Garden of Eden, Noah and the Tower of Babel – are again from the Coxie workshop.

Back down the corridor is the **Zodiac Room**, ornamented by an astrological frieze, an ingenious 1920s reconstruction of a sixteenth-century fresco, as well as another series of biblical tapestries. The northeast corner towers contain the private royal apartments. The **chapel**, rebuilt in 1602, looks onto the king's bedchamber, while the walls of the **study**, with its fine floor and stucco decorations, are a mini-art gallery in themselves, crammed with works by Dutch and Flemish artists, among them a Rubens sketch and a painting by the younger Brueghel. The seventeenth-century **Bird Room**, named after the wooden birds that used to hang from the ceiling, leads on to the **Eagle Room**, the old court of justice, with a Rubens portrait of Prince Władysław Waza. Last comes the large **Senators' Hall**, originally used for formal meetings of the Senate in the days when Kraków was still the capital, which houses a collection of tapestries illustrating the story of Noah and the Ark, another impressive coffered ceiling and a sixteenth-century minstrel's gallery still used for the occasional concert.

The Skarbiec

If you've got the stamina, the next thing to head for is the **Skarbiec** (Royal Treasury and Armoury; same ticket and hours as Komnaty Królewskie) in the northeast corner of the castle (entrance on the ground floor). The paucity of crown jewels on display, however, is testimony to the ravages of the past. Much of the treasury's contents had been sold off by the time of the Partitions to pay off marriage dowries and debts of state. The Prussians did most of the rest of the damage, purloining the coronation insignia in 1795, then melting down the crown and selling off its jewels. The vaulted Gothic **Kazimierz Room** contains the finest items from a haphazard display of lesser royal possessions including rings, crosses and the coronation shoes and burial crown of Sigismund August. The oldest exhibit is a fifth-century ring inscribed with the name "MARTINVS", found near Kraków.

The prize exhibit in the next-door **Jadwiga and Jagiełło Room** is the solemnly displayed *Szczerbiec*, a thirteenth-century copy of the weapon used by Bolesław the Brave during his triumphal capture of Kiev in 1018, used from then on in the coronation of Polish monarchs. Like other valuable items in the collection here, the sword was taken to Canada during World War II for safekeeping. The other two exhibits here are an early-sixteenth-century sword belonging to Sigismund the Old and the oldest surviving royal banner, made in 1533 for the coronation of Sigismund August's third wife, Catherine von Habsburg. In the following room are a variety of items connected with **Jan Sobieski**, most notably the regalia of the Knights of the Order of the Holy Ghost sent to him by the pope as thanks for defeating the Turks at Vienna in 1683. Things get more military from here on. The next barrel-vaulted room contains a host of finely crafted display weapons, shields and helmets, while the final **Armoury Room** is dedicated to serious warfare, with weapons captured over five centuries from Poland's host of foreign invaders, including copies of the banners seized during the epic Battle of Grunwald (1410), a fearsome selection of huge double-handed swords and a forbidding array of spears with weird and wonderful spikes on top.

The Sztuka Wschodu and Wawel Zaginiony

The **Sztuka Wschodu** exhibition (Orient of the Wawel; same hours as the Komnaty Królewskie; 6zł, free on Wed), housed in the older west wing of the castle, focuses on Oriental influences in Polish culture. The first floor has an interesting section on early contacts with Armenia, Iran, Turkey, China and Japan, but the main "influences" displayed here seem to be war loot from the seventeenth-century campaigns against the Turks. The centrepiece is a collection of **Turkish tents and armour** captured after the Battle of Vienna, with a prize bust of Sobieski swathed in emperor-like laurels in attendance. Other second-floor rooms display an equally sumptuous assortment of Turkish and Iranian carpets, banners and weaponry seized during the fighting – the sixteenth-century **Paradise carpet** must have gone very nicely in the royal front room.

The **Wawel Zaginiony** exhibition (Lost Wawel; Mon, Wed, Thurs & Sat 9.30am–3pm; Fri 9.30am–4pm, Sun 10am–3pm; 6zł, free on Wed), beneath the old kitchens, south of the cathedral, takes you past the excavated remains of the hill's most ancient buildings, including the foundations of the tenth-century **Rotunda św. Feliksa i Adaukta** (Rotunda of SS. Felix and Adauctus), the oldest known church in Poland. A diverse collection of medieval archeological finds is displayed in the old coach house.

Around Wawel

Back out through the castle entrance and into the main square, the western section contains a set of foundations, all that remains of two Gothic churches (św. Michala and św. Jerzego, or St Michael's and St George's) raised in the fourteenth century but demolished by the Austrians in the early 1800s, along with the surrounding buildings, and a well-tended garden. Beyond the ruins, it's worth taking in the view over the river from the terrace at the western edge of the hill. If you're feeling energetic, you could, instead of returning directly to town, clamber down the steps to the **Smocza Jama** (Dragon's Cave; May–Sept daily 10am–5pm; 3zł) at the foot of the hill – the legendary haunt of Krak (see p.401) and the medieval site of a fishermen's tavern, now guarded by an aggressive-looking bronze dragon that used to entertain tourists by belching a brief blast of fire every couple of minutes – although it has been remarkably quiet of late. It's still very popular with the school parties that descend here in droves from the castle, snapping up trinkets from the massed ranks of souvenir sellers. From the Dragon's Cave, a walk west along the bend of the river towards the **Dębnicki bridge** is rewarded by an excellent view back over the castle. Alternatively, if you fancy a longer walk, stroll south along the riverbank a kilometre or so to Piłsudski Bridge and on into Kazimierz (see below). Clearly visible across the other side of the river is the new **Centrum Sztuki i Techniki Japońskiej Manggha** at Konopickiej 26 (Manggha Japanese Cultural Centre; Tues–Sun 10am–6pm, 8zł) initiated by, among others, film-maker Andrzej Wajda, and opened amid much public fanfare in November 1994. A large, elegant building designed by Aratolsozaki of the Los Angeles Art Gallery and Barcelona Olympic Stadium fame, the centre houses the extensive collection of Japanese art amassed by Feliks Jasieński (aka Manggha), Poland's leading nineteenth-century Japanologist and art collector, notably a valuable collection of woodcuts. Downstairs, there's a large performance hall used mainly for concerts, part of a leading new cultural attraction in the city. The Centre's terrace café, a popular meeting place, offers a good view onto the river and Wawel Hill.

Finally, if the idea of a boat trip appeals, the **barge** moored by the riverbank, a little way south of the dragon, offers hour-long trips along the river throughout the day (May–Sept; last departure 5.30pm), and there are also trips to Bielany (see p.449). Moored next to the barge is a floating **restaurant and bar**.

Kazimierz, the ghettoes and Płaszów

(The) Jews are gone. One can only try to preserve, maintain and fix the memory of them – not only of their struggle and death (as in Warsaw and Auschwitz), but of their life, of the values that guided their yearnings, of the international life and their unique culture. Cracow was one of the places where that life was most rich, most beautiful, most varied, and the most evidence of it has survived here.

Henryk Halkowski, a surviving Kraków Jew. Extracted from *Upon the Doorposts of Thy House* by Ruth Ellen Gruber (Wiley).

South from Wawel Hill lies the **Kazimierz** district, originally a distinct town named after King Kazimierz, who granted the founding charter in 1335. Thanks to the acquisition of royal privileges, the settlement developed rapidly, trade centring around a market square almost equal in size to Kraków's. The main influence on the character of Kazimierz, however, was King Jan Olbracht's decision to move Kraków's already significant **Jewish population** into the area from the ul. św. Anny district in 1495.

In tandem with Warsaw, where a **ghetto** was created around the same time, Kazimierz grew to become one of the main cultural centres of Polish Jewry. Jews were initially limited to an area around modern-day ul. Szeroka and Miodowa, and it was only in the nineteenth century that they began to spread into other parts of Kazimierz. By this time there were ghettoes all over the country, but descriptions of Kazimierz in Polish art and literature make it clear that there was something special about the headily Oriental atmosphere of this place.

The soul of the area was to perish in the gas chambers of nearby Auschwitz, but many of the buildings, synagogues included, have survived. Walking round the streets today, you feel the weight of an absent culture. Yiddish inscriptions fronting the doorways, an old pharmacy, a ruined theatre: the details make it easier to picture what has gone than wandering around the drab postwar housing estates covering the former Warsaw Ghetto.

Recent years have seen a marked revival of life and activity in Kazimierz. Long-neglected buildings are finally being renovated, many with financial assistance from the worldwide Jewish community, and the area has seen a marked

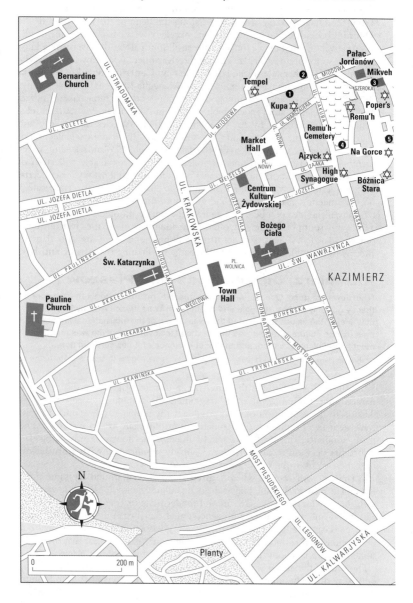

increase in visitors, in part thanks to Steven Spielberg's film *Schindler's List*, much of which was filmed in and around Kazimierz, in part to the growing number of Jews drawn to this erstwhile centre of European Jewish culture. Modern Kazimierz is a strange mixture of gentrified tourist suburb and bohemian inner-city area. As well as hotels and restaurants aimed squarely at richer tourists, cafés and bars patronized by sassy young Krakovians are increasingly colonizing Kazimierz's old tenement houses. Above all today's Kazimierz

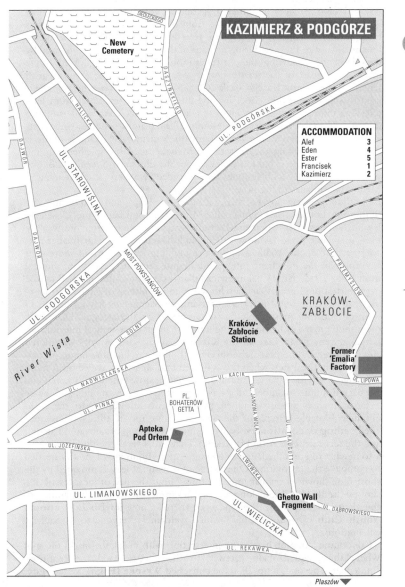

is a place to enjoy, as well as to ponder the more profound aspects of Poland's Jewish heritage.

There's a Kazimierz branch of the Kraków **tourist information** office at ul. Jozefa 7 (Mon–Fri 10am–4pm), and signboard-maps marked with tourist sights are planted at regular intervals throughout the district.

Along Ulica Józefa

Kazimierz is a ten-minute walk south of the Wawel (alternatively take tram #3, #9, #11 or #13) along ul. Stradomska and its continuation, ul. Krakówska, which formerly separated the ghetto from the rest of the city. The obvious route into the ghetto is along **ulica Józefa**, so named following Emperor Joseph II's visit to the area during his tour of the regions of Poland annexed by the Habsburgs following the First Partition (1772). Walking along Józefa towards the heart of the ghetto proper, you pass no. 11, the former parish school of the nearby Bożego Ciała (Corpus Christi) church, whose students used to supplement the school income by extorting a transit fee from Jews travelling into the city centre. Here, as elsewhere in the area, wandering into the often dilapidated **courtyards** leading off the main street gives you a feeling of the atmosphere of the vanished ghetto. A memorable example of this is the **courtyard** linking Józefa with ul. Meiselsa, used by Spielberg for the scenes depicting the expulsion of Jews from the ghetto in *Schindler's List*, the whitewashed walls, cobblestones and arcaded wooden attics lending a Mediterranean aura to the place.

Continuing along Józefa, turn left into ul. Kupa and you'll find the **Synagoga Izaaka** (Isaac Synagogue; Mon–Fri & Sun 9am–7pm, closed on Jewish holidays; 6zł), a graceful Baroque structure named after the wealthy local merchant, Isaac Jakubowicz (in Yiddish, reb Ajzyk) who financed its construction in the 1630s. Getting the building started proved more of a handful than the merchant anticipated: despite securing permission directly from King Władysław IV, Jakubowicz's plans were forcefully opposed by the parish priest of Corpus Christi, who wrote to the bishop of Kraków protesting that it would result in priests carrying the sacraments having to pass in front of, and thus presumably be contaminated by, a synagogue. Thankfully the bishop proved rather more enlightened than his ecclesiastical inferior, and building went ahead. Like all the Kazimierz synagogues, Ajzyk's was looted and destroyed by the Nazis, the surviving hull of the building being partially restored in the 1950s when it was turned into an artist's workshop. A more thorough renovation, started in the mid-1980s, is now functionally complete. Set back from the street behind a walled gate, the relatively modest and sedate exterior focuses around a raised twin staircase leading up to the main entrance. Notable features of the synagogue interior are the fabulous stuccoed **ceiling decoration**, probably from the workshop of Giovanni Falconi, and the reconstructed Aron Ha Kodesh. That said, overall the building retains a somewhat disembodied, empty feeling – more funds are obviously needed to complete the restoration. One source of revenue at least is provided by the short film, shown at regular intervals throughout the day, of local Jewish life shot by the BBC in 1936 along with scenes from the wartime dismantling of the ghetto. Next door to the synagogue there's a new **Jewish Educational Youth Club** (☎012/429 3657) which welcomes everyone to its Sabbath celebrations.

Continuing along ul. Józefa, the intersection with ul. Jakuba marks the spot where the guarded main gateway to the ghetto stood for centuries. Immediately beyond, at no. 38, is the buttressed **Wysoka (High) Synagogue**, built in the late 1550s, and so named because the synagogue was located on the first floor of the building, the ground floor being occupied by shops, replaced today by storerooms. Devastated by the Nazis, the building was renovated in the 1960s and turned into a conservation workshop, a function it still retains. Despite talk of the Jewish community reclaiming use of the building, there's little sign of restoration work on it beginning yet, lack of funds being as usual the main obstacle. The entrance to the building is from a staircase next door (no. 40). Inside the synagogue (the place is generally closed, access being totally dependent on someone being around to let you in), there's precious little of the original decoration left – the sumptuous stuccoed Renaissance vaulting of the building was completely destroyed by the Nazis – the Aron Ha Kodesh still there in the wall near the entrance being one of the very few exceptions.

Around Ulica Szeroka

Further east along ul. Józefa brings you out onto ul. Szeroka (Wide Street), a broad open space whose numerous synagogues constituted the focus of religious life in the ghetto. On the southern side of this truncated square stands the **Stara Synagoga** (Old Synagogue), the grandest of all the Kazimierz synagogues and the earliest surviving Jewish religious building in Poland. Modelled on the great European synagogues of Worms, Prague and Regensburg, the present Renaissance building was completed by Mateo Gucci in the 1570s, replacing an earlier brick building destroyed, like much of the surrounding area, by a fire in 1557. The synagogue's story is closely entwined with the country's history. It was here, for example, that Kościuszko came to rally Kraków Jews in 1794 in support of armed resistance to the Partitions, a precedent followed by the Kazimierz rabbi Ber Meissels during the uprisings of 1831 and 1863. President Ignacy Mościcki made a symbolically important state visit to the synagogue in 1931, a move designed to demonstrate official amity with the country's Jewish population. Predictably, the Nazis did a thorough job of destroying the place. Following the war, the painstaking process of refashioning the building on the lines of Gucci's graceful original structure was initiated. The rebuilt synagogue was subsequently converted into a **museum** of the history and culture of Kraków Jewry (Wed & Thurs 9am–3.30pm, Fri 11am–6pm, Sat & Sun 9am–3pm; closed first Sat & Sun of the month when it opens Mon & Tues 9am–3.30pm instead). Nazi destruction was thorough, so the museum's collection of art, books, manuscripts and religious objects has a slightly cobbled-together feel to it, though there's an interesting and evocative set of photos of life in the ghetto before World War II. The wrought-iron *bimah* in the centre of the main prayer hall is original, the masterful product of a sixteenth-century Kraków workshop. In tandem with the general revival of interest in Jewish Kraków, the synagogue now plays host to an increasing number of temporary exhibitions relating to the history and culture of Polish Jewry, as well as providing one of the central locations for the annual summer **Jewish Cultural Festival** (see box, p.442).

On the east side of Szeroka, no. 22 formerly housed the **Na Górce Synagogue**, associated with Rabbi Nathan Spira, a celebrated seventeenth-century cabbalist scholar, the tercentenary of whose death was the occasion for a major commemoration in Kazimierz in 1933. This and the surrounding houses were originally owned by the Jekeles family, one of the wealthiest merchant dynasties in Kazimierz and founders of the Isaac Synagogue (see opposite). The synagogue has been converted into a smart bank, an encouraging sign of economic confidence in the development potential of the area.

One of the major Jewish communities in Poland for much of the last six centuries, the Jews of Kraków occupy a significant place in the history of the city. The first Jews settled in Kraków in the second half of the **thirteenth century**, a small community establishing itself on ul. św. Anny, then known as ul. Żydowska (Jewish street), in today's university district, with a synagogue, baths and cemetery beyond the city walls. By the **fourteenth century**, the community still numbered no more than a couple of hundred people, but the **fifteenth century** it was enlarged by an influx of Jews from all over Europe, notably Bohemia, Germany, Italy and Spain, fleeing growing persecution and discrimination in their homelands. Significant numbers of Jews were by now setting up home south of the Stare Miasto in Kazimierz, building their own ritual baths, marketplace and a synagogue (the predecessor of the Stara Synagoga that you can still see standing today), and shifting the focus of community life away from the traditional areas of settlement around ul. św. Anny. It was a process completed in 1495, when a serious fire in the city was blamed on the Jews, provoking their expulsion from the Stare Miasto – thus swelling the ranks of those in Kazimierz.

Economically, the Reformation era was a time of significant growth for the city, a development in which Jews participated actively, as goldsmiths, publishers, furriers and butchers especially. Culturally the **sixteenth century** was also something of a golden age for Jewish culture in Kraków, with local Talmudic scholars and the books produced on the printing presses of Menachim Meisler and others enjoying high international prestige. As a mark of their growing authority, rabbis and elders of the Kraków community were chosen to represent Małopolska on the Council of the Four Lands (see box, pp.306–307) when it met for the first time in Lublin in 1581. The ghetto area was expanded in 1583, and again in 1603, attaining a considerable size which it retained for the next two centuries, with a fence and stone wall along ul. Józefa separating it from the rest of Kazimierz.

Economically, the community's heyday came to a end with the Swedish invasions (known popularly as the "Swedish Deluge") of the mid-**seventeenth century**, when Charles X's troops occupied the city and systematically destroyed large parts of it. By 1657, the ghetto population of around 4500 had declined by two-thirds, many Jews having emigrated to other parts of the country, notably the new capital Warsaw, in search of better times. Throughout the **eighteenth century**, the age-old struggle for economic ascendancy between Jewish and Gentile merchants and craftspeople continued apace, as elsewhere, culminating in the issue of an edict severely curtailing Jews' economic freedoms and even, in 1776, an order for them to leave Kazimierz altogether. The Austrian occupation of Kraków in 1776 in the wake of the First Partition temporarily put a lid on local squabbling. The Austrians' initial move was to incorporate the whole of Kraków directly into Austrian territory, abolishing the separate judicial status of Kazimierz and all other outlying districts in the process.

Under the terms of a **nineteenth-century** statute promulgated in the wake of the establishment of the Free City of Kraków (1815–46), the ghetto was officially liquidated and the walls separating it torn down, with a direct view to encouraging assimilation among the Jewish population. Jews were now permitted to live anywhere in Kazimierz, and with special permits, duly granted to merchants and craftsmen, to reside throughout the city area. It was another almost fifty years, however, before they were granted the right to vote in elections to the Austro-Hungarian Diet, eventually also benefiting from the Habsburg declaration of equal rights for all Jewish subjects of the empire.

The latter part of the nineteenth century was marked by a fierce struggle for influence among rival sections of the Jewish community in Kraków. On one side stood the assimilationists, favouring progressive integration of Jewish culture, and in some radical instances, even religion, into mainstream Catholic society, often accompanied by a noticeable hint of Polish nationalism. On the other stood the ranks of conservative

Orthodox Jewry, zealously committed to the preservation of a radically distinct way of life. In Kraków, as elsewhere, the European-wide upsurge in anti-Semitism in the closing years of the century led to a marked dampening of support for the assimilationist programme, a trend exacerbated by intensifying economic competition between Gentiles and Jews in which the latter generally appeared to come out best. The early **twentieth century** was also a period of growing political activity, with the formation of several Jewish political parties, notably the first Zionist groupings.

The period following the end of **World War I** and the regaining of national independence was one of intense population growth in Jewish Kraków, the community rising from 45,000 people in 1921 to nearly 57,000 a decade later, and over 64,000 on the eve of the Nazi invasion of Poland. Most, but by no means all, of Kraków's Jews lived in Kazimierz. The inward-looking and mostly poor Hassidim dominated the synagogues, prayer houses and Talmudic schools of the quarter, while the more integrated, upwardly mobile sections of the community moved out into other city districts, the Stare Miasto included, and increasingly adopted the manners and educational habits of their Gentile neighbours. This was a period of rich cultural activity, notably in the Jewish Theatre, established in 1926 in southern Kazimierz, the biggest star being the legendary Ida Kamińska, still remembered today as one of the great prewar Polish actresses. Contemporary accounts make it clear that Kazimierz possessed a memorable and unique atmosphere, the predominantly poor but intensely vibrant Jewish community carrying on unchanged the traditions of its forebears, seemingly oblivious to the increasingly menacing world outside it.

Following the **Nazi invasion** of Poland, Kraków was occupied by Wehrmacht units on September 6, 1939, and within days the Nazi Security Police issued an order directing all Jewish-owned commercial enterprises to be daubed with a Star of David. A month later, the General Government was established with its capital in Kraków, and the new Nazi governor Hans Frank arrived to take over. A series of increasingly restrictive laws began to affect Jews. From the end of November, 1939, all Jews were required to wear the notorious blue and white armbands, and in May 1940, Frank embarked on a drive to enforce this edict, a campaign that continued through the winter.

From here on the situation deteriorated. In March 1941, an official ghetto area was established. Located in the Podgórze district, south of Kazimierz across the river, the ghetto was surrounded and effectively sealed off by two-metre-high walls. Through the rest of the year an increasingly ruthless schema developed. Jews from the area surrounding Kraków were herded into the cramped and insanitary ghetto area, and from June 1942 onwards, fearsome and bloody mass deportations from the ghetto to Bełzec concentration camp and eventually Auschwitz-Birkenau, began. Compounding the torture and destruction, a new forced labour camp was set up in November 1942 at Płaszów, just south of the ghetto (see p.445).

In a final determined drive, a major SS operation on March 14, 1943 removed or murdered the remains of the ghetto population. Those not killed in cold blood on the streets were either marched out to Płaszów or transported to the gas chambers of Auschwitz. Thus was nearly seven hundred years of Jewish presence in Kraków uprooted and effectively destroyed. Under the ruthless rule of its notorious commander **Amon Goeth**, Płaszów was transformed into a murderous work camp where those who didn't die from hunger, disease and exhaustion were regularly finished off at whim by the twisted Goeth himself, who was later caught, tried and eventually executed in Kraków in September 1946. In January 1945, with Soviet forces rapidly advancing west, many of the surviving camp inmates were moved to Auschwitz (the workers at Oskar Schindler's factory excepted), and the site dynamited by the camp guards.

In many ways, the **postwar history** of Kraków's Jews parallels that of other Polish cities with notable prewar Jewish communities. By the end of 1945, roughly 6000

continued overleaf

Set back from the square, behind a gated yard, at no. 16 is the former **Synagoga Poppera** (Popper or Stork's Synagogue), a typical brick structure raised in the 1620s by another wealthy local merchant family. These days it houses a youth cultural centre, open unpredictably, every trace of its original purpose having been erased by the Nazis. On the far northern corner of the square, stands the old community bathhouse and *mikveh*, now a café-restaurant.

Straddling the intersection with ul. Miodowa at the top of the square, is an old merchant's house known as **Pałac Jordanów** (Jordan's Palace). The building now houses the Jordan (Mon–Sat 10am–6pm, Sun 10am–4pm), a cultural centre-cum-bookshop established by an enterprising local resident, an exemplary model of sensitivity and commitment to reviving interest in Jewish Kazimierz. As well as a good range of publications relating to Jewish life in Kraków and Poland generally, and a pleasant, animated café, the centre offers guided **walking tours** (groups and individuals) round the area, the basic ghetto tour lasting 3 hours (25zł per person, minimum 3 people). The options include a "Schindler's List Tour", its popularity matched by what some will regard as the exploitive morality of such an enterprise. All the guides speak English and generally know their stuff pretty well, and you can take things as fast or as slowly as you like. You need to book at least a day in advance for all tours (☎012/429 1374).

Moving round the top of the square, the tiny **Synagoga Remu** (Remu'h Synagogue) at ul. Szeroka 40 (Mon–Fri & Sun 9am–4pm), is one of two still functioning in the quarter. Built in 1557 on the site of an earlier wooden synagogue, it was ransacked by the Nazis and restored after the war. It's named after Moses Isserles, also known as Rabbi Remu'h, an eminent Polish writer and philosopher and the son of the synagogue's founder. On Fridays and Saturdays, the small local congregation is regularly swelled by the increasing number of Jews visiting Poland these days. Behind the synagogue is the Remu'h **cemetery**, established twenty or so years earlier, and in use till the end of the eighteenth century, after which it was supplanted by the New Cemetery (see opposite). Many of the gravestones were unearthed in the 1950s having been covered with a layer of earth in the interwar years – a saving grace, as the rest of the cemetery was smashed up by the Nazis during the occupation. One of the finest is that of Rabbi Remu'h, its stele luxuriously ornamented with plant motifs. Just inside the entrance, tombstones torn up by the Nazis have been collaged together to form a high, powerful Wailing Wall.

Around Ulica Miodowa

West of Szeroka, along ul. Miodowa, on the corner of ul. Podbrzezie, is the **Synagoga Templu** (Tempel Synagogue), a magnificent, Neo-Renaissance construction founded in the 1860s by the local Association of Progressive Jews, with whose modernist, reforming theology it was long identified. This is the second of the two synagogues in Kazimierz still used for worship today. The synagogue interior is a grand affair, the large central hall surrounded by the women's gallery, erected on decorated iron supports, and graced by ornate wall decorations and some lavish stuccowork in the ceiling. In the centre sits the *bimah*, and beyond it the white marble altar, separated from the main body of the interior by a decorated screen wall. Illuminating the whole building is a glowing set of 36 stained-glass windows restored in the 1970s, and visible only from the inside, featuring geometrical motifs alongside characteristic floral and plant designs. Opening hours are unpredictable, as the synagogue is closed for renovation, with no clear date for completion. At least during regular work hours, however, a small contribution to the caretaker should grant you access. When work's finished the place is likely to be stunning.

Southeast of here, ul. Warszauera brings you to the **Synagoga Kupa** (Kupa Synagogue), built in the 1640s with funds collected from the local community. The first of the synagogues to be reopened as a functioning religious building after World War II, it's again not easy to get in to see this one without prior arrangement. If the caretaker is around to let you in, the renovated interior shows few traces of its former character, the only surviving decoration being the zodiacal paintings covering the ceiling and beams of the gallery, and a seventeenth-century stone plaque below one of the windows. The exterior of the building stands flush against the old defensive walls of the area which you can see from around the corner on ul. Kupa.

Continuing west along ul. Warszauera brings you to plac Nowy, the **former Jewish marketplace** and still referred to popularly as such. In the middle of the bustling square, stands the old round covered market hall, little changed in appearance from its previous Jewish incarnation, when the building housed its own ritual slaughterhouse.

West of the square along ul. Meiselsa, is the sparkling new **Jewish Cultural Centre** at no. 17 (Centrum Kultury Żydowskiej; Mon–Fri 10am–6pm, Sat & Sun 10am–2pm; ☏012/430 6452), a clear expression of the revival of interest in Kazimierz. Located on the site of a former prayer house, the smart new centre was opened in November 1993, complete with plush conference rooms, library and other support facilities. After a slow start the place seems to be finding its feet among the local community, although it's aimed more at visitors. Regular conferences and exhibitions make it always worth looking in to see what's going on, especially if it's hot, when the soothing air conditioning and genteel café-bar provide a welcome respite from the rigours of the city. Overall there's no doubting the serious intentions of the organizers, who describe their central aim as being to "ensure that the experience of Kazimierz is an encounter with the presence of Jewish culture". If future plans to develop a kosher restaurant, offices and eventually a hotel materialize, the centre looks set to become a major fixture in the district.

Finally, through the tunnel underneath the rail track at the far eastern end of ul. Miodowa lies the **Nowy Cmentarz** (New Cemetery; Mon–Fri, Sun & Jewish holidays 9am–6pm; entrance through no. 55), a little-visited site that succeeded the Remu'h as the main Jewish burial site in the early 1800s. The contrast between the two places is striking. A quiet, brooding place of leafy, overgrown walkways and crumbling clusters of ornately carved monuments and tombstones, the cemetery is among the most powerful testaments to Jewish life in the district. In among the mausoleums of the great and good of Habsburg-era Kazimierz, for example, you'll find memorials erected after World War II by relatives of those who perished in the concentration camps, many of them simple tablets recording the names and dates of murdered family members. To the right of the entrance gate stands a memorial to local victims of the Holocaust.

Western Kazimierz

As the presence of several churches indicates, the western part of Kazimierz was the part where non-Jews tended to live. Despite its Baroque overlay, which includes some ornately carved choir stalls and a boat-shaped pulpit complete with rigging, the interior of the Gothic **Kościół Bożego Ciała** (Church of Corpus Christi), on the corner of ul. Bożego Ciała, retains early features including stained-glass windows installed around 1420, tranquil cloisters and well-tended gardens. The Swedish king Carl Gustaf is supposed to have used the building as his operational base during the mid-seventeenth-century siege of the city. The high church looks onto **plac Wolnica**, the old market square of Kazimierz, now much smaller than it used to be, thanks to the houses built along the old trade route through it in the nineteenth century.

The fourteenth-century **town hall**, later rebuilt, stands in what used to be the middle of the square, its southern extension an overambitious nineteenth-century addition. It now houses the largest **ethnographic museum** in the country (Mon 10am–6pm, Wed–Fri 10am–3pm, Sat & Sun 10am–2pm; 4zł; free on Sun). The collection focuses on Polish folk traditions, although there's also a selection of artefacts from Siberia, Africa, Latin America and various Slav countries. A detailed survey of life in rural Poland includes an intriguing section devoted to ancient folk customs and an impressive collection of costumes, painting, woodcarving, fabrics and pottery – an excellent introduction to the fascinating and often bizarre world of Polish folk culture.

Two more churches west of the square are worth looking in on. On ul. Skałeczna stands fourteenth-century **Kościół św. Katarzyny** (St Catherine's Church), founded by King Kazimierz for Augustine monks imported from Prague. The large basilican structure covered by an expansive roof is a typical and structurally well-preserved example of Kraków Gothic, though the bare interior has suffered everything from earthquakes to the installation of an Austrian arsenal. The Gothic vestibule on the southern side of the church features some delicate carved stonework, while the adjoining cloisters contain some notable surviving fragments of the original Gothic murals. Further down the road is the **Pauline church and monastery**, perched on a small hill known as **Skałka** (the Rock). Tradition connects the church with St Stanisław, the bishop of Kraków, whose martyrdom by King Bolesław the Bold in 1079 is supposed to have happened here. Conscious of the symbolic position the canonized martyr grew to assume in the medieval tussle for power between Church and State, later kings made a point of doing ritual penance at the site following their coronation. An altar to the popular saint stands in the left aisle of the remodelled Baroque church, and underneath you can see the block on which he's supposed to have been beheaded. Underneath the church is a **crypt** cut into the rock of the hill, which was turned into a mausoleum for famous Poles in the late nineteenth century. Eminent artists, writers and composers buried here include Kraków's own Stanisław Wyspiański, composer Karol Szymanowski and the medieval historian Jan Długosz.

The wartime ghetto

Following an edict from Hans Frank, in March 1941 the entire Jewish population of the city was crammed into a tiny **ghetto** over the river, south of Kazimierz, in the area around modern-day plac Bohaterów Getta. It was sealed off by high walls and anyone caught entering or leaving unofficially was summarily executed. After waves of deportations to the concentration camps, the ghetto was finally liquidated in March 1943, thus ending seven centuries of Jewish life in Kraków.

The story of the wartime ghetto shot to prominence in 1994 due to Steven Spielberg's film *Schindler's List*, based on Thomas Keneally's prize-winning book recounting the wartime exploits of Oskar Schindler, a German industrialist who saved the lives of hundreds of ghetto inhabitants. In search of authenticity, Spielberg shot the majority of the film in and around the area, sometimes using the original, surviving buildings, as in the case of the old Emalia factory, in other cases, re-creating from scratch, for example the Płaszów camp, built in an old quarry in the south of the area. Inevitably, the success of Spielberg's film has spawned a crop of enterprises bent on exploiting the attendant tourist potential. While some may question the ethics of tourist exploitation of Holocaust memory, this needs to be balanced against the undoubted and welcome interest in Jewish culture and history that the film has generated.

It's relatively easy to detect signs of past Jewish presence in what is now a quiet, rather run-down suburban district, and there is no shortage of local guides on hand to help. The most obvious is the **Apteka Pod Orłem** (Pharmacy under the Eagles – the old ghetto pharmacy) on the southwest corner of plac Bohaterów, now a museum (Tues–Fri 10am–4pm, Sat 10am–2pm; 2zł) containing a photographic and documentary record of life (and death) in the wartime ghetto and Płaszów camp. Its wartime proprietor Dr Pankiewicz was the only non-Jewish Pole permitted to live in the ghetto, and the exhibition touches on the sensitive question of Polish wartime aid to Jews, notably the role of Pankiewicz himself in assisting the ghetto population, as testified to in letters from the Yad Vashem Centre in Jerusalem displayed among the exhibits. The building at no. 6, on the other side of the square, was the headquarters of the Jewish Combat Organization (ŻOB) which continued operating until the ghetto's liquidation. Jews were regularly deported en masse from the square to the extermination camps of Treblinka and Auschwitz-Birkenau.

At the bottom of ul. Lwówska, which runs southeast of the square, there's a short fragment of the **ghetto wall**. West of the square on ul. Węgierska is the burnt-out shell of the old Jewish theatre, while around the corner on ul. Jozefinska, today's state mint turns out to be the former **Jewish bank**. Casting further out in the district, the **Emalia enamel factory** run by Oskar Schindler, these days producing electronic component parts, still stands on ul. Lipowa (no. 4), east of the rail track. If you want to, you can look around the factory (with permission from the caretaker), many of whose features you'll recognize if you've seen the film. There's also a small exhibition displayed just inside the entrance to the building.

Płaszów concentration camp

As well as imprisoning people in the ghetto, the Nazis also relocated many Jews to the **concentration camp at Płaszów**, built near an old Austrian hill fort a couple of kilometres south of Kazimierz. Levelled after the war, the camp's desolate hilltop site is now enclosed by fields and concrete residential blocks. Although local guidebooks often fail to mention the site, it is marked on the large *Kraków: plan miasta* city map by two "Pomnik Martyrologii" symbols, just above the junction of ul. Kamienskiego and ul. Wielicka.

To get here, take a local train (Tarnów direction) to Płaszów station or walk from Podgórze (20min), down to ul. Wielicka and cross over the road. The mortuary that served the Jewish cemetery before the war used to stand on the corner of ul. Jerozolimska. Scramble about in the undergrowth just beyond this and you'll find the remains of the camp gate, blown up by the retreating Nazis in January 1945, and the remains of quarries dug by camp inmates. The villa occupied by camp commander Amon Goeth still stands on ul. Jerozolimska, now occupied by a local resident. From here it's a ten-minute walk along paths through the overgrown surroundings to the brow of the hill and the large **monument** to the victims of the camp erected in the 1960s, clearly visible from the road below. Close to it stands a smaller memorial plaque encased in a stone obelisk put up by the city's Jewish community. Unlike its officially sanctioned neighbour, the plaque dedication recalls the fact that the majority of those who were incarcerated and died in Płaszów were Jewish.

Like many Nazi concentration camps, the site has an eerie, wilderness atmosphere, all the more so for the lack of buildings. Scratch beneath the surface of the grass-covered mounds and you'll find shards of pottery, scraps of metal and cutlery – tell-tale evidence of its wartime use.

Zwierzyniec and beyond

Moving west of Wawel along the loop of the river, you soon enter the Zwierzyniec district, one of the city's oldest suburbs and the home of several Kraków traditions, notably the custom of constructing *szopki* (cribs) at Christmas and the Lajkonik ceremony (see "Festivals", p.460).

Perched at the edge of the river, the **Norbertine church and monastery** is a fortified thirteenth-century structure, with a fine Romanesque portal (all that remains of the original building) and a restful Neoclassical interior. Used by the nuns living in the complex, it's a good spot for a quiet moment away from the city bustle. The church isn't often open, though, so it's best to visit around the time of services – 5pm is generally a good bet. The annual Lajkonik pageant, believed to have been initiated by the nuns, starts from outside the complex.

Just up the hill from here is the **Kościół Salvatora** (Church of the Saviour), one of the oldest in the city. Built on the site of a pagan Slav temple, excavations have revealed three earlier Romanesque churches, the oldest dating back to around 1000 AD. Continue up the hill and after fifteen minutes you'll reach the edge of **Błonia**, the largest green expanse in the city. Originally a marshy bog, the area was subsequently drained and has served all manner of uses, from medieval football field to the site of the huge open-air Masses during Pope John Paul II's politically charged visits to Poland in 1979, 1983 and 1987, each of which attracted as many as two million people.

The Kościuszko Mound

A three-hundred-metre-high hill stands roughly 3km west of the city centre, capped by a memorial mound erected in the 1820s in honour of Poland's greatest revolutionary hero, **Tadeusz Kościuszko**. A veteran of the American War of Independence, Kościuszko returned to Poland to lead the 1794 insurrection against the Partitions. For Poles he is the personification of the popular insurrectionary tradition that involved peasants as well as intellectuals (see box on p.448).

The **mound** itself is a latterday example of a peculiar Kraków phenomenon – a series of cone-shaped hills built by local people probably for pagan rituals, the oldest dating back to the seventh century. This mound was added onto the hill by the patriotic citizenry of Kraków in the 1820s, using earth from Kościuszko's battle sites, both from Poland and (reputedly) from the United States. Access to this section of the hill is via an effusive **museum** of Kościuszko memorabilia (Tues–Sun 10am–4pm: access to the mound May–Sept 9am–sunset, Oct–Apr 10am–sunset), adjoined by the tiny neo-Gothic **Chapel of Blessed Bronisława**. The climb up the mound is fairly steep, but worth it for the panoramic views from the top, even reaching as far as the Tatra mountains on really clear days. You certainly won't be alone up here, as the mound has been a popular local outing spot ever since it was first raised. Back down the slope, just up the road from the museum is a large brick fortress built by the city's Austrian rulers in the 1850s. These days it houses the local RFM radio station – hence the plac Paul McCartney outside – and a swish **hotel and restaurant**, the *Pod Kopcem* (see p.410). If you're in need of refreshment but don't want to blow your money in these pricey surroundings the terrace café up on the ramparts, open till sunset, makes a good alternative, as well as offering further enjoyable views. Lower down, the deer roaming about the hillside are a surprising sight so close to a city centre, although the polluted grass can't be doing them much good.

From the city centre (pl. Matejki) bus #100 runs to the hotel (about 30min), but if you feel like a walk out of town you can cross the **Błonia** and then, crossing a couple of roads, follow one of the overgrown pathways up the slopes – a good two-hour trek.

Las Wolski and the Piłsudski Mound

For a more extended bout of countryside, you could take an hour's walk west from the Kościuszko mound to the wonderful stretch of woodland known as **Las Wolski**, a popular area for picnics and day outings with city residents. There's a small **zoological gardens** and hearty **restaurant** at the centre. A little further on through the woods, 500m to the north, stands another mound, raised in the late 1930s, this one erected, in emulation of Kościuszko's, to the interwar era national leader **Józef Piłsudski** (1867–1935). The mound was wilfully neglected during the postwar era by communist authorities uncomfortable with the man's political legacy, and in 1953 the granite memorial plaque placed on the summit was summarily removed using a tank. Calls for the mound's rehabilitation gathered pace during the 1980s, and in 1990 an ambitious restoration project received official support. After a few years of rebuilding work the mound is now in much better shape, a newly restored granite memorial included. As with its neighbour eastwards it affords some fine views over the city. Bus #134 runs from the city centre to the mound (40min).

The university conference centre

East of the edge of the Las Wolski about 5km west of the centre along ul. Księcia Józefa, up ul. Jodłowa and a steep climb of the hill north through the woods takes you up to the main **university conference centre**. The first building you encounter is the elegant palatial structure that the city's Nazi wartime ruler Hans Frank planned to convert into his personal residence. Round the back of the main building there's a bar-restaurant, *U Ziyada* (☎012/421 9830 or 421 9831), that's popular with city folk as an out-of-town dining and drinking spot, especially during the summer. And understandably so: the main balcony offers a superb vantage point from which to take in the tranquil rural surroundings. In good weather, the views south are fantastic, with the Tatras visible in the distance on a really clear summer's day, and it's hard to believe you're

What Adam Mickiewicz is to the Polish literary Romantic tradition, **Tadeusz Kościuszko** is to its heroic military counterpart. Swashbuckling leader of armed national resistance in the early Partition years, Kościuszko was also a noted radical whose espousal of the republican ideals of the French Revolution did little to endear him to fellow aristocrats, but everything to win over the hearts and minds of the oppressed Polish peasantry. As the string of US towns and streets named after him testify, Kościuszko is also almost as well known in the USA as within Poland itself on account of his major role in the **American War of Independence**, in thanks for which he was made both an honorary American citizen and brigadier general in the US Army.

The bare bones of Kościuszko's life story revolve round a fabulously contorted series of battles, insurrections, revolutions and impossible love affairs. An outstanding student from the start, he fled to Paris in 1776 to escape from the general whose daughter he tried to elope with, continuing on to America, where he joined up with the independence forces fighting the British. In the following five years he was right in the thick of things, helping to bring about the capitulation of the British forces under General Burgoyne at Saratoga (Oct 1778), and involved in both the important **Battle of the Ninety-Six** and the lengthy blockade of **Charleston** (1781).

Returning to Poland in 1784, he finally gained military office in 1789 after a lengthy period out in the political cold, simultaneously failing (again) to win the consent of a general whose eighteen-year-old daughter he had fallen in love with. Kościuszko's finest hour, though, came in 1792 with the tsarist army's invasion of Poland following the enactment of internal reforms intended to free the country from Russian influence. After the bloody **Battle of Dubienka** (July 1792), Kościuszko was promoted to general by King Stanisław Poniatowski, also receiving honorary French citizenship from the newly established revolutionary government in Paris. From enforced exile in Saxony, Kościuszko soon returned to Poland at the request of the expectant insurrectionary army, swearing his famous **Oath of National Uprising** before a huge crowd assembled on the Rynek Główny in Kraków in March 1794.

The immediate results of Kościuszko's assumption of leadership were spectacular. A disciplined army largely comprising scythe-bearing peasants won a famous victory over Russian forces at the **Battle of Racławice** (April 1794). In a bid to gain more volunteer peasant recruits, Kościuszko issued the **Połaniec Manifesto** (May 1794), offering amongst other things to abolish serfdom, a radical move resisted by aristocratic supporters. Retreating to Warsaw, the embattled Polish forces held out for two months against the combined might of the Prussian and Russian armies, Kościuszko himself leading the bayonet charges at a couple of critical junctures. After inciting an insurrection in the Wielkopolska region that forced Prussian forces to retreat temporarily, Kościuszko was finally beaten and taken prisoner by the Russians at Maciejowice, an event that led to the collapse of the national uprising.

Imprisoned in St Petersburg and by now seriously ill, Kościuszko was freed in 1796 and returned to the USA to an enthusiastic reception in Philadelphia, soon striking up what proved to be a lasting friendship with Thomas Jefferson. The last decades of Kościuszko's life were marked by a series of further disappointments. He revisited France in 1798 in the hope that Napoleon's rise might presage a revival of Polish hopes, but refused to participate in Napoleon's plans, having failed to gain specific political commitments from Bonaparte with regard to Poland's future. Remaining studiously aloof from French advances, Kościuszko was again approached for support after Bonaparte's fall in 1814, this time from the unlikely quarter of the Russian emperor Alexander I, who atttempted to gain his approval for the new Russian-ruled **Congress Kingdom** established at the Congress of Vienna (1815). Uncompromising republican to the last, the radical conditions he put forward met with no response. Embittered, Kościuszko retired to Switzerland, where he died in 1817. Two years later the legendary warrior's remains were brought to Kraków and buried among the monarchs in the vaults of Wawel. Reviving a pagan Polish burial custom, the people of the city raised the **memorial mound** to him you can still visit today.

still relatively close to the city centre. Unless you have your own transport, you'll have to rely on a taxi to get here – if the driver doesn't know the way, "Instytut Badań Polonijnych" should do the trick; the cost of the journey (approximately 40zł each way) is more than justified by the experience.

Bielany

A couple of kilometres further west of the city brings you to the Bielany district. Perched high up on the southwest edge of the Las Wolski, overlooking the river, is the monumental **Camadulensian church and monastery** (8am–6pm). The only way to get here if you don't have your own transport is to take tram #2 from the train station to the Zwierzyniec terminus, and change to bus #109, #209, #229 or #239, alighting at the Srebrna Góra stop, from where it's a fifteen-minute walk up the hill to the church complex. It's a popular place for outings, so follow the crowds if in doubt.

A walled walkway brings you to the entrance to the complex, through which you're confronted by the huge, crumbling facade of the monastery church, the high central section flanked by a pair of equally imposing square towers. The spacious interior of the church consists of a soaring barrel-vaulted nave lined by a series of ornate chapels, the most notable of which, the **chapels of św. Benedykta** (St Benedict) and **św. Romualda** (St Romuald), feature a lavish series of paintings by the artist Tommaso Dolabella depicting the lives of the saints. A little behind the entrance is the tomb of the church's founder, Mikołaj Wolski, crown marshal of Poland in the early 1600s, placed here, it is said, so that churchgoers will walk over it – a stirring example of the humility the Camadolese aim to inculcate among their members.

The monks follow a strict routine of prayer and worship, so the chances are you'll catch them intoning plainsong from the raised, partially hidden gallery behind the altar. With the monks chanting in the background, a visit down into the **crypt**, where the bodies of deceased hermits are stored in coffinless niches, sealed and then exhumed eighty years later for their skeletons to be displayed, is an eerie, not to say chilling experience. Bear in mind, too, that the church complex is supposedly only open to men, except during Sunday Mass and on religious holidays, although this doesn't seem to deter the unisex crowd of visitors, mostly Poles, you'll find trekking around the place throughout the summer. Despite its relative proximity to the city, the Bielany complex feels light years away from the world at large.

The Camadolese Order

Of all the monastic orders present in Poland today, few could claim, or wish, to match the **Camadolese Order** for asceticism. Founded in Italy in the second century AD by **Saint Romuald** (c.950–1027), the ultra-ascetic practices of the Camadolese, which include minimal contact between the monks, who live in their own separate hermitages, a vegetarian diet and little connection with the outside world, attracted Polish champions of the Counter-Reformation, who invited them to settle in Poland, notably at **Bielany**. This they did, starting in the early 1600s, and they still retain a presence in the country, with two communities continuing to function. Well-known in Polish Catholic circles for their grim motto, "Memento Mori" ("Remember that you must die"), the hermits don't actually sleep in wooden coffins, as popular rumour has it, though they do preserve the skulls of their long-deceased brethren, as proudly displayed in the crypt at Bielany. However, the order's appeal seems to be on the wane. Apart from the two houses in Poland, there are known to be only six other Camadolese hermitages left worldwide, four in Italy and two, somewhat improbably, in Colombia.

The outskirts

If Wawel Hill and the main square are quintessential old Kraków, the steel mills, smokestacks and grimy housing blocks of **Nowa Huta**, 10km to the east of the city centre, are the embodiment of the postwar communist dream, and any Krakowiak will want to show them to you.

South of the city, a fifteen-kilometre bus ride offers a glimpse of an earlier industrial past in the form of the medieval **Wieliczka salt mine**, a beautiful, UNESCO-listed site that demands a visit. **Tyniec**, 15km southwest of the city, out along the river, is a fine Benedictine abbey, which holds organ recitals during the summer.

Nowa Huta and Mogiła

Raised from scratch in the late 1940s on the site of an old village, the vast industrial complex of **Nowa Huta** now has a population of over 200,000, making it by far the biggest suburb, while the vast steelworks accounts for more than fifty percent of the country's production. One of the epicentres of Solidarity-era opposition activity and all-round resistance to communist rule, it's worth visiting for the insights it offers into the working-class culture of postwar Poland as well as the immense ecological problems facing parts of the country. Indeed, there's good reason for saying that you haven't done justice to the city until the smokestacks and decaying housing estates of Nowa Huta figure alongside the historic treasures of the Stare Miasto in your impressions of the place.

From Kraków city centre, it's a forty-minute tram journey (#4, #9, #15 or #22) to **plac Centralny**, a typically grey, monumental slab of Socialist Realist architecture, now bereft of its statue of Lenin, which was replaced in 1990 by a small replica of the Gdańsk Crosses. From here, seemingly endless streets of residential blocks stretch out in all directions – a bigger contrast with the medieval city centre would be hard to imagine. East along the main road, al. Jana Pawła II, are the mills known for decades as the **Lenin Steelworks**, since renamed the Sendzimir Works, and still employing upwards of 10,000 people. The complex faced an uncertain future in the immediate post-communist period, due both to its role as a major environmental polluter, and its greedy reliance on government subsidues to remain in business. Such is Nowa Huta's importance as an employer, however, that it would be political suicide for any Polish government to allow it to go under.

For the time being, restructuring, and the securing of foreign loans (loans more often than not guaranteed by jittery Polish governments), have helped turn Nowa Huta into one of the more profitable steelworks in Poland – but further investment in new machinery will be needed if it is to retain this position into the future. On the pollution front, significant reductions in the steelworks' hazardous emission levels have been achieved through decreased production combined with the introduction of new smoke filters on the main chimneys.

In keeping with the antireligious policies of the postwar government, churches were not included in the original construction plans for Nowa Huta. After years of intensive lobbying, however, the ardently Catholic population eventually got permission to build one in the 1970s. The **Arka** (the colloquial name for Kościół NMP, or Church of Our Lady) in the northern Bienczyce district, is the result – an amazing ark-like concrete structure encrusted with mountain pebbles. Go there any Sunday and you'll find it packed with steelworkers and their families decked out in their best, a powerful testament to the seemingly unbreakable Catholicism of the Polish working class. To get there, take tram #5 from Kraków train station to al. Kocmyrzowska, then walk north up ul. Obrońców Krzyża.

The other local church, the large **Kościół św. Maximiliana Kolbego** (Maximilian Kolbe Church) in the Mistrzejowice district, was consecrated by Pope John Paul II in 1983, a sign of the importance the Catholic hierarchy attaches to the loyalty of Nowa Huta. Kolbe, canonized in 1982, was a priest sent to Auschwitz for giving refuge to Jews; in the camp, he took the place of a Jewish inmate in the gas chambers. Trams #1, #16 and #20 from plac Centralny all pass by the building.

In total contrast to these recent constructions, a mile east of plac Centralny off al. Jana Pawła II stands the Cistercian monastery of **Mogiła**, a world away from the bustle of Nowa Huta. Bus #153 passes right by. Built around 1260 on the regular Cistercian plan of a triple-aisled basilica with series of chapels in the transepts, the Abbey Church, one of the finest examples of Early Gothic in the region, is a tranquil, meditative spot, the airy interior graced with a fine series of Renaissance murals. What you won't find any longer is the late-medieval paper mill built by the Order on the banks of the nearby River Dłubnia, which exported its products all the way into Russia. Across the road is the Church of St Bartholomew, one of the oldest wooden churches in the country, with an elaborately carved doorway from 1466 and a Baroque belfry

Tyniec

Within easy striking distance of the city centre, 15km west along the river, is the village of **TYNIEC**. City bus #112, which departs from Rynek Dębnicki, west of Wawel across the river, takes you here, as do excursion boats from below Wawel in summer (see p.435), a nice trip provided you don't inspect the water too carefully.

The main attraction is the abbey of **Tyniec**, an eleventh-century foundation that was the Benedictines' first base in Poland. Perched on a white limestone cliff on the edge of the village, the abbey makes an impressive sight from the riverbank paths. The farm plots and traditional wooden cottages dotted around the village lend the place a rural feel at odds with its location so close to the city centre, and it's a popular place for a Sunday afternoon stroll.

The original Romanesque abbey was rebuilt after the Tatars destroyed it during the 1240 invasion, and then completely remodelled in Gothic style in the fifteenth century, when the defensive walls were also added. The interior of the church subsequently endured the familiar Baroque treatment, but bits of the Gothic structure are left near the altar and in the adjoining (but usually off-limits) cloisters. From June to August the church holds a series of high-quality **organ concerts** during which the cloisters are opened. For a bite to eat *Na Piaski*, a basic bar in the village, is about the only option.

Wieliczka

Fifteen kilometres southeast of Kraków is the **salt mine** at **WIELICZKA** (Kopalnia Soli "Wieliczka"), a unique phenomenon described by one eighteenth-century visitor as being "as remarkable as the Pyramids and more useful". Today it's listed among UNESCO's World Cultural Heritage monuments. Salt deposits were discovered here as far back as the eleventh century, and from King Kazimierz's time onwards, local mining rights, and hence income, were strictly controlled by the Crown. As mining intensified over the centuries, a huge network of pitfaces, rooms and tunnels proliferated – nine levels in all, extending to a depth of 327m with approximately 300km of tunnels stretching over an area some 10km wide. The future of the mine became uncertain following a serious bout of **flooding** in September 1992, when a huge river of water began pouring into the complex through an abandoned mine passageway some 170m underground. The town of Wieliczka, much of which is built over the mines, was also badly affected: walls collapsed, cracks appeared in the fabric of the local monastery, and the train tracks running through the centre of town shifted, causing Kraków–Wieliczka train services to be suspended (they didn't start up again until the middle of 2001). With the site made safe again, scaled-down mining continues today, and there's a sanatorium 200m down to exploit the supposedly healthy saline atmosphere. The mines are popular with Polish and foreign tourists, so be prepared for crowds in summer.

Privately owned **minibuses** run direct to Wieliczka salt mine from outside Kraków train station – although departures may depend on how many tourists are around. Otherwise, you can take a local Kraków-Wieliczka **train** – there are plenty of them – which will drop you off a little way from the mine, but it isn't difficult to locate the pit's solitary chimney and squeaky conveyor belt; follow the "Muzeum" signs.

The mine

Entrance to **the mine** (mid-April to mid-Oct daily 7.30am–7.30pm; mid-Oct to mid-April Tues–Sun 8am–4pm; 29zł; Ⓦ www.kopalnia.pl) is by guided tour only, in groups of thirty or so. In summer English-language tours set off quite regularly; in winter you may have to follow a Polish-language tour. You can always buy the English-language guidebook available at the ticket office. Be prepared for a bit of a walk – the tour takes two hours, through nearly two miles of tunnels.

A clanking lift takes you down in complete darkness to the first of the three levels included in the **tour**, at a depth of 65m (if you're unlucky, you may have to walk the whole way down to the bottom level and up again). The rooms and passageways here were hewn between the seventeenth and nineteenth centuries, and whereas the lower sections are mechanized, horses are still partly used to pull things around on the top three levels. Many of the first-level chambers are pure green salt, including one dedicated to Copernicus, which he is supposed to have visited.

The further you descend, the more spectacular and weird the chambers get. As well as underground lakes, carved chapels and rooms full of eerie crystalline shapes, the second level features a chamber full of jolly salt gnomes carved in the 1960s by the mineworkers. The star attraction, **Blessed Kinga's Chapel**, completed in the early part of the nineteenth century, comes on the bottom level, 135m down: everything in the ornate fifty-metre-long chapel is carved from salt, including the stairs, bannisters, altar and chandeliers. The chapel's acoustic properties – every word uttered near the altar is audible from the gallery – has led to its use as a concert venue, and even, of late, as a banquet hall, ex-US president George Bush Senior being one of the first to be feted with a feast in his honour in 1995, a token of thanks for his support for anti-pollution measures in the city. Recent events have included performances of Zbigniew Preisner's film scores for Kieślowski's internationally renowned *Red*, *White* and *Blue* trilogy. A **museum**, also down at the lowest level, documents the history of the mine, local geological formations, and famous visitors such as Goethe, Balzac and the emperor Franz Josef.

Eating and drinking

Kraków's burgeoning tourist status has given rise to a decent selection of **restaurants**, with new places springing up every week. For the moment, however, keep in mind that demand is also high, and for the top-notch places, booking is essential. In general, you'll need to turn up early to eat; this is not a late-night city as far as food is concerned. The inexorable rise of foreign tourism has however made considerable dents on local drinking patterns, with the typically central European habit of daytime and early evening socializing in cafés now augmented by a new-found enthusiasm for the drink-and-dance-til-dawn lifestyles common to Western cities.

There is a good deal happening on the cultural front, with one of the best **theatre** groups in Europe, a long-established **cabaret** tradition and numerous **student events**. The compact size of Kraków's city centre and the presence of the university gives a general buzz that's largely absent in other large Polish cities, Warsaw included.

For local **listings** and general information, the monthly *Karnet* (see p.405) is invaluable, although Polish-language sources like *Gazeta Wyborcza* and *Aktivist* (see p.405) can't be beaten for the full low-down on what's going on.

Restaurants and snack bars

The city's choice of restaurants has grown by leaps and bounds in the post-communist era, with new places springing up – and others disappearing – all the time, to an extent that even locals find a little disorientating. Happily, a number of traditional, canteen-style **milk bars** (*bar mleczny*, or *jadłodajnia* as they're more commonly known in Kraków) have survived in the city, offering trusty Polish favourites (notably *pierogi*, *barszcz* and *placki*) at mouth-watering prices. Traditional Polish fare tempered by splashes of European cuisine – Western and Central – also predominates in the more mainstream **restaurants**, although Kraków's Jewish past seems to have rubbed off on some of the better places, with dishes like jellied carp and various versions of *gefillte fisch* appearing on menus. This is especially true of the establishments in the Kazimierz district, most of which are angled towards the new influx of tourists eager to explore Jewish heritage. In addition, there's a growing selection of ethnic restaurants to choose from, not yet the equivalent of Warsaw but certainly a big improvement on even a couple of years ago.

Places at the lower end of the scale, not always distinguishable from fast-food joints, are still generally a bargain, while, at the top, you can expect to pay at least as much as equivalents back home. We've provided telephone numbers for those places where you really need to make **reservations**.

You'll have no trouble picking up a hamburger or **snack** in the city centre – Western-style **fast-food** joints (with a number of big-league franchises, *McDonald's* included) have moved in on the Stare Miasto area in a major way. In addition, numerous hole-in-the-wall joints dole out kebabs, pizza slices and hot dogs, often well into the early hours.

Cheap

Akropol ul. Grodzka 9. Passable Greek takeaway and sit-down place, offering filling portions. Till 1am.

Bar Grodzki ul. Grodzka 47. Trusty and cheap *jadłodajnia* midway between the Rynek and the Wawel, an excellent place to sample *placki* (potato pancakes) topped with goulash or mushrooms. Till 7pm.

Bistro Stop ul. św. Tomasza 24. Small and homely *jadłodajnia* with a smaller range than other milk bar-style places, but more in the way of salads. Mon–Fri till 7pm, Sat till 4pm. Closed Sun.

Caffeteria Pod Błękitnym Kotem ul. Poselska 9. Bijou café serving up a selection of standard milk-bar fare but in daintier portions. Also does good coffee. Open till 10pm.

Cechowa ul. Jagiellońska 11. Handy if you're in the university area, with excellent pancakes and a fast lunchtime service.

Cyklop ul. Mikołajska 16 ☎012/421 6603. Good-quality pizza joint, and popular as a consequence.

Also does takeaway. Till 10pm.

Dworzanin ul. Floriańska 19. Brash grill and salad bar in the front room, traditional milk bar serving ultra-cheap *pierogi* and *bigos* in the back. Till 8pm.

Ekologiczny Bar Wegetariański MOMO ul. Dietla 49. Imaginative range of Mediterranean/Eastern veggie food, with good salads and healthy sweets. Till 8pm.

Grace Pizzeria ul. św. Jana 1. Functional, unatmospheric but reliable source of cheap pizzas (also takeaways), with another branch at ul. Sienna 15. Till 10.30pm.

Kramy Dominikańskie ul. Stolarska 8/10. No-nonsense grilled pork chops, *pierogi* and the like. Worth knowing about because it's open till 3am.

Kuchcik ul. Jagiellońska 12. Down-to-earth milk bar offering good-quality Polish cuisine (the *bigos* and *pierogi* are particularly good) in a centre-of-town location. Mon–Fri till 6pm.

Pod Aniołkami ul. Szewska 14. Useful and popular pizza parlour, just off the Rynek to the west. Till 10pm.

Pod Temidą ul. Grodzka 43. Ultra-traditional, functional and cheap milk bar much used by the local student population. Till 8pm.

Różowy Słoń ul. Sienna 1. Café-type snack bar, with humorous comic-book decor. Big choice of both sweet and savoury pancakes. Another site opposite the opera house at ul. Szpitalna 38. Till 9pm.

Svensson ul. Długa 12. Popular Swedish-owned takeaway, good for lunchtime Scandinavian *pierogi* (long thin affairs, quite unlike their Polish counterparts) or salad. Mon–Fri from 10am until food runs out.

U Babci Maliny, ul. Sławkowska. The Rolls-Royce of milk bars, housed in the basement of the Polish Academy of Sciences (PAN) building; cheap range of typical home-made Polish cheapies, as well as fancier dishes like wild boar and duck. Mon–Fri till 7pm, Sat & Sun till 5pm.

U Pani Stasi ul. Mikołajska 18. A small, privately owned fast-food joint, east of the Rynek. Popular with students and offering home cooking including excellent *pierogi*. It's hidden from the street, but the queues are conspicuous. Mon–Fri from 12.30pm until the food runs out: definitely for lunchtimes only.

Vega ul. św. Gertrudy 7. Comfy vegetarian café-restaurant offering an excellent choice of cheap and healthy eats along with a good salad selection. Open till 9pm. Additional branches at ul. Krupnicza 22 (till 10pm) and in Kazimierz at ul. Szeroka 3 (till 11pm).

Zakątek ul. Grodzka 2. Good-quality salad and sandwich bar in a handy location. Hidden away at the end of the courtyard. Mon–Sat till 8.30pm. Closed Sun.

Moderate

Alef ul. Szeroka 17 ☎012/421 3870. A well-established, cosy café/restaurant done up to look like a traditional mid-nineteenth-century Kazimierz parlour offering a selection of Jewish and Polish cuisine. Frequent live music. Till 10pm.

Ariel ul. Szeroka 18 ☎012/421 7920. A long-standing café/restaurant in the heart of the Kazimierz district, a glitzy place with a mixed Polish/Jewish menu. Live music most evenings. Till midnight.

Arka Noego ul. Szeroka 2. Café-restaurant inside the Landau/Jordan Palace aimed squarely at the tourists, and serving Polish-Jewish food. Backyard terrace makes a nice place to sit out in summer. Till 10pm.

Balaton ul. Grodzka 37. Good but cramped Hungarian restaurant in uninspiring surroundings; be prepared for a wait, especially in summer. Till 10pm.

Bombay Tandoori ul. Mikołajska 18. Intimate, place with a menu limited to a small range of typical Indian-restaurant classics, but standards are high and there are a couple of vegetarian choices. Till 11pm.

Cherubino ul. św. Tomasza 2. Popular place run by the owner of *Pod Aniołami* – dependable Polish and Italian cuisine in fancy surroundings, but not wildly expensive. Till 11pm.

Chimera ul. św. Anny 3. Solid Polish meat and fowl dishes in the intimate main dining room, cheap salads and snacks in the downstairs cellar. Till midnight.

Chłopskie Jadło ul. św. Agnieszki 1 ☎012/421 8520. Rootsy re-creation of an old-time Polish country inn with a fine range of calorific traditional specialities on offer. The atmosphere is hearty and informal, and there are plenty of cheap dishes on the menu alongside some top-notch, pricey specialities. Already a tourist-group favourite, so booking is advisable in season. Also at ul. św. Jana 3. Till midnight.

CK Dezerterzy ul. Bracka 6. Comfortable, bistro-style place offering a quality selection of regular Polish favourites, from *pierogi*, *bigos* and the like to more substantial meat and fish dishes. Till midnight.

Corleone ul. Poselska 19. New Italian restaurant with good pasta and excellent salads, in an enjoyable backstreet location. Till midnight.

Da Pietro Rynek Główny 17. Best of the new Italian restaurants in town, in a medieval cellar below a courtyard off the main square. Reasonably priced pasta and salads. Till midnight.

Guliwer ul. Bracka 6 ☎012/430 2466. Stylishly decorated rustic bistro with a not-entirely French menu, but still good value for money. Till 11pm.

Hawełka Rynek Główny 34. Large dining room with straight-backed chairs and Matejko reproductions on the walls, offering a solid range of Polish food. Angled at tourists, but prices are not too high, unless you go for the game dishes. Till 11pm.

Hoang Hai ul. Stradomska 13. Vietnamese-Chinese fare and friendly service, on the road leading from the Wawel towards Kazimierz. Till 9.30pm.

Klezmer Hois ul. Szeroka 6 ☎012/411 1245. Well regarded Polish-Jewish restaurant with yet more of the nostalgic nineteenth-century decor that seems de rigeur for Kazimierz eateries. Till 11pm.

Kurza Stopka pl. Wszystkich Świętych 9. Poultry specialities with a long-standing reputation among local residents. Potato pancakes with goulash are another house favourite. Till 11pm.

Lemon ul. Floriańska 53. Serbian-Balkan grill food in a glass-fronted pavilion just off the main tourist thoroughfare. Till 11pm.

Na Kazimierzu ul. Szeroka 39. Smart new kosher café/restaurant in the recently renovated building next to the Remu'h synagogue. Till 10pm.

Orient Express ul. Poselska 22 ☎012/422 6672. Moderately priced new eatery on the vintage train theme, faux Agatha Christie decor included. The Central European section of the rail line dominates the menu. Till 11pm.

Smak Ukraiński ul. Kanonicza 15. Reasonably priced and friendly place on the way to the Wawel, featuring tasty Ukrainian fare. Till 9pm.

Staropolska ul. Sienna 4. Slightly old-fashioned venue just off the Rynek, with the emphasis on traditional pork and poultry dishes. Nothing special, but it's reliable and not too pricey. Till 10pm.

Szuflada ul. Wiślna 5 ☎012/423 1334. Reasonably priced place with modern European menu, whose appeal centres on creatively quirky surrealist decor – chair people, flying zebras and the like. Back-room jazz bar is good too. Till 1am.

Taco Mexicano ul. Poselska 20. Passable, moderately priced Mexican restaurant in lively surroundings. Open till 11pm.

Taco Mexicano Casa Susana Rynek Główny 19. A wider, slightly more authentic choice of dishes than the other Mexican restaurants in town, relaxing atmosphere and good service. Till 11pm.

Expensive

A Dong ul. Brodzińskiego 3 ☎012/656 4872. Upscale Vietnamese venture marooned in Podgórze, but worth seeking out for the city's best Asian food. Open till 11pm.

Copernicus ul. Kanonicza 16 ☎012/431 1044. Plush hotel restaurant offering an imaginative European-Polish mix, and a wider range of animals than elsewhere – hare, pheasant and venison are usually on the menu. Till 11pm.

Cyrano de Bergerac ul. Sławkowska 26 ☎012/411 7288. Smart, high-quality new French restaurant, popular with local gastronomes, too, so booking is recommended. Till midnight. Closed Sun.

Elektor ul. Szpitalna 28 ☎012/423 2314. Swish new hotel restaurant offering a mix of Polish and French dishes. Live classical music. Booking recommended in summer. Open till midnight.

Krew i Róża ul. Grodzka 9 ☎012/429 6187. Fancy new central place run by the successful Chłopskie Jadło team. The interior decor of Bosch/Memling-style fantasy pieces is an attractive enough distraction from the stiff price tab. Accent on classic Polish cuisine; try roast pheasant if you're pushing the boat out. Till midnight.

La Fontaine ul. Sławkowska 1 ☎012/431 0955, ⓦwww.lafontaine.com.pl. Newish restaurant with attentive service, imaginative French-Polish mix, and a good local reputation with local foodies. Till 11pm.

Osorya ul. Jagiellońska 5 ☎012/292 8020. Chintzy clutter of furnishings make for an atmospheric place to feast upon dishes such as duck breast, or sirloin rolled in bacon. Till midnight.

Paese ul. Poselska 24 ☎012/421 6273. Tastefully decorated Corsican place with beautifully prepared dishes, popular with the city smart set. Open till midnight.

Pod Aniołami ul. Grodzka 35 ☎012/421 3999. Recently opened medieval cellar restaurant that's already gained a reputation as one of the city's premium-quality Polish speciality venues, offering all manner of trout, lamb, pork, duck and grill dishes. Booking recommended. Till midnight.

Pod Różą ul. Floriańska 14. Expensive but good-quality hotel restaurant serving standard Polish fare.

Pod Gruszką, ul. Szczepańska 1 ☎012/422 8896. Solid centre-town upstairs restaurant attached to the Kraków Journalists Foundation: a good choice of traditional Polish dishes and very reasonable prices. Till 11pm.

Tetmajerowska Rynek Główny 34 ☎012/422 0631. Smart Polish restaurant in fin-de-siècle setting decorated by the artist of same name, in the same building as the Hawełka (see above). Good food, even better service. Booking advisable in summer. Till 11pm.

Villa Decjusza ul. 28 Lipca 17a ☎012/425 3521,

ⓦwww.willa-decjusza.restauracje.com. Ultra-smart and correspondingly pricey cellar restaurant favoured by local and visiting politicians, in the cellar of the recently renovated Villa Decjusza – hence the cod Renaissance decor. Well out of town in the Wola Justowska district. Booking essential. Till midnight.

Wierzynek Rynek Główny 15 ☎012/422 1035. Kraków's most famous restaurant. On a good night it's among the best in the country with specialities like mountain trout and the house *wierzynek* dish, though standards have been erratic of late. Prices remain very reasonable at around 60zł–75zł a head for main course and drink. Booking is pretty essential if you want a table inside in the evening: the outside terrace has a faster turnover and you may well be lucky. Till 10.30pm.

Cafés and bars

Cafés proliferate in and around the city centre, almost all those on the square adding on an impromptu outdoor terrace section in summer (regulation-issue plastic chairs and Western-brand name sunshades in all but the older-established places). Especially in the evenings, these make nice places in which to soak up the atmosphere, with the additional distraction of the assortment of roving buskers vying for the tourist złoty. **Bars** have made major inroads over the past few years, most obviously in the Stare Miasto area: where you do your drinking has become a question of choice rather than necessity. While youthful, trendier places dominate there are plenty of alternatives, with some of the nicest watering holes tucked away in courtyards off the Rynek Główny. Cafés tend to close at around 10-11pm, although many of the soundproofed cellar bars keep serving well after midnight, and a growing number of nightclubs keep going until dawn.

Cafés

Botanika ul. Bracka 9. Daytime sandwich bar transformed into smartish café-bar in the evenings. All-metal furnishings add a touch of quirkiness. Occasional live music. Till 11pm.

Carmel Coffee ul. św. Krzyża 12. Comfy chairs, *belle-époque* furniture and good coffee. Till midnight.

Esplanada ul. św. Tomasza 30. Sober, book-lined interior with a winning selection of coffees and pastries. Till 10pm

Europejska Rynek Główny 36. Smart modern café with indifferent service; its main plus is the terrace view onto the square. Till midnight.

Graffiti ul. św. Gertrudy 5. Elegant café, despite the name, that looks like a nineteenth-century parlour, next to the Wanda cinema and frequented by an agreeable thirtysomething crowd. Cinematic posters on the wall, and excellent film screenings (summer weekends only) in the garden. Till midnight.

Gołębnik ul. Gołębia 5. Small pleasant tea house with art exhibitions by local artists.

Herbaciarnia No. 1 ul. św. Tomasza 5. Large selection of teas; also good for breakfast. Till midnight.

Jama Michalika ul. Floriańska 45. Famous and atmospheric old café-cum-cabaret, opened in 1895 and a famous Młoda Polska haunt – worth dropping in at for the furnishings alone (see also "Theatre, cabaret and cinema", p.458).

Loch Camelot, ul. św Tomasza 17. Pricey but well-located new place with themed wood furnishings, homely decor, and downstairs cellar which sometimes hosts concerts and cabaret (see p.458) – the kind of place that foreigners patronize in the hope that it will turn them into an instant Krakowiak. Good breakfast buffets, lunches and sweets (try the *szarlotka* – apple pie). Till midnight.

Noworolski Rynek Główny 1/3. Traditional square-side café with wonderfully restored Art Nouveau interior, that's been popular with Krakowiaks ever since the late nineteenth century. The place where elderly matrons come to dutifully nibble their way through fancy pastries. Till midnight.

Pożegnanie z Afryką ul. św. Tomasza 21. Specialist branch of the *Out of Africa* chain, with an extensive variety of quality caffeine injections. Its deserved popularity makes for occasional queues. Till 10pm.

Redolfi Rynek Główny 37/39, near the corner with ul. Sławkowska. A cosy haunt with a splendid Art Nouveau interior; the coffee's better than usual too. Till 11pm.

U Literatów ul. Kanonicza 7. Worth seeking out for its pleasant, tranquil back courtyard. Also does food until 9pm.

U Zalipianek ul. Szewska 24. Traditional *kawiarna* decked out with folksy motifs serving up tea, coffee and cakes to Kraków ladies of a certain age. Lovely terrace overlooking the Planty. Till 10pm.

Vis-à-vis Rynek Główny 29, Basic, functional

café-bar on the main square long favoured by Polish artists, nowadays somewhat lagging behind in the style stakes. Till 10pm.

Bars

Alchemia ul. Estery 5. Darkly atmospheric, candle-lit café-pub in the heart of Kazimierz. You'll see bohemians, fashionably arty types and local Kazimierz drinkers lounging around in its suite of four rooms. Small selection of baguettes for the hungry.

Black Gallery ul. Mikołajska 24. Cellar bar with rough-hewn walls and industrial furnishings. Good vibes and a crowded dance floor downstairs, soothing shrub-enclosed patio out the back.

Bull Pub ul. Mikołajska 2. Relaxing, if rather bland, tourist joint with pictures of fox-hunting types on the wall. Of all the pubs in central Kraków, this is the one most likely to show mid-week European soccer matches on the telly.

Café Numero Rynek Główny 6. Small, stylish place with low-key lighting, soothing jazzy music, and outdoor seating in a high-walled courtyard. Decent place for a daytime coffee as well as a relaxing night-time drink.

Dom Wina ul. Pijarska 11. Currently the city's only real wine bar. Decent range of reasonably priced vintages on offer, and a relaxed atmosphere.

Dym ul. św. Tomasza 11. Narrow coffee bar-cum-drinking den with artfully distressed walls and a similar-looking clientele. Jazz on the sound system and outdoor terrace.

Klub Kulturalny ul. Szewska 25. Laid-back studenty cellar with lots of cosy nooks, and a cutting-edge dance culture music policy. Try not to stare too long at the swirly floor mosaics if you've had one too many.

Kredens Rynek 12. Lively café-bar with outdoor seating in the courtyard, and sweaty cellar hosting late-night drinking and dancing to a feel-good mixture of pop tunes old and new.

Maska ul. Jagiellońska 5. Art Deco café-bar housed in the Stary theatre, a popular hang-out for actors and arty locals.

Paparazzi ul. Mikołajska 9. Smart pub with big cocktail menu and pictures of celebrities on the wall – and trendily dressed wannabes crowding round the bar.

Pod Jaszczurami Rynek Główny 8. Large student pub (the bouncers sometimes turn away people without university IDs, so have your excuses ready) with warm, salmony-pink decor and a stage at one end of the room – frequently used for concerts, literary readings and DJ events.

Pod Jemiołą ul. Floriańska 20. Tiny bar with rough-hewn rustic decor and a local reputation for studied decadence. An eclectic blend of pleasing beats (anything that isn't top-40 radio fodder, basically) on the sound system, and courtyard seating in summer. Initially a little difficult to find: look for the sign advertising the adjacent "Arsenal" militaria shop.

Pod Papugami Irish Pub ul. św. Jana 18. Lively place occupying a warren of underground rooms stuffed with old motorcycles and other collectable junk.

RE ul. Mikołajska 5. Cellar bar with mildly alternative leanings (i.e you're unlikely to hear techno on the sound system), offering a big outdoor garden terrace, and frequent live music – a schedule of what's on should be posted outside.

Roentgen pl. Szczepański 3. Deep, smoky cellar hang-out favoured by local alternative types, improbably located in the basement of a fertility clinic. Acid jazz, drum 'n' bass and other nonmainstream styles on the sound system, and DJs at the weekends.

Shakesbeer ul. Gołębia 2. City-centre pub with rather un-pub-like decor, which looks like something out of an interior design magazine. Refined place to down a few pints.

Singer ul. Estery 20. Stiflingly smoky retro café-bar in Kazimierz that's established itself as something of an "in the know" tourist favourite. Name refers to the old tailors' sewing machines that serve as tables.

Entertainment, nightlife, festivals and shopping

Even if you don't speak the language, some of Kraków's **theatrical events** are well worth catching. In addition to consulting the city's listings magazines (see "Information" p.405), look in at the Cultural Information Centre (see p.405) which, as well as making bookings, produces *Karnet*, a monthly calendar with comprehensive listings of events. It's as well to bear in mind that during the summer months everything sells out fast. For **rock** or vaguely alternative events, check the listings magazines, or look out for fly posters around town and in the record shops. The best place to track down information on the **gay scene** in Kraków is the Ⓦ www.http//gayeuro.com/krakow/ site. A couple of places in town worth checking out are *Hades*, a bar/nightclub on ul. Starowiślna, near the river, the *Biedna* restaurant on ul. Bracka and the *Jama Michalika* café (see p.456).

Theatre, cabaret and cinema

Ever since Stanisław Wyspiański and friends made Kraków the centre of the **Młoda Polska** movement at the beginning of the twentieth century, many of Poland's greatest actors and directors have been closely identified with the city. Until his death in December 1990, the most influential figure on the scene was avant-garde director **Tadeusz Kantor**, who used the Cricot 2 theatre at ul. Kanonicza 5 as the base for his visionary productions. While the theatre itself has since been dissolved part of the building has been transformed into a centre – known as the Cricoteka – devoted to documenting the man's life and work, open to the public (☎012/422 8332).

Stary Teatr, the city's premium drama venue, currently stages performances at three different sites: the main stage at ul. Jagiellońska 1, and studio settings at ul. Sławkowska 14 and Starowiślna 21 (box office for all three venues at Jagiellońska 1; Tues–Sat 10am–1pm & 5–7pm; ☎012/422 4040, Ⓦ www.stary-teatr.krakow.pl). The company in residence places a strong emphasis on the visual aspects of performance, making their productions (mostly reinterpretations of Polish and foreign classics) unusually accessible. They've built up an international following from appearances at the Edinburgh Festival and other prestigious events.

Of the city's other fifteen or so other theatres, the splendid Teatr im J. Słowackiego on plac św. Ducha (☎012/423 1700), modelled on the Paris Opéra, is the biggest and one of the best known, with a regular diet of **classical Polish drama** and **ballet**, plus occasional opera. Check too the STU, al. Krasińskiego 16 (☎012/422 2744), which tends to specialize in the latest productions of **contemporary drama**; the Bagatela, ul. Karmelicka 6 (☎012/292 7219, Ⓦ www.bagatela.krakow.pl), where you might encounter anything from Ray Cooney to Anton Chekhov; and the Groteska, ul. Skarbowa 2 (☎012/633 3762, Ⓦ www.groteska.pl), a **mime** and **puppet theatre** that puts on children's productions.

Cabaret

Cabaret is also an established feature of Kraków, with a tradition of productions laced with thinly veiled political satire stretching back to Habsburg days, when poets and artists associated with the Młoda Polska movement established the Zielony Balonik (Green Balloon) cabaret in order to provide a showcase for satirical sketches, improvised drama and song. The tradition revived in communist times with the creation of the Piwnica Pod Baranami in 1956, an initially student-run affair that endured to become Kraków's longest running and best-loved cabaret. The *Pod Baranami*, at Rynek Główny 27 (☎012/423 0732), is still going strong today; its main rivals are the Cabaret Jama Michalika, ul. Floriańska 45 (☎012/422 1561); and Loch Camelot, ul. św. Tomasza 17 (☎012/421 0123) – the latter established in 1992 in order to revive the traditions of the original Zielony Balonik. Check with the information centres for current details: when they are performing – usually at the weekend – tickets sell out fast, so unless you've been lucky enough to get hold of one by booking, your only option is to turn up at the door and hope to be able to get in on spec.

Cinema

Central Kraków's main **cinemas**, the Apollo, Sztuka and Reduta, are all grouped together on the corner of ul. św Tomasza and ul. św. Jana (for programme details for all three call ☎012/421 4199 or check ⊛www.ars.pl), and show current mainstream movies and a few art-house choices. Other central places include Wanda, ul. św. Gertrudy 5 (☎012/422 1455), for mainstream films; and Pod Baranami, Rynek 27 (☎012/423 0768), for art-house movies. The *Graffiti* café (see p.456) shows films in an outdoor courtyard on summer weekends.

Classical music

For classical concerts, the **Filharmonia Szymanowskiego** (box office Mon–Fri 2–7pm, Sat from 1hr before concerts; ☎012/422 9477, ⊛www.filharmonia.dnd.com.pl), ul. Zwierzyniecka 1, is home of the Kraków Philharmonic, one of Poland's most highly regarded orchestras. Following a major fire in December 1991, which gutted the building, destroying the main concert hall and its valuable organ in the process, the building has been totally renovated and the orchestra is back in business, offering a regular service of high-quality concerts.

The **Capella Cracoviensis**, the city's best-known choir, based at the Filharmonia, gives fairly regular concert performances at churches and other venues around the city – check the local listings for details. Large-scale **opera** performances – mostly, but not always in Polish – are put on fairly regularly at the **Teatr im J. Słowackiego** (check listings or call the theatre box office – see opposite – for details of performances).

Clubs and discos

The city's growing nightlife scene is well represented in the host of cellar bars around the Rynek and in the Stare Miasto which stay open until the early hours to accommodate a mixture of drinkers and dancers. Most of these places pull in a wide ranging hedonistic crowd by playing a mixture of current pop hits and disco oldies – for more discerning clubbing, there are a number of specialist venues around town which offer different styles of music on different nights of the week. In addition there are a number of student clubs operating around the city – unpredictable, not always easy to find but generally worth the effort.

As far as live music is concerned, **jazz** has a long tradition in Kraków and is generally easier to find than rock – although it's worth checking listings or looking out for posters on the off-chance that there's something going on.

Harris Piano Jazz Bar Rynek Główny 28. Upmarket Western-style piano jazz bar popular with Kraków yuppies. Live jazz most evenings. Open till midnight, 2am at weekends.
Indigo ul. Floriańska 26. Cosy basement pub with a jazz theme, with cool sounds on the sound system or on stage; details of upcoming gigs are usually posted on the door. Till 3am.
Jazz Rock Café ul. Sławkowska 12. Not the smoky saxophone-tooting haunt the name sug-

gests – but a disco-pub where young Cracovians bop to anything from Britney to Boney M.
Kornet al. Krasińskiego 19. Dedicated if somewhat staid jazz club near the *Cracovia* hotel. Regular live gigs, including house band Wed and Fri. Open till 11pm.
Miasto Krakoff ul. Łobzowska 3. Mecca for serious clubbers and gig-addicts, with retro-industrial decor, and a regular programme of events – look out for posters.

Music Bar 9 ul. Szewska 9. Central cellar disco packed with a youthful hedonistic set grooving to an unsophisticated pop-techno mix.

Orlik ul. Oleandry 1. Club nights, occasional jazz, rock or ethno evenings in the Rotunda cultural centre right next door to the *Żaczek* student hostel. Also functions as daytime bar and internet café.

Pasja ul. Szewska 5. Classic Polish-style disco popular with a youthful fun-seeking crowd.

Pewex ul. św. Tomasza 11A. cellar bar with a few kitschy decor touches, a tiny dance floor and a couple of adjacent chill-out rooms. Relaxed and friendly venue for non-mainstream clubbing (music can be anything from reggae to house).

Pod Papugami ul. Szpitalna 1. Not to be confused with the bar of the same name. Regular disco open till late at weekends.

Rotunda ul. Oleandry 1. Large student club/centre right next door to *Orlik* (see above). Occasional live gigs, jazz and themed club nights.

Stacja Woodstock ul. Kurniki 3. Cellar-bound rock club near the bus station which regales an easy-going crowd of local hairies with classic rock/metal discos, and frequent live gigs by local cover bands.

U Muniaka ul. Floriańska 3. Formerly adventurous jazz venue now catering mainly to the tourist groups, with predictable consequences for the type of live acts on show. Open Wed–Sun till midnight.

Uwaga Mały Rynek 3. Funkily decorated subterranean hole bombarding arty bohemian punters with a selection of frenetic dance beats.

Festivals, events and activities

June is the busiest month for festivities, with four major events: the **Kraków Days** (a showcase for a range of concerts, plays and other performances), the **Jewish Cultural Festival**, the **Folk Art Fair** and the **Lajkonik Pageant**. The last, based on a story about a raftsman who defeated the Tatars and made off with the khan's clothes, features a brightly dressed Tatar figure leading a procession from the Norbertine Church in the western district of Zwierzyniec to the Rynek. The costume used in the ceremony was created by Stanisław Wyspiański (see p.426), the original of which is displayed in the Muzeum Historyczne Krakowa (see p.413).

Over the **Christmas** period, a Kraków speciality is the construction of intricately designed Nativity scenes or *szopki*. Unlike traditional cribs elsewhere, these amazing architectural constructions are usually in the form of a church (often based upon Mariacki), built with astounding attention to detail from everyday materials – coloured tinfoil, cardboard and wood. A special exhibition of the best prize-winning works is displayed at the Muzeum Historyczne Kraków a on Rynek Główny (see p.413), which lasts until the end of January. Some of the best examples from recent years are kept in the permanent exhibitions on the upper floor of the museum, while older *szopki* can be seen in the ethnographic museum. You can see some of the oldest fourteenth-century *szopki* all year round in the Kościół św. Andrzeja (see p.426).

Other cultural events include the **organ concerts** at Tyniec (see p.451) from June to August, and at various of the city's churches in April. The **Graphic Art Festival**, held from May to September in even-numbered years, is a crowd-puller, too. And finally, on a rather smaller scale, there's an annual **International Short Film Festival** (May–June).

Wisła Kraków are one of the oldest **soccer** clubs in the country, topping the league table eight times – they were champions in 1999 and 2001. They play at the Wisła Stadium, ul. Reymonta, in the western Czarna Wieś district (a 25min walk from the Rynek; otherwise bus #144 passes close by). Their bitter rivals, Cracovia, were the first soccer team ever to be formed in Poland (and were the pope's favourite boyhood club), but are currently languishing in the third division – their stadium is just beyond the *Cracovia* hotel on al. Focha.

For those who fancy a dip, the Park Wodny **swimming pool**, 5km northeast of the centre at ul. Dobrego Pasterza 126 (daily 7am–11pm; ☎012/413

7399), is the city's main aquatic indoor playground. Take bus #129 from the train station.

Shopping

The city centre's inexorable return to the moneyed heart of central Europe is eloquently expressed in the range of shops in the centre, with several commerce-oriented streets, notably **ulica Floriańska**, gradually acquiring the affluent-looking boutiques and other consumerist hallmarks of the average Western European city. **Ulica Szewska** is also a good street for boutiques as well as more traditional Polish clothes shops. Even by Polish standards, though, **opening hours** are a bit eccentric. Most places don't open till 10 or 11am, closing around 7pm (bakeries are usually an exception), so if you're planning shopping tours, check the opening times first. Galerija Centrum, on the corner of ul. św. Anny and the Rynek, is the biggest of the downtown department stores.

Kraków has plenty of useful **bookshops**. By far the best is the Empik megastore on Rynek Główny, where you'll find a selection of international magazines, English-language guidebooks and novels, and a good map section. Sklep Podróżnika, ul. Jagiellońska 6, is also good for guidebooks and maps. Places which tend to stock English-language titles include Akademicka, ul. św. Anny 6, one of the main university bookshops; Hetmańska, Rynek Główny 17; and Columbus, ul. Grodzka 60. Antykwariat, ul. św. Tomasza 26, is the place to browse for rare and secondhand volumes. The best places for **records** and **CDs** are Empik (see above) and Muzyczna, Rynek Główny 36. Desa, ul. Grodzka 8, is a general **antique** shop; while Postery Gallery, ul. Stolarska 8, sells good reproductions of historical poster art.

For a taste of a more customary postwar Polish style of shopping, the street traders' **market**, it's worth making your way into the **Kleparz** district fifteen minutes' walk north of the Rynek Główny. Rynek Kleparski, just across ul. Basztowa, offers a mixed jumble of Poles and former Soviet citizens touting an imaginative variety of wares, anything from home-picked fruit and veg to books, bootleg cassettes, Soviet army uniforms, moonshine and dubiously antique bric-a-brac. Heading towards the north along shop-lined ul. Długa brings you to the larger plac Nowy Kleparz, surrounded by an array of cheap secondhand and cut-price shops.

Finally, if you need a **late-night store**, the following are open 24 hours a day: A & C, ul. Starowiślna 1; Delicje, Rynek Kleparski 5; and Oczko, ul. Podwale 6.

Listings

Airlines Austrian Airlines, ul. Krakowska 41 ☎012/429 6666; British Airways, ul. św. Tomasza 25 ☎012/422 8621 or 422 8645; LOT, ul. Basztowa 15; ☎012/422 4215; SAS, ul. Kapitana Medweckiego ☎012/285 5008.
American Express In the Orbis office (see Travel Agents, below).
Bike rental At the Żaczek student hostel, al. 3 Maja 5, for 3zł per hour. May–Sept.
Banks, money and exchange ATM machines are found in innumerable locations on and around Rynek Główny. Bank Narodowy, ul. Basztowa 20, and PKO, Rynek Główny 31, exchange travellers' cheques but it can be a very slow process. In

addition, PKO do cash advances on the major international credit cards. Orbis (see Travel Agents, below), also changes cheques but charges a hefty commission. Cash transactions get a lower rate of exchange. Private *kantors*, usually open during regular business hours, remain one of the best options for straight currency exchanges as they usually charge no commission.
Bus tickets Available in advance from Orbis (see Travel Agents, below). Buying international tickets in summer can involve hours of queueing. For international routes, try Orbis (see above), Sinbad, inside the bus station ☎012/421 0240; or Jordan,

ul. Sławkowska 12 ☎ 012/422 2033. Bus information is available on ☎ 9433 or ☎ 012/422 2021.

Car rental Ann Rent A Car, at the airport ☎ 012/639 3249, ⊛ www.ann-rent-a-car.com.pl; Avis, ul. Lubicz 23 ☎ 012/629 6108, ⊛ www.avis.pl; Europcar, ul. Krowoderska 58 ☎ 012/633 7773, ⊛ www.europcar.com; Hertz, at the *Cracovia* hotel, see p.409 ☎ 012/429 6262. Airport delivery on request.

Consulates Denmark, ul. Floriańska 37 ☎ 012/421 7120; Russia, ul. Westerplatte 11 ☎ 012/422 8388); Ukraine, ul. Krakowska 41 ☎ 012/656 2336; UK, ul. św. Anny 9 ☎ 012/421 7030; USA, ul. Stolarska 9 ☎ 012/429 6655.

Emergencies Ambulance ☎ 999; police ☎ 997; fire ☎ 998. Don't expect to get an English speaker on any of these numbers.

Hospitals Kraków lacks a central general hospital – they're mostly geared to dealing with specific complaints – so ring the information line on ☎ 012/422 0511 to find which one you need, or call an ambulance on ☎ 999.

Internet access New places are opening up all the time: try *Cyberland*, ul. św. Jana 6 (in the Ars cinema complex; 10am–midnight); *e-network.pl*, Sienna 14 (24hr); *Garnet*, Florianska 14 (24hr); *Internet Club InterMark*, Floriańska 30 (daily 10am–midnight); or *Looz*, ul. Mikołajska 13 (Sun–Thurs 10am–midnight, Fri & Sat 10am–8am; ⊛ www.looz.com.pl). Prices hover between 4 and 6zł per hour.

Laundry There's a laundry in the basement of the *Piast* student hostel (see p.411). For dry cleaning go to Betty Clean, ul. Długa 17.

Pharmacies Useful central pharmacies include Grodzka, ul. Grodzka 26 (Mon–Fri 8am–9pm, Sat 9am–4pm, Sun 10am–5pm); and Pod Złotą Głową, Rynek 13 (Mon–Fri 9am–9pm, Sat 9am–4pm). Pharmacies stay open 24hr according to a rota;

check the information posted in their windows, or call ☎ 012/422 0511, to find out which one is on duty.

Phonecards Available from the Telekomunikacja Polska (TKP) main office, Rynek Główny 17, along with a growing number of local shops.

Photographic supplies Digital Photo Express, Grodzka 38, will print your holiday snaps as well as offering the whole range of professional processing services. Sells all kinds of film.

Post offices and mail The main post office is at ul. Wielopole 2; has poste restante, phone and fax services (Mon–Fri 7.30am–10.30pm, Sat 8am–2pm, Sun 9–11am). The branch just outside the train station has one counter open 24hr. For express mail, try EMS, in the main post office ☎ 012/422 6696; DHL, ul. Balicka 79 ☎ 012/636 8994; or TNT, ul. Pleszowska 29 ☎ 012/415 6030.

Radio The local RMF station (70.06FM), eastern Europe's first independently owned radio setup, based inside the *Pod Kopcem* hotel, broadcasts throughout southern Poland: it has English-language news bulletins five times a day from Monday to Saturday (8.30am, 10.30am, 3.30pm, 5.30pm and 9pm), and BBC news at 9pm on Sundays.

Taxis There are plenty of companies to choose from. Dependable options include Wawel Taxi ☎ 9666; Radio Taxi ☎ 919; Euro Taxi ☎ 9664; or Metro Taxi ☎ 9667.

Train tickets are available from the Orbis office at Rynek Główny 41 and in the train station. Expect queues at the international ticket desk. For train enquiries, call ☎ 9436 or ☎ 012/624 1436.

Travel agents Orbis, Rynek Główny 41 (☎ 012/422 9180) are good for bus and train tickets; Almatour, Grodzka 2 (☎ 012/422 4668), specialize in youth travel and sell ISIC cards; Express Travel, ul. św. Gertrudy 23 (☎ 012/292 0525), operate bus tours to local attractions; as do Jordan, ul. Długa 9 (☎ 012/421 2125).

Małopolska

The name **Małopolska** – literally Little Poland – in fact applies to a large swath of the country, for the most part a rolling landscape of traditionally cultivated fields and quiet villages. It's an ancient region, forming, with Wielkopolska, the early medieval Polish state, though its geographical divisions, particularly from neighbouring Silesia, are a bit nebulous. The bulk of Małopolska proper sits north of Kraków, bounded by the Świętokrzyskie Mountains to the north and the broad range of hills stretching down from

Częstochowa to Kraków – the so-called Szlak Orlich Gniazd (Eagles' Nest Trail) – to the west.

North of Kraków, into the Małopolska heartlands, towns such as **Pinczów**, **Szydłów** and **Jędrzejów** offer rewarding insights into the Jewish-tinged history of the region, while **Kielce**, a largish industrial centre and the regional capital, provides a good stepping-off point for forays into the **Świętokrzyskie**, called mountains but really no more than high hills, though still enjoyable walking territory. The ruins of the once grand Krzyżtopor Castle, near Opatów, are among the best and most memorable in the country. **Częstochowa**, the only other city of the region, is famous as the home of the Black Madonna, which draws huge crowds for the major religious festivals and annual summer pilgrimages from all over the country. Pope John Paul II is a native of the region, too, and his birthplace at **Wadowice** has become something of a national shrine, while the Catholic trail continues to the west at **Kalwaria Zebrzydowska**, another pilgrimage site.

Due west of Kraków at **Oświęcim** is the **Auschwitz-Birkenau** concentration camp, preserved more or less as the Nazis left it.

Oświęcim: Auschwitz-Birkenau

Seventy kilometres west of Kraków, **OŚWIĘCIM** would in normal circumstances be a nondescript industrial town – a place to send visitors on their way without a moment's thought. The circumstances, however, are anything but normal here. Despite the best efforts of the local authorities to cultivate and develop a new identity, the town is indissolubly linked with the name the Nazi occupiers of Poland gave the place – Auschwitz.

△ Auschwitz

Following the country's conquest in 1939, many of the largest and most murderous of the **Nazis' concentration camps** were established in Poland. The camps described in detail in this book – Auschwitz, Majdanek and Stutthof – are easily accessible to travellers visiting Kraków, Lublin and Gdańsk. Others, with no less hideous a history, are more difficult to get to. For those wanting to visit them, the other major camps are:

Bełżec Close to the Ukrainian border, some 40km southeast of Zamość. The death camp at Bełżec, a small country town with its own Jewish population, was established in January–February 1942 as an extension of a labour camp opened in May 1940. The camp rapidly began its murderous and clinically planned business, using six gas ovens to dispose of its victims at the rate of 4500 a time. By the time the Nazis began liquidating the camp in December 1942, a process completed in spring 1943 (when the whole site had been obliterated and reforested), it is estimated that some 600,000 Roma and Jews, principally from the Lublin region, Lwów (L'viv), Kraków, Germany, Austria, Hungary, Romania and Czechoslovakia, had been murdered. The monument to the Jews murdered here was built in the 1960s on the former site of the camp.

Chełmno Nad Nerem (Cumhof). Established in December 1941 on the banks of the River Ner, 50km northwest of Łódź, this was the first death camp built by the Nazis in Poland, and was liberated in 1945. An estimated 340,000 were murdered here, the majority Polish Jews. Traces of the camp remain alongside an official monument to its victims. The camp was a key subject of Claude Lanzemann's controversial documentary *Shoah*.

Rogoźnica (Gross-Rosen). On the road between Legnica and Świdnica in Silesia this was one of the earliest forced labour/concentration camps, established in August 1940, and liquidated in March 1945. A monument now stands to the 40,000 people who perished here.

Sobibór Seventy kilometres east of Lublin, right up by the Belarus border, this death camp was set up in March 1942 as part of the increasingly desperate Nazi drive towards the Final Solution. It was dismantled by the Nazis in October 1943, following an inmates' revolt led by a Soviet Jewish POW officer (about 300 escaped), by which time an estimated 250,000 inmates – mostly Jews from Poland, Ukraine, Holland, France and Austria – had been murdered, most of them in the camp's gas chambers. A commemorative monument as well as a mound of ashes made from burnt corpses has been erected on the former camp site.

Treblinka Roughly 100km northeast of Warsaw on the eastern edges of Mazovia, the camps (known simply as Treblinka "I" and "II") were built along the borderline agreed between Germany and the Soviet Union prior to their joint invasion of Poland in September 1939. Treblinka was shut down by the Nazis in late 1943, by which time an estimated 800,000 people – Jews, Roma, Poles and many others – had perished in its gas chambers. A Museum of Remembrance was established in the early 1960s, with a large monument commemorating the inmates' uprising of August 1943.

Some history

Following the Nazi invasion of Poland in September 1939, Oświęcim and its surrounding region were incorporated into the domains of the Third Reich and the town's name changed to **Auschwitz**. The idea of setting up a concentration camp in the area was mooted a few months later by the Breslau (Wrocław) division of the SS, the official explanation being the overcrowding in existing prisons in Silesia combined with the political desirability of a campaign of mass-arrests throughout German-occupied Poland to round up all potentially "troublesome" Poles. After surveying the region, the final choice of location fell on an abandoned Polish army barracks in Oświęcim, then an insignificant rural town well away from major urban settlements – and prying eyes – on the borders of Silesia and Małopolska. As Himmler himself was later to explain, Auschwitz was chosen on the clinically prosaic grounds that it was a "convenient location as regards communication, and because the area can be easily sealed off".

Orders to begin work on the camp were finally given in April 1940, the fear-some **Rudolf Höss** was appointed its commander, and in June of that year, the Gestapo sent the first contingent of around seven hundred prisoners, mainly Jews, to the new camp from nearby Tarnów. As the number of inmates swelled rapidly, so too did the physical size of the camp, as Auschwitz was gradually, but methodically, transformed from a detention centre into a full-scale death camp. The momentum of destruction was given its decisive twist by Himmler's decision in 1941 to make Auschwitz the centrepiece of Nazi plans for the Final Solution, the Nazis' attempt to effect the elimination of European Jewry by systematically rounding up, transporting and murdering all the Jews in Reich territories. To this end a second camp, **Birkenau**, was set up a couple of kilometres from the main site, with its own set of gas chambers, crematoria and eventually even its own railway terminal to permit the "efficient" dispatch of new arrivals to the waiting gas chambers.

By the end of 1942, **Jews** were beginning to be transported to Auschwitz from all over Europe, many fully believing Nazi propaganda that they were on their way to a new life of work in German factories or farms – the main reason, it appears, that so many brought their personal valuables with them. The reality, of course, couldn't have been more different. After a train journey of any-thing up to ten days in sealed goods wagons and cattle trucks, the dazed sur-vivors were herded up the station ramp, whereupon they were promptly lined up for inspection and divided into two categories by the SS: those deemed "fit" or "unfit" for work. People placed in the latter category, up to seventy-five per-cent of all new arrivals, according to Höss's testimony at the Nuremberg trials, were told they would be permitted to have a bath. They were then ordered to undress, marched into the "shower room" and gassed with **Zyklon B** cyanide gas sprinkled through special ceiling attachments. In this way, up to two thou-sand people were killed at a time (the process took 15–20 minutes), a murder-ously efficient method of dispatching people that continued relentlessly throughout the rest of the war. The greatest massacres occurred from 1944 onwards, after the special railway terminal had been installed at Birkenau to per-mit speedier "processing" of the victims to the gas chambers and crematoria. Compounding the hideousness of the operation, SS guards removed gold fill-ings, earrings, finger rings and even hair – subsequently used, amongst other things, for mattresses – from the mass of bodies, before incinerating them. The cloth from their clothes was processed into material for army uniforms, their watches given to troops in recognition of special achievements or bravery.

The precise numbers of people murdered in Auschwitz-Birkenau between the camp's construction in 1940 and final liberation by Soviet forces in January 1945 has long been a subject of dispute, often for reasons less to do with a con-cern with factual accuracy than "revisionist" neo-Nazi attempts to deny the historical reality of the Holocaust. Though the exact figure will never be known, in reputable historical circles it's now generally believed that some-where between one and a half and two million people died in the camp, the vast majority (85–90 percent) of whom were Jews, along with sizeable contin-gents of Romanies (Gypsies), Poles, Soviet POWs and a host of other European nationalities.

To describe **Auschwitz-Birkenau** as a "museum" seems morally shocking: strictly speaking, however, the description is correct, if a museum is understood to be a place where objects are chosen, arranged and displayed with a purpose. In the first place, what the visitor to Auschwitz-Birkenau sees today does not reflect the way the camp developed under the Nazis, or the camp that the Soviet liberators found in January 1945. Many important sections of the site, for example, have been altered, destroyed or allowed to fall into ruin. Some cases in point are the entrance kiosk of today's parking lot, originally the site of the main entrance to the camp – not as is commonly assumed, the gate bearing the notorious "*Arbeit Macht Frei*" inscription; the visitors' complex next to the parking lot, originally the reception centre for camp inmates; and, most importantly, the crematorium just outside the fence of the main **Auschwitz** site – a partially reconstructed replica of the ruined original the camp guards hastily blew up, along with other incriminating evidence, prior to evacuating the site. This is not to suggest any similarity of intention with those neo-Nazi groups and revisionist historians who use discrepancies between the original Auschwitz camp plan and today's site as "evidence" to support their Holocaust denials. It is to recognize that from the outset the purpose of preserving Auschwitz had more to do with memory and bearing witness than the straight presentation of objective historical fact – and rightly so, many will feel.

Further, although it is Auschwitz that official tours and guidebooks mostly focus on, it was in **Birkenau** that the vast majority of the killing (mostly of Jews) occurred – a result, some would argue, of the postwar "museum" planners' focus on presenting and preserving sites connected with Polish martyrdom, and a phenomenon perpetuated to this day in the minority of visitors who make it to Birkenau. Third, and most shamefully, until the 1990s officially produced information about the camps downplayed, or to be more accurate, perhaps, omitted to make adequate mention of the specifically Jewish-related aspects of the genocide enacted in the camp.

The immediate context for the glaring omission of the **Jewish perspective** in official communist-era Polish guidebooks and tours of the concentration camps was straightforwardly political. For Poland's postwar communist regime, like those in other East European countries, the horrors of World War II were a constant and central reference point. Following the official Soviet line, the emphasis was on the war as an antifascist struggle, in which good (communism and the Soviet Union, represented by the new postwar governments) had finally triumphed over evil (fascism and Nazi Germany).

This interpretation provided an important legitimizing prop for the new regimes. The Soviet Union, aided by loyal national communists, were the people who had liberated Europe from Hitler, and as inheritors of their antifascist mantle, the newly installed communist governments sought to portray themselves as heirs to all that was noble and good. In this schematic view of the war, there was no room for details of the racial aspects of Nazi ideology – people were massacred in the camps because fascists were butchers, not because the victims were Jews or Poles or Romanies. Hence the camps were opened up first and foremost as political monuments to the victims of fascism rather than to the Holocaust. The official decree establishing the museum in 1947 captures the ideological leavening succinctly: "On the site of the former Nazi concentration camp, a monument to the martyrdom of the Polish nation and of other nations is to be erected for all time to come."

Recognizing the sensitivities that continue to surround these issues, Poland's post-communist authorities have shown far greater willingness than their predecessors to acknowledge the specifically anti-Semitic dimensions of Nazi devastation. Along with "revised" figures for the numbers of deaths at Auschwitz and Birkenau, official guidebooks to the camp now state clearly that the vast majority of the victims were Jews, and signs give greater prominence to the specifically Jewish aspects of the genocide practised here.

In the broader sweep of Polish–Jewish relations, the biggest running sore of recent years in relation to Auschwitz-Birkenau has been the controversy over the **Carmelite Convent** established in 1984, flush against the walls of Auschwitz, in a building once used by the Nazis as a storehouse for Zyklon B gas crystals. In 1987, following sustained protests from the World Jewish Congress and other concerned organizations over what was viewed as a misconceived and offensive attempt to "baptize" and appropriate the Holocaust for religious ends, the Roman Catholic hierarchy consented to the removal of the convent. Following the nuns' failure to meet the agreed deadline, the dispute flared up in the summer of 1989. Jewish activists from the USA and Israel staged a series of protests at the site under an international media spotlight. Local residents reacted furiously (and on occasions, violently) to what were interpreted as hostile foreign intrusions into Church life. Cardinal Glemp suggested that a world Jewish media conspiracy was being directed against the Church, a remark that provoked several noted Polish-Catholic intellectuals to censure him publicly. In turn, it could be argued that Jewish reactions showed little sympathy for or understanding of the widespread Polish perception of Auschwitz as a symbol of national suffering, at Auschwitz, in particular, and under the Nazis in general, and of the more than three million Gentile Poles killed during the Nazi occupation.

All in all, the dispute over the convent provoked much sadness and bitterness, needlessly retarding the slow and often painful process of promoting and reordering Polish-Jewish relations. The collective sigh of relief when the nuns finally moved to the new site designated for them in summer 1993 was audible, not least as their continuing failure to budge had for a while threatened to result in a Jewish boycott of official ceremonies marking the fiftieth anniversary of the 1943 Warsaw Ghetto Uprising. The convent is now located next to the **Centre for Information, Dialogue and Prayer** established in 1992, on a site 1km southwest of the camp, which aims to provide a space for reflection and discussion on the meaning and legacy of the Holocaust, in particular a place of encounter between locals and Jewish visitors to the camps.

A further twist to the camp's history came during the ceremonies held to mark the **fiftieth anniversary of the liberation of Auschwitz-Birkenau** in January 1995. Once again, an event intended to demonstrate memory and unity threatened to be overshadowed by disputes. Angered by what they saw as a failure to accord Jewish sufferings in Auschwitz their proper place in the two-day commemorations, Jewish participants organized their own emotionally charged act of remembrance at the camp the day before the official ceremony. In his speech at the ceremony the next day, attended by a host of world political and religious leaders, President Lech Wałęsa, stung by the perceived slight, deviated from his prepared text to acknowledge the unique and specific suffering of Jews – the first time he had ever done so in public.

A virtual rerun of the convent controversy occurred in 1998, when radical Catholic nationalist groups began planting a sea of **crucifixes** around an eight-metre cross just beyond the camp's southern perimeter. Erected to commemorate Karol Wojtyła's visit to the camp in 1979, the cross had always been tolerated by Jewish organizations. The emergence of hundreds of smaller crosses around it was, however, another matter. The Polish authorities battled to defuse the dispute by attempting to secure the crosses' removal via legal expropriation of the land on which they were placed, but this hasn't prevented further – albeit sporadic – outbreaks of cross-planting near the site.

The latest controversy to affect Auschwitz involves the establishment of a **buffer zone** around the camp, within which all commercial activities that could compromise the dignity of the site are to be prohibited. In 1999 the Polish government decreed that the zone would occupy a hundred-metre radius around the boundaries of the camp. Members of the Jewish community nevertheless pointed out that a

continued overleaf

Auschwitz-Birkenau in postwar Poland contd.

UNESCO-sponsored agreement dating from 1979 had envisaged a zone 500m deep, and began to campaign for the 1979 agreement's ratification. The existence of any kind of buffer zone was profoundly unpopular with the inhabitants of **Zasole**, the 10,000-strong Oświęcim suburb which directly borders on the Auschwitz site. The bar on commercial activity was seen by them as an unfair imposition on an area of town that is already marked by economic stagnation and high unemployment. Things came to a head in early 2001, when a popular **disco**, crassly situated near the camp in a building once used by the Nazis to store clothes and other belongings stolen from inmates, was closed down by the regional governor of Małopolska – over the heads of the Zasole council. The Oświęcim authorities are currently working on an urban development plan that will respect the five-hundred-metre zone while providing room for the economic development of Zasole at the same time – predictably, many in Zasole regard this as a sellout. The difficult and emotionally charged issue of Polish-Jewish relations looks set to remain in the headlines for some time to come.

The physical scale of the Auschwitz-Birkenau camp is a shock in itself. Most visitors, though, see only the main Auschwitz section of the complex. This, however, was only one component of the hideous network of barracks, compounds, factories and extermination areas. It is only in visiting Birkenau, roughly 3km down the road from Auschwitz, that you begin to grasp the full enormity of the Nazi death machine.

Practicalities

To get to Auschwitz-Birkenau from Kraków by **train**, services to Oświęcim are fairly frequent (6 daily from Kraków central station; 12 from Płaszów station). Return services can be inconvenient, though, which combined with the decreasing number of departures as the morning progresses makes an early start a good idea. Overall, it's definitely advisable to check current timetables before setting out. **Buses** run less frequently and several terminate at the main bus terminal 2km east of the centre of Oświęcim. Either way, it's a ninety-minute journey.

Most people choose to visit Auschwitz first (the site of the main "museum" displays), before heading for Birkenau, 3km to the northwest. From Oświęcim station, it's a twenty-minute walk (turn right outside the train station and follow the signs) or short bus ride (numerous municipal services make the journey; details are posted at the train station exit) to the gates of Auschwitz. An hourly bus service operates between Auschwitz and Birkenau (April–Sept only; 2zł); otherwise taxis are available, or you can walk there in 35 minutes. You can then catch the hourly bus back to Auschwitz, followed by a municipal bus back to the train station – or simply walk direct from Birkenau to the train station (30min). As you can appreciate from the above, **walking** the whole circuit (train station–Auschwitz–Birkenau–train station) can be time-consuming, but many people prefer to do it this way, because it gives them time to ponder the enormity of what it is they're visiting. Bear in mind however that you'll be walking along unshaded asphalt all the way – not particularly comfortable in high summer.

The trip back to Kraków can be done by either train or bus – departures for the latter are from the terminal opposite the train station in Oświęcim. Departures are a bit unpredictable, particularly during the afternoons, so you'd be well advised to check both sets of timetables on arrival in the town.

In the unlikely event that you'd want a **place to stay** over, you have several options. The church-run *Centrum Dialogu i Modlitwy* (Centre for Dialogue and Prayer) at ul. św. M. Kolbego 1 (☎033/843 1000; ❸, reductions for students), used by visiting pilgrim and tour groups, is peacefully located ten minutes' walk south of the Auschwitz site. The *Międzynarodowy Dom Spotkań Młodzieży*, ul. Legionów 11 (☎033/843 2107, ⊛www.mdsm.pl; ❸), due east of the train station, and within walking distance of Auschwitz, is an International Youth Meeting Centre run by a reconciliatory German Protestant organization and offers decent accommodation in en-suite doubles, triples and quads, although it's often booked to capacity by groups. Hotels include the *Olimpijski*, opposite the main bus station at ul. Chemików 2a (☎033/842 3841; ❹), and the *Glob*, just outside the train station at ul. Powstanców Śląskich 16 (☎033/843 3999; ❹), both of which are reasonably businesslike options with average en-suites. All these places have their own restaurants or canteens, while the large **cafeteria** inside the Auschwitz camp area also provides basic meals.

Auschwitz-Birkenau is unfathomably shocking. If you want all the specifics on the camp, you can pick up a detailed official **guidebook** (3zł; in English and other languages) with maps, photos and a horrendous array of statistics, along with other volumes detailing aspects of its history. Alternatively, you can join a **guided group**, often led by former inmates (40zł per person; apply at the clearly signed desk inside the entrance). It's important to remember that both sites are as much living memorials as museums, visited by many people – both Polish and foreign – whose relatives were murdered here, a fact testified to in the mass of candles, flowers and notes you'll find at such places as the execution wall and the crematoria. Although the ban on children under thirteen entering the complex has been lifted – even school parties visit Auschwitz now – you'd be well advised to consider seriously before exposing young people to such a potentially traumatizing experience.

Auschwitz

Most of the Auschwitz camp buildings, the barbed-wire fences, watchtowers, and the entrance gate inscribed "*Arbeit Macht Frei*" ("Work Makes Free") have been preserved as the **Museum of Martyrdom** (daily: June–Aug 8am–7pm; May & Sept 8am–6pm; April & Oct 8am–5pm; Jan, Feb & late Dec 8am–3pm; March & Nov–Dec 15 8am–4pm; free). What you won't find here any longer, though, are the memorial stone and succession of plaques placed in front of and around the camp by the postwar communist authorities claiming that four million people died in a place officially described as an "International Monument to Victims of Fascism". In a symbolic intellectual clean-up, the inflated numerical estimates were removed and the lack of references to the central place of **Jews** in the genocide carried out in Auschwitz-Birkenau were remedied in 1990 at the orders of the International Committee set up to oversee the running of the site.

The **cinema** is a sobering starting point. The film shown was taken by the Soviet troops who liberated the camp in May 1945 – its harrowing images of the survivors and the dead aimed at confirming for future generations what really happened. The board outside lists timings for showings in different languages, although you can pay for a special showing of the English-language version (15zł). The bulk of the **camp** consists of the prison cell blocks, the first section being given over to "exhibits" found in the camp after liberation. Despite last-minute destruction of many of the thirty-five **storehouses** used for the possessions of murdered inmates, there are rooms full of clothes and suitcases, toothbrushes, dentures, glasses, a huge collection of shoes and a huge mound of women's hair – 70 tonnes of it. It's difficult to relate to the scale of what's shown.

Block 11, further on, is where the first experiments with Zyklon B gas were carried out on Soviet POWs and other inmates in 1941. Between two of the blocks stands the flower-strewn **Death Wall**, where thousands of prisoners were summarily executed with a bullet in the back of the head. As in the other concentration camps, the Auschwitz victims included people from all over Europe – over twenty nationalities in all. Many of the camp barracks are given over to **national memorials**, moving testimonies to Nazi actions throughout occupied Europe as well as the sufferings of inmates of the different countries – Poles, Russians, Czechs, Slovaks, Norwegians, Turks, French, Italians and more. The exhibitions haven't changed much over the years and the displays are starting to fade with age – notably the obviously outdated "Yugoslav" memorial, which contains a highly inappropriate lionization of Tito's wartime partisan movement and next to nothing about Auschwitz. This section is closed between October and April, except for those on guided tours.

Another, larger, barrack, no. 27 (open year-round), is labelled simply "**Jews**". There's a long, labyrinthine display of photographs inside, although they're left, unlabelled, to speak for themselves. The atmosphere is one of quiet reverence, in which the evils of Auschwitz are felt and remembered rather than detailed and dissected. On the second floor, there's a section devoted to Jewish resistance both inside and outside the camp, some of which was organized in tandem with the Polish AK (Armia Krajowa), or Home Army, some entirely autonomously. A simple tablet commemorates Israeli President Chaim Herzog's visit here in 1992.

Despite the strength and power of this memorial, some still find it disconcerting to see it lumped in among the others, as if Jews were just another "nationality" among many to suffer at the hands of the Nazis. Despite other recent changes in the way events in Auschwitz are officially presented, this is one aspect of the old-style presentation of the Jewish dimension of the camp that you may feel has still not been fully addressed.

The prison blocks terminate by the **gas chambers** and the ovens where the bodies were incinerated. "No more poetry after Auschwitz", in the words of the German philosopher Theodor Adorno.

Birkenau

The **Birkenau camp** (same hours) is much less visited than Auschwitz, though it was here that the majority of captives lived and died. Covering some 170 hectares, the Birkenau camp, at its height, comprised over three hundred buildings, of which over sixty brick and wood constructions remain; the rest were either burnt down or demolished at the end of the war, though in most instances you can still see their traces on the ground – visible along with the rest of the camp from the top of the tower above the entrance gate, which you can climb. Walking through the site, stretching into the distance are row upon row of barracks, fenced off by barbed wire and interspersed with watchtowers. Mostly built without foundations onto the notoriously swampy local terrain, these are the pitiful dwellings in which tens of thousands (over 100,000 at the camp's peak in August 1944) lived in unimaginably appalling conditions. Not that most prisoners lived long. Killing was the main goal of Birkenau, most of it carried out in the huge **gas chambers** at the far end of the camp, damaged but not destroyed by the fleeing Nazis in 1945. At the height of the killing, this clinically conceived machinery of destruction gassed and cremated sixty thousand people a day.

Most of the victims arrived in closed **trains**, mostly cattle trucks, to be driven directly from the rail ramp into the gas chambers. Rail line, ramp and sidings are all still there, just as the Nazis left them. In the dark, creaking huts the pitiful bare bunks would have had six or more shivering bodies crammed into each level. Wander round the barracks and you soon begin to imagine the absolute terror and degradation of the place. A monument to the dead, inscribed in ten languages, stares out over the camp from between the twisted ruins of the gas chambers and crematoria. Eerily, beyond the monument in the far northern corner of the camp area is a pond where piles of human ashes from the crematoria were deposited, its water still a murky grey.

Kalwaria Zebrzydowska and Wadowice

Southwest of Kraków are two places of great religious significance to Poles: **Kalwaria Zebrzydowska**, a centre of pilgrimage second only to Częstochowa, and **Wadowice**, birthplace of Karol Wojtyła, now Pope John Paul II. Numerous local buses work the Kraków–Kalwaria–Wadowice route, ensuring that you can combine both destinations in an easy day-trip from the city.

Kalwaria Zebrzydowska

Nestled among hills some 30km southwest of Kraków, the town of **KALWARIA ZEBRZYDOWSKA** looks and feels like a footnote to its main attraction: a historic hilltop centre of religious pilgrimage. Reached via the road leading south off the curiously empty Rynek from behind the parish church, with a steepish half-kilometre climb to the top, the large complex contains a Bernardine monastery, Church of the Virgin and a Via Dolorosa built by the Zebrzydowski family in the early seventeenth century, following a vision of three crosses here on the family estate. Miracles followed and the country's first and best-known Calvary grew to become one of its most popular sites of pilgrimage.

Before construction began, the Zebrzydowskis sent an envoy to Jerusalem for drawings and models of the holy places. Thus many of the **chapels** built across the nearby hills are modelled on buildings in the holy city. In addition to the main Via Dolorosa, a sequence of Marian Stations was added in the 1630s, including a "House of Mary", the **Kościół Grobu Matki Bożej** (Church of the Tomb of Mary), housing a tomb of the Virgin built in the form of a large domed sarcophagus, and a string of other chapels and buildings – a 3km circuit all told. The towering main **Bazylika Matki Bożej** (Basilica of the Virgin) is a familiar Baroque effusion, with a silver-plated Italian figure of the Virgin standing over the high altar. The object that inspires the greatest devotion, however, is the **painting** of the Virgin and Child in the Zebrzydowski chapel, said to have been shedding tears at regular intervals since the 1640s. The pope (who grew up 15km away in Wadowice) used to be a regular visitor to the shrine, and you'll usually find pilgrims buzzing among the customary ranks of snack bars and trinket stalls that line the approach to the basilica.

The site always has its crowds, but they are at their most intense during **August**, the traditional time of pilgrimage throughout the country, particularly during the **Festival of the Assumption** (Aug 15) and at **Easter**, when the Passion Plays are performed here on Maundy Thursday and Good Friday, with the vast accompanying crowds processing solemnly around the sequence of chapels in which the events of Holy Week are fervently re-enacted. The heady atmosphere of collective catharsis accompanying these events offers an insight into the inner workings of Polish Catholicism. To anyone from more sober northern climes, the realism (figures are tied on crosses, while spectators are dressed as Romans) can all be very perplexing, even frightening; however, gruesome enactments of the Crucifixion are an established feature of peasant Catholic festivals throughout Europe.

Due to its proximity to Kraków, Kalvaria isn't the kind of place where many people stay overnight, and **accommodation** options are correspondingly thin on the ground. The Dom Pielgrzyma, ul. Bernardyńska 46 (☎033/876 5539), is a Church-run place offering basic doubles with shared facilities (❶) and several larger dorms (21zł per person), although there's a 9.30pm curfew. The *Stadion* (also sometimes known as the *Sportowy*), ul. Mickiewicza 16 (☎033/876 6492), is a sports hotel a short walk north of the Rynek which has triples and quads for about 25zł per person, all without shower. For a bite to **eat** the choices are the *Żarek*, immediately north of the Rynek on ul. Jagiellońska, the *Korona*, on ul. 11 Listopada, ten minutes' walk east of the Rynek, and the *Torino*, a basic café-bar on the Rynek itself.

Wadowice

Fourteen kilometres further west is the little town of **WADOWICE**, whose rural obscurity was shattered by the election of local boy **Karol Wojtyła** to the papacy in October 1978. Almost instantly the town became a place of pilgrimage, with the souvenir industry quick to seize the opportunities.

The train and bus stations are on the eastern side of the town, from where it's a ten-minute walk to the elegantly paved and flowerbedded market square. Main point of reference here is the onion-domed **parish church**, where Karol Wojtyła was baptized in 1920. Most visitors gravitate towards the Chapel of the Virgin Mary on the left-hand side of the entrance, site of a nineteenth-century image of the Virgin to which Karol Wojtyła prayed regularly as a schoolboy. Behind the church, the old **town hall** now houses a museum (Mon–Thurs 9am–3pm; Fri 9am–4.30pm, Sat 10am–2pm, Sun 11am–3pm; 2zł) with changing exhibitions on local history. A few steps away from the museum at ul. Kościelna 7 is the **pope's birthplace**, a simple two-room apartment where he spent the first 18 years of his life. It has now been turned into a shrine-like **museum** (Tues–Sun 9am–1pm & 2–6pm; free), packed with pictures illustrating the pontiff's early life. It's far too small to cope with the coach parties that regularly descend on the place, so be prepared for a bit of a crush.

For a **place to stay**, your best bets are the *Dom Pielgrzyma* hostel, which offers dorms and simple doubles south of the square at Fatimska 90 (☎033/873 1200; ❷); and the *Podhalanin* **hotel**, an army-owned rest home at the north end of town on the Oswiecim road at ul. Wojska Polskiego 17 (☎033/823 3817; ❸), and offering acceptable en-suites. Wadowice has one culinary claim to fame in the shape of the **Kremówka Wadowicka**, a deliciously wobbly slice of creamy custard that is sold at all the town's cafés – *Cukierna Beskidzka*, just off the main square on ul. Jagiellońska, is one of the best places to try it. For more substantial eating, the *Piwnica* **restaurant**, also on Jagiellońska, serves up good, inexpensive pork and fish dishes in an attractive cellar. *Kawiarna Galicja*, right next to the pope's birthplace on Kościelna, is a relaxing place for civilized **drinking**.

Babia Góra national park and beyond

The southwesternmost part of Małopolska forms part of the Beskid mountain chain, with by far the most notable part being the **Babia Góra** massif. It's the second smallest of Poland's national parks, though arguably the one most prized

△ The summit of Giewont, Tatra Mountains

by naturalists, being of sufficient importance to be included on UNESCO's World Biosphere list (you can find information about it at Ⓦ www.bpn.babia-gora.pl). Much loved by Poles, who visit the area in droves, the area as a whole is still relatively undiscovered by foreigners. A specific characteristic of the region is the way that the vegetation forms distinct vertical bands. Up to a height of 1150m, it's thickly wooded, particularly with beech, fir and spruce trees, which then give way to spruce and rowans. There follows a sector of dwarf mountain pines, while the highest areas have only grasses, mosses and lichen among the loose boulders. Hundreds of different plant species grow in the massif, which is also inhabited by 115 different kinds of bird and a number of wild animals, including lynxes, wolves and brown bears.

West of the park area, on the border with Silesia, Żywiec, famous for its beer, is a pleasant place to while away a few hours, benefiting from a favourable location in a broad valley at the foot of three mountain chains, the Beskid Mały to the northeast, the Beskid Śląski to the north and west, and the Beskid Żywiecki to the south.

Zawoja and around

The gateway to the national park is ZAWOJA, a straggling community situated on the banks of the Skamica, around 65km from Kraków. Its residents claim that it stretches 12km from end to end, making it the longest village in Poland, and perhaps even in Europe. It's a bucolic place largely unspoiled by tourism, and – in contrast to other Polish highland resorts – there's no real village centre boasting tourist services, cafés and shops. There's a limited amount of skiing activity in winter, with a number of slopes suitable for beginners and unambitious intermediates on the southwest fringes of the village; at other times Zawoja is an oasis of rustic peace.

There's no rail line, but direct **buses** run from Kraków, Katowice and Bielsko-Biała – as well as from Wadowice, 70km to the north. Most buses terminate at Zawoja–Policzne at the extreme south of the resort, near the entrance to the national park – this is the best place to get off if a day out in the hills is all you require. If you're interested in a **place to stay** in Zawoja, it's worth alighting at Zawoja-Centrum, 6km before Zawoja-Polanicze, where the local **tourist office** (Mon–Fri 9am–5pm; Ⓦ www.zawoja.pl) will direct you towards private rooms (❶). Most of the village's accommodation options and shops are grouped around Zawoja-Widły, midway between Centrum and Polanicze. Best of the places to stay in Widły is probably the *Krokus* (☎033/877 5140; ❸), a family-run pension that offers tidy en-suites with TV; although the plainer en-suites on offer at the nearby *Zawojanka* (☎033/877 5122; ❷) will suffice providing it's not overrun by school groups. Both the Zawojanka and the *Diablak*, also in Widły (☎033/877 5126), offer accommodation in five- or six-person dorms from 15zł per person. *Camping Rafako* (☎033/877 5176), also in Widły, has all-year bungalows (❷). There's a scattering of snack bars in Widły, and the hotels also offer food, although *Jadło pod Lipami*, just uphill from the main road, is the best place in which to sample good home cooking.

Walking in the park

The easiest approach to Babia Góra is from the Zawoja-Polanicze car park, which lies on the Zawoja-Jablonka road. On foot, it can be reached by the **blue trail**, leading gently upwards from the village through the woods to the *Markowe Szczawiny* **refuge** (☎033/877 5105), which serves hot meals and has dormitory accommodation. If time is limited, it's best to switch here to the **yellow trail**, which takes you directly up to **Diablak** (1725m), the highest peak in the range, enabling you to see a good cross-section of scenery en route – beware that there's one place on this route where you have to make a fixed ladder ascent. From the top, which forms part of the international boundary with Slovakia, there's a sweeping panoramic **view** that stretches on (the regrettably few) clear days as far as the Tatras. It's then a comfortable descent back to the car park by the **red trail**; this offers the best views of the main peak, and should be used in both directions if you're at all wary of sheer drops. If you have more time at your disposal, you can see the whole massif in one long day by continuing west from the summit of Diablak along the green trail, switching to the red to go back to the refuge, then returning to Zawoja by the black trail.

Zubrzyca Górna

It's also worth making a detour to the village of **ZUBRZYCA GÓRNA**, about 4km south of the car park, and also accessible along the green trail. At the northernmost fringe of the village is the **ethnographical park** (Tues–Sun: April 15–Sept 15 9am–3pm; Sept 16–April 14 9am–2.30pm; 2zł), an impressive, well-maintained open-air museum of the region's traditional local architecture.

Żywiec

About 50km west of Zawoja by road – though less than half that as the crow flies – is **ŻYWIEC**, which is also readily accessible by train from any of the major cities in this corner of Poland. The town enjoys a certain international fame courtesy of its **brewery**, which annually produces over thirty million litres of what's generally agreed to be the best **beer** in Poland. Until the end of the communist era, you were far more likely to find Żywiec beer on the shelves of a British or American supermarket than you were anywhere in Poland, most of it being exported in order to obtain desperately needed hard currency. Nowadays their lager-style brew is served in cafés and bars all over Poland. If you can find it their **porter** – a darker, stronger beer less commonly available – is also well worth trying. Beer aside, Żywiec is an attractive place to break your journey – you'll get good **views** of the surrounding mountains from the shore of the often dried-up reservoir at the northern end of town.

The Town

Żywiec's **castle** (Tues–Fri 9am–3pm, Sat & Sun 10am–2pm; 3zł) was founded by the dukes of Oświęcim in the fifteenth century, gaining a handsome arcaded courtyard in the Renaissance period. In the nineteenth century, it was heavily restored by the Habsburgs, who also built the pristine white **palace** opposite, the object of a slow-moving restoration programme. There's a generally tranquil café, the *Zamkowa*, in the castle courtyard, while the huge park to the south is well worth a stroll, even if it's just to see the whimsical eighteenth-century **Chinese tea house**.

Just to the east of the palace is the **Kościół Mariacki** (St Mary's Church), which would be an unremarkable Gothic building with standard Baroque furnishings were it not for the imperious galleried Renaissance tower, which provides a landmark from all over town. On the main street, ul. Kościuszki, immediately north of the church, is the local **museum** (Tues–Fri 9am–4pm, Sat 10am–3pm, Sun 10am–2pm; 5zł), housed in a Baroque mansion, and boasting a fine collection of *górale* folk crafts and costumes. The only other sight worth mentioning is the rustic wooden **Kościół św. Krzyża** (Church of the Holy Cross) on ul. Świętokrzyska, just off the western end of ul. Kościuszki.

Practicalities

Both the **train** and **bus stations** are located on the opposite side of the River Soła from the town centre, which is a ten-minute walk away along ul. Marchewskiego. The **tourist office** is on the Rynek, at no. 12 (☎033/861 4310). **Hotel** options in town are scarce: the *Nad Sołą*, ul. Tetmajera 75 (☎033/861 0310; ❸), is probably your best bet, a medium-sized modern place squarely aimed at business types, although it's hard to find – near the river 2km south of the centre. The only central option is the *Roma*, ul. Kościuszki 12 (☎033/861 0443; ❷), which only has six rooms and is often full. The **youth hostel** is right next to the station at ul. Ks. Słonki 4 (☎033/861 2639), while the **campsite**, *Dębina*, is well to the south of town, at ul. Kopernika 4 (☎033/861 4888), near the Sporysz train station.

There are several decent **restaurants** along the main drag, ul. Kościuszki, and another good one, *Ratuszowa*, on the corner of the market square at ul. Mickiewicza 1 – an eclectic place which serves up anything from Polish to Chinese. Every August, there's a **festival** of local folklore when you'll see colourful traditional costumes being worn, the women's outfits especially rich in lace and embroidery.

The Ojców Valley and the Szlak Orlich Gniazd

To the northwest of Kraków, the **Ojców Valley** offers an easy respite from the rigours of the city. This deep limestone gorge of the River Prądnik has a unique microclimate and an astonishingly rich variety of plants and wildlife, virtually all of it now protected by the **Ojców national park** (information at ⓦ www.ojcowskipn.prv.pl), one of the country's smallest and most memorable protected regions. With an attractive and varied landscape of scenic river valley, twisted rock formations, peaceful forests and a rich and varied flora, the nineteen-square-kilometre park makes a beautiful and easily accessible area for a day's trekking, particularly in September and October, when the rich colours of the Polish autumn are at their finest. Anyone considering giving the park the attention it deserves should pick up the *Ojówski Park Narodowy* map (1:22,500), widely available both in Kraków and on arrival in Ojców.

The valley also gives access to the most southerly of the **castles** built by King Kazimierz to defend the southwestern reaches – and most importantly, the trade routes – of the country from the Bohemian rulers of Silesia. Known as the **Szlak Orlich Gniazd** (Eagles' Nest Trail), these fortresses are strung along the hilly ridge extending westwards from Ojców towards Częstochowa.

Ojców and into the valley

The principal point of access to the river gorge is **OJCÓW**, 25km from Kraków (and served by most – but not all – Kraków–Olkusz buses), the national park's only village and filled to bursting with local school groups in season. Developed as a low-key health resort in the mid-nineteenth century, it's a delightful village, with wooden houses straggling along a valley floor framed by deciduous forest and craggy limestone cliffs. Just beyond the car park where buses stop is a small **natural history museum** (mid-May to mid-Nov Tues–Sun 9am–4.30pm; mid-Nov to mid-May Tues–Fri 8am–3pm; 2zł), where you'll find mammoth tusks, the jaws of prehistoric cave bears, and a modest collection of stuffed local fauna. Immediately beyond is the PTTK **regional museum** (Mon–Fri 9am–3pm; 2zł), located above the Ojców post office, which contains prints of the village as it looked in the nineteenth century, and a corner stacked with local folk costumes, notable for the extravagantly embroidered and beaded women's jackets. Overlooking the village to the north is a fine, ruined **castle** (April–Oct Tues–Sun 10am–4.45pm, stays open later at the height of summer; 1.50zł), the southern extremity of the Szlak Orlich Gniazd and an evocative place in the twilight hours, circled by squadrons of bats. There's not much of the castle left, apart from two of the original four-teenth-century towers, the main gate entrance and the walls of the castle chapel. There are excellent views over the winding valley, and a path through the woods which leads up to the Złota Góra campsite and restaurant (see below). A few hundred metres north up the valley from Ojców castle is the curious spectacle of the **Kaplica na Wodzie** (Wooden Chapel) straddling the river on brick piles. This odd site neatly circumvented a nineteenth-century tsarist edict forbidding religious structures to be built "on solid ground", part of a strategy to subdue the intransigently nationalist Catholic Church. These days, it's only open for visits between Masses on Sundays.

Heading south from the village takes you through a small gorge lined with strange rock formations, most famous of which, about 15 minutes out from the village, is the Krakowska Brama (Kraków Gate), a pair of rocks which seem to form a huge portal leading to a side valley. Before reaching the Krakowska Brama you may well be enticed uphill to the right by a (black-waymarked) path to the **Jaskinia Łokietka** (Łokietka Cave; late April to mid-Nov: daily 9.30am–4.30pm; 5zł), some thirty minutes' distant, the largest of a sequence of chambers burrowing into the cliffs outside Ojców. According to legend it was here that King Władysław the Short was hidden and protected by loyal local peasants following King Wenceslas of Bohemia's invasion in the early four-teenth century. Around 250m long, the rather featureless illuminated cave is a bit of a let-down if you've come expecting spectacular stone and ice forma-tions. Individual travellers will have to wait to join a guided group before being allowed inside.

Ojców practicalities

There's a PTTK **information office** (Mon–Fri 9am–3pm; ☏012/389 2036) next to the car park which can help you find a place to stay, and a souvenir shop in the same building which sells maps. The Ojcowianin travel agency, in the same building as the PTTK museum (☏012/389 2089), also has informa-tion on rooms. Alternatively, it's usually fairly easy to rent a room in someone's house in the village by asking around, though things get pretty full up in the summer season. The only **hotel** option in easy striking distance is the basic *Zosia* (☏012/389 2008; ❷) in Złota Góra, a kilometre northwest of the castle up the hill road through the forest. There's a **campsite** a couple of hundred metres beyond the *Zosia*, as well as a **restaurant**, the *Zajazd*, which does good trout. Back down in Ojców, the *Pod Kazimierza* café-restaurant mops up many of the day-trippers.

Pieskowa Skała

If the weather's fine and you're up for walking the nine-kilometre road and footpath from Ojców, **PIESKOWA SKAŁA**, home to the region's best-known and best-preserved castle, is an enjoyable and trouble-free piece of hik-ing. Direct buses also run from Kraków (45min) via Ojców. A few kilometres north of Ojców the marked path (red trail) takes you through the tiny village of **Grodzisko**, just north of the main road. The tiny late-seventeenth-century **chapel** here was built on the site of a convent established here in the early 1300s by King Władysław the Short (1306–33) under the patronage of his saintly sister, Salomea. Figures of both founder and patroness adorn the walls of this fine Baroque construction. Added curiosity value is provided by the stone carving of an elephant carrying an obelisk-shaped object on its back, located round the back of the chapel.

Roughly 4km on along the roadside path the castle approach is signalled by an eighteen-metre limestone pillar known locally as **Maczuga Herkulesa** (Hercules' Club) rearing up in front of you, beyond which you can see the castle. Long the possession of the Szafraniec family, the **castle** (courtyard 8am–8pm; free) is in pretty good shape following extensive recent renovation, the fourteenth-century original having been rebuilt in the 1580s as an elegant Renaissance residence. As at Wawel, the most impressive period feature is the delicately arcaded courtyard, a photogenic construction that's a regular feature in travel brochures. Don't expect to enjoy it undisturbed, however: for most of the summer the place positively hums with tourist traffic, which can make a visit a stamina-depleting experience.

The castle **museum** (Tues–Fri 10am–3.30pm, Sat & Sun 10am–5.30pm; 7zł) is divided into two main exhibitions, one covering the history of the building, the other illustrating the development of European art from the Middle Ages to the nineteenth century, drawing extensively on Wawel's Muzeum Narodowe collection. The roomful of Gothic pieces includes some fine carved wooden statues of the saints by unknown local artists, a fifteenth-century tapestry from Tournai and some sturdy chests from the mid-1400s. The second-floor Baroque rooms continue the period furniture theme, sumptuously decorated Flemish and Dutch tapestries lining the walls, the most notable among them depicting a series of heroic scenes from the life of Alexander the Great. Completing the trail through art history, there are rooms devoted to Rococo, Neoclassicist and Biedermeier art and furniture, the last in particular sporting a fine collection of period exhibits.

To finish off a visit, head for the **restaurant** at the top of one of the fortified towers, serviced by waitresses in regional costume. In summer they put tables out on the roof terrace, from where you can enjoy a fine view over the valley, and, if you're lucky, some excellent local trout.

The end of the trail

The remaining castles of the Szlak Orlich Gniazd are very ruined, but dramatic, seeming to spring straight out of the Jurassic rock formations. You really need your own vehicle to follow the whole route as, although all the castles are accessible by bus, you'll experience long waits and frequent detours, and it's unlikely you'd be able to find anywhere to stay. However, the most impressive of the other castles are also the easiest to get to. At **OGRODZIENIEC**, some 35km north of Pieskowa Skała on the main road to Olkusz (served by bus from Kraków), the ruin you see today was built during Kazimierz the Great's reign and remodelled into a magnificent Renaissance residence reputedly the equal of Wawel, before being ravaged by the Swedes in 1655. **ZAWIERCIE** preserves only the substantial shell of a frontier fortress.

The most accessible castle in the trail, after Pieskowa Skała, is at **OLSZTYN**, just a few kilometres southeast of the city boundaries of Częstochowa, to which it's linked by several buses an hour (#58 or #67; 30min). The **castle** here, which dominates the surrounding landscape, is the one generally used to promote the route on tourist brochures and posters – understandably so, given its dramatic location on the limestone cliffs, a steepish eastwards climb from the village. Built in the mid-1300s by King Kazimierz III, like many others of its kind Olsztyn castle was laid to waste during the Swedish "Deluge" of the 1650s. Though impressive enough, the remains you see today only hint at past glories. Unusually, the castle was laid out in two parts, with a round watchtower crowning one outcrop of rock, and a keep on top of another; from the ruins of each there's a superb view over the whole upland region, the effect heightened by the winds buffeting the place most of the time. Down in the village there are a scattering of tourist-oriented **places to eat**, including the *Piccolo* and *Pod Zamkiem* restaurants, both on ul. Zamkowa, the approach to the castle, as well as a number of more basic places on and around the Rynek. The only accommodation currently on offer is the seasonal **campsite** off ul. Zielona, 10 minutes' walk southeast of the Rynek.

Częstochowa

To get an understanding of the central role that Catholicism still holds in contemporary Poland, a visit to **CZĘSTOCHOWA** is essential and, for many people, an extraordinary experience. The hilltop monastery of **Jasna Góra** (Bright Mountain) is one of the world's greatest places of pilgrimage, and its famous icon, the **Black Madonna**, has drawn the faithful here over the past six centuries – reproductions exist in almost every Polish church.

The special position that Jasna Góra and its icon hold in the hearts and minds of the majority of Poles is the product of a rich web of history and myth. It's not a place you can react to dispassionately, indeed it's hard not to be moved as you overhear troupes of pilgrims breaking into hymn as they shuffle between the Stations of the Cross, or watch peasants praying mutely before the icon they've waited a lifetime to see. One thing that will strike you here, as the crowds swell towards an approaching festival, is the number of excited teenagers in attendance, all treating the event with the expectation you'd find at an international rock concert.

Central to this nationwide veneration is the tenuous position Poland has held on the map of Europe; at various times the Swedes, the Russians and the Germans have sought to annihilate it as a nation. Each of these traditional and non-Catholic enemies has laid siege to Jasna Góra, yet failed to destroy it, so adding to the icon's reputation as a miracle-worker and the guarantor of Poland's very existence.

The regular influx of pilgrims to Częstochowa means that you might have problems finding somewhere to stay in town. Luckily it's an easy day-trip from Kraków thanks to good rail connections. Buses also run daily from Katowice, Kraków, Łódź and Warsaw.

Some history

The hill known as Jasna Góra was probably used as part of the same defensive system as the castles along the Szlak Orlich Gniazd. In the **fourteenth century**, it came under the control of Ladislaus II, whose main possession was the independent duchy of Opole on the other side of the Silesian frontier. In 1382, he founded the monastery here, donating the miraculous icon a couple of years later. Ladislaus spent his final years imprisoned in his own castle, having fallen into disgrace for trying to prevent the union with Lithuania. Nevertheless, the monastery quickly attracted pilgrims from a host of nations and was granted the special protection of the Jagiellonian and Waza dynasties, though it was not until the **fifteenth century** that a shrine of stone and brick was built.

In the first half of the **seventeenth century**, the monastery was enclosed by a modern fortification system as a bulwark of Poland's frontiers – and its Catholic faith – at a time of Europe-wide political and religious conflicts. Its worth was proved in the six-week-long siege of 1655 by the Swedes, who failed to capture it in spite of having superior weapons and almost 4000 troops ranged against just 250 defenders. This sparked off an amazing national fight-back against the enemy, who had occupied the rest of the country against little resistance, and ushered in Poland's short period as a European power of the first rank.

In the early **eighteeth century** the Black Madonna was crowned Queen of Poland in an attempt by the clergy to whip up patriotism and fill the political void created by the Russian-sponsored "Silent Sejm", which had reduced the nation to a puppet state. Jasna Góra was the scene of another heroic defence in 1770, when it was held by the Confederates of Bar against greater Russian forces, and retained by them until after the formal partitioning of Poland two years later. Częstochowa was initially annexed by Prussia, but after a few years as part of Napoleon's Duchy of Warsaw, it served as a frontier fortress of the Russian Empire for more than a century. It was incorporated into the new Polish state after **World War I**, when the icon's royal title was reaffirmed.

Towards the end of **World War II**, Soviet troops defused bombs left by the retreating Nazis that might finally have destroyed the monastery. They later had cause to regret their actions, as although Częstochowa itself developed into a model communist industrialized city, Jasna Góra became a major focus of opposition to the communist regime. The Church skilfully promoted the pilgrimage as a display of patriotism and passive resistance, a campaign that received a huge boost in 1978 with the election of Karol Wojtyła, archbishop of Kraków and a central figure in its conception, as **Pope John Paul II**. His

devotion to this shrine ensured worldwide media attention for Poland's plight; as a consequence, praying at Jasna Góra has become an essential photo-opportunity for the new breed of democratic politicians.

The town

Other than Jasna Góra, Częstochowa has very few sights, although the broad tree-lined boulevards at least give the heart of the city an agreeably spacious, almost Parisian feel. On pl. Biegańskiego, just off al. NMP, is the district **museum** (Tues, Thurs, Fri & Sat 8.30am–4pm, Wed 10.30am–5.30pm, Sun 10am–4pm; 3zł), which has a decent archeology section plus the usual local history displays. If you want to continue with the ecclesiastical theme, you can visit the small Baroque **Kościół św. Barbary** (St Barbara's Church) to the south of Jasna Góra, allegedly the place where the Black Madonna was slashed (see box, p.483); **Kościół św. Jakuba** (St James's Church), opposite the town hall on al. NMP, a tsarist-era Orthodox building converted into a Catholic place of worship following the attainment of independence in 1918; and the **cathedral**, east of the train station on ul. Krakowska, a vast, soulless neo-Gothic structure built – but never fully completed – in the early 1900s.

Near the suburban station of Raków, reached by any southbound tram, is an important **archeology reserve** (Tues–Sat 9am–3pm, subject to random closures), with 21 excavated graves from the Lusatian culture of the sixth and seventh centuries BC.

Jasna Góra

A dead straight three-kilometre-long boulevard, al. Najświętszej Marii Panny (usually abbreviated as NMP), cuts through the heart of Częstochowa, terminating at the foot of **Jasna Góra**. On most days, ascending the hill is no different from taking a walk in any other public park, but the huge podium for open-air Masses gives a clue to the atmosphere here on the major Marian **festivals** – May 3, August 15, August 26, September 8 and December 8 – when up to a million pilgrims converge, often in colourful traditional dress. Many come on foot, and every year, tens of thousands make the nine-day walk from Warsaw to celebrate the Feast of the Assumption.

The monastery

Although there's relatively little of the souvenir-peddling tackiness found in Europe's other leading Marian shrines, Jasna Góra could hardly be called beautiful: its architecture is generally austere, while the defensive walls give the hill something of a fortress-like feel. **Entry** is still via four successive gateways, each one of which presented a formidable obstacle to any attacker. As you wander around the complex you'll notice two key components of the pilgrimage experience – redemption and commerce. At every turn you'll find confessionals at which the faithful eagerly queue, while numerous **offering boxes** outside key doorways and dedicated to one saint or another, comfortably finance the upkeep of the spectacle. To deal with the visiting hordes there's a visitor **information centre** immediately inside the complex entrance (daily: May–Sept 7.30am–7pm; Oct–April 8am–5pm), run by nuns and usefully complete with an ATM bank machine.

The best way to begin an exploration is by ascending the 100-metre-high **tower** (May–Sept daily 8am–4pm), a pastiche of its eighteenth-century predecessor, which was destroyed in one of the many fires which have plagued the monastery. An earlier victim was the monastic **church**, which has been transformed from a Gothic hall into a restrained Baroque basilica, now without pews, to make room for more pilgrims. Not that it's without its exuberant features, notably the colossal high altar in honour of the Virgin and the two sumptuous family chapels off the southern aisle, which parody and update their royal counterparts in the Wawel cathedral in Kraków.

Understandably, the **Kaplica Cudownego Obrazu** (Chapel of the Miraculous Image), a separate church in its own right, is the focal point of the monastery. It's also the only part to retain much of the original Gothic architecture, though its walls are so encrusted with votive offerings and discarded crutches and leg-braces that this is no longer obvious. Masses are said here almost constantly but you'll have to time it right if you want a view of the **Black Madonna** (see box opposite), a sight that should not be missed. Part of the time the icon is shrouded by a screen, each raising and lowering of which presumably exists to add a certain dramatic tension and is accompanied by a solemn trumpet fanfare. When it's on view (Mon–Fri 6am–noon & 1–9pm, Sat & Sun 6am–1pm & 2–9pm) you only get to see the faces and hands of the actual painting (the Virgin's countenance being famously dour) as the figures of the Madonna and Child are always "dressed" in varying sets of jewel-encrusted robes that glitter all the more impressively against the black walls. Whatever your views on the validity of pilgrimages, veneration of a miraculous wonder or Church-engineered money-making device, you cannot fail to be impressed by the sheer devotion that the icon inspires in the hearts and minds of most Poles.

Other sites in the complex fail to hold the resonance of the chapel, although between them they help to flesh out the site's history. To the north of the chapel, a monumental stairway leads to the **Knights' Hall**, the principal reception room, adorned with flags and paintings illustrating the history of the monastery. There are other opulent Baroque interiors, notably the **refectory**, whose vault is a real *tour de force*, and the **library**. However, you'll have to enquire at the information office by the main gateway for permission to see them, as they are normally closed to the public.

The museums

Jasna Góra's treasures are kept in three separate buildings. The most valuable liturgical items can be seen in the **Skarbiec** (Treasury; daily 9am–5pm) above the sacristy, entered from the southeastern corner of the ramparts. There's usually a long queue for entry, so be there well before it opens.

At the southwestern end of the monastery is the **Arsenał** (daily 9am–5pm), devoted to the military history of the fortress and containing a superb array of weapons, including Turkish war loot donated by King Jan Sobieski. Alongside is the **Muzeum Sześćsetlecia** (600th Anniversary Museum; daily 9am–5pm), which tells the monastery's story from a religious standpoint. Exhibits include the seventeenth-century backing of the Black Madonna, which illustrates the history of the picture, and votive offerings from famous Poles, prominent among which is Lech Wałęsa's 1983 Nobel Peace Prize, along with the oversize pen he used to sign the landmark August 1980 Gdańsk Agreements (see "History" in Contexts p.692). Completing the displays is the **Sala Maryjna** (Marian Hall; daily same hours), a collection of contemporary artists' impressions of the Black Madonna and similarly iconic representations of the pope.

Finally, it's worth strolling around the ramparts to the eastern end of the complex, which is where the big festival Masses are celebrated before the mass of pilgrims assembled in the park below, as evidenced by the large rock-stadium-style platform in place during the spring and summer.

The Black Madonna

According to tradition, the **Black Madonna** was painted from life by **St Luke** on a beam from the Holy Family's house in Nazareth. This explanation is accepted without question by most believers, though the official view is kept deliberately ambiguous. Scientific tests have proved the icon cannot have been executed before the sixth century, and it may even have been quite new at the time of its arrival at the monastery. Probably Italian in origin, it's a fine example of the hierarchical **Byzantine style**, which hardly changed or developed down the centuries. Incidentally, the "black" refers to the heavy shading characteristic of this style, subsequently darkened by age and exposure to incense.

What can be seen today may well be only a copy made following the picture's first great "miracle" in 1430, on the occasion of its theft. According to the official line, this was the work of followers of the Czech reformer Jan Hus, but it's more likely that political opponents of the monastery's protector, King Władysław Jagiełło, were responsible. The legend maintains that the picture increased in weight so much that the thieves were unable to carry it. In frustration, they slashed the Virgin's face, which immediately started shedding blood. The icon was taken to Kraków to be restored, but in memory of the miracle, two wounds (still visible today) were scratched into the left cheek of the Madonna.

Sceptics have pointed out that during the Swedish siege, usually cited as the supreme example of the Black Madonna's miracle-working powers, the icon had been moved to neutral Silesia for safekeeping. Yet, such was its hold over the Polish imagination, that its future seemed to occasion more anguished discussion at the time of the Partitions than any other topic. In the present day, the pope's devotion to the image has helped to focus the world's attention on Poland, simultaneously supplying ample fodder for the more archaic and nationalistic strains of Polish Catholicism.

Practicalities

The main exit of Częstochowa's ultramodern train station brings you out onto a neat plaza bordered by the bus station to the south. Turn right onto al. Wolności to reach the town's main artery, al. NMP. The well-stocked and well-organized **tourist information centre** is at al. NMP 65 (Mon–Fri 9am–5pm, Sat 9am–2pm; ☎034/368 2260, ⓦwww.czestochowa.um.gov.pl). The most convenient **hotels** are those beside the train station (leave the station via the eastern exit, following the signs for ul. Piłsudskiego, to save yourself a circuitous walk): the *Polonia,* ul. Piłsudskiego 9 (☎034/324 6832; ❹), recently refurbished but still decidedly old-style; and the nearby *Ha Ga* in a converted residential block at ul. Katedralna 9 (☎034/324 6173; en-suites with TV ❸, rooms with shared facilities ❷) – both are very popular with pilgrim groups and can be hard to get a room in, especially on spec. At the foot of Jasna Góra is the *Patria,* ul. J. Popiełuszki 2 (☎034/324 7001, ⓔpatria@orbis.pl; ❽), a luxurious Orbis-run place much used by foreign tour groups. The *Sekwana,* ul. Wieluńska 24 (☎034/324 8954; ❺), is a small, French-owned hotel in a good location immediately north of the monastery complex.

As you'd expect, there's a fair choice of **hostel** accommodation, much of it geared specifically to pilgrims and based in the environs of the monastery – although bear in mind that these places tend to have 10–11pm curfews. Cheapest of these is *Hala Noclegi,* ul. Klasztorna 1 (☎034/365 6668 ext. 224; 15zł per person) right beneath the monastery's southwest corner, offering basic dorm beds with cold-water basins. If it's full an alternative is the large *Dom Rekolekcyjny,* ul. św. Barbary 43 (☎034/324 1177; 20zł per person), also run by sisters, a short walk south of the monastery complex. The most popular option however is the huge and well-organized *Dom Pielgrzyma* at ul. Wyszyńskiego 1 (☏034/324 7011), north of the car park on the west side of the monastery, where you can stay in four-person dorms (20zł per person) or prim en-suite doubles (❷). Most convenient of the **youth hostels** is a spartan affair a couple of blocks north of al. NMP at Jasnogórska 84/96 (☏034/324 3121). There's a **campsite**, *Camping Oleńka*, with a few bungalows (❶) in an ideal spot on the west side of the monastery's car park at ul. Oleńki 10/30 (☏034/324 7495). If you're driving, it's well signposted on the town approaches, until you get to the crucial last turning, between apartment buildings, into ul. Oleńki. Check the map on p.426.

For **eating** and drinking, there's a large choice of places along al. NMP and near the station, many of them basic snack-bar or fast-food joints. The *Dom Pielgrzyma* hostel, just outside the Jasna Góra complex, has a sizeable self-service café-restaurant catering for the needs of most day-trippers. Restaurants are gradually improving, both in range and quality. *Malibu*, al. NMP 55, is a café-bar that also does grills and steaks at reasonable prices; *Stacherczak*, ul. Racławicka 3, is a popular, reasonably priced Chinese restaurant that doubles as a student music club at weekends. The *Polonus*, al. NMP 73/75, is a good place to sample Polish meat and fish in semi-formal surroundings; although it can't compare with the standards offered by the restaurant of the *Sekwana* hotel, a smartish French place that's about as good as it currently gets in the city. *Café Milano*, al. NMP 59, is the place to go for a decent espresso, ice cream and cakes.

For **drinking**, *Pod Gruszką*, al. NMP 37, in a courtyard off the main street, is a decent café-bar popular with a local student crowd, which also has a small but tempting range of salads. *Prohibicja*, on the corner of Racławicka and Dąbrowskiego, is a stylish bar with a 1920s speakeasy theme, a wide range of cocktails, and excellent food.

North of Kraków

Travelling north from Kraków on the road to Kielce and Warsaw, you soon find yourself in the heartlands of Małopolska, dominated by sleepy rural towns and a colourful patchwork quilt of traditional strip-farmed fields. The towns of **Jędrzejów**, **Pińczów** and **Szydłów** all offer a characteristic rural Polish combination of historical curiosity and comparative contemporary anonymity. If you've no need to hurry your journey north, they make an enjoyable diversion, with transport connections, chiefly by bus, relatively problem-free.

Jędrzejów

Forty kilometres north of Kraków, **JĘDRZEJÓW** is, in most respects, another sleepy provincial outpost of Małopolska, a two-bit town used as a convenient stopping-off point on the main Kraków–Kielce road which bisects it.

The reason most visitors, mainly Polish, come here is for the **Muzeum Zegarów Słonecznych** (Sundial Museum; Tues–Sun: May–Sept 9am–4pm; Oct–April 9am–3pm: compulsory guided tours on the hour every hour, last tour one hour before closing; 5zł), an eccentric setup housing one of the top three gnomonic collections in the world (the other two are in Chicago and Oxford), based on the notable collection of three hundred or so sundials amassed by local enthusiast Dr Tadeusz Przypkowski and left to the museum established in his house after his death in 1962.

What sounds like a potentially less than thrilling proposal turns out to be well worth a visit. Dials of every shape, size and construction are gathered here, the oldest dating back to the early 1500s. Highlights of the collection include a group of attractive sixteenth- and seventeenth-century ivory pocket sundials, a set of Asian instruments and an eccentric piece from the mid-1700s that comes complete with a small cannon tuned to fire on the hour at one o'clock every afternoon. The rest of the museum is taken up with Przypkowski's more rambling collections of stuffy old furniture, books, art, clocks, watches and old bottles.

The other object of note in town is the impressive Cistercian **abbey** about 2km west of the centre along ul. 11 Listopada. One of the group of Cistercian foundations established in the region in the early 1200s, the imposing twin-towered Romanesque basilica was remodelled a number of times over the centuries, the final product being the largely late-Baroque interior of today, featuring some ornate wall and altar paintings and lavishly carved choir stalls. Virtually the only feature reminding you of the church's architectural origins is the distinctive cross-ribbed vaulting developed by the Cistercians. Very little of the original monastic buildings survives, the main exception being sections of the Gothic cloisters, which the resident parish priest will show you on request. Among the abbey's former residents is **Wincenty Kadłubek** (1161–1223), bishop of Kraków and author of the *Chronica Polonorum*, the first written chronicle of Polish history. His remains are contained in a diminutive Baroque coffin housed in a side chapel off the abbey's southern aisle.

Practicalities

Jędrzejów's location on the main Kraków–Kielce road means that getting in and out of the place is relatively easy: buses and trains run to both destinations at fairly frequent intervals. The **bus** and **train stations** are next to each other roughly 2km west of the main square along ul. Przypkowskiego.

In the unlikely event of you wanting to stay here, the only central **accommodation** option is the *Hotel Zacisze*, west of the main square at Piłsudskiego 4 (☎041/386 1825; ❷), which offers a small number of simple doubles and quads – all of which share facilities. The only **restaurant** worth venturing into is the *Zodiak*, at ul. Partyzantów 3, just south of the Rynek.

Pińczów

Southeast of Jędrzejów, 28km along the quiet backroads of Małopolska, the contemporary rural anonymity of **PIŃCZÓW** belies the town's notable historical role. The old limestone quarries in evidence around the town were long an important source of stone for church building throughout the country. Along with nearby Raków (see p.488), Pińczów rose to prominence during the latter half of the sixteenth century as one of the chief centres of Protestant agitation in Reformation-era Poland, a group of Calvinist divines establishing an academy and a printing press responsible, among other things, for publication of the first Polish grammar in 1568. The town and surrounding region's resistance-minded streak surfaced again during the latter stages of World War II, when local partisan units were so successful at clearing Nazi troops out of the area that the town gained the nickname "The Republic of Pińczów", though not surprisingly they were unable to prevent the wholesale removal of the substantial Jewish population that had lived here for centuries.

Most of the town's collection of historic monuments are ranged on or around the Rynek, the usual small town square with all main roads leading onto it. On the west side of the Rynek stands the **parish church**, started in the 1430s but only completed two centuries later. While elements of the original Gothic design survive in the exterior of the church, the interior is the standard ornate Baroque including an array of sumptuous side altars, carved choir stalls and an overpowering high altar. The adjoining building, the former Pauline monastery, houses the local **museum** (Tues 8am–3pm, Wed & Thurs 8am–4pm, Fri–Sun 10am–3pm; 2zł), a ramshackle collection of historical exhibits and local archeological finds enlivened by a small but interesting set of exhibits relating to the history of the town's Jewish population.

A few minutes' walk from the square down ul. Klasztorna is the former **synagogue**, a large cube-shaped brick structure built in the late 1600s and set back from the street. Despite being looted and damaged by the Nazis during World War II, the empty remaining shell of the building is nevertheless in better condition than many others, mainly thanks to the restoration work that seems to have been carried out intermittently. If the funds ever materialize, there are plans to turn the place into a museum. A plaque on one of the outside walls commemorates the town's Jewish community – still a rarer occurrence than it ought to be in Poland. The wall separating the synagogue from the street contains pieced-together fragments of tombstones from the local Jewish cemetery.

If you don't mind an uphill scramble, the **Kaplica św. Anny** (Chapel of St Anne), clearly visible on a hillside overlooking the Rynek, is a fine Renaissance structure, probably designed by Santa Gucci – one of several period Italian architects drawn to Pinczów by the town's ample supply of raw building materials – and one of the few examples of a freestanding chapel in the country. The chapel isn't often open, however, which means you may have to content yourself with admiring the twin-domed structure from the outside, along with the views over the surrounding countryside.

Practicalities

The bus station is five minutes' walk south of the Rynek on ul. Partyzantów, with frequent servies to Kielce and less frequently to Jędrzejów. The only **places to stay** in town are the *Hotel MOSIR*, ul. Pałęki 26 (℡041/357 2044; ❶), offering simple showerless rooms – mostly doubles and triples – ten minutes' walk south of the Rynek, the lakeside **camping** site nearby (same tel); and a seasonal **youth hostel** at ul. Szkolna 2 (℡041/357 2844). The options for food are similarly limited – a couple of basic **restaurants** on the Rynek, including the smoky *Uśmiech*, will serve you up a regular *kotlet schabowy*, an alternative being the *Manhattan* at ul. Krótka 3, off the west side of the Rynek.

Szydłów

First impressions of **SZYDŁÓW**, 50km east of Jędrzejów, are less than promising. Perched atop a hill amid undulating Małopolska farmlands, this half-deserted rural backwater is certainly not a place to head for in search of action. What makes a visit here worthwhile, however, is the remnants of the fortified Gothic architectural complex built by King Kazimierz the Great in the mid-fourteenth century.

Though the road takes you up around the top of the town, the principal entrance to the Stare Miasto is through the Brama Krakowska (Kraków Gate), a towering structure enhanced by the attic added in the late 1500s. Despite wartime devastation of the town, substantial sections of the fortifications, notably the walls, have survived essentially intact. Clambering around the chunky stone battlements, you sense that King Kazimierz, an indefatigable builder of castles, was a man who put security first. Certainly, the defences he raised here were enough to see Szydłów through the depredations and invasions that ruined many neighbouring towns in later centuries. A fair bit of the castle itself survives, too, notably a solid-looking tower that's now the town **museum** (May–Sept: Tues, Thurs–Sun 8am–3.30pm, Sat & Sun 10am–2pm; Oct–April: Tues–Sun 8am–3.30pm 4zł), housing a low-key collection of local artefacts and historical finds.

West across the wide, open square, stuck out on the far edge of the medieval complex is the **synagogue**, a large structure surrounded by heavy stone buttresses. One of the oldest synagogues in the country and built, according to local legend, at the instigation of Esterka, King Kazimierz's fabled Jewish mistress, the building is currently closed up and empty, waiting for someone to stump up the money to do something with it.

Despite being torched by the Nazis in 1944, the Gothic **parish church**, north of the Rynek, retains a few elements of its original decoration, notably the tryptych on the main altar. **Wszystkich Świętych** (All Saints' Church), marooned outside the main city walls across the road from the Kraków Gate, fared little better, though you can still see sections of the original Gothic polychromy on the walls.

Buses serving Kielce and Jędrzejów run from the stop on the main square, There's nowhere decent to stay in town, and eating opportunities are limited to the basic café and snack-bar places on the square.

Kielce and northern Małopolska

Most people see nothing more of the northern reaches of Małopolska than the glimpses snatched from the window of a Warsaw–Kraków express train – a pity, because the gentle hills, lush valleys, strip-farmed fields and tatty villages that characterize the region are quintessential rural Poland. The main town is **Kielce**, roughly halfway between Warsaw and Kraków, but the real attraction for visitors lies in rambling about in the **Świętokrzyskie** – so-called mountains that are, in reality, more of a hill-walkers' range. Lovers of castles will not want to miss the magnificent ruins at **Krzyżtopór**, while south of Kielce, the **Jaskinia Raj** (Raj Cave), **Chęciny** and the *skansen* at **Tokarnia** make enjoyable excursions, the latter being one of the best of the country's numerous open-air folk architecture museums. They're all in relatively easy striking distance of the city, making it feasible, given an early start, to combine all three in a day's outing.

Heading north along the main road to Warsaw, through the attractive Małopolska countryside, there are a couple of minor stops worth considering: the Cistercian abbey at **Wąchock** and the old *shtetl* of **Szydłowiec**, which has one of the largest remaining Jewish cemeteries in the country.

Kielce

KIELCE, the regional capital, is nothing much to look at, having undergone the standard postwar development, but it has a relaxed, down-at-heel, rural atmosphere. Long the chosen summer residence of the bishops of Kraków, who furnished the city with its main architectural attractions, the town retains little more than echoes of its grander past. Its place in the postwar record is assured, as the site of the infamous **July 1946 pogrom** when over forty Jewish survivors of the Nazi terror were murdered by locals inflamed by rumours of the attempted ritual murder of a Gentile child. On a more contemporary note, the economic transformations of the post-communist era are beginning to show through – albeit much more slowly than in Kraków – in the increasing tally of new shops, cafés and restaurants in evidence in the city centre.

The Polish Brethren

Among the sects that emerged in Reformation-era Poland to challenge Catholic dominance of religious sympathies the **Polish Brethren** occupy a notable place. Also known by a cluster of other names – Arians, Racovians and Socinians being the commonest variants – this loose cluster of like-minded radically dissenting thinkers crystallized into a distinctive group following the establishment of an academy in 1570 at **Raków**, a minor provincial centre 12km north of Szydłow, under the protection of Michał Sienicki, an aristocratic patron and early disciple.

Theologically speaking, what marked the Brethren out from the Calvinists and other Protestant schools developing in Poland at the time was their decisive rejection of the traditional Orthodox doctrines of the Trinity and the divinity of Christ. A leading figure in the development of the Brethren's doctrines was **Fausto Sozzini** (Socinius) who settled in Raków in 1579. Socinius was particularly successful in the spreading of Arian doctrines among the Polish aristocracy. These doctrines were collected in the **Racovian Catechism**, published in Polish in 1605, and subsequently translated into Latin, German and eventually English (1652). Such was the notoriety (and popularity) of the catechism by this stage, that Oliver Cromwell ordered local sheriffs to confiscate the entire print run of the first English edition and burn it as soon as it arrived from the Continent.

In practical terms, the Brethren espoused a religiously based communism of the kind advocated by the Diggers and other radical sects a century later in Cromwellian-era England. The structure of the settlement at Raków was determined by a thoroughgoing pacifism, shared manual labour, the complete abolition of social hierarchy and the denial of the authority of the state. From simple beginnings, the Raków Academy grew into a centre of international repute, with over 1000 students by the beginning of the seventeenth century, and its printing presses churning out a steady stream of tracts and catechisms. The model of the academy proved attractive to many and was duplicated elsewhere in the territories of the Polish-Lithuanian Commonwealth, most notably at **Nowogródek** in present-day Belarus.

For all the religious tolerance exhibited in Poland during the Reformation era – "the land without bonfires" as it was popularly known – the Arians were regarded by many as having gone a theological and political step too far. As the one sect explicitly excluded from the provisions of the **Confederation of Warsaw** (1573) regarding religious tolerance in the Commonwealth, they remained constantly open to the threat of persecution, though instances of martyrdom actually proved remarkably few and far between. In the end, though, under pressure from all sides, the state authorities decided to act, closing first the academy at Nowogródek in 1618 and then the centre at Raków in 1638, following a vote in the Sejm occasioned by news that students had destroyed a roadside crucifix. Deprived of their bases, the Brethren retreated into the countryside, continuing their activities, but never fully regaining the heights of influence and renown they had previously enjoyed.

Though Arianism eventually faded as a religious force in Poland, its ideas continued to find resonance in later centuries. In particular, the Polish Brethren are often regarded as precursors of the **Unitarianism** that flourished (often, but not always, minus the social egalitarianism) among the Presbyterians and other nonconformist churches in England and the United States in the nineteenth century, crystallizing in the formation and development of the modern Unitarian church.

As to **modern Raków**, there's little left by way of traces of the Brethren or their academy except a couple of distinctively shaped whitewashed houses built as living quarters for students at the academy.

The City

All the monuments worth seeing are concentrated around a relatively small central area, bisected by ul. Sienkiewicza, the main city street. North of Sienkiewicza is the pleasant main **Rynek**, lined with crumbling eighteenth- and nineteenth-century mansions, one of which (no. 3/5) houses a **regional museum** (Tues & Thurs–Sun 9am–4pm; 4zł), with a fairly forgettable collection of local archeological finds and ethnographic exhibits. More diverting are the occasional exhibitions of contemporary Polish art that visit the museum throughout the year, generally in summer.

South of Sienkiewicza, on another square, pl. Zamkowy, you'll find the **cathedral** – Romanesque, lost in the later Baroque reconstruction – highlights of the murky interior being a fine Renaissance monument in red marble to a female member of the local Zebrzydowski family, sculpted by Il Padovano, a sumptuous early Baroque high altarpiece from the workshops of Kraków, and some elaborate Rococo decorative carvings in the choir stalls. During major religious festivals, the square east of the cathedral is packed with smartly dressed locals, many in regional folk costume, processing solemnly around the square.

A short way west of the cathedral is the **Pałac Biskupów Krakowskich** (Kraków Bishop's Palace), an impressive early Baroque complex, built on a closed axial plan mimicking the layout of a period north Italian villa supplemented, as in Wawel Castle, by features such as a sturdy-looking roof adjusted to the demands of a northern climate. Constructed in the late 1630s as a residence for the bishops of Kraków, under whose ecclesiastical jurisdiction the

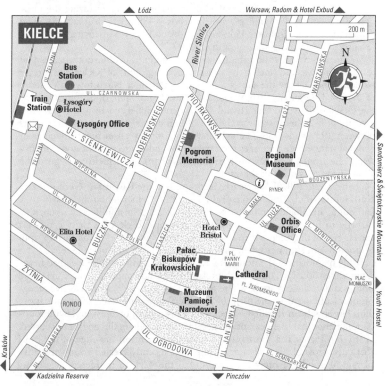

city and surroundings fell, up until the late eighteenth century, the palace now houses another **regional museum** (Wed–Sun 9am–4pm, plus May–June & Sept–Oct Tues 10am–6pm; 5zł), this time among the country's weightier ones.

A mazey selection of ground-floor and upstairs rooms are taken up with an extensive collection of **Polish art** from the seventeenth century onwards. As often in such museums, the early works are effectively an extended portrait gallery of the Polish aristocracy, alongside the usual selection of patriotic favourites such as Kościuszko and Prince Józef Poniatowski. The nineteenth- and twentieth-century rooms contain a notable selection of Młoda Polska movement-era art, including works by Wyspiański, some typically distorted, dreamlike Witkiewicz compositions and a diverting group of self-portraits by Małczewski. On a military note, the museum's collection of swords and other weapons of war from across the centuries culminates in the Piłsudski sanctuary, established in the venerated prewar leader's honour, a few years after his death in 1935, and kept pretty much the same ever since.

Most rooms of the **upper floor** comprise the former bishop's apartments, adorned with a sumptuous array of period furnishings, several of them still retaining their original decoration. The most notable feature here is the decorated high ceilings with intricately painted larch beams and elaborate friezes running around the tops of the walls. The finest example of this effect is in the **Great Dining Hall**, the frieze here consisting of a mammoth twin-level series of portraits of Kraków bishops and Polish monarchs. A number of apartments display some striking ceiling paintings from the workshop of Thomas Dolabella, notably the **Senatorial Hall** in the west wing, featuring the ominous *Judgement of the Polish Brethren* (see box p.488), with a grand, sweeping depiction of scenes from the Polish–Swedish and Polish–Muscovite wars of the seventeenth century in the adjoining room.

Working your way round the back of the museum to the south brings you to ul. Zamkowa, and one of the more something sights of Kielce, the former **prison** at no. 3, now the site of a **Museum Pamięci Narodowej** (Museum of National Remembrance; Wed, Sat & Sun 10am–5pm; donation). Used by the Gestapo in World War II, and subsequently inherited by the communist security police, the prison was the site of innumerable torturings and murders between 1939 and 1956. The cells have been preserved in pretty much their original state – note the cages built over the windows to prevent notes or anything else from being passed outside to those prisoners lucky enough to be allowed some exercise in the yard.

Further south still, ul. Kaczmarka leads south to the **Rezerwat Geologiczny Kadzielnia** (Kadzielnia Geological Reserve), a former limestone quarry now laid out as an (albeit scruffy) park. With bleak crags surrounded by scrub, it's a surprise to find such a seemingly wild landscape so close to a city centre. At the far end of the reserve is an open-air concert venue, the "amphitheatre", put to good use in summer when various cultural events take place here.

While memories of the notorious **Kielce Pogrom** may have weighed heavily in wider postwar Polish–Jewish relations (see box opposite), the same could not be said in the city itself, where for many years there was no effective recognition of the event in the form of an official monument or commemoration. This has now been rectified – albeit at the instigation of a private Jewish foundation, rather than the city authorities. The house where the pogrom occurred, at no. 7/8 Planty, is a short walk west of the square on the edge of the canal that cuts across ul. Sienkiewicza. It displays a recently erected commemorative plaque in Polish, Hebrew and English "to the 42 Jews murdered . . . during anti-Semitic riots" – a commendably honest description of an event of which some in Poland would prefer not to be reminded. Other sites of historic Jewish interest are the former synagogue on al. IX Wieków Kielc, now an archive building, and the crumbling **cemetery** some way south of the centre in the Pakosz district (bus #4 passes fairly close by – get off on ul. Pakosz), where around a hundred gravestones are still standing, along with a dignified monument to local victims of the Holocaust.

The Kielce Pogrom

Kielce has achieved notoriety in postwar Poland as the site of the infamous **July 1946 pogrom**. Inflamed by rumours of the attempted ritual murder of an eight-year-old Gentile Polish child, elements of the local populace attacked buildings occupied by Jewish survivors of the Nazi terror, killing 42 people and wounding another forty over a period of hours, with no sign of intervention from the local police. Following a summary trial conducted shortly afterwards by secret police under the leadership of Edmund Kwasek, a notorious Stalinist-era butcher, nine of the twelve people rounded up and tried were found guilty of the killings and executed by firing squad. In customary communist-era fashion all questions concerning, for example, the precise circumstances surrounding the pogrom or the security forces' failure to prosecute the local alcoholic whose claim that his son had been abducted sparked the killings – a story he himself later admitted to have fabricated – were met with a deafening silence. A defining moment in the development of postwar Polish-Jewish relations, the Kielce pogrom long constituted a blank spot in both local memory and official political discourse.

In symbolic terms, this has now been partially remedied by the commemorative plaque to the victims placed at the actual site of the massacre along with a series of **official apologies** and acts of public contrition that took place on the fiftieth anniversary of the pogrom in July 1996. Politically, however, the issue continues to rankle. The report of the posthumous official commission of enquiry, released in 1997 after five years' sifting of the evidence, stopped short of pronouncing definitively on the question of ultimate responsibility for the killings. And while Kwasek has finally admitted that those brought to trial were simply picked up at random, many of the broader issues surrounding the pogrom remain unanswered. As a result, the **conspiracy theories** of various hues that have long formed the bedrock of public discussion of the event continue to hold sway. The official line during the communist era – still heard on occasion – suggests that the pogrom was the work of the armed anticommunist opposition still active in the surrounding region in 1946. By contrast, anticommunist-oriented public opinion tends toward the thesis that the Polish communist party instigated the killings in a bid to distract public opinion from the rigged summer 1946 referendum used to legitimize the party's subsequent assumption of political power, and held only a few days prior to the killings. Predictably, some more right-wing groups like to point the finger at "Zionist organizations" who are supposed to have engineered the whole thing with the intention of discrediting Poland in the outside world. On a more positive note, the commission did at least categorically reject one of the more outlandish theories, to the effect that events in Kielce were engineered by Soviet security forces as part of an attempt to encourage Holocaust survivors to emigrate to Palestine – at this stage the official Moscow line favoured the establishment of an independent Jewish state under Soviet influence. In addition, the commission asked local authorities to examine the evidence submitted to the commission with a view to prosecuting named local officials at the time for acts of gross negligence and incompetence – a valedictory admission that whatever the remaining uncertainties, the authorities come out of the whole affair pretty appallingly.

Practicalities

The town's **train station and bus station** – the latter a marvellously frivolous circular building resembling the kind of flying saucers imagined by 1950s sci-fi comic-book writers – are close by each other on the west side of town, a ten-minute walk down ul. Sienkiewicza into the centre. There's a 24-hour **left-luggage** office (*przechowalnia bagażu*) in the train station if you're just passing through.

There's a friendly **tourist information centre** in the town hall at Rynek 1 (Mon–Sat 10am–5pm; ☏041/367 6436, ✉itkielce@poczta.onet.pl), which can help you to find accommodation, provide brochures and city maps, and advise on routes into the Góry Świętokrzyskie mountains (see p.495). There's a smallish selection of **accommodation** from which to choose, most of it directed towards commercial travellers and boasting prices to match. The only budget alternatives are the scattering of **private rooms** (mostly in the outskirts; ❷) on offer from the tourist office, and the year-round **youth hostel** at ul. Szymanowskiego 5 (☏041/342 3735), 1km east of the city centre (bus #21 from the train station). The tourist office will also tell you if any student hostels are open to tourists over the summer.

Following a recent overhaul and change of management, the *Łysogóry*, ul. Sienkiewicza 78 (☏041/366 2511, ⓦwww.lysogory.com.pl; ❼), opposite the train station, has upgraded itself to an upper-bracket **hotel** aimed at the business market. The dilapidated but central *Hotel Bristol*, ul. Sienkiewicza 21 (☏041/368 2460; ❻) could certainly use similar attention, though its restaurant is still fairly respectable. The *Elita*, ul. Równa 4a (☏041/344 2230, ⓦwww.jandb.com.pl; ❻), is a small, new, privately run hotel with comfortable, well-kept rooms and in walking distance south of the stations. The *Exbud*, ul. Manifestu Lipcowego 34 (☏041/332 6360, ⓦwww.exbud.com.pl; ❼), is a towering business-oriented place offering all the creature comforts, 2km northeast of the centre on the Warsaw road.

The cafés and snack bars grouped around pl. Wolności are the best places to grab a quick bite to eat. Among the **restaurants**, the *Bartosz*, just off pl. Wolności on Bartosza Głowackiego, is the best source of cheap Polish stodge, although it closes at 7pm. For more relaxed dining, the popular *Winnica*, ul. Winnicka 4, has some good traditional Ukrainian dishes, notably the soups (although beware the dreaded house "dance band" at weekends); while the restaurant of the *Hotel Exbud* (see above) is widely considered to be the best place for international food, excellent service and prices that won't break the bank. *Asean*, Rynek 14, is the best of the Vietnamese restaurants, although the similar *A Dong Quan*, round the corner at Duża 5, is slightly cheaper and is correspondingly popular with discerning locals.

Of the **bars** and **cafés**, the *Pożegnanie z Afryką*, on ul. Leśna, serves the quality coffees that are the chain's hallmark. *Pub Studencki Tunel*, ul. Duża 7, is pretty much what it says it is – a long, low basement bar attracting a relaxed young crowd; while the nearby *Jazz Club*, ul. Duża 9, is a step up in the style stakes, and often features live music, although be prepared to blag your way in after 10pm, when (officially at least) it becomes a members' club.

The Jaskinia Raj

Ten kilometres south of Kielce, and roughly 1km west of the main Kraków road, is the **Jaskinia Raj** (Raj Cave; April–Nov Tues–Sun 10am–5pm; compulsory guided tours in Polish only; 8zł), one of the myriad underground formations dotted around southern Poland, principally in central-northern

Małopolska and the Tatras. Only discovered in 1964, the "Paradise Cave" (Jaskinia Raj) as it's popularly known, rapidly established itself as a local favourite, and particularly in summer, droves of school buses and day-trippers descend on the place. If you want to avoid the crowds, you'd be well advised to get there early. The **bus** (#31 from Kielce) drops you on the main road, from where you walk to the main car park and on along a wooded path to the ticket office-cum-café/museum at the cave entrance.

Only a stretch of 150 metres inside the caves is open to visitors, but it's a spectacular enough experience comprising a series of **chambers** filled with a seemingly endless array of stalagmites, stalactites and other dreamlike dripstone formations. It's now been established that Neanderthals inhabited the caves as long as 50,000 years ago – these days the wintertime occupants are mainly bats – and scientific research carried out here continues to unearth archeologically significant finds such as a recently discovered stockade constructed from reindeer antlers. Some of the finds are on display in the small museum attached to the ticket office at the cave entrance. If you want to stop over, there's a basic **hotel**, the *Zajazd Raj* (☎041/346 5127; ❸) close to the car park, which has its own restaurant.

Chęciny

Five kilometres further south along the Kraków road (at the end of the #31 bus route), the little town of **CHĘCINY** makes for an interesting historical diversion. A sleepy provincial town nestled peacefully at the foot of the overlooking hill, and focused around a characteristic open square, the town looks and feels like the kind of place where nothing much has or is ever going to happen. Though there's not a great deal to see, as often, an awareness of historical context lends places like this their peculiar aura of poignancy mingled with charm. For centuries Chęciny, like many towns in the surrounding area, was a typical Polish *shtetl*, with Jews making up more than half the population. The Jews are gone now, but the buildings they created remain – synagogue, merchant houses, cemetery – in silent testimony to their age-long presence. Look carefully at some of the houses on and around the square, for example, and you can still see the spot on the doorpost where the *mezuzah* ripped out by the Nazis once sat.

On one side of the square stands the Parish **Kościół św. Jozefa** (St Joseph's Church), an unremarkable place notable mainly for its organ, built in the 1680s and still functioning with the help of its intricate original mechanical action. A short walk along ul. Długa is the former **synagogue**, a characteristically solid brick structure with a two-tiered roof built in the early seventeenth century. Like many former synagogues this is now a cultural centre, but as with all too many other former Jewish places of worship, a few decorative features apart there's been little attempt to preserve anything of the original features of the building, the main prayer hall now functioning as a weekend disco complete with glittering lights illuminating the empty frame of the Aron Ha Kodesh. More encouragingly, the place has recently acquired a sign that at least indicates its previous function.

If you're feeling reasonably fit it's worth scrambling up the hill behind the square to the imposing **castle ruins** perched at the top (Tues–Sun 9am–6pm; 1zł). Completed in the 1310s for King Władysław I and remodelled three centuries later, following major destruction by the Swedes, this strategically significant outpost was eventually allowed to slide into ruin. All that remains today is the polygonal plan of the outer wall, the main gate and a couple of towers, which you can wander around freely. What really makes the trek up worthwhile is the excellent views over the surrounding countryside, with Kielce, and on a clear day, the Świętokrzyskie Mountains visible in the distance. Scrambling down the hill right of the castle brings you to the evocative **Jewish cemetery**, crumbling and overgrown, but with a fair number of carved tombstones still in evidence.

For an overnight stay you're limited to the rudimentary **youth hostel** at ul. Białego Zagłębia 1 (☎041/315 1068); or the *Franciskański Osrodek Rekolekcyjny*, ul Franciskańska 10 (☎041/315 1069, ✉fran@kielce.opoka.org.pl) in Fransiscan monastery buildings in triples or multi-bed dorms. For a bite to eat, about your only option is the **bar** at ul. Łokietka 26, a short way down the hill from the Rynek, a local beer- and vodka-swiller's haunt that provides the bare culinary minimum.

Tokarnia

A further 7km south from Chęciny is the outstanding museum of folk architecture, or **skansen** (April–Oct Tues–Sun 10am–5pm; Nov–March Mon–Fri 9am–2pm; 6zł) at **TOKARNIA**. The open-air museum is visible from the road, up on the hillside, though signposting is almost nonexistent: if you're travelling by bus (from Kielce, take buses heading for Jędrzejów via Chęciny) ask the driver for the *skansen* and you'll be dropped close by. In summer a basic café operates in the house at the entrance to the area.

The main idea of a *skansen* is to provide a showcase for rural architecture and customs, in many cases all but disappeared now, and on this score the Tokarnia site succeeds admirably. Established in the 1970s, and still adding to its collection of buildings, the *skansen* is one of the largest and best in the country. Well laid out, with all the buildings grouped according to surrounding regions of Małopolska, this museum provides an enjoyable survey of local architectural traditions. Helpfully, there's a brief guide in each building in English, French and German outlining its traditional use, and, if your Polish is up to it, a devoted contingent of women from local villages there to fill you in on all the details. They're justly proud of their particular building, and in customary rural fashion, in no hurry to see you move on, so be prepared to spend at least a couple of minutes paying each structure the required respect.

The thatched and shingle-roofed buildings assembled here encompass the full range of rural life, with an emphasis on traditional farmsteads, from relatively prosperous setups – the more religious pictures on display the wealthier the family – to the dwellings of the poorest subsistence farmers. Great care and attention has been paid to re-creating the interiors as they would have been in the early part of the century and beyond, with many of the houses containing an amazing array of old wooden farm implements, kitchen utensils and tools used in traditional crafts such as ostlery, shingling, brewing, woodcarving, herbal medicinal preparations and candle-making. Additionally, there are a number of other buildings such as a wonderful old windmill, a pharmacy and a fine mid-nineteenth-century *dwór* of the kind inhabited by relatively well-off *szchlachta* families from Chopin's generation and beyond up until World War II. The contrast between its size and opulence and the other ruder dwellings on display is striking, reflecting the grinding poverty and endemic inequalities of rural Polish society that were a major factor in the successive waves of emigration to the New World from the latter part of the last century on into the 1930s.

The Góry Świętokrzyskie and beyond

In this low-lying region, the **Góry Świętokrzyskie**, only 600m at maximum, appear surprisingly tall. Running for almost 70km east from Kielce, the mountains' long ridges and valleys, interspersed with isolated villages, are popular and rugged hiking territory, the core of the range now protected within a national park area. During World War II the area was a centre of armed resistance to the Nazis: a grim, essentially factual account of life in the resistance here is given in Primo Levi's book *If Not Now, When*, in which he refers to the area as the Holy Cross Mountains – a literal translation of their Polish name.

The Łysogóry

Twenty kilometres east of Kielce is the **Łysogóry** (Bald Mountain) range – more glorified hills than mountains in reality – a fifteen-kilometre-long stretch of scenic hilltop forest interspersed with twisted outcrops of broken quartzite that's a popular destination with day-trippers and hikers alike. The whole range is encompassed within the limits of the national park, which explains the abundant wildlife in evidence in the forests. The place to head for is **ŚWIĘTY KRZYŻ**, one hour by bus from the main Kielce station (5 daily, from 7am). The journey takes you along the edge of the range and eventually up a scenic mountainside road to the edge of the **Świętokrzyskie national park**, stopping at a car park near the foot of Łysa Gora (595m). Immediately beyond the car park is the *Jodłowy Dwór* **hotel** (☎041/302 5028, ✉jodlowy_dwor@pro .onet.pl; ❸), a reasonable overnighter with en-suite rooms and its own restaurant.

The bus continues through the park (the only vehicle allowed to do so), but you're better off walking from here, through the protected woodland habitat of a range of birds and animals, including a colony of eagles. The marked path leads to a clearing – from where you can pick up the road again – then past a huge TV mast to the **abbey** (30min), established up here by Italian Benedictines in the early twelfth century. The buildings have changed beyond recognition, about the only remnant of the original foundation being the abbey church's Romanesque doorway. The isolated mountain site, however, maintains an ancient feel; the abbey itself replaced an earlier pagan temple, traces of which were discovered nearby some years ago. On a more sombre

note, the abbey buildings were turned into a prison following the enforced dissolution of the Benedictine order in 1825, and it remained so up until 1945, having been used by the Nazis as a concentration camp for Soviet POWs. Just how appalling conditions were then is indicated by photographs in the old monastery building of camp signs (in Russian and German) forbidding cannibalism.

The abbey **museum** (daily: May–Aug 10am–5pm; April, Sept & Oct 10am–4pm; Nov–March 9am–3pm; 4zł) houses one of the country's best natural history collections, covering every aspect of the area's wildlife, with exhibits ranging from butterflies and snakes to huge deer and elk. There's a good view down into the valley below the edge of the abbey, and you can also see some of the large tracts of broken stones that are a distinctive glaciated feature of the hilltops.

The trail continues due east down the mountain, passing after about 400m another path off to the left, which takes you in about five minutes to an overgrown Soviet war cemetery; last resting place of many inmates of the Święty Krzyż abbey. Back on the main trail, another 2km walk brings you to the village of **NOWA SŁUPIA**. The principal point of interest here is the **Muzeum Starożytnego Hutnictwa** (Museum of Ancient Metallurgy; Tues–Sun 9am–4pm; 5zł), located on the site of iron-ore mines and smelting furnaces developed here as early as the second century AD, as evidenced by the impressive array of primitive ironworks unearthed around here during the past few decades: for nearly a thousand years, it seems, this was the site of one of Europe's biggest ironworks. From Nowa Słupia you can take a bus back to Kielce, or climb back up and catch one from Święty Krzyż. For **accommodation** in Nowa Słupia there's a year-round **youth hostel**, near the museum at ul. Świętokrzyska 64 (☎041/317 7016); and a nearby **campsite** (May–Sept; ☎041/317 7085) that has a few cheap cabins on offer as well as a restaurant.

The highest point of the Łysogóry is a summit known as **Łysica** (611m) at the western end of the range, a legendary witches' meeting place with an excellent viewpoint. If you set out for Nowa Słupia by bus from Kielce early enough in the day you'll have time to take in the village museums before **hiking** the marked path up to Święty Krzyż and along the ridge to Łysica, continuing 2km down the woodland, past memorials to resistance fighters hunted down by the Nazis, to the village of **ŚWIĘTA KATARZYNA** – a total hike of 18km. From here you can catch the bus back to Kielce before the end of the day. In Święta Katarzyna itself, there's a **convent** that's been home to an enclosed order of Bernardine nuns since the fifteenth century. If you turn up during daylight hours you can usually peer in at the church. In summer there's a PTTK-run **information kiosk** on the village's main street. If you want to stay over it's a choice between the *Baba Jaga*, ul. Kielecka 18 (☎041/311 2226; en-suites ❸, rooms with shared facilities ❶), a basic **hotel** with its own restaurant; the roomier and slightly more comfortable *Jodelka*, ul. Kielecka 3 (☎041/311 2111; en-suites ❷, rooms with shared facilities ❸); and a year-round **youth hostel** (☎041/311 2206).

Opatów

Some 60km east of Kielce on the Lublin road, beyond the outer reaches of the Świętokrzyskie Mountains, the little town of **OPATÓW** is as somnolent a place as you would expect in these parts. Yet the town has known better days, originally developing out of its position on one of the major medieval trading routes east into Russia. Badly mauled during the Tatar raids of Poland (1500–1502), Opatów was purchased and subsequently fortified by Chancellor

Krzysztof Szydłowiecki (see p.499).The Stare Miasto complex grouped around the long square at the top of the hill and surrounded by walls is what remains of the chancellor's development of the town.

As often, the most notable building is the **parish church** on the main square, dedicated to St Martin, a towering three-aisled Romanesque basilica raised in the mid-twelfth century and remodelled in later centuries. A few features of the original Romanesque decoration survive, notably the main doorway, the dual windows in the south tower and some frieze decoration on the facade. These aside, the thing to look out for is the group of Szydłowiecki family **tombs**, especially that of Chancellor Krzysztof. Executed, like the others in the group, in the 1530s by a duo of Italian architects from the court at Wawel, the tomb has a powerful bronze bas-relief of the citizens of Opatów mourning the chancellor's death – a moving tribute to a man whose family name had died out by the end of the century owing to a persistent failure to produce male heirs.

One section of the square is crisscrossed by a honeycomb of underground **tunnels** and **cellars**, a throwback to the town's merchant past, originally used for storing goods sold in the local market. It's now possible to visit the cellars – ask at the PTTK office on the square, which organizes guided visits underground when demand is sufficient.Ten minutes' walk away, back down the hill, through the Brama Warszawska (Warsaw Gate) and across the River Opatówka, is the **Bernardine church**, an ornate late-Baroque structure with a fine high altarpiece that replaced the earlier fifteenth-century church destroyed by Swedish troops during the invasions of the mid-1650s.

The **bus station**, in the centre of town, has good connections to nearby Sandomierz and reasonable ones to Kielce. The only **accommodation** options to speak of are a basic PTTK hostel, ul. Obronców Pokoju 16 (☎015/868 2778; ❶) and a seasonal youth hostel at ul. Cmielowska 2 (☎015/868 2374), while for simple meals there are a couple of **restaurants** on the main square.

Krzyżtopór

Despite its dilapidated state the **Krzyżtopór castle**, near the village of Ujazd, 15km southwest of Opatów on the road to Staszów, is one of the most spectacular ruins in Poland (buses from Opatów cover the route). Nothing in the surrounding landscape prepares you for the mammoth building that suddenly rears up over the skyline. Even then, it's not until you actually enter the castle compound (Tues–Sun 10am–4pm, often longer during summer months) that you really begin to get a handle on the scale of the place, a magnificent ruin still bearing many hallmarks of the considerable architectural ingenuity that went into designing and constructing the complex.

The history of the castle is a textbook case of grand aristocratic folly. Built at enormous expense for Krzysztof Ossoliński, the governor of Sandomierz province, by Italian architect Lorenzo Muretto, and completed in 1644, only a year before Ossoliński's death, the castle was thoroughly ransacked by the Swedes only a decade later, a blow from which it never really recovered, despite being inhabited by the Ossoliński family up until the 1770s. Plans to resurrect the castle have come and gone over time, the latest initiative being a somewhat uncertain bid to revive the place as a tourist attraction.

The basic **layout** of the castle comprises a star-shaped set of fortifications surrounding a large inner courtyard, and within this, a smaller elliptical inner area. The original architectural conception mimicked the calendar at every level: thus there were four towers, representing the seasons, twelve main walls for the months, 52 rooms for the weeks, 365 windows for the days, and even an additional window for leap years, kept bricked up when out of sync with the calendar. Ossoliński's passion for horses was accommodated by the network of stables, some 370 in all, built underneath the castle, each equipped with its own mirror and marble manger. While remnants of the stables survive, the same can't be said for the fabled dining hall in the octagonal entrance tower, originally dominated by a crystal aquarium built into the ceiling.

Carved on the entrance tower before the black marble portal are a large cross (*krzyż*) and an axe (*topór*), a punning reference to the castle's name, the former a symbol of the Catholic Church's Counter-Reformation, of which Ossoliński was a firm supporter, the latter part of the family coat of arms. Inside the complex, you're inevitably drawn to wandering around the rather unstable nooks and crannies of the castle. The longer you stay, the more the sheer audacity and expanse of the place hits home, in particular, the murky ruins of the cellars, which seem to go on for ever. With the high inner walls towering above as you descend into the bowels of the building, it's easy to understand why the castle has generated its fair share of legends, notably that of the lady and knight said to prowl the ramparts by moonlight, the knight being Krzysztof Baldwin, the second lord of the castle killed by a Tatar archer.

Most people move straight on after visiting, though such is the magic of the place, that don't be surprised if you end up spending longer here than you planned. If you want to stay the night, the building in front of the castle entrance offers basic overnight **accommodation** and **snacks**, and there's the additional option of camping in the castle grounds.

Wąchock

The only reason for going to **WĄCHOCK**, 44km north of Kielce (and getting there certainly constitutes something of a detour from the main Radom–Warsaw road) is to visit the town's Cistercian **abbey**. One of the major Cistercian centres in Poland, the monastery is also widely regarded as one of the finest and best-preserved monuments of Romanesque architecture in the country. Built by the group of Burgundian monks who settled here in 1179 at the invitation of Gedko, bishop of Kraków, the complex was completed in 1239, probably by Italian masons whose leader, Maestro Simon, carved his name on the facade of the church. The monks of the Cistercian community give **guided tours** round the abbey, mostly to prearranged tourist groups, which you are welcome to tag along with: otherwise the brothers are happy to let people come in and look around the church and main sections of the cloister during specified **opening hours** (Mon–Sat 9am–noon & 1–5pm, Sun 2–5pm).

Just five minutes' walk from the main square, entrance to the complex is through the main abbey door, where you'll need to make yourself known at the reception desk. Opposite is a small **museum** devoted to the history of the place, including its role in the exploits of the Polish insurgents who fought Russian troops from their bases in the surrounding hills during the failed 1863 Uprising against tsarist rule. The original Romanesque interior design of the basilica-shaped **abbey church**, topped with a high tower, has largely been submerged under a mass of florid Baroque ornamentation, though the cross-ribbed vaulting characteristic of Cistercian architecture is still in evidence. On into the adjoining monastic complex, the most notable features are two well-preserved original Romanesque sections of the **cloisters**, much of which was remodelled in the sixteenth and seventeenth centuries. The **chapter house**, in the eastern section, is the real showstopper. Its exquisitely proportioned cross-ribbed vaulting is divided into nine sections interspersed with a sequence of arches supported by four columns, whose capitals are ornamented with intricately carved floral decoration, also gracing the surrounding walls. On the south side of the cloister, the **refectory** also features more soothing cross-ribbed vaulting and decorative carved stonework, the atmosphere of the place suggestive of the calming rhythms of the monastic life practised here for centuries.

For places to stay, the only current option in town is a summer-only **youth hostel**, ul. Kościelna 10, while for a bite to eat, there are a couple of basic **restaurants/cafés** on and around the Rynek, none of them memorable. There's a reasonably frequent though slow-paced **bus** service to and from Kielce, terminating at Wąchock's Rynek.

Szydłowiec

Forty-five kilometres north of Kielce, **SZYDŁOWIEC** is exactly the kind of dusty Stare Miasto most people whizz through on the way to and from Kraków, but there's enough worth seeing in its small, but nonetheless enjoyable, set of historical monuments to justify a brief stopover.

A placid central Rynek provides the focal point of the town, dominated by a fine **town hall**, substantially renovated since the late 1980s, a robust early-seventeenth-century construction topped with a high tower, the attic's arcaded decorative frieze emphasizing the influence of Kraków's Sukiennice on the style of construction. There's a pleasant café in the cellars underneath the building that also holds occasional concerts and other cultural events. Off the southern side of the Rynek stands the late-Gothic **Kościół św. Zygmunta** (Church of St Sigismund), with accompanying belfry, completed in the early 1500s, and mercifully spared the usual later Baroque accretions. Notable features of the largely well-preserved original interior include the sumptuous early-seventeenth-century **high altar**, a fine carved **Coronation of the Virgin** from 1531 and, most striking of all, the late-Gothic polyptych housed in the presbytery. Produced by one of the prolific Kraków workshops of the period, the central panel illustrates the Assumption of the Virgin, with the twelve Apostles gathered round the empty tomb of the resurrected Christ. Below them kneel the figures of the Szydłowiec family, the town founders and financial patrons of the church. Mikołaj Szydłowiecki, royal chancellor until his death in 1532, is commemorated in a fine marble tablet executed by Bartolomeo Berecci of Wawel cathedral fame.

Half a kilometre west of the Rynek is the town **castle**, a dilapidated old pile surrounded by a stagnant moat, built for Chancellor Szydłowiecki in the 1510s, overhauled a century later and, by the look of things, allowed to sink gracefully into decline ever since. Much of the castle is closed to visitors, the major exceptions being the cobbled inner courtyard and a **Muzeum Ludowych Instrumentów Muzycznych** (Museum of Folk Instruments; Tues–Fri 9am–3.30pm, Sat 10am–5.30pm; entrance from the south side of the building; 3zł), which houses an enjoyable selection of musical accoutrements ranging from fiddles, accordions, hurdy-gurdies and bagpipes to more exotic creations such as animal-shaped whistles and percussion instruments of all shapes and sizes.

Jews formed a sizeable percentage of the town population up until the liquidation of the Nazi-established ghetto here in January 1943, when they were deported en masse to Treblinka. Echoes of their presence revolve around the former **synagogue**, now a library, on ul. Grabarskiej, near the old Jewish-run brewery on ul. Sowińskiego, and most powerfully of all in the **cemetery**, out at the end of ul. Wschodnia, on the edge of town near the Radom road. One of the largest and most impressive such sites left in Poland, a walk through the walled, overgrown burial ground, where over 3000 tombstones are still standing, the oldest dating back to the late eighteenth century, uncovers numerous examples of the elaborately carved floral and symbolic motifs typical of Jewish *matzevot* in Poland and elsewhere in east-central Europe. A memorial near the main cemetery gate commemorates the 16,000 Jews deported from the town in 1943.

Practicalities

The **bus station** is a short walk north of the Rynek, on the main Radom road, with regular services to and from Radom and less frequent connections with Kielce. Buses also run to Skarżysko-Kamienna where you can change for the better service to Kielce. Unless you're really desperate, you won't want to stay here for the night: the **accommodation** options are a basic youth hostel at ul. Kolejowa 26a (⬭048/617 1295); and the *Motel Iguś*, out on the Radom road at ul. Kościuszki 261 (⬭048/617 4551; ❸). The only **restaurants** worth speaking of, the *Ratuszowa* on the Rynek, and the *Biesiadia* on the way to the Jewish cemetery, are extremely simple.

Podhale and the Tatras

Ask Poles to define their country's natural attractions and they often come up with the following simple definition: the lakes, the sea and the mountains. The mountains consist of an almost unbroken chain of ridges extending the whole length of the southern border, of which the highest, most spectacular and most revered are the **Tatras** – or **Tatry** as they're known in Polish. Eighty kilometres long, with peaks rising to over 2500m, the Polish Tatras are actually a relatively small part of the range, most of which rises across the border in Slovakia. As the estimated three million annual tourists show, however, the Polish section has enough to keep most people happy: high peaks for dedicated mountaineers, excellent trails for hikers, cable cars and creature comforts for day-trippers, and ski slopes in winter. What used to be a prime Eastern Bloc holiday region is now being transformed into something of a Western tourist enclave, the legions of East Europeans that used to descend on **Zakopane** rapidly being replaced by new hordes of Italians, French – and increasingly English – taking advantage of the low cost of holidaying in the Polish mountains.

Podhale – the Tatra foothills, beginning to the south of Nowy Targ – is a sparsely populated region of lush meadows, winding valleys and old wooden villages. The inhabitants of Podhale, the **górale**, are fiercely independent mountain farmers, known throughout Poland for their folk traditions. The region was "discovered" by the Polish intelligentsia in the late nineteenth century and the *górale* rapidly emerged as symbols of the struggle for independence, the links forged between intellectuals and local peasants presaging the anticipated national unity of the post-independence era. As in other neglected areas of the country, the poverty of rural life led thousands of *górale* to emigrate

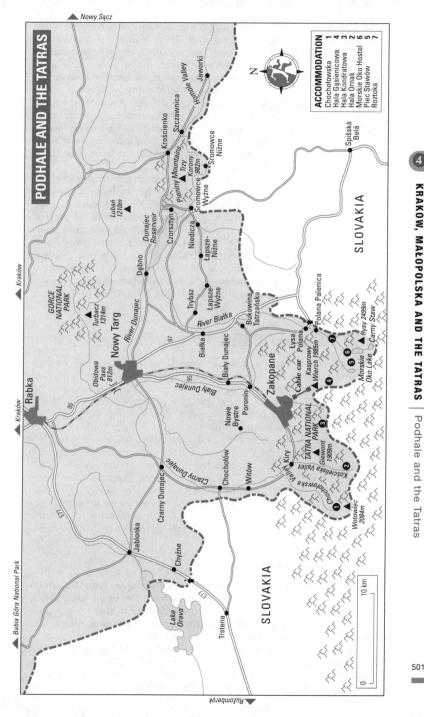

ACCOMMODATION
Chochołowska	1
Hala Gąsienicowa	4
Hala Kondratowa	3
Hala Ornak	2
Morskie Oko Hostel	6
Piec Stawów	5
Roztoka	7

Nowy Sącz

N

Kraków

Kraków

Babia Góra National Park

Ružomberok

SLOVAKIA

SLOVAKIA

Jaworki

Homole Valley

Szczawnica

Kroscienko

Pieniny Mountains

Trzy Korony 982m

Stromowce Nizne

Stromowce Wyzne

Spisská Belá

Czorsztyn

Niedzica

Lapsze-Nizne

Lapsze Wyzne

Trybsz

Dunajec Reservoir

Lubań 1210m

Debno

River Dunajec

Nowy Targ

GORCE NATIONAL PARK

Turbacz 1314m

River Białka

Bukowina Tatrzańska

Białka

Biały Dunajec

Bialy Dunajec

Poronin

Nowe Bystre

Obidowa Pass 812m

Rabka

Czarny Dunajec

Chochołów

Witów

Kiry

Chochołowska Valley

Kościeliska Valley

TATRA NATIONAL PARK

Giewont 1909m

Wotowiec 2084m

Zakopane

Cable car

Kasprowy Wierch 1985m

Lysa Polana

Polana Palenica

Rysy 2499m

Czarny Staw

Morskie Oko Lake

7

6

5

4

3

2

1

Jabłonka

Chyżne

Czarny Dunajec

Lake Orava

Trstena

10 km

0

to the United States in the 1920s and 1930s. The departures continue today, with at least one member of most households spending a year or two in Chicago, New York or other US Polish émigré centres, returning with money to support the family and, most importantly, build a house.

Since the demise of communism, the traditional bonds between Podhale and the rest of the country have been shaken by what many locals see as central government's insensitivity to their specific concerns. Tensions surfaced following Solidarity's refusal to adopt a popular *górale* community leader as their main candidate in the elections of summer 1989, choosing instead a union loyalist. Subsequent governments have shown somewhat more concern for regional sensitivities, encouraged, no doubt, by the economic benefits to be reaped from its burgeoning tourist development.

Despite the influx of holiday-makers, the *górale* retain a straight-talking and highly hospitable attitude to outsiders. If you're willing to venture off the beaten track, away from the regular tourist attractions around Zakopane, there's a chance of real and rewarding contacts in the remoter towns and villages. The *górale* are also the guardians of one of Poland's most vibrant folk music traditions, retaining an appetite for the kind of rootsy, fiddle-driven dance music that has all but died out in the lowlands. Traditional bands regularly appear at local festivities and weddings (which are usually a high-profile component of any given Saturday), and also appear regularly in the bars and restaurants of Zakopane – which is also a good place to seek out CDs and tapes of the music.

South to Zakopane

From Kraków, the main road south heads through the foothills towards **Zakopane**, the main base for the Tatras. Approaching the mountains the road runs through a memorable landscape of gentle valleys, undulating slopes and strip-farmed fields. Along the route you'll see plenty of houses built in the distinctive pointed Podhale style – newer houses have tin roofs, the older ones are decorated wooden structures – as well as wayside Catholic shrines and farming people dressed in the equally distinctive local costume. In addition, now, there's a sizeable contingent of privately run roadside restaurants and bed-and-breakfast places – heralded by "*noclegi*" (rooms) signs – established in the wake of the country's current economic transition. Most buses, and visitors, run straight through, though it can be pretty slow going – usually around two hours – but, with a little time on your hands, it's worth considering a couple of breaks in your journey. A warning for motorists: watch out for cows – and drunks – careering out into the road. Accidents are common.

Rabka and the Gorce

The climb begins as soon as you leave Kraków, following the River Raba from Myślenice to Lubień and then on, with the first glimpses of the Tatras ahead, to **RABKA**, around 60km from the city. This is a quiet little town, with a beautiful seventeenth-century **church** at the base of a hill, now housing a small **ethnographic museum** (Tues–Sun 9am–4pm; 3zł).

Surrounding Rabka is a mountainous area known as the **Gorce**, much of it national park land. It's fine, rugged hiking country, with paths clearly signposted, and offers a less-frequented, and more easy-going alternative to the more demanding Tatras. There are **trails** to several mountain-top hostels: *Luboń*

Wielki (1022m), *Maciejowa* (815m), *Groniki* (1027m) and – highest and best of all – *Turbacz* (1310m), a solid six-hour walk east of town. Before setting out, pick up the **map** *Beskid Makowski (Beskid Średni* 1:75,000) available locally.

If the idea of a **stay** appeals, there are several options in Rabka, including the *Anna*, ul. Nowy Świat 27 (℡018/267 7477; ❹), whose comfortable rooms boast TV and shower; and the *Hanusia*, ul. Bystra 18 (℡018/267 7547; ❸), a *pensjonat* 1km from the train station.

Nowy Targ

From Rabka the road continues over the **Obidowa Pass** (812m), then down onto a plain crossed by the Czarny Dunajec river and towards Podhale's capital, **NOWY TARG** (New Market). The oldest town in the region, established in the thirteenth century, the key attraction of this squat, undistinguished place – the home of many a Polish-American – is, as the name suggests, a **market**, held each Thursday (and increasingly at weekends too) on a patch of ground just east of the centre. Once an authentic farmers' event, with horse-drawn carts lining the streets was done here, accompanied by a lot of serious animal trading stalls laden with local produce and crafts. Of late, however, both the character and the appeal of the market has been diminished by a glut of Western consumer goods and, although the folsky items are still here, you'll have to search a bit harder to find them. For visitors, the main shopping attractions are the chunky sweaters that are the region's hallmark – prices are lower and the quality generally better here than in either Kraków or Zakopane. Be prepared to haggle for anything you buy (wool and crafts especially), and arrive early if you want to get any sense of the real atmosphere. The market has also been invaded by droves of Russians, Ukrainians and Slovaks, the latter turning up weekly by the busload to benefit from the relatively cheaper prices in Poland, their booty duly wafted through the laxly policed crossings along the Slovak border. By 10am or so, with business done, most of the farmers retreat to local cafés for a hearty bout of eating and, especially, drinking.

There's no point in staying in Nowy Targ when a range of far more enticing mountain destinations are so close at hand, and once you've had a browse round the market, you'd be well advised to move on.

The Lenin Trail

Nowy Targ marks the starting point of an unofficial **Lenin Trail**: the old prison just beyond the southeast corner of the main square is where he was briefly interned on suspicion of spying in 1914. The Bolshevik leader had already been a full-time resident of the Podhale region for over a year, renting a room in the village of Biały Dunajec, just north of Zakopane. The locality had several advantages for Lenin: it was near enough to the tsarist border for him to retain contact with his revolutionary colleagues, and the area's reputation as a health resort attracting all manner of sickly looking intellectuals ensured that his presence here was unlikely to attract the unwelcome curiosity of the locals. He drank coffee and read the papers in Zakopane's main society hangout of the time, *Café Trzaski* – an establishment that sadly no longer exists. After his brief spell in prison he relocated to Switzerland, from where he returned to Russia in 1917 in order to take command of the Revolution.

In 1947 a **Lenin Museum** was opened in the village of Poronin, between Biały Dunajec and Zakopane, but it closed its doors for good in 1990, with most of its artefacts being shunted off to the Museum of Socialist Realism in Kozłowka palace. The house where Lenin lived in Biały Dunajec still stands, although the owners shun publicity in the hope that it won't become a target for tourists.

Zakopane and around

South of Nowy Targ, the road continues another 20km along the course of the Biały Dunajec before reaching the edges of **ZAKOPANE**, a major mountain resort, crowded with visitors throughout its summer **hiking** and winter **skiing** seasons. It has been an established attraction for Poles since the 1870s, when the purity of the mountain air began to attract the attention of doctors and their consumptive city patients. Within a few years, this inaccessible mountain village of sheep farmers was transformed, as the medics were followed by Kraków artists and intellectuals, who established a fashionable colony in the final decades of Austro-Hungarian rule. A popular holiday centre ever since, Poles began discovering the place en masse in the 1920s and 1930s, and in the postwar era the town grew to become one of the country's prime tourist hotspots. In step with the growing influx of foreigners, drawn by the lure of the mountains (and what remain by Western standards bargain prices), Zakopane has of late begun to acquire the hollow, overdeveloped feel of a major European tourist trap. It's a must for the wonderful setting and access to the peaks, but the distinctive traditional *górale* architecture of much of the town is being increasingly submerged in the welter of commercial developments.

Arrival, information and accommodation

The **bus** and **train stations** are both a ten-minute walk east of the main street, ul. Krupówki. Some private buses to Kraków pick up and drop from a stop on ul. Kościuszki, just west of the stations. The **tourist office**, housed in a wooden chalet a few steps west of the stations at ul. Kościuszki 17 (daily: July–Aug & Dec–April 8am–8pm; rest of the year 9am–5pm; 018/☎201 2211), is a helpful source of information on the whole area; ask here about anything concerning staying in Zakopane or seeing the Tatras, including maps and guides; alternatively, check out ⓦwww.zakopane.pl. The Tatrzański Park Narodowy, or Tatra **national park office**, at Chałubińskiego 44 (daily 8am–4pm; ☎018/206 3799, Ⓔkozica@tpn.zakopane.pl), is an essential source of expert information if you're planning a serious mountain trek.

Note that **parking** can be a bit of a problem for motorists these days in the increasingly congested town centre. Your best bets are the couple of parking lots on al. 3 Maja, directly east of ul. Krupówki. Alternatively, the hotels and *pensjonaty* mentioned below all have parking facilities.

Accommodation

Zakopane is increasingly well served with a wide range of accommodation, although it's still worth booking rooms well in advance in midsummer or during the skiing season. Particularly during *ferie*, the traditional two-week break for schoolchilden (usually the last week in January and first week in February), everything on offer is booked solid.

You can book **private rooms** (❷) and pensions (❹) through the tourist office (see above), and a number of private travel agents in town – the most helpful being Kozica, operating out of a hut 200m west of the bus station along ul. Kościuszki; PTTK, Krupówki 12 (☎018/201 2429); Redykołka, Kościeliska 1 (☎018/201 3253, ⓦwww.tatratours.pl); and Tatra Club, Krupówki 36 (☎018/201 2931).

Zakopane's all-year **youth hostel**, downhill from the bus station at ul. Nowotarska 45 (☎018/206 6203), has some en-suite doubles (❸), doubles with shared facilities (❷), and dorm rooms from 25zł per person. For **campers** there

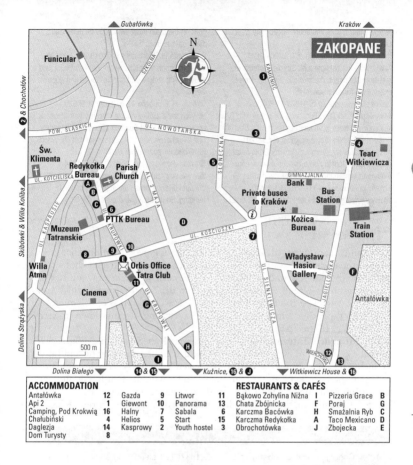

▲ Gubałówka   Kraków ▲

ZAKOPANE

N

Funicular

◄ & Chochołów

Św. Klimenta

Redykołka Bureau   Parish Church

Muzeum Tatranskie

PTTK Bureau

Willa Atma

Orbis Office
Tatra Club

Cinema

Teatr Witkiewicza

Bank

Private buses to Kraków   Bus Station

Kožica Bureau   Train Station

Władysław Hasior Gallery

Antałówka

Skibówki & Willa Koliba ◄

Dolina Strążyska ◄

0   500 m

Dolina Białego ▼   ⑭ & ⑮ ▼   ▼ Kuźnice, ⑯ & ⓙ   ▼ Witkiewicz House & ⑯

ACCOMMODATION					
Antałówka	12	Gazda	9	Litwor	11
Api 2	1	Giewont	10	Panorama	13
Camping, Pod Krokwią	16	Halny	7	Sabala	6
Chałubiński	4	Helios	5	Start	15
Daglezja	14	Kasprowy	2	Youth hostel	3
Dom Turysty	8				

RESTAURANTS & CAFÉS			
Bąkowo Zohylina Niżna	I	Pizzeria Grace	B
Chata Zbójnicka	F	Poraj	G
Karczma Bacówka	H	Smażalnia Ryb	C
Karczma Redykołka	A	Taco Mexicano	D
Obrochotówka	J	Zbojecka	E

are two sites: *Camping Pod Krokwią*, (☎018/201 2256), ul. Żeromskiego, across from the bottom of the ski jump on the east side of town; and *Za Strugiem*, ul. Za Strugiem 39 (☎018/201 4566), a thirty-minute walk west of the centre. The **hotels** listed below can be subject to considerable price hikes during high season.

Antałówka ul. Wierchowa 3 ☎018/201 3271, ✉antalowka@polskietatry.pl. Biggish concrete hotel with servicable en-suites, ideally located a short uphill walk away from the bus station and town centre. Excellent views over town and mountains. ⑤

Api 2 Kamieniec 13a ☎018/206 2931, ⓦwww.api.zakopane.top.pl. Cosy pension north of the stations with smallish en-suites with TV and a decent breakfast. ④

Chałubiński ul. Chramcówki 15 ☎018/206 8061, ⓦwww.chalubinski.ceti.com.pl. Big place just north of the stations with a hotel section offering reasonably comfy en-suites, and an old-fashioned rest-home section with rooms – anything from doubles to quintuples – with shared facilities. ②–④

Daglezja ul. Piłsudskiego 14 ☎018/201 4041, ⓦwww.daglezja.com.pl. Well-equipped, medium-size, and rather swanky modern hotel with sauna and solarium on site. ⑦

Dom Turysty ul. Zaruskiego 5 ☎018/206 3281, ⓦwww.domturysty.zakopane.pl. Cheap central hotel with a safe car park and attractive setting. Gets a lot of students in season. En-suites, rooms with shared facilites, and some dorms (30zł per person). ③–④

Gazda al. Zaruskiego 2 ☎018/201 5011. Central hotel with decent-quality en-suites with TV, facilities for the disabled and a reasonable restaurant. ⑤

Giewont ul. Kościuszki 1 ☎018/201 2011, ⓦwww.giewont.net.pl. Orbis hotel, right in the centre. Often has rooms spare outside the high season. **⑤**

Halny ul. Sienkiewicza 6a ☎018/201 2041, ✉halny@regle.zakopane.pl. Simple socialist-era rest-home between the stations and the centre, offering no-frills en-suites. **③**

Helios ul. Stołeczna 2a ☎018/201 3808, ⓦwww.polhotels.com. Functional en-suites with TV in a concrete block, with facilities for the disabled. **⑥**

Kasprowy Polana Szymaszkowa ☎018/201 4011, ✉kasprowy@orbis.pl. Luxury Orbis hotel west of town, looking onto the mountains, complete with swimming pool and tennis courts. **⑦**

Litwor ul. Krupówki 40 ☎018/261 7190, ⓦwww.litwor.pl. Modern and rather stylish hotel right on the main strip, with good facilities and a dinky on-site pool. **⑦**

Panorama ul. Wierchowa 6 ☎018/201 5081. A sizeable concrete neighbour to the *Antałówka* (see above), with simple unfussy en-suites and good views. **⑤**

Sabala ul. Krupówki 11 ☎018/201 5092, ⓦwww.sabala.zakopane.pl. Ultramodern place occupying the 1894 building of one of Zakopane's first ever hotels, the Staszeczkówka. Lovely, wood-furnished en-suites with TV. **⑦**

Start ul. Piłsudskiego 22 ☎018/206 1394, ⓦwww.start.zakopane.pl. Unexciting but reliable cheapie offering en-suites in a plain concrete building. Some triples and quads. **③**

The Town

Zakopane's main street, **ul. Krupówki**, is a bustling pedestrian precinct given over to the traditional assortment of restaurants, cafés and souvenir shops, now spiced by the newly acquired collection of Western-style takeaway joints, delis and billiard halls. Uphill, the street merges into **ul. Zamoyskiego**, which runs on out of town past the fashionable *fin-de-siècle* wooden villas of the outskirts, while in the other direction, it follows a rushing stream down towards Gubałówka Hill (see p.511).

The **Muzeum Tatrzanskie** (Tatra Museum; Tues–Sun 9am–3.30pm; 3zł), near the centre of ul. Krupówki, covers local wildlife, ethnography and history, including a section on the wartime experiences of the *górale*, who were brutally punished by the Nazis for their involvement with the Polish resistance and cross-mountain contacts with the Allied intelligence. The museum is dedicated to T. Chałubinski, the doctor who "discovered" Zakopane in the 1870s.

Karol Szymanowski

After Chopin, **Karol Szymanowski** (1882–1937) is Poland's greatest composer, forging his own distinctive style in an exotic and highly-charged mix of orientalism, opulence and native folk music. Always striving to find a national voice, he feared provincialism – "Poland's national music should not be the stiffened ghost of the polonaise or mazurka . . . Let our music be national in its Polish characteristics but not falter in striving to attain universality."

From the 1920s Szymanowski spent much time in **Zakopane** and became a key member of a group of intellectuals (including the artist and playwright Witkacy) who were enthused by the folklore of the Tatras and dubbed themselves "the emergency rescue service of Tatra culture". Among Szymanowski's works that show a direct influence of Tatra music are the song cycle *Sęopiewnie* (1921), the *Mazurkas* for piano (1924–25) and, above all, the ballet *Harnasie* (1931) which is stuffed full of outlaws, features a spectacular highland wedding and boasts authentic *górale* melodies in orchestral garb.

Alongside two violin concertos and his *Symphony Song of the Night*, Szymanowski's greatest work is the **Stabat Mater** (1926), which draws on the traditions of old Polish church music and is a stunning choral work of great economy and austere beauty. After many years of ill health, Szymanowski died of tuberculosis in 1937 and received an illustrious state funeral with the Obrochta family, one of the leading *górale* bands, playing around his tomb in the Skałka church in Kraków.

Towards the northern end of Krupówki, ul. Kościeliska veers off towards an area liberally sprinkled with traditional buildings, kicking off with the wooden **Kościół św Klimenta** (Church of St Clement). The low-ceilinged interior gves off an attractive piney smell, and holds several examples of a popular local form of folk art – devotional paintings on glass, in this case depicting the Stations of the Cross. Outside in the graveyard lie the tombs of many of the town's best-known writers and artists, among them that of **Stanisław Witkiewicz** (1851–1915), who developed the distinctive Zakopane architectural style based on traditional wooden building forms. The houses he built – all steep pointy roofs and jutting attic windows – went down a storm with a pre-World War I middle class who were crazy for all things rustic. Witkiewicz's memorial in the cemetery is a typical mixture of thoughtful design and woodworking craft: a smooth totem pole in which a niche bears a wooden statuette of a pensive Christ with his head in his hands – a traditional folk depiction of the Saviour assuming responsibilty for the world's troubles. There's also a commemorative tablet to Witkiewicz's equally famous son, **Witkacy** (see box, overleaf), standing by his mother's grave. Alongside the famous are the graves of old *górale* families, including well-known local figures such as the skier Helena Marusarzówna, executed by the Nazis for her part in the resistance.

Just beyond the church stands the **Willa Koliba**, Witkiewicz's first architectural experiment, and now a **Muzeum Stylu Zakopańskiego** (Museum of the Zakopane Style; Wed–Sat 9am–5pm, Sun 9am–3pm; 4zł). Starting off with a ground-floor display of the folk crafts from which Witkiewicz got his inspiration, the exhibition moves on to the kind of furniture that he set about designing – chunky chairs adorned with squiggly details in an engaging mixture of Art Nouveau and folkloric forms. There's also a scale model of Witkiewicz's greatest architectural creation, the Willa Pod Jodłami, an extraordinarily intricate wooden house which brings to mind a Scandinavian timber church redesigned as a country mansion – enjoy the model while you're here, because it's difficult to get close up to the real thing (see below). Finally there's a marvellous collection of Witkacy's often deranged pastel portraits, including a lot of distorted, angular depictions of the people – mostly women – who featured prominently in his circle.

Moving back towards Krupówki and turning south down ul. Kasprusie soon leads to the **Willa Atma**, a traditional-style villa and longtime home of composer **Karol Szymanowski** (see box, opposite), now a museum dedicated to its former resident (Tues–Sun 10am–4pm).

East of the main drag, near the bus and train stations, a wooden building at ul. Jagiellońska 18b – it's just off the road in a side alley – houses the **Hasior** gallery (Wed–Sat 11am–6pm, Sun 9am–3pm), presenting the work of one of the country's key postwar artists, **Władysław Hasior** (1928-1999). Building installations from piles of junk, or constructing pseudo-religious banners from pieces of metal, Hasior was typical of many Polish artists of the 1960s and 1970s in developing a quirky and often subversive form of sculpture that had little to do with the ideological dictates of the Party.

Bystre, Jaszczurówka and Swibówki

The southeastern fringes of town contain a couple of Witkiewicz's best-known creations. The **Willa Pod Jodłami** in the suburb of **BYSTRE**, 2km from the centre, is now in private hands and is hard to get a good look at, so you'd be well advised to press on 1.5km further east to the **wooden chapel** at **JASZCZURÓWKA** (hourly buses to Brzeziny pass by), a fairy-tale structure encrusted with folksy ornamentation. The traditional *górale* woodcraft from which Wirkiewicz took his inspiration is convincingly demonstrated in the brace of wooden churches and chapels that can be seen in and around the town area. Particularly worth visiting is the **Sanktuarium Matki Bożej Fatimskiej** (Sanctuary of Our Lady of Fatima) at **SWIBÓWKI**, a thirty-minute walk west of town along ul. Kościeliska, which also has a remarkable chapel at the rear of the main church complex.

Witkacy

Stanisław Ignacy Witkiewicz (1885–1939) – **Witkacy** as he's commonly known – is the most famous of the painters, writers and other artists associated with Zakopane. Born in Warsaw, the son of **Stanisław Witkiewicz**, the eminent painter and art critic who created the so-called Zakopane Style of primitivist wooden architecture, it was in the artistic ferment of turn-of-the-twentieth-century Zakopane that Witkacy spent much of his early life. After quitting Zakopane following his fiancée's suicide, in 1914, Witkacy joined an expedition to New Guinea and Australia led by a family friend, the celebrated anthropologist Bronisław Malinowski, and returned to a Europe on the verge of war. With the outbreak of World War I, the reluctant Witkacy, a Russian passport-holder, was compelled to travel to St Petersburg to train as an infantry officer. In the event, Witkacy's time in Russia proved influential to his artistic development. As well as experimenting with hallucinogenic drugs he began studying philosophy, a pursuit which strongly influenced the subsequent development of his work and art.

After surviving the war physically if not mentally unscathed, Witkacy re-established himself in Zakopane in 1918. From then on he developed his bubbling artistic talents in a host of directions, the most significant being **art**, **philosophy**, **drama** and **novel writing**. During the following fifteeen years or so, Witkacy produced over twenty plays, many of which were premiered in Zakopane by his own theatre company, formed in 1925, with several productions being staged in the epic surroundings of Morskie Oko Lake. An exponent of an avant-gardist theory of drama that extolled the virtues of "pure form" over content, Witkacy wrote dramas that are generally bizarre, almost surrealist pieces spiced up with large dollops of sex and murder. Cold-shouldered by uncomprehending 1920s Polish audiences, the Witkacy dramatic oeuvre was rediscovered – and banned for some time by communist authorities – in the 1950s, since when it's consistently ranked among the most popular in the country.

Artistically, Witkacy's main interests revolved around the famous **studio** he set up in Zakopane, where he churned out hundreds of portraits, many commissioned, of his friends and acquaintances from the contemporary artistic world. A dedicated drug-experimenter, Witkacy habitually noted, in the corner of the canvas, which drug he had been taking when painting; the self-portraits in particular reveal a disturbed, restless aesthetic sensibility. Witkacy's **novels** – by common consent almost untranslatable – are similarly fantastic doom-laden excursions into the wilder shores of the writer's consciousness, a graphic example being *Nienasycenie* ("Insatiability", 1930), which revolves around an epic futuristic struggle between a Poland ruled by the dictator Kocmołuchowicz ("Slovenly") and communist hordes from China hell-bent on invading Europe from the east.

In a sense, reality fulfilled Witkacy's worst apocalyptic nightmares. Following the Nazi invasion of Poland in 1939, the artist fled east. On learning that the Soviets were also advancing into Poland in the pincer movement agreed under the terms of the notorious Molotov-Ribbentrop Pact, a devastated Witkacy committed suicide, a legendary act that ensured his place in the pantheon of noble patriots, as well as that of great artists, in the eyes of the nation.

Eating, drinking and entertainment

Eating is never a problem in Zakopane. If you want a snack there are plenty of cafés, fast-food joints and streetside *zapiekanki* merchants to choose from, with many vendors along ul. Krupówki. **Restaurants** are plentiful, too, with a rash of places on the main street offering local food in faux-rustic surroundings – often with live folk music accompaniment. A local product worth trying at least once is the bun-shaped **sheep's milk cheeses** you see on sale all over town: try a small one first, because they're not to everyone's taste. **Bars and nightlife** are a growing feature of the town centre, though many of the venues are pretty tacky. Out of season, things are relatively quiet by 10pm.

Restaurants

Bankowo Zohylina Niżna ul. Piłsudskiego 6. Folk-style restaurant in a log building serving up hearty Polish cuisine.

Chata Zbójnicka (Robbers' Hut) ul. Jagiellońska. Restaurant just uphill from the road, decked out as a mock mountain-smuggler's den complete with log fire, and serving traditional *górale* fare. The *baranina* (roast lamb) – typical of the regional cuisine – is worth a try.

Karczma Bacówka ul. Krupówki 61. Standard Polish cuisine in a touristy, pine-furnished interior. Good for either a quick bowl of *bigos* or a more leisurely meal.

Karczma Redykołka corner of ul. Krupówki and ul. Kościeliska. A touristy traditional-style inn with waitresses dressed in local costume serving some *górale* specialities.

Obrochtówka ul. Kraszewskiego 10a. Reasonably priced and the best of the traditional-style restaurants – the *placki* (potato pancakes) in particular are excellent. Folk music some evenings.

Pizzeria Grace ul. Krupówki 2. Quick-and-easy pizzeria in a fast-foodish surroundings.

Poraj ul. Krupówki 50. Good Polish food in one of many such places along the main drag.

Smażalnia Ryb ul. Krupówki 8. Simple fish-fry place on the main drag, with al-fresco seating beside a babbling brook.

Taco Mexicano ul. Kościuski 9a. Satisfying if slightly bland range of Mexican favourites, in a pleasingly intimate suite of rooms.

Zbojecka ul. Krupówki 30. Cellar bar-restaurant on the main strip with large wooden benches draped with sheepskins, meaty grill food, and folk music live (or loud pop on the sound system, depending on your luck).

Cafés and bars

There are innumerable **drinking** dens on and around the main street, most of which succeed in sweeping in thirsty tourists due to their central location rather than any inherent atmosphere. One of the nicest places to kick off an evening is *Anemon*, Krupówki 38, a relaxing place which succeeds in being a cosy pub without trying to ape international styles. *Café Sanacja*, hidden in a small plaza just off Krupówki, attracts a laid-back clientele with its intimate atmosphere and nostalgic, interwar decor; while *Paparazzi*, a smartish cellar pub just off the main street at Galicy 8, caters for the dedicated late-night beer drinkers as well as the cocktail crowd. *Rockus*, Zaruskiego 5, underneath the Dom Turysty, is a rock-pop disco bar popular with a teen crowd, and decorated with portraits of rock greats – and Franz Kafka.

Entertainment

Entertainment varies according to season. Founded in memory of the man who staged many of his own plays here, the **Teatr im. Stanisława Witkiewicza**, at ul. Chramcówki 15 (box office in the PTTK travel agency; Mon–Fri 10am–4pm, Sat 10am–2pm; ☎018/206 3281, ⊛www.witkacy .zakopane.pl), north of the train station, stages a regular variety of performances (including a lot of Witkacy pieces, but also featuring twentieth-century greats like Miller and Camus) throughout the year – check with the tourist offices for current details. The biggest cultural event, however, is the annual international **festival of mountain folklore** held since the late 1960s, and now occupying the prime tourist season mid-August spot. A week-long extravaganza of concerts, music competitions and street parades, alongside the sizeable contingent of local *górale* ensembles, the festival draws highlander groups from a dozen or so European countries. The timing means hefty crowds are guaranteed, and there's enough going on to keep most people happy. Along with the summer musical events in the Pieniny region further east you won't get a better chance to sample the tub-thumping exuberance of a *górale* choir dressed to the nines, whooping their way through a string of joyous mountain melodies. Other local cultural events of note are the **Karol Szymanowski Music Days** held every July, featuring classical concerts by Polish and guest foreign artists in and around the town, and an **art film festival**, held every other March.

Adventure sports around Zakopane

Poles have been enjoying the winter **ski slopes** in Zakopane for as long as there's been a resort, and in the case of the *górale*, for a good deal longer. The winter season traditionally runs from December to March, though the snow has been very unpredictable in recent years. Slopes in the area vary greatly in difficulty and quality. In accordance with international standards, they are graded black, red, blue and green in order of difficulty, with the cross-country routes marked in orange. Many otherwise closed areas of the national park are open to skiers once the snows have set in, but you must remember to avoid the avalanche (*lawina*) areas marked on signs and maps, and check conditions before leaving the marked routes.

The most popular runs are on **Nosal** and **Kasprowy Wierch**, as these are the ones with ski lifts. From the village of Kuźnice (a few minutes by bus from the centre of Zakopane) you can travel by vintage gondola (over 60 years old but still reliable) to the top of Kasprowy Wierch (1967m) and ski back down to the village (5–7km, depending which trails you use) or ski to one of the surrounding valleys, Goryczkowa or Gąsienicowa, from where you can take the lift back up again. Tickets up in the gondola cost 20zł and can be bought in advance in Zakopane. The Nosal slope is short and steep (650m with a 233m height difference), while on the other side of town Gubałówka offers a much gentler slope reached by funicular. It's south-facing, so you can rent beach chairs (even in winter) and sunbathe on its slopes. You can also get **skiing lessons** – the instructors at the Nosal ski school speak English and charge 50–60zł per hour. **Ski rental** costs about 35zł per day.

Mountain-biking is a popular summertime pursuit, with legions of enthusiastic bikers heading for the slopes. After an initial flush of enthusiasm, the national park authorities woke up to the environmental threats posed by unregulated biking access to the slopes, and there are now five designated **cycle routes** within the park area: around Morskie Oko; up to Hala Gąsienicowa; to Kałatówki; along the Kościeliska and Chochołowska valleys; and up to Droga pod Reglami. In addition, there are a number of cycle routes in the hills north of Zakopane – some 650km of them in total. You can **rent mountain bikes** at a number of places around town, including Bzyck, ul. Krupówki 37 (☎018/201 4707), Rent a Bike, ul. Sienkiewicza 37 (☎018/206 4266), and the *Pod Krokwią* campsite. Bike rental costs around 50zł a day.

Paragliding, is also popular, though it's confined to areas outside the national park, including the Nosal slope, Gubałówka and Wałowa Góra. If you've never tried it before, there are several instructors in town who also rent all the necessary gear. Try Air Sport, ul. Strążyska 13 (☎018/201 3311, ⊛www.air-sport.zakopane.pl).

Finally, there's a **toboggan run** (*rynna*) on the Gubałówka slope. Rides down the 750-metre-long slide reach speeds of up to 40kph, and cost around 30zł a time.

Listings

American Express c/o Orbis, ul. Krupówki 22.
Mon–Fri 8am–6pm, Sat 8am–noon.
Banks PKO Bank, ul. Gimnazjalna 1 (Mon–Fri 10.15am–2.30pm), and Pekao, ul. Gimnazjalna 1; both accept travellers' cheques. There are also plenty of ATMs in town.
Hospital ul. Kamieniec 10 ☎018/206 2021.

Left luggage At the bus station (8am–7pm); and at the train station (24hr, with an unpredictable lunchtime pause).
Pharmacy ul. Krupówki 37 & 39; ul. Witkiewicza 3.
Police The police station is at ul. Jagiellońska 12.
Post office The main office is at ul. Krupówki.
Taxi ☎018/2087 or ☎9621.

Around Zakopane

If hiking in the Tatras proper sounds too energetic, there are a number of easy and enjoyable **walks** in the foothills and valleys surrounding Zakopane. A useful **map** to look out for is *Tatry i Podhale* (1:75,000).

Gubałówka Hill

There's an excellent view of the Tatras from the top of **Gubałówka Hill** (1120m) to the west of town (follow ul. Krupówki out from the centre). However, it's very popular, as you'll see from the long queues for the **funicular** (July & Aug 7am–9pm, Sept–June 8am–5pm; 14zł return). Walking up is possible, though strenuous (1hr). From the summit, a good day reveals the high peaks to the south in sharp relief against clear blue mountain skies. Most people linger a while over the view, browse in the souvenir shops and head back down again, but the long wooded hill ridge is the starting point of several excellent **hikes**, taking you through characteristic Podhale landscape.

To the west, from the top of the funicular, past the refreshment stop, the **trails** begin as a single path, which soon divides. Continue south along the ridge and you gradually descend to the Czarny Dunajec valley (black route), ending up at the village of **WITÓW**, around two hours' walking in all; buses back to Zakopane take fifteen minutes. Alternatively, take the north fork and it's a four-hour hike to the village of **CHOCHOŁÓW**, with its fine wooden houses and church; you can get here by two routes, either following the track (which soon becomes a road) through the village of Dzianisz, or taking the cross-country route marked *Szlak im. Powstania Chochołowskiego* on the *Tatry i Podhale* **map**.

East of the funicular, the main path leads to **PORONIN**, on the Zakopane–Kraków road, a once sleepy village now disfigured by uncontrolled holiday villa construction. A steep climb up the marked path east of the village takes you to a hilltop area with wonderful views. Continue east from here and you come to **BUKOWINA TATRZAŃSKA**, a largish village with buses back to Zakopane (15min), and the usual gaggle of **pensjonaty** in the ❸-❹ range if you want to stay.

Dolina Białego and Dolina Strążyska

For some easy and accessible valley hiking, Dolina Białego and Dolina Strążyska each provide a relaxed long afternoon's walk from Zakopane; taken together they would make an enjoyable and not over-strenuous day's outing.

Leaving Zakopane to the south, along ul. Strążyska, you reach **Dolina Strążyska** after around an hour's walk. At the end of the valley (3hr) you can climb to the **Hala Strążyska**, a beautiful high mountain pasture (1303m); the **Siklawica waterfall**, on the way, makes an enjoyable rest point, a stream coursing down from the direction of Giewont. The views are excellent too, with Mount Giewont (1694m) rearing up to the south, and to the north a wonderful panorama of Zakopane and the surrounding countryside. Walk east along the meadow to the top of **Dolina Białego** and you can descend the deep, stream-crossed valley, one of the gentlest and most beautiful in the region, continuing back to the outskirts of Zakopane (6–7hr in total).

Dolina Chochołowska and Dolina Kościeliska

Two of the loveliest valleys of the area are **Dolina Chochołowska** and **Dolina Kościeliska**, both a bus ride west of town and offering an immensely enjoyable and rewarding full day's hiking excursion. It would also be possible to combine the two, staying at the *Chochołowska* hostel (see below) or one of the mountain/shepherds' huts along the way, some of which are marked on the map. For the latter, the *Hajduk* **pension** (☎018/207 0075; ❶) in Kiry (see below) makes an excellent overnight base.

Dolina Chochołowska, the longest valley in the region, follows the course of a stream deep into the hills. From Zakopane, take a bus toward Polana Huciska, a couple of kilometres into the valley. From the car park at the head of the valley, it's a good hour's walk to the *Chochołowska* hostel, beautifully situated overlooking the meadows, with the high western Tatras and the Czech border behind. A clandestine meeting between the pope and Lech Wałęsa took place here in 1983 and is commemorated by a tableau on the wall. The steep paths up the eastern side lead to ridges that separate the valley from Dolina Kościeliska – one path, from a little way beyond the car park, connects the two valleys, making the cross trip possible.

Dolina Kościeliska is a classic beauty spot, much in evidence on postcards of the region. To get here, take the bus to the hamlet of **KIRY** and set off down the stone valley track ahead. For around 50zł a horse-drawn cart will run you down the first section of the valley to a point known as Polana Pisana, but from here on it's walkers only. A distinctive feature of Kościeliska is the caves in the limestone cliffs – once the haunts of robbers and bandits, legend has it. Take a detour off to the left from Polana Pisana – marked *jaskinia* (caves) – and you can visit various examples, including **Jaskinia Mrożna**, where the walls are permanently encased in ice.

Beyond Polana Pisana, the narrow upper valley is a beautiful stretch of crags, gushing water, caves and greenery reminiscent of the English Lake District, leading to the *Hala Ornak* **hostel**, a popular overnight stop with a **restaurant**. Day walkers return back down the valley to take the bus back to Zakopane, but if you want to continue, two marked paths lead beyond the hostel: the eastern route takes you the short distance to **Smreczyński Staw** (1226m), a tiny mountain lake surrounded by forest; the western route follows a high ridge over to Dolina Chochołowska – a demanding walk only for the fit.

The Tatras

Poles are serious mountaineers, with an established network of climbing clubs, and it's in the Tatras that everyone starts and the big names train. Most of the peaks are in the 2000–2500m range, but these unimpressive statistics belie their status, and their appearance. For these are real mountains, snowbound on their heights for most of the year and supporting a good skiing season in December and January. They are as beautiful as any mountain landscape in northern Europe, the ascents taking you on boulder-strewn paths alongside woods and streams up to the ridges, where grand, windswept peaks rise in the brilliant alpine sunshine. Wildlife thrives here: the whole area was turned into a national park in the 1950s and supports rare species such as lynx, golden eagles and brown bear, and there's a good chance of glimpsing them.

The steadily increasing volume of climbers, walkers and skiers using the slopes is having its effect on the area though, and in a bid to generate funds for local environmental protection, the park authorities have now imposed a (nominal) entry charge on all visitors entering the park area, collected at booths at the main access points to the mountains. Groups of ten people or more must have an official guide, arranged, unless you're part of a pre-booked touring group, through the park offices in Zakopane (see p.504). Tussles between the conservationist-minded park authorities and local tourism developers are also holding back **skiers**, in an attempt to protect the rich flora of the slopes, and the authorities have steadfastly refused to countenance the building of any further facilities, such as new ski lifts, within the territory of the park.

Though many of the peak and ridge climbs are for experienced climbers only, much is accessible to regular walkers, with waymarked paths which give you the top-of-the-world exhilaration of bagging a peak. For skiers, despite the relative paucity of lifts and hi-tech facilities, there are some high-quality pistes, including a dry slope running down from peaks such as **Kasprowy Wierch** and the very steep **Nosal** (see box p.510).

Afraid of their citizens catching "the Polish disease" (Solidarity), the Czechs virtually closed this part of the border in 1980, and for the next ten years, hikers were confronted with the somewhat comical sight of uniformed police sweating it out over the mountain passes. Things have eased up these days, with the current editions of the *Tatry i Podhale* **map** showing cross-border walks in great detail, though the border police are still in evidence and a number of official crossing points remain mysteriously closed to foreigners (see Basics, pp.14–15 for details). Where crossing is permitted, most foreigners just need a passport stamp, however, and the new political climate means that exploration of the whole Tatra region is possible for the first time since the war.

Hiking in the Tatras

It is as well to remember that the Tatras are an alpine range and as such demand some respect and preparation. The most important rule is to stick to the marked paths, and to arm yourself in advance with a decent **map**. The best is the *Tatrzański Park Narodowy* (1:30,000), which has all the paths accurately marked and colour-coded. You will probably want the English version, *The Tatra National Park*. This map has all you'll need – including estimated times between various points – but an alternative is the *Polskie Tatry* **guidebook**, available in English and going into detail about the main hiking routes. All the above are available from shops in Zakopane; one book you should consider picking up before you leave home is *The High Tatras* (Cicerone Press) written jointly by an Englishman and a Slovak woman, an authentic guide to hikes in the mountains aimed at the serious enthusiast. Remember never to leave the tree line (about 2000m) unless visibility is good, and when the clouds close in, start descending immediately.

Overnighting in the PTTK-run **huts** dotted across the mountains is an experience in itself. There are seven of them in all, clearly marked on the *Tatra National Park* map (for up-to-date information on openings, check at the national park office in Zakopane). In summer, the huts are packed with student backpackers from all over the country, and are an ideal place to mix in, preferably over a bottle of vodka. As they generally can't afford the beds, they kip down on the floor, and if it's really crowded you'll probably be joining them. **Food** is basic, but pricey for Poles, and most bring their own. Even if you don't want to lug large weights around the mountaintops, a supply of basic rations is a good idea as well as water. **Camping** isn't allowed in the national park area, and **rock-climbing** only with a permit – ask at the park offices (see above) for details. For anyone attempting more than a quick saunter, the right **footwear and clothing** are, of course, essential. Lastly, take a **whistle** – blow six times every minute if you need help.

The **weather** is always changeable, and you should not venture out without waterproofs and sturdy boots: most rain falls in the summer, when there may also be thunderstorms and even hail- and snow-showers. Even on a warm summer's day in the valleys, it can be below freezing at the peaks. Set out early (the weather is always better in the morning), and tell someone when and where you're going – a **weather information** service is available on ☎018/206 3019. The number of the **mountain rescue service** (Tatrzańskie Ochotnicze Pogotowie Ratunkowe) is ☎018/206 3444, though don't expect much English to be spoken.

In addition, respect the **national park rules**: don't leave any rubbish, keep to the marked paths and don't pick flowers or disturb the wild animals.

Routes

The easiest way up to the peaks is by **cable car** (July & Aug 7.30am–8pm, Sept–June 8am–5pm; 28zł return) from the hamlet of **KUŹNICE**, a three-kilometre walk or bus journey south from Zakopane along the Dolina Bystrego. In summer, the cable car is a sell-out, making advance booking at the Orbis office a virtual necessity, unless you're prepared to turn up before 8am. For the journey down, priority is always given to people who've already got tickets, but return tickets only allow you two hours at the top – this is fine if you only want to get up to Kasprowy Wierch (see below), but no good if you're planning more extended hiking. One way of avoiding the biggest queues is to make the ascent on Sunday mornings when the majority of Poles are likely to be at Mass.

Kasprowy Wierch and descents to Kuźnice

The cable car ends near the summit of **Kasprowy Wierch** (1985m), where weather-beaten signs indicate the border with Slovakia. From here, many day-trippers simply walk back down to Kuźnice through the Hala Gąsienicowa (2hr). An equally popular option is to walk up and return by cable car (2hr 30min). A rather longer alternative is to strike west to the cross-topped summit of **Giewont** (1894m), the "Sleeping Knight" that overlooks Zakopane (allow 2hr for this). Watch out if it's been raining, however, as the paths here get pretty slippery and are very worn in places. The final bit of the ascent is rocky with secured chains to aid your scramble to the top. From the summit, topped with a tall cross, the views can be spectacular on a good day. For the return, head down to Kuźnice through the Dolina Kondratowa past the *Hala Kondratowa* hostel (allow 40min to get to the hostel, then a further hour to get to the village). This downward journey is fairly easy going and the whole trip is quite feasible in a day if you start out early.

The Orła Perć and Morskie Oko

East of Kasprowy Wierch, the walking gets tougher. From **Świnica** (2300m), a strenuous ninety-minute walk, experienced hikers continue along the **Orła Perć** (Eagles' Path), a challenging, exposed ridge with spectacular views. The *Pięc Stawów* **hostel**, in the high valley of the same name, provides overnight shelter at the end (4hr).

From the hostel you can hike back down Dolina Roztoki to **Łysa Polana**, a border-crossing point with Slovakia in the valley (2hr), and get a bus back to Zakopane. An alternative is to continue east to the lake of **Morskie Oko** (Eye of the Sea; 1399m; 1hr 30min). Encircled by precipitous sheer cliff faces and alpine forest, this large glacial lake is one of the Tatras' big attractions, and one of the most popular day-trip destinations for tourists staying in Zakopane. Most people begin the journey by car or bus rather than on foot, following the road that loops east then south from Zakopane, passing through Poronin before climbing up into the Tatra foothills. It's a spectacular journey at times, with a road following a mountain ridge whose forest cover occasionally parts to reveal superb views of the Tatras. After descending towards the border crossing at Łysa Polana, the road continues a few more kilometres to its final destination, a large car park surrounded by snack stalls at **Polana Palenica**. From the car park, a fairly obvious track leads past a national park booth (charging the 2zł entrance fee to the park) and climbs slowly through the trees towards Morskie Oko, which is some 9km (1hr 45min) uphill. Horse-drawn carts (25zł per person) are on hand to ferry those tourists who can't face the walk.

The *Morskie Oko* hostel, situated by the side of the lake, serves up decent grilled-sausage-type fare, and provides a convenient base for the ascent of **Rysy** (2499m), the highest peak in the Polish Tatras. Closer to hand, on the same red-marked route is **Czarny Staw** (1580m), a lake that if anything, appears even chillier than Morskie Oko.

East of the Tatras

East of the Tatras, the mountains scale down to a succession of lower ranges – *beskidy* as they're known in Polish – stretching along the Slovak border. The walking here is less dramatic than in the Tatras, but excellent nonetheless, and the locals are a good bunch too, including *górale* and a long-established Slovak minority. The highlights of the region are the **Pieniny**, mountains hard by the Slovak border, and a raft run through the **Dunajec Gorge**, far below.

Transport in this little-known region can be a bit of a struggle, away from the immediate vicinity of **Szczawnica**, a spa town that makes the best base for exploring the Pieniny.

The Spisz region

The road east from Nowy Targ to Szczawnica is one of the most attractive in the country, following the broad valley of the Dunajec through the **Spisz**, a backwoods region whose villages are renowned for their wooden houses, churches and folk art. Annexed by Poland from the newly created Czechoslovak state in 1920, for centuries it was part of the semi-autonomous province of Spis (Slovak)/Spisz (Polish)/Zips (German) that formed part of the Hungarian kingdom. The old aura of a quiet rural backwater remains, the region's Slovak minority bearing testimony to its historic borderland position. Buses cover the route four or five times a day.

DĘBNO, 14km from Nowy Targ, boasts one of the best-known **wooden churches** in the country, a shingled, steep-roofed larch building, put together without using nails and surrounded by a charming wicket fence, with a profile vaguely reminiscent of a snail. Inside, the full length of walls and ceiling is covered with exuberant, brilliantly preserved fifteenth-century polychromy and **woodcarving.** The subjects are an enchanting mix of folk, national and religious motifs, including some fine hunting scenes and curiously Islamic-looking geometric patterns. In the centre of the building, fragments survive of the original rood screen, supporting a tree-like cross, while the original fifteenth-century altarpiece triptych features an unusually militant-looking St Catherine. In addition, there's a fine carved statue of St Nicholas, a medieval wooden tabernacle and some banners reputedly left by Jan Sobieski on his return from defeating the Turks in Vienna in 1683. The church is usually open during daylight hours; if not, local enquiries may reveal the whereabouts of the priest (who lives just over the road), who will probably open things up. For an overnight stay, there's a **youth hostel** (July–Aug) in the village.

Immediately east of Dębno lies the **Dunajec reservoir**, a controversial hydro-electric project which was opposed by many environmentalists before the valley – and a couple of its villages – were finally subsumed by water in 1997. The reservoir's dam saved much of the downriver settlements from floods later the same year, significantly decreasing the project's unpopularity with the locals. A minor road branches off to follow the southern banks of the river before arriving at Niedzica (see below), although most traffic sticks to the high ground north of the water, arriving after 12km at the turn-off to **CZORSZTYN**. Lying 2km south of the main road, this small village is overlooked by a memorable, if very ruined, **castle**. From its heights you get sweeping **views** over the valley and to the castle of Niedzica across the mouth of the Dunajec Gorge.

Niedzica and west along the Slovak border
NIEDZICA lies just across the gorge from Czorsztyn, but it's a roundabout trip by road, which involves heading back to Dębno, or southeast towards Sromowce. By public transport, Niedzica is served by bus from Nowy Targ.

The village occupies a strategic position at a major confluence of the Dunajec with a large tributary plunging down from Slovakia. Control of this valley and the border territory explains the presence of the **castle**, perched above the river. Originally raised in the fourteenth century as a stronghold on the Hungarian border, it was reconstructed in its current Renaissance style in the early 1600s, and today lies under threat from the hydroelectric scheme, which some experts believe will erode its rock foundations. It today houses the castle **museum** (Tues–Sun 9am–5pm; 4zł), with displays on the stronghold's history and a strong collection of local folk crafts. A Tintin-like folk tale associates the castle with the Incas. The wife of the last descendant of the Inca rulers allegedly lived here in the late eighteenth century, and left a hidden document detailing the legendary Inca treasure buried in Lake Titicaca in Peru – a document supposedly discovered in 1946. If you want a **place to stay**, there's the *Hotel Pieniny*, ul. Kanada 38 (☎018/262 9383, ✉pieniny@zzw-niedzica.com.pl; en-suites ❸, rooms with shared facilities ❷), or the *Pensjonat Chata Spiska*, Pod Sosnami (☎018/262 9403, ✉niedzica@ns.onet.pl; ❺), a cosy place with folksy wooden interiors.

To the west of Niedzica, a little-frequented backroad winds its way towards Nowy Targ and Zakopane through the heart of the Spisz. Most villages here were effectively cut off from the outside world well into the nineteenth century, and serfdom was only abolished here in 1931. It still feels like another world, particularly in villages like **TRYBSZ** and **ŁAPSZE** which have Slovak populations. If you get the chance, visit on a Sunday morning, when you may catch the music of the excellent local choirs. The churches in both villages are equally enjoyable – the one in Trybsz is a wooden construction whose interior is lined with a fine sequence of mid-seventeenth-century frescoes illustrating biblical scenes and the lives of the saints in colourful, naive relief.

The Pieniny

A short range of Jurassic limestone peaks, rearing above the spectacular Dunajec Gorge, the **Pieniny** offer some stiff hillwalking, but require no serious climbing to reach the 1000-metre summits. Jagged outcrops are set off by abundant greenery, the often humid mountain microclimate supporting a rich and varied flora. Like the Tatras, the Pieniny are an officially designated national park and have a network of controlled paths. The detailed *Pieniński Park Narodowy* (1:22,500) **map** is useful and is available in most tourist offices and bookshops.

The main range, a ten-kilometre stretch between Czorsztyn and Szczawnica, is the most popular hiking territory, with the peaks of Trzy Korony (Three Crowns; 982m) the big target.

The principal southern point of access to the park is Sromowce-Kąty (also the starting point for rafting trips on the Dunajec Gorge, see below), 10km southeast of Krośnica, where there's a tourist **information point** and a national park **ticket office** (2zł), accessible by five buses a day from Nowy Targ. Most hikers however start explorations of the Pieniny from Krościenko, which is served by the more frequent services operating the Nowy Targ-Szczawnica bus route.

Krościenko and the Trzy Korony

The town of **KROŚCIENKO**, a one-hour bus ride east of Nowy Targ, is a dusty, unexciting little place which would hardly merit a stopoff were it not the main starting point for **hikes** to the Trzy Korony (see below). The **PTTK office**, in the centre at ul. Jagiellońska 65 (☎018/262 3059), doles out private rooms (❷); and there's the *Hanka* holiday home at no. 55 in the same street (☎018/262 5528; ❷) – although Szczawnica, 4km down the road (see overleaf) is a better place to stay.

From the bus stop in the middle of Krościenko you can follow the signs – and in summer the packs of hikers – south on the yellow route. The path soon begins to climb through the mountainside woods, with plenty of meadows and lush clearings on the way. Around two hours from Krościenko, you'll reach **Okrąglica**, the highest peak of the **Trzy Korony**, via some chain-bannistered steps. On a clear day there's an excellent view over the whole area: the high Tatras off to the west, the slopes of Slovakia to the south, and the Dunajec Gorge far below.

Many hikers take the same route back, but two alternatives are worth considering. One is to walk to Szczawnica (p.518), a two- or three-hour trip. Head back along the route you came as far as Bajków Groń (679m), about three-quarters of the way down, and from there follow the blue path across the mountains south to Sokolica and down to the river, where you can get a boat across to the *Orlica* hostel. The other, if you want to combine the walk with the Dunajec Gorge, is to descend the mountain southwest to Sromowce Kąty (3hr), one of the two starting points for the raft trip upriver (see below).

The Dunajec Gorge

Below the heights of the Pieniny the fast-moving Dunajec twists and turns below great limestone rockfaces and craggy peaks. The river is a magnet for **canoeists**, who shoot fearlessly through the often powerful rapids; for the less intrepid, the two- to three-hour **raft trip** provides a gentler though thoroughly enjoyable version of the experience. Tourists have been rafting down these waters since the 1830s, a tradition derived in turn from the ancient practice of floating logs downriver to the mills and ports. Contrary to what the tourist brochures lead you to believe, this is not exactly white-water rafting – the journey is smooth-going, giving you the chance to appreciate the scenic surroundings of forest, fields and sheer limestone crags – the real pluses of the experience.

Run by the Polskie Stowarzyszenie Flisaków Pienińskich (Association of Pieniny Raftsmen; ☎018/262 9721, ⓦwww.flisacy.com.pl), the trips begin at **KĄTY**, a few hundred metres east of Sromowce Wyżne; regular buses run to Kąty from Szczawnica and Nowy Targ.

Weather and water levels permitting, the rafting season runs from early May to late October, operating 8am to 5pm between May and August; finishing at 4pm in September and 2pm in October. In season, rafts leave as soon as they're full, and the earlier you get here the less likely it is you'll have to queue up. Rafts run to Szczawnica at the eastern end of the gorge, where a courtesy bus will bring you back to Kąty if you so desire. Individual travellers should expect to pay about 40zł per person, although it's worth bearing in mind that most of the travel agents in Zakopane offer trips, which usually include a stop-off at Niedzica castle as well – excursions cost anything between 70-150zł depending on whether food is laid on.

The rafts are sturdy log constructions, made of five pontoons held together with rope and carrying up to ten passengers, plus two navigators (in traditional Pieniny costume). Here, as further east, the river forms the border with Slovakia, and at several points, Slovak villages face their Polish counterparts across the banks, with their own rafters and canoeists hugging the southern side of the river. After plenty of sharp twists and spectacular cliffs, the rafts end up at Szczawnica, from where buses return to Kąty until 4pm, from a stop a few minutes' walk from the landing stage.

Szczawnica

Sited on the edge of the sparkling River Dunajec below the peaks of the Pieniny, **SZCZAWNICA** is a highly picturesque example of the small spa resorts strung out in the steep valleys east of the Tatras. Once patronized by Nobel Prize-winning novelist Henryk Sienkiewicz, it's still the most visited town in the region, crowded through the summer with all types of mountain holiday-makers: canoeists setting off down the gorge, hikers heading off to the hills, industrial workers recuperating in the sanatoria.

Buses run here from both Nowy Targ (40km) and, on a slightly roundabout route, from Zakopane (50km), dropping you in the centre of town, by the river. From here it's a short walk up to the bustling square, and the staid health establishments of the **upper town**. In the communist era, Szczawnica's alkaline springwater was consumed by miners and steelworkers, now replaced by the regular brand of health-seeking tourists, Polish and foreign; casual visitors are free to wander in and sample the waters. There's little else to see in town, unless you happen to be around during *górale* folk events. The attraction for most foreign visitors lies in getting out to explore the Pieniny and the Dunajec Gorge.

You can get up onto an eastern spur of the Pieniny by taking the **chairlift** (July–Aug & Dec–April) just below the main street to the 722-metre-high Góra Palenica, which provides excellent views of the valley. There's a short downhill run and a modest snowboard park here in winter, although it's nothing for the serious winter sportsperson to get excited about.

The chairlift terminal is also the starting point for the Dunajec Gorge **foot-** and **cycle-path**, which runs westwards along the south bank of the river, crossing over into Slovakia after 3km (the border is open to walkers and cyclists until 8pm in summer, 5pm in winter), and continuing for another 9km along the banks of the gorge as far as Červeny Klåštor, the main Slovakian starting point for rafting trips. You can rent bikes at the chairlift terminal.

You should at least follow the path for the 2km it takes you to reach the west end of Szczawnica village; here you get excellent **views** of the sheer cliffs marking the eastern end of the Dunajec Gorge, from which the bobbing forms of rafts emerge at regular intervals.

Practicalities

Tourist information duties are currently carried out by the PTTK office, ul. Główna 1 (Mon–Fri 8am–3pm; ☎018/262 2332), which sells hiking maps and books private rooms (❶) – otherwise, just look out for *noclegi* signs. **Hotel** accommodation comes in all shapes and sizes; in the upper part of the resort, *Górnik*, Zdrojowa 4 (☎018/262 2411, ⓦwww.sanatoriumgornik.com.pl) is a workers' rest-home with a mixed bag of en-suites (❺) and rooms with shared facilities (❷); while *Hamernik*, ul. Kowalczyk 3b (☎018/262 1301; ❸), is a charming chalet-style pension. Handy for the lower part of town is the recently renovated *Hotel Pod Kolejką*, right by the chairlift terminal at Główna 7 (☎018/262 2724; ❹). A more spartan alternative is the *Orlica* PTTK **hostel** at ul. Pienińska 12 (☎018/262 2248), right on the edge of the gorge, a kilometre south of the raft disembarkation point. You can **camp** at the *Orlica*, or at *Pole Namiotowe* (literally "tent site"), Pienińska 6.

The *Halka* **restaurant**, on the main street at ul. Główna 2, is a cheap source of no-nonsense Polish nosh – otherwise there are loads of snackbars along the main strip.

The Pieniny górale highlanders

Like the Podhale, the Pieniny region is populated by **górale highlanders** who for much of the century have been migrating to the United States in great numbers; it's not uncommon to come across broad Chicago accents in the villages. To the outsider, the main distinction between the Podhale and Pieniny clans is the colours of their **costumes** – the reds, browns and blacks of the western Podhale giving way to the purple-blues of the Pieniny decorated jackets. Like their Podhale neighbours, the *górale* of the Pieniny dress up traditionally on Sundays and for other major community events – weddings, festivals and the like. The men's costume consists of tight-fitting woollen trousers decorated with coloured strips of embroidery (*parzenice*), high leather cummerbund-type bands round the waist, decorated jackets and waistcoats and a feather-topped hat. The women wear thin woollen blouses, thickly pleated skirts festooned with flowers and brightly coloured headscarves. The men also go in for thick embossed leather shoes (*kierpce*) of the type you can pick up in the tourist shops. Besides costume, the clans have their own distinct **dialects**, and even Polish-speakers find it hard to follow a Pieniński in full swing.

Music is the most accessible aspect of their culture. In summer, you may well catch vocal ensembles at open-air folk evenings held in Szczawnica or Krościenko – a good excuse for everyone to dress up and sing their hearts out. While the harmonies and vocal style are similar in both *górale* regions, the Pieniński make more use of instruments – violins and a thumping bass in particular – to create a sound that has marked similarities to Slovak and Hungarian country styles. The visiting crowds are overwhelmingly Polish at these traditional old-time romps, and for the atmosphere alone it's well worth joining them.

Dolina Homole and Jaworki

A short local excursion worth considering is to the **Dolina Homole**, 8km east of Szczawnica. This is a peaceful valley of wooded glades and streams, and you can walk up to the surrounding hilltops in less than two hours. There's a PTTK campsite up here too.

From Szczawnica, it's a fifteen-minute bus ride east to the village of **JAWORKI**, starting point for the walk and an interesting example of the ethnic and religious twists characterizing the eastern hill country. At first sight, the late eighteenth-century **church**, a cavernous construction with an elaborately decorated balcony, looks like a regular Catholic building, but a glance at the iconostasis behind the altar indicates a different history. Although now Roman Catholic, it was originally a Uniate *cerkiew*, in what was the westernmost point of Lemk settlement in Poland (see box pp.368–369). Today only a couple of Lemk families remain. If you find the church closed, ask for the key from the house next door. A basic **bar/restaurant** (closed Mon) in the village serves fine fish dishes and Okocim beer.

Travel details

Trains

Częstochowa to: Katowice (hourly; 1–2hr); Kielce (10 daily; 2hr); Kraków (1 daily; 2–3hr); Łódź (8 daily; 2–3hr); Warsaw (8 daily; 3–4hr).
Kielce to: Częstochowa (10 daily; 2hr); Katowice (4 daily; 4hr); Kraków (5 daily; 2–3hr); Łódź (1 daily; 4hr); Lublin (4 daily; 5–6hr); Warsaw (12 daily; 3–4hr).
Kraków to: Białystok (1 daily; 10hr); Bydgoszcz (3 daily; 7–9hr); Częstochowa (8 daily; 2–4hr); Gdańsk (3 daily; 5–11hr); Katowice (15 daily; 1hr 30min–2hr); Kielce (11 daily; 2–3hr); Krynica (8 daily; 5–6hr); Lublin (3 daily; 5–7hr); Nowy Sącz (9 daily; 3–4hr; 1 express); Poznań (6 daily; 7–8hr); Przemyśl (10 daily; 3–5hr; 1 express); Rzeszów (10 daily; 2–3hr); Szczecin (5 daily; 12–14hr); Tarnów (10 daily; 2hr); Warsaw (15 daily; 2hr 30min–6hr; expresses every hour from 6.15am–12.15pm, every 2hrs 2.15–6.15pm); Wrocław (12 daily; 4–6hr); Zakopane (10 daily; 2–5hr; 1 express).
Zakopane to: Częstochowa (3 daily; 7–8hr; sleepers); Gdańsk (1 daily; 12hr; sleeper); Katowice (2–4 daily; 4–6hr); Kraków (15 daily; 3–5hr); Warsaw (2 daily; 5–12hr).

Buses

Kielce to: Kraków (7 daily; 2hr 30min); Łódź (7 daily; 3hr); Sandomierz (3 daily; 2hr); Święty Krzyż (5 daily; 1hr); Warsaw (4 daily; 4hr).
Kraków to: Cieszyn (7 daily; 3hr); Kalvaria Zebrzydowska (every 30min; 40min); Kielce (7 daily; 2hr 30min); Nowy Targ (12 daily; 1–2hr); Ojców (Mon–Fri 8 daily, Sat & Sun 6 daily; 45min); Sandomierz (2 daily; 4–5hr); Oświęcim-Auschwitz (9 daily; 1hr 30min); Tarnów (15 daily; 1hr–1hr 30min); Wadowice (every 30min; 1hr 20min); Zakopane (12 daily; 2hr 30min–3hr); Zamość (2 daily; 6–8hr).
Nowy Targ to Niedzica (5 daily; 40min); Sromowce Kąty (5 daily; 1hr); Szczawnica (10 daily; 1hr).
Szczawnica to: Jaworki (Mon–Fri 10 daily, Sat & Sun 7 daily; 20min).
Wadowice to : Bielsko-Biała (hourly; 1hr 15min); Kalvaria Zebrzydowska (every 30min; 40min); Kraków (every 30min; 1hr 20min); Zawoja (2 daily; 1hr 20min).
Zakopane to: Bielsko-Biała (3 daily; 2hr 30min–4hr); Katowice (2 daily; 4hr); Kraków (12 daily; 2hr 30min–3hr); Lublin (1 daily; 8hr); Nowy Sącz (3 daily; 1–2hr); Nowy Targ (every 30min; 40min); Polana Palenica (Jul–Aug 20 daily, June & Sept 12 daily, Oct–May 6 daily; 45min); Rzeszów (1 daily; 3–4hr); Szczawnica (5 daily; 1hr 20min); Warsaw (1 daily; 8–9hr).

Flights

Kraków to: Gdańsk (1 daily; 2hr); Warsaw (1–3 daily; 1hr).

International flights

Kraków to: Amsterdam (1 daily; 3hr 20min); Berlin (1 daily; 1hr 30min); Frankfurt (1 daily; 2hr), London (1 daily; 3hr 30min); New York (4 weekly; 14hr); Paris (4 weekly; 3hr 20min), Rome (3 weekly; 3hr 10min), Vienna (1 daily; 1hr 20min) and Zürich (1 daily; 2hr).

International trains

Kraków to: Berlin (2 daily; 9hr); Bratislava (1 daily; 8hr), Bucharest (1 daily; 25hr); Budapest (1 daily; 11hr); Kiev (1 daily; 22hr); Odessa (1 daily; 26hr); Prague (1 daily; 8hr 30min); Vienna (2 daily; 7hr).

International buses

Kraków to: Berlin (1 daily; 12hr); Budapest (2 weekly; 10hr); London (1 daily; 28hr); Paris (1 daily; 25hr); Rome (1 daily; 25hr); Vienna (1 daily; 10hr).

Silesia

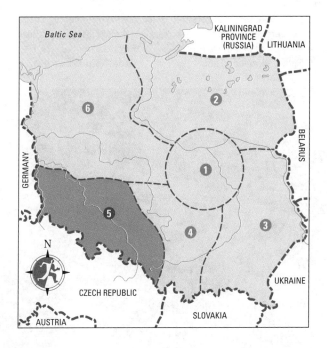

Baltic Sea

KALININGRAD
PROVINCE
(RUSSIA)

LITHUANIA

BELARUS

GERMANY

N

CZECH REPUBLIC

AUSTRIA

SLOVAKIA

UKRAINE

Highlights

Silesia

n Poland it's known as *Śląsk*, in the Czech Republic as *Slezsko*, in Germany as *Schlesien*: all three countries hold part of the frequently disputed province that's called in English **Silesia**. Since 1945, Poland has had the best of the argument, holding all of it except for a few of the westernmost tracts, a dominance gained as compensation for the Eastern Territories, which were incorporated into the USSR in 1939 and never returned.

Silesia presents a strange dichotomy. On the one hand it offers some of the most bewitching countryside in the whole of Poland, thanks in large part to the fir-clad mountains and rippling hills that form the province's border with the Czech Republic. On the other hand Silesia is notoriously scarred by ill-planned industrial development, its lowland regions peppered with bleak grey towns – especially the huge **Katowice** conurbation in the southeast.

Best place to begin exploring the region is Silesia's chief city, **Wrocław**, an enticing cosmopolitan centre which combines modern commercial bustle with the attractions of a medieval Stare Miasto. The landscape around Wrocław is largely made up of level, undramatic arable terrain, and it's best to make a beeline for the mountains to the south and west – where the Sudeten chain contains some of the most popular recreation areas in the country. Of these, the **Karkonosze national park** is the easiest to reach from Wrocław, with the regional centre of **Jelenia Góra** providing access to the skiing and hiking resorts of **Karpacz** and **Szklarska Poręba**. Slightly further east, the **Kłodzko region**'s outlying massifs provide some of Poland's best walking country, with refined old health resorts like **Kudowa-Zdroj**, **Lądek-Zdrój** and **Międzygórze** offering everything from spa treatments to winter sports. In the extreme southeastern corner of Silesia, and usually accessed from Katowice, the **Beskid mountains** fold their limbs around the up-and-coming ski resort of **Szczyrk** and the futuristic rest-cure hotels of **Ustroń**.

Accommodation price codes

The accommodation listed in this book has been given one of the following price codes, based, unless stated otherwise, on the cost of the cheapest double room in high season. For more details see p.39.

❶ under 60zł	❹ 120–160zł	❼ 300–400zł
❷ 60–90zł	❺ 160–220zł	❽ 400–600zł
❸ 90–120zł	❻ 220–300zł	❾ over 600zł

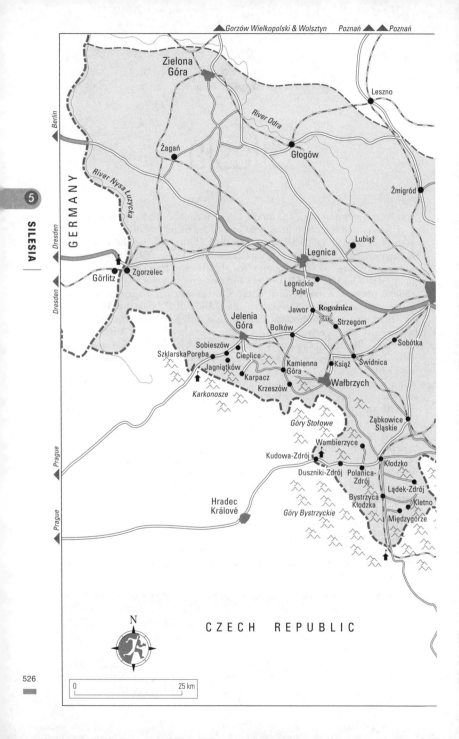

Zielona
Góra

Leszno

Berlin ◄

River Odra

Żagań

Głogów

Żmigród

River Nysa Łużycka

GERMANY

Dresden ◄

Lubiąż

Legnica

Görlitz   Zgorzelec

Legnickie
Pole

Dresden ◄

Jawor   Rogoźnica

Jelenia
Góra   Bolków   Strzegom

Sobótka

Sobieszów
SzklarskaPoręba   Cieplice   Kamienna   Książ   Świdnica
Jagniątków   Góra
Karpacz   Wałbrzych

Krzeszów

Karkonosze

Ząbkowice
Śląskie

Góry Stołowe

Wambierzyce

Kudowa-Zdrój
Kłodzko

Duszniki-Zdrój   Polanica-
Zdrój

Prague ◄   Lądek-Zdrój
                            Bystrzyca   Kletno
Hradec   Kłodzka
Králové   Góry Bystrzyckie   Międzygórze

Prague ◄

N

CZECH   REPUBLIC

526

0   25 km

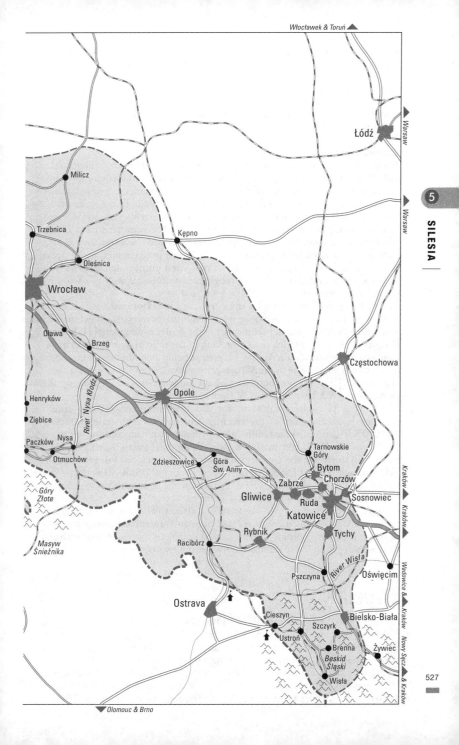

Travelling from one mountain region to another you'll pass through old ducal capitals like as **Legnica**, **Świdnica**, **Brzeg**, **Opole** and **Cieszyn**. The last one possesses an attractive small-town air, while some of the others seem indifferent to their historical heritage. Many of the province's finest surviving monuments are to be found in these towns; other slightly less accessible sights are the medieval fortifications of **Paczków**, south of Wrocław, and the Baroque monasteries of **Legnickie Pole** and outstanding **Krzeszów**, both in the west of the province.

Some history

Along with Wielkopolska and Małopolska, Silesia was a key component of the early Polish nation. Following the collapse of the country's monarchical system, the duke of Silesia, a member of the Piast dynasty, sometimes served as Poland's uncrowned king. However, this system fell by the wayside in the wake of the Tatar invasions in the thirteenth century, and the duchy was divided into **Lower** and **Upper Silesia**, the northwestern and southeastern parts of the province respectively. As the succeeding dukes divided their territory among their sons, Silesia became splintered into eighteen principalities: hence what you see today is the legacy of a series of pint-sized former capitals, each with its fair share of churches and other religious institutions as well as a few surviving castles and palaces.

As each line died out, its land was incorporated into **Bohemia**, which eventually took over the entire province when the Piasts were extinguished in 1675 – by which time it had itself become part of the Austrian-dominated **Habsburg Empire**. In 1740, Frederick the Great, king of the militaristic state of **Prussia**, launched an all-out war on Austria, his pretext being a dubious claim his ancestors had once had to one of the Silesian principalities. After changing hands several times, all but the southern part of the province was taken over by the Prussians in 1763, becoming part of Bismarck's Germany in 1871.

In 1921 a plebiscite resulted in the industrial heartlands of the eastern province becoming part of the recently resurrected Polish state. A further 860,000 Silesians opted for Polish rather than German nationality when given the choice in 1945, and displaced Poles from the Eastern Territories were brought in to replace the Germans who were now evacuated from the region. Yet, although postwar Silesia has developed a strongly Polish character, people are often bilingual and some consider their prime loyalty to lie with Silesia rather than Poland. It was only as a result of international pressure that the German government decided not to stake a claim to Silesia as part of the unification talks; notwithstanding the November 1990 treaty confirming the borders, the issue will probably only be buried completely when Poland manages to close the gap in living standards between the two countries.

Wrocław

Lower Silesia's historic capital, **WROCŁAW** is the fourth-largest city in Poland with a population of 664,000. There's an exhilarating big city feel to it, yet behind this animated appearance lies an extraordinary story of ruin and regeneration. Its special nature comes from the fact that it contains the souls of two great cities. One of these is the city that has long stood on this spot, Slav by origin but for centuries German (who knew it as Breslau). The other is **Lwów** (now L'viv), capital of the Polish Ukraine, which was annexed by the

Soviets in 1939 and retained by them in 1945. After the war, its displaced population was encouraged to take over the severely depopulated Breslau, which had been confiscated from Germany and offered them a ready-made home.

Part re-creation of Lwów, part continuation of the tradition of Breslau, postwar Wrocław has a predominantly industrial character. However, there's ample compensation for this in the old city's core. The multinational influences which shaped it are graphically reflected in its architecture: the huge Germanic brick **Gothic churches** that dominate the Stare Miasto centre are intermingled with Flemish-style Renaissance mansions, palaces and chapels of Viennese Baroque, and boldly utilitarian public buildings from the early years of the twentieth century. The tranquillity of the parks, gardens and rivers – which are crossed by over one hundred **bridges** – offers a ready escape from the urban bustle, while the city has a vibrant cultural scene, its **theatre** tradition enjoying worldwide renown.

Some history

The origins of Wrocław are unknown. There may well have been a community here in Roman times, but the earliest documentary evidence is a ninth-century record of a Slav market town called **Wratislavia** situated on a large island at the point where the sand-banked shallows of the River Odra were easily crossed. Subsequently, this became known as **Ostrów Tumski** (Cathedral Island) in honour of the bishopric founded here in 1000 by Bolesław the Brave.

German designs on Wratislavia came to the fore in 1109, when the army of Emperor Henry V was seen off by Bolesław the Wrymouth. The site of the battlefield became known as **Psie Pole** (Dogs' Field), which today is one of the city's five administrative districts; the name supposedly arose because the Germans retreated in such chaos that they could not retrieve their dead, leaving the carcasses to the local canine population.

This proved to be only a temporary setback to German ambitions. Immediately after the creation of the duchy of Lower Silesia on the death of Bolesław the Wrymouth in 1138, German settlers were encouraged to develop a new town on the southern bank of the river. Destroyed by the Tatars in 1241, this was soon rebuilt on the grid pattern which survives to the present day. In 1259 the city, now known as **Breslau**, became the capital of an independent duchy. It joined the Hanseatic League, and its bishop became a prince of the Holy Roman Empire of Germany, ruling over a territory centred on Nysa.

The duchy lasted only until 1335, when Breslau was annexed by the **Bohemian kings**, who had sufficient clout to rebuff Kazimierz the Great's attempts to reunite it with Poland. During the two centuries of Bohemian rule the mixed population of Germans, Poles and Czechs lived in apparent harmony, and the city carried out the construction of its huge brick churches. Most of these were transferred to Protestant use at the Reformation, which managed to take root even though the Bohemian crown passed in 1526 to the staunchly Catholic **Austrian Habsburgs**. However, Breslau paid heavily for the duality of its religious make-up during the Thirty Years' War, when its economy was devastated and its population halved.

The years of Austrian rule saw Breslau become increasingly Germanized, a process accelerated when it finally fell to Frederick the Great's **Prussia** in 1763. It became Prussia's most important city after Berlin, gaining a reputation as one of the most loyal linchpins of the state during the Napoleonic wars, when the French twice occupied it, only to be driven out. In the nineteenth

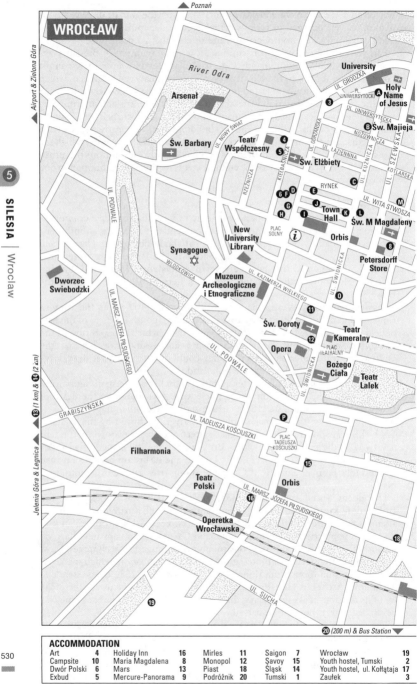

SILESIA | Wrocław

5

WROCŁAW

▲ Poznań

River Odra

University

UL GRODZKA

Airport & Zielona Góra ▲

Arsenał

PL.
UNIWERSYTECKI Ⓐ

Holy
Name
of Jesus

③

Św. Barbary

Teatr
Współczesny

UL. NOWY ŚWIAT

RZEŹNICZA

④

⑤

KIEŁBAŚNICZA

UL. ODRZAŃSKA

UL. UNIWERSYTECKA

Ⓑ Św. Majieja

NOŻOWNICZA

UL. ŁAZIENNA

Św. Elżbiety

RYNEK

Ⓒ

UL. KUŹNICZA

KOTLARSKA

UL. SZEWSKA

Ⓔ

UL. WITA STWOSZA

Ⓜ

⑥ Ⓓ

UL. PODWALE

Ⓖ

Ⓗ

Ⓙ

Ⓘ

Town
Hall

Ⓚ

Ⓛ

Św. M Magdaleny

Synagogue
✡

WŁODKOWICA

New
University
Library

PLAC
SOLNY

ⓘ

Orbis

⑧

Dworzec
Swiebodzki

Muzeum
Archeologiczne
i Etnograficzne

UL. KAZIMIERZA WIELKIEGO

Petersdorff
Store

Jelenia Góra & Legnica ▲ ⑬ (1 km) & ⑭ (2 km) ▲

UL. MARSZ. JÓZEFA PIŁSUDSKIEGO

Ⓞ

UL. ŚWIDNICKA

⑪

Św. Doroty

⑫

Opera

Teatr
Kameralny

PLAC
TEATRALNY

UL. PODWALE

Bożego
Ciała

Teatr
Lalek

UL. ŚWIDNICKA

GRABISZYŃSKA

UL. TADEUSZA KOŚCIUSZKI

Ⓟ

PLAC
TADEUSZA
KOŚCIUSZKI

Filharmonia

⑮

Teatr
Polski

Orbis

⑯

UL. MARSZ. JÓZEFA PIŁSUDSKIEGO

⑱

Operetka
Wrocławska

UL. SUCHA

⑲

⑳ (200 m) & Bus Station ▼

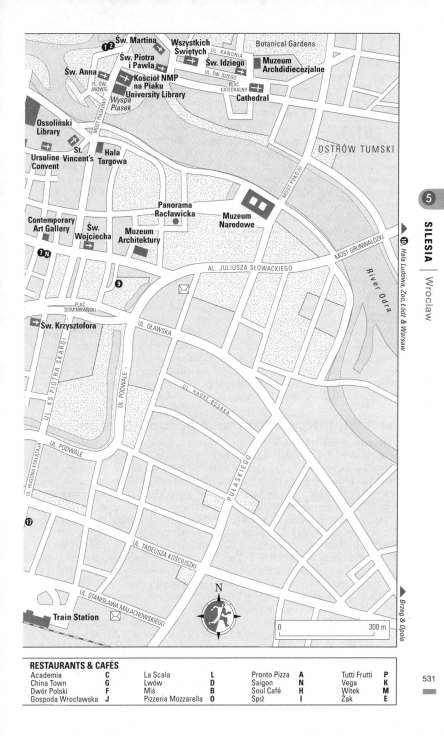

Św. Martina

Wszystkich
Świętych

UL. KANONIA

Botanical Gardens

Św. Piotra
i Pawła

Św. Idziego

Muzeum
Archdidiecezjalne

Św. Anna

PL. ŚW.
JADWIG

Kościół NMP
na Piaku

UL. ŚW. IDZEGO

University Library

Wyspa
Piasek

PLAC
KATEDRALNY

Cathedral

Ossoliński
Library

MOST PIASKOWY

OSTRÓW TUMSKI

St.
Ursuline Vincent's
Convent

Hala
Targowa

MOST POKOJU

Contemporary
Art Gallery

Św.
Wojciecha

Panorama
Racławicka

Muzeum
Narodowe

Muzeum
Architektury

MOST GRUNWALDZKI

AL. JULIUSZA SŁOWACKIEGO

River Odra

PLAC
DOMINIKAŃSKI

Św. Krzysztofora

UL. OŁAWSKA

UL. KS PIOTRA SKARGI

UL. PODWALE

UL. HAUKE-BOSAKA

UL. PODWALE

UL. HUGONA KOŁŁATAJA

PUŁASKIEGO

UL. TADEUSZA KOŚCIUSZKI

N

UL. STANISŁAWA MAŁACHOWSKIEGO

Train Station

0   300 m

Brzeg & Opole

RESTAURANTS & CAFÉS

Academia	**C**	La Scala	**L**	Pronto Pizza	**A**	Tutti Frutti	**P**
China Town	**G**	Lwów	**D**	Saigon	**N**	Vega	**K**
Dwór Polski	**F**	Miś	**B**	Soul Café	**H**	Witek	**M**
Gospoda Wrocławska	**J**	Pizzeria Mozzarella	**O**	Spiż	**I**	Żak	**E**

century it grew enormously with the Industrial Revolution, becoming one of the largest cities of the German nation.

After World War I, Breslau's **Polish community** held a series of strikes in protest at their exclusion from the plebiscite held elsewhere in Silesia to determine the boundaries of Poland. Being only twenty thousand strong and outnumbered by thirty to one, their actions made little impact. Nor did Breslau figure among the targets of Polish leaders when looking for possible gains at the expense of a defeated Nazi Germany. In the event, they gained it by default. The Nazis made the suicidal decision, on retreating from the Eastern front, to turn the entire city into a fortress. It managed to hold out for four months against the Red Army, only capitulating on May 6, the day before the unconditional surrender. However, street fighting had left seventy percent of the city in ruins, with three-quarters of the civilian population having fled west.

The subsequent **return to Poland** of this huge city, rechristened with the modern Polish version of its original name, shocked the Germans more than any other of their many territorial losses. Its second transformation occurred much faster than that of seven centuries earlier: over the next few years, most of the remaining German citizens were shunted westward, while the inhabitants of Lwów were transferred here across Poland, bringing many of their institutions with them.

A relatively modest amount of government aid was made available for the **restoration of the city**, much of which remained in ruins for decades. Nonetheless, a distinctive and thoroughly Polish city has gradually emerged, one whose revival finally seemed complete in the 1980s when its population level surpassed the prewar figure of 625,000. Wrocław's riverbank areas suffered serious damage in 1997, when disastrous **flooding** threatened much of southwestern Poland and the Czech Republic, although the affected areas were speedily patched up, and you won't see much evidence of it today.

Arrival, information and getting around

The main **train station**, Wrocław Główny – a mock-Moorish structure that is itself one of the city's sights – faces the broad boulevard of ul. Józefa Piłsudskiego, about fifteen minutes' walk south of the centre. The main **bus station** (Dworzec PKS) is on ul. Sucha, at the back of the train station. Bus #406 runs roughly once an hour between the bus station and the **airport**, which lies in the suburb of Strachowice, 10km west of the centre.

The **tourist information** office at Rynek 14 (Mon–Fri 9am–5pm, Sat 10am–2pm; ☏071/344 3111) has maps and leaflets, and can advise on accommodation. Although updated less frequently than its sister publications in Warsaw and Kraków, *Wrocław in Your Pocket* (6zł; ⓦwww.inyourpocket.com), available from kiosks and bookstores, is an indispensable guide to the city's restaurant and bar scene and includes the usual wealth of practical tips. If your Polish is up to it, there is plenty of listings information in the monthly *Informator Wrocławski*, available at newsstands. Otherwise, you can find information online at ⓦwww.wroclaw.pl, ⓦwww.wroclaw.com or ⓦwww.um.wroc.pl.

Trams cover almost the entire built-up area of Wrocław; the #0, a circular route round the central area, makes an easy introduction to the city. A pair of historic trams, known as *Jaś i Małgosia* (Hänsel and Gretel) run throughout the summer. Tram and bus **tickets** cost 1.80zł each; express line bus tickets cost 2.50zł; and night services are 3.60zł. Tickets are purchased from kiosks and shops displaying the MPK (local transport authority) sign.

Accommodation

Wrocław has **accommodation** to suit every taste and pocket, although the central hotels are increasingly charging Western prices, forcing budget travellers out towards the suburbs, or into the city's two hostels. There is no especially busy time of year, and most of the business-oriented hotels offer significant weekend reductions – be sure to ask when you phone. Avoid the (allegedly) three-star hotels near the train station like the *Europejski* and the *Polonia* – unless you delight in being overcharged for crummy communist-era accommodation.

The most central **youth hostel** is a couple of minutes' walk north of the main station at ul. Hugona Kołłątaja 20 (℡071/343 8856). It's a rather soulless place, offering mixed six-bed rooms or twenty-bed dorms, but it's equipped with clean showers and toilets. Beds are 30zł each, but there's a 10am–5pm lockout and a 10pm curfew. Much preferable is the new **HI hostel** occupying one wing of the *Hotel Tumski* (see overleaf; ℡071/322 6099; Ⓦwww.hotel-tumski.com.pl), which offers cramped but modern dorms for 35zł per person.

There's a **campsite** with chalets (❷) to rent on the east side of town near the Olympic Stadium at al. Ignacego Paderewskiego 35 (May–Sept; ℡071/348 46 51) – tram #17 from the train station.

Around the train station

Holiday Inn ul. Piłsudskiego 49/57 ℡071/787 0000, Ⓦwww.holiday-inn.pl/wroclaw. The top business address in town, with the standards of comfort and service that you would expect at this price. Big weekend discounts. ❾

Piast ul. Piłsudskiego 98 ℡071/343 0033. Conveniently situated opposite the train station, but be prepared for tired-looking musty rooms, and a certain amount of noise from the nearby main road and from other guests. Acceptable for a short stay. Doubles with shared facilities as well as those with, with en-suite bathrooms. ❸–❹

Podróżnik ul. Sucha 1-11 ℡071/373 2845. Simple no-frills place situated above the bus station's ticket hall, offering neat, if smallish, en-suites. ❹

Savoy pl. Kościuszki 19 ℡071/340 3219. Simple en-suite rooms located midway between the train station and the Stare Miasto. Fills up fast due to its attractive pricing, so ring in advance. ❹

Wrocław ul. Powstańców Śląskich 7 ℡071/372 4466, Ⓔhwroclaw@orbis.pl. The most prestigious of the Orbis group of hotels in town, located a short distance southwest of the main train station. Rooms are up to international business standard, with air conditioning, minibar and satellite TV. Indoor swimming pool on site. ❼

The Stare Miasto centre

Art ul. Kiełbaśnicza 20 ℡071/378 7100, Ⓦwww.arthotel.wroc.pl. Stylish and comfortable downtown hotel, offering en-suite rooms with satellite TV and minibar. ❽

Dwór Polski ul. Kiełbaśnicza 2 ℡071/372 3415, Ⓔdworpol@wr.onet.pl. Small and classy establishment offering quality service and twenty well-equipped, slightly old-fashioned double rooms or suites. ❼

Exbud ul. Kiełbaśnicza 24–25 ℡071/34 10916, Ⓦwww.exbud-hotel.wroc.pl. Bright, fully equipped rooms in a modern building, just off the main square. ❽

Maria Magdalena ul. św. Marii Magdaleny 2 ℡071/341 0898, Ⓦwww.hotel-mm.com.pl. Spanking new and rather plush hotel with all the creature comforts, a stone's throw from the Rynek. ❽

Mercure-Panorama pl. Dominikański 1 ℡071/323 2700, Ⓔpanorama@orbis.pl. Flashy glass-and-steel four-star, conveniently located on the eastern side of the Stare Miasto centre. A reasonable business-standard choice. ❽

Mirles ul. Kazimierza Wielkiego 45 ℡071/341 0873. One of the few inexpensive choices in the city centre, housed on the top floor of a building that looks a bit like a nineteenth-century office block. Modernized two- and three-bed rooms with shared facilities. Booking essential. ❸

Monopol ul. Modrzejewskiej 2 ℡071/343 7041, Ⓔmonopol@orbis.pl. Least expensive of the city's Orbis hotels, a good-looking *fin-de-siècle* establishment with a wonderful atmosphere of faded grandeur. Rooms come with creaky parquet floors, a range of olde-worlde furnishings – and satellite TV. En-suites as well as rooms with shared bathrooms. ❹–❼

Saigon ul. Wita Stwosza 22/23 ℡071/344 2881. Good-value establishment above the eponymous Vietnamese restaurant right in the centre of the

Stare Miasto. Rooms are plain but cosy and come with shower, phone and TV. ❻

Tumski Wyspa Słodowa 10 ☎071/322 6099, ⓦwww.hotel-tumski.com.pl. Brand new hotel just north of the town centre enjoying a quiet riverside location on Wyspa Piasek. Pristine pastel-coloured rooms with shower and TV. ❻

Zaułek pl. Uniwersytecki 15 ☎071/341 0046, ⓦwww.hotel.uni.wroc.pl. Charming university-run place with intimate feel. En-suite rooms with TV and minibar come with chintzy wallpaper and homely pine furnishings. ❼

Out of the centre

Mars ul. Żelazna 46 ☎071/365 2000. Refurbished tower block 2km southwest of the centre, with sparsely furnished but spick-and-span rooms. One WC/bathroom shared between every two rooms. Tram #5 from opposite the train station to the Pereca stop. ❸

Śląsk ul. Oporowska 62 ☎071/365 2002. Sports hotel in a park 3km southwest of the main train station and served by trams #4, #5 and #20. Rooms come with showers and TV or shared facilities . ❷–❹

The City

Wrocław's **central area**, laid out in the usual grid pattern, is delineated by the **River Odra** to the north and by the bow-shaped **ul. Podwale** to the south – the latter following the former fortifications whose defensive moat, now bordered by a shady park, still largely survives. The main concentration of shops and places of entertainment is found at the southern end of the centre and in the streets leading south to the train station. Immediately bordering the Odra at the northern fringe of the centre is the **university quarter**. Beyond are a number of peaceful traffic-free islets, formerly sandbanks where the shallow river was once forded, and now linked to each other and to the mainland by graceful little bridges which add a great deal to the city's appeal. The southern part of the much larger island of **Ostrów Tumski**, further east, is the city's ecclesiastical heart, with half a dozen churches and its own distinctive hubbub. Further north is an area of solidly nineteenth-century tenements, while the city's main green belt lies off the eastern side of the island.

The Rynek

Fittingly, the core of the Stare Miasto's grid is occupied by the vast space of the **Rynek**, its centre taken up by the superb edifice of the **town hall** and surrounded for the most part by the equally grandly renovated facades of former town houses. No longer a place of commerce, it's now a tourist and leisure-oriented zone, given over mainly to museums, restaurants, alfresco cafés, bookshops and, a telling new development, antique shops.

Among the cluster of modern buildings to the rear of the New Town Hall is the celebrated **Laboratory Theatre** founded by **Jerzy Grotowski**. For two decades this was one of the most famous centres for experimental drama in the world, although it was dissolved following Grotowski's emigration to Italy in 1982. In its place is a research institute devoted to Grotowski's work, and you can see an exhibition on the original theatre if you ask at the offices down the alley to the left. The tiny studio theatre, on the second floor of the building, is still used for experimental performances by visiting actors: check the billboard outside for details.

Of the mansions lining the main sides of the Rynek, those on the south and western sides are the most distinguished and colourful. Among several built in the self-confident style of the Flemish Renaissance, no. 2, the **Pod Gryfami** (Griffin House), is particularly notable. No. 5, with a reserved Mannerist facade, is known as the **Dwór Wazów** (Waza Court), in honour of the tradition that it was the place where King Zygmunt Waza stayed during secret negotiations for his marriage to Anna von Habsburg. The mansion's cellars have been converted into the *Dwór Polski* restaurant, (see "Restaurants", p.544).

Next door, at no. 6, is the **Pod Złotym Słońcem** (House of the Golden Sun), behind whose Baroque frontage is a suite of Renaissance rooms containing the **Muzeum Sztuki Medalierskiej** (Museum of the Art of Medal Making; Tues–Sat 11am–5pm, Sun 10am–6pm; 4zł); its shop sells examples of the craft. The last striking house in the block is no. 8, again Baroque but preserving parts of its thirteenth-century predecessor; it's known as the **Pod Siedmioma Elektorami** (House of the Seven Electors), a reference to the seven grandees superbly depicted on the facade who elected the Holy Roman emperor, Leopold I. A black Habsburg eagle cowers menacingly over the building's doorway.

The town hall

The magnificent **town hall**, symbol of the city for the last seven centuries, was originally a modest one-storey structure erected in the wake of the ruinous Tatar sacking and progressively expanded down the years. Its present appearance dates largely from the fifteenth-century high point of local prosperity, when the south aisle was added and the whole decorated in an elaborate late-Gothic style. The international mix of stylistic influences reflects the city's status as a major European trading centre, creating one of the city's finest and most venerable buildings.

The **east facade** is the one which catches the eye and figures in all Wrocław's promotion material. It features an astronomical clock from 1580 and an elaborate central gable decorated with intricate terracotta patterns and exquisite pinnacles. In contrast, the west facade (the main entrance) is relatively plain, save for the octagonal Gothic belfry with its tapering Renaissance lantern. The intricate carvings embellishing the **south facade** are worthy of more protracted scrutiny, lined up between the huge Renaissance windows crowned with their spire-like roofs. Along its length are filigree friezes of animals and foliage as well as effigies of saints and knights, mostly nineteenth-century pastiches, overshadowed by an old crone and a yokel.

Relieved of its municipal duties by the adjoining nineteenth-century offices, the town hall now serves as the city museum, or **Muzeum Miejskie** (Ⓦ www.muzeum.miejskie.wroclaw.pl; Tues–Sat 11am–5pm, Sun 10am–6pm; 5zł), although it's the largely unaltered interior itself which constitutes the main attraction. If you've an interest in the precise chronology of the building's components, check out the colour-coded plan just inside the main doorway on the right.

The kernel of the town hall, dating back to the 1270s, is the twin-aisled **Burghers' Hall** situated on the ground floor, just past the rather cute sculpture of a bagpipe-playing bear – a representation from a seventeenth-century legend. Not only the venue for important public meetings and receptions, the hall also did service throughout the week as a covered market, functioning as such for 450 years. The next part to be built, at the very end of the thirteenth century, was the **Bailiff's Room** immediately to the east, which was the office and courtroom of the official who governed the city in the duke's name. Over the centuries, it gained an extravagant vault and a couple of doorways in Renaissance and Neoclassical styles, one of which leads to a small meeting room fitted with a huge ceramic-tiled heater and adorned with portraits of former mayors and other civic dignitaries.

A tasteless nineteenth-century marble staircase decorated with an illuminating 1927 reproduction map of the fifteenth-century island town of "Breslau" leads upstairs to the resplendent three-aisled **Knights' Hall**, often the scene of temporary exhibitions. The keystones of the hall's vault are highly inventive, some of them character studies of all strata of society, while heavy oak wardrobes and chests from subsequent centuries line the otherwise empty hall. Even more richly decorated is the coffer-ceilinged oriel window, which gives a Renaissance flourish to the otherwise Gothic character.

At the far end of the hall are two stone portals, the one on the right (usually closed) adorned with hairy wild men. The left doorway gives access to the **Princes' Room**, a pure example of fourteenth-century Gothic with a vault resting on a single central pillar. It was originally built as a chapel, but takes its name from its later use as a meeting place for the rulers of Silesia's principalities. Today it's a repository for various municipal treasures of religious and secular silverware. From here you can visit the warmly wood-panelled **Alderman's Office** and the adjacent **Strong Room**, with displays of ancient coins and the heavy stamps used to make them.

West of the Rynek

The southwest corner of the Rynek leads to a second, much smaller square, **plac Solny**. Its traditional function as a market has been recently revived, with the salt from which the market takes its name now replaced by flowers. Most of the buildings offer substantially less sensory delight, dating back no further than the early nineteenth century, with pride of place taken by the Neoclassical **old stock exchange**, which occupies most of the southern side of the square.

Just off the northwest corner of the Rynek are two curious Baroque houses known as **Jaś i Małgosia**, (Hänsel and Gretel), linked by a gateway giving access to the **Kościół św. Elżbiety** (St Elizabeth's Church). Proving that brick need not be an inherently dull material, this is the most impressive of Wrocław's churches. Since the mid-fifteenth century its huge ninety-metre **tower**, under construction for 150 years, has been the city's most prominent landmark. Originally a lead-sheeted spire added another 36m to the steeple's height, but this overambitious pinnacle was blown down by storms a year after completion and never rebuilt. Ill fortune has continued to dog the church, which having been destroyed by a hailstorm in 1529 was burnt out under suspicious circumstances in 1976. Restoration work has now at last been completed, and the lofty, bright interior is well worth a peek.

Facing the inner ring road just west of here is the only other block of old **burghers' houses** surviving in the city. Across the road and down ul. Antoniego Cieszyńskiego is the **arsenal** at no. 9, originally sixteenth-century but considerably altered by the Prussians a couple of hundred years later. It now provides a rather splendid home to both the **Muzeum Miltariów** (Military Museum; Tues–Sat 11am–5pm, Sun 10am–6pm; 5zł), which displays a bristling selection of medieval swords and pikes as well as uniforms throughout the ages, and the **Muzeum Archeologiczne** (Archeology Museum; Tues–Sat 11am–5pm, Sun 10am–6pm; 5zł), with a relatively undramatic, though well-presented, collection of medieval finds, and a scale model of Ostrów Tumski as it looked in the twelfth century.

On the next street to the south, ul. Mikołaja, stands the Gothic church of **Cerkiew św. Barbary** (St Barbara's Church), which has been given to Russian Orthodox exiles from Lwów. If you come here on Saturday evening or on Sunday morning you can hear their gravely beautiful sung services, which last for well over two hours. At other times, only the chapel entered from the cemetery on the north side of the church is open.

Two streets further to the south is the plain Baroque **Kościół św. Antoniego** (St Anthony's Church), immediately to the east of which is the maze-like former **Jewish quarter**, whose inhabitants fled or were driven from their tenements during the Third Reich, never to return. It seems that the postwar authorities have always been unsure as to how to react to this embarrassing legacy of the city's German past: a recent Polish guidebook to Wrocław makes no mention of the quarter's existence nor of the city's Ukrainian connection. The Neoclassical **synagogue**, tucked away on a tiny square halfway down ul. Włodkowica on the right-hand side, is currently the subject of intensive restoration work. Another poignant reminder of the Judaic heritage is the **Jewish cemetery**, south of the main train station at ul. Ślężna 113, on the route of trams #9 and #19. However, although this is now officially recognized as a historical site of considerable significance, access is possible only at weekends.

South of the Rynek

Immediately to the east of the Jewish quarter lies a part of the city built in obvious imitation of the chilly classical grandeur of the Prussian capital, Berlin. Indeed it was Carl Gotthard Langhans, designer of the Brandenburg Gate, who built the Neoclassical palace on the northern side of ul. Kazimierza Wielkiego, now the **Nowa Biblioteka Uniwersytecka (**New University Library). He also had a hand in the monumental **Pałac Królewski** (Royal Palace) on the opposite side of the street. The central block of this is now the **Muzeum Etnograficzne** (Ethnographic Museum; Tues–Sun 10am–4pm; 4zł, free on Sat) which has a large collection of dolls in traditional dresses from around the world – a good place to visit if you're with children.

The royal flavour of this quarter continues in a different vein with the lofty Gothic church of **Kościół św. Doroty** (St Dorothy's Church), also known as the "Church of Reconciliation". This was founded in 1351 by Charles IV, king of Bohemia and the future Holy Roman emperor, in thanks for the conclusion of his negotiations with Kazimierz the Great, which secured Bohemia's rule over Silesia in return for a renunciation of its claim to Poland. Unlike most of Wrocław's other brick churches, this stayed in Catholic hands following the Reformation, becoming a Franciscan monastery. Its interior was whitewashed and littered with gigantic altars in the Baroque period, giving it a relatively opulent appearance in comparison to its neighbours which still bear the hallmarks of four centuries of Protestant sobriety.

Behind St Dorothy's stands the **Opera Dolnośląska** (Lower Silesian Opera House), built by Carl Ferdinand Langhans in a faithful continuation of his father's Neoclassical style. Facing it is another example of fourteenth-century Gothic, **Kościół Bożego Ciała** (Corpus Christi), distinguished by the delicate brickwork of its facade, porch and gable, and by the elaborate interior vaulting.

East of the Rynek

Returning to ul. Kazimierza Wielkiego and proceeding east, you come to the part-Gothic, part-Renaissance **St Christopher's church**, used by the small minority of German-speaking Protestants who remain here. Behind it stretches the vast esplanade of **pl. Dominikański**. Until 1945 there was a heavily built-up quarter on this spot, but this was so badly damaged in street fighting at the war's end that it was completely razed. There's some compensation for this loss in the unusually wide **view** of the old city which has been opened up as a result. Between here and the Rynek, at the junction of ul. Oławska and ul. Szewska, is a classic of twentieth-century design, the former **Petersdorff store** by Erich Mendelsohn. Built in 1927 and used for retail purposes ever since, it's the only one of several stores by the great German Expressionist architect to have survived, its counterparts all having fallen victim to modernization. The concrete and glass building relies for its effect on the interplay between the bold horizontals of the main street fronts and the dramatically projecting cylinder on the corner.

The twin-towered **Kościół św. Marii Magdaleny** (St Mary Magdalene's Church), a block north of here, is another illustration of the seemingly inexhaustible diversity of Wrocław's brick churches: this fourteenth-century example is unusual in having flying buttresses, giving it a French feel. Like the Kościół św. Elżbiety, two slender spires originally capped the towers, but were dismantled and replaced with Baroque domes to escape their neighbour's fate. A bevy of funeral plaques and epitaphs from the fifteenth to eighteenth centuries lines its exterior, though the most striking adornment is the twelfth-century Romanesque sandstone **portal** on the south side. This masterpiece of Romanesque carving, dating from 1180, (and whose tympanum has been moved for conservation to the Muzeum Narodowe) came from the demolished abbey of Ołbin in the north of the city which was dissolved in 1546 to strengthen the city's defences. The church is also notable as being the site of the first Protestant sermon to be held in Wrocław in 1523 during the earliest days of the Reformation.

Moving due east from here along ul. Wita Stwosza soon leads to the **Galeria Awangarda** at no. 32 (Tues–Thurs 11am–7pm, Fri noon–8pm, Sat & Sun noon–6pm; prices vary), Wrocław's leading contemporary gallery, and a good place to catch high-profile exhibitions of Polish and international art. The building itself is worth a look, incorporating the surviving Neoclassical facade of a bombed-out nineteenth-century town house into a modern, glass-and-steel pavilion. Beyond here ul. Wita Stwosza opens out onto pl. Dominikański, at the northern end of which lie the buildings of the **Dominican monastery** centred on the thirteenth-century **Kościół św. Wojciecha** (St Adalbert's Church), which is embellished with a fine brickwork gable and several lavish Gothic and Baroque chapels. A couple of blocks east, the gargantuan former **Bernardine monastery** stands in splendid isolation; there's a particularly fine view of its barn-like church from the park beyond. The last important example of Gothic brickwork in the city, the monastery was begun in the mid-fifteenth century and finished only a few years before the Reformation, whereupon it was dissolved and the church used as a Protestant parish church. Severely damaged during the war, the church and cloisters have been painstakingly reconstructed to house the somewhat misleadingly named **Muzeum Architektury** (Museum of Architecture Tues–Sun 10am–4pm; 2zł). In fact, this is a fascinating documentary record, using sculptural fragments and old photos, of the many historic buildings in the city which perished in the war.

Panorama Racławicka

Wrocław's best-loved sight, the **Panorama Racławicka** (Panorama of the Battle of Racławice; May–Sept daily 9am–5pm; Oct–April Tues–Sun 10.30am–3.30pm; 16zł) is housed in a specially designed rotunda in the park by the Bernardine monastery. Looking like a gargantuan wicker basket rendered in concrete, the building contains a truly enormous painting, 120m long and 15m high, commissioned in 1894 to celebrate the centenary of the defeat of the Russian army by the people's militia of Tadeusz Kościuszko near the village of Racławice, between Kraków and Kielce. Ultimately this triumph was in vain: the third and final Partition of Poland, which wiped it off the map altogether, occurred the following year. Nonetheless, it was viewed a century later by patriots of the still subdued nation as a supreme example of national will and self-sacrifice, which deserved a fitting memorial.

For a few decades, panorama painting created a sensation throughout Europe and North America, only to die abruptly with the advent of the cinema. In purely artistic terms, most surviving examples are of poor quality, but this one is an exception, due largely to the participation of **Wojciech Kossak**, one of the most accomplished painters Poland has produced.

The subsequent **history of the painting** is a remarkable saga which mirrors the fate of Poland itself. Despite an attempt by Polish-Americans to buy it and have it shipped across the Atlantic, it was placed on public view in Lwów, which was then part of Austria – the only one of the Partitioning powers that would have tolerated such nationalist propaganda. It remained there until 1944, when it was substantially damaged by a bomb. Although allocated to Wrocław, as the cultural heir of Lwów, it was then put into storage – officially because there were no specialists to restore it and no money to build the structure the painting would need. The truth was that it was politically unacceptable to allow Poles to glory in their ancestors' slaughter of Russians.

That all changed with the events of 1980. Within five years the painting had been immaculately restored and was on display in a snazzy new building, with much attention being paid to a natural foreground of soil, stones and shrubs, which greatly adds to the uncanny appearance of depth. It's one of Poland's most popular tourist attractions, an icon second only in national affection to the Black Madonna of Jasna Góra (see p.483). Poles flock here in their droves, and during term-time there are regular school outings to see it. Visitors are admitted at thirty-minute intervals, and are supplied with headphones with English-language commentary and appropriate sound effects. Afterwards you can study the scale model of the battlefield downstairs at leisure.

The Muzeum Narodowe

At the opposite end of the park is the ponderously Prussian neo-Renaissance home of the **Muzeum Narodowe** (National Museum; Tues–Wed & Fri–Sun 10am–4pm, Thurs 9am–4pm; 6zł; free on Thurs), which unites the collections of Breslau and Lwów. An important collection of medieval stone **sculpture**, housed on the ground floor, includes the delicately linear carving of *The Dormition of the Virgin* which formed the tympanum of the portal of Kościół św. Marii Magdaleny. The other major highlight is the poignant early-fourteenth-century **tomb** of Henryk the Righteous, one of the earliest funerary monuments to incorporate the subsequently popular motif of a group of weeping mourners.

On the first floor, one wing is devoted to an impressive display of Silesian **polychrome wood sculptures**. The most eye-catching exhibits are the colossal late-fourteenth-century statues of saints from Kościół św. Marii Magdaleny, their raw power compensating for a lack of sophistication. More pleasing are the many examples of the "Beautiful Madonnas" that were for long a favourite subject in central European sculpture: a particularly fine example is the one made in the early fifteenth century for the cathedral.

The **foreign paintings** in the opposite wing include few worth seeking out. Among these are Cranach's *Eve*, originally part of a scene showing her temptation of Adam which was cut up and repainted as two portraits of a burgher couple in the seventeenth century. *The Baptism of Christ* is a fine example of the art of Bartholomeus Spranger, the leading exponent of the erotic style favoured at the imperial court in Prague at the turn of the seventeenth century.

One of the star pieces in the comprehensive collection of **Polish paintings** on the top floor is the amazingly detailed *Entry of Chancellor Jerzy Ossoliński into Rome in 1633* by Bernardo Bellotto, best known for his documentary record of eighteenth-century Warsaw (see p.91). The other leading exhibit here is an unfinished blockbuster by Matejko, *Vows of King Jan Kazimierz Waza*. Set in Lwów Cathedral, it illustrates the monarch's pledge to improve the lot of the

△ Jaszczurowka Chapel

peasants at the end of the war against his invading Swedish kinsmen. Other works to look out for are Piotr Michałowski's *Napoleon on Horseback*, the *Fatherland Triptych* by Jacek Małczewski, and some mountainscapes by Wojciech Gerson. A number of galleries are devoted to contemporary **arts and crafts**, much of it surprisingly daring for work executed under communist rule. Władysław Hasior (see p.507) is well represented with a clutch of his often facile, often disturbing, installations from the late Sixties, and there's an impressive contingent of larger-than-life male figures, looking something like a Chinese emperor's terracotta army, courtesy of Magdalena Abakanowicz, Poland's best-known living sculptor.

The university quarter

Wrocław's academic quarter can be reached in just a few minutes from the Rynek by way of ul. Kuźnicza, but the most atmospheric approach is to walk there from the Muzeum Narodowe along the south bank of the Odra, for a series of delightful **views** of the ecclesiastical quarter opposite.

Overlooking the Piaskowski Bridge is the **Hala Targowa** (Market Hall), a preformed concrete update of the brick church idiom built in 1908. Most days it's piled with irresistible food and other commodities. From this point, the triangular-shaped university quarter, jam-packed with historic buildings, is clearly defined by two streets, ul. Uniwersytecka to the south and ul. Grodzka, which follows the Odra.

Along the northern side of the former are three religious houses. First is **Kościół św. Wincentego** (St Vincent's Church), founded as a Franciscan monastery by Henryk the Pious not long before his death at the Battle of Legnica (see p.548). One of the grandest of the city's churches, it was severely damaged in the war and rebuilt in 1991. Inside, several altarpieces by the renowned Silesian artist, Michael Willmann, have been returned to their former glory, while its Baroque monastic buildings overlooking the Odra are now used by the university. Henryk also founded the **Ursuline convent** alongside, which served as the mausoleum of the Piasts, who ruled the city during its period as an independent duchy.

Last in the row is the fourteenth-century **Kościół św. Macieja** (St Matthew's Church), containing the tomb and memorial portrait of the city's most famous literary figure, the seventeenth-century mystic poet Johann Scheffler – better known as **Angelus Silesius** ("the Silesian Angel"), the pseudonym he somewhat immodestly adopted after his conversion to Catholicism. Facing the south side of the church is the Renaissance Palace of the Piasts of Opole, while across ul. Szewska is the Baroque residence of their cousins from Brzeg-Legnica; both are now used by the university.

Behind St Matthew's stands one of Wrocław's most distinguished buildings, the domed **Ossoliński** library. Originally a hospital, it was erected in the last quarter of the seventeenth century and designed by the Burgundian architect Jean Baptiste Mathey. The library collections are another legacy from Lwów, where they were assembled by the family whose name they still bear. Among the many precious manuscripts is the original of the Polish national epic, Mickiewicz's *Pan Tadeusz*. However, you will only be able to see it during special exhibitions; the rest of the time it is closed to visitors.

The elongated pl. Uniwersytecki begins on the southern side with a dignified eighteenth-century palace, **Dom Steffensa**, again owned by the university. Facing it is one of the most obviously Austrian features of the city, the **Kościół Najświętszego Imienia Jezus** (Church of the Blessed Name of Jesus), built in the Jesuit style at the end of the seventeenth century, one of the rash of Counter-Reformation religious buildings in the Habsburg lands. Its most arresting feature is the huge allegorical ceiling fresco by the most celebrated Austrian decorative painter of the day, Johann Michael Rottmayr.

Adjoining the church is the 171-metre-long facade of the Collegium Maximum of the **university**, founded in 1702 by Emperor Leopold I. The wide entrance portal bears a balcony adorned with statues symbolizing various academic disciplines and attributes; more can be seen high above on the graceful little tower.

A frescoed staircase leads up to the main assembly hall or **Aula Leopoldina** (daily 10am–3.30pm; 3zł). The only historic room which remains in the huge building, it's one of the greatest secular interiors of the Baroque age, fusing the elements of architecture, painting, sculpture and ornament into one bravura whole. Lording it from above the dais is a statue of the founder, armed, bejewelled and crowned with a laurel. The huge illusionistic **ceiling frescoes** by Christoph Handke show the *Apotheosis of Divine and Worldly Wisdom* above the gallery and auditorium, while the scene above the dais depicts the university being entrusted to the care of Christ and the Virgin Mary. On the wall spaces between the windows are richly framed oval portraits of the leading founders of the university, while the jambs are frescoed with trompe l'oeil likenesses of the great scholars of classical antiquity and the Middle Ages.

Wyspa Piasek, Ostrów Tumski and beyond

From the Market Hall, the Piaskowski Bridge leads you out to the sandbank of **Wyspa Piasek**, with a cluster of historic buildings crammed together in the centre. The first you come to on the right-hand side is the **university library**, installed in an Augustinian monastery which was used as the Nazi military headquarters. Beside it is the fourteenth-century **Kościół NMP na Piasku** (Church of St Mary on the Sands), dull on the outside, majestically vaulted inside. The aisles have an asymmetrical tripartite rib design known as the Piast vault, which is peculiar to this region. In the south aisle is the Romanesque tympanum from the previous church on the site, illustrating the dedication by its donor, Maria Włast. Across the road stands the Baroque **Kościół św. Anny** (St Anne's Church), now used by a Ukrainian Orthodox (Uniate) community from Lwów (see p.356), while at the far end of the islet are two old **mills**, known as *Maria i Feliks*.

Ostrów Tumski

The two elegant little painted bridges of Most Młyński and Most Tumski connect Wyspa Piasek with **Ostrów Tumski**. For those not already sated by medieval churches, there's a concentration of five more here, beginning just beyond Most Tumski with the fifteenth-century **Kościół św. Piotra i Pawła** (Church of SS Peter and Paul), behind which is the squat hexagonal **Kościół św. Marcina (St Martin's Church)** of a couple of centuries earlier. As you cross the bridges, you can still see sandbags and other makeshift defences dotted along the riverbanks: the severe floods of 1997 threatened at one point to engulf this part of the city.

Far more prepossessing than these is the imperious **Kosciół św. Krzyża** (Holy Cross Church), which, with its massive bulk, giant buttresses and pair of dissimilar towers, looks like some great fortified monastery of definitive Silesian Gothic. In fact, it's really two churches, one on top of the other. The lower, originally dedicated to St Bartholomew, is more spacious and extensive than an ordinary crypt, but lacks the exhilarating loftiness of its partner upstairs. The complex was founded in 1288 by Duke Henryk the Righteous as his own mausoleum, but his tomb has now been removed to the Muzeum Narodowe. A highly elaborate Baroque monument to **św Jan Nepomuk** stands in the square outside; his life is illustrated in the column bas-reliefs.

Ulica Katedralna leads past several Baroque palaces (among which priests, monks and nuns are constantly scuttling) to the slender twin-towered **Katedra św. Jana** (Cathedral of St John). A wall mural on the right-hand side of the street, featuring the papal arms, marks the visit of Pope John Paul II to the city in 1997. Grievously damaged in 1945, the cathedral has been fully restored to its thirteenth-century form – it was Poland's first cathedral built in the Gothic style, completed in 1272. The one exterior feature of note is the elaborate **porch**, though its sculptures, with the exception of two delicate reliefs, are mostly replicas from the last century. Three chapels behind the high altar make a visit to the dank and gloomy interior worthwhile, reminiscent of the relatively unadorned English equivalents from the same era. On the southern side, **St Elizabeth's chapel** dates from the last two decades of the seventeenth century, its integrated architecture, frescoes and sculptures created by Italian followers of Bernini. Next comes the Gothic **lady chapel**, with the masterly Renaissance funerary plaque of Bishop Jan Roth by Peter Vischer of Nuremberg. Last in line is the **Corpus Christi chapel**, a perfectly proportioned and subtly decorated Baroque gem, begun in 1716 by the Viennese court architect Fischer von Erlach.

Opposite the northern side of the cathedral is the tiny thirteenth-century **Kościół św. Idziego** (St Giles's Church), the only one in the city to have escaped destruction by the Tatars, and preserving some finely patterned brickwork. Down ul. Kanonia, the **Muzeum Archidiecezjalne** (Archdiocesan Museum; Tues–Sun 9am–3pm; 2zł) at no. 12 has a sizeable and ramshackle collection of sacred artefacts. By now you'll be craving for some relief from cultural indigestion; escape from the same street into the **botanical gardens** at ul. Sienkiewicza 6 (Mon–Fri 8am–5pm), established in the Odra's former riverbed at the beginning of the twentieth century when a municipal ornamentation programme of the city was undertaken.

Ulica Szczytnicka leads east to the elongated avenue of pl. Grunwaldzki, which gained notoriety in 1945 when it was flattened into an airstrip to allow the defeated Nazi leaders to escape. At its southern end is the most famous of the city's bridges, **Most Grundwaldzki**, built in 1910.

East of Ostrów Tumski

Wrocław's most enticing stretch of greenery is the **Park Szczytnicki**, east of Ostrów Tumski, on the route of trams #1, #2, #4, #10 and #12. Its focal point is the **Hala Ludowa**, a huge hall built in 1913 to celebrate the centenary of the liberation of the city from Napoleon. Designed by the innovative Max Berg, it combines traditional Prussian solidity with a modernistic dash – the unsupported 130-metre-wide dome is an audacious piece of engineering even by present-day standards, used for trade fairs and sporting events, with the occasional exhibition. Around the Hala Ludowa are a number of striking colonnaded pavilions; these were built a few years earlier by Berg's teacher Hans Poelzig, who was responsible for making the city a leading centre of the *Deutscher Werkbund*, the German equivalent of the English Arts and Crafts Movement.

In the same park is a work by a yet more famous architect: the box-like **Kindergarten** with peeling whitewash is eastern Europe's only building by Le Corbusier. Along with the huge steel needle beside the hall, this is a legacy of the Exhibition of the Regained Territories, held here in 1948. Other delights in the park include an amphitheatre, a Japanese garden and pagoda, an artificial lake and hundreds of different trees and shrubs – including oaks that are more than six hundred years old. Best of all is a sixteenth-century **wooden church**, brought here from Kędzierzyn in Upper Silesia. Its tower is particularly striking, especially the lower storey with its highly distinctive log construction, a form normally associated with the Ukraine. Across the road lie some **zoological gardens** (summer 9am–6pm; winter 9am–5pm; 8zł), with the largest collection of formerly wild animals in Poland.

Eating, drinking and entertainment

Wrocław has a good selection of **places to eat**, most of which are within the old central area. Most restaurants are open until 10 or 11pm unless otherwise stated, and we've included telephone numbers of places where booking is advisable. **Drinking** and **nightlife** in the city are improving too: both ul. Tadeusza Kościuszki and the Rynek are humming with activity until well past midnight in summer, and the student area at the end of ul. Kuźnicza remains lively until the early hours. Note that addresses below with "Rynek–Ratusz" denote the central buildings of the market square, while those with "Rynek" refer to the periphery.

Cafés and snack bars

Miś ul. Kuźnicza 48. Traditional, milk bar-style canteen always packed with students. Till 6pm Mon–Fri, 5pm on Sat. Closed Sun.

Soul Café pl. Solny 4. Relaxing, upmarket place serving up dainty canapés and fancy cakes. Till 10pm.

Tutti Frutti pl. Kościuszki 1/4. Large downtown café with summer terrace offering ice cream, cakes, pancakes, and decent coffee. Also serves up egg-and-bacon breakfasts and hearty Polish lunches.Till 10pm.

Vega Rynek-Ratusz 27a. Good, inexpensive vegetarian haunt with plant-filled interior just to the right of the town hall's famous facade. Till 7pm Mon–Fri, 5pm at weekends.

Witek Wita Stwosza 41. Tiny café with tiny fast-food menu; but people queue out the door to snap up the toasted cheese-and-mushroom sandwiches. Till 7pm Mon–Fri, 6pm Sat. Closed Sun.

Restaurants

Academia ul. Kuźniczka 65/66. Bar-restaurant with cool modernist interior serving up modern brasserie food like flans and salads.

China Town Rynek 7. Bright, breezy and popular Chinese restaurant in the "Pod Błikitnym Słońcem" passage, with good prices.

Dwór Polski Karczma Piastów ul. Kiełbaśnicza 6/7. The "Burghers' Restaurant", entered from the first street west of the Rynek, is a good place for typical Polish cooking at reasonable prices.

Gospoda Wrocławska Sukiennice 6. Fine, traditional food in an olde-worlde wooden-beamed interior. Attentive service accompanies higher-than-average prices.

La Scala Rynek 38. Moderately priced Italian restaurant on the Old Town Square. Open till midnight.

Lwów Rynek 4. Ukrainian-Polish menu offering hearty meat-based main courses, and a good range of pancakes for afters. Cosy dining room upstairs, outdoor terrace in summer.

Pizzeria Mozarella ul. Świdnicka 26. Reasonable sit-down pizzeria on the main downtown street, which also does decent pasta, lasagne and salads.

Pronto Pizza pl. Uniwersytecki 7. Small, unpretentious place opposite the university doling out quick and cheap pizza and pasta dishes to impoverished scholars.

Saigon ul. Wita Stwosza 22/23. Vietnamese food aimed at European tastes in the hotel of the same name. The kitsch decor makes it a nice change.

Spiż Rynek-Ratusz 2. Restaurant-cum-superior-pub incorporating Poland's first boutique brewery, with a strong dark beer, a light Pils, and a tangy wheat beer all brewed on the premises. You can even get beer soup.

Żak Rynek-Ratusz 9. Moderately upscale place with a good range of grilled meats and fondues, and a nice outdoor terrace – also a good spot for a drink.

Bars and pubs

Golden Corner Ruska 1–2 (entrance round the corner on Kiełbaśniczej). Lively pub in a long cellar broken up into several small areas, catering for teens and early-twenty-somethings eager to dance to chart hits as the night wears on.

Gumowa Róża ul. Wita Stwosza 32. A cosy

labyrinth of underground rooms in the basement of the Awangarda gallery (entrance from alley round the back), catering for an easy-going, arty clientele.

John Bull pl. Solny 6/7. Moderately faithful imitation of a British pub, attracting enough of the local beautiful people to prevent it from becoming a chintzy tourist trap.

Kalogródek ul. Kuźnica 29b. Beer garden long popular with students from the nearby university, with outdoor tables and benches arranged on terraces overlooking a little plaza.

Liverpool Świdnicka 37. Dark, roomy, neon-lit place with themed DJ nights and occasional live bands.

Pod Kalamburem ul. Kuźnica 29a. Bar located between the Rynek and the university quarter, with beautiful Jugendstil decor and some lethal cocktails.

Pod Papugami Sukiennice 9a. Brash bar decorated in mixture of industrial and gothic styles, popular with hedonistic yuppies. Live music and dancing some nights.

Ragtime pl. Solny 17. Upscale café-bar stuffed with jazz memorabilia, and featuring live jazz a couple of times per week. Also a good – if expensive – place to eat.

Rura Łazienna 4 ⓦwww.rura.wroc.pl. Music club with a long bar for boozing and chatting upstairs, and a table-strewn cellar with a stage often occupied by blues or jazz bands downstairs.

Uni-café pl. Uniwersytecki 11. Popular student hang-out in the shadow of the great university facade.

Entertainment and festivals

The number and variety of **nightspots** in Wrocław has improved immensely in recent years, although venues tend to come and go. The tourist office will have details of which places are currently open – otherwise look out for posters or trawl through the pages of *Co Jest Grane* – the **listings** supplement given away free with Friday editions of the *Gazeta Wyborcza* newspaper. Current town-centre venues include *Pięć Nutek*, Podwale 37/38, a smallish cellar club that caters for specialist musical tastes (altrnative rock, reggae, drum'n'bass and so on) as well as hosting regular live gigs; and *Strefa Radia Kolor*, pl. Nowy Targ, a vast bomb shelter of a place which offers more mainstream dance music and live appearances by moderately successful Polish rock/pop acts. Gigs and raves regularly take place in *Wagon*, located in the former Dworzec Świebodzki train station on the western fringes of the Stare Miasto. Look out too for alternative rock gigs and themed DJ nights at *Madness Music Club*, 300m southeast of the bus station at ul. Hubska 6.

Main venue for classical **drama** in Wrocław is the Teatr Polski, ul. Gabrieli Zapolskiej 3 (☎071/343 8789); and its subsidiary Teatr Kameralny, ul. Świdnicka 28 (☎071/344 6201). The traditions of Jerzy Grotowski's famous studio theatre live on in the shape of the Jerzy Grotowski Centre of Creation and Theatrical and Cultural Research, Rynek-Ratusz (☎071/343 4267), which organizes workshops, performances, and occasional concerts; while the Teatr Współczesny, ul. Rzeźnicza 12 (☎071/358 8922), is the best place to go for contemporary Polish work as well as modern international plays in Polish translation. Teatr Lalek, ul. Braniborska 59 (☎071/373 5695), is a celebrated **puppet theatre**: book well in advance for its regular weekend shows, which are invariably sold out. The city's annual **drama festivals** include one devoted to monologues in January, and a contemporary Polish play season in May and June.

There's a similarly wide choice in **classical music**. Both the Opera Dolnośląska (Lower Silesian Opera), ul. Świdnicka 35 (box office at ul. Mazowiecka 17; ☎372 4357, ⓦwww.opera.ies.com.pl), and the Operetka Wrocławska, ul. Piłsudskiego 72 (☎071/343 5652), maintain high standards, yet tickets (rarely in excess of 30zł) are easy to obtain. Orchestral concerts and recitals take place regularly at the Filharmonia, ul. Piłsudskiego 19 (☎071/343 8528).

Central **cinemas** showing mainstream Hollywood movies with a smattering of art films are Atom, Piłsudskiego 74, and Warszawa, Piłsudskiego 64.

Wrocław hosts two contrasting **international music festivals** each year: the renowned Jazz on the Odra (Jazz nad Odrą) in May, and Wratislavia Cantans, devoted to oratorios and cantatas, in September. There's also a festival of early music at the beginning of December. The tourist office will have details.

Listings

Airlines LOT, ul. Piłsudskiego 36.

Books and maps Empik, on the north side of the Rynek, has the best all-round selection of foreign magazines, maps and English-language paperbacks. Księgarna Podróżnika, Wita Stwosza 19/20, is a specialist map shop that stocks just about everything you might need.

Car rental Avis, ul. Piłsudskiego 46 ☎071/372 3567, ⓦwww.avis.pl; and Joka, *Hotel Europejski*, Piłsudskiego 88 ☎071/781 8188, ⓦwww.joka.com.pl.

Internet access Adan, ul. Ruska 40/41 (daily 9am–11pm); *W Sercu Miasta*, Przejście Żelaźnicze

8, Rynek (daily 10am–midnight). Expect to pay 6zł/hr.

Left luggage At bus station (daily 8am–10pm).

Pharmacy Apteka, Wita Stwosza 3, is open 24hr.

Post Office Outside the train station at Piłsudskiego 12 (Mon–Fri 8am–8pm).

Taxis There are central ranks opposite *Monopol* hotel, and on ul, Wita Stwosza outside the Kościół św. Marii Magdaleny.

Travel Agents Orbis, Rynek 29, sells bus, train and plane tickets, as well as handling car rental; PTTK, Rynek Ratusz 11/12, has hiking information.

Lower Silesia

Once outside Wrocław, the northwestern swath of Silesia – known as **Lower Silesia** – is not an area of outstanding touristic interest, and you'd be best advised to move quickly towards the mountains of the south and east if time in this part of Poland is limited. Despite a scattering of semi-industrial towns, Lower Silesia is predominantly rural, with the River Odra and its tributaries draining some of the most productive agricultural land in the country. The scenery doesn't offer any surprises, being at its best around the isolated massif to the southwest, and the belts of deep forest in the northwest. Despite the lack of a real focus for visitors, a number of settlements here make worthwhile stopoffs if you're passing through the region – either because of their historical significance or due to their possession of the odd architectural monument of note. Due to the extensive **public transport** network, Wrocław itself makes a perfectly adequate touring base, though there's plenty of **accommodation** elsewhere should you prefer to stay in a more tranquil location.

Ślęża and Sobótka

The flatness of the plain south of the Odra is abruptly broken some 30km from Wrocław by an isolated outcrop of rocks with two peaks, the higher of which is known as **Ślęża** (718m). One of the most enigmatic sites in Poland, Ślęża was used for pagan worship in Celtic times, and was later settled by the Slav tribe after whom the mountain – and Silesia itself – are named.

Ślęża is normally approached from **SOBÓTKA**, which is on the rail line and some bus routes to Świdnica. Between the bus terminal and the train station is the Gothic parish church, outside which stands the first of several curious ancient **sculptures** to be seen in the area – consisting of one stone placed across another, it's nicknamed *The Mushroom*. On the slopes of Ślęża, there's a large and voluptuous statue of a woman with a fish, while the summit has a carved lion on it. Exactly what these carvings symbolize is not known: some certainly postdate the Christianization of the area, but that hasn't prevented their association with pagan rites. It's not exactly a place to look for quiet mystery however, being enormously popular with day-trippers and often teeming with busloads of schoolkids.

Five separate **hiking trails** traverse the hillsides, some of them stony, so it's wise to wear sturdy shoes. More than an hour is necessary for the busiest stretch, the direct ascent from Sobótka to the top of Ślęża by the route indicated by yellow signs. The summit is spoiled by a number of ugly buildings including the inevitable television tower, while the neo-Gothic chapel is a poor substitute for the castle and Augustinian monastery which once stood here. Recompense is provided in the form of an extensive panoramic view including, on a clear day, the Karkonosze and Kłodzko highlands to the south and west.

Should you wish to stay, there is one acceptable **hotel** in Sobótka, the *Pod Misiem*, ul. Mickiewicza 7/9 (☎071/316 2035; ❷), which has a small number of doubles but mostly deals in dorm-style triples (30zł per person); and a **hostel** on Ślęża itself, the *Na ślęży* (☎017/344 4752), which is usually occupied by groups. At Sulistrowice, 2km to the south, there's a **campsite** (☎071/316 2151) with chalets (❶). The Pod Misiem has a decent restaurant, and you'll find a couple of **snack bars** on Sobótka's main square.

Trzebnica

TRZEBNICA, 24km north of Wrocław, has a long and distinguished history, having been granted a charter in 1250 by Duke Henryk III, so making it one of Silesia's oldest recorded towns. It was his marriage to the German princess St Hedwig (known in Poland as Jadwiga) which was largely responsible for shifting Silesia towards a predominantly German culture, setting the trend for the next six centuries.

The couple established a **Cistercian convent** in the town in 1202, the sole monument of note. Built in the plain style favoured by this order – still Romanesque in shape and feel, but already with the Gothic pointed arch and ribbed vault – it was progressively remodelled and now has a predominantly Baroque appearance evident in its main feature, the **Basilica of St Jadwiga**. A survival from the original building is the **portal**, which was found during excavation work and re-erected, half-hidden, to the left of the porch. Its sculptures, showing King David playing the harp to Bathsheba attended by a maidservant, are notably refined thirteenth-century carvings. The northern doorway also survives, but is of a lower standard of workmanship.

Inside the church, every column features a sumptuous Baroque altarpiece, while, to the right of the choir, the **St Hedwig's chapel**'s resplendent gilt and silver altar almost outshines the main item. The princess, who spent her widowhood in the convent, was canonized in 1267, just 24 years after her death, whereupon this chapel was immediately built in her memory. In 1680, her simple marble and alabaster sepulchral slab was incorporated into a grandiose tomb, whose sides are lined with sacred statuary while Jadwiga clutches a model of the basilica. At the same time, a considerably less ostentatious memorial to her husband was placed in the choir, its entrance guarded by statues of St Hedwig and her even more celebrated niece, St Elizabeth of Hungary.

You're unlikely to want a **place to stay** in Trzebnica, but the *Hotel Pod Płatanami*, ul. Kilińskiego 2 (☎071/312 0980; ❷), will do the honours if you get stuck. The *Ratuszowa* **restaurant**, Rynek 4, is a conveniently central place to eat.

Lubiąż

Set close to the north bank of the Odra, 51km west of Wrocław (regular daily buses) and signposted off the Wrocław–Zielona Góra road, the quiet village of

LUBIĄŻ stands in the shadow of a **Cistercian abbey** that ranks as one of the largest and most impressive former monastic complexes in central Europe. Originally founded by the Benedictines in the first half of the twelfth century, it was taken over by the Cistercians a generation later.

Although resting on medieval foundations, the appearance of the complex – laid out in the ground plan of a squared-off figure 6 – is one of sober Baroque: the community flourished in the aftermath of the disastrous Thirty Years' War, and was able to build itself palatial new headquarters, with over three hundred halls and chambers. Silesia's greatest painter, **Michael Willmann** (see p.561), lived here for over four decades, carrying out a multiplicity of commissions for the province's religious houses, and was interred in the church's crypt. However, prosperity was short-lived: decline began in 1740, when Silesia came under the uncompromisingly Protestant rule of Frederick the Great's Prussia, and continued until the monastery was dissolved in 1810. Since then, the complex has served as a mental hospital, stud farm, munitions factory, labour camp and storehouse, in the process drifting into a state of semi-dereliction. After the fall of communism, the Lubiąż Fund was established to attract foreign capital to renovate the site.

What has undoubtedly the potential to become one of Poland's leading tourist attractions has the merest trickle of visitors. At present, given the continued renovation of the interior, the main reason for making a visit is to appreciate the colossal exterior – something that would stand out in any capital city let alone lost here in the Silesian countryside. Most impressive, and readily accessible by walking through the gatehouse, is the 223-metre-long **facade**, whose austere economy of ornament is interrupted only by the twin towers of the church at the point where the figure 6 plan joins back onto itself. The church interior (currently inaccessible) was unfortunately stripped of most of its rich furnishings during World War II, and a few small frescoes on the cupola of scenes from the lives of ss Benedict and Bernard are all that remain of Willmann's extensive decorative scheme. Only parts of the rest of the abbey are open (Tues–Sun: Jul–Aug 9am–5pm; Sept–June 10am–3pm; 5zł), but you should be able to see a number of beautifully restored rooms decorated in the Baroque style, including the showpiece Knights' Hall (Sala Książęca).

Legnica and Legnickie Pole

On April 4, 1241 the Tatar hordes – having ridden five thousand miles from their Mongolian homelands and ravaged everything in their path – won a titanic battle 60km west of Wrocław against a combined army of Poles and Silesians, killing its commander, Duke Henryk the Pious. Silesia's subsequent division among Henryk's descendants into three separate duchies began a process of dismemberment which was thereafter to dog its history. One of the new capitals was **LEGNICA**, a fortified town a few kilometres from the battlefield, one of the few in the area to have escaped destruction. It remained a ducal seat until the last of the Piasts died in 1675, but by then its role as their main residence had been taken over by Brzeg.

Although often ravaged by fires and badly damaged in World War II, Legnica has maintained its role as one of Silesia's most important cities, and is nowadays a busy regional centre of 110,000 inhabitants preserving a wide variety of monuments. The most interesting of these relics, a castle and three churches, are set at the cardinal points around the city centre, now comprising undeveloped open spaces and residential concrete blocks – the legacy of Legnica's wartime ruin.

The Town

If you're arriving by train or bus, the main sights can be covered by a circular walk in an anticlockwise direction from the stations, which are just over the road from each other. Following ul. Dworcowa (between the stations) to the right, you shortly come to the wide pl. Zamkowy, with the early-fifteenth-century **Brama Głogowksa** (Głogów Gate) one of only two surviving parts of the city wall and standing in isolation, and the enormous **castle** behind.

The latter is a bit of a mishmash and now houses administrative offices, with no worthwhile interiors open to inspection, apart from the chapel. Nonetheless, it has some interesting features, particularly the **gateway** in the form of a triumphal arch, the only surviving part of the Renaissance palace built here. All that remains of the earlier defensive castle, long since replaced by a Romantic pseudo-fortress designed by the great Berlin architect Karl Friedrich Schinkel, is two heavily restored towers; the higher octagonal, the lower cylindrical and ringed by a crenellated balcony capped by an octagonal tower.

Continuing down ul. Nowa, which offers the best overall view of the castle, you arrive at ul. Partyzanów, the axis of a well-preserved Baroque quarter. On the right are the Jesuit buildings including the **Kościół św. Jana** (St John's Church) with its massive facade, appearing all the more impressive for being confined to a narrow street. Protruding from the eastern side of the church, its orientation and brick Gothic architecture looking wholly out of place, is the presbytery of the thirteenth-century Franciscan Monastery which formerly occupied the spot. It owes its survival to its function as the Piast mausoleum: inside you'll see several sarcophagi, plus Baroque frescoes illustrating the history of Poland and Silesia under the dynasty.

Another fine Baroque palace, the **Rycerska** academy, can be found in ul. Chojnowska, the street immediately behind the church. Here also is the late-fourteenth-century **Chojnow** tower plus a small section of the medieval wall.

This same street runs into the elongated **Rynek**, which has lost much of its character: the two rows of historic buildings placed back-to-back along the central part of the square are now set off by functional modern dwellings which have transformed the Rynek into an undistinguished public space. Eight arcaded Renaissance houses, all brightly coloured and a couple decorated with reliefs, have managed to preserve a little old-time character. These are charming narrow-gabled burgher residences, two of them with sgraffito embellishments; note in particular the lovely "Quail basket" house with its cylindrical bay window.

At the end of this block is the **Stary Ratusz** (Old Town Hall), a restrained Baroque construction, while behind stands the **theatre**, built in the first half of the nineteenth century in a style reminiscent of a Florentine palazzo. There's also a fine eighteenth-century fountain dedicated to Neptune.

From this point, and probably long before, you can't miss the huge twin-towered **Katedra św. Piotra i Pawła** (Cathedral of SS Peter and Paul), with its rich red-brick neo-Gothic exterior, stylistically matched by the arcaded turn-of-the-twentieth-century buildings facing it on the corner of the Rynek. Two lovely fourteenth-twentieth-century portals have survived: the northern one, featuring a tympanum of *The Adoration of the Magi* flanked by statues of the church's two patrons, overshadows the more prominent facade doorway with its *Madonna and Child*. The furnishings of the interior, which largely retains its original form, range from a late-thirteenth-century font with bronze bas-reliefs to an elaborately carved Renaissance pulpit and a typically theatrical Baroque high altar.

Ulica Piotra i Pawła leads back to the train station via pl. Mariacki, with the brick Gothic **Kościół Mariacki** (St Mary's Church), whose gaunt exterior brings to mind military rather than ecclesiastical architecture. Notwithstanding its dedication, it's still the place of worship of the remnant of the Protestant community, who were in a majority here until 1945.

Practicalities

The **train station** lies to the northeast of the old city centre, with the **bus station** just over the road. Legnica's **hotels** boil down to the *Cuprum*, Skarbowa 2 (☎076/851 2280; ❻), right by the castle and featuring comfy en-suite rooms with TV; and the cheaper and considerably dowdier *Narol* near the stations at Gliwicka 1 (☎076/862 6927; ❶).

There are several moderately priced **restaurants** in town: the popular *Adria*, Rynek 9, includes Indian as well as Polish specialities; the *Tivoli*, southwest of the Rynek at ul. Złotoryjska 31, offers good Polish cooking with some passable veggie options, but closes at 9pm. There are plenty of **bars** around the centre: the *Sunlight Music Club*, ul. Orła Białego 3, has a certain tacky charm and stays open late at weekends.

Legnickie Pole

LEGNICKIE POLE, 11km southeast of Legnica, stands on the site of the great battleground; it can be reached by any bus going to Jawor, or by the municipal services #9, #16, #17 and #20. Extensive repair work was carried out in 1991 on the village's principal buildings in conjunction with the 750th anniversary of the battle.

A church was erected on the spot where Henryk the Pious' body was found (according to tradition, his mother, later St. Jadwiga of Trzebnica, was only able to identify the headless corpse from his six-toed foot), and in time this became a Benedictine monastery – said to be the stone chapel facing the abbey complex. A Protestant parish for four centuries, the church now houses the **Muzeum Bitwy Legnickiej** (Museum of the Battle of Legnica; Wed–Sun 11am–5pm; 4zł, free on Wed), which includes diagrams and mock-ups of the conflict and a copy of Henryk's tomb (the original is in Wrocław's Muzeum Narodowe; see p.539). Outside the museum are several large wooden carvings commissioned for the 750th anniversary, including depictions of a wily Tatar archer and Henryk's severed head.

The Benedictines, who were evicted during the Reformation, returned to Legnickie Pole in the early eighteenth century and constructed the large **Kościół św. Jadwigi** (St Jadwiga's Church) directly facing the museum. It was built by **Kilian Ignaz Dientzenhofer**, the creator of much of Prague's magnificent Baroque architecture. His characteristic use of varied geometric shapes and the interplay of concave and convex surfaces is well illustrated here. The interior of the church (usually closed outside Mass times; ask at the museum and they may unlock it) features an oval nave plus an elongated apse and is exceptionally bright, an effect achieved by the combination of white walls and very large windows. Complementing the architecture are the bravura **frescoes** covering the vault by the Bavarian **Cosmos Damian Asam**. Look out for the scene over the organ gallery, which shows the Tatars hoisting Henryk's head on a stake and celebrating their victory, while the duke's mother and wife mourn over his body.

Since the second dissolution of the monastery in 1810, the **monastic buildings** (currently a women's hospice) have been put to a variety of uses. For nearly a century they served as a Prussian military academy; its star graduate was Paul von Hindenburg, German commander-in-chief during World War I and president from 1925 until his death in 1934.

Legnickie Pole has a cheap **motel** at ul. Kossak-Szczuckiej 7 (☎076/858 2094; en-suites ❸, rooms with shared facilities ❷), which also has a **restaurant**; and at the edge of the village is the only **campsite** (June–Sept; ☎076/858 2397) in the Legnica area, with four-person chalets for 70zł.

Zielona Góra

Occupying the northwestern corner of Lower Silesia, straddling the railway line between Wrocław and Berlin, 100,000-strong **ZIELONA GÓRA** was little damaged in World War II, and preserves an eclectic mixture of the kind of downtown buildings which have all but disappeared in other Polish towns. It's a patchwork of the architectural styles practised in turn-of-the-twentieth-century Germany, with the solidly historicist Wilhelmine rubbing shoulders with the experimental forms of Jugendstil. There are also a few older landmarks in the midst of these, including a couple of towers surviving from the fifteenth-century ramparts, the Gothic Church of St Hedwig and the much-remodelled Renaissance Town Hall in the centre of the Rynek. Most imposing of all is the **Kościół Matki Boskiej Częstochowskiej** (Church of Our Lady of Częstochowa), an eighteenth-century example of the Silesian penchant for half-timbered ecclesiastical buildings. The nearby **regional museum**, al. Niepodległości 15 (Wed–Fri 11am–5pm, Sat 10am–3pm, Sun 10am–4pm; 4zł) contains an overview of the local **wine**-making industry – Zielona Góra being the only place in Poland where this tipple is produced.

Zielona Góra's adjacent **train** and **bus stations** are on the northeastern edge of the centre, a fifteen-minute walk from the central Rynek. The PTTK office, just north of the Rynek at ul. Kupiecka 17 (Mon–Fri 7.30am–3.30pm; ☎068/325 5491) is currently doing the honours as the town's **tourist information office**, but is short of brochures and English-speakers. Orbis obviously think well of Zielona Góra, as they have an expensive **hotel** here, the *Polan*, a couple of blocks east of the stations at ul. Staszica 9a (☎068/327 0091, ✉polan@orbis.pl; ❽). Alternatively, there's a brace of less expensive establishments; the *Śródmiejski*, right in the town centre at ul. Żeromskiego 23 (☎068/325 4471; ❸–❺ depending on whether you get new furniture and sat-TV or not); and the much smaller *Pod Lwem*, near the stations at ul. Dworcowa 14 (☎068/324 1055; ❸). There's an all-year **youth hostel** with space for **camping**, just to the southeast of the station at ul. Wyspiańskiego 58 (☎068/327 0840). To get there, turn left outside the station and walk under the flyover, take the first right up the hill and, passing the *Polan*, turn left at the lights into ul. Wyspiańskiego – altogether about a twenty-minute walk.

Zielona Góra has a truly international choice of good-value **restaurants**, with an Indian-Thai mix at *Indyska*, Stary Rynek; anything from Italian to Chinese at *To Tu*, immediately south of the Rynek at pl. Pocztowy 17; and a wider European range at *Figaro*, some way west of the Rynek at al. Wojska Polskiego 114a. For great Polish food try *Nieboska Komedia*, just northeast off the Rynek at al. Niepodległości 3/5.

Żagań

Some 50km southwest of Zielona Góra, and reachable from there by train or bus, is the old ducal capital of **ŻAGAŃ**. It suffered badly in World War II, when it gained international notoriety as the site of the Nazi prisoner-of-war camp, Stalag VIIIC, a real-life break-out from which provided the inspiration for the film *The Great Escape*. Although the town centre has been partially restored, it stands very much in the shadow of what was an exceptionally illustrious past for such a small town: the duchy was once conferred on Albrecht von Waldstein (aka Wallenstein), the military genius who had commanded the imperial forces in the Thirty Years' War; the astronomer Johannes Kepler passed the last two years of his life there, as Wallenstein's guest; while the great French novelist Stendhal was a later resident.

Starting at the western end of the compact centre, you first see the finest of the half-dozen historic churches, **Kościół Mariacki** (St Mary's Church), formerly part of an Augustinian monastery. Originally a high-gabled Gothic hall church from the fourteenth century, its interior, which boasts a beautiful Renaissance altar dedicated to the Holy Trinity, was completely remodelled in the Baroque epoch. Further east is the first of two large market squares, the Stary Rynek, lined with a number of sixteenth- and seventeenth-century burghers' mansions, and the Gothic **town hall**, to which a Florentine-style loggia was appended last century. Beyond is the larger New Rynek, with the Jesuit Church on the north side. Set in a park just to the south is the **palace**, begun in the Renaissance period by order of Wallenstein, but mostly built in an Italianate Baroque style later in the seventeenth century. It was badly desecrated during World War II, when its rich interiors were destroyed; it's now used as a cultural centre.

On ul. Lotników Alianckich in the suburb of Stary Żagań is the site of **Stalag VIIIC**, today designated the **Muzeum Martyrologii Alianckich Jeńców Wojennich** (Museum of Martyrology; daily 10am–5pm; donation requested). Some 200,000 prisoners from all over the world, most of them officers, were incarcerated here. Although the camp itself was totally razed after the war, a monument commemorates those who were killed, while a special museum room displays prisoners' beds along with samples of their hair, glasses, clothes and documents, plus photographs and a model of how the camp once looked.

Practicalities

Best value of Żagań's **hotels** is the parkside *Młynówka,* ul. Żelazna 2a (☎068/377 3074; ❸), a black and white building situated in the park behind the palace. Alternatives are the more upmarket *Nadbrodzański,* just over the river at pl. Kilińskiego 1 (☎068/377 3447; ❹); and the basic *Dom Turysty* (☎068/377 3467; ❸), a gloomy proposition set in the courtyard of pl. Klasztorny bordered by the brooding hulk of Kościół Mariacki. There is also a **youth hostel** at ul. X-lecia 19 (☎068/377 3235) with basic dorm rooms and a sun lounge.

The best **place to eat** is the *Nadbrodzański's* restaurant; otherwise try *Kepler* at Rynek 27; or the good-value *Tropik* on the opposite side of the square at Rynek 8/9. Each May, the Crystal Room in the palace is put to appropriate use as the venue for the main local **festival**, the All-Polish Dance Competition.

Jelenia Góra and around

Some 110km southwest of Wrocław, **JELENIA GÓRA** is the gateway to one of Poland's most popular holiday and recreation areas, the **Karkonosze national park**. Its name means "Deer Mountain", but the rusticity this implies is scarcely reflected in the town itself which has been a manufacturing centre for the past five centuries. Founded as a fortress in 1108 by King Bolesław the Wrymouth, Jelenia Góra came to prominence in the Middle Ages through glass and iron production, with high-quality textiles taking over as the corner-stone of its economy in the seventeenth century. With this solid base, it was hardly surprising that, after it came under Prussian control, the town was at the forefront of the German Industrial Revolution.

The Town

Thankfully Jelenia Góra's present-day factories have been confined to the peripheries, leaving the traffic-free historic centre remarkably well preserved. Even in a country with plenty of prepossessing central squares, the **plac Ratuszowy** is an impressive sight. Not the least of its attractions is that it's neither a museum piece nor the main commercial centre: most of the businesses are restaurants and cafés, while the tall mansions are now subdivided into flats. Although their architectural styles range from the late Renaissance via Baroque to Neoclassical, the houses form an unusually coherent group, all having pastel-toned facades reaching down to arcaded fronts at street level. Occupying the familiar central position is the large mid-eighteenth-century **town hall**, its unpainted stonework providing an apposite foil to the colourful houses.

To the northeast of pl. Ratuszowy rises the slender belfry of the Gothic parish **church**. Epitaphs to leading local families adorn the outer walls, while the inside is chock-full of Renaissance and Baroque furnishings. Yet another eye-catching tower can be seen just to the east, at the point where the main shopping thoroughfare, ul. Marii Konopnickiej, changes its name to ul. 1 Maja. Originally part of the sixteenth-century fortifications, it was taken over a couple of centuries later to serve as the belfry of **Kaplica św. Anny** (St Anne's Chapel). The only other survivor of the town wall is the tower off ul. Jasna, the street which forms a westward continuation of pl. Ratuszowy.

Continuing down ul. 1 Maja, you come in a couple of minutes to the Baroque **Kaplica NMP** (Chapel of St Mary); it's normally kept locked, but if you happen to be here on a Sunday morning you can drop in to hear the fervent singing of its Russian Orthodox congregation. At the end of the street, enclosed in a walled park-like cemetery, is another Baroque church, **Kościół św. Krzyża** (Holy Cross Church), built in the early eighteenth century by a Swedish architect, Martin Franze, on the model of St Catherine's in Stockholm. Though sober from the outside, the double-galleried interior is richly decorated with trompe l'oeil frescoes.

From the bustling ul. Bankowa which skirts the Stare Miasto to the south, ul. Jana Matejki leads to the **district museum** at no. 28 (Tues, Thurs & Fri 9am–3.30pm, Wed, Sat & Sun 9am–4.30pm; 3zł, free on Wed) at its far end, just below the wooded Kościuszki Hill. Apart from temporary exhibitions, the display space here is given over to the history of **glass** from antiquity to the present day, with due emphasis on local examples and a particularly impressive twentieth-century section.

There is a useful **museum** about the Karkonosze national park at ul. Chałubińskiego 23 (Tues–Sun 10am–4pm; 2zł) for those planning to visit it, providing some advance information on what you can see there and how to get around. The display of old postcards provides a nostalgia-tinged view of the region's popularity as a health tourism destination in Wilhelmine Germany.

For the best **viewpoint** in town, head west from pl. Ratuszowy along ul. Jasna, then cross ul. Podwale and continue down ul. Obrońców Pokoju into the woods and over the bridge. Several paths lead up the hill, which is crowned with an outlook tower that's permanently open. From the top there's a sweeping view of Jelenia Góra and the surrounding countryside.

Practicalities

The main **train station** is about fifteen minutes' walk from the centre, at the east end of ul. 1 Maja. Local buses plus a few services to nearby towns leave from the bays in front, but the **bus station** for all intercity departures is at the opposite end of town off ul. Obrońców Pokoju. Given the existence of plentiful buses to the nearby mountain resorts of Karpacz and Szklarska Poręba, it's unlikely that you'll want to stay in Jelenia Góra, although the helpful **tourist office** at ul. 1 Maja 42 (Mon–Fri 9am–6pm, Sat 10am–2pm; ☎075/767 6925, ⓦwww.sudety.it.pl) will find you a **hotel** bed in town – or in the spa suburb of Cieplice (see below) if you do. Of the central establishments, the *Europa*, ul. 1 Maja 16 (☎075/764 7231; en-suites ❺, rooms with shared facilities ❸) is ideally central but a little musty; preferable are the nearby *Jelonek*, ul. 1 Maja 5 (☎075/764 6541; ❺) a small, comfortable place in a Baroque town house (the lower floor of which has been colonized by *Pizza Hut*); or the snazzier but equally small *Baron*, which manages to squeeze swish bright rooms into a historic building just off the main Rynek at ul. Grodzka 4 (☎075/752 5391; ❻). Only if the latter is full is it worth stepping up to the Orbis-run, 180-room *Jelenia Góra*, 2km south of town on the road to Kowary and Karpacz at ul. Sudecka 63 (☎075/764 6481, ⓔjgora@orbis.pl; ❼). The *Park*, just down the road from the *Jelenia Góra* on ul. Sudecka 42 (☎075/752 6942; ❷), has clean en-suites and also has year-round **camping** facilities. There's an all-year **youth hostel** at ul. Bartka Zwyci*izcy 10 (☎075/752 5746).

Of the **snack bars** along the main street, *Spaghetteria al Dente*, ul. 1 Maja 33, serves up palatable pasta and risotto dishes for next to nothing. There are numerous **cafés** and **restaurants** grouped around the main square, most offering outdoor seating and cheap, reasonable food. *Smok* at no. 15 has a limited but tasty menu of Chinese fare; while *Pokusa*, at no. 12, concentrates on hearty Silesian beef and pork dishes. Best of the lot is probably *Kurna Chata* at no. 22, serving up inexpensive home cooking in a cosy spot underneath the arcades.

Cultural life centres on the Secessionist-style **Cyprian Norwid Theatre** at al. Wojska Polskiego 38 (box office Tues–Fri 3–6pm & 1hr before performances; ☎075/764 7273), whose main drama season is in the autumn. For **classical music**, try the Filharmonia Dolnośląska, Pilsudskiego 60 (☎075/752 6095).

Jelenia Góra hosts concerts of chamber and organ music in July, while early to mid-August sees a **festival** of street theatre. Lot, Pocztowa 11 (☎075/767 6370) is the best of the **cinemas**.

Cieplice Śląskie-Zdrój

The municipal boundaries of Jelenia Góra have been extended to incorporate a number of communities to the south, nearest of which is the old spa town of **CIEPLICE ŚLĄSKIE-ZDRÓJ**, 8km away. Although it has a number of modern sanatoria, along with concrete apartment blocks in the suburbs, Cieplice still manages to bask in the aura of an altogether less pressurized age. To catch this atmosphere at its most potent, attend one of the regular concerts of **Viennese music** in the spa park's delightful Neoclassical **theatre**.

The broad main street of Cieplice is designated as a square – pl. Piastowski. Its main building is the large eighteenth-century **Schaffgotsch** palace, named after the German grandees who formerly owned much of the town. There are also a couple of Baroque **parish churches** – the one for the Catholics stands in a close at the western end of the street and is generally open, whereas its Protestant counterpart to the east of the palace is locked except on Sunday mornings.

A walk south through the Park Norweski, which continues the spa park on the southern side of the River Podgórna, brings you to the small **Muzeum Przyrodnicze** (Natural History Museum; Tues–Fri 9am–3pm, Sat & Sun 9am–4pm; 3zł, free on Sun) housed in the so-called Nordic Pavilion. Inside the wooden building, erected here last century, you'll find cases of butterflies as well as the stuffed avians in which the museum specializes.

Practicalities

Local **bus** #9 from Jelenia Góra passes through the centre of Cieplice; #7, #8 and #15 stop on the western side of town, while #4, #13 and #14 stop on the eastern side. Cieplice is also the place where the roads to Karpacz and Szklarska Poręba separate: buses to both places pass through the town.

The **tourist office**, pl. Piastowski 36 (Mon–Fri 9am–5pm, Sat 10am–2pm; ☎075/755 8844, ⓦwww.sudety.it.pl), will fix you up with **private rooms** (❶) in town or direct you towards the **hotels**, of which the most central is the Cieplice, ul. Cervi 11 (☎075/755 1041; ❸), offering a mixed bag of dowdy and renovated rooms right by the spa park. The nearby *Venus* **pension**, ul. Cervi 19 (☎075/755 7880; ❷), offers a bit more in the way of intimate charm. The **campsite**, *Rataja*, at ul. Rataja 9 (☎075/755 2566), is near the Orle train station 4km southwest of town, on the routes of buses #7 and #15.

In the assembly rooms beside the spa theatre there's a good **café** with a cold buffet service and dancing in the evenings, and there's a decent **milk bar** at the western end of pl. Piastowski. There's a good traditional Polish **restaurant** at pl. Piastowski 26, and a pizzeria, the *Mafioso*, next door.

Sobieszów

Buses #7, #9 and #15 all continue the few kilometres south to **SOBIESZÓW**. Once again, there are two Baroque **parish churches**, both located off the main ul. Cieplicka: the Protestant one is appropriately plain, while the Catholic is exuberantly decorated. In an isolated location on the southeastern outskirts is the **regional museum** (Tues–Sun 9am–4pm; 2zł), with displays on the local geology, flora and fauna.

From here, red and black trails offer a choice of ascents to the castle of **Chojnik** (Tues–Sun 9am–4pm; 3.50zł), which sits resplendently astride the wooded hill of the same name. It's actually much further from town than it appears – allow about an hour for the ascent. Founded in the mid-fourteenth century, the castle is celebrated in legend as the home of a beautiful man-hating princess who insisted that any suitor had to travel through a treacherous ravine in order to win her hand. Many perished in the attempt: when one finally succeeded, the princess chose to jump into the ravine herself in preference to marriage. The castle was badly damaged in 1675, not long after the addition of its drawbridge and the Renaissance ornamentation on top of the walls. Yet, despite its ruined state, enough remains to give a good illustration of the layout of the medieval feudal stronghold it once was, with the added bonus of a magnificent **view** from the round tower.

The castle houses a **restaurant** and **tourist hostel** (☎075/755 3535) with dorm beds from 20zł per person, though the relative solitude afforded by its isolated position is the sole reason for staying.

The Karkonosze

The mountains of the **Karkonosze** are the highest and best-known part of the chain known as the Sudety, which stretches 300km northwest from the smaller Beskid range, forming a natural border between Silesia and Bohemia. Known for its raw climate, the predominantly granite Karkonosze range rises abruptly on the Polish side, and its lower slopes are heavily forested with fir, beech, birch and pine, though these are suffering badly from the acid rain endemic in central Europe. At around 1100m, these trees give way to dwarf mountain pines and alpine plants, some of them exotic to the region.

Primarily renowned as **hiking** country, these moody, mist-shrouded mountains strongly stirred the German Romantic imagination and were hauntingly depicted by the greatest artist of the movement, Caspar David Friedrich. From the amount of German you hear spoken in the resorts, it's clear that the region offers a popular and inexpensive vacation for its former occupants – and the Polish tourist authorities certainly aren't complaining.

Lying just outside the park's boundaries, the two sprawling resorts of **Szklarska Poręba** and **Karpacz** have expanded over recent years to meet this need, and nowadays constitute well-equipped bases from which to embark on summer hiking and winter skiing expeditions. As the area is relatively compact – the total length of the Karkonosze is no more than 37km – and the public transport system good (if circuitous), there's no need to use more than one base. The upper reaches of the Karkonosze have been designated a **national park** (entry 3zł per day), but as elsewhere, this label does not guarantee an unequivocal vision of natural splendour. If you're not into extended walking or off-road biking, a **chairlift** ascent up to the summits will make an enjoyable day's excursion.

The 1:30,000 **map** of the park, available from kiosks and travel offices, shows all the paths and viewpoints and is a must if you intend doing any serious walking. Like all mountain areas, the range is notorious for its changeable weather; take warm clothing even on a sunny summer's day. **Mist** hangs around on about three hundred days in the year, so always stick to the **marked paths** and don't expect to see much.

Szklarska Poręba

SZKLARSKA PORĘBA lies 18km southwest of Jelenia Góra and just to the west of a major international road crossing into the Czech Republic. It can be reached from Jelenia Góra either by train, depositing you at the station on the northern heights of the town, or by bus, whose terminus is at the eastern entrance to the resort.

You might prefer to walk the last few kilometres of the bus route from Piechowice (which also has a train station); although not actually in the National Park, this offers some fine scenery. The road closely follows the course of the **Kamienna**, one of the main streams rising in the mountains, which is joined along this short stretch by several tributaries, in a landscape reminiscent of the less wild parts of the Scottish highlands. Many of the best vistas are to be had from the road itself, which has an intermittent lane set aside for walkers; the views from the hiking trails are obscured by trees most of the time. However, you do need to make a detour down one of the paths in order to see the **Szklarka** waterfall, situated in a beautiful canyon setting. The point to turn off is easy to find, as it's usually thronged with souvenir sellers.

The Kamienna slices Szklarska Poręba in two, with the main streets in the valley and the rest of the town rising high into the hills on each side. It's well worth following the stream all the way through the built-up part of the resort, as there follows another extremely picturesque stretch on the far side of the centre, with some striking rock formations (the **Kruce Skalny**) towering above the southern bank.

From the busy town the quickest way up to the summits is by **chairlift** (late April to mid-Oct & Dec to early April daily 9am–4.30pm; 24zł return), which goes up in two stages and terminates a short walk from the summit of **Szrenica** (1362m). Its departure point is at the southern end of town: from the bus station, follow ul. 1 Maja, then turn right into ul. Turystyczna, continuing along all the way to the end, following green then black markers. From the top of the lift, you can walk back down or, more ambitiously, follow the ridge east to the sister peak of Snieżka and the resort of Karpacz beneath it (see below), a good day's walking.

Over on the northern side of town, the **Hauptmann House** at ul. 11 Listopada 23 (Dom Hauptmana; Tues, Thur & Fri 9am–3.30pm, Wed, Sat & Sun 9am–4.30pm; free) remembers the German novelist and playwright Gerhard Hauptmann, one of the many artists and writers who spent their holidays in Szklarska at the close of the nineteenth century. It was here that Hauptmann wrote much of *The Weavers*, a drama of Silesian industrial life that helped bag the Nobel Prize for Literature in 1912. Photographs and manuscripts recall the author's career, and there's also a collection of pieces from the local Huta Julia glass works, source of the region's lead crystal.

Practicalities

As you'd expect, Szklarska Poręba has a great variety of accommodation. Online information is available at Ⓦwww.szklarskaporeba.pl, while the **tourist information centre** at ul. Jedności Narodowej 3 (Mon–Fri 8am–6pm, Sat & Sun 9am–7pm; ☎075/717 2494, Ⓔit@szklarskaporeba.pl) has access to over thirty **pensions** (❷–❹) offering good-value accommodation, often involving worthwhile half-board deals. They also have a team of **guides** if you want assistance getting up and down the misty mountains.

Good-value **hotels** include the Eden, ul. Okrzei 13 (☎075/717 2181; ❸) a big modern house offering en-suites with TV just south of the centre; and the nearby Scots, ul. Kilińskiego 11a (☎075/717 3737; ❹), a rustic place with cosy en-suite rooms above a pub. Carmen, near the Szrenice lift at ul. Broniewskiego 8 (☎075/717 2558, Ⓔmolcarmen@go2.pl; ❹), is a largish pension with well-appointed en-suites; while sauna, gym and covered pool are on offer at the four-star *Hotel Bornit*, ul. Mickiewicza 21 (☎075/753 9503, Ⓦwww.bornit.hotel.pl; ❻), a glass-fronted monolith overlooking the town centre from a hillside perch just to the west. The **youth hostel** is a long way northeast of the centre at ul. Piastowska 1 (☎075/717 2141), on the wrong side of town for the best walks, but it is open all year. Most central of the **campsites** is the *Pod Mostem* at Gimnazijalna 5 (☎075/717 3062), just west of the bus station; further afield, the *Południowy Stok* on the northwest fringes of the resort at ul. Batalionów Chłopskich 12 (☎075/717 2129), is open all year and has four-person chalets for around 80zł.

There's a cluster of inexpensive snack huts at the foot of the Szrenica chairlift; otherwise the central ul. Jedności Narodowej offers the main concentration of **places to eat**. *Diavolo* at no. 26 specializes in tasty pizzas, *pierogi* and pancakes; while *Fantazija*, at no. 14, is better for more substantial meat and fish dishes – the latter also does good coffee and ice cream in the café section. *Krysztal*, ul. 1 Maja 19, is the place to go for traditional Polish nosh followed by a spot of old-time dancing.

Karpacz and around

KARPACZ, 15km south of Jelenia Góra and linked to it by at least twenty buses a day, is an even more scattered community than Szklarska Poręba, occupying an enormous area for a place with only a few thousand permanent inhabitants. It's a fairly characterless place if the centre of town is all you see, but the sheer range of easily accessible hikes in the neighbouring mountains make this the most versatile of Silesia's highland resorts.

Much of Karpacz is built along the main road, ul. 3 Maja (ul. Karkonoska in its upper reaches), which stretches and curves uphill for some 5km. Most tourist facilities are located in **Karpacz Dolny** (Lower Karpacz), at the lower, eastern end of the resort, although **Karpacz Górny** (Upper Karpacz), up the valley to the west, has its fair share of hotels and pensions. In between lies the **Biały Jar** roundabout (named after the next-door *Biały Jar* hotel), which is the main starting point for most of the hiking trails.

The Town

Located in the upper reaches of Karpacz Górny and clearly visible from the main road is the most famous, not to say curious, building in the Karkonosze – the **Wang Chapel** (Mon–Sat 9am–6pm, Sun 11.30am–6pm; 3.5zł). Girdled at a discreet distance by souvenir stalls and snack bars, this twelfth-century wooden church with Romanesque touches boasts some wonderfully refined carving on its portals and capitals, as well as an exterior of tiny wooden tiles giving it a scaly, reptilian quality. It stood for nearly six hundred years in a village in southern Norway, but by 1840, it had fallen into such a state of disrepair that the parishioners sought a buyer for it. Having failed to interest any Norwegians, they sold it to one of the most enthusiastic architectural conservationists of the day, King Friedrich Wilhelm IV of Prussia. He had the church dismantled and shipped to this isolated spot, where it was meticulously reassembled over a period of two years. The stone tower added at the beginning of the twentieth century is the only feature which is not original, and looks conspicuously inappropriate. In deference to Friedrich Wilhelm's wishes, the chapel is still used on Sunday mornings for Protestant worship; there are also organ recitals on alternate Sundays in summer.

The only other sightseeing attraction in town is the small **Muzeum Sportu i Turystyki** (Museum of Sport and Tourism; Tues, Wed, Fri–Sun 9am–4pm, Thurs 11am–6pm; 3zł), housed in an alpine chalet at ul. Kopernika 2 in Karpacz Dolny. Inside you'll find a selection of archaic bobsleighs and crampons and, upstairs, a room full of lace, carved furniture and traditional dress, as well as a model of Chojnik castle. Below the museum is the valley of the Dolna, which offers a superb **view** over the national park.

Hiking in the park

Before undertaking any day-walks in this area it's worth getting yourself a copy of the 1:30,000 *Karpacz i Okolice* **map**, if you haven't already got the national park map mentioned on p.556. It includes a plan of the town and is sold at the tourist information Centre (see p.557).

Booths next to the Wang Chapel and the Biały Jar roundabout sell entrance **tickets** to the national park (3zł). Biały Jar is the more popular entrance point to the park, not least because it's twenty minutes' walk from the lower station of the **chairlift** (8am–5pm) which leads up towards Kopa (1375m), just twenty minutes from the Karkonosz's high point of Śnieżka (see below).

A short detour west from the lift station takes you to the upper of two **waterfalls** on the River Łomnica, which rises high in the mountains and flows all the way through Karpacz, defining much of the northern boundary of the town, as well as the course of ul. Konstytucji 3 Maja, which follows a largely parallel line. The second waterfall, below Biały Jar on a path waymarked in red, is less idyllic, having been altered to form a dam.

The most popular goal for most walks is the summit of **Śnieżka**, at 1602m the highest peak in the range and sometimes covered with snow for up to six months of the year. Lying almost due south of Karpacz, it can be reached by the **black trail** in about three hours from the *Biały Jar*, or in about forty minutes if you pick up the trail at the top of the Kopa chairlift. From the chairlift you pass through the Kocioł Łomniczki, whose abundant vegetation includes Carpathian birch, cloves, alpine roses and monk's hood. Access to the actual summit is by either the steep and stony "Zigzag Way" (the red trail) which ascends by the most direct method, or the easier "Jubilee Way" (the blue route), which goes round the northern and eastern sides of the summit. At the top is a large modern weather station-cum-snack bar, where you can get cheap hot **meals**; refreshments are also available in the refuges on Kopa and *Pod Śnieżka*, and at the junction of the two trails.

The **red trail** also serves the summit. From Biały Jar it follows the stream to the chairlift terminal and then forks right near the *Orlinek* hotel onto an unmade track which climbs steadily for forty minutes to a junction with a yellow path and a refuge. The path continues above the tree line and after some steeper zigzags reaches the *Pod Śnieżka* refuge, another forty minutes later: the refuge is less than fifteen minutes above the Kopa chairlift terminal, following the black waymarkers. From here the side-trip east to the summit of Śnieżka takes twenty minutes by the "Zigzag Way". On a clear day, the **view** from Śnieżka stretches for 80km, embracing not only other parts of the Sudety chain in Poland and the Czech Republic, but also the Lausitz mountains in Germany.

Once at the summit, it's worth following the red trail immediately to the west above two glacial **lakes**, Mały Staw and Wielki Staw just above the tree line. Assuming you don't want to continue on to Szklarska Poręba, you can then descend by the black trail and switch to the blue, which brings you out at Karpacz Górny. If you're feeling energetic you might like to go a bit further along the red trail and check out the Słonecznik and the Pielgrzymy **rock formations** thereafter descending by the yellow and later blue trails back to Karpacz Górny. If the above routes seem too strenuous, a satisfyingly easy alternative is to take the blue trail from the Karpacz Górny to the *Samotnia* refuge on the shore of Mały Staw, a round trip taking about three hours.

Practicalities

Most **buses** from Jelenia Góra terminate at Biały Jar (picking up and dropping off at numerous stops along ul. 3 Maja on the way), although some continue all the way to Karpacz Górny. Bearing in mind that it can take an hour to walk from one end of the resort to the other, these buses represent a useful way of shuttling up and down the resort once you get established.

You can also get to Karpacz by **train**, although it's probably not worth the bother: there are only two painfully slow services a day from Jelenia Góra, and Karpacz's train station is at the extreme eastern end of the resort, from where everything lies a stiff walk uphill.

Information about **private rooms** (❷) and **pensions** (❷–❹) is available from the **tourist office** at ul. Konstytucji 3 Maja 25a (Mon–Fri 8.30am–4.30pm; ☏075/761 9453, Ⓦwww.karpacz.pl) in Karpacz Dolny. There's a well-equipped Orbis **hotel** in Karpacz Dolny, the modern 300-bed *Skalny*, ul. Obrońców Pokoju 3 (☏075/752 7000, Ⓔskalny@orbis.pl; ❻) although it loses out in terms of atmosphere to some of the smaller, more intimate upscale hotels emerging in town: *Klub Holandia*, midway between Karpacz Dolny and Biały Jar at 3 Maja 67 (☏075/761 0982; ❻); and the *Rezydencja*, in Karpacz Dolny at ul. Parkowa 6 (☏075/761 8020; ❻), whose understated plushness makes it the cosiest place to stay in town. Less pricey places in Dolny include the *Kolorowa*, ul. Konstytucji 3 Maja 58 (☏0075/761

9503; ❺), a large pension on the main strip with a loyal German clientele and a good restaurant; and the *Bacówki*, opposite the Skalny at ul. Obrońców Pokoju 6a (☎075/761 9764; ❸), which basically consists of a cluster of dinky wooden huts, with bathrooms shared between every two or three rooms.

Karpacz is full of places where you can refuel after a hard day in the hills, with the stretch of ul. Konstitucji 3 Maja just west of the tourist office boasting a particularly generous selection of **eating** and **drinking** venues. *Rubenzal*, ul. Konstitucji 3 Maja 51, is a small hut serving up cheap *pierogi, bigos* and other filling Polish staples; *Pizzeria Verdi*, on the opposite side of the road, offers a good range of thin-crust pies in stylish surroundings; and *Karczma Śląska*, just off the main drag at Rybacka 1, is an inexpensive source of grilled pork dishes. The nearby restaurant of the *Kolorowa* hotel offers a similarly meaty menu but with more choice and slightly higher prices. *Country Grill*, ul. Obrońców Pokoju 6a, is a ranch-like place next to the *Bacówki* where you can eat traditional Polish food and sink numerous beers in a vast wooden stable.

Between the Karkonosze and the Kłodzko valley

In the stretch of land between the *Karkonosze* mountains and Silesia's other main recreation area – the *Kłodzko* valley to the southeast – lie several historic towns, most of them connected with the former **Duchy of Świdnica**, which lasted only from 1290 to 1392 but exerted a profound influence on Silesian culture. With the exception of the city of Wałbrzych, a truly horrible example of Poland's post-World War II industrial development, it's a delightfully rustic corner of Silesia to travel through, consisting largely of rolling arable land fringed by sizeable patches of forest. Although Wałbrzych is an important transport hub lying on the Wrocław–Jelenia Góra rail line, road travellers can avoid it altogether by following the main roads to Świdnica (easily accessible by bus from Jelenia Góra, Wrocław and Kłodzko) just to the north.

Krzeszów

The village of **KRZESZÓW**, lies in the shade of a huge **abbey** complex which ranks, historically and certainly artistically, among the most exceptional monuments in Silesia. Situated some 46km southeast of Jelenia Góra it's some way south of the main Świdnica-bound route, but you won't regret making the effort to visit the place – to get there by public transport, catch a bus from Jelenia Góra to the grubby textile town of Kamienna Góra and change there.

The abbey was originally founded in 1242 by Benedictines at the instigation of Anne, widow of Henryk the Pious. However, they stayed for less than half a century; the land was bought back by Anne's grandson, Bolko I of Świdnica, who granted it to the Cistercians and made their church his family's mausoleum. Despite being devastated by the Hussites and again in the Thirty Years' War, the abbey flourished, eventually owning nearly 300 square kilometres of land, including two towns and forty villages. This economic base funded the complete rebuilding in the Baroque period, but not long afterwards the community went into irreversible decline as the result of the confiscation of its lands during the Silesian Wars.

For over a century the buildings lay abandoned, but in a nicely symmetrical turn of events they were reoccupied by Benedictine monks from Prague in

1919, with a contingent of nuns joining them after World War II. Restoration work is now largely completed, with both the main churches returned to an outstanding condition. That you should find such an architecturally impressive institution dominating this tiny Silesian village only adds to its splendour.

The two churches are very different in size and feel. The smaller and relatively plainer exterior of the two, **Kościół św. Jozefa** (St Joseph's Church), was built in the 1690s for parish use. In replacing the medieval church, its dedication was changed to reflect the Counter-Reformation cult of the Virgin Mary's husband, designed to stress a family image which was overlooked in earlier Catholic theology. Inside, the blue-veined marble and high windows give a bright impression with the newly renovated altar resplendent in the typically Baroque style. The magnificent **fresco cycle** in which Joseph – previously depicted by artists as a shambling old man – appears to be little older than his wife and is similarly transported to heaven, is a prime artistic expression of this short-lived cult. Executed with bold brushwork and warm colours, it is the masterpiece of **Michael Willmann**, an East Prussian who converted to Catholicism and spent the rest of his life carrying out commissions from Silesian religious houses. On the ceiling, Willmann continued the family theme with various biblical genealogies.

Built in the grand Baroque style, the monastic **church** was begun in 1728 and finished in just seven years – hence its great unity of design, relying for effect on a combination of monumentality and elaborate decoration. Its most striking feature is undoubtedly its imposing **facade**, with gravity-defying statues of various religious figures filling the space between the two domed towers.

Inside, the three altarpieces in the transept are all Willmann's work, but the most notable painting is a Byzantine icon which has been at Krzeszów since the fourteenth century. The nave ceiling frescoes illustrate the life of the Virgin, and thus form a sort of counterpoint to those in the parish church; that in the south transept shows the Hussites martyring the monks. From the south transept you pass into the Piast **mausoleum** behind the high altar. This is kept open when tourist groups are around (which is quite frequently in summer); at other times you'll have to persuade a monk or nun to open it up. Focal point of the chapel is the grandiose coloured marble monument to Bernard of Świdnica, to each side of which are more modest Gothic sarcophagi of Bolko I and II. The history of the abbey is told in the frescoes on the two domes.

There's a **snack bar** in the car park opposite the abbey's entrance. For an **overnight stay** the *Betlejem* pension (☎075/742 2324; ❶–❷), signposted 2km south of town, makes an idyllic retreat – a *drzewnianka* (wooden chalet) situated in the woods, which you'll find hard to leave. Adjacent to the building is the little-known *Pawilion na Wodzie* (Water Pavilion), a former summer house for Krzeszów's bishops, which the owners of the house will show you around for a small fee. A less memorable night can be spent at one of the two pensions in Kamienna Góra: the *Pan Tadeusz*, ul. Legnicka 2e (☎075/744 5227; ❷), little more than a converted modern house signposted close to the traffic lights on the Bolków road out of town; and the slightly more charming and central *Krokus* at ul. Parkowa 16 (☎075/744 3514; ❹).

Bolków, Jawor and Strzegom

The very name of **BOLKÓW**, 35km east of Jelenia Góra on the road to Świdnica, proclaims its foundation by the first duke of Świdnica, Bolko I. Although a ruin, his **castle** (Tues–Fri 9am–3pm, Sat 8am–3pm, Sun 9am–4pm; 2zł) is still an impressive sight, rising imperiously above the little town. Later converted into a Renaissance palace, it passed into the control of the monks of Krzeszów, and was finally abandoned after their Napoleonic suppression. A section of the buildings has been restored to house a small museum on the history of the town, and you can ascend the tower for a fine panoramic view. Below it is the old well, now a wish-fulfilling repository for near worthless old złoty notes.

There's little to see in the lower town, though the gaudily painted Gothic parish church and the sloping Rynek have a certain charm. The town has two **hotels**, *Bolków*, ul. Sienkiewicza 17 (☎075/741 3341), with a mixture of refurbished ensuites (❹) and simpler rooms with shared facilities (❷); and the somewhat simpler *Panorama* at ul. Mickiewicza 6 (☎075/741 3444; ❷). The *Bolków* boasts an excellent **restaurant**; and you'll find a cluster of **cafés** on the Rynek.

Jawor

Some 20km north of Bolków, on the main road to Legnica, lies the somewhat larger town of **JAWOR**, which was formerly the capital of one of the independent Silesian duchies. It preserves a fair number of colourful Renaissance and Baroque town houses, many of them on the small arcaded Rynek from which erupts the neo-Renaissance bulk of the **town hall** nicely complementing its tower, retained from its fourteenth-century Gothic predecessor. A somewhat later Gothic style is evident in **Kościół św. Marcina** (St Martin's Church), a fine hall design, with varied furnishings including Renaissance choir stalls and a Baroque high altar. Behind the church, a hole in the epitaph-laden brick wall leads to some even older, rubbish-strewn ruins.

From the Rynek, ul. Grundwalska heads northwest through pl. Wolności. On the far side, a gate leads to the town's most historically if not necessarily visually intriguing monument, the barn-like, timber-framed **Kościół Pokoju** (Church of Peace). Its name derives from the Peace of Westphalia of 1648, which brought to an end the morass of religious and dynastic conflicts known as the Thirty Years' War, though the name could equally well apply to the tranquil setting outside the old town walls. The church was one of three (two of which survive) that Silesia's Protestant minority were allowed to build following the cessation of hostilities, and both the material used – wood and clay only, no stone or brick – and the location outside the town centre were among the conditions laid down by the ruling Habsburg emperor. Designed by an engineer, Albrecht von Säbisch, the church was cleverly laid out in such a way that an enormous congregation could be packed into a relatively modest space, an effect illustrated even more clearly in its more charismatic counterpart in Świdnica (see p.564).

You can catch a bite to eat at the *Ratuszowa* **restaurant** at Rynek 5: otherwise, there's no great reason to hang around.

Strzegom

East of Bolków the main road to Świdnica continues through undulating terrain, passing a turn-off after 10km to the town of **STRZEGOM**, a further 10km to the north. It's regarded by some as Silesia's oldest town, and might well be among the oldest in Poland. A long-established source of granite extracted from nearby quarries, it nevertheless preserves few suggestions of its antiquity. Approaching from afar you can't miss the huge Gothic bulk of its **Bazylika św. Piotra i Pawła** (Basilica of SS Peter and Paul), built from the local rock with more readily workable sandstone tympanums illustrating *The Last Judgement* (with what seems like an excess of Apocalyptic Horsemen) and on the southern porch, *The Dormition of the Virgin*.

Książ

One of the best-preserved castles in Silesia – and the largest hilltop fortress in the country – is to be found in **KSIĄŻ**, just off the main Jelenia Góra–Świdnica route, reached by a minor road which branches south at the village of Świebodzice, 20km east of Bolków. By **public transport** your best bet is to carry on to Świdnica, from where minibus #31 (destination Wałbrzych) from outside the train station runs to within a ten-minute walk of the castle. If you're travelling by rail, aim for Wałbrzych and catch municipal bus #8, which drops you right at the foot of your destination (Zamek Książ).

Before you the majestic **castle** (May–Sept Tues–Fri 10am–5pm, Sat & Sun 10am–6pm; April & Oct Tues–Sun 10am–4pm; Nov–March Tues–Sun 10am–3pm; 7zł) sits on a rocky promontory surrounded on three sides by the Pełcznica river's ravine. Despite a disparity of styles taking in practically everything from the thirteenth-century Romanesque of Duke Bolko I's original fortress to idealized twentieth-century extensions, it makes as impressive a sight as you'll get in Silesia's war- and industry-ravaged environs. Partially transformed into a bomb-proof bunker for Hitler during the war, the castle was subsequently occupied by the Soviet army and what they and the Germans hadn't pillaged was picked away by nearby residents until the local authorities took it upon themselves to restore the site. At present, the condition of the four hundred room castle might be described as "stabilized", undertaking a variety of roles including bar, restaurant, art gallery, hotel and historic tourist attraction. However this lack of identity, added to the freedom to wander around the deserted corridors (possibly a result of contradictory signposting) makes for an agreeable visit.

If you do decide to visit, make sure you splash out for the escorted ascent of the main **tower**, which takes about 25 minutes. Built over the original core of Bolko's citadel, ascending the ever-diminishing staircase to the Baroque lantern is like climbing through centuries of Książ's past. On the way the guide will point out salient details which include Gothic elements and graffiti from the wartime and Soviet occupants. From the top, the view across the terracotta-tiled roofs and forest to the surrounding hills will absorb you while you catch your breath with the guide pointing out distant hills from where V2 rockets were fired on England over fifty years ago.

Back at ground level are some rather staid exhibitions of contorted glass at which the Poles excel, along with the customary collection of historical artefacts. By far the finest interior is the **Maximilian Hall**, a piece of palatial Baroque complete with carved chimneypieces, gilded chandeliers, a fresco of Mount Parnassus and colourful marble panelling. Either side of the hall are salons which continue the ornamentation with colour-themed decor.

The basement houses an inexpensive **restaurant**, while on the other side is an authentically cramped beer cellar which leads onto an attractive terrace. This western side of the castle, clad in thick ivy, but not even a century old, overlooks the small French ornamental gardens and the entrance to what are presumably the vestiges of Hitler's bunker – a few poorly lit concrete-lined corridors leading nowhere. Occupying some outbuildings close to the entrance gate, the *Książ* **hotel** (☎074/843 2798; renovated en-suites ❺, rooms with shared facilities ❶) makes an inexpensive and unusual place to spend the night.

Świdnica

Although visible as a collection of ever-familiar smokestacks when approached by road, **ŚWIDNICA**, 16km northeast of Wałbrzych and for centuries Silesia's second most important city, is blessed by the fact that it suffered little damage in World War II. Today the town still manages to preserve some of the grandeur of a former princely capital, resulting in an attractive Silesian town with a tangible self-confidence.

Although Świdnica's period of independent glory – coming soon after its twelfth-century foundation – was short-lived, the town continued to flourish under Bohemian rule. Not only was it an important centre of trade and commerce, it ranked as one of Europe's most renowned brewing centres, with its famous *Schwarze Schöps* forming the staple fare of Wrocław's best-known tavern and exported as far afield as Italy and Russia.

The lively **Rynek** is predominantly Baroque, though the core of many of the houses is often much older. Two particularly notable facades are at no. 7, known as **The Golden Cross**, and no. 8, **The Gilded Man**. In the central area of the square are two fine fountains and the handsome early-eighteenth-century **town hall**, which preserves the tower and an elegant star-vaulted chamber from its Gothic predecessor.

Kościół św. Stanisława i Wacława

Off the southeastern corner of the Rynek, the main street, ul. Długa, curves gently downhill. The view ahead stretches past a number of Baroque mansions to the majestic **belfry** – at 103m the second-highest in Poland – of the Gothic parish **Kościół św. Stanisława i Wacława** (Church of SS Stanisław and Wenceslas). Intended as one of a pair, the tower was so long under construction that its final stages were finished in 1613, long after the Reformation. This incomplete nature is visible from the strikingly unsymmetrical facade where the matching right side is conspicuous by its absence. Nevertheless, the extant facade, in front of which stands a Baroque statue of St Jan Nepomuk, is impressive enough, featuring a sublime late-Gothic relief of *St Anne, the Virgin and Child*. Around the early-fifteenth-century portals, the two patrons occupy a privileged position in the group of Apostles framing the Madonna – notice also the relief to the right of a man being thrown from a bridge for some arcane felony.

After the Thirty Years' War the church was given to the Jesuits, who carried out a Baroque transformation of the **interior**, respecting the original architecture while embellishing it to give a richer surface effect. A massive high altar with statues of the order's favourite saints dominates the east end; the organ with its carvings of the heavenly choir provides a similar focus to the west, while the lofty walls were embellished with huge Counter-Reformation altarpieces, some of them by Willmann.

The Kościół Pokoju

Set in a quiet walled close ten minutes' walk north of the Rynek, the **Kościół Pokoju** (Church of Peace) was built in the 1650s for the displaced Protestant congregation of SS Stanisław and Wenceslas, according to the conditions on construction applied at Jawor (see p.562) a few years before and to plans drawn up by the same engineer. Although the smaller of the two, it is the more accomplished: indeed, it's considered by some to be the greatest timber-framed church ever built. At first sight, the rusticity of the scene, with its shady graveyard, seems to be mirrored in the architecture, but it's actually a highly sophisticated piece of design. Over 3500 worshippers could be seated inside, thanks to the double two-tiered galleries: all would be able to hear the preacher, and most could see him.

The whole appearance of the church was sharply modified in the eighteenth century, as the Protestant community increased in size and influence after Silesia came under the rule of Prussia. A domed vestibule using the hitherto banned materials was added to the west end, a baptistry to the east, while a picturesque group of **chapels and porches** was tagged on to the two long sides of the building. The latter, recognizable today by their red doorways, served as the entrances to the private boxes of the most eminent citizens whose funerary monuments are slowly crumbling away on the exterior walls. At the same time, the church was beautified inside by the addition of a rich set of furnishings – pulpit, font, reredos and the large and small organs.

Practicalities

From the **train** and **bus stations** it's a couple of minutes' walk east to the Rynek. The **tourist information centre**, right on the Rynek at ul. Wewnętrzna 2 (Mon–Fri 9am–5pm, Sat 8am–4pm; ☎074/852 0290, ✉swidnicainftur@poczta.onet.pl), can direct you towards the town's **accommodation** possibilities, which kick off with the swish and comfortable *Hotel Park*, a short walk south of the bus and train stations at ul. Pionerów 20 (☎074/853 7098; ❻). The *Piast*, situated just west of the Rynek at ul. Kotlarska 11 (☎074/852 3076; ❺), also offers cosy if slightly dowdy en-suites; while a cheaper option is the *Sportowy*, 1km southeast of the centre at ul. Śląska 31 (☎074/852 2532), which has a mixture of en-suites (❸) and rooms with shared facilities (❷). As for **eating**, the nameless milk bar at Rynek 18 is the best daytime source of good, cheap Polish food; otherwise the *Royal Prince*, down by the train station at pl. Grunwaldzki 11, offers some similarly inexpensive Polish options alongside Italian and Chinese dishes; while the *Stylowa*, a couple of blocks northwest of the Rynek at ul. ks. Bolka 14, has food with a Hungarian slant. The restaurants of the *Park* and *Piast* hotels are worth considering for slap-up Polish nosh. Best of the central **drinking** options are the *Highlander*, on the corner of pl. Grunwaldzki and ul. Wałbrzyska; and the *Czerwony Gryf*, diagonally opposite the train station on al. Niepodległości.

The Ziemia Kłodzka

Due south of Wrocław is a rural area of wooded hills, gentle valleys and curative springs that provides a timely antidote to the heavy industry which blights much of lowland Silesia. Known as the **Ziemia Kłodzka** (Kłodzko Region) after its largest town, it's surrounded on three sides by the Czech Republic with which the Sudety mountains form a natural frontier.

A popular holiday area for insolvent Silesians looking for a break from the industrial conurbations, you may not find many of the five **spa resorts** (identified by the suffix *–zdrój*) as appealing as they sound. The gracious prewar days when "taking the waters" was a fashionable indulgence are long gone, and although the spas have recently started to respond to new opportunities in tourism, a sense of faded grandeur still prevails. If you're heading for the Czech Republic then a visit to one or two and a quick swig of the effervescent local tonic won't ruin your day.

In the hills above these resorts are some fine **hiking routes** passing through landscapes dotted with sometimes bizarre rock outcrops. A network of marked paths covers the entire region, in which there are several separate ranges; the best are found in the southeast of the area, taken up by the **Masyw Śnieżnika**. This specific area is as yet little touched by the more rapacious tourist development elsewhere and is a worthwhile destination for spending a few quiet days in the hills. The red and yellow 1:90,000 *Ziemia Kłodzka* **map**, easily available from local bookshops, is an essential companion.

Accommodation throughout the Kłodzko region is plentiful, although the bigger resorts tend to fill up with partying youngsters in high summer. Nevertheless it's possible to stay here very cheaply, with the custom-built **pensions** offering particularly good value. For **getting around**, buses, which eventually get to even the smallest villages, or hitching are your best bets; picturesque rail lines hug the valleys, but train stations are usually on the outskirts of the towns.

Kłodzko

Spread out beneath the ramparts of a stolid Prussian fortress, the thousand-year-old town of **KŁODZKO** was for centuries a place of strategic importance and today its Stare Miasto still retains some of the charm of its medieval origins – a rarity in Silesia, which makes a stopover here rewarding. Situated on the main trade route between Bohemia and Poland, until the eighteenth-century Prussian takeover, Kłodzko's ownership fluctuated between the adjacent nations. Indeed at one point the town belonged to the father of Adalbert, the Czech saint who was to have a crucial impact on the development of the early Polish nation (see p.412).

Kłodzko's bus station is the main public transport hub for the whole region, linking the settlements of the Ziemia Kłodzka with Świdnica to the northwest and Paczków and Nysa to the east. However there's not a great choice of accommodation in town, so you're best advised to head for one of the spa resorts, like Kudowa-Zdrój, if you're going to be staying in this part of Silesia for any length of time.

The Town

From the main train and bus stations situated side by side in the centre of town, the best way to enjoy an exploration of the attractive **Stare Miasto** is to cross the steel-girder bridge beside the prominent *Hotel Astoria* which brings you into ul. Grottgera. At the end of this street you'll find the main survivor of the town's medieval fortifications, the Gothic **bridge**, adorned in the Baroque period by a collection of sacred statues who still manage to look pleadingly heavenward despite centuries of weathering.

On the opposite bank, grand nineteenth-century mansions rise high above the river. Passing them, you ascend to the sloping Rynek (known as plac Bolesława Chrobrego) which has a number of fine old houses from various periods, an undistinguished nineteenth-century Town Hall and an ornate Baroque fountain which looks up to the fortress's walls. Greatly extended by the Prussians in the eighteenth century from earlier defensive structures built on the rocky knoll, the squat **fortress** (Tues–Sun 9am–6pm; 5zł) lost its reputation for impregnability when captured by the all-conquering army of Napoleon in 1807. As with other historical monuments which have suffered the vagaries of several disparate owners, the fortress nowadays has become a repository for a variety of objects from old fire engines to contemporary local glassware, and you can even learn to abseil in one of the courtyards. However, most visitors come here for the stronghold's extensive network of **tunnels** (guided tours daily 9am–6pm; 5zł) which were excavated by prisoners of war during the Prussian era, and today still entail a fair amount of crawling around in semi-darkness while the guide rattles through his spiel.

During the last war the fortress was used as a prison camp and in one of the many galleries you'll find a memorial to the thousands of prisoners who perished here. Near the uppermost terrace a small chamber also houses a genuinely chilling sculpture which further commemorates the wartime dead. Nearby is the **viewpoint** over the town's roofscapes to the hills beyond; it bears a striking resemblance to the comparable, if somewhat grander, panorama from Grenoble's similar fort in southeastern France.

By the entrance of the fortress is the northern aperture of the **Podziemna Trasa,** yet another underground passage (daily 9am–6pm; 5zł), this 600-metre example making an unusual and blissfully cool way of passing under the Stare Miasto on a hot summer's day. There are various instruments of torture to see along the way, including miniature French guillotines and even more barbaric Prussian methods of execution. The exit brings you out just below a small square in which stands one of the finest Baroque church interiors in Poland. Kłodzko's parish **Kościół NMP** (Church of Our Lady) really should not be missed and will have avid church-spotters drooling in the aisles. Outside, the Gothic building's shell remains remarkably well preserved, but inside, two and a half centuries of Baroque ornamentation were undertaken with such zeal that you hardly know where to rest your eyes. Barely a surface is left without some kind of embellishment in gold, marble or paint, giving a busy impression that either fills you with awe or gives you a headache. One of the many things to look out for is the fourteenth-century tomb of the founder, Bishop Ernst of Pordolice, which somehow managed to survive the desecrations of the Hussites five centuries ago.

Leaving the church square to the west and following ul. Łukasiewicza to no. 4, brings you to the **Muzeum Ziemi Kłodzkiej** (Kłodzko Regional Museum; Tues–Fri 10am–3.30pm, Sat & Sun 11am–4pm; 2zł, free on Sun) whose sole redeeming feature, apart from the occasional concert recitals in the adjacent hall, is the exhaustive assembly of over four hundred clocks located on the top floor. The collection is based on the fruits of the Świedbodzia and Srebrna Góra **clock** factories and displays everything from ancient astronomical devices, working grandfather and irritating cuckoo clocks, to porcelain-backed kitchen clocks. One small dark room features a mirrored floor reflecting a ceiling covered in still more clocks.

Practicalities

Kłodzko Miasto **train station**, which is beside the **bus station**, is only a few minutes' walk from the centre; this station is also the best place to catch trains heading south, and to the two spa valleys to the east and west. The main station, Kłodzko Główny, is over 2km north and only worth using if you're heading to Wrocław or Jelenia Góra. The rather excellent **tourist office**, located on the southwestern corner of the town hall at pl. Chrobrego 1 (Mon–Fri 9am–6pm, Sat 10am–2pm; ☎074/865 8970, ⊛www.ziemiaklodzka.it.pl or ⊛www.powiat.klodzko.pl), can fill you in on accommodation possibilities throughout the region. The PTTK office at Wita Stwosza 1 (Mon–Thur 8am–4pm, Fri 8am–6pm, Sat 9am–1pm; ☎074/867 3740) is the place to buy local hiking **maps**.

Of the **hotels**, *Astoria* on pl. Jedności (☎074/867 3035; ❸) is easy to find, being right opposite the bus and train stations, although its roomy en-suites are on the tatty side. The *Marhaba* at ul. Daszyńskiego 16 (☎074/865 9933, ⓔsnieznik@netgate.com.pl; ❸), five minutes' walk west of the bus station just over the modern bridge and on the right, offers smaller, but slightly smarter rooms. There is a **youth hostel** 1km north of the centre at ul. Nadrzeczna 5 (☎074/867 2524), which will put you up for under 20zł a head.

The International-Tunisian fare on offer at the **restaurant** of the *Marhaba* is worth a try; otherwise you'll find all the eating and drinking options you need around the main square. *Romana*, on the east side of the town hall, serves up a decent pizza as well as tasty pancakes and ice cream, and has outdoor, fountain-side seating in summer. *U Ratusza*, on the other side of the town hall at pl. Chrobrego 3, is the place to go for a slap-up Polish meal.

Wambierzyce

Heading west from Kłodzko on the main road to Prague are a string of **spa towns**. The first of these, **Polanica-Zdrój**, is not worth the detour in its own right, but a right turn at the west end of town leads 9km to the village of **WAMBIERZYCE** (buses from Polanica-Zdrój or Kłodzko), another tiny rural settlement set out of all proportion to the huge religious institution found there.

The Baroque **basilica**, perched above a broad flight of steps above the village square has been the site of pilgrimages since 1218, when a blind man regained his sight by praying at a statue of the Virgin Mary enshrined in a lime tree. Pilgrimages ensued over the following centuries with the shrine growing ever bigger on the donations of its visitors. The impressive monumental facade of the basilica is all that remains of the third shrine built here at the end of the seventeenth century, the main body of the building collapsing soon after completion, at which point it was rebuilt with the interior you see today. The basilica is circumvented by a broad ambulatory with a variety of chapels and grottoes representing the Stations of the Cross. The small nave of the basilica is a fairly reserved octagon hung with altarpieces by Michael Willmann, while the all-important pulpit gets the usual excess of ornamentation. On the ceiling is a fresco depicting an angel passing the design for the basilica to the local people, its anticipated form appearing as a ghostly image on the hill behind them. The oval chancel has a cupola illustrating the fifteen Mysteries of the Rosary with a magnificent silver tabernacle from Venice bearing the miraculous image, accompanied by a profusion of votive offerings encased at its side.

Found all around the town are nearly one hundred **shrines** depicting further scenes from the Passion, culminating appropriately at **Calvary**, the wooded hill facing the basilica up which lead a long series of steps lined by still more shrines. Halfway up on the left is the **Szopka** (Tues–Sun 10am–1pm & 2–4pm), a large mechanical contraption from the early nineteenth century that presents biblical and everyday local scenes, laid out like miniature theatre sets.

There's a comfy **hotel**, the *Wambierzyce*, on the main square at pl. NMP 1 (☎074/871 9186, ⓦwww.hotel-wambierzyce.com.pl; ❹), which also has a reasonable **restaurant**.

Duszniki-Zdrój

Back on the main Prague road, continuing 10km west of Polanica-Zdrój brings you to the much older spa resort of **DUSZNIKI-ZDRÓJ**, which has a little more going for it than the younger Polanica. The town is best known for its **Chopin Musical Festival** held here in the first half of August each year, an event which commemorates the concerts given by the sixteen-year-old composer during a convalescence in 1826. This, and the unusual industrial museum (see opposite), add to the usual charms of a spa.

Duszniki is divided by the Wrocław–Prague road with the **train station** to the north and the Stare Miasto and spa quarter located on the south side. On the **Rynek**, Renaissance and Baroque styles are mingled with less edifying postwar additions, with one of the old town houses bearing a plaque recording Chopin's stay. Leaving the market square to the east down ul. Kłodzko, you pass the parish **Kościół św. Piotra i Pawła** (Church of SS Peter and Paul), an externally bland example of early-eighteenth-century Baroque with two unusually ornate pulpits inside. One is shaped like a whale, with the creature's gaping maw forming a preaching platform – a zany stylistic reference to the Jonah story which is occasionally found in other Polish churches.

At the bottom of the same street is the **Muzeum Papiernictwa** (Museum of the Paper Industry; Tues–Fri 9am–5pm, Sat & Sun 9am–3pm; 6zł), which occupies a large paper mill dating from the early seventeenth century and constitutes the town's chief curiosity. One of Poland's most precious industrial buildings, its fine half-timbering, sweeping mansard roof, novel domed entrance turret and crude gable end add up to an eye-catching if understated piece of Baroque architecture.

The town's spa park lies over to the southwestern side of the Rynek, a long stretch of tree-shaded walkways that culminates after about 1km with an ensemble of nineteenth-century buildings including the **Chopin Palace** (Dworek Chopina) – a dinky Neoclassical pavilion that holds recitals throughout the summer season, including those connected with the Chopin Festival.

Practicalities

The the **train station** lies to the north of the Wrocław–Prague road. Duszniki-Zdrój isn't as animated as Kudowa-Zdrój further down the road, but if you want to stay here the **tourist office**, Rynek 9 (Mon–Fri 8am–5pm, Sat 8am–2pm; ☎074/866 9413), will direct you towards the town's private rooms (❶) and pensions (❸). There's a lot of simple, socialist-era rest homes around town, of which the *Polonez*, ul. Zdrojowa 38 (☎074/866 9226; ❸), is a cheap and cheerful example. Of the newer **hotels**, the *Fryderyk*, ul. Wojska Polskiego 10 (☎074/866 0488, ⓦwww.fryderyk.com.pl; ❺), offers snazzy en-suites in an attractive *belle-époque* building.

West to Kudowa-Zdrój and the Góry Stołowe

Leaving Duszniki and heading towards the Czech frontier, you pass through the village of **SZCZYTNA**, where a glass factory produces more of Silesia's famous crystal. You might be intrigued by the impressive neo-Gothic **castle** situated near the summit of **Szczytnik** (589m), south of town, but it's actually some kind of children's home and not open to visitors. However, a winding road leads up the hill to a fine viewpoint over the valley below.

KUDOWA-ZDRÓJ lies at the foot of the Góry Stołowe and Wzgórza Lewińskie, 16km west of Duszniki and a couple of kilometres before the crossing into the Czech Republic. Its **springs** were discovered in 1580, and two centuries later the first spa building was erected, so creating the beginnings of today's resort. More than any of the other resorts, Kudowa preserves the feel of the bygone days when it was patronized by the internationally rich and famous, and today it continues to prosper albeit on a more prosaic level. It remains one of the most popular health resorts anywhere in Poland, but charmingly under-commercialized. A decent choice of accommodation and proximity to the Góry Stołowe help to make Kudowa-Zdrój the most likely place to base yourself in the Ziemia Kłodza.

Grand old villas set in their own grounds give Kudowa its erstwhile aristocratic air, yet it has no obvious centre other than the **spa park**. Here the huge domed **pijalnina** (pump room) houses the venerated marble fountain from which issue hot and cold springs. Nearby a stall cashes in on visitors' sentimentality, selling the pipe-like *kóbki*, small flattened jugs with swan-necked spouts, from which the surprisingly refreshing water – slightly sweet and carbonated – is traditionally imbibed. Adjacent to the pump room is a concert hall where a festival celebrating the music of Stanisław Moniuszko takes place each July. Sharing the nationalist outlook of Chopin, his compatriot and contemporary, Moniuszko's music has never caught on abroad to anything like the same extent, although you'll see a few bars of his music set into the amusingly kitschy "sheet music" railings installed around town. The spacious spa park's appeal continues with well-kept flowerbeds and over three hundred different species of tree and shrub.

Practicalities

Buses deliver you to ul. 1 Maja on the northeastern side of the town centre, from where it's a short walk back the way you came to the centrally placed **tourist office**, ul. Zdrojowa 42 (Mon–Fri 9am–5pm, Sat 10am–2pm; ☎074/866 1387, ⓦwww.kudowa.pl), which has a full list of private rooms (❷) and pensions (❸) in town. A lot of Kudowa-Zdrój's rest homes are run by the FWP (a workers' holiday association that dates back to the old regime), whose central reception desk in the *Bajka* hotel, ul. Zdrojowa 36 (☎074/866 1261), will fix you up with a simple no-frills room in one of their properties from 25zł per person. Decent **hotels** offering functional en-suites include the *Kosmos* at ul. Mariana Buczka 8a (☎074/866 1511; ❸); and the *Gwarek* at ul. Słowackiego 10 (☎074/866 1890; ❷), although you'll find more in terms of cosiness and atmosphere in the cluster of pensions just up from the bus station. Among the latter, *Kaprys*, Sikorskiego 2 (☎074/866 1663; ❷), is a medium-sized place with simple en-suite doubles, triples and quads; *Renia*, Sikorskiego 4 (☎074/866 1867; ❸), offers four rooms and an intimate B&B feel; and *Scaliano*, Sikorskiego 6 (☎074/866 1867; ❹), is a sizeable family-run hotel offering neat en-suites with TV. The *OSiR* sport hotel, ul. Łąkowa 12 (☎074/866 17 08; ❷), is in a scruffy area 1km west of town just off the main Prague road, but it does have a **hostel** section (20zł per person) and a **campsite** in the grounds.

Most characterful place to eat in Kudowa is the rustic-style *W Starym Młynie*, 1km west of town along ul. nad Potokiem, where you can eat heartily on meaty Polish staples. Similar fare can be sampled at central establishments like *Kosmiczna*, ul. Zdrojowa 41; and the nearby *Piekełko*, ul. Moniuszki 2 – both of which feature dining and dancing to an accompaniment of synthesizer-driven easy listening tunes. *Amfora*, on the way to the bus stop at ul. 1 Maja 11, offers a similarly Polish repertoire but without the music. *Café Domek*, Zdrojowa 34, serves up decent pizzas and ice cream on a big outdoor terrace, and is also a relaxing place for a **drink**. The other night-time drinking venues are down by the pump house, where you'll find *Raj*, favoured by an older crowd who like to dance to evergreen music under a mirrorball; and the next-door *Palma*, a stylish café-bar with correspondingly trendier clientele.

Into the Góry Stołowe

Rising above 900m and almost as flat as their name suggests, the **Góry Stołowe** (Table Mountains) are not the most enticing range in the Kłodzko region, but do have some extraordinary rock formations which can be appreciated in a full day's walk from Kudowa.

Starting from Kudowa, the green trail leads north to the outlying hamlet of **Czermna**, only thirty minutes from town, where the **Kaplica Czaszek** (Chapel of Skulls; daily 10am–1pm & 2–5pm) contains a macabre scene which threatens to undo the curative effects of Kudowa's springs. Its walls and ceiling are decorated with over three thousand skulls and crossed bones from the dead of various wars and epidemics. The chapel's priest, with the help of his devoted grave-digger, amassed the collection during the last decades of the eighteenth century. Their own remains are set in a glass case by the altar and thousands more skulls are stashed in the crypt. In fact ossuaries are common in central Europe, often based on the belief that having one's bones stored in a suitably holy site will increase the chances of enjoying a favourable afterlife.

The trail then goes northeast to the first of several fantastic rock formations in the range, the **Błędne Skały** (Erratic Boulders), where it twists and turns, squirming through narrow gaps between gigantic rocks. It then continues via Pasterka to the village of **Karłów**, from where a climb of nearly seven hundred steps leads to the **Szczeliniec Wielki**, the highest point in the range at 919m. Here the rocks have been weathered into a series of irregular shapes nicknamed "the camel", "the elephant", "the hen", and so on. There's a small entrance fee once you get to the top where a café offers refreshments, then you follow the trail which goes down through a deep chasm, on to a viewpoint and back by a different route.

From Błędne Skały the **red trail** leads directly to Karłów continuing east 5km to the largest and most scattered group of rocks in the area, the **Skalne Grzyby** (Petrified Mushrooms), rocks whose bases are worn away by uneven erosion producing the top-heavy appearance their name suggests.

If you want to tackle either Szczeliniec Wielki or the Skalne Grzyby without walking all the way from Kudowa, then consider catching a bus as far as Karłów (May–Sept 5 daily), and starting from there.

South of Kłodzko: Międzygórze and the Masyw Śnieżnika

At the southeastern corner of the Kłodzko region is the enticing **Masyw Śnieżnika**, the best of whose scenery can be seen in a good day's walk and which unlike the overrun Karkonosze to the west, seems to be pleasingly ignored by the crowds. The main jumping-off point is the charming hill resort of **Międzygórze** (Among the Hills), a dead end 30km southeast of Kłodzko and well served by buses.

Midway down the valley south of Kłodzko, some 15km away, is **BYSTRZY-CA KŁODZKA**, its peeling medieval core reminiscent of a charismatically decayed Mediterranean town. This impression is particularly strong if you cross over the river to get a magnificent full-frontal view of the town's tier-like layout, which on a sunny day looks more like southern France than Poland. First appearances can be deceptive however – the briefest of wanders around Bystrzyca's tatty streets will be enough to convince you that it was a mistake to break your journey here. Although the friendly **tourist office** at ul. Rycerskiej 20 (Mon–Fri 8.30am–6.30pm, Sat 10am–3pm, Sun 10am–2pm; ☏074/811 3731) will try and persuade you otherwise, it's best to continue southwards towards Międzygórze.

Międzygórze

Lying at the head of a wooded valley east of Bystrzyca, **MIĘDZYGÓRZE** is one of the quieter, more pleasant corners of the Kłodzko region – well worth a couple of days' stay if rustic peace and hiking opportunities are what you need. The village is characterized by the **drzewnianki** (wooden villas) built to serve as rest homes at the beginning of the nineteenth century. Ramshackle affairs with carved balustrades, neo-Gothic turrets and creaky interiors, they're still in use as tourist accommodation today.

Built around a central T-junction, the village is easy to find your way around. Five minutes' walk west of the junction, steps descend from the *Nad Wodospadem* hotel to a 27m-high **waterfall**, surrounded by deep forest. On the far side of the waterfall paths ascend towards the **Ogród Bajek** (Fantasy Garden) about twenty minutes away, a hilltop garden designed by local forester Izydor Kriesten before World War II, and restored by the PTTK in the 1990s. It's an altogether charming spot consisting of huts constructed from roots, branches and cones, each of which is inhabited by an assemblage of gnomes and model animals.

Accommodation in Międzygórze's *drzewnianki* (❶) is handled by the FWP, whose central reception is just uphill from the T-junction at ul. Sanatoryjna 2 (daily 8am–6pm; ☎074/813 5109). Of the **hotels**, the frumpy en-suites at the *Nad Wodospadem* at the western entrance to the village (☎074/813 5120; ❷) are somewhat eclipsed by the modern, avocado-coloured affairs at the central *Pensjonat Millennium*, ul. Wojska Polskiego 9 (☎074/813 5287, ⓦwww.millennium.maxi.pl; ❸). The *Wilczy Dol*, right on the T-junction (☎074/813 5286, ⓦwww.wilczy.dol.maxi.pl), has dorm beds from 15zł per person.

Both the *Millennium* and the *Nad Wodospadem* have decent **restaurants**. A marvellously laid-back place to hang out is the café of the *Wilczy Dol* (see above), with graffiti-style decor, tasty snacks, and alternative music on the sound system – outdoor gigs are sometimes organized in summer.

Walking in the Masyw Śnieżnika

Bang in the middle of Międzygórze, there's a signpost bristling with boards indicating the many waymarked tracks in the area. One particularly good walk follows the waymarked **red trail**, which rises steeply through lovely wooded countryside for about three hours, leading to the *Na Śnieżniku* **refuge** (☎074/813 5130), an isolated PTTK hostel which offers dorm beds and also serves inexpensive homely meals. From here it's then a much gentler ascent to the flat summit of **Śnieżnika** (1425m), the highest point in the Kłodzko region, set right on the Czech border.

From the summit it's worth descending north by the yellow trail towards Kletno, which will bring you in about an hour to the Bear's Cave, or **Jaskinia Niedźwiedzia** (daily except Mon & Thurs: May–August 9am–4.40pm; Feb–April & Sept–Nov 10am–4.40pm). Discovered in 1966 during quarrying, the cave takes its name from the bear fossils discovered there. Bats still inhabit the cave which boasts the usual anthropomorphically wondrous stalactites and stalagmites. Visits are by guided tour only, with group numbers limited to fifteen people, exploring 600m of cave in about 40 minutes. You can also get to the cave directly from Międzygórze, without scaling any mountains, in about two hours.

From the cave, another kilometre's walk brings you to the village of **KLETNO**, which has a couple of snack bars, a bus service to Kłodzko via Stronie Śląskie and Lądek-Zdrój, and hostel-style **accommodation** in the *Centre for Ecology and Ecotourism* at Kletno Górne 17 (☎074/814 1388). There's another hostel 3km down the road at Kletno 8 (☎074/814 1358).

Lądek-Zdrój and beyond

Returning to Bystrzyca Kłodzka, a scenic drive winds back up into the hills directly east of town. Climbing up through forested slopes and emerging from the trees, the narrow road reaches a **pass** where it's worth stopping to appreciate the superb panorama around you. Descending down the other side, the valley unfolds revealing an isolated Lutheran chapel near the village of Sienna, and brings you to the pleasant town of **Stronie Śląskie** (terminus of the rail line from Kłodzko) whose Sudety glassworks have managed not to turn the place into the usual eyesore.

Eight kilometres further north is the spa resort of **LĄDEK-ZDRÓJ**, where, according to tradition, the waters were known for their healing properties as early as the thirteenth century, when the bathing installations were allegedly destroyed by the Tatars. They've certainly been exploited since the late fifteenth century, and in later years attracted visitors as august as Goethe and Turgenev. Today the town, strung out along the river Biała Ladecka, retains a charm that the more popular western spa resorts cannot match.

Centrepiece of the grandiose Neoclassical **spa buildings** at the east end of town is the main sanatorium, a handsome domed building evoking the heyday of the spa, and hereabouts you'll find the odd villa still surviving from that era. In the older part of town, about a kilometre to the west, a mid-sixteenth-century stone **bridge** can still be seen, decorated with statues of religious figures. The town's spacious **Rynek** features some Baroque-fronted houses, all facing the octagonal tower of the town hall.

Tourist information duties are handled by the **PTTK**, near the spa quarter at ul. Kościuszki 44 (Mon–Fri 8am–3pm; ☎074/814 6255). As for **accommodation**, the FWP office, Paderewskiego 5 (☎074/814 6272), will find you a room in one of the resort's rest homes for 35zł per person. The *Hotel Lido*, ul. Kościuszki 23a (☎074/814 7165; ❹), has reasonable en-suites with TV; and there's a **youth hostel** (☎074/814 6645) in the outlying hamlet of Stojków, 3km to the south – although you'll have to walk there if you don't have your own transport. For **eating**, standard and inexpensive Polish fare is on offer at both the restaurant of the *Lido* and the *Polska Chata*, ul. Kościuszki 5.

Immediately to the east of the town, the **Góry Złote** (Golden Mountains) offer some good hiking routes. Check out the blue trail which leads southeast of the town, ascending within an hour to a ruined medieval castle near the summit of **Karpień** (776m), via a series of oddly weathered rocks so often found throughout the region.

Leaving Lądek and heading north, the road continues winding through the forests where you'll encounter soot-spewing trucks transporting rubble from the region's quarries to the processing plants. Soon the road decends swiftly to the town of **Złoty Stok**, sat on the edge of the interminable plain which stretches, with only modest variations in elevation, all the way to the Baltic.

Paczków to Nysa

Heading east from the Kłodzko region, you traverse the undulating plateau of Upper Silesia, which stretches down to the Beskid Mountains. The route runs through a string of small fortified towns associated for most of their history with the bishops of Wrocław, who ruled an independent principality here from 1195 until its dissolution by Prussia in 1810. Like much of southern Silesia, it's an entrancing landscape of rolling farmland broken up by forest, largely unaffected by significant industrial development. The terrain levels out a bit towards Nysa, where most of the surrounding fields are given over to the cultivation of rapeseed, producing a blaze of bright yellow ground cover in the early summer.

Buses operating the Kłodzko–Paczków–Nysa route present your best way of **getting around**; placing the region within easy day-trip range of the Ziemia Kłodzka. Should you be approaching from the north, Nysa is well connected by bus to Wrocław and Opole. Trains trundle through the region on their way from Kłodzko to Katowice, but they're both slow and infrequent.

Paczków

In contrast to its neighbours, the quiet little market town of **PACZKÓW**, 30km east of Kłodzko, has managed to preserve its medieval fortifications almost intact – hence its designation as "Poland's Carcassonne". In reality, Paczków is hardly in that league, but has the advantage of being untouched by the hands of Romantically inclined nineteenth-century restorers, as well as being generally overlooked by crowds of tourists.

Nowadays, the mid-fourteenth-century **ramparts** form a shady promenade around the centre of the Stare Miasto; their visual impact is diminished by the enveloping later buildings, though it's a wonder that the town managed to grow so much without their demolition. As it is, nineteen of the twenty-four towers survive, as does nearly all of the original 1350 metres of wall, pierced by three barbicans: the square Wrocław Gate of 1462 and the cylindrical Ząbkow and Kłodzkego gates from around 1550.

The area within the walls, spread across a gentle slope, consists of just a handful of streets, but is centred on a large **Rynek**. In the familiar off-centre position is the **town hall**, so comprehensively rebuilt in the twentieth century that only the belfry of its Renaissance predecessor is left.

Rearing up behind the Rynek stands the attention-grabbing form of **Kościół św. Jana** (St John's Church), a strongly fortified part of the town's defences. With a central tower jazzed up with crenellations resembling molar teeth, it looks more like the kind of fortress the Venetians would have built in the Adriatic than a parish church in central Silesia. Inside, the box-like geometry of the design is particularly evident, with the chancel the same length as the main nave.

Practicalities

Paczków has two **hotels**. The *Korona*, ul. Wojska Polskiego 31 (☎077/431 6177; ❷) lies outside the ramparts on a street leading directly off the southeastern side of the Rynek. One kilometre south of town, just off the Nysa road, the *Energopol*, ul. Chrobrego 2 (☎077/431 6298; ❷), is a former workers' hostel which makes up for its undistinguished prefabs with friendly service and good value. There's also a **campsite** on the southwestern fringes of town at ul. Jagiellońska 6 (☎077/431 6813). As far as **places to eat** are concerned, there are a number of cafés around the Rynek offering simple snacks; and a cheap, satisfying pizzeria, the *Monika*, on ul. Sienkiewicza, with outdoor seating in the shadow of the town walls.

Otmuchów

OTMUCHÓW, 14km east of Paczków, was the original capital of the prince-bishopric. In the centre of town is the **castle**, nowadays a hotel but originally twelfth-century Romanesque, which guarded an extensive fortification system now all but vanished. It was transformed into a palace in the sixteenth century, and in 1820 was sold to Wilhelm von Humboldt, founder of the university of Berlin and architect of Prussia's educational system. He lived here in retirement, the liberal views he had championed having fallen from official favour.

The castle tower is sometimes open to tourists in the summer, but times are unpredictable. It's worth making your way up here however, if only to linger in the well-tended garden of the castle hotel.

On the Rynek is the Renaissance **town hall**, adorned with a beautifully elaborate, double-faced sundial mounted on a corner of the building. The square slopes upwards to a well-kept floral garden and the parish **church**, a very central-European-looking Baroque construction with a customary twin-towered facade. Recently renovated to perfection by German capital (a practice now occurring throughout the former German territories of post-communist Poland), its ample interior is richly decorated with stuccowork by Italian craftsmen and large painted altarpieces, including several by Michael Willmann.

The *Zamek* **hotel** in the castle (☎077/431 4691, ⓦ www.zamek.otmuchow,pl; ❺) offers rather cosy rooms furnished in a jumble of styles, although be warned that some of the singles come with shared bathroom facilities. To eat in Otmuchów, the **café-restaurant** *Herbowa* in the castle takes some beating, offering classic Polish dishes in formal, starched-napkin surroundings. The *Merkury*, facing the town hall at ul. Zamkowa 2, has a big choice of inexpensive pizzas and salads.

Nysa

The name of **NYSA**, 12km east of Otmuchów, has become synonymous with the trucks made here for export all over Eastern Europe. Yet industry is a relative newcomer to this town which, in spite of the devastation of 1945, still preserves memories of the days when it basked in the fanciful title of "the Silesian Rome", a reference to its numerous religious houses and reputation as a centre of Catholic education. It came to the fore when the adoption of the Reformation in Wrocław forced the bishops to reside outside the city; they then built up Nysa, the capital of their principality for the previous couple of centuries, as their power base. With its sprinkling of architectural monuments left stranded in a sea of postwar concrete, Nysa is a place for a brief wander rather than a protracted stay.

The Town

From both the bus and train stations, bear right along the edge of the park, then turn left into ul. Kolejowa which leads in a straight line towards the centre. On the way, you pass the fourteenth-century **Brama Wrocławska** (Wrocław Gate), an unusually graceful piece of military architecture with wrought-iron dragons' heads acting as gutter flues, left stranded by the demolition of the ramparts. It's a tantalizing reminder of Nysa's long role as a border fortress: first fortified in the twelfth century by Bolesław the Wrymouth in his struggles against his Bohemian-backed brother Zbigniew.

Having lost its town hall and all but four of its old houses during the war, Nysa's vast **Rynek** is nevertheless not as bad as you might expect, with a few flowerbeds and benches on which repose the town's idle, weary and inebriate. Particularly attractive is the jolly seventeenth-century **Waga Miejska** (Weigh House), which looks as if it belongs somewhere in the Low Countries.

Off the northeastern side of the Rynek is the **Katedra św. Jakuba** (St James's Cathedral) which long served the exiled bishops. Put up in just six years in the 1420s, it was comprehensively flattened during World War II, and faithfully reconstructed soon afterwards. It's a fine example of the hall church style, with nave and aisles of equal height – a design much favoured in Germany but rare in Poland. Entering through the graceful double portal, it's the spareness of the lofty thirty-metre interior which makes the strongest impression. So crushing is the weight of the vault that many of the uncomfortably slender octagonal brick pillars visibly bow under the strain. The chapels provide the only intimate note: fenced off by wrought-iron grilles, they feature funerary plaques and monuments to the bishops and local notables. Outside, the church's detached stone **belfry** was abandoned after fifty years' work and further damaged during the war, after which it seems to have been left to its own devices.

South of St James's lies the well-preserved if generally deserted Baroque episcopal quarter. The **Pałac Biskupi** (Bishops' Palace), reached down ul. Jarosławka at no. 11, is now fitted out as a surprisingly good local **museum** (Tues 9am–5pm, Wed–Fri 9am–3pm, Sat & Sun 10am–3pm; 3zł, free on Sat), with well-documented exhibits on the history of Nysa. Inside you'll find spacious displays of sixteenth- to eighteenth-century engravings, several pictures of Nysa's postwar ruin, including a shrapnel-damaged 1574 weather vane, as well as fragments from irreparable buildings. There's also a model of the town as it was three hundred years ago, various secular and religious treasures and perhaps best of all, some wonderfully chunky carved and inlaid Baroque furniture, including a few huge wardrobes it would take a crane to shift and on which you could justifiably observe "they don't make them like that anymore".

Immediately west of here lies the complex of Jesuit buildings in pl. Solny, which kick off with the white-walled **Kościół NMP** (Church of Our Lady), its austerity is softened by some recently discovered ceiling frescoes and a beautiful eighteenth-century silver tabernacle at the high altar. Adjoining it is the famous **Carolinum College**, whose luminaries included the Polish kings Michał Korybut Wiśniowiecki and Jan Sobieski.

South of the Rynek, the only other reminder of "the Silesian Rome" is the **Klasztor Bożogrobców** (Monastery of the Hospitallers of the Holy Sepulchre). This order moved to Nysa from the Holy Land at the end of the twelfth century, but the huge complex you see today dates from the early eighteenth century. It's now a seminary, and you have to ask at the reception on ul. św. Pawła to get into the magnificent Baroque **Kościół św. Piotra i Pawła** (Church of SS Peter and Paul) on the parallel ul. Bracka. Passing a rather creepy Eye of Providence looking down on you in the courtyard, you'll soon have your efforts rewarded. The resplendent interior features gilt capitals, a multicoloured marble altar that's one of the best for miles, and a reproduction of the Holy Sepulchre in Jerusalem. There's also a cycle of highly theatrical frescoes by the brothers Christoph Thomas and Felix Anton Scheffler.

Heading northwest from the Rynek along ul. Krzywoustego brings you to the **Brama Ziębicka** (Ziębicka Gate), a plain brick tower standing in the middle of a roundabout. You can climb up its 150 steps for a couple of złoty.

Practicalities

The **bus** and **train stations** are at the eastern side of the town. Nysa's one central **hotel**, the *Piast*, right by the Ziębicka Gate at ul. Krzywoustego 14 (☎077/433 4084, ✉hotelpiast@poczta.onet.pl; ❺), offers comfy en-suites and Eighties decor. Otherwise, there's the *Navigator*, a friendly, upscale B&B 300m west of the Rynek at ul. Wyspiańskiego 11 (☎077/433 4170; ❸), and the *Garnizonowy*, over the river just north of the centre at ul. Kościuszki 4 (☎077/433 1035), offering spartan doubles (❶) or rooms with shower (❷).

The best **restaurants** are the *Capri*, a snazzy pizzeria at Rynek 35; and the *Kama*, close by at Rynek 32–35, which offers good Polish fare with some worthwhile vegetarian options. The Polish cooking at the *Hotel Piast* restaurant is also reasonable, and it's open till midnight.

Brzeg

A worthwhile stopover for a few hours between Wrocław and Opole is the old ducal seat of **BRZEG**, an easily manageable and agreeable market town with an impressive array of monuments. Originally a fishing village on the bank (*brzeg*) of the Odra, Brzeg was documented in the early thirteenth century as having a **castle** associated with the Piast dynasty. In 1311 it became a regional capital in the continuing subdivision of Silesia, and ousted Legnica as the main residence of the court. The Piasts remained there until 1675 when the family, a prominent dynasty throughout the recorded history of Poland, finally died out.

The Town

Next to the **castle** (see below) is the superbly renovated Jesuit **Kościół św. Krzyża** (Church of the Holy Cross), which dates back to the turn of the eighteenth century. Sober enough from the outside, its single interior space is encrusted with Rococo decorations with an illusionist altar replacing the usual epic construction. Across from the palace stands the Piast **college**, which was built some thirty years later. It has suffered even more from the vagaries of time and now houses a police academy.

Back towards the centre is the **town hall**, which belongs to the same architectural school as the palace, and again is an adaptation of an older structure, from which the tall belfry survives. It consists of two long parallel buildings, each terminating in a tower crowned by a bulbous Baroque steeple, joined together by the triple-gabled facade, although this all makes it sound much more impressive than it actually is. Further on towards the bus and train stations is the Rynek, centred on the fourteenth-century **Kościół św. Mikołaja** (St Nicholas's Church), its twin towers rebuilt last century and linked by an unusual arched bridge. The interior is startlingly spacious and boasts a varied collection of finely carved memorial plaques of prominent families. To the left of the altar is a carved wooden **triptych** presenting mysterious medieval interpretations of various biblical events, while the opposite side offers a rather wily depiction of the Matka Boska Częstochowska; certainly an improvement on the po-faced original venerated in Częstochowa (see p.483).

The castle

Brzeg's most historic area lies by the park a few minutes northwest of the town centre, close to the river. Seen from its spacious square, the **castle** (Tues & Thurs–Sat 10am–4pm, Wed 10am–6pm; 4zł), though fondly referred to locally as the "Silesian Wawel" (Wawel being the famous castle in Kraków; see p.428), is a bit of an anticlimax: predominantly Renaissance, with the Gothic presbytery of St Hedwig's (the mausoleum of the Piasts), plus various misjudged additions that have all but ruined any visual integrity. Badly damaged by Frederick the Great's troops in 1741, the palace was relegated for the next century and a half to the status of an arsenal. Only in the last decade has restoration returned parts of the structure to something like their former glory, which, in the case of the interior Renaissance sections, is something special. Built in the 1530s by a team of Italian masons, Brzeg became the prototype for a whole series of palaces in Poland, Bohemia, northern Germany and Sweden.

The extravagantly rich **gateway** is perhaps the finest Renaissance feature, modelled on Dürer's woodcut of a triumphal arch in honour of Emperor Maximilian. Above, in a shameless piece of self-glorification, are portrait figures of Duke George II and his wife, Barbara von Brandenburg. At the same level are pairs of knights whose coats of arms include those of Brzeg, Legnica and the Jagiellonian monarchs of Poland – the last, given that Silesia had not been a part of Poland for the past three centuries, being an expression of unrequited loyalty. Two tiers of busts above the windows trace the duke's genealogy, beginning with what appears as a rather regal interpretation of the peasant Piast at the upper left-hand corner. On the left rises the Lwów Tower, a survival of the medieval castle, along with part of its fortifications.

To some extent, the three-storey **courtyard** does indeed resemble the much larger Wawel palace in Kraków, above all in the lofty arcades. However, its carved decoration ultimately gives it a different character, with the heraldic motif continued on the more modest interior gate and antique-style medallions to the sides of the arcades.

The halls of the second floor have been adapted to house the **Silesian Piast Museum**, which frequently contains exhibits from the Muzeum Narodowe in Wrocław.

Practicalities

The **train** and **bus stations** are both just a few minutes' walk south of the town centre. The accommodation situation in town is pretty desperate, with the *Piast* **hotel**, situated near the station on the way to the town centre at ul. Piastowska 14 (☎077/416 2027; en-suites ❺, rooms with shared facilities ❷), currently representing the only reliable central choice. The classiest **restaurant** remains the *Ratuszowa* in the town hall cellars, which is an excellent source of good, medium-price food.

In late May, Brzeg's castle, town hall and churches are put to impressive use for a four-day-long international **festival** of classical music.

Opole

If you're planning on spending a fair amount of time in Silesia, chances are you'll end up in **OPOLE** sooner or later. Situated in the very heart of the province, midway down the train line between Wrocław and Katowice, and within easy reach of Nysa, the Kłodzko region and Częstochowa, the city makes a convenient touring base. Though ravaged by scores of fires throughout its history, the centre presents a well-balanced spread of old and new, ringed by a green belt and with the unsightly industrial installations banished to the outskirts.

One of Opole's main assets is its setting on the banks of the Odra. The river divides to form an island, the **Wyspa Pasieka**, which was inhabited in the ninth century by a Slavic tribe called the Opolanes. Bolesław the Brave established the island as a fortress, but it subsequently became divorced from its mother country, serving as the capital of a Piast principality from 1202 until this particular line died out in 1532.

The city and the highly productive agricultural land around were understandably coveted by the Polish state after World War I, but Opole voted to remain part of Germany in the plebiscite of 1921, subsequently becoming the capital of the German province of Upper Silesia. In contrast to most other places ceded to Poland after World War II, the Opole region has retained a sizeable **German** minority, an asset that can be admitted now that Germany has surrendered its territorial claims to this area.

The City

The hub of Opole has long moved from the Wyspa Pasieka to the right bank of the Odra, where the central area is laid out on a gridiron pattern. Nonetheless, the island in many ways makes a chronologically correct place to begin an exploration.

The island

Of the four **bridges** crossing the arm of the river, look out for the second as you move northwards from the train station, one of several structures in Opole built around 1910 in the Secessionist style. Arched like a bridge in a Japanese garden, this steel construction was made so cheaply that it was once known as the Groschen Bridge after the smallest coin then in circulation. It bears the curious coat of arms of the city, showing half an eagle and half a cross: the local Piasts allowed one side of the family's traditional blazon to be replaced by a

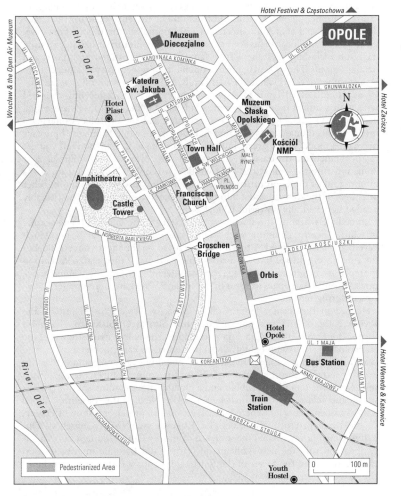

symbol of the city's acquisition of a relic of the True Cross. Halfway across the bridge, take a glance in either direction; the thick lining of willow trees along the bank give an uncannily rural impression light years away from its urban location.

The medieval Piast **castle** certainly hasn't been done any favours by the city planners, its surviving **round tower** now partly hidden behind ugly 1930s council offices that were built over the ruins. In summer you can climb to the top of the tower for a view of the city. The castle's grounds have been converted into a park with a large artificial lake sporting fountains and an open-air amphitheatre, the setting for the **Festival of Polish Song** – the Polish pop industry's most important annual showcase – held each June. Continuing north along ul. Piastowska, you get a good view of the Stare Miasto on the opposite bank, lined with a jumble of riverside buildings.

The city centre

Returning across the Odra by ul. Zamkowa, you soon arrive at the Franciscan **church**, a much-altered Gothic construction chiefly remarkable for the richly decorated Chapel of St Anne, erected in 1309, off the southern side of the nave. Endowed by the local Piasts to serve as their **mausoleum**, it has an exquisite star vault including keystones of the family eagle and painted with floral and heraldic motifs. The two magnificent double tombs were carved around 1380 by a member of the celebrated Parler family. Although he was still alive, an effigy of Duke Bolko III was made to accompany that of his recently deceased wife, with a similar monument created in belated memory of his two ancestral namesakes. The retable is from a century later, and shows Bolko I offering a model of this monastery to St Anne and the Virgin, while Ladislaus II presents her with a model of the great church of Jasna Góra in Częstochowa. If you get to the Franciscan **monastery**, just around the corner on pl. Wolności 2, at 2pm, and ring the bell at the little window, a monk will lead you on a 45-minute tour of the **catacombs**, which contain the unadorned coffins of other members of the dynasty and a number of fourteenth-century frescoes, notably a faded but tragically powerful *Crucifixion*.

Immediately beyond the Franciscan monastery is the buzzing **Rynek**, some of whose cheerful mansions were badly damaged in World War II, but which have been deftly restored. A **town hall** has stood on the square since 1308, but the fine tower you see today – a wonderful pastiche of the Palazzo Vecchio in Florence – originates from an early-nineteenth-century neo-Renaissance design, being rebuilt true to form in the mid-1930s when it unexpectedly collapsed during repairs.

Housed in the former Jesuit College at ul. św. Wojciecha 13 just off the Rynek is the district museum, or **Muzeum Śląska Opolskiego** (Tues–Fri 9am–3.30pm, Sat 10am–3pm, Sun noon–5pm; 3zł), whose main strength is the archeology section, with exhibits from prehistoric to early medieval times. Also worth looking out for are some attractive tinted photographs from earlier this century showing the castle making way for the council offices, the town hall's tower reduced to a pile of rubble, and a chilling monochrome shot of Opole's synagogue ablaze on the *Kristallnacht* of 1938. Next to the museum, a broad stairway ascends to a hill where St Adalbert used to preach as bishop of Prague, Opole being part of his diocese. The **Kościół św. NMP** (Church of Our Lady), which now occupies the spot, was originally Gothic, though this is hardly apparent from the neo-Romanesque facade and Baroque interior decorations. Beyond are the tower of the fourteenth-century fortress and remains of the sixteenth-century town wall.

The cathedral quarter

From the Rynek, ul. Książat Opolskich leads to the cathedral of **Katedra św. Jakuba** (St James's Cathedral), mixing fourteenth-century Gothic and nineteenth-century imitation with the usual Baroque excesses. Raised to the status of a cathedral only a couple of decades ago, the church, which soars with Gothic verticality, is chiefly famous for the allegedly miraculous, jewel-encrusted icon to the right of the main altar – the *Opole Madonna* crowned by a gaggle of gaily cavorting cherubs.

The **Muzeum Diecezjalne** (Diocesan Museum; Tues & Thurs 10am–noon & 2–5pm; 3zł) is located in a block of modern buildings at the beginning of ul. Kardynała Kominka. Opened in 1987 largely as a result of voluntary effort, it was the object of considerable local pride as the first non-state museum in postwar Poland and one whose display techniques put the nationally owned collections to shame. Leaflets are available in English and German describing the exhibits, all from churches in the Opole region. On the ground floor are several outstanding Gothic sculptures, including an *Enthroned Madonna* in the Parler style. Upstairs, pride of place is taken by the fourteenth-century reliquary made to house Opole's fragment of the True Cross; there's also a lovely *Virgin and Child* attributed to Fra Filippo Lippi. The small room next door features gifts to adorn the *Opole Madonna* presented by worthies ranging from King Jan Sobieski to the present pope. Imaginative exhibitions of contemporary religious art are also featured.

The Muzeum Wsi Opolskiej

By the side of the main road to Wrocław, 8km west of the city centre at ul. Wrocławska 174, reached by bus #5 from the main bus station, is the excellent open-air Opole village museum, or **Muzeum Wsi Opolskiej** (Tues–Sun 10am–6pm; 5zł). Some sixty examples of the wooden rural architecture of the region have been erected here, many grouped in simulation of their original environment. Particularly notable is the wooden church from Gręboszów built in 1613, a typical example of what is still the main place of worship in a few Silesian villages. Other highlights are a windmill and an eighteenth-century water mill in full working order, as well as an orchard full of beehives built in the same rustic idiom.

Practicalities

Opole's main **train** and **bus** stations are at the southern end of town close to the centre, just a few minutes along ul. Wojciecha Korfantego from the Wyspa Pasieka. It is perhaps the best-signposted town in Poland, telling you not only the names of streets but what hotels and sights lie along them. The **tourist office** at ul. Krakowska 15 (Mon–Fri 9am–5pm; ⓣ077/451 1987, ⓔpromocja@um.opole.pl) will give you the low-down on local **accommodation** possibilities – although there's a shortage of budget-oriented places in town. Of the inexpensive places, the small and friendly *Zacisze*, just east of the historic quarters at Grunwaldzka 28 (ⓣ077/454 2304; ❹), offers a mixture of rooms with en-suite or shared facilities just east of the town centre; while the recently renovated *Festival*, 1km northeast of the Rynek at ul. Oleska 86 (ⓣ077/455 6017, ⓔhotelfestival@com.pl; ❻), is already edging towards business standard. Plusher still are the *Weneda*, just east of the train and bus stations at ul. 1 Maja 77 (ⓣ077/453 6513, ⓦwww.hotel-weneda.opole.pl; ❻); the revamped Orbis-run *Hotel Opole*, conveniently located close to the train station at ul. Krakowska 59 (ⓣ077/451 8100, ⓔopole@orbis.pl; ❻); and the *Piast*, ul. Piastowska 1 (ⓣ077/454 9710; ❼), which has a pleasant terrace overlooking the river. The **youth hostel** is to the rear of the main train station at ul. Struga 16 (July &

Aug; ☎077/454 3352). The nearest **campsite** is 5km northeast of town on the Kluczbork road, next to the bathing beach at Lake Turowa – Kluczbork-bound buses pass by.

Opole has many excellent **restaurants**. Reliable Polish fare is available from the dimly atmospheric *Skorpion*, ul. Książąt Opolskich 6; while *U Mnicha*, Ozimska 10, serves up a mixture of domestic and Middle-Eastern grill dishes in a rough-hewn cellar done up with hi-tech fittings. There's the cheap *Express Pizzeria* at ul. Reymonta 14, and the *Grabówska* creperie, near the river at ul. Mozarta 2, serves the best pancakes in Silesia.

In summer the Rynek is alive with people **drinking** into the early hours: try the excellent *Maska*, a lively pub-style venue at Rynek 4 which also does restaurant-quality food. Elsewhere, there's the *Highlander* at ul. Szpitalna 3, where you can play darts and admire the mock tartan kilts of the waiters; and the *Pub pod Smokiem*, a pleasant summer-evening spot at the tip of Wyspa Pasieska on ul. Ostrowek.

Opole is reasonably well served with cultural diversions. There are two **cinemas**: the Odra at ul. Ozimska 4 and the Kraków at ul. Katowicka 69. The main **theatre** is the J. Kochanowski at pl. Teatralny 12, and there's a **puppet theatre** at pl. Kopernika 1.

Góra Świętej Anny

Forty kilometres southeast of Opole, conspicuous on its 410-metre hill, is the village of **GÓRA ŚWIĘTEJ ANNY** (St Anne's Hill). Associated with the cult of St Anne, mother of the Virgin Mary, it's one of the most popular places of **pilgrimage** in Poland and is the scene of colourful processions on July 26 each year. Although the cult of St Anne is long established in Silesia, Góra Świętej Anny's status as a major pilgrimage shrine dates back only to the mid-seventeenth century, when a Franciscan **monastery** was built to replace a modest Gothic votive chapel. As is the case with Jasna Góra, its popularity is intimately associated with Polish nationalism, fanned by the fact that the monks have been expelled three times (as a result of the policies of Napoleon, Bismarck and Hitler). For five days in May 1921, the village was the scene of bitter fighting following the Upper Silesia plebiscite, which left it in German hands. Ill-feeling has persisted: it was only in 1989 that the outlawing of Masses in German, introduced when the monks returned in 1945 in retaliation for previous bans on Polish services, was rescinded.

The church, decorated in a restrained Baroque style, houses the source of the pilgrimage, a tiny miraculous statue of *St Anne with the Virgin and Child*, high above the main altar. An unassuming piece of folksy Gothic carving, it's usually decked out in gorgeous clothes. Below the monastery buildings is the mid-eighteenth century **Calvary**, an elaborate processional way with 33 chapels and shrines telling the story of the Passion. A large and less tasteful **Lourdes grotto** was added as the centrepiece in 1912.

Outside major church festivals, however, it's a moribund little place, the antithesis of the relentlessly busy Jasna Góra and not really worth the detour unless you've your own transport. Getting here by public transport is a long-winded process best done by taking a train from Opole to the hideously industrialized Zdzieszowice and then covering the remaining 6km on foot or by bus. You'll find a small shop in the town square below the church and the tidy *Anna* **pension** on the main road a short distance away at ul. Leśnicka 7 (☎077/461 5412; ❷). There is, however, a **youth hostel** at ul. Szkolna 1 (☎077/461 5473), and the *Pod Górą Chelmską* **hotel** and roadhouse, half a kilometre southeast of town at ul. Leśnicka 26a (☎077/461 5484; ❸).

Katowice and around

The southeastern corner of Silesia is dominated by an almost continuously built-up conurbation of about a dozen towns, which begins around 65km southeast of Opole and rejoices in the collective name of **GOP** (Górnośląski Okręg Przemysłowy, or Upper Silesian Industrial District). Two million inhabitants make this the most densely populated part of the country, with 400,000 in the largest city, **KATOWICE** – an important rail hub providing easy onward connections to Kraków, Częstochowa and Bielsko-Biała.

The region's rich mineral seams have been extensively mined since the Middle Ages – nearly a tenth of the world's known coal exists here, but it wasn't until the nineteenth-century **industrial revolution** that the area became heavily urbanized. In 1800, Katowice had just 500 inhabitants. Fifty years later, its population was a still modest 4000 before Upper Silesia mushroomed into the powerhouse of the Prussian state, in tandem with the broadly similar Ruhr at the opposite end of the country.

With a population composed almost equally of Germans and Poles (and with many of mixed blood), the fate of the area became a hot political issue after World War I – and one that was to be of far more than local significance (see box, overleaf, for the full story). In the communist period, the conurbation maintained its high-profile position, thanks to the ideological stress placed on heavy industry. Workers here enjoyed a privileged position; mining wages, for example, were three times the national average income.

Given the factory-filled appearance of the GOP's urban landscape, and the catastrophic **pollution** produced by its heavy industries, it's a region unlikely to appear on any but the most eccentric tourist itineraries. Many of the less profitable factories closed down in the 1990s, reducing environmental problems but adding to the ranks of local unemployed. However Katowice's big population and excellent communicatons have made it an obvious target for foreign investment, and those travellers who stop off here will find that a sense of big-city bustle coexists with the inexcapable aura of post-industrial decay.

Despite the presence of a full symphony orchestra in Katowice, the GOP's most important contribution to modern Polish culture has probably been its **football** teams – with the likes of GKS Katowice, Ruch Chorzów and Gornik Zabrze regularly tasting top-level success. The Polish national team often plays here, and English fans may wish to forget that Katowice was the scene of a famous 0-2 defeat in 1973 that helped to confirm England's decline as a footballing power – and effectively ended the international career of World Cup-winning captain Bobby Moore. The Poles, meanwhile, went on to enjoy a golden decade of international success.

The Town

Although Katowice is notoriously low on sightseeing attractions, those with time to kill could do worse than peep into the **Muzeum Śląskie** (Museum of Silesia; Tues–Fri 10am–5pm, Sat & Sun 1am–4pm; 3zł), just north of the Rynek, which harbours a reasonable collection of Polish art. From here you can't miss Katowice's most alluring building, the futuristic sports hall known as the **Spodek** ("flying saucer"), a dark, domed structure presiding above the road intersection to the north. Rock fans from all over southern Poland flock here to attend major gigs – numerous big names from the West have appeared here in recent years.

In the aftermath of World War I, the dispute between Poland and Germany over the ownership of **Upper Silesia** represented the first reasonably successful attempt by the international community at providing an enduring, if not permanent, solution to a potentially explosive problem by means of mediation rather than through military force.

Following Germany's wartime defeat, the Allies at first intended to transfer the whole of Upper Silesia to the newly resurrected Poland, which would otherwise have been a poor agricultural country with no industrial base. Polish spokesmen stressed their historical claim on the territory and on its demographic make-up, although the latter couldn't be quantified exactly. Strongly partisan support for the transferral of sovereignty came from France, which wished to weaken Germany as much as possible and establish a strong ally to its east. This rather unnerved the British, ever anxious about the balance of power in Europe and concerned at the potential danger of French hegemony. They gradually came to back the ferocious German backlash against the proposed change in ownership, believing that it was in Europe's best interests for industries to be left in the hands of the nation that had developed them, rather than being handed over to a new country with no business experience: Prime Minister Lloyd George went so far as to suggest that allocating Upper Silesia to Poland was like giving a clock to a monkey.

As the Allies dragged their feet on the issue, Upper Silesia remained the one unresolved question on the now much-changed map of Europe. Frustrated at the lack of progress, the Poles staged **insurrections** in 1919 and 1920. Eventually, the Allies decided to test popular feelings by means of a **plebiscite**, which was held in March 1921. This was won by the Germans by 707,000 votes to 479,000, but the result was discredited by the fact that a large number (thought to be around 182,000) of former citizens were temporarily shipped back from their new homes elsewhere in Germany. Support for continued German sovereignty was strongest in the industrial communities closest to Poland, making the solution of partition seemingly intractable, particularly as it was taken for granted that the conurbation could not be divided satisfactorily.

In May 1921, a third insurrection led to the **occupation** of the territory by the Polish army. Realizing the need for a quick solution, the Allies referred the matter to the **League of Nations**, the body newly established to promote world peace. The neutral observers who were assigned to the task decided that **partition** was the only fair solution, and used the plebiscite returns as the basis for determining the respective shares of the carve-up. By the **Geneva Convention on Upper Silesia** of 1922, which ran to 606 articles, the Germans retained two-thirds of the land and three-fifths of the population, but an international boundary was cut through the industrial conurbation, a somewhat Solomonic solution which left Poland with the vast majority of the coal mines and blast furnaces. However, in what was itself a radical and previously untried experiment, the area was kept as an economic unit, with guarantees on the movement of goods, material and labour, the provision of public services and the rights of individuals who found themselves living under an alien flag.

Despite dire predictions to the contrary, the agreement endured for the full fifteen years it was scheduled to operate. The Poles proved perfectly capable of running what had previously been German industrial concerns, and the presence of an international frontier did not impede the conurbation's productivity. Admittedly there was a persistent flow of grievances, mostly from the Germans, who conveniently forgot that they had managed to hold on to a good deal of valuable territory which they'd come close to losing. However, the country's new democratic leaders felt duty bound to stop short of calling for a return of the lost portion, and, had it not been for the advent of Hitler, the League's audacious solution might well have survived indefinitely.

Practicalities

Should you make an overnight stay in town, there are three inexpensive **hotels** conveniently close to the train station. A couple of minutes' walk west, at ul. Dworcowa 9, is the *Centralny* (☎032/253 9041; ❹), and a few minutes further on, the *Śląski* at ul. Mariacka 15 (☎032/253 7011; ❹). Just behind the station you'll also find the *Polonia* at ul. Kochanowskiego 3 (☎032/251 2850; ❹). The *Silesia*, near the bus station at ul. Piotra Skargi 2 (☎032/596211; ❼) is the best of the downtown business-oriented places.

Katowice's all-year **youth hostel** is about fifteen minutes' walk north of the train station at ul. Sokolska 26 (☎032/59 6487). **Camping** in Katowice might sound paradoxical, but diehards will find a site southwest of the city centre by a lake at ul. Murckowska 6 (mid-May to late Sept; ☎032/255 5388) and reached by bus #4.

Many of the best **eating** venues are to be found on two pedestrianized streets near the station; ul. Stawowa and ul. Wawelka, where you'll find numerous pizzerias and snack outlets. The *Bodega*, Stawowa 10, offers a range of European cuisine in a cosy candle-lit ambience; while the *Café Gaudi*, Wawelska 2, serves up cakes and ice cream in a florid interior inspired by the Barcelona-based architect.

Tarnowskie Góry

From a tourist point of view, the only worthwhile town north of Katowice is **TARNOWSKIE GÓRY**, some 20km away on the far side of the conurbation. It's a place with a far more venerable history: silver and lead deposits were discovered in the thirteenth century and it was given an urban charter and mining rights in the sixteenth by the dukes of Opole. Some idea of its underground wealth is given in a document dated 1632, listing twenty thousand places where minerals could be exploited.

The principal reason for coming here is to see two historic **mine** sites, one of which, while not quite matching the famous salt mines of Wieliczka (see p.451), makes an intriguing excursion underground. Both sites are a walkable couple of kilometres south and west of the town centre; an inexpensive map from the PTTK office (see overleaf) will make things clear, although some street names have since been changed.

The mines

The first of the sites, the **Kopalnia Staszica** at ul. Sześć Boże 52 (Staszica Mine and Museum; Mon–Fri 8am–2pm, Sat & Sun 9am–3pm; 11zł per person, plus 22zł for a guide), is the more educational, but less interesting of the two. To get here, leave town on the main Gliwice road, go through the lights and take the second left into ul. Jedności Robotniczej and you'll find the mine a little further on on the left – altogether about thirty minutes' walk. Dating back to medieval times, the mine was formerly worked for silver, lead and copper, and in the small museum you'll see the old equipment, plus models of how the mine was operated and water levels controlled. The highlight, though, is a motorboat trip along the flooded drainage tunnels which were excavated as needs arose; dozens of kilometres of passageways undermine the entire area.

A large wall map explains the connection between the mine and the **Sztolnia Czarnego Pstrąga** (Black Trout Shaft; Mon–Fri 8am–dusk, Sat & Sun 11am–3pm; reservations necessary at weekends on ☎032/285 2981; 8zł per person plus 16zł for a guide), 3km away on the western side of town. It takes its name from the eponymous fish which occasionally get into the tunnels from the rivers into which they drain. If coming from the town centre, walk west past the park along ul. Kard. S. Wyszyńskiego, cross the lights and continue down the hill. You'll see the signs to the left before a Lutheran chapel. If you have a car, leave it at the edge of the woods and walk down to the nearest of the two entrances; "Szyb Sylvester". Outside, a blackboard will indicate the times of the half-hourly excursions to the other entrance, "Szyb Ewa", 600m away through the woods. Once inside, you descend down a vertical shaft and make a spooky journey by boat along one of the former drainage channels.

Perhaps the best thing about the tour is the utterly convincing optical illusion that's played on you as you approach your steel canoe. As soon as the boat gets underway the guide rattles affably through his routine, barely pausing for breath, while heaving the entourage of up to eight vessels along the walls with his arms. Passing through rock-hewn "gates", associated legends are recounted; at one point any woman wanting to find a husband within the year is invited to rap on the wall.

Practicalities

Tarnowskie Góry is reached from Katowice in about an hour by **train** with the station located a couple of minutes' walk east of the central Rynek. Best source of **information** is the office of the SMZT (Stowarzyszenie Miłośników Ziemi Tarnogorskiej, or Friends of the Tarnowskie Góry Region; Mon–Fri 7.30am–3.30pm; ℡032/285 4996), on the way towards the Kopalnia Staszica at ul. Gliwicka 2; although the PTTK office, just south of the Rynek at at ul. Górnicza 7 (Mon–Fri 8am–4pm; ℡032/285 4891), may be of some use.

Accommodation really boils down to the *Olimpijski hotel* at ul. Korczaka 23 (℡032/285 4524; ❸) and the *Mirage*, out on the Gliwice road at ul. Gliwicka 126 (℡032/285 8323; ❺). There's one decent **restaurant**, the *Pod Sztolnią* on ul. Janasa.

South of Katowice

Directly south of Katowice the outstanding castle museum in the charming town of **Pszczyna** makes an unmissable stopover on the way to the hills of the **Beskid Śląski**, just south of the twin towns of **Bielsko-Biała**. Although lacking the grandeur of the nearby Tatra Mountains, the region's highlands are worth investigating on your way to the Czech Republic, not least for the chance to experience the undeveloped charm of the border-divided town of **Cieszyn**. There are regular bus and train services from Katowice to Bielsko-Biała, from where the Beskid resort of **Szczyrk** and Cieszyn are easily accessible, although the latter town can also be reached directly from Katowice by bus.

Pszczyna

About forty minutes from Katowice by train, or the same number of kilometres by road is the small town of **PSZCZYNA**, a world away from the conurbation's industrial squalor. If Nysa is the "Silesian Rome" and Paczków "Poland's Carcassonne" then the **castle** (Tues & Sat 10am–3pm, Wed–Fri 9am–3pm, Sun 10am–4pm; 7zł), just off the town's market square, might with the same inflated logic elevate Pszczyna to "Silesia's Versailles".

Originating as a Piast hunting lodge in the twelfth century, it was successively expanded and rebuilt in the Gothic and Renaissance styles before gaining its largely Baroque appearance following a fire, with other features added in the nineteenth century. In 1946, it was opened as a museum of some of Poland's finest historical artefacts, many rescued from Silesian stately homes ruined by the war. These are set among tasteful period furnishings in a slowly growing number of rooms refurbished to the stunning level of detail of their eighteenth-century heyday.

Begin by slipping whatever footwear you have on into the compulsory slippers in which you slide round the display.

The collection starts off on the ground floor with an array of hunting trophies including a wild boar leaping out of the wall and a rather more docile European bison (ask at the town tourist office about the **bison reserve** – *reserwat żubrów* – in nearby Jankowice; bison rearing was begun in the region by Duke Jan Henryk von Hochberg XI in 1865, and now about 50 bison live in the 800-hectare reserve), while neatly arranged expositions of European and Oriental armour fill the adjacent rooms.

The works of obscure German and Flemish painters are found in the **Great Hall**, which offers a fine display of Baroque and Regency furniture under a superbly gilded stucco ceiling. Ascending the aptly named Grand Staircase bordered by its stone balustrade, past a green serpentine vase used to hold wine at feasts, tapestries with stucco borders and marble sculptures, you reach the residential part of the castle. Private apartments designed for Princess Daisy von Pless, an English lady from the Cornwallis-West family who married Prince Hans Heinrich XV in 1891, witnessed by the Prince of Wales, the future King Edward VII, have been carefully preserved and restored, and there are lovely portraits of Princess Daisy, who became a great favourite. Those with a taste for the bizarre will enjoy the "English lavatory" in Princess Daisy's bathroom, with hand rests in the shape of snakes made of green marble.

The highlight, however, comes when you have passed through the Prince's apartments and library and reach the stunning **Chamber of Mirrors**. At each end of the hall, huge mirrors in gilded brass frames create an impression of a much larger room, embellished by crystal chandeliers hung from a ceiling depicting a swirling sky. Splendidly ornate balconies look down onto the chamber from the second floor, while murals depicting the four seasons and the signs of the zodiac are squeezed in between the gilded stucco decoration. The rows of period chairs filling the chamber are used during the monthly chamber music recitals held here. Make sure you see it from the balcony above as well as from below.

Subsequent rooms include an Art Nouveau dining room, a mirror gallery, and a charming billiard-room. The final point of interest inside is the **Hunting Room**'s barrel vaulting which hints at the castle's origins and is hung with still more antlers.

The handsome late-eighteenth-century **Rynek** in front of the palace is lined with fine mansions and a bright white Baroque-fronted Protestant Church with an incompatibly plain, bright interior. Ulica Parkowa, a block north of ul. Dworcowa, the road between the town centre and the station, is more a track through the park than a road, and it leads to a small **skansen** (Wed–Sun 10am–3pm; 4zł) of reassembled rural buildings containing carriages, a sleigh and an old hearse.

Practicalities

You'll find the **train** and **bus stations** located a kilometre east of the town's Rynek. The best place to **stay the night** is the excellent-value *Hotel Retro* on ul. Warowna 31 (☎032/210 2245, ✉retro@ka.onet.pl; ❹), where en-suite doubles come with phone, satellite TV and minibar; there's also a sauna and solarium on site. Cheaper beds are on offer at the more basic PTTK **tourist hostel**, ul. Bogedaina 16 (☎032/210 3833; ❸), which has the customary mixture of en-suites and rooms with shared bathrooms.

Numerous snack bars and open-air refreshment points liven up the Rynek, and there are plenty of **cafés** and **bars** in which to eat and drink on ul. Piastowska, the pedestrianized street leading off the Rynek's northeast corner: try the *Pizzeria Primavera* at Piastowska 14, the *Restauracja Kasztelanska* round the corner on ul. Bendarska, or the *Michalika* at Dworcowa 11.

Bielsko-Biała

A further 25km south of Pszczyna, at the foot of the Beskid Śląski ranges, lies **BIELSKO-BIAŁA**, two formerly separate towns, united in 1951. Now forming one seamless whole around the River Biała which formerly divided them, the two towns spent most of their history in different countries – Bielsko belonged to the duchy of Cieszyn, which in due course became part of Bohemia, whereas Biała was part of the Oświęcim duchy, which fell to the Polish crown in the fifteenth century.

Both towns flourished in the late nineteenth century, thanks to their high-quality textile products, and the cityscape today, like its northern English counterparts, is dominated by the imposing buildings of that period. Nevertheless, it's a place from which to catch buses to Cieszyn or Szczyrk rather than stick around – Bielsko which lies on the west bank of the river, has a particularly down-at-heel feel, and although Biała, over to the east, has been spruced up in recent years, it's not one of the most charming spots that Poland has to offer.

The Town

Arriving at the main bus or train stations, it's a fifteen-minute walk to **Bielsko**'s centre down ul. 3 Maja, a broad boulevard lined with the turn-of-the-twentieth-century tenements so characteristic of the city. It ends at the busy pl. Bolesława Chrobrego, above which lie the half-abandoned streets and alleys which define Bielsko's Stare Miasto centre. A couple of blocks south of the small **Rynek**, on ul. Schodowa, is the unusual **Katedra św. Mikołaja** (St Nicholas's Cathedral), dating from early this century. The tall belfry, flanked by two smaller towers, could be described as an Escheresque vision of the Italian Renaissance and provides the city with its most visually striking landmark. The interior is less enthralling, featuring a number of impressive Secessionist stained-glass windows. North of the Rynek is a quiet district where you'll come across the occasional turn-of-the-twentieth-century mansion decorated with floral window boxes and, in **plac Luthra**, underlining the historical strength of Protestantism in these parts, the country's only statue of **Martin Luther**. Behind him stands a typically angular Evangelical church dating from 1782, with its traditionally light but spartan interior ending in an altar so underplayed it might not be there.

Just east of pl. Chrobrego, **Biała**'s centre provides a complete contrast to Bielsko, its bustling streets lined with cafés and gleaming shop fronts. Just north of the coffee-and-cream coloured neo-Renaissance town hall, pl. Wojska Polskiego is a pleasant broad square on whose northeastern corner stand two of the town's best-preserved Secessionist buildings side by side. The **Pod Żabami** (House of Frogs) is so named because of the amusing reliefs seen round the corner, dating from the late eighteenth century. Over the doorway repose two smartly-dressed and rather self-satisfied frogs puffing on a pipe and strumming a mandolin while two beetles scurry across the wall.

At the extreme southeastern edge of the urban area, reached by bus #24, you'll find the formerly separate village of **Mikusowice** whose wooden

Kościół św. Barbary (St Barbara's Church) is the finest example of this highly distinctive form of vernacular architecture to be found in the region. Built at the end of the seventeenth century, the church is strikingly geometric, with a square tower and nave and a hexagonal chancel, while its skyline, with bulbous bell turrets and steeply pitched shingle roofs, is aggressively picturesque. The interior was adorned a generation after its construction with a series of naive wall paintings illustrating the legend of its patron saint. There's also a lovely fifteenth-century carving of the Madonna and Child in the left aisle.

Practicalities

The main **bus** and **train stations** are in the northern part of Bielsko. There's plenty of **accommodation** in town, beginning with the top-of-the-range *Park Hotel Vienna*, north of town on the Szczyrk road at ul. Bystrzańka 48 (☎033/812 0500, ✆www.vienna.pl; ❽). More convenient for the centre is the *Hotel Prezydent*, ul. 3 Maja 12 (☎033/822 7211, ✉prezydent@pol.pl; ❼), although the well-equipped rooms are a bit on the dowdy side. Cheaper options include the *Olimp*, ul. Rychlińskiego 19 (☎033/814 7509; ❹); and the *PTTK Dom Turysty*, just uphill from the stations at ul. Krasińskiego 38 (☎033/812 3019), which has a couple of doubles (❷) as well as dorm beds for 25zł per person. There's a **youth hostel** at ul. Komorowicka 25 (☎033/816 7466).

There's a wide range of places to **eat and drink**: *Bar Orientalny*, occupying the ground floor of the House of Frogs, is a cheap, reliable Chinese place; while *Pizzeria Margerita*, ul. Cechowa 8, has the best range of pizzas. Good traditional Polish fare can be had in the *Restauracja Patria*, ul. Wzgórze 19, which stays open after midnight at weekends. *Kawiarna Papuga*, near pl. Luthra at Frycza Modczewskiego 8, is a good place for a civilized drink.

It's worth seeing what's on at the Banialuka theatre at ul. Mickiewicza 20 (☎033/815 0915) – it's the national **puppet theatre**, and in May during even-numbered years an international **puppet festival** is held here.

Szczyrk and the Beskid Śląski

Immediately south of Bielsko-Biała lies the small Silesian section of the **Beskid**, an archetypal central European mountain landscape characterized by fir-clad slopes reaching up towards bald summits. Within Poland, it's a popular holiday area with **SZCZYRK**, the main resort 15km southwest of Bielsko-Biała (from which there are frequent bus connections), offering an an ever-widening range of places to stay. In winter the combination of guaranteed snowfall and steep slopes provides the country's most demanding **downhill skiing**, considered superior, if less varied, to its Tatran equivalents. In summer it is full of hikers moving between chalet hostels on the slopes. It is a region of wooden churches, folk costumes, occasional castles and manageable hikes. If you're heading for the hills by foot or mountain bike, the locally available *Beskid Śląski i Żywiecki* (1:75,000) **map** will come in very handy.

Fifteen minutes' walk south of the bus station (see below), an all-year-round two-stage **chairlift** (Wyciąg; 8.30am–5.30pm; return 16zł) runs to the summit of **Skrzyczne** (1245m), the highest peak in the range. In summertime it's used by bucket-swinging bilberry pickers who comb the slopes and sell their produce by the roadsides on either side of town. From the summit you'll face the 1117m peak of Klinczok with the conurbation of Bielsko-Biała beyond. There's also the usual refuge and restaurant up here. The energetic alternative is to slog up either the blue or the green trail for a couple of hours from Szczyrk. The latter continues south to Barania Góra (1220m), the source of the

River Wisła, Poland's greatest waterway which winds a serpentine 1090km course through Kraków, Warsaw and Toruń before disgorging itself into the Baltic near Gdańsk.

Practicalities

Szczyrk is a long, straggling village with a **bus station** placed roughly at the midpoint of its single street. New arrivals should get off the bus here – otherwise they'll end up several kilometres away at the final stop, which is in Szczyrk's southernmost reaches.

As far as **information** goes, your best bet is to check out the Polish-language site ⓦ www.szczyrk.com.pl. **Accommodation** in Szczyrk, however, is easy to find. The Beskidy travel agency, just south of the bus station at ul. Myśliwska 4 (ⓣ033/817 8878), will direct you towards private rooms (❶) and *pensjonaty* (❸) as well as selling local hiking maps. The centrally located *PTTK Dom Turysty*, ul. Górska 7 (ⓣ033/817 8578, ⓔ turysta@szczyrk.com.pl), offers doubles (❷) as well as dorms from 20zł per person. *Pensjonat Koliba*, right by the Skrzyczne chairlift at ul. Skośna 17 (ⓣ033/817 9930; ❹) is a good-value source of simple en-suites with TV and breakfast; while the *Hotel Beskidek*, ul. Górska 7A (ⓣ033/817 8411; ⓦ www.szczyrk.com.pl/beskidek; ❹), offers slightly plusher quarters, right next to a short slalom course. Better still is the *Klimczok*, 3km west of the centre at Poziomkowa 20 (ⓣ033/828 1400, ⓦ www.klimczok.pl; ❽), which looks like a cross between an alpine chalet and a corporate headquarters and is very much the winter resort-hotel of choice, featuring restaurant, pub, swimming pool and disco. The *Skalite* **campsite** at ul. Kempingowa 2 (ⓣ033/817 8760) is clearly visible from the roadside when entering the village from the Bielsko-Biała direction.

Plenty of snack bars line Szczyrk's main road, and there are several good **restaurants** specializing in filling Polish cuisine: notably the *Maxim* at ul. Beskidzka 87, and the elegant *Senator* at ul. Myśliwska 8. *Green Pub*, midway between the centre and the Skrzyczne chairlift, serves up decent pizza and spaghetti, and is also the best place in town to sink a pint; and the *Hacjenda Pub*, opposite the bus station, sometimes has rock/pop gigs.

Wisła and around

From Barania Góra, there's a choice of marked descents to **WISŁA**, an unpretentious health resort favoured by holiday-makers from the Katowice conurbation who can't afford to stay in Szczyrk. It can also be reached by bus from either Cieszyn or Szczyrk – the latter route makes a scenic, looping circuit through the valleys and passes of the range.

Another long, thin village that clings to either side of the main road up the valley, Wisła itself is a surprisingly charmless place – a socialist era, concrete resort full of low cost, low quality accommodation. Wisła's principal modern-day claim to fame is that it's the home town of Adam Małysz, the ski jumper who dominated the world rankings in 2001, becoming a national folk hero in the process – the village's shops are full of Małysz-related souvenirs. One other possible reason to linger is provided by the **Muzeum Beskidzkie** (Beskid Museum; Tues, Thurs & Fri 9am–3pm, Wed 9am–5pm, Sat & Sun 10am–2pm; 3zł), just off the main square), where you'll find agricultural implements, folk costumes, and examples of the goatskin bagpipes on which the local herders used to tootle away. The Wiślańska Strzecha restaurant, in the museum yard, is a good place to catch a bite to eat before moving on.

The best **hike** from here is southwest via the yellow trail to **Stożek** (978m), a fine vantage point which forms part of the border with the Czech Republic, and which has a pleasant chalet-type **hostel** near the summit, the *Schronisko na Stożku*.

Ustroń and Brenna

Ten kilometres downstream from Wisła and likewise served by bus from Cieszyn, the spa resort of **USTROŃ** is at first sight a futuristic looking place, with a cluster of glass-fronted, pyramid-shaped hotels sprouting from the forested hillside on the eastern side of town. Down on the dusty main road that forms Ustroń's centre, things are a little more prosaic, with the customary gaggle of uninviting cafés and cheap shops. The park on the east side of the main road harbours the **Muzeum Hutnictwa i Kuźnictwa** (Museum of Metallurgy; Tues 9am–5pm, Wed–Fri 9am–2pm, Sat 9am–1pm, Sun 9.30am–1pm; 3zł), where ancient steam-hammers and various water-powered things provide mute testimony to Ustroń's erstwhile role as a major iron-working centre.

Hikers are drawn to Ustroń by its proximity to one of the most popular peaks in the Beskids, **Równica** (884m), just to the east. It can be reached by the red trail, or you can try to negotiate a vehicle up the tortuous mountain road. A second recommended hike in the area is southwest from Ustroń by the blue route to **Czantoria** (995m), another summit right on the Czech frontier.

The **tourist office** (Mon–Fri 8am–4pm; Sat 9am–1pm; ☎033/854 2653), right next door to the **bus station** at Rynek 2, will sort you out with a **private room** in the centre of Ustroń (❶), or send you up to one of the pyramid-shaped **hotels** (❸), which are a bit scruffier up-close than they appear to be from afar. One of the best of the latter is the *Narcyz*, ul. Zdrojowa 9 (☎033/854 3595, ⓦwww.narcyz.com.pl; ❹), which boasts en-suites with TV, and also rents out mountain bikes. A swankier choice, down by the museum, is the new *Hotel Ustroń*, ul. Hutnicza 7 (☎033/854 2205, ⓔustron@animus.pl; ❻), which also has a rather plush **restaurant**. For cheaper food, the unnamed grill hut on the opposite side of the road to the bus station serves up excellent grilled fish.

On the eastern side of Równica, on the bank of the River Brennica, lies **BRENNA**, the most secluded resort in the range. The course of the river has been terraced here, and there are good opportunities for bathing; there's also an open-air theatre which is used for regional song and dance events at weekends throughout the summer. Accommodation options revolve around numerous **pensions**, including the simple, homely *Hawana*, ul. Jatny 34 (☎033/853 6729, ⓔhawana@bb.onet.pl; ❷); and the slightly more upscale *Malwa*, ul. Jatny 11 (☎033/853 6493, ⓦwww.malwa.pl; ❹), a spacious place with nice en-suites.

Cieszyn

Straddling the Czech frontier 35km west of Bielsko-Biała, the divided town of **CIESZYN** somehow managed to escape wartime ruin and today retains a charming centre of somewhat faded buildings. It's one of the region's most attractive old towns and is well worth a visit if coming from or going to the Czech Republic. The ancient town, established nearly twelve centuries ago, was claimed by both Czechoslovakia and Poland following the break-up of the Habsburg Empire after World War I. In 1920 the Conference of Ambassadors decided on using the River Olza as the new frontier, making the eastern part of the town Polish and the opposite side (known as Český Těšín) Czech. Ignoring the fact that people of mixed ethnicity were living all over town, no attempt was made to rationalize the nationality problem, and until recently, estranged nationals could only visit their former homeland with special passes. The exception was All Saints' Day, when the border was thrown open.

Nowadays the frontier at the town centre bridge flows freely in both directions.

The central **Rynek**, with the eighteenth-century town hall, stands at the highest point of the central area. Just off the southwest corner of the square is the Gothic **Kościół św. Marii Magdaleny** (Church of St Mary Magdalene), containing a mausoleum of yet more Piast dukes who established an independent principality here in 1290.

The main street, ul. Głęboka, lined with some of the most imposing mansions, sweeps downhill from the Rynek towards the river. If you take ul. Sejmowa to the left and then the first turning right, you'll find yourself on ul. Trzech Braci ("Street of the Three Brothers"). Here stands the **well** associated with the legend of the town's foundation. In the year 810, the three sons of King Leszko III met up at this spring after a long spell wandering the country. They were so delighted to see each other again that they founded a town named "I'm happy" (*cieszym się*). From the foot of ul. Głęboka, it's only a few paces along ul. Zamkowa to the Most Przyjazni, the **frontier post** for the crossing over to the Czech part of town, although most cars use the viaduct to the north for speedier transit avoiding the town centre. The pedestrian crossing from the Czech Republic back to Poland is about 700m upstream across Most Wolności.

On the west side of ul. Zamkowa rises a hill crowned by a fourteenth-century Gothic **tower** (daily: April–Oct 9.30am–5pm; Nov–March 9.30am–3pm), the only surviving part of the Piast palace. From the top, there's a superb view over both sides of the town and the Beskidy beyond. Alongside stands one of the oldest surviving buildings in Silesia, the **Kaplica św. Mikołaja** (Chapel of St Nicholas), a handsome Romanesque rotunda dating back to the eleventh century, with the vestiges of a contemporaneous well in front of it. Also on the hill are a Neoclassical hunting palace and a "ruined" Romantic folly among the trees. Other than that, idle ambling might lead you to the Baroque-towered Protestant **Church of Jesus**, visible on the hill just east of the centre. Inside, its statues of the four Evangelists crowd over the altar and liven up the otherwise plain interior.

Practicalities

Cieszyn's **bus** and **train stations** are centrally located about ten minutes' walk east of the Rynek, where the well-organized Miejskie Centrum Informacji, the **tourist office** (Mon 10am–6pm, Tues–Sat 8am–6pm; ☎033/852 3050, ⓦwww.um.cieszyn.pl), which is at no. 1, will provide you with pretty much everything you need to know about the town. The PTTK office at Głęboka 56 (Mon & Thurs 8am–5pm, Tues, Wed & Fri 8am–3pm, Sat 8am–noon) sells a reasonable range of local maps. For simple, no-frills **accommodation** you could do worse than try the soulless but habitable *Gambit*, ul. Bucewicza 18 (☎033/852 0651, ⓦwww.hotelgambit.com.pl; en-suites ❸, rooms with shared facilities ❶); or the marginally smarter *Akademicus* at Paderewskiego 6 (☎033/852 1100; ❸), where all the rooms come with en-suite facilities. A step up in the style stakes are the *Gościniec pod Kurantem*, ul. Srebrna 7 (☎033/851 8522; ❹), a cosy guesthouse in an alleyway off the Rynek; and the Orbis-run *Halny*, a business-oriented hotel 2km north of the centre at ul. Motelowa 21 (☎033/852 0451, ⓔmcieszyn@orbis.pl; ❻).

There are plenty of **places to eat** on and around the main square: *Bar Żak*, Rynek 20, doles out inexpensive pizzas and milk-bar-style dishes; while *Gospoda Pod Dobrą Datą*, Rynek 15, has a wider range of more substantial Polish dishes. *Starówka*, downhill from the Rynek at ul. Mennicza 20, is a cosier, more upmarket place to feast on well-prepared meat and fish, and also has a nice garden. Among the **cafés**, *Pod Arkadami*, Rynek 4, serves up some of the best ice cream; *Herbaciarna Mak*, Głęboka 31, is a cosy refuge in which to partake of speciality teas and cakes; and *Bar Premiera*, ul. Aleksandra Fredry 3, is the place to sample sweet and savoury crepes. The Celtic-themed *Highlander* is the best of a cluster of night-time **drinking** venues just off the Rynek on ul. Zielona. *Club Piwnica*, underneath the *Targowa* restaurant at Stary Targ 1, occasionally hosts **live jazz**.

Travel details

Trains

Cieszyn to: Bielsko-Biała (8 daily; 1hr).

Jelenia Góra to: Bydgoszcz (1 daily; 8hr; couchettes); Częstochowa (2 daily; 6hr); Gdańsk (1 daily; 10hr; couchettes); Kalisz (4 daily; 5hr–6hr 30min); Katowice (3 daily; 7hr); Kielce (1 daily; 8hr; couchettes); Kłodzko (4 daily; 2hr); Kraków (2 daily; 9–10hr; couchettes); Leszno (3 daily; 4–5hr); Łódź (4 daily; 6hr 30min–9hr); Lublin (1 daily; 11hr 30min; couchettes); Opole (4 daily; 4hr–4hr 30min); Poznań (4 daily; 5hr–6hr 30min); Szczecin (1 daily; 9hr; couchettes); Szklarska Poręba (7 daily; 1hr 30min); Wałbrzych (23 daily; 1hr); Warsaw (4 daily; 8hr 30min–9hr 30min); Wrocław (12 daily; 2hr–2hr 30min); Zielona Góra (2 daily; 4hr 30min–5hr 30min).

Katowice to: Białystok (2 daily; 6–8hr; couchettes); Bielsko-Biała (every 30min; 1hr 30min–2hr 30min); Bydgoszcz (4 daily; 5–7hr; couchettes); Częstochowa (26 daily; 1hr 30min–2hr); Gdańsk (6 daily; 6hr 30min–9hr; couchettes); Jelenia Góra (3 daily; 7hr); Kielce (11 daily; 2hr 30min–3hr 30min); Kołobrzeg (1 daily 11hr 30min; couchettes); Kraków (36 daily; 1hr 30min–2hr); Legnica (7 daily; 4–7hr); Leszno (7 daily; 4hr 30min–5hr); Łódź (8 daily; 3hr 30min–5hr); Lublin (5 daily; 6–7hr); Nysa (4 daily; 4hr); Olsztyn (2 daily; 8hr 30min–11hr); Opole (23 daily; 2hr); Poznań (15 daily; 5–7hr); Przemyśl (7

daily; 5hr 30min); Pszczyna (every 30min; 1hr–1hr 30min); Rzeszów (8 daily; 4–5hr); Słupsk (1 daily; 13hr; couchettes); Szczecin (5 daily; 9–10hr); Świnoujście (3 daily; 10hr–11hr 30min); Wałbrzych (3 daily; 6hr); Warsaw (17 daily; 3hr 30min–5hr); Wrocław (21 daily; 2–3hr); Zakopane (3 daily; 5–7hr; couchettes); Zamość (2 daily; 8–10hr); Zielona Góra (4 daily; 5–6hr).

Wrocław to: Białystok (2 daily; 10hr 30min–13hr; couchettes); Bydgoszcz (6 daily; 4–5hr); Częstochowa (6 daily; 3–4hr); Gdańsk (7 daily; 6hr–7hr 30min; couchettes); Jelenia Góra (12 daily; 2hr–2hr 30min); Kalisz (3 daily; 2hr–2hr 30min); Katowice (21 daily; 2–3hr); Kielce (3 daily; 5hr–6hr 30min); Kłodzko (7 daily; 2hr 30min); Kołobrzeg (2 daily; 8–10hr); Kraków (17 daily; 4–6hr); Legnica (22 daily; 1hr); Leszno (27 daily; 1hr–1hr 30min); Łódź (14 daily; 4–6hr); Lublin (3 daily; 8hr 30min–9hr 30min; couchettes); Olsztyn (2 daily; 7hr 30min–10hr; couchettes); Opole (42 daily; 1hr–1hr 30min); Poznań (26 daily; 2hr); Przemyśl (5 daily; 8hr 30min; couchettes); Rzeszów (6 daily; 7hr; couchettes); Słupsk (2 daily; 9–10hr); Szczecin (11 daily; 6hr–7hr 30min; couchettes); Świnoujście (3 daily; 7–8hr); Wałbrzych (20 daily; 1hr 30min); Warsaw (16 daily; 6–7hr; couchettes); Zakopane (1 daily; 8hr 30min; couchettes); Zielona Góra (10 daily; 2–3hr).

Buses

Bielsko-Biała to: Cieszyn (20 daily; 1hr); Kraków (16 daily; 3hr); Szczyrk (every 30min; 40min); Wisła (3 daily; 1hr 10min); Zakopane (3 daily; 3hr 30min); Żywiec (hourly; 40min).

Brzeg to: Nysa (2 daily; 2hr).

Cieszyn to Bielsko-Biała (20 daily; 1hr); Brenna (hourly; 1hr); Katowice (10 daily; 2hr 30min); Kraków (6 daily; 4hr); Ustroń (every 30min; 30min); Wisła (every 30min; 45min).

Jelenia Góra to: Bolków (8 daily; 50min); Kamienna Góra (8 daily; 55min); Karpacz-Biały Jar (every 30min; 40min); Kłodzko (2 daily; 3hr 20min); Legnica (12 daily; 2hr); Świdnica (6 daily;

1hr 50min); Szklarska Poręba (hourly; 45min).

Katowice to: Bielsko-Biała (12 daily; 1hr 45min); Cieszyn (10 daily; 2hr 30min); Kłodzko (1 daily; 5hr).

Kłodzko to: Kudowa-Zdrój (hourly; 1hr 10min); Lądek-Zdrój (hourly; 50min); Katowice (1 daily; 5hr); Międzygórze (6 daily; 1hr 20min); Nysa (7 daily; 1hr 20min); Opole (3 daily; 3hr 40min); Packów (12 daily; 40min); Świdnica (6 daily; 1hr 50min).

Kudowa-Zdrój to: Karłów (May–Sept: 5 daily; 20min); Katowice (1 daily; 6hr); Kłodzko (hourly; 1hr 10min).

Opole to: Kłodzko (3 daily; 3hr 40min); Nysa (12 daily; 2hr 20min).
Wrocław to: Karpacz (2 daily; 4hr); Kudowa-Zdrój

(5 daily; 3hr 30min); Legnica (hourly; 1hr 30min); Nysa (10 daily; 2hr 45min); Świdnica (6 daily; 1hr 30min); Trzebnica (hourly; 50min).

International trains

Katowice to: Berlin (1 daily; 8hr); Prague (3 daily; 4hr 30min), Vienna (1 daily; 9hr).
Wrocław to: Berlin (1 daily; 6hr); Budapest (1

daily; 11hr); Dresden (4 daily; 5hr); Prague (3 daily; 6hr 30min).

SILESIA | Travel details

Wielkopolska and
Pomerania

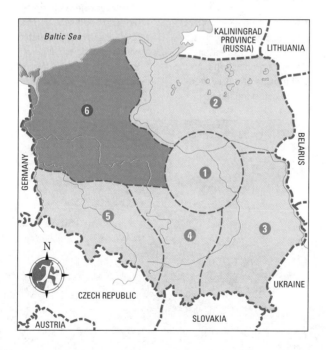

CHAPTER 6

Highlights

* **Poznań** Wielkopolska's bustling commercial and cultural capital is also home to the wonderful, leafy cathedral district of Ostrów Tumski. **P.528**

* **Wielkopolska national park** This wonderfully tranquil area of forests and lakes tops the list of potential daytrips from Poznan. **P.557**

* **Gniezno** An easy-going provincial town which was for centuries the seat of Poland's archbishops, and is still the site of a truly wonderful cathedral. **P.563**

* **Biskupin** Take the narrowguage train from Źnin to visit this re-constructed Iron Age village, situated amidst a rolling rural landscape. **P.565**

* **Łeba** A characterful coastal village-cum-beach resort, right next door to the alluring dune-scapes of the Slowinski national park. **P.589**

* **Międzyzdroje** A charming, old fashioned seaside spa town, conveniently located within striking distance of the thickly-forested Woliński national park. **P.591**

Wielkopolska and Pomerania

Wielkopolska and **Pomerania**, the two northwest regions of the country, constitute a large swath of modern Poland. Geographically speaking it's a fairly unified area, much of which is made up of flat arable land, although there are thick belts of forest in the north and west. However, the feel and history of the two provinces remain highly distinct. Wielkopolska formed the core of the original Polish nation and has remained identifiably Polish through subsequent centuries, despite long periods of German rule; Pomerania, by contrast, bears the imprint of the Prussians, who lorded it over this area from the early eighteenth century through to 1945 – the province only became Polish after 1945, and "Lower Pomerania", to the west of Świnoujście, remains German territory. The proximity of Germany has continued to exert a strong influence over the two regions, particularly with the removal of communist-era border restrictions in 1990, and the massive increase in cross-border traffic and trade. The impact of German investment in the area is most evident in **Poznań**, a burgeoning business centre that is also western Poland's major urban tourist draw.

Wielkopolska's regional capital is **Poznań**, an attractive and vibrant city famed within the country for the 1956 riots which were the first major revolt against communism. As well as offering a lot in the way of urban sightseeing, it's also a good place from which to explore the woods of the **Wielkopolska national park** just to the south, a rare region of wilderness in this heavily agricultural belt. To the east of Poznań lies **Gniezno**, the ancient seat of Poland's first ruling dynasty, the Piasts, and still the ecclesiastical capital of Poland, full of seminaries and trainee priests. In the environs of Gniezno

Accommodation price codes

The accommodation listed in this book has been given one of the following price codes, based, unless stated otherwise, on the cost of the cheapest double room in high season. For more details see p.39.

❶ under 60zł
❷ 60–90zł
❸ 90–120zł
❹ 120–160zł
❺ 160–220zł
❻ 220–300zł
❼ 300–400zł
❽ 400–600zł
❾ over 600zł

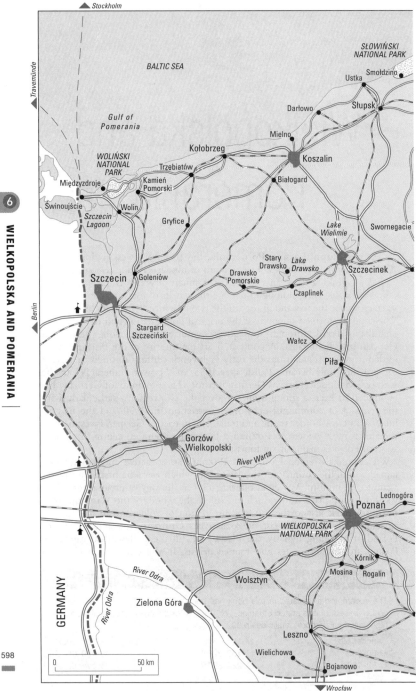

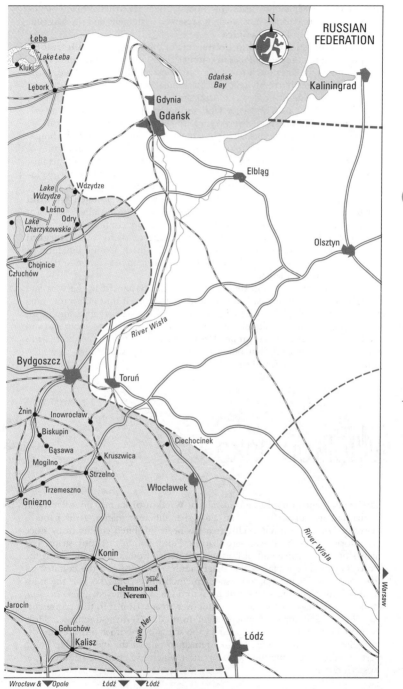

Łeba
Lake Łeba
Kluki
Lębork

RUSSIAN
FEDERATION

N

Gdańsk
Bay

Kaliningrad

Gdynia
Gdańsk

Elbląg

Lake
Wdzydze
Wdzydze

Olsztyn

Leśno
Odry
Lake
Charzykowskie

Chojnice
Człuchów

River Wisła

Bydgoszcz

Toruń

Żnin
Inowrocław
Biskupin
Ciechocinek
Gąsawa
Mogilno
Kruszwica
Strzelno
Włocławek
Trzemeszno
Gniezno

Konin

River Wisła

Chełmno nad
Nerem

Warsaw

Jarocin

Gołuchów
Kalisz

River Ner

Łódź

Wrocław & ▼Opole   Łódź ▼   ▼Łódź

lie several worthwhile historical sights, notably the reconstructed Iron Age village of **Biskupin**, Poland's most ancient preserved settlement, and the Museum of the First Piasts at **Lake Lednica**.

The main focus for tourists in **Pomerania** is the string of **seaside resorts** that pull in large numbers of Poles in summer, their glorious white sand beaches sweeping away far enough to enable you to escape the crowds. Due to the Pomeranian coast's northerly latitudes the holiday season is rather short here; but in July and August hordes of tourists arrive to soak up what sun there is, with fish-and-chip stalls and beer tents springing up to service basic gastronomic needs. Although relatively quiet, spring and early autumn can be rewarding times to visit, especially if beach strolling – rather than sunbathing – is your thing. The fishing village of **Łeba**, gateway to the famed sand dunes of the **Słowiński national park**, is the place to aim for in eastern Pomerania, although any number of other charming beachside settlements await exploration nearby. Over to the west, the island of **Wolin** offers yet more in the way of fine sands, as well as the European bison reserve in the forested **Woliński national park**. Inland Pomerania is peppered with grey, rather downbeat towns which serve as useful nodal points for transport connections but offer little else. However several architectural nuggets stand out: **Stargard Szczeciński** harbours some fine examples of the brick Gothic buildings so typical of the Baltic lands, and **Kamień Pomorski** is an old lagoon settlement with a wonderful cathedral.

The big industrial cities in this part of Poland – **Szczecin** in the west and **Bydgoszcz** over to the east – are never likely to make it into Polish tourism's Top Ten, but shouldn't be overlooked entirely: both possess an appealing urban vigour, and a wealth of cultural diversions. Stretched out between Szczecin and the Bydgoszcz, the Pomeranian **lakeland** is less known than its counterpart in Mazury (see Chapter 2), but offers a few low-key lakeside resorts as well as enjoyable recreation for cyclists and hikers.

Wielkopolska

The ever so gently undulating landscape of **Wielkopolska** may not offer much drama, but its human story is an altogether different matter, as its name – "Greater Poland" – implies. This area has been inhabited continuously since prehistoric times, and it was here that the Polish nation first took shape. The names of the province and of Poland itself derive from a Slav tribe called the **Polonians**, whose leaders – the **Piast** family – were to rule the country for five centuries. Their embryonic state emerged under Mieszko I in the midtenth century, but the significant breakthrough was achieved under his son, Bolesław the Brave, who gained control over an area similar to that of present-day Poland, and made it independent from the German-dominated Holy Roman Empire. Though relegated to the status of a border province by the mid-eleventh century, Wielkopolska remained one of the indisputably Polish parts of Poland, resisting the Germanization which swamped the nation's other western territories.

The major survival from the early Piast period is at **Lake Lednica**, located just west of **Gniezno**, the first city to achieve dominance before decline brought about the consolation role of Poland's ecclesiastical capital. It was quickly supplanted as the regional centre by nearby **Poznań**, which has retained its position as one of Poland's leading commercial cities.

Even older than either of these is **Kalisz**, which dates back at least as far as Roman times, while the region's prehistoric past is vividly represented at the Iron Age village of **Biskupin**, a halfway point on the **narrow-gauge rail line** that rattles along between the town of **Żnin** and the village of Gąsawa. Another town in the province which has played an important part in Polish culture, albeit at a later date, is **Leszno**, once a major Protestant centre. Yet this is predominantly a rural province, and perhaps its most typical natural attraction is the **Wielkopolska national park**, epitomizing the region's glaciated landscape.

As elsewhere in Poland, there are plentiful trains and buses, even to the smallest outpost, with the former usually having the edge in terms of speed and convenience.

Poznań

Thanks to its position on the Paris–Berlin–Moscow rail line, and as the one place where all international trains stop between the German border and Warsaw, **POZNAŃ** is many visitors' first taste of Poland. In many ways it's the ideal introduction, as no other city is more closely identified with Polish nationhood. *Posnania elegans Poloniae civitas* ("Poznań, a beautiful city in Poland"), the inscription on the oldest surviving depiction of the town, has been adopted as a local catchphrase to highlight its unswerving loyalty to the national cause over the centuries. Nowadays it's a city of great diversity, encompassing a tranquil cathedral quarter, an animated centre focused on one of Europe's finest squares and a dynamic business district whose trade fair is the most important in the country. A brace of fine museums and a wealth of nightlife opportunities ensure that a couple of days are well spent here – it may be a big city, but most of its primary attractions are grouped in a central, walkable core that is in places free from traffic. Outside the central area the rattle of trams and tyres on cobbled streets makes it a noisy but invigorating place. It's also a good base from which to explore the region's other key attractions, with regular trains running to the Wielkopolska national park, Gniezno and beyond.

Some history

In the ninth century the Polonians founded a castle on a strategically significant island in the River Warta, and in 968 Mieszko I made this one of the two main centres of his duchy, and the seat of its first bishop. The settlement that developed here was given the name **Ostrów Tumski** (Cathedral Island), which it still retains.

Although initially overshadowed by Gniezno, Poznań did not follow the latter's decline after the court moved to Kraków in the mid-thirteenth century. Instead, it became the undisputed capital of Wielkopolska and the main bastion of Poland's western border. The economic life of the city then shifted to the west bank of the river, adopting the familiar grid pattern around a market square which remains to this day. Poznań's prosperity soared as it profited from the fifteenth-century decline of both the Teutonic Order and the Hanseatic League, and the city became a key junction of European trade routes as well as a leading centre of learning.

Along with the rest of the country, regression inevitably set in with the ruinous Swedish Wars of the seventeenth and eighteenth centuries. Revival of sorts came during the Partitions period, when Poznań became the Prussian city of Posen; sharing in the wealth of the Industrial Revolution, it also consolidated its reputation as a rallying point for **Polish nationalism**, resisting Bismarck's Germanization policy and playing an active role in the independence movements. An uprising in December 1918 finally forced out the German occupiers, ensuring that Poznań would become part of the resurrected Polish state.

Poznań's rapid expansion during the interwar period has been followed by accelerated growth, doubling in population to its present level of almost 600,000, and spreading onto the right bank of the Warta. The city's association with the struggle against foreign hegemony – this time Russian – was again demonstrated by the **food riots** of 1956, which were crushed at a cost of 74 lives. These riots are popularly regarded as the first staging post towards the formation of Solidarity 24 years later.

As well as being a vibrant university town, modern Poznań is a brash, self-confident commercial centre revelling in its key position on the Berlin-Warsaw road and rail routes. Above all it is known for the international **trade fairs** held on the exhibition grounds just west of the train station – a tradition begun when the Great East-German Exhibition was held here in 1908, restarted by the Poles in 1921, and now symbolic of the city's post-communist economic dynamism. You can check out more on this at ⓦwww.mtp.com.pl.

Arrival, information and city transport

The main **train station**, Poznań Główny, is 2km southwest of the historic quarter; the front entrance, not immediately apparent, is situated between platforms 1 and 4, but the nearest tram station is reached from the western exit beyond platform 7 (if in doubt, follow the *Mcdonald's* signs) which leads out onto ulica Głogowska. Tram #5 heads from here to al. Marcinkowskiego, 300m short of the main Rynek; while tram #8 delivers you pl. Ratajskiego in the western part of the downtown area. The **bus station** is five minutes' walk to the east of the train station along ul. Towarowa. Bus #59 serves the **airport** in the suburb of Ławica, 7km west of the centre.

Visitors have the luxury of two tourist offices which have a wealth of pamphlets and maps for sale and will give out information on accommodation. There's a **city information centre** (Centrum Informacji Miejskiej, or CIM; Mon–Fri 10am–7pm, Sat & Sun 10am–5pm; ☏061/9431) beside the Empik store on the corner of Ratajczaka and 27 Grudnia; and a Poznań regional **tourist information centre** at Stary Rynek 59 (Mon–Fri 9am–5pm, Sat 10am–2pm; ☏061/852 6156).

The city is well served by a dense and efficient network of **tram** and **bus** routes, with services running from about 5.30am until 10.45pm – after which infrequent night buses run on selected routes. Tickets (bought from kiosks) cost 1zł for a trip of 10 minutes or under, 2zł for a trip of 30 minutes.

Accommodation

Poznań has a fair range of accommodation, but **hotels** tend to be overpriced for what they offer – and rates can rise by an additional fifty percent or more during trade fairs, which take place at regular intervals throughout the year except in July and August (the rates quoted below are for non-trade fair periods). There's an acute shortage of inexpensive hotel accommodation, and those on a tight budget will be dependent on the city's **youth hostels**, or on **private rooms** (❷), which are available from the 24-hour Globtour office in the main hall of the train station (private rooms available up until 10pm) or from the Biuro Zakwaterowania (Accommodation Bureau; Mon–Fri 8am–6pm, Sat 9am–2pm; ☎061/866 3560), just across the road from the train station's western exit at Głogowska 16.

Hostels and campsites

The handiest of the **hostels** is five minutes' walk west of the train station at ul. Berwińskiego 2/3 (6–10am & 5–10pm; ☎061/866 4040; trams #3, #5, #8 and #11 pass by). Like many Polish hostels it's housed in a grim-looking nineteenth-century building, and is spartan if perfectly clean inside, offering beds in four-person dorms for 20zł a head. Slightly comfier is the hostel 2.5km north of the train station at Drzymały 3 (6–10am & 5–10pm; ☎061/848 5836; tram #11 to the Nad Wierzbakiem stop), which has some double rooms (❷) as well as dorm beds for 25zł per person.

As in every university town, **student dorms** during the summer vacation (roughly July–Aug) are a good bet. One of the tourist offices (see opposite) will know which of the dorms are open to tourists.

The nearest **campsite** is the *Malta* (☎061/876 6203, ✉camping@ malta.poznan.pl), situated 2km east of the centre at the northeastern end of the eponymous lake, although its luxury two- to four-person bungalows, complete with satellite TV (❻), are more expensive than some downtown hotel rooms. Tram #8 from the train station passes along Warszawska (get off after passing the Novotel on your right), a good 600m north of the site.

Hotels

Central

Dom Turysty Stary Rynek 91, entrance round the side on Wroniecka ☎061/852 8893, ⓦwww.dom-turysty-hotel.com.pl. PTTK-run hotel occupying a reconstructed eighteenth-century palace right on the main hotel square. The only hotel that doesn't raise its prices during trade fairs, the smallish rooms come with 1970s-era furnishings but are clean and comfortable throughout. There are some simple hostel-style triples and quads, although most rooms are doubles, which either come with en-suite facilities or with shared bathrooms. ❹–❺

Ikar ul. Kościuszki 118 ☎061/857 6705, ⓦwww.hotelikar.com.pl. A rather soulless-looking multistorey concrete building, but the rooms are comfortable and come with fridge and satellite TV. Sizeable weekend discounts. ❼

Lech ul. św. Marcin 74 ☎061/853 0151, ⓦwww.hotel-lech.poznan.pl. One of a pair of long-established hotels right in the heart of town which claim 3-star status without really delivering it. Rooms come with standard, socialist-era brown-carpet colour schemes, but the en-suite bathrooms are new. The hotel also offers a two-person apartment with a mirror above the bed, should you feel the need. ❺

Poznań pl. Gen. Andersa 1 ☎061/858 7000, ✉hpoznan@orbis.pl. Located just 1km south of the city centre, but still well within walking distance, this high-rise building is the flagship of Orbis's concrete fleet. Ruinous rates during fair periods but big weekend reductions at other times of year. ❼

Royal ul. św. Marcin 71 ☎061/858 2300, ⓦwww.hotel-royal.com.pl. Characterful, recently renovated place with bags of quirky charm, tucked into a quiet courtyard just off Poznań's main downtown street. The rooms (all en-suite with TV) are on the small side but are cosily furnished in warm colours. Many of the doubles are L-shaped, making it impossible to push the twin beds together, so you'll need to specify a double bed if that's what you want. ❻

Rzymski al. Karola Marcinkowskiego 22 ☎061/852 8121. Spruced-up hotel with a good restaurant and just a couple of minutes' walk from the Stary Rynek. Uninspiring but adequate rooms with shower and TV. ❺

Wielkopolska ul. św. Marcin 67 ☎061/852 7631. Good location directly across the street from the *Lech*, and similarly old-fashioned. Ponderously furnished but acceptably clean and comfortable.

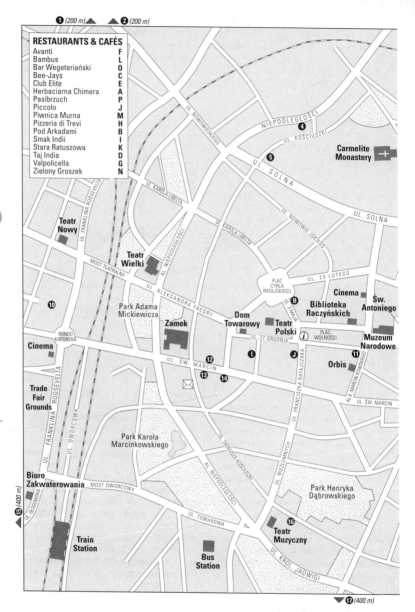

RESTAURANTS & CAFÉS

Avanti	F
Bambus	L
Bar Wegeteriański	O
Bee-Jays	C
Club Elite	E
Herbaciarna Chimera	A
Pasibrzuch	P
Piccolo	J
Piwnica Murna	M
Pizzeria di Trevi	H
Pod Arkadami	B
Smak Indii	I
Stara Ratuszowa	K
Taj India	D
Valpolicella	G
Zielony Groszek	N

Rooms with en-suite shower and WC as well as those with shared bathrooms. ⑤–⑥

Out of the centre

Meridian ul. Litewska 22 ☎061/847 1564. Expensive private hotel in a tranquil setting by a lake in Park Sołacki, 2km northwest of the centre. Rooms are en-suite with minibar. Half-price weekend deals are sometimes offered if the hotel isn't full. Tram #11 from the train station passes nearby. ⑦

Merkury ul. Franklina Roosevelta 20 ☎061/855 8000, ℮merkury@orbis.pl. Comfortable if slightly characterless Orbis hotel, close to the train station and trade fair buildings. ⑦

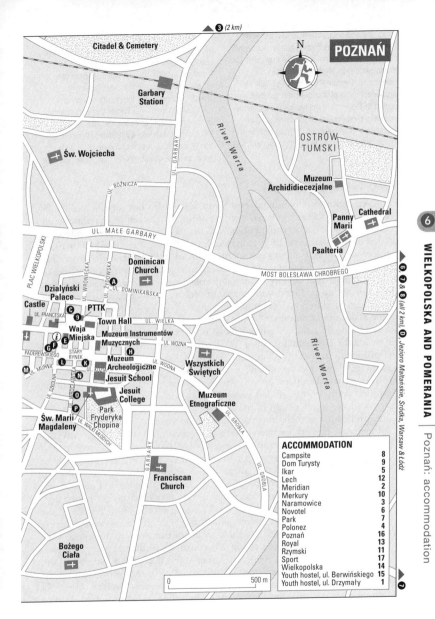

POZNAŃ

Citadel & Cemetery

Garbary Station

Św. Wojciecha

UL. BOŻNICZA

River Warta

UL. GARBARY

OSTRÓW TUMSKI

Muzeum Archididiecezjalne

Panny Marii

Cathedral

Psalteria

UL. MAŁE GARBARY

PLAC WIELKOPOLSKI

Dominican Church

UL. DOMINIKAŃSKA

MOST BOLESŁAWA CHROBREGO

Działyński Palace

Castle

UL. FRANCESKA

PTTK

Town Hall

UL. WIELKA

Waja Miejska

Muzeum Instrumentów Muzycznych

UL. WOZNA

PADEREWSKIEGO

STARY RYNEK

Muzeum Archeologiczne

UL. WODNA

Wszystkich Świętych

River Warta

Jesuit School

Jesuit College

Muzeum Etnograficzne

Św. Marii Magdaleny

Park Fryderyka Chopina

UL. WILKI MŁODYCH

UL. GROBLA

Franciscan Church

UL. GROBLA

GARBARY

Bożego Ciała

ACCOMMODATION

Campsite	8
Dom Turysty	9
Ikar	5
Lech	12
Meridian	2
Merkury	10
Naramowice	3
Novotel	6
Park	7
Polonez	4
Poznań	16
Royal	13
Rzymski	11
Sport	17
Wielkopolska	14
Youth hostel, ul. Berwińskiego	15
Youth hostel, ul. Drzymały	1

0   500 m

Naramowice ul. Naramowicka 150 ☎061/822 7443. Comparatively good-value two-star hotel 3km north of the Rynek, offering simple en-suite rooms. Reached by bus #51 from the main (northern) entrance of the train station. ❺

Novotel ul. Warszawska 64/66 ☎061/877 0011, ⓔnpoznan@orbis.pl. Plush Orbis motel situated in

parkland 2km east of the centre, a short walk from the northern shores of Lake Maltańskie. Off the main E30 Warsaw road. ❽

Park ul. Majakowskiego 77 ☎061/879 4081, ⓦwww.hotel-park.com.pl. German-owned business hotel on the southern bank of Lake Maltańskie 2km east of the city centre. Prices for

rooms and food are comparable with its Orbis rivals, but it surpasses them in quality. Rooms with lakeside views are more expensive than those on the landward side. Weekend reductions. ❽
Polonez al. Niepodległości 36 ☎061/864 7100, ⓔpolonez@orbis.pl. Another Orbis establishment, located to the north of the centre. It's a concrete, expensive monster like all the others, and with the range of boutiques and services on offer it can at times look more like a shopping mall than a hotel. ❼

Sport Hotel ul. Chwiałkowskiego 34 ☎061/833 0591, ⓦwww.posir.poznan.pl. Former budget hotel twenty minutes' walk south of the centre, totally revamped in 2001. The management have gone for sparse modernist minimalism rather than chintzy plushness, and the results look good. All rooms are en-suite with TV, and there are twenty-percent reductions at weekends. Take tram #6 or #12 from Most Dworcowy (2 stops) or the bus station (1 stop) to al. Królowej Jadwigi, then walk south past the derelict sports stadium for 5min. ❺

The Stary Rynek

For seven centuries the distinguished **Stary Rynek** has been the hub of life in Poznań, even if these days it has lost its position as the centre of political and economic power. Archetypally Polish, with the most important public buildings sited in the middle, it was badly damaged during the last war, subsequently gaining the sometimes overenthusiastic attentions of the restorers. However only die-hard purists will be upset by this, as it's now among the most attractive of Poland's rejuvenated old city centres and makes you appreciate what a fine idea the town square is. Lined with a characterful mixture of facades – some in muted greys and browns, others in bright pastel colours – it is at its best in the spring and summer months, when pavement cafés and beer bars, basking under a forest of loudly-coloured parasols, burst out onto its cobbled central area.

Outside the **town hall** stands a fine Rococo **fountain**, alongside a copy of the **pillory** in its traditional location. Still in the centre of the Rynek, running southwards from the town hall, is a colourful line of buildings known as **Houses of the Keepers**, once home of the market traders, many of whom sold their wares in the arcaded passageways on either side. The present structures, each varying in height from its neighbour by a few inches, date from the sixteenth century and are thus the oldest in the square.

Immediately behind the western side of the town hall is the **Waga Miejska** (Weigh House), once the most important public building in this great trading centre; what you see today is a reproduction of the original, the work of Quadro. Adjoining it to the south is the sternly Neoclassical **Odwach** (Guardhouse), a single-storey pavilion built for the "defence and decoration" of the city in the 1780s, and surmounted by a pair of distinctly unmilitary-looking female figures blowing trumpets. Closing off the southern side of the central Rynek are two low concrete buildings – ugly structures erected during the communist period which add the only discordant notes to the square. One of them is now the **Wielkopolskie Muzeum Wojskowe** at Stary Rynek 9 (Wielkopolska Museum of Arms; Tues noon–6pm, Wed, Fri & Sat 9am–4pm, Sun 10am–3pm; 5zł), a dreary display of weaponry in the province, from the Middle Ages onwards. The other houses the **Arsenal Gallery** (Tues–Sat 11am–6pm, Sun 10am–3pm; prices differ according to what's on), the prime venue in the city for changing exhibitions of contemporary art.

Many a medieval and Renaissance interior lurks behind the Baroque facades of the **gabled houses** lining the outer sides of the Stary Rynek, most of them shops, restaurants, cafés or antique shops. On the eastern side, at no. 45 is the **Muzeum Instrumentów Muzycznych** (Museum of Musical Instruments; Tues & Sat 11am–5pm, Wed & Fri 10am–4pm, Sun 10am–3pm; 5.50zł), the only collection of its kind in Poland. Its exhibits range from folk instruments from all over the world, through Chopin memorabilia to a vast array of violins. The last is a reminder that every five years the city hosts the Wieniawski International Violin Competition, one of the most prestigious events for young virtuosi (next due in 2006).

The western side of the square is almost equally imposing, above all because of the massive green and white **Działyński Palace** at no. 78, its facade topped by a monumental swan which cranes its neck down towards the square. Cultural soirées took place here in the nineteenth century, helping to keep Polish-language culture alive in what was a Prussian-governed city. The houses at the extreme ends of this side were the homes of prominent Poznań personalities. Number 71 belonged to Jan Chróściejewski, twice the mayor of the city around 1600 and the author of the world's first book on children's diseases. Giovanni Battista Quadro lived in no. 84, and a statue of the architect, sketchbook in hand, occupies a niche in the facade. Its interior houses the **Muzeum Literackie im. Henryka Sienkiewicza** (Henryk Sienkiewicz Literature Museum; Mon–Fri 10am–5pm; 3zł). Although Poland's most celebrated novelist (see box overleaf) had only a rather tenuous connection with Poznań – he penned a couple of short stories while staying at the *Hotel Bazar* (now a clothes shop) on al. Marcinkowskiego – this is the most important museum dedicated to his life and works, largely due to the energies of Poznań-based Sienkiewicz enthusiast Ignacy Moś. Inside lies a straightforward words-and-pictures account of the author's life, accompanied by first editions of his works in innumerable languages.

The Ratusz

The **Ratusz** (town hall) is in every way predominant. Originally a two-storey Gothic brick structure, it was radically rebuilt in the 1550s by Giovanni Battista Quadro of Lugano, whose turreted facade gives it a Moorish feel. The arcaded eastern facade presents the building at its most vivacious, its lime-green pilasters framing a frieze of Polish monarchs, who are accompanied here by portraits of statesmen and poets from ancient Greece and Rome – a propagandist attempt to present Poland's rulers as the guardians of classical wisdom. Every day at noon, the effigies of two goats emerge onto the platform of the **clock** above the facade and butt their heads twelve times. This commemorates the best-known local legend in which the two animals locked horns on the steps of the town hall, and thereby drew attention to a fire which had just begun there, so saving the city from a potentially disastrous conflagration. In thanks, the goats were immortalized in the city's coat of arms, as well as in this timepiece. Other sides of the building are inscribed with the words of Polish Renaissance sages, to which post–World War II restorers were forced to add extracts from the communist constitution.

The interior is now the **Muzeum Historii Miasta Poznania** (Museum of the History of Poznań; Mon & Tues 10am–4pm, Wed–Fri noon–6pm, Sat 9am–4pm, Sun 10am–3pm; 5.50zł), though this is less educational than it sounds, and the main reason for entering is to see the building itself. Surviving from the Gothic period the vaulted **cellars** were transformed into a prison in the sixteenth century; they now contain the earliest objects in the display, notably items excavated on Ostrów Tumski and the medieval pillory. However, the most impressive room is the Renaissance **great hall** on the first floor, dating from 1555. Its coffered vault bears polychrome bas-reliefs which embody the exemplary civic duties and virtues through scenes from the lives of Samson, King David and Hercules. The southern section by the staircase depicts astrological and bestial figures (including a rather fantastical rhino), while the marble busts of Roman emperors around the walls are reminders of the weighty tradition of municipal leadership. The top floor continues with a display of local treasures, portraits and old postcards, enlivened by temporary exhibitions on local history.

West of the Stary Rynek

Just to the west of the Stary Rynek stands a hill with remnants of the inner circle of the **medieval walls**. This particular section guarded what was once Zamek Przemysława, the castle and seat of the rulers of Wielkopolska. Modified down the centuries and almost completely destroyed in 1945, a part has been restored to house the **Muzeum Sztuk Użytkowych** (Museum of Decorative Arts; Tues, Wed, Fri & Sat 10am–4pm, Sun 10am–3pm; 5.50zł). This features an enjoyable collection from medieval times to the present day, while the Gothic cellars are used for exhibitions of the work of contemporary Polish artists.

Below the hill is the Baroque **Kościół św. Antoniego** (Church of St Anthony), its interior decorated by the Franciscan brothers Adam and Antonin Swach, the former a painter, the latter a sculptor and stuccoist. The church's most eye-catching corner is the sumptuous Chapel of the Virgin Mary on the left-hand side of the main altar, where a small image of the saint is buried in a dark wooden frame decorated with bold geometric designs in gold and silver. Cherubs roam across pink and golden skies in the dome above. Round by the main altar, the ornate choir stalls appear to be resting on subdued dragons.

Henryk Sienkiewicz (1846–1916)

Outside Poland, **Henryk Sienkiewicz**'s reputation has rested largely on *Quo Vadis?*, an epic on the early Christians in the decadent days of the Roman Empire, which won him the 1905 **Nobel Prize for Literature** and quickly became a favourite subject with movie moguls. Yet the huge popular success of this led, after the author's death, to the almost total international neglect of the remainder of his colossal oeuvre, which, even in hopelessly inadequate translations, had marked him out as Poland's answer to Charles Dickens.

Born in the Podlasie region to a minor aristocratic family of Tatar origin, Sienkiewicz began his career as a **journalist** and **short story writer**, the culmination of which was a trip to the United States in 1876–77, where he worked in a short-lived Polish agricultural commune in California. Here he wrote *Letters from America* (containing vivid descriptions of such diverse subjects as New York City and the Indian campaigns), and the burlesque novella *Charcoal Sketches*, a satire on rural life in Russian Poland. On his return home, he drew on his experiences of émigré life in *American Stories*, which include his one work in this genre which frequently turns up in literary anthologies, *The Lighthouse Keeper*. These were followed by the despairing novella *Bartek the Conqueror*, the finest of a number of works set in the Poznań region – which, being under Prussian control, made a safer medium for the nationalist message of an author subject to Russian censors.

Thereafter, Sienkiewicz changed tack, reviving what was then regarded as the outmoded form of the **historical epic**. His vast trilogy *With Fire and Sword*, *The Deluge* and *Fire in the Steppe* is set against the heroic backdrop of Poland's seventeenth-century wars with the Cossacks, Swedes and Turks. It is remarkable for its sure sense of structure, employing a permanent set of characters – whose language is skilfully differentiated according to their class and culture – with plentiful genealogical digressions and romantic interludes to break the unfolding of the main plot. Historical realism, however, was sacrificed in favour of Sienkiewicz's own Catholic, nationalist, chivalrous and anti-intellectual outlook. Despite its non-Polish setting, *Quo Vadis?*, which followed the trilogy, was always regarded as a fable about the country's oppression under the Partitions, emphasized by the fact that two of the

From here it's only a short walk round the corner to the vast elongated space of **plac Wolności**, which formerly bore the name of Napoleon, then Kaiser Wilhelm, only gaining its present designation – Freedom Square – after the Wielkopolska uprising in 1918. Here stands another seminal centre of the fight to preserve Polish culture, the **Biblioteka Raczyńskich** (Raczyński Library), founded in the early nineteenth century to promote Polish-language learning and literature, and still functioning as a library. Architecturally, it's one of the most distinguished buildings in the city, erected in the 1820s in cool Neoclassical style, the elegant Corinthian pillars of its colonnaded southern facade presiding serenely over the square.

The Muzeum Narodowe
Directly facing the Raczyński Library is the doomily dark-grey facade of the ill-named **Muzeum Narodowe** (National Museum; Tues 10am–6pm, Wed & Fri 9am–5pm, Thur 10am–4pm, Sat 10am–7pm, Sun 11am–4pm; 7zł). At present it's more of a gallery, with one of the few important displays of old master paintings in Poland.

The **Italian** section begins with panels from Gothic altarpieces by artists such as Bernardo Daddi and Lorenzo Monaco, and continues with Renaissance pieces such as Bellini's *Madonna and Child with Donor* and Bassano's *At Vulcan's Forge*. Prize exhibit of the gallery's small but choice **Spanish** section is

leading characters are Lygians – inhabitants of what subsequently became the heartlands of Poland. Ironically, it is really one of Sienkiewicz's weaker works, irredeemably marred by its maudlin sentimentality, for all its mastery of narrative, description and characterization. He showed a greater concern for historical accuracy in his final epic, *The Teutonic Knights*, in which Poland's plight was reflected in the clearest and most relevant parallel from the past.

Sienkiewicz also produced a couple of novels with contemporary settings, *Without Dogma* and *The Połaniecki Family*. These helped to increase his cult status in **nationalist circles**, and political activity, boosted by the international celebrity status bestowed by *Quo Vadis?*, became increasingly important to him after the turn of the twentieth century. On the outbreak of World War I Sienkiewicz moved to Switzerland where, along with the pianist Ignacy Jan Paderewski, he was instrumental in setting up the **Polish National Committee**, which in due course came to be recognized by the Western allies as a provisional government. However, he did not live to play the direct political role that might otherwise have fallen to him when Poland was resurrected at the end of the war.

Always an important part of the curriculum in Polish schools, Sienkiewicz has made something of a comeback in recent years, with the Polish film industry turning his ouevre into a cinematic gold mine. Veteran director Jerzy Hoffman, who had already filmed creditable adaptations of *The Deluge* and *Fire in the Steppe* in the Sixties and Seventies, set the ball rolling with a lavish big-screen version of *With Fire and Sword* in 1999. It was the most expensive Polish film ever made at the time, and soon became the most succesful, garnering an incredible seven million paying viewers. The film failed to make a big impact abroad, but video and DVD versions (complete with English subtitles) are available in big-city media stores in Poland should you wish to see what all the fuss was about. A celluloid version of Sienkiewicz's *In Desert and Wilderness*, a children's adventure story set in Africa, was one of the big box office hits of 2001 (and came complete with soundtrack album and picture-book spin-offs); while a new Polish version of *Quo Vadis* (a grandiose affair whose budget already surpasses that of *With Fire and Sword*) is currently in production. Sienkiewicz, it seems, is here to stay.

Zurbarán's *Madonna of the Rosary*. This Counter-Reformation masterpiece was part of a cycle for the Carthusian monastery at Jerez, and features actual portraits of the silent monks. By the same artist is *Christ at the Column*, a sharply edged work from the very end of his career, and there are also a couple of notable works by his contemporary Ribera. Highlights of the extensive display of **Low Countries** art include an affectionate *Madonna and Child* attributed to Massys and the regal *Adoration of the Magi* by Joos van Cleve.

The **Polish** canvases are an anticlimax, but look out for the room dedicated to the inconsistent Jacek Malczewski, the historical scenes by Jan Matejko, the landscapes of Wojciech Gerson and the subdued portraits of Olga Boznańska. You can also see examples of a uniquely Polish art: portraits of sixteenth-century nobles painted on sheet metal, which were placed on the deceased's coffin. It's well worth checking to see what's on in the new north wing of the gallery, the venue for high-profile touring exhibitions.

Beyond Plac Wolności

Moving into the business and shopping thoroughfares which branch out west from pl. Wolności, you shortly come to the **Teatr Polski**, a charming wedding cake of a building at ul. 27 Grudnia. Erected in the 1870s by voluntary contributions, this was yet another major cultural institution during the Partitions period: the uphill nature of this struggle is reflected in the inscription on the facade – *Narod Sobie*, or "The Nation by Itself". Overlooking the busy junction at the end of the street is the city's most distinguished postwar building, the **Dom Towarowy** department store – Poznań's version of Harrods or Bloomingdales. Built in the mid-1950s, it's an imposing ten-storey cylinder constructed round a hollow core in which a spiral staircase unfolds.

An insight into the curious dichotomy of life during the Partitions is provided by the large buildings standing further to the west, which reflect the self-confidence of the German occupiers in the first decade of the twentieth century. Ironically, many of these cultural establishments and administration offices were taken over just a few years after they were built by an institution with very different values, the new University of Poznań. The most imposing of the group, the huge neo-Romanesque **Kaiserhaus**, had an even more dramatic change of role. Built in imitation of the style favoured by the Hohenstaufen emperors of early medieval Germany, it was intended to accommodate the Kaiser whenever he happened to be in town. Renamed the **Zamek**, it's now a vibrant cultural centre which provides an umbrella for all manner of activities – including rock concerts in the courtyard round the back. In the park beyond are two huge crucifixes bound together with heavy rope, forming a **monument** to the victims of the Poznań food riots of June 1956. The riots – and their brutal suppression by the security forces – sent shockwaves through Polish society, precipitating the return to power of the reform-minded communist Władisław Gomułka. The lesson that workers' protests could make and break regimes was not lost on future generations, helping to precipitate the rise of Solidarity in 1980. It was during Solidarity's extraordinary period of power and influence in communist Poland – before the declaration of martial law in December 1981 – that the monument was unveiled in June 1981, marking the 25th anniversary of the riots.

South and east of the Stary Rynek

Returning to the Stary Rynek and continuing along ul. Wodna brings you to the **Pałac Górków** (Górka Palace) at no. 27, which still preserves its intricate Renaissance portico and sober inner courtyard. The mansion now houses the **Muzeum Archeologiczne** (Archeology Museum; Tues–Fri 10am–4pm, Sat

10am–6pm, Sun 10am–3pm; 3zł), where the displays are short on aesthetic appeal but commendably thorough. They trace the history of the region from the time of the nomadic hunters who lived here between 15,000 and 8000 BC, all the way to the early feudal society of the seventh century AD, and give an account of the latest archeological research in the region.

Ulica Świętosławska ends in a cluster of gloriously salmon-coloured former Jesuit buildings, the finest examples of Baroque architecture in the city. The end of this street is closed by the facade of **Kościół Farny św. Marii Magdaleny**, understatedly known as the parish church, completed just forty years before the expulsion of the Jesuits in 1773. Its magnificently sombre interior is all fluted columns with gilded capitals, monumental sculptures, large altarpieces framed by twisted columns and rich stuccowork, in the full-blown Roman manner. Over the high altar is a painting illustrating a legendary episode from the life of St Stanisław. Then a bishop, he was accused by King Bolesław the Generous of not having paid for a village he had incorporated into his territories. In order to prove his innocence, the saint resurrected the deceased former owner of the land to testify on his behalf. It's the one church in town worth seeing and makes a fitting place in which to enjoy **organ recitals**, which usually take place at noon on Saturdays – check inside the church for details of additional performances.

Across the road is the **Jesuit school**, now one of Poland's main ballet academies; take a peek at its miniature patio, an architectural gem. To the east of the church is the front section of the **Jesuit college**, currently the seat of the city council. The Jesuits have returned to Poznań, though they were unable to reclaim the buildings they created. Instead, they now occupy the oldest left-bank building, the **Dominican church** to the northeast of the Stary Rynek. Despite a Baroque recasing, this still preserves original Romanesque and Gothic features, as well as a stellar-vaulted Rosary chapel.

The late-Baroque **Kościół Wszystkich Świętych** (All Saints' Church), almost due east of the Stary Rynek, is the epitome of a Lutheran church, with its democratic central plan layout and overall plainness. Yet although it survives as an almost complete period piece, the exodus of virtually all the Protestants this century means that it's now used for Catholic worship, as is evidenced by the jarring high altar.

At no. 25 on the adjacent ul. Grobla is the former lodge of the freemasons, now the **Muzeum Etnograficzne** (Ethnographical Museum; Tues, Wed, Fri & Sat 10am–4pm, Sun 10am–3pm; 5.5zł), with some interesting carvings, ceramics and musical instruments. Further south you'll see the twin-towered Baroque church of the **Franciscan monastery**, which has been gleamingly restored by the monks who repossessed it following its wartime use as a warehouse. Built in 1473 and destroyed by the Swedes two hundred years later, photographs in the vestibule show the church before, during and after the war when the Franciscans completed their masterful repair. What you see now is a gleaming bright interior of white and gold with shades of ochre and Rococo flourishes.

North of the Stary Rynek

The northern quarters are best approached from pl. Wielkopolski, a large square now used for markets. From here ul. Działowa passes two churches facing each other on the brow of the hill. To the right is the Gothic **Kościół św. Wojciecha** (St Adalbert's Church), chiefly remarkable for its little seventeenth-century wooden belfry which somehow got left on the ground in front of the brick facade. Opposite, the handsome Baroque facade of the **Carmelite monastery** reflects a more complete image. Further uphill are the most exclusive cemeteries in Poznań, reserved for people deemed to have made a valu-

△ Wicker beach shelters

able contribution to the life of Wielkopolska, as well as a monument to the defenders of the city in 1939.

Beyond, al. Niepodległości ascends to the vast former citadel. This Prussian fortress was levelled after the war to make a **memorial garden** in honour of the six thousand Russians and Poles who lost their lives in the month-long siege which led to its capture. Most of them are buried here in the vast, park-like cemeteries ranged across the southern side of the hill, while to the south-east are the graves of British and Commonwealth soldiers.

Ostrów Tumski and the right bank

From the left bank the Most Bolesława Chrobrego (Great Bridge) crosses to the holy island of **Ostrów Tumski**, a world away in spirit, if not in distance, from the hustle of the city (trams #1, #4 and #8 go over the bridge.) Only a small portion of the island is built upon, and a few priests and monks comprise its entire population. Lack of parishioners means that there's not the usual need for evening Masses, and after 5pm the island is a ghost town.

The first building you see is the late-Gothic **psalteria**, characterized by its elaborate stepped gable. It was erected in the early sixteenth century as a residence for the cathedral choir. Immediately behind is an earlier brick structure, the **Kościół Panny Marii** (Church of Our Lady). This seemingly unfinished and unbalanced small church was given supposedly controversial stained glass and murals after the war. A couple of minutes' walk north of the cathedral is the **Archdiocesan Museum** (Muzeum Archidiecezjalne; Mon–Sat 9am–3pm; 3zł), located at ul. ks. Ignacego Posadzego 2, with a spread of sculptures, treasure and some rather fine religious art that ought to be on show somewhere more prominent.

The Basylika św. Piotra i Pawła

The streets of the island are lined with handsome eighteenth-century houses, all very much in the shadow of the **Basylika św. Piotra i Pawła** (Basilica of SS Peter and Paul), one of Poland's most venerated cathedrals. Over the centuries the brickwork exterior succumbed to Baroque and Neoclassical remodellings but when much of this was stripped by wartime devastation, it was decided to restore as much of the Gothic original as possible. Unfortunately, the lack of documentary evidence for the eastern chapels meant that their successors had to be retained. The Baroque spires on the two facade towers and the three lanterns around the ambulatory, which give a vaguely Eastern touch, were also reconstructed. Indeed it is the view onto this end of the building which offers its most imposing, if misleading aspect.

Inside, the basilica is impressive, but not outstanding as befits its pre-eminent status among the nation's places of worship. The **crypt**, entered from below the northern tower, has been extensively excavated, uncovering the thousand-year-old foundations of the pre-Romanesque and Romanesque cathedrals which stood on the site – two models depict their probable appearance. Also extant, though isolated by grilles as if they were the Crown Jewels, are parts of the sarcophagi of the first two Polish kings, Mieszko I and Bolesław the Brave. Their remains currently rest in the **Golden Chapel** behind the altar. Miraculously unscathed during the war, this hyper-ornate creation, representing the diverse if dubious tastes of the 1830s, is the antithesis of the plain architecture all around it. Its decoration is a curious co-operation between mosaic artists from Venice (who created the patterned floor and the copy of Titian's *Assumption*) and a painter and a sculptor from the very different Neoclassical traditions of Berlin, although the untutored eye is unlikely to spot any stylistic discord.

Of the many other **funerary monuments** which form one of the key features of the cathedral, that of Bishop Benedykt Izdbieński, just to the left of the Golden chapel, is notable. This was carved by Jan Michałowicz, the one native Polish artist of the Renaissance period who was the equal of the many Italians who settled here. The other outstanding tomb is that of the Górka family, in the Holy Sacrament chapel at the northern end of the nave, sculpted just a few years later by one of these itinerant craftsmen, Hieronimo Canavesi. Other **works of art** to look out for are the late-Gothic carved and gilded high altar triptych from Silesia, the choir stalls from the same period and fragments of sixteenth-century frescoes, notably a cycle of the Apostles on the south side of the ambulatory.

Śródka

Crossing Most Mieska I brings you to the right-bank suburb of **Śródka**, the second-oldest part of the city, whose name derives from the word for Wednesday – market day here in medieval times. Though there's nothing special to see, something of the atmosphere of an ancient market quarter survives in the quiet streets immediately north of the main thoroughfare. Just beyond is another distinct settlement, known as **Komandoria** after the commanders of the Knights of Saint John of Jerusalem, who settled here towards the end of the twelfth century. The late Romanesque church of this community, **Kościół św. Jana** (St John's Church), survives with Gothic and Baroque additions and now stands in splendid isolation on the far side of the **Rondo Śriódka**, a busy traffic roundabout.

Jezioro Maltańskie

Immediately southeast of Rondo Śriódka, paths lead down to the western end of **Jezioro Maltańskie** (Lake Malta), the city's most popular summertime playground. This two-kilometre-long stretch of water, built to accommodate rowing regattas and surrounded by footpaths, is where Poznań folk come to walk, cycle, rollerblade, and practise their pram-pushing skills. Most people gravitate towards the eastern end of the lake, where there are a couple of grassy strands equipped with concrete bathing piers, alongside children's play areas, a dry-ski slope, and an all-weather toboggan run. With a gaggle of stands doling out beer, sausage and ice cream, it's a vibrant and colourful place to spend a weekend afternoon. Just beyond the lake's eastern shore is a wooded park crisscrossed by marked walking trails. A few minutes' walk within the park lies the boundary of the sizeable, open-plan **Nowe Zoo** (New Zoo; daily 9am–7pm; 6zł), which stretches eastwards for a further 1.5km. A **narrow-gauge rail line** especially designed for children (every 30min 10am–6pm May–Sept; 5zł) runs from Rondo Śriódka to the zoo, running alongside the northern shore of the lake on the way.

Eating and drinking

There's a constantly growing range of restaurants, cafés and bars in what is a fast-changing city – although many new establishments go out of fashion within months of opening. Most eating and drinking takes place around the Rynek or in neighbouring alleys such as Wrocławska, Wodna and Woźna; and you'll rarely have to travel outside the walkable confines of the town centre in search of an evening out. Restaurants are usually open until 11pm or midnight; while bars are much more flexible with their opening hours, keeping going until 2 or 3am at weekends, but closing up early during the week if not enough customers show up. Note that Poznań is a major brewing centre, and that its **beers**, Ratusz and (especially) Lech, are not the inferior products their price tags would suggest.

Cafés and snack bars

Avanti Stary Rynek 76. Ever-popular spaghetti house and snack bar that continues to offer good value, despite the antiseptic fast-food surroundings. French fries and salads too. Till 11pm.

Bar wegeteriański ul. Wrocławski 21. Good, cheap vegetarian food in a subterranean daytime café a stone's throw from the Rynek. Mon–Fri till 6pm, Sat till 2pm, closed Sun.

Herbaciarna Chimera ul. Dominikańska 7. Refined tea-shop-cum-café with a wide range of brews and some fancy snacks – such as deep-fried camembert – and salads. Till midnight.

Pasibrzuch ul. Wrocławska 23. Cheap canteen food in bright, minimalist surroundings. Till 10pm.

Piccolo ul. Ratajczaka 37 & ul. Rynkowa 1. Filling, cheap bowls of spaghetti and a small salad bar. Not one for the pasta purists perhaps, but outstanding value. Till 9pm.

Pod Arkadami pl. C. Ratajskiego 10. Lashings of cheap and wholesome Polish food in simple milk-bar surroundings. Mon–Fri till 7pm, Sat & Sun till 5pm.

Zielony Groszek ul. Paderewskiego 11. Tiny café just round the corner from the Rynek offering sandwiches and a small range of Polish staples. Good place to slurp down a plateful of *pierogi* (ravioli-like dough parcels stuffed with meat) before hitting the pubs. Till 10pm.

Restaurants

Bambus Stary Rynek 64/5. Central location for Chinese food, in a smart restaurant with formal service. Good food, but at a price.

Bee-Jays Stary Rynek 87. Brash modern restaurant occupying attractive barrel-vaulted rooms on the main square. Eclectic selection of ribs, Tex-Mex, and a few Indian dishes on the menu. Big outdoor terrace in summer.

Club Elite Stary Rynek 2. Subterranean haunt with friendly service and tasty Polish food.

Estella, ul. Garbary 41. Upmarket Italian establishment open until midnight.

Piwnica Murna ul. Murna 3. Attractive candle-lit cellar just round the corner from the Stary Rynek with live jazz and blues some nights. A good selection of grills and salads, and a good place for a drink too.

Pizzeria di Trevi ul. Wodna 7. Just off the Stary Rynek, and offering basic inexpensive pizzas in pleasant surroundings.

Pod Koziolkami Rynek 92. Smartish grill restaurant serving up generous platefuls of steak and other meats, along with a decent range of salads.

Smak Indii ul. Kantaka 3. Downtown Indian restaurant with a good range of moderately priced fare, including several vegetarian options.

Stara Ratuszowa Stary Rynek 55. Expensive place offering solid Polish fare, although you pay for the atmosphere – heavy on solid furniture and dark drapes – rather than the food. Expect to pay the equivalent of £12/US$20 for a three-course meal. Open till 1am.

Taj India ul. Wiankowa 3. On the eastern shores of Lake Maltańskie, offering good-quality Indian food, and open until midnight.

Valpolicella ul. Wrocławska 7. Cosy, intimate venue for a good quality Italian meal washed down with decent wine. A good place for scampi.

Bars and pubs

Blue Note ul. św. Marcin 80/82, entrance round the side on Kościuszki ⓦ www.bluenote.info .poznan.pl. Jazz club underneath the Zamek cultural centre with two tiers of seating. Frequent gigs (rock as well as jazz) and club nights, when you may have to pay a cover charge.

Chelsea London Pub ul. Wodna 5. Smallish drinking venue just east of the main square, with a cosy living-room feel.

Harry's Pub Stary Rynek. Lively town-centre bar that mixes fun-pub brashness with woody, folksy furnishings. Also does decent steak-and-chips-style grub.

O'Morgan's Pub ul. Wielka 7. Irish-run basement bar crammed with wooden benches and tables. Nothing much in the way of decor, but seems to attract a relaxed fun-loving crowd. Occasional live music and dancing.

Pod Aniołem ul. Wrocławska 8. Stylish, comfortable café-bar in an atmospheric old building. Good place for an intimate evening drink.

Pod Zielonym Abażurem ul. św. Marcin 28. Relaxed café-bar in a courtyard just off the street, with a jumble of potted plants and homely *objets d'art*. A bit like having a drink in a quirky friend's flat.

W Starym Kinie ul. Nowowiejskiego 8. Dimly lit, comfy and relaxing place with moderately bohemian clientele and a soothing soul/jazz/reggae mix on the sound system.

Za Kulisami ul. Wodna 24. Café-bookshop not far from the Stary Rynek, with dinky wooden tables set out beside the bookshelves. Equally good for a daytime drink or an evening boozing session.

Entertainment and nightlife

There's always a great deal going on in Poznań when it comes to highbrow culture. **Tickets** to performances are easy to come by, with prices rarely exceeding 25zł even for the best seats. For details of what's on track down a copy of *iks* (4zł), a monthly **listings** booklet whose inner pages carry an English-language calendar of events, available from newsstands or from the city information centre. A more up-to-the-minute – albeit Polish-language – source of information is the Friday edition of the *Gazeta Wyborcza* newspaper, which carries full cinema, concert and club listings in the *Co jest grane* supplement.

The Teatr Polski, ul. 27 Grudnia 8/10 (box office Tues–Sat 10am–7pm, Sun 4–7pm; ☎061/852 5627), presents classic **drama**; while the Teatr Nowy, ul. Dąbrowskiego 5 (box office Tues–Sat 1–7pm, Sun 4–7pm; ☎061/848 4885), specializes in modern fare. **Opera** is performed at the Teatr Wielki, ul. Aleksandra Fredry 9 (box office Mon–Sat 1–7pm, Sun 4–7pm; ☎061/852 8291); while the Polski Teatr Tańca, ul. Kozia 4 (box office Tues–Sun 1–6pm; ☎061/852 42 41), is the home of the Balet Poznański and offers varied **dance** programmes. **Orchestral concerts** are held at the Filharmonia Poznańska, ul. św. Marcin 81 (box office daily 1pm–6pm; ☎061/853 6935); while the Akademia Muzyczna, ul. św. Marcin 87 (☎061/856 8900) puts on a regular programme of **chamber music**. **Musicals** are put on at the Teatr Muzyczny, ul. Niezłomnych 1a (box office Tues–Fri 10am–7pm, Sat & Sun 2hr before performance; ☎061/852 3267), while **puppet shows** are among the attractions at the Teatr Animacji in the Zamek cultural centre at ul. św. Marcin 80/82 (box office Tues–Sun 10am–noon & 2–5pm; ☎061/853 6964).

There are a dozen **cinemas** in town, most showing the latest releases with Polish subtitles, so you can enjoy the film and learn a few Polish expletives on the way. The most central theatres are the Apollo, ul. Ratajczaka 18; the Gwiazda, al. Marcinkowskiego 18; the Pałacowe, ul. św. Marcin 80/82; and the Muza, ul. św. Marcin 30. Handiest of the new multiplexes is the Multikino, just south of the centre at ul. Królowej Jadwigi 51.

Many of Poznań's central bars feature DJs and dancing at the weekend. In addition there are a growing number of **clubbing** venues to choose from – look out for street posters, or consult *Gazeta Wyborcza* on Fridays, to find out what's on. In the centre, both *Best*, ul. św. Marcin, and *Galaxy*, Stary Rynek 87/88, dish out a no-nonsense diet of mainstream techno and hits from the last few decades. For the more discerning, *Klub Mo*, 500m north of the Rynek at Bóźnicza 5, is more likely to feature cutting-edge dance music, reggae, or alternative rock. Of the student clubs outside the centre, *Cicibór*, 2km north of the centre at ul. Piątkowska 80a (tram #11 to the end), concentrates on mainstream hits and oldies; while *Eskulap*, about 1km west of Rondo Kaponera at Przybyszewskiego 39, is more specialized, with different styles of music (hip-hop, drum'n'bass and other genres) on different nights.

On a more tradional note, the St John's Fair (Jarmark Świętojański), is a handicrafts **fair** of many years' standing, with stalls occupying the Stary Rynek in the days leading up to St John's Day (June 21). St Martin's Day (Nov 11) is marked by the mass-consumption of *rogale świętomarcińskie*, locally produced croissant-like pastries which can be bought in local bakeries and food shops.

Lech Poznań, once giants of first division **football** but now struggling to stay in the second division, play at the Lech stadium, west of the centre at ul. Bułgarska 5/7 (tram #13 from Rondo Kaponera).

Listings

Airlines LOT, ul. Pekary 6 ℡061/858 5500; SAS, at the airport ℡061/847 5036.

Books and maps The Empik store on the corner of ul. 27 Grudnia and ul. Ratajczaka (Mon–Sat 9am–10pm, Sun 9am–4pm) has the best overall selection of maps, English-language magazines and books. Globtrotter, just off the northern side of the Rynek at ul. Żydowska 1, is a specialist store for maps and guidebooks.

British Council At ul. Ratajczaka 39 (Mon–Fri 10am–6pm, Sat 10am–2pm). Reading room with English-language newspapers.

Car rental Borexpo, ul. św. Marcin 24 ℡061/851 5123; Hertz, in the *Hotel Poznań*, pl. Gen. Henryka Dąbrowskiego 1 ℡061/833 2081.

Hospital ul. Chełmońskiego 20 ℡061/866 0066.

Internet access *Internet Club*, ul. Garncarska 10; and *Klik*, Jaskółcza.

Left luggage at the train station (24hr) and at the bus station (8am–10pm).

Pharmacies There's a 24hr pharmacy at ul. 23 Lutego 13.

Post office Main office at ul. Kościuszki 77 (Mon–Fri 7am–9pm, Sat 8am–7pm, Sun 10am–7pm). The train station branch, just outside the western entrance at Głogowska 17, is open 24hr.

Taxis ℡919 or ℡9622.

Travel agents Orbis, ul. Marcinkowskiego 21 ℡061/853 2052, deals with international bus, train and air tickets.

Around Poznań

It's simple to escape from the big-city feel of Poznań, as its outskirts soon give way to peaceful agricultural villages set in a lake-strewn landscape. Within a 25-kilometre radius of the city is some of the finest scenery in Wielkopolska, along with two of Poland's most famous **castles**, which, if you have a car, combine to make a full day's excursion. If you're dependent on public transport, you'll probably have to devote a day to each of them.

Kórnik

Twenty-two kilometres southeast of Poznań on the main road to Katowice, the lakeside village of **KÓRNIK** is the site of one of the great castles of Wielkopolska. There are regular services from Poznań's main **bus** station; don't go by **train**, as the station is 4km from the village.

Kórnik has an appealing rural feel, consisting essentially of one long main street, ul. Poznańska, along which you'll find a few restaurants and snack bars. This street culminates in a market square by the red-brick **parish church** which contains tombs of the **Górka** family, the first owners of the village.

The Górkas built their **castle** (March–Nov Tues–Sun 9am–5.30pm; 8zł) at the extreme southern edge of the village in the fourteenth century. A fragment of the original survives, as does the medieval layout with its moat, but the castle was rebuilt in neo-Gothic style in the nineteenth century by Italian and German craftsmen including Karl Friedrich Schinkel, best known for his Neoclassical public buildings in Berlin. However, his designs were considerably modified, and credit for the final shape of the castle is due to the owner, Tytus Działyński, whose aim was as much to show off his collection of arms and armour, books and *objets d'art* as to provide a luxurious home for himself.

In contrast to the affected grandeur of the exterior, with its mock defensive towers and Moorish battlements (most evident on the south side, opposite the entrance) the interior is rather more intimate. On the ground floor it's the decorative parquet flooring and Regency furniture which catch the eye. The **drawing room** with its superb gilded ceiling and huge carved wooden portal bears Działyński's coat of arms, and none other than Chopin once ran his fingers across the keyboard of the nearby grand piano. The spacious **Black**

Hall, with its slender white vaulting, gives a hint of the Moorish excesses upstairs, while next door, the **dining room** returns to a medieval European theme with its wooden coffered ceiling displaying heralds of almost the entire fifteenth-century Polish nobility. On the first floor is the one really theatrical gesture, the **Moorish Hall**, which attempts to mimic Granada's Alhambra. Here Działyński displayed his collection of antique Polish armour and weapons including an impressive feather-peaked suit once worn by a hussar and a cannon bearing the pretentious inscription: *ultima ratio regis* (a king's last resort).

To see all sides of the castle's exterior, you have to visit the **arboretum** (May–Oct daily 9am–5pm; 3zł). Originally in the formal French style, this was transformed in the seemingly arbitrary manner of a *jardin anglais*. There are over two thousand species of trees and shrubs, from all corners of the world including China, Korea and America, as well as a Gothic-Moorish view of the castle's south facade. The lakeside offers an even more pleasant stroll, particularly the western bank with its fine distant views.

Rogalin

With your own transport, it's easy to combine a visit to Kórnik with a look round the palace at **ROGALIN**, a hamlet 10km to the west on the road to Mosina. With only three buses a day from Poznań, those dependent on public transport will have to check times carefully in advance.

The **palace** (Tues–Sat 10am–4pm, Sun 10am–6pm; 8zł, free on Thurs) was the seat of many Polish nobles from the eminent Poznań family, the Raczyńskis. It's one of Poland's finest mansions, a truly palatial residence forming the axis of a careful layout of buildings and gardens. Built in a style which shows the earlier Baroque tastefully blending with the prevailing Neoclassical, the gleaming middle block centring the facade still remains closed pending renovation of the interior. In the meantime, you can visit the restored rooms in the two bowed **wings**, which feature some fine furniture including a lovely lyre cabinet as well as portraits of illustrious Raczyńskis, most notably a sinister depiction of Roger who's buried in the chapel (see below) and a far more agreeable looking Anna Raczyńska. Best of all is the **art gallery** (marked "Galeria Obrazów") off the southern side, a well-laid-out collection of nineteenth-century Polish and German works. Jacek Malczewski was a frequent guest at Rogalin and his works are well represented here, as are those of **Jan Matejko**, his epic *Virgin of Orleans* taking up an entire wall.

Fronting the palace courtyard is a long forecourt, to the sides of which are the stables and **coach house**, the latter now a repository of carriages once used by owners of this estate, along with the last horse-drawn cab to operate in Poznań. Passing outside the gates, a five-minute walk brings you to the unusual **chapel** which undertakes the duties of a parish church and mausoleum of the now defunct Raczyńskis. Set peacefully at the side of the road, it's a copy of one of Europe's best-preserved Roman monuments, the Maison Carrée in Nîmes, but built in a startlingly pink sandstone.

At the back of the main palace is an enclosed and rather neglected *jardin français*. More enticing is the English-style park beyond, laid out on the site of a primeval forest. This is chiefly remarkable for its **oak trees**, three of the most ancient of which have been fenced off for protection and are known as the "Rogalin Oaks". Among the most celebrated natural wonders of Poland, they are at least one thousand years old – and thus of a similar vintage to the Polish nation itself. Following World War II they became popularly known as Lech, Czech and Rus, after the three mythical brothers who founded the Polish, Czech and Russian nations; with all due modesty, the largest is designated as Rus.

There's a **restaurant** and bar by the road, opposite the entrance to the palace, and an upmarket **hotel** (☎061/813 8030; ❻) in the palace grounds. Significantly cheaper is the **youth hostel** at ul. Poznańska 3 (☎061/813 8038), which has dorm beds for 15zł per person.

Wielkopolska national park

The only area of protected landscape in the province, the **Wielkopolska national park** occupies an area of some 100 square kilometres to the south of Poznań. Unspoiled by any kind of development, it's a popular day-trip destination from the regional capital. Formed in geologically recent times, it's a post-glacial landscape of low moraines, gentle ridges and lakes. Half the park is taken up by forest, predominantly pine and birch planted as replacements for the original hardwoods.

Access to the park from Poznań is fairly easy, with about 14 daily **trains** (the slow *osobowy* services from Poznań to Leszno or Wrocław) passing through a sequence of settlements on the eastern fringes of the park – Puszczykowo, Puszczykówko and Mosina – from where you can pick up hiking trails into the park itself. The western border of the park is served by the Poznań–Wolsztyn rail line (some of the five daily services are still pulled by antiquated steam engines from the Wolsztyn depot; see p.621), which passes through the trailhead town of Stęszew. Catching a train to the eastern side of the park, walking across it, and returning to Poznań from Stęszew (or vice versa), makes for a perfectly feasible day-trip. It's also increasingly popular to cross the park by bike (trails open to cyclists have orangey-red waymarks), although as yet there's nowhere in the vicinity of the park where you can actually hire one. The settlements around the park are nothing much to shout about, and it seems wise to head back to Poznań in the evening rather than opting to stay here.

Fifteen kilometres south of Poznań, the twin villages of **PUSZCZYKOWO** and **PUSZCZYKÓWKO** lie on the west bank of the snaking river Warta, both serving as the starting points for trails heading into the northern section of the park. Puszczykówko is marginally the more appealing of the two, if only because it's the site of the **Muzeum Arkadego Fiedlera** (Arkady Fiedler Museum; May–Oct Tues–Sun 9am–5pm; 3zł), located just east of the station in the former house of the prolific Polish travel writer. Fiedler's first book was an account of a rafting trip down the River Dniester in 1926, and after a spell in the RAF, he went on to enjoy a postwar career as one of the most popular travel writers in the Eastern Bloc, churning out books on his experiences in Africa, South America and the East. The museum is full of the personal nick-nacks brought back from his sojourns abroad, while the delightful garden boasts an impressive array of replica Aztec, Olmec and other sculptures – the whole ensemble presided over by a haughty Easter Island head.

Another 2km south of Puszczykówko is **MOSINA**, a small and rather dreary town which is nevertheless the best starting point for exploring the eastern reaches of the park (see "Walking in the park", overleaf). It's also the site of a reasonable **hotel** and **restaurant** in the shape of the *Morena*, ul. Konopnickiej 1 (☎061/813 2746; ❷–❸), just west of the town centre on the main road to Stęszew, which has en-suites and rooms with shared facilities.

Over on the other side of the park, thirteen kilometres west of Mosina, the equally nondescript town of **STĘSZEW** is another potential base for **staying** in the area; with *Motel 2000*, south of the centre at ul. Kościańska 89 (☎061/813 4400; ❹), which is clean and comfortable but lacks atmosphere; and a **campsite** (☎061/813 4061), set on the banks of Lake Lipno just to the

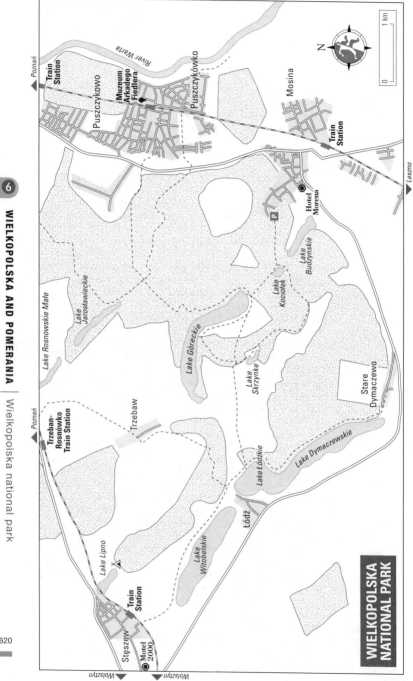

WIELKOPOLSKA
NATIONAL PARK

N

0   1 km

Poznań

Train
Station

River Warta

Puszczykowo

Muzeum
Arkadego
Fiedlera

Puszczykówko

Mosina

Train
Station

Leszno

P

Hotel
Morena

Lake
Budzynskie

Lake
Kociołek

Lake Rosnowskie Małe

Lake
Jarosławieckie

Lake Góreckie

Lake
Skrzynke

Stare
Dymaczewo

Trzeban-
Rosnówko
Train Station

Trzebaw

Poznań

Lake Łódżkie

Lake Dymaczewskie

Łódż

Lake Lipno

Lake
Witobelskie

Train
Station

Stęszew

Motel
2000

Wolsztyn

Wolsztyn

northeast at ul. Chrobrego 81. There are a couple of cafés on the Rynek; otherwise the restaurant of the *Motel 2000* is your best bet for a meal.

Walking in the park

Exploring the park, it's best to stick to the three official **hiking paths**, which are generally well marked and unstrenuous. Each takes several hours to cover its entire length, though it's easy enough to switch from one to the other – the best idea if you're restricted for time.

Walking **from Mosina** gets you into the best of the terrain quickly. Heading out of town on the road to Stęszew, turning right at the *Hotel Morena*, and then turning left at the top of the hill (waymarks – red for cyclists and blue for walkers – point you in the right direction), brings you to a car park and picnic site overlooking the park (and offering one of the park's few panoramic views). From here the path descends to the small heart-shaped Lake Kociołek, which is beautifully shaded by trees. If your plan is to cross the park to Stęszew, your best bet is to follow the blue trail from here, which leads north round the lake before continuing through the forest to the southern end of Lake Góreckie. It then climbs through thick woods before passing through open countryside to Lake Łódźkie, on the far side of which – off the trail but on the main road – is the hamlet of Łódź, clustered around a seventeenth-century wooden church. The route then leads along the northern shore of Lake Witobelskie to Stęszew.

The **red trail** runs south along the shore of Lake Kociołek before travelling circuitously uphill, skirting the small Lake Skrzynka just before crossing the blue trail. It arrives at the bend in the sausage-shaped Lake Góreckie, from where there's a view across to an islet with a ruined castle – a former fortress of the Działyński family, and a meeting point for the Polish insurgents of 1863. The path then leads halfway round the perimeter of the lake as far as Jeziory, where there's another car park plus a restaurant and café. Two separate red paths proceed to Puszczykówko, while a third follows the long northerly route to Puszczykowo via Lake Jarosławieckie.

The **black trail** begins at the station of **Trzebaw-Rosnówko** (just north of Stęszew; it's also on the Poznań–Wolsztyn rail line), then traverses the fields to the hamlet of Trzebaw, before continuing through the woods to Lake Łódźkie. It then follows the eastern bank of this lake and its much longer continuation, Lake Dymaczewskie – which together make up the largest stretch of water in the park – before ending at Stare Dymaczewo on the Mosina–Stęszew road. In many ways this is the least convenient place at which to end up: buses between Mosina and Stęszew are so infrequent that you'd probably save time by backtracking on foot and making your way out of the park by another route.

Southern Wielkopolska: Wolsztyn, Leszno and Kalisz

Those with a nostalgia for the days of steam should make tracks for the little lakeside town of **WOLSZTYN**, 75km southwest of Poznań, the only remaining rail depot in Europe that still uses steam locomotives to haul passenger services – which currently run to Poznań, Leszno and Zbaszynek. It's something that the local railway staff are incredibly proud of, and at the time of writing there are no plans to phase out this seemingly anachronistic service. Pride of the local fleet is the green-liveried *Piękna Helena* ("Beautiful Helena"), built for the Polish state railways in 1936 and still going strong. Often seen pulling the 9.05am service from Poznań to Wolsztyn, she's also a much-valued show-piece, periodically trundling around Europe to represent Poland at various railway nostalgia events. Wolsztyn is a popular destination for train enthusiasts from nearby Germany, and in addition to the timetabled daily services, a parade of steam locomotives is staged at Wolsztyn station every year on the first Saturday of May – extra trains are laid on from Poznań on the day. Holidays tailored to railway enthusiasts, which can include the opportunity to learn how to drive an engine, are organized by the UK-based Wolsztyn Experience, 20 Whitepit Lane, Flackwell Heath, High Wycombe, Bucks HP10 9HS (ⓌW www.wolsztynexperience.org.uk). If you want more information on the Wolsztyn-based locomotives, then websites like ⓌW www.polrail.com and ⓌW www.parowozy.com.pl are a useful resource.

Spread out to the north of the train and bus stations, the centre of Wolsztyn itself has a few fine buildings, notably a Baroque church with an impressive frescoed vault. At the end of the main street, at ul. 5 Stycznia 34, is the Muzeum Roberta Kocha (Robert Koch Museum; Tues–Fri 9am–4pm, Sat & Sun 10am–2pm; 2zł), occupying the home of this artist, one of the best Poland ever produced, who died in Auschwitz. It's his sculptures which stand out, notably the large reliefs on the rear of the house and the classically inspired portrait busts in the garden (just about visible from the back when the museum is closed) – mostly replicas of works destroyed by the Nazis.

Leaving the museum through the garden brings you to the shore of Lake Wolsztyn, where there's a small sandy beach and secluded lakeside paths leading off in either direction. Walking westwards and following the shore through wooded parkland brings you after fifteen minutes or so to a **skansen** (Tues–Fri 9am–5pm, Sat 10am–5pm, Sun noon–5pm; closed Dec & Jan; 3zł), which boasts a small but impressive collection of sturdy traditional farm buildings, each topped by a thick thatch of reeds taken from the nearby lake.

Practicalties

Train and bus stations are located together on the southern side of the town centre. Cheapest place to stay in town is the *OSiR* sports **hotel** opposite the *skansen* (☎068/384 3663), a utilitarian block with simple doubles with sink (❶) and some en-suites (❷). Moving up in price, the *Kaukaska*, just west of the train station at ul. Poniatowskiego 19 (☎068/347 2852; ❹), offers smart modern en-suites with TV. There's a **campsite** next door to the *OSiR* hotel.

The al-fresco **cafés** by the beach offer the best places to grab a quick meal and a drink in summer; otherwise the **restaurant** of the *Kaukaska* offers the best range of food.

Leszno

One of the places served by Wolsztyn's steam trains is **LESZNO** some 40km to the southeast, which also lies on the main road and rail routes linking Poznań to Wrocław. Nowadays a sleepy market town, it hardly hints at the glittering role it has played in Poland's history. Its entire early story is bound up with one of the country's most remarkable dynasties, the Leszczyński family, who founded Leszno in the late fourteenth century. The last of the male line, **Stanisław Leszczyński**, deposed the hated Augustus the Strong of Saxony to become king of Poland in 1704, only to be overthrown by the same rival six years later. He briefly regained the throne in 1733, but met with far more success in exile in France, marrying his daughter to Louis XV, and himself becoming duke of Lorraine and gaining a reputation as a patron of the arts.

The Town

The handsome cobbled **Rynek** is ringed by predominantly Neoclassical buildings with the odd Baroque facade surviving the Swedish Wars that left Leszno in ruins. The colourist approach favoured by the architects – prominent among whom was the Italian Pompeo Ferrari – is shown to best effect in the salmon pink tones of the recently spruced-up **town hall**.

Just south of the Rynek, the exterior of the twin-towered **Kościół św. Mikołaja** (St Nicholas's Church) strikes a more typically sombre note. Its interior, on the other hand, displays a good example of Rococo ornamentation – the florid style of late Baroque's death throes. On each side of the altar are the huge, seemingly unpainted monuments to the Leszczyńskis. A fascinating contrast with this richness is provided by the clean, sober lines of the **Kościół św. Krzyża** (Church of Holy Cross), a couple of minutes' walk to the southwest on pl. Metziga. The church is surrounded by the ornate remains of crumbling epitaphs set in its perimeter walls, while a collection of small memorial obelisks from the late eighteenth century further commemorate the passing of Leszno's prominent families. Inside the vestibule a life-size angel bears a huge shell; an unusual vessel for holy water.

On the same square, shaded by a huge oak tree, is the regional museum, or **Muzeum Okręgowe** (Tues noon–5pm, Wed–Fri 9am–2pm, Sat & Sun 10am–2pm), a miscellaneous local collection, featuring several coffins bearing sculpted reliefs of the deceased, and a room devoted to Comenius of the Bohemian Brethren (see box, below). A few streets east of here, off ul. Bolesława Chrobrego, is the brick **Kościół św. Jana** (Church of St John), aesthetically unremarkable but semi-interesting as the place where the Bohemian Brethren held their services.

Practicalities

The **train** and **bus stations** lie just west of Leszno's main street, ul. Słowiańska, which drives north to meet the Rynek. Once you've pottered around Leszno's town centre you'd be wise to move on, although the **tourist office**, Słowiańska 24 (Mon–Fri 9am–5pm, Sat 9am–3pm; ☎065/529 8191) will guide you towards the town's limited accommodation possibilities should you wish to stay; you can also get online information at ⓦ www.leszno.pl.

The *Centralny* **hotel** at ul. Słowiańska 30 (☎065/520 2217; ❺) is a handily placed if somewhat overpriced source of uninspiring en-suite rooms; more expensive still is the *Akwawit*, ul. św. Jozefa 5 (☎065/529 3781, ⓦwww.akwav-it.com.pl; ❽), at the far end of the flyover (visible from the train and bus stations) on the west side of town, which exudes an aura of plush modernity and boasts an adventure swimming pool next door. The *Vienawa* **restaurant** on the northern side of the Rynek offers well-presented Polish fare at reasonable prices; it also boasts a cosy ground-floor pub.

Kalisz

At the extreme southeastern corner of Wielkopolska, midway between Poznań and Łódź, lies the industrial town of **KALISZ**. Almost universally held to be Poland's oldest recorded city, it was referred to as Calissia by Pliny in the first century and was described in the second century as a trading settlement on the "amber route" between the Baltic and Adriatic. Though apparently inhabited without interruption ever since, it failed to develop into a major city. Built around an attractive Rynek and its surrounding grid of cobbled alleys, Kalisz makes for a convenient stopover if you're passing through, especially if you're on the way to the palace at Gołuchów (see opposite).

The Town

As the train and bus stations are 3km from the centre of the city you'll need to catch a bus in; see "Practicalities", opposite, for details. On the way in, along ul. Górnośląska and ul. Śródmiejska, you'll pass two space-age churches that shoot up from parallel boulevards – contemporary symbols of the key role of Catholicism in modern Poland.

Kalisz's pleasant if unspectacular Rynek centres on a large Neoclassical **town hall**. Down ul. Kanonicka at the northwestern end of the square is the brick Gothic **Kościół św. Mikołaja** (Church of St Nicholas), which has been subject to a fair amount of neo-Gothic tinkering, though for once this is not entirely to its disadvantage. Inside, the prize item is the altarpiece of *The Descent from the Cross*, brought here from Rubens' workshop in Antwerp. Located just off the southeastern corner of the Rynek is a smaller square which lies in front of the **Kościół Franciszkanów** (Franciscan Church), an older and simpler example of Gothic brickwork, but with generous Baroque interior decorations – unfortunately it's usually locked.

From here, it's just a short walk north to ul. Kolegialna, which defines the eastern perimeter of the Stare Miasto. Along it you'll pass the long facade of the **Jesuit college**, a severe Neoclassical composition incorporating a finely carved Renaissance portal. The only part of the building that visitors are allowed to enter is the church, which follows the plain Mannerist style of the Jesuits' most important church, the Gesu in Rome. Immediately beyond the college, standing beside the surviving fragment of the city's ramparts, is the single-towered **collegiate church**, a more adventurous example of late-eighteenth-century Baroque which includes parts of its Gothic predecessor. The interior bristles with works of art, the most notable of which is a Silesian polyptych from around 1500 – but unfortunately again, only the vestibule is normally kept open.

Ten minutes' walk southwest of the centre, across the River Prozna, is the **Muzeum Ziemi Kaliskiej** (Museum of the Kalisz Region; Tues, Thurs, Sat & Sun 10am–2.30pm, Wed & Fri noon–5pm; 3zł) at Kościuszki 12, which displays locally excavated Roman and Neolithic artefacts rarely seen elsewhere in Poland.

Practicalities

Both the **train** and **bus** stations are to be found 3km from the centre at the southwestern end of the city. To reach the centre, take buses #2, #11, #12, #15, #18 or #19 from the stop on the main road outside the bus station – all these end up on pl. św. Jozefa just east of the main Rynek. There's a helpful **tourist office** one block northwest of the Rynek at ul. Gabarska 2 (Mon–Fri 10am–5pm, Sat 10am–2pm; ☎062/757 3267).

Accommodation options include *U Bogdana*, ul. Legionów 15-17 (☎062/753 0823; ❷), which offers simple rooms with shared bathrooms in a residential block about 100m north of the train and bus stations. Moving upmarket, the *Calisia*, 500m southwest of the Rynek at ul. Nowy Świat 1-3 (☎062/767 9100; ❻, sizeable weekend discounts), has smart en-suites with TV; while the Orbis-run *Prosna*, 2km southwest of the centre near the stations at ul. Górnośląska 53/55 (☎062/768 9100, ✉prosna@orbis.pl; ❻), is a satisfactory if bland source of business-standard comforts.

For a quick bite to **eat** or **drink**, there are plenty of places around the Rynek. *Kawarnia Italia* on the eastern side of the square is the best place for cakes and ice cream. *Nem Nan Khong*, just west of the Rynek on Piskorzewska, offers cheap and tasty Thai snacks; while *Piwnica Ratuszowa*, Rynek 20, concentrates on stolid Polish staples.

Gołuchów

Twenty kilometres from Kalisz on the main road to Poznań, and reached by frequent Poznań-bound buses from the main bus station, the village of **GOŁUCHÓW** would be a place you'd whizz through were it not for its **Palace**, the one outstanding monument in the Kalisz area.

It began as a small defensive castle, built for Rafał Leszczyński of the famous Leszno family in 1560. Early the following century, his son Wacław completely transformed it into a palatial residence worthy of a man who had risen to be royal chancellor. Like the Polish state itself, it gradually fell into ruin. In 1853 it was bought by Tytus Działyński, the owner of Kórnik (see p.617), as a present for his son Jan, who married Izabella, daughter of the formidable Adam Czartoryski. While her husband languished in exile for his part in the 1863 Uprising, Izabella devoted herself to re-creating the glory of the castle, eventually opening it as one of Poland's first museums. Rather than revert to the Italianate form of the original, she opted for a distinctively French touch – with its steeply pitched roofs, prominent chimneys, pointed towers and graceful arcaded terrace, the palace looks like a passable pastiche of something you might find in the Loire Valley.

The small **apartments** (tour Tues–Sun 10am–4pm, last admission 3.15pm; 5zł) are crammed with paintings and *objets d'art*. Highlight of the display is some magnificent antique vases – just part of an assembly whose other items are now kept in the Muzeum Narodowe in Warsaw. After the guided tour you can wander off to the two rooms under the stairway, in which changing exhibitions from the castle's collection of engravings are held.

The landscaped **park** surrounding the palace contains a **café** and an uninspiring **Muzeum Leśnictwa** (Museum of Forestry; Tues–Sun 10am–3pm; 2.50zł). Near here you'll also come across Izabella's neo-Baroque funerary chapel, and on the outskirts of the park you can find a bison farm.

If you want a **place to stay**, the *Dom Pracy Twórcej* **hotel** at ul. Borowskiego 2 (☎062/761 7111; ❸), offers plainish but adequate en-suite rooms. Otherwise there's a **campsite** (☎062/761 8281), which is well signposted from the main road. Eating possibilities are limited to the village's single **restaurant**, which serves up a satisying range of Polish standards.

Gniezno and around

Despite the competing claims of Poznań, Kruszwica and Lednica, **GNIEZNO**, 50km east of Poznań, is generally credited as the first capital of Poland, a title based on the dense web of myth and chronicled fact that constitute the story of the nation's earliest years. Nowadays Poland's ecclesiastical capital has the feel of a quiet but charming small town, but there are sufficient historical attractions here to make Gniezno well worth a couple of days' stay. It's also an excellent base from which to visit places featured on the so-called **Szlak Piastowski** (Piast Route), a tourist trail between Poznań and Inowrocław which highlights salient locations associated with the Piast dynasty. Most important of these is the medieval archeological site at **Lake Lednica** (also the site of a large ethnographic museum), which is only a few minutes' journey from town by bus.

Some history

Lech, the legendary founder of Poland, supposedly came across the nest (*gniazdo*) of a white eagle here; he founded a town on the spot, and made the bird the emblem of his people, a role it still maintains. Less fancifully, it's known for sure that Mieszko I had established a court here in the late tenth century, and that in the year 1000 it was the scene of a turning point in the country's history.

The catalyst for this, ironically enough, was a Czech, **św. Wojciech** (St Adalbert), the first bishop of Prague. Unable to cope with the political demands of his office, he retired to a monastery, but later bowed to pressure from Rome to take up missionary work. In 997 he set out from Gniezno to evangelize the Prussians, a fierce Baltic tribe who lived on Poland's eastern borders – and who quickly dispatched him to a martyr's death. In order to recover the body, Mieszko I's son, **Bolesław the Brave**, was forced to pay Wojciech's weight in

gold, an astute investment as it turned out. At the pope's instigation, Emperor Otto III made a pilgrimage to Gniezno, bringing relics with him which would add to the site's holiness. Received in great splendour, he crowned Bolesław with his own crown, confirming Poland as a fully fledged kingdom and one which was independent of the German-dominated Holy Roman Empire. Furthermore, Gniezno was made the seat of Poland's first archbishopric; Wojciech's brother Radim was the first to be appointed to the post.

Gniezno was soon replaced as capital by the more secure town of Kraków, and although it made a partial recovery in the Middle Ages, it never grew very big. Nevertheless, it has always been important as the official seat of the primate of Poland. Throughout the period of elected kings, the holder of this office functioned as head of state during each interregnum, and it is still one of the most prestigious positions in the land. In recent times, the Gniezno archbishopric has been coupled to that of Warsaw, with the primate tending, for obvious reasons, to spend far more time in the capital. The pressures this caused led in 1992 to Gniezno losing its historic role as the primate's seat in return for its own full-time archbishop, though it will permanently regain the honour on the retirement or death of the present incumbent, Cardinal Glemp.

The City

The compactness of Gniezno is immediately evident: from either the train or bus station, it's only a few minutes' walk straight down ul. Lecha to ul. Bolesława Chrobrego, the quiet end of a main thoroughfare that boasts several refurbished pastel-coloured buildings. In ten minutes you pass into the pedestrianized section of this street, which ends up at the quiet, cobbled **Rynek**.

There are three Gothic churches worth a quick look. Just off the southern side of the Rynek is the **Kościół św. Trójcy** (Church of the Holy Trinity), partly rebuilt in the Baroque style following a fire, beside which stand the only surviving remains of the city walls. Off the opposite side of the Rynek towers the **Franciscan church**, while further to the north is **Kościół św. Jana** (St John's Church). The latter, a foundation of the Knights Templar, preserves fourteenth-century frescoes in its chancel and has carved bosses and corbels depicting virtues and vices.

The cathedral

Northwest from the Rynek down ul. Tumska lies Gniezno's episcopal quarter, and protruding fittingly above it is the **cathedral** in whose forecourt stands a statue of Bolesław the Brave. Reminiscent of Poznań Cathedral, the basic brick structure was built in the fourteenth century in the severest Gothic style, but was enlivened in the Baroque period by a ring of stone chapels and by the addition of steeples to the twin facade towers. Entering the cathedral by the west door and following the ambulatory in an anticlockwise direction takes you past a sequence of richly decorated chapels, in which many of Poland's primates are buried, although most are usually only visible from behind locked grilles. Behind the high altar lies the silver **shrine of św. Wojciech,** the martyr seen here reclining on his sarcophagus. The work of Gdańsk craftsman, Peter van Rennen, the shrine is surrounded by figures representing the different social classes, along with depictions of the chief events of św. Wojciech's life. The shrine itself is housed in a huge and recently re-gilded frame flanked by arches of black and white marble. Other monuments to prominent local clerics and laymen can be seen throughout the cathedral. One which may catch your attention is that to **Primate Stefan Wyszyński**, in the north side of the ambulatory (see box overleaf).

In the history of communist Europe, there is nothing remotely comparable to the career of Stefan Wyszyński, who adapted the traditional powers of the primate of Poland to act as spokesman and regent of his people.

Wyszyński's early ministry was centred in Włocławek, where he was ordained in 1924, quickly establishing a reputation in the social field. He spent the war years in the **underground resistance movement**, having been saved from the German concentration camps, which accounted for most of his colleagues in Włocławek, through the prompt action of his bishop, who had ordered him to leave the town. He returned as head of the Włocławek Seminary in 1945 before enjoying a meteoric rise through the church hierarchy, being appointed bishop of Lublin the following year, and elevated to the archdiocese of Gniezno and the title of **Primate of Poland**, in 1948.

The elimination of Poland's formerly substantial Jewish, Orthodox and Protestant minorities as a result of World War II and its aftermath meant that nearly 98 percent of the population professed **Catholicism**, as opposed to the prewar figure of 75 percent. At the same time, however, organized religion came under threat from communist atheism. Matters came to a head with the Vatican's worldwide decree of 1949, which ordered the withholding of sacraments to all communist functionaries and sympathizers: this caused particular tensions in Poland, where the new administration, particularly in rural areas, was dependent on practising Catholics. Wyszyński reached a compromise agreement with the government the following year whereby the affairs of Church and State were clearly demarcated.

This cosy relationship did not last long: a wave of Stalinist **repression** in 1952–3 led to the end of religious instruction in schools, the usurpation of most of the Church's charitable activities, and to the imprisonment and harassment of thousands of priests. As a culmination, the bishop of Kielce was sentenced to twelve years' imprisonment on charges of espionage. Wyszyński's protests led to his own **arrest**, and he was confined to the Monastery of Komańcza in the remote Bieszczady Mountains. The detention of a man widely regarded as possessing saintly qualities had the effect of alienating the regime even further from the bulk of the populace, and Wyszyński acted as the symbolic figurehead of the unrest which reached crisis proportions in 1956.

Wyszyński was released later that year as part of the package – which also included the return of Gomułka to power – forestalling the Soviet invasion which would almost certainly have ensued had a political breakdown occurred. From then on, the communists were forced to accept the **special status** of the Catholic Church in Polish society, and they were never afterwards able to suppress it: in 1957, Wyszyński was allowed to travel to Rome to receive the cardinal's hat he had been awarded five years previously. Under his leadership – which, from a theological point of view, was extremely conservative – Poland came to be regarded as the most fervently Catholic nation in the world, with the Jasna Góra pilgrimage (see p.54) promoted as the central feature of national consciousness. Wyszyński's sermons, often relayed from every pulpit in the country, became increasingly fearless and notable for such pronouncements as his celebrated claim that "Polish citizens are slaves in their own country".

Although Wyszyński did not live to see the collapse of the communist regime against which he had fought so doggedly, his last years were ones of unbridled triumph. The standing to which he had raised Poland within the Roman Catholic faith was given due reward in 1978, when his right-hand man, Karol Wojtyła – once courted by the communists as a potentially more malleable future primate – leapfrogged over him to become the first-ever Polish pope. Then, at the very end of his life, the government was forced to yield to him as a powerbroker at the heart of the **Solidarity** crisis. When Wyszyński died, he was rewarded with a **funeral** matched in postwar Europe only by those of the victorious war leaders, Churchill and de Gaulle; the country came to a standstill as even his communist opponents were prominent in paying their last respects.

Just past the primate's tomb is another porch which leads to the *skarby*, or **treasury** (Tues–Sun 9am–4pm; 10zł) where several of Poland's earliest manuscripts are kept. The most beautiful of these is the eleventh-century *Golden Codex*, made for Gniezno at Reichenau in southwestern Germany, the most inventive centre of European book illumination at the time. A far simpler Gospel book from a couple of centuries earlier has annotations by Irish missionaries, which has prompted the suggestion that it was the Irish who converted the Polish tribes. Although not formally open to the public, objects including illuminated manuscripts are occasionally exhibited at the information kiosk on the opposite side of the nave. Near here is the entrance to the newly restored **crypt**, final resting place of former primates with evidence of the Romanesque foundations as well as some relics predating that time. Other valuable treasures are kept in the **archdiocesan museum** (daily 10am–4pm; 5zł), housed in one of the cluster of buildings to the north of the cathedral at ul. Kolegiaty 2, the star item being a chalice said to have belonged to św. Wojciech.

The cathedral's monumental highlight is the magnificent pair of **bronze doors** located at the entrance to the southern aisle. Unfortunately the doors are frequently locked away out of sight, although a replica is housed in the Muzeum Pociątków Państwa Polskiego (see below). Hung around 1175 and an inevitable influence on van Rennen, these are among the finest surviving examples of Romanesque decorative art, and are unique in Poland. Wojciech's life from the cradle to beyond the grave is illustrated in eighteen scenes, going up the right-hand door and then down the left, all set within a rich decorative border. Quite apart from their artistic quality, the doors are remarkable as a documentary record: even the faces of the villainous Prussians are based on accurate observation. Unfortunately, until the things are properly lit, the detail described above is difficult to distinguish, although buying the colour guide (see below) certainly helps. Passing through the doorway reveals the intricate **portal** on the other side. Though its tympanum of *Christ in Majesty* is orthodox enough, the carvings of griffins and the prominent mask heads give it a highly idiosyncratic flavour.

At the souvenir kiosk on the south aisle you can buy a glossy if rather skimpy trilingual **guide** (including English) on the cathedral.

Lake Jelonek

Just west of the cathedral is Lake Jelonek, a peaceful spot with a wonderful view of the town. Overlooking its far bank, but more easily approached via the main road, is a large modern building containing a college and the **Muzeum Pociątków Państwa Polskiego** (Museum of the Origins of the Polish State; Tues–Sun 10am–5pm; 6zł). This contains some immensely dull archeological finds from various Wielkopolska sites on the entrance floor, along with changing art exhibitions upstairs. Much more worthwhile is the absorbing display of artefacts and thirty-minute audiovisual presentation downstairs (English commentary available on request) which elaborates on the development of medieval life in Wielkopolska and the significance of the Piast dynasty.

Practicalities

The **train** and **bus** stations are side by side about 500m south of the centre – walk straight down ul. Lecha to ul. Bolesława Chrobrego, which terminates at the Rynek.

Cheapest of the **hotels** is the *Orzeł*, situated right next to a speedway oval at ul. Wrzesinska 25 (☎061/426 4925; ❷–❸), offering simple but clean rooms in a frumpy part of town some 20 minutes' walk south of the centre. More expen-

WIELKOPOLSKA AND POMERANIA | Gniezno: practicalities

sive but still representing great value is the friendly, charming and superbly central *Pietrak*, in the middle of the pedestrianized area at ul. Chrobrego 3 (☎61/426 1497; ⑤), which has comfortable en-suite rooms with satellite TV and minibar, and a big buffet breakfast. If the Pietrak is full you can always try the *Lech*, fifteen minutes' walk northeast of the centre at ul. Jolenty 5 (☎61/426 2385, ⑤426 1294; ⑤), an uninspiring but habitable 1970s-era hotel with plain en-suites, where guests can use the nearby swimming pool and fitness centre; or the snazzier *Gewert*, slightly further out in the same direction at ul. Paczkowskiego 2 (☎61/428 2375; ⑤; buses #9 or #17 from Dworcowa to Budowlanych), which has lovely bright en-suites with TV, although it is in an area of scruffy towerblocks 1.5km from the centre. The **youth hostel**, close to the stations at ul. Pocztowa 11 (on the top floor; ☎061/426 2780), is a welcoming place with few rough edges.

There's a cluster of pleasant **restaurants** with outdoor seating in the centre of town on the pedestrianized section of ul. Bolesława Chrobrego. The *Pietrak* hotel (see above), which seems to have a monopoly on the best things in central Gniezno, houses a cheap, fast and cheerful grill bar on the ground floor, and a more formal, starched-tablecloth restaurant with an international menu in the cellar. *Pizzeria Verona*, Chrobrego 1, is a trusty and cheap place for a quick bite; while *Złoty Smok*, a few steps off the west side of the Rynek, offers good, inexpensive Chinese food in unpretentious surroundings.

For **drinking**, there's a brace of outdoor bars in the Rynek in summer; although the *Pub* opposite the *Pietrak* is the most comfortable of the central bars. *Music Pub Wieża*, occupying the base of an old water tower out beyond the *Lech* hotel at ul. Żwirki i Wigury 29, has a grassy outdoor terrace and hosts occasional gigs – worth heading out for if you see fly-posters around town. The *Internet Pub* on Podgórna is the place to check your **emails**.

Lake Lednica

One of the most worthwhile excursions you're likely to make in this corner of Poland is to the slender **Lake Lednica**, 18km west of Gniezno and easily reached from there by taking any Poznań or Pobiediska-bound bus. Site of a tenth-century courtly residence equal in importance to Gniezno, the lake is now the site of both an absorbing archeological site and one of the largest *skansens* in the country. The bus stop is just by the access road to the museums (you'll probably catch sight of the sign advertising the Wielkopolski Park Etnograficzny), just west of the turnoff to Dziekanowice. Driving from Poznań it's the second turn left after the three roadside windmills.

From the road end it's a ten-minute walk north to the **Wielkopolski Park Etnograficzny** (Wielkopolska Ethnographic Park; mid-April to end April & Jul–Oct Tues–Sat 9am–5pm, Sun 10am–5pm; May–June Tues–Sat 9am–6pm, Sun 10am–6pm; Nov Tues–Sat 9am–3pm, Sun 10am–3pm; 7zł), an open-air museum consisting of about fifty traditional rural buildings from the last 250 years or so – including windmills, a Baroque cemetery chapel with all its furnishings, and several farmsteads. Some of the more eye-catching of the latter belonged to the Wielkopolska Dutch – immigrants from the Low Countries who were encouraged to settle here in the seventeenth and eighteenth centuries because of their superior knowledge of land irrigation techniques. They built solid, prosperous-looking farmhouses with red-tiled roofs, unlike their Polish neighbours, who preferred thatch. The Dutch were long ago assimilated by the Polish and German-speaking communities in the region.

From the *skansen*, continue north through the village of Dziekanowice and turn left at the T-junction to reach the disparate tourist complex known as the

Muzeum Pierwszych Piastów na Lednicy (Museum of the First Piasts at Lednica; May–June 9am–6pm; mid-April to end April & July–Oct: 9am–5pm; mid-Feb to mid–April & Nov: 9am–3pm; Dec–Jan closed; 8zł). Just beyond the village you'll come across the museum's cash desk and a small exhibition hall filled with replica tenth-century arms and armour. From here it's another ten-minute walk to the impressive wooden gateway (whose upper storey turns out to be a snack bar) that marks the entrance to the core of the site. Another exhibition room houses a small collection of domestic artefacts, including combs carved from animal bones and silver bowls which presumably served as the early Piasts' tableware. Once you've perused these it's a good idea to take the chained daily **ferry** (every 30min 9am–5pm;) to **Ostrów Lednicki**, the largest of the three tiny islands in Lake Lednica, where it's believed that Mieszko I once held court.

This unlikely site, uninhabited for the last six centuries, was once a royal seat equal to Poznań and Gniezno in importance – **Bolesław the Brave** was born here, and it may also have been where his coronation by Emperor Otto III took place, rather than in Gniezno. It began life in the ninth century as a fortified town covering about a third of the island and linked to the mainland by a jetty. In the following century, a modest **palace** was constructed, along with a church: the excavated remains only hint at its former grandeur, but the presence of stairways prove it was probably at least two storeys high. By the landing jetty a model of the former settlement gives an idea of how it may have looked, surrounded by the still extant earth ramparts from which now flutters a Polish flag. The buildings were destroyed in 1038 by the Czech Prince Brzetysław, but the church was rebuilt soon afterwards, only gradually to fall into disuse, along with the town itself. For centuries the island served as a cemetery, only to be lulled out of its sleep by tourism.

Żnin

Forty kilometres north of Gniezno on the Bydgoszcz road (and reached by hourly buses) the small town of **Żnin** would be ordinarily unremarkable were it not for two major attributes – the ageing **narrow-gauge rail line** that meanders for 12km through the pastures south of town to the village of Gąsawa, and the reconstructed Iron Age settlement of **Biskupin** which lies along the route. In between Żnin and Biskupin, a small railway museum in the village of **Wenecja** adds to the list of attractions. The narrow-guage line still operates a limited tourist–oriented service, and presents the most enjoyable way of reaching Venecja and Biskupin in summer – otherwise, a combination of local buses and walking will enable you to see the sites and still get back to Gniezno by nightfall.

Żnin

ŻNIN is a place from which to catch services to Biskupin rather than a tourist town in its own right. Luckily, the train, bus and narrow-gauge stations are all within 100m of each other on the northeastern side of town. It's a good idea to head for the narrow-gauge station first in order to check the timetable: if there are no convenient services running that day, then consider catching a bus to Gąsawa, from where you can walk to Biskupin in about 30 minutes.

If you have time to kill in Żnin, head a block south of the train and bus stations to find ul. 700-lecia, which winds towards a neat and unassuming Rynek.

At the far end of the square stands the octagonal brick **tower** of the demolished fifteenth-century town hall, whose interior has been fitted out as the local **museum** (Tues–Fri 9am–4pm, Sat 9am–3pm, Sun 10am–3pm; 3zł) – a far from captivating selection of local crafts and other oddments. Immediately beyond here lies the fair-sized **Lake Czaple**, the grassy shores of which make for an attractive walk.

There are a few reasonable **accommodation** options: the *Basztowy*, near the Rynek on ul. 700-lecia a (☎052/302 0006, ⊕www.hotel-basztowy.com.pl; ❺), is the most comfortable and central of the hotels; while the *Martina*, 2km north of the centre at ul. Mickiewicza 37 (☎052/302 8733; ❹) has parking facilities, a sauna and cupboard-sized rooms; and the PTTK *Dom Turysty*, beside the lake at ul. Szkolna 16 (☎052/302 0113; ❶) has sparsely furnished rooms with shared facilities. The **restaurant** of the *Hotel Basztowy* offers solid Polish fare; while *Vito*, on the corner of Lewandowskiego and ul. 700-lecia, serves up snack meals, has good ice cream, and is a decent place to drink.

The Żnin–Gąsawa narrow-gauge rail line

The **Żnin–Gąsawa narrow-gauge rail line** has been running for over a century, although it has long since ceased to be a meaningful means of public transport for the locals, and now functions almost exclusively as a tourist attraction. The railway has retained one fully operational steam engine, although it only sees action on selected summer weekends, and all other services are hauled by aesthetically less appealing diesels. There are five daily Żnin–Gąsawa services between mid-June and September; two or three daily from May to mid-June and October to mid-November. Additional departures are often laid on for tour groups, and individual travellers are allowed to tag along if space allows – so it always pays to ask the station staff. The journey to Biskupin takes about fifty minutes, with trains barely exceeding walking pace, but the trip – through gently rolling countryside dotted with silver-blue lakes – is definitely worthwhile.

The train rattles noisily through hay fields and vegetable patches, its second stop, **WENECJA**, being the halfway point. This hamlet's name is the Polish word for Venice, fancifully justified by the fact that it is almost surrounded by water, lying as it does between two lakes. To the left of the station are the remains of the fourteenth-century **castle** of Mikołaj Nałęz, a notoriously cruel figure known as the "Devil of Wenecja". Only the lower parts of the walls survive. On the opposite side of the tracks is the open-air **Muzeum Kolei Wąskotorowej** (Narrow-Gauge Railway Museum; daily: April–Oct 9am–6pm; Nov–March 10am–2pm; 4zł), exhibiting a motley collection of undersized engines and rolling stock which once served the area.

From Wenecja the train continues along the edge of Lake Biskupin and stops right outside the entrance to the settlement a few minutes later. If you miss a train, you can walk from Wenecja to Biskupin in about 30 minutes.

Biskupin

The Iron Age village of **BISKUPIN**, 30km north of Gniezno, is one of the most evocative archeological sites in Europe. Discovered in 1933, when a schoolmaster noticed some hand-worked stakes standing in the reeds at the lakeside, excavations commenced the following year until experts from Warsaw soon pronounced that the site had been a **fortified village** of the Lusatian culture, founded around 550 BC and destroyed in tribal warfare some 150 years later. The subsequent uncovering of the settlement has thrown fresh light on the tribal life of the period, enabling the solution of many previously unresolved questions.

The site

In contrast to the overcautious approach that makes so many famous archeological sites disappointing to non-specialists, it was decided to take a guess and reconstruct the palisade, ramparts and part of the village. The price to be paid for this approach is evident at the entrance to the **archeological park** (daily: mid-April to Sept 8am–7pm; Oct 8am–6pm subject to weather), with souvenir and snack bars lining the car park on the other side of the tracks.

From the entrance, it's best to go straight ahead past a re-erected eighteenth-century cottage and start with the **museum**, which provides a pretty good introduction to the site as a whole. Inside you'll find all manner of objects dug up here – tools, household utensils, weapons, jewellery, ornaments and objects for worship, some thought to be ten thousand years old. The exhibits are all superbly mounted and lit, and are accompanied by English-language captions. Piecing together the evidence, archeologists have been able to draw a picture of a society in which hunting had been largely superseded by arable farming and livestock breeding. Their trade patterns were surprisingly extensive – their iron seems to have come from Transylvania, and there's an intriguing group of exhibits imported from even further afield, the most exotic being some Egyptian beads. Most remarkable of all was the tribe's prowess in building, as can be seen in the model reconstruction of the entire village. Beyond the museum buildings is an enclosure for **tarpans**, miniature working horses which have evolved very little since the time of the settlement.

Backtracking to the cottage and turning right, it's only a couple of minutes' walk down the path to the **reconstructed site**. The foreground consists of the uncovered foundations of various buildings, some from as late as the thirteenth century; of more interest are re-creations of the Iron Age buildings – although only a section of each has been built, and not exactly on their former site, it requires little imagination to picture what the whole must have looked like.

The **palisade** was particularly ingenious: it originally consisted of 35,000 stakes grouped in rows up to nine deep and driven into the bed of the lake at an angle of 45 degrees. It acted both as a breakwater and as the first line of the fortifications. Immediately behind was a circular **wall** of oak logs guarded by a tall watchtower: the latter is the most conjectural part of the whole restoration project. Inside the defences were a ring road plus eleven symmetrical streets, again made of logs and filled in with earth, sand and clay; the **houses** were grouped in thirteen terraces ranged from east to west to catch the sun. An entire extended family would live in each house, so the population of the settlement probably numbered over a thousand. As you can see from the example open for inspection, each house had two chambers: pigs and cattle – the most important privately owned objects – were kept in the lobby, while the main room, where the family slept in a single bed, was also equipped with a loft for the storage of food and fuel.

The *Diabeł Wenecki* pleasure boat offers thirty-minute **cruises** on the lake (Tues–Sat 9am–5pm, Sun 9am–4pm), allowing you to view the site from the water.

In an unintentional parody of the Iron Age village, a sizeable settlement of timber-built **snack-huts** has grown up around the car park at the site's entrance; here you can feast on anything from pork chops to pancakes before moving on. If you've missed the last **train**, some (but not all) Żnin–Gąsawa **buses** pass the site entrance, although perhaps the easiest thing to do is walk uphill to Gąsawa (30min), from where you can catch regular buses plying the Gniezno–Bydgoszcz route.

Trzemeszno to Inowrocław

Once you've seen Gniezno, Lednica and Biskupin, the rest of eastern Wielkopolska is a bit of a let-down, characterized by a string of unassuming, semi-industrialized towns which have little in the way of attention-grabbing appeal. However there's many an architectural gem hidden away in the region, together with plentiful reminders of the **Piast** dynasty – certainly enough to structure an itinerary around if you have time to spare. There's not much in the way of tourist facilities or urban thrills in the region – so it's a good idea to treat Gniezno as your most likely touring base. If you're travelling by **public transport**, Trzemeszno, Mogilno and Inowrocław are easily reached by bus and train from Gniezno; Inowrocław bus station is the most convenient jumping-off point for Strzelno and Kruszwica.

Trzemesno

Sixteen kilometres east of Gniezno, the Szlak Piastowski (Piast Route) winds through **TRZEMESZNO**, now a lightly industrialized town that was founded, according to tradition, by św. Wojciech (St Adalbert). It can be reached either by bus from Gniezno or Baltic-bound train – the latter involving a 3km walk south to the town.

The ancient church that św. Wojciech is said to have established was succeeded by a Romanesque structure, parts of which are incorporated in the town's main sight, the Baroque **basilica**. From the outside it appears merely pleasingly rotund, but once inside you'll find a revelation of light and colour that – if you've developed a taste for Baroque church interiors – is well worth the break in your journey. In this instance it's the superb **paintings** in the dome and along the transept that for once take the attention away from the central altar, under which an effigy of Wojciech reposes. The ceiling frescoes vividly depict three crucial scenes from the saint's life and death: his vicious slaying by the Prussian pagans; the retrieval of his remains for their weight in gold, with Wojciech now just a few body parts on a scale; and his eventual entombment in the basilica.

Right opposite the church is the central but run-down **hotel** *Czeremcha* (☎052/315 4386; ❷) at pl. Kilińskiego 9. There's a **restaurant** at the *Czeremcha*, and the *Pałuchanka* on pl. Kilińskiego is also passable.

Strzelno

More of the Szlak Piastowski's artistic treasures are found 17km east of Mogilno in the sleepy town of **STRZELNO**. Both the **bus and train stations** lie at the southwestern fringe of town; from there, walk straight ahead, turning left up ul. Ducha to reach the rather unprepossessing main square. Continuing down to the right brings you to two outstanding Romanesque buildings.

The **Klasztor św. Trójcy** (Monastery of the Holy Trinity) is a typically Polish accretion: brick Gothic gables and a monumental Baroque facade sprout from a late-twelfth-century Romanesque shell. After the war, some of the interior plasterwork was removed to reveal, in well-nigh perfect condition, three original nave **pillars**. Two of these, adorned with figurative carvings, are crafted with a delicacy found in few other European sculptures of the period; a third is quite plain. Another slimmer column of almost equal quality forms the sole support of the vault of the somewhat neglected chapel of St Barbara, to the right of the altar over which hangs a huge crown.

Beside the monastery church stands the slightly older little red sandstone **Kaplica św. Prokopa** (Chapel of St Procopius). In contrast to its neighbour, this has preserved the purity of its original form, its half-round tower perfectly offset against the protruding rotund apses to a most pleasing effect. It's kept locked, but you could ask in the Klasztor św. Trójcy or the buildings alongside for a look inside. Incidentally, the churches are not the earliest evidence of worship on this site: the large stone boulder in front of them is thought to have been used for pagan rites.

There's a small **hotel**, the *Dom Wycieczkowy*, at pl. Daszyńskiego 1 (☎052/318 9237; ❷–❸), offering a choice between serviceable en-suites or spartan rooms with shared facilities. The unpretentious *Piastowska* **restaurant** at ul. św. Ducha 34, serves up basic Polish fare at cheap prices.

Kruszwica

The Szlak Piastowski (Piast Route) moves on to **KRUSZWICA**, a town surrounded by grain silos and ugly factories about 16km northeast of Strzelno. Standing at the head of the pencil-slim **Lake Gopło**, the largest of all western Poland's lakes, Kruszwica is enshrined in Polish folklore as the cradle of the Piast dynasty.

The **bus station** is located at the northwestern fringe of the town. From here, walk ahead to the main street, ul. Niepodległości. This leads to a spacious but unremarkable Rynek, just east of which is a bridge over the lake.

The shady tree-lined peninsula immediately to the south of this is a popular tourist spot, as evidenced by the presence of a number of snack stands. It's dominated by a brick octagon known as the **Mysia Wieża**, or Mouse Tower. Allegedly, this was where a notorious rodent feast took place (see box below); in fact, ironically enough, it was part of a castle built by the last of the Piast dynasty, Kazimierz the Great. During the summer season, you can climb to the top for a sweeping view down the length of Lake Gopło, on which hour-long **cruises** operate aboard the *Rusałka*.

Kruszwica's only other historic monument is the early-twelfth-century **collegiate church**, situated on the eastern shore – coming from town take the first left after the bridge and continue for a kilometre. A grim granite basilica with three apses, it has been stripped of most of its later accretions, except for the brick Gothic tower, and gives a good impression of what an early Christian church may have once looked like. Supposedly occupying the miraculous site of Piast's cottage, it served as a cathedral for the first half-century of its life, before being supplanted by Włocławek.

The legend of the foundation of the Piast dynasty

The legend goes that the **descendants of Lech** were ousted as the nation's rulers by the evil Popiel family. To ensure there was no competition for his succession, the last King Popiel killed all his male kin except his own children, then established himself at a castle in Kruszwica, where he subjected his people to a reign of terror. One day, SS John and Paul came in the guise of poor travellers, but the king refused them hospitality and they were forced to lodge with a peasant named **Piast**. They baptized him and his family, and predicted that he would be first in a long line of monarchs, whereupon they vanished. Shortly afterwards, the Poles rose up against their evil ruler. He took refuge in his castle tower, where he was eventually devoured by rats. The people then chose the worthy Piast as his successor.

Should you need a **place to to stay** there's the *Hotel Sportowy Gopło* at ul. Poznańska 17 (☎052/351 5233; ❷), which offers prim en-suite doubles, and some much cheaper, dorm-like triples and quads. The only **restaurant** worth mentioning is the inevitably named *Piastowska*, on ul. Niepodległości, offering an enticing range of Polish and Ukrainian food.

Inowrocław

The easternmost extent of the Szlak Piastowski comes 15km north of Kruszwica at **INOWROCŁAW**, a nineteenth-century spa town subsequently blighted by twentieth-century industrialization and pollution. The town's erstwhile popularity as a place to take the cure is reflected in the grand turn-of-the-twentieth-century buildings erected along the town's main axis, ul. Królowej Jadwigi, which are now re-emerging from decades of neglect in their full colourful pomp.

In the heart of the Stare Miasto, just south of the Rynek down ul. Paderewskiego and then right, is **św. Mikołaja** (St Nicholas), a Gothic parish church with Renaissance and Baroque additions. Inside, the vault's ribs lead down to murals depicting key events from the Bible – starting with Adam and a shame-faced Eve's explusion from the Garden.

The town's main monument is the **Kościół Zwiastowania NMP** (Church of the Annunciation), a contemporary of the Romanesque basilicas in Strzelno and Kruszwica, albeit one heavily altered. A Romantic spire was added last century along with an attractive interior paint job similar to that in Włocławek's Kościół św. Jana. It occupies a pleasantly landscaped position in a park, a few minutes' walk east of the big roundabout which lies between the compact commercial centre and the bus and train stations, respectively ten and fifteen minutes' walk to the north.

Given Inowrocław's industrial appearance, it's unlikely to rate as an overnight stop, and there are in any case plentiful onward **train** connections to Bydgoszcz (see p.638) and Toruń (p.210). If you're stuck, the *Hotel Bast*, ul. Krolowej Jadwigi 35 (☎052/357 2024; ❺), has overpriced doubles with shared facilities (❺), and some dowdy en-suites (❼). Dorm beds are available from the *OsiR* **hostel** 1km west of the centre at ul. Wierzbińskiego 9 (☎052/357 6730). The restaurant of the *Bast* is probably your best place for a decent meal.

Pomerania (Pomorze)

Pomerania's long, sandy coastline is its major attraction, and a couple of days holed up on the Baltic here is one of the most pleasant ways of unwinding that the country can offer. Less known but equally appealing, especially travelling by bike, is the inland forested lake district, with its Prussian peasant villages and conspicuous absence of heavy industry.

Bydgoszcz, a major industrial city with a small historic centre, serves as the gateway to the lakes to the north, but it's only attractive in parts, and you may only want to make use of it for changing trains or buses. Best base and transport hub in the lake district is **Szeczinek**, on the shores of Lake Welimie, although **Lake Drawsko**, bordered by the settlements of **Czaplinek** and **Stary Drawsko**, is probably the region's single most enticing stretch of water. On the coast there are plenty of resorts to choose from: **Łeba** manages to combine fishing-village atmosphere with fine beaches and the **Słowiński National Park**; low-key resorts like **Ustka**, **Darłówko** and **Mielno** preserve something of their genteel nineteenth-century character; while to the west many of the finest beaches are found around **Kołobrzeg** and on the islands of **Wolin** and **Uznam**. Just inland, a chain of towns from **Kamień Pomorski** to **Stargard Szczeciński** provide a modicum of architectural attractions, all of which are readily accessible from the great port of **Szczecin**, Pomerania's largest city and historic capital, and today a bustling urban centre.

A brief history of Pomerania

In prehistoric times the southern Baltic coast was inhabited by the Celts, who were later displaced by a succession of Germanic tribes. By the end of the fifth century they too had been ousted by Slav people known as the **Pomorzanie**, relics of whose settlements are preserved on Wolin island, in the west of the region. The lands of the Pomorzanie were in turn conquered by the Piast **King Mieszko I**, who took Szczecin in 979 – a campaign that is cited by the Poles in support of their claim to ownership of this often disputed territory. Thereafter the picture gets more complicated. Throughout the medieval era, Pomerania evolved as an essentially independent dukedom ruled by a local Slav dynasty commonly called the **Pomeranian princes**, who nonetheless owed loyalty to the Polish monarch. Eastern Pomerania was conquered by the Teutonic Knights in 1308, and was later known as Royal Prussia; this part of the region returned to the Polish sphere of influence under the terms of the 1466 Treaty of Toruń (see p.211).

The ethnic mix of the region played a dominant part in governing its allegiances. While a Slav majority retained its hold on the countryside, heavy German colonization of the towns inexorably tilted the balance of power to the territorially ambitious Brandenburg margraviate. In line with the westward drift, the Pomeranian princes finally transferred formal allegiance to the Holy Roman Empire in 1521, and the inroads of the Reformation further weakened the region's ties with Catholic Poland, which anyway was more interested in its eastern borderlands than its western terrains. In 1532, the ruling Gryfit dynasty divided into two lines, and their territory was partitioned along a line west of the Odra delta: the larger eastern duchy was henceforth known as Hinter Pomerania; the small one to the west as Lower or Hither Pomerania. None of the latter's territory has ever subsequently formed part of Poland.

Control of the region was fiercely disputed during the **Thirty Years' War**, with the Swedes taking over all of Lower Pomerania, plus some of the coastline of Hinter Pomerania. The Treaty of Westphalia of 1648 formalized the division of the latter, whose capital, Szczecin/Stettin, thereby became part of Sweden. Following the departure of the Swedes in the 1720s, **the Prussians** reunited Lower and Hinter Pomerania into a single administrative province, and during the Partitions were able to join it up with their territories to the east by the annexation of Royal Prussia. Their control over the region was undisturbed until after the Versailles Treaty of 1919, when a strip of Pomerania's eastern fringe was ceded to Poland, some of it forming part of the notorious "Polish Corridor". Nearly all of the territory of the old duchy of Hinter Pomerania was **allocated to Poland** in 1945, as part of the compensation deal for loss of the Eastern Territories to the Soviet Union. Mass emigration of the area's German population, which started during the final months of the war, gathered apace after the transfer of sovereignty; in their place came displaced Polish settlers, mostly from the east.

Transport links within Pomerania are good: there's a reasonable train service that runs parallel to the coast on the Gdańsk–Szczecin line, including one international train to Berlin, with local connections up to the coastal resorts and buses for excursions inland into the countryside. If you're approaching the Pomeranian coast from the northeast, east, then Gdynia (see Chapter 2) offers the best in the way of bus connections.

Bydgoszcz

BYDGOSZCZ is a sprawling industrial city, developed around a fortified medieval settlement strategically located on the River Brda, shortly before its confluence with the Wisła. Growth took off at the end of the eighteenth century when, as the Prussian town of Bromberg, it became the hub of an important waterway system due to the construction of a canal linking the Wisła to the Odra via the rivers Brda, Noteć and Warta. Unlike much of the region to the north, it has been Polish since 1920, when it was ceded by Germany and incorporated into the province of Poznań. During World War II, the city suffered particularly badly at the hands of the Nazis: mass executions of civilians followed its fall, and by the end of the war over fifty thousand people – a quarter of the population – had been murdered, with many of the rest deported to labour and concentration camps.

Despite the inevitable signs of decay in the communist-era suburbs, modern Bydgoszcz has the feel of a dynamic, self-confident city, and it's a good place in which to recharge your urban batteries if you've been out in the sticks for a while. It has fast public transport links with the historic town of Toruń (see Chapter 2) to the east, and is also the place from which to catch buses to Szczecinek in the Pomeranian lake district to the northwest.

The City

As ever, the focal point of the medieval centre is the **Stary Rynek** on the south bank of the Brda, a relatively unassuming square that nevertheless boasts a clutch of Baroque and Neoclassical mansions, newly done up in pastel greens and pinks. A typical communist-style **monument** to the victims of Nazism overshadows the vast bulk of the **Jesuit college**, which closes the west side of the square, with another fine frontage along ul. Jezuicka. Begun at the end of the seventeenth century, this was for long the town's leading educational establishment, now used as municipal offices.

In a secluded corner just to the north is the red-brick fifteenth-century **Kościół Farny** (Parish Church). This has recently been raised to the status of a co-cathedral, though its dimensions and appearance are more modest than those of many a village church. Nonetheless, its exterior is graced by a fine Gothic gable, while inside, among the usual Baroque ornamentation, is the sixteenth-century high altar of *The Madonna with the Rose*. The church overlooks **Wyspa Młynska**, a small island situated at the point where the River Brda separates into several little channels. Crossed by dainty bridges and overlooked by old half-timbered granaries and red-brick warehouses, these slow-flowing waterways make up an area that has been fancifully styled as the Bydgoszcz Venice. One of the warehouses, tucked away at the northern end of Wyspa Młynska, holds the **town museum** (Tues–Wed 9am–5pm, Thurs–Sat 10am–4pm, Sun 10am–2pm; 4zł), with displays on the history of the town, including archive material on the Nazi atrocities. A couple of blocks south of the Rynek lies ul. Długa, the main shopping street, recently re-cobbled and planted with Victorian-style wrought-iron lamps in a rather tasteful attempt to bestow on the city centre a modicum of *belle-époque* sheen.

Crossing over to the northern bank, you come to the former **Kościół Klarysek** (Convent Church of the Poor Clares), a curious amalgam of late Gothic and Renaissance, with later alterations. Its conventual buildings now contain the **district museum** (Tues–Fri 10am–4pm, Sat–Sun noon–4pm; 3zł), devoted mostly to the work of the eclectic local artist Leon Wyczółkowski. Running north then east from here is the rather grand thoroughfare of ul. **Gdańska**, lined with an impressive sequence of imposing nineteenth-century office blocks, many of which have been throughly restored in the last few years. Spinning off Gdańska towards the train station is **Dworcowa**, a narrow, cobbled street that seems to have changed little since the mid-1900s, and boasts some (sadly unrestored) Art Nouveau facades at nos. 45, 47 and 49.

Five blocks east of here is a historical curiosity which rewards the short detour – the basilica of **St Vincent de Paul**, a vast circular brick church self-consciously modelled on the Pantheon in Rome and capable of accommodating twelve thousand worshippers. Its construction was a direct result of the town's change in ownership from Protestant Prussia to Catholic Poland, which necessitated a much larger space for the main feast days than the small existing churches were able to provide. Passing through the brick-columned portico into the basilica the vast space beneth the dome momentarily distracts you, but after a while the lack of a focal point makes itself felt, and it dawns that the circular design is better used in stadiums, not churches. One thing the basilica has got going for it is a rather snazzy collection of Art Deco-esque pine confessionals.

There's a **railway museum** (Tues–Fri noon–5pm, Sat 10am–2pm; 3zł) by the station at ul. Zygmunta Augusta 7, an engaging if small collection which can't compare with the display at Wenecja (see p.632).

Practicalities

The **train station** is located to the northwest of the city centre: a fifteen-minute walk straight down ul. Dworcowa brings you out onto Gdańska (or tram #1, #2, #4 or #8), from where it's a short hop over the river to the Stary Rynek. Bydgoszcz's bus station is 1km east of the centre along Jagiellońska. There's a **tourist office** (Mon–Fri 9am–5pm; ☎052/345 4785) just across from the train station at ul. Zygmunta Augusta 10; online information can be found at ⓦ www.bydgoszcz.com.

Generally speaking **accommodation** gets more promising (and more expensive) the further away you are from the train station. The *Asystenta*, near at hand at ul. Dworcowa 79 (☎052/322 0631; ❸), has adequate but spartan rooms with bathrooms in the hallway; while the almost adjacent *Centralny*, ul. Dworcowa 85 (☎052/322 8876; ❺), is a touch more salubrious, but is overpriced for what it offers. A little further down the road, the soaring concrete *Brda*, ul. Dworcowa 94 (☎052/322 4061, ⓦ www.hotelbrda.com.pl; ❻), offers serviceable en-suites with TV, and offers weekend discounts. In the heart of town just behind the Rynek, the *Hotel Ratuszowy*, ul. Długa 37 (☎052/322 8861, ⓦ www.hotelratuszowy.com.pl; ❻), is cramped but comfortable and superbly located. The Orbis-run *Pod Orłem*, al. Gdańska 14 (☎052/583 0530, ⓔ podorlem@orbis.pl; ❽), has been refurbished and now relives its *fin-de-siècle* elegance; while the gleaming new *City Hotel*, ul. 3 Maja 6 (☎052/325 2500,

@www.cityhotel.bydgoszcz.pl; ❽), exudes an atmosphere of cool minimalist haughtiness. The **youth hostel** is a couple of minutes' walk from the train station at ul. Józefa Sowińskiego 5 (☏052/322 7570).

There's a wide range of **eating** possibilities; *Baalbek*, just off the Rynek at Magdzińskiego 3, serves up cheap and tasty *szaszłyk* and souvlakia takeaways; while *Pizzeria Capri*, also near the Rynek at Niedzwiedzowa 9, offers a decent range of pies in more comfortable, sit-down surroundings. *Piwnica Ratuszowa*, Jezuitska 16, is the handiest central place in which to treat yourself to lashings of meat-heavy Polish food. Tasty and moderately priced Indian dishes are on offer at the *Sogo Indyjska*, ul. Dworcowa 50. If you're splashing out, try hotel restaurants like the *Chopin* in the *City Hotel* at ul. 3 Maja 6 (☏052/22 8841), which has an outstanding range of international cuisine and a good choice of vegetarian options – expect to pay around 110zł for a three-course meal without drinks.

The Rynek area is awash with both daytime and evening **drinking** venues. *Café Reggiano Emilia*, on the northern side of the Rynek, is a comfy place from which to watch the world go by, and does excellent ice cream. Cosy pub-style bars within easy reach include *Amsterdam*, on the south side of the Rynek, and *Mefisto* and *Tuba Bar* just off the Rynek to the east. In summer, the deck of a green barge moored on the River Brda, just by the town's central bridge, is transformed into a vast beer garden. *Hysteria*, Dworcowa 13, is the main venue for Friday night pack-em-in techno **clubbing**; although a much more alternative crowd hangs out at *Mózg*, Gdańska 10 (entrance down the Parkowa side street), a rambling café-cum-music club which is one of the major venues in this corner of Poland for jazz and rock gigs.

The *Remiza Internet Pub*, near the train station at Dworcowa 83 (3pm till last guest), is exactly what it says: a place where you can surf the net and enjoy a beery session while you're at it.

For more high-brow **entertainment**, the Filharmonia Pomorska, just east of ul. Gdańska at ul. Karola Libelta 16 (box office daily noon–6pm), is the main **musical** venue; as well as regular concerts, it features a fortnight-long classical festival each September. The main **theatre** is the nearby Teatr Polski, al. Mickiewicza 2 (box office Tues–Sun 3–7pm; ☏52/321 1238, @www.psi.com.pl/TP). Opera Nova at ul. Gdańska 20 (box office Mon–Thurs 3–6.30pm, Sun 9–11am; www.opera.bydgoszcz.pl) is the venue for **opera**.

The Pomeranian lakeland

The **Pomeranian lakeland** lies over to the northwest of Bydgoszcz, centred on the resort town of **Szczecinek**. It is an area of low undulating hills smothered by bygone glaciers, patches of pine and birch forest and quiet, tree-lined roads linking small market towns separated by over a thousand lakes. After blossoming as a workers' holiday retreat about a generation ago, the area stagnated as a tourist destination in the early 1990s, but is now undergoing a modest revival. It's not nearly as developed as the Masurian lakes in the east of the country, and can't offer as much in the way of tourist facilities. The fish-fry stalls and beer huts which characterize the rest of Polish seaside and lakeland tourism are conspicuous by their absence here, and you might find the region's rustic laid-back feel correspondingly soothing.

Many of the Poles who come here are content to park up at the few **lakeside resorts** where the accommodation tends to be concentrated, although activities such as riding, sailing and hiking are beginning to emerge as major draws. The region's gentle gradients, quiet villages and lack of heavy traffic make a lovely if undemanding location for a **cycling tour**, although even fat-tyred mountain bikes might find some of the sandy forest tracks hard work.

Bydgoszcz and Szczecin are the best places from which to catch **buses** into the area; in addition, **trains** working the Poznań–Kołobrzeg route trundle through Szczecinek.

Two good **maps** cover the entire area in detail: the green PPWK 1:300,000 *Kaszuby, Kujawy, Wielopolska* sheet #2 covers the eastern lake district from Poznań to Gdańsk, and the same scale *Pomorze, Wielkopolska* sheet #1 takes you west to Szczecin and the German border. They're usually available in the bigger bookshops and Empik stores.

Chojnice and the Eastern Lake District

Some 50km north of Bydgoszcz, near Lake Charzykowskie, lies **CHOJNICE**, a quiet, unpretentious place where you may find yourself waiting for buses towards the more appealing lakes just to the north. The **bus** and **train stations** are both next to each other just over 1km southeast of the town's dusty, open square – the setting for its main bit of animation, a weekly market, when the streets are filled with traders. Architecturally, the town has a few reminders of its past as the last Polish stronghold of the Teutonic Knights, although Chojnice also bears the ignominious distinction of being the first town to be attacked by the Nazis on September 1, 1939. The most impressive old building is the **town hall** whose stepped gable looks down on the Rynek. Sections of the town walls have also survived the battering of the centuries, most notably the five-storey **Brama Czuchołowoska** (Czuchołow Gate), off the western edge of the Rynek, which houses a **museum** (Tues–Sat 11am–4pm; 2zł) displaying an unexceptional array of historical items.

Lake Charzykowskie

Northwest of Chojnice, a series of lakes and waterways extends for an unbroken 60km towards the edges of Kashubia (see p.199). The relaxed rural pace encourages a gentle exploration of a couple of days. Equipped with your own tent and a modicum of discretion you can pretty much camp for free (bearing in mind the usual precautions for fire). Otherwise there are several cheap small hotels en route.

From Chojnice, the place to head for is **Lake Charzykowskie**, at whose southern end is the village of **CHARZYKOW**, a five-kilometre bus ride from Chojnice. There are a couple of **hotels**, including *Pod Żaglami* at ul. Długa 71A (☎052/398 8135; ❸), which also has a café and **restaurant**. There's also a **campsite** by the lake. Driving north from here through scented forests of pine and beech, the road crosses an isthmus separating Lake Charzykowskie from Lake Karsińskie, at whose northern end is the pleasant resort village **SWORNEGACIE**. Once the site of a twelfth-century Augustinian and later Cistercian monastery, these days the devotion leans firmly towards waterborne recreation – pedalos, canoes and kayaks can be rented near the bridge for about 30zł per hour. Opposite the eighty-year-old neo-Baroque church you'll find the *Wagant* **restaurant** with the well-equipped *JOSK* **holiday resort** up the small hill (☎052/398 1337), which contains a small pension (❹) as well as chalets (❷) and boat rental.

From Swornegacie you can wind your way along a variety of routes to the small working village of **LEŚNO** 20km northeast, with its seventeenth-century church shell disclosing some modest Baroque details. It is the oldest wooden church in the province, with a shingle roof. There's an archeological site in the centre of the village, dating back through the medieval era to the Iron Age of the fourth century BC, which includes a stone circle similar to that at Odry (see below).

Odry

Just outside the village of **ODRY**, 20km northeast of Chojnice (and served by sporadic **buses** from Koszalin or Chojnice), a wooded nature reserve hides a well-preserved megalithic site. A sequence of irregular **stone circles** and overgrown burial mounds, it covers an area about half the size of a football pitch. It has been dated to the first or second century, though little is known of its origins. To find the clearing in which it stands isn't easy, adding to the enjoyment of the site when you finally arrive; before setting out from the village ask directions for the *Kręgi Kamieniece*.

Roads (but not public transport) lead northwest from Odry towards Wdzydze Kiszewskie (p.201) and the Kashubian lakes (see Chapter 2).

The Western Lake District: Szczecinek and Czaplinek

One of the most popular lakeland bases is the town of **SZCZECINEK**, in the relatively more visited western lake district. A modern and rather over-functional holiday centre on the Koszalin–Poznań road, it stands by **Lake Wielimie**, where formerly grand mansions hint at the town's bygone heyday. At its centre stands a tidy modern Rynek overlooked by a castellated red-brick town hall. Just off the square, the town **museum** (Wed–Sun 10am–4pm; 1zł) is more noteworthy for being arranged in three storeys of a tall narrow tower than for the quality of the exhibits – mostly pot and weapon fragments from Dark-Age Slav settlements in the area. Beyond here, neat lakeside gardens stretch out along the shore, with a municipal beach about 1km to the southeast and a shady waterfront promenade stretching to the northwest.

Szczecinek's **bus station** is about 400m northwest of the main square; the **train station** is some 2km to the southeast, from where municipal buses take you into the centre. The **tourist office** (Mon–Fri 7am–3pm; ☎094/374 9100), just behind the central Rynek at pl. Wolności 18, can guide you towards private rooms and pensions (❷). Best value of the **hotels** is provided by the *Pojezierze*, Wyszyńskiego 69a (☎094/374 3341; ❹), a large 1970s-era place on the main road through town, offering no-nonsense but homely en-suites with TV. An added veneer of comfort is provided by the *Resiedence*, Lelewela 12 (☎094/372 3370, ℱ372 3393; ❻), a large modern lakeside house about 1km north of the centre, with simple but tastefully furnished rooms; although it can't compete in the style stakes with the *Żółty Dom*, Ordona 11 (☎94/372 3482, ℱ372 3481; ❻), a refurbished villa on the lakefront just west of the centre whose rooms boast classy, colour-supplement interiors. You'll also find a **youth hostel** at ul. Armii Krajowej 29 (☎094/374 3505), and a **campsite** on ul. Kościuszki (☎094/374 4399).

Quick and cheap **meals** can be had at the uncomplicated and cramped *Pizzeria Primavera*, in a courtyard behind the Rynek at pl. Wolnosci 18; or the more comfortable *U Kwaka* at Wyszyńskiego 13, which serves up kebabs and other grilled meats in a pub-like interior. More substantial fare is on offer at the *Grand Café* on the Rynek, which concentrates on stolid pork- or chicken-and-chips meals; or *Jolka*, a smart pavilion on the lakefront at the end of

Ordona, about 1000m north from the centre, which is a good place to sample fresh fish. The roomy *Europa'b* on the Rynek is the most convivial of the **bars**.

Czaplinek and Lake Drawsko

Forty kilometres west of Szczecinek lies **Lake Drawsko**, one of the largest Pomeranian lakes, a tranquil expanse of deep, clear water some 10km in length. In summer you'll find groups of Polish canoeists powering their way through the area: if you feel like joining them, there are rental facilities in the Drawsko area's main town, Czaplinek. Walking is wonderful, too, with paths rambling off through the lakeside woods for miles in all directions.

Squatting above the southern shores of Lake Drawsko is **CZAPLINEK**, an early Slav stronghold eventually wrested into the Brandenburg domains from the Teutonic Knights. The town has a drowsy charm about it and tourism doesn't seem to have much affected the easy-going life of the place. From the main square, where Szczecin–Szczecinek buses stop, streets slope down towards the town's only real attraction, the lakefront itself, a tranquil tree-shaded area punctuated by the odd canoe and boat-rental outlet. A lakeside **path** heads north towards the town beach about 1500m from the centre, before continuing onwards past a couple more bathing areas attached to the campsites on the northern fringes of town. It becomes a wilder woodland walk the further north you go, with trees crowding in on all sides, parting occasionally to reveal startlingly beautiful lakeside vistas. The path eventually emerges on the main road just short of Stary Drawsko (see below).

Accommodation includes the *Hotel Pomorski*, Jagiellońska 11 (☎94/375 5444; ❹), an uninspiring modern block with serviceable en-suites; and the altogether superior *Elektor*, Rynek 4 (☎94/375 5086, ⓦwww.bci.pl/elektor; ❻). Best of the lakeside **campsites** is 1km north of town at ul. Drahimska 79/81 (☎094/375 5168) with a small beach and a jetty.

With regular connections to and from Szczecin and Szczecinek), **buses** present the best way of getting in and out of town; the **train station** is about 3km south of the village, and only sporadically served by bus.

Stary Drawsko

Six kilometres north of Czaplinek and overlooked by the ruins of a fourteenth-century castle, **STARY DRAWSKO** is a bucolic village lying on a neck of land between lakes Drawsko to the west and Żerdno to the east. However it's difficult to get to the shore of either lake, as so much of the shore is in private hands, unless you choose to stay at the *Kleofas* holiday home (☎094/375 8877; ❹), which has huts with en-suite showers and TV, and a private beach with boat rental facilities. *Chata Toniego* (☎094/375 8879; ❹) is a pleasant pension in the nearby hamlet of Nowe Drawsko, 3km to the west.

Łeba and around

Of all the Pomeranian seaside resorts, **ŁEBA** is the most celebrated; an attractive old fishing settlement presiding over kilometre upon kilometre of irresistable dune-backed beaches. Small enough to preserve a village-like feel, it nevertheless receives enough visitors in summer to generate an invigorating holiday bustle. The bigger of the local **dunes** (*wydmy*), just west of town in the **Slowinski national park**, form one of Poland's prime natural attractions, and attract hordes of sightseers as a result. There are plenty of unspoiled Baltic pine forests and silvery sands nearby if you want to escape the crowds.

The village

The **village** itself is set a kilometre back from the sea: dunes and beaches cover the original site of the settlement, which was forced to move inland in the late sixteenth century because of shifting sands. Both buses and trains drop you two blocks west of ul. Kościuszki, the main street running down the middle of the resort, which is still lined with several of the one-storey, brick-built fishermen's houses once common to the region. A little way further north Kościuszki bridges a canalized branch of the River Łeba, where trawlers and pleasure boats moor, before veering eastwards and becoming Nadmorska, a shoreside avenue which leads to the bigger hotels and campsites. In summer the area is busy with cheerful holiday-makers heading for the unbroken sandy **beaches** that are widely regarded as among the cleanest on the Baltic coast. Poles aren't the only people who have enjoyed the bracing location: wandering through the park that provides the main approach to the beaches from Nadmorska, you'll pass the summer house once used by Nazi propaganda chief Josef Goebbels.

Another stretch of beach to the west of town can be accessed by walking down ul. Turystyczna, which heads west from the train and bus stations, and passes a swanky new yachting marina and the turn-off to Rąbka (see p.646) before arriving at another clutch of beachside campsites. Round the back of the PTTK campsite, just before the access to the beach, a path leads off into the forest towards the meagre ruins of **Kościół św. Mikołaja** (St Nicholas's Church), a lone reminder of the village's former location.

Practicalities

Regular **buses** and **trains** run to Łeba from the provincial town of Lębork just to the south, which stands on the main road and rail routes connecting Gdańsk in the east with Słupsk (see p.648) and Koszalin (p.650) to the west. There are also direct buses to Łeba from **Gdynia** (see chapter 2). Other than checking out ⓦwww.leba.pl, you can get information just round the corner from the train and bus stations, where the public library on ul. 11 Listopada holds the Biuro Promocji Miasta Łeby, the local **tourist office** (summer Mon–Fri 8am–4pm, Sat & Sun 10am–1pm; winter closed Sat & Sun; ☎059/866 2565), which will help you find a **place to stay** in one of the innumerable private rooms (❷) and pensions (❷–❸). Two other bureaus doling out rooms for similar prices are Przymorze, opposite the train station at Dworcowa 1 (☎059/866 1360, ⒺPrzymorze@poczta.onet.pl); and Centrum turystyczne Łeba (☎059/866 2277), a couple of blocks east at Kościuszki 64. If these are shut, most of the houses along Nadmorska and the surrounding streets display "*poko-je*" signs indicating vacancies.

Among the handily placed **pensions**, *Pod Krokodylem*, Turystyczna 7 (☎059/866 2105; ❸), is a good source of simple rooms just west of the train and bus stations on the road to Rąbka; while *Anna*, ul. Dworcowa (☎059/866 1371; ❹), is a largish place right by the station with balconied rooms and a neat garden out front. *Kowelin*, just off the main street at Nad Ujściem 6 (☎059/866 1440 or 866 1466; ❸), is one of the better-value **hotels**, offering smallish en-suites with TV, most of which have balconies; while *Wodnik*, Nadmorska 10 (☎059/866 1366, ⓦwww.maxmedia.pl/wodnik; ❺) is a larger concrete affair consisting of several pavilions a short walk from the beach; all rooms have TV and telephones. For a minor splash-out consider the charming *Neptun* at ul. Sosnowa 1 (☎059/866 1432 or 866 2331, ⓦwww.infocity.com.pl/neptun; ❼), a hundred-year-old villa with a mock castle-turret that was turned into a factory-owned rest home after World War II, when it lost much of its *belle-époque* sheen. Renovated and turned into a plush hotel in the 1990s, it's right on the beach, surrounded by pines, and has an outdoor swimming pool.

For **campers** – and there are plenty of them in summer – there are several sites along ul. Turystyczna and ul. Nadmorska, all close to the beaches, and a number of them rent chalets too. Best of the bunch are *Ambre* on Nadmorska (☎059/866 2472), a large, well-organized place stretched out beneath birch trees, and the PTTK site at the far end of Turystyczna, right beside the beach.

There's a surfeit of **snack bars** selling locally caught fried fish (*smażona ryba*); one of the best is the canal-side *Taverna Rybacka Konopa*, just off the main street on Wybreże, a big shed filled with wooden tables offering excellent battered halibut alongside grilled salmon and trout. Of the **restaurants**, *Pizzeria* on Wojska Polskiego opposite the Rybak cinema is tiny but has a generous range of thin-crust pies, and a small outdoor terrace; while the more elegant *BD*, Kościuszki 35, offers a wide choice of well-presented meat and fish dishes in comfortable surroundings, and also does breakfasts. The restaurant of the *Neptun* hotel serves up international and Polish food in a formal, starched-napkin ambience. The bakeries at Kościuszki 25 and 46 are the best places to find takeaway pastries and cakes.

You can **drink** in any of the fish-fry venues, although the *Viking Bar*, near the bridge at the beginning of the Rąbka road, is the place where most of the visiting Varsovians tend to hang out. *Café Mozart*, at the western end of Wojska Polskiego, has an unpretentious upstairs disco which attracts an amiable cross-section of after-hours drinkers.

Słowiński national park

West of Łeba is Jezioro Łebsko, or Lake Łebsko, the largest of several lagoons separated from the sea by a belt of mobile **sand dunes** that form the centre of **Słowiński national park**, one of the country's most memorable natural attractions, special enough to be included in UNESCO's list of world Biosphere Reserves. The park gets its name from the **Slovincians**, a small ethnic group of Slav origin who, like their neighbours the Kashubians, have retained a distinctive identity despite centuries of Germanization.

This area is an ornithologist's paradise, with over 250 **bird** species either permanently inhabiting the park or using it as a migratory habitat. The 600 scenic lakes attract fishing, whilst the postglacial lakes incorporated into the river systems have created excellent canoe trails. Both activities are very popular here.

> ### Fauna in Słowiński national park
>
> **Birds** in the park are classified into three main groups: nesting, migratory and wintering species. Nesters include such rare species as the white-tailed eagle, crane, eagle owl and black stork. It's also a popular area for the more common white stork: you're bound to encounter the sight of a stork nesting atop a telegraph pole before long. During the late autumn migration period you'll see large flocks of wild geese winging over the lakes, and in winter you'll find ducks and other fowl from the far north of Europe sheltering here on the warmer southern shores of the Baltic – velvet scoters, mergansers, auks and whooper swans included.
>
> **Mammals** are numerous too, the shores of the lakes harbouring deer and boar, with elks, racoons and badgers in the surrounding woods. Shy red squirrels are a common sight in among the trees surrounding Łeba, while foxes emerge at night to scour the village's rubbish bins.

Geomorphically speaking this is an unusual region: the shallow lagoons covering the central part of the park once formed a gulf, which the deposition of sand eventually isolated from the sea. Between them a narrow spit of land emerged roughly two thousand years ago, whose dense original covering of oak and beech forests was gradually eroded by intensive animal grazing and tree felling, the forests disappearing under the dunes that overran the thirty-kilometre spit. Abandoned to the elements by its few original human inhabitants, during World War II the expanse of shifting, undulating sand provided an ideal training ground for units of Afrika Korps, who drilled here in preparation for the rigours of Rommel's North African campaigns. In the latter stages of the war the spit west of Łeba was turned into a rocket research station: the missiles tested here were close cousins of the fearsome V1 and V2 rockets that later bombarded London.

Park access

The eastern entrance to the park is at **RĄBKA**, a small holiday village on the shores of Lake Łebsko, a twenty-minute walk west of Łeba itself. To get there, leave Łeba via ul. Turystyczna and take the signed left turn about 1km out of town, or take one of the **boats** or tourist "**trains**" (electric buses, really) that leave in season from the bridge over the River Łeba at Turystyczna's eastern end. Rąbka itself is nothing more than a short line of houses and a couple of snack bars backing onto the lake, the shores of which are covered with thick reeds, making access to the water difficult, but providing ideal cover for the birds: sanctuaries at several points protect the main breeding sites.

The **pathway to the dunes** begins on Rąbka's western edge, where a kiosk sells **tickets** to the park (8am–dusk; 2zł) as well as local maps. Innumerable forms of **transport** are on offer to those who are too pressed for time to walk all the way to the dunes: horses and carts (20zł per person), tourist trains (3zł) and chauffered golf carts (10zł) await outside the park entrance, and there are infrequent boats from Rąbka's landing stage in season, although by far the most popular option is to rent a bike in Rąbka (4–6zł an hour). While boat passengers glide across Lake Łebsko, those going by land proceed through thick forest down a narrow metalled road built by the German military in World War II to serve the rocket research station – you'll see a couple of cone-headed concrete pillboxes standing guard beside the route.

Vyrzutnia

Three kilometres west of Rąbka lies a small clearing known as **Vyrzutnia** ("Launchpad"), the site of the World War II base where the German military experimented with various forms of rocket between 1943 and 1945 – part of Hitler's strategy of producing terror weapons that would give Germany a psychological advantage over its adversaries. A museum (April–Oct daily 9am–5pm; 5zł) built inside one of the observation bunkers contains sepia photographs of prewar Łeba, alongside diagrams of the rockets developed here by Hitler's scientists. The first of these was the stumpy, five-and-a-half-metre-long *Rheintochter* (Rhine Daughter), although this was soon superseded by the much larger *Rheinbote* (Rhine Messenger), a sleek eleven-metre affair that closely resembles the ground-to-air missiles in use today. Despite over eighty test launches, the *Rheinbote* never saw active service, the Germans instead opting for the V2 rockets that were developed by a separate team at Peenemünde in eastern Germany. Outside the bunker is one of the launchpads themselves – a concrete pit topped by rails onto which a rocket gantry was wheeled. There are a few rusting fragments of a *Rheintocher* lying around in the nearby sands, together with a complete Soviet rocket of the 1950s, brought here from elsewhere and built to almost exactly the same design as the *Rheinbote* – an eloquent demonstration of how Nazi technology was eagerly adopted by the Cold War superpowers after 1945.

The park dunes

Passengers on boats and tourist trains (but not those in traps, golf carts or on pushbikes) have to disembark at Vyrzutnia and proceed to the dunes on foot, following a path which forges westwards through deep forest for a further 2km before emerging at the base of the **Biała Góra** (White Mountain), the first – and, with an altitude of 40m, the highest – of the **dunes**, which stretch westwards for about 5km.

Even a brief hike will give you the flavour of the terrain, though. Dried by the sun and propelled by the wind, the dunes migrate over 10m per year on average, leaving behind the broken tree stumps you see along the path. Out in the middle of the dune area, there's a desert-like feeling of desolation with the sands rippling in the wind giving an eerie sense of fluidity.

Crossing the dunes northwards will bring you down onto the seashore within a few minutes: from here you can walk back to Łeba along the beach (8km) if you don't fancy returning the way you came. If you're feeling up to a sterner challenge you could walk in the opposite direction by following a marked path along the beach and then inland to the village of Smołdzino (see below) 12km to the southwest, although there are no buses back to Łeba from here.

Kluki and Smołdzino

Twenty kilometres southwest of Łeba, on the southern edge of Lake Łebsko and at the end of a minor road, is the little Slovincian village of **KLUKI**, which is accessible by occasional bus from Słupsk (see p.648) or by lake cruiser from Łeba in the summer months. Entirely surrounded by woods, Kluki has a *skansen* of Slovincian timber-framed architecture (mid-May to Sept Tues–Sun 9am–4pm; Oct to mid-May Tues–Sun 9am–3pm); you'll see similar, if more dilapidated, buildings still in use in several villages all over the region.   .

A further 10km west of Kluki lies **SMOŁDZINO,** the site of the park's natural history museum, the **Muzeum Przyrodnicze Słowińskiego Parku Narodowego** (daily 9am–5pm; 4zł), which contains an extensive display of the park's flora and fauna; the park offices here can provide you with detailed information about the area, including advice on bird-watching around the lake. Just to the west of the village is the 115-metre-high **Rowokół Hill**, whose observation tower affords a panoramic view over the entire park area. There's a summer-only **youth hostel** (no tel) in the village, and some private rooms – although there's no accommodation bureau, so you'll have to try your luck by looking for *pokoje* signs.

The central Pomeranian coast

West of Łeba lies a string of seaside resorts, commencing with laid-back, relatively relaxing places like **Ustka**, **Darłowo** and **Mielno**, and culminating with unwieldy **Kołobrzeg**, a major venue for mass tourism Polish style. Lying just inland are the regional administrative centres of **Słupsk** and **Koszalin** – important transport hubs which you'll pass through en route to the coastal settlements, but hardly worthy of an overnight stop in their own right.

Słupsk

Continuing southwest through lush farming country along the sub-coastal back-road, the next place of any significance is **SŁUPSK**, 40km from Łeba, an early Slav settlement that was ruled by Pomeranian princes and Brandenburg margraves for much of its history. What little there is worth seeing in the town can be covered in an hour or two. By the banks of the River Słupia on the south-eastern fringe of the centre, the Renaissance castle on Zamkowa houses the **Muzeum Pomorza Środkowego** (Museum of Central Pomerania; July–Aug daily 10am–5pm; Sept–June Wed–Sun 10am–4pm; 4zł). Alongside displays of local ethnography, there's a large collection of modern Polish art, most notably the distorted caricatures and self-portraits of Stanisław Ignacy Witkiewicz – the avant-garde artist and playwright who committed suicide soon after the start of World War II (see box on p.508). The old castle **mill** opposite is one of the earliest specimens of its kind in the country, packed with more folksy exhibits (same times), while the reconstructed Gothic **Dominican church** has a fine Renaissance altarpiece and the tombs of the last Pomeranian princes.

Słupsk's **train station**, with the **bus station** just opposite, is at the west end of Al. Wojska Polskiego, the kilometre-long boulevard leading to the centre. There are onward services to Darłowo, while buses to Ustka leave from a stop on Al. Wojska Polskiego just round the corner. There's a useful **tourist information centre** at ul. Wojska Polskiego 16 (Mon–Fri 9am–5pm; ☎ & ℱ 059/842 0791), and a couple of decent downtown **hotels** if you need to stay. The *Hotel PTTK*, ul. Szarych Szeregów 1 (☎059/842 2902; ❷–❸), is an unassuming but good-value place just over the Słupia river from the centre; while the *Zamkowy*, near the castle at ul. Dominikańska 9 (☎059/842 5294; ❹), has slightly plusher en-suites with TV. Best **place to eat** in town is the *Pod Kluką*, east of the PTTK hotel at ul. Kaszubska 22, a good place to enjoy moderately priced Polish fare in traditional surroundings.

Ustka

Twenty kilometres northwest of Słupsk (and accessible by bus or local train) is **USTKA**, a one-time member of the Hanseatic League that's become an established member of the bucket-and-spade league for well over a century. A largely modern town with shipyards straddling the mouth of the river Słupia, Ustka's lack of architectural personality is in large part alleviated by its beaches, as good as any on the Baltic coast, which stretch east of town towards Słowiński national park.

From the **port** a seaside promenade heads eastwards along the town's principal beach. Here you'll find a few stretches of manicured park, and the usual grouping of unpretentious cafés and ice-cream stalls, although it's worth continuing eastwards to where the wilder, duney, forest-backed parts of the beach are to be found. Behind the promenade are several half-timbered nineteenth-century **villas**, sole reminders of the time when Ustka – then known as Stolpmünde – was a favoured watering hole of the Prussian elite.

Practicalities

Ustka's **bus station** is just off the main street, Marynarki Polskiej; the **train station** is a block away to the east on ul. Dworcowa. Follow Marynarki Polskiej northwards to reach the port. The **tourist office** at Marynarki Polskiej 87 (July–Aug daily 8am–7pm; Sept–June Mon–Fri 8am–4pm; ☎059/814 7170) organizes accommodation in the town's innumerable private

6

rooms and pensions – the eastern end of the resort around ul. Rybacka is the best place to look for *noclegi* signs if you arrive late. There's also a growing number of modern, medium-sized **hotels**, notably the *Rejs*, Marynarki Polskiej 51 (☎059/814 78 50; ❺), built in imitation of the half-timbered structures that once characterized the region, and boasting smart, chic en-suites; and the *Dajana*, right on the seafront promenade at Chopina 9 (☎059/814 48 65; ❼; 50 percent reductions out of season), where rooms come with soothing pastel colours and pine furnishings.

Fried fish is freely available from the pavilions along the promenade: one of the best is *Korsarz*, at the western end, an engagingly tacky place with plastic sharks hanging from the ceiling. A more upmarket take on the fish theme is offered by *Sedme Niebo*, attached to the *Hotel Rejs*, a classy joint with low-key lighting and formal service. Best of a rash of **pizzerias** along Marynarki Polskiej is *Tawerna Kapitańska* (also known as *Bar Italia*), offering thin-crust pizzas and reasonable pasta dishes in no-nonsense surroundings.

Darłowo and beyond

A more attractive proposition than Ustka is **DARŁOWO**, 40km further west and a couple of kilometres inland on the River Wieprza, reached by a couple of buses a day from Ustka and more frquent services from Słupsk. The beaches north of the town, around the coastal suburb of Darłówko, are as popular as any, and Darłowo itself has an engaging historic core.

The **Rynek** here is the site of a gracefully reconstructed **town hall**, complete with its Renaissance doorway and a rather cleverly designed fountain. On one side of the Rynek sits the Gothic **Kościół NMP** (St Mary's Church) an attractive brick building with a relatively restrained Baroque interior overlay. Inside there's an eighteenth-century wooden pulpit decorated with scenes from the Last Judgement; in among a clutch of royal tombs located beneath the tower is that of the notorious King Erik VII (1397–1459), a local-born aristocrat who acceded to the thrones of Denmark, Sweden and Norway, and married Henry V of England's daughter Phillipina – whom he later tired of and banished to a nunnery. Deposed in 1439 he returned to Darłowo and lived out the last years of his life here as the duke of Słupsk, living off piracy in the Baltic Sea.

South of the Rynek lies the well-preserved fourteenth-century **castle** of the Pomeranian princes, now home to **Muzeum Regionalne** (Regional Museum; mid–June to end of Aug Mon–Fri 10am–5.30pm, Sat & Sun 10am–3.30pm; Sept to mid–June daily 10am–1.30pm; 6zł) which contains exhibits on local folklore as well as furnishings from the castle itself – notably the ornate seventeenth-century limewood pulpit which once graced the castle chapel.

About 400m northeast of the Rynek along ul. Ojca Damiana Tyneckiego is the extraordinary white-walled **Kaplica św. Gertrudy** (St Gertrude's Chapel), a twelve-sided seventeenth-century structure which squats beneath a tapering, inverted ice-cream cone of a roof covered in slender wooden shingles. The galleried interior is decorated with pictures of shoes and boots donated by pious tradesmen – St Gertrude being, among other things, the patron saint of cobblers.

Darłówko and Iwięcino

On the coast 3km west of Darłowo (and reached by regular shuttle service from the bus station) lies **Darłówko**, a low-rise, leafy resort straddling the mouth of the Wieprza. Clogged by fishing boats, the river is spanned by a pedestrian **drawbridge**, whose control tower – a mushroom-shaped affair resembling something out of a 1960s sci-fi movie – is very much a local attraction. There are the usual expanses of sand backed by woods, making this as restful a place as any if you're in need of a seaside breather.

If you've a car it's worth taking the backroads west from Darłowo, which pass through an attractive open landscape of fields, woods and quiet old Pomeranian villages. The sagging timber-framed farm buildings are still just about standing, as in several cases are the similarly aged brick churches. A charming example is at **IWIĘCINO**, a tiny village halfway between Darłowo and Koszalin. The fourteenth-century structure features a faintly painted wooden ceiling and sixteenth-century pews, a delicate Renaissance altarpiece and a splendid late-Baroque organ.

Practicalities

Darłowo's **bus station** is just west of the town centre: walk down Boguslawa X-ego and cross the river to reach the **Rynek**. The local **tourist office** in Darłowo's castle (see above; same hours; ☎094/314 3051) can help out with details of private rooms and pensions in both Darłowo and Darłówko. Of Darłowo's **accommodation** options, the *Irena*, midway between the bus station and the Rynek at ul. Wojska Polskiego 64 (☎094/314 3692; ❹), and the *Hotel nad Wieprzą*, just west of the centre at ul. Traugutta 6 (☎094/314 3657; ❹), are both medum-sized places that provide reasonable en-suite rooms. There's more variety however in Darłówko, where you can choose between plain but cosy pensions like the *Albatros*, ul. Wilków Morskich 2 (☎094/314 3220; ❸); hotels like the *Nord*, ul. Plazowa 4 (☎094/314 4351; ❹), which has comfortable en-suites; or plusher affairs like the Klub Plaza, ul. Słowiańska 3 (☎094/314 3120; ❺), whose rooms come with TV. There's a **campsite** midway between Darłowo and Darłówko at ul. Conrada 20 (☎094/314 2872).

There's a single rather basic pizzeria on Darowo's Rynek, but few other **places to eat**. There are numerous snack stalls in Darówko in season, doling out the usual ice cream, fish snacks and beer.

Koszalin

As even the determinedly upbeat tourist brochures tacitly admit, **KOSZALIN**, the bustling provincial capital 25km west of Darłowo, isn't the sort of place that gets the crowds shouting. The Stare Miasto was badly damaged during 1945, and much of the centre was rebuilt in utilitarian style in the years that followed. Set back some 10km from the sea, Koszalin is certainly not a holiday resort – but you're likely to pass through its bus and train stations if you're heading for the beaches at nearby Mielno, Unieście and Kołobrzeg.

There's the customary scattering of sights here if you have time to kill between connections. The modern flagstoned **Rynek** contains one of the strangest examples of Polish Sixties architecture – an orange and blue town hall that was considered the epitome of cool modernity when it was first built. Just south of the square is **Katedra Mariacka** (St Mary's Cathedral), an imposing, oft-remodelled Gothic structure with a few pieces of original decoration, notably a large fourteenth-century crucifix and a scattering of Gothic statuary, originally from the main altarpiece and now incorporated into the stalls, pulpit and organ loft. The nineteenth-century water mill facing the Stare Miasto walls from the corner of ul. Młyńska houses the **Muzeum Okręgowie** (Regional Museum; Tues–Sun 10am–4pm; 5zł) at no. 38, with a varied collection of folk art, archeological finds and other regional miscellany. The most interesting part is the reconstructed thatched farmhouse in the museum yard, a fine example of the sturdy peasant architecture characteristic of the Pomeranian coastal region.

The train and bus stations are both ten minutes' walk west of the Rynek. The local **tourist office** at ul. Dworcowa 10 (Mon–Fri 8am–5pm; ☎094/342 7399) will help out with information on the neighbouring resorts. If you get stuck in Koszalin, your best bets for **accommodation** are the rather delapidated *Turystyczny*, just east of the Rynek at ul. Głowackiego 7 (☎094/342 3004; ❷), which has simple rooms with shared bathrooms; or the considerably plusher *Arka*, between the stations and the Rynek at ul. Zwycięstwa 20 (☎094/342 7911; ❼), a Western businessmen's favourite.

For a **place to eat**, the *Maredo*, Zwycięstwa 13, serves up Polish staples in a bright fast-food atmosphere; while the *Bar-Pizzeria* on the northeastern corner of the Rynek serves up unsophisticated if satisfying thin-crust pies.

Mielno and Unieście

Bus #1 from Koszalin train station departs every thirty minutes or so for the resort of **MIELNO** some 12km northwest of town, a long, straggling beachside settlement that extends as far as **UNIEŚCIE** (where most buses terminate), the next village to the east. Formerly the main port for Koszalin, Mielno is now one of the quieter, more laid-back resorts on the coast, although the presence of a large saltwater lake just inland from the beach ensures a steady influx of yachtspeople on summer weekends.

It's best to get off the bus at the western entrance to the resort, from where ul. 1 Maja leads down to a seaside promenade overlooked by a smattering of *belleépoque* holiday villas – including some attractively rickety timber constructions. It will take you roughly half an hour to walk from here to Unieście, which has a comparatively sleepy, village-like feel, with wooden fishing boats parked up on its dune-fringed beach. The sands are more unspoilt (and more deserted) the further east you go – once you've cleared Unieście, it's 10km to the next habitation.

The **tourist office** just by the bus stop in Mielno (Mon–Fri 9am–5pm; ☎094/318 9955) will have details of private rooms (❶) and pensions (❷) throughout the two villages. Well placed for the quiet end of the beach is the *Eden* **hotel**, an incongruously alpine-looking building at the far end of Unieście at Morska 20 (☎094/318 9735; ❶), with sparsely furnished but eminently bearable rooms with shared facilities. Midway between Mielno and Unieście, the smallish *Czarny Staw*, ul. Chrobrego 11 (☎094/318 9835; ❷) is a good-value source of plain en-suites. At the other end of the scale, the *Willa Milenium*, in the centre of Mielno at ul. 1 Maja 10 (☎94/318 9674; ❻), is a modern place aping the half-timbered style of the nearby villas, and comes with all the creature comforts.

For **camping** *Bulaj*, at the western end of Unieście, occupies a grassy site right by the lake. For **eating**, *Café Flayn*, at the point where ul. 1 Maja meets the sea, is a bright pavilion filled with leafy houseplants and boasting a terrace both front and back – a great place for a fishy fry-up or just a drink.

Kołobrzeg

A forty-kilometre bus or train ride west of Koszalin, **KOŁOBRZEG** is Poland's largest Baltic holiday metropolis, a beach resort and health spa rolled into one that attracts over a million visitors a year. However it is also the country's most urbanized resort: most of its hotels look as if they've escaped from a big-city housing project, and the line of greying sanatoria along the seafront convey little sense of Riviera panache. **Tourism** here is organized on an industrial scale, and there's a corresponding lack of the informal, pension-style lodgings you'll find in smaller coastal places. Points in the town's favour include the beach, which is as good as any in the region, and the kind of year-round facilities (such as shops, restaurants and bars) that are often lacking in its sleepier Pomeranian neighbours.

The Stare Miasto and the beach

Much of the town centre is modern; an area of pedestrianized streets and plazas, lined with brightly painted apartments and office blocks built in imitation of the Hanseatic town houses of old. Dominating the skyline however is the collegiate **Kościół Mariacki** (St Mary's Church), originally built as a simple Gothic hall, but extended in the fifteenth century with the addition of star-vaulted aisles, adding to the impression of depth and spaciousness. A particularly striking effect was achieved with the façade, whose twin towers were moulded together into one vast solid mass of brick. Many of the furnishings perished in the war, but some significant items remain, notably several Gothic triptychs and a fourteenth-century bronze font.

To the north stands the other key public building, the **town hall**. A castellated Romantic creation incorporating some of its fifteenth-century predecessor, it was built from designs provided by the great Berlin architect Karl Friedrich Schinkel.

However it's the **beach** that the visitors come for, and throughout the summer you'll find throngs of Polish holiday-makers soaking up the sun on the main strand. There's 1.6km of beach to lie on, complete with deck chairs, wicker cots, parasols and rowing boats for rent. There's plenty of scope for a decent stroll, with a **promenade** running the length of the beach and a pier towards the western end. Beyond the pier stands a tall brick **lighthouse** (daily 9am–7pm; 2zł) offering good views of the surrounds, and a stone monument commemorating "Poland's Reunion with the Sea", a highly symbolic event which took place here in 1945. With the German withdrawal from Kołobrzeg in March, a band of Polish patriots gathered on the beach to hurl a wedding ring into the sea, thereby marking Poland's re-marriage to a stretch of coast that had for so long been in German hands.

Practicalities

Kołobrzeg's **train** and **bus** stations are next to each other on ul. Kolejowa. The town centre lies ten minutes' to the south along ul. Dworcowa, while the seafront is an equal distance to the north.

The best source of **tourist information** is the PTTK office (Mon–Fri 7.30am–3.30pm, plus July–Aug Sat & Sun 8am–noon; ☎094/352 3287), housed in the remains of a medieval city fortification, the Baszta Prochowa (Gunpowder Tower), at ul. Dubois 20. You can pick up town maps and book private **rooms** (❶) here. The *Relaks* at ul. Kościuszki 24 (☎094/352 7735; ❹), is one of the few pleasant pensions in town, offering en-suite rooms with balconies near the eastern end of the beach, and a nice garden with kiddies' swings. Of the high-rise hotels, the *Medyk*, some way from the sea on the southern fringes of the centre at ul. Szpitalna 7 (☎094/352 3450; ❸), is largely patronized by health-spa tourists, but offers reasonable standards for the price; while the *Bałtyk*, ul. Bałtycka 17/18 (☎094/352 8040; ❹), has one of the best beachside positions. The *New Skanpol*, down the road from the station at ul. Dworcowa 10 (☎094/352 8211; ❻), is the best of the downtown business choices. The *Baltic* **campsite**, 1500m east of the stations at ul. IV Dywizji Wojska Polskiego 1 (☎094/352 4569), is beside a wooded park ten minutes' walk from the sea.

For **eating**, there are numerous excellent fish-and-chip bars along the seafront, some of which – notably *U Jana* at ul. Morska 6 – are quite swish-looking places sited in stylish plate-glass pavilions. For a more leisurely sit-down meal, the *Karczma Monte Christo*, near the sea at Morska 7c, features a faux-rustic, wooden-bench interior and succulent grilled dishes – steaks, pork chops and fish. In the modern town centre, the *Tawerna u Jensa*, ul. Gierczak 26, serves up Polish standards alongside wild boar and game in a rather formal-looking subterranean dining room – although you can sit outside in the summer. Cheap and tasty pizzas can be had at the *Bella Italia*, ul. Gierczak 27.

Kołobrzeg is not short of **drinking** venues. The hotel cafés along the seafront are the places to go if you fancy a spot of "proper" dancing to evergreen tunes; otherwise, the best of the bars are in the modern centre. *Café Mariacka*, Mariacka 16a, functions as both daytime café and night-time drinking den, and has the feel of a cosy living room; while *Zezem*, round the corner at Giełdowa 8a, is a small and friendly cellar bar with a limited choice of Mexican snacks. *Fiddlers Green*, Dubois 16, is a smart and slightly upmarket little pub with Irish brews on tap. Otherwise, try the *Taverna*, ul. Tarnopolska 1c, the *Saxofon*, Mariacka 9, or the *Pod Papugami*, ul. Girczak 44.

Trzebiatów, Gryfice and Goleniów

Moving on from Kołobrzeg, the choice is between continuing west along the coastal area by bus, or heading southwest towards Szczecin, a journey more conveniently made by train. The former is the more obviously attractive option, but if heading for Szczecin you have a chance to see the towns of **Trzebiatów**, **Gryfice** and **Goleniów**, all once prominent members of the **Hanseatic League**. For all their former prosperity however, their churches and fortifications offer the only tangible reminder of their heyday; all three towns are now in varying stages of neglect.

Trzebiatów

By far the most attractive of the trio, **TRZEBIATÓW** lies on the banks of the Baltic-bound River Rega, just under 30km from Kołobrzeg. It's a place where time seems to have gone backwards, transforming a well-heeled trading town into a straggling agricultural village with a pronounced rural air. A good deal of imagination is required to visualize this sleepy Polish backwater as it was four hundred years ago when it played a key role in the Reformation. Johannes Bugenhagen, who spent nearly two decades as rector of its Latin School, became one of Luther's leading lieutenants, returning in 1534 to persuade the Pomeranian Assembly, which had specially convened here, to adopt the new faith throughout the province.

Trzebiatów's skyline is dominated by the magnificent tower of **Kościol Mariacki** (St Mary's), one of the most accomplished Gothic churches in the region, crowned with the unusual combination of a brick octagon and a lead spire. In it hang two historic bells – one, named Gabriel, is from the late fourteenth century; the other, known as Mary, dates from the early sixteenth century. The building's interior is chiefly notable for its clear architectural lines and uncluttered appearance which, like the German epitaphs on the walls, are evidence of the four centuries it spent in Protestant hands.

Close to the church is the Rynek, in the centre of which stands the recently renovated **town hall**, constructed in the sober Baroque style favoured in northern German lands. One or two Gothic houses line the square, their appearance heightened by the presence of so many undistinguished newer buildings. Just off the southern side is the abandoned chapel of **św. Ducha** (the Holy Ghost), the setting for the Assembly which decided to introduce the

Reformation into Pomerania. At the end of the street you can see the rotund **Kaszana** bastion, and **town walls**, a significant stretch of which still survives. Much of this fortification work dates from the fifteenth century, when Trzebiatów was engaged with an at-times violent dispute with Gryfice over navigation rights on the Rega river.

Heading east towards the station from the centre you'll cross a **stone bridge** built in 1905 – a stylish, Secession-influenced structure decorated with hospitable-looking fishes.

Both the **bus** and **train stations** are located outside the built-up part of town, about ten minutes' walk to the east. The only decent place to eat is the unpretentious first-floor *Ratuszowa* **restaurant** on the Rynek, but it closes at 7pm.

Gryfice

About 20km up the Rega from Trzebiatów is **GRYFICE**, a slightly larger town with a decidedly more urban feel to it. German commentators on Pomerania are readily stirred to anger at the mere mention of its name: the town was taken undamaged by the Red Army in 1945, only to be set ablaze soon afterwards, and was later used as the site of a penal camp in which a large number of civilians were detained.

The Gothic **Kościół Mariacki** (Church of St Mary) is a copybook example of the Baltic style, notable chiefly for its sturdy single western tower and its finely detailed portals, many of which have since been bricked up. Inside you'll find some good Baroque furnishings, in particular the pulpit and the high altar. The surviving parts of the **fortifications** – the Stone Gate, the High Gate and the Powder Tower – can be seen towards the river to the east.

Goleniów

The largest and liveliest town of the group is **GOLENIÓW**, 55km southwest of Gryfice. It's an important rail junction, the meeting point of the line between Kołobrzeg and Szczecin with those to Kamień Pomorski and Świnoujście. Among its few assets is its situation in the middle of the **Puszcza Goleniowska**, a vast forested area which stretches almost all the way up to Wolin – a particularly scenic journey by train.

Goleniów's main church, **Kościół św. Katarzyny** (St Catherine's Church), is imposing largely owing to extensive remodelling last century when the tower was added – today its brick columns bow visibly under the strain. Nearby are the **town walls**, whose surviving towers and gateways make a nicely varied group, with the showpiece being the **Brama Wolińska** (Wolin Gate), an elaborate building in its own right now housing a cultural centre. Also worth a look is the timber-framed **granary** standing all alone on the banks of the River Ina.

Kamień Pomorski

Some 60km west of Kołobrzeg lies the quiet little waterside town of **KAMIEŃ POMORSKI**, an atmospheric Pomeranian centre which demands a visit for its fine cathedral and agreeable setting. Travelling by car along the main routes it's easy to miss this town, since it's not on the major coastal road to Świnoujście. Public transport is another matter however; there are good bus connections with Kołobrzeg, Międzyzdroje, Świnoujście and Szczecin, rendering Kamień an easy stopoff.

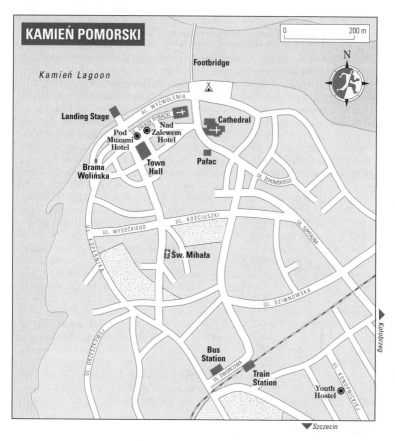

KAMIEŃ POMORSKI

0   200 m

N

Kamień Lagoon

Footbridge

Landing Stage

AL. WYZWOLENIA

Nad Zalewem Hotel

Pod Muzami Hotel

Cathedral

Brama Wolińska

Town Hall

Pałac

UL. ŻEROMSKIEGO

UL. KOŚCIUSZKI

UL. WYSOCKIEGO

UL. KOPERNIKA

Św. Mihała

UL. SZYMANA

UL. DZIWNOWSKA

Kołobrzeg

UL. ORZESZKOWEJ

Bus Station

UL. DWORCOWA

Train Station

Youth Hostel

UL. KONOPNICKIEJ

Szczecin

The town's **history** began in the ninth century, when a port was established here on the River Dziwna, a short stretch of water connecting the huge Zalew Szczeciński, or Szczecin Lagoon, with the smaller Zalew Kamieński, or Kamień Lagoon – all of which are part of the delta formed by the Odra as it nears its mouth at the Gulf of Pomerania. By the late twelfth century, Kamień was significant enough to be appointed as the seat of the bishopric of West Pomerania, a position it kept for nearly four hundred years, while by the late 1300s it felt rich enough to join the Hanseatic League. The Swedes seized the town during the Thirty Years' War, but by the late seventeenth century it had been appropriated by the Brandenburg rulers, not coming under Polish control until after World War II. Despite extensive wartime damage, Kamień Pomorski seems to have come out better than most towns in the area: concrete buildings fill in the huge gaps between the occasional burghers' mansions, yet there's enough of the older architecture to retain a sense of times past.

The Town

All Kamień's sights are on and around the **Rynek** whose north edge looks out onto the lagoon. The fifteenth-century **town hall**, in the middle, is a careful reconstruction, its brick archways rising to a stepped and curvilinear Baroque gable at each end – a rarely seen combination. Parts of the walls ringing the Stare Miasto have survived, notably the **Brama Wolińska** west of the square, an imposing Gothic gateway, surrounded by apartment buildings.

East of the square stands the **cathedral**, retaining its Romanesque features at ground level, but otherwise the customary mass of brickwork is in the Gothic idiom. Construction of the brick and granite basilica began in the 1170s, following the creation of the Kamień bishopric, with many subsequent additions over the following centuries. Inside the cathedral, you're enveloped by majestic Gothic vaulted arches; the presbytery is older, and covered with flowing early-thirteenth-century decoration. Other sections of the earliest polychromy are tucked away in corners around the transept, including a stern *Christ Pantocrator* and a fine *Crucifixion* that was uncovered in the 1940s. The focus of attention, though, is the superb fifteenth-century triptych gracing the altar, the most outstanding of many such Gothic pieces in the building – the rest are in the **sacristy museum**. A central *Coronation of Mary* is surrounded by scenes from the lives of the saints, most notably John Chrysostom, to whom the building is dedicated. To the right of the altar is another finely sculpted Romanesque portal, leading to the sacristy.

The cathedral's most famous feature, however, is its massive Baroque **organ**, at the back of the building, its forest of silver pipes and exuberant detail crowned by a procession of dreamy gilded saints. As you approach from the nave, a portrait of the instrument's creator, a local bishop by the name of Bogusław de Croy i Archot, stares down on the congregation from a cherub-encircled frame. In July the cathedral hosts an **International Organ and Chamber Music Festival**, with concerts every Friday – details from the Biuro Katedralny opposite. To complete the ensemble, across pl. Katedralny is the **Pałac Biskupski** (Bishop's Palace), a stately, late-Gothic structure with a finely carved attic.

Downhill from the cathedral lie the grassy banks of the **lagoon**. There's no real beach here, but it's a relaxing place to stretch your legs, and there's a footbridge leading over to a tranquil, reedy area on the opposite bank.

Practicalities

All Kamień's sights are a straightforward ten-minute walk north of the **bus** and **train stations**. Central Kamień can boast two exceedingly cosy medium-sized **hotels**, both of which feature en-suite rooms with TV: the *Pod Muzami*, on the corner of the main square at Gryfitów 1 (☎91/382 2240; ❹), is in an old half-timbered building but has bright modern interiors; while the next-door *Staromiejski Nad Zalewem*, Rybacka 3 (☎91/382 2644; ❹), goes for a plusher, chintzier style. There's a **campsite** by the lagoon at al. Wyzwolenia 2 (☎091/382 0076).

For **eating**, you'll find the customary gaggle of snack bars and fish-fry huts down by the water's edge. For more substantial food try the restaurants in the *Hotel Pod Muzami* on the Rynek, or the *Ratuszowa* by the town hall.

Wolin

Across the water from Kamień Pomorski is **WOLIN**, the first of two large, heavily indented islands that separate the Szczecin Lagoon from the Gulf of Pomerania. The gap dividing Wolin from the mainland is at times so narrow that it's often described as a peninsula rather than an island; indeed, roads are built directly over the River Dziwna in two places – near its mouth at Dzwinów, some 12km from Kamień, and at **Wolin town** towards the island's southern extremity, where it is also forded by the rail line from Szczecin. From Kamień, you can choose to approach by either of these two roads, the only ones of significance on the island. They converge at the seaside town and hiking centre of **Międzyzdroje**, before continuing onwards to the western extremity of the island and **Świnoujście** an engaging mixture of bustling port, health spa and beach resort.

The island, which is 35km long and between 8km and 20km across, offers a wonderfully contrasted landscape of sand dunes, lakes, forest, meadows and moors. Part of its dramatic **coastline** – undoubtedly its most memorable feature – has attracted crowds of holiday-makers since the nineteenth century; it is likely to be heavily developed in the future, but in the meantime it remains relatively unspoilt. A sizeable portion of the island is under protection as a national park, and you really need to take time to hike if you want to appreciate it to the full.

Wolin Town

Squatting beside the Dzwina river on the island's southeastern tip, the town of **WOLIN** occupies the site of one of the oldest Slav settlements in the country. According to early chronicles, a pagan tribe known as the Wolinians established themselves here in the eighth century, developing one of the most important early Baltic ports, and carrying on a healthy trade with the Vikings. A temple to Światowid and to Trzygłów, a triple-headed Slav deity, existed here until the early twelfth century, and was presumably destroyed by the Christian Poles only when they captured the stronghold.

Echoes of the town's pagan past are present in the totem-like reconstructed wooden figures dotted around close to the water, all depicting Slav gods. The ruins of the medieval **Kościół św. Mikołaja** (Church of St Nicholas), just up from the main square, show echoes of a Christian past too. Recent excavations have uncovered plentiful evidence of the Wolinian settlement: you can see their discoveries in the local **museum** (Tues–Sun 9am–4pm; 2zł) on the main road at the eastern end of town. The road bridge linking Wolin to the mainland provides a good vantage point from which to survey the narrow **Dziwna channel**, packed with shoals of small fishing vessels on calm days.

Wolin town lacks a beach, and isn't the most convenient of access points to the national park, so you're unlikely to need to stay here. If you do, the *Wineta* **hotel** on the main road through town (☎091/326 1884; ❸) will sort you out with a room. **Buses** on the Świnoujście–Szczecin route pick up and drop off on Wolin's main street; the train station is a short distance to the east.

Międzyzdroje

By far the best base for exploring the island is **MIĘDZYZDROJE**, which offers easy access to a long sandy beach and the best hiking trails in the area. A favourite Baltic resort with the prewar German middle class, it went downmarket with its transferral to Poland, but is now one of the west Baltic's busiest resorts. New hotels are springing up in the beachside areas, and the number of German and Scandinavian visitors is on the increase. However the centre of town remains a laid-back, far from overdeveloped place, its streets filled with trade union-owned sanatoria and holiday homes. It may not look all that snazzy a place to the outsider, but Międzyzdroje was traditionally one of the places where Polish TV and film stars spent their holidays. A modicum of showbiz glitter still exists in the shape of the **Festiwal Gwiazd** (Star Festival) at the beginning of July, when a horde of minor celebrities and their hangers-on descend on town to attend public film screenings and concerts, and generally hang out.

The centre of town, 1km inland from the sea, revolves around **plac Neptuna**, a modern, pedestrianized, café-filled square which brings to mind the mall-like plazas of Mediterranean holiday resorts. Immediately to the south is the main traffic thoroughfare, ul. Niepodległości, which is overlooked by the national park museum, the **Muzeum Przyrodnice Wolińskie o Parku Narodowego** (Tues–Sat 9am–5pm; 2zł) – a well-presented display of the island's flora and fauna which is well worth visiting before heading off into the park itself.

It's a ten-minute walk northwards from pl. Neptuna to ul. Bohaterów Warszawy, the **promenade** which stretches for some 4km along the shore. Its focal point is the nineteenth-century **pier**, the entrance to which is framed by an imposing pair of domed pavilions now occupied by ice-cream kiosks. The first one hundred metres or so of the pier is covered by a canopy, forming an arcade-like space filled with cafés and boutiques selling beach gear.

The bison reserve

Wolin's densely wooded national park (see opposite) starts right on the outskirts of Międzyzdroje, and one of the park's principal attractions – the European **bison reserve** (Tues–Sun 10am–6pm; 5zł) – lies a twenty-minute walk away from the town centre. To get there, head uphill from the PTTK office on ul. Niepodległości and follow the signs. You'll pass through a national park entrance gate after about five minutes – beyond which a trail leads through deep forest to the reserve itself. The reserve was set up a couple of decades ago to reintroduce animals to a habitat where they hadn't been seen since the 1300s. A breeding programme was started by introducing stock from the much larger bison reserve in Białowieża in eastern Poland (see p.283). You can see several of the beasts from a distance, and the reserve is also home to a few wild deer, some eagles and a clutch of amusing wild boars who loll about in the mud, twitching their prodigious snouts.

Practicalities

The **train station** is at the southeastern fringe of town, five minutes' walk uphill from the centre, while **buses** pick up and drop off closer to the centre, on ul. Niepodległości.

The PTTK office at the junction of Niepodległości and Kolejowa (Mon–Fri 7am–5pm, Sat 9am–1pm; ☎091/328 0462) sells maps and gives **information** on routes into the park, and might direct you towards private rooms (❶), although you'll probably have to look round town on your own – the streets behind the seafront are the best places to start. The PTTK has a **hotel** above the office (☎091/328 0382; ❷) offering clean but plain rooms with shared bathrooms; and a better-equipped annexe, nearer the beach at ul. Dąbrówski 11 (☎091/328 0929; ❹), which has en-suites. The *Marina*, Gryfa Pomorskiego 1 (☎91/328 0449 or 328 2382, ⓦwww.miedzyzdroje.to.jest.to/marina; ❺), is a smart new building on the main road through town providing smallish but extremely cosy en-suite rooms with TV. You'll get similar standards of comfort at the *Perła*, Pomorska 7 (☎91/328 1303; ❺), a spanking new pension just off the promenade a little to the east of the pier; the *Aurora*, Bohaterow Warszawy 17 (☎91/328 1248, ⓦwww.miedzyzdroje.to.jest.to/aurora; ❻), whose higher prices are justified by its pier-side position; and the *Slavia*, ul. Promenada Gwiazd 34 (☎091/328 0098; ❻), whose balconies have sea views. If you want to stay in unbridled comfort, the *Amber Baltic*, ul. Bohaterów Warszawy 26a (☎091/328 0800, ⓦwww.hotel-amber-baltic.pl; ❸), charges international prices for facilities that include golf, bowling, tennis and surfing, plus an outdoor swimming pool. Best of the **campsites** is the *Gromada*, ul. Bohaterów Warszawy 1 (☎091/328 0779), at the western end of the seafront.

The *Cukierna Marczello* **café** at pl. Neptuna 3 does the best pastries and cakes in town and has decent coffee. For something more substantial, the *Carmen* **restaurant**, immediately opposite, serves up satisfying platters of Polish meat-and-potatoes cuisine. You'll find several fish-and-chip stalls along the seafront promenade, and an inexpensive Chinese fast-food joint in the shape of *Ti Li*, just west of the pier at Bohaterow Warszawy 16. For **drinking**, the café-bars on the pier (most of which also serve pizza and other snacks) fill up on summer weekends, although the best all-year-round venue is *Roza Wiatrow* at plac Neptuna 7, a smart, cosy pub with nautical prints and model boats stashed around the place.

Woliński national park

Woliński national park is an area of outstanding natural interest: apart from its richly varied landscapes, it is the habitat of over two hundred different types of bird – the sea eagle is its emblem – and numerous animals such as red and fallow deer, wild boar, badgers, foxes and squirrels. It would take several days to cover all its many delights, but a good cross-section can be seen without venturing too far from Międzyzdroje. Alternatively, take a bus or train going in the direction of Wolin town, or a bus going towards Kamień or Kołobrzeg, and alight at any stop: you'll soon find signs enabling you to pick up one of the colour-coded trails. A good aid to walking in this region is the 1:75,000 *Zalew Szczeciński* **map** which has all the paths clearly marked; it's readily available in Międzyzdroje, notably from the national park museum (see opposite).

The trails

Some of the most impressive scenery in the park can be seen by following the **red trail** along its eastward stretch from Międzyzdroje, which passes for a while directly along the beach. You soon come to some awesome-looking tree-crowned **dunes**, where the sand has been swept up into cliff-like formations up to 95m in height – the highest to be seen anywhere on the Baltic. Quite apart from its visual impact, much of this secluded stretch is ideal for a spot of swimming or sunbathing away from the crowds. After a few kilometres, the markers point the way upwards into the forest, and you follow a path which skirts the tiny Lake Gardno before arriving at the village of **WISEŁKA**, whose setting has the best of both worlds, being by its eponymous lake, and above a popular stretch of beach. Here there's a restaurant, snack bars, and several shops. The trail continues east through the woods and past more small lakes to its terminus at **KOŁCZEWO**, set at the head of its own lake, and the only other place along the entire route with refreshment facilities. From either here or Misełka, you can pick up a bus back to Międzyzdroje.

Also terminating at Kołczewo is the **green trail**: if you're prepared to devote a very long day to it, you could combine this with the red trail in one circular trip. The trail begins in Międzyzdroje and passes by the bison reserve (see opposite) before continuing its forest course, emerging at a group of glacial lakes around the village of Warnowo (which can also be reached directly by train), where there's another reserve, this time for mute swans. Five lakeshores are then skirted en route to Kołczewo.

The third route, the **blue trail**, follows a southerly course from Międzyzdroje's train station, again passing through wooded countryside before arriving at the northern shore of the Szczecin Lagoon. Following this to the east, you traverse the heights of the Mokrzyckie Góry, then descend to the town of Wolin.

Finally, the western section of the **red trail** follows the coast for a couple of kilometres, then cuts straight down the narrow peninsula at the end of the island to the shore of the islet-strewn Lake Wicko Wielkie, before cutting inland to Świnoujście.

Świnoujście

Across the water from Wolin on the western tip of the island of Uznam, the bustling fishing port, naval base and beach resort of **ŚWINOUJŚCIE** is a popular entry point into Poland, thanks to the passenger ships which sail here from Sweden and Denmark. It's also 3km away from the land border with Germany (there's a crossing open to pedestrians and cyclists, but not cars), to whom the vast bulk of the island of Uznam belongs.

Świnoujście's international **ferry terminal**, together with both the **bus** and **train stations**, is stranded on the eastern bank of the Świna estuary – which seperates Uznam from Wolin. A half-hourly car ferry (on which pedestrians travel free) runs over to the centre of town, which lies on the western bank. The town centre is fairly nondescript, and it's best to head directly to the town's superb white-sand **beach** – which lies twenty minutes' northwards on the far side of the spacious **spa park**. Once you reach the shore, you'll probably be drawn in to the endless stream of strollers passing along the pedestrianized ul. Żeromskiego, which runs from east to west along the seafront, passing neat flowerbeds and stately seaside villas on the way.

The **tourist office**, just west of the ferry landing at pl. Słowiański 15 (Mon–Fri 9am–5pm; ☎091/322 4999; ✉cit@fornet.com.pl) can direct you towards private rooms (**②**) and pensions (**③**). Cheapest of the **hotels** is the *Dom Rybaka* at Wybrzeże Władysława IV 22 (☎091/321 2943; **②**), which offers rooms with shared facilities overlooking the harbour. There's a lot more choice nearer the seafront however: *Hutnik*, Żeromskiego 15 (☎091/321 5411; **③**), has simple ensuites in a beachside building dripping with *fin-de-siécle* style; while the more up-to-date *Filla*, Żeromskiego 16 (☎091/321 2619, ⓦhttp://uznam.top.pl/~allbud/) is an affordable apartment hotel offering cosy quarters with kitchenettes (**④**). The *Atol*, just behind the promenade at Orkana 3 (☎91/321 3010, ⓦwww.hotel-atol.com.pl; **②**), is one of the better new hotels in town, offering pastel-coloured en-suites, a sauna, and a list of former guests that rejoices in top showbiz mastodons like Boney M and Smokie.

There's an HI **youth hostel** at Gdyńska 26 (☎091/327 0613), about 1km southwest of the tourist office – and hence a good half-hour's walk from the seafront – but it does boast a few double rooms (**①**) as well as dorms. The *Relax* **campsite** is more handily located at ul. Słowackiego 1 (☎091/321 3912), between the spa park and the beach, and has chalets (**②**).

To **eat**, you could do worse than head for *Gryf*, an enormous bench-filled yard on the seafront promenade serving up tasty grilled fish; *Pizzeria Muszla*, about 200m further east, is a slightly more stylish sit-down venue which has some good pasta dishes. The restuarant of the *Polaris* hotel, Sowackiego 33, is a plush and formal place in which to feast on classic fish and meat dishes, but remains affordable. For **drinking**, *Jazz Café Casablanca*, near the tourist office on pl. Słowiański, has a touch more style than the al-fresco beer bars on the seafront promenade. **Nightlife** centres around old-time dancing in the larger hotels, or more frenetic physical jerks in the summer-only disco-bars on the seafront.

Moving on from Świnoujście, there are regular **train** and **bus** services to Szczecin, and a summer only **hydrofoil** service that runs across the lagoon to Szczecin three times a day. In addition there are daily car ferries to Ystad, Malmö and Copenhagen, and passenger boats (intended for day-trippers, really) to the nearby German beach resorts of Ahlbeck, Bansin and Heringsdorf.

Szczecin

The largest city in northwestern Poland, with 400,000 inhabitants, **SZCZECIN** sprawls around the banks of the Odra in a tangle of bridges, cranes and dockside machinery: a city with a long maritime and shipbuilding heritage. It's a gruff, workaday city that bares few of its charms to the passing visitor. However it's also a fast-paced, fast-changing place that boasts a clutch of cultural diversions, not to mention an impressive collection of bars. It's also an important transport hub: the western half of Poland's Baltic coastline is served by regular buses and trains from here, as is the Pomeranian lakeland to the east.

The Slav stronghold established here in the eighth century was taken by the first Piast monarch, Mieszko I, in 967 – a point much emphasized in Polish histories. From the early twelfth century, Szczecin became the residence of a local branch of Piast princes, rulers of Western Pomerania, but German colonists were already present in force by the time the city joined the Hanseatic League in the mid-thirteenth century. The next key event was the port's capture by the Swedes in 1630, after which it was held by them for nearly a century. Sold to the Prussians in 1720, it remained under Prussian rule until 1945, when it became an outpost on Poland's newly established western frontier. With the border just west of the city limits and Berlin – for which Stettin/Szczecin used to be the port – only a couple of hours away by car or train, the German presence is still palpable.

Wartime pummelling destroyed most of the old centre, which never received quite the same restorative attention as some less controversially Polish cities. There is no Rynek or pedestrianized town centre any longer, although a distinctly Parisian radial pattern of streets survives in what has become the main part of the city. Despite its size, there isn't that much to take in – a full day is enough to cover all the main sights.

Arrival and information and accommodation

The central **train station** and the nearby **bus terminal** are located near the water's edge, from where it's a fifteen-minute walk (or a quick tram ride) north up the hill to the town centre. There are **left-luggage** facilities in the pedestrian underpass beneath the train station's ticket hall (daily 6am–midnight). For details of the comprehensive bus and tram **city transport** routes you'll need to get hold of a copy of the red Szczecin town map – available from the tourist office (see below) as well as most bookstores. Bus and tram tickets, bought from kiosks, cost 1.50zł for 20 minutes of travel, 2.50zł for 1hr.

Szczecin **airport** – chiefly dedicated to internal flights but with some international services – is in fact located at Goleniów (☎182 864), 45km north of the city, with bus services to and from the LOT office at al. Wyzwolenia 17.

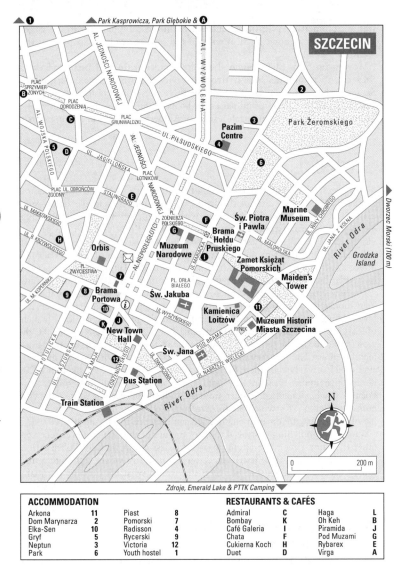

Zdroje, Emerald Lake & PTTK Camping ▼

ACCOMMODATION					RESTAURANTS & CAFÉS			
Arkona	11	Piast	8		Admiral	C	Haga	L
Dom Marynarza	2	Pomorski	7		Bombay	K	Oh Keh	B
Elka-Sen	10	Radisson	4		Café Galeria	I	Piramida	J
Gryf	5	Rycerski	9		Chata	F	Pod Muzami	G
Neptun	3	Victoria	12		Cukierna Koch	H	Rybarex	E
Park	6	Youth hostel	1		Duet	D	Virga	A

The municipal **tourist office**, which occupies a squat circular pavilion at al. Niepodległości 1 (Mon–Fri 9am–5pm; ☎091/434 0440), gives advice on accommodation, and sells **town maps**.

Accommodation

There's a fair spread of **accommodation** in town, ranging from the most luxurious international-class hotels to a couple of post-communist fleapits, and even in high summer you shouldn't have too much trouble finding a bed for the night. Prices include breakfast unless otherwise stated.

Almatur, ul. Bohaterów Warszawy 83 (Mon–Fri 9am–5pm; ☎091/484 43 55), will be able to tell you which **student hostels** in Szczecin are open to tourists over the summer.

Hotels

Arkona ul. Panieńska 10 ☎091/488 026, ✉arkona@orbis.pl. Overpriced Orbis concrete block with not-quite groovy 1970s-era furnishings. Nice location below the castle, just behind the old town hall. ⑥

Dom Marynarza ul. Malczewskiego 10/12 ☎091/424 0001. Moderately priced but well-equipped slab of concrete just to the north of Park Żeromskiego, about 2km from the centre, offering en-suites with TV. ⑤

Elka-Sen ul. 3 Maja 1A ☎091/433 5604. Charming little place in a converted hospital basement, handy for both the city centre and the stations. Rooms are on the cramped side but come with colourful furnishings and en-suite shower. Reserve in advance if possible. ④

Gryf al. Wojska Polskiego 49 ☎091/433 4566. Dowdy downtown hotel on a busy thoroughfare, with a mixture of dingy unrefurbished rooms with shared facilities, and bright modern en-suites with TV. No breakfast. ③–⑤

Neptun ul. Matejki 18 ☎091/488 3883, ✉neptun@orbis.pl. Luxury Orbis joint on the west side of Park Żeromskiego. ⑦

Park ul. Plantowa 1 ☎094/488 1524. Newish hotel offering modern en-suites attractively decorated in pastel colours, and with comparatively roomy bathrooms. More intimate in feel than the other business-standard hotels, and the location – right in the middle of Park Żeromskiego – is a major plus. ⑦

Piast pl. Zywciestwa 3 ☎091/433 6662.

Unrenovated downtown hotel offering gloomy rooms with tatty furnishings. Acceptable for a one-night stay. Rooms with en-suite bath as well as those with shared facilities. No breakfast. ③

Pomorski pl. Brama Portowa 4 ☎091/433 6151. Ideally central, but rooms are sparsely furnished and unkempt. A short-stay bolt-hole, nothing more. En-suites and rooms with shared facilities. No breakfast. ②–③

Radisson pl. Rodła 10 ☎091/359 5595. Gleaming custom-built luxury hotel with its own casino, nightclub, fitness centre and swimming pool along with all the other upmarket facilities expected by its largely expense-account clientele. ⑨

Rycerski ul. Potulicka 1/3 ☎091/445 2413. Smart, fully renovated place right in the heart of town, offering en-suite tuel-suites with TV. ⑥

Victoria pl. Batorego 2 ☎091/434 3855. Comfortable medium-sized hotel in refurbished nineteenth-century building within easy striking distance of train and bus stations. ⑥

Hostels and campsites

Ul. Monte Cassino 19a ☎091/422 4761. Comfortable and friendly hostel situated just north-west of the centre, past the south end of ul. M. Kopernika. Handy for Szczecin's parks. Tram #3 to pl. Rodła, then tram #1 to the Piotra Skargi stop.

PTTK Camping ul. Przestrzenna 23 ☎091/460 1165. In Dąbie, 3km east of town – take the local train to Szczecin-Dąbie station, followed by bus #56, #62 or #79. Open May–Sept; tent space and chalets (②) available.

The City

The medieval **Stare Miasto**, laid out on a slope on the left bank of the Odra, was heavily bombed in the last war. Restoration work on the showpiece buildings went on until the 1980s, with the gaps either left vacant or filled by drab modern housing. While you're walking around you'll notice very few people and a distinct lack of shops in this area; **commercial** life shifted west a kilometre to a part of town which survived in better shape. This was laid out towards the end of the nineteenth century in the Parisian manner, with broad boulevards radiating out from pl. Grunwaldzki, the vicarious heart of Szczecin.

The commercial centre

Ascending ul. Dworcowa from the train station, you soon see some of the massive late-nineteenth- and early-twentieth-century Prussian buildings so characteristic of the heart of the city. Commanding the heights is the bulky red-brick frame of the neo-Gothic new **town hall**, now the seat of the maritime authorities. Across the street, steps lead up to the former **Savings Bank**, a Jugendstil fantasy, whose slender tower and decorative facades seem to echo the faintly oriental gothic flavour of that architectural style.

At the top of ul. Dworcowa is the traffic-engulfed square named after the **Brama Portowa** (Harbour Gate), not so much a gate as two ornate Baroque gables linked by a long hall, built by the Prussians in 1725 to mark their purchase of the city. Immediately to the west of the gateway is the largest and busiest of the squares, pl. Zwycięstwa, on which stand a couple of turn-of-the-twentieth-century churches which have successively served the local garrison. Leading off to the north is al. Niepodległości, the city's main thoroughfare, on whose western side stand two more of the big Prussian public buildings – the post office, still fulfilling its original function, and the administration building of the Pomeranian district, which has been taken over by the displaced Savings Bank.

Św. Jakuba and around

Heading east from the Brama Portowa to the river, ul. Kardynała Wyszyńskiego brings you to the **Katedra św. Jakuba** (St James's Cathedral), a massive Gothic church grievously damaged in 1945, and the subject of over-expedient restoration (including some concrete windows) which was only completed in 1982, an event celebrated by its elevation to the seat of a bishop the following year. The oldest parts of the church date back to the fourteenth century and are the work of Hinrich Brunsberg, the finest of the specialist brickwork architects of the Baltic lands. The hall design he used here is notable for its consummate simplicity. In the middle of the following century, the single **tower** was constructed to replace the previous pair; this is now only half of its prewar height of 120m, having been rebuilt minus the spire and further trivialized with the addition of a clock. Its five-and-a-half-tonne bell now hangs in a frame outside, as does a memorial to Carl Loewe, one of the great ballad composers and singers of the nineteenth century, who was for several decades the church's organist and music director. Today the building's profile is rather plain, with it's bulky exterior best appreciated coming up ul. Kardynała Wyszyńskiego from the river, although to the rear of the church you'll find a pretty little Gothic rectory.

On pl. Orła Białego, the square on the north side of the cathedral, is the Baroque **Pod Globusem Palace**, originally built for the ruler of the Prussian province of Pomerania and now used as the medical academy. Across from it, part obscured by a willow tree, stands an intriguing **fountain** adorned with the eponymous white eagle (*biały orzeł*) overlooking a group of satyrs who gurgle stoically into an enormous clam. Hidden among the trees at the cathedral end of the square is another piece of Baroque frippery, a statue of the goddess Flora.

The lower town

Down ul. Wyszyńskiego towards the river, you come on the right-hand side to the oldest surviving building in Szczecin, the Franciscan monastery of **św. Jana** (St John), part of which dates back to the thirteenth century. Its distinctive feature is its geometric inconsistency showing that medieval builders could and did get their calculations wrong. The chancel is an irregular decagon, yet has a seven-part vault, while the later nave adjoins at an oblique angle, its off-centre vaulting a vain attempt to align the bays with the aisle windows. It's a rare example of a building that was never rebuilt properly but never quite collapsed: looking inside you can see the alarmingly warped columns braced by a network of steel girders.

Immediately east of here lies the Stary Rynek, where concrete blocks and vacant lots rub shoulders with several reconstructed burghers' houses gaudily decked out in bright blue and orange colour schemes. By far the most personable of Szczecin's buildings is the gabled **old town hall** in the Rynek's centre, an artful reconstruction of the fourteenth-century original, probably designed by Hinrich Brunsberg, which was flattened in the war. The restorers opted to return it to something like its original appearance, preserving only one Baroque gable while presumably managing to artfully incorporate the lopsidedness of an aged building. These days the building serves as a small **Muzeum Historii Miasta Szczecina** (Museum of the History of Szczecin; Wed & Fri 9am–3.30pm, Tues, Thurs, Sat & Sun 10am–5pm; 4zł).

The only burgher's mansion still standing in Szczecin is the mid-sixteenth-century **Kamienica Loitzów** (Loitz House), just uphill at the corner of ul. Kurkowa, a tower-type residence of a prominent local banking and trading dynasty. Further down the same street are two other rare medieval survivors, a grange and the municipal weigh house. Of the once formidable fifteenth-century fortification system, almost nothing remains save the appropriately graceful **Maiden's Tower**, now stranded between the castle and a network of interchanges funnelling the city's traffic over the river.

Zamek Książąt Pomorskich

By now you'll have spotted the **Zamek Książiżąt Pomorskich** (Castle of the Pomeranian Princes) commanding views of the river from its hillside perch. A Slav fortified settlement on this spot was replaced in the mid-fourteenth century by a stone structure, the oldest section of the current building. The whole thing was given a Renaissance enlargement in the late sixteenth century, and again remodelled in the 1720s. Princes and dukes aside, the building has been used as a brewery, office block, barracks and anti-aircraft emplacement – the last function being the direct cause of its flattening in an air raid in 1944. Reconstruction continued into the 1980s, since when it's been turned into a museum and cultural centre. The **Muzeum Zamkowe** (Castle Museum; Tues–Sun: July–Aug 10am–6pm; Sept–June 10am–4pm; 6zł) occupies a few vaults, displaying a few repaired sarcophagi as well as photographs of the castle's restoration from postwar ruin. The chapel on the ground floor of the north wing is now a concert hall. In the east wing, much of the exterior decoration has been reworked with the addition of a few more faux concrete windows and the castle's distinctive clock; most of this section is now occupied by a cinema and other cultural facilities. If you're here in summer, you might get to hear an open-air concert in the castle courtyard.

After a visit to the castle **café** – a popular rendezvous point – it's worth climbing the two hundred or so steps up the *wieża*, or **bell tower** (same hours as museum; 2zł) for the view over the city, port and surroundings. You'll notice a striking absence of industrial chimneys; instead church spires and dockside cranes pierce the skyline.

North of the castle

Immediately to the west of the castle is ul. Farna, where the residence of the commandant formerly stood. This was the birthplace in 1729 of Sophie von Anhalt-Zerbst, a princess of a very minor German aristocratic line who has gone down in history as **Empress Catherine the Great of Russia**. A character of extreme ruthlessness – she deposed her own husband, and was probably behind his subsequent murder – her reputation has always been a matter of controversy. Among her "achievements" was a considerable imperialistic expansion, one manifestation of which was a leading role in the three Partitions that wiped Poland off the map. That her native city is now Polish is truly ironic.

A couple of blocks further west is ul. Staromłyńska, at the corner of which rises an elegant Baroque palace, formerly the Pomeranian parliament and now home of a section of the **Muzeum Narodowe** at no. 27 (National Museum;

Tues & Thurs 10am–5pm, Wed & Fri 9am–3.30pm, Sat & Sun 10am–4pm; 10zł). The ground floor features several important Polish artists, most notably Waliszewski, Zofia Stryjenska and the broodingly introspective Jacek Małczewski. Upstairs there's an even mushier collection of paintings by local artists on sea-based themes, although the fine Baroque-era furniture is worth an admiring look. Older works are displayed in the annexe across the street. On the ground floor here is an impressive display of medieval Pomeranian **sculpture**. Highlights include the thirteenth-century columns, topped with delicately carved capitals, from the monastery of Kołbacz; a monumental wooden sacromenteum of the same period from Wolin; and several expressively carved and painted mid-fifteenth-century triptychs from Pomerania. Upstairs, later sections emphasize Polish painters, with a token German work occasionally thrown in.

Across the broad open space of pl. Żołnierza Polskiego is the Baroque **Brama Hołdu Pruskiego** (Gate of Prussian Homage), whose design, with reliefs of military trophies, echo those of the Brama Portowa. Its interior is now used for changing exhibitions of the work of contemporary painters and photographers. Facing it to the east is the beguiling fourteenth-century **Kościół św. Piotra i Pawła** (Church of SS Peter and Paul) a Gothic church built on the site of one established by Polish missionaries in the early twelfth century. In a rich ensemble of original ornamental detail the most striking elements are the seventeenth-century memorial tablets, the German inscriptions reminding you of the city's Teutonic heritage, and the unusual wooden vaulting.

On the north side of the church, ul. Małopolska leads to **Wały Chrobrego**, a leafy promenade commanding an expansive panorama of the Odra river and the industrial suburbs on the far shore. The promenade – conceived as a showpiece of muscular civic architecture by Szczecin's pre-World War I German masters – is lined with an imposing sequence of prestigous public buildings. The largest of these, fronted by a grandiose staircase which leads down to a riverside terrace, now houses the **Muzeum Morskie** (Marine Museum; Tues, Thurs, Sat & Sun 10am–5pm, Wed & Fri 9am–3.30pm; 6zł). Inside lies a wealth of material on seafaring Slavs and Celts, with graphic displays from the Stone, Iron and Bronze Ages. Huge arrow-covered maps delineate bygone migrations, while upstairs a gallery is devoted to objects from classical antiquity. However, most impressive and unexpected is an inspired ethnographic exhibition with detailed dioramas of a Dogon village in Mali, a shoreside equivalent from the Ivory Coast and, in the next room, some creepy West African statues, fetishes and carved masks. On the next floor, a Papuan village gets the same treatment, although the budget or the enthusiasm seems to have waned at the rather feeble rendition of a Buddhist temple.

A block to the north of the museum lies the leafy **Park Żeromskiego**, the only significant stretch of park in the centre. Over beyond the western side of the park on pl. Rodła looms the **Kompleks Pazim** (Pazim Centre), a clutch of steel-framed, blue glass buildings that contains a hotel (the *Radisson*; see p.663), shopping centre and business complex. Thrown up since the fall of communism, the Centre gives this part of Szczecin a rather showy but anachronistic look, as if a piece of contemporary Chicago has been dropped into nineteenth-century Europe.

The harbour

Szczecin is one of the largest ports on the Baltic, with a highly developed shipping industry, and you'll appreciate the essence of the city more fully if you take a **boat trip** round the port and harbour. Excursions, lasting just over an hour, leave from the **Dworzec Morski** terminal, northeast of Wały Chrobrego

(☎091/433 2818). Ask here about the boat and hydrofoil services across the vast Szczecin Lagoon to Świnoujście (see p.660).

The outskirts

Despite the patchily built-up character of its centre, Szczecin has plenty of stretches of greenery, which are ideal for a quick break from the urban bustle, particularly on summer evenings. Just to the north of the centre is the **Park Kasprowicza**, which can be reached on trams #1 or #9 or by walking up al. Jedności Narodowej from the centre. After first negotiating the ornamental flowerbeds at the park's southern end, you soon reach the huge triple-eagle monument made to commemorate the fortieth anniversary of the outbreak of World War II, symbolizing the three generations of Poles who lost their lives. Proceeding northwestwards through the park, the **Ogród Dendrologiczny** (Dendrological Garden) on the east bank of the narrow Lake Rusałka contains over two hundred species of trees and shrubs, including a host of exotic varieties, such as Californian redwoods. Beyond the lake, tree-lined paths continue towards **Park Głębokie**, a full 5km out of the centre (and also reached by riding trams #1 and #9 to the Głębokie terminus), arranged around the sausage-shaped lake of the same name. This is a much wilder, less developed area, perfect for tranquil woodland walks.

The most distinctive park in the city is that in the eastern suburb of **Zdroje**, reached by a slow train or buses. Here you'll find a number of hiking trails, a couple of restaurants, and the **Jezioro Szmaragdowe** (Emerald Lake), which was created in the 1920s by flooding a former quarry; you can go for a swim here, or simply admire the play of light on its deep green waters.

Eating, drinking and entertainment

The gastronomic situation in Szczecin is as varied as in any other big Polish city, with a reasonable number of places offering good-quality Polish food, alongside a growing number of ethnic alternatives. Most restaurants stay open till 11pm, with one or two remaining open into the early hours. We've included the telephone numbers of those restaurants where reservations are advised.

Despite the rash of outdoor beer stalls that fill al. Żołnierza Polskiego in summer, there are no real nighttime strolling areas in Szczecin, and most people aim for a particular bar rather than crawling from one to the other. Fortunately, there are loads of good **pubs** and **bars** in the main downtown area, with new ones opening up all the time – many of them also serve up good food.

Restaurants and cafés

Admirał ul. Monte Cassino 37 ☎091/434 2815. *The* place to go to for seafood, but on the expensive side.

Bombay ul. Partyzantów 1. Upmarket Indian restaurant a few steps south of the Brama Portowa, with exemplary service and a reasonably authentic menu, including some vegetarian dishes – although the spice level is on the bland side.

Café Galeria Mariacka. Stylish café-restaurant down a side street near the Brama Hołdu Pruskiego, with salads, sandwiches and a range of contemporary European mains. Also does breakfast from 10am.

Chata pl. Hołdu Pruskiego 8 ⊕www.chata.com.pl. Best place in town for traditional Polish food, offer-

ing roast duck, wild boar and pheasant alongside traditional porky standards. Lots of homely wooden furniture, and folksy paintings on the wall. More expensive than average but not prohibitively so. Deservedly popular with the foreign contingent.

Cukiernia Koch ul. Wojska Polskiego 4. Prime downtown venue for relaxing over a cup of coffee or pigging out on the decadent range of pastries and cakes. There's another branch at Wyzwolenia 14.

Duet, ul. Bogusława 1/2. Relaxing café with a wide choice of teas, cakes and ice creams.

Haga ul. Sienna 10. Dutch-style pancake restaurant with a good location opposite the old town hall, and excellent food. Over-lit modernist interior makes it an unatmospheric venue for a drawn-out evening repast.

Oh Keh ul. Piastow 1. The kind of place that can't decide whether it's a restaurant, or a bar that does food: smallish but satisfying range of Tex-Mex dishes, and wide choice of imported bottled beers.

Piramida ul. Niepodległości 2. Grill house with Middle Eastern theme: a frieze of larger-than-life ancient Egyptians on the rear wall sets the tone. Splash out on steaks, or opt for cheaper eat-in or take-out kebabs and *shawarma*.

Pod Muzami pl. Żołnierza Polskiego 2. Long-established restaurant serving up mid-priced European fare in a place that looks like an old-fashioned nightclub: a basement with mauve decor, mirror ball and dancefloor. DJs or show bands play golden oldies.

Rybarex ul. Obrońców Stalingradu 5a. Inexpensive fish bar with a wide and adventurous selection of dishes: ideal for fast lunchtime service. Closes at 7pm Mon–Fri, at 5pm on Sat. Closed Sun.

Virga Park Głębokie. Five kilometres northwest of the centre, just behind the terminus of trams #1 and #9: the ideal stopoff after an afternoon walking in the nearby woods of Park Głębokie. Solid and not-too-expensive veal-and-pork repertoire, in a cosy room decorated with kooky ceramics and glassware.

Bars

Brama Jazz Café pl. Hołdu Pruskiego 1. Chic, barrel-vaulted space situated right inside the Brama Hołdu Pruskiego, usually with art exhibits on the walls. Good choice of baguettes and salads if you're hungry. Frequent live jazz. Outdoor terrace in summer.

Café Prawda Wielka Odrzańska 20. Cool bar for cool people on the riverfront just behind the Old Town Hall. Minimalist decor, cutting-edge techno in the background, and a basement bar where DJs play at weekends.

Christopher Columbus Wały Chrobrego. Curving timber-and-glass pavilion on a leafy promenade, enjoying good views of the riverfront down below. Plenty of outdoor seating: a good place to spend a summer afternoon.

Hormon corner of pl. Odrodzenia and al. Piłsudskiego ⓦ www.hormon.szczecin.art.pl. Spacious bare-brick cellar welcoming a trendy cross-section of teens and twenty-somethings. DJs or live bands provide entertainment at the weekends, when there's an entrance fee.

Irish Pub Dublin ul. Kaszubska 57. Prime place for a relaxing drink immediately north of the Brama Portowa, with dark wood furnishings, mini-mal lighting, and unobtrusive music. Hearty meat dishes, and a good choice of salads on the menu.

Nautilus Pub ul. Jana z Kolna 7. Lively riverside pub with lots of outdoor seating, next to the Dworzec Morski. Turquoise colour scheme and odd bits of boat hanging from the ceiling help to hammer home the nautical theme. Extensive food menu.

Piano al. Piłsudskiego 28. Comfortable and atmospheric watering hole whose furnishings feature lots of rough wood and rope: it's a bit like being below decks in a sailing ship.

Rocker Club ul. Partyzantów 2. Large, pub-style basement bar a block south of the Brama Portowa, with middle-of-the-road rock music either on tape or performed by local cover bands. Entrance fee on gig nights.

Nightlife and entertainment

For **clubbing**, *Rzeczywistość*, al. Wojska Polskiego 20, is the main venue for mainstream techno events; while *Kubuś* north of the centre at ul. Chopina 55a (buses #51 and #78) is a raucous, friendly student club with an unself-consciously poppy range of music. *Trans*, southwest of the centre at al. Powstańców Wielkopolskich 20, is another student club, but with a much more eclectic programme of DJ events and gigs. Another place with regular live music is *Słowianin*, a municipally funded cultural centre just above the bus station on ul. Korzeniowskiego which acts as an umbrella for all kinds of alternative activities and indie gigs – you'll recognize it from the psychedelic portraits of the Beatles and other idols graffitied onto the outside walls.

The Filharmonia Szczecińska, pl. Armii Krajowey 1 (☎091/422 0589), has a regular programme of **classical music** concerts, while operas and operettas are performed in the opera house at ul. Korsarzy 34 (☎091/480 0340). Szczecin's main **theatre** is the Teatr Polski, ul. Swarożyca 3 (☎091/433 0090), although the Teatr Wspólczesny, Wały Chrobrego 3 (☎091/434 2451) offers a wider range of modern Polish drama. **Puppet shows** are held at the Teatr Lalek Pleciuga, ul. Kaszubska 9 (☎091/434 1002). You'll find a cluster of multiplex **cinemas** around the south end of al. Wojska Polskiego.

The Friday edition of *Gazeta Wyborcza* is the best source of **listings** information. **Annual events** include the Days of the Sea in June, which feature yacht races, parades, and performances of sea shanties; a contemporary painting festival in July; and a festival of Orthodox church music in November.

Listings

Airlines LOT, ul. Wyzwolenia 17 ☎091/433 5058.
Books and Newspapers English-language press at Empik, on the corner of al. Wojska Polskiego and pl. Zwycięstwa.
Cinemas Colosseum, ul. 5 Lipca; Delfin, ul. Piłsudskiego 40/42; Kosmos, al. Wojska Polskiego 8.
Ferries Polska Żegluga Baltycka, ul. Wyszynskiego 26 (☎091/488 0945, ⓦwww.pol-ferries.com) and Unity Line, pl. Rodła 8 (☎091/359 5654, ⓦwww.unityline.pl), sell tickets for services from Świnoujście to Denmark and Sweden.
Hospital Pomorski Akademii Medycznej, al. Unii Lubelskiej 1. Tram #1 or #9.
Internet access *Portal*, ul. Kaszubska 52, south off pl. Wycięstwa, entrance in the yard round the back of the building (daily 10am–midnight).
Left luggage At the train station (see p.661).
Pharmacy There's a 24hr Apteka at ul. Więckowskiego 12, north off pl. Wycęstwa.
Post Office Main office at ul. Bogurodzicy 1 (Mon–Fri 8am–8pm, Sat 9am–2pm).
Travel Agents Orbis, pl. Zwycięstwa 1 (☎091/434 4425), handles international plane and bus tickets. Interglobus, at the train station (☎091/485 0422), deal in bus tickets to Germany, Britain and other European destinations.

Stargard Szczeciński

Some 35km southeast of Szczecin, on the Bydgoszcz road, lies **STARGARD SZCZECIŃSKI**, the town which briefly became the capital of Pomerania during the seventeenth-century occupation of Szczecin by the Swedes. Situated on the River Ina, a tributary of the Odra, Stargard owed its early development to its position on the old trade routes to and from the Baltic. Nowadays primarily an industrial centre, it suffered severe damage in World War II, but a trio of spectacular medieval buildings survived. They're definitely worth seeing if you're passing through the area: once you have had a quick look around the Rynek however, Stargard's modern concrete heart is unlikely to detain you further.

The Stare Miasto

Arriving at the train station, or the bus station to its rear, it's just a few minutes' walk east down ul. Kardynała Wyszyńskiego to the **Stare Miasto**. This nestles behind fifteenth-century brick walls some four metres thick, of which substantial sections remain, including five towers and four gateways. The shady **Park Chrobrego** has been laid out as a promenade along the western side, containing the longest surviving portion of the ramparts. Following ul. Chrobrego downhill from here, you come to the River Ina, where down to the left stands the most impressive survivor of the fortification system, the **Brama Młyńska** (Mill Gate). This is a covered bridge under which boats could pass, protected by a mighty pair of battlemented octagonal towers topped with sharply pointed steeples.

The **Rynek**, which occupies an unusually off-centre location towards the southeastern end of the Stare Miasto, about five minutes' walk from the Mill Gate, has a number of impressive reconstructed burghers' houses. At the corner stands the renovated **town hall**, a plain Renaissance structure featuring a superbly curvaceous gable adorned with colourful terracotta tracery. Next to it is the **guard house**, whose open arcades and loggia suggest the Mediterranean rather than the Baltic. Together with the **Waga Miejska** (Weigh House) next door, it houses the local **museum** (Tues–Sun 10am–4pm; 4zł; free on Sun).

Next to the town hall stands the magnificent **Kościoł Mariacki** (Church of Our Lady), one of the most original and decorative examples of the brickwork Gothic style found in the Baltic lands, probably the work of Hinrich Brunsberg and commissioned around 1400. The two towers, with their glazed green and white ceramics, can be seen from all over the town: the southern one, topped with a fancy gable and flanked by a luscious coat of ivy, resembles a great tower-house; its higher northern counterpart is a truly bravura creation, topped by four chimney-like turrets and a great central octagon, itself crowned in the Baroque era with a two-storey copper lantern. As a fittingly small-scale contrast, the east end and the protruding octagonal chapel dedicated to the Virgin show off the decorative potential of carved brick. The interior was impressively repainted in the nineteenth century and features an earlier and quite over-the-top illusionist altarpiece.

With innumerable **trains** and **buses** heading back to Szczecin you shouldn't need to stay in Stargard. There are two conveniently central **hotel** options however: the simple *Staromiejski*, which offers unadorned rooms with shared facilities in a converted apartment building by the Mill Gate on ul. Spichrzowa 2 (℡092/577 2223; **❸**); and the nearby *Hotel PTTK*, ul. Kuśnierzy 5 (℡092/578 3191), which has en-suites (**❹**) or rooms with shared facilities (**❷**). The *Ratuszowa* in the Rynek's shopping centre is the most convenient **place to eat**, offering Polish standards in unassuming surroundings.

Travel details

Trains

Bydgoszcz to: Częstochowa (5 daily; 5hr); Gdańsk (hourly; 2hr); Kołobrzeg (8 daily; 4hr 30min); Kraków (3 daily; 7–8hr); Łódź Kaliska (11 daily; 3–4hr); Poznań (11 daily; 2–4hr); Szczecin (2–3 daily; 4–6hr); Toruń (hourly; 40min); Warsaw (6 daily; 4–5hr).

Gniezno to Bydgoszcz (10 daily; 50min); Gdynia (8 daily); Inowrocław (20 daily; 55min); Mogilno (20 daily; 30min); Poznań (20 daily; 45min–1hr 5min); Toruń (6 daily; 1hr 30min–2hr); Wrocław (6 daily).

Kalisz to: Białystok (1 daily; 8hr); Jelenia Góra (4 daily; 5hr–6hr 30min); Legnica (5 daily; 4–5hr); Leszno (3 daily; 2hr 50min); Lublin (3 daily; 7hr); Łódź (half-hourly; 1hr 30min–2hr); Poznań (6 daily; 3hr); Szczecin (2 daily; 6hr); Warsaw (11 daily; 3hr–4hr 30min); Wrocław (14 daily; 2hr–3hr 30min); Zielona Góra (3 daily; 4–5hr).

Kamień Pomorski to: Szczecin (3 daily; 2hr 30min).

Kołobrzeg to: Bydgoszcz (6 daily; 5hr); Gdańsk (3 daily; 4–5hr); Gryfice (5 daily; 1hr 20min); Koszalin (9 daily; 1hr); Poznań (4 daily; 5–6hr); Szczecin (1 daily; 4–5hr); Trzebiatow (5 daily; 40min); Warsaw (3 daily; 8–10hr).

Leszno to: Bydgoszcz (5 daily; 3hr 30min–4hr 30min); Kalisz (3 daily; 2hr 50min); Łódź (3 daily; 4hr); Poznań (half-hourly; 40min–1hr 10min); Wrocław (26 daily; 1hr 30min–2hr).

Lębork to: Łeba (2 daily; 35min).

Międzyzdroje to Szczecin (20 daily; 1hr 40min–2hr); Świnoujście (20 daily; 20–30min).

Poznań to: Białystok (1 daily; 10hr 30min; couchettes); Bydgoszcz (12 daily; 2hr–2hr 30 min); Częstochowa (8 daily; 4hr); Gdańsk (8 daily; 4hr); Gniezno (hourly; 55min); Inowrocław (12 daily; 1hr 50min); Jelenia Góra (5 daily; 5–6hr); Kalisz (6 daily; 3hr); Katowice (15 daily; 5–6hr); Kołobrzeg (5 daily; 5hr); Kraków (8 daily; 6hr 35min); Leszno (half-hourly; 1hr–1hr 30min); Łódź (7 daily; 4–5hr); Olsztyn (4 daily; 4hr 30min–6hr); Opole (9 daily; 3hr 30min–4hr 30min); Przemyśl (3 daily; 11–13hr; couchettes); Rzeszów (3 daily; 10–11hr; couchettes); Słupsk (5 daily; 5–6hr); Szczecin (18 daily; 3–4hr); Świnoujście (7 daily; 4–5hr); Toruń (8 daily; 2hr 30min–3hr); Warsaw (20 daily; 4–5hr); Wrocław (26 daily; 2hr–3hr 30min); Zakopane (2 daily; 11–13hr; couchettes); Zielona Góra (6 daily; 2hr 30min–3hr).

Słupsk to: Gdańsk (12 daily; 2–3hr); Kołobrzeg (Jul–Aug 6 daily, rest of year 2 daily; 2hr–2hr 30min); Koszalin (hourly; 1hr); Szczecin (9 daily; 3–4hr); Ustka (8 daily; 25min).

Świnoujście to: Kraków (2 daily; 12–13hr; couchettes); Poznań (7 daily; 4–5hr); Szczecin (18 daily; 2hr–2hr 30min); Warsaw (3 daily; 8–10hr, couchettes).

Szczecin to: Bydgoszcz (2 daily; 4–5hr); Gdańsk (5 daily; 5–6hr); Kamień Pomorski (3 daily; 2hr 30min); Kołobrzeg (1 daily; 4–5hr); Koszalin (6 daily; 3–4hr); Kraków (5 daily; 10–11hr); Łódź (3 daily; 6–7hr); Poznań (12 daily; 3–4hr); Słupsk (9 daily; 3–4hr); Świnoujście (20 daily; 2hr–2hr 30min); Warsaw (5 daily; 5–8hr; couchettes).

Szczecinek to: Chojnice (6 daily); Czaplinek (8 daily; 1hr); Kołobrzeg (6 daily; 2hr–2hr 30min); Poznań (6 daily; 4hr).

Żnin to Inowrocław (6 daily; 45min).

Buses

Bydgoszcz to: Chełmno (12 daily; 1hr); Chojnice (8 daily; 2hr); Gniezno (8 daily; 2hr 20min); Szczecinek (5 daily; 2hr 50min); Toruń (hourly; 50min); Żnin (8 daily; 1hr 15min).

Darłowo to: Kołobrzeg (3 daily; 2hr); Koszalin (10 daily; 1hr 5min); Słupsk (7 daily; 1hr 15min–2hr); Ustka (2 daily; 1hr).

Gdynia to: Łeba (July–Aug 4 daily; Sept–June 1 daily; 1hr 50min–2hr 30min); Międzyzdroje (2 daily; 7hr).

Gniezno to: Bydgoszcz (8 daily; 2hr 20min); Gąsawa (8 daily; 50min); Mogilno (6 daily; 50min); Trzemeszno (8 daily; 30min); Żnin (8 daily; 1hr 5min).

Kamień Pomorski to: Kołobrzeg (7 daily; 1hr 45min); Międzyzdroje (July–Aug 12 daily; Sept–June 9 daily; 1hr); Stargard Szczeciński (2 daily; 3hr); Szczecin (6 daily; 2hr 30min); Świnoujście (July–Aug 16 daily; Sept–June 9 daily; 1hr 20min); Wolin (12 daily; 40min).

Kołobrzeg to: Darłowo (3 daily; 2hr); Kamień Pomorski (7 daily; 1hr 45min); Koszalin (20 daily; 50min); Poznań (3 daily; 6hr); Trzebiatow (24 daily; 45–55min).

Koszalin to: Darłowo (10 daily; 1hr 5min); Kołobrzeg (20 daily; 50min); Mielno (every 30min; 20min); Szczecinek (10 daily; 2hr 10min); Unieście (every 30min; 25min).

Łeba to: Gdynia (July–Aug 4 daily, Sept–June 1 daily; 1hr 50min–2hr 30min); Lębork (12 daily; 30min); Rowy (Jul–Aug 2 daily; 1hr); Słupsk (6 daily; 1hr 50min); Ustka (Jul–Aug 2 daily; 1hr 15min).

Międzyzdroje to: Gdańsk (1 daily; 7hr 40min); Gdynia (2 daily; 7hr); Kamień Pomorski (July–Aug 12 daily; Sept–June 9 daily; 1hr); Szczecin (3 daily; 2hr 15min); Świnoujście (Jul–Aug 20 daily; Sept–June 12 daily; 20min).

Poznań to: Gołuchow (8 daily; 2hr 30min); Kalisz (8 daily; 3hr).

Słupsk to: Darłowo (7 daily; 1hr 15min–2hr); Łeba (6 daily; 1hr 50min); Koszalin (12 daily); Kołobrzeg (4 daily); Ustka (every 30min–hour; 30min).

Świnoujście to: Międzyzdroje (Jul–Aug 20 daily; Sept–June 12 daily; 20min); Szczecin (3 daily; 2hr 35min).

Szczecin to: Czaplinek (3 daily; 2hr 45min); Międzyzdroje (3 daily; 2hr 15min); Stargard Szczeciński (hourly; 50min); Świnoujście (3 daily; 2hr 35min); Szczecinek (Mon–Fri 3 daily; Sat 2 daily; Sun 1 daily; 3hr 40min).

Szczecinek to: Bydgoszcz (5 daily; 2hr 50min); Chojnice (2 daily; 2hr); Czaplinek (12 daily; 50min–1hr); Koszalin (10 daily; 2hr 10min); Szczecin (3 daily; 3hr 35min).

Ustka to: Darłowo (2 daily; 1hr); Koszalin (2 daily; 2hr 5min); Łeba (Jul–Aug 2 daily;); Słupsk (every 30min–hour; 30min).

Żnin to: Bydgoszcz (8 daily; 1hr 15min); Gąsawa (every 30min; 20min); Gniezno (8 daily; 1hr 5min); Inowrocław (8 daily; 30min).

International trains

Poznań to Berlin (6 daily; 4hr 30min).

Szczecin to Berlin (1 daily; 3hr 30min).

International ferries

Świnoujście to: Ahlbeck (Jun–Sept; 8 daily; 15min); Bansin (June–Sept; 3 daily; 25min); Copenhagen (5 weekly; 9hr); Heringsdorf (June–Sept; 3 daily; 20min); Malmö (1 daily; 10hr); Ystad (1 daily; 9hr).

contexts

contexts

CONTEXTS

History

No other European country has had so chequered a history as Poland. At its mightiest, it has been a huge commonwealth stretching deep into the Baltics, Russia and the Ukraine; at its nadir, it has been a nation that existed only as an ideal, its neighbours having on two occasions conspired to wipe it off the map. Yet, for all this, a distinctive Polish culture has survived and developed without interruption for more than a millennium.

The beginnings

The great plain that is present-day Poland, stretching from the River Odra (or Oder) in the west all the way to the Russian steppes, has been inhabited since the Stone Age. For thousands of years it was home to numerous tribes – some nomadic, others settlers – whose traces have made Poland a particularly fruitful land for archeologists. Lying beyond the frontiers of the Roman Empire, it did not sustain anything more socially advanced than a tribal culture until a relatively late date.

The exact period when this plain was first settled by Slav tribes is uncertain, but it may have been as late as the eighth century. Although diffuse, the various **Slav** groups shared a common culture – certainly to a far greater extent than is true of the Germanic tribes to the west – and the Polish language can be said to have existed before the Polish state.

It was the **Polonians** (the "people of the open fields"), based on the banks of the River Warta between Poznań and Gniezno, who were ultimately responsible for the forging of a recognizable nation, which thereafter bore their name. From the early ninth century, they were ruled by the **Piast** dynasty, whose early history is shrouded in legend but emerges into something more substantial with the beginnings of recorded history in the second half of the tenth century.

In 965, the Piast **Mieszko I** married the sister of the Duke of Bohemia and underwent public baptism, thus placing himself under the protection of the papacy. Mieszko's motives appear to have been political: Otto the Great, the Holy Roman Emperor, had extended Germany's border to the Odra and would have had little difficulty in justifying a push east against a pagan state. By 990, Mieszko had succeeded in uniting his tribal area, henceforth known as Wielkopolska (Great Poland), with that of the Vistulanian tribe, which took the name of Małopolska (Little Poland). Silesia, settled by yet another Slav tribe, became the third component of this embryonic Polish state.

Mieszko's policies were carried to their logical conclusion by his warrior son **Bolesław the Brave**. In 1000, the Emperor Otto III was dispatched by the pope to pay tribute to the relics of the Czech saint, Adalbert, which Bolesław had acquired. During his stay, the emperor crowned Bolesław with his own crown, thus renouncing German designs on Polish territory. Subsequently, Bolesław established control over Pomerania, Kujawy and Mazovia; he also gained and lost Bohemia and began Poland's own easterly drive, pushing as far as Kiev. The name "Poland" now came into general use, and its status as a fully fledged kingdom was underlined by Bolesław's decision to undergo a second coronation in 1022.

Piast Poland

By the middle of the eleventh century, Małopolska had become the centre of the nation's affairs and Kraków had replaced Gniezno as capital, owing to Wielkopolska's vulnerability to the expansionist Czechs and Germans. Political authority was in any case overshadowed by the power of the Church: when **Bishop Stanisław** of Kraków was murdered in 1079 on the orders of **Bolesław the Generous**, the clergy not only gained a national saint whose cult quickly spread, but also succeeded in dethroning the king.

In the early twelfth century, centralized monarchical power made a comeback under **Bolesław the Wrymouth**, who regained Pomerania – which had become an independent duchy – and repulsed German designs on Silesia. However, he undid his lifetime's work by his decision to divide his kingdom among his sons: for the rest of the century and beyond, Poland lacked central authority and was riven by feuds as successive members of the Piast dynasty jostled for control over the key provinces. Pomerania fell to Denmark, while Silesia began a long process of fragmentation, becoming increasingly Germanic.

In 1225 **Duke Konrad of Mazovia**, under threat from the heathen Prussians, Jacwingians and Lithuanians on his eastern border, invited the **Teutonic Knights**, a quasi-monastic German military order, to help him secure his frontiers. The knights duly based themselves in Chełmno, and by 1283 they had effectively eradicated the Prussians. Emerging as the principal military power in northern Europe, the knights built up a theocratic state defended by some of the most awesome castles ever built, ruthlessly turning on their former hosts in the process. They captured the great port of Gdańsk in 1308, renaming it Danzig and developing it into one of Europe's richest mercantile cities. At the same time, German peasants were encouraged to settle on the fertile agricultural land all along the Baltic. Poland was left cut off from the sea, with its trading routes severely weakened as a result.

If the Teutonic Knights brought nothing but disaster to the Polish nation, the effects of the **Tatar invasions** of 1241–42 were more mixed. Although the Poles were decisively defeated at the **Battle of Legnica**, the Tatars' crushing of the Kiev-based Russian empire paved the way for Polish expansion east into White and Red Ruthenia (the forerunners of Belarus and Ukraine), whose principalities were often linked to Poland by dynastic marriages. On the down side, the defeat spelt the beginning of the end for Silesia as part of Poland. It gradually split into eighteen tiny duchies under the control of Bohemia, then the most powerful part of the Holy Roman Empire.

It was only under the last Piast king, **Kazimierz the Great** (1333–70), that central political authority was firmly re-established in Poland. Kraków took on some aspects of its present appearance during his reign, being embellished with a series of magnificent buildings to substantiate its claim to be a great European capital. It was also made the seat of a university, the first in the country and before long one of the most prestigious on the continent. Kazimierz's achievements in domestic policy went far beyond the symbolic: he codified Poland's laws, created a unified administrative structure with a governor responsible for each province, and introduced a new silver currency.

With regard to Poland's frontiers, Kazimierz was a supreme pragmatist. He secured his borders with a line of stone castles and formally recognized Bohemia's control over **Silesia** in return for a renunciation of its claim to the Polish crown. More reluctantly, he accepted the existence of the independent state of the Teutonic Knights, even though that meant Poland was now land-locked. To compensate, he extended his territories east into **Red Ruthenia** and **Podolia**, which meant that, although the Catholic Church retained its prominent role, the country now had sizeable Eastern Orthodox and Armenian minorities.

Even more significant was Kazimierz's encouragement of **Jews**, who had been the victims of pogroms all over Europe, often being held responsible for the Black Death. A law of 1346 specifically protected them against persecution in Poland and was a major factor in Poland's centuries-long position as the home of the largest community of world Jewry.

The Jagiellonians

On Kazimierz's death, the crown passed to his nephew **Louis of Anjou**, king of Hungary, but this royal union was short-lived, as the Poles chose Louis' younger daughter **Jadwiga** to succeed him in 1384, whereas her sister ascended the Hungarian throne. This event was important for two reasons. First, it was an assertion of power on the part of the aristocracy and the beginnings of the move towards an elected monarchy. Second, it led soon afterwards to the most important and enduring alliance in Polish history – with Lithuania, whose grand duke, Jogaila (henceforth known to history by his Polish name, **Jagiełło**), married Jadwiga in 1386. Europe's last pagan nation, Lithuania, had resisted the Teutonic Knights and developed into an expansionist state which now stretched from its Baltic homeland all the way to the Crimea.

After Jadwiga's death in 1399, Jagiełło ruled the two nations alone for the next 45 years, founding the Jagiellonian dynasty – which was to remain in power until 1572 – with the offspring of his subsequent marriage. One of the first benefits of the union between the two countries was a military strength capable of taking the offensive against the Teutonic Knights, and at the **Battle of Grunwald** in 1410, the order was defeated, beginning its long and slow decline. A more decisive breakthrough came as a result of the **Thirteen Years' War** of 1454–66. By the **Treaty of Toruń**, the knights' territory was parti-tioned: Danzig became an independent city-state, run by a merchant class of predominantly German, Dutch and Flemish origins, but accepting the Polish king as its nominal overlord; the remainder of the knights' heartlands around the Wisła (Vistula) became subject to Poland under the name of Royal Prussia; and the order was left only with the eastern territory thereafter known as Ducal Prussia or East Prussia, where it established its new headquarters in the city of Königsberg.

Towards the end of the fifteenth century, Poland and Lithuania began to face new dangers from the east. First to threaten were the **Crimean Tatars**, whose menace prompted the creation of the first Polish standing army. A far more serious threat – one which endured for several hundred years – came from the **Muscovite tsars**, the self-styled protectors of the Orthodox faith who aimed to "liberate" the Ruthenian principalities and rebuild the Russian empire which had been destroyed by the Mongol Tatars. The Jagiellonians countered by building up their power in the west. The Bohemian crown was acquired by clever politicking in 1479 after the religious struggles of the Hussite Wars; that of Hungary followed in 1491. However, neither of these unions managed to last.

The Renaissance and Reformation

The spread of **Renaissance** ideas in Poland – greatly facilitated by the country's Church connections with Italy – was most visibly manifested in the large number of Italianate buildings constructed throughout the country, but science and learning also prospered under native Polish practitioners such as **Nicolaus Copernicus**.

This period saw a collective muscle-flexing exercise by the Polish nobility (*szlachta*). In 1493, the parliament, or **Sejm**, was established, gaining the sole right to enact legislation in 1505 and gradually making itself an important check on monarchical power.

The **Reformation** had a far greater impact on Poland than is often admitted by Catholic patriots. Its most telling manifestation came in 1525, with the final collapse of the Teutonic Order when the grand master, Albrecht von Hohenzollern, decided to accept the new Lutheran doctrines. Their state was converted into a secular duchy under the Polish crown but with full internal autonomy – an arrangement that was to be disastrous for Poland in the long term, but which removed any lingering military strength from the order. Lutheranism also took a strong hold in Danzig and the German-dominated cities of Royal Prussia, while the more radical Calvinism won many converts among the Lithuanian nobility. Poland also became home for a number of refugee sects: along with the acceptance already extended to the Jewish and Orthodox faiths, this added up to a degree of religious tolerance unparalleled elsewhere in Europe.

The Republic of Nobles

Lacking an heir, the last of the Jagiellonians, **Sigismund August**, spent his final years trying to forge an alliance strong enough to withstand the ever-growing might of Moscow. The result of his negotiations was the 1569 **Union of Lublin**, whereby Poland, Royal Prussia, Livonia (subsequently part of Latvia) and Lithuania were formally merged into a commonwealth. Although each part of the commonwealth retained certain autonomous privileges, it was to all intents and purposes a unified Polish state from now on, ruled over by an integrated, Polish-speaking nobility. In the same year the Sejm moved to Warsaw, a more central location for the capital of this new agglomeration; its capital status became official in 1596.

On the death of Sigismund August in 1572, the royal chancellor, **Jan Zamoyski**, presided over negotiations which led to the creation of the so-called **Republic of Nobles** – thenceforth kings were to be elected by an assembly of the entire nobility, from the great magnates down to holders of tiny impoverished estates. On the one hand this was a major democratic advance, in that it enfranchised about ten percent of the population, by far the largest proportion of voters in any European country; but on the other hand it marked a strengthening of a feudalistic social system. Capitalism, then developing in other European countries, evolved only in those cities with a strong German or Jewish **burgher** class (predominantly in Royal Prussia), which remained isolated from the main power structures of Polish society.

In 1573, the Frenchman **Henri Valois** was chosen as the first elected monarch, and, as was the case with all his successors, was forced to sign a document which reduced him to a managerial servant of the nobility. The nobles also insisted on their **Right of Resistance** – a licence to overthrow a king who had fallen from favour. The Sejm had to be convened at two-yearly intervals, while all royal taxes, declarations of war and foreign treaties were subject to ratification by the nobles.

Although candidates for the monarchy had to subscribe to Catholicism, the religious freedom that already existed was underpinned by the **Compact of Warsaw** of 1573, guaranteeing the constitutional equality of all religions. However, the Counter Reformation left only a few Protestant strongholds in Poland: a large section of the aristocracy was reconverted, while others who had recently switched from Orthodoxy to Calvinism were persuaded to change allegiance once more. The Orthodox Church was further weakened by the schism of 1596, leading to the creation of the Uniate Church, which recognized the authority of Rome. Thus Poland gradually became a fervently Catholic nation once more.

The Republic of Nobles achieved some of its most spectacular successes early on, particularly under the second elected king, the Transylvanian prince **Stefan Bathory**. Having carried out a thorough reform of the army, he waged a brilliant campaign against the Russians in 1579–82, neutralizing this particular threat to Poland's eastern borders for some time to come.

The Waza dynasty and its aftermath

The foreign policy of the next three elected monarchs, all members of the Swedish **Waza dynasty**, was less fortunate. **Sigismund August Waza**, the first of the trio, was a Catholic bigot who soon came into conflict with the almost exclusively Protestant population of his native land and was deposed from the Swedish throne in 1604. Though his ham-fistedness meant that Poland now had a new (and increasingly powerful) enemy, he continued as the Polish king for the next 28 years, having fought off a three-year-long internal rebellion.

In 1618, Ducal Prussia was inherited by the elector of Brandenburg, **John Sigismund von Hohenzollern**, who set about weakening Poland's hold on the Baltic seaboard. A couple of decades later, the Hohenzollerns inherited much of Pomerania as well, with another section being acquired by Sweden. Poland managed to remain neutral in the calamitous series of religious and dynastic conflicts known as the **Thirty Years' War**, from which Sweden emerged as Europe's leading military power.

The reign of the third of the Wazas, **Jan Kazimierz**, saw Poland's fortunes plummet. In 1648, the year of his election, the Cossacks revolted in the Ukraine, eventually allying themselves with the Russian army, which conquered eastern Poland as far as Lwów. This diversion inspired the Swedes to launch an invasion of their own, known in Polish history as the **Swedish Deluge** ("Potop"), and they soon took control of the remainder of the country. A heroic fightback was mounted, ending in stalemate in 1660 with the **Treaty of Oliwa**, in which Poland recovered its former territories except for Livonia. Three years earlier, the Hohenzollerns had wrested Ducal Prussia from the last vestiges of Polish control, merging it with their other territories to form the state of Brandenburg-Prussia (later shortened to Prussia).

As well as the territorial losses suffered, these wars had seen Poland's population reduced to four million, less than half its previous total. A further crucial development of this period had been the first use in 1652 of the **liberum veto**, whereby a single vote in the Sejm was enough to stall any piece of legislation. Once established, the practice soon became widespread in the protection of petty interests, and Poland found itself on the slippery slope towards ungovernability. This process was hastened when it was discovered that one dissenter was constitutionally empowered to object not only to any particular measure, but to dissolve the Sejm itself – and in the process repeal all the legislation it had passed. Meanwhile, the minor aristocracy gradually found themselves squeezed out of power, as a group of a hundred or so great magnates gradually established a stranglehold.

Jan Sobieski

Before repeated use of the liberum veto led to the final collapse of political authority, Poland had what was arguably its greatest moment of glory in international power politics – a consequence of the Ottoman Turks' attempt to advance from the Balkans into central Europe. They were eventually beaten back by the Poles, under the command of **Jan Sobieski**, at the **Battle of Chocim** (in southwestern Ukraine) in 1673 – as a reward for which Sobieski was elected king the following year. In 1683 he was responsible for the successful defence of Vienna, which marked the final repulse of the Turks from western Europe.

However, Poland was to pay a heavy price for the heroism of Sobieski, who had concentrated on the Turkish campaign to the exclusion of all other issues at home and abroad. His relief of Vienna exhausted Poland's military capacity while enabling Austria to recover as an imperial power; it also greatly helped the rise of the predatory state of Prussia, which he had intended to keep firmly in check. His neglect of domestic policy led to the liberum veto being used with impunity, while Poland and Lithuania grew apart as the nobility of the latter engaged in a civil war.

The decline of Poland

Known as "**Augustus the Strong**" owing to his fathering of over 300 children, Sobieski's successor, **Augustus Wettin**, was in fact a weak ruler, unable to shake off his debts to the Russians who had secured his election. In 1701, Friedrich III of Brandenburg-Prussia openly defied him by declaring Ducal Prussia's right to be regarded as a kingdom, having himself crowned in Königsberg. From then on, the Hohenzollerns plotted to link their territories by ousting Poland from the Baltic; in this they were aided by the acquisition of most of the rest of Pomerania in 1720. Augustus's lack of talent for power politics was even more evident in his dealings with Sweden, against whom he launched a war for control of Livonia. The conflict showed the calamitous decline of Poland's military standing, and the victorious Swedes deposed Augustus in 1704, securing the election of their own favoured candidate, **Stanisław Leszczyński**, in his place.

Augustus was reinstated in 1710, courtesy of the Russians, who effectively reduced Poland to the role of a client state in the process. The "**Silent Sejm**" of 1717, which guaranteed the existing constitution, marked the end of effective parliamentary life. The Russians never hesitated to impose their authority, cynically upholding the Republic of Nobles as a means of ensuring that the liberal ideals of the Age of Reason could never take root in Poland and that the country remained a buffer against the great powers of western Europe. When Leszczyński won the election to succeed Augustus the Strong in 1733, they intervened almost immediately to have him replaced by the deceased king's son, who proved to be an even more inept custodian of Polish interests than his father. Leszczyński was forced into exile, spending the last thirty years of his life as the duke of Lorraine.

In 1740, Frederick the Great launched the **Silesian Wars**, which ended in 1763 with Prussia in control of all but a small part of the province. As a result, Prussia gained control over such parts of Poland's foreign trade as were not subject to Russia. The long-cherished ambition to acquire Royal Prussia and thus achieve uninterrupted control over the southern coast of the Baltic was Frederick's next objective.

When the younger Augustus Wettin died in 1763, the Russians again intervened to ensure the election of **Stanisław-August Poniatowski**, the former lover of their empress, Catherine the Great. However, Poniatowski proved an unwilling stooge, even espousing the cause of reform. Russian support of the Orthodox minority in Poland led to a growth of Catholic-inspired nationalism, and by obstructing the most moderately liberal measures, Russian policy led to an outbreak of revolts. By sending armies to crush these, they endangered the delicate balance of power in Eastern Europe.

The Partitions

Russia's Polish policy was finally rendered impotent by the revolt of the **Confederacy of Bar** in 1768–72. A heavy-handed crackdown on these reformers would certainly have led to war with Prussia, probably in alliance with Austria; doing nothing would have allowed the Poles to reassert their national independence. As a compromise, the Russians decided to support a Prussian plan for the **Partition of Poland**. By a treaty of 1772, Poland lost almost thirty percent of its territory. White Ruthenia's eastern sectors were ceded to Russia, while Austria received Red Ruthenia plus Małopolska south of the Wisła – a province subsequently rechristened Galicia. The Prussians gained the smallest share of the carve-up in the form of most of Royal Prussia, but this was strategically and economically the most significant.

Stung by this, the Poles embarked on a radical programme of reform, including the partial emancipation of serfs and the encouragement of immigration from the three empires which had undertaken the Partition. In 1791, Poland was given the first codified **constitution** in Europe since classical antiquity and the second in the modern world, after the United States. It introduced the concept of a people's sovereignty, this time including the bourgeoisie, and adopted a separation of powers between executive, legislature and judiciary, with government by a cabinet responsible to the Sejm.

This was all too much for the Russians, who, buying off the Prussians with the promise of Danzig, invaded Poland. Despite a tenacious resistance under **Tadeusz Kościuszko**, erstwhile hero of the American War of Independence, the Poles were defeated the following year. By the **Second Partition** of 1793, the constitution was annulled; the Russians annexed the remaining parts of White and Red Ruthenia, with the Prussians gaining Wielkopolska, parts of Mazuria and Toruń in addition to the star prize of Danzig. This time the Austrians held back and missed out on the spoils.

In 1794, Kościuszko launched a national insurrection, achieving a stunning victory over the Russians at the **Battle of Racławice** with a militia largely composed of peasants armed with scythes. However, the rebellion was put down, Poniatowski forced to abdicate, and Poland wiped off the map by the **Third Partition** of 1795. This gave all lands east of the Bug and Niemen rivers to Russia, the remainder of Małopolska to Austria, and the rest of the country, including Warsaw, to Prussia. By an additional treaty of 1797, the partitioning powers agreed to abolish the very name of Poland.

Napoleon and the Congress of Vienna

Revolutionary France was naturally the country that Polish patriots looked to in their struggle to regain national independence, and Paris became the headquarters for a series of exiles and conspiratorial groups. Hopes eventually crystallized around **Napoleon Bonaparte**, who assumed power in 1799, but when three Polish legions were raised as part of the French army, Kościuszko declined to command them, regarding Napoleon as a megalomaniac who would use the Poles for his own ends.

Initially, these fears seemed unfounded: French victories over Prussia led to the creation of the **Duchy of Warsaw** in 1807 out of Polish territory annexed by the Prussians. Although no more than a buffer state, this seemed an important first step in the re-creation of Poland and encouraged the hitherto uncommitted **Józef Poniatowski**, nephew of the last king and one of the most brilliant military commanders of the day, to throw in his lot with the French dictator. As a result of his successes in Napoleon's Austrian campaign of 1809, part of Galicia was ceded to the Duchy of Warsaw.

Poniatowski again played a key role in the events of 1812, which Napoleon dubbed his "**Polish War**" and which restored the historic border of Poland-Lithuania with Russia. The failure of the advance on Moscow, leading to a humiliating retreat, was thus as disastrous for Poland as for France. Cornered by the Prussians and Russians near Leipzig, Poniatowski refused to surrender, preferring to lead his troops to a heroic, suicidal defeat. The choice faced by Poniatowski encapsulated the nation's hopeless plight, and his act of self-sacrifice was to serve as a potent symbol to Polish patriots for the rest of the century.

The **Congress of Vienna** of 1814–15, set up to organize post-Napoleonic Europe, decided against the re-establishment of an independent Poland, mainly because this was opposed by the Russians. Instead, the main part of the Duchy of Warsaw was renamed the **Congress Kingdom** and placed under the dominion of the Russian tsar. The Poznań area was detached to form the Grand Duchy of Posen, in reality no more than a dependency of Prussia. Austria was allowed to keep most of Galicia, which was governed from Lwów (renamed Lemberg). After much deliberation, it was decided to make Kraków a city-state and "symbolic capital" of the vanished nation.

The struggle against the Partitions

The most liberal part of the Russian Empire, the Congress Kingdom enjoyed a period of relative prosperity under the governorship of **Adam Czartoryski**, preserving its own parliament, administration, educational system and army. However, this cosy arrangement was disrupted by the arch-autocrat **Nicholas I**, who became tsar in 1825 and quickly imposed his policies on Poland. An attempted **insurrection** in November 1830, centred on a botched assassination of the tsar's brother, provoked a Russian invasion. Initially, the Polish army fared well, but it was handicapped by political divisions (notably over whether the serfs should be emancipated) and lack of foreign support, despite the supposed guarantees provided by the Vienna settlement. By the end of the following year, the Poles had been defeated; their constitution was suspended and a reign of repression began. These events led many to abandon all nationalist hopes: the first great wave of Polish **emigration**, principally to America, began soon after.

An attempted insurrection against the Austrians in 1846 also backfired, lead-ing to the end of Kraków's independence with its reincorporation into Galicia. This setback was a factor in Poland's failure to play an active role in the European-wide revolutions of 1848–49, though by this time the country's plight had attracted the sympathy of the emergent socialist movements. Karl Marx and Friedrich Engels went so far as to declare that Polish liberation should be the single most important immediate objective of the workers' movement. The last major uprising, against the Russians in 1863–64, attracted the support of Lithuanians and Galicians but was hopelessly limited by Poland's lack of a regular army. Its failure led to the abolition of the Congress Kingdom and its formal incorporation into Russia as the province of "Vistulaland". However, it was immediately followed by the **emancipation of the serfs**, granted on more favourable terms than in any other part of the tsarist empire – in order to cause maximum ill-feeling between the Polish nobility and peasantry.

Following the crushing of the 1863–64 rebellion, the **Russian sector** of Poland entered a period of quiet stability, with the abolition of internal tariffs opening up the vast Russian market to Polish goods. For the next half-centu-ry, Polish patriots, wherever they lived, were concerned less with trying to win independence than with keeping a distinctive culture alive. In this they were handicapped by the fact that this was an era of great empires, each with many subjugated minorities whose interests often conflicted: Poles found themselves variously up against the aspirations of Lithuanians, Ukrainians and Czechs. They had the greatest success in Galicia, because they were the second largest ethnic group in the Habsburg Empire, and because the Habsburgs had a more lax attitude towards the diversity of their subjects. The province was given powers of self-government and, although economically backward and ruled by a reactionary upper class, flourished once more as a centre of learning and the arts.

Altogether different was the situation in **Prussia**, the most efficiently repres-sive of the three partitioning powers. It had closely followed the British lead in forging a modern industrial society, and Poles made up a large percentage of the workforce in some of its technologically most advanced areas, notably the rich minefields of Upper Silesia. The Prussians, having ousted the Austrians from their centuries-long domination of German affairs, proceeded to exclude their rivals altogether from the united Germany they created by 1871, which they attempted to mould in their own Protestant and militaristic tradition.

For the Poles living under the Prussian yoke, the price to be paid for their relative prosperity was a severe clampdown on their culture, seen at its most extreme in the **Kulturkampf**, whose main aim was to crush the power of the Catholic Church, with a secondary intention of establishing the unchallenged supremacy of the German language in the new nation's educational system. It misfired badly in Poland, giving the clergy the opportunity to whip up support for their own fervently nationalistic brand of Catholicism.

Meanwhile, an upturn in political life came with the establishment, in response to internal pressure, of representative assemblies in Berlin, Vienna and St Petersburg. Towards the end of the century, this led to the formation of various new Polish **political parties** and movements, the most important of which were: the Polish Socialist Party (PPS), active mainly in the cities of Russian Poland; the Nationalist League, whose power base was in the peripheral provinces; the Peasant Movement of Galicia; and the Christian Democrats, a dominant force among the Silesian Catholics.

The resurrection of Poland

World War I smashed the might of the Russian, German and Austrian empires and allowed Poland to rise from the dead. Desperate to rally Poles to their cause, both alliances in the conflict made increasingly tempting offers: as early as August 1914 the Russians proposed a Poland with full rights of self-government, including language, religion and government, albeit one still ultimately subject to the tsar.

When the German and Austrian armies overran Russian-occupied Poland in 1916, they felt obliged to trump this offer, promising to set up a Polish kingdom once the war was over. The foundations of this were laid immediately, with the institution of an interim administration – known as the **Regency Council** – and the official restoration of the Polish language. Even though carried out for cynical reasons, these initial steps were of crucial importance to the relaunch of a fully independent Poland, a notion which had soon gained the support of the US President Woodrow Wilson and of the new Bolshevik government in Moscow.

Meanwhile, two bitter rivals had emerged as the leading contenders for leadership of the Polish nation. **Józef Piłsudski**, an impoverished noble from Lithuania and founding member of the PPS, had long championed a military solution to Poland's problems. During the war, his legions fought on behalf of the Germans, assuming that the defeat of the Russians would allow him to create the new Polish state on his own terms. In this, he favoured a return to the great tradition of ethnic and religious diversity of centuries past. **Roman Dmowski**, leader of the Nationalist League, represented the ambitions of the new middle class and had a vision of a purely Polish and staunchly Catholic future, in which the Jews would, as far as possible, be excluded. He opted to work for independence by exclusively political means, in the hope that victory over Germany would lead the Western allies to set up a Polish state under his leadership.

In the event, Piłsudski came out on top: the Germans, having held him in internment for well over a year, released him the day before the armistice of

November 11, 1918, allowing him to take command of the Regency Council. He was sworn in as head of state three days later. Dmowski had to accept the consolation prize of head delegate to the Paris Peace Conference, though his associate, the concert pianist **Ignacy Jan Paderewski**, became the country's first prime minister.

Poland redefined

The new Poland lacked a defined territory. Initially, it consisted of the German and Austrian zones of occupation, centred on Warsaw and Lublin, plus Western Galicia. Wielkopolska was added a month later, following a revolt against the German garrison in Poznań, but the precise frontiers were only established during the following three years on an ad hoc basis. Yet, though the Paris Conference played only a minor role in all this, it did take the key decision to give the country access to the sea by means of the **Polish Corridor**, a strip of land cut through the old Royal Prussia, which meant that East Prussia was left cut off from the rest of Germany. Despite intense lobbying, it was decided to exclude Danzig from the corridor, on the grounds that its population was overwhelmingly German; instead, it reverted to its former tradition as a city-state – an unsatisfactory compromise that was later to have tragic consequences.

The **Polish-Soviet War** of 1919–20 was the most significant of the conflicts that crucially determined the country's borders. Realizing that the Bolsheviks would want to spread their revolution to Poland and then to the industrialized West, Piłsudski aimed to create a grouping of independent nation-states stretching from Finland to Georgia to halt this new expansionist Russian empire. Taking advantage of the civil war between the Soviet "Reds" and the counter-revolutionary "Whites", his army marched deep into Belarus and the Ukraine. He was subsequently beaten back to Warsaw, but skilfully regrouped his forces to pull off a crushing victory and pursue the Russians eastwards, regaining a sizeable chunk of the old Polish-Lithuanian commonwealth's eastern territories in the process, an acquisition confirmed by the **Treaty of Riga** in 1921.

At the very end of the war, Piłsudski seized his home city of **Wilno** (Vilnius), which had a mixed Polish and Jewish population, but was claimed by the Lithuanians on the grounds that it had been their medieval capital. Other border issues were settled by plebiscites organized by the League of Nations, the new international body set up to resolve such matters. In the most significant of these, Germany and Poland competed for Upper Silesia. The Germans won, but the margin was so narrow that the League felt that the distribution of votes justified the partition of the province. Poland gained most of the Katowice conurbation, thus ensuring that the country gained a solid industrial base.

The interwar years

The fragility of the new state's political institutions became obvious when Piłsudski refused to stand in the 1922 presidential elections on the grounds that the office was insufficiently powerful. Worse, the victor, **Gabriel Narutowicz**, was hounded by the Nationalists for having won as a result of votes cast by "non-

Poles", and was assassinated soon afterwards. For the next few years, Poland was governed by a series of weak governments presiding over hyperinflation, feeble attempts at agrarian reform and a contemptuous army officer class.

In May 1926, Piłsudski staged a military coup, ushering in the so-called **Sanacja** regime, named after a slogan proposing a return to political "health". Piłsudski functioned as the state's commander-in-chief until his death in 1935, though he held no formal office after an initial two-year stint as prime minister. Parliamentary life continued, but opposition was emasculated by the creation of the so-called **Non-Party Bloc for Co-operation with the Government**, and disaffected groups were brought to heel by force if necessary.

Having a country led by **Stalin** on one frontier was bad enough; when **Hitler** seized power in Germany in 1933, Poland was a sitting target for two ruthless dictators, despite managing to sign ten-year nonaggression pacts with each. Hitler had always been open about his ambition of wiping Poland off the map again, regarding the Slavs as a race who were fit for no higher role than to be slaves of the Aryans. He also wanted to unite all ethnic Germans under his rule: a foreign policy objective that was quickly put into effect by his annexation of Austria in March 1938 and of parts of Czechoslovakia – with British and French connivance – in September of the same year. As Hitler's attentions turned towards Poland, his foreign minister Joachim von Ribbentrop and his Soviet counterpart Vyacheslav Molotov concluded the notorious **Nazi–Soviet Pact** in August 1939, which allowed either side to pursue any aggressive designs without the interference of the other. It also included a secret clause which agreed on a full partition of Poland along the lines of the Narew, Wisła and San rivers.

World War II

On September 1, 1939, Hitler invaded Poland, beginning by annexing the free city of Danzig, thereby precipitating **World War II**. The Poles fought with great courage, inflicting heavy casualties, but were numerically and technologically in a hopeless position. On September 17, the Soviets invaded the eastern part of the country, claiming the share-out agreed by the Nazi–Soviet Pact. The Allies, who had guaranteed to come to Poland's defence, initially failed to do so, and by the end of the first week in October the country had capitulated. A government-in-exile was established in London under **Władysław Sikorski**.

Millions of civilians – including virtually every Jew in Poland – were to be slaughtered in the Nazi **concentration camps** that were soon being set up in the occupied territory. And as this was going on, Soviet prisoners were being transported east to the **Gulag**, while wholesale murders of the potentially troublesome elements in Polish society were being carried out, such as the massacre of **Katyn**, where 4500 officers were shot.

Nazi control of western Poland entailed further territorial dismemberment. Some parts of the country were simply swallowed up by the Reich, with north-western districts forming part of the newly created Reichgau of Danzig-West Prussia, and west-central territories around Poznań being absorbed into the Warthegau. Everything else – Warsaw and Kraków included – was placed under a German-controlled administration known as the **Gouvernement Generale**, an ad hoc structure designed to exploit the economic and labour potential of Poland while the war lasted. Poles everywhere were subjected to dislocation and

hardship. Those living in the Warthegau were forced to emigrate to the Gouvernement Generale in an attempt to Germanize the province; while those in Danzig-West Prussia fared slightly better, and were allowed to stay where they were providing they adopted German names and passports.

The Nazi invasion of the Soviet Union in June 1941 prompted Stalin to make an alliance with Sikorski, ushering in a period of uneasy co-operation between

Soviet forces and the Polish resistance, which was led by the **Home Army** (AK). The Red Army's victory at Stalingrad in 1943 marked the beginning of the end for the Nazis, but it enabled Stalin to backtrack on promises made to the Polish government-in-exile. At the **Tehran Conference** in November he came to an arrangement with Britain and America with regard to future spheres of influence in Europe, making it almost inevitable that postwar Poland would be forced into the Soviet camp. He also insisted that the Soviet Union would retain the territories it had annexed in 1939. Allied support for this was obtained by reference to the current border's virtual coincidence with the so-called Curzon Line, which had been drawn up by a former British Foreign Secretary in 1920 in an unsuccessful attempt at mediation in the Polish–Soviet War.

During the **liberation of Poland** in 1944, any possibility of reasserting genuine Polish control depended on the outcome of the uprising in Warsaw against the Nazi occupiers. On July 31, with the Soviets poised on the outskirts of the city, the Home Army was forced to act. The Red Army lay in wait during the ensuing bloodbath. When the insurgents were finally defeated at the beginning of October, Hitler ordered that the city be razed before leaving the ruins to the Red Army. In early 1945, as the Soviets pushed on through Poland, the Nazis set up last-ditch strongholds in Silesia, but these were overrun by the time of the final armistice in April.

No country suffered so much from World War II as Poland. In all, around 25 percent of the population died, and the whole country lay devastated. Moreover, although the Allies had originally gone to war on its behalf, it found itself reduced in size and shifted west across the map of Europe by some 200 kilometres, with its western frontier fixed at the lines of the Odra and Nysa rivers. Stalin had in effect achieved his twin aims of moving his frontiers and his sphere of influence well to the west.

The losses in the east – including Lwów and Wilno, both great centres of Polish culture – were painful, and involved the transfer of millions of people across the country in the following two years. There were compensations, however: Pomerania and the industrially valuable Silesia were restored after a gap of some seven centuries; and the much-coveted city of Danzig, which had been detached since its seizure by the Teutonic Knights, was also returned – and, as Gdańsk, it was later to play a major role in postwar Polish history.

The rise of Polish communism

The Polish communists took power, not through popular revolution, as their Soviet counterparts had – nor even with significant public support, as the Czech communists had – but through the military and political dictate of an occupying force. Control was seized by the **ZPP** (Union of Polish Patriots), an organization formed by Stalin in 1943 from Polish exiles and Russian placemen with polonized names. As the Red Army drove the Germans west, the ZPP established a Committee for **National Liberation in Lublin**, under the leadership of **Bolesław Bierut**. This was to form the core of the Polish government over the next few years.

Political opposition was fragmented and ineffectual. From the government-in-exile, only a single prominent figure returned to Poland after 1945 – **Stanisław Mikołajczyk**, leader of the prewar Peasants' Party. He was to leave again in 1947, narrowly avoiding imprisonment.

The Polish communists and socialists who had remained in Poland during the war now regrouped. The communists, though suspicious of Moscow, joined the ZPP to form the **Polish Workers' Party** under general secretary **Władisław Gomułka**, as the socialists attempted to establish a separate party. Meanwhile, the Soviets ran the country as an outlying province, stripping factories of plant and materials, intimidating political opponents, and orchestrating the brutal suppression of a nationalist uprising in the western Ukraine by the Polish army, in what is referred to as the **Civil War** (1945–47).

The economic and political framework of Poland was sealed by the elections of 1947. The communists and socialists, allied as the **Democratic Bloc**, won a decisive victory over their remaining opponents through an extended campaign of political harassment and manipulation. After the forcible merger of the socialists and communists in 1948 as the **PZPR** (Polish United Workers' Party), it only remained for the external pressures of the emerging Cold War to lock Poland completely into the Soviet sphere of influence and the Soviet model of economic and political development.

The transformation of Poland

Polish history from 1947 to 1955 can only be understood against the backdrop of the developing **Cold War**. After the Berlin Blockade (1948), the formation of NATO (1949) and the rearmament of the German Federal Republic, the Soviet Union regarded a stable, communist Poland as an essential component of its defence. The realpolitik of Soviet foreign policy was not lost on the Polish communists, who, though subordinate in many areas, retained a degree of independence from Moscow. Thus, while foreign policy was determined by Moscow, and Poland joined the Warsaw Pact on its formation in 1955, some leeway remained in domestic policy. For example, First Secretary Gomułka, although deposed and arrested in 1951, was not executed, unlike other disgraced leaders in Eastern Europe. Nor were the purges of the Party and the suppression of civil opposition as savage as elsewhere.

Nonetheless, the new Constitution of 1952 enshrined the leading role of the **PZPR** in every aspect of Polish society, designating the country as the Polish People's Republic (PPR). Further, while the trappings of elections and a two-house parliament were retained, the other parties – the Democratic Party (SD) and the reconstituted Peasants' Party (ZSL) – were under the effective political control of the PZPR. Real power lay with the Politburo, Central Committee and the newly formed economic and administrative bureaucracies. Only the **Catholic Church**, although harassed and extensively monitored by the authorities, retained a degree of independence as a political and cultural organization – its defiance characterized by the primate, **Cardinal Wyszyński**, arrested in 1953 for "anti-state" activities and imprisoned for three years.

Nationalization continued throughout this period, accelerated through the first **Three Year Plan** (1947–50) and the first **Six Year Plan** (1950–56). Although the former retained some emphasis on the role of private ownership, the thrust of both was towards the collectivization of agriculture and the creation of a heavy industrial base. Collectivization proved impossible in the absence of the sort of force used by Stalin against the Kulaks: the programme slowed in the mid-1950s and was tacitly abandoned thereafter. Industrially the plans proved more successful: major iron and steel industries were established, mining extensively exploited in Silesia and an entire shipbuilding industry developed along the Baltic coast – most notably in Gdańsk. There were, inevitably, costs: standards of living remained almost static, food was scarce, work was long, hard and often dangerous, and unrestrained industrialization resulted in terrible pollution and despoilation of the land. Perhaps the most significant achievement of the period was the creation of an urban industrial working class for the first time in Polish history. Paradoxically, these very people proved to be the backbone of almost every political struggle against the Party in the following decades.

1956 – the Polish October

In Poland, as in Hungary, 1956 saw the first major political crisis of the communist era. Faction and dissension were already rife, with intellectuals calling for fundamental changes, splits within the Party leadership and increasing popular disenchantment with the excesses of Stalinism. In February 1956 **Khrushchev** made his famous "secret" speech to the Twentieth Congress of the Soviet Communist Party, denouncing Stalin and his crimes: for Bolesław Bierut, president and first secretary of the PZPR, as for other Eastern European leaders, the speech was a bombshell, unmasking the lie of the absolute correctness of Stalin's every act. Reform-minded members of the Party in Poland were the first to make copies available in the West, but for Bierut and the hardline leadership it was the end: Bierut died directly after the Congress, many suspecting that he had committed suicide.

Then in June, workers in Poznań took to the streets over working conditions and wages. The protest rapidly developed into a major confrontation with the authorities, and in the ensuing street battles with the army and security police up to eighty people were killed and many hundreds of others wounded. Initial government insistence that "imperialist agents" had instigated the troubles gave way to an admission that some of the workers' grievances were justified and that the Party would try to remedy them.

The Poznań riots further divided an alarmed and weakened Party. Hardliners pushed for Defence Minister General Rokossowski to take over the leadership, but it was **Gomułka**, with his earnest promises of reform, who carried the day. In October, the Party plenum elected Gomułka as the new leader, without consulting Moscow. An enraged Khrushchev flew to Warsaw to demand an explanation of this unprecedented flouting of the Kremlin's authority. East German, Czech and Soviet troops were mobilized along Poland's borders, in response to which Polish security forces prepared to defend the capital. Poland held its breath as Gomułka and Khrushchev engaged in heated debate over the crisis. In the end, Gomułka assured Khrushchev that Poland would remain a loyal ally and maintain the essentials of communist rule. Khrushchev returned to Moscow, Soviet troops withdrew, and four days later Gomułka addressed a huge crowd in Warsaw as a national hero. The **Soviet invasion of Hungary** to crush the national uprising there in early November 1956 provided a clear reminder to Poles of how close they had come to disaster.

The **Polish October**, as it came to be known, raised high hopes of a new order, and initially those hopes seemed justified. Censorship was relaxed, Cardinal Wyszyński was released and state harassment of the Church and control over the economy eased. A **cultural thaw** encouraged an explosion of creativity in art and theatre – much of it wildly experimental – and opened the doors to "decadent" Western preoccupations such as jazz and rock and roll. But the impetus for **political reform** quickly faded, and the 1960s saw a progressive return to centralized planning, a stagnant economy and sporadic attempts to reassert some measure of control over an increasingly disaffected populace.

1970–1979: from Gomułka to Gierek

The final days of the Gomułka years were marked by a contrast between triumph in foreign policy and the harsh imposition of economic constraint. Pursuing his policy of Ostpolitik, **Willy Brandt** – SPD chancellor of the German Federal Republic – visited Poland in December 1970 and laid to rest some of the perennial concerns of postwar Polish foreign policy. In signing the **Warsaw Treaty**, West Germany recognized Poland's current borders and opened full diplomatic relations. And in an emphatic symbolic gesture, Brandt knelt in penance at the monument to those killed in the Warsaw Ghetto Uprising.

A few days later, on December 12, huge food price rises were announced, provoking a simmering **discontent** that was to break out in strikes and demonstrations along the Baltic coast, centring on Gdańsk. When troops fired on demonstrators, killing many, the protests spread like wildfire, to the point of open insurrection (Gomułka's Defence Minister, a certain **Wojciech Jaruzelski**, was to be put on trial for the killings some twenty years later). A traumatized Central Committee met five days before Christmas, hurriedly bundling Gomułka into retirement and replacing him as first secretary with **Edward Gierek**, a member of the Party's reformist faction in the 1960s. Price rises were frozen and wage increases promised, but despite a Christmas calm, strikes broke out throughout January 1971, with demands for free trade unions and a free press accompanying the more usual economic demands. Peace was only restored when Gierek and Jaruzelski went to the Gdańsk shipyards by taxi to argue their case and admit their errors to the strikers.

The Gierek period marked out an alternative route to social stability. Given access to Western financial markets by Brandt's reconciliation, the Gierek government borrowed heavily throughout the **early 1970s**. Food became cheaper and more plentiful as internal subsidies were matched by purchases from the West and the Soviet Union. Standards of living rose and a wider range of consumer goods became more freely available. However, the international economic recession and oil crises of the mid-Seventies destroyed the Polish boom at a stroke. Debts became impossible to service, new loans harder to obtain, and it became apparent that earlier borrowing had been squandered in unsustainable rises in consumption or wasted in large-scale projects of limited economic value.

By **1976** the wheel had turned full circle with remarkable rapidity. The government announced food price rises of almost treble the magnitude of those proposed in the early Seventies. This time the ensuing strikes were firmly repressed and many activists imprisoned, and it is from this point that one can chart the emergence of the complex alliance between Polish workers, intellectuals and the Catholic Church. In response to the imprisonment of strikers, the KOR (Committee for the Defence of Workers) was formed. Comprising **dissident intellectuals**, it was to provide not only valuable publicity and support for the opposition through Western contacts, but also new channels of political communication through underground **samizdat** publications, plus a degree of strategic sophistication that the spontaneous uprisings had so far lacked.

But perhaps even more decisive was the election of **Karol Wojtyła**, archbishop of Kraków, as Pope John Paul II in 1978. A fierce opponent of the communist regime, he visited Poland in 1979 and was met by the greatest public gatherings that Poland had ever seen. For the Polish people he became a symbol of Polish cultural identity and international influence, and his visit provided a public demonstration of their potential power.

1980–1989: Solidarity

Gierek's announcement of 100-percent price rises on foodstuffs in July 1980 led to more strikes, centring on the **Gdańsk shipyards**. Attempts by the authorities to have a crane operator, Anna Walentynowicz, dismissed for political agitation intensified the unrest. Led by a shipyard electrician, **Lech Wałęsa**, the strikers occupied the yards and were joined by a hastily convened group of opposition intellectuals and activists, including future prime minister **Tadeusz Mazowiecki**. Together they formulated a series of demands – the so-called **Twenty-one Points** – that were to serve not only as the principal political concerns of the Polish opposition, but to provide an intellectual template for every other oppositional movement in Eastern Europe.

Demands for popular consultation over the economic crisis, the freeing of political prisoners, freedom of the press, the right to strike, free trade unions and televised Catholic Mass were drawn up along with demands for higher wages and an end to Party privileges. Yet the lessons of Hungary in 1956 and Czechoslovakia in 1968 had been learnt, and the opposition was careful to reiterate that they "intended neither to threaten the foundations of the Socialist Republic in our country, nor its position in international relations".

The Party caved in, after protracted negotiations, signing the historic **Gdańsk Agreements** in August 1980, after which free trade unions, covering over 75 percent of Poland's 12.5 million workforce, were formed across the country, under the name **Solidarność – Solidarity**. Gierek and his supporters were swept from office by the Party in September 1980, but the limits of Solidarity's power were signalled by an unscheduled Warsaw Pact meeting later in the year. Other Eastern European communist leaders perceptively argued that Solidarity's success would threaten not only their Polish counterparts' political futures, but their own as well. Accordingly, Soviet and Warsaw Pact units were mobilized along Poland's borders. The Poles closed ranks: the Party reaffirmed its Leninist purity, while Solidarity and the Church publicly emphasized their moderation.

Throughout 1981 deadlock ensued, while the economic crisis gathered pace. Solidarity, lacking any positive control over the economy, was only capable of bringing it to a halt, and repeatedly showed itself able to do so. **General Jaruzelski** took control of the Party in July 1981 and, in the face of threats of a general strike, continued to negotiate with Solidarity leaders, but refused to relinquish any power. A wave of strikes in late October 1981 were met by the imposition of **martial law** on December 12, 1981: occupations and strikes were broken up by troops, Solidarity was banned, civil liberties suspended and union leaders arrested. However, these measures solved nothing fundamental, and in the face of creative and determined resistance from the now underground Solidarity movement, still actively supported by large segments of the populace, martial law was lifted in the wake of Pope John Paul II's second visit to his home country in 1983.

The period 1984 to 1988 was marked by a final attempt by the Jaruzelski government to dig Poland out of its economic crisis. The country's debt had risen to an astronomical $39 billion, wages had slumped, and production was hampered by endemic labour unrest, the cutting edge of what throughout the 1980s remained Eastern Europe's most organized and broadly based opposition movement. In 1987, Jaruzelski submitted the government's programme of price rises and promised democratization to a referendum. The government lost, the real message of the vote being a rejection not merely of the programme but of the notion that the Party could lead Poland out of its crisis. As the Party's route lay blocked by popular disenchantment, the opposition's opened up after major strikes in May 1988.

Jaruzelski finally acknowledged defeat after a devastating second wave of strikes in August of that year and called for a "courageous turnaround" by the Party, accepting the need for talks with Solidarity and the prospect of real **power sharing** – an option of political capitulation probably only made possible by the election of Gorbachev as general secretary in the Kremlin.

1989–1990: the new Poland

The **round-table talks** ran from February to April 1989, the key demands being the absolute acceptance of the legal status of Solidarity, the establishment of an independent press and the promise of what were termed semi-free elections. Legalization of Solidarity was duly agreed, opposition newspapers were to be allowed to publish freely and all 100 seats of a reconstituted upper chamber, the Senate, were to be freely contested. In the lower house of parliament, the Sejm, 65 percent of seats were to be reserved for the PZPR and its allied parties, with the rest openly contested.

The communists suffered a humiliating and decisive defeat in the consequent elections held in July 1989, whereas Solidarity won almost every seat it contested. Thus while the numerical balance of the lower chamber remained with the PZPR, the unthinkable became possible – a Solidarity-led government. In the end, the parties which had previously been allied to the PZPR broke with their communist overlords and voted to establish the journalist **Tadeusz Mazowiecki** as prime minister in August 1989, installing the first non-communist government in Eastern Europe since World War II. Subsequently the PZPR rapidly disintegrated, voting to dissolve itself in January 1990 and then splitting into two notionally social democratic currents.

The tasks facing Poland's new government were formidable: economic dislocation, political volatility and a rapidly changing scene in the rest of Eastern Europe. For the most part, the government retained a high degree of support in the face of an austerity programme far stiffer than anything proposed under the communist regime.

President Wałęsa and the first free elections

Lech Wałęsa, long out of the main political arena, forced the pace in the presidential election of 1990, calling for the removal of Jaruzelski, a faster pace of reform and a concerted effort to remove the accumulated privileges of the senior Party men. Against him stood Prime Minister Mazowiecki and the previously unknown **Jan Tymiński**, a Canadian-Polish businessman employing free-market rhetoric and Western-style campaigning techniques. Although clearly in the lead in the first round of voting in December 1990, Wałęsa was required to face a second round against Tymiński. Mazowiecki, having finished a disappointing third, then resigned as prime minister, taking the whole government with him. Wałęsa won the second round comfortably.

In January 1991 Wałęsa appointed as prime minister **Jan Krzysztof Bielecki**, a leading intellectual force within Solidarity. This appointment was symptomatic of the country's changing political and social climate: a business-oriented liberal from Gdańsk, Bielecki represented the new technocratic elite already making rapid headway in the "new Poland". Significantly, Bielecki retained the services of Leszek Balcerowicz as finance minister, a move indicative of the new government's continuing commitment to economic reform.

Throughout 1991 the government's tough **austerity programme** continued to dominate the national agenda, with steadily rising prices, rocketing unemployment and continued government spending cuts making heavy inroads into the pockets and lives of ordinary Poles. Internationally, however, Balcerowicz's tough policies gained the support of the Western financial institutions, a fact that found practical expression in a landmark agreement with the **International Monetary Fund** (IMF) on a fifty-percent reduction of Poland's estimated 33 billion dollars of official debt.

Elections – the first fully free ones since World War II – were held in October 1991. The campaign itself was a fairly tame affair, the most notable feature being the spectacular array of parties (nearly seventy in total) taking part, including everyone from national minorities like the Silesian Germans to the joke Beer Lovers' Party as well as a bewildering array of old-time opposition factions, religiously based parties, nationalists and one-off independents.

However the hyper-proportional electoral system, with no percentage entry hurdles, was a recipe for **political factionalism** and fragmentation: 29 parties entered the new Sejm, the highest scorer, the Democratic Union (UD), gaining a meagre 14 percent of the alarmingly low (43 percent) turnout. Bielecki resigned, and after a two-month period of confusion, Wałęsa called on Jan Olszewski, a lawyer and prominent former dissident, to form a new coalition government.

The new centre-right **coalition government** put together by Olszewski adopted an increasingly aggressive stance on the subject of "decommunization", pushing for the unmasking of public figures suspected of having collaborated with the security services during the communist era. The question of **lustration** – the exclusion from public life of those had compromised themselves under the previous regime – has been a controversial issue in Poland ever since, largely because of the potentially huge number of people who could be targeted in this way. It cetainly cost Oleszewski his job, ousted by a no-confidence vote in June 1992. His successor was **Halina Suchocka** of the Democratic Union, Poland's first woman prime minister. Her new cabinet embraced everyone from the Catholic rightists of the Christian National Association (ZChN) to members of her own left-liberal-inclined UD, a consummate piece of political bargaining and compromise that surprised many observers accustomed to the infighting and posturing endemic to Polish political life.

The Suchocka government

In many respects, the **Suchocka government** proved surprisingly successful and cohesive. Domestically its most important achievement was a social pact over wage increases, concluded between government and trade unions (the remnants of declining Solidarity included) in autumn 1992 after a major wave of strikes – a temporary resolution, at least, of an issue that has regularly threatened to derail Poland's post-communist reform project. On the darker side, the increasingly powerful role of **the Church** in Poland's political and social life came well to the fore, above all in the heated national debate sparked by government moves to criminalize abortion, a move supported strongly by the Catholic Church but opposed by many within the country, as well as by Western institutions like the Council of Europe.

The issue that caused the Suchocka government most trouble was the vexed issue of large-scale **privatization**. The Sejm threw out a bill designed to privatize over six hundred major state enterprises in March 1993, and despite the adoption of a compromise solution a month later, the whole thing was derailed by Solidarity MPs, who led a vote of no-confidence over the government's handling of economic policy.

President Wałęsa called for fresh **elections** in September 1993, which resulted in victory for a coalition between the former-communist Democratic Left Alliance (SLD) and the Peasants' Party (PSL), which won nearly 36 percent of the vote. Due to the adoption of a new electoral system which specified that parties needed to win at least five percent of the vote in order to secure representation in the Sejm, scores of parties failed to make it into parliament, despite receiving a total of nearly 35 percent of the vote between them. While the scale of the SLD-PSL victory surprised many both inside and outside the country, few doubted that, as in several other post-communist countries, discontent with the decline in popular living standards stemming from the economic reform programmes lay behind the election of a reformed-communist-led government.

The conflict with Wałęsa

The new government, led by PSL leader **Waldemar Pawlak**, affirmed its commitment to continued market reforms, but at the same time pledged to do more to address its negative social effects. However, serious outbreaks of SLD-PSL infighting weakend Pawlak's authority, and a new wave of public-sector strikes initiated by a revived Solidarity in the early spring damaged the government's standing still further.

Ultimately, however, the conflict that most undermined Pawlak's government was a prolonged tussle with President Lech Wałęsa. Frustrated by the left's electoral success and what he (correctly) perceived to be his own increasing political marginalization, Lech Wałęsa engaged the government in a struggle over proposed constitutional amendments that aimed to transfer responsibility for ratifying government appointments from the president to the Sejm. In late 1994 Wałęsa demanded the resignation of Defence Minister Admiral Piotr Kołodziejcyk for his supposed failure to carry out reforms of the military. Pawlak caved in and dismissed Kołodziejcyk, though for the next two months the two were unable to agree on who should succeed the admiral.

Seemingly intent on confrontation, in January 1995 Wałęsa attacked new government legislation raising personal income tax levels and urged a campaign of popular tax refusal. In the end it was left to a constitutional tribunal to rule that the president had acted unconstitutionally, and Wałęsa was compelled to approve the new tax law. The showdown came in February, when Wałęsa demanded Pawlak's resignation and threatened to dissolve parliament if he was not replaced immediately. Incensed by this blatant display of presidential arrogance, the Sejm voted to initiate **impeachment proceedings** against Wałęsa should he make good his threats. A full-scale crisis was prevented by Pawlak's eventual decision to quit, to be replaced in early March by the SLD's Józef Oleksy, speaker of the Sejm, who proceeded to form a new government based on the same coalition of the SLD, PSL and independents.

The 1995 presidential elections

The focus of political attention now shifted towards the November presidential elections, the first since Wałęsa assumed office in 1990. Early opinion polls pointed to Wałęsa's deep unpopularity among an electorate weary of his seemingly unquenchable appetite for political intrigue. This time Wałęsa's main rival was the SLD's **Aleksander Kwaśniewski**, a polished, smooth-talking character who knew how to win over audiences potentially alienated by his ex-communist political record. By talking of Poland's future as a speedily modernizing country, Kwaśniewski won over the both the young and the emergent middle classes, who clearly preferred consensus and stability to the divisive leadership style of Lech Wałęsa.

Following a final campaign marked by some pretty gruesome mudslinging, Kwaśniewski carried the day by a slim margin of 52 percent to Wałęsa's 48, on a 68 percent voter turnout. A chastened Wałęsa made little effort to hide his anger at the result, and the final weeks of his presidency were marked by further characteristically intemperate outbursts, notably his refusal to attend Kwaśniewski's swearing-in ceremony just before Christmas.

There was one final act of vengeance left, however. Days before stepping down from office, the minister of internal affairs, Andrzej Milczanowski, a Wałęsa appointee, released documents reportedly suggesting that Prime Minister Józef Oleksy was suspected of having collaborated with the KGB. Despite Oleksy's persistent denials, political pressure forced him to resign in late January. The SLD's **Włodzimierz Cimoszewicz**, a lawyer and former justice minister, took over.

The post-Wałęsa era

The Cimoszewicz administration retained essential continuity with the Oleksy government, and the major storms appeared to have subsided. However the opposition remained deeply unhappy with the effective monopoly of state power now exercised by the former-communists, and 1996 witnessed strenuous attempts by the centre-right parties to unite against the "red threat" persistently trumpeted by Wałęsa. The fruit of their labours was the formation of the **Solidarity Election Action** (AWS) coalition in June 1996. This was a makeshift alliance of some 25 parties, comprising such heavyweights as Solidarity, the Centre Agreement (PC) and the Christian National Union (ZChN), alongside a string of minor rightist groupings. Despite its inherent fractiousness the AWS succeeded in making rapid political headway, not least due to the astute leadership of Solidarity chairman Marian Krzaklewski, who soon emerged as the coalition's leading public figure.

Meanwhile Cimoszewicz's government was putting in a mixed performance. Despite the inconclusive results of a national referendum on privatization held in February 1996 – fewer than the requisite 50 percent of the voting population bothered to participate – the government proceeded to enact legislation designed to facilitate further sell-offs of state enterprises.

The focus of national attention swung firmly away from politics following the severe **floods** that swept across southern Poland in July 1997. At least 55 people died, over 140,000 were evacuated from their homes and cities such as Wrocław suffered extensive damage, prompting the temporary adoption of emergency measures and an influx of aid from international sources. The government came in for severe criticism for what was perceived as a failure to act decisively in response to the floods, and in August it barely survived a PSL-sponsored vote of no confidence.

The late 1990s

The September 1997 **elections** handed victory to the Solidarity-led AWS with 34 percent of the vote, although they found themselves in need of **coalition partners** to be able to form a government. After lengthy negotiations a deal was finally hammered out with the centre-right Freedom Union (UW), led by Leszek Balcerowicz, and the smaller right-wing Movement for the Reconstruction of Poland (ROP). The new government was led by Jerzy Buzek, a veteran Solidarity activist from Silesia who owed his elevation to Krzaklewski's decision to forgo the premiership and concentrate instead on the presidential elections scheduled for 2000.

The new government's programme blended the old with the new. Some **policies**, such as emphasis on rapid integration into NATO and the EU, continuing privatization and reform of government structures suggested continuity with the previous government. Other components, notably Buzek's pledge to promote Christian beliefs and "family values" – a familiar leitmotif of conservative Catholic agitprop – indicated real differences in ideological background and approach. The ethical differences rapidly made themselves felt, too. In December the new Sejm accepted a **Constitutional Tribunal** ruling overturning the liberalized abortion law passed the previous year in the face of fierce Church criticism and widespread centre-right political opposition. The following month the Concordat with the Vatican regulating Church-State relations, whose formal ratification had hitherto been stalled by the SLD and its allies, was finally voted into law.

Despite the conciliatory, confidence-building style of Buzek himself, his government was ultimately hamstrung by the split between the Balcerowicz faction, which was committed to an ongoing programme of free market reforms and public spending cuts, and those closer to Solidarity, who favoured a less radical style. The economic growth of the mid-1990s was beginning to slow down by the end of the decade, unemployment was rising, and those in work were frustrated by having to put up with negligible pay rises from one year to the next. In these conditions, the SLD – guided by affable former Politburo member **Leszek Miller** – bounced back into popular affections.

The new millennium

The first test of the SLD's resurgent popularity came with the **presidential elections** of October 2000. The incumbent, SLD-supported **Aleksander Kwaśniewski**, had represented the interests of his country with much more dignity than his crotchety predecessor Lech Wałęsa, and possessed an accessible blokeishness that appealed strongly to the average Pole on the street. Most importantly, he was seen as a consensus-building national figurehead who resisted the temptation to interfere too much in day-to-day politics. Even Kwaśniewski's gaffes, such as appearing slightly the worse for drink at a ceremony commemorating the victims of the Katyn forest massacre, failed to dent his popularity.

Faced by such a formidable opponent, Kwaśniewski's main rival, the AWS's **Aleksander Krzaklewski**, didn't stand a chance. The only highlight of a lacklustre campaign was the AWS camp's decision to release a two-year-old piece of video footage which showed the president – who had just arrived at an official function by helicopter – encouraging an aide to kiss the ground, pope-style, in an attempt to raise a chuckle from the assembled dignatories. Most mainstream Poles were publicly critical of Kwaśniewski's crass behaviour, but privately found it all rather amusing – needless to say, the attempted slur backfired on the AWS.

Kwaśniewski's subsequent **landslide victory** left the AWS-led government in disarray. The unpopularity brought on the government by the radical economic reform espoused by the Freedom Union prompted many prominent right-wingers to defect to a new, more moderate, centre-right political grouping called the **Civic Platform**. Buzek's lame-duck government limped gamely on into 2001, but all kinds of unexpected things went wrong: a much-vaunted reform of the **state pension system** resulted in farce when the computer system intended to run it failed to function. Billions of złotys went unaccounted for, causing genuine distress and outrage among employees.

The death warrant of the AWS-led government was delivered by the very organization whose interests it had been formed to promote. In May 2001, **Solidarity** finally faced up to the dilemma which had been dogging its leaders throughout the previous decade: how could a movement which had been formed to defend workers' rights continue to participate in right-of-centre governments whose policies repeatedly conflicted with workers' interests? Desperate to retain the confidence of its core membership, Solidarity decided to withdraw from the AWS in order to concentrate on its role as a trade union.

Transfixed by visions of rats and sinking ships, a sorry-looking AWS mounted an unconvincing campaign for the **parliamentary elections** of September 2001. Profiting from government mistakes rather than presenting a radically different programme of its own, the SLD cruised effortlessly to victory, winning forty-five percent of the vote – although this was not enough to ensure an absolute majority in the Sejm. Both the AWS and the Freedom Union were wiped out entirely, failing to achieve the five percent of the vote necessary to win parliamentary representation, and were replaced by the Civic Platform as the main voice of right-of-centre Poland. The new administration, headed by Leszek Miller and including Włodzimierz Cimosziewicz as foreign minister, still needed parliamentary allies in order to ensure a workable majoriy in the Sejm, and opted for an unlikely coalition with **Samoobrana** (Self-Defence), a peasants'-rights party led by **Andrzej Lepper**, a maverick populist notorious for his controversial and often antidemocratic outbursts.

Fractured by political infighting, the political right in Poland may well take many years to reorganize itself into a credible force. However the policies it pioneered throughout the 1990s remain at the centre of Polish political life. Despite its communist past, the SLD has no choice but to remain committed to the triple strategy of loyalty to NATO, accession to the EU, and economic austerity at home. A disciplined party packed with pragmatists and suave careerists, the SLD may indeed prove more effective at achieving these goals than any of its predecessors in government.

Poland in the world

The twin goals of membership of NATO and the European Union have been the dominant themes of the country's foreign policy throughout the post-1989 period. Initially, **membership of NATO** appeared to be the least likely of the two ambitions to be realized, but throughout the 1990s the weak international position of Russia – the country most threatened by NATO enlargement – allowed Poland unexpected freedom of manoeuvre. In January 1994, Poland signed up to the organization's newly formed Partnership for Peace Agreement, and – together with the Czech Republic and Hungary – was officially invited to join the organization three years later, despite considerable Russian grumbling. All three were formally accepted into the alliance in March 1999, one month ahead of NATO's fiftieth anniversary celebrations.

Membership of NATO has been broadly popular with the Polish public, not least because it seems to offer the country cast-iron protection against any future resurgence of Russian power. Possessing by far the biggest army in east-central Europe, Poland already sees itself is a key player in the Western alliance – a role that it will undoubtedly seek to develop further in the future. However it remains to be seen whether the improvement in relations between NATO and Russia witnessed in the wake of the **September 11 attacks** will bring added security to the Poles, or merely increase their fears of being marginalized in a world run by powers greater than themselves.

Poland's drive to gain **membership of the EU** has been far from straightforward – not least because existing EU members themselves have been slow to agree on when, and how, future enlargement should take place. EU leaders met in Nice in November 2000 to lay down ground rules for the admittance of Poland and other candidates from eastern Europe, but the precise timetable for this remains unclear. The Polish government's official position – that Poland will be ready for EU membership by 2003 – is tempered by the realization that the organization itself may be far from ready to receive them.

The picture is further complicated by the existence of an **anti-EU lobby** in Poland itself – combining everyone from farmers worried about exposure to EU agricultural competition to a nationalist-religious coalition wary of the effects of secular Western values on the nation's moral fibre. Particular hostility is aroused by the fact that EU membership will allow foreigners to buy Polish land – a possibility that provokes much gnashing of teeth in the west and north of the country, where it is feared that German firms and individuals will snap up properties in areas where they once held sway. The Germans themselves are less than sanguine about Polish membership, fearing that this will prompt a mass migration of unemployed Poles seeking job opportunities west of the border. There are already suggestions that Polish accession to the EU will be accompanied by a whole raft of special conditions, including a seven-year moratorium on the free movement of Polish labour, and an even longer period during which other EU nationals will be banned from buying Polish property. With fewer than fifty percent of Poles expressing outright enthusiasm for EU membership, the SLD government will have to tread very carefully in its negotiations with Brussels if it hopes to keep the whole process on track.

From dissent to democracy

Poland's modern political transformation can be attributed to many factors, first and foremost the concerted efforts of the oppositional triad – unique in east-central Europe – of Church, workers (Solidarity) and intellectuals. In the following excerpt from her book, *Poles Apart* (see "Books", p.733), Irish journalist Jaqueline Hayden, a seasoned visitor to Poland, profiles Janek and Krystyna Lityńska, a couple whose lives exemplify in many respects the struggles that have given birth to a new political order in the country.

Reluctant Heroism

Krystyna Litynska is always quick to point out that she was interned for ten weeks after martial law while many of her friends served much lengthier sentences. But though the duration was shorter the long-term effects of that two-and-a-half month incarceration have remained with her to this day. The 13th of December 1981 was bitterly cold, like any other winter night in Warsaw. It was not a night to huddle in a freezing cold barracks with no blankets, running water, light or heating. Unwilling to glorify her experience, Krystyna is almost matter-of fact in her description of the tuberculosis she contracted as a result of her period in Olszynka women's prison. Perhaps one side-effect of the mass communication of the horrors of war and torture is to lessen the impact of the withdrawal of basic human rights, wrongful imprisonment and non-violent inhuman treatment. It appears to make even the victims unwilling to complain lest it appear that they seek to compare their treatment with that meted out by more gruesome or brutal regimes.

The night of 13 December is in the same category as the day of the assassination of President John F. Kennedy for most Poles. Everyone remembers where they were and what they were doing. Rumours of a possible Soviet intervention or military clamp-down had been circulating on and off since the strikes began in July and August 1980. Tensions rose and eased, hopes ran high, and then low. But in a country where people had grown used to living on a knife edge and where people had begun to regard Solidarity's power as real rather than symbolic the coup d'etat in the end came as a surprise.

By the autumn of 1981 Krystyna and Jan had moved from his mother's apartment into a rented flat in a housing scheme, built for army and police families, on the outskirts of Warsaw. Given their political activity, the occupation of most of their neighbours was a bit unfortunate. The couple's relations with the secret policeman who lived opposite were not good. They had deteriorated rapidly after he stuffed their keyhole with a sealing agent in protest at the caterwauling of their dog, Pilsudski (named after Marshall Josef Pilsudski, because of the dog's likeness to the controversial dictator).

In recalling the events of 13 December, Krystyna remembers hurling abuse at the secret policeman as she was led past him on her way to the police car.

In retrospect she felt she had been unfair because he had had the courage to confront the arresting officers. Neighbours told her that he had called after them: "So now you're taking women." Later she found out that his son-in-law, like many other sons and daughters, was active in Solidarity.

The first inkling Krystyna and Jan had that something was wrong was when they tried to telephone a cab for a friend who was about to leave their flat. It is not unusual, even today, to have difficulty phoning from one side of Warsaw to another. So, when neither his own nor a neighbour's phone upstairs worked, Jan left the building and went to another block in the hope that he could make the connection through a different exchange network. By the time it dawned on him that the phones were not working anywhere, the police were already knocking on their door. When Krystyna opened it, she was grabbed by the throat and pushed inside. In the struggle that ensued, she asked for a search warrant. "This time," the secret policeman told her politely, "we will not be searching your flat. Pack your bags, Pani Krystyna and wear something warm. It is very cold out tonight." It was only when he entered the hallway of his own apartment block that Jan saw what was happening. He ran upstairs to a third-floor flat where some friends lived, but before he was able to jump out of the window the door was bashed in by a crowbar and he was nabbed before he could escape. Hearing the shouting upstairs, Krystyna ran up to find Jan being pulled downstairs by the police, who were so angry about their near miss that they were going to take him away wearing only his shirt and slippers. In the mêlée that followed Krystyna remembers being pulled off Jan by a huge Ubek (policeman) with flat eyes. It was then that she broke her golden rule of not reacting or showing emotion in the presence of "them". So, as she shouted to all around her that they were "sons of bitches" she was nearly strangled by the furious Ubek with the funny eyes.

Eventually they packed their bags in peace. The police tried to remain polite and kept a decent distance while the neighbours hung around the landings so as to get a good view of the goings on. Both remember being more worried about what would happen to their dog than about what the night held in store for them. In a country where queueing for food was the most important daily chore, Jan remembers how awful it was to have to leave behind them a five-pound tin of ham which he had been given as a present. There was no bread in the house so they couldn't even make sandwiches.

Krystyna remembers how strange the atmosphere was when they arrived at Wilcza Street police station. The place was packed with all their friends who were greeting each other. "The whole thing was very dramatic but in a serious way." The first group she saw included a famous theatre director who was hand-cuffed to his son. At about five in the morning the first transport of women left the station en route to the women's prison. Looking out of the window of the police van, Krystyna saw a huge phalanx of ZOMO (riot police) guarding Solidarity headquarters in the centre of Warsaw. It is an image that is indelibly printed on her memory. Later, as the van moved towards the outskirts of the city, she watched as column after column of tanks slowly lumbered snake-like towards Warsaw, intent on strangling Solidarity's newly won freedom.

When her group reached the prison, it was obvious that the women guards did not know how to act towards the rather cosmopolitan and unusual batch of newly arrived prisoners. For a start they seemed unsure about how they should address them. "Pani" is a term of politeness not normally afforded the criminal community in Poland, so the guards avoided direct references alto-gether at first. The scene degenerated into complete farce when it was realized that one of Poland's most famous stage and film actresses, Halina Mikolajska, was about to be incarcerated in a barracks with no heat, window panes, water, blankets or light. As the revered actress was being led down to her new accommodation, an enthralled warder urged her to mind the icy steps as well as enthusiastically telling Ms Mikolajska how delighted she was to meet her and how much she admired her work. In fact the actress was made of stern stuff. Since she had first became involved in KOR [Workers Defence Committee – opposition group formed in 1976 to defend striking workers that grew to become the intellectual nucleus for Solidarity] in 1977, she had grown used to being the victim of the secret police's dirty tricks department. She often found the keyholes in her apartment blocked with glue or her car sprayed with noxious chemicals. And of course she had suffered the hardest cut of all; she had on occasion been banned from working. Krystyna remembers her with great affection as a "real", as opposed to a political, Catholic. She was a believer in the fullest sense.

Olszynka prison had until the previous March been used as a barracks. Since then it had been left vacant and ready but without running water, heating or light. When the women arrived, there was dust and dirt everywhere. There were seven bunk beds in their room. There were no blankets despite the freezing weather, so on that first night the women huddled under filthy mattresses to try and keep warm. It took three days for the prison authorities to organize a water supply. While Krystyna and her thirteen companions waited for the authorities to get organized, they gathered snow to flush the toilet which was behind a screen in the corner of the room. Slowly over the following days, lights and blankets began to appear...

Krystyna refers to Olszynka prison as the "health farm". When she was released, having been diagnosed as suffering from tuberculosis, she weighed forty-five kilos. "There was no temptation to eat. Breakfast and supper were the same, with bread, margarine and fifth-grade jam which came off a block. Dinner or lunch was either pea, cabbage or Scotch broth. Sometimes the barley stew had fragments of bacon in it with tufts of hair stuck to it. You can imagine the effect on our stomachs."

Given the nature of the women involved it is not surprising that many ex-internees shrug off the experience. Krystyna's cell adopted a non-conformist approach to dealing with the prison authorities. "If you rebel, you automatically acknowledge their power and authority. If you ignore them you win." So, roll-call, where the warders tried to impose some sort of military regime, became hysterical, with women shouting out that nobody had escaped that night. Like many other women who were interned or jailed, Krystyna's memories are of the camaraderie and spirit that developed between them. Perhaps it was fortuitous that Christmas followed less than two weeks after the mass arrests.

The Christmas holiday is celebrated with particular emphasis on tradition in Poland. After the fast on Christmas Eve, families start their festivities when the first star appears in the sky with a meal that has come from the sea, the woods, the mountains and the fields. Presents are then exchanged after midnight Mass. But on Christmas Eve 1981, Krystyna and her cell mates had what she describes as "a very elegant supper" of boiled eggs. Because it is regarded as a potential narcotic, prisoners are not normally allowed tea, but Regina Litynska, Krystyna's mother-in-law, had sent in a parcel with tea, sardines and a jumper. So, that night, the women celebrated by drinking, what the authorities judged to be a terribly dangerous brew.

Behaving and acting normally was the essence of the KOR philosophy of opposition. Celebrating Christmas as best they could was much more than an attempt to keep their spirits high: the women were defying, by ignoring it, the attempt to crush their spirit of opposition. They even managed to adorn their quarters with a symbolic Christmas tree. On one of the daily walks around the quadrangle one of the women found a spiky twig which she brought back with her. And with great ingenuity they used the cotton wool from some Red Cross sanitary towels and some silver paper from their cigarette allowance to decorate their little bare twig. Then by "recycling" the packaging and the tinsel paper from their Cosmos cigarettes, Krystyna's adept colleagues made themselves a set of playing cards using the rocket on the back as the standard image and drawing the faces of the cards on the front: "We drew our King to look like Jaruzelski. I remember that we played a lot of Patience."

On New Year's Eve, they were allowed a great privilege. The lights, which normally went out at nine o'clock were left on until ten. Krystyna remembers it as being a funny night: "We had three liqueur chocolates between seven of us. The next day was my birthday. I actually got presents. A Solidarity badge and ring were smuggled into the prison. I was delighted."

★★★★★

Coming out of jail or any confinement can be a frightening experience. It was doubly so in Krystyna's case. Her husband was still interned as were many of her friends. She knew she was blacklisted and would be unable to get a job. She was not even sure where she could stay: "Inside the rules were clear cut. Outside there was a world without a future for me." Because she was ill, the authorities decided not to transfer Krystyna to Rakowiecka Street prison...

For at least a year after her release, Krystyna had a large shadow on her lung and was registering a high temperature every day. She was receiving treatment for tuberculosis but nothing improved her condition. When after three months in Warsaw's respiratory hospital the doctors decided to operate for suspected cancer, Krystyna thought better of it and signed herself out. She is convinced that she took the right decision.

Krystyna Litynska is an able and talented psychologist. Now that Poland is free, she is much sought after and was at one point running two separate psychiatric facilities. But from the time of her association with Jan in 1975, she was blacklisted and found it very difficult to get work officially after the middle of 1976. Following her release in March 1982 it took her over a year to find what she calls a "real" job.

While she was imprisoned Krystyna received just two letters from Jan. One had been brought to her by a priest, while his mother brought another during a visit. Like so many other men grabbed in the Warsaw region that apocryphal night Jan was taken to Bialolenka internment camp just outside Warsaw. It was there that Krystyna headed as soon as she was able just after her own release. "It was a Garden of Eden," Jan recalls, by comparison with the conditions he experienced later in Warsaw's main prison on Rakowiecka Street. There is almost a nostalgia in his tone when he describes life at Bialolenka. Because it was an internment camp the Bialolenka regime was less harsh and provided reasonable library facilities for the inmates. Jan also remembers that the company was good. After all he was among friends. However, once he was served with a warrant charging him with treason in September 1982, Jan was moved to Rakowiecka Street, where life became much tougher on every level: "It was far worse to be taken from Bialolenka to Rakowiecka than to be taken there from freedom." For the first three months he was allowed no visits at all and received post only after seven weeks. Krystyna describes that period as "very nasty: the minimum sentence he faced was five years and because he was charged with treason, the possibility of a death sentence was on our minds all of the time."

For Krystyna, this period was one of constant organizing: "It takes so much time when a person is in jail. First, letters have to be written to arrange visits and parcels. In the political cases the letters have to go to the censor so that takes even more time. Then, because he was trying to study, I had to ask the prosecutor for permission to get certain books in for him. The men were allowed a three-kilo parcel per month, so I had to try and get the best, the most nutritious food, into the parcels. That was not easy with all the shortages at the time. He was having a lot of problems with his teeth so I wanted to get him vitamins."

With so many people interned or imprisoned, lots of families found themselves involved in organizing visits, petitions and food parcels. In fact it had the opposite effect to the one desired by the government. People who were not overtly political became part of a network of support activity which by its very nature had political overtones. So, while a clandestine underground was slowly establishing itself furtively, on the surface of Polish society, old ladies, brothers and sisters, fathers and mothers crossed backwards and forwards over cities and countryside carrying food parcels for the "boys" (and girls). In their attempt to destroy Solidarity, the government gave the union what it needed to become invincible. It gave Solidarity a common mythology.

But, of course, while history tends to look at the political dimension of important events, for those involved there is also the very human reality of their experience. "Jail cemented our relationship. It was Janek's fourth time inside. I felt he really needed me. I felt very responsible. When you're on the outside, you feel obliged to carry on no matter what's going on inside oneself. You've got to provide comfort. Letters become very important for both people. I wrote a sort of diary for Janek. Love returns when people are in jail. During the Solidarity period (before martial law) we were ships in the night. Then there was a terrible longing."

In June 1983, Jan's mother Regina went to see the Interior Minister, General Czeslaw Kiszczak, and asked him to allow her son to attend the First Holy Communion of his daughter, Basha: "Basically the cops just arrived at the door and there was Janek. There were guests everywhere. All those people, it was quite frightening for someone who had been locked up for so long in a tiny cell. I hardly got a chance to talk to him." Krystyna remembers that many of their friends were saying they would try and get him taken into hospital so that he would not have to go back to Rakowiecka. "But in the end Janek said that it was up to me to decide whether he should go underground or not."

When Jan disappeared there was a national alert and because his photograph was posted everywhere he had to change his appearance rapidly. That was actually quite difficult in his case. Jan Litynski is a slight man with very distinct mannerisms. When he speaks, the thoughts and words shoot like bullets from a rapid fire machine gun. He never sits still. And in those rare moments when he does he is either chain smoking or repeatedly wrapping a lock of hair around his finger. He is just like a sprint athlete straining on the blocks in the excruciating moment before the starter pistol relieves the tension.

But with the aid of a beard, new glasses and a suit, something he was not used to, Jan took on a new persona. He was one of the most successful members of Solidarity's underground. He was never re-arrested and remained in hiding until September 1986, when after a general amnesty for political prisoners, he came out, along with the other last remaining underground activist, to a joint press conference of both groups. Nearly five years of his life had passed by since martial law.

The underground period has had important political ramifications. By its very existence it maintained a beacon of hope but, more importantly, its existence eventually forced the one-party state into a position where it tacitly accepted the reality of an opposition.

For Krystyna Litynska it was not a very happy time: "I very rarely met Janek. It was too dangerous. I was watched all of the time. The arrangements to go and see him were incredible. I only saw him once or twice every three months or so. Before he came out I hadn't seen him for six months – that was from March to September. That was too long. Jail is much better for a relationship than being underground. When one's husband is in jail, you still get to see him, even if it is through a glass window. But then you feel useful. You're participating and involved. The underground had a bad effect on marriages. One learns to live independently. One develops one's own life, has one's own responsibilities. If a person didn't detach a little they'd become psychologically unwell."

Though Jan Litynski was a leader among activists, his road to internment and arrest after martial law mirrored that of many others of his generation. After he went to Warsaw University in 1983 to study mathematics he became involved in the numerous political discussion clubs that were springing up all over the place in those years. One of the most famous groups was organized by Adam Michnik (later an MP and editor of *Gazeta Wyborcza*). Its title translates into "the club of the searchers for diversity". Like Litynski, Michnik came from both a communist and Jewish background and was later to become one of the most important interpreters of modern Polish history. Ludka Wujec, now a prominent member of the Democratic Union, has known Jan since he was five: "I suppose up to about 1968, perhaps it was earlier, Janek wanted to fix socialism. The word 'reformer' is a difficult one here, but basically most of the people involved in those discussion groups were moving in the direction of rejecting the system. But at the time they perceived themselves as operating from within it." The authorities dubbed them the "March Commandos" and the name stuck.

Essentially the groups were made up in the main of young Marxist intellectuals who were struggling to find socialism in the so called socialist state in which they lived. Jan says that he was influenced by the thinking of October '56 when for a brief period it looked as if a brand of liberal communism was about to sweep through Poland. That short flirtation with workers' councils and talk of liberal economics ended with the rehabilitation of Gomulka, though it took a little while for Poles to realize that Wladyslaw Gomulka was not some great reforming knight in shining armour: "I felt that there had never been real socialism in Poland because socialism was based on a combination of workers ruling and democracy. During 1964 and 1965 both Jacek Kuron and Karol Modzelewski had been jailed for their writing. We were studying their texts and believed in a society based on a series of links between worker self governing enterprises and democracy. The problem was that we had no contact with the workers but we certainly had a lot of contact with the lack of democracy. It was a long process, but the more we read and the more we analyzed Marxism, the more we questioned why democracy had to be limited to the proletariat. When you're young and you've read right through Marxist literature and you've worked out that it doesn't hold water you try and work out where the mistake happened. Then eventually you realize that the big mistake was at the beginning."

Jan was twenty-two when he was arrested following the student protests after the closure of the play *Forefather's Eve* [performed in May 1968]. Sentenced to two and a half years for supposedly setting up an illegal organization, Jan ended up serving a year and a half in Rakowiecka Street prison. The jailings and persecution of both the Jews and the intelligentsia in 1968 galvanized a whole network of people, including lecturers and students, into an opposition stance. It also provided those who were jailed with credibility in the eyes of people who might otherwise have been dismissive of the activities of young hothead students. It would, however, be difficult to be dismissive of one-, two- and three-year jail sentences.

Jan is quite philosophical about his experience of imprisonment: "It either breaks you and your character is gone for the rest of your life or else you stick it out. I had known that I had taken a certain course in life. I knew what the risks were. I thought I was doing what was right and just. If your attitude is that going to jail is the end of your life, that you are losing today, tomorrow and the future, then you'll break down." Jan quotes the robust and colourful Jacek Kuron, who was no stranger to Polish jails: "When you get involved you have to measure your arse up to the accused's bench. If you think it fits, continue."

From that point on, there was no doubt that Jan Litynski's posterior measured up. "It is important to understand that what the government engaged in during 1968 was one of the nastiest campaigns against the Jews and against the intelligentsia in the history of Poland." As someone who was a member of both groups, Jan was now clearly identified as being opposed to "them". Because he had been kicked out of the university in March, Jan had been unable to sit the exams in June. When he was released in 1969 he found work as a barman and as a metal grinder as well as working at a shoe factory. Eventually he was able to get a job more commensurate with his skills at a computer centre where he worked as a programmer.

Jan never thought of leaving Poland, but many others did. Those who stayed found that the base of opposition within which they operated was broadening. From the outside it looked as if two extremes had joined forces. In reality as long as there was just one foe there was little to separate the aims of the Catholic intellectuals who began to cooperate with the Marxist and former Marxist dissidents whose characters had been moulded by the '68 experience. It would, however, be the late seventies before this new rainbow coalition of thinkers was able to put its theories of worker support and stimulation into practice. In the meantime the martyred workers in Gdansk, bloodied but victorious after their opposition to the Christmas 1970 food price increases, were creating their own mythology of heroic resistance. And though the intellectuals played no role in Gdansk, it was, combined with the events of '68, the end for many of any residual belief that the system was reformable.

Looking back at the sequence of events one could be forgiven for thinking that the Party almost connived in the making of the opposition. In its proposed changes to the Constitution in 1975, the Party attempted to have its leading role and the special relationship with the Soviet Union formally enshrined. The move resulted in a series of protests against the changes... And so when, in June 1976, Edward Gierek decided that the Polish economy could not sustain the food price freeze any longer, the workers once again resisted. This time however they did not have to fight alone.

Krystyna remembers the night the massive food hikes were announced very clearly. "It was hot and Midsummer's Eve and ... many people were having parties. The windows were open, so we could hear all the radios. The prime minister was making a speech announcing the huge increases. It was very dramatic because they'd been frozen for so long. There had been gossip, but it was a shock. The next day the protests began at the Ursus factory. A big crowd marched off to the nearby railway lines and dug up the sleepers. It stopped the Paris–Moscow express. A wave of strikes followed. At Radom workers set fire to the local party headquarters. After that it spread all over the country. The government reacted with incredible brutality. There were murders and terrible beatings. Workers were literally terrified. Many were made to run through a 'path of good health'. That was two lines of truncheon-wielding cops. In Radom it was particularly bad. There was incredible terror there. People were being thrown out of their jobs under paragraph 52, which allowed the authorities to sack a worker who was absent without leave." What would later be known as an intervention committee then became active on an ad hoc basis. In the beginning its activities were unstructured: "It was all very spontaneous. It was an effort to help those who'd been imprisoned. Their families were normally very afraid and didn't know what to do. Often they were even afraid to come forward when help was offered. Basically we started going to the places where there'd been trouble, to places where people had been sacked or beaten up and we tried to help. Janek went to Radom very early on. He gathered information about what was going on and tried to help get people out of jail. Then after there was a series of suspicious deaths at militia stations, he began writing articles based on the information he had gathered." Ludka Wujec was with a group of intellectuals who attended the trials of those charged with offences after Ursus: "When we saw how helpless the families were, how frightened they were, we just spontaneously approached them and raised money, there and then in the corridor at the court. There were no leaders at Ursus. These people had been picked out of the crowd for punishment. They were entitled to a state appointed defence lawyer, but we got our own lawyers to help on a voluntary basis. It was the beginning of an organized network of help. We learned a lot from the workers we met. We heard a lot about arrests, sackings and all kinds of illegal procedures."

Very shortly after the protests Jan, along with several other activists, began publishing an information bulletin detailing what was happening, where, and to whom. That "Information Bulletin" was probably the first of the literally hundreds of dirty grey sheets that would play a vital role in counteracting the government's disinformation activities. That the pen is mightier than the sword is a truism but if it had ever required verification the period following Radom and Ursus which culminated in Solidarity's victory in August 1980 would surely be proof enough.

As the contacts were made and the truth was outed it became clear that spontaneous help was not enough. It needed an umbrella under which to operate. And so, in September, a diverse group of intellectuals got together calling themselves, at first, the Workers' Defence Committee (later, the Social Self-Defence Committee). Well known and respected economists, writers, lecturers, former communists and former pre-war socialists headed the list of KOR's members in the hope that they would afford protection to the less well known activists who were working at the grassroots level to help the workers. However, it would soon become clear that no amount of moral authority would keep Adam Michnik, Jacek Kuron, Jan Litynski or indeed many other young KOR activists out of jail.

Krystyna remembers 1977 as a tragic year but Jan points out that it was also the year of KOR's first success: "First of all Janek was sacked from his job at the computer centre in February. So from then on, I was trying to earn a living for both of us. It was not easy because I was blacklisted as well. On 12 March my mother died. On 14 May a student activist, Stanislaw Pyjas, was killed in a militia station in Cracow. They said he fell down the stairs, but they killed him.

Then on the 19th, Janek was arrested. I think about fourteen other KOR members were arrested at the same time. From then on the searches at the flat were regular. They (the secret police) would often follow me. They'd walk just a couple of metres behind me." But as Jan emphasizes, the year was not all bleak. On 22 July, Independence Day, the government announced an amnesty and thus avoided the embarrassment of a series of trials of martyrs.

Within a month of his release Jan was busy establishing Robotnik which played a key role in fostering self-organization among workers. Over the next few years he travelled all over Poland gathering information, giving information and forging contacts between the intellectuals and the rank-and-file factory workers. He was particularly involved in the mining towns of Silesia and was later to be one of Walbrzych's first freely elected members of parliament.

★★★★★

Meeting Jan and Krystyna Litynski was a milestone in my life. The meeting made me do what young people often don't have time to do. It made me stop and think. I had arrived at Warsaw's somewhat undistinguished airport on an afternoon in late July 1980. In my notebook I had what turned out to be a fairly comprehensive list of KOR's most famous members. That, as I remember, was about the height of my organization. Having got through the agony and fear of being identified as a journalist travelling on a visitor's visa, I was delighted at having crossed the first hurdle. Being a bit of a prude I was somewhat put out when I was informed at the student hostel where I was to stay that because they were full I would have to share the room with three men. There were not even curtains between the beds. In my confused expectations of the trip I had anticipated all sorts of cloak and dagger scenarios straight out of Freddie Forsyth. But none of his anti-heroes had to undress underneath a blanket. Having mumbled my goodbyes to my new Swedish room-mates I set off to find the great and famous Jacek Kuron. Needless to say KOR's ebullient guru was not at home. In his place I found an intense young German who announced himself to be in the middle of a major thesis on Polish dissidence. This young man, sensing that I was in a bit of a muddle, suggested that I go over and see Jan Litynski. More importantly, he added that I should meet his wife Krystyna, who spoke English...

That first evening, I sat on the bed-cum-settee in the corner of the sitting room on Wyzwolenia Street, sipping lemon tea and explaining who I was, and why I had come. Amid the constant interruption of the telephone and door bell I listened as Krystyna told me about the series of strikes which were breaking out all over Poland. As the hours passed I listened as she both received and passed on information about strikes, plans and meetings. By the time Jan returned to the flat, she had already promised me that I could travel with him wherever he went. What is more, she would not hear of me staying at the hostel. The offer of a corner on her floor was more wonderful than the promise of a four-poster bed. I was bowled over by their kindness. Over the next couple of weeks I travelled with Janek to the mining towns of Silesia for meetings with workers who were trying to set up alternative trade union structures, and to places like Cracow for secret meetings between intellectual activists and workers from the Nowa Huta steel works which is nearby. In Warsaw I was secretly introduced to worker leader Zbigniew Bujak in a safe flat. He was constantly on the move that July and August as the arrest and harassment of activists increased and the tension heightened. On and off over the period I became conscious of the presence of shadows when I moved around with Jan.

In the days immediately before and of course after the Gdansk strike the secret police presence became frightening. For the Litynskis, it was part of their normal life experience. I am not ashamed to say that I was terrified...

What impressed me about Jan and Krystyna was the knowledge that they had never thought of leaving Poland. In a Western country this couple would have had a secure income and a good lifestyle. In Poland they lived with Jan's mother in a cramped flat. Though enormously talented they had difficulty getting suitable work because of their politics. When Krystyna did get a job, it was at a clinic two hours away from her home. And after all of that travelling she had to queue for basic food stuffs like countless other Polish women. Both were regularly harassed and intimidated. Their home was repeatedly searched. Jan, was by then, very familiar with conditions in Polish jails. But never once had I heard them proffer information about their personal troubles and hardships. They certainly never moaned. Talking to them I realized that they were firmly focused on their political goals. Years later, when I talked to them about martial law, about jail and about the underground years, their attitude was still the same. Incredibly they simply weren't bitter.

Jan's attitude to "them" (the Party) has more than likely kept him sane through many difficult experiences: "I don't feel any bitterness. Why should I? All my life I've been a vulture on them. As a totality I can't tolerate them but I've rarely had a personal feeling of hate to an individual." Jan explains that there was not any big decision to become political: "Being a dissident is about the choice of a certain style of life. It does require courage but that was not a problem for me."

Krystyna was twenty-five when she met Janek in 1974: "I was bookish, but not sheltered. My family was too big and too poor for any of us to be sheltered. My sisters, my brothers, we saw how hard our parents worked. They fought hard for our existence. I met Janek at an important time in my life when I was deciding what I should do with myself. I was working out what I wanted from life. He stepped out of a different world. All his friends had been together since '68. I began to hear about anti-Semitism, about people who were leaving the country or had left. I began to meet people who were names from another world. I began to open my eyes and see and understand things completely differently."

I remember being struck by how difficult it was to categorize Jan and Krystyna's politics. And, as I've mentioned earlier, that was a problem the whole world faced when Solidarity failed to fit into a neatly defined pigeonhole. In The Captive Mind, Czeslaw Milosz highlights the unreality of many western Marxists who refused, even at the height of Stalinism, to acknowledge that in practice the Marxist model was not working out in Eastern Europe. Jan and Krystyna were well used to meeting ardent young communists from the United States, Germany or Britain who had to perform mental cart-wheels in order to retain their belief following a visit to Poland.

Unlike many people in the west who took a political stand on places like Poland, Cambodia or Angola, politics was not an abstract, idealistic or doctrinaire thing for them. They were living the reality of Utopian socialism but were far too intelligent to think that its political opposite alone was the cure for Poland's ills. In a sense then it was impossible to politically define Jan and Krystyna and many people like them, because politics, as defined in terms of right and left did not come into the frame in pre-1989 Poland. For Krystyna, like Janek, the dissident road is a question of choice: "If you looked at Radom, at Ursus and at what happened to people there. If you looked at their suffering and at how people lived, if you come from a poor family yourself and know how difficult life can be, and then if you look at 'them', at the secret police and think of the obscenities they whisper in your ear, you have to turn. It is not a political thing, it is basically about human sensitivity. Things are either right or wrong. It starts as a moral thing but then one's actions become political. You've no choice."

By 1978, Krystyna was well and truly aware of the consequences of her choice. She remembers that in one week their flat was searched twice: "There was one day – a very important day for me. In many ways it was a milestone. The police arrived at about five-thirty or six in the morning. I was on the afternoon shift at the clinic which was outside of Warsaw. The job was very important to me, I really wanted to get there. Normally the men who searched were very polite. There were four or five of them this time. They searched our tiny flat for hours. I had just had a tooth removed and I was still bleeding. The police were drunk and unpleasant. I was nervous and upset. The older man, the one in charge of the search, agreed in the end to let me go to work. So he drove me to where I got the works' bus and waited until I'd got on. It is very hard to explain how I felt. Nobody would have understood my feelings. What could I have said had I not been able to get to work. With the secret police shadowing me, I felt as if I was in a ghetto. I was alone. It was so different after the strikes, after Solidarity and martial law. In 1982 people would have understood if I'd explained what had happened. But in 1978, if I'd said anything, people would have been too frightened to help me."

While it might have been the Pope who began the breakdown of the sense of individual isolation in Polish society, and though it was Solidarnosc that gave birth to the individual's sense of power within a mass movement, it was "they", the Party, with the introduction of martial law, who generalized the dissident experience. It was not a simple case of creating martyrs and heroes. Solidarity at its height had ten million members. That was nearly a third of the total population. By resorting to martial law in order to deal with a situation it felt it could no longer control, the Party declared war on a huge section of Polish society. In doing so it turned dissidence into a mass movement. Jan Litynski sees 13 December as "a farce. Everything had been said and done, everything had changed and they were returning to their old ways." And what for? Over the next five years the Polish economy continued to deteriorate while the Party exercised power for power's sake. Eventually with the threat of economic collapse looming, the Party chose to recognize the existence of an opposition, by offering to share responsibility if not power. Jaruzelski's coup d'etat was eventually brought down by the sterility of the power it sought to maintain.

In "the new reality", as Krystyna likes to call post-communist Poland, she has been busy working both in the field of psychiatric care as well as working for various academic institutions. Jan is an MP and chaired the important Parliamentary Commission on Social Policy until the return of the post-communist coalition government in September 1993. Both are acutely aware of the range of complex problems Poland now faces: "In socialist countries in the past, there was secret police and harassment but there was also a funny sense of safety. Big Daddy was always there to look after you. With no official unemployment, people were always sure of being paid. Now everyone has to be his own Big Daddy. Today the enemy is gone and people aren't sure who the new enemy is. As a nation we're having to learn how to deal with different political views and to learn political language. People are having to learn how to relate to people that they disagree with politically. There are so many new questions and problems. In the past there was just one ideology. One was either for it or against it. Now we're trying to find out what we meant when we said that we wanted a 'civil society'. What does it mean? It is not just the economy that has to be built. We have to establish new health, education and social security structures. We have to decide what kind of political model we want to operate in Poland. Should we have a strong President? Should parliament play the role it has been playing since the first elections?"

But whatever the problems, Krystyna is sure that she now lives in a real world where people are responsible for themselves: "Life is much safer in one way, but in another way people here are very afraid of the future. Now everything depends on oneself. For me personally things are better. We have more money. It is good to have a husband who is bringing in a salary. I'm not the only one responsible anymore. We have our own flat. It is not big, but we're not living with my mother-in-law. But the best thing of all is the knowledge that I can walk down the street and not be afraid of the secret police. I'm not afraid of searches anymore and of course it is like being in paradise to read a free press."

In 1991 President Lech Walesa gave a speech to the European Parliament in which he virtually told the West that it had a moral obligation to financially support Poland because it had rid itself of its communist manacles. So what?, was the response from Western business interests who would have preferred to hear what Walesa had to say about the progress the country was making in completing the transformation of the economy. Jan Litynski feels that people find it difficult to move on and respond to the rapidly changing world in which the whole of Eastern Europe finds itself: "People here saw communism as a sort of cancer. They thought that if you operated and removed it, that afterwards, everything would be okay." Lech Walesa knows full well that the battle was only beginning when the communists fell, but in continuing the rhetoric, albeit abroad, of looking for adulation and support simply for removing communism, he is copperfastening a false expectation that the changes will be rapid and painless. Another side effect of seeing the future through the eyes of the past is to inhibit political development and growth.

Jan is no longer comfortable being described as a dissident. He wants to leave that old battle behind him and start building "the new reality". For him that means many things, including the view that anticommunist witch-hunting is divisive, and a diversion from real political progress. But it is not just the communist past that should be jettisoned according to this view. Jan knows that hankering after Solidarity's halcyon days is perverting the development of parliamentary democracy: "Of course we all grew out of a movement of protest. But things are more complex now and some of us have moved on." The split within Solidarity was a painful one. Jan now acknowledges that thinking that the union would remain undivided was probably naive. He now thinks that it was also wishful thinking to hope that post-communist political activity would develop through a social movement. He is critical of the role of the various Solidarity offshoots which entered parliament: "In the past the workers and of course, Solidarity, were to the forefront in the call for change. Now they're a very conservative force. They're now the biggest obstacle on the road to change." At the heart of what Jan is saying is the view that the political game must be played within parliament, that the players must move in from the streets. "It is more pleasant to be in a mass movement, to be without responsibility, than to have to deal with reality. Fighting for power isn't nice but it is real."

It is somewhat ironic that the political party which is loudest in its opposition to what it regards as the diversionary rhetoric of decommunization is the one whose most prominent members were almost martyred by the Party. Jan Litynski belongs to the secular and liberal end of the Democratic Union, born out of the grouping which supported Poland's first non-communist premier, Tadeusz Mazowiecki, when he ran against Lech Walesa for the Presidency. In crude terms, that battle was waged between populist and sober politics: "The party was created, it evolved around the defence of the liberal changes that were introduced by Tadeusz Mazowiecki's first government. In simple terms we backed Balcerowicz [Leszek Balcerowicz, deputy premier and architect of the first economic reform plan]. The best way to characterize the Democratic Union is to say that it has a sober way of thinking. We're not populist. We believe in a step by step evolutionary approach to the economy. We don't believe in short cuts or miracles. There is no getting away from hardship during the short term. We believe that the flow of money within the economy has to be strictly controlled. Otherwise inflation is inevitable. On the other hand, many of us would be Keynesian if the conditions existed." In other words Jan's wing of the party believes in a capitalist market economy with a "human face".

With many of the most famous names from KOR and the Young Poland Movement now involved in UD, it is largely a party of the intelligentsia. It is going after the middle class voter, a category that up until recently did not exist in Poland. The old school of secular dissidents generally looked West rather than East for inspiration. Today UD supports membership of the European Community and shies away from nationalist or xenophobic rhetoric.

★★★★★

I visited Poland during the first, partially free, elections in 1989. This was how I began one newspaper article: "There are two gold leaf invitations pinned to the kitchen door of the Litynski flat on Filtrowa Street. One invites 'Mr Jan Litynski MP and Mrs Litynski' to meet the American Ambassador, while the other is from the Indian Embassy. This would not be unusual were it not for the fact that, as a dissident and founder of Solidarity, Jan Litynski spent the years between 1981 and 1986 either in jail or in hiding." The invitation contrasted starkly with the dark days of martial law when Krystyna had fashioned a Christmas tree from a fallen twig and the cotton wool from a sanitary towel. The Litynskis had come in from the cold.

"Reluctant Heroism" is reprinted by permission of Irish Academic Press, Dublin.

Polish music

Traditional music in Poland isn't exactly a widespread living tradition. The country has Westernized rapidly and the memory of communist fakelore has tainted people's interest in the genuine article. But in certain pockets, Poland boasts some of the most distinctive sounds in Europe, and the experience of a *górale* (highland) wedding – fired by furious fiddling, grounded by a sawing cello and supercharged with vodka – is unforgettable. Simon Broughton, editor of *Songlines* magazine, outlines the background and highlights some of the new developments.

Roots and development

In Poland, as elsewhere in eastern Europe, an interest in folklore emerged in the nineteenth century, allied to aspirations for national independence – folk music and politics in the region often have symbiotic links. The pioneering collector of songs and dances from all over the country was **Oskar Kolberg** (1814–90). His principal interest was in song, and it's thought that during the nineteenth century instrumental music was fairly primitive with dramatic developments occurring only in the last one hundred and fifty years or so. From the early years of this century gramophone recordings were made, and by 1939 substantial archives had been amassed in Poznań and Warsaw. Both collections were completely destroyed during **World War II** and scholarly collecting had to begin anew in 1945. The wartime annihilation and shifting of ethnic minorities in Poland also severely disrupted the continuity of folk traditions. The postwar communist regimes throughout eastern Europe endorsed folk culture as far as it could be portrayed as a cheerful espousal of healthy peasant labour, but each regime adopted a different approach. What survives today is sometimes in spite of, but largely a result of, those policies. At one extreme, Bulgaria strongly encouraged amateur grass-roots music; on the other, Czechoslovakia effectively sanitized its folk music to irrelevance. Poland adopted something close to the Czech approach, but allowing enough slack for a few local bands to keep some genuine traditions going.

The official face of Poland's folk culture was presented by professional folk troupes – most famously the **Mazowsze** and **Śląsk ensembles** – who gave (and still give) highly arranged and polished virtuoso performances: middle-of-the-road massed strings and highly choreographed twirls, whoops and foot stamping. The repertoire was basically core Polish with, perhaps, a slight regional emphasis (the Mazowsze territory is around Warsaw, the Śląsk around Wrocław), but the overall effect was homogenization rather than local identity. The groups were regularly featured on radio and TV and they had their audience. Smaller, more specialized groups, like Słowianki in Kraków, were also supported and kept closer to the roots, but for the most part the real stuff withered away as the image of folk music became tarnished by the bland official ensembles.

Polish dances

Thanks to Chopin, the **mazurka** and **polonaise** (*polonez*) of central Poland are probably the best-known dance forms and are at the core of the folk repertoire. Both are in triple time with the polonaise generally slower and more stately than the mazurka. In fact there are really three types of mazurka, the slower *kujawiak*, medium tempo *mazur* and faster *oberek*. The polonaise is particularly associated with the more ceremonial and solemn moments of a wedding party. It was taken up by the aristocracy from a slow walking dance (*chodzony*), given a French name identifying it as a dance of Polish origin and then filtered back down to the lower classes. In addition to the triple-time dances of central Poland, there are also some characteristic five-beat dances in the northeastern areas of Mazury, Kurpie and Podlasie.

As you move south, somewhere between Warsaw and Kraków, there is a transitional area where the triple-time dances of central Poland give way to the duple-time dances of the south like the **krakowiak** and **polka**. Generally speaking the music of central Poland is more restrained and sentimental than that of the south, which is wilder and more full-blooded. The *krakowiak* is named after the city of Kraków and the polka is claimed by both the Poles and the Bohemians as their own, although it was in Bohemia that it became most widely known. Of course, all these dances are not confined to their native areas, but many have become staples across the country and abroad. **Weddings** are the main occasion for traditional music, but in an agrarian country where barely eight percent of the land was collectivized, important annual events like the **harvest festival** (*dozynki*) have persisted as well.

Folk music today

Today, with the notable exception of the Tatra region and a few other pockets, traditional music has virtually ceased to function as a living tradition and has been banished to regional **folk festivals**. Several of these are very good indeed, with the Kazimierz Festival at the end of June foremost amongst them (see box overleaf). But the best way to hear this music is at the sort of occasion it was designed for – a **wedding** (*wesele*), for instance, where lively tunes are punched out by ad hoc groups comprising (nowadays) clarinet, saxophone, accordion, keyboard and drums. At country weddings there is often a set of traditional dances played for the older people, even when the rest of the music is modern. In the rural areas people tend to be hospitable and welcoming and, once you've shown a keen interest, an invitation is often extended. Typically, the areas where the music has survived tend to be the remoter regions on the fringes – Kurpie and Podlasie in the northeast, around Rzeszów in the southeast (where the *cimbały* – hammer dulcimer – is popular in the local bands), and the Podhale and highland regions in the Tatras along the southern border. But this isn't the whole story.

It's always worth contacting the Polish National Tourist Office (see p.28) in your home country for confirmation of the events and dates listed below: they can often provide an extensive run-down of annual festivals and cultural events. If you can navigate your way through Polish websites, then both www.independent.pl and www.etno.terra.pl carry festival dates and line-ups.

Bielsk Podlaski Festiwal Kultury Ukraińskiej na Podlasiu (Festival of Ukrainian Culture in Podlasie). Traditional music and dances from Ukrainian communities on both sides of the border. Held during late October in venues in both Bielsk Podlaski and nearby Białystok. Contact the Bielski Dom Kultury, ul. 3. Maja 2, 17-100 Bielsk Podlaski (Ⓦhttp://republika.pl/podlaska-jesien).

Giżycko Mazovia Folk Festival. Traditional Polish music held in late July with a Mazovian bias, performed in an outdoor amphitheatre in Giżycko's Boyen Fortress. Contact: Giżycko Centrum Kultury, ul. Konarskiego 8, 11-500 Giżycko (Ⓣ087/428 1637, Ⓔgck@webmedia.pl).

Gorzów Wielkopolski Romane Dywesa (Festival of Gypsy Music). Out by the German border 120km west of Poznań, held in early July. Contact Stowarzyszenie Twórców i Przyciól Kultury Cygańskiej, ul. Łokietka 28/4a, 66-400 Gorzów Wielkopolski (Ⓣ095/722 5582; or try the municipal website Ⓦwww.gorzow.pl).

Kazimierz Dolny The Festival of Folk Bands and Singers (last weekend in June) is Poland's biggest traditional music festival. Contact Wojewódzki Dom Kultury, ul. Dolna Panny Marii 3, 20-010 Lublin (Ⓣ081/532 4207, Ⓕ532 3775).

Kraków Festival of Jewish Music & Culture. A well-established event held late every June. Draws top-line international kletzmer acts as well as local bands. Contact the Centrum Informacji Kulturalnej (Cultural Information Centre), ul. św. Jana 2, 31-100 Kraków Ⓣ012/421 7787, Ⓦwww.karnet.krakow.2000 or Ⓦwww.krakow.2000.pl; or the Jewish Cultural Centre, ul. Meiselsa 17, 31-100 Kraków Ⓣ012/430 6452.

Kraków Rozstaje Festival. Traditional music in early September, from Małopolska as well as Poland's central European neighbours. Contact the Centrum Informacji Kulturalnej (see above; Ⓦwww.krakow2000.pl/rozstaje).

Krotoszyn Folk Festival. World music from Cuba to the Carpathians, in a small town midway between Poznań and Wrocław, held in late July. Contact Krotoszyński Ośrodek Kultury, ul. 56 Pułku Piechoty Wlkp. 18, 63-700 Krotoszyn (Ⓣ062/725 4278, Ⓔkokrot@poczta.onet.pl).

Lublin Mikołajke (St Nicholas' Festival). Held in early December, traditional Polish music festival that mixes serious ethnological intent with good hedonistic fun. Organized by the same people who run contemporary folk band Orkiestra św. Mikołaja. Contact Orkiestra św. Mikołaja, Chata Żaka, ul. Radziszewskiego 16, 20-

Podhale music

Podhale, the district around Zakopane, is home to the **górale** (highland) people and has the most vibrant musical tradition in the country. It has been one of Poland's most popular resort areas for years and is in no way remote or isolated. The Podhale musicians are familiar with music from all over the country and beyond, but choose to play in their own way. This sophisticated approach is part of a pride in Podhale identity which probably dates from the late nineteenth century when several notable artists and intellectuals (including the composer **Karol Szymanowski**, see p.506) settled in Zakopane and enthused about the music and culture. Music, fiddlers and dancing brigands are as essen-

031 Lublin (☎081/533 3201; ⊕www.mikolaje.lublin.pl).

Nowy Sącz Festiwal w Krajobrazie (Festival in the Landscape). A coming together of both ethnic and experimental electronic acts in mid-July, with concerts usually taking place in an open-air amphitheatre in the town park. Contact Galeria Stary Dom, ul. Pijarska 13, 33-300 Nowy Sącz (☎018/444 1699).

Ostrów Wielkopolski Folk Festival. Eclectic late-August bash offering everything from authentic Polish roots music to dub reggae. Ostrów is a middle-of-nowhere town just southwest of Kalisz (see p.624), and accessible from either Poznań or Wrocław by train. Contact Folk Fest, ul. Mickiewicza 26, 46-320 Praszka (⊕www.otofolkfest.prv.pl).

Rzeszów Festiwal Polonijnych Zespołów Folklorystycznych (World Festival of Polonia Folklore). A triennial international bash bringing together music and dance ensembles from the worldwide Polish diaspora. Next due in July 2002 and 2005. Contact Wspólnota Polska, Krakowskie Przedmieście 64, 00-071 Warsaw; ☎022/635 0440, ⊕www.wspolnota-polska.org.pl).

Warsaw Dom Tańca (Dance House). Warsaw organization that arranges folk dance evenings open to all, as well as folk concerts. However it has changed venue many times in recent years; contact the Warszawski Ośrodek Kultury, ul. Elektoralna 12, Warsaw ☎022/870 0384), or try sites such as ⊕www.etno.terra.pl or ⊕www.domtanca.art.pl for details.

Żywiec Międzynarodowe Spotkania Folklorystyczne (International Folk Meetings) (July–Aug), and the Festiwal Górali Polskich (Festival of Polish Highland Music). Held in July and August, both feature many of the acts who go on to appear in Zakopane (see above). Contact Żywiec tourist office, Rynek 12, 34-300 Żywiec (☎033/861 4310, ⊕www.zywiec.pl).

Ząbkowice Śląskie Folk Fiesta. A late June/early July world music festival with a healthy mix of Polish and foreign groups, in a small town 25km northeast of Kłodzko (see p.566). Contact: Ząbkowicki Ośrodek Kultury, Rynek 24, 57-200 Ząbkowice Śląskie (☎074/815 1381, ⊕http://fiesta.netgate.com.pl).

Zakopane Międzynarodowy Festiwal Folkloru Ziem Gorskich (International Festival of Highland Folklore). Sizeable gathering of traditional Polish and international groups strutting their stuff in a vast marquee in the town centre during August. Details from the Zakopane tourist office at ul. Kościuszki 17, 34-500 Zakopane (☎021/201 2211, ⊕www.zakopane.pl/festiwal).

Zydnia Vatra Festival of Łemk & Ukrainian Culture. A big event in the Łemk/Ukrainian cultural calendar, attracting thousands of people and a wide range of groups from Poland, Slovakia, Ukraine, Romania and Yugoslavia. Held in late July right out in the Beskid Niski, just southeast of Gorlice (see p.379).

tial to the image of Podhale life as the traditional costumes of tight felt trousers, broad leather belts with ornate metal clasps and studs, embroidered jackets and black hats decorated with cowrie shells. This music has more in common with the peasant cultures along the Carpathians in Ukraine and Transylvania than the rest of Poland. While traditional music in lowland Poland has tended to keep its simple drone accompaniment (where it survives at all), in Podhale there's a strong chordal harmony – probably a result of the intellectual presence.

The typical **Podhale ensemble** is a string band (the clarinets, saxophones, accordions and drums that have crept in elsewhere in Poland are much rarer here) of a lead violin (*prym*), a couple of second violins (*sekund*) playing accompanying chords and a three-stringed cello (*bazy*). The music is immediately identifiable by its melodies and playing style. The tunes tend to be short-winded, angular melodies in an unusual scale with a sharpened fourth. This is known to musicians as the "Lydian mode" and gives rise to the Polish word **lidy-zowanie** to describe the manner of singing this augmented interval. The fiddlers typically play these melodies with a "straight" bowing technique – giving the music a stiff, angular character as opposed to the swing and flexibility of the more usual "double" bowing technique common in eastern Europe and typified by gypsy fiddlers. The straining high male vocals which kick off a dance tune are also typical. At the heart of the repertoire are the **ozwodna** and **krzesany** couple dances, both in duple time. The first has an unusual five-bar melodic structure and the second is faster and more energetic. Then there are the showy **zbójnicki** (Brigand's Dances) which are the popular face of Podhale culture – central to festivals and demonstrations of the music. Danced in a circle by men wielding small metal axes (sometimes hit together fiercely enough to strike sparks), they are a celebration of the *górale* traditions of brigandage, with colourful robberies, daring escapes, festivities and death on the gallows for anti-feudal heroes. "To hang on the gibbet is an honourable thing!" said the nineteenth-century *górale* musician Sabała, "They don't hang just anybody, but real men!"

The songs you are most likely to hear as a visitor to Zakopane are those about the most famous brigand of them all, **Janosik** (1688–1713). Musically they are not Podhale in style, but are lyrical ballads with a Slovakian feel, and countless tales of the region's most famous character are sung on both sides of the border. The most played songs are *Idzie Janko* and *Krywan* – and the tune for the former seems to be used for many other Janosik songs as well. The latter is not actually about the brigand, but one of the Tatra's most celebrated mountains.

The mountain regions around Podhale also have their own, if less celebrated, musical cultures. To the west there is **Orawa**, straddling the Polish/Slovak border and the Beskid Żywieckie to its north, with an annual festival in the town of Żywiec itself. To the east of Zakopane, the music of the **Spisz** region has more Slovak bounce than the Podhale style and boasts an excellent fiddle-maker and musician in Woytek Łukasz. Even if you don't make it to a highland wedding, music is relatively accessible in **Zakopane**. Many of the restaurants have good bands that play certain nights of the week; there are occasional stage shows and there's the Festival of Highland Folklore in August.

Ethnic minorities

Since the political changes of the 1980s, there's been something of a revival in the music of some of the national minorities living in Poland. There is now a more liberal climate in which to express national differences and travel is easier across the borders between related groups in Lithuania, Belarus and Ukraine. Poland's **Boyks** and **Łemks** are ethnically and culturally linked to Ukrainians and the Rusyns of Slovakia, and their music betrays its eastern Slavonic leanings in its choral and polyphonic songs. Boyk and Ukrainian groups are now a regular feature of the Kazimierz Festival. Look out for the group led by singer **Roman Kumłuk** who, with fiddler **Wołodymyr Bodnaruk**, performs music of the **Hucul** people of the Carpathian mountains. You can hear the common heritage with certain types of Romanian, Ukrainian and Jewish music. The singer **Maria Krupowiec**, born in

Górale weddings

Górale weddings are often held in the local fire station, where there's room enough for feasting and dancing – plus it provides useful extra income for the fire brigade. It is here that the family members assemble and the couple are lectured by the leader of the band on the importance of the step they are taking – an indication of how integral the band is to the event. Then comes the departure for the church in a string of horse-drawn carriages – the band in one, the bride in another and the groom following in one behind. At the front, the **pytacy**, a pair of outriders on horseback, shout rhymes to all and sundry. The band play the couple into the wooden church and, from the gallery inside the church, keep going while communion takes place. Then it's back to the fire station for the party.

The band will keep going for hours, substituting different players from time to time to give themselves a short break. Quite unexpected until you get used to it is the way the *górale* dances and songs are superimposed, often with no relation to each other. A fast up-tempo dance will be in progress when suddenly a group of women will launch into a slow song seemingly oblivious to the other music – the tensions between the instrumental music and song are both calculated and fascinating.

Among the dances the local *ozwodne* and *krzesane* figure highly, begun by one of the men strutting over to the band and launching into the high straining vocals that cue the tune. The man then draws a girl onto the floor, dances a few steps with her before handing her over to the man on whose behalf he originally selected her. All this is part of a carefully structured form that culminates late in the evening with the ritual of the *cepiny* (or *cepowiny* as it's known in Podhale), the "capping ceremony". This is a peasant rite of passage that happens all over Poland, when the bride has a scarf tied round her head symbolizing her passage from the status of a single to a married woman.

The music whirls on throughout the night and extends well beyond the Podhale repertoire, with romantic waltzes and *mazurkas*, fiery polkas and *czardasz* – tunes that you might hear in northern Poland, Slovakia, Hungary or Romania, but always given a particular Podhale accent. The *górale* people are famed for keeping themselves to themselves and mistrusting outsiders, but there's no blinkered puritanism. They take and enjoy what they want from outside, confident and proud of the strength of what they have.

Vilnius, Lithuania, but raised in Poland, has sung Lithuanian, Belarusian and Polish songs exploring the connections and differences between them.

World War II saw the effective extermination of Jewish life and culture in Poland along with the exuberant and melancholy **klezmer** music for weddings and festivals that was part of it. The music had its distinctive Jewish elements, but drew heavily on local Polish and Ukrainian styles. Thanks to emigration and revival, the music now flourishes principally in the US and is barely heard in Poland except at the annual Festival of Jewish Culture in Kraków. The city is, though, home to its own klezmer band, **Kroke**. This trio, led by violinist **Tamasz Kukurba**, started off playing schmaltzy standards, but has evolved into an inventive and exciting band who've proven their ability on tour (at the Womad festivals held worldwide, for example). Two of the band's members are Jewish, although one of them didn't discover the fact until they'd been playing klezmer for several years – which says something about the pressure to assimilate in postwar Poland.

CONTEXTS | Polish folk music

Traditional

Gienek Wilczek's Bukowina Band *Music of the Tatra Mountains* (Nimbus, UK). Gienek is an eccentric peasant genius taught by Dziadonka, a notorious female brigand of Podhale who had learned from Bartuś Obrochta, the favoured *górale* fiddler of Szymanowski. His playing is eccentric with a richly ornamented, raw but inspirational sound.

Sowa Family Band *Songs and Music from Rzeszów Region* (Polskie Nagrania, Poland). A wonderful disc of authentic village dances from a family band with over 150 years of recorded history. The 1970s recordings are rather harsh, but splendid all the same. Sadly, the band is no longer playing.

Trebunia Family Band *Music of the Tatra Mountains* (Nimbus, UK). A great sample of *górale* music recorded not in a cold studio session, but at an informal party to bring that special sense of spontaneity and fun. Wild playing from one of the region's best bands and well recorded. Fiddler Władysław Trebunia is the father-figure and the band includes his son Krzysztof (who often leads in his own right), daughter Hania and several other family members.

Trebunia Family *Polish Highlanders Music* (Folk, Poland). This is the Trebunia's own label version of their *górale* music. There's terrific repertoire and playing, but it suffers from a touch too much reverb and not enough of the fun that makes the Nimbus recording so good.

Various *Polish Folk Music: Songs and Music from various Regions* (Polskie Nagrania, Poland). An excellent cross-section of music from eight different regions all over the country, from Kashubia in the north to Podhale in the south. Recordings from Polish radio giving the perfect overview.

Various *Poland: Folk Songs and Dances* (AIMP/VDE-Gallo, Switzerland). A more "hardcore" selection of field recordings compiled by Anna Czekanowska. Includes some recent recordings of music by ethnic minorities. Good notes.

Various *Polish Village Music: Historic Polish-American Recordings 1927–1933* (Arhoolie, US). Recordings from old 78s of Polish bands recently arrived in the US. Most still have a great down-home style. *Górale* fiddler Karol Stoch ("Last Evening in Podhale") was the most highly regarded of his day and the first to record commercially. His music sounds astonishingly similar to that which can still be heard in the region today. Not true for the bands from elsewhere in Poland. Very good notes and translations.

Various *Pologne: Danses* (Arion, France). The cover makes it look like one of those appalling "folklorique" ensembles, but this is actually a very good collection of instrumental polkas, *obereks* and other dances from southeastern Poland. Two family bands from Rzeszów district and the third, the celebrated Pudełko family, from Przeworsk. Includes several solo tracks on the *cimbały* hammer dulcimer. Excellent notes.

Various *Pologne: Instruments populaires* (Ocora, France). Predominantly instrumental music ranging from shepherds' horns and flutes, fiddles and bagpipes to

Revival and new music

It is perhaps not over-optimistic to sense a slight picking up of interest in Polish traditional music as the exhortations of the sanitized troupes slip further into the distance. In the western region of Wielkopolska there's been something of a revival in **bagpipe** (*kozio* – literally "goat") playing, a tradition reaching back to the Middle Ages in Eastern Europe. And in the last few years

small and medium-sized ensembles. A compilation, by Maria Baliszewska, of field recordings of the real thing in the best Ocora tradition. Good notes.

Various *Sources of Polish Folk Music* (Polish Radio Folk Collection, Poland). An excellent ten-volume series issued by Polish Radio, documenting Polish folk music with recordings from the 1960s to the mid-90s, many of them recorded at the Kazimierz Festival. Each disc focuses on a different area and comes with good notes in Polish and English on the characteristics of the region, the vocal and instrumental music and biographies of the musicians. Vol 1: Mazovia; Vol 2: Tatra Foothills; Vol 3: Lubelskie; Vol 4: Małopolska Północna; Vol 5: Wielkopolska; Vol 6: Kurpie; Vol 7: Beskidy; Vol 8: Krakowskie Tarnowskie; Vol 9: Suwalskie Podlasie; Vol 10: Rzeszowskie Pogórze. Contact: Polskie Radio SA, Biuro Promocji i Handlu, al. Niepodległości 77/85, 00-977 Warszawa, Poland ℗022/645 5901.

Contemporary

Brathanki *Ano!* (Columbia, Poland). Traditional *górale* folk music reinvented as major-label pop, but delivered with enough verve and humour to win over all but the most die-hard traditionalists. This album was one of the biggest commercial successes of 2000, and Brathanki have been well-nigh unavoidable on Polish radio and TV ever since.

Golec uOrkiestra *Golec uOrkiestra* (Program, Poland). The Golec brothers adopt a similar approach to Brathanki in writing accessible pop songs in *górale* style. However there's something rawer, rootsier and funkier in their brass-driven sound. Massively popular but well-respected with it, the uOrkiestra were paid the compliment – or indignity – of having George W. Bush Junior quote their song lyrics during a keynote speech in Warsaw in spring 2001.

Kwartet Jorgi *Jam* (Jam, Poland; available from Jam Phone Co in Poland ℗22/83 0021). This is the quartet's first release from 1990, featuring lots of old tunes collected by Kolberg. The Jewish-sounding *Ubinie* tune seems to tie in with the Chagall picture on the cover.

Kwartet Jorgi *Kwartet Jorgi* (Polskie Nagrania, Poland). Their second CD is a release of older material recorded in 1988. It ventures more widely in repertoire with Irish and Balkan tunes as well as excursions into what sounds like medieval jazz.

Namysłowski Jazz Quartet & Kapela Góralska (ZAIKS/BIEM, Poland). This Trebunia jazz collaboration, featuring the doyen of Polish saxophonists, is well worth hearing. If you are in Zakopane be sure to pick up a cassette.

Twinkle Brothers and Trebunia Family *Twinkle Inna Polish Stylee: Higher Heights* and *Comeback Twinkle 2* (Ryszard Music, Poland; available from Caston distribution in Poland on ℗27/642 3221). The intriguing sounds of "góralstafarianism".

a few good contemporary folk groups have emerged. Not surprisingly, some of the most interesting developments have come out of Podhale and in particular the **Trebunia** family band of Poronin. Here the stern fiddler Władysław Trebunia and his son Krzysztof are both preservers of and experimenters with the tradition, as well as being leaders of one of the very best wedding bands around. In 1991 they joined up with reggae musician Norman "Twinkle" Grant to produce two albums of **Podhale reggae**, or perhaps more accurately, reggae in a Polish style. Surprising as it might seem, once you get used to the rigid beat imposed on the more flexible Polish material, the marriage works rather well and there are interesting parallels between Rasta and Pod-hale concerns. In 1994, the Trebunias teamed up on another project with one of Poland's leading jazz musicians, saxophonist Zbigniew Namysłowski. Here the usual *górale* ensemble meets saxophone, piano, bass and drums in an inventive romp through classic Podhale hits such as Zbójnicki tunes, Krywan and Idzie Janko.

Elsewhere, contemporary folk bands to look out for are the Lublin-based **Orkiestra Św. Mikołaja** and, particularly, the **Kwartet Jorgi**. Although based in Poznań, the group takes its music from all round Poland and beyond, with many of the tunes coming from the nineteenth-century collections of **Oskar Kolberg**. The group's leader, Maciej Rychły, plays an amazing range of ancient Polish bagpipes, whistles and flutes which are sensitively combined with guitars, cello and drums. The music isn't purist, but is inventive and fun and shows how contemporary Polish folk music can escape the legacy of sanitized communist fakelore. In a similar spirit, following the Hungarian **táncáz** ("dancehouse") movement, a Dom Tańca has been started in Warsaw to play and teach authentic Polish folk dances. This is the place to go to learn your *mazurkas* and *obereks*.

Current trends

The growing popularity of the mix-and-match approach of **world music** has had a considerable impact on the Polish folk scene, encouraging young urban Poles to dabble in traditional music from around the globe – and rediscovering their own folk heritage in the process. Not only has this led to an increase in the number and popularity of folk-oriented festivals (see box pp.716–717), it has also led to the emergence of a lot of new music. The tradition of experimentation pioneered by the Trebunia-Twinkle partnership was continued by other acts throughout the 1990s: Scandinavian-Polish act **De Press** produced an infectiously punky folk-rock fusion, while the more ethereal **Karpaty Magiczne** created their own genre of arty ethno chill-out music involving anything from dulcimers to digeridoos. In 1999 an album bringing together Serbian composer **Goran Bregovic** and Polish rock diva **Kayah** (entitled *Kayah and Bregovic*) was a massive hit in Poland – and even though it consisted of Balkan-inspired material rather than Polish songs, it was of inestimable importance in building an audience for folk-rock crossover music in general. The main beneficiary of this was **Brathanki**, a group from southern Poland who mixed frenetic *górale* tunes with modern pop-rock guitar riffs, and sold copies of their debut album *Ano!* by the bucketload. The success of their second album, *Pa-Ta-Taj!* (2001), seemed to confirm their status as one of the country's major pop acts. They were joined in the nation's affections by the **Golec uOrkiestra**, led by two brothers, Paweł and Lukasz (a trumpeter and trombonist) from the Żywiec region. Like Brathanki, the uOrkiestra base their repertoire on the swirling dance music of the *górale* tradition, this time adding a punchy, brass-band feel – spiced up by the occasional Latin twist. Neither the Golec brothers nor Brathianki have been warmly embraced by the folk purists (and there are suggestions that Brathanki "borrowed" some of their melodies from an uncredited Hungarian composer), but there's no doubt that they've brought both media fashionability and record-industry money to the world of Polish folk – thereby creating a wider field of opportunity for others.

With thanks to Krzysztof Cwizewicz

Walking in the Tatras

The pine-forested slopes and glacier-carved ridges of the Polish Tatra Mountains are by far the most spectacular and challenging mountain walking area in the country. Travel writer and enthusiastic hiker Chris Scott visited the region twice in 1991. The following piece is an account of his contrasting experiences in summer and on his return in winter.

The area within the **Tatrzański Park Narodowy** (Tatras National Park or TPN) encompasses peaks in the 1800–2100m range from the less visited western frontier ridge past the cable car station at Kasprowy Wierch (1985m), midway along the park's southern flank. East of Kasprowy, the park's most frequently visited summit, are the Wysokie or High Tatras, including the demanding Orła Perć and inaccessible Liptowskie Mury ridges; the latter end at the 2499m peak of Rysy, the highest in Poland. Best of all, the small park provides seven hostels ranging from diminutive "Hansel and Gretel" cabins to grand interwar lodges in the main valleys leading north from the border, and comes complete with a well-developed network of clearly waymarked tracks crisscrossing the entire area.

The colours of the tracks detailed below refer to their corresponding waymarks on trees and signposts in the Tatras National Park and on the yellow 1:30,000 tourist **map** that covers the park.

★★★★★

A few years ago I visited the Tatras, having taken the bus from Dover to Kraków, a surprisingly effortless thirty-hour journey. Once in Kraków, a week's wages converted into what was then two and a half million złotys, a huge wad of low-value notes which the recent currency revisions have thankfully eliminated. First impressions of the country contradicted the drab visions of austerity then associated with Poland. Although poverty was still endemic, the commerce – or "handel", for which the Poles are well known – thrived in all forms, with shops replete with an unexpected variety of food at prices around a quarter of those in England.

Just a dollar's worth of złotys secured a seat on the next bus leaving for Zakopane from where next morning, loaded with sausage and bread, I set off south to Kuźnice and the start of the black trail which winds west through the forested foothills to the beautiful valley, Dolina Chochołowska. Mistakenly presuming I'd chosen a moderate introduction for my first hill-walking in ten years, I in fact found myself panting and sweating in the 30°C heat. Closer scrutiny of the excellent TPN tourist map available in Zakopane revealed that far from being a "low-level introductory route", the black track laboriously climbed and descended successive spurs between the valleys running north off the main ridge, rather than simply slowly gaining height and maintaining it. This, combined with a hot summer's day and full camping gear saw me relish the refreshment at each valley-bed stream before commencing yet another slog up into the woods and over the next spur. The plunge pool at the Wodospad Siklawica (Siklawica Waterfall) was thronged with sunbathers and their gambolling children, while all along the way, similarly casually attired Poles bade me "Cześć", the customary salute meted out to passing walkers. Indeed, it soon became clear that an unusually broad cross-section of society was on the march in the Tatras. Most prolific were keen school-aged kids sporting ex-army rucksacks and clumpy boots, oblivious to the wonders of modern lightweight gear but enjoying themselves nonetheless.

By the time I reached the Dolina Kościeliska, the contour-mashing trudge had worn me out and so I decided to investigate the promising-sounding Jaskina Mrozna (Frozen Cave) a short distance up the valley. On the way *górale* (pronounced "gouraleh"), the indigenous mountain folk of the Tatras, dressed traditionally in their white felt outfits, ferried tourists up and down the valley in horse-drawn carts. A popular Polish folk song relates the pitiful plight of the proud and distinctive *górale*, forced to seek work in the despised factories of the lowlands, their days of shepherding and guiding in the hills having come to an end.

Dumping my overloaded pack in some ferns, I skipped weightlessly up to the cave entrance and enjoyed a blissfully refrigerated grope through the dimly lit tunnel that was only truly appreciated once I emerged back into the late-afternoon heat. Deciding I'd had enough for one day, I made one final climb up the blue track to the clearing on top of Polana Stoły where I flopped down exhaustedly on the grass.

By late next afternoon I found myself camped above the treeline on a spur beneath Wołowiec, the 2063m peak on the frontier ridge in the park's southwestern corner. Perplexed at the lack of fellow campers, I later realized that the practice is forbidden in the park and anyway, the hostels (*schroniska*) or basic refuges (*szałasy*) are much more enjoyable places to spend the night. Nevertheless, my borrowed tent successfully beat off a convoy of ensuing thunderstorms and by nine next morning I'd passed over the summit of Wołowiec, descending to the Jamnickie Stawy (lakes) on the Slovak side of the frontier; an infringement of cross-border etiquette, but the only source of water nearby. Wisps of the previous night's storm trailed from the surrounding peaks as I washed and fed myself, while *świstaki* – beaver-like rodents similar to Alpine marmots – scurried from burrow to burrow. Once I was back on the main frontier ridge, it was a straightforward walk west along the red track over a succession of 2000m summits to Starorobociański Wierch (2176m) at which point the next 10km of the frontier ridge remain out of bounds to all except the wildlife. Instead, the path turns north along the Ornak ridge, for me an excruciatingly protracted and waterless six-kilometre slog down to the Ornaczańska hostel. Set at the head of the Dolina Kościeliska, whose lower reaches I'd crossed a couple of days ago, the large timber cabin was packed to the gills with hard-up but cheerful teenagers making their own sandwiches and tea in an attempt to save what was, to me, the negligible expense of a cooked meal. Kids sat around on tables singing along to a strumming guitar, or repairing ageing equipment until lights-out came, and those who could not afford bunks unrolled their sleeping bags on the tables and benches.

Next morning I decided that hostels were far preferable to further illicit camping, so I returned to Zakopane, diverting to make a torchlit crawl through the unmarked interior of Jaskina Mylna about which I'd been told the night before. Back in town a cheap guesthouse performed the role of a left-luggage office while I headed back to Kuźnice and up the yellow track to the ample Murowana hostel, ideally placed for excursions into the High Tatras visible to the southeast. Again I met up with gregarious Polish youths who quizzed me about life in England and explained their frustration with the government austerity measures distancing them further from the increasing range of imported commodities.

Next morning I and a small group of disparate hikers headed up the blue track, passing Czarny Staw (Black Lake) before the steep ascent up to the Orła Perć, a dramatic ridge of jagged 2300m peaks that requires a steady head for heights and includes several exposed sections safeguarded by chains and rails. Indeed, even getting onto the ridge required occasional clambering hand over hand up fixed chains until we reached the saddle. From here a wonderful panorama spread out east down the upper reaches of the Dolina Pięciu Stawów Polskich (Valley of the Five Polish Lakes), wrapped in a horseshoe of 2000m-high ridges. A hard-earned four-kilometre descent brought us to the isolated cabin situated by the lowest lake where some of the group continued on down the Dolina Roztoki and the bus to Zakopane. If the other hostels had been crowded, this one was positively sinking into its foundations with the weight of its guests. Dinners were passed over the heads jammed along the benches and by night-time every body-sized flat surface was covered in recumbent figures.

The next afternoon was spent basking by the lakeside of Morskie Oko (Eye of the Sea), one of the Tatras' most famous landmarks, chatting with a couple of Danes I'd met a few days earlier. Situated below the towering walls of the Liptowskie Mury ridge, which defines the Slovak border, the lake is dominated by the bare slopes of Rysy, Poland's highest peak. Its summit was my destination the following day, and following a frosty night bivouacked by the shores of a higher lake, a clear dawn start saw the arduous scramble up the peak completed by 8am. Sitting with satisfaction on the cemented summit block inscribed with "P" on one side and "CH" (a relic of the days when this was Czechoslovakia) on the other, I looked out over the distant farmlands of the Slovak and Polish republics which surrounded me. Over the Liptowskie Mury, a helicopter was performing a recovery exercise or possibly an early rescue, and clambering down from the summit block I was dismayed to encounter three smartly uniformed soldiers, armed with heavy rifles and radios. A short chat with them revealed that the ascent of Rysy was a tiresome but regular task undertaken for the security of the forthcoming weekend's hikers.

Back in Zakopane, I became the victim of a bizarrely premeditated overnight robbery by the over-friendly weirdo with whom I shared my room – an instance of Poland's opportunistic crime epidemic to which foreign visitors are especially vulnerable. Fortunately, the landlady was so distraught by this event that she gave me the fare back to Kraków where I picked up my bus home.

*****

Four months later, on Christmas Eve, a friend and I tramped by torchlight through the snow to the grand alpine hostel at the head of the Dolina Chochołowska, arriving just as the festive feast laid on for the guests was being cleared away.

With borrowed or home-made ice axes and crampons, and inexpensive Polish down jackets, we were hoping to repeat my west–east traverse of the previous summer, conditions permitting. However, next day an attempt to get up to Wołowiec was soon aborted when, exhausted by repeated falls through deep snow, we were beaten back by the biting winds once out on the bare slopes. Acknowledging that the short winter days made a walk along the exposed frontier ridge too risky, we instead walked back down the valley and took the yellow track east through the thick forests leading up to the Iwaniacka Pass and down to the Ornaczańska hostel into which I'd stumbled exhausted a few months earlier in T-shirt and shorts. One thing all of the Tatras' hostels share in common is a robust central heating system that's more than capable of putting up with the severest Polish winter. Following a typically crowded but affable evening, we walked back down the Kościeliska, passing the Mrozna Cave, and turned east along the black and yellow tracks. These led us close to the 1909m summit of Giewont, whose twenty-metre-high steel crucifix is visible from all over Zakopane. From Giewont we slid semi-controllably down into the Dolina Kondratowa, using our ice axes as brakes, and were soon stamping the snow off our boots outside the idyllically situated Kondratowa hostel, a small log cabin only a couple of kilometres beneath the Czerwone Wierchy (Red Peaks) on the frontier ridge, which was at this point again open to walkers. With an eye out for the weather, we precooked some food for tomorrow's anticipated walk along the ridge to Kasprowy Wierch, and squeezed two-to-a-bunk, ready for an early start. Next day dawned clear and so we set off up the Dolina Sucha Kondracka, occasionally sinking through the soft snow up to our chests, although as the slope steepened conditions improved and we doggedly kicked our way up to Suchy Wierch Kondracki (1890m) where a furious wind all but blew us back down. Crawling along the knife-edge ridge with thought-provoking drops down into the valleys was a little more difficult than we had planned, as we occasionally lost the track and clambered around the ice-clad precipices of the Suche Chuby. Any intentions we may have had about undertaking the difficult traverse of the Orła Perć were soon brought into perspective as we completed the broad climb up to Kasprowy Wierch, site of a cable-car station adjacent to a huge mountain-top restaurant. Unfortunately for those who had struggled up here along the paths from Zakopane, this was closed, but the hall provided welcome shelter from the storm building up outside. Groups of cheerful but underdressed Poles huddled together, stamping their numbed feet and re-wrapping sodden scarves around their heads. One of them begged to buy one of our sandwiches, before we all set off down the valley into the fading light and a lull in the blizzard. If most mountain accidents occur during final descents then here were several waiting to happen, as the frozen but happy day-trippers slithered down the slopes hand in hand, laughing uproariously and singing refrains from their favourite ballads. When Bob's ice axe pick separated from its shaft while breaking a controlled slide, we accepted the limitations of our home-welded ironwear and said goodbye to the snowbound Tatras.

Chris Scott

Books

A vast amount of writing both from and about Poland is available in English, and the quantity increased at an accelerated pace with the advent of the post-communist regime.

Most of the books listed below are in print, and those that aren't (listd as "o.p.") should be easy enough to track down in secondhand bookshops; where two publishers are given, the first is British, the second US. In the UK, the best source for Polish books is the Polish-run Orbis Books, 66 Kenway Rd, London SW5 ORD (☎020 7370 2210), which also stocks a large selection of photo albums (many out of print) from Poland itself.

Travel writing and guidebooks

Anne Applebaum *Between East and West* (Papermac). Well-informed, vividly written account of British-based US journalist's travels through the eastern Polish borderlands. Starting from Kaliningrad and moving down through Lithuania, Belarus, Ukraine and Moldova, Applebaum's broad-ranging cultural-historical frame of reference means the book suffers less than others from being too close to immediate events.

Karl Baedeker *Northern Germany; Southern Germany and Austria; Russia* (all o.p.). Staple finds in secondhand shops, the old nineteenth- and early twentieth-century Baedekers are always fascinating, but never more so than in the case of Poland, which was then under Partition. A strong German bias is evident in the first two books, with Polish elements often ignored or glossed over; even in the later editions there's not the slightest anticipation of Poland's possible re-emergence as a nation.

Hilaire Belloc *Return to the Baltic* (Constable, o.p.). Whimsical account of Belloc's travels through Denmark, Sweden and Poland – he clearly felt more at home among his fellow Catholics in Warsaw and Kraków than in Lutheran Scandinavia.

Tim Burford *Hiking Guide to Poland and Ukraine* (Bradt Publications). Thoroughly researched guide to hiking in the region.

Alfred Döblin *Journey to Poland* (I.B. Tauris/Paragon House, both o.p.). Döblin, best known for his weighty Expressionist novels, visited the newly resurrected Polish state in 1923, primarily to seek out his Jewish roots, though he himself was non-practising, and was later to convert to Catholicism. The result is a classic of travel literature, full of trenchant analysis and unnervingly prophetic predictions about the country's future, interspersed with buttonholing passages of vivid descriptive prose (see p.154).

Ruth E. Gruber *Jewish Heritage Travel: A Guide to East-Central Europe* and *Upon the Doorposts of Thy House: Jewish Life in East-Central Europe Yesterday and Today* (both Wiley, o.p.). The first title is a useful country-by-country guide to Jewish culture and monuments of the region. The practical information tends to be basic, verging on the hieroglyphic, so will need supplementing for the serious searcher. The more discursive *Upon the Doorposts of Thy House* gives Gruber the space she needs to stretch out and really get into her subject. The sections on Auschwitz and Kraków's Kazimierz district are masterly, thought-provoking essays.

Eva Hoffman *Exit into History: A Journey through the New Eastern Europe* (Minerva/Penguin USA). US journalist of Polish Jewish origin returns to her roots on a journey through the early 90s post-communist landscape. Inevitably already dated, but the sections on Poland stand out for their combination of shrewd political insight and human warmth.

Joram Kagan *Poland's Jewish Heritage* (Hippocrene). A useful summary of the Jewish sites of Poland, along with an outline history.

Philip Marsden *The Bronski House: A Return to the Borderlands* (Flamingo/Arcade). Sensitively written account of the author's journey to the Polish/Belarusian borderlands in the company of Zofia Ilińska, an aristocratic former resident returning for the first time in fifty years.

Rory McLean *Stalin's Nose* (Flamingo). One of the best of the flurry of accounts of "epic" journeys across post-communist east-central Europe. The author's quirky brand of surrealist humour enlivens the trip, which takes in obvious Polish stopoffs, Auschwitz and Kraków, en route for Moscow.

Colin Saunders and Renata Narozna *The High Tatras* (Cicerone). Detailed and comprehensive recent guide to the ins and outs of scaling the Tatras. For dedicated hikers and climbers.

Miriam Weiner *Jewish Roots in Poland: Pages from the Past and Archival Inventories* (YIVO/Routes to Roots Foundation). Monumental coffee-table-sized guide to all aspects of Polish Jewry, the fruit of years of meticulous and painstaking trailing through archival sources – and the country itself – by its US-based author.

History

Chimen Abramsky, **Maciej Jachimczyk** and **Antony Polonsky** (eds.) *The Jews in Poland* (Basil Blackwell/Blackwell Publishing). Historical survey of what was for centuries the largest community of world Jewry.

Neal Ascherson *The Struggles for Poland* (Pan, o.p./Random House, o.p.). Ascherson's book was designed to accompany the Channel 4 TV series and its focus is squarely on the twentieth century, with just a thirty-page chapter on the previous thousand years. For most general readers, though, this is the best possible introduction to modern Polish history and politics.

Norman Davies *The Heart of Europe: A Short History of Poland* (OUP/OUP). A brilliantly original treatment of modern Polish history, beginning with the events of 1945 but looking backwards over the past millennium to illustrate the author's

ideas. Scrupulously gives all points of view in disentangling the complex web of Polish history.

Norman Davies *God's Playground* (2 vols; OUP/Columbia UP). A masterpiece of erudition, entertainingly written and pretty much definitive for the pre-Solidarity period.

Norman Davies *White Eagle, Red Star: The Polish Soviet War, 1919–20* (Orbis Books/Hippocrene). Fascinating account of a little-known but critically important episode of European history, at a time when Lenin appeared ready to export the Soviet Revolution into Europe.

Norman Davies and **A. Polonsky** (eds.) *Jews in Eastern Poland and the USSR 1939–49* (Macmillan). Meticulously researched and well-written account of the fate of eastern Europe's largest Jewish population in time of war.

Wacław Jedrzejewicz *Piłsudski* A Life for Poland (Hippocrene).

Comprehensive biography of the enigmatic military strongman.

Paul Latawski (ed.) *The Reconstruction of Poland 1914–23* (Palgrave). Useful set of essays on the run-up to and early period of inter-war Polish independence. Good on the nationalist leader Roman Dmowski and the minorities issue.

Czesław Miłosz *The History of Polish Literature* (California UP). Written in the mid-1960s, it is however still the standard English-language work on the subject, informed by the author's consummate grasp of the furthest nooks and crannies of Polish literature.

Krystyna Olzer (ed.) *For Your Freedom and Ours* (F. Ungar). Anthology of Polish political writings over the centuries with an emphasis on progressive traditions. Some stirring pieces from Kościuszko ("The Polanic Manifesto"), Piłsudski and the World War II Polish resistance among others. A useful reference book.

Bianka Pietrow-Ennker *Women in Polish Society* (Columbia UP). Intriguing collection of academic essays on the prominent but under-recognized role of women in Partitions-era Poland. Radical feminist its perspective isn't, however.

Józef Piłsudski *Memoirs of a Polish Revolutionary and Soldier* (Faber & Faber, o.p./ AMS Press). Lively stuff from Lech Wałęsa's hero, who – after a dashing wartime career – was Poland's leader from 1926 to 1934.

Iwo Pogonowski *Jews in Poland: A Documentary History* (Hippocrene). Thorough if idiosyncratically presented account of Polish Jewry from the earliest times up until the present day – not too many axes to grind either. Contains an intriguing selection of old prints from everyday life in the ghettos, *shtetls* and synagogues.

Antony Polonsky (ed.) *The Jews in Old Poland 1700–1795* (I.B. Tauris); *Studies From Polin: From Shtetl to Socialism* (Littman). The first is an informative, wide-ranging set of historical essays by a combined team of Polish and Israeli scholars covering Jewish life in Poland from earliest times up to the end of the Partitions era. The second, a collection of essays drawn from the learned journal of the Oxford Institute for Polish-Jewish Studies, covers diverse aspects of Polish Jewish history, politics, literature and culture. Doesn't shrink from the more controversial and sensitive topics either.

Adam Zamoyski *The Polish Way* (John Murray/Hippocrene Books). The most accessible history of Poland, going up to the end of the communist regime. Zamoyski is an American émigré Pole, and his sympathies – as you would expect in a member of one of Poland's foremost aristocratic families – are those of a blue-blooded nationalist. His more recent *The Last King of Poland* (Phoenix/Wiedenfield and Nicholson, o.p.), is a readable biography of doomed monarch Stanisław Antoni Poniatowski.

World War II and the Holocaust

Alan Adelson and Robert Lapides *The Łódź Ghetto – Inside a Community under Siege* (Penguin, o.p./Penguin USA, o.p.). Scrupulously detailed narrative of the 200,000-strong ghetto, with numerous personal memoirs and photographs.

Janina Bauman *Winter in the Morning* (Virago/Free Press); *A Dream of Belonging* (Virago, o.p./Trafalgar Square). Bauman and her family survived the Warsaw Ghetto, eventually leaving the country following the anti-Semitic backlash of 1968. Winter is a delicate and moving account of life and death in the ghetto. Less dramatic but equally interesting, *Belonging*, the second volume of her autobiography, tells of life in the communist party and disillusionment in the early postwar years.

Jan Ciechanowski *The Warsaw Uprising of 1944* (CUP, o.p.). Compelling, day-by-day account – the best of many on this subject.

Martin Gilbert *The Holocaust* (HarperCollins). The standard work, providing a trustworthy overview on the slaughter of European Jewry – and the crucial role of Poland, where most Nazi concentration camps were sited.

Geoffrey Hartman (ed.) *Holocaust Remembrance: The shapes of memory* (Blackwell, o.p.). Wide-ranging collection of essays by artists, scholars and writers on diverse aspects of contemporary remembrance of the Holocaust. A number of chapters on Polish themes, including useful pieces on Lanzemann's *Shoah*, Auschwitz and the construction of the Jewish memorials in Poland.

Gustaw Herling *A World Apart* (OUP, o.p./Arbor House, o.p.). Account of deportation to a Soviet labour camp, based on the author's own experiences.

Rudolf Höss *Death Dealer: Memoirs of the SS Kommandant at Auschwitz* (Da Capo). Perhaps the most chilling record of the barbarity: a remorseless autobiography of the Auschwitz camp commandant, written in the days between his death sentence and execution at Nürnberg.

Stefan Korbonski *The Polish Underground State* (Hippocrene). Detailed account of the history and inner workings of the many-faceted Polish wartime resistance by a leading figure of the time. Korbonski has produced a number of other books on related themes, notably Fighting Warsaw, an account of the 1944 Warsaw Uprising drawing on his own experience.

Dan Kurzman *The Bravest Battle* (Pinnacle, o.p./Putnam, o.p.).

Detailed account of the 1943 Warsaw Ghetto Uprising, conveying the incredible courage of the Jewish combatants.

Primo Levi *If This is a Man* (Everyman); *The Truce* (Everyman); *Moments of Reprieve* (Penguin/Penguin US); *The Drowned and the Saved* (Abacus/Vintage Books); *The Periodic Table* (Penguin/Schocken Books); *If Not Now, When?* (Penguin/Penguin USA). An Italian Jew, Levi survived Auschwitz because the Nazis made use of his training as a chemist in the death-camp factories. Most of his books, which became ever bleaker towards the end of his life, concentrate on his experiences during and soon after his incarceration in Auschwitz, analysing the psychology of survivor and torturer with extraordinary clarity. *If Not Now, When?* is the story of a group of Jewish partisans in occupied Russia and Poland: giving plenty of insights into eastern European anti-Semitism, it's a good corrective to the mythology of Jews as passive victims.

Betty Jean Lifton *Janusz Korczak: The King of the Children* (St Martins/Farrar, Straus & Giroux). Biography of the Jewish doctor who died in Treblinka with the orphans for whom he cared. He was the eponymous subject of an Andrzej Wajda film.

Richard C. Lukas *The Forgotten Holocaust* (Hippocrene). Detailed study of Nazi atrocities against Polish Gentiles which, in the author's view, were every bit as barbaric as against their Jewish counterparts.

Jan Nowak *Courier for Warsaw* (Collins Harvill, o.p.). Racily written memoir of the Polish underground resistance.

Emmanuel Ringelblum *Polish-Jewish Relations during the Second World War* (Northwestern UP). Penetrating history of the Warsaw Ghetto focusing on the vexed issue of Polish–Jewish wartime relations. Written from the inside by the prominent prewar Jewish historian – history recorded as it was occurring. Tragically, only a portion of Ringelblum's own writings and the extensive Ghetto archives he put together were recovered after 1945.

Saul Rubinek *So Many Miracles* (Penguin, o.p./Penguin US, o.p.). Rubinek's interviews with his parents about their early life in Poland and survival under Nazi occupation make a compelling piece of oral history, and one that paints a blacker than usual picture of Polish-Jewish relations.

Art Spiegelman *Maus* (Penguin/Pantheon Books). Spiegelman, editor of the cartoon magazine *Raw*, is the son of Auschwitz survivors. *Maus* is a brilliant comic-strip exploration of the ghetto and concentration camp experiences of his father, recounted in flashbacks. The story runs through to Art's father's imprisonment at Auschwitz; subsequent chapters of the sequel – covering Auschwitz itself – have been printed in recent editions of *Raw*, now available as a separate book, *Maus II* (Penguin). In 2001, *Maus* was published in Poland to great acclaim – despite the fact that the Polish characters in the book are depicted as pigs.

Wladyslaw Szpilman *The Pianist* (Penguin/Picador USA). Wartime memoirs of concert pianist and composer Szpilman (1911–2000), who miraculously survived the Warsaw Ghetto. Originally published as *Smięc Miasta* (Death of a City) in 1945, Szpilman's book was initially buried by a postwar Polish regime unwilling to recognize the full extent of Jewish suffering in World War II. Now available again in both Polish and English versions, *The Pianist* has already made it onto celluloid courtesy of Kraków ghetto survivor Roman Polański.

Carl Tighe *Gdańsk: National Identity in the German-Polish Border Lands* (Pluto). Alternatively titled *Gdańsk: the Unauthorised Biography*, an apt description of a fascinating history of a city that Poles and Germans have tussled over for centuries. Studiously avoiding the pro- or anti-Polish/German dichotomy that bedevils many interpretations, the author sets out to capture the unique story of the Gdańsk/Danzig citizenry, arguing that claims of real Polish or German identity tell us more about the needs of latterday nationalists than the cultural complexities of the past.

The Warsaw Ghetto (Interpress, Warsaw). Official state publication, issued in several languages, that documents the destruction of the capital's Jewish population.

Harold Werner *Fighting Back: A Memoir of Jewish Resistance in World War II* (Columbia UP). Gripping, straightforwardly written account of the author's experiences as a member of a Jewish partisan unit fighting against the Nazis in wartime Poland.

Politics and society

Timothy Garton Ash *The Polish Revolution: Solidarity 1980–82* (Penguin/Vintage Books o.p.); *The Uses of Adversity* (Penguin/Vintage Books, o.p.); *We The People: The Revolution of 89* (Penguin/Vintage Books, o.p.). Garton Ash was the most consistent and involved Western reporter on Poland in the Solidarity era, displaying an intuitive grasp of the Polish mentality. His *Polish Revolution* is a vivid record of events from the birth of Solidarity – a story extended in the climactic events of 1989, documented as an eyewitness in Warsaw, Budapest, Berlin and Prague.

Misha Glenny *The Rebirth of History: Eastern Europe in the Age of Democracy* (Penguin, o.p./Penguin

US). One chapter deals with Poland, homing in on the economic and political difficulties of post-communist reconstruction.

Jaqueline Hayden *Poles Apart: Solidarity and the New Poland* (Irish Academic Press). Personal account of political developments in Poland from August 1980 up to the election of the SLD-led government in 1993 by an Irish journalist who visited the country throughout the period. The format – a series of extended interviews with key opposition figures, tracing their lives and political development – offers an interesting overview that combines the personal with the political. See pp.701–713 for an extract from the book.

Paul Latwski (ed.) *The Reconstruction of Poland 1914–23* (Macmillan, o.p.). Wide-ranging set of academic essays focusing on the lead-up to the country's (re)achievement of independence, and subsequent struggles with new-found statehood, particularly the sensitive question of minorities. Useful annexe of period documents.

Jan Josef Lipski *A History of KOR – The Committee for Workers' Self-Defence* (University of California Press).

Detailed history of a key 1970s opposition movement regarded as one of Solidarity's main inspirations. A resistance veteran and leading light in KOR, Lipski shows how it developed ideas and strategies of nonviolence and an "independent civil society" as a response to totalitarianism. A demanding but worthwhile read.

Grazyna Sikorska *Jerzy Popiełuszko, a Martyr for Truth* (Fount, o.p./Eerdmans, o.p.). Hagiographic biography of the murdered Catholic priest and national hero.

Radek Sikorski *The Polish House: An Intimate History Of Poland* (Weidenfeld & Nicolson, o.p.). Highly personalized and passionately penned account of modern Polish history by former Solidarity activist, UK exile and jounalist who rose briefly to the heights of deputy defence minister in 1992, aged 29. Author's trenchantly anticommunist views begin to grate after a while, but overall you'd be hard put to find a better insider's introduction to contemporary realities.

Stewart Steven *The Poles* (Collins Harvill, o.p.). Excellent journalistic account of all aspects of society in early-1980s Poland.

Essays and memoirs

Kazimierz Brandys *Warsaw Diary 1977–81* (Chatto, o.p./Vintage, o.p.); *Paris, New York: 1982–84* (Random House, o.p.). The *Warsaw Diary* by this major Polish journalist and novelist brilliantly captures the atmosphere of the time, and especially the effect of John Paul II's first papal visit in 1979. During martial law, possession of this book carried an automatic ten-year sentence. Paris/New York powerfully traces his early life in imposed exile while continually reflecting on developments at home.

Adam Czerniawski *Scenes from a Disturbed Childhood* (Serpent's Tail, o.p.). Uplifting, entertainingly writ-

ten account of a childhood spent escaping the traumas of World War II – to Turkey and an Arab school in Palestine, before ending up with his impoverished upper-class family in southeast England. A welcome addition to wartime émigré memoir literature.

Hans Magnus Enzensberger *Europe, Europe* (Pantheon/Alfred Knopf). A *tour de force* from the German anarchist, delving outside the mainstream to answer the question "What is Europe?" The section on Poland is a wonderfully observant roam around the main cities in 1986.

Granta 30: New Europe! (Penguin, o.p./Penguin US o/p).

Published at the beginning of 1990, this state-of-the-continent anthology includes Neil Ascherson on the eastern Polish borderlands and a series of brief reactions to events from a dozen or so European intellectuals.

Zbigniew Herbert *Barbarian in the Garden* (Harcourt/Harcourt). Stirring, lyrical set of essays on Mediterranean themes by the noted recently deceased Polish poet, with 1960s post-Stalinist-era Poland – the period when they were written – a recurring background presence.

Eva Hoffman *Lost in Translation* (Minerva, o.p./Penguin US). Wise, sparklingly written autobiography of a Polish Jew centring, as the title suggests, around her experience of emigration from Kraków to North America in the 1960s. Plenty of insights into the postwar Jewish/Eastern Europe émigré experience.

Eva Hoffman *Shtetl: The Life And Death Of A Small Town* and *The World Of Polish Jews* (Vintage, o.p./Houghton Mifflin Company). Imaginative, well-researched reconstruction of life in a typical prewar Polish *shtetl*. Good on broader issues of Polish–Jewish relations, although her carefully balanced conclusions have come in for predictable criticism from those who say it paints too rosy a picture of the prewar period.

Lynne Jones *States of Change – A Central European Diary* (Merlin, o.p.). Highly personal account, wandering mainly through Poland and paying special attention to the alternative scene of punks, greens, anarchists, peaceniks, etc.

Ryszard Kapuscióski *Shadow of the Sun* (Penguin/Alfred Knopf). For many years Kapuscióski was the only full-time Polish foreign correspondent, and he's best known for his trilogy on the dictators of Iran, Angola and Ethiopia. His latest book, a collection of sketches of African politics, offers many wry insights into his native land.

Adam Michnik *Letters From Prison* (University of California Press). Collection of writings by prominent opposition intellectual and editor of the *Gazeta Wyborcza*, once Solidarity's house newspaper, now critical of (and disowned by) Wałęsa. The essay "A New Evolutionism" is a seminal piece of new political writing, and the more historical pieces are fascinating, too.

Czesław Miłosz *The Captive Mind* (Penguin/Vintage Books); *Native Realm* (Penguin/University of California Press); *Beginning with my Streets* (I. B. Tauris/Farar, Strauss and Giroux). The first is a penetrating analysis of the reasons so many Polish artists and intellectuals sold out to communism after 1945, with four case-studies supplementing a confession of personal guilt. *Native Realm*, the unorthodox autobiography of the years before Miłosz defected to the West, is especially illuminating on the Polish-Lithuanian relationship. The last is a wide-ranging collection of essays by the Nobel Prize-winning author, including an invigorating set of pieces revolving around Wilno (Vilnius), the author's boyhood home and spiritual mentor in later life.

Toby Nobel Fluek *Memoirs of my Life in a Polish Village 1930–39* (Hamish Hamilton, o.p./Random House, o.p.). Touching memoir of a young Jewish girl growing up in a village near Lwów in the 1930s. Plenty of insights into the traditional prewar Polish rural way of life, enhanced by the author's simple but evocative illustrations.

Barbara Porajska *From the Steppes to the Savannah* (Random House, o.p.). Simply written yet informative memoir of one of the hundreds of Poles deported to Kazakhstan and other parts of Soviet Asia following the Soviet annexation to eastern Poland in 1939. Like many others, too, the author finally made it to Britain, via adventures in Iran and East Africa.

Theo Richmond *Konin: A Quest* (Vintage/Vintage Books). Moving account of a British Jew's tireless quest to trace his family roots in a small town in western Poland that also displays a strong feel for the broader historical and political context.

Tim Sebastian *Nice Promises* (Chatto and Windus, o.p.). Former Warsaw BBC correspondent's reflections on the early 1980s in Poland. Chatty, anecdotal stuff, but plenty of insights into the politics and spirit of the times.

Teresa Torańska *Oni: Poland's Stalinists Cross-Examined* (HarperCollins, o.p.). Interviews with Polish communists and Party leaders from the Stalinist era carried out during the Solidarity era by investigative journalist Torańska. The result is a fascinating insight into how Stalin established Soviet control over Eastern Europe, and Poland in particular.

Lech Wałęsa *The Struggle and the Triumph: An Autobiography* (Arcade). Ghostwritten, it would seem, by a Solidarity committee, in the years before Lech split the party and created his own role as "axe-wielding" president.

Culture, art and architecture

F.C. Anstrutter *Old Polish Legends* (Hippocrene). Entertaining retellings of some of the best-known traditional Polish tales and legends, including the legends of Krakus, Wanda and most famously, the story of the trumpeter of Kraków *hejnał* fame.

Adam Bujak *Kraków* (Sport y Turystyka, Poland). Beautiful collection of photographs of the city and its surroundings by one of Poland's premier contemporary photographers.

David Buxton *The Wooden Churches of Eastern Europe* (CUP, o.p.). Wonderful illustrations of Poland's most compelling architectural style. Well worth hunting out in libraries: it will make you want to traipse around Silesia, the Bieszczady Mountains and Czech borderlands.

Huit Siècles d'Eglises Polonaises: le Cas du Ermland (Romain Pages Editions, France). Beautifully photographed French album of the distinctive church architecture of the Warmia region of northeast Poland, including useful background text.

Les Icones de Pologne (Editions de Cerf/Arkadia, o.p.). Good repro-

ductions of most of the major icons from Poland's regional museums. Scour the *antiquariats* of the big cities for a copy.

Oleh Iwanusiw *Church In Ruins* (St Sophia Association of Ukrainian Catholics in Canada). Painstakingly compiled and well-produced photographic record of Orthodox and Greek Catholic churches in the Przemyśl region, complete with an account of the current state of (dis)repair of every building as of 1987. Hard to get hold of, but with luck you might be able to pick up a copy at the Icon Museum in Przemyśl.

Sophie Knab *Polish Customs, Traditions & Folklore* (Hippocrene). Compendium of Polish folklore grouped according to months of the year and central rites of passage. A delight for anthropologists as much as anyone interested in delving into what lies behind ethnographic exhibits on show in regional museums throughout the country.

Jan Kott (ed.) *Four Decades of Polish Essays* (Northwestern UP). Culture-based anthology – on art, literature, drama, plus politics – that features most of the major intellectual names of postwar Poland.

Anna Nietksza *Impresje Polskie* (Fundacja Buchnera, Poland). Excellent set of photographic portraits of contemporary Poland, taking in everything from rural life and industrial landscapes to the face of the emerging post-communist social order. Accompanying booklet with summary captions in English and German. Widely available in Poland.

The Polish Jewry: History and Culture (Interpress, Warsaw). Wide-ranging collection of essays and photographs on all aspects of culture – from customs and family life to theatre, music and painting. A beautiful production.

Polish Realities *The Arts in Poland 1908–89* (Third Eye Centre, Glasgow). Excellent anthology of essays on all aspects of cultural life in Poland in the 1980s – architecture and youth culture alongside the obvious pieces on film, literature and theatre – which accompanied a major season of events in Glasgow under the same title. A testimony to the city's special links with Poland.

Reise nach Masuren (Rautenberg Verlage). One of the large series of photo albums based on East Prussian

memorabilia, produced by the German Rautenberg publishing house. Despite some dubious *alte Heimat* politics that occasionally steer dangerously close to straightforward revanchism, these volumes are nevertheless infused with a clear love of the old East Prussian territories, and the photographs of the region are some of the best around.

Roman Vishniac *Polish Jews – A Pictorial Record* (Schocken). Haunting selection of pictures by the legendary photographer, evoking Jewish life in the *shtetls* and ghettos of Poland immediately before the outbreak of World War II. A good introduction to the great man's work if you can't get hold of *A Vanished World* (Penguin, o.p.), the acclaimed album that brings together most of the 2000 or so photos from Vishniac's travels through Jewish Poland.

Tomasz Wiśniewski *Jewish Białystok and Surrroundings in Eastern Europe* (Ipswich). Encyclopedic survey of the wealth of prewar Jewish architecture in the eastern borderlands, much of it destroyed but with a significant number of buildings still surviving. Great for exploring the Białystok-Tykocin region.

Polish fiction

Shmuel Yozef Agnon *A Simple Story* (Schocken/Syracuse University Press); *Dwelling Place of My People* (Scottish Academic Press, o.p.). Agnon, Polish-born Nobel Prize-winner and father-figure of modern Hebrew literature, sets *A Simple Story* in the Jewish communities of the Polish Ukraine, belying its title by weaving an unexpected variation on the traditional Romeo-and-Juliet-type tale of crossed lovers. In Dwelling Place he recalls his childhood in Poland, in a series of highly refined stories and prose poems.

Jerzy Andrzejewski *Ashes and Diamonds* (Northwestern UP). Spring 1945: resistance fighters,

communist ideologues and black-marketeers battle it out in small-town Poland. A gripping account of the tensions and forces that shaped postwar Poland, and the basis for Andrzej Wajda's film of the same title.

Asher Barash *Pictures from a Brewery* (Peter Owen, o.p.). Depiction of Jewish life in Galicia, told in a style very different from the mythic, romantic approach favoured by Agnon.

Tadeusz Borowski *This Way for the Gas, Ladies and Gentlemen* (Penguin/Penguin US). These short stories based on his Auschwitz experiences marked Borowski out as the great literary hope of communist Poland, but he committed suicide soon after their publication, at the age of 29.

Joseph Conrad *A Personal Record* (Penguin). An entertaining, ironic piece of "faction" about Conrad's family and his early life in the Russian part of Partition Poland, addressing the painful subjects of his loss of his own country and language.

Ida Fink *A Scrap of Time* (Penguin, o.p./Northwestern UP). Haunting vignettes of Jews striving to escape the concentration camps – and of the unsung Polish Gentiles who sheltered them.

Adam Gillon (ed.) *Introduction to Modern Polish Literature* (Hippocrene). An excellent anthology of short stories and extracts from novels, many of them (eg Reymont's *The Peasants*) out of print in English.

Witold Gombrowicz *Ferdydurke* (Yale UP); *Pornografia* (Boyars); and *The Possessed* (Boyars). The first two experimentalist novels concentrate on humanity's infantile and juvenile obsessions, and on the tensions between urban life and the traditional ways of the countryside. *The Possessed* explores the same themes within the more easily digestible format of a Gothic thriller.

Marek Hłasko *The Eighth Day of the Week* (Northwestern UP/Greenwood Publishing); *Killing the Second Dog* (Minerva, o.p./Cane Hill Press, o.p.); and *Next Stop – Paradise & the Graveyard* (Greenwood Publishing). Poland's "Angry Young Man", Hłasko articulated the general disaffection of those who grew up after World War II, his bleak themes mirrored in a spare, taut prose style.

Pawel Huelle *Who Was David Weiser?* and *Moving House* (both Bloomsbury/Harcourt). The first is the well-translated first novel by a young Gdańsk-born writer, centring on an enigmatic young Jewish boy idolized by his youthful contemporaries: author's themes and style show an obvious debt to fellow Danziger Günter Grass. Huelle's magic-realist propensities are further developed in Moving House, his latest work to be translated, a marvellous collection of short stories, with the intersecting worlds of Polish and German/ Prussian culture again providing the primary frame of reference.

Tadeusz Konwicki *A Minor Apocalypse* (Dalkey Archive Press); *A Dreambook for our Time* (Penguin, o.p./Dalkey Archive Press); *The Polish Complex* (Penguin US, o.p.). A convinced Party member in the 1950s, Konwicki eventually made the break with Stalinism; since then a series of highly respected novels, films and screenplays have established him as one of Poland's foremost writers. Describing a single day's events, *A Minor Apocalypse* is narrated by a character who constantly vacillates over his promise to set fire to himself in front of the Party headquarters. *Dreambook* is a hard-hitting wartime tale, while *The Polish Complex* is a fascinating, often elusive exploration of contemporary life in Poland. Like Miłosz and many others who grew up in Wilno, now the capital of Lithuania, Konwicki betrays a yearning for a mystic homeland.

Janusz Korczak *King Matty the First* (Hippocrene). Written by the famous Jewish doctor who died, along with his orphans, at Treblinka, this long children's novel, regarded as the Polish counterpart of *Alice in Wonderland*, appeals also to adults through its underlying sense of tragedy and gravitas.

Stanisław Lem *Return from the Stars* (Mandarin, o.p.); *Tales of Pirx the Pilot* (Harcourt); *His Master's Voice* (Harvest Books/Northwestern UP). The only recent Polish writing to have achieved a worldwide mass-market readership, Lem's science fiction focuses on the human and social predicament in the light of technological change.

Czesław Miłosz *The Seizure of Power* (Faber, o.p.); *The Issa Valley* (Penguin/Farrar, Straus and Giroux). *The Seizure of Power*, the first book by this Nobel Prize-winning writer, is a wartime novel, while the semi-autobiographical Issa Valley is a wonderfully lyrical account of a boy growing up in the Lithuanian countryside.

Jan Potocki *The Manuscript Found at Saragossa: Ten Days in the Life of Alphonse von Worden* (Penguin). A self-contained section of a huge unfinished Gothic novel written at the beginning of the nineteenth century by a Polish nobleman: a rich brew of picaresque adventures, dreams, hallucinations, eroticism, philosophical discourses and exotic tales.

Bolesław Prus *Pharaoh* (Hippocrene); *The Doll* (Central European UP/OUP). The first, a late nineteenth-century epic, set in ancient Egypt, offers a trenchant examination of the nature of power in a society that was of more than passing relevance to Partition-era Poland. *The Doll* is a notable new translation of probably the most famous of the "Polish Tolstoy's" lengthier works, complete with a useful introduction by the noted poet and critic Stanisław Barańczak. Widely regarded as one of the great nineteenth-century social novels, this is a brilliantly-observed story of obsessive love against the backdrop of a crisis-ridden *fin-de-siècle* Warsaw.

R. Pynsent and S. Kanikova (eds.) *The Everyman Companion to East European Literature* (Dent). The Polish section combines thoughtful introductory essays on the place of literature and writers in the national consciousness. Includes short extracts from works by major artists (Prus, Witkiewicz, Mickiewicz), a literary itinerary through the country and a brief authors' A–Z.

Władysław Reymont *The Peasants*; *The Promised Land* (both o.p.). Reymont won the Nobel Prize for *The Peasants*, a tetralogy about village life (one for each season of the year), but its vast length has led to its neglect outside Poland. *The Promised Land*, which was filmed by Wajda, offers a comparably unromanticized view of industrial life in Łódź.

Bruno Schulz *Street of Crocodiles* (Penguin/Penguin US) and *Sanatorium under the Sign of the Hourglass* (Picador/Houghton Mifflin). These kaleidoscopic, dream-like fictions, vividly evoking life in the small town of Drohobycz in the Polish Ukraine, constitute the entire literary output of their author, who was murdered by the SS.

Henryk Sienkiewicz *Quo Vadis?* (Hippocrene); *Charcoal Sketches and Other Tales* (Angel, o.p.); *With Fire and Sword*; *The Deluge*; and *Fire in the Steppe* (Hippocrene). Sienkiewicz's reputation outside Poland largely rests on *Quo Vadis?* (which won him the Nobel Prize), treating the early Christians in Nero's Rome as an allegory of Poland's plight under the Partitions. Until recently, Sienkiewicz's other blockbusters existed only in inadequate and long out-of-print translations, but the Polish–American novelist W.S. Kuniczak has recently rendered the great trilogy about Poland's seventeenth-century wars with the Swedes, Prussians, Germans and Turks into English in a manner that at last does justice to the richly crafted prose of the originals. If the sheer size of these is too daunting, a more than adequate taste of the author's style can be had from the three novellas in the *Charcoal Sketches* collection, which focus on the different classes of nineteenth-century Polish rural society with a wry wit and a sense of pathos.

Isaac Bashevis Singer *The Magician of Lublin* (Penguin/Buccaneer Books, o.p.); *The Family Moskat*

(Vintage/Farrar, Straus and Giroux, o.p.); *Collected Stories* (Penguin/Farrar, Straus and Giroux); *The Slave* (Penguin/Farrar, Straus and Giroux); *Satan in Goray* (Vintage/Farrar, Straus and Giroux); *The King of the Fields* (Penguin, o.p./Farrar, Straus and Giroux). Singer, who emigrated from Poland to the USA in the 1930s, writes in Yiddish, so his reputation rests largely on the translations of his novels and short stories. Only a selection of his vast output is mentioned here. *The Magician of Lublin* and *The Family Moskat*, both novels set in the ghettos of early twentieth-century Poland, are masterly evocations of life in vanished Jewish communities. *The Slave* is a gentle yet tragic love story set in the seventeenth century, while *Satan in Goray* is a blazing evocation of religious hysteria in the same period. His penultimate work, *The King of the Fields*, re-creates the early life of the Polish state, and is his only novel without a Jewish emphasis.

Andrzej Szczypiorski *The Beautiful Mrs Seidemann* (Phoenix/Grove-Atlantic). Best-selling novel by prominent contemporary Polish writer who survived both the Warsaw Uprising and subsequently the concentration camps. The story centres around a Jewish woman who uses her wits – and beauty – to survive the Nazis. Stirringly written, though the fatalistic historical musings (he's obviously got a foreign audience in mind) become increasingly oppressive as the book progresses.

Stanisław Ignacy Witkiewicz *Insatiability* (Northwestern UP). Explicit depiction of artistic, intellectual, religious and sexual decadence against the background of a Chinese invasion of Europe. The enormous vocabulary, complicated syntax and philosophical diversions don't make an easy read, but this is unquestionably one of the most distinctive works of twentieth-century literature.

Polish poetry

S. Barańczak and C. Cavanagh (eds.) *Spoiling Cannibal's Fun: Polish Poetry of the Last Two Decades of Communist Rule* (Northwestern UP). Representative anthology of recent Polish poetry with informative introductory essay by co-editor and translator Stanisław Barańczak, one of the country's pre-eminent émigré literary figures whose poems are also featured in this volume.

Susan Bassnett and Piotr Kuhiwczak (eds.) *Ariadne's Thread: Polish Women Poets* (Dufour Editions). Poems by eight distinctive contemporaries, ranging from reinterpretations of classical myth to the horrors of torture.

Adam Czerniawski (ed.) *The Burning Forest* (Bloodaxe Books). Selected by one of Poland's leading contemporary poets, this anthology covers Polish poetry from the laconic nineteenth-century verses of Cyprian Norwid, through examples of Herbert, Rożewicz and the editor, up to young writers of the present day.

Zbigniew Herbert *Selected Poems* (W.W. Norton); *Report from the Besieged City* (OUP, o.p./HarperCollins, o.p.). Arguably the greatest contemporary Polish poet, with a strong line in poignant observation; intensely political but never dogmatic. The widespread international mourning occasioned by Herbert's death in 1998 confirmed the man's special place in contemporary literary affections.

Adam Mickiewicz *Pan Tadeusz* (Hippocrene); *Konrad Wallenrod* and *Grażyna* (both University Press of America). Poland's national epic, set among the gentry of Lithuania at the time of the Napoleonic invasion, is here given a highly effective verse translation. In contrast to the self-delusion about Polish independence shown by the characters in *Pan Tadeusz, Konrad Wallenrod* demonstrates how that end can be achieved by stealth and cunning; like *Grażyna*, its setting is Poland-Lithuania's struggle with the Teutonic Knights.

Czesław Miłosz *New and Collected Poems* (Penguin/HarperCollins). A writer of massive integrity, Miłosz in all his works wrestles with the issues of spiritual and political commitment; this collection encompasses all his poetic phases, from the Surrealist of the 1930s to the émigré sage of San Francisco.

Czesław Miłosz (ed.) *Polish Postwar Poetry* (California UP). Useful anthology selected and mostly translated by Miłosz, with an emphasis on poetry written after the thaw of 1956. The closer you get to the 1980s the grittier and more acerbic they become, as befits the politics of the era.

Tadeusz Różewicz *Conversations with the Prince* (Anvil Press, o.p.). These uncompromising verses, rooted in everyday speech, are among the most accessible examples of modern Polish poetry.

Anna Swir *Fat Like the Sun* (Women's Press, o.p.). Selection from a leading feminist poet.

Wisława Szymborska *People on the Bridge* (Forest Books). For some time virtually the only volume of poems by the 1996 Nobel Prize-winning Polish author available in English. Szymborska remains one of the most distinctive modern (female) voices, translated here by fellow poet, Adam Czerniawski. Of the volumes to appear in the wake of the Nobel award, *View With a Grain of Sand* (Faber and Faber/Harcourt) is an excellent introduction to the Szymborska oeuvre; *Poems New and Collected 1957–1997* (Faber and Faber/Harcourt), is a large, well-translated selection of her poems spanning the last four decades: *Sounds, Feelings, Thoughts: Seventy Poems* (Princeton UP), a reissue, covers similar territory, albeit less comprehensively.

Aleksander Wat *Selected Poems* (Penguin, o.p.). Dating from Wat's middle and later years, these wide-ranging poems, with their predominant tone of despair at the century's excesses, make a fascinating contrast to the Futurist short-story fantasies he wrote in the interwar period.

Karol Wojtyła *Easter Vigil and Other Poems* (Hutchinson, o.p./Random House, o.p.). Pope John Paul II followed a sideline career in poetry throughout his priesthood. This selection casts light on the complex private personality of a very public figure.

Polish drama

Solomon Anski *The Dybbuk*, included in *Three Great Jewish Plays* (Applause). Written by a prominent member of the Jewish socialist movement, this drama of divine justice is the masterpiece of Yiddish theatre. Also included in the anthology is a work on a similar theme, *God of Vengeance* by Scholem Asch.

Daniel Gerould (ed.) *The Witkiewicz Reader* (Quartet, o.p./Northwestern UP). Painstakingly compiled and well-translated anthology of writings by the great artist/philosopher/dramatist covering the various stages of Witkiewicz's development, from the early plays via explicitly drug-induced musings through to later philosophical and literary critical pieces.

Witold Gombrowicz *The Marriage; Operetta;* and *Princess Ivona* (all Boyars/Northwestern UP). Three plays exploring similar themes to those found in Gombrowicz's novels.

Tadeusz Kantor *Wielopole/Wielopole*

(Marian Boyars). One of the most successful products of Poland's experimental theatre scene, complete with a lavish record of its production plus the author/director's rehearsal notes.

Sławomir Mrożek *Tango* (Cape, o.p./Grove, o.p.); *Vatzlav* (Applause, o.p.); *Striptease, Repeat Performance and The Prophets* (Applause, o.p.). Mrożek is the sharpest and subtlest satirist Poland has produced, employing nonsensical situations to probe serious political issues.

Tadeusz Różewicz *The Card Index*; *The Interrupted Act and Gone Out*; *Marriage Blanc and The Hunger Artist Departs* (all Marion Boyars). The best works by an unremittingly inventive experimentalist.

Juliusz Słowacki *Mary Stuart* (Greenwood Press, o.p./Greenwood Publishing, o.p.). Słowacki ranks second only to Mickiewicz in Polish esteem, but his reputation hasn't travelled. Nonetheless, this is a fine example of Romantic drama, set against the backdrop of the murders of David Rizzio and Mary's husband, Henry Darnley.

Stanisław Ignacy Witkiewicz *The Madman and the Nun, The Water Hen & The Crazy Locomotive* (Applause). Witkiewicz created a Theatre of the Absurd twenty years before the term came into common use through the work of Ionesco and Beckett. This volume makes the ideal introduction to the versatile avant-garde painter, novelist and playwright.

Literature by foreign writers

Isaac Babel *Red Cavalry*, from *Collected Stories* (Penguin/Penguin US). A collection of interrelated short stories about the 1919–20 invasion of Poland, narrated by the bizarrely contradictory figure of a Jewish Cossack communist, who naturally finds himself torn by conflicting emotions.

Günter Grass *The Tin Drum* (Minerva/Random House); *Dog Years* (Minerva/Harcourt); *Cat and Mouse* (Minerva/Harcourt). These three novels, also available in one volume as the *Danzig Trilogy* (Harcourt/Fine Communications), are one of the high points of modern German literature. Set in Danzig/Gdańsk, where the author grew up, they hold up a mirror to the changing German character this century. The later *The Call of the Toad* (Minerva/Harcourt), provides a satirical commentary on post-communist Polish and German attitudes towards the same city's past.

Gerhart Hauptmann *The Weavers* (Methuen, o.p) in the UK; published as part of *Three Plays* (Waveland Press) in the US.. Set against the background of a heroic but inevitably futile mid-nineteenth-century uprising by the Silesian weavers against the mill owners, this intense drama gained its reputation as the first "socialist" play by having a collective rather than a single protagonist.

E.T.A. Hoffmann *The Jesuit Chapel at G*, in *Six German Romantic Tales*, Angel Books/Dufour Editions); *The Artushof*, in *Tales of Hoffmann* (Penguin/Penguin US). Hoffmann began writing his masterly stories of the macabre while a bored civil servant in Prussian Poland; these are two with a specifically Polish setting.

Thomas Keneally *Schindler's List* (Hodder and Stoughton/Simon and Schuster). Originally entitled *Schindler's Ark* before becoming the subject of Spielberg's film, this powerful, 1982 Booker Prize-winning novel, is based on the life of Oskar Schindler, a German industrialist who used his business operations to shelter thousands of Jews.

Leon Uris *Mila 18* (Bantam

Books). Stirring tale of the Warsaw Ghetto Uprising – Mila 18 was the address of the Jewish resistance militia's HQ.

Film

Krzysztof Kieślowski and **Krysztof Piesiewicz** *Decalogue* (Faber and Faber). Transcripts of the internationally acclaimed series of films, set in a Warsaw housing estate, featuring tales of breaches of the Ten Commandments.

Brian McIlroy *World Cinema: Poland* (Flicks Books, o.p.). In-depth study of the Polish film scene including interviews, biographies and plenty of black and white stills.

Andrzej Wajda *Double Vision: My Life in Film* (Faber and Faber, o.p./Henry Holt, o.p.). Autobiography of Poland's most famous director; rather more rewarding than some of his later celluloid creations.

language

language

Language

P olish is one of the more difficult European languages for English speakers to learn. Even so, it is well worth acquiring the basics: not only is Polish beautiful and melodious, but a few words will go a long way. This is especially true away from the major cities where you won't find a lot of English spoken. Knowledge of German, however, is quite widespread.

The following features provide an indication of the problems of Polish grammar. There are three genders (masculine, feminine and neuter) and no word for "the". Prepositions (words like "to", "with", "in" etc) take different cases, and the case changes the form of the noun. Thus, "miasto" is the Polish for "town", but "to the town" is "do miasta" and "in the town" is "w mieście". You don't have to learn this sort of thing off by heart, but it can be useful to be able to recognize it.

Finally, a brief word on how to address people. The familiar form used among friends, relations and young people is "ty", like French "tu" or German "du". However, the polite form which you will usually require is "Pan" when addressing a man and "Pani" for a woman ("Sir" and "Madam"). *Always* use this form with people obviously older than yourself, and with officials.

The *Rough Guide to Polish* **phrasebook** has a more detailed selection of useful terms.

Pronunciation

While Polish may look daunting at first, with its apparently unrelieved rows of consonants, the good news is that it's a **phonetic language** – ie it's pronounced exactly as spelt. So once you've learnt the rules and have a little experience you'll always know how to pronounce a word correctly.

Stress:
Usually on the penultimate syllable, eg Warsza**wa**, przyja**ciel**, **ma**tka.

Vowels:
a: as "a" in "cat".
e: "e" in "neck".
i: "i" in "Mick", never as in "I".
o: "o" in "lot", never as in "no" or "move".
u: "oo" in "look".
y: unknown in Standard English; cross between "e" and Polish "i", eg the "y" in the Yorkshire pronunciation of "Billy".

There are three specifically Polish vowels:
ą: nasalized – like "ong" in "long" or French "on".
ę: nasalized – like French "un" (eg Lech Wałęsa).
ó: same sound as Polish "u".

Vowel combinations include:

ie: pronounced y-e, eg "nie wiem" (I don't know): ny-e vy-em (not nee-veem).
eu: each letter pronounced separately, eg "E-u-ropa" (Europe).
ia: rather like "yah", eg "historia" (history): histor-i-yah.

Consonants:

Those which look the same as English but are different:
w: as "v" in "vine", eg "wino" pronounced "vino" (wine).
r: trilled (as in Scottish pronunciation of English "r").
h: like the "ch" in Scottish "loch".
Some consonants are pronounced differently at the end of a word or syllable:
b sounds like p, d like t, g like k, w like f.

Polish-specific consonants include:
ć and **ci**: "ch" as in "church".
ł: "dark l" sounding rather like a "w".
ń and **ni**: "soft n", sounding like "n-ye", eg "koń" (horse): kon-ye.
ś and **si**: "sh" as in "ship".
ź and **zi**: like the "j" of French "journal".
ż and **rz**: as in French "g" in "gendarme". (Note that the dot over the z is sometimes replaced by a bar through the letter's diagonal.)

Consonantal pairs:

cz: "ch" (slightly harder than "ć" and "ci").
sz: "sh" (ditto "ś" and "si").
dz: "d" as in "day" rapidly followed by "z" as in "zoo", eg "dzwon" (bell): d-zvon. At the end of a word is pronounced like "ts" as in "cats".
dź: "d-sh", eg "dźungla" (jungle): d-shun-gla.
dż: sharper than the above; at the end of a word is pronounced like "ć" (ch).
szcz: this fearsome-looking cluster is easy to pronounce – "sh-ch" as in "pushchair", eg "szczur" (rat): sh-choor.

Useful words and phrases

Words

Tak – Yes	**Dosyć** – Enough
Nie – No/not	**Tam** – Over there
Proszę – Please/you're welcome	**Ten/ta/to** – This one (masc/fem/neuter)
Proszę bardzo – More emphatic than "proszę"	**Tamten/tamta/tamto** – That one (masc/fem/neuter)
Dziekuję/dziekuję bardzo – Thank you	
Gdzie – Where	**Wielki** – Large
Kiedy – When	**Mały** – Small
Dlaczego – Why	**Więcej** – More
Ile – How much	**Mniej** – Less
Tu/tam – Here, there	**Mało** – A little
Teraz – Now	**Dużo** – A lot
Później – Later	**Tani** – Cheap
Otwarty – Open	**Drogi** – Expensive
Zamknięty – Closed/shut	**Dobry** – Good
Wcześniej – Earlier	**Zły/niedobry** – Bad

Gorący - Hot
Zimny - Cold
Z - With

Bez - Without
W - In
Dla - For

Phrases

Dzień dobry - Good day; hello
Dobry wieczór - Good evening
Dobra noc - Good night
Cześć! - "Hi!" or "'Bye" (like Italian "ciao")
Do widzenia - Goodbye
Przepraszam - Excuse me (apology)
Proszę Pana/Pani - Excuse me (requesting
  information)
Jak się masz? - How are you? (informal)
Jak się Pan/Pani ma? - How are you? (formal)
Dobrze - Fine
Czy Pan/Pani mówi po angielsku? - Do you
  speak English?
Rozumiem - I understand
Nie rozumiem - I don't understand
Nie wiem - I don't know
Proszę mówić trochę wolniej - Please
  speak a bit more slowly
Nie mówię dobrze po polsku - I don't speak
  Polish very well
Co to znaczy po polsku? - What's the Polish
  for that?

Jestem tu na urlopie - I'm here on holiday
Jestem Brytyjczykiem/Brytyjką - I'm British
  (male/female)
Irlandczykiem/Irlandką - Irish
Amerikaniem/Amerikanką - American
Kanadyjczykiem/Kanadyjką - Canadian
Australyjczykiem/Australyjką - Australian
Mieszkam w . . . - I live in . . .
Dzisiaj - Today
Jutro - Tomorrow
Pojutrze - Day after tomorrow
Wczoraj - Yesterday
Chwileczkę - Moment!/Wait a moment
Rano - In the morning
Po południu - In the afternoon
Wieczorem - In the evening
Gdzie jest . . . ? - Where is . . . ?
Jak dojechać do . . . ? - How do I get
  to . . . ?
Która (jest) godzina? What time is it?
Jak daleko jest do . . . ? - How far is it
  to . . . ?

Accommodation

Hotel Hotel
Noclegi Lodgings
Czy jest gdzieś tutaj hotel? Is there a hotel
  nearby?
Czy Pan/Pani ma pokój? Do you have a
  room?
Pojedynczy pokój Single room
Podwójny pokój Double room
Będziemy jedną dobę For one night (doba: 24
  hours)
Dwie noce Two nights
Trzy noce Three nights
Tydzień A week
Dwa tygodnie Two weeks
Pokój z łazienką With a bath
Z prysznicem With a shower
Z balkonem With a balcony
Z ciepłą wodą Hot water
Z bieżące wodą - Running water
Ile kosztuje? - How much is it?

To drogo - That's expensive
To za drogo - That's too expensive
Czy to obejmuje śniadanie? - Does that
  include breakfast?
Czy nie ma tańszego? - Do you have any-
  thing cheaper?
Czy mogę zobaczyć pokój? - Can I see the
  room?
Dobrze, wezmę - Good, I'll take it
Mam rezerwację - I have a booking
Czy możemy tu rozbić namiot? - Can we
  camp here?
Czy jest gdzieś tutaj camping? - Is there a
  campsite nearby?
Namiot - Tent
Schronisko - Cabin
Schronisko młodziezowe - Youth hostel
Proszę o jadłospis - The menu, please
Proszę o rachunek - The bill, please

Travelling

Auto – Car
Samolot – Aircraft
Rower – Bicycle
Autobus – Bus
Prom – Ferry
Pociąg – Train
Dworzec, samochód, stacja – Train station
Autobusowy – Bus station
Taksówka – Taxi
Autostop – Hitchhiking
Piechotą – On foot
Proszę bilet do . . . – A ticket to . . . , please
Bilet powrotny – Return
W jedną stronę – Single
Proszę z miejscówką – I'd like a seat
  reservation

Kiedy odjeżdża pociąg do Warszawy? –
  When does the Warsaw train leave?
Czy muszę się przesiadać? – Do I have to
  change?
Z jakiego peronu odjedzie pociąg? – Which
  platform does the train leave from?
Ile to jest kilometrów? – How many kilome-
  tres is it?
Ile czasu trwa podróż? – How long does the
  journey last?
Jakim autobusem do . . . ? – Which bus is it
  to . . . ?
Gdzie jest droga do . . . ? – Where is the
  road to . . . ?
Następny przystanek, proszę – Next stop,
  please

Signs

Wejście; wyjucie – Entrance; exit/way out
Wstęp wzbroniony – No entrance
Toaleta – Toilet
Dla panów; męski – Men
Dla pan; damski – Women
Zajęty – Occupied
Wolny – Free, vacant
Przyjazd; odjazd – Arrival; departure (train, bus)
Przylot; odlot – Arrival; departure (aircraft)
Remont – Closed for renovation/stocktaking
Ciągnąć; pchać – Pull; push
Nieczynny – Out of order; closed (ticket coun-
  ters, etc)

Peron – Platform
Kasa – Cash desk
Stop – Stop
Granica międzynarodowa – Polish state
  frontier
Rzeczpospolita Polska – Republic of Poland
Uwaga; baczność – Beware, caution
Uwaga; niebezpieczeństwo – Danger
Policja – Police
Informacja – Information
Nie palić; palenie wzbronione – No
  smoking
Nie dotykać – Do not touch

Driving

Samochód, auto – Car
Na lewo – Left
Na prawo – Right
Prosto – Straight ahead
Parking – Parking
Objazd – Detour
Koniec – End (showing when a previous sign
  ceases to be valid)
Zakaz wyprzedzania – No overtaking

Benzyna – Petrol/gas
Stacja benzynowa – Petrol/gas station
Olej – Oil
Woda – Water
Naprawić – To repair
Wypadek – Accident
Awaria – Breakdown
Ograniczenie prędkości – Speed limit

Days, months and dates

Poniedziałek – Monday
Wtorek – Tuesday
Środa – Wednesday
Czwartek – Thursday
Piątek – Friday

Sobota – Saturday
Niedziela – Sunday
Styczeń – January
Luty – February
Marzec – March

Kwiecień – April
Maj – May
Czerwiec – June
Lipiec – July
Sierpień – August
Wrzesien – September
Październik – October
Listopad – November

Grudzień – December
Wiosna – spring
Lato – summer
Jesień – autumn
Zima – winter
Wakacje – holidays
Święto – bank holiday

Numbers

Jeden – 1
Dwa – 2
Trzy – 3
Cztery – 4
Pięć – 5
Sześć – 6
Siedem – 7
Osiem – 8
Dziewięć – 9
Dziesięć – 10
Jedenaście – 11
Dwanaście – 12
Trzynaście – 13
Czternaście – 14
Piętnaście – 15
Szesnaście – 16
Siedemnaście – 17
Osiemnaście – 18
Dziewiętnaście – 19

Dwadzieścia – 20
Trzydzieści – 30
Czterdzieści – 40
Pięćdziesiąt – 50
Sześćdziesiąt – 60
Siedemdziesiąt – 70
Osiemdziesiąt – 80
Dziewięćdziesiąt – 90
Sto – 100
Dwieście – 200
Trzysta – 300
Czterysta – 400
Pięćset – 500
Sześćset – 600
Siedemset – 700
Osiemset – 800
Dziewięćset – 900
Tysiąc – 1000
Milion – 1,000,000

Food and drink

Common terms

Antrykot/wołowy – Mixed
Filiżanka – Cup
Gotowany – Boiled
Grill/z rusztu – Grilled
Jadłospis – Menu
Kolacja – Dinner
Kwąuny – Sour
Łyżka – Spoon
Marynowany – Pickled
Mielone – Minced
Na zdrowie! – Cheers!
Nadziewany – Stuffed
Nóż – Knife

Obiad – Lunch
Śniadanie – Breakfast
Świeży – Fresh
Słodki – Sweet
Smacznego! – Bon appetit!
Surowy – Raw
Szaszłyk – Grilled
Szklanka – Glass
Sznycel – Escalope/schnitzel
Talerz – Plate
Wegetariański – Vegetarian
Widelec – Fork

Basic foods

Bułka – Bread rolls
Chleb – Bread

Chrzan – Horseradish
Cukier – Sugar

Dró b – Poultry
Frytki – Chips/French fries
Jajko – Egg
Jarzyny/warzywa – Vegetables
Kanapka – Sandwich
Kołduny – Dumplings stuffed with meat
Kotlet – Cutlet
Makaron – Macaroni
Masło – Butter
Mięso – Meat
Ocet – Vinegar
Olej – Oil

Owoce – Fruit
Pieczeń – Roast meat
Pieczyste – Steak
Pieprz – Pepper
Potrawy jarskie – Vegetarian dishes
Ryby – Fish
Ryż – Rice
Śmietana – Cream
Sól – Salt
Surówka – Salad
Zupa – Soup

Soups

Barszcz czerwony (z pasztecikem) –
  Beetroot soup (with pastry)
Barszcz ukraiński – White borsch
Bulion/rosół – Bouillon
Chłodnik – Sour milk and vegetable cold soup
Kapuśniak – Cabbage soup
Kartoflanka – Potato soup
Krupnik – Barley soup
Zurek – Sour cream soup

(zupa) Cebulowa – Onion soup
(zupa) Fasolowa – Bean soup
(zupa) Grochowa – Pea soup
(zupa) Grzybowa – Mushroom soup
(zupa) Jarzynowa – Vegetable soup
(zupa) Ogórkowa – Cucumber soup
(zupa) Owocowa – Cold fruit soup
(zupa) Pomidorowa – Tomato soup

Meat, fish and poultry

Baranina – Mutton
Bażant – Pheasant
Befsztyk – Steak
Bekon boczek – Bacon
Cielęcina – Veal
Dziczyzna – Game
Dzik – Wild boar
Gęś – Geese
Golonka – Leg of pork
Indyk – Turkey
Kaczka – Duck
Karp – Carp
Kiełbasa – Sausage

Kotlet schabowy – Pork cutlet
Kurczak – Chicken
Łosoś – Salmon
Makrela – Mackerel
Pstrąg – Trout
Śledź – Herring
Salami – Salami
Sardynka – Sardine
Sarnina – Elk
Wątróbka – Liver with onion
Węgorz – Eel
Wierprzowe – Pork
Wołowe – Beef

Fruit and vegetables

Ananas – Pineapple
Banan – Banana
Ćwikła/buraczki – Beetroot
Cebula – Onion
Cytryna – Lemon
Czarne jagody borówki – Blackberries
Czarne porzeczki – Blackcurrant
Czereunie – Cherries
Czosnek – Garlic
Fasola – Beans
Groch – Peas

Gruszka – Pears
Grzyby/pieczarki – Mushrooms
Jabłko – Apple
Kalafior – Cauliflower
Kapusta – Cabbage
Kapusta kiszona – Sauerkraut
Kompot – Stewed fruit
Laskowe/orzechy – Almonds
Maliny – Raspberries
Marchewka – Carrots
Morele – Apricots

Ogórek - Cucumber
Ogórki - Gherkins
Orzechy włoskie - Walnuts
Papryka - Paprika
Pomarańcze - Orange
Pomidor - Tomato

Śliwka - Plum
Szparagi - Asparagus
Szpinak - Spinach
Truskawki - Strawberries
Winogrona - Grapes
Ziemniaki - Potatoes

Cheese

Bryndza - Sheep's cheese
Oscypek - Smoked goats' cheese
Twaróg - Cottage cheese

(ser) Myśliwski - Smoked cheese
(ser) Tylżycki - Cheddar cheese

Cakes and desserts

Ciastko - Cake
Ciasto drożdżowe - Yeast cake with fruit
Czekolada - Chocolate
Galaretka - Jellied fruits
Lody - Ice cream

Makowiec - Poppyseed cake
Mazurek - Shortcake
Pączki - Doughnuts
Sernik - Cheesecake
Tort - Tart

Drinks

Cocktail mleczny - Milk shake
Gorąca czekolada - Drinking chocolate
Herbata - Tea
Kawa - Coffee
Koniak - Cognac/brandy (imported)
Miód pitny - Mead
Mleko - Milk
Napój - Bottled fruit drink
Piwo - Beer
Sok - Juice

Sok pomarańczowy - Orange juice
Sok pomidorowy - Tomato juice
Spirytus - Spirits
Winiak - Polish brandy
Wino - Wine
Wino słodkie - Sweet wine
Wino wytrawne - Dry wine
Woda - Water
Woda mineralna - Mineral water
Wódka - Vodka

Glossaries

General terms

ALEJA - Avenue (abbreviation al.).
BIURO ZAKWATEROWAŃIA - Accommodation office.
BRAMA - Gate.
CERKIEW - (pl. *cerkwie*) Orthodox church, or a church belonging to the Uniates (Greek Catholics), a tradition loyal to Rome but following Orthodox rites that dates back to the 1595 Act of Union (see box on p.000).
CMENTARZ - Cemetery.
DOLINA - Valley.

DOM - House.
DOM KULTURY - Cultural House, a community arts and social centre.
DOM WYCIECZKOWY - Cheap, basic type of hotel.
DROGA - Road.
DWÓR - Country house traditionally owned by member of the *szlachta* class.
DWORZEC - Station.
GŁÓWNY - Main – as in Rynek Główny, main square.

GÓRA – (pl. *góry*) Mountain.
GRANICA – Border.
JEZIORO – Lake.
KANTOR – Exchange office.
KAPLICA – Chapel.
KAWIARNIA – Café.
KATEDRA – Cathedral.
KLASZTOR – Monastery.
KOŚCIÓŁ – Church.
KSIĄDZ – Priest.
KSIĄŻĘ – Prince, duke.
KSIĘGARNIA – Bookshop.
KRAJ – Country.
LAS – Wood, forest.
MASYW – Massif.
MIASTO – Town. (Stare Miasto – Old Town; Nowe Miasto – New Town.)
MOST – Bridge.
NARÓD – Nation, people.
NYSA – River Neisse.
ODRA – River Oder.
OGRÓD – Gardens.
PAŁAC – Palace.
PIWNICA – Pub.
PLAC – Square.
PLAŻA – Beach.
POCZTA – Post office.
POGOTOWIE – Emergency.
POKÓJ – (pl. *pokóje*) Room.
POLE – Field.
PROM – Ferry.
PRZEDMIEŚCIE – Suburb.
PRZYSTANEK – Bus stop.

PUSZCZA – Ancient forest.
RATUSZ – Town Hall.
RESTAURACJA – Restaurant.
RUCH – Chain of newpaper kiosks also selling public transport tickets.
RYNEK – Marketplace, commonly the main square in a town.
RZEKA – River.
SEJM – Parliament.
SHTETL – Yiddish name for a rural town, usually with a significant Jewish population.
SKAŁA – Rock, cliff.
SKANSEN – Open-air museum with reconstructed folk architecture and art.
STOCZNIA – Shipyards.
ŚWIĘTY – Saint (abbreviation Św.).
STAROWIERCY – (Old Believers) Traditionalist Russian Orthodox sect, small communities of which survive in east Poland.
STARY – Old.
SZLACHTA – Term for the traditional gentry class, inheritors of status and land.
ULICA – Street (abbeviation ul.).
WOJEWÓDZTWO – Administrative district.
WIEŚ – (pl. *wsie*) Village.
WIEŻA – Tower.
WINIARNIA – Wine cellar.
WISŁA – River Vistula.
WODOSPAD – Waterfall.
WZGÓRZE – Hill.
ZAMEK – Castle.
ZDRÓJ – Spa.
ZIEMIA – Region.

Art and architecture

AISLE – Part of church to the side of the nave.
AMBULATORY – Passage round the back of the altar, in continuation of the aisles.
APSE – Vaulted termination of the altar end of a church.
ARON HA KODESH – Place in synagogue for keeping the scrolls of the Torah (law), conventionally in the form of a niche in the eastern wall.
BAROQUE – Exuberant architectural style of the seventeenth and early eighteenth centuries, characterized by ornate decoration, complex spatial arrangement and grand vistas. The term is also applied to the sumptuous style of painting of the same period.
BASILICA – Church in which nave is higher than the aisles.

BIMAH – Raised central platform in a synagogue containing the pulpit from which the Torah is read.
BLACK MADONNA – National icon, an image of the Virgin and Child housed in the Jasna Góra monastery in Częstochowa.
CAPITAL – Top of a column, usually sculpted.
CHANCEL – Section of the church where the altar is situated, usually the east end.
CHOIR – Part of church in which service is sung, usually beside the altar.
CRYPT – Underground part of a church.
FRESCO – Mural painting applied to wet plaster, so that colours immediately soak into the wall.
GOTHIC – Architectural style with an emphasis on verticality, characterized by pointed arch

and ribbed vault: introduced to Poland in the thirteenth century, surviving in an increasingly decorative form until well into the sixteenth century. The term is also used of paintings and sculpture of the period.

HALL CHURCH – Church design in which all vaults are of approximately equal height.

ICONOSTASIS – Screen with a triple door separating the sanctuary from the nave in Uniate and Eastern Orthodox churches.

JUGENDSTIL – German version (encountered in western Poland) of Art Nouveau, a sinuous, highly decorative style of architecture and design from the period 1900–15.

MANNERISM – Deliberately over-sophisticated style of late-Renaissance art and architecture.

MANSARD – Curb roof in which each face has two slopes, with the lower one steeper than the upper.

MATZEVAH – An upright traditional Jewish tombstone adorned with inscriptions and symbolic ornamentation.

MEZUZAH – Scroll containing handwritten parchment scrolls of the scriptures, traditionally placed in a small case and fixed on the righthand doorpost of a Jewish house.

MŁODA POLSKA – (Young Poland) Turn-of-the-twentieth-century cultural movement centred on Kraków.

NAVE – Main body of the church, generally forming the western part.

NEOCLASSICAL – Late-eighteenth- and early-nineteenth-century style of art and architecture returning to classical models as a reaction against Baroque and Rococo excesses.

POLYPTYCH – Painting or carving on several hinged panels.

RENAISSANCE – Italian-originated movement in art and architecture, inspired by the rediscovery of classical ideals.

ROCOCO – Highly florid, light and graceful style of architecture, painting and interior design, forming the last phase of Baroque.

ROMANESQUE – Solid architectural style of the late-tenth to mid-thirteenth centuries, characterized by round-headed arches and geometrical precision. The term is also used for paintings of the same period.

ROMANTICISM – Late-eighteenth- and nineteenth-century movement, rooted in adulation of natural world and rediscovery of the country's rich historic heritage, strongly linked in Poland to the cause of national independence.

SECESSIONIST – Style of early-twentieth-century art and architecture, based in Germany and Austria, which reacted against academic establishments.

STUCCO – Plaster used for decorative effects.

TRANSEPT – Arms of a cross-shaped church, placed at ninety degrees to nave and chancel.

TRANSITIONAL – Architectural style between Romanesque and Gothic.

TRIPTYCH – Carved or painted altarpiece on three panels.

TROMPE L'OEIL – Painting designed to fool the onlooker into believing that it's actually three-dimensional.

History and politics

ARIANS – Radical Protestant grouping that gained a strong footing in the Reformation-era Polish-Lithuanian Commonwealth.

AUSTRO-HUNGARIAN EMPIRE – Vast Habsburg-ruled domain incorporating most of central Europe, enlarged to include Polish province of Galicia during the Partition period.

BALCEROWICZ, LESZEK – Finance minister following the 1989 elections. Responsible for introducing the country's post-communist programme of radical, free-market economic reform. Currently head of the National Bank of Poland.

BIELECKI, JAN – Solidarity adviser and young technocrat, based in Gdańsk; was prime minister from December 1990 to November 1991.

BUZEK, JERZY – Prime minister in the AWS-led centre-right coalition from 1997 to 2001. Founder member of Solidarity who comes from the southwest of the country. Buzek was the country's first non-Catholic political leader.

CHRISTIAN NATIONAL UNION (ZChN) – Most important of the Catholic-based political parties formed in the early post-communist era.

CITIZENS MOVEMENT-DEMOCRATIC ACTION (ROAD) – Coalition of intellectuals and former Solidarity activists formed to oppose Wałęsa's Centre Agreement. Key figures included the then prime minister Mazowiecki, Adam Michnik, Zbigniew Bujak and Bronisław Geremek. Became Democratic Union in 1991.

COMMONWEALTH – Union of Poland, Lithuania, Royal Prussia and Livonia (Latvia); formed by Lublin Union (1569), it lasted until the Third Partition of 1795.

CONGRESS KINGDOM OF POLAND – Russian-ruled province of Poland established in 1815, following the Congress of Vienna.

DEMOCRATIC LEFT ALLIANCE (SLD) – Alliance of SdRP (Social Democracy of the Republic of Poland) and other former-communist forces. Effectively successor to the now defunct communist party (PZPR), from whose ranks both current prime minister Leszek Miller, and the president, Aleksander Kwaśniewski, are drawn. Under pragmatic leader Leszek Miller, the SLD won a landslide victory at the elections of September 2001 to become the dominant force in Polish politics.

DEMOCRATIC UNION (UD) – Centrist political party which attracted strong support among former Solidarity intellectuals, now merged in the Freedom Union.

DUCAL PRUSSIA – (East Prussia) The eastern half of the territory of the Teutonic Knights, converted into a secular duchy in 1525 and divided in 1945 between Poland and the Soviet Union.

EMIGRACJA – Commonly used Polish term for the worldwide Polish community living outside the country.

FREEDOM UNION (UW) – Unia Wolności. Main centrist/liberal party founded as a successor to the UD when it merged with a smaller liberal party in 1994. Currently headed by a coterie of heavyweight former dissidents including Bronisław Geremek and 1995 presidential candidate manqué Jacek Kuroń.

GALICIA – Southern province of Poland including Kraków incorporated into Austro-Hungarian Empire during the Partition period, granted autonomy in latter half of nineteenth century.

GEREMEK, BRONISŁAW – Medieval historian at Warsaw University who acted as adviser to Wałęsa and the Solidarity movement. Elected leader of the Solidarity group in parliament after the June 1989 elections but resigned in November 1990. A key figure in the Freedom

Union since its inception, he was the country's (widely respected) Foreign Minister in the AWS-led government of 1997-2001.

GIEREK, EDWARD – Leader of the communist party in the 1970s, until removed following the strikes of summer 1980.

HABSBURG – The most powerful imperial family in medieval Germany, operating from a power base in Austria. Subsequently gave their name to the agglomeration of lands, centred on Austria, known as the Habsburg Empire.

HANSEATIC LEAGUE – Medieval trading alliance of Baltic and Rhineland cities, numbering about a hundred at its fifteenth-century peak. Slowly died out in seventeenth century with competition from the Baltic nation-states and rise of Brandenburg-Prussia.

HASSIDISM – Mystical religious and social movement founded by Israel ben Elizer (1700–1760) known as Baal Schem Tov. Hassidism opposed rabbinical Judaism and preached joy in life through religious ecstasy, dance and song.

HETMAN – Military commander; a state officer in the Polish-Lithuanian Commonwealth era.

HOLY ROMAN EMPIRE – Name of the loose confederation of German states (many now part of Poland) which lasted from 800 until 1806.

JAGIELLONIAN – Dynasty of Lithuanian origin which ruled Poland-Lithuania from 1386 to 1572.

JARUZELSKI, WOJCIECH – General of the armed forces, called in by the Party in 1981 to institute martial law and suppress Solidarity. His subsequent flexibility and negotiating skill helped to usher in democracy and he became president after the June 1989 elections, until the election of Wałęsa in December 1990.

KULTURKAMPF – Campaign launched by German Chancellor Bismarck in the 1870s, aimed at suppressing Catholic culture (including the Polish language) inside German territories.

KUROŃ, JACEK – Veteran opposition activist and key figure in Solidarity movement; served as minister of labour in the Mazowiecki government, returning to the same position in the Suchocka administration. Stood as the Freedom Union's official candidate in the 1995 presidential elections.

KWAŚNIEWSKI, ALEKSANDER – Former communist government minister of sport in the 1980s, elected as president in November 1995. Cuts a confident eloquent figure, who despite political divisions over his communist background has hitherto demonstrated a deft ability to act as "president of the whole nation".

LUSTRATION – Term applied to the controversial process of excluding from public life those supposed to have collaborated with the communist-era security services.

MARTIAL LAW – Military crackdown instigated by General Jaruzelski in December 1981 and remaining in effect until summer 1983.

MAZOWIECKI, TADEUSZ – Catholic lawyer and journalist and longtime adviser to Solidarity. Country's first post-communist prime minister who ran unsuccessfully for president against Wałęsa in December 1990.

MICHNIK, ADAM – Warsaw academic and leading Solidarity theoretician and activist. Chief editor of *Gazeta Wyborcza*, the country's biggest-selling daily newspaper, ever since it was set up in 1989.

NAZI–SOVIET PACT (or MOLOTOV–RIBBENTROP PACT) – 1939 agreement between Nazi Germany and the Soviet Union, which contained a secret clause to eliminate Poland from the map.

ODER-NEISSE LINE – Western limit of Polish territory set by Yalta Agreement, 1945.

PARTITION PERIOD – Era from 1772 to 1918, during which Poland was on three occasions divided into Prussian, Russian and Austrian territories.

PIASTS – Royal dynasty which forged the Polish state in the tenth century and ruled it until 1370; branches of the family continued to hold principalities, notably in Silesia, until 1675.

POLISH UNITED WORKERS PARTY (PZPR) – Former communist party who disbanded themselves in January 1990, the majority forming a new Social Democratic Party (the SdRP, see under "Post-communists" below).

POLONIANS – Slav tribe which formed the embryonic Polish nation.

POST-COMMUNISTS – Blanket term used to describe the parties and groupings emerging from the ashes of the Polish communist party (Polish United Workers Party or PZPR), which was dissolved in January 1990.

Principal successor to the PZPR is the SdRP (the full title is "Social Democracy of the Republic of Poland"), a leading force in the coalition government that ruled the country 1993–97. The post-communist label is also used to refer to the Democratic Left Alliance (see separate entry), of which the SdRP is a member.

PRUSSIA – Originally a Slavic eastern Baltic territory, now divided between Poland and the Russian Federation. It was conquered by the Teutonic Knights in the thirteenth century and acquired in 1525 by the Hohenzollerns, who merged it with their own German possessions to form Brandenburg-Prussia (later shortened to Prussia).

ROUND TABLE AGREEMENT – Pathbreaking bipartisan agreement between Jaruzelski's communist government and the Solidarity opposition in spring 1989, leading to the elections in June of that year.

ROYAL PRUSSIA (or WEST PRUSSIA) – Territory centred on the Wisła delta, originally the easternmost sector of Pomerania, renamed after its capture from the Teutonic Knights in 1466.

RUTHENIA – A loose grouping of principalities, part of which formed Poland's former Eastern Territories.

SARMATISM – Seventeenth-century Polish aristocratic cult based on the erroneous notion that they were directly descended from the Sarmatians, a nomadic people who lived on the northern shores of the Black Sea during the time of the Roman Empire.

SOLIDARITY (SOLIDARNOŚĆ) – The eastern bloc's first independent trade union, led by Lech Wałęsa, suppressed under martial law and re-legalized in 1989, before forming the core of the new democratic government. Subsequently irrevocably split into pro- and anti-Wałęsa factions, it enjoyed something of a renaissance in the mid-1990s, providing the backbone of the Solidarity Election Action (AWS), an alliance of right-wing parties formed in June 1996 to contest the 1997 parliamentary elections. Solidarity left the AWS in 2001, ostensibly to concentrate on its role as a trade union again.

SUCHOCKA, HALINA – Lawyer from Poznań chosen as Poland's first ever woman prime minister in summer 1992. A popular, if somewhat aloof figure.

TATARS - Mongol tribe who invaded Poland in the thirteenth century, some of them settling subsequently.

TEUTONIC KNIGHTS - Quasi-monastic German military order who conquered parts of the eastern Baltic, establishing their own independent state 1226–1525.

TZADDIK - Charismatic Hassidic religious teacher and leader belonging to hereditary dynasty.

UNIATES - (also known as Greek Catholics) Eastern-rite Christians who, following the Union of Brest (1595), formally accepted the Pope's authority, though they retained many Orthodox rites. Within modern Poland, Uniates comprise a mixture of Ukrainians, Łemks and Boyks.

WAŁĘSA, LECH - Shipyard electrician who led strikes in the Gdańsk shipyards in 1980, leading to the establishment of the independent trade union, Solidarity, of which he became chairman. In this role, he opposed the communist government throughout the 1980s, and led negotiations in the Round Table Agreement of 1989. Following the June 1989 elections, he parted company with many of his former Solidarity allies, forcing a presidential contest, which he won in December 1990. Defeated in the next presidential elections (Nov 1995), since when he's kept a – by his standards at least – relatively low political profile. Awarded the Nobel Peace Prize in 1983.

WAZA - (Vasa) Swedish royal dynasty which ruled Poland 1587–1668.

WORKERS' DEFENCE COMMITTEE (KOR) - Oppositional group formed in the mid-1970s, regarded by many as a precursor to Solidarity.

YALTA AGREEMENT - 1945 agreement between the victorious powers that established Poland's (and Europe's) postwar borders, without necessarily consulting those it affected.

Street names

The stars from the pantheon of Polish communist iconography after whom many streets were named after **World War II** have now largely disappeared. Since the **Solidarity** election victory of 1989 a systematic renaming of streets has been carried out, though in classic Polish style it took local authorities a lot longer to agree on new names than in, say, the neighbouring Czech and Slovak republics, the whole process being held up by interminable local infighting. It's not the first time such a process has occurred either: nineteenth-century Russian and German street names were replaced by Polish ones after **World War I**, which themselves came down following the Nazi wartime occupation. Many older streets have simply reverted to their prewar names, the new ones showing a marked preference for **Catholic** identification. Remember that street names always appear in their genitive or adjectival form, eg Franciscan Street is Franciszkańska, Piłsudski Street is Piłsudskiego and Mickiewicz Street Mickiewicza.

General Władysław Anders (1892–1970) - Renowned military figure who led the Polish troops who were exiled to Siberia at the start of World War II and later returned to fight on the Allied side in the Middle East, then in Europe.

Armii Krajowej (AK) - The Home Army, forces of the wartime Polish resistance.

Józef Bem (1794–1850) - Swashbuckling military figure who participated in the 1848 "Springtime of the Nations" in both Austria and Hungary.

General Zygmunt Berling (1896–1980) - First commander-in-chief of communist-sponsored Polish forces in the Soviet Union.

Bohaterów Getta - Heroes of the Ghetto, in memory of the April 1943 Warsaw Ghetto Uprising against the Nazis.

Tadeusz Bór-Komorowski (1895–1966) - Commander of AK (Home Army) forces during the 1944 Warsaw Uprising.

Władysław Broniewski (1897–1962) - Early socialist adherent of Piłsudski's World War I Legions, revolutionary poet and famously unreformed drunkard.

Fryderyk Chopin (1810–49) (also sometimes spelt "Szopen" in Polish) - Celebrated Romantic-era composer and pianist, long a national icon (see p.136).

Chrobrego - Refers to Bolesław Chrobry (Bolesław the Brave), first king of Poland and the man who established the country as a definite independent state.

Maria Dąbrowska (1889–1965) - Fine modern Polish writer best known for her epic novels.

Aleksander Fredro (1793–1876) - Popular dramatist, especially of comedies.

Grunwald - Landmark medieval battle (1410) where combined Polish-Lithuanian forces thrashed the Teutonic Knights.

Jan Kasprowicz (1860–1926) - Popular peasant-born neo-Romantic poet and voluminous translator of Western classics into Polish.

Jan Kochanowski (1530–84) - Renaissance-era poet, the father of the modern Polish literary canon.

Maksymilian Kolbe (1894–1941) - Catholic priest martyred in Auschwitz, canonized by Pope John Paul II.

Maria Konopnicka (1842–1910) - Children's story writer of the nineteenth century, adherent of the "Positivist" School which developed in reaction to the traditional national preference for Romanticism.

Mikołaj Kopernik (1473–1543) - Indigenous name of the great astronomer known elsewhere as Copernicus, who spent much of his life in the Baltic town of Frombork.

Tadeusz Kościuszko (1746–1817) - Dashing veteran of the American War of Independence and leader of the 1794 Insurrection in Poland (see p.448).

Józef Ignacy Krasicki (1735–1801) - Enlightenment-era poet-bishop of Warmia, dubbed the "Polish Lafontaine".

Zygmunt Krasiński (1812–59) - Author of Nieboska Komedia, one of the trio of Polish Romantic messianic greats.

Józef Kraszewski (1812–87) - Hugely popular historical novelist. His novels (over 200 of them) cover everything from the early Piasts to the Partition era.

6 Kwietnia (6 April) - Date of the Battle of Racławice, where Kościuszko's largely peasant army defeated the tsarist forces in 1794.

11 Listopada (11 November) - Symbolically important post-World War I Polish Independence Day.

29 Listopada - Start of (failed) November 1830 Uprising against the Russians.

1 Maja - Labour Day.

3 Maja - Famous democratic Constitution of 1791.

9 Maja - Polish "V" Day – the Russian-declared end of World War II – one day after Britain and other western European countries.

Jan Matejko (1838–93) - Patriotic *fin-de-siècle* painter closely associated with Kraków, where he lived most of his life.

Adam Mickiewicz (1798–1855) - The Romantic Polish poet, a national figure considered kosher by just about everyone, former communist leaders included (see p.00).

Stanisław Moniuszko (1819–72) - Romantic composer of patriotic operas, popular in Poland but little known elsewhere.

Gabriel Narutowicz (1865–1922) - First president of the Second Polish Republic, assassinated a few days after his nomination.

Ignacy Paderewski (1860–1941) - Noted pianist and composer who became the country's first prime minister post-World War I and the country's regaining of independence.

Jan Paweł II - The incumbent Catholic pontiff and Polish national hero. Many streets are now renamed after Pope John Paul II.

Józef Piłsudski (1867–1935) - One of the country's most venerated military-political figures, key architect of the regaining of independence after World War I, and national leader in the late 1920s and early 1930s.

Józef Poniatowski (1767–1813) - Nephew of the last Polish king who fought in numerous Polish and Napoleonic campaigns: an archetypal Polish military-Romantic hero.

Jerzy Popiełuszko - Radical Solidarity-supporting priest murdered by the Security Forces in 1984, and since elevated to the ranks of national martyrs.

Bolesław Prus (1847–1912) - Positivist writer, best known for quasi-historical novels such as *Pharaoh* and *Lalka* (*The Doll*).

Kazimierz Pułaski (1747–79) - Polish-American hero of the US War of Independence.

Mikołaj Rej (1505–69) - So-called "Father of Polish Literature", one of the first to write in the language.

Władysław Reymont (1867–1925) - Nobel Prize-winning author of *The Peasants* and *The Promised Land*.

Henryk Sienkiewicz (1846–1916) - Stirring historical novelist who won the Nobel Prize for his epic *Quo Vadis*?

15 Sierpnia - Date of the Battle of Warsaw (August 1920) that halted the Soviet offensive against Poland, popularly known as the "miracle on the Vistula".

Władysław Sikorski (1881–1943) - Prewar Polish prime minister and wartime commander-in-chief of Polish forces in the West.

Marie Skłodowska-Curie (1867–1934) - Nobel Prize-winning scientist and discoverer of the radioactive elements radium and polonium.

Juliusz Słowacki (1809–49) - Noted playwright and poet, one of the three Polish Romantic greats.

Jan Sobieski (1635–96) - Quintessentially Polish king famous for his celebrated rescue of Vienna (1683) from the Ottoman Turks.

Bohaterów Stalingradu - "Heroes of Stalingrad", a reference to the turning point in the defeat of Nazi Germany; less common than it was, but one of the few communist names to survive.

22 Styczni - Date of the start of January Uprising of 1863 against the Russians.

Karol Świerczewski (1897–1947) - One of the few communist figures to survive the post-1989 street name clearout (not everywhere though), a fact probably explained by his role in the controversial 1947 "Operation Vistula" (see p.368).

Świętego Ducha - Holy Spirit, generally used in square names.

Świętej Trójcy - Holy Trinity – another self-explanatory Catholic favourite.

Karol Szymanowski (1882–1937) - Noted modern Polish classical composer, a long-time Zakopane resident.

Kazimierz (Przerwa) Tetmajer (1865–1940) - Turn-of-the-twentieth-century Neo-Romantic poet, part of the Kraków-based Młoda Polska school.

Westerplatte - The Polish garrison the attack on whom by the Nazis in September 1939 signalled the start of World War II.

Wilsona - After US President Woodrow Wilson, who supported the cause of Polish independence at the Versailles Conference (1919).

Stanisław Ignacy Witkiewicz (1885–1939) - Maverick modernist artist and writer whose plays anticipated postwar Theatre of the Absurd.

1 Września - Start of World War II – the September 1939 Nazi invasion of Poland.

Stanisław Wyspiański (1867–1907) - Renowned Młoda Polska era poet, playwright and painter best known for his plays *Wesele* (*The Wedding*) and *Wyzwolenie* (*Liberation*).

Kardynał Stefan Wyszyński (1901–81) - Tenacious postwar Catholic primate of Poland, figurehead of popular resistance to communism.

Wszystkich Świętych - All Saints – a popular Catholic festival.

Stefan Żeromski (1864–1925) - One of the most renowned Polish novelists, a Neo-Romantic writer best known for his historical novel *Popioły* (*The Ashes*).

Town names

Because Poland's borders have changed so often, many of its towns, including virtually all which were formerly German, have gone under more than one name. What follows is a checklist of names most of which can now be regarded as historical. The letters in parenthesis identify the language of the non-Polish form: G=German, OS=Old Slav, C=Czech, R=Russian, U=Ukrainian, L=Lithuanian, E=English.

Barczewo - Wartenburg (G)
Biała - Biala (G)
Bielsko - Bielitz (G)
Bierutowice - Brückenberg (G)
Bolków - Bolkenhain (G)
Braniewo - Braunsberg (G)
Brzeg - Brieg (G)
Brześć - Brest (E), Briest (R)
Brzezinka - Birkenau (G)
Bydgoszcz - Bromberg (G)

Bystrzyca Kłodzka - Habelschwerdt (G)
Chełmno - Kulm (G)
Chmielno - Ludwigsdorf (G)
Chojnice - Kornitz (G)
Cieplice Śląskie-Zdrój - Bad Warmbrunn (G)
Cieszyn - Teschen (G)
Czaplinek - Tempelburg (G)
Dąbie - Altdamm (G)
Darłowo - Rügenwaldermünde (G)
Darłówko - Rügenwalde (G)

Dobre Miasto - Guttstadt (G)
Duszniki-Zdrój - Bad Reinerz (G)
Elbląg - Elbing (G)
Ełk - Lyck (G)
Frombork - Frauenburg (G)
Gdańsk - Gyddanyzc (OS), Danczik, Dantzig,
  Danzig (G), Dantsic (E)
Gdynia - Gdingen (OS), Gottenhafen (G)
Gierłoz - Görlitz (G)
Giżycko - Lötzen (G)
Głogów - Glogau (G)
Gniezno - Gnesen (G)
Goleniów - Gollnow (G)
Góra Świętej - Anny Sankt Annaberg (G)
Grudziądz - Graudenz (G)
Grunwald - Tannenberg (G), Zalgiris (L)
Gryfice - Greifenberg (G)
Hel - Hela (G)
Henryków - Heinrichau (G)
Inowrocław - Hohensalza (G)
Iwięcino - Eventin (G)
Jagniątków - Agnetendorf (G)
Jawor - Jauer (G)
Jelenia - Góra Hirschberg (G)
Kadyny - Cadinen (G)
Kamień Pomorski - Cammin (G)
Kamienna - Góra Landeshut (G)
Karłów - Karlsberg (G)
Karpacz - Krummhübel (G)
Kartuzy - Karthaus (G)
Katowice - Kattowitz (G)
Kętrzyn - Rastenburg (G)
Kłodzko - Glatz (G)
Kluki - Klucken (G)
Kołczewo - Kolzow (G)
Kołobrzeg - Kolberg (G)
Koszalin - Kösel (G)
Kraków - Cracow (E), Krakau (G)
Kruszwica - Kruschwitz (G)
Krzeszów - Grüssau (G)
Książ - Fürstenstein (G)
Kudowa-Zdrój - Bad Kudowa (G)
Kwidzyn - Marienwerder (G)
Lądek-Zdrój - Bad Landeck (G)
Łeba - Leba (G)
Legnica - Liegnitz (G)
Legnickie Pole - Wahlstatt (G)
Leszno - Lissa (G)
Lidzbark Warmiński - Heilsberg (G)
Łódź - Litzmannstadt, Lodsch (G)
Lubiąż - Leubus (G)
Lwów - Lemberg (G), Lvov (R), L'viv (U)
Malbork - Marienburg (G)

Międzygórze - Wölfesgrund (G)
Międzyzdroje - Misdroy (G)
Mikołajki - Nikolaiken (G)
Milicz - Militsch (G)
Morąg - Mohrungen (G)
Mrągowo - Sensburg (G)
Nysa - Neisse (G)
Oleśnica - Oels (G)
Oliwa - Oliva (G)
Olsztyn - Allenstein (G)
Olsztynek - Hohenstein (G)
Opole - Oppeln (G)
Orneta - Wormditt (G)
Oświęcim - Auschwitz (G)
Otmuchów - Ottmachau (G)
Paczków - Patschkau (G)
Pasłęk - Preussich Holland (G)
Polanica-Zdrój - Bad Altheide (G)
Poznań - Posen (G)
Pszczyna - Pless (G)
Reszel - Rössel (G)
Ruciane-Nida - Niedersee (G)
Słupsk - Stolp (G)
Smołdzino - Schmolsin (G)
Sobieszów - Hermsdorf (G)
Sobótka - Zobten (G)
Sopot - Zoppot (G)
Sorkwity - Sorquitten (G)
Stargard Szczeciński - Stargard (G)
Strzegom - Striegau (G)
Strzelno - Strelno (G)
Świdnica - Swidnitz, Schweidnitz (G)
Święta Lipka - Heiligelinde (G)
Świnoujście - Swinemünde (G)
Szczecin - Stettin (G)
Szczecinek - Neustettin (G)
Szklarska Poręba - Schreiberhau (G)
Sztutowo - Stutthof (G)
Tarnowskie Góry - Tarnowitz (G)
Toruń - Thorn (G)
Trzebiatów - Treptow (G)
Trzebnica - Trebnitz (G)
Trzemeszno - Tremessen (G)
Ustka - Stolpmünde (G)
Wałbrzych - Waldenburg (G)
Wambierzyce - Albendorf (G)
Warszawa - Warsaw (E), Warschau (G)
Węgorzewo - Angerburg (G)
Wilkasy - Wolfsee (G)
Wilno - Vilnius (L)
Wisełka - Neuendorf (G)
Wisła - Weichsel (G)
Włocławek - Leslau (G)

Wolin - Wollin (G)
Wrocław - Breslau (G), Wratislavia (OS),
    Vratislav (C)
Ząbkowice Śląskie - Frankenstein (G)
Żagań - Sagan (G)

Ziębice - Münsterberg (G)
Zielona Góra - Grünberg (G)
Żmigród - Trachenberg (G)
Żukowo - Zuchau (G)
Żywiec - Saybusch (G)

Acronyms and organizations

ALMATUR - Official student organization and travel office.

IT (Informator Turystyczny) - Tourist information office.

NBP (Narodowy Bank Polski) - Polish National Bank.

ORBIS - Former state travel agency, now privatized; abroad, Orbis offices are called POLORBIS in some (but not all) countries.

PKO (Polska Kasa Oszczędności) - State savings bank.

PKP (Polskie Koleje Państwowe) - State railways.

PKS (Polska Komunikacja Samochodowa) - State bus company.

PTTK (Polskie Towarzystwo Turystyczno-Krajoznawcze) - Tourist agency – Polish Tourism and Nature Lovers' Association.

PZMot (Polski Związek Motorowy) - National motorists' association.

PZPR (Polska Zjednoczona Partia Robotnicza) - Polish communist party – now defunct.

index

and small print

Index

Map entries are in colour

INDEX

763

K

L

Twenty Years of Rough Guides

In the summer of 1981, Mark Ellingham, Rough Guides' founder, knocked out the first guide on a typewriter, with a group of friends. Mark had been travelling in Greece after university, and couldn't find a guidebook that really answered his needs. There were heavyweight cultural guides on the one hand – good on museums and classical sites but not on beaches and tavernas – and on the other hand student manuals that were so caught up with how to save money that they lost sight of the country's significance beyond its role as a place for a cool vacation. None of the guides began to address Greece as a country, with its natural and human environment, its politics and its contemporary life.

Having no urgent reason to return home, Mark decided to write his own guide. It was a guide to Greece that tried to combine some erudition and insight with a thoroughly practical approach to travellers' needs. Scrupulously researched listings of places to stay, eat and drink were matched by careful attention to detail on everything from Homer to Greek music, from classical sites to national parks and from nude beaches to monasteries. Back in London, Mark and his friends got their Rough Guide accepted by a farsighted commissioning editor at the publisher Routledge and it came out in 1982.

The Rough Guide to Greece was a student scheme that became a publishing phenomenon. The immediate success of the book – shortlisted for the Thomas Cook award – spawned a series that rapidly covered dozens of countries. The Rough Guides found a ready market among backpackers and budget travellers, but soon acquired a much broader readership that included older and less impecunious visitors. Readers relished the guides' wit and inquisitiveness as much as the enthusiastic, critical approach that acknowledges everyone wants value for money – but not at any price.

Rough Guides soon began supplementing the "rougher" information – the hostel and low-budget listings – with the kind of detail that independent-minded travellers on any budget might expect. These days, the guides – distributed worldwide by the Penguin group – include recommendations spanning the range from shoestring to luxury, and cover more than 200 destinations around the globe. Our growing team of authors, many of whom come to Rough Guides initially as outstandingly good letter-writers telling us about their travels, are spread all over the world, particularly in Europe, the USA and Australia. As well as the travel guides, Rough Guides publishes a series of dictionary phrasebooks covering two dozen major languages, an acclaimed series of music guides running the gamut from Classical to World Music, a series of music CDs in association with World Music Network, and a range of reference books on topics as diverse as the internet, pregnancy and unexplained phenomena. Visit **www.roughguides.com** to see what's cooking.

Rough Guide credits

Text editor: Geoff Howard
Series editor: Mark Ellingham
Editorial: Martin Dunford, Jonathan Buckley, Jo Mead, Kate Berens, Ann-Marie Shaw, Helena Smith, Judith Bamber, Orla Duane, Olivia Eccleshall, Ruth Blackmore, Claire Saunders, Gavin Thomas, Alexander Mark Rogers, Polly Thomas, Joe Staines, Richard Lim, Duncan Clark, Peter Buckley, Lucy Ratcliffe, Clifton Wilkinson, Alison Murchie, Matthew Teller, Fran Sandham (UK); Andrew Rosenberg, Stephen Timblin, Yuki Takagaki, Richard Koss (US)
Production: Susanne Hillen, Andy Hilliard, Link Hall, Helen Prior, Julia Bovis, Michelle Draycott, Katie Pringle, Mike Hancock, Zoë Nobes, Rachel Holmes, Andy Turner

Cartography: Melissa Baker, Maxine Repath, Ed Wright, Katie Lloyd-Jones
Picture research: Louise Boulton, Sharon Martins, Mark Thomas
Online: Kelly Cross, Anja Mutic-Blessing, Jennifer Gold, Audra Epstein, Suzanne Welles, Cree Lawson (US)
Finance: John Fisher, Gary Singh, Edward Downey, Mark Hall, Tim Bill
Marketing and Publicity: Richard Trillo, Niki Smith, David Wearn, Chloë Roberts, Claire Southern, Demelza Dallow (UK); Simon Carloss, David Wechsler, Kathleen Rushforth (US)
Administration: Tania Hummel, Julie Sanderson (UK); Hunter Slaton (US)

Publishing information

This ninth edition published May 2002 by Rough Guides Ltd,
62–70 Shorts Gardens, London WC2H 9AH
4th Floor, 345 Hudson St, New York, NY 10014
Distributed by the Penguin Group
Penguin Books Ltd,
80 Strand, London WC2R ORL
Penguin Putnam, Inc.
345 Hudson Street, NY 10014, USA
Penguin Books Australia Ltd,
487 Maroondah Highway, PO Box 257, Ringwood, Victoria 3134, Australia
Penguin Books Canada Ltd,
10 Alcorn Avenue, Toronto, Ontario, Canada M4V 1E4
Penguin Books (NZ) Ltd,
182–190 Wairau Road, Auckland 10, New Zealand
Typeset in Bembo and Helvetica to an original design by Henry Iles.
Printed in Italy by LegoPrint S.p.A

Acknowledgements

Jonathan Bousfield would like to thank James Howard; Elizabeth and David Bousfield; Christina and Malcolm Martin; Mark Lenzi; Johanna Mazurek; and Geoff Howard for editorial services above and beyond the call of duty.

The editor and authors would like to thank Link Hall for assured layout; David Price for sure-footed proofreading; Maxine Repath, Ed Wright and Katie Lloyd-Jones for all things cartographic; Sharon Martins for making picture research fun; Louise Boulton for another fine cover design; Annie Shaw for much-appreciated help; and Bridgit and Brenda at North South Travel, without whom Jonathan would never have reached Poland.

Readers' letters

Many thanks to all the readers who wrote in with their comments and suggestions about the previous edition (apologies for any omissions or misspellings): David Crosbie; Mr Dunn; Elaine Hewson; Edward W. Kornowski; Katarzyna Kozanecka; Monica Mackaness and Jon Garrett; Clive Mather; Barbara Ramsbottom; Chris Sielski; and Tal Stein.

Photo credits

around the world

in twenty years

London Mini Guide ★ London Restaurants ★ Los Angeles ★ Madeira ★
Madrid ★ Malaysia, Singapore & Brunei ★ Mallorca ★ Malta & Gozo ★ Maui
★ Maya World ★ Melbourne ★ Menorca ★ Mexico ★ Miami & the Florida
Keys ★ Montréal ★ Morocco ★ Moscow ★ Nepal ★ New England ★ New
Orleans ★ New York City ★ New York Mini Guide ★ New York Restaurants
★ New Zealand ★ Norway ★ Pacific Northwest ★ Paris ★ Paris Mini Guide
★ Peru ★ Poland ★ Portugal ★ Prague ★ Provence & the Côte d'Azur ★
Pyrenees ★ The Rocky Mountains ★ Romania ★ Rome ★ San Francisco ★
San Francisco Restaurants ★ Sardinia ★ Scandinavia ★ Scotland ★
Scottish Highlands & Islands ★ Seattle ★ Sicily ★ Singapore ★ South Africa,
Lesotho & Swaziland ★ South India ★ Southeast Asia ★ Southwest USA ★
Spain ★ St Lucia ★ St Petersburg ★ Sweden ★ Switzerland ★ Sydney ★
Syria ★ Tanzania ★ Tenerife and La Gomera ★ Thailand ★ Thailand's
Beaches & Islands ★ Tokyo ★ Toronto ★ Travel Health ★ Trinidad &
Tobago ★ Tunisia ★ Turkey ★ Tuscany & Umbria ★ USA ★ Vancouver ★
Venice & the Veneto ★ Vienna ★ Vietnam ★ Wales ★ Washington DC ★
West Africa ★ Women Travel ★ Yosemite ★ Zanzibar ★ Zimbabwe

also look out for our maps,
phrasebooks, music guides
and reference books